T0348759

Handbook of
ECONOMIC
FORECASTING

VOLUME 2A

Handbook of
ECONOMIC
FORECASTING

VOLUME 2A

Edited by

GRAHAM ELLIOTT

ALLAN TIMMERMANN

Amsterdam • Boston • Heidelberg • London • New York • Oxford
Paris • San Diego • San Francisco • Singapore • Sydney • Tokyo
North Holland is an imprint of Elsevier

ELSEVIER

North Holland is an imprint of Elsevier
Radarweg 29, Amsterdam, 1043 NX, The Netherlands
The Boulevard, Langford Lane, Kidlington, Oxford, OX5 1GB, UK

Notices
Knowledge and best practice in this field are constantly changing. As new research and experience broaden our understanding, changes in research methods, professional practices, or medical treatment may become necessary.

Practitioners and researchers must always rely on their own experience and knowledge in evaluating and using any information, methods, compounds, or experiments described herein. In using such information or methods they should be mindful of their own safety and the safety of others, including parties for whom they have a professional responsibility.

To the fullest extent of the law, neither the Publisher nor the authors, contributors, or editors, assume any liability for any injury and/or damage to persons or property as a matter of products liability, negligence or otherwise, or from any use or operation of any methods, products, instructions, or ideas contained in the material herein.

Library of Congress Cataloging-in-Publication Data

A catalog record for this book is available from the Library of Congress

British Library Cataloguing-in-Publication Data

A catalogue record for this book is available from the British Library

For information on all North Holland publications
visit our website at http://store.elsevier.com

ISBN: 978-0-444-53683-9

Printed in Great Britain
13 14 15 16 17   9 8 7 6 5 4 3 2 1

This book is dedicated to Clive W.J. Granger and Halbert L. White, Jr.

CONTENTS

8. Forecasting the Price of Oil   427

Ron Alquist, Lutz Kilian, and Robert J. Vigfusson

9. Forecasting Real Estate Prices   509

Eric Ghysels, Alberto Plazzi, Rossen Valkanov and Walter Torous

INTRODUCTION TO THE SERIES

The aim of the *Handbooks in Economics* series is to produce Handbooks for various branches of economics, each of which is a definitive source, reference, and teaching supplement for use by professional researchers and advanced graduate students. Each Handbook provides self-contained surveys of the current state of a branch of economics in the form of chapters prepared by leading specialists on various aspects of this branch of economics. These surveys summarize not only received results but also newer developments from recent journal articles and discussion papers. Some original material is also included, but the main goal is to provide comprehensive and accessible surveys. The Handbooks are intended to provide not only useful reference volumes for professional collections but also possible supplementary readings for advanced courses for graduate students in economics.

Kenneth J. Arrow and Michael D. Intriligator

CONTRIBUTORS

Chapter 1
Jon Faust
Johns Hopkins University
Jonathan H. Wright
Johns Hopkins University

Chapter 2
Marco Del Negro
Federal Reserve Bank of New York
Frank Schorfheide
University of Pennsylvania

Chapter 3
Marcelle Chauvet
University of California
Simon Potter
Federal Reserve Bank of New York

Chapter 4
Marta Bańbura
European Central Bank
Domenico Giannone
Université libre de Bruxelles
Michele Modugno
Université libre de Bruxelles
Lucrezia Reichlin
London Business School

Chapter 5
Volker Wieland
Goethe University of Frankfurt
Maik Wolters
University of Kiel

Chapter 6
David Rapach
John Cook School of Business
Guofu Zhou
Olin School of Business

Chapter 7
Gregory Duffee
Johns Hopkins University

Chapter 8
Ron Alquist
Bank of Canada
Lutz Kilian
University of Michigan
Robert J. Vigfusson
Federal Reserve Board

Chapter 9
Eric Ghysels
University of North Carolina
Alberto Plazzi
University of Lugano and Swiss Finance Institute
Rossen Valkanov
University of California
Walter Torous
Massachusetts Institute of Technology

Chapter 10
Peter Christoffersen
University of Toronto
Kris Jacobs
University of Houston
Bo Young Chang
Bank of Canada

Chapter 11
Erik Snowberg
Caltech
Justin Wolfers
University of Michigan
Eric Zitzewitz
Dartmouth College

SECTION *I*

Macro Forecasting

CHAPTER 1

Forecasting Inflation

Jon Faust and Jonathan H. Wright

Department of Economics, Johns Hopkins University, Baltimore MD 21218, USA

Contents

Abstract

This chapter discusses recent developments in inflation forecasting. We perform a horse-race among a large set of traditional and recently developed forecasting methods, and discuss a number of principles

Handbook of Economic Forecasting, Volume 2A
ISSN 1574-0706, http://dx.doi.org/10.1016/B978-0-444-53683-9.00001-5

that emerge from this exercise. We find that judgmental survey forecasts outperform model-based ones, often by a wide margin. A very simple forecast that is just a glide path between the survey assessment of inflation in the current-quarter and the long-run survey forecast value turns out to be competitive with the actual survey forecast and thereby does about as well or better than model-based forecasts. We explore the strengths and weaknesses of some specific prediction methods, including forecasts based on the Phillips curve and based on dynamic stochastic general equilibrium models, in greater detail. We also consider measures of inflation expectations taken from financial markets and the tradeoff between forecasting aggregates and disaggregates.

Keywords

Survey forecasts, Nowcasting, Shifting endpoints, Shrinkage, Inflation compensation, Disaggregate forecasts

1. INTRODUCTION

Long-term nominal commitments such as labor contracts, mortgages and other debt, and price stickiness are widespread features of modern economies. In such a world, forecasting how the general price level will evolve over the life of a commitment is an essential part of private sector decision-making. The existence of long-term nominal obligations is also among the primary reasons economists generally believe that monetary policy is not neutral, at least over moderate horizons. While macroeconomists continue to debate whether these non-neutralities give rise to beneficially exploitable trade-offs for monetary policymakers, the recent New Keynesian formulation of optimal policy has raised the prominence of inflation forecasting in policymaking (Woodford, 2003).

Central banks aim to keep inflation stable, and perhaps also to keep output near an efficient level. With these objectives, the New Keynesian model makes explicit that optimal policy will depend on optimal forecasts (e.g., Svensson, 2005), and further that policy will be most effective when it is well understood by the general public. These results helped bolster a transparency revolution in central banking. A centerpiece of this revolution has been the practice of central banks announcing forecasts of inflation and other key variables. This practice was initiated by "inflation targeting" central banks who generally released forecasts in quarterly "Inflation Reports." The Fed (the U.S. central bank formally called the Federal Reserve System) lagged behind other central banks in joining this practice, but now publishes quarterly forecasts for inflation and other macroeconomic variables. The costs and benefits of transparency are widely debated, but the need for a central bank to be concerned with inflation forecasting is broadly agreed. In short, inflation forecasting is of great importance to households, businesses, and policymakers.

This chapter reviews the state of the art in inflation forecasting. A significant part of our review involves simply rounding up and summarizing the performance of the myriad forecasting models and methods that have been proposed. Now is a particularly good time for such a review, as there has been an explosion in the number and variety of methods in recent years. Along with a number of traditional time series models, a host of new methods for use with large numbers of predictors have recently come to the fore. There are many newly popular forecast combination techniques. Financial markets have also provided new assets (indexed-linked bonds, inflation derivatives), the prices of which may contain clearer forward-looking information about inflation than was available from previously existing assets. Further, with the pathbreaking work of Smets and Wouters (2003, 2007), structural economic models have – for the first time since the 1970s – been put forward as serious forecasting models.

Finally, the creation of a number of vintage datasets in recent years makes possible quasi-realtime comparisons of proposed methods. By a quasi-realtime forecast we mean a model-based forecast for some point in time in the past based only on data that was available to forecasters at that time. These data allow us to ask whether a new method could, in principle, have been used to improve on the best forecasts that were actually made in real time.

One principal aim, then, in this chapter is to round up the traditional and newer methods and compare their strengths and weaknesses, paying close attention where possible to data vintage issues. Many elements of this review are present in excellent forecasting papers in the recent literature. Few papers, however, do a comprehensive review, and the results in some cases seem to be sensitive to the particulars of the exercise. Thus, pulling things together on as consistent a basis as possible is of some value.

We go beyond mere review, however, following some themes that have emerged in several recent papers. Based on our reading of these themes, we argue that a more fundamental re-think of the topic of inflation forecasting is called for. One motivation for this re-think is that subjective inflation forecasts of inflation seem to outperform model-based forecasts in certain dimensions, often by a wide margin. This is in stark contrast to the results for, say, GDP forecasting where trivially simple time series models often perform similarly to the best subjective forecasts over any but the shortest horizons.

Thus, the chapter begins by attempting to isolate the apparent source of the advantage of subjective forecasts so that we can attempt to bring that information into the model-based forecasts. We note that the forecast path over, say, eight quarters involves two boundary values: the path starts at a nowcast of where inflation is right now and it ends somewhere close to an estimate of what we will call the local mean inflation rate. There are good reasons reviewed below why the subjective forecasters outperform most conventional models regarding both boundary values. The advantage of the subjective methods historically seems to be largely due to the choice of boundary values.

If we accept this conclusion, it is natural to consider ways of giving the standard forecasting models the advantage of good boundary values. Given good boundaries could the models come closer to or surpass subjective forecasts? Our results here are basically negative. The methods that work well essentially choose some smooth path between the boundaries, and end up being about equivalent. One can do much worse by giving the model too much flexibility to fit sampling fluctuations. Every model constrained in a heavy-handed way performs about equally well given good boundary values. Less constrained methods often do worse, and never do appreciably better.

Overall, the big roundup of methods says that you should choose the two boundary values astutely and, given these values, effectively ignore most information that might lead you to deviate from a smooth path between the boundaries.

There is one important difference between inflation forecasting by a central bank and inflation forecasting by the public, which is worth stressing at the outset. Unlike the public, the central bank has control over monetary policy, which in turn affects inflation. So the central bank's inflation forecast depends on what they expect their own policy actions to be. The central bank could integrate over this uncertainty – giving an unconditional forecast. Or the central bank could condition its forecast on a particular path of interest rates – such as unchanged interest rates or a path implied by futures quotes. The Federal Reserve's Greenbook forecast and the Bank of England forecasts are both conditional forecasts. If one takes the conditioning seriously, this poses a substantial obstacle to assessing the quality of these forecasts (Faust and Wright, 2008). In this chapter, we nevertheless treat all forecasts as though they are unconditional forecasts.

The plan for the remainder of this chapter is as follows. Section 2 contains our review of forecasting methods, and our comparison of them on U.S. data. In Section 3, we analyze forecasts of inflation extracted from financial market variables linked explicitly to inflation. These assets have not been traded long enough for inclusion in our broad review of forecasting methods, so we treat them separately. Section 4 discusses some other topics – the construction of inflation density forecasts, forecasting aggregates directly versus aggregating forecasts of components, and issues of forecasting core versus headline inflation. Section 5 gives a comparison of a few inflation forecasting methods for some international data. Section 6 concludes.

2. APPROACH FOR OUR GENERAL REVIEW

In this section, we describe the set-up for our broad review of forecasting methods.

2.1. A Triply Great Sample and its Problems

As is generally the case in macroeconomics, the choice of sample period for our forecast comparison exercise is constrained by data availability. In practice, the available data do not allow us to start the forecast evaluation exercises before about 1980.[1] Thus, the feasible span for forecast evaluation is something like 1980 to the present. This includes about a

---

[1] This is because of the forecasts that we wish to evaluate. Naturally some forecasts could be considered over much longer periods.

20-year period known as the Great Moderation, bookended by two short and distinctly immoderate subsamples: the end of the Great Inflation and the recent Great Recession. Thus, while all three parts of the sample are Great in some way, the sample as a whole presents some serious challenges.

It is well known that U.S. inflation was much more quiescent and harder to forecast during the Great Moderation period from, say, 1985 to 2007, than during the period before (e.g., Stock and Watson (2007)). Up until the financial crisis, it might have been fashionable to presume that the Great Moderation period would continue indefinitely, and thus focusing on the Great Moderation sample period might have seemed most relevant to the project of forecasting going forward.

Even during the Great Moderation, the "good luck or good policy" debate (e.g., Stock and Watson, 2003a; Ahmed et al., 2004) makes clear that the foundations for presuming that the Great Moderation would last forever were rather shaky. Of course, now we must add "bad policy" to the list of explanations for the extended buoyant period, and we have little firm basis for treating the Great Moderation sample as "the new normal."

At present, it is a question of fundamental importance whether "the new normal" will be a pattern more like the pre-Great Moderation period, the Great Moderation, or perhaps some third pattern such as the path followed by Japan during the "lost decade(s)."

One might make an argument that all three periods in our available sample should be pooled. After all, the ideal would be to have a forecasting model that performs well across the board and in all conditions. Of course, this may be an unattainable ideal. Our best macroeconomic theories are generally viewed as first order approximations around some steady-state. Similarly, our parsimonious (often linear) time series models are probably best viewed as local approximations to some more complicated process.

In this view, it would be natural, as a first goal, to choose forecasting models that perform well in something we might call "normal times," leaving periods far from the steady-state to be studied separately. While it may be hard to define "normal times," it is clear that the extreme periods that bookend our largest available sample are not normal times.

We take a pragmatic approach to this issue. We omit the unusual period of the early 1980s (which would be especially unrepresentative in including the end, but not the start, of the Great Inflation). However, we include data spanning the recent crisis, during which inflation behavior has not been as extreme (if we were modeling output growth or bank lending, our approach might be different). Thus, our baseline results for forecast evaluation are for the period 1985 Q1 to 2011 Q4. We also report separate results, excluding the recent crisis. While including the crisis raises root mean square prediction errors (RMSPEs) across the board, the basic conclusions about relative forecast accuracy that we emphasize are unaffected by inclusion or exclusion of this period.

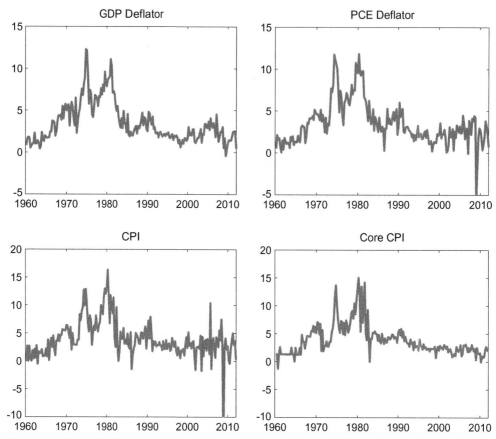

Figure 1.1 Annualized inflation rates. *Notes:* Quarter-over-quarter inflation rates corresponding to various price indexes (2011Q4 vintage data).

2.2. Measures of Inflation

We will focus on prediction of quarterly inflation as measured by the GDP deflator,[2] the personal consumption expenditures (PCE) deflator, the Consumer Price Index (CPI), and core CPI (CPI excluding food and energy). Inflation rates are computed as $\pi_t = 400 \log(p_t/p_{t-1})$ where p_t is the underlying price index. CPI data are of course available at the monthly frequency, but our focus throughout this chapter is on quarterly data (using end-of-quarter CPI values). Figure 1.1 shows the evolution of these four inflation measures over the past half century. They tend to move together, but differences in composition and likely aggregation biases mean, however, that their short-run and even long-run behavior may differ.[3] Still, a slowly moving trend component – rising in the Great Inflation, and

---

[2] GNP deflator prior to 1992.

[3] For example, CPI inflation tends to be about 0.3 percent per annum higher than PCE inflation, because the regular CPI index does not use chain weighting, and so has a well-known upward substitution bias.

falling over subsequent decades – can clearly be seen for all four inflation measures. This slowly-varying trend is a recurrent theme of a large recent macroeconomic literature, much of which does not focus narrowly on the forecasting question. Many authors, including Sims (1993), Kozicki and Tinsley (2001,2005), Gürkaynak et al. (2005), Cogley and Sargent (2005), Cogley and Sbordone (2008), De Graeve et al. (2009), Cogley et al. (2010), Stock and Watson (2010), van Dijk et al. (2011), Gonzáles et al. (2011), Clark (2011), Clark and Doh (2011), Dotsey et al. (2011) and Wright (forthcoming) have all emphasized the need to take account of slowly varying perceptions of long-run inflation objectives in forecasting inflation, understanding the term structure of interest rates, and/or modeling the relationship between inflation and economic slack.

In our forecast evaluations, forecast errors are calculated as actual minus forecast value, but for variables that are repeatedly and indefinitely revised with evolving definitions, an issue arises as to what to treat as the actual. Revisions to CPI and core CPI inflation are trivial; but revisions to the other inflation measures are large,[4] and include benchmark revisions, which incorporate conceptual and definitional changes. It makes little sense to evaluate whether judgmental or time series models predict definitional changes, and the Greenbook, in particular, explicitly does not attempt to do so. Thus, we follow Tulip (2009) and Faust and Wright (2009) in measuring actual realized inflation by the data as recorded in the real-time dataset of the Federal Reserve Bank of Philadelphia two quarters after the quarter to which the data refer.

2.3. Metrics and Inference

Our main results are for RMSPEs. More specifically, we compute quasi-realtime recursive out-of-sample RMSPEs. Out-of-sample accuracy is considered because parameter estimation error and structural breaks (as surveyed by Giacomini and Rossi (forthcoming)) often mean that good in-sample fit fails to translate into out-of-sample forecasting performance.[5] We generally present RMSPEs relative to a benchmark (detailed later). The benchmark is in the denominator so that numbers less than one indicate that the alternative model outperforms the benchmark.

Assessing the statistical significance of any deviations in relative RMSPEs from unity raises some knotty econometric questions in the case where the forecasting models being compared are nested. Clark and McCracken (2009a, forthcoming) provide thorough discussions of the issues. One might think of the hypothesis as being that the smaller model is correctly specified in population. In this case, the two models are the same under the null. When viewed as a test of the null hypothesis that the small model is correct in population,

---

[4] Croushore (2008) discusses data revisions to PCE inflation especially around 2003 when Federal Reserve officials were concerned about a very low level of inflation that subsequently got revised away.

[5] We emphasize that there is no such thing as a truly out-of-sample forecast evaluation, because the models that are considered in such an exercise are always the outcome of a data mining process conducted, if not by the individual researcher, then by the economics profession as a whole.

the test of Diebold and Mariano (1995) has a non-standard asymptotic distribution, and alternatives such as the test of Clark and West (2007) are often used instead, as they are close to being correctly sized.

The null hypothesis for the Clark and West (2007) test, however, is not that the two nested models have equal RMSPE in the current sample size, but rather that the small model is correctly specified and so the two models have equal RMSPE in population. We instead prefer to think of the relevant hypothesis as being that the two models have equal *finite-sample* forecast accuracy.[6] Clark and McCracken (forthcoming) find that comparing the Diebold and Mariano (1995) test statistic to standard normal critical values gives a test of the null hypothesis of equal finite-sample forecast accuracy (in both the nested and non-nested cases) that has size fairly close to the nominal level, provided that the standard errors use the rectangular window with lag truncation parameter equal to the forecast horizon, and the small-sample adjustment of Harvey et al. (1997) is employed. This is the approach that we adopt throughout this chapter.

We would note two further caveats on our use of the Diebold and Mariano (1995) test. First, the results that we appeal to strictly apply to a comparison among primitive forecasting *models*. We will however be using them to compare forecast *methods* that each combine multiple models. Second, the presence of data revisions presents some potential to add to size distortions (Clark and McCracken (2009b, forthcoming)). However, for two of our inflation measures (CPI and core CPI), data revisions are trivial. As we find about as many rejections of the null of equal forecast accuracy for these inflation measures as for the others (PCE and GDP deflator inflation), we suspect that data revisions do not lead our tests of equal finite-sample accuracy seriously astray.

2.4. Forecasts

We focus on prediction of quarterly inflation rates made in the middle month of each quarter. We consider forecasts for the current quarter (horizon $h = 0$) and subsequent quarters. The first set of forecasts is made in February 1985; the final one is made in November 2011. For the most part (and unless explicitly noted otherwise) we perform a quasi-realtime forecasting exercise, using the vintage datasets from the database maintained by the Federal Reserve Bank of Philadelphia. We also make use of the vintage Greenbook databases used in Faust and Wright (2009). When using vintage data, our timing convention is based on the Federal Reserve Bank of Philadelphia's real-time dataset. Only data that were available in the middle of the second month of each quarter are included in forecasting. Since our forecasts are dated in the middle month of quarter, t, in all cases, the published inflation data go through the previous quarter $t - 1$.

---

[6] To see the difference, consider the case where the restricted model has one highly informative predictor and the alternative model adds another 50 that add some very modest forecasting power. Owing to the effects of parameter estimation error, one would expect to find that the bigger model has substantially higher RMSPE in small sample sizes. The important distinction between population and finite-sample predictive accuracy was discussed in Inoue and Kilian (2004).

We prefer to forecast single-quarter inflation rates rather than cumulative inflation rates over longer periods, because it makes it easier to see how the predictability varies with horizon. In contrast, inflation from the last quarter to, say, four quarters hence conflates short- and longer-term inflation predictions. We consider forecasts for the current quarter (horizon $h = 0$) and for the next eight quarters ($h = 1, 2, \ldots, 8$).

2.5. A Roundup of Forecasting Models

In this section, we describe the set of methods for forecasting inflation, π_t, that we shall evaluate. We consider a few models with purely stationary specifications for inflation. These models however imply, by construction, that the forecast of inflation converges to the unconditional mean as the horizon gets large. For example, long-horizon forecasts of inflation made in recent years using stationary models estimated on a period covering the Great Inflation have been over 4 percent. These seem unreasonable forecasts, and they result from ignoring the slowly-varying trend in inflation that is evident in Figure 1.1.

As a device to capture this varying local mean, we measure the trend level of inflation, τ_t, using the most recent 5-to-10-year-ahead inflation forecast from Blue Chip – Blue Chip has asked respondents to predict the average inflation levels from 5 to 10 years, hence twice a year, since 1979.[7] Prior to 1979, we have no source of long-run survey inflation expectations, and so use exponential smoothing[8] of real-time inflation data instead as a crude proxy. Then we define the inflation "gap" as $g_t = \pi_t - \tau_t$, and consider models in which g_t is treated as stationary, and for forecasting purposes, τ_t is assumed to follow a random walk. This idea of forecasting inflation in "gap" form around some slowly-varying local mean has been found to be quite successful (Kozicki and Tinsley, 2001, Stock and Watson, 2010; Cogley et al., 2010 and Clark, 2011). It controls for a low-frequency component that is evidently quite important in the behavior of inflation over the last few decades. Some analysts interpret the trend as representing agents' perceptions of the Fed's long-run inflation target, which in this view must have shifted over time, owing to changes in the Fed's preferences and also in its credibility. We also consider other non-stationary specifications for inflation and subjective forecasts. In all, we consider the following set of competing forecasting methods:

1. **Direct forecast (Direct).** For each horizon h, we run the regression $\pi_{t+h} = \rho_0 + \Sigma_{j=1}^{p}\rho_j\pi_{t-j} + \varepsilon_{t+h}$ and use this to obtain the forecast of π_{T+h}.
2. **Recursive autoregression (RAR).** We estimate $\pi_t = \rho_0 + \Sigma_{j=1}^{p}\rho_j\pi_{t-j} + \varepsilon_t$. The h-period forecast is constructed by recursively iterating the one-step forecast forward. If the AR model is correctly specified, then the AR forecast will asymptotically

---

[7] The Blue Chip survey asks respondents for predictions of GDP deflator and CPI inflation only. We use the GDP deflator inflation projection as the trend measure for PCE inflation and use the CPI inflation projection as the trend measure for core CPI inflation.

[8] For any time series, $z(t)$, the exponentially smoothed counterpart, $z^{ES}(t)$, satisfies the recursion $z^{ES}(t) = \alpha z^{ES}(t-1) + (1-\alpha)z(t)$, where α is the smoothing parameter, set to 0.95 throughout this chapter.

outperform the direct benchmark, but the direct forecast may be more robust to mis-specification, as discussed by Marcellino et al. (2006). Like direct autoregression, this does not impose a unit root on the inflation process.

3. A Phillips-curve-motivated forecast (PC). The Phillips curve is the canonical eco-nomically motivated approach to forecast inflation (Phillips, 1958; Gordon, 1982; 1998; Brayton et al., 1999; Stock and Watson 1999, 2009, and many others). For each h, we estimate $\pi_{t+h} = \rho_0 + \Sigma_{j=1}^{p} \rho_j \pi_{t-j} + \lambda u_{t-1} + \varepsilon_t$, where u_{t-1} is the unem-ployment rate in quarter $t-1$, and use this to forecast π_{T+h}. Phillips curve forecasts are sometimes interpreted more broadly, replacing the unemployment rate with other economic activity measures, such as the output gap, industrial production growth, or marginal cost.

4. A random walk model. We consider two variants on this. The pure random walk model (RW) takes π_{T-1} as the forecast for π_{T+h}, $h = 0, \ldots, 5$. The closely-related forecast for inflation considered by Atkeson and Ohanian (2001) (RW-AO) instead takes $\frac{1}{4}\Sigma_{j=1}^{4}\pi_{T-j}$ as the forecast for π_{T+h}.

5. An unobserved component stochastic volatility model (UCSV). The model is univari-ate: $\pi_t = \tau_t + \eta_t^T$ and $\tau_t = \tau_{t-1} + \eta_t^P$ where η_t^T is $iidN(0, \sigma_{T,t}^2)$, η_t^P is $iidN(0, \sigma_{P,t}^2)$, $\log(\sigma_{T,t}^2) = \log(\sigma_{T,t-1}^2) + \psi_{1,t}$, $\log(\sigma_{P,t}^2) = \log(\sigma_{P,t-1}^2) + \psi_{2,t}$ and $(\psi_{1,t}, \psi_{2,t})'$ is $iidN(0, 0.2I_2)$. The forecast of π_{T+h} is the filtered estimate of τ_T. If the variances of η_t^T and η_t^P were constant, then this would be an integrated moving average (IMA) model. Stock and Watson (2007) find that the UCSV model provides good forecasts for inflation.

6. The autoregression in gap form (AR–GAP). For each horizon h, we estimate the regression $g_{t+h} = \rho_0 + \Sigma_{j=1}^{p}\rho_j g_{t-j} + \varepsilon_{t+h}$. We then iterate this forward to provide a forecast of g_{T+h} and add τ_T back to the forecast to get the implied prediction of inflation, treating the trend as a random walk. Henceforth, all the time series predictions that we consider are in "gap" form – they yield a forecast of g_{T+h}, to which we add back the final observation on the trend to get the implied prediction of inflation.

7. The "fixed ρ" forecast. We assume that the inflation gap is an AR(1) with a fixed slope coefficient, ρ, which is set to 0.46. This is in turn the slope coefficient from fitting an AR(1) to the 1985Q1 vintage of GDP deflator inflation from 1947Q2 to 1959Q4. Thus, the model is $g_t = \rho g_{t-1} + \varepsilon_t$, and absolutely no parameter estimation is involved. This can in turn be used to obtain a forecast of g_{T+h} and, adding τ_T back to the forecast, gives the implied prediction of inflation.

8. A Phillips curve forecast in "gap" form (PC-GAP). We apply the Phillips curve not to inflation, but to the inflation gap, g_t. For each h, we estimate $g_{t+h} = \rho_0 + \Sigma_{j=1}^{p}\rho_j g_{t-j} + \lambda u_{t-1} + \varepsilon_t$, where u_{t-1} is the unemployment rate in quarter $t-1$, and use this to

forecast g_{T+h} and hence π_{T+h}. Phillips curves applied to the inflation gap have been considered by Stock and Watson (2010) and Koenig and Atkinson (2012).

9. A Phillips curve forecast in "gap" form with a time-varying NAIRU (PCTVN-GAP). For each h, we estimate $g_{t+h} = \rho_0 + \Sigma_{j=1}^{p}\rho_j g_{t-j} + \lambda(u_{t-1} - u_{t-1}^*) + \varepsilon_t$, where u_t^* is an estimate of the NAIRU. We use the most recent 5-to-10-year-ahead Blue Chip survey forecast for the unemployment rate as the estimate of the time-varying NAIRU. This goes back to 1979 — before this we use exponential smoothing of the real-time realized unemployment rate instead.

10. A term structure VAR based forecast (Term Structure VAR). Macro–finance models aim to characterize the joint dynamics of Treasury yields and macroeconomic variables (Ang and Piazzesi, 2003; Diebold et al., 2006). A simple way of operationalizing this (following Diebold and Li, 2006) is to fit a Nelson–Siegel yield curve to the term structure of interest rates at the end of each quarter, specifying that the yield on a zero-coupon bond of maturity n is

$$y_t(n) = \beta_{1t} + \beta_{2t}\left(\frac{1 - e^{-\lambda n}}{\lambda n}\right) + \beta_{3t}\left(\frac{1 - e^{-\lambda n}}{\lambda n} - e^{-\lambda n}\right), \qquad (1)$$

where λ is treated as fixed at 0.0609. The coefficients β_{1t}, β_{2t}, and β_{3t} have interpretations as the level, slope, and curvature of yields. The underlying zero–coupon yields for this exercise are from the dataset of Gürkaynak et al. (2007). We can then fit a VAR(1) to β_{1t}, β_{2t}, β_{3t}, the inflation gap, and the unemployment rate. Vector autoregressions of this sort are familiar in the macro–finance term structure literature (see, for example, Joslin et al., 2010).[9]

11. A forecast based on VAR with time-varying parameters (TVP-VAR). This is a VAR(2) in inflation, the unemployment rate and Treasury bill yields in which the intercept and slope coefficients are allowed to drift slowly over time, as in Primiceri (2005). The parameters follow random walks with stochastic volatility. This can be thought of as a multivariate generalization of the UCSV model.[10]

12. Equal-weighted averaging (EWA). This and the next two methods assessed are *large dataset methods*. We constructed a dataset of 77 predictors at the quarterly frequency, listed in Table 1.1. All of the series are available from 1960Q1 through to the end of the sample, and as such constitute a balanced panel. As is usual, the series were transformed such that the transformed series (levels, logs, log differences etc.) are arguably stationary. Unfortunately, unlike the rest of our forecasting exercise, these

---

[9] Some authors impose no-arbitrage restrictions rather than estimating an unrestricted VAR, as we do here. Joslin et al. (forthcoming) however argue that the imposition of these no-arbitrage restrictions is empirically inconsequential.

[10] Cogley and Sbordone (2008) estimate the parameters of a structural New-Keynesian Phillips curve by matching the coefficients of a reduced form VAR with time-varying parameters. Inflation forecasts from the New-Keynesian Phillips curve model are thus designed to be close to those from the VAR with time-varying parameters.

Table 1.1 Variables and Transformations in Our Large Dataset

Variable	Transform	Variable	Transform
Average Hourly Earnings: Construction	DLN	Payrolls: Goods-Producing	DLN
Average Hourly Earnings: Manufacturing	DLN	Payrolls: Government	DLN
Average Weekly Hours	Level	Payrolls: Information Services	DLN
Average Weekly Hours: Overtime	Level	Payrolls: Leisure	DLN
Civilian Employment	DLN	Payrolls: Natural Resources	DLN
Real Disposable Personal Income	DLN	Payrolls: Other Services	DLN
New Home Starts	Log	Payrolls: Professional	DLN
Housing Starts: 1-Unit Structures	Log	Payrolls: Retail Trade	DLN
Housing Starts: 5 + Unit Structures	Log	Payrolls: Total Private Industries	DLN
Housing Starts in Midwest	Log	Payrolls: Trade, Transportation	DLN
Housing Starts in Northeast	Log	Payrolls: Wholesale Trade	DLN
Housing Starts in South	Log	Real GDP	DLN
Housing Starts in West	Log	Real Consumption	DLN
Industrial Production Index	DLN	Real Durables Consumption	DLN
IP: Business Equipment	DLN	Real Consumption (Services)	DLN
IP: Consumer Goods	DLN	Real Residential Investment	DLN
IP: Durable Consumer Goods	DLN	Real Non-residential Investment	DLN
IP: Durable Materials	DLN	Real Government Spending	DLN
IP: Final Products (Market Group)	DLN	Real Exports	DLN
IP: Materials	DLN	Real Imports	DLN
IP: Non-durable Consumer Goods	DLN	Federal Funds Rate	FD
IP: Non-durable Materials	DLN	3 Month Treasury Bill Yield	FD
ISM Manufacturing: PMI Index	Level	1 Year Yield	FD
ISM: Employment Index	Level	3 Year Yield	FD
ISM: Inventories Index	Level	5 Year Yield	FD
ISM: New Orders Index	Level	10 Year Yield	FD
ISM: Production Index	Level	AAA Corporate Yield (Moody's)	FD
ISM: Prices Index	Level	BAA Corporate Yield (Moody's)	FD
ISM: Supplier Deliveries Index	Level	3 Month Bill/Fed Funds Spread	Level
Total Non-farm Payrolls: All Employees	DLN	1 Year/3 Month Bill Spread	Level
Civilians Unemployed - 15 Weeks	DLN	3 Year/3 Month Bill Spread	Level
Civilians Unemployed for 15–26 Weeks	DLN	5 Year/3 Month Bill Spread	Level
Civilians Unemployed for 27 Weeks +	DLN	10 Year/3 Month Bill Spread	Level
Civilians Unemployed for 5–14 Weeks	DLN	AAA/10 Year Bill Spread	Level
Civilians Unemployed <5 Weeks	DLN	BAA/AAA Spread	Level
Civilian Unemployment Rate	FD	Excess Stock Market Return	Level
Non-farm Payrolls: Construction	DLN	SMB Fama French Factor	Level
Payrolls: Education	DLN	HML Fama French Factor	Level
Payrolls: Financial Activities	DLN		

Notes: Transformations are DLN: first difference of logs; FD: first differences.

data are *not* real-time. Instead, a single recent vintage of data is used for the large dataset methods.[11] However, real-time forecasting exercises with large datasets have been considered (Bernanke and Boivin, 2003; Faust and Wright, 2009), and those studies found that the relative performance of large dataset and simpler forecasting methods is not greatly affected by whether one uses real-time data or a single vintage of revised data. We first estimate and forecast using n simple models, each of the form $g_{t+h} = \rho_0 + \Sigma_{j=1}^{p} \rho_j g_{t-j} + \beta_i x_{i,t-1} + \varepsilon_{it+h}$ for $i = 1, \ldots n$ where $x_{i,t}$ is the value of the ith predictor in the large dataset at time t. Letting $\hat{g}_{T+h}^{i}$ be the forecast of g_{T+h} from the ith model, the EWA forecast of the inflation gap is $n^{-1} \Sigma_{i=1}^{n} \hat{g}_{T+h}^{i}$. This method was first proposed by Bates and Granger (1969) and its surprising empirical success is part of the folklore of forecasting. Stock and Watson (2003b) among others find continuing support for the folklore.

13. Bayesian model averaging (BMA). In this method, described in more detail by Wright (2009a), we assign a prior over the parameters of the n models used in EWA, just described; and a flat prior that each model is equally likely to be true. The prior for the model parameters follows Fernandez et al. (2001). Write each model as $g_{t+h} = \lambda_i' w_{i,t} + \varepsilon_{it}$, where $\varepsilon_{it} \sim N(0, \sigma^2)$, let the prior for λ_i conditional on σ be $N(\bar{\lambda}, \phi(\sigma^2 \Sigma_{t=1}^{T} w_{i,t} w_{i,t}')^{-1})$ and the marginal prior for σ be proportional to $1/\sigma$. The models are then estimated and the forecast from each is evaluated at the posterior mean for the parameters. Finally, these n forecasts are then combined in a weighted average with weights determined by the posterior probability that each model is correct. The prior has a hyperparameter, ϕ, that determines how much the model weights are likely to vary from equal weighting. We set $\phi = 2$.

The theoretical justification of this method relies on strictly exogenous regressors and iid errors – assumptions that are patently false in our application. Earlier work (Koop and Potter, 2003 and Wright, 2009a) shows that the method works well in cases like the one at hand, however, and we simply view BMA as a pragmatic shrinkage device.

14. Factor augmented vector autoregression (FAV). This uses the VAR $\xi_t = \mu_0 + \Sigma_{j=1}^{p} \mu_j \xi_{t-j} + \varepsilon_t$, where $\xi_t = (g_t, z_{1t}, z_{2t}, \ldots z_{mt})'$ and $\{z_{it}\}_{i=1}^{m}$ are the first m principal components of $\{x_{it}\}_{i=1}^{n}$, with the predictors first standardized to have mean zero and unit variance. The model can be estimated and iterated forward to provide a forecast of g_{T+h}. This method was proposed by Bernanke et al. (2005).

15. The Dynamic Stochastic General Equilibrium (DSGE) model of Smets and Wouters. Our choice of the Smets–Wouters (2007) model is due to its iconic nature, the existence of a body of prior results and the pragmatic fact that compiling a real-time dataset for the more elaborate models has not been done and would be very expensive. There

---

[11] The problem could be dealt with by using the vintage datasets of Faust and Wright (2009), but those datasets come from the Greenbook process and the forecast period would have to end outside the 5-year embargo for those forecasts.

are, of course, many versions of DSGE models and it might be nice to include more recent models and even the larger models in use at the Federal Reserve Board.

We base our DSGE forecasts on the real-time exercise conducted by Edge and Gürkaynak (2010). They created, and graciously made available to all, vintage datasets for the Smets–Wouters model for the period 1992 to 2009. We augment these vintage datasets with data from the vintage Greenbook databases used in Faust and Wright (2009), allowing us to extend the exercise back to 1985 Q1 as with our other models. The Smets–Wouters model gives forecasts for GDP deflator inflation alone.

In the baseline case, we follow Edge and Gürkaynak (2010) in using the Bayesian prior specified by Smets and Wouters to re-estimate the model by Markov Chain Monte Carlo for each vintage of the data. We take as forecasts the mean of the predictive density for inflation taking the full posterior distribution of the model parameters into account. We also investigated forming forecasts treating the parameters as fixed at the posterior mode, but found that this gave similar results.

The Smets–Wouters model is a stationary specification. However, the prior mean for the steady-state inflation rate is 2.5 percent, and so long-horizon forecasts for inflation from this model do not necessarily have to be close to the sample mean at the time that the forecast is being made (unlike for methods 1–3 above).

16. The Dynamic Stochastic General Equilibrium with shifting local mean (DSGE-GAP). It is hard to evaluate a model estimated by Bayesian methods on a quasi-realtime basis, as the choice of priors was inevitably influenced by the data observed at the time that the model is first proposed. As a crude device to mitigate this potential for "lookback" bias in forecasting with the Smets–Wouters model, we also consider a modification of this forecasting method in which the prior mean for the steady-state of inflation is set to our real-time measure of the local mean of inflation, τ_t.

17. Finally, we consider three fully real-time judgmental forecasts, each of which incorporates an immense range of information processed through an economics-influenced subjective filter:

    i. Blue Chip survey (BC). Blue Chip provides a forecast of both the GDP deflator and CPI. The AR-GAP benchmark forecast is affected by long-term Blue Chip survey predictions, but at least for the horizons for which they are available, one might just want to use the Blue Chip projections directly. Blue Chip forecasts are released at the start of each month. For each quarter, we take the second Blue Chip forecast, which is always released before the time at which our forecasts are being made (the middle of the middle month of the quarter).

    ii. Survey of Professional Forecasters (SPF). The SPF also provides quarterly GDP deflator and CPI forecasts. These are released at the start of the middle month of each quarter, again just before the time at which our forecasts are being made.

    iii. The Fed staff's Greenbook forecast. The Greenbook provides GDP deflator, CPI and CPI-Core forecasts. While the Greenbook forecast is informed by myriad small-scale and large-scale models, it is ultimately a judgmental forecast (Reif-schneider et al., 1997). The forecast is made once per FOMC meeting. To align these Greenbook forecasts with the rest of our exercise, we simply choose the Greenbook closest to, but before, the middle of the middle month of the quarter. The Greenbook forecast is conditioned on a particular path for the policy interest rate over the forecast horizon – which is not meant to be a prediction of that policy rate. That makes it a conditional forecast, as noted in the introduction. However, in evaluating the forecasts, we shall assess the Greenbook in exactly the same way as all the other forecasts, neglecting the effect of this conditioning. The available evidence indicates that all these judgmental forecasts do remarkably well, generally dominating model-based forecasts (Ang et al., 2007; Faust and Wright, 2009; Croushore, 2010) – even when the models are chosen *ex post* in light of known behavior of inflation in the forecast period.

In most proposed models, p lags of inflation (or the inflation gap) are included on the right-hand-side. We select p using the Bayes Information Criterion in the AR-GAP model, and use the *same* number of lags in all the other models that have p lags of inflation or the inflation gap (methods 1, 2, 3, 6, 8, 9, 12, 13 and 14 as listed above).[12]

The above set of models is a fairly comprehensive list of the sort of models that have appeared in the literature. But it is of course far from exhaustive. Other methods that have been proposed include threshold models (Dotsey et al., 2011), LASSO methods that do prediction and variable selection jointly (Bai and Ng, 2008), bootstrap aggregation (Inoue and Kilian, 2008) and household survey expectations (Inoue et al., 2009). There is moreover one additional natural family of forecasting approaches and that involves some sort of direct extraction of an inflation forecast from inflation-related financial market variables. These are treated separately in Section 3 due to the limited available sample.

2.6. Results of the Forecast Comparison Exercise

We can then evaluate the competing forecasts in terms of their real-time recursive out-of-sample RMSPEs. The results for all four inflation measures are shown in Table 1.2. All RMSPEs are reported relative to the benchmark of the "fixed ρ" forecast (an AR(1) in gap form with a fixed slope coefficient). A relative RMSPE below 1 means that the forecast is doing better than the benchmark. We pick this benchmark because it is very simple, yet is still amazingly hard to beat by much. We also assess the statistical significance of the deviations in relative RMSPEs from unity, using the test of Diebold and Mariano (1995), as discussed earlier.

The entries in Table 1.2 are mostly above 1, indicating that the AR in gap form with a fixed slope coefficient gives better out-of-sample forecasts than most alternatives.

---

[12] There is some evidence that BIC does best for direct forecasts while AIC does best for iterated forecasts (Inoue and Kilian, 2006; Marcellino et al., 2006).

Table 1.2 RMSPE of Selected Inflation Forecasts

Horizon	0	1	2	3	4	8
Panel A: GDP Deflator						
Direct	1.06**	1.00	0.96	1.04	1.09	1.34***
RAR	1.06**	1.02	1.01	1.17***	1.24***	1.53***
PC	1.07*	1.03	1.01	1.08	1.14*	1.41***
RW	1.19***	1.17**	1.09	1.04	1.06	1.25*
RW–AO	0.95	0.90*	0.91	0.94	0.96	1.05
UCSV	0.98	0.96	0.91	0.91	0.94	1.07
AR–GAP	1.03	0.97	0.95*	1.01	1.05	1.18***
PC–GAP	1.04	1.02	1.03	1.10*	1.17**	1.33***
PCTVN–GAP	1.04	1.02	1.03	1.10*	1.17**	1.30***
Term Structure VAR	1.07**	1.12**	1.16***	1.25***	1.32***	1.50***
TVP-VAR	0.99	0.94	0.95	0.94	1.00	1.21
EWA	1.02	0.94*	0.91**	0.97	1.01	1.15***
BMA	1.00	0.91**	0.89***	0.97	1.09	1.19**
FAVAR	1.02	1.03	1.07	1.06	1.13**	1.26***
DSGE	1.06	1.02	1.06	1.08	1.08	1.16
DSGE–GAP	1.02	0.95	0.97	0.98	0.97	1.05
BC	0.81***	0.85***	0.87***	0.90***	0.94**	
SPF	0.82***	0.84***	0.86***	0.88***	0.91**	
GB	0.84*	0.83**	0.82**	0.81**	0.82**	
Fixed ρ+ nowcast	0.81***	0.93***	0.97**	1.00	1.00	1.00
Panel B: PCE Deflator						
Direct	1.13**	1.18**	1.22*	1.24**	1.16**	1.32***
RAR	1.13**	1.21**	1.18*	1.22***	1.17**	1.33***
PC	1.14**	1.21**	1.24*	1.27**	1.19**	1.33***
RW	1.23***	1.35**	1.32*	1.38**	1.28**	1.4*
RW–AO	1.10**	1.08	1.07	1.07	1.04	1.16*
UCSV	1.06*	1.07	1.06	1.09	1.06	1.17
AR–GAP	1.09**	1.12**	1.13*	1.14***	1.10***	1.23***
PC–GAP	1.09**	1.14**	1.16**	1.19***	1.18***	1.35***
PCTVN–GAP	1.10**	1.15**	1.17**	1.20***	1.18***	1.32***
Term Structure VAR	1.08***	1.11***	1.12***	1.18***	1.21***	1.38***
TVP-VAR	1.13**	1.18*	1.18*	1.14*	1.10	1.29*
EWA	1.08**	1.12**	1.13	1.13**	1.08***	1.22***
BMA	1.08**	1.12**	1.14	1.14***	1.12***	1.31***
FAVAR	1.04	1.13**	1.12**	1.15***	1.14***	1.25***

(Continued)

Table 1.2 *Continued*

Horizon	0	1	2	3	4	8
Panel C: CPI						
Direct	1.02	1.10*	1.18**	1.23***	1.15***	1.23***
RAR	1.02	1.15*	1.11**	1.16***	1.13***	1.21***
PC	1.04	1.12*	1.19**	1.24***	1.16***	1.22***
RW	1.28**	1.40**	1.34**	1.46***	1.34**	1.51**
RW-AO	1.03	1.07*	1.07*	1.09**	1.07*	1.12*
UCSV	0.96	1.01	1.03	1.07**	1.03	1.10***
AR-GAP	1.00	1.06	1.10**	1.13***	1.11***	1.16***
PC-GAP	1.01	1.07*	1.12**	1.15***	1.15***	1.22***
PCTVN-GAP	1.02	1.09**	1.14***	1.16***	1.16***	1.22***
Term Structure VAR	1.00	1.06*	1.12***	1.15***	1.20***	1.23***
TVP-VAR	1.11	1.34	1.28	1.15**	1.40	1.48
EWA	0.99	1.06	1.10*	1.11***	1.09***	1.15***
BMA	1.02	1.09*	1.12*	1.12***	1.13***	1.19***
FAVAR	0.98	1.12**	1.12***	1.13***	1.14**	1.18***
BC	0.8**	0.98	1.00	0.97	0.99	
SPF	0.78**	0.97	1.00	0.99	0.99	
GB	0.82***	1.05	1.03	1.01	0.99	
Fixed ρ+ nowcast	0.80**	1.00	1.01	1.00**	1.00	1.00***
Panel D: Core CPI						
DAR	1.05	1.06*	1.20***	1.39***	1.38***	1.76***
RAR	1.05	1.11***	1.54***	1.73***	1.71***	2.13***
PC	1.09*	1.09	1.22***	1.41***	1.40***	1.77***
RW	1.17***	1.09	1.06	1.17**	1.11	1.13
RW-AO	0.97	0.97	0.98	0.97	0.98	1.08
UCSV	0.98	0.95	0.94	0.99	0.98	1.04
AR-GAP	1.10**	1.14***	1.24***	1.42***	1.45***	1.69***
PC-GAP	1.17***	1.24***	1.35***	1.55***	1.57***	1.82***
PCTVN-GAP	1.19***	1.27***	1.38***	1.56***	1.60***	1.83***
Term Structure VAR	1.38***	1.60***	1.64***	1.69***	1.77***	1.95***
TVP-VAR	1.03	1.00	0.95	0.98	0.98	1.23
EWA	1.04	1.08**	1.16**	1.32***	1.35***	1.60***
BMA	1.05	1.11***	1.16**	1.38***	1.45***	1.65***
FAVAR	1.21***	1.35***	1.32***	1.40***	1.65***	1.77***
GB	0.95	0.91*	0.88*	0.89*	0.87*	

Notes: This table reports the pseudo-out-of-sample recursive RMSPE of alternative *h*-quarter-ahead forecasts of four inflation measures (quarter-over-quarter), all relative to the benchmark of an AR(1) in "gap" form with a fixed slope coefficient. All forecasts are fully real-time, except for the large dataset methods (EWA, BMA, FAVAR), which use revised data on the predictors. The sample consists of data as observed in 1985Q1-2011Q4, with data going back to 1960Q1 in all cases. Cases in which the relative root mean square prediction error is significantly different from one at the 10, 5 and 1 percent significance levels are denoted with one, two and three asterisks, respectively. These are based on the Diebold and Mariano (1995), implemented as described in the text.

Simple time series methods that treat inflation as a stationary process – the direct forecast, the autoregression, and the Phillips Curve – do especially badly relative to the benchmark. The forecasts in gap form fare better. Still, most of the time, the "fixed ρ" benchmark does a bit better than the other forecasts in gap form, including the Phillips curve gap forecasts (PC-GAP and PCTVN-GAP). There are some cases in which other alternatives beat the benchmark, including the term structure VAR, or model averaging methods (equal-weighted or BMA), but the improvements are not great (at the very best about a 10 percent reduction in RMSPE), nor are these gains consistent across inflation measures or forecast horizons. Within the model averaging methods, Bayesian model averaging has a slight edge over equal-weighted model averaging in most, but not all, cases. Meanwhile, the forecasting performance of the factor augmented VAR is less good; the forecasting performance of factor-based models for inflation (and growth) seems to be fragile and dependent on the precise variables used in the large dataset (Faust and Wright, 2009). The Atkeson–Ohanian version of the random walk forecast and the UCSV and TVP-VAR forecasts, which are all non-stationary, generally do reasonably well, with performance comparable to the benchmark.

The DSGE model provides some of the better forecasts for GDP deflator inflation in Table 1.2. The observation that DSGE models that are competitive with alternatives has been made by Smets and Wouters (2003,2007), Edge and Gürkaynak (2010), Edge et al. (2010) and Kwon (2011) and this observation that DSGE models (incorporating certain frictions) can provide forecasts with reasonable accuracy has greatly enhanced their appeal to central banks around the world. Still, even these forecasts have RMSPE that is higher than the simple "fixed ρ" benchmark at all horizons. The DSGE-GAP model does a bit better; its forecast accuracy is roughly on a par with the simple benchmark.

2.7. Four Principles

We see four key principles emerging from our forecast comparison exercise:

2.7.1. Subjective Forecasts Do Best

The very best forecasts in Table 1.2 are the subjective ones: Blue Chip, SPF and Greenbook. Indeed, these are the only forecasts that consistently significantly improve on our simple benchmark. The fact that purely subjective forecasts are in effect the frontier of our ability to forecast inflation has been found by a number of recent papers (Ang et al., 2007; Faust and Wright, 2009; Croushore, 2010). Perhaps it should not be too surprising – private sector and Fed forecasters have access to econometric models, but add expert judgment to these models. Relative to the benchmark, the subjective forecasts give reductions in RMSPE of up to 25 percent. This means that they are doing far better than direct, RAR and PC forecasts for inflation. Within the set of subjective forecasts, the Greenbook seems to have a small edge (consistent with Romer and Romer, 2000), although this result is known to be somewhat dependent on the sample period. Note that in this exercise, the Blue Chip and SPF forecasts span the financial crisis and the accompanying severe recession, while the Greenbook forecasts end in 2006. Atkeson and Ohanian (2001) found that the random walk forecast did better than the Greenbook in a particular sample with one observation per year from 1983 to 1995, but that result appears to be special to the precise sample period (Faust and Wright, 2009).

Thus our first principle is that purely judgmental forecasts of inflation are right at the frontier of our forecasting ability. This in turn has substantive implications for empirical work beyond just the narrow question of forecast accuracy. It suggests that a useful way of assessing models is by their ability to match survey measures of inflation expectations (e.g., Del Negro and Eusepi, 2011). And it implies that in estimating forward-looking macroeconomic models, it may be better to treat survey forecasts as direct measures of expected future inflation (e.g., Adam and Padula (2003)), instead of the more commonly-used method of replacing expected inflation with future realized values and then using instrumental variables (Gali and Gertler, 1999).[13]

The next three principles shed some additional light on the advantage of the subjective forecasts and on whether further modeling work can erode this advantage.

2.7.2. Good Forecasts Must Account for a Slowly Varying Local Mean

All of the models that perform reasonably well have some method for taking account of a slowly evolving local mean for inflation. The models based on stationary specifications for inflation do consistently less well than models in gap form and three of the non-stationary models are among the best performers. During recent years, the stationary models have generated unreasonably high forecasts of inflation at longer horizons because inflation has been persistently below the full-sample average.

The evident desirability of using models that account for a slowly-varying trend naturally raises the question of the appropriate measurement of the trend component of inflation, τ_t. We have adopted the approach of using long-run survey expectations (Clark, 2011; Kozicki and Tinsley, 2012; Wright, forthcoming); but one might also measure the trend by exponential smoothing, or by measuring the permanent component from the UCSV model (following Stock and Watson, 2010). Any of these will capture the low-frequency shifts in inflation. Figure 1.2 plots three different real-time measures of the long-run trend inflation: the 5-to-10-year-ahead Blue Chip survey forecast, real-time exponentially smoothed inflation and the permanent component from the UCSV model. All share the same trend, but the survey forecasts declined more rapidly in the late 1980s and early 1990s than exponentially smoothed inflation. This suggests that in this case the subjective forecasters were quicker to realize the ongoing disinflation than

---

[13] See Kleibergen and Mavroeidis (2009) and Rudd and Whelan (2005) for discussion of the econometric problems that can arise with the instrumental variables approach.

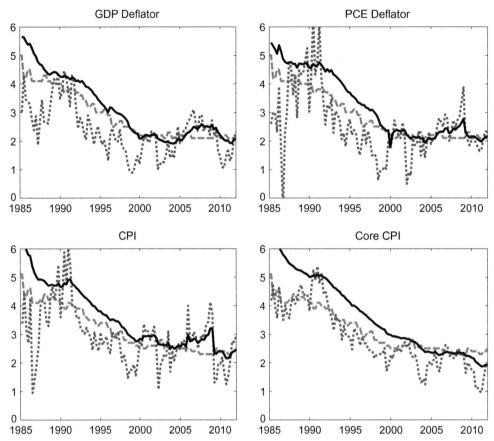

Figure 1.2 Alternative measures of trend inflation. *Notes:* Red dashes: 5-to-10-year-ahead Blue Chip inflation projections (GDP deflator for the upper panels, CPI for the lower panels). Blue dots: the UCSV trend inflation series, i.e., the real-time filtered estimates of the final level of the permanent component of each of the four inflation measures. Black solid line: exponentially smoothed real-time inflation, using each of the four inflation measures, and a smoothing coefficient of 0.95. (For interpretation of the references to color in this figure legend, the reader is referred to the web version of this book.)

one could have divined from the other methods, which essentially extrapolate recent inflation.[14]

We re-did all our gap forecasts using exponential smoothing to measure trend inflation in place of the long-run survey value, but found that this typically made the inflation forecasts less accurate. This brief exploration by no means demonstrates that subjective forecasts of the local mean inherently dominate their model-based counterparts. However, if these low-frequency shifts mainly involve fundamental change in the economy or

---

[14] Also, the trend from the UCSV model is a good bit less smooth than either the long-range Blue Chip survey forecast or exponentially smoothed inflation.

policymaking environment, there are reasons to believe that parsimonious econometric models based on standard determinants of inflation may have difficulty capturing all the relevant information. For example, a change in the long-run inflation target of the central bank might well be announced, but at the time of announcement this information would not be in the conventional determinants of inflation. This is one interpretation of the superior performance of the survey-based trend measure during the disinflation from the early 1980s peak.

Our second principle is that every inflation forecast for horizons longer than one or two quarters hence should involve some mechanism for capturing low-frequency local mean dynamics. Long-horizon survey forecasts seem to represent a good way of doing this.

2.7.3. The Nowcast

For horizon zero, the nowcast for all three subjective methods have RMSPEs around 20 percent smaller than the very best of the model-based forecasts (which already use the subjective information on the local mean from long-horizon survey forecasts). Where does the nowcasting advantage come from? One thing is clear from our experience observing the nowcasting process at the Fed and from our discussions with professional forecasters: nowcasting and backcasting in practice involve a very different process from forward-looking forecasting. This is because the relevant information set regarding the current quarter is generally much different from that for future quarters. Often a large portion of the source data for inflation are available before the official data are released; thus, a nowcasting exercise can in part involve replicating the data construction agency. Further, often there will have been special events such as hurricanes, dock strikes, special sales programs by auto manufacturers, etc., in the current quarter that are known and that can be directly accounted for in some way in making the nowcast. A specific recent example is that when Vancouver hosted the Winter Olympics in 2010, there was an enormous spike in lodging prices in Vancouver, and the Bank of Canada took this special information into account in its nowcast for Canada-wide inflation.[15]

We do not intend to take a strong position on whether the nowcasting embedded in subjective forecasts could be rendered entirely systematic so that we could remove the word "subjective." Perhaps some of the recently proposed mixed-frequency nowcasting models that have been proposed (e.g., Giannone et al., 2008; Andreou et al., 2008; Banbura et al., forthcoming) could achieve this, or at least get close. On the other hand, we suspect that an econometric model rich enough to systematically take account of all possible special factors that might be present in a given quarter would be unwieldy and not cost-effective.

---

[15] We are grateful to Sharon Kozicki for this example.

Part of the benefit of Greenbook and other judgmental forecasts at longer horizons flows from their advantage in measuring the current state of the economy [as suggested by Sims (2002), Giannone et al. (2008), Faust and Wright (2009)]. Fortunately, as Faust and Wright (2009) argue, we can easily give any model forecast the benefit of a good nowcast by simply augmenting the predictor database for each model with a high quality nowcast – bring all predictor data series up to the current quarter based on a good nowcast and then compare all the models' forecasting ability, having given all an equal footing on the nowcast.

Our third principle is that good forecasts begin with high quality nowcasts.

2.7.4. Heavy Shrinkage in the Use of Information Improves Inflation Forecasts

Table 1.2 includes the relative RMSPEs for GDP deflator and CPI inflation using an AR(1) model in gap form with a fixed slope coefficient (the "fixed ρ" method), but using the Blue Chip current-quarter nowcast as a jumping-off point. This is a trivial way to take account of the importance of the second and third principles. We use the Blue Chip projections for nowcasting, because they are available at the highest frequency, and are thus least likely to be stale, and also because they are available for the entire forecast period, whereas the Greenbook is not available for the last 5 years. Unfortunately, we do not have a Blue Chip nowcast for PCE deflator or core CPI inflation. So the "fixed ρ + nowcast" method is available only for GDP deflator and CPI inflation.

We can view this forecast path as having two boundaries – the forecast starts at the Blue Chip nowcast and converges at long horizons to the local mean estimated from Blue Chip. Our first two principles determine the boundary conditions, and the forecast path simply involves exponential decay from one boundary toward the other. This forecast turns out to do very well. At horizon 0 it is (by construction) the same as the Blue Chip forecast, which has excellent accuracy. But by getting the jumping-off point right, it also improves forecast accuracy at horizons 1 and 2, at least for GDP deflator inflation.

Indeed any of forecasting methods 1–10 above can be implemented using the current-quarter jumping-off point, based on Blue Chip nowcasts.[16] The DSGE forecasts can also be implemented using the current-quarter jumping-off point.[17] Table 1.3 reports the relative RMSPEs of these forecasts, all relative to the benchmark of the "fixed ρ" method starting from the current-quarter Blue Chip nowcast.

All of the models in gap form considered in Table 1.3 are effectively glide paths from the nowcast to the local mean. But the benchmark is different from the other forecasts in

---

[16] We do not have nowcasts for all the predictors in the large dataset in this chapter, so it is not possible to give the large dataset methods the advantage of a good nowcast. This problem could be dealt with by using the vintage datasets used in Faust and Wright (2009), but those datasets come from the Greenbook process and the forecast period would have to end outside the 5-year embargo for Greenbook forecasts.

[17] We have nowcasts only for some of the variables that are used in the DSGE model. What we do is to use the DSGE model to construct current-quarter forecasts, and replace these with nowcasts, where those are available, before constructing forecasts at longer horizons.

Table 1.3 RMSPE of Selected Inflation Forecasts Using Blue Chip Nowcasts as Jumping-Off Point

Horizon	0	1	2	3	4	8
Panel A: GDP Deflator						
Direct	1	0.98	0.95	1.02	1.07	1.32***
RAR	1	0.98	0.96	1.14***	1.22***	1.50***
PC	1	0.98	0.98	1.04	1.11*	1.39***
RW	1	0.93**	0.87**	0.92	0.94	1.06
RW–AO	1	0.95	0.88**	0.90	0.94	1.06
UCSV	1	0.95	0.89*	0.90*	0.92	1.04
AR–GAP	1	0.99	0.97	0.99	1.05**	1.18***
PC–GAP	1	1.01	1.02	1.07	1.14**	1.32***
PCTVN–GAP	1	1.01	1.02	1.07	1.15**	1.30***
Term Structure VAR	1	1.06*	1.11**	1.19***	1.27***	1.46***
TVP–VAR	1	0.95	0.89*	0.87**	0.92	1.09
DSGE	1	0.88**	0.92	1.01	1.02	1.13
DSGE–GAP	1	0.88***	0.89*	0.96	0.97	1.05
BC	1	0.91***	0.90***	0.91***	0.94**	
SPF	1.02	0.90***	0.88***	0.88***	0.91**	
GB	0.97	0.89*	0.84**	0.81**	0.82**	
Panel B: CPI						
DAR	1	1.13**	1.06*	1.07*	1.06**	1.14***
RAR	1	1.13**	1.06**	1.09**	1.1***	1.19***
PC	1	1.14**	1.06*	1.08*	1.06*	1.13***
RW	1	1.08*	1.08*	1.09*	1.07*	1.07
RW–AO	1	1.09*	1.09**	1.09**	1.07*	1.15*
UCSV	1	1.01	1.02	1.04*	1.02	1.07*
AR–GAP	1	1.08**	1.05**	1.07**	1.07**	1.16***
PC–GAP	1	1.08**	1.07***	1.09***	1.11***	1.23***
PCTVN–GAP	1	1.09**	1.08***	1.09***	1.12***	1.23***
Term Structure VAR	1	1.04	1.10***	1.15***	1.18***	1.23***
TVP–VAR	1	1.15*	1.25*	1.16**	1.09*	1.28
BC	1	0.98	1.00	0.98	0.99	
SPF	0.97***	0.97	1.00	0.99	0.99	
GB	0.99	1.05	1.02	1.02	0.99	

Notes: As for Table 1.2, except that the Blue Chip current-quarter forecast is treated as the final observation for all forecasts except the SPF and the Greenbook. The table shows RMSPEs relative to the benchmark of an AR(1) in "gap" form with a fixed slope coefficient, using the Blue Chip nowcast. By construction, the relative RMSPEs for the current quarter are all equal to 1 (except for the SPF and the Greenbook). Blue Chip nowcasts are only available for GDP deflator and CPI inflation.

that it has only one parameter, and that parameter is fixed independently of the data used in the remainder of the forecasting exercise. Yet all the models in gap form, even given the nowcast, struggle to do better than this benchmark. Some alternative model-based forecasts do a bit better in some cases, but the improvements are small and inconsistent.[18] In other words, we simply ask the Blue Chip survey "Where are we now?" and "Where will we be in 5–10 years?" This is a very draconian form of shrinkage that uses no data and no subjective views to directly inform the answer to "where will we be in 1 quarter, or 2, or …, 8?" Yet, the resulting forecast is close to the frontier of predictive performance.

Note that the UCSV forecast also does quite well relative to the alternatives, especially when it is given a good nowcast. Remember that the UCSV model is a univariate model involving only inflation. The UCSV forecast essentially involves taking current inflation, filtering out the bit that is taken to be purely transitory, and taking whatever is left as the forecast of inflation for all horizons. Viewed from the standpoint of the boundary conditions discussion, the forecast path for the UCSV model with nowcast starts with the Blue Chip nowcast and then for all other horizons jumps immediately to its estimate of the local mean. Thus, like the benchmark model, the UCSV makes no attempt to exploit *any* information regarding the path between the boundary conditions. The Atkeson–Ohanian random walk forecast can be thought of as doing a similar filtering exercise.

Our point is that these models seem to have a useful approach to measuring the local mean and nowcasting, but they essentially eschew any other ambitions. One might have hoped that they would provide a starting point for finding even better models that make more savvy use of the myriad available data series in order to forecast how inflation will evolve between the boundary conditions, but Table 1.3 shows that this is broadly incorrect. Once one has a good estimate of the local mean and a good nowcast, it is difficult to find any way to constructively use additional information from a model.

Thus our fourth principle is that heavy-handedness helps (H^3). Draconian restrictions (or shrinkage, or use of very informative priors) are generally required to get models close to the frontier of inflation forecasting performance.

At first sight, it might seem surprising or even worrisome that we can do little better in forecasting inflation than choosing a fixed glide path that moves quite quickly from an initial condition toward the local mean. But, observed by Edge and Gürkaynak (2010), if monetary policy is mainly directed toward offsetting deviations in inflation from a slowly-moving target, then deviations in inflation from that target should short-lived.

We now turn to some additional topics relating to our forecast comparison exercise.

2.8. Inflation Forecasts and the Financial Crisis

Inflation was volatile during the recent financial crisis and its aftermath (as can be seen in Figure 1.1). As discussed earlier, this poses a dilemma of whether or not to include this period in a forecast evaluation exercise. In Table 1.4 we report the RMSPEs of all the forecasts for GDP deflator inflation, relative to the benchmark of a fixed ρ forecast in gap

---

[18] Table 1.3 also reports results for the subjective forecasts. The Blue Chip, SPF and Greenbook forecasts do better than the benchmark for GDP deflator inflation at one- to four-quarter-ahead horizons, by anything from 6 to 23 percent. Thus, for GDP deflator inflation, the benefit of subjective forecasts is not solely the result of getting the boundaries right. However, the benchmark and subjective forecasts have almost identical accuracy for CPI inflation.

Table 1.4 RMSE of GDP Deflator Inflation Forecasts over the Pre-Crisis Period

Horizon	0	1	2	3	4	8
Direct	1.06*	0.98	0.93	0.97	1.03	1.27***
RAR	1.06*	1.01	0.98	1.13**	1.20**	1.49***
PC	1.07*	0.99	0.95	1.00	1.06	1.34***
RW	1.16**	1.14*	1.03	0.95	0.98	1.17
RW–AO	0.96	0.86**	0.86*	0.87*	0.90	1.00
UCSV	0.98	0.92	0.86*	0.84*	0.88	1.03
AR–GAP	1.03	0.95	0.93**	0.97	1.03	1.18***
PC–GAP	1.04	0.99	0.98	1.05	1.13*	1.32***
PCTVN–GAP	1.04	0.99	0.98	1.05	1.12*	1.30***
Term Structure VAR	1.06*	1.11**	1.16***	1.24***	1.31***	1.48***
TVP–VAR	1.02	0.95	0.89	0.86**	0.90	1.05
EWA	1.02	0.94*	0.91**	0.94*	1.00	1.15**
BMA	1.01	0.91*	0.87***	0.93*	1.02	1.12*
FAVAR	1.03	1.00	1.02	1.06	1.13*	1.28***
DSGE	1.07	1.04	1.07	1.07	1.06	1.13
DSGE–GAP	1.02	0.97	0.97	0.96	0.94	1.00
BC	0.86**	0.85***	0.87***	0.90**	0.93**	
SPF	0.85**	0.83***	0.84***	0.86***	0.89**	
GB	0.84*	0.83**	0.82**	0.80**	0.81**	
Fixed ρ+ nowcast	0.86**	0.93***	0.98**	1.00	1.00	1.00

Note: As for Table 1.2, except that only forecasts made for 2007Q3 and earlier are included.

form, over a pre-crisis sample. Table 1.4 is therefore just like Table 1.2, except that only forecasts that were made for quarters 2007Q3 and earlier are included. As it turns out, perhaps surprisingly, the relative RMSPEs in the pre-crisis sample (Table 1.4) are very similar to those in the full sample (Table 1.2). Thus inclusion of the financial crisis does not materially change our conclusions as to the relative average accuracy of competing forecast methods for GDP deflator inflation. The same is true for the other three inflation measures (pre-crisis results for these are not shown, to conserve space). It is also true for methods using a nowcast.

2.9. How Different are the Better Model Forecasts?

Table 1.5 shows the correlations of nine good forecasts for GDP deflator inflation, at the four-quarter-ahead horizon. These forecasts are all roughly comparable in their *average* predictive performance. It might be that they are quite different forecasts and just so happen to give the same average forecast accuracy. Or, their comparable performance might owe to their being roughly the same forecast. Which it is matters a great deal – to the extent that they are fundamentally different forecasts, we might want to find some way of combining them to produce a more accurate prediction, or might be interested in characterizing the circumstances under which one forecast does particularly well.

Table 1.5 Correlations among Selected Inflation Forecasts

	Fixed ρ	PC-GAP	VAR	EWA	BMA	BC	SPF	DSGE	DSGE-GAP
Panel A: GDP Deflator									
Fixed ρ	1.00	0.78	0.80	0.89	0.82	0.96	0.94	−0.08	0.50
PC-GAP	0.78	1.00	0.96	0.90	0.89	0.84	0.84	0.22	0.62
VAR	0.80	0.96	1.00	0.85	0.85	0.85	0.85	0.12	0.55
EWA	0.89	0.90	0.85	1.00	0.93	0.91	0.90	0.18	0.66
BMA	0.82	0.89	0.85	0.93	1.00	0.84	0.84	0.17	0.63
BC	0.96	0.84	0.85	0.91	0.84	1.00	0.98	0.01	0.55
SPF	0.94	0.84	0.85	0.90	0.84	0.98	1.00	0.02	0.54
DSGE	−0.08	0.22	0.12	0.18	0.17	0.01	0.02	1.00	0.81
DSGE-GAP	0.50	0.62	0.55	0.66	0.63	0.55	0.54	0.81	1.00
Panel B: PCE Deflator									
Fixed ρ	1.00	0.80	0.80	0.85	0.51				
PC-GAP	0.80	1.00	0.96	0.92	0.92				
VAR	0.80	0.96	1.00	0.84	0.84				
EWA	0.85	0.92	0.84	1.00	0.96				
BMA	0.81	0.92	0.84	0.96	1.00				
Panel C: CPI									
Fixed ρ	1.00	0.79	0.72	0.83	0.73	0.96	0.94		
PC-GAP	0.79	1.00	0.87	0.92	0.90	0.83	0.84		
VAR	0.72	0.87	1.00	0.68	0.73	0.77	0.78		
EWA	0.83	0.92	0.68	1.00	0.92	0.82	0.83		
BMA	0.73	0.90	0.73	0.92	1.00	0.72	0.71		
BC	0.96	0.83	0.77	0.82	0.72	1.00	0.99		
SPF	0.94	0.84	0.78	0.83	0.71	0.99	1.00		
Panel D: Core CPI									
Fixed ρ	1.00	0.88	0.80	0.97	0.94				
PC-GAP	0.88	1.00	0.97	0.95	0.91				
VAR	0.80	0.97	1.00	0.89	0.85				
EWA	0.97	0.95	0.89	1.00	0.98				
BMA	0.94	0.91	0.85	0.98	1.00				

Notes: This table shows the correlations among selected out-of-sample forecasts of each of the four inflation indicators considered in this chapter.

Consistent with Sims (2002), Table 1.5 shows that most of the forecasts are highly correlated with each other.

The exceptions to this result of high correlation are the DSGE forecast (which has little correlation with other alternatives over the full sample period) and the DSGE-GAP forecast (which has moderate correlation with other alternatives). Figure 1.3 plots the DSGE, DSGE-GAP and AR-GAP four-quarter-ahead forecasts for GDP deflator

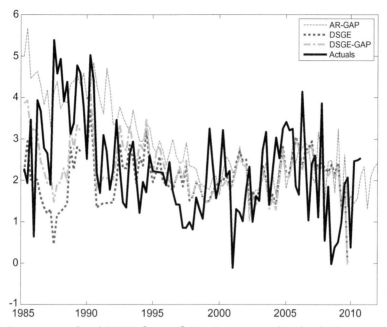

Figure 1.3 Four-quarter-ahead GDP Deflator Inflation Forecasts and Realized Values. *Notes:* The forecasts extend through 2011Q4, but realized values are only available for forecasts made in 2010Q2 and earlier (given the convention of defining realized values as the data as observed in the middle of the second quarter after the quarter to which the data refer).

inflation, along with the subsequent actual realized values, shifted back four quarters, so that the forecasts and actuals would coincide if the forecast were perfect. The DSGE forecast bounces around 2.5 percent for the whole sample, which is the prior mean for steady-state inflation in this model. Meanwhile, the AR–GAP forecasts share the downward trend of long-run Blue Chip survey forecasts. Thus, the AR–GAP and DSGE forecasts have different trending behavior, and that's why they are effectively uncorrelated with each other in the full sample. The DSGE-GAP forecast, which has a prior mean centered around the most recent long-run Blue Chip survey forecasts, not surprisingly picks up some of the downward trend in these survey projections. It has consequently a higher correlation with the AR–GAP and other forecasts. Indeed, from the mid 1990s to the financial crisis, the DSGE, DSGE-GAP and AR–GAP forecasts do not just have comparable RMSPEs – they are strikingly similar forecasts.

The high correlation between forecasts means that, while there could be some scope for improving predictive accuracy by forecast combination, it cannot be the magic bullet. Aiolfi et al. (2010) consider combinations of various survey and time series forecasts. They find that there can be some gains from such combinations, but survey forecasts are still hard to beat. To illustrate this point, we consider forecasts that put weight λ on the Blue

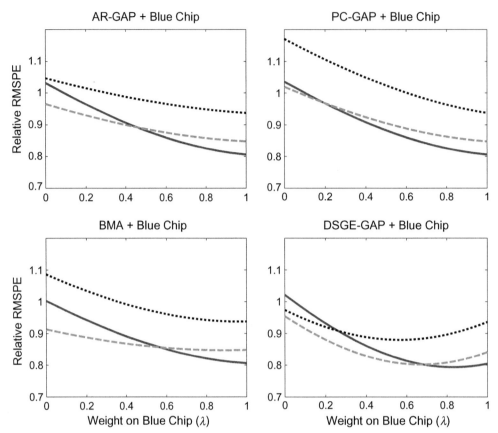

Figure 1.4 Relative RMSPEs of combination forecasts. *Notes:* In each panel a combination forecast was formed that places weight λ on the Blue Chip forecast and 1 − λ on some econometric forecast (real-time forecasts made 1985Q1-2011Q4). The blue solid line, red dashed line and black dotted line refer to current-quarter, one-quarter-ahead and four-quarter-ahead forecasts, respectively. (For interpretation of the references to color in this figure legend, the reader is referred to the web version of this book.)

Chip prediction and 1 − λ on some other forecast. Figure 1.4 plots the relative RMSPEs of these survey + time series forecasts against the weight λ (for GDP deflator inflation at various forecast horizons). In most cases, the optimal weight on the survey forecast turns out to be 1. The only exception to this is that at some horizons, even though the Blue Chip forecast is more accurate than the DSGE-GAP model, a combination can do a little better than even the Blue Chip projection.

2.10. A Comment on the DSGE Model Forecasts

A long period of DSGE model refinement using the postwar sample preceded Smets and Wouters finding a particular DSGE model with forecasting performance on a par with standard benchmarks. This was a remarkable and important achievement. The results of this chapter suggest, however, that there is still more to understand about the DSGE model forecast accuracy. From the standpoint of the economics profession we may hope that the solid performance is due to the fact that the model correctly captures important economic relations. From a skeptical scientific perspective, however, this remains far from clear.

The results earlier in this section give us reason to believe that part of the advantage of the DSGE model stems from use of a prior for steady-state inflation specified in light of the full estimation sample – a prior that probably was at odds with what most agents actually expected at the time. More broadly, it's very hard to imagine a fully real-time assessment of the Smets–Wouters model. Unlike a simple time series model, it involves many specification decisions and choices about the prior. We would like to know how the model would have fared if *all* these choices had been made in real-time. But in the model that we have, these choices – with the possible exception of the steady-state inflation prior – are made in light of the full estimation sample.[19]

Further, a main result in our study is that very heavy-handed restrictions improve forecast accuracy over less restricted models. In short, we need models that keep the forecast from following the sample too closely. In our view it is an open question whether the DSGE model performance stems not from being "right" in some meaningful economic sense, but simply from being heavy-handed. Cynically, one can point out that fitting poorly is one way to avoid overfitting. More generously, the model may amount to a way to choose an arbitrary glide path between two end points. Any such glide path does pretty well, but doing well thereby need not be seen as much support for any particular economic story.

2.11. The Phillips Curve

Our results for the Phillips curve models are not very supportive, consistent with the available evidence on the forecasting performance of the Phillips curve, which is mixed and sensitive to the sample period (Brayton et al., 1999; Liu and Rudebusch, 2010; Stock and Watson, 2009). There is plentiful evidence of a tradeoff between slack and inflation (e.g., Stock and Watson, 2010 and Meier, 2010). Another example is that at the time of writing the euro-zone countries with the highest unemployment are exhibiting the most disinflation. Still, none of this translates into clear and consistent improvements in out-of-sample forecast accuracy. In our experience, defenders of the Phillips curve models often react to negative results by arguing that non-linearities may render the model more useful for forecasting in some periods than in others.

Standard theory gives good reasons for possible non-linearity in the Phillips curve, so these protests should be taken seriously. Filardo (1998) and Barnes and Olivei (2003) have posited a non-linearity in the Phillips curve whereby it should be most useful for

---

[19] Tetlow and Ironside (2007) is a useful reminder of how revisions to model specification can be at least as important as revisions to data.

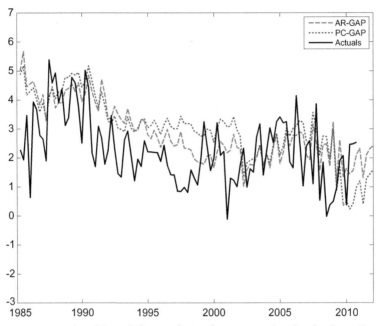

Figure 1.5 Four-quarter-ahead GDP deflator inflation forecasts and realized values. *Notes:* The forecasts extend through 2011Q4, but realized values are only available for forecasts made in 2010Q2 and earlier (given the convention of defining realized values as the data as observed in the middle of the second quarter after the quarter to which the data refer).

forecasting inflation when unemployment is cyclically high. Stock and Watson (2010) and Dotsey et al. (2011) find some support for this view. Ball et al. (1988) have considered versions of the Phillips curve in which it flattens at low levels of inflation. That would suggest that Phillips curve should give larger improvements in forecast inflation at times when the inflation rate is relatively high.

To examine the forecasting performance of the Phillips curve over time in more detail, Figure 1.5 plots the PC–GAP and AR–GAP four-quarter-ahead forecasts for GDP deflator inflation, along with the subsequent actual realized values, again shifted back four quarters, so that the forecasts and actuals would coincide if the forecast were perfect. Indeed, it can be seen that there were periods in which inclusion of the AR–GAP turned out to be closer to the mark than the PC–GAP forecast. This is true in the mid to late 1990s, when the low level of unemployment led the PC–GAP forecast to project a rise in inflation that never occurred. It is also true at the end of the sample, where inflation came in higher than would be predicted by the PC–GAP forecast [see Ball and Mazumder (2011)]. On the other hand, there are episodes where the PC–GAP forecast did well, including around the business cycle peak in 1990 and around the year 2000.

2.12. Conditional Forecast Comparisons

Claims that a particular forecast (such as the Phillips curve) may work better at some times than at others motivate us to consider conditional forecast comparisons. In the comparison between any two forecasts, one might ask the question of whether one forecast is better *conditional* on some other variable. In principle, two forecasts could be equally good on average, but one forecast could be better than the other under certain conditions (Giacomini and White, 2006). The question can be posed in two different ways. We might ask if one forecast is better than another conditional on some variable that was known at the time that the forecast was made. Of course, if one forecast is better than another only conditional on some other observed variable, then this must indicate that both forecasting models are in some way misspecified and that some kind of non-linearity is called for, but implementing this may be too ambitious. Alternatively, we might ask if one forecast is better than another conditional on some variable that is not yet known when the forecast is made. For example, we might ask if one forecast is better than another if the forecast turns out to refer to a period during a recession. Although this does not give a direct strategy for improving forecast accuracy, the question might still be of interest if the user of the forecast has a loss function that penalizes forecast misses at some times more than at others. For example, the central bank may be particularly averse to large forecast errors if they happen during recessions.

We consider both questions. Table 1.2 showed that over the last quarter century, it was hard to do much better than the "fixed ρ" forecast. But we can also compare the out-of-sample relative RMSPEs of the forecasts *conditional* on the forecast being made at a time of cyclically high inflation or cyclically high unemployment.

We define a period of cyclically high inflation as being one where the average of inflation over the previous four quarters is above the trend. Following Stock and Watson, we define the unemployment gap as the difference between the real-time unemployment rate and the real-time average unemployment rate over the previous 12 quarters. We then define a period of cyclically high unemployment as one in which this unemployment gap exceeds 0.5 percent. One might think of this as a proxy for NBER recession quarters, but it is a fully real-time measure, whereas the NBER peaks and troughs are called only well after the fact. Also, this criterion is a bit less stringent than the NBER recession dates. Over our sample, there are three periods of elevated unemployment using this definition: from 1990Q4 to 1993Q1, from 2001Q4 to 2003Q4 and from 2008Q3 to 2011Q1.

Tables 1.6 and 1.7 show the out-of-sample relative RMSPEs of GDP deflator inflation forecasts conditional on the forecast being made at times of cyclically high inflation/ unemployment, respectively. As can be seen in Table 1.6, the ability of the Phillips curve, or other forecasting methods, to outperform the AR-GAP benchmark is about the same at times of cyclically high inflation as it is in the sample as a whole. The results in Table 1.7 are a little more encouraging. It seems to be slightly easier to beat the AR-GAP benchmark at times of high unemployment. In particular, Phillips curve forecasts, give

Table 1.6 RMSPE of GDP Deflator Inflation Forecasts
Forecasts Made During Periods of Elevated Inflation

Horizon	0	1	2	3	4	8
Direct	1.12**	1.13**	1.11	1.39**	1.38***	1.66***
RAR	1.12**	1.15**	1.16	1.42**	1.43***	1.74***
PC	1.15**	1.19**	1.17**	1.47***	1.48***	1.78***
RW	1.31***	1.34***	1.27	1.37***	1.29***	1.43***
RW–AO	0.92	1.01	1.01	1.10*	1.11***	1.21***
UCSV	0.94	1.05	1.03	1.12*	1.13***	1.24***
AR–GAP	1.05	1.06	1.03	1.20**	1.16***	1.22***
PC–GAP	1.08	1.12*	1.09*	1.27***	1.30***	1.43***
PCTVN–GAP	1.06	1.09	1.04	1.19***	1.20***	1.31***
Term Structure VAR	1.17***	1.19*	1.11	1.26***	1.33***	1.54***
TVP–VAR	0.91	1.00	1.03	1.01	1.08	1.23***
EWA	1.02	1.02	0.98	1.10***	1.05	1.12***
BMA	1.01	0.97	0.98	1.12***	0.94	1.00
FAVAR	0.92	1.04	1.00	0.88*	0.86*	1.06*
DSGE	1.07*	1.04	1.15	1.22	1.08*	1.26***
DSGE–GAP	1.06*	1.01	1.10	1.12	1.00	1.12*
BC	0.88	0.94	0.94	0.99	1.01	
SPF	0.89	0.91*	0.87**	0.96*	1.01	
GB	1.43**	0.87	0.98	1.14*	1.05	
Fixed ρ+ nowcast	0.88	0.98	0.98	1.00	1.01***	1.00

Notes: As for Table 1.2, except that only forecasts made during periods of elevated inflation are considered.

small improvements in forecasting inflation. The term structure VAR also does better in this subsample than in the sample period as a whole. However, the improvements are not very big, and this exercise is based on quite a small sample size. In several cases the relative RMSPEs are not significantly different from one. Although the evidence is tantalizing, and highly relevant to the current situation, it is hard to have great confidence that the PC-GAP will continue to deliver better inflation forecasts in future periods of cyclically high unemployment.

We also evaluated the RMSPEs of inflation forecasts conditional on the forecast referring to a period in the 3 years immediately after an NBER business cycle trough. In contrast to the results in Tables 1.6 and 1.7, this is an example of conditioning on a variable known only after the fact. Results are reported in Table 1.8. There is some slight evidence that the predictability of inflation is higher in the early stages of expansions than at other times. But the improvement in forecast accuracy is not great. We did the same exercise for the 3 years immediately before an NBER business cycle peak, and for NBER recessions. The results are not reported, but the "fixed ρ" benchmark was even harder to beat in these periods.

Table 1.7 RMSPE of GDP Deflator Inflation Forecasts
Forecasts Made During Periods of Elevated Unemployment

Horizon	0	1	2	3	4	8
Direct	1.10**	1.03	1.03	1.10	1.16*	1.32***
RAR	1.10**	1.06	1.09	1.25**	1.31***	1.48***
PC	1.10**	1.07	1.08	1.12	1.17*	1.26***
RW	1.25***	1.28***	1.28*	1.07	1.19**	1.42*
RW-AO	0.94	0.98	1.04	1.05	1.03	1.08
UCSV	0.96	1.05	1.00	0.95	0.99	1.07
AR–GAP	1.07**	0.98	0.98	1.02	1.06**	1.19***
PC–GAP	1.05	1.01	1.05	1.08	1.11	1.12*
PCTVN-GAP	1.05	1.01	1.05	1.06	1.10	1.11
Term Structure VAR	1.04	0.95	1.02	1.04	1.12	1.23***
TVP-VAR	0.96	0.96	1.09	1.07	1.19	1.55
EWA	1.04	0.90	0.88*	0.92	0.99	1.13**
BMA	1.02	0.83**	0.82**	0.93	1.22	1.33
FAVAR	1.05	1.08	1.18	0.94	1.06	1.23**
DSGE	1.07	1.12	1.02	0.87	0.83	0.78
DSGE-GAP	1.05	1.05	0.96	0.84	0.79	0.93
BC	0.73**	0.78**	0.83*	0.86**	0.88*	
SPF	0.75**	0.76**	0.79**	0.82**	0.83*	
GB	0.61**	0.74*	0.81	0.77	0.70	
Fixed ρ + nowcast	0.73**	0.89*	0.96*	1.00	1.00	1.00

Notes: As for Table 1.2, except that only forecasts made during periods of elevated unemployment are considered.

Overall, we have found only weak evidence for improved forecastability of inflation relative to the "fixed ρ" benchmark, even when we condition on other variables.

2.13. Time-Varying Predictability

Closely related to the idea of assessing the performance of a forecast relative to a benchmark conditional on some other variable, one might also ask if the forecast does better than a benchmark *over a certain period of time*. Giacomini and Rossi (2010) propose a "fluctuations test" which uses the test statistic of Diebold and Mariano (1995), but computed over m-year rolling windows. They derive the asymptotic distribution of the maximum value of this statistic, over all possible windows. The null hypothesis is that the forecast *never* beats the benchmark. Rossi and Sekhposyan (2010) apply this test to forecasting CPI inflation. They find that certain variables – such as industrial production and capacity utilization – had significant predictive power for future inflation in the early 1980s, but that it subsequently disappeared.

Table 1.8 RMSPE of GDP Deflator Inflation
Forecasts Made for Periods During the Early Stages of Expansions

Horizon	0	1	2	3	4	8
Direct	1.13**	1.06	0.99	1.17	1.24**	1.56***
RAR	1.13**	1.09	1.02	1.32***	1.37***	1.66***
PC	1.16**	1.10	1.07	1.22	1.30***	1.67***
RW	1.20**	1.29**	1.14	1.14	1.23*	1.45***
RW-AO	1.01	0.94	0.98	1.05	1.04	1.13
UCSV	1.02	1.00	0.94	0.95	1.02	1.16*
AR-GAP	1.09*	1.02	0.96	1.07	1.10**	1.24***
PC-GAP	1.11	1.04	1.05	1.15	1.22**	1.44***
PCTVN-GAP	1.13*	1.06	1.05	1.12	1.17	1.34***
Term Structure VAR	1.06	0.99	0.98	1.08	1.23**	1.55***
TVP-VAR	1.10	0.98	1.03	1.08	1.19	1.51*
EWA	1.08	0.97	0.88**	0.96	1.01	1.16***
BMA	1.02	0.85**	0.8**	0.96	1.21	1.28
FAVAR	1.24**	1.16	1.17	0.96	1.03	1.16***
DSGE	1.02	1.00	0.96	1.01	0.90	0.91
DSGE-GAP	1.00	0.97	0.91*	0.96	0.84	0.87
BC	0.90	0.81**	0.83*	0.85**	0.90*	
SPF	0.89	0.80**	0.79**	0.80**	0.86	
GB	0.84	0.91	0.82	0.80	0.74	
Fixed ρ+ nowcast	0.90	0.90***	0.98**	1.00	1.00	1.00

Notes: As for Table 1.2, except that only forecasts made for one of the 12 quarters after business cycle troughs are considered.

2.14. Alternative Measures of Forecast Quality

In this chapter, we focus on assessing forecast quality by RMSPEs. Some researchers prefer instead to use more general loss functions (Patton and Timmermann, 2007), such as the asymmetric LINEX loss function. At least from the perspective of forecasting inflation in a central bank, or a similar public policy environment, we are a little skeptical that there would be a large and systematic preference for overpredicting inflation rather than underpredicting it (or vice versa). However, if one wishes to assess forecast quality using absolute prediction error, or an asymmetric loss function, that is of course possible too.

Another way of assessing forecast quality is to run a forecast efficiency regression, projecting the forecast errors onto variables that were known at the time that the forecast was being made, such as the forecast itself. [20] This is not a horse race between two forecasts.

---

[20] A special case is the Mincer–Zarnowitz regression, which is most often written as a regression of the variable to be forecast on the forecast itself; efficiency requires the intercept and slope to be zero and one respectively. This is algebraically equivalent to requiring both intercept and slope coefficients to be zero in a regression of the forecast error on the forecast itself.

Rather it is a test of the null hypothesis that a particular forecast is giving the conditional expectation of the future value of the variable at the time that the projection is being made.[21] Clearly the null is rejected if the regression coefficients are significantly different from zero; in this case, there exists in principle some way of correcting the forecast to make it more accurate. Romer and Romer (2000) and Patton and Timmermann (2012) are among the authors who have applied tests of this sort to the Greenbook and other growth and inflation forecasts. Patton and Timmermann consider a variant of the test which evaluates the hypothesis of forecast efficiency at multiple horizons jointly (increasing power) and they find evidence against the efficiency of the Greenbook inflation forecasts. This implies that there is some scope to improve on Greenbook forecasts, despite their low RMSPEs.[22]

Patton and Timmermann (2012) also show that forecast rationality under quadratic loss implies certain bounds on the second moments of forecasts and forecast errors across horizons, and develop tests of these variance bounds. Again they find evidence against the rationality of Greenbook forecasts. For example, the variance of a rational forecast ought to be decreasing in the forecast horizon, but Patton and Timmermann (2012) document that the variance of Greenbook forecasts for GDP deflator inflation is actually *increasing* in the forecast horizon.

3. MARKET-BASED MEASURES OF THE INFLATION OUTLOOK

For over a decade, the U.S. Treasury has issued Treasury inflation-protected securities (TIPS): debt securities for which the coupon and principal payments are indexed to the CPI, in addition to conventional nominal bonds. Comparing the yields on these two types of Treasury bonds allows us to compute measures of *inflation compensation* or *breakeven inflation*, defined as the rate of inflation that would give investors the same return at maturity on a nominal security and an indexed security.[23] They are often interpreted as *market-based measures of inflation expectations* and receive enormous attention from policymakers and in the press. The idea of being able to read inflation expectations directly out of market prices has long held an allure for economists and central bankers – indeed this was one of the motivations for issuing TIPS in the first place (Greenspan, 1992; Campbell and Shiller, 1996 and Bernanke and Woodford, 1997). We will argue that, while

---

[21] If the forecaster has quadratic loss, the forecast efficiency regression tests whether this loss function is being minimized, but this does not apply to other loss functions (Elliott, Komunjer and Timmermann (2005)).

[22] It is important to bear in mind that even if such a test results in a rejection of the null hypothesis of forecast efficiency, this does not necessarily mean that some other forecast will be more accurate in terms of *out-of-sample* predictive ability. Croushore (2012) and Arai (2012) discuss using the Patton and Timmermann (2012) test to adjust Greenbook forecasts.

[23] Smoothed yield curves have been fitted to both the nominal and TIPS coupon securities (Gürkaynak et al. (2007, 2010)) and can be used for computing inflation compensation (or forward inflation compensation) at different maturities.

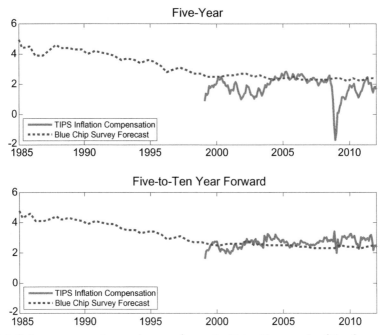

Figure 1.6 Inflation compensation and survey forecasts. *Notes:* The panels of the figure show TIPS-based inflation compensation at 5- and 5-to-10-year forward horizons and the corresponding maturity Blue Chip survey CPI forecasts. The TIPS-based inflation compensation series are from the dataset of Gürkaynak et al. (2010): these data are available only back to 1999.

direct high-frequency market-based information is valuable, interpreting these spreads as pure measures of inflation expectations is wrong and potentially dangerous.

Figure 1.6 plots the 5- and 5-to-10-year-ahead forward rates of inflation compensation from TIPS. They are quite volatile, especially during the acute phase of the recent financial crisis – if taken literally as inflation forecasts, they would lead policymakers to be in a constant state of panic, at some times about excessively high inflation, and at other times about excessively low inflation. This figure also shows the corresponding-maturity survey forecasts of inflation, from Blue Chip. These trended downwards during the 1990s, but have been very flat over the past decade. Unfortunately, it would take a very long sample to directly evaluate the RMSPEs of these different long-term inflation forecasts, which we clearly do not have.

However, it seems clear that forward inflation compensation from TIPS is too volatile to represent a rational forecast of the long-run expected level of inflation, or the implicit inflation target of the central bank. We can be more precise about this following a line of reasoning proposed by Gürkaynak et al. (2010). If a 5-to-10-year forward rate of inflation compensation really is the rational expectation of inflation in the long-run, then it should be a martingale. Otherwise, the expectation of the long-run expectation of inflation tomorrow would differ from the long-run expectation of inflation today, which

Table 1.9 Volatility of Changes in Five-To-Ten-Year Forward Inflation Compensation at Selected Horizons

Horizon	Standard Deviation (Basis Points)	Variance Ratio Statistic
One day	5.1	
One month	21.4	−1.38
Three months	27.8	−2.34**
Six months	33.9	−2.13**

Notes: This table shows the standard deviation of 1-day and 1-, 3- and 6-month changes in the 5-to-10-year forward rate of inflation compensation. They are computed assuming 22 days per month. The variance ratio statistic is the heteroskedasticity robust test statistic of Lo and Mackinlay (1988) and has a standard normal asymptotic distribution. The sample period is from the start of 1999 to the end of 2011. One, two and three asterisks denote significance at the 10, 5 and 1 percent significance levels respectively.

is impossible by the law of iterated expectations. And if forward inflation compensation is a martingale, then the volatility of k-period changes in forward inflation compensation must be k times the volatility of one-period changes. This can in turn be tested using the variance ratio test of Lo and Mackinlay (1988). Table 1.9 shows the standard deviation of 1-day and 1-, 3- and 6-month changes in 5-to-10-year forward inflation compensation, along with variance-ratio test statistics. Under the martingale hypothesis, the variance-ratio test statistics have a standard normal asymptotic distribution.[24] However, we see in Table 1.9 that the test rejects in the left tail, meaning that the volatility of longer-term changes in inflation compensation is too small relative to the volatility of daily changes for 5-to-10-year forward inflation compensation to be a martingale.

Thus, the spreads between nominal and index-linked debt embody inflation expectations, but their interpretation is evidently also complicated by inflation risk premia, and by the different liquidity of nominal and TIPS securities.[25] Normally, one would expect the inflation risk premium to drive TIPS yields down relative to their nominal counterparts, causing inflation compensation to widen. Meanwhile, one would expect the liquidity premium to drive the less liquid TIPS yields up relative to their nominal counterparts, causing inflation compensation to narrow. Both of these effects are presumably time-varying. As can be seen in Figure 1.6, 5-year inflation compensation is typically below the survey expectation, perhaps because the liquidity premium is the dominant effect. On the other hand, 5-to-10-year forward inflation compensation is typically above the survey expectation. Perhaps this is because the liquidity premium is to some extent "differenced out" in the forward rate whereas investors are willing to pay a large risk premium to compensate for inflation risk over longer horizons. Term structure models can be used

[24] The test statistic is $z^*(q)$ in the notation of Lo and MacKinlay. This test allows for time-varying conditional heterokedasticity.

[25] The same conclusion is reached by Pflueger and Viceira (2011), who instead use predictive regressions to show that the excess returns on a long-nominal and short-TIPS portfolio are time-varying.

to attempt to decompose inflation compensation into inflation expectations, liquidity premia, and inflation risk premia (see, for example, D'Amico et al., 2010 and Joyce et al., 2010). The resulting inflation expectations are far more stable than raw inflation compensation, but the available sample size is too short to evaluate these as inflation forecasts.

3.1. New Inflation Derivatives

Recently some other alternative market-based inflation measures have developed. There is now an over-the-counter market in inflation swaps. These are contracts where one party agrees to pay an interest rate on a notional underlying principle that is fixed at the start of the contract, while the other party agrees to pay the realized inflation rate on that same notional principle. Only the net of the two amounts actually changes hands. Under risk-neutrality, the fixed rate should equal expected inflation over the life of the contract.

Figure 1.7 plots the 10-year inflation swaps rate along with the ten-year rate of TIPS inflation compensation. The two have generally moved together, with the swaps rate being slightly higher.[26] They diverged noticeably in late 2008, in the most severe part of the financial crisis. Campbell et al. (2009), Hu and Worah (2009) suggest a rather technical explanation for this. Parties had lent money to Lehman in the collateralized repo market. Following the demise of Lehman, this collateral had to be sold. A good part of the collateral was in TIPS, which are comparatively illiquid. The prices of TIPS bonds fell and their yields rose, as the collateral had to be sold at firesale prices, even more than would be explained by the obviously disinflationary impact of the financial crisis and the resulting recession. The swaps market was apparently not affected in the same way, or at least not to the same extent. In any event, Figure 1.7 should cast considerable doubt on the idea of reading inflation expectations directly from either bond spreads or inflation derivatives. Haubrich et al. (2008) consider a term structure model using TIPS, inflation swaps, realized inflation data and surveys jointly to infer a measure of inflation expectations.

There are also short-horizon inflation swaps which provide information about investors' assessment of short-run inflation prospects, although again these are not pure inflation expectations. Figure 1.8 shows the time series of 1-year-ahead inflation swap rates, the shortest maturity that is available. Subsequent realized CPI inflation is also shown in the figure, shifted back 1 year, so that the forecasts and actuals would coincide if the forecast were perfect. The inflation swap rates are available only back to 2005, and so it is still too soon to assess their performance as predictors of inflation. However, looking at Figure 1.8, we can say that while these short-term inflation swap rates may be telling us something

---

[26] Fleckenstein et al. (2010) discuss the fact that inflation swap rates are higher than the spread between nominal and TIPS bond yields. They interpret this as representing an anomaly in the pricing of TIPS. But as the inflation swaps market is quite small, it would seem to us more natural to view it as an anomaly in the pricing of inflation swaps. In a bit more detail, customers in the inflation swaps market almost uniformly want to buy insurance against inflation. Inflation swaps dealers must hedge this risk, and they do so using TIPS and nominal Treasuries. We interpret the relatively high inflation swap rates as the "fee" that dealers require to provide this insurance service.

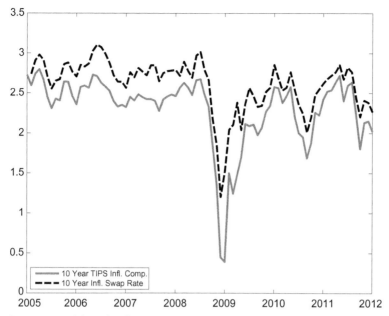

Figure 1.7 Ten-year TIPS-based inflation compensation and inflation swap rates. *Notes:* The TIPS-based inflation compensation series are from the dataset of Gürkaynak et al. (2010). The inflation swap rates are from Bloomberg.

about near-term inflation expectations, they appear to move almost in lockstep with *past* inflation.

Very recently, inflation options have started to be actively traded. These take the form of caps and floors. A simple cap is a contract which entitles the holder to receive a payment at maturity that is a fraction $\max((1+\pi)^n - (1+s)^n, 0)$ of a notional underlying principle, where π is the realized average inflation rate over the life of the contract, s is a strike price, and n is the life of the contract in years. The holder must pay an up-front fee for this contract. Inflation floors are similar, except that the holder receives a payoff when inflation turns out to be particularly low. The prices of these derivatives can be used to reverse-engineer investors' probability density for inflation, under the assumption that investors are risk-neutral. Kitsul and Wright (2012) find that during recent years these option-implied densities have implied non-negligible odds of both deflation and fairly high inflation (greater than 4 percent), even over 5- and 10-year horizons. But of course investors are not risk-neutral, and they may be willing to pay a premium to hedge against the risks of both deflation and a sharp pickup in inflation. While inflation caps and floors do not provide physical density forecasts, except under risk neutrality, they do tell us something about the inflation concerns of some investors.[27]

---

[27] TIPS actually contain an option-like feature. The principal repayment at maturity will be the *greater* of the nominal face value and the face value adjusted for inflation over the life of the security. This can be used to back out the

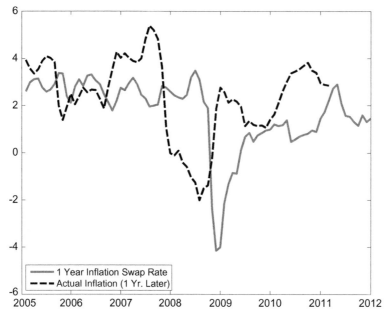

Figure 1.8 One-year inflation swap rates and realized inflation. *Notes:* The figure shows the 1-year inflation swap rates, from Bloomberg. Subsequent realized values (of headline CPI inflation) are also shown: these are plotted against the month at which the forecast was made. Thus, perfect foresight forecasts would by construction line up perfectly with the subsequent realized values.

4. OTHER TOPICS

4.1. Density Forecasts

Only the most foolishly overconfident forecasters claim to have perfect foresight. A point forecast of inflation without some measure of associated uncertainty is arguably of little value. Meanwhile, a density forecast gives a complete characterization of the beliefs of the forecaster about future inflation prospects. One particular special case of a density forecast that is of particular topical interest is estimating the probability of deflation, as policymakers are worried that this might result in a spiral in which falling prices push real interest rates up, depressing aggregate demand, and putting further downward pressure on prices. One can also construct measures of the risk of excessively low (or high) inflation, given a specification of the users' preferences (Kilian and Manganelli (2007, 2008)).

One way of constructing a density forecast is to take any point forecast and assume that the errors are homoskedastic. Assuming normality, one would take the point forecast ±1.96 standard deviations, or one could instead take the percentiles of the distributions of the historical errors and add those onto the point forecasts (Reifschneider and Williams, 2000). This latter approach is also taken in the density forecasts included in the Greenbook

implied probability of deflation (Wright, 2009b; Christensen et al., 2011), although these calculation again assume risk–neutrality.

since 2004. The difficulty with an exercise like this is that it assumes that the errors are always drawn from the *same* distribution, which in turn renders the whole density forecasting problem a rather uninteresting extension point forecasting. But the volatility of shocks to both output growth and inflation clearly vary over time. Indeed, the motivating example for Rob Engle's pathbreaking work on volatility clustering (Engle, 1982) was inflation, although these methods are now more widely applied to asset price returns. A density forecast ought therefore to aspire to be more informative than simply adding and subtracting constants from the point forecasts.

A number of such approaches have been proposed for constructing density forecasts for inflation. One is to use univariate or VAR forecasts, but with GARCH effects, stochastic volatility, or breaks in variance (Giordani and Söderlind, 2003; Stock and Watson, 2007; Groen, Paap and Ravazzolo, 2009 or Clark, 2011). Another is to use quantile regressions, in which the model specifies not the conditional mean of inflation, but rather some conditional quantiles (Manzan and Zerom, 2009) – the different quantiles may exhibit different sensitivity to the predictors. And a third way is to use survey density forecasts, or the density forecasts provided by central banks. Since 1968, the Survey of Professional Forecasters has asked respondents to assign probabilities to inflation falling into a number of bins, which represents a simple density forecast, discussed and evaluated by Diebold et al. (1999). More recently, the ECB Survey of Professional Forecasters (ECB-SPF) has obtained density forecasts at short and long –horizons for euro-zone inflation. The Bank of England has produced density forecast ("fan charts") in its quarterly Inflation reports since 1997 (Britton et al., 1998; Clements, 2004). The Bank of England constructs these densities using a three parameter functional form for the density, and sets the parameters (effectively mean, volatility, and skewness) judgmentally. Appropriately, the SPF, ECB-SPF and Bank of England inflation density forecasts all widened out substantially during the recent financial crisis.

As an illustration of questions that may be addressed with density forecasts, we use real-time estimation of the UCSV model to construct probabilities of average inflation (GDP deflator) over the next 2 years being above 4 percent (top panel) or below 0 percent (bottom panel) from 1985Q1 to 2011Q4. These probabilities are shown in Figure 1.9. The probability of a sustained period of excessively high inflation was elevated in the early part of the sample, but then declined and has remained near zero since then. The probability of sustained deflation remained below 10 percent throughout the sample, even during the financial crisis. That's because the variance of the permanent component of inflation in the UCSV model is estimated to be very small at the end of the sample period.

4.2. Forecasting Aggregates or Disaggregates?

A long-standing question is whether it is better to forecast inflation aggregates directly, as we have done so far in this chapter, or to forecast the disaggregated inflation rates, and then aggregate these forecasts. Theoretically, if the data generating process is known, then aggregating disaggregate forecasts must be at least as good as constructing the aggregate

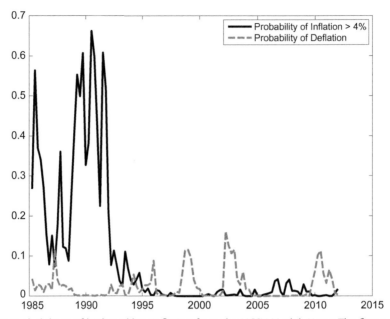

Figure 1.9 Probabilities of high and low inflation from the UCSV Model. *Notes:* The figure shows the probability of GDP deflator inflation being above 4 percent or below 0 percent on average over the subsequent 2 years. These are obtained from real-time estimation of the unobserved components stochastic volatility model of Stock and Watson (2007), applied to GDP deflator inflation.

forecast directly (Lütkepohl, 1987). But, when the data generating process has to be estimated, then it is possible for the direct aggregate forecast to be more accurate, because it entails the estimation of fewer parameters. If the disaggregates all have similar dynamics, then we might expect forecasting aggregates to work best in small samples. On the other hand, if the disaggregates have very persistent properties, then we would expect aggregation of disaggregate forecasts to do better. In the end, it is an empirical question as to which of these two methods is more accurate. Hubrich (2005) compares these two approaches to forecasting euro area inflation, and finds that neither method necessarily works better. Bermingham and D'Agostino (2011) are more supportive of aggregating disaggregate forecasts.

In this chapter, we illustrate the trade-offs between forecasting inflation aggregates directly and forecasting the disaggregates, by considering the real-time forecasting of overall CPI inflation. One innovation relative to the existing work on comparing these two alternative forecasting strategies is that our forecasts are all in gap form, in keeping with a main theme of this chapter. The forecasts that we consider are as follows:

1. An AR-GAP forecast for overall CPI inflation. This method thus uses aggregates to forecast aggregates. The lag order is determined by the Bayes Information Criterion.

2. An AR–GAP forecast for overall CPI inflation using an AR(1) with a slope coefficient fixed at 0.46 (as in the "fixed ρ" forecasts discussed earlier).

3. As in method 1, except using a separate univariate autoregression for the food, energy and core (i.e., ex-food-and-energy) CPI inflation disaggregates. All disaggregates are expressed in gap form, relative to the overall CPI inflation trend. These give forecasts of the disaggregates, which can then be combined, using real-time CPI weights, to obtain an implied forecast for overall CPI inflation.

4. As in method 3, except imposing that the slope coefficients in the autoregressions for food and energy inflation are both equal to zero. This imposes that food and energy inflation have no persistence.

5. As in method 4, except imposing that core inflation is an AR(1) with a slope coefficient fixed at 0.46.

6. A VAR in the food, energy and core CPI inflation disaggregates. This VAR provides forecasts of disaggregates which can then be combined to obtain the implied forecast for overall inflation.

7. A VAR in overall CPI inflation, and food and energy disaggregates, used to forecast overall inflation. This provides a direct forecast of aggregate inflation, but uses the disaggregated variables to do so. The idea of projecting aggregates onto disaggregates was proposed by Hendry and Hubrich (2011), who found that it may be a promising direction, especially if the researcher combines the information in the disaggregates judiciously, perhaps using model selection procedures.

Table 1.10 shows the RMSPE of all of these forecasts. The VARs (methods 6 and 7) and the univariate autoregression for overall CPI inflation all have roughly comparable performance. Fitting univariate autoregressions to the three components separately (method 3) fares a bit better at short horizons. But our main finding is that heavy-handedness helps. The AR–GAP forecast for overall CPI inflation with a fixed slope coefficient does better than the unrestricted AR–GAP model. Within the disaggregate forecasts, restricting the slope coefficients for food and energy inflation to be zero improves forecast accuracy. Adding in the restriction that core inflation is an AR(1) with a fixed slope coefficient helps further, and in fact gives the best forecasts for overall CPI inflation.[28] The argument of Lütkepohl (1987) for aggregating disaggregate forecasts is right, but the benefits are easily swamped by parameter estimation error. It is by imposing parameter restrictions (that are obviously not literally correct) that we are able to get some gain out of a "bottom up" forecasting strategy.

   Managing headline (i.e., total) inflation is presumably the appropriate ultimate objective of the central bank – people consume food and energy, and it seems hard to imagine a substantive rationale for why these should matter less than other elements of the

---

[28] This is still true in a sample that ends before the financial crisis, but the gains from treating food and energy inflation as transitory are smaller in this earlier sample.

Table 1.10 Comparison of Aggregate and Disaggregate Forecasts of Total CPI

	h = 0	h = 1	h = 2	h = 3	h = 4	h = 8
AR in aggregates	2.65	2.68	2.70	2.80	2.75	2.83
– Fixed ρ	2.66	2.53	2.44	2.48	2.48	2.43
Univariate ARs in disaggregates	2.53	2.56	2.59	2.70	2.74	2.78
– No persistence in food and energy	2.47	2.51	2.55	2.64	2.64	2.65
– Fixed slopes	2.44	2.44	2.45	2.47	2.48	2.43
VAR in disaggregates	2.71	2.80	2.65	2.70	2.70	2.73
VAR in aggregates and disaggregates	2.71	2.83	2.66	2.70	2.71	2.73

Notes: This table reports the pseudo-out-of-sample recursive RMSPE of alternative *h*-quarter-ahead forecasts of total CPI inflation (quarter-over-quarter; annualized percentage points). The sample consists of data vintages from 1985Q1 to 2011Q4, with the data going back to 1960Q1 in all cases. The alternative forecasting methods considered are (i) an AR fitted to total CPI inflation, (ii) an AR(1) fitted to total inflation imposing that the slope coefficient is 0.46, (iii) univariate autoregressions in core, food and energy inflation, with the resulting forecasts combined using real-time CPI weights, (iv) univariate autoregressions in core, food and energy inflation imposing that the slope coefficients on food and energy are zero, (v) univariate autoregressions in core, food and energy with fixed slope coefficients, imposing that the slope coefficients are 0.46, 0 and 0, respectively, (vi) a VAR in core, food and energy inflation, and (vii) a VAR in overall, food and energy inflation. In all cases, all inflation series are used in gap form, relative to the trend in overall CPI inflation.

consumption basket. Nonetheless, the Fed pays most attention to core inflation rather than headline inflation, arguing that food and energy components in headline inflation are overwhelmingly transitory. The point is discussed in Blinder (1997), who indeed defines a concept of core inflation as the part of inflation that has some persistence. Decomposing CPI into food, energy and all other items appears to be a useful way of splitting out more- and less-persistent inflation fluctuations.

4.3. Using Core Forecasts as Headline Forecasts

Indeed, if we treat the food and energy components of inflation as pure noise, with no pass-through into core prices, then any model estimation ought to be applied to core inflation even if prediction of total inflation is our end-objective. If food and energy are pure noise, then the population projection coefficients from regressions of core and total inflation onto explanatory variables are exactly the same, but the former are just estimated more precisely. As a result, even if we want to predict total inflation, we are better off forecasting core inflation and then using this as if it were a prediction of total inflation.[29]

Table 1.11 evaluates how this strategy works in practice. The table reports the out-of-sample RMSPEs of forecasts of core CPI inflation when used as predictions of subsequent total CPI inflation, relative to the benchmark of applying the same forecasting method directly to total CPI inflation. Most relative RMSPEs in Table 1.11 are slightly below 1,

---

[29] See Faust and Wright (2011) for further discussion of the idea that predictive regressions should be estimated removing any purely unforecastable components from the left-hand-side variable.

Table 1.11 RMSPEs of Core CPI Forecasts Evaluated as Forecasts of Total CPI

	$h = 0$	$h = 1$	$h = 2$	$h = 3$	$h = 4$	$h = 8$
Direct	0.90	0.89	0.88	0.88	0.95	0.93
RAR	0.90	0.86	0.97	0.96	0.98	0.99
PC	0.89	0.88	0.88	0.88	0.95	0.93
Random Walk	0.74	0.70	0.77	0.74	0.76	0.71
AR-GAP	0.94	0.94	0.96	0.97	1.01	0.99
PC-GAP	0.93	0.94	0.96	0.97	1.00	0.98
PCTVN-GAP	0.93	0.94	0.96	0.97	1.00	1.00
Term Structure VAR	0.96	1.01	1.02	1.01	1.01	0.98
EWA	0.93	0.93	0.94	0.96	1.00	0.99
BMA	0.91	0.89	0.92	0.94	0.96	0.96
FAVAR	0.93	0.92	0.98	0.98	0.97	1.00

Notes: This table reports the pseudo-out-of-sample recursive RMSPE of h-quarter-ahead forecasts of core CPI inflation (quarter-over-quarter), evaluated as predictors of total CPI inflation, relative to the RMSPE of the corresponding direct forecasts of total CPI inflation. The sample consists of data vintages from 1985Q1 to 2011Q4, with the data going back to 1960Q1 in all cases.

indicating that forecasting core inflation may indeed be appropriate, even if the end-goal is predicting total inflation.

4.4. Alternative Inflation Measures

CPI inflation excluding food and energy seems to be useful as a predictor of future total inflation. There are a number of alternative inflation indices that one might use for similar reasons. Bryan and Cecchetti (1994) advocated using median CPI inflation (across components) as a measure of core inflation.[30] Cutler (2001) and Bilke and Stracca (2007) have both constructed price indices that weight the components by their persistence. Detmeister (2011, 2012) considers the usefulness of a number of variants on core inflation, evaluated as predictors of future total inflation. Bryan and Meyer (2010) decompose overall CPI inflation into the inflation associated with goods that have relatively sticky/flexible prices. They find a more pronounced tradeoff between slack and inflation when inflation is measured from the "flexible prices" CPI, which could potentially turn out to be useful for inflation forecasting.

5. INTERNATIONAL INFLATION FORECASTS

In this section, we briefly consider the forecasting of consumer price inflation in a few large foreign countries: Canada, Germany, Japan, and the United Kingdom. Analysis

---

[30] Ball and Mazumder (2011) noted that median CPI inflation declined more distinctly than total inflation (or even than inflation excluding food and energy) during the Great Recession.

of the foreign experience is useful because it increases our effective sample size. In this respect, it is useful that Germany, Japan, and the U.K. all had substantially different inflation experiences to the U.S. over the last half century. For example, the rise in inflation in the late 1970s was considerably more muted in Germany than in the U.S. Also, inflation remained quite high in the UK into the early 1990s, well after the Great Inflation had subsided in most other developed countries. And, at the time of writing, Japan is experiencing a slow but sustained and pernicious deflation that has already lasted for more than a decade.

For the international forecast comparison, we use only *ex-post* revised data,[31] and consider only a small subset of the methods that we applied to the main forecast comparison using U.S. data in Section 2. For the foreign countries, we only consider the direct forecast, the two random walk forecasts (RW and RW-AO), the UCSV forecast, the Phillips curve (PC) forecast, the autoregression in gap form (AR-GAP), the "fixed ρ" forecast, and the Phillips curve forecast in gap form (PC-GAP). For the last three of these forecasts, the inflation trend is measured from the most recent 5-to-10-year-ahead inflation forecast from Consensus Forecasts – a multi-country macroeconomic survey analogous to Blue Chip for the U.S.

The models are estimated on quarterly data from 1960Q1 through to 2011Q4. We consider recursive pseudo-out-of-sample forecasts for the current and subsequent quarters using all these methods, with the first forecast made in 1985Q1. We evaluate the competing forecasts in terms of their RMSPEs, relative to the benchmark of the "fixed ρ" forecast (the AR(1) in gap form with a fixed slope coefficient). The results are reported in Table 1.12.

The results are qualitatively similar to those that we earlier found for the U.S. in Section 2. The "fixed ρ" benchmark – that is a glide-path from the most recent observation to an estimate of the local mean – is hard to beat by much. The relative RMSPEs are statistically significantly less than one in only a few cases. Even in these cases, they are around 0.9, corresponding to a 10 percent improvement relative to a very simple baseline. The pure random walk forecast does not do well: quarter-over-quarter inflation is too noisy to be a good estimate of the local mean. However, the other methods that allow for some non-stationarity in inflation – the "fixed ρ" benchmark forecasts, the Atkeson-Ohanian version of the random walk forecast, and the UCSV, AR-GAP and PC-GAP forecasts – are all about equally good. The forecasts that are based on treating inflation as a stationary process (direct and PC) do particularly badly at longer horizons, except perhaps for Germany. Germany has had more stable inflation dynamics over the last half century than the U.S., Canada, Japan, or the U.K., and so it is perhaps not surprising that allowing for a time-varying local mean is less critical for Germany than it is for the other

---

[31] Most countries outside the U.S. report only inflation data without seasonal adjustment. The seasonal patterns in price data are however important. We therefore adjusted our inflation data for Canada, Germany, Japan, and the United Kingdom using the X12 seasonal adjustment filter.

Table 1.12 RMSPE of International Inflation Forecasts

Horizon	0	1	2	3	4	8
Panel A: Canada						
Direct	1.04	1.11**	1.17**	1.10*	1.06	1.16**
RW	1.27***	1.36***	1.28**	1.39***	1.26**	1.22**
RW-AO	1.02	1.07	1.03	1.03	1.02	1.01
UCSV	0.97	1.04	1.05	1.05	1.01	0.99
PC	1.04	1.11*	1.16**	1.09	1.05	1.16***
AR-GAP	1.00	1.04	1.06	1.03	1.02	1.08**
PC-GAP	0.96	0.99	0.98	0.95	0.95	1.00
Panel B: Germany						
Direct	1.01	0.95	0.98	1.00	0.99	1.12*
RW	1.15**	1.12*	1.07	1.22**	1.12	1.34**
RW-AO	1.01	0.96	0.96	1.02	1.04	1.16*
UCSV	0.98	0.96	0.96	1.01	0.97	1.13
PC	0.97	0.90*	0.92	0.96	0.94	1.05
AR-GAP	0.99	0.94	0.96	0.98	0.96	1.02
PC-GAP	1.01	0.94	0.95	1.00	0.98	1.14
Panel C: Japan						
Direct	1.04	1.05	1.19***	1.42***	1.40***	1.55***
RW	1.15***	1.09	0.99	1.13	1.00	1.10
RW-AO	0.93*	0.89**	0.86*	0.88	0.85*	0.95
UCSV	0.91***	0.87**	0.85**	0.89	0.84*	0.91
PC	0.97	0.96	1.00	1.17	1.16	1.50*
AR-GAP	0.92***	0.87***	0.85***	0.88***	0.86***	0.87***
PC-GAP	0.97	0.92	0.92	1.06	1.00	1.22
Panel D: United Kingdom						
Direct	1.04	1.07	1.10	1.24**	1.19	1.39**
RW	1.15*	1.12	1.04	1.16	1.14	1.18
RW-AO	0.97	0.91	0.88	0.90	0.93	1.03
UCSV	0.95	0.90	0.88	0.93	0.93	1.03
PC	1.14**	1.25**	1.48***	1.76***	1.78**	2.38***
AR-GAP	0.99	0.99	0.95	1.01	0.98	1.05*
PC-GAP	1.04	1.04	1.06	1.20*	1.19*	1.32***

Notes: This table reports the pseudo-out-of-sample recursive RMSPE of alternative h-quarter-ahead forecasts of consumer price inflation (quarter-over-quarter) in four countries, all relative to the benchmark of an AR(1) in "gap" form with a fixed slope coefficient. Revised seasonally adjusted data were used. The sample is 1960Q1-2011Q4; the first pseudo-out-of-sample forecasts are made in 1985Q1, using data up to and including 1984Q4. Cases in which the relative root mean square prediction error is significantly different from one at the 10, 5 and 1 percent significance levels are denoted with one, two and three asterisks, respectively. These are based on the two-sided test of Diebold and Mariano (1995), implemented as described in the text.

countries. The performance of the forecasts based on Phillips curve relationships is not terribly encouraging. For example, the PC-GAP forecast does worse than the "fixed ρ" benchmark for some country/horizon combinations, and never does much better.

The most natural interpretation for why the "fixed ρ" benchmark generally does so well is that central banks use monetary policy to push inflation back to target fairly quickly. If so, one would expect the benchmark to do less well in countries or at times where central banks have been less successful in this pursuit. It is noteworthy that for Japan, the AR-GAP, RW-AO, and UCSV model give 5–16 percent reductions in RMSPE relative to the "fixed ρ" benchmark. Moreover, these improvements in forecast accuracy are statistically significant in some cases.[32] The fact that our benchmark seems a little easier to beat for Japan may be a reflection of the difficulty that the Bank of Japan has experienced in eliminating deflation.

Our results in Table 1.12 do not include judgmental forecasts of inflation, except of course that we use long-run surveys to measure the inflation trend. [33] Groen, Kapetanios and Price (2012) evaluated judgmental forecasts of inflation for the United Kingdom. They compared the Bank of England inflation forecasts with those from a range of econometric models. They found that the Bank of England forecast consistently did best, but that it did so mainly by incorporating judgment about the long-run value of inflation. This is again entirely consistent with our results for the U.S.

6. CONCLUSIONS

In this chapter, we have discussed a numbers of methods for forecasting inflation. We find that judgmental forecasts (private sector surveys and the Greenbook) are remarkably hard to beat. But we don't necessarily even need the whole term structure of judgmental inflation forecasts. If we just take the current-quarter and long-run survey forecasts, then a very simple glide path between these two boundary conditions – that doesn't involve any parameter estimation – turns out to be a surprisingly competitive benchmark.

In many forecasting contexts, very simple methods that limit or avoid parameter estimation turn out to work shockingly well. For example, Meese and Rogoff (1983) found that the driftless random walk is an excellent predictor of exchange rates. We find that in much the same way, extremely simple inflation forecasts – that however take account of nowcasting and secular changes in the local mean inflation rate – are just about the best that are available. If monetary policy mainly is directed toward smoothly

---

[32] The AR-GAP model has two estimated parameters: the intercept and the slope coefficient. Note that the estimate of the intercept coefficient is negative for Japan in recent years.

[33] Most central banks produce judgmental inflation forecasts. There are also several surveys for countries outside the U.S., such as the ECB-SPF. Consensus Forecasts is however the only survey that is of global scope, and it does not include forecasts of quarter-over-quarter inflation that we study in this chapter. For this reason, we don't include it in our forecast comparison.

eliminating deviations of inflation from some slowly-moving target, this result might be about what we should expect.

ACKNOWLEDGMENTS

We are grateful to two anonymous referees, Todd Clark, Joseph Haubrich, Kirstin Hubrich, Sharon Kozicki, Evan Koenig, Lutz Kilian, Barbara Rossi, Ellis Tallman and Alan Timmermann for their very helpful comments on earlier drafts, and to Lu Xu for research assistance. All errors are our sole responsibility.

REFERENCES

Adam, Klaus, Padula, Mario, 2003. Inflation dynamics and subjective expectations in the United States. Working Paper.

Ahmed, Shagil, Levin, Andrew T., Wilson, Beth Anne, 2004. Recent improvements in US macroeconomic stability: good policy, good practices, or good luck? Review of Economics and Statistics 86, 824–832.

Aiolfi, Marco, Capistran, Carlos, Timmermann, Allan, 2010. Forecast Combinations. In: Clements, Michael P., Hendry, David F. (Eds.), Oxford Handbook of Economic Forecasting. Oxford University Press, Oxford.

Andreou, Elena, Ghysels, Eric, Kourtellos, Andros, 2008. Should macroeconomic forecasters look at daily financial data? Working Paper.

Ang, Andrew, Piazzesi, Monika, 2003. A no-arbitrage vector autoregression of term structure dynamics with macroeconomic and latent variables. Journal of Monetary Economics 50, 745–787.

Ang, Andrew, Bekaert, Geert, Wei, Min, 2007. Do macro variables, asset markets or surveys forecast inflation better? Journal of Monetary Economics 54, 1163–1212.

Arai, Natsuki, 2012. Using forecast evaluation to improve accuracy of the greenbook forecast. Working Paper.

Atkeson, Andrew, Ohanian, Lee E., 2001. Are Phillips curves useful for forecasting inflation? Federal Reserve Bank of Minneapolis Quarterly Review 25, 2–11.

Bai, Jushan, Ng, Serena, 2008. Forecasting economic time series using targeted predictors. Journal of Econometrics 146, 304–317.

Ball, Laurence, Mazumder, Sandeep, 2011. Inflation dynamics and the great recession. Brookings Papers on Economic Activity 1, 337–387.

Ball, Laurence, Mankiw, N. Gregory, Romer, David, 1988. The new Keynesian economics and the output-inflation trade-off. Brookings Papers on Economic Activity 1, 1–65.

Banbura, Marta, Giannone, Domenico, Modugno, Michele, Reichlin, Lucrezia, 2012. Nowcasting, forthcoming. In: Timmermann Allan, Elliott, Graham (Eds.), Handbook of Economic Forecasting, vol. 2. Elsevier, Amsterdam.

Barnes, Michelle L., Olivei, Giovanni P., 2003. Inside and outside bounds: threshold estimates of the Phillips curve, New England Economic Review, 1–18.

Bates, John M., Granger, Clive W.J., 1969. The combination of forecasts. Operations Research Quarterly 20, 451–468.

Bermingham, Colin, D'Agostino, Antonello, 2011. Understanding and forecasting aggregate and disaggregate price dynamics, ECB Working Paper 1365.

Bernanke, Ben S., Boivin, Jean, 2003. Monetary policy in a data-rich environment. Journal of Monetary Economics 50, 525–546.

Bernanke, Ben S., Woodford, Michael, 1997. Inflation forecasts and monetary policy. Journal of Money, Credit and Banking 29, 653–684.

Bernanke, Ben S., Boivin, Jean, Eliasz, Piotr, 2005. Measuring monetary policy: a factor augmented vector autoregressive (FAVAR) approach. Quarterly Journal of Economics 120, 387–422.

Bilke, Laurent, Stracca, Livio, 2007. A persistence-weighted measure of core inflation in the Euro area. Economic Modelling 24, 1032–1047.

Blinder, Alan S., 1997. Commentary on "Alternative Strategies for Aggregating Prices". Federal Reserve Bank of Saint Louis Review 3, 139–142.

Brayton, Flint, Roberts, John. M., Williams, John C., 1999. What's happened to the Phillips curve? FEDS Discussion Paper, 99–49.

Britton, Erik, Fisher, Paul, Whitley, John, 1998. The inflation report projections: understanding the fan chart. Bank of England Quarterly Bulletin 38, 30–37.

Bryan, Michael F., Cecchetti, Stephen G., 1994. In: Gregory Mankiw N. (Ed.), Measuring Core Inflation in Policy. Chicago University Press, Chicago.

Bryan, Michael F., Meyer, Brent, 2010. Are some prices in the CPI more forward looking than others? We think so. Federal Reserve Bank of Atlanta Economic Commentary, 2010–2.

Campbell, John Y., Shiller, Robert J., 1996. A Scorecard for Indexed Government Debt. National Bureau of Economic Research Macroeconomics Annual. MIT Press.

Campbell, John Y., Shiller, Robert J., Viceira, Luis M., 2009. Understanding inflation-indexed bond markets. Brookings Papers on Economic Activity 1, 79–120.

Christensen, Jens H.E., Lopez, Jose A., Rudebusch, Glenn D., 2011. Extracting deflation probability forecasts from Treasury yields. Federal Reserve Bank of San Francisco. Working Paper, 2011–10.

Clark, Todd E., 2011. Real-time density forecasts from VARs with stochastic volatility. Journal of Business and Economic Statistics 29, 327–341.

Clark, Todd E., McCracken, Michael W., 2009a. Nested forecast model comparisons: a new approach to testing equal accuracy. Federal Reserve Bank of Kansas City. Working Paper, 2009–11.

Clark, Todd E., McCracken, Michael W., 2009b. Tests of equal predictive ability with real-time data. Journal of Business and Economic Statistics 27, 441–454.

Clark, Todd E., McCracken, Michael W., forthcoming. Advances in forecast evaluation. In: Timmermann, Allan, Elliott, Graham, (Eds.), Handbook of Economic Forecasting, vol. 2. Elsevier, Amsterdam.

Clark, Todd E., Taeyoung, Doh, 2011. A bayesian evaluation of alternative models of trend inflation. Working Paper.

Clark, Todd E., West, Kenneth D., 2007. Approximately normal tests for equal predictive accuracy in nested models. Journal of Econometrics 138, 291–311.

Clements, Michael P., 2004. Evaluating the Bank of England density forecasts of inflation. Economic Journal 114, 855–877.

Cogley, Timothy, Sargent, Thomas J., 2005. Drifts and volatilities: monetary policies and outcomes in the post World War II US. Review of Economic Dynamics 8, 262–302.

Cogley, Timothy, Sbordone, Argia M., 2008. Trend inflation, indexation, and inflation persistence in the New Keynesian Phillips curve. American Economic Review 98, 2101–26.

Cogley, Timothy, Primiceri, Giorgio, Sargent, Thomas J., 2010. Inflation-gap persistence in the US. American Economic Journal: Macroeconomics 2, 43–69.

Croushore, Dean 2008. Revisions to PCE inflation measures: implications for monetary policy. Working Paper.

Croushore, Dean, 2010. An evaluation of inflation forecasts from surveys using real-time data. BE Journal of Macroeconomics, Contributions 10.

Croushore, Dean, 2012. Comment on "Forecast Rationality Tests Based on Multi-Horizon Bounds". Journal of Business and Economic Statistics 30, 17–20.

Cutler, Joanne, 2001. A new measure of core inflation in the UK. Working Paper.

D'Amico, Stefania, Kim, Don H., Wei, Min, 2010. Tips from TIPS: the informational content of Treasury inflation-protected security prices, FEDS Discussion Paper, 2010-19.

De Graeve, Ferris, Emiris, Marina, Wouters, Rafael, 2009. A structural decomposition of the US yield curve. Journal of Monetary Economics 56, 545–559.

Del Negro, Marco, Eusepi, Stefano, 2011. Fitting observed inflation expectations. Journal of Economic Dynamics and Control 35, 2105–2131.

Detmeister, Alan K., 2011. The usefulness of core PCE inflation measures, FEDS Discussion Paper, 2011-56.

Detmeister, Alan K., 2012. What should core inflation exclude? FEDS Discussion Paper, 2012-43.

Diebold, Francis X., Li, Canlin, 2006. Forecasting the term structure of government bond yields. Journal of Econometrics 130, 337–364.

Diebold, Francis X., Mariano, Roberto S., 1995. Comparing predictive accuracy. Journal of Business and Economic Statistics 13, 253–263.

Diebold, Francis X, Tay, Anthony S., Wallis, Kenneth F., 1999. Evaluating density forecasts of inflation: the survey of professional forecasters. In: Engle, Robert F., White, Halbert, (Eds.), "Cointegration, Causality, and Forecasting: A Festschrift in Honour of Clive W.J. Granger". Oxford University Press, Oxford.

Diebold, Francis X., Rudebusch, Glenn D., Aruoba, S. Boragan, 2006. The macroeconomy and the yield curve: a dynamic latent factor approach. Journal of Econometrics 131, 309–338.

Dotsey, Michael, Fujita, Shigeru, Stark, Tom, 2011. Do Phillips curves conditionally help to forecast inflation. Working Paper.

Edge, Rochelle, Gürkaynak, Refet S., 2010. How useful are estimated DSGE model forecasts for central bankers. Brookings Papers on Economic Activity 2, 209–244.

Edge, Rochelle, Kiley, Michael T., Laforte, Jean-Philippe, 2010. A comparison of forecast performance between Federal Reserve staff Forecasts, simple reduced-form models, and a DSGE model, Journal of Applied Econometrics 25, 720–754.

Elliott, Graham, Ivana Komunjer, Allan Timmermann, 2005. Estimation and testing of forecast rationality under flexible loss. Review of Economic Studies 72, 1107–1125.

Engle, Robert F., 1982. Autoregressive conditional heteroskedasticity with estimates of the variance of United Kingdom inflation. Econometrica 50, 987–1007.

Faust, Jon, Wright, Jonathan H., 2008. Efficient forecast tests for conditional policy forecasts. Journal of Econometrics 146, 293–303.

Faust, Jon, Wright, Jonathan H., 2009. Comparing Greenbook and reduced form forecasts using a large real-time dataset. Journal of Business and Economic Statistics 27, 468–479.

Faust, Jon, Wright, Jonathan H., 2011. Efficient prediction of excess returns. Review of Economics and Statistics 93, 647–659.

Fernandez, Carmen, Ley, Eduardo, Steel, Mark F.J., 2001. Model uncertainty in cross-country growth regressions. Journal of Applied Econometrics 16, 563–576.

Filardo, Andrew J., 1998. New evidence on the output cost of fighting inflation. Federal Reserve Bank of Kansas City Economic Review (3rd quarter), pp. 33–61.

Fleckenstein, Matthias, Longstaff, Francis A., Lustig, Hanno, 2010. Why does the Treasury issue TIPS? The TIPS-Treasury bond puzzle. NBER Working Paper, 16358.

Gali, Jordi, Gertler, Mark, 1999. Inflation dynamics: a structural econometric analysis. Journal of Monetary Economics 44, 195–222.

Giacomini, Raffaella, Rossi, Barbara, 2010. Forecast comparisons in unstable environments. Journal of Applied Econometrics 25, 595–620.

Giacomini, Raffaella, Rossi, Barbara, 2012. Advances in forecasting under model instability, forthcoming. In: Timmermann, Allan, Elliott, Graham, (Eds.), Handbook of Economic Forecasting, vol. 2. Elsevier, Amsterdam.

Giacomini, Raffaella, White, Halbert, 2006. Tests of conditional predictive ability. Econometrica 74, 1545–1578.

Giannone, Domenico, Reichlin, Lucrezia, Small, David, 2008. Nowcasting GDP: the real time informational content of macroeconomic data releases. Journal of Monetary Economics 55, 665–676.

Giordani, Paolo, Söderlind, Paul, 2003. Inflation forecast uncertainty. European Economic Review 47, 1037–1059.

Gonzáles, Andrés, Hubrich, Kirstin, Teräsvirta, Timo, 2011. Forecasting inflation with gradual regime shifts and exogenous information. ECB Working Paper, 1363.

Gordon, Robert J., 1982. Inflation, flexible exchange rates, and the natural rate of unemployment. In: Baily, Martin N. (Ed.), Workers, Jobs and Inflation. The Brookings Institution, Washington.

Gordon, Robert J., 1998. Foundations of the goldilocks economy: supply shocks and the time-varying NAIRU. Brookings Papers on Economic Activity 2, 297–333.

Greenspan, Alan, 1992. Statement to the Congress, Federal Reserve Bulletin, 603–607.

Groen, Jan J.J., Kapetanios, George, Price, Simon, 2009. A Real time evaluation of Bank of England forecasts of inflation and growth. International Journal of Forecasting 25, 74–80.

Groen, Jan J.J., Paap, Richard, Ravazzolo, Francesco, 2009. Real-time inflation forecasting in a changing World. Federal Reserve Bank of New York Staff Reports, 388.

Gürkaynak, Refet S., Sack, Brian P., Swanson, Eric T., 2005. The sensitivity of long-term interest rates to economic news: evidence and implications for macroeconomic models. American Economic Review 95, 425–436.

Gürkaynak, Refet S., Sack, Brian P., Wright, Jonathan H., 2007. The US Treasury yield curve: 1961 to the present. Journal of Monetary Economics 54, 2291–2304.

Gürkaynak, Refet S., Sack, Brian P., Wright, Jonathan H., 2010. The TIPS yield curve and inflation compensation. American Economic Journal: Macroeconomics 2, 70–92.

Harvey, David I., Leybourne, Stephen J., Newbold, Paul, 1997. Testing the equality of prediction mean squared errors. International Journal of Forecasting 13, 281–291.

Haubrich, Joseph G., Pennacchi, George G., Ritchken, Peter H., 2008. Estimating real and nominal term structures using Treasury yields, inflation, inflation forecasts, and inflation swap rates. Federal Reserve Bank of Cleveland Working Paper 2008-10.

Hendry, David, Hubrich, Kirstin, 2010. Combining disaggregate forecasts or combining disaggregate information to forecast an aggregate. Journal of Business and Economic Statistics 29, 216–227.

Hu, Gang, Worah, Mihir, 2009. Why TIPS real yields moved significantly higher after the Lehman Bankruptcy. PIMCO, Newport Beach, California.

Hubrich, Kirstin, 2005. Forecasting Euro area inflation: does aggregating forecasts by HICP component improve forecast accuracy? International Journal of Forecasting 21, 119–136.

Inoue, Atsushi, Kilian, Lutz, 2004. In-sample or out-of-sample tests of predictability: which one should we use? Econometric Reviews 23, 371–402.

Inoue, Atsushi, Kilian, Lutz, 2006. On the selection of forecasting models. Journal of Econometrics 130, 273–306.

Inoue, Atsushi, Kilian, Lutz, 2008. How useful is bagging in forecasting economic time series? a case study of US CPI inflation. Journal of the American Statistical Association 103, 511–522.

Inoue, Atsushi, Kiraz, Fatma B., Kilian, Lutz, 2009. Do actions speak louder than words? household expectations of inflation based on micro consumption data. Journal of Money, Credit and Banking 41, 1331–1363.

Joslin, Scott, Priesbsch, Marcel, Singleton, Kenneth J., 2010. Risk premiums in dynamic term structure models with unspanned macro risks. Working Paper.

Joslin, Scott, Le, Anh, Singleton, Kenneth J., forthcoming. Why Gaussian macro-finance term structure models are (nearly) unconstrained factor-VARs. Journal of Financial Economics.

Joyce, Michael, Lildholdt, Peter M., Sorensen, Steffen, 2010. Extracting inflation expectations and inflation risk premia from the term structure: a joint model of the UK nominal and real yield curves. Journal of Banking and Finance 34, 281–94.

Kilian, Lutz, Manganelli, Simone, 2007. Quantifying the risk of deflation. Journal of Money, Credit and Banking 39, 561–590.

Kilian, Lutz, Manganelli, Simone, 2008. The central banker as a risk manager: estimating the Federal Reserve's preferences under Greenspan. Journal of Money, Credit and Banking 40, 1103–1129.

Kitsul, Yuriy, Wright, Jonathan H., 2012. The Economics of options-implied inflation probability density functions. NBER Working Paper 18195.

Kleibergen, Frank, Mavroeidis, Sophocles, 2009. Weak instrument Robust tests in GMM and the new Keynesian Phillips curve. Journal of Business and Economic Statistics 27, 293–311.

Koenig, Evan F., Atkinson, Tyler, 2012. Inflation, slack and fed credibility. Dallas Fed Staff Paper, 16.

Koop, Gary, Potter, Simon, 2003. Forecasting in large macroeconomic panels using Bayesian model averaging. Federal Reserve Bank of New York Staff Report, 163.

Kozicki, Sharon, Tinsley, Peter A., 2001. Shifting endpoints in the term structure of interest rates. Journal of Monetary Economics 47, 613–652.

Kozicki, Sharon, Tinsley, Peter A., 2005. What do you expect? imperfect policy credibility and tests of the expectations hypothesis. Journal of Monetary Economics 52, 421–447.

Kozicki, Sharon, Tinsley, Peter A., 2012. Effective use of survey information in estimating the evolution of expected inflation. Journal of Money, Credit and Banking 44, 145–169.

Kwon, So Jung, 2011. Can judgmental forecasts help DSGE forecasting? Working Paper.

Liu, Zheng, Rudebusch, Glenn D., 2010. Inflation: mind the gap. Federal Reserve Bank of San Francisco Economic Letter, 2010-02.

Lo, Andrew W., Mackinlay, A. Craig, 1988. Stock prices do not follow random walks: evidence from a simple specification test. Review of Financial Studies 1, 41–66.

Lütkepohl, Helmut, 1987. Forecasting Aggregated Vector ARMA Processes. Springer Verlag, Berlin.

Manzan, Sebastiano, Zerom, Dawit, 2009. Are macroeconomic variables useful for forecasting the distribution of US inflation? Working Paper.

Marcellino, Massimo, Stock, James H., Watson, Mark W., 2006. A comparison of direct and iterated multistep AR methods for forecasting macroeconomic time series. Journal of Econometrics 135, 499–526.

Meese, Richard A., Rogoff, Kenneth, 1983. Empirical exchange rate models of the seventies? Do they fit out of sample? Journal of International Economics 14, 3–24.

Meier, André, 2010. Still minding the gap – inflation dynamics during episodes of persistent large output gaps. IMF Working Paper, 10-189.

Patton, Andrew J., Timmermann, Allan, 2007. Properties of optimal forecasts under asymmetric loss and nonlinearity. Journal of Econometrics 140, 884–918.

Patton, Andrew J., Timmermann, Allan, 2012. Forecast rationality tests based on multi-horizon bounds. Journal of Business and Economic Statistics 30, 1–17.

Pflueger, Carolin E., Viceira, Luis M., 2011. Inflation-indexed bonds and the expectations hypothesis. Annual Review of Financial Economics 3, 139–158.

Phillips, A. William, 1958. The relationship between unemployment and the rate of change of money wages in the United Kingdom 1861–1957. Economica 25, 283–299.

Primiceri, Giorgio E., 2005. Time varying structural vector autoregressions and monetary policy. Review of Economic Studies 72, 821–852.

Reifschneider, David L., Williams, John C., 2000. Three lessons for monetary policy in a low-inflation era. Journal of Money, Credit and Banking 32, 936–966.

Reifschneider, David L., Stockton, David J., Wilcox, David W., 1997. Econometric models and the monetary policy process. Carnegie Rochester Series on Public Policy 47, 1–37.

Romer, Christina D., Romer, David H., 2000. Federal reserve information and the behavior of interest rates. American Economic Review 90, 429–457.

Rossi, Barbara, Sekhposyan, Tatevik, 2010. Have economic models' forecasting performance for US output growth and inflation changed over time, and when? International Journal of Forecasting 26, 808–835.

Rudd, Jeremy, Whelan, Karl, 2005. New tests of the new-Keynesian Phillips curve. Journal of Monetary Economics 52, 1167–1181.

Sims, Christopher A., 1993. A nine-variable probabilistic macroeconomic forecasting model. In: Stock, James H., Watson, Mark (Eds.), NBER Studies in Business: Business Cycles, Indicators, and Forecasting, vol. 28. National Bureau of Economic Research, Cambridge.

Sims, Christopher A., 2002. The role of models and probabilities in the monetary policy process. Brookings Papers on Economic Activity 2, 1–40.

Smets, Frank, Wouters, Raf, 2003. An estimated stochastic dynamic general equilibrium model of the Euro area. Journal of the European Economic Association 1, 1123–1175.

Smets, Frank, Wouters, Raf, 2007. Shocks and frictions in US business cycles: a Bayesian DSGE approach. American Economic Review 97, 586–607.

Stock, James H., Watson, Mark W., 1999. Forecasting inflation. Journal of Monetary Economics 44, 293–335.

Stock, James H., Watson, Mark W., 2003a. Has the business cycle changed? evidence and explanations. Federal Reserve Bank of Kansas City Symposium: Monetary Policy and Uncertainty, Jackson Hole, Wyoming.

Stock, James H., Watson, Mark W., 2003b. Forecasting output and inflation: the role of asset prices. Journal of Economic Literature 41, 788–829.

Stock, James H., Watson, Mark W., 2007. Has inflation become harder to forecast? Journal of Money, Credit and Banking 39, 3–34.

Stock, James H., Watson, Mark W., 2009. Phillips curve inflation forecasts. In: Fuhrer, Jeffrey, Kodrzycki, Yolanda, Little, Jane, Olivei, Giovanni (Eds.), Understanding Inflation and the Implications for Monetary Policy. MIT Press, Cambridge.

Stock, James H., Watson, Mark W., 2010. Modeling inflation after the crisis. In: Macroeconomic Challenges: The Decade Ahead, Federal Reserve Bank of Kansas City Economic Policy Symposium.

Svensson, Lars E.O., 2005. Monetary policy with judgment: forecast targeting. International Journal of Central Banking 1, 1–54.

Tetlow, Robert J., Ironside, Brian, 2007. Real-time model uncertainty in the United States: the fed, 1996–2003. Journal of Money, Credit and Banking 39, 1533–1849.

Tulip, Peter, 2009. Has the economy become more predictable? changes in Greenbook forecast accuracy. Journal of Money, Credit and Banking 39, 1217–1231.

Van Dijk, Dick, Koopman, Siem Jan, van der Wel, Michel, Wright, Jonathan H., 2011. Forecasting interest rates with shifting endpoints. Working Paper.

Woodford, Michael, 2003. Interest and Prices: Foundations of a Theory of Monetary Policy. Princeton University Press, Princeton, New Jersey.

Wright, Jonathan H., 2009a. Forecasting US inflation by Bayesian model averaging. Journal of Forecasting 28, 131–144.

Wright, Jonathan H., 2009b. Comment on "Understanding inflation-indexed bond markets". Brookings Papers on Economic Activity 1, 126–38.

Wright, Jonathan H., forthcoming. Evaluating real-time VAR forecasts with an informative democratic prior. Journal of Applied Econometrics.

CHAPTER 2

DSGE Model-Based Forecasting

Marco Del Negro* and Frank Schorfheide†

*Research Department, Federal Reserve Bank of New York, 33 Liberty Street, New York, NY 10045, USA
†Frank Schorfheide: Department of Economics, 3718 Locust Walk, University of Pennsylvania, Philadelphia, PA 19104-6297, USA

Contents

Handbook of Economic Forecasting, Volume 2A
ISSN 1574-0706, http://dx.doi.org/10.1016/B978-0-444-53683-9.00002-7

Abstract

Dynamic stochastic general equilibrium (DSGE) models use modern macroeconomic theory to explain and predict comovements of aggregate time series over the business cycle and to perform policy analysis. We explain how to use DSGE models for all three purposes – forecasting, story-telling, and policy experiments – and review their forecasting record. We also provide our own real-time assessment of the forecasting performance of the Smets and Wouters (2007) model data up to 2011, compare it with Blue Chip and Greenbook forecasts, and show how it changes as we augment the standard set of observables with external information from surveys (nowcasts, interest rates, and long-run inflation and output growth expectations). We explore methods of generating forecasts in the presence of a zero-lower-bound constraint on nominal interest rates and conditional on counterfactual interest rate paths. Finally, we perform a post-mortem of DSGE model forecasts of the Great Recession, and show that forecasts from a version of the Smets–Wouters model augmented by financial frictions and with interest rate spreads as an observable compare well with Blue Chip forecasts.

Keywords

Bayesian analysis, Conditional forecasts, DSGE models, External information, Financial frictions, Forecast accuracy, Great recession, Monetary policys shocks

1. INTRODUCTION

The goal of this chapter is to provide an illustrative overview of the state-of-the-art of forecasting with dynamic stochastic general equilibrium (DSGE) models and to improve upon existing techniques. DSGE models use modern macroeconomic theory to explain and predict co-movements of aggregate time series over the business cycle. The term *DSGE model* encompasses a broad class of macroeconomic models that spans the standard neoclassical growth model discussed in King et al. (1988) as well as New Keynesian monetary models with numerous real and nominal frictions that are based on the work of Christiano et al. (2005) and Smets and Wouters (2003). A common feature of these models is that decision rules of economic agents are derived from assumptions about preferences, technologies, and the prevailing fiscal and monetary policy regime by solving intertemporal optimization problems. As a consequence, the DSGE model paradigm delivers empirical models with a strong degree of theoretical coherence that are attractive as a laboratory for policy experiments. A review of the most recent developments in the literature on New Keynesian monetary DSGE models is provided by Christiano et al. (2010).

In empirical work, DSGE models are frequently estimated with Bayesian methods (see, for instance, An and Schorfheide (2007a) or Del Negro and Schorfheide (2010) for a review), in particular if the goal is to track and forecast macroeconomic time series. Bayesian inference delivers posterior predictive distributions that reflect uncertainty about latent state variables, parameters, and future realizations of shocks conditional on the available information. Estimated DSGE models are increasingly used by central banks around the world as tools for macroeconomic forecasting and policy analysis. Examples of such models include the small open economy model developed by the Sveriges Riksbank (Adolfson et al., 2007a,b), the New Area-Wide Model developed at the European Central

Bank (Coenen et al., 2008; Christoffel et al., 2011), and the Federal Reserve Board's Estimated, Dynamic, Optimization-based model (Edge et al., 2009).

This chapter has a methodological and a substantive dimension. On the methodological side, we provide a collection of algorithms that can be used to generate forecasts with DSGE models. This collection includes algorithms to generate draws from the posterior distribution of DSGE model parameters, the distribution of future observations conditional on current information (predictive distribution, in short), the predictive distribution conditional on external nowcasts and short-run interest rate expectations, and the predictive distribution conditional on interest-rate paths reflecting alternative monetary policy scenarios. A particular emphasis is given to methods that allow the user to incorporate external information into the DSGE-model-based forecasts. This external information could take the form of forecasts for the current quarter (nowcasts) from surveys of professional forecasters, short-term and medium-term interest rate forecasts, or long-run inflation and output-growth expectations. We also study the use of unanticipated and anticipated monetary policy shocks to generate forecasts conditional on desired interest rate paths.

On the substantive side, we are providing detailed empirical applications of the forecasting methods discussed in this chapter using U.S. macroeconomic time series. We begin by comparing the accuracy of real-time forecasts from a small-scale New Keynesian DSGE model and the Smets and Wouters (2007) model to the accuracy of forecasts published in the Federal Reserve Board of Governors so-called "Greenbook" and professional forecasts published in the Blue Chip survey. Using our algorithms, we then show how the forecast performance of DSGE models can be improved by incorporating data on long-run inflation expectations as well as nowcasts from the Blue Chip survey. We also show that data on short- and medium-horizon interest rate expectations improves the interest rate forecasts of the Smets–Wouters model with anticipated monetary policy shocks, but has some adverse effects on output growth and inflation forecasts. In several instances, the use of external information requires small changes to the DSGE model, typically the incorporation of additional structural shocks that absorb otherwise unexplained variation in the external information. We propose modifications that can be easily incorporated in any DSGE model. Throughout this chapter we focus on informal RMSE comparisons rather than formal tests of predictive ability. The design of such tests is discussed in detail in the surveys by West (2006) and Clark and McCracken (2012).

To illustrate forecasting conditional on a interest rate path we generate DSGE model forecasts as of May 2011 and compare the evolution of output growth, inflation, and interest rates under the DSGE model's predicted interest rate path to a hypothetical path along which interest rates stay at 25 basis points until the second quarter of 2012. Finally, in the context of interval and density forecasting we study the real-time forecasting performance of the Smets–Wouters model and a DSGE model with financial frictions during the 2008–2009 recession.

While most of the algorithms that are presented in this chapter are not new, many of the substantive applications are novel. First, our forecast accuracy comparisons include data from the Great Recession – the most significant macroeconomic event in the past quarter of a century – while most previous studies only use data from the Great Moderation period. Also, to our knowledge, this is the first study that documents the forecast error reduction achievable by the use of long-run inflation expectations data that carefully compares the accuracy of DSGE model forecasts generated with and without conditioning on external nowcasts, that assesses the effect of incorporating interest-rate expectations via anticipated monetary policy shocks. Finally, we are the first to conduct a "post-mortem" of DSGE-based forecasting during the Great Recession, and to examine the relative forecasting performance of models with and without financial frictions during this episode. This analysis points out the importance of incorporating the real-time information contained in interest rate spreads for forecasting.

Our findings can be summarized as follows: for nowcasts and short-run forecasts DSGE models are at a disadvantage compared to professional forecasts, but over the medium and long-run DSGE model forecasts for both output and inflation become competitive with – if not superior to – the Blue Chip consensus forecasts. For interest rate forecasts the DSGE models are generally of inferior accuracy relative to the Blue Chip consensus. Our empirical analysis also shows that expanding the set of observables beyond the usual macroeconomic time series commonly used in DSGE model estimation can lead to a substantial improvement in forecasting performance, especially during particularly important episodes such as the Great Recession.

The standard set of observables has two important limitations. The first is timeliness: National Income and Product Accounts (NIPA data) are only available with a lag, and therefore the DSGE econometrician lacks information about the current state of the economy. We show that incorporating nowcast information from private forecasters can ameliorate this problem, leading to better short-term forecasts. This finding confirms the "folklore" among DSGE model forecasters in central banks, who routinely use nowcasts from judgemental forecasters in their projections. The improvement in forecast accuracy at short horizons does not translate into substantially different medium and long-run forecasts, however. The second limitation concerns the breadth of the information set. Financial market variables such as spreads may capture information about the state of the economy that is not contained in the standard observables. Similarly, surveys about interest rates or 10-year inflation expectations can inform the econometrician about the short and medium run intentions of policy makers (e.g., capture information in policy announcements such as the "considerable period," "measured pace," "extended period," etc.), or longer run changes in the policy stance, respectively.

Before delving into the details, we will take a step back and discuss why we think that forecasting with DSGE models is a useful enterprise. A macroeconomic forecaster can in principle choose from a large pool of econometric models. Some models are univariate, others are multivariate; some are linear, others are non-linear; some are based on economic theory whereas others simply exploit correlations in the data. Empirical DSGE models are multivariate, in most instances they are linearized, and they build upon modern dynamic macroeconomic theory which emphasizes intertemporal decision making and the role of expectations. The benefit of building empirical models on sound theoretical foundations is that the model delivers an internally consistent interpretation of the current state and future trajectories of the economy and enables a sound analysis of policy scenarios. The potential cost is that theory-implied cross-coefficient restrictions might lead to a deterioration in forecast performance.

While a decade ago the costs outweighed the benefits, the scale has tipped in favor of DSGE models in recent years. First, DSGE models have been enriched with endogenous propagation mechanisms, e.g., Christiano et al. (2005), and exogenous propagation mechanisms, e.g., Smets and Wouters (2003, 2007), which allow the models to better capture the autocovariance patterns in the data. Second, as demonstrated in Section 5, DSGE models can be easily modified to incorporate external information into the forecasts, both real-time information about the current state of the economy as well as information about its long run trends. Real-time information is interpreted by the models as information about the realization of the structural shocks, and is useful to improve the accuracy of short-horizon forecasts. Moreover, long-run inflation expectations can be used to anchor long-horizon forecasts of nominal variables.

The case for DSGE model forecasting ultimately rests on the fact that these models provide a good package. Granted, there exist time series models that generate more accurate univariate forecasts of output growth and inflation, but these models might miss co-movements between these two variables. Bayesian VARs, discussed in detail in Karlsson (2012), tend to be good multivariate forecasting models but it is difficult to identify more than one or two structural shocks and to provide a narrative for the current and future state of the economy. Moreover, VARs typically do not have enough structure to generate predictions about anticipated changes in interest rates. Dynamic factor models are able to extract information from a large cross section of macroeconomic variables and to explain the co-movements among these series as being generated by a low-dimensional vector of latent variables. While the forecasting record of these models is strong, the policy experiments that could be carried out with these models are very limited. Finally, none of the aforementioned models would allow the user to measure the degree of distortion in the economy that ought to be corrected through monetary policy.

Estimated DSGE models can perform a lot of tasks simultaneously. They generate multivariate density forecasts that reflect parameter and shock uncertainty. They provide a device for interpreting the current state and the future path of the economy through the lens of modern dynamic macroeconomics and provide decompositions in terms of structural shocks. Moreover, the models enable the user to generate predictions of the effect of alternative policy scenarios. While a successful decathlete may not be the fastest runner or the best discus thrower, he certainly is a well-rounded athlete.

The remainder of this chapter is organized as follows. Section 2 provides a description of the DSGE models used in the empirical analysis of this chapter. The mechanics of generating DSGE model forecasts within a Bayesian framework are described in Section 3. We review well-known procedures to generate draws from posterior parameter distributions and posterior predictive distributions for future realizations of macroeconomic variables. From these draws one can then compute point, interval, and density forecasts. The first set of empirical results is presented in Section 4. We describe the real-time data set that is used throughout this chapter and examine the accuracy of our benchmark point forecasts. We also provide a review of the sizeable literature on the accuracy of DSGE model forecasts. Documenting the accuracy of DSGE model predictions is not just important from a forecasting perspective, but it can also be viewed as part of a general evaluation strategy for dynamic macro models. In fact, Smets and Wouters's (2003, 2007) success of generating DSGE model forecasts that are competitive with forecasts from large Bayesian VARs convinced many researchers and policymakers that DSGE models are indeed empirically viable.

The accuracy of DSGE model forecasts is affected by how well the model captures low frequency trends in the data and by the extent to which important information about the current quarter (nowcast) is incorporated into the forecast. In Section 5 we introduce shocks to the target-inflation rate, long-run productivity growth, as well as anticipated monetary policy shocks into the (Smets and Wouters, 2007) model. With these additional shocks, we can use data on inflation, output growth, and interest rate expectations from the Blue Chip survey as observations on agents' expectations in the DSGE model and thereby incorporate the survey information into the DSGE model forecasts. We also consider methods of adjusting DSGE model forecasts in light of Blue Chip nowcasts. In Section 6 we provide a critical assessment of using unanticipated and anticipated monetary policy shocks to generate forecasts conditional on a desired interest rate path.

Up to this point we have mainly focused on point forecasts generated from DSGE models. In Section 7 we move beyond point forecasts. We start by using the DSGE model to decompose the forecasts into the contribution of the various structural shocks. We then generate density forecasts throughout the 2008–2009 financial crisis and recession, comparing predictions from a DSGE model with and without financial frictions. We also present some evidence on the quality of density forecasts by computing probability integral transformations. Finally, Section 8 concludes and provides an outlook. As part of this outlook we discuss forecasting with non-linear DSGE models and point the reader to several strands of related literature in which forecasts are not directly generated from DSGE models but the DSGE model restrictions nonetheless influence the forecasts.

Throughout this chapter we use the following notation. $Y_{t_0:t_1}$ denotes the sequence of observations or random variables $\{y_{t_0}, \ldots, y_{t_1}\}$. If no ambiguity arises, we sometimes drop the time subscripts and abbreviate $Y_{1:T}$ by Y. θ often serves as generic parameter vector, $p(\theta)$ is the density associated with the prior distribution, $p(Y|\theta)$ is the likelihood function, and $p(\theta|Y)$ the posterior density. We use *iid* to abbreviate independently and identically distributed and $N(\mu, \Sigma)$ denotes the normal distribution with mean μ and variance-covariance matrix Σ. Finally, $\mathcal{I}\{x \geq a\}$ is the indicator function equal to one if $x \geq a$ and equal to zero otherwise.

2. THE DSGE MODELS

We consider three DSGE models in this chapter. The first model is the Smets and Wouters (2007), which is based on earlier work by Christiano et al. (2005) and Smets and Wouters (2003) (Section 2.1). It is a medium-scale DSGE model, which augments the standard neoclassical stochastic growth model by nominal price and wage rigidities as well as habit formation in consumption and investment adjustment costs. The second model is obtained by augmenting the Smets–Wouters model with credit frictions as in the financial accelerator model developed by Bernanke et al. (1999) (Section 2.2). The actual implementation of the credit frictions closely follows (Christiano et al., 2009). Finally, we consider a small-scale DSGE model, which is obtained as a special case of the Smets and Wouters (2007) model by removing some of its features such as capital accumulation, wage stickiness, and habit formation (Section 2.3).

2.1. The Smets–Wouters Model

We begin by briefly describing the log-linearized equilibrium conditions of the (Smets and Wouters, 2007) model. Long-run growth in this model is introduced through a total factor productivity process $\ln A_t = (1 - \alpha)\gamma t + \tilde{z}_t$, where $\tilde{z}_t$ follows the autoregressive law of motion

$$\tilde{z}_t = \rho_z \tilde{z}_{t-1} + \sigma_z \varepsilon_{z,t}. \tag{1}$$

Here α is the capital share in the Cobb–Douglas production function of intermediate goods producers and γ turns out to be the average growth rate of the economy. We deviate from Smets and Wouters (2007) in that we detrend the model variables that are subject to growth by $Z_t = e^{\gamma t + \frac{1}{1-\alpha}\tilde{z}_t}$ instead of $e^{\gamma t}$. The growth rate of Z_t in deviations from γ, denoted by z_t, follows the process:

$$z_t = \ln\left(Z_t/Z_{t-1}\right) - \gamma = \frac{1}{1-\alpha}(\rho_z - 1)\tilde{z}_{t-1} + \frac{1}{1-\alpha}\sigma_z \epsilon_{z,t}. \tag{2}$$

As explained in detail in Del Negro and Schorfheide (2010), this alternative detrending makes it possible to express almost all equilibrium conditions in a way that encompasses both the trend-stationary total factor productivity process in Smets and Wouters (2007) ($0 \leq \rho_z < 1$), as well as the case where technology follows a unit root process ($\rho_z = 1$).

All variables in the subsequent equations are appropriately detrended and expressed in log deviations from their non-stochastic steady state. Steady state values are denoted by *-subscripts and steady state formulas are provided in a Technical Appendix (available upon request). The consumption Euler equation takes the form:

$$c_t = -\frac{(1 - he^{-\gamma})}{\sigma_c(1 + he^{-\gamma})}\left(R_t - \mathbb{E}_t\left[\pi_{t+1}\right] + b_t\right) + \frac{he^{-\gamma}}{(1 + he^{-\gamma})}\left(c_{t-1} - z_t\right)$$
$$+ \frac{1}{(1 + he^{-\gamma})}\mathbb{E}_t\left[c_{t+1} + z_{t+1}\right] + \frac{(\sigma_c - 1)}{\sigma_c(1 + he^{-\gamma})}\frac{w_* L_*}{c_*}\left(L_t - \mathbb{E}_t\left[L_{t+1}\right]\right), \quad (3)$$

where c_t is consumption, L_t is labor supply, R_t is the nominal interest rate, and π_t is inflation. The exogenous process b_t drives a wedge between the intertemporal ratio of the marginal utility of consumption and the riskless real return $R_t - \mathbb{E}_t\left[\pi_{t+1}\right]$, and follows an AR (1) process with parameters ρ_b and σ_b. The parameters σ_c and h capture the relative degree of risk aversion and the degree of habit persistence in the utility function, respectively. The next condition follows from the optimality condition for the capital producers, and expresses the relationship between the value of capital in terms of consumption q_t^k and the level of investment i_t measured in terms of consumption goods:

$$q_t^k = S'' e^{2\gamma}(1 + \beta e^{(1-\sigma_c)\gamma})\left(i_t - \frac{1}{1 + \beta e^{(1-\sigma_c)\gamma}}\left(i_{t-1} - z_t\right)\right.$$
$$\left. - \frac{\beta e^{(1-\sigma_c)\gamma}}{1 + \beta e^{(1-\sigma_c)\gamma}}\mathbb{E}_t\left[i_{t+1} + z_{t+1}\right] - \mu_t\right), \quad (4)$$

which is affected by both investment adjustment cost (S'' is the second derivative of the adjustment cost function evaluated at the steady state) and by μ_t, an exogenous process called "marginal efficiency of investment," which affects the rate of transformation between consumption and installed capital (see Greenwood et al. (1998)). The latter, called $\bar{k}_t$, indeed evolves as

$$\bar{k}_t = \left(1 - \frac{i_*}{\bar{k}_*}\right)\left(\bar{k}_{t-1} - z_t\right) + \frac{i_*}{\bar{k}_*}i_t + \frac{i_*}{\bar{k}_*}S'' e^{2\gamma}(1 + \beta e^{(1-\sigma_c)\gamma})\mu_t, \quad (5)$$

where $i_*/\bar{k}_*$ is the steady state ratio of investment to capital. μ_t follows an AR (1) process with parameters ρ_μ and σ_μ. The parameter β captures the intertemporal discount rate in the utility function of the households. The arbitrage condition between the return to capital and the riskless rate is:

$$\frac{r_*^k}{r_*^k + (1 - \delta)}\mathbb{E}_t\left[r_{t+1}^k\right] + \frac{1 - \delta}{r_*^k + (1 - \delta)}\mathbb{E}_t\left[q_{t+1}^k\right] - q_t^k = R_t + b_t - \mathbb{E}_t\left[\pi_{t+1}\right], \quad (6)$$

where r_t^k is the rental rate of capital, r_*^k its steady state value, and δ the depreciation rate. Capital is subject to variable capacity utilization u_t. The relationship between $\bar{k}_t$ and the amount of capital effectively rented out to firms k_t is

$$k_t = u_t - z_t + \bar{k}_{t-1}. \quad (7)$$

The optimality condition determining the rate of utilization is given by

$$\frac{1-\psi}{\psi}r_t^k = u_t, \tag{8}$$

where ψ captures the utilization costs in terms of foregone consumption. From the optimality conditions of goods producers it follows that all firms have the same capital–labor ratio:

$$k_t = w_t - r_t^k + L_t. \tag{9}$$

Real marginal costs for firms are given by

$$mc_t = w_t + \alpha L_t - \alpha k_t, \tag{10}$$

where α is the income share of capital (after paying markups and fixed costs) in the production function.

All of the equations so far maintain the same form whether technology has a unit root or is trend stationary. A few small differences arise for the following two equilibrium conditions. The production function is:

$$y_t = \Phi_p\left(\alpha k_t + (1-\alpha)L_t\right) + \mathcal{I}\{\rho_z < 1\}(\Phi_p - 1)\frac{1}{1-\alpha}\tilde{z}_t, \tag{11}$$

under trend stationarity. The coefficient Φ_p reflects the presence of fixed costs in the production function of the intermediate goods producers. The term $(\Phi_p - 1)\frac{1}{1-\alpha}\tilde{z}_t$ drops out if technology has a stochastic trend, because in this case one has to assume that the fixed costs are proportional to the trend. Similarly, the resource constraint is:

$$y_t = g_t + \frac{c_*}{y_*}c_t + \frac{i_*}{y_*}i_t + \frac{r_*^k k_*}{y_*}u_t - \mathcal{I}\{\rho_z < 1\}\frac{1}{1-\alpha}\tilde{z}_t. \tag{12}$$

The term $-\frac{1}{1-\alpha}\tilde{z}_t$ disappears if technology follows a unit root process. Government spending g_t is assumed to follow the exogenous process:

$$g_t = \rho_g g_{t-1} + \sigma_g \varepsilon_{g,t} + \eta_{gz}\sigma_z \varepsilon_{z,t}.$$

Finally, the price and wage Phillips curves are, respectively:

$$\pi_t = \frac{(1 - \zeta_p \beta e^{(1-\sigma_c)\gamma})(1 - \zeta_p)}{(1 + \iota_p \beta e^{(1-\sigma_c)\gamma})\zeta_p((\Phi_p - 1)\epsilon_p + 1)}mc_t$$

$$+\frac{\iota_p}{1 + \iota_p \beta e^{(1-\sigma_c)\gamma}}\pi_{t-1} + \frac{\beta e^{(1-\sigma_c)\gamma}}{1 + \iota_p \beta e^{(1-\sigma_c)\gamma}}\mathbb{E}_t\left[\pi_{t+1}\right] + \lambda_{f,t}, \tag{13}$$

and

$$w_t = \frac{(1 - \zeta_w \beta e^{(1-\sigma_c)\gamma})(1 - \zeta_w)}{(1 + \beta e^{(1-\sigma_c)\gamma})\zeta_w((\lambda_w - 1)\epsilon_w + 1)} \left(w_t^h - w_t\right)$$
$$- \frac{1 + \iota_w \beta e^{(1-\sigma_c)\gamma}}{1 + \beta e^{(1-\sigma_c)\gamma}} \pi_t + \frac{1}{1 + \beta e^{(1-\sigma_c)\gamma}} \left(w_{t-1} - z_t - \iota_w \pi_{t-1}\right)$$
$$+ \frac{\beta e^{(1-\sigma_c)\gamma}}{1 + \beta e^{(1-\sigma_c)\gamma}} \mathbb{E}_t \left[w_{t+1} + z_{t+1} + \pi_{t+1}\right] + \lambda_{w,t}, \tag{14}$$

where ζ_p, ι_p, and ϵ_p are the Calvo parameter, the degree of indexation, and the curvature parameters in the Kimball aggregator for prices, and ζ_w, ι_w, and ϵ_w are the corresponding parameters for wages. The variable w_t^h corresponds to the household's marginal rate of substitution between consumption and labor, and is given by:

$$w_t^h = \frac{1}{1 - he^{-\gamma}} \left(c_t - he^{-\gamma} c_{t-1} + he^{-\gamma} z_t\right) + \nu_l L_t, \tag{15}$$

where ν_l characterizes the curvature of the disutility of labor (and would equal the inverse of the Frisch elasticity in absence of wage rigidities). The mark-ups $\lambda_{f,t}$ and $\lambda_{w,t}$ follow exogenous ARMA (1,1) processes

$$\lambda_{f,t} = \rho_{\lambda_f} \lambda_{f,t-1} + \sigma_{\lambda_f} \varepsilon_{\lambda_f,t} + \eta_{\lambda_f} \sigma_{\lambda_f} \varepsilon_{\lambda_f,t-1}, \quad \text{and}$$
$$\lambda_{w,t} = \rho_{\lambda_w} \lambda_{w,t-1} + \sigma_{\lambda_w} \varepsilon_{\lambda_w,t} + \eta_{\lambda_w} \sigma_{\lambda_w} \varepsilon_{\lambda_w,t-1},$$

respectively. Last, the monetary authority follows a generalized feedback rule:

$$R_t = \rho_R R_{t-1} + (1 - \rho_R) \left(\psi_1 \pi_t + \psi_2 (y_t - y_t^f)\right)$$
$$+ \psi_3 \left((y_t - y_t^f) - (y_{t-1} - y_{t-1}^f)\right) + r_t^m, \tag{16}$$

where the flexible price/wage output y_t^f obtains from solving the version of the model without nominal rigidities (that is, Eqs. (3) through (12) and (15)), and the residual r_t^m follows an AR (1) process with parameters ρ_{rm} and σ_{rm}.

The SW model is estimated based on seven quarterly macroeconomic time series. The measurement equations for real output, consumption, investment, and real wage growth, hours, inflation, and interest rates are given by:

$$\begin{aligned}
\textit{Output growth} \quad &= \gamma + 100 \left(\Delta y_t + z_t\right) \\
\textit{Consumption growth} &= \gamma + 100 \left(\Delta c_t + z_t\right) \\
\textit{Investment growth} \quad &= \gamma + 100 \left(\Delta i_t + z_t\right) \\
\textit{Real Wage growth} \quad &= \gamma + 100 \left(\Delta w_t + z_t\right), \\
\textit{Hours} \quad &= \bar{l} + 100 l_t \\
\textit{Inflation} \quad &= \pi_* + 100 \pi_t \\
\textit{FFR} \quad &= R_* + 100 R_t
\end{aligned} \tag{17}$$

where all variables are measured in percent, Δ is the temporal difference operator, π_* and R_* measure the steady state level of net inflation and short-term nominal interest rates, respectively, and $\bar{l}$ captures the mean of hours (this variable is measured as an index). The priors for the DSGE model parameters is the same as in Smets and Wouters (2007), and is summarized in Panel I of Table 2.1. We will comment on procedures to elicit prior distributions in Section 3.1 and illustrate in Section 5.1 that the prior choice can be very important for the forecasting performance of the DSGE model.

2.2. A Medium-Scale Model with Financial Frictions

We now add financial frictions to the SW model building on the work of Bernanke et al. (1999), Christiano et al. (2003), DeGraeve (2008), and Christiano et al. (2009). This amounts to replacing (6) with the following conditions:

$$E_t \left[\tilde{R}_{t+1}^k - R_t \right] = b_t + \zeta_{sp,b} \left(q_t^k + \bar{k}_t - n_t \right) + \tilde{\sigma}_{\omega,t} \tag{18}$$

and

$$\tilde{R}_t^k - \pi_t = \frac{r_*^k}{r_*^k + (1-\delta)} r_t^k + \frac{(1-\delta)}{r_*^k + (1-\delta)} q_t^k - q_{t-1}^k, \tag{19}$$

where $\tilde{R}_t^k$ is the gross nominal return on capital for entrepreneurs, n_t is entrepreneurial equity, and $\tilde{\sigma}_{\omega,t}$ captures mean-preserving changes in the cross-sectional dispersion of ability across entrepreneurs (see Christiano et al. 2009) and follows an AR (1) process with parameters ρ_{σ_ω} and σ_{σ_ω}. The second condition defines the return on capital, while the first one determines the spread between the expected return on capital and the riskless rate.[1] The following condition describes the evolution of entrepreneurial net worth:

$$\begin{aligned} \hat{n}_t = \zeta_{n,\tilde{R}^k} \left(\tilde{R}_t^k - \pi_t \right) - \zeta_{n,R} \left(R_{t-1} - \pi_t \right) + \zeta_{n,qK} \left(q_{t-1}^k + \bar{k}_{t-1} \right) + \zeta_{n,n} n_{t-1} \\ - \frac{\zeta_{n,\sigma_\omega}}{\zeta_{sp,\sigma_\omega}} \tilde{\sigma}_{\omega,t-1}. \end{aligned} \tag{20}$$

In addition, the set of measurement equations (17) is augmented as follows

$$\text{Spread} = SP_* + 100\mathbb{E}_t \left[\tilde{R}_{t+1}^k - R_t \right], \tag{21}$$

where the parameter SP_* measures the steady state spread. We specify priors for the parameters SP_*, $\zeta_{sp,b}$, in addition to ρ_{σ_ω} and σ_{σ_ω}, and fix the parameters $\bar{F}_*$ and γ_* (steady state default probability and survival rate of entrepreneurs, respectively). A summary is provided in Panel V of Table 2.1. In turn, these parameters imply values for the parameters of (20), as shown in the Technical Appendix. We refer to the DSGE model with financial frictions as SW-FF.

---

[1] Note that if $\zeta_{sp,b} = 0$ and the financial friction shocks are zero, (6) coincides with (18) plus (19).

Table 2.1 Priors for the Medium-Scale Model

	Density	Mean	St. Dev.		Density	Mean	St. Dev.
Panel I: SW Model							
Policy Parameters							
ψ_1	Normal	1.50	0.25	ρ_R	Beta	0.75	0.10
ψ_2	Normal	0.12	0.05	ρ_{r^m}	Beta	0.50	0.20
ψ_3	Normal	0.12	0.05	σ_{r^m}	InvG	0.10	2.00
Nominal Rigidities Parameters							
ζ_p	Beta	0.50	0.10	ζ_w	Beta	0.50	0.10
Other "Endogenous Propagation and Steady State" Parameters							
α	Normal	0.30	0.05	π^*	Gamma	0.62	0.10
Φ	Normal	1.25	0.12	γ	Normal	0.40	0.10
h	Beta	0.70	0.10	S''	Normal	4.00	1.50
ν_l	Normal	2.00	0.75	σ_c	Normal	1.50	0.37
ι_p	Beta	0.50	0.15	ι_w	Beta	0.50	0.15
r_*	Gamma	0.25	0.10	ψ	Beta	0.50	0.15
(Note $\beta = (1/(1 + r_*/100)))$							
$\rho s,\ \sigma s,\ and\ \eta s$							
ρ_z	Beta	0.50	0.20	σ_z	InvG	0.10	2.00
ρ_b	Beta	0.50	0.20	σ_b	InvG	0.10	2.00
ρ_{λ_f}	Beta	0.50	0.20	σ_{λ_f}	InvG	0.10	2.00
ρ_{λ_w}	Beta	0.50	0.20	σ_{λ_w}	InvG	0.10	2.00
ρ_μ	Beta	0.50	0.20	σ_μ	InvG	0.10	2.00
ρ_g	Beta	0.50	0.20	σ_g	InvG	0.10	2.00
η_{λ_f}	Beta	0.50	0.20	η_{λ_w}	Beta	0.50	0.20
η_{gz}	Beta	0.50	0.20				
Panel II: SW with Loose π_* Prior ($SW - Loose$)							
π^*	Gamma	0.75	0.40				
Panel III: Model with Long Run Inflation Expectations ($SW\pi$)							
ρ_{π^*}	Beta	0.50	0.20	σ_{π^*}	InvG	0.03	6.00
Panel IV: Model with Long Run Output Expectations ($SW\pi Y$)							
ρ_{z^p}	Beta	0.98	0.01	σ_{z^p}	InvG	0.01	4.00
Panel V: Financial Frictions ($SW - FF$)							
SP_*	Gamma	2.00	0.10	$\zeta_{sp,b}$	Beta	0.05	0.005
ρ_{σ_w}	Beta	0.75	0.15	σ_{σ_w}	InvG	0.05	4.00

Notes: The following parameters are fixed in (Smets and Wouters, 2007): $\delta = 0.025$, $g_* = 0.18$, $\lambda_w = 1.50$, $\varepsilon_w = 10$, and $\varepsilon_p = 10$. In addition, for the model with financial frictions we fix $\bar{F}_* = .03$ and $\gamma_* = .99$. The columns "Mean" and "St. Dev." list the means and the standard deviations for Beta, Gamma, and Normal distributions, and the values s and v for the Inverse Gamma (InvG) distribution, where $p_{\mathcal{IG}}(\sigma|v, s) \propto \sigma^{-v-1} e^{-vs^2/2\sigma^2}$. The effective prior is truncated at the boundary of the determinacy region. The prior for $\bar{l}$ is $\mathcal{N}(-45, 5^2)$.

2.3. A Small-Scale DSGE Model

The small-scale DSGE model is obtained as a special case of the SW model, by removing some of its features such as capital accumulation, wage stickiness, and habit formation. After setting $h = 0$ and eliminating the shock b_t the consumption Euler equation simplifies to:

$$c_t = \mathbb{E}_t \left[c_{t+1} + z_{t+1} \right] - \frac{1}{\sigma_c} \left(R_t - \mathbb{E}_t \left[\pi_{t+1} \right] \right). \tag{22}$$

After setting the capital share α in the production function to zero, the marginal costs are given by the wage: $mc_t = w_t$. In the absence of wage stickiness the wage equals the households' marginal rate of substitution between consumption and leisure, which in equilibrium leads to $w_t = c_t + \nu_l L_t$. In the absence of fixed costs ($\Phi_p = 1$) detrended output equals the labor input $y_t = L_t$. Overall, we obtain

$$mc_t = c_t + \nu_l y_t. \tag{23}$$

The Phillips curve simplifies to

$$\pi_t = \frac{(1 - \zeta_p \beta)(1 - \zeta_p)}{(1 + \iota_p \beta)\zeta_p} mc_t + \frac{\beta}{1 + \iota_p \beta} \mathbb{E}_t \left[\pi_{t+1} \right] + \frac{\iota_p}{1 + \iota_p \beta} \pi_{t-1}. \tag{24}$$

We assume that the central bank only reacts to inflation and output growth and that the monetary policy shock is iid. This leads to a policy rule of the form

$$R_t = \rho_R R_{t-1} + (1 - \rho_R) \left[\psi_1 \pi_t + \psi_2 (y_t - y_{t-1} + z_t) \right] + \sigma_R \epsilon_{R,t}. \tag{25}$$

Finally, the aggregate resource constraint simplifies to

$$y_t = c_t + g_t. \tag{26}$$

Here we have adopted a slightly different definition of the government spending shock than in the SW model.

The model is completed with the specification of the exogenous shock processes. The government spending shock evolves according to

$$g_t = \rho_g g_{t-1} + \sigma_g \epsilon_{g,t}. \tag{27}$$

Since the small-scale model does not have a strong internal propagation mechanism and cannot generate serially correlated output growth rates, we slightly generalize the technology process from an AR (1) process to an AR (2) process

$$\tilde{z}_t = \rho_z (1 - \varphi)\tilde{z}_{t-1} + \varphi \tilde{z}_{t-2} + \sigma_z \epsilon_{z,t}, \tag{28}$$

which implies that the growth rate of the trend process evolves according to

$$z_t = \ln \left(Z_t / Z_{t-1} \right) - \gamma = (\rho_z - 1)(1 - \varphi)\tilde{z}_{t-1} - \varphi(\tilde{z}_{t-1} - \tilde{z}_{t-2}) + \sigma_z \epsilon_{z,t}.$$

The innovations $\epsilon_{z,t}$, $\epsilon_{g,t}$, and $\epsilon_{R,t}$ are assumed to be iid standard normal.

The small-scale model is estimated based on three quarterly macroeconomic time series. The measurement equations for real output growth, inflation, and interest rates are given by:

$$
\begin{aligned}
\textit{Output growth} &= \gamma + 100 \ (\Delta y_t + z_t) \\
\textit{Inflation} &= \pi_* + 100\pi_t \\
\textit{FFR} &= R_* + 100R_t
\end{aligned}
\tag{29}
$$

where all variables are measured in percent and π_* and R_* measure the steady state level of inflation and short-term nominal interest rates, respectively. For the parameters that are common between the SW model and the small-scale model we use similar marginal prior distributions as listed in Table 2.1. The additional parameter φ_z has a prior distribution that is uniform on the interval $(-1, 1)$ because it is a partial autocorrelation. The joint prior distribution is given by the products of the marginals, truncated to ensure that the DSGE model has a determinate equilibrium.

3. GENERATING FORECASTS WITH DSGE MODELS

Before examining the forecast performance of DSGE models we provide a brief overview of the mechanics of generating such forecasts in a Bayesian framework. A more comprehensive review of Bayesian forecasting is provided by Geweke and Whiteman (2006). Let θ denote the vector that stacks the DSGE model parameters. Bayesian inference starts from a prior distribution represented by a density $p(\theta)$. The prior is combined with the conditional density of the data $Y_{1:T}$ given the parameters θ, denoted by $p(Y_{1:T}|\theta)$. This density can be derived from the DSGE model. According to Bayes Theorem, the posterior distribution, that is the conditional distribution of parameters given data, is given by

$$
p(\theta|Y_{1:T}) = \frac{p(Y_{1:T}|\theta)p(\theta)}{p(Y_{1:T})}, \quad p(Y_{1:T}) = \int p(Y_{1:T}|\theta)p(\theta)d\theta,
\tag{30}
$$

where $p(Y_{1:T})$ is called the marginal likelihood or data density. In DSGE model applications it is typically not possible to derive moments and quantiles of the posterior distribution analytically. Instead, inference is implemented via numerical methods such as MCMC simulation. MCMC algorithms deliver serially correlated sequences $\{\theta^{(j)}\}_{j=1}^{n_{sim}}$ of n_{sim} draws from the density $p(\theta|Y_{1:T})$.

In forecasting applications the posterior distribution $p(\theta|Y_{1:T})$ is not the primary object of interest. Instead, the focus is on predictive distributions, which can be decomposed as follows:

$$
p(Y_{T+1:T+H}|Y_{1:T}) = \int p(Y_{T+1:T+H}|\theta, Y_{1:T})p(\theta|Y_{1:T})d\theta.
\tag{31}
$$

This decomposition highlights that draws from the predictive density can be obtained by simulating the DSGE model conditional on posterior parameter draws $\theta^{(j)}$ and the observations $Y_{1:T}$. In turn, this leads to sequences $Y^{(j)}_{T+1:T+H}, j = 1, \ldots, n_{sim}$ that represent draws from the predictive distribution (31). These draws can then be used to obtain numerical approximations of moments, quantiles, and the probability density function of $Y_{T+1:T+H}$. In the remainder of this section, we discuss how to obtain draws from the posterior distribution of DSGE model parameters (Section 3.1) and how to generate draws from the predictive distribution of future observations (Section 3.2).

3.1. Posterior Inference for θ

Before the DSGE model can be estimated, it has to be solved using a numerical method. In most DSGE models, the intertemporal optimization problems of economic agents can be written recursively, using Bellman equations. In general, the value and policy functions associated with the optimization problems are non-linear in terms of the state variables, and the solution of the optimization problems requires numerical techniques. The implied equilibrium law of motion can be written as

$$s_t = \Phi(s_{t-1}, \epsilon_t; \theta), \tag{32}$$

where s_t is a vector of suitably defined state variables and ϵ_t is a vector that stacks the innovations for the structural shocks.

In this chapter, we proceed under the assumption that the DSGE model's solution is approximated by log-linearization techniques and ignore the discrepancy between the non-linear model solution and the first-order approximation. In fact, in Section 2 we presented the DSGE models in terms of log-linearized equilibrium conditions. These equilibrium conditions form a system of linear rational expectations difference equations that generically could be written as

$$\Gamma_0(\theta)s_t = \Gamma_1(\theta)s_{t-1} + \Psi(\theta)\epsilon_t + \Pi(\theta)\eta_t, \tag{33}$$

where η_t is a vector of rational expectations forecast errors. In order to cast the equilibrium conditions presented in Section 2 into the canonical form (33), one has to introduce forecast errors for variables that appear in expectation terms, e.g., $\eta^x_t = x_t - \mathbb{E}_{t-1}[x_t]$.

A solution algorithm for (33) is provided in Sims (2002).[2] In a nutshell, it amounts to expressing η_t as a function of ϵ_t subject to the constraint that the law of motion of s_t is non-explosive. This solution takes the form

$$s_t = \Phi_1(\theta)s_{t-1} + \Phi_\epsilon(\theta)\epsilon_t. \tag{34}$$

The system matrices Φ_1 and Φ_ϵ are functions of the DSGE model parameters θ, and s_t spans the state variables of the model economy, but might also contain some redundant

---

[2] There exist many alternative algorithms for linear rational expectations systems in the literature. Each algorithm uses a slightly different canonical form of the difference Eq. (33) as a starting point.

elements that facilitate a simple representation of the measurement equation:

$$y_t = \Psi_0(\theta) + \Psi_1(\theta)t + \Psi_2(\theta)s_t. \tag{35}$$

Equations (34) and (35) provide a state-space representation for the linearized DSGE model. This representation is the basis for the econometric analysis. If the innovations ϵ_t are Gaussian, then the likelihood function $p(Y_{1:T}|\theta)$ can be evaluated with a standard Kalman filter.

We now turn to the prior distribution represented by the density $p(\theta)$. An example of such a prior distribution is provided in Table 2.1. The table characterizes the marginal distribution of the DSGE model parameters. The joint distribution is then obtained as the product of the marginals. It is typically truncated to ensure that the DSGE model has a unique solution. DSGE model parameters can be grouped into three categories: (i) parameters that affect steady states; (ii) parameters that control the endogenous propagation mechanism of the model without affecting steady states; and (iii) parameters that determine the law of motion of the exogenous shock processes.

Priors for steady state related parameters are often elicited indirectly by ensuring that model-implied steady states are commensurable with pre-sample averages of the corresponding economic variables. Micro-level information, e.g., about labor supply elasticities or the frequency of price and wage changes, is often used to formulate priors for parameters that control the endogenous propagation mechanism of the model. Finally, beliefs about volatilities and autocovariance patterns of endogenous variables can be used to elicit priors for the remaining parameters. A more detailed discussions and some tools to mechanize the prior elicitation are provided in Del Negro and Schorfheide (2008).

A detailed discussion of numerical techniques to obtain draws from the posterior distribution $p(\theta|Y_{1:T})$ can be found, for instance, in An and Schorfheide (2007a) and Del Negro and Schorfheide (2010). We only provide a brief overview. Because of the non-linear relationship between the DSGE model parameters θ and the system matrices $\Psi_0, \Psi_1, \Psi_2, \Phi_1$ and Φ_ϵ of the state-space representation in (34) and (35), the marginal and conditional distributions of the elements of θ do not fall into the well-known families of probability distributions. Up to now, the most commonly used procedures for generating draws from the posterior distribution of θ are the Random-Walk Metropolis (RWM) Algorithm described in Schorfheide (2000) and Otrok (2001) or the Importance Sampler proposed in DeJong et al. (2000). The basic RWM Algorithm takes the following form.

Algorithm 1.   Random-Walk Metropolis (RWM) Algorithm for DSGE Model.

1. *Use a numerical optimization routine to maximize the log posterior, which up to a constant is given by* $\ln p(Y_{1:T}|\theta) + \ln p(\theta)$. *Denote the posterior mode by* $\tilde{\theta}$.
2. *Let* $\tilde{\Sigma}$ *be the inverse of the (negative) Hessian computed at the posterior mode* $\tilde{\theta}$, *which can be computed numerically.*
3. *Draw* $\theta^{(0)}$ *from* $N(\tilde{\theta}, c_0^2 \tilde{\Sigma})$ *or directly specify a starting value.*

4. For $j = 1, \ldots, n_{sim}$: draw ϑ from the proposal distribution $N(\theta^{(j-1)}, c^2\tilde{\Sigma})$. The jump from $\theta^{(j-1)}$ is accepted ($\theta^{(j)} = \vartheta$) with probability $\min\{1, r(\theta^{(j-1)}, \vartheta|Y_{1:T})\}$ and rejected ($\theta^{(j)} = \theta^{(j-1)}$) otherwise. Here,

$$r(\theta^{(j-1)}, \vartheta|Y_{1:T}) = \frac{p(Y_{1:T}|\vartheta)p(\vartheta)}{p(Y_{1:T}|\theta^{(j-1)})p(\theta^{(j-1)})}. \qquad \square$$

If the likelihood can be evaluated with a high degree of precision, then the maximization in Step 1 can be implemented with a gradient-based numerical optimization routine. The optimization is often not straightforward because the posterior density is typically not globally concave. Thus, it is advisable to start the optimization routine from multiple starting values, which could be drawn from the prior distribution, and then set $\tilde{\theta}$ to the value that attains the highest posterior density across optimization runs. In some applications we found it useful to skip Steps 1 to 3 by choosing a reasonable starting value, such as the mean of the prior distribution, and replacing $\tilde{\Sigma}$ in Step 4 with a matrix whose diagonal elements are equal to the prior variances of the DSGE model parameters and whose off-diagonal elements are zero.

While the RWM algorithm in principle delivers consistent approximations of posterior moments and quantiles even if the posterior contours are highly non-elliptical, the practical performance can be poor as documented in An and Schorfheide (2007a). Recent research on posterior simulators tailored toward DSGE models tries to address the shortcomings of the "default" approaches that are being used in empirical work. An and Schorfheide (2007b) use transition mixtures to deal with a multi-modal posterior distribution. This approach works well if the researcher has knowledge about the location of the modes, obtained, for instance, by finding local maxima of the posterior density with a numerical optimization algorithm. Chib and Ramamurthy (2010) propose to replace the commonly used single block RWM algorithm with a Metropolis-within-Gibbs algorithm that cycles over multiple, randomly selected blocks of parameters. Kohn et al. (2010) propose an adaptive hybrid Metropolis–Hastings samplers and (Herbst, 2010) develops a Metropolis-within-Gibbs algorithm that uses information from the Hessian matrix to construct parameter blocks that maximize within-block correlations at each iteration and Newton steps to tailor proposal distributions for the various conditional posteriors.

3.2. Evaluating the Predictive Distribution

Bayesian DSGE model forecasts can be computed based on draws from the posterior predictive distribution of $Y_{T+1:T+H}$. We use the parameter draws $\{\theta^{(j)}\}_{j=1}^{n_{sim}}$ generated with Algorithm 1 in the previous section as a starting point. Since the DSGE model is represented as a state-space model with latent state vector s_t, we modify the decomposition of the predictive density in (31) accordingly:

$$p(Y_{T+1:T+H}|Y_{1:T}) \tag{36}$$
$$= \int_{(s_T,\theta)} \left[\int_{S_{T+1:T+H}} p(Y_{T+1:T+H}|S_{T+1:T+H})p(S_{T+1:T+H}|s_T, \theta, Y_{1:T})dS_{T+1:T+H} \right]$$
$$\times p(s_T|\theta, Y_{1:T})p(\theta|Y_{1:T})d(s_T, \theta).$$

This predictive density reflects three sources of uncertainty. First, there is parameter uncertainty, captured by the posterior distribution $p(\theta|Y_{1:T})$. Second, since some of the states s_t, e.g., shock processes and certain endogenous state variables such as the capital stock, are unobserved and the dimension of s_t can be larger than the dimension of y_t, there is uncertainty about s_T conditional on $Y_{1:T}$. This uncertainty is captured by the density $p(s_T|\theta, Y_{1:T})$. Third, there is uncertainty about the future realization of shocks that determine the evolution of the states. This uncertainty is captured by $p(S_{T+1:T+H}|s_T, \theta, Y_{1:T})$. Since (35) excludes measurement errors the density $p(Y_{T+1:T+H}|S_{T+1:T+H})$ is simply a point mass. Draws from the predictive density can be generated with the following algorithm:

Algorithm 2.   Draws from the Predictive Distribution. *For $j = 1$ to n_{sim}, select the j'th draw from the posterior distribution $p(\theta|Y_{1:T})$ and:*

1. *Use the Kalman filter to compute mean and variance of the distribution $p(s_T|\theta^{(j)}, Y_{1:T})$. Generate a draw $s_T^{(j)}$ from this distribution.*

2. *A draw from $p(S_{T+1:T+H}|s_T, \theta, Y_{1:T})$ is obtained by generating a sequence of innovations $\epsilon_{T+1:T+H}^{(j)}$. Then, starting from $s_T^{(j)}$, iterate the state transition equation (34) with θ replaced by the draw $\theta^{(j)}$ forward to obtain a sequence $S_{T+1:T+H}^{(j)}$:*

$$s_t^{(j)} = \Phi_1(\theta^{(j)})s_{t-1}^{(j)} + \Phi_\epsilon(\theta^{(j)})\epsilon_t^{(j)}, \quad t = T+1, \dots, T+H.$$

3. *Use the measurement equation (35) to obtain $Y_{T+1:T+H}^{(j)}$:*

$$y_t^{(j)} = \Psi_0(\theta^{(j)})+\Psi_1(\theta^{(j)})t+\Psi_2(\theta^{(j)})s_t^{(j)}, \quad t = T+1, \dots, T+H. \qquad \square$$

Algorithm 2 generates n_{sim} trajectories $Y_{T+1:T+H}^{(j)}$ from the predictive distribution of $Y_{T+1:T+H}$ given $Y_{1:T}$. The algorithm could be modified by executing Steps 2 and 3 m times for each j, which would lead to a total of $m \cdot n_{sim}$ draws from the predictive distribution. A point forecast $\hat{y}_{T+h}$ of y_{T+h} can be obtained by specifying a loss function $L(y_{T+h}, \hat{y}_{T+h})$ and determining the prediction that minimizes the posterior expected loss:

$$\hat{y}_{T+h|T} = \text{argmin}_{\delta\in\mathbb{R}^n} \int_{y_{T+h}} L(y_{T+h}, \delta)p(y_{T+h}|Y_{1:T})dy_{T+h}. \tag{37}$$

The most widely-used loss function for the evaluation of DSGE model forecasts is the quadratic forecast error loss function

$$L(y, \delta) = tr[W(y - \delta)'(y - \delta)],$$

where W is a symmetric positive-definite weight matrix and $tr[\cdot]$ is the trace operator. Under this loss function the optimal predictor is the posterior mean

$$\hat{y}_{T+h|T} = \int_{y_{T+h}} y_{T+h} p(y_{T+h}|Y_{1:T}) dy_{T+h} \approx \frac{1}{n_{sim}} \sum_{j=1}^{n_{sim}} y_{T+h}^{(j)}, \tag{38}$$

which can be approximated by a Monte Carlo average. While it is compelling to assume that actual macroeconomic forecasters and central bankers operate under much more complex loss functions, there does not exist a widely-agreed-upon alternative. For this reason we focus in Sections 4 and 5 on RMSEs as a measure of forecast performance.

Pointwise (meaning for fixed h rather than jointly over multiple horizons) $1 - \alpha$ credible interval forecasts for a particular element $y_{i,T+h}$ of y_{T+h} can be obtained by either computing the $\alpha/2$ and $1-\alpha/2$ percentiles of the empirical distribution of $\{y_{i,T+h}^{(j)}\}_{j=1}^{n_{sim}}$ or by numerically searching for the shortest connected interval that contains a $1 - \alpha$ fraction of the draws $\{y_{i,T+h}^{(j)}\}_{j=1}^{n_{sim}}$. By construction, the latter approach leads to sharper interval forecasts.[3] These credible intervals are often plotted as "fan charts," such as those shown in the Monetary Policy Reports of inflation targeting central banks like the Riksbank or the Bank of England. In order to obtain the full density of the forecasts one can apply a kernel estimator (see Silverman (1986) for an introduction) to the set of draws $\{y_{i,T+h}^{(j)}\}_{j=1}^{n_{sim}}$.

The posterior mean predictor can alternatively be calculated based on the following decomposition:

$$\mathbb{E}[y_{T+h}|Y_{1:T}] = \int \mathbb{E}[y_{T+h}|\theta, Y_{1:T}] p(\theta|Y_{1:T}) d\theta.$$

In the linear state-space model given by (34) and (35)

$$\mathbb{E}[y_{T+h}|\theta, Y_{1:T}] = \Psi_0(\theta) + \Psi_1(\theta)(T+h) + \Psi_2(\theta)[\Phi_1(\theta)]^h \mathbb{E}[s_T|\theta, Y_{1:T}].$$

In turn, Algorithm 2 simplifies considerably. In Step 1 the forecaster only has to calculate the mean $\mathbb{E}[s_T|\theta, Y_{1:T}]$ with the Kalman filter and in Step 2 $\mathbb{E}[y_{T+h}|\theta, Y_{1:T}]$ can be computed directly.

As a short-cut, practitioners sometimes replace the numerical integration with respect to the parameter vector θ in Algorithm 2 by a plug-in step. Draws from the plug-in predictive distribution $p(y_{T+1:T+H}|\hat{\theta}, Y_{1:T})$ are obtained by setting $\theta^{(j)} = \hat{\theta}$ in Steps 2 and 3 of the algorithm. Here $\hat{\theta}$ is a point estimator such as the posterior mode or the posterior mean. While the plug-in approach tends to reduce the computational burden, it does not deliver the correct Bayes predictions and interval and density forecasts will

---

[3] In general, the smallest (in terms of volume) set forecast is given by the highest-density set. If the predictive density is uni-modal the second above-mentioned approach generates the highest-density set. If the predictive density is multi-modal, then there might exist a collection of disconnected intervals that provides a sharper forecast.

understate the uncertainty about future realizations of y_t. However, to the extent that the posterior distribution is concentrated near $\hat{\theta}$, the results obtained from the plug-in approach can be very similar to the results from the full Bayesian analysis. For instance, in Figures 2.13 and 2.14 of Section 7.2 we will plot quantiles of predictive densities based on the full Bayesian analysis. When we compared them to quantiles obtained under the plug-in approach, we found them to be very similar.

4. ACCURACY OF POINT FORECASTS

We begin the empirical analysis with the computation of RMSEs for our DSGE models. The RMSEs are based on a pseudo-out-of-sample forecasting exercise in which we are using real-time data sets to recursively estimate the DSGE models. The construction of the real-time data set is discussed in Section 4.1. Empirical results for the small-scale DSGE model of Section 2.3 are presented in Section 4.2. We compare DSGE model-based RMSEs to RMSEs computed for forecasts of the Blue Chip survey and forecasts published in the Board of Governors' Greenbook. A similar analysis is conducted for the SW model in Section 4.3. Finally, Section 4.4 summarizes results on the forecast performance of medium-scale DSGE models published in the literature.

4.1. A Real–Time Data Set for Forecast Evaluation

Since the small-scale DSGE model is estimated based on a subset of variables that are used for the estimation of the SW model, we focus on the description of the data set for the latter. Real GDP (GDPC), the GDP price deflator (GDPDEF), nominal personal consumption expenditures (PCEC), and nominal fixed private investment (FPI) are constructed at a quarterly frequency by the Bureau of Economic Analysis (BEA), and are included in the National Income and Product Accounts (NIPA).

Average weekly hours of production and non-supervisory employees for total private industries (PRS85006023), civilian employment (CE16OV), and civilian non-institutional population (LNSINDEX) are produced by the Bureau of Labor Statistics (BLS) at the monthly frequency. The first of these series is obtained from the Establishment Survey, and the remaining from the Household Survey. Both surveys are released in the BLS Employment Situation Summary (ESS). Since our models are estimated on quarterly data, we take averages of the monthly data. Compensation per hour for the non-farm business sector (PRS85006103) is obtained from the Labor Productivity and Costs (LPC) release, and produced by the BLS at the quarterly frequency.

Last, the federal funds rate is obtained from the Federal Reserve Board's H.15 release at the business day frequency, and is not revised. We take quarterly averages of the annualized daily data and divide by four. All data are transformed following (Smets and

Wouters, 2007). Specifically:

$$
\begin{array}{ll}
\textit{Output growth} & = 100 * \Delta LN((GDPC)/LNSINDEX) \\
\textit{Consumption growth} & = 100 * \Delta LN((PCEC/GDPDEF)/LNSINDEX) \\
\textit{Investment growth} & = 100 * \Delta LN((FPI/GDPDEF)/LNSINDEX) \\
\textit{Real wage growth} & = 100 * \Delta LN(PRS85006103/GDPDEF) \\
\textit{Hours} & = 100 * LN((PRS85006023 * CE16OV/100)/LNSINDEX) \\
\textit{Inflation} & = 100 * \Delta LN(GDPDEF) \\
\textit{FFR} & = (1/4) * FEDERAL\ FUNDS\ RATE.
\end{array}
$$

Here Δ denotes the temporal difference operator. In the estimation of the DSGE model with financial frictions we measure *Spread* as the annualized Moody's Seasoned Baa Corporate Bond Yield spread over the 10-Year Treasury Note Yield at Constant Maturity. Both series are available from the Federal Reserve Board's H.15 release. Like the federal funds rate, the spread data are also averaged over each quarter and measured at the quarterly frequency. Spread data are also not revised.

Many macroeconomic time series get revised multiple times by the statistical agencies that publish the series. In many cases the revisions reflect additional information that has been collected by the agencies, in other instances revisions are caused by changes in definitions. For instance, the BEA publishes three releases of quarterly GDP in the first 3 months following the quarter. Thus, in order to be able to compare DSGE model forecasts to real-time forecasts made by private-sector professional forecasters or the Federal Reserve Board, it is important to construct vintages of real–time historical data. We follow the work by Edge and Gürkaynak (2010) and construct data vintages that are aligned with the publication dates of the Blue Chip survey and the Federal Reserve Board's Greenbook/Tealbook.

Whenever we evaluate the accuracy of Blue Chip forecasts in this chapter, we focus on the so-called Consensus Blue Chip forecast, which is defined as the average of all the forecasts gathered in the Blue Chip Economic Indicators (BCEI) survey. The BCEI survey is published on the 10th of each month, based on responses that have been submitted at the end of the previous month. For instance, forecasts published on April 10 are based on information that was available at the end of March. At the end of March the NIPA series for the first quarter of the current year have not yet been published, which means that the DSGE model can only be estimated based on the fourth quarter of the previous year.

While there are three Blue Chip forecasts published every quarter, we restrict our attention to the months of April, July, October, and January. Our selection of Blue Chip dates maximizes the informational advantage for the Blue Chip forecasters, who can in principle utilize high-frequency information about economic activity in the previous quarter. For instance, a forecaster who constructs a forecast at the end of March for the April 10 Blue Chip survey release has access to high-frequency information, e.g., daily interest rates and monthly unemployment and inflation measures, for the first quarter. As a consequence, reported accuracy differentials between DSGE model and professional nowcasts (Sections 4.2 and 4.3) can be viewed as upper bounds. Moreover, the improvements in DSGE model forecasting performance achieved by incorporating external nowcasts (Section 5.3) can also be interpreted as upper bounds. The first forecast origin considered in the subsequent forecast evaluation is January 1992 and the last one is April 2011. The estimation sample for the January 1992 DSGE model forecast ends in 1991:Q3 and the first forecast (nowcast) is for 1991:Q4.

The Greenbook/Tealbook contains macroeconomic forecasts from the staff of the Board of Governors in preparation for meetings of the Federal Open Market Committee (FOMC). There are typically eight FOMC meetings per year. For the comparison of Greenbook versus DSGE model forecasts we also only consider a subset of four Green-book publication dates, one associated with each quarter: typically from the months of March, June, September, and December.[4] We refer to the collection of vintages aligned with the Greenbook dates as Greenbook sample. The first forecast origin in the Green-book sample is March 1992 and the last one is September 2004, since the Greenbook forecasts are only available with a 5-year lag. Table 2.2 summarizes the Blue Chip and Greenbook forecast origins in 1992 for which we are constructing DSGE model fore-casts. Since we always use real–time information, the vintage used to estimate the DSGE model for the comparison to the March 1992 Greenbook may be different from the vin-tage that is used for the comparison with the April 1992 Blue Chip forecast, even though in both cases the end of the estimation sample for the DSGE model is T=1991:Q4.

The Blue Chip Economic Indicators survey only contains quarterly forecasts for one calendar year after the current one. This implies that on January 10 the survey will have forecasts for eight quarters, and only for six quarters on October 10. When comparing forecast accuracy between Blue Chip and DSGE models, we use seven- and eight-quarter ahead forecasts only when available from the Blue Chip survey (which means we only use the January and April forecast dates when computing eight-quarter ahead RMSEs). For consistency, when comparing forecast accuracy across DSGE models we use the same approach (we refer to this set of dates/forecast horizons as the "Blue Chip dates"). Similarly, the horizon of Greenbook forecasts also varies over time. In comparing DSGE model and Greenbook forecast accuracy we only use seven- and eight-quarter ahead whenever available from both.

For each forecast origin our estimation sample begins in 1964:Q1 and ends with the most recent quarter for which a NIPA release is available. Historical data were taken from the FRB St. Louis' ALFRED database. For vintages prior to 1997, compensation and population series were unavailable in ALFRED. In these cases, the series were taken from Edge and Gürkaynak (2010).[5] In constructing the real time data set, the release of one

---

[4] As forecast origins we choose the last Greenbook forecast date before an advanced NIPA estimate for the most recent quarter is released. For instance, the advanced estimate for Q1 GDP is typically released in the second half of April, prior to the April FOMC meeting.

[5] We are very grateful to Rochelle Edge and Refet Gürkaynak for giving us this data, and explaining us how they constructed their data set.

Table 2.2 Blue Chip and Greenbook Forecast Dates for 1992

Forecast Origin		End of Est.	Forecast			
Blue Chip	Greenbook	Sample *T*	*h* = 1	*h* = 2	*h* = 3	*h* = 4
Apr 92	Mar 92	91:Q4	92:Q1	92:Q2	92:Q3	92:Q4
Jul 92	Jun 92	92:Q1	92:Q2	92:Q3	92:Q4	93:Q1
Oct 92	Sep 92	92:Q2	92:Q3	92:Q4	93:Q1	93:Q2
Jan 93	Dec 92	92:Q3	92:Q4	93:Q1	93:Q2	93:Q3

series for a given quarter may outpace that of another. For example, in several instances, Greenbook forecast dates occur after a quarter's ESS release but before the NIPA release. In other words, for a number of data vintages there is, relative to NIPA, an extra quarter of employment data. Conversely, in a few cases NIPA releases outpace LPC, resulting in an extra quarter of NIPA data. We follow the convention in Edge and Gürkaynak (2010) and use NIPA availability to determine whether a given quarter's data should be included in a vintage's estimation sample. When employment data outpace NIPA releases, this means ignoring the extra observations for hours, population, and employment from the Employment Situation Summary. In cases where NIPA releases outpace LPC releases, we include the next available LPC data in that vintage's estimation sample to "catch up" to the NIPA data.

There is an ongoing debate in the real-time literature whether forecast errors should be computed based on the most recent vintage or the so-called "first final" data release, which for output corresponds to the Final NIPA estimate (available roughly 3 months after the quarter is over). The forecast error statistics below are based on actuals that are obtained from the most recent vintage of each data series. The argument in favor of using the most recent data vintage is that it is likely to be closer to the "true" actual. Advocates of the "first final" approach, on the other hand, tend to point out that professional forecasters often get evaluated based on how well they predict the initial data release. We therefore also show forecast errors based on both methods for some of the experiments and found that the general conclusions about the forecast performance of DSGE models are not affected by the choice of actuals.

Finally, the various DSGE models only produce forecasts for per-capita output, while Blue Chip and Greenbook forecasts are in terms of total GDP. When comparing RMSEs between the DSGE models and Blue Chip/Greenbook we therefore transform per-capita into aggregate output forecasts using (the final estimate of) realized population growth.[6]

---

[6] Edge and Gürkaynak (2010) follow a similar approach, except that their population "actuals" are the "first finals," consistently with the fact that they use "first finals" to measure forecast errors.

4.2. Forecasts from the Small-Scale Model

We begin by comparing the point forecast performance of the small-scale DSGE model described in Section 2.3 to that of the Blue Chip and Greenbook forecasts. RMSEs for output growth, inflation, and interest rates (Federal Funds) are displayed in Figure 2.1. Throughout this chapter, GDP growth, inflation, and interest rates are reported in Quarter-on-Quarter (QoQ) percentages. The RMSEs in the first row of the figure are for forecasts that are based on the information available prior to the January, April, July, and October Blue Chip publication dates over the period from 1992 to 2011. The RMSEs in the bottom row correspond to forecasts generated at the March, June, September, and December Greenbook dates over the period from 1992 to 2004.

The small-scale model attains a RMSE for output growth of approximately 0.65%. The RMSE is fairly flat with respect to the forecast horizon, which is consistent with the low serial correlation of U.S. GDP growth. At the nowcast horizon ($h = 1$), the Blue Chip forecasts are much more precise, their RMSE is 0.42, because they incorporate information from the current quarter. As the forecast horizon increases to $h = 4$ the RMSEs of the DSGE model and the Blue Chip forecasts are approximately the same. The accuracy of inflation and, in particular, interest rate forecasts of the small-scale DSGE model is decreasing in the forecast horizon h due to the persistence of these series. The inflation RMSE is about 0.25% at the nowcast horizon and 0.35% for a 2-year horizon. For the Federal Funds rate the RMSE increases from about 0.15 to 0.5. The inflation and interest rate Blue Chip forecasts tend to be substantially more precise than the DSGE model forecasts both at the nowcast as well as the 1–year horizon.

In comparison to the Greenbook forecasts the output growth forecasts of the small-scale DSGE model are more precise for horizons $h \geq 3$. Moreover, the inflation forecast of the DSGE model at the nowcast horizon is about as precise as the Greenbook inflation nowcast, but for horizons $h \geq 1$ the Greenbook forecasts dominate. We do not report RMSEs for Greenbook interest rate projections because these were not available from either the FRB St. Louis' ALFRED or the Philadelphia Fed's Real-Time data sets. Moreover, the Greenbook interest rate projections are conceptually different from DSGE model or Blue Chip interest forecasts, since these are an important input for interest-rate decision of the FOMC. In general the DSGE model forecast errors are smaller for the Greenbook sample than for the Blue Chip sample. This differential is caused by the large forecast errors during the 2008–2009 recession.

Underlying the computation of the DSGE model forecast error statistics is a recursive estimation of the model parameters. The sequence of parameter estimates contains a wealth of information about macroeconomic stability and the evolution of policy trade-offs over time. However, given this chapter's focus on forecast performance, we will not study the evolving parameter estimates. Instead we refer the interested reader to Canova (2009), who reports rolling estimates for a small-scale New Keynesian DSGE model and uses them to study explanations for the Great Moderation.

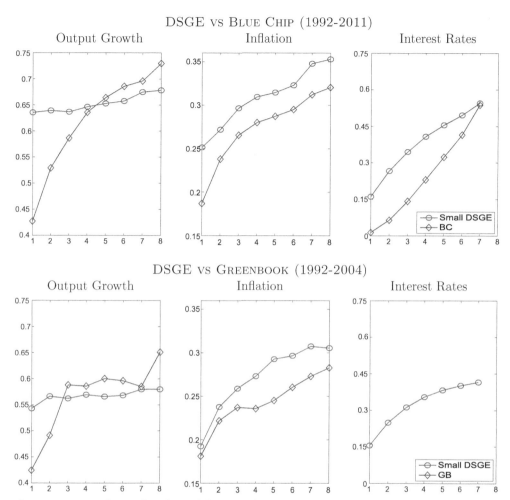

Figure 2.1 RMSEs for small-scale model. *Notes:* The top and bottom panels compare the RMSEs for the Small-Scale DSGE model (circles) with the Blue Chip (blue diamonds, top panel) and Greenbook (green diamonds, bottom panel) for one through eight quarters ahead for output growth, inflation, and interest rates. All variables are expressed in terms of QoQ rates in percentage. Section 4.1 provides the details of the forecast comparison exercise. (For interpretation of the references to color in this figure legend, the reader is referred to the web version of this book.)

4.3. Forecasts from the Smets–Wouters Model

We proceed by computing forecast error statistics for the SW model reviewed in Section 2.1. The results are reported in Figure 2.2. The top panels provide a comparison to Blue Chip forecasts from 1992 to 2011 and the bottom panels a comparison to Greenbook forecasts from 1992 to 2004. The accuracy of the output growth forecasts from the SW model is commensurable with the accuracy of the forecasts generated by the

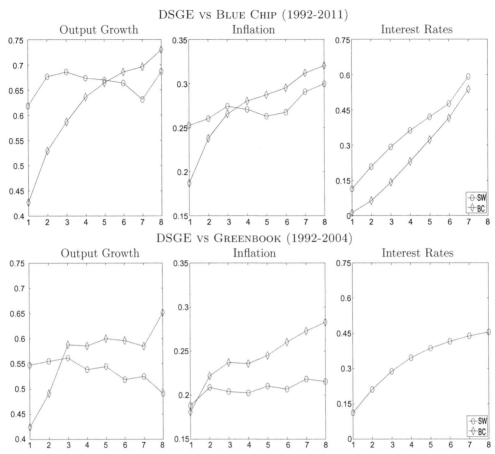

Figure 2.2 RMSEs for SW model. *Notes:* The top and bottom panels compare the RMSEs for the SW DSGE model (circles) with the Blue Chip (blue diamonds, top panel) and Greenbook (green diamonds, bottom panel) for one through eight quarters ahead for output growth, inflation, and interest rates. All variables are expressed in terms of QoQ rates in percentage. Section 4.1 provides the details of the forecast comparison exercise. (For interpretation of the references to color in this figure legend, the reader is referred to the web version of this book.)

small-scale DSGE model. However, for $h > 1$, the inflation forecasts of the SW model are more precise than the inflation forecasts of the small-scale model, which can be attributed to a more sophisticated Phillips curve relationship and the presence of wage stickiness. The SW interest rate forecasts are slightly more accurate in the short run but slightly less precise in the long run. In the short-run the Blue Chip forecasts of output growth and inflation are more precise than the forecasts from the SW model, but for horizons $h = 5$ to $h = 8$, the DSGE model dominates. As in the case of the small-scale DSGE model, the SW model forecast errors are smaller for the Greenbook sample than for the Blue Chip sample. Except in the very short-run, the SW model produces more precise point forecasts of output growth and inflation than the Greenbook, with the difference being more notable for inflation.

In addition to RMSE statistics for individual time series one can also consider multivariate forecast error statistics such as the log determinant of the forecast error covariance matrix of a vector of time series. The so-called "ln-det" statistic had been proposed by Doan et al. (1984). The eigenvectors of the forecast error covariance matrix generate linear combinations of the model variables with uncorrelated forecast errors. The determinant equals the product of the eigenvalues and thereby measures the product of the forecast error variances associated with these linear combinations. The more linear combinations exist that can be predicted with small forecast error variance, the smaller the ln-det statistic. We did compute ln-det statistics for joint forecasts of output growth, inflation, and interest rates both for the SW model as well as for the Blue Chip forecasts. The results are consistent with the RMSE statistics depicted in Figure 2.2: in the short-run the Blue Chip forecasts dominate, whereas for $h > 4$ the DSGE model forecasts are preferable. In the remainder of this chapter we focus on RMSEs for individual series rather than the ln-det summary statistic.

Up to this point we considered multi-step-ahead forecasts of growth rates (of output and prices) and levels (interest rates) in period $T + h$. Alternatively, the model can be used to forecast *average* growth rates and *average* levels over periods $T + 1$ to $T + h$. In many instances, forecasts of averages might be more appealing than forecasts of a growth rate between period $T + h - 1$ and $T + h$.[7] RMSEs associated with forecasts of averages tend to have a different profile as a function of h. To fix ideas, suppose that y_t, say inflation, evolves according to an AR (1) process

$$y_t = \theta y_{t-1} + u_t, \quad u_t \sim iidN(0, 1), \quad 0 < \theta < 1. \tag{39}$$

To simplify the exposition, we will abstract from parameter uncertainty and assume that θ is known. The time T h-step forecast of y_{T+h} is given by $\hat{y}_{T+h|T} = \theta^h y_T$. The h-step ahead forecast error is given by

$$e_{T+h|T} = \sum_{j=0}^{h-1} \theta^j u_{T+h-j}. \tag{40}$$

In turn, the population RMSE is given by

$$\sqrt{\mathbb{E}[e_{T+h|T}^2]} = \sqrt{\frac{1 - \theta^{2h}}{1 - \theta^2}} \longrightarrow \frac{1}{\sqrt{1 - \theta^2}} \text{as } h \to \infty. \tag{41}$$

---

[7] Of course, one could also forecast differences in log levels between period T and $T + h$, which would be the average growth rate over that time span multiplied by h. However, in our experience, policy discussions tend to focus on forecasts of average growth rates rather than changes in log levels.

If θ is close to zero, the RMSE as a function of h is fairly flat, whereas it is strongly increasing for values of θ close to one. The RMSEs associated with the DSGE model forecasts aligned with the Blue Chip publication dates in the top panels of Figure 2.2 are broadly consistent with this pattern. The serial correlation of output growth and inflation is fairly small, which leads to a fairly flat, albeit slightly increasing RMSE function. Interest rates, on the other hand, follow a highly persistent process ($\theta \approx 1$), which generates RMSEs that are essentially linearly increasing in the forecast horizon.

The error associated with a forecast of an h-period average is given by

$$\bar{e}_{T+h|T} = \frac{1}{h} \sum_{s=1}^{h} \left(\sum_{j=0}^{s-1} \theta^j u_{T+s-j} \right) = \frac{1}{h} \sum_{j=0}^{h-1} \frac{1-\theta^{j+1}}{1-\theta} u_{t+h-j}. \tag{42}$$

The second equality is obtained by re-arranging terms and using the formula $\sum_{s=0}^{j-1} \theta^s = (1-\theta^j)/(1-\theta)$. The resulting population RMSE is given by

$$\sqrt{\mathbb{E}[\bar{e}_{T+h|T}^2]} = \frac{1}{\sqrt{h(1-\theta)^2}} \sqrt{1 - 2\theta \frac{1-\theta^h}{h(1-\theta)} + \theta^2 \frac{1-\theta^{2h}}{h(1-\theta^2)}}. \tag{43}$$

Thus, the RMSE of the forecast of the h-period average decays at rate $1/\sqrt{h}$. Based on results from the Blue Chip sample, we plot RMSEs for the forecasts of average output growth, average inflation, and average interest rates in Figure 2.3. In assessing the empirical results, it is important to keep in mind that the population RMSE calculated above abstracts from parameter uncertainty and potential misspecification of the forecasting model. The GDP growth and inflation RMSEs for the DSGE model are indeed decreasing in the forecast horizon. The interest rate RMSEs remain increasing in h, but compared to Figure 2.2 the slope is not as steep. Since the Blue Chip forecasts are more precise at short horizons, the averaging favors the Blue Chip forecasts in the RMSE comparison.

Finally, Figure 2.4 uses "first final" as actual in the computation of forecast error. RMSEs for both output and inflation are a bit lower than those shown in Figure 2.2, but the overall conclusions are unchanged. The RMSEs for the federal funds rate are of course identical to those in Figure 2.2 as this series is not revised.

4.4. Literature Review of Forecasting Performance

By now there exists a substantial body of research evaluating the accuracy of point forecasts from DSGE models. Some of the papers are listed in Table 2.3. Many of the studies consider variants of the (Smets and Wouters, 2003, 2007) models. Since the studies differ with respect to the forecast periods, that is, the collection of forecast origins, as well as the choice of data vintages, direct comparisons of results are difficult. Smets and Wouters (2007) report output growth, inflation, and interest rate RMSEs of 0.57%, 0.24%, and 0.11%

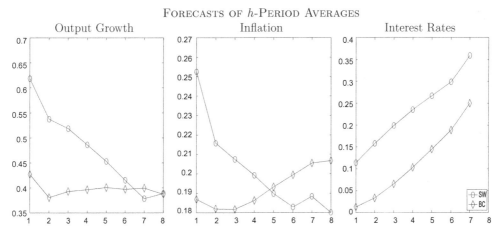

Figure 2.3 RMSEs for SW model vs Blue Chip: forecasting averages. *Notes:* The figure compares the RMSEs for the SW DSGE model (circles) with the Blue Chip forecasts (blue diamonds) for one through eight quarters-ahead averages for output growth, inflation, and interest rates.All variables are expressed in terms of QoQ rates in percentage. Section 4.1 provides the details of the forecast comparison exercise. (For interpretation of the references to color in this figure legend, the reader is referred to the web version of this book.)

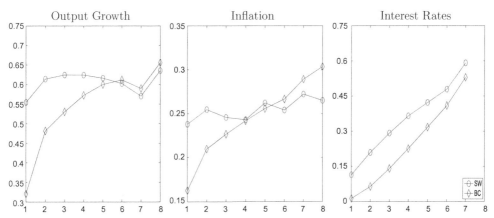

Figure 2.4 RMSEs for SW model vs Blue Chip: using first finals as actuals. *Notes:* The top and bottom panels compare the RMSEs for the SW DSGE model (circles) with the Blue Chip (blue diamonds, top panel) and Greenbook (green diamonds, bottom panel) for one through eight quarters ahead for output growth, inflation, and interest rates. All variables are expressed in terms of QoQ rates in percentage, and the RMSEs are computed using the "first final" vintage as the measure of actuals. Section 4.1 provides the details of the forecast comparison exercise. (For interpretation of the references to color in this figure legend, the reader is referred to the web version of this book.)

QoQ. The forecast period considered by Smets and Wouters (2007) ranges from 1990:Q1 to 2004:Q2 and is comparable to our Greenbook sample. The corresponding RMSEs obtained in our analysis in Section 4.3 using real–time data are 0.55%, 0.19%, and 0.11%.

Table 2.3 A Sample of Studies Reporting RMSEs for Medium-Scale DSGE Models

Study	Forecast Origins	Real Time
Rubaszek and Skrzypczynski (2008)	1994:Q1–2005:Q3	Yes
Kolasa et al. (2010)	1994:Q1–2007:Q4	Yes
DeGraeve et al. (2009)	1990:Q1–2007:Q1 (h = 1)	No
Wolters (2010), Del Negro-Schorfheide Model	1984:Q1–2000:Q4	Yes
Wolters (2010), Fuhrer-Moore Model	1984:Q1–2000:Q4	Yes
Wolters (2010), SW Model	1984:Q1–2000:Q4	Yes
Wolters (2010), EDO Model	1984:Q1–2000:Q4	Yes
Edge and Gürkaynak (2010)	1992:Q1–2004:Q4	Yes
Edge et al. (2009)	1996:Q3–2002:Q4	Yes
Smets and Wouters (2007)	1990:Q1–2004:Q4 (h = 1)	No
Del Negro et al. (2007)	1985:Q4–2000:Q2 (h = 1)	No
Schorfheide et al. (2010)	2001:Q1–2007:Q4 (h = 1)	No

In order to make the RMSE results comparable across studies we generate forecasts from a simple AR(2), using the variable definitions, forecast origins, and estimation samples that underly the studies listed in Table 2.3. We chose an AR(2) model as a benchmark because it is easy to estimate and tends to perform better than widely-used no-change forecasts, in particular at longer horizons. In particular, we use real-time data whenever the original study was based on real-time data and we use the corresponding vintage for studies that were based on the analysis of a single vintage. The AR(2) model is estimated using Bayesian techniques with the improper prior $p(\sigma^2) \propto (\sigma^2)^{-1}$, where σ^2 is the innovation variance.

Figure 2.5 depicts RMSE ratios for DSGE model forecasts versus AR(2) forecasts. Each cross corresponds to one of the studies listed in Table 2.3. A value less than one indicates that the RMSE of the DSGE model forecast is lower than the RMSE of the benchmark AR(2) forecast. The solid lines indicate RMSE ratios of one. The top panels summarize the accuracy of output growth and inflation forecasts, whereas the bottom panels summarize the accuracy of interest rate and inflation forecasts. In general, the DSGE models perform better at the $h = 4$ horizon than at the one-quarter-ahead horizon as there are fewer observations in the upper-right quadrant.

While the one-step-ahead output growth forecasts from the DSGE models are by and large at par with the AR(2) forecasts, the bottom left panel indicates that the DSGE model inflation and interest rate forecasts in general tend to be worse than the AR(2) forecasts. At the 1-year horizon, more than half of the DSGE model output growth forecasts are more accurate than the corresponding AR(2) forecasts. One outlier (the RMSE ratio is close to 2.0) is the output growth RMSE reported in Del Negro et al. (2007), which is computed from an infinite-order VAR approximation of the state-space representation of the DSGE model. Growth rate differentials between output, investment, consumption, and real wages might contribute to the poor forecast performance of the DSGE model. Finally, about half of the estimated DSGE models considered here are able to produce inflation and interest rate forecasts that attain a lower RMSE than the AR(2) forecasts.

Our interpretation of Figure 2.5 is that DSGE model forecasts can be competitive in terms of accuracy with simple benchmark models, in particular for medium-run forecasts. This statement, however, has two qualifications. First, the DSGE model needs to be carefully specified to optimize forecast performance. Second, if the AR(2) model is replaced by a statistical model that is specifically designed to forecast a particular macroeconomic time series well, DSGE model forecasts can be dominated in terms of RMSEs by other time series models.

For comparison, RMSE ratios for some of the key models studied in this handbook chapter are summarized in Table 2.4. The *Small DSGE* and the *SW* models are the specifications that were used to generate the forecasts in Sections 4.2 and 4.3. The RMSE ratios for output growth are around 1.08. The inflation RMSE ratios range from 0.80 (SW

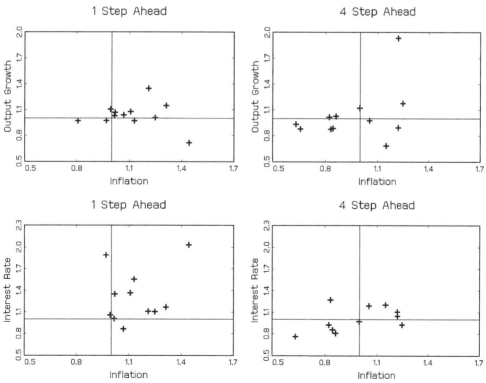

Figure 2.5 RMSEs reported in the literature. *Notes:* Figure depicts RMSE ratios: DSGE (reported in various papers)/AR(2) (authors calculation). As indicated in Table 2.3 the forecast periods differ across studies. Detailed information about the calculation of the RMSE ratios is provided in Appendix 8.3.

Table 2.4 RMSE Ratios Relative to AR(2) Model

Model	Sample	Output Growth	Inflation	Interest
		$h = 1$		
Small DSGE	Blue Chip	1.09	0.99	1.30
SW		1.06	0.99	0.92
SWπ		1.00	0.95	0.95
SWπ now		0.74	0.76	0.10
Small DSGE	Greenbook	1.08	0.98	1.31
SW		1.07	0.95	0.90
SWπ		1.01	0.92	0.98
SWπ now		0.89	0.83	0.08
		$h = 4$		
Small DSGE	Blue Chip	1.00	0.91	0.89
SW		1.04	0.80	0.79
SWπ		0.96	0.78	0.75
SWπ now		0.96	0.76	0.67
Small DSGE	Greenbook	1.10	0.91	0.83
SW		1.06	0.95	0.81
SWπ		1.01	0.72	0.76
SWπ now		1.00	0.70	0.67

Notes: Small DSGE is model described in Section 7.2 used for forecasting in Section 4.2; *SW* is the Smets-Wouters model described in Section 2.3 and studied in Section 4.3; *SWπ* is the Smets-Wouters model with time-varying inflation target (see Section 5.1); *SWπ now* is the Smets-Wouters model with time-varying inflation target and external nowcasts (see Section 5.3).

model, $h = 4$, Blue Chip sample) to 0.99 (SW model, $h = 1$, Blue Chip sample) and the interest rate RMSE ratios range from 0.79 (SW model, $h = 4$, Blue Chip sample) to 1.31 (Small DSGE, $h = 1$, Greenbook sample). Thus, overall the forecast performance of the benchmark models considered here is commensurable with the performance reported in the literature. In Table 2.4 we also report RMSE ratios for a version of the Smets–Wouters model that exploits information in long-run inflation expectations (SWπ, see Section 5.1) and a version that incorporates information from inflation expectations and external nowcasts (SWπ now. These specifications will be introduced in Section 5.3). The low RMSE ratios for SWπ and SWπ now foreshadow an important empirical finding: the use of external information can drastically improve the forecast performance of DSGE models.

Many of the papers in the DSGE model forecasting literature offer direct comparisons of DSGE model forecasts to other forecasts. Edge and Gürkaynak (2010) compare univariate forecasts from the SW model estimated with real-time data against forecasts obtained from the staff of the Federal Reserve, the Blue Chip survey, and a Bayesian vector autoregression (VAR). Based on RMSEs, they conclude that the DSGE model delivers forecasts that are competitive in terms of accuracy with those obtained from the alternative prediction methods. Comparisons between DSGE model and professional forecasts are also reported in Wieland and Wolters (2011, 2012). The evidence from Euro Area data is similar. Adolfson et al., 2007a assess the forecasting performance of an Open Economy DSGE model during the period of 1994–2004 based on RMSEs, log determinant of the forecast-error covariance matrix, predictive scores, and the coverage frequency of interval forecasts. Overall, the authors conclude that the DSGE model compares well with more flexible time series models such as VARs.

Christoffel et al. (2011) examine the forecasting performance of the New Area Wide Model (NAWM), the DSGE model used by the European Central Bank. The authors evaluate the model's univariate forecast performance through RMSEs and its multivariate performance using the ln–det statistic. They find that the DSGE model is competitive with other forecasting models such as VARs of various sizes. The authors also find that the assessment of multivariate forecasts based on the ln–det statistic can sometimes be severely affected by the inability to forecast just one series, nominal wage growth.

The Bayesian VARs that serve as a benchmark in the aforementioned papers typically use a version of the Minnesota prior that is not optimized with respect to its empirical performance. For instance, these priors exclude some of the dummy observations described in Sims and Zha (1998) and more recently discussed in Del Negro and Schorfheide (2010) that generate *a priori* correlations among VAR coefficients and have been found useful for prediction. Del Negro and Schorfheide (2004) and DSSW compare the forecasting performance of DSGE models to Bayesian VARs that use prior distributions centered at the DSGE model restrictions, varying the variance of the prior and hence the weight placed on the DSGE model restrictions. Both papers find that the resulting DSGE-VAR forecasts significantly better than the underlying DSGE model.

In addition to comparing point forecasts across different models, Edge and Gürkaynak, (2010) also examine the overall quality of DSGE model forecasts. To do so, they estimate regressions of the form

$$y_{i,t} = \alpha^{(h)} + \beta^{(h)}\hat{y}_{i,t|t-h} + e_t^{(h)}. \tag{44}$$

If the predictor $\hat{y}_{i,t|t-h}$ is the conditional mean of $y_{i,t}$ then the estimate of $\alpha^{(h)}$ should be close to zero and the estimate of $\beta^{(h)}$ close to one. In the simple AR (1) example in Eq. (39) of Section 4.3 the residual $e_t^{(h)}$ would be equal to the h-step-ahead forecast error $e_{t|t-h}$ in (40) and the population R^2 of the regression (44) would be θ^{2h}. For inflation forecasts of varying horizons h, Edge and Gürkaynak, (2010) find that $\alpha^{(h)}$ is significantly positive, $\beta^{(h)}$ is significantly less than one, and R^2 is near zero. The output growth forecasts are better behaved in that the authors are unable to reject the hypotheses that $\alpha^{(h)} = 0$ and $\beta^{(h)} = 1$. Moreover, R^2 is between 0.07 and 0.2. The fairly low R^2 is qualitatively consistent with the low persistence in inflation and output growth during the forecasting period.

Herbst and Schorfheide (2011) examine whether the realized pseudo-out-of-sample RMSE of DSGE model forecasts is commensurable with the RMSE that would be expected given the posterior distribution of DSGE model parameters. By simulating the estimated DSGE model and then generating recursive forecasts on the simulated trajectories, one can obtain a DSGE model-implied predictive distribution for RMSEs. The authors find that for a small-scale DSGE model, similar to the model of Section 2.3, the actual RMSEs of output and inflation forecasts are within the bands of the predictive distribution. The actual interest rate RMSEs, on the other hand, exceed the predictive bands, indicating a deficiency in the law of motion of the interest rate. For the Smets and Wouters (2007) model, the inflation and interest rate RMSEs fall within the bands of the predictive distribution, but the realized output growth RMSE is smaller than the RMSE predicted by the model. A possible explanation is that some of the estimated shock processes are overly persistent because they need to absorb violations of the balanced growth path restrictions of the DSGE model. This would lead to excess volatility in the simulated output paths.

To summarize, the empirical evidence in the literature suggests that DSGE model forecasts are comparable to standard autoregressive or vector autoregressive models but can be dominated by more sophisticated univariate or multivariate time series models. Nonetheless DSGE models present advantages relative to reduced form models as tools for predictions because they provide an intelligible economic story for their projections, as we mentioned in the introduction and will discuss in more detail in Section 7. Moreover, these models also provide a framework for policy analysis. In the forecasting context this is important as they can be used to make projections based on alternative paths for the policy instrument (see Section 6).

5. DSGE MODEL FORECASTS USING EXTERNAL INFORMATION

In the previous section we generated baseline forecasts from two DSGE models. For the small-scale model these forecasts were based on output growth, inflation, and interest rate data. For the SW model we also used data on consumption, investment, hours worked, and real wages. However, these series reflect only a subset of the information that is available to a forecaster in real time. While quarterly NIPA data are released with a lag of more than 4 weeks, other series, e.g., interest rates, are observed at a much higher frequency and without publication lag. Thus, in this section we present methods of improving DSGE model forecasts by incorporating what we call external information. This external information can take various forms. We consider long-run inflation expectations (Section 5.1), long-run output growth expectations (Section 5.2), nowcasts of output and inflation from professional forecasters (Section 5.3), as well as expectations of the short-term interest rate over various horizons (Section 5.4).

Two different approaches of incorporating the external information are considered. First, in Sections 5.1, 5.2, and 5.4 we treat some of the (rational) expectations held by agents within the DSGE model as observable and equate them with multi-step forecasts published by the Blue Chip survey. Discrepancies between DSGE-model implied expectations and professional forecasts are bridged by introducing additional structural shocks into the DSGE models presented in Section 2: shocks to the target inflation rate, the growth rate of technology, and anticipated monetary policy shocks. We have chosen the additional shocks to provide a mechanism that can plausibly capture the otherwise unexplained variance in the additional expectation series. Second, in Section 5.3 we consider methods that amount to interpreting nowcasts from professional forecasters as a noisy measure of (or as news about) current quarter macroeconomic variables. In turn, the external nowcasts provide information about the exogenous shocks that hit the economy in the current quarter and thereby alter the DSGE model forecasts. These methods do not require the DSGE model to be modified and augmented by additional structural shocks.

5.1. Incorporating Long-Run Inflation Expectations

The level of inflation and interest rates has shifted substantially in the post-war period. In our DSGE models the estimated target inflation rate roughly corresponds to the sample average of the inflation rate. If the sample includes observations from the 70s and 80s, then this sample average tends to be higher than what can be thought of as a long-run inflation target of the past decade, which is around 2%. In turn, this leads to a poor forecast performance.

In Figure 2.6 we are plotting the RMSE of the output growth, inflation, and interest rate forecasts from the SW model under the prior distribution used in Smets and Wouters (2007) as well as an alternative prior. The original prior for the quarterly steady state inflation rate used by Smets and Wouters (2007) is tightly centered around 0.62% (which is about 2.5% annualized) with a standard deviation of 0.1%. Our alternative prior is centered at 0.75% and is less dogmatic with a standard deviation of 0.4% (see Panel II of Table 2.1). We refer to the model with "loose" prior as SW-Loose. Under the (Smets and Wouters, 2007) prior the estimated target inflation rate is around 2.7% to 3.0%, whereas the "loose" prior yields posterior estimates in the range of 4% to 5%. As a consequence, the medium-run forecast accuracy is worse for the SW-Loose model than for the SW model, in particular for inflation but also for interest rates and output growth.

The forecast inaccuracy caused by the gradual decline of inflation and interest rates post 1980 had been recognized by Wright (2011), who proposed to center the prior distribution for the vector of long-run means in a Bayesian VAR at the 5-to-10-year expectations of professional forecasters. This approach turned out to be particularly helpful for inflation forecasts, because of the ability of survey forecasts to capture shifting end points. Faust and Wright (2011) use a similar approach to improve inflation forecasts from a DSGE model. Instead of simply centering a tight prior for π_* with hindsight, they center the prior at the most recent long-run inflation forecast.

We follow a different route. In order to capture the rise and fall of inflation and interest rates in the estimation sample, we replace the constant target inflation rate by a time-varying target inflation. While time-varying target rates have been frequently used for the specification of monetary policy rules in DSGE model (e.g., Erceg and Levin (2003) and Smets and Wouters (2003), among others), we follow the approach of Aruoba

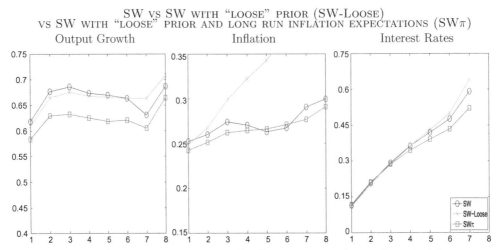

SW vs SW with "loose" prior (SW-Loose)
vs SW with "loose" prior and long run inflation expectations (SWπ)

Figure 2.6 Using inflation expectations. *Notes:* The figure compares the one through eight quarters-ahead RMSEs for the SW DSGE model (SW, circles) with the SW model with a "loose" prior on the parameter π_* (SW-Loose, crosses) and the SW model with observed long run inflation expectations (SWπ, squares) for output growth, inflation, and interest rates. The comparison is done for the same vintages/forecast dates as the Blue Chip/DSGE comparison discussed in Section 4.3. All variables are expressed in terms of QoQ rates in percentage. Section 4.1 provides the details of the forecast comparison exercise.

and Schorfheide (2011) and Del Negro and Eusepi (2011) and include data on long-run inflation expectations as an observable into the estimation of the DSGE model. At each point in time, the long-run inflation expectations essentially determine the level of the target inflation rate. To the extent that long-run inflation expectations at the forecast origin contain information about the central bank's objective function, e.g., the desire to stabilize inflation at 2%, this information is automatically included in the forecast. Clark (2011) constructs a Bayesian VAR in which variables are expressed in deviations from long-run trends. For inflation and interest rates these long-run trends are given by long-horizon Blue Chip forecasts and the VAR includes equations that capture the evolution of these forecasts. Our treatment of inflation in the DSGE model bears similarities to Clark's (2011) VAR.

More specifically, for the SW model the interest-rate feedback rule of the central bank (16) is modified as follows:[8]

$$R_t = \rho_R R_{t-1} + (1 - \rho_R)\left(\psi_1(\pi_t - \pi_t^*) + \psi_2(\gamma_t - \gamma_t^f)\right) \tag{45}$$

$$+\psi_3\left((\gamma_t - \gamma_t^f) - (\gamma_{t-1} - \gamma_{t-1}^f)\right) + r_t^m.$$

[8] We follow the specification in Del Negro and Eusepi (2011), while Aruoba and Schorfheide (2011) assume that the inflation target also affects the intercept in the feedback rule.

The time-varying inflation target evolves according to:

$$\pi_t^* = \rho_{\pi^*}\pi_{t-1}^* + \sigma_{\pi^*}\epsilon_{\pi^*,t}, \tag{46}$$

where $0 < \rho_{\pi^*} < 1$ and $\epsilon_{\pi^*,t}$ is an iid shock. We follow Erceg and Levin (2003) and model π_t^* as following a stationary process, although our prior for ρ_{π^*} will force this process to be highly persistent (see Panel III of Table 2.1). The assumption that the changes in the target inflation rate are exogenous is, to some extent, a short-cut. For instance, the learning models of Sargent (1999) or Primiceri (2006) would suggest that the rise in the target inflation rate in the 1970s and the subsequent drop is due to policy makers learning about the output-inflation trade-off and trying to set inflation optimally. We are abstracting from such a mechanism in our specification. The set of measurement equations (17) is augmented by

$$\pi_t^{O,40} = \pi_* + 100\mathbb{E}_t \left[\frac{1}{40} \sum_{k=1}^{40} \pi_{t+k} \right] \tag{47}$$

$$= \pi_* + \frac{100}{40}\Psi_2(\theta)_{(\pi,.)}(I - \Phi_1(\theta))^{-1} \left(I - [\Phi_1(\theta)]^{40} \right) \Phi_1(\theta)s_t,$$

where $\pi_t^{O,40}$ represents observed long-run inflation expectations obtained from surveys (in percent per quarter), and the right-hand-side of (47) corresponds to expectations obtained from the DSGE model (in deviation from the mean π_*). The second line shows how to compute these expectations using the transition equation (34) and the measurement equation for inflation. $\Psi_2(\theta)_{(\pi,.)}$ is the row of $\Psi_2(\theta)$ in (35) that corresponds to inflation.

The long-run inflation forecasts are obtained from the Blue Chip Economic Indicators survey and the Survey of Professional Forecasters (SPF) available from the FRB Philadelphia's Real-Time Data Research Center. Long-run inflation expectations (average CPI inflation over the next 10 years) are available from 1991:Q4 onwards. Prior to 1991:Q4, we use the 10-year expectations data from the Blue Chip survey to construct a long time series that begins in 1979:Q4. Since the Blue Chip survey reports long-run inflation expectations only twice a year, we treat these expectations in the remaining quarters as missing observations and adjust the measurement equation of the Kalman filter accordingly. Long-run inflation expectations $\pi_t^{O,40}$ are therefore measured as

$$\pi_t^{O,40} = (\text{10-YEAR AVERAGE CPI INFLATION FORECAST} - 0.50)/4,$$

where 0.50 is the average difference between CPI and GDP annualized inflation from the beginning of the sample to the 1992, the starting point for our forecasting exercise, and where we divide by 4 since the data are expressed in quarterly terms.

Importantly from a real-time forecasting perspective, the inflation expectation data used in the DSGE model estimation is available to both Blue Chip and Greenbook forecasters by the time they make their forecasts. The timing of the SPF Survey is geared to the release of the BEA's Advance NIPA report, which is released at the end of the first month of each quarter. This implies that, for instance, when producing DSGE forecasts with $T = 1991$:Q4 we use long-run inflation expectation data that is public by the end of January 1992, that is, well before the associated Greenbook and Blue Chip forecasts are made (March and April 1992, respectively, see Table 2.2).

The modified SW model with time-varying inflation target and inflation expectation data, henceforth SWπ, is recursively estimated on the real-time data vintages and forecast RMSEs are plotted in Figure 2.6. While the inflation RMSEs associated with forecasts from the SWπ model are only slightly lower than those of the SW model, the former is much more appealing because it is not based on a prior distribution that from an *a priori* perspective is rather tight. Moreover, the SWπ is much more flexible. If the average level of inflation as well as inflation expectations will rise again in the future, then the estimated inflation target will increase and the forecasts will adapt to a higher level of inflation. The use of a time-varying inflation target also improves the long-run interest rate forecasts and, interestingly, leads to a substantial reduction in the RMSE of the output growth forecasts compared to the benchmark SW model.

5.2. Incorporating Output Expectations

Over the past six decades the U.S. economy has experienced several shifts in the long-run growth rates of productivity and output, e.g., the productivity slowdown of the 1970s. While the changes in long-run growth rates are not as pronounced as the changes in the inflation rate during the late 1970s and early 1980s, capturing low frequency movements in productivity growth is potentially important for DSGE model forecasts of output. Thus, we now introduce long-run output growth expectations as an observable variable in the DSGE model following the same approach we used for the long-run inflation expectations in Section 5.1.

The measurement equations are augmented with an expression equating the model-implied long-run output expectation with the long-run growth forecasts from the Blue Chip Economic Indicators survey:

$$Growth_t^{O,40} = \gamma + 100\mathbb{E}_t \left[\frac{1}{40} \sum_{k=1}^{40} (y_{t+k} - y_{t+k-1} + z_{t+k}) \right], \qquad (48)$$

where $Growth_t^{O,40}$ represents the observed long-run-growth expectation (in percent per quarter) obtained from the two surveys and the right-hand-side of (48) is the corresponding expectation computed from the DSGE model. Ten-year GDP forecasts are given in aggregate annualized growth rates. They are transformed into quarterly per capita rates using the 5-year (backward looking) moving average of the population series from the

ESS Household Survey:

$$Growth_t^{O,40} = \text{10-YEAR AVERAGE GDP GROWTH FORECAST}/4$$
$$- 100 * (LN(LNSINDEX/LNSINDEX(-20))/20).$$

In order to generate time-variation in the DSGE model's implied long-run output growth expectations we introduce very persistent changes to the growth rate of productivity in the SW model described in (2). Specifically, we assume that z_t, the growth rate of the stochastic trend Z_t in deviations from γ, follows the process:

$$z_t = \log(Z_t/Z_{t-1}) - \gamma = \frac{1}{1-\alpha}(\rho_z - 1)\tilde{z}_{t-1} + \frac{1}{1-\alpha}\sigma_z\epsilon_{z,t} + z_t^p, \qquad (49)$$

where

$$z_t^p = \rho_{z^p} z_{t-1}^p + \sigma_{z^p}\epsilon_{z^p,t}. \qquad (50)$$

The prior for ρ_{z^p} is chosen to ensure that the local level process z_t^p is highly persistent (see Panel IV of Table 2.1). This kind of specification is also widely used in the long-run risk literature. In Bansal and Yaron's (2004) endowment economy consumption growth follows a local-level process and Croce (2008) assumes that productivity growth is subject to persistent shocks in order to generate realistic asset-pricing implications for a production economy.

As in Section 5.1, we recursively re-estimate the DSGE model with time-varying productivity growth. RMSEs for the SWπ model versus the DSGE model with inflation and output expectations, denoted by SWπY, are depicted in Figure 2.7. Unlike the incorporation of long-run inflation expectations, the use of long-run output growth expectations does not lead to an improvement in the forecast performance of the DSGE model except for investment growth.[9] Output, inflation, consumption, and real wage growth forecasts deteriorate, albeit the deterioration in inflation is very small. For instance, while the SWπ model attains an RMSE for output growth of 0.58% at $h = 1$ and 0.67% at $h = 8$, the corresponding RMSEs for the SWπY model are 0.65% and 0.70%. In terms of percentage increase in RMSE, the largest drop in forecast accuracy occurs for consumption at $h = 2$. The inclusion of long-run output growth expectations increases the RMSE by about 12% from 0.64 to 0.72. Since the use of long-run output growth expectations was not successful we subsequently focus on model specifications that ignore this information.

5.3. Conditioning on External Nowcasts

As explained in Section 4.1, the NIPA data that enter the estimation of the DSGE model only become available with a lag of more than 4 weeks. During this time period, a lot of

---

[9] A similar finding is reported in Wright's (2011) VAR study. While centering the prior distribution for the intercept in the inflation equation at the long-run inflation expectation lead to substantial RMSE reductions, a similar centering for the intercept prior in the output equation did not reduce the forecast error.

other important information about the state of the economy is released, e.g., interest rates, unemployment rates, inflation data. Some of this information is implicitly incorporated in the current quarter forecasts surveyed by Blue Chip because the professional forecasters included in the survey are not required to use quarterly-frequency time series models and also can make subjective adjustments to model-based forecasts in view of high frequency economic data.

This leaves us with two options. We could enlarge the set of measurement equations and possibly shorten the time period t in the DSGE model from quarterly to monthly or weekly, such that the state-space model given by (34) and (35) can be linked to a broader set of variables, some of which are observable at higher frequency than quarterly. Such an approach would build on the work by Boivin and Giannoni (2006), who proposed

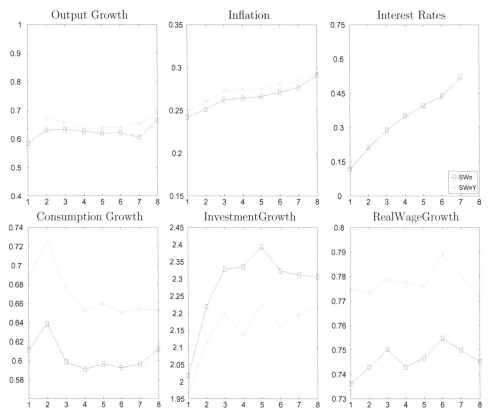

Figure 2.7 Using inflation and output expectations. *Notes:* The figure compares the one through eight quarters-ahead RMSEs for the SW with long run inflation expectations (SWn) vs SW with long run inflation and output growth expectations (SWnY) for output growth, inflation, interest rates, consumption, investment, and real wage growth. The comparison is done for the same vintages/forecast dates as the Blue Chip/DSGE comparison discussed in Section 4.3. All variables are expressed in terms of QoQ rates in percentage. Section 4.1 provides the details of the forecast comparison exercise.

to restrict the factor law of motion in a large-scale dynamic factor model to a DSGE model-implied state transition equation (34). While this approach is conceptually elegant, it is computationally cumbersome, despite some recent advances in Kryshko (2010). Alternatively, we could use an external model that uses high-frequency current quarter information to generate nowcasts and then essentially feed these nowcasts as observations into the DSGE model.

In this section we pursue the second option and use the now casts obtained from the Blue Chip survey to improve the forecasts from the SWπ DSGE model. We proceed in four steps. First, the timing of the nowcast release is described. Second, we consider two approaches of incorporating external information: (i) nowcasts are interpreted as noisy measures of variables dated $T + 1$ (recall that T corresponds to the end of estimation sample and beginning of forecasting origin); (ii) nowcasts are interpreted as news about $T + 1$ data. We provide algorithms to generate draws from the predictive density of the DSGE models under these two interpretations of external information. Third, using the noise interpretation, nowcasts are incorporated into forecasts from the SWπ model. Finally, we discuss alternative methods that have been proposed in the literature.

To fix ideas, the timing of the DSGE model forecasts and the Blue Chip nowcasts for the year 1992 is illustrated in Table 2.5. Columns 1 and 2 of Table 2.5 are identical to Columns 1 and 3 of Table 2.2. Consider for instance the forecast origin that corresponds to the July 1992 Blue Chip release. Due to the timing of the NIPA GDP release the estimation sample ends in 1992:Q1. In our notation, the first quarter of 1992 corresponds to period T. We modify the DSGE model forecast by incorporating the nowcast for 1992:Q2 ($T + 1$) published in July 1992. To fix notation, assume that the variables used for the DSGE model estimation are partitioned into $y'_{T+1} = [y'_{1,T+1}, y'_{2,T+1}]$, where $y_{1,T+1}$ is the subvector for which external information z_{T+1} is available. The $T + 1$ subscript highlights that the information in z pertains to $t = T + 1$ variables.

To understand how external information alters the DSGE model forecasts, consider the following factorization of the one-step-ahead predictive density:

Table 2.5 Blue Chip Forecast Dates and Nowcast Information for 1992

Forecast Origin	End of Est. Sample T	External Nowcast $T + 1$	Forecast	
			$h = 1$	$h = 2$
Apr 92	91:Q4	92:Q1 based on Apr 92 BC	92:Q1	92:Q2
Jul 92	92:Q1	92:Q2 based on Jul 92 BC	92:Q2	92:Q3
Oct 92	92:Q2	92:Q3 based on Oct 92 BC	92:Q3	92:Q4
Jan 93	92:Q3	92:Q4 based on Jan 93 BC	92:Q4	93:Q1

$$p(y_{T+1}|Y_{1:T}) = \int_{\theta} \left[\int_{s_T, s_{T+1}} p(y_{T+1}|s_{T+1}, \theta) p(s_T, s_{T+1}|\theta, Y_{1:T}) d(s_T, s_{T+1}) \right]$$
$$p(\theta|Y_{1:T}) d\theta. \tag{51}$$

We adopted the timing convention that the Blue Chip nowcasts z_{T+1} become available after period T, but prior to the release of y_{T+1}. In view of (51), z_{T+1} provides information about the latent states (s_T, s_{T+1}) and the DSGE model parameters θ. Thus, $p(s_T, s_{T+1}|\theta, Y_{1:T})$ and $p(\theta|Y_{1:T})$ should be replaced by $p(s_T, s_{T+1}|\theta, Y_{1:T}, z_{T+1})$ and $p(\theta|Y_{1:T}, z_{T+1})$, respectively. In the remainder of this section we focus on $p(s_T, s_{T+1}|\theta, Y_{1:T}, z_{T+1})$, assuming that

$$p(\theta|Y_{1:T}, z_{T+1}) \approx p(\theta|Y_{1:T}). \tag{52}$$

Thus, unlike in the work on conditional forecasting with Bayesian VARs by Waggoner and Zha (1999), we disregard the information contents of the external nowcasts with respect to the model parameters θ. This assumption is compelling in applications in which the information in the sample $Y_{1:T}$ and prior distribution strongly dominates the information contained in z_{T+1}. For the SWπ model considered below, the shortest estimation sample contains about 110 observations for eight macroeconomic time series, whereas z_{T+1} is comprised of only one observation for three time series.

We now turn our attention to the construction of $p(s_{T+1}, s_T|\theta, Y_{1:T}, z_{T+1})$. Since we adopted the convention that z_{T+1} provides information about $y_{1,T+1}$ we can write without loss of generality

$$y_{1,T+1} = z_{T+1} + (y_{1,T+1} - z_{T+1}) = z_{T+1} + \eta_{T+1}. \tag{53}$$

An assumption about the joint distribution of z_{T+1} and η_T determine the joint distribution of $y_{1,T+1}$ and z_{T+1}. For now, we consider two specific assumptions that we classify as *Noise* and *News*. Under the *Noise* assumption the external information z_{T+1} is interpreted as a noisy measure of $y_{1,T+1}$, that is

$$\text{Noise}: \quad z_{T+1} = y_{1,T+1} - \eta_{T+1}, \quad y_{1,T+1} \perp \eta_{T+1}. \tag{54}$$

Here η_{T+1} is a measurement error that is independent ($\perp$) of the actual value $y_{1,T+1}$. Under the *News* assumption it is the nowcast z_{T+1} that is independent of the error term η_{T+1}

$$\text{News}: \quad y_{1,T+1} = z_{T+1} + \eta_{T+1}, \quad z_{T+1} \perp \eta_{T+1}. \tag{55}$$

Such a correlation structure arises if, for instance, z_{T+1} is a conditional expectation of $y_{1,T+1}$ given $Y_{1:T}$ and other information.

The *Noise* assumption can be easily incorporated into the Kalman-filter-based analysis of the DSGE model. After the time T Kalman filter iterations have been completed and $p(s_T|Y_{1:T}, \theta)$ has been computed, (54) is used as period $T+1$ measurement equation. This leads to the following algorithm:

Algorithm 3.   Draws from the Predictive Distribution Conditional on External Nowcast (Noise Assumption). *For $j = 1$ to n_{sim}, select the j'th draw from the posterior distribution $p(\theta|Y_{1:T})$ and:*

1. *Use the Kalman filter to compute mean and variance of the distribution $p(s_T|\theta^{(j)}, Y_{1:T})$.*
2. *In period $T + 1$ use Eq. (54) as measurement equation for the nowcast z_{T+1} assuming $\eta_{T+1} \sim N(0, \sigma_\eta^2)$. Use the Kalman filter updating to compute $p(s_{T+1}|\theta^{(j)}, Y_{1:T}, z_{T+1})$ and generate a draw $s_{T+1}^{(j)}$ from this distribution.*
3. *Draw a sequence of innovations $\epsilon_{T+2:T+H}^{(j)}$ and, starting from $s_{T+1}^{(j)}$, iterate the state transition equation (34) forward to obtain the sequence $S_{T+2:T+H}^{(j)}$.*
4. *Use the measurement equation (35) to compute $Y_{T+1:T+H}^{(j)}$ based on $S_{T+1:T+H}^{(j)}$.*   □

So far, we have assumed that the external information only pertains to observations dated $T + 1$. Algorithm 3 has a straightforward generalization to the case in which the external information spans multiple horizons, e.g., $T + 1, \ldots, T + \bar{H}$. Denoting this information by $Z_{T+1:T+\bar{H}} = \{z_{T+1}, \ldots, z_{T+\bar{H}}\}$, Step 2 can be replaced by using the simulation smoother described in Carter and Kohn (1994) to generate a draw $S_{T+1:T+\bar{H}}^{(j)}$ from $p(S_{T+1:T+\bar{H}}|\theta^{(j)}, Y_{1:T}, Z_{T+1:T+\bar{H}})$. Associated with each simulated sequence of latent states $S_{T+1:T+\bar{H}}^{(j)}$ is a sequence of structural shocks $\epsilon_{T+1:T+\bar{H}}^{(j)}$. The distribution of the structural shocks conditional on the external information no longer mean zero. Thus, an external nowcast of output growth that is different from the DSGE model forecast might be rationalized by a particular combination of structural shocks, such as technology or monetary policy shocks.[10]

According to the *News* assumption in (55), the nowcast is interpreted as a predictive distribution for $y_{1,T+1}$ that incorporates both the information $Y_{1:T}$ used in the DSGE model estimation as well as some additional, not explicitly specified information that has been processed by the professional forecasters included in the Blue Chip survey. We will describe an algorithm that is based on the following representation of the predictive density

$$p(y_{T+1}|Y_{1:T}, z_{T+1}) = \int_\theta \left[\int_{\tilde{y}_{1,T+1}} p(y_{T+1}|s_{T+1}, \theta)p(s_{T+1}|\tilde{y}_{1,T+1}, Y_{1:T}, \theta) \right. \tag{56}$$

$$\left. \times \; p(\tilde{y}_{1,T+1}|Y_{1:T}, z_{T+1})d\tilde{y}_{1,T+1} \right] p(\theta|Y_{1:T})d(\theta, s_{T+1}).$$

We assume that conditional on the Blue Chip nowcast $Y_{1:T}$ contains no additional information that is useful for predicting $y_{1,T+1}$, that is,

$$p(\tilde{y}_{1,T+1}|Y_{1:T}, z_{T+1}) = p(\tilde{y}_{1,T+1}|z_{T+1}) \tag{57}$$

---

[10] Beneš et al. (2008) interpret the likelihood of the structural shocks that are needed to attain the path of observables implied by the external information as a measure of how plausible this external information is in view of the model.

and the density on the right-hand-side is given by (55). The density $p(s_{T+1}|\tilde{\gamma}_{1,T+1}, Y_{1:T}, \theta)$ in (56) captures the information about the latent state s_{T+1}, accounting through $\tilde{\gamma}_{1,T+1}$ for the information contained in z_{T+1}. Since the DSGE model is represented as a linear Gaussian state-space model, the one-step-ahead forecast generated by (56) of $\gamma_{1,T+1}$ equals z_{T+1}. The following algorithm implements the conditional forecast.

Algorithm 4.   Draws from the Predictive Distribution Conditional on External Nowcast (News Assumption). *For $j = 1$ to n_{sim}, select the j'th draw from the posterior distribution $p(\theta|Y_{1:T})$ and:*

1. *Use the Kalman filter to compute mean and variance of the distribution $p(s_T|\theta^{(j)}, Y_{1:T})$.*
2. *Generate a draw $\tilde{\gamma}_{1,T+1}^{(j)}$ from the distribution $p(\tilde{\gamma}_{1,T+1}|Y_{1:T}, z_{T+1})$ using (55), assuming $\eta_{T+1} \sim N(0, \sigma_\eta^2)$.*
3. *Treating $\tilde{\gamma}_{1,T+1}^{(j)}$ as observation for $\gamma_{1,T+1}$ use the Kalman filter updating step to compute $p(s_{T+1}|\theta^{(j)}, Y_{1:T}, \tilde{\gamma}_{1,T+1}^{(j)})$ and generate a draw $s_{T+1}^{(j)}$ from this distribution.*
4. *Draw a sequence of innovations $\epsilon_{T+2:T+H}^{(j)}$ and, starting from $s_{T+1}^{(j)}$, iterate the state transition equation (34) forward to obtain the sequence $S_{T+2:T+H}^{(j)}$.*
5. *Use the measurement equation (35) to obtain $Y_{T+1:T+H}^{(j)}$ based on $S_{T+2:T+H}^{(j)}$.*

Using (57) in Step 2 of Algorithm 4, we impose that $\tilde{\gamma}_{1,T+1} \sim N(z_{T+1}, \sigma_\eta^2)$. This step can be modified to allow for a more general conditional distribution of $\tilde{\gamma}_{1,T+1}$. For instance, instead of imposing that the conditional mean of $\tilde{\gamma}_{1,T+1}$ equals the Blue Chip nowcast z_{T+1}, one could use a weighted average of the Blue Chip nowcast and the one-step-ahead DSGE model forecast from $p(\gamma_{1,T+1}|Y_{1:T}, \theta)$. Hard conditioning on external nowcasts, i.e., imposing the equality $\gamma_{1,T+1} = z_{T+1}$, can be implemented by setting $\sigma_\eta^2 = 0$. In this case Algorithms 3 and 4 are identical. Finally, note that the mean forecast obtained under the *News* assumption (with $\sigma_\eta^2 > 0$) always coincides with the mean forecast obtained under hard conditioning (that is, setting $\sigma_\eta^2 = 0$). This is because the updating equation that determines the mean of $p(s_{T+1}|\theta^{(j)}, Y_{1:T}, \tilde{\gamma}_{1,T+1}^{(j)})$ in Step 3 of Algorithm 4 is linear in $\tilde{\gamma}_{1,T+1}^{(j)}$. The predictive distribution is, of course, more diffuse.

We now use Algorithm 3 to incorporate information from Blue Chip nowcasts of output growth, inflation, and interest rates into the DSGE model forecasts. We refer to the resulting forecasts as SWπ-now. The vector of measurement errors σ_η^2 in (54) associated with the Blue Chip nowcasts are calibrated to match the size of the nowcast error (that is, the Blue Chip RMSE for $h = 1$ in Figure 2.2). Figure 2.8 depicts RMSEs for SWπ and SWπ-now forecasts as well as the Blue Chip forecasts. The top panels of the figure depict RMSEs for output growth, inflation, and interest rates, which are the three series for which we add external information. At the nowcast horizon $h = 1$ the RMSEs associated with SWπ-now and Blue Chip forecasts are essentially identical and dominate the SWπ forecasts by a considerable margin. The nowcasts reduce the RMSEs of output

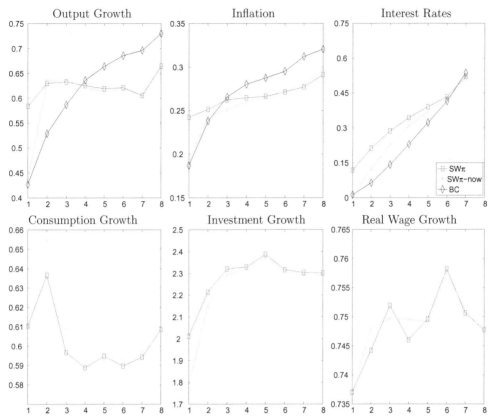

Figure 2.8 Using inflation expectations and external nowcasts. *Notes:* The figure compares the one through eight quarters-ahead RMSEs for Blue Chip (diamonds), the SW model with observed long run inflation expectations (SWπ, squares) and the SW model with observed long run inflation expectations and output growth, inflation, and interest rate nowcasts (SWπ-now, crosses) for output growth, inflation, interest rates, consumption, investment, and real wage growth. The comparison is done for the same vintages/forecast dates as the Blue Chip/DSGE comparison discussed in Section 4.3. All variables are expressed in terms of QoQ rates in percentage. Section 4.1 provides the details of the forecast comparison exercise.

growth forecasts horizon $h = 1$ from 0.58% to 0.43%, but essentially have no effect on RMSEs for $h > 1$. At horizons $h = 2$ and $h = 3$ the Blue Chip forecasts dominate the SWπ-now forecasts. This ranking is reserved for horizons $h > 3$.

The positive effect of the external information on inflation and interest rate forecasts is more persistent. For instance, for $h = 1$ the interest rate RMSE is reduced from 0.12 (SWπ) to 0.01 (SWπ-now). For $h = 4$ the RMSE is lowered from 0.35 (SWπ) to 0.31 (SWπ-now). For horizons $h = 2$ to $h = 5$ the Blue Chip interest rate forecasts remain more accurate than the SWπ-now forecasts. For inflation, on the other hand, SWπ predictions weakly dominate Blue Chip forecasts at all horizons. Although the Blue Chip nowcasts include no information about consumption and investment growth, we observe a RMSE reduction for $h = 1$. To the extent that the joint predictive distribution correctly captures non-zero correlations between output, inflation, and interest rates on the one hand and consumption and investment growth on the other hand, information about the first set of variables can sharpen the predictions for the second set of variables. We also generated forecasts based on Algorithm 4. Since the RMSE graphs look essentially identical to those depicted in Figure 2.8, we are not reporting them separately in this chapter.

A number of alternative approaches of incorporating external information in DSGE model forecasts have been considered in the literature. Herbst and Schorfheide (2011) take the output of a simulator that generates draws from the unconditional predictive density, e.g., Algorithm 2, and use Kernel weights to convert draws from the unconditional predictive density into draws from a conditional predictive density. This non-parametric approach can in principle be applied to draws from any kind of joint predictive distribution to hard-condition on $y_{1,T+1} = z_{T+1}$. A benefit of the Kernel-based method is that the posterior distribution of θ is also implicitly updated[11] in light of the external information z_{T+1}, without having to explicitly evaluate the augmented likelihood $p(z_{T+1}, Y_{1:T}|\theta)$. However, if the dimension of z_{T+1} is moderately large or if the external nowcast lies far in the tails of the model-implied predictive distribution $p(Y_{1,T+1}|Y_{1:T})$ a precise Kernel-based approximation of the conditional distribution could require a large number of draws from the predictive distribution $p(y_{T+1:T+H}|Y_{1:T})$.

While the approach in Herbst and Schorfheide (2011) leads to hard conditioning, i.e., fixing the conditioning variables at a particular value, Robertson et al., (2005) propose a non-parametric method that allows users to soft-condition on external information. Rather than imposing that $y_{1,T+1} = z_{T+1}$, the authors' goal is to impose the restriction $\mathbb{E}[y_{1,T+1}] = z_{T+1}$. Building on insights from the empirical likelihood literature, see Owen (2001), the authors apply an exponential tilting procedure to the draws from the unconditional predictive distribution $p(Y_{T+1:T+H}|Y_{1:T})$. Each draw $Y_{T+1:T+H}^{(j)}$ receives a weight w_j such that the empirical distribution associated with the weighted draws minimizes the Kullback–Leibler distance to the unweighted empirical distribution subject to the moment constraint $\sum_{j=1}^{n_{sim}} w_j y_{1,T+1}^{(j)} = z_{T+1}$. The procedure allows the user to remain agnostic about all aspects of the distribution of η_{T+1} in (55), except the constraint $\mathbb{E}[\eta_{T+1}] = 0$.

Monti (2010) develops an approach of incorporating external professional forecasts into a DSGE model, which combines aspects of what we previously referred to as news and noise assumption. She assumes that the professional forecasters have additional information (news) about the structural shocks that are hitting the economy in the current period. However, the professional forecasters also add some personal judgment to their forecasts which works like a noise term. Monti (2010) derives a set of measurement equations for current period observations and multi-step professional forecasts and estimates

---

[11] For instance, $p(y_{2,T+1}|z_{T+1}, Y_{1:T}) = \int p(y_{2,T+1}|z_{T+1}, Y_{1:T}, \theta) p(\theta|z_{T+1}, Y_{1:T}) d\theta$. Thus, θ is averaged with respect to the posterior distribution that also conditions on z_{T+1}.

the DSGE model on this joint information. Rather than conditioning on external fore-casts, Giannone et al., (2010) directly incorporate monthly information in the estimation of a DSGE model. In a nutshell, the authors first estimate the DSGE model parameters based on the usual quarterly observations and then transform the state-transition equations to monthly frequency. In addition to the usual quarterly variables, the authors then also use monthly variables to make inference about the current state of the economy and to improve the accuracy of short-horizon forecasts.

5.4. Incorporating Interest Rate Expectations

Discrepancies between DSGE model-based interest rate forecasts on the one hand and external forecasts or financial-market based expectations of future interest rates pose a challenge for the DSGE model analysis, in particular, if it is evident that the latter are more accurate than the former. The state-space representation of the DSGE model given by (34) and (35) implies that

$$\mathbb{E}[y_{t+h}|s_t] = \psi_0(\theta) + \Psi_1(\theta)(t+h) + \Psi_2(\theta)[\Phi_1(\theta)]^h s_t.$$

Thus, adding observations that are equated with the DSGE model-implied expectations of endogenous variables generates a singularity problem because there are fewer shocks in the model than observables in the measurement equation. In Section 5.1 we overcame the singularity problem by adding an additional structural shock to the model: we replaced the constant target inflation rate by a stochastically varying target inflation rate which was driven by a new innovation $\epsilon_{\pi^*,t}$. We followed a similar approach in Section 5.2 by adding a shock to the growth rate of technology. In this section we will introduce so-called anticipated monetary policy shocks to absorb discrepancies between observed and DSGE-model-implied interest rate expectations. However, unlike in Sections 5.1 and 5.2, due to data limitations we do not re-estimate the DSGE model recursively with observations on interest-rate expectations. We simply use the posterior of the SWπ model and incorporate the additional information when generating the forecast.

Equation (16) characterizes the monetary policy rule for the SW model with constant target inflation rate and (45) is the modified version with the time-varying inflation target. The disturbance r_t^m captures deviations from the systematic part of the policy rule. While in many DSGE models these deviations are assumed to be iid, the SW model allows for a serially correlated process:

$$r_t^m = \rho_{r^m} r_{t-1}^m + \sigma_{r^m} \epsilon_t^m. \tag{58}$$

We now augment the process r_t^m by anticipated shocks that capture future expected deviations from the systematic part of the monetary policy rule:

$$r_t^m = \rho_{r^m} r_{t-1}^m + \sigma_{r^m} \epsilon_t^m + \sum_{k=1}^{K} \sigma_{r^m,k} \epsilon_{k,t-k}^m, \tag{59}$$

where the policy shocks $\epsilon_{k,t-k}^m$, $k = 1, \ldots, K$, are known to agents at time $t - k$, but affect the policy rule with a k period delay in period t. Thus, agents are assumed to expect certain deviations from the systematic part of the interest-rate feedback rule several quarters in advance.

To the extent that the SWπ-now model with a policy rule given by (45) and (58) is unable to match the observed interest rate expectations in the data (see Figure 2.8), the anticipated monetary policy shocks can absorb the discrepancies between actual and DSGE model-implied expectations. As central banks around the world have been experimenting with so-called forward guidance, that is, sending signals about the future path of interest rates, we would expect the external interest rates forecasts to become more accurate and the use of anticipated shocks to rationalize the interest rate expectations in DSGE models to become attractive and plausible.

It is convenient to express the anticipated shocks in recursive form. For this purpose, we augment the state vector s_t with $\bar{H}$ additional states $v_t^m, \ldots, v_{t-\bar{H}}^m$ whose law of motion is as follows:

$$v_{1,t}^m = v_{2,t-1}^m + \sigma_{r^m,1}\epsilon_{1,t}^m, \quad v_{2,t}^m = v_{3,t-1}^m + \sigma_{r^m,2}\epsilon_{2,t}^m, \quad \cdots \quad v_{K,t}^m = \sigma_{r^m,K}\epsilon_{K,t}^m \quad (60)$$

and rewrite the process r_t^m in (59) as

$$r_t^m = \rho_{r^m} r_{t-1}^m + \sigma_{r^m}\epsilon_t^m + v_{1,t-1}^m. \quad (61)$$

It is easy to verify that $v_{1,t-1}^m = \sum_{k=1}^K \sigma_{r^m,k}\epsilon_{k,t-k}^m$, that is, $v_{1,t-1}^m$ is a "bin" that collects all anticipated shocks that affect the policy rule in period t. The model's solution can then again be expressed in terms of the transition equation (34).

While one could in principle estimate the anticipated shock model based on an augmented data set that includes interest rate expectations, we start from estimates of the SWπ model based on $Y_{1:T}$ and then switch to the anticipated shocks model, denoted by SWπR-now, to generate forecasts. This shortcut facilitates the comparison between forecasts from the SWπ-now and the SWπR-now because the forecasts are generated based on the same posterior distribution of DSGE model parameters θ.[12] The timing of the forecasts and the external information is explained in Table 2.6. The first three columns are identical to Columns 1 to 3 of Table 2.5. Consider the forecast origin that corresponds to the July 1992 Blue Chip release. The July 10 Blue Chip Economic Indicator survey is based on forecasts that were generated at the end of June. At this point, the forecasters essentially know the average interest rate for 1992:Q2, which is period $T + 1$. We interpret Blue Chip interest forecasts for 1992:Q3 through 1993:Q2 as observations of interest rate expectations $R_{T+2|T+1}^e$ to $R_{T+5|T+1}^e$:

$$R_{T+1+k|T+1}^e = R_* + \mathbb{E}_{T+1}\left[R_{T+1+k}\right], \quad k = 1, \ldots. \quad (62)$$

---

[12] We do not have estimates for the standard deviations $\sigma_{r^m,k}$ of the anticipated shocks. In the implementation, we assume that these shocks have the same standard deviation as the contemporaneous shock: $\sigma_{r^m,k} = \sigma_{r^m}$.

Table 2.6 Blue Chip Forecast Dates and Nowcast Information and Interest Rate Expectations for 1992

Forecast Origin	End of Est. Sample T	External Nowcast $T + 1$	Interest Rate Exp. $R^e_{T+2|T+1}, \ldots, R^e_{T+5|T+1}$	Forecast $h = 1$	$h = 2$
Apr 92	91:Q4	92:Q1 based on Apr 92 BC	92:Q2–93:Q1	92:Q1	92:Q2
Jul 92	92:Q1	92:Q2 based on Jul 92 BC	92:Q3–93:Q2	92:Q2	92:Q3
Oct 92	92:Q2	92:Q3 based on Oct 92 BC	92:Q4–93:Q3	92:Q3	92:Q4
Jan 93	92:Q3	92:Q4 based on Jan 93 BC	93:Q1–93:Q4	92:Q4	93:Q1

R_* is the steady state interest rate and $\mathbb{E}_{T+1}[R_{T+1+k}]$ is the DSGE model-implied k-period–ahead interest rate expectation.

Federal funds rate expectations are taken from Blue Chip Financial Forecasts survey, which is published on the first of each month.[13] They are given in annual rates and are transformed in the same manner as the interest rate series in the estimation sample:

$$R^e_{T+1+k|T+1} = \text{BLUE CHIP } k\text{-QUARTERS AHEAD FFR FORECAST}/4.$$

Since Blue Chip Financial Forecasts extend to at most two calendar year including the current one, the horizon k for the interest forecasts varies from seven to five quarters, depending on the vintage. We use all available data. In addition to the interest rate expectations, we also incorporate the Blue Chip nowcasts into the forecasting procedure, using the *Noise* approach described in Section 5.3. This leads to the following algorithm to generate draws from the predictive distribution:

Algorithm 5.   Draws from the Predictive Distribution Conditional on External Nowcast (Noise Assumption) and Interest Rate Expectations. *For $j = 1$ to n_{sim}, select the j'th draw from the posterior distribution $p(\theta|Y_{1:T})$ and:*

1. *Based on the DSGE model without anticipated shocks, use the Kalman filter to compute mean and variance of the distribution $p(s_T|\theta^{(j)}, Y_{1:T})$.*

2. *Forecast the latent state s_{T+1} based on T information using the DSGE model without anticipated shocks.*

3. *Switch to DSGE model with anticipated shocks. Augment the state vector by the additional state variables $v^m_{1,t}, \ldots, v^m_{K,t}$. Set mean and variances/covariances of these additional states to zero. Denote the augmented state vector by $\tilde{s}_t$.*

4. *Adjust the measurement equation such that it lines up with the available Blue Chip nowcasts, z_{T+1}, as well as the interest rate expectations $R^e_{T+2|T+1}, \ldots, R^e_{T+5|T+1}$. Use the Kalman*

---

[13] There is a 10-day gap between the BCFF and the BCEI survey, so the two are not quite based on the same information set. Also, the survey participants are not the same, although there is a substantial overlap. We ignore these differences. We thank Stefano Eusepi and Emanuel Mönch for providing us with this data, and their RA, Jenny Chan, for helping us find out how they were constructed.

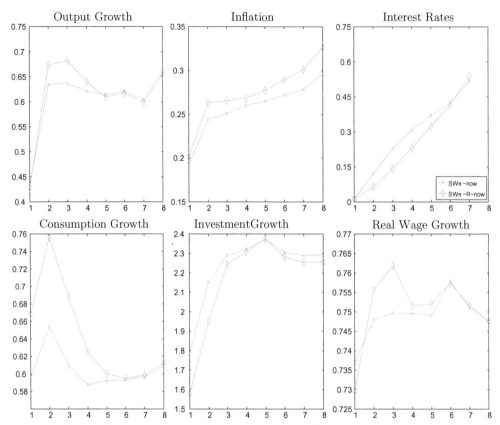

Figure 2.9 Using inflation expectations, external nowcasts, and interest rate expectations. *Notes:* The figure compares the one through eight quarters-ahead RMSEs for the SW model with observed long run inflation expectations and output growth, inflation, and interest rate nowcasts (SWπ-now, crosses) and the SW model with observed long run inflation and interest rate expectations and nowcasts (SWπR-now, diamonds) for output growth, inflation, interest rates, consumption, investment, and real wage growth. The comparison is done for the same vintages/forecast dates as the Blue Chip/DSGE comparison discussed in Section 4.3. All variables are expressed in terms of QoQ rates in percentage. Section 4.1 provides the details of the forecast comparison exercise.

filter updating to compute $p(\tilde{s}_{T+1}|\theta^{(j)}, Y_{1:T}, z_{T+1}, R^e_{T+2|T+1}, \ldots, R^e_{T+5|T+1})$ Generate a draw $\tilde{s}^{(j)}_{T+1}$ from this distribution.

5. Draw a sequence of innovations $\epsilon^{(j)}_{T+2:T+H}$ and, starting from $\tilde{s}^{(j)}_{T+1}$, iterate the state transition equations of the DSGE model forward to obtain a sequence $\tilde{S}^{(j)}_{T+2:T+H}$.

6. Use the measurement equation to obtain $Y^{(j)}_{T+1:T+H}$ based on $\tilde{S}^{(j)}_{T+1:T+H}$.

In Figure 2.9 we compare forecasts from the SWπ-now model, which only utilizes current quarter interest rates, and the model that utilizes interest rate expectations up to four quarters ahead, SWπR-now. The interest-rate expectations modify the DSGE model forecasts in two ways, broadly corresponding to the endogenous and exogenous component of monetary policy. If survey interest rate forecasts differ from the DSGE model forecasts, it must be because either (i) the market's perception of the state of the economy is different from that of the DSGE econometrician (and hence entails a different policy response) or (ii) because the market anticipates deviations from the policy rule in the future (due to, say, changes in FOMC language). Formally, the use of interest-rate expectations in the measurement equation affects the inference about the latent state $\tilde{s}_{T+1}$ in Step 4 of Algorithm 5. This latent state vector has two components, namely s_{T+1} and the additional state variables $v_{k,t}^m$, $k = 1, \ldots, K$, specified in (60). Since the anticipated monetary policy shocks only affect the exogenous component of the monetary policy rule, the output growth, inflation, and interest rate dynamics generated by the reversion of s_{T+1} to its steady state of zero are the same as in the SWπ-now model. However, the inferred period $T + 1$ level of the state vector can be different if we use information on expected interest rates (endogenous component). In addition, the forecasts of the SWπ-R-now model are influenced by the impulse-responses to the anticipated monetary policy shocks (exogenous component) that align the model-based interest rate forecasts in period $T + 1$ with the observed interest rate expectations.

The use of interest-rate expectations reduces the RMSE for the Federal Funds rate for horizon $h = 2$ to $h = 5$. For instance, while the RMSE associated with the SWπ-now model is 0.23% for $h = 2$, it drops to 0.14% if interest rate expectations are included. Unfortunately, the interest rate expectations have an adverse effect on output growth and inflation forecasts. For instance, at $h = 3$ the output growth RMSE rises from 0.63% to 0.68% and the inflation RMSE increases from 0.25% to 0.27%. While consumption and real wage growth forecasts also deteriorate over the two- to five-quarter horizon, only the investment growth forecast improves. For $h = 2$ the investment growth RMSE for the SWπ-now model is 2.15% whereas it is only 1.95% for the SWπR-now model. While it is difficult to disentangle which feature of SWπR-now is responsible for the observed deterioration in the forecast performance, we provide a detailed discussion of responses to anticipated monetary policy shocks in the next section.

6. FORECASTS CONDITIONAL ON INTEREST RATE PATHS

In this section we are generating forecasts conditional on a particular interest path. In particular, we assume that in periods $t = T + 1, \ldots, T + \bar{H}$ the interest rate takes (in expectation or actually) the values $\bar{R}_{T+1}, \ldots, \bar{R}_{T+\bar{H}}$, where $\bar{H} \leq H$. We consider two methods: using unanticipated monetary policy shocks (Section 6.2) and using anticipated monetary policy shocks (Section 6.3). Before engaging in conditional forecasting, we briefly review the effects of monetary policy shocks in a simple DSGE model (Section 6.1) and provide impulse response functions for the SWπ model. At last, we provide an empirical illustration of conditional forecasting (Section 6.4).

6.1. The Effects of Monetary Policy Shocks

In order to understand the effects of unanticipated and anticipated monetary policy shocks, we begin by solving an analytical example.[14] The subsequent example is based on a further simplification of the small-scale model presented in Section 2.3. The simplified version of the model consists of the linearized Euler equation:

$$y_t = \mathbb{E}[y_{t+1}] - (R_t - \mathbb{E}[\pi_{t+1}]), \tag{63}$$

a Phillips curve,

$$\pi_t = \beta\mathbb{E}[\pi_{t+1}] + \kappa y_t, \tag{64}$$

and a monetary policy rule with unanticipated and anticipated monetary policy shocks:

$$R_t = \frac{1}{\beta}\pi_t + \epsilon_t^R + \sum_{k=1}^{K}\epsilon_{k,t-k}^R. \tag{65}$$

As in Section 5.4, we use $\epsilon_{k,t-k}^R$ as a shock that is realized in period $t - k$ and affects the interest rate k periods later. The inflation coefficient in the policy rule is restricted to be equal to $1/\beta$, which facilitates the analytical solution of the model.

We first determine the law of motion of output. The Euler equation (63) implies that output is the sum of expected future real rates. Of course future real rates are endogenous and further manipulations are needed to express output as the sum of expected future monetary policy shocks. Using (65) to eliminating the nominal interest rate from the Euler equation yields

$$y_t = \mathbb{E}_t[y_{t+1}] - \left(\frac{1}{\beta}\pi_t - \mathbb{E}_t[\pi_{t+1}]\right) - \epsilon_t^R - \sum_{k=1}^{K}\epsilon_{k,t-k}^R. \tag{66}$$

The restriction imposed on the inflation coefficient in the monetary policy rule implies that we can express next period's real return on a nominal bond as a function of current output. More specifically, we can re-write the Phillips curve (64) as

$$\frac{1}{\beta}\pi_t - \mathbb{E}[\pi_{t+1}] = \frac{\kappa}{\beta}y_t \tag{67}$$

and combine (67) with (66) to obtain

$$y_t = \mathbb{E}[y_{t+1}] - \frac{\kappa}{\beta}y_t - \epsilon_t^R - \sum_{k=1}^{K}\epsilon_{k,t-k}^R. \tag{68}$$

Defining $\psi = (1 + \kappa/\beta)^{-1}$ and solving (68) forward yields

$$y_t = -\psi\mathbb{E}_t\left[\sum_{j=0}^{\infty}\psi^j\left(\epsilon_{t+j}^R + \sum_{k=1}^{K}\epsilon_{k,t+j-k}^R\right)\right].$$

---

[14] See also Milani and Treadwell (2011) for a discussion and some empirical results.

Since the expected value of $\epsilon^R_{k,t+j}$ is zero for $j > 0$ we deduce

$$y_t = -\psi \left(\epsilon^R_t + \sum_{k=1}^{K} \epsilon^R_{k,t-k} + \sum_{j=1}^{K} \sum_{k=j}^{K} \psi^j \epsilon^R_{k,t+j-k} \right). \tag{69}$$

This equation implies that the impulse response function for a K-period anticipated shock takes the form

$$\frac{\partial y_{t+h}}{\partial \epsilon^R_{K,t}} = \frac{\partial y_t}{\partial \epsilon^R_{K,t-h}} = -\psi^{1+K-h}, \quad h = 0, \ldots, K \tag{70}$$

and is zero thereafter. The anticipated monetary policy shock raises the expected real return on government bonds and through the consumption Euler equation leads to a decrease in output. Output drops upon impact. Since $0 < \psi < 1$ the output effect increases over time and peaks at $-\psi K$ periods after impact, before it drops to zero.

The law of motion of inflation can be obtained by solving (64) forward. After calculating $\mathbb{E}_t[y_{t+i}]$ based on (69), it can be shown that inflation has the representation

$$\pi_t = -\kappa\psi \left(\epsilon^R_t + \sum_{k=1}^{K} \epsilon^R_{k,t-k} + \sum_{j=1}^{K} \sum_{k=j}^{K} \psi^j \epsilon^R_{k,t+j-k} \right) \tag{71}$$

$$-\kappa\psi \sum_{i=1}^{K} \beta^i \left(\sum_{k=i}^{K} \epsilon^R_{k,t+i-k} + \sum_{j=1}^{K} \sum_{k=j+i}^{K} \psi^j \epsilon^R_{k,t+i+j-k} \right).$$

It can be verified that inflation responds to a K-period anticipated shock according to

$$\frac{\partial \pi_{t+h}}{\partial \epsilon^R_{K,t}} = \frac{\partial \pi_t}{\partial \epsilon^R_{K,t-h}} = -\kappa\psi \left(\psi^{K-h} + \beta^{K-h} + \psi^{K-h} \sum_{i=1}^{K-1-h} \left(\frac{\beta}{\psi} \right)^i \right), \quad h = 0, \ldots, K, \tag{72}$$

where $\beta/\psi = \beta + \kappa$. Inflation also drops on impact of the anticipated monetary policy shock and remains below steady state until period $t + K$, after which it reverts to zero. The shape of the inflation response depends on whether $\beta + \kappa$ is less than or greater than unity. Finally, the law of motion of the interest rates is obtained by plugging (71) into the monetary policy rule (65). The anticipated future increase in interest rates leads to a drop in interest rates prior to $h = K$ because the central bank lowers interest rates in response to the below-target inflation rate.

We now compute impulse response functions of interest rates, output growth, and inflation to an unanticipated and an anticipated contractionary policy shock based on the estimated SWπ model. This model exhibits more elaborate dynamics than the simple analytical model. The impulse response functions depicted in Figure 2.10 are computed using the posterior mode estimates from the May-2011 vintage. The anticipated shock is

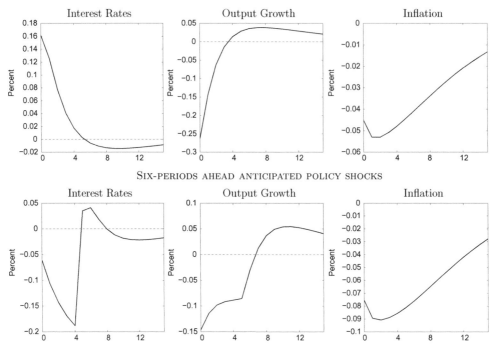

Figure 2.10 Impulse responses to anticipated and unanticipated policy shocks. *Notes:* The figure shows the impulse response functions of interest rates, output growth, and inflation to a one-standard deviation unanticipated (top panel) and anticipated (bottom panel) policy shock. The anticipated shock is known to agents six periods in advance. The impulse responses are computed using the modal estimates for the last available vintage (May 2011) for model SWπ.

known to the agents in the model $k = 6$ periods in advance. The size of both shocks is the same, and equal to the estimated standard deviation of the unanticipated shocks.

The response to the unanticipated monetary policy shock (top panels) follows the familiar pattern. Interest rates rise by about 16 bp, whereas output falls by 25 bp upon impact. Over time, output growth reverts back to zero and eventually becomes negative, as the long-run effect of an unanticipated shock on the level of output is zero. Inflation falls by 5 bp and slowly reverts back to zero. The strong response of output relative to inflation is a reflection of the magnitude of estimated nominal rigidities in the model.

As foreshadowed by the analytical calculations, the effect of the anticipated policy shock is quite different from the response to the unanticipated shock. To understand the pattern it is helpful to reconsider (70) and (72). Upon impact, the anticipated monetary policy shock lowers output and inflation, and via the systematic part of the monetary policy rule also interest rates. This pattern is also evident in the bottom panels of Figure 2.10. Output and inflation drop by 15 bp and 8 bp, respectively, interest rates fall by 5 bp due to the endogenous policy response. In the simple analytical model output keeps on falling after the impact of the anticipated policy shock because $0 < \psi < 1$. This implies that output growth remains negative, which we also see in Figure 2.10. According to (72) the shape of the inflation response is ambiguous. The SWπ produces a hump-shaped response that reaches its trough at $h = 2$. The interest rate jumps after six periods, when the anticipated deviation from the rule is actually realized. Unlike the simple analytical model, the SWπ model has endogenous state variables, which generate fairly persistent dynamics even after the policy shock is realized.

Generally, the effect of the anticipated shock on output is much more persistent than that of the unanticipated shock. Since inflation depends on the present discounted value of future marginal costs, this persistence implies that the impact on inflation is almost twice as strong, even though the size of the shock is the same. After having examined the responses to unanticipated and anticipated monetary policy shocks, we now turn to the problem of generating forecasts conditional on a desired interest-rate path by the central bank.

6.2. Using Unanticipated Shocks to Condition on Interest Rates

Many central banks generate model-based forecasts conditional on hypothetical interest rate paths. One popular scenario in policy discussions is the constant-interest-rate scenario which assumes that the nominal interest rate stays fixed at its current level over the forecast horizon. Since in DSGE models as well as vector autoregressive models interest rates are endogenous, it is by no means guaranteed that the model predicts the interest rate to be constant. For concreteness, suppose that the current level of the nominal interest rate is 2% and the posterior mean predictions for periods $T+1$ and $T+2$ are 2.25% and 2.50%, respectively. In this case, a constant-interest rate path would, in the logic of the DSGE model, require an intervention that lowers the interest rate by 25 bp in period $T+1$ and by 50 bp in period $T+2$.

One approach of generating forecasts conditional on hypothetical interest rate with DSGE models is to utilize a sequence of unanticipated monetary policy shocks as in Leeper and Zha (2003) and Smets and Wouters (2005). Mechanically, it is straightforward to compute such forecasts. Without loss of generality assume that the interest rate R_t is ordered first in the vector y_t, that is, $y_{1,t} = R_t$. Moreover, use $\epsilon_t^{<-p>}$ to denote the sub-vector of ϵ_t that contains all structural innovations, except for the monetary policy innovation that is used to attain the desired interest rate path. Lastly, assume that the monetary policy shock ϵ_t^p is ordered first, such that $\epsilon_t = [\epsilon_t^p, \epsilon_t^{<-p>'}]'$. Typically, the policy shock ϵ_t^p would correspond to a short-lived deviation from the systematic part of the monetary policy rule, but in the SWπ model ϵ_t^p could also correspond to the innovation of the target-inflation process.

Let $\bar{R}_{T+1}, \ldots, \bar{R}_{T+\bar{H}}$ denote the desired interest rate path, where $\bar{H} \leq H$. Using the unanticipated monetary policy shocks we can modify the predictive density in two ways. We consider two cases. In Case (i) the predictive density is modified such that the interest rate R_{T+h} on average is equal to $\bar{R}_{T+h}$ for $h = 1, \ldots, H$. Alternatively, in Case (ii) the predictive density is modified such that $R_{T+h} = \bar{R}_{T+h}$ with probability one.

The following algorithm can be used to generate draws from the predictive distribution conditional on the desired interest rate path. Only Step 3 of the algorithm differs for Cases (i) and (ii). In Case (ii), the monetary policy shocks ϵ_t^p are computed as a function of the non-policy shocks $\epsilon_t^{<-p>}$, whereas in Case (i) the non-policy shocks are set to zero when computing ϵ_t^p.

Algorithm 6.   Draws from the Counterfactual Predictive Distribution via Unanticipated Shocks. *For $j = 1$ to n_{sim}, select the j'th draw from the posterior distribution $p(\theta|Y_{1:T})$ and:*

1. *Use the Kalman filter to compute mean and variance of the distribution $p(s_T|\theta^{(j)}, Y_{1:T})$. Generate a draw $s_T^{(j)}$ from this distribution.*

2. *Draw a sequence of innovations $\epsilon_{T+1:T+H}^{<-p>(j)}$ for the non-policy shocks.*

3. **Case (i):** $\mathbb{E}[R_t|Y_{1:T}] = \bar{R}_t$. *Compute the sequence $\bar{\epsilon}_t^{p(j)}, t = T+1, \ldots, T+\bar{H}$ as follows. For $t = T+1$ to $t = T+\bar{H}$: Determine $\bar{\epsilon}_t^{p(j)}$ as the solution to*

$$\bar{R}_t = \Psi_{1.,1}(\theta^{(j)}) + \Psi_{1.,1}(\theta^{(j)})t + \Psi_{1.,2}(\theta^{(j)}) \left(\Phi_1(\theta^{(j)})s_{t-1} + \Phi_\epsilon(\theta^{(j)})[\bar{\epsilon}_t^{p(j)}, 0]' \right),$$

iterating s_t forward according to $s_t = \Phi_1 s_{t-1} + \Phi_\epsilon[\bar{\epsilon}_t^{p(j)}, 0]'$.

Case (ii): $R_t = \bar{R}_t$ **with probability one.** *Compute the sequence $\bar{\epsilon}_t^{p(j)}, t = T+1, \ldots, T+\bar{H}$ as follows. For $t = T+1$ to $t = T+\bar{H}$: Determine $\bar{\epsilon}_t^{p(j)}$ as the solution to*

$$\bar{R}_t = \Psi_{1.,1}(\theta^{(j)}) + \Psi_{1.,1}(\theta^{(j)})t + \Psi_{1.,2}(\theta^{(j)}) \left(\Phi_1(\theta^{(j)})s_{t-1} + \Phi_\epsilon(\theta^{(j)})[\bar{\epsilon}_t^p, \epsilon_t^{<-p>(j)}]' \right),$$

iterating s_t forward according to $s_t = \Phi_1 s_{t-1} + \Phi_\epsilon[\bar{\epsilon}_t^p, \epsilon_t^{<-p>(j)}]'$.

4. *Starting from $s_T^{(j)}$, iterate the state transition equation (34) forward to obtain the sequence $S_{T+1:T+H}^{(j)}$:*

$$s_t^{(j)} = \Phi_1(\theta^{(j)})s_{t-1}^{(j)} + \Phi_\epsilon(\theta^{(j)})[\epsilon_t^{p(j)}, \epsilon_t^{<-p>(j)'}]', \quad t = T+1, \ldots, T+H.$$

For $t = T+1, \ldots, T+\bar{H}$ use $\epsilon_t^{p(j)} = \bar{\epsilon}_t^p$ obtained under Case (i) or (ii) above. For $t > T+\bar{H}$, generate a draw $\epsilon_t^{p(j)} \sim N(0,1)$.

5. *Use the measurement equation (35) to compute $Y_{T+1:T+H}^{(j)}$ based on $S_{T+1:T+H}^{(j)}$.*   □

There are two conceptual drawbacks associated with the use of unanticipated monetary policy shocks. First, if the interest rate path $\bar{R}_{T+1:T+\bar{H}}$ is credibly announced by the central bank, then the deviations from the systematic part of the monetary policy rule are not *unanticipated*. Consequently, the use of unanticipated monetary policy shocks might lead to inaccurate predictions. Second, suppose that the interest rate path is not announced to the public but its implementation requires a sequence of strongly positively correlated unanticipated monetary policy shocks. Over time, the agents in the DSGE model might be able to detect the persistence in the deviation from the systematic part of the monetary policy rule and suspect that the policy rule itself might have changed permanently, which, in turn, creates an incentive to update decision rules. Of course, none of this is captured in the DSGE model itself. Leeper and Zha (2003) recommend to analyze the effect of monetary policy interventions with unanticipated shocks only if the interventions are modest. Here modest essentially means that in a larger model in which agents assign positive probability to occasional shifts in policy regimes, the intervention would not trigger the learning mechanism and lead the agent to believe that the policy regime has shifted.

6.3. Using Anticipated Shocks to Condition on Interest Rates

More recently, the literature has considered the use of anticipated monetary policy shocks to generate forecasts conditional on an interest rate path that deviates from the model-implied path, e.g., Laseen and Svensson (2011), Blake (2012), and Milani and Treadwell (2011). This approach is appealing because several central banks have changed their communication strategy and started to announce interest rate paths. Consider the modified policy rule (59) that includes anticipated shocks $\epsilon^R_{k,t-k}$ as discussed in Section 5.4.

Suppose that after time T shocks are realized, the central bank announces the interest rate path. For the agents the announcement in a one-time surprise in period $T + 1$, which corresponds to the realization of a single unanticipated monetary policy shock ϵ^R_{T+1} and a sequence of anticipated shocks

$$\epsilon^R_{1:K,T+1} = \left[\epsilon^R_{1,T+1},\ \epsilon^R_{2,T+1},\ \ldots,\ \epsilon^R_{K,T+1}\right]',$$

where $K = \bar{H} - 1$. Notice that unlike in Section 6.2 all policy shocks that are used to implement the interest rate path are dated $T + 1$. We will subsequently use ϵ_t to denote the vector that collects the innovations of the unanticipated shocks (both policy and non-policy shocks) and $\epsilon^R_{1:K,t}$ the vector of anticipated policy shocks. In slight abuse of notation, we denote the expanded state vector that includes cumulative effects of anticipated shocks, see (60), also by s_t and use the same notation for the state transition equation, which is now driven by the combined innovation vector $[\epsilon'_t, \epsilon^{R'}_{1:K,t}]'$. The following algorithm determines the time $T + 1$ monetary policy shocks as a function of the desired interest rate sequence $\bar{R}_{T+1}, \ldots, \bar{R}_{T+\bar{H}}$ to generate predictions conditional on an announced interest rate path. The announced interest rate path will be attained in expectation.

Algorithm 7.   Draws from the Counterfactual Predictive Distribution via Anticipated Shocks. *For $j = 1$ to n_{sim}, select the j'th draw from the posterior distribution $p(\theta|Y_{1:T})$ and:*

1. *Use the Kalman filter to compute mean and variance of the distribution $p(s_T|\theta^{(j)}, Y_{1:T})$. Generate a draw $s_T^{(j)}$ from this distribution.*
2. *Draw a sequence of innovations $\epsilon^{(j)}_{T+1:T+H}$.*

3. *Consider the following system of equations, omitting the $\theta^{(j)}$ argument of the system matrices:*

$$\bar{R}_{T+1} = \Psi_{1.,0} + \Psi_{1.,1}(T+1) + \Psi_{1.,2}\Phi_1 s_T$$
$$+ \Psi_{1.,2}\Phi_\epsilon [\underbrace{\bar{\epsilon}^R_{T+1}, 0, \ldots, 0, \bar{\epsilon}^{R'}_{1:K,T+1}}_{\epsilon'_{T+1}}]'$$

$$\bar{R}_{T+2} = \Psi_{1.,0} + \Psi_{1.,1}(T+2) + \Psi_{1.,2}(\Phi_1)^2 s_T$$
$$+ \Psi_{1.,2}\Phi_1\Phi_\epsilon [\underbrace{\bar{\epsilon}^R_{T+1}, 0, \ldots, 0, \bar{\epsilon}^{R'}_{1:K,T+1}}_{\epsilon'_{T+1}}]'$$

$$\vdots$$

$$\bar{R}_{T+\bar{H}} = \Psi_{1.,0} + \Psi_{1.,1}(T+\bar{H}) + \Psi_{1.,2}(\Phi_1)^{\bar{H}} s_T$$
$$+ \Psi_{1.,2}(\Phi_1)^{\bar{H}-1}\Phi_\epsilon [\underbrace{\bar{\epsilon}^R_{T+1}, 0, \ldots, 0, \bar{\epsilon}^{R'}_{1:K,T+1}}_{\epsilon'_{T+1}}]'$$

This linear system of $\bar{H}$ equations with $\bar{H}$ unknowns can be solved for $\bar{\epsilon}^R_{T+1}$ and $\bar{\epsilon}^R_{1:K,T+1}$.

4. *Starting from $s_T^{(j)}$, iterate the state transition equation (34) forward to obtain a sequence $s_{T+1:T+H}^{(j)}$:*

$$s_t^{(j)} = \Phi_1(\theta^{(j)}) s_{t-1}^{(j)} + \Phi_\epsilon(\theta^{(j)})[\underbrace{\epsilon_t^R, \epsilon_t^{<-R>'}, \epsilon_{1:K,t}'}_{\epsilon_t'}]', \quad t = T+1, \ldots, T+H,$$

where (i) $\epsilon_t^{<-R>} = \epsilon_t^{<-R>(j)}$ for $t = T+1, \ldots, T+\bar{H}$ (we are using simulated values throughout); (ii) $\epsilon_{T+1}^R = \bar{\epsilon}^R_{T+1}$ and $\epsilon_t^R = \epsilon_t^{R(j)}$ for $t = T+2, \ldots, T+\bar{H}$ (use solved-for value in period $T+1$ and simulated values thereafter); (iii) $\epsilon_{1:K,T+1}^R = \bar{\epsilon}^R_{1:K,T+1}$ and $\epsilon_{1:K,t}^R = 0$ for $t = T+2, \ldots, T+\bar{H}$ (use solved-for values in period $T+1$ and zeros thereafter).

5. *Use the measurement equation (35) to compute $y_{T+1:T+H}^{(j)}$ based on $s_{T+1:T+H}^{(j)}$.*   □

To shed some light on the algorithm it is instructive to revisit the analytical example of Section 6.1. For $K = 1$ output, inflation, and interest rates are given by

$$y_t = -\psi\left(\epsilon_t^R + \epsilon_{1,t-1}^R + \psi\epsilon_{1,t}^R\right) \tag{73}$$
$$\pi_t = -\kappa\psi\left(\epsilon_t^R + \epsilon_{1,t-1}^R + (\psi+\beta)\epsilon_{1,t}^R\right)$$
$$R_t = \psi\epsilon_t^R + \psi\epsilon_{1,t-1}^R - \frac{1}{\beta}\kappa\psi(\psi+\beta)\epsilon_{1,t}^R.$$

Suppose that the central bank wants to raise interest rates by 25 basis points (bp) for periods $T+1$ and $T+2$. The unanticipated policy shock ϵ_{T+1}^R and the anticipated policy shock $\epsilon_{1,T+1}^R$ are determined by solving the system

$$\bar{R}_{T+1} = 0.25 = \psi \epsilon^R_{T+1} - \frac{1}{\beta} \kappa \psi (\psi + \beta) \epsilon^R_{1,T+1}$$

$$\bar{R}_{T+2} = 0.25 = \psi \epsilon^R_{1,T+1}.$$

For $\kappa = 0.1$ and $\beta = 0.99$, which leads to $\psi = 0.91$, the second equation implies that the anticipated policy shock needs to be equal to $\epsilon^R_{1,T+1} = 0.275$. The anticipated shock lowers the interest rate in the first period by 2.5 bp. To compensate for this effect, the unanticipated monetary policy shock has to be equal to 30 bp. Once the policy shocks have been determined, Algorithm 7 amounts to simulating the system (73) holding the time $T + 1$ monetary policy shocks fixed.

One can also solve for the effect of a policy that raises interest rates 25 bp above the steady state level in periods $T + 1$ and $T + 2$ in an alternative manner. Since there is no persistence in the model, the economy returns to the rational expectations equilibrium in period $t = T + 3$. Thus, in the absence of further shocks $y_{T+3} = \pi_{T+3} = R_{T+3} = 0$. In turn, $\mathbb{E}_{T+2}[y_{T+3}] = \mathbb{E}_{T+2}[\pi_{T+3}] = 0$. The Euler equation (63) for period $T + 2$ implies that output is determined by $y_{T+2} = -R_{T+2}$. Using $\mathbb{E}_{T+2}[\pi_{T+3}] = 0$ once more, the Phillips curve (64) implies that $\pi_{T+2} = \kappa y_{T+2}$. Now that period $T + 2$ output and inflation are determined, (63) and (64) can be solved to find y_{T+1} and π_{T+1} conditional on R_{T+1}. The solution is identical to the one obtained with the anticipated monetary policy shocks.

The effect of keeping the interest rate constant at, say $\bar{R} = 25$ bp, for an extended period of time can be determined by proceeding with the backward solution of the difference equations:

$$y_{t-j} = y_{t-j+1} - \bar{R} + \pi_{t-j+1}, \quad j = 0, 1, \ldots, K$$
$$\pi_{t-j} = (1 + \beta)\pi_{t-j+1} + y_{t-j+1} - \bar{R}$$

As explained in detail in Carlstrom et al. (2012) the backward iterations generate explosive paths for output and inflation which leads to potentially implausibly large initial effects of extended periods of fixed interest rates. In larger systems the explosive roots could also be complex such that fixed interest rates cause oscillating dynamics. Carlstrom et al. (2012) interpret the explosive dynamics as a failure of New Keynesian monetary DSGE models. This sentiment is shared by Blake (2012), who proposes an alternative method of simulating DSGE models conditional on an interest rate path that is pre-determined for $\bar{H}$ periods. His solution involves a modification that introduces indeterminacy into the model and then selects an equilibrium path that delivers *a priori* reasonable responses.

In sum, it remains an open research question how to best generate DSGE model forecasts conditional on a fixed interest rate paths. While, the use of anticipated shocks is appealing at first glance and easy to implement, it might produce unreasonable dynamics. We view this as a reason to exercise caution when generating predictions of interest rate announcements and recommend to carefully examine the responses to anticipated monetary policy shocks before engaging in this type of policy analysis.

6.4. Forecasting Conditional on an Interest Rate Path: An Empirical Illustration

Figure 2.11 provides an example of forecasting conditional on an interest rate path, where the new path is implemented via anticipated policy shocks using Algorithm 7. The figure shows the May-2011 vintage data for interest rates, output growth, and inflation (black lines), the DSGE model mean forecasts for these variables conditional on the Blue Chip expectations for the FFR (red solid lines), and the forecasts conditional on the announcement that the quarterly FFR will instead be 0.25% for the next four quarters (red dashed lines). The exercise is conducted with model SWπR.

The left panel shows the expected interest rate path pre- and post-intervention. The pre-intervention interest rate forecast (solid) incorporates the market Federal Funds rate expectations for the subsequent six quarters, as measured by the Blue Chip forecasts available on May 10, 2011. Markets expect the interest rate to remain at (or near) the effective zero lower bound through the end of 2011, and liftoff to occur only in 2012:Q1. The post-intervention path (dashed line) captures the effect of an hypothetical announcement by the monetary authorities that they intend to raise rates immediately. Specifically, the intervention consists of an announcement at the beginning of period $T + 1$ (2011:Q2 in our case) that the quarterly FFR will be 0.25% (1% annualized) for the next four quarters (through 2012:Q1). In terms of the model mechanics, such an announcement amounts to a vector of time $T+1$ unanticipated and anticipated shocks computed in such a way to obtain $R_{T+1} = \mathbb{E}_{T+1}[R_{T+2}] = .. = \mathbb{E}_{T+1}[R_{T+4}] = 0.25$, as described in Algorithm 7.

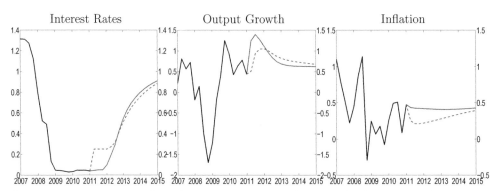

Figure 2.11 Forecasting conditional on an interest rate path. *Notes:* The figure shows the May 2011 vintage data for interest rates, output growth, and inflation (black lines), the DSGE model mean forecasts for these variables conditional on the Blue Chip expectations for the FFR (red solid lines), and the forecasts conditional on the announcement that the quarterly FFR will instead be .25% over the next four quarters (red dashed lines). The exercise is conducted with model SWπ. (For interpretation of the references to color in this figure legend, the reader is referred to the web version of this book.)

Consistent with the impulse responses shown in Figure 2.10, the announcement that policy will be more contractionary than expected leads to lower inflation and lower output growth. The effect of the announcement on output growth is front-loaded, as we discussed in Section 6.1. On impact (2011:Q2) the difference between the solid and dashed lines is about 75 basis points, that is, roughly 3% annualized. The difference narrows over the following two quarters and is about zero in 2012:Q1, even though the difference in interest rates in that quarter is almost as large as it was in 2011:Q2. After 2012:Q1 output growth following the contractionary announcement is actually higher than otherwise. This is not surprising in light of the fact that monetary policy is still neutral in this model. Slower growth in the short-run must be compensated by higher growth later, since eventually the effect of the announcement on the level of output must be zero. Nonetheless the post-intervention *level* of output remains below the pre-intervention level at least through 2015, leading to lower real marginal costs and lower inflation, as shown in the last panel of Figure 2.11.

7. MOVING BEYOND POINT FORECASTS

Thus far this chapter has focused on point forecasts generated from DSGE models and on how to improve their accuracy by using external information. For the remainder of this chapter we will explore other aspects of DSGE model forecasts. First, an important feature that distinguishes DSGE models from many other time series models is that DSGE models attribute macroeconomic fluctuations to orthogonal structural shocks. Thus, the models can provide decompositions of historical time series as well as the predicted path of the economy. We illustrate the use of shock decompositions in Section 7.1. Second, the algorithms described in the preceding sections generate draws from the predictive distribution which can be used to obtain interval or density forecasts, as discussed in Section 3.2. In Section 7.2 we generate real-time density forecasts from the SWπ model as well as the DSGE model with financial frictions introduced in Section 2.2 and examine the extent to which the forecasts capture the evolution of output growth and inflation during the 2008–2009 recession. Third, in Section 7.3 we examine more systematically whether DSGE model density forecasts are well calibrated in the sense that stated probabilities are commensurable with actual frequencies.

7.1. Shock Decompositions

DSGE models deliver a structural interpretation for both the history and the forecasts of macroeconomic time series. Figure 2.12 displays so-called shock decompositions for output growth and inflation, that illustrate the contribution of the various structural shocks to the historical and projected evolution of the two series. Before discussing the results in detail, we present the algorithm that is used to construct the decomposition.

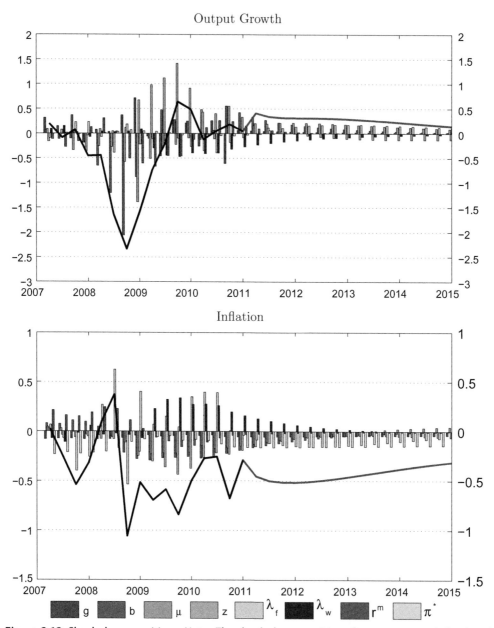

Figure 2.12 Shock decompositions. *Notes:* The shock decompositions for output growth (top) and inflation (bottom) are computed using model SWπ estimated on the last available vintage (May 2011). The black and red lines represent the data and the forecasts, both in deviation from the steady state. The colored bars represent the contribution of each shock to the evolution of the variables. (For interpretation of the references to color in this figure legend, the reader is referred to the web version of this book.)

Algorithm 8. Draws from the Posterior Distribution of a Shock Decomposition.

For $j = 1$ to n_{sim}, select the j'th draw from the posterior distribution $p(\theta|Y_{1:T})$ and:

1. *Use the simulation smoother[15] to generate a draw $(s_0^{(j)}, \epsilon_{1:T}^{(j)})$ from the distribution $p(s_0, \epsilon_{1:T}|Y_{1:T}, \theta^{(j)})$.*
2. *For each structural shock $i = 1, \ldots, m$ (which is an element of the vector s_t):*

    (a) *Define a new sequence of innovations $e_{1:T}^{(j)}$ (e_t is of the same dimension as ϵ_t) by setting the i'th element $e_{i,t}^{(j)} = \epsilon_{i,t}^{(j)}$ for $t = 1, \ldots, T$ and $e_{i,t}^{(j)} \sim N(0, \sigma_i^2)$ for $t = T+1, \ldots, T+H$. All other elements of the vector $e_t^{(j)}$ are set equal to zero for $t = 1, \ldots, T+H$.*

    (b) *Starting from $\tilde{s}_0 = s_0^{(j)}$, iterate the state transition equation (34) forward using the innovations $e_{1:T+H}^{(j)}$ to obtain the sequence $\tilde{S}_{1:T+H}^{(j)}$.*

    (c) *Use the measurement equation (35) to compute $\tilde{Y}_{1:T+H}^{(j)}$ based on $\tilde{S}_{1:T+H}^{(j)}$.* $\square$

In practice, researchers sometimes take some or all of the following short-cuts: the parameter draws $\theta^{(j)}$ are replaced by the posterior mean or mode, say $\hat{\theta}$; draws of $(s_0^{(j)}, \epsilon_{1:T}^{(j)})$ are replaced by the mean of the distribution $p(s_0, \epsilon_{1:T}|Y_{1:T}, \hat{\theta})$; and future values of $e_{i,t}$ (Step 2(a)) are set to zero. According to the logic of the model the smoothed innovations $\epsilon_{i,t}$ should be homoskedastic and uncorrelated across i. Faust and Gupta (2012) conduct posterior predictive checks and find for an estimated version of the SW models that these properties are not always satisfied, indicating deficiencies in the model specification.

The shock decomposition for output growth and inflation in Figure 2.12 is obtained from the SWπ model based on the May-2011 data vintage and provides an interpretation of the 2008–2009 recession through the lens of a DSGE model. The black and red lines represent the data and the forecasts, both in deviations from the steady state. The colored bars represent the contribution of each shock in the model to the evolution of the historical and the projected path of the two series. The bars in Figure 2.12 show the posterior mean of the output generated with Algorithm 8. The two shocks chiefly responsible for the drop in output (top panel of Figure 2.12) are shocks that captures imperfections in financial markets, namely the discount rate (b) and the marginal efficiency of investment (μ) shocks.

As discussed in Smets and Wouters (2007), the discount rate shock has similar effects as a shock to the external finance premium in a model with explicit financial frictions as in Section 2.2. This is evident from the no-arbitrage condition (18). All else equal, a negative b shock coincides with an increase in the expected return of capital. Likewise, an increase in the riskiness of entrepreneurial projects (positive $\tilde{\sigma}_\omega$ shock) raises the spread between the expected return on capital and the riskless rate. The μ shock captures, in a broad sense, the headwinds from the crisis. More precisely, the shock shifts the efficiency

---

[15] See, for instance, the textbook by Durbin and Koopman (2001) for a detailed discussion on how to simulate smoothed states and state disturbances.

with which savings are turned into future capital, and therefore serves as a proxy for the efficiency of financial intermediation (see Justiniano et al. (2009)).

Wage mark-up (λ_w) and monetary policy (r^m) shocks also play a significant role in the 2008–2009 recession. Wage mark-up shocks capture imperfections in the labor market, whereas the monetary policy shocks capture unanticipated deviations from the systematic part of the interest rate feedback rule. During the recession output and inflation were very low compared to their target value. According to the systematic part of the interest-rate feedback rule nominal interest rates should have been below zero during this period. Since the linearized version of the DSGE model ignores the zero-lower-bound constraint on the nominal interest rate, contractionary monetary policy shocks are necessary to rationalize the observed 25 bp interest rates. The contractionary monetary policy shocks contributed to the depth of the recession. Finally, positive productivity shocks are the main drivers of the recovery in GDP after the trough, which is consistent with the behavior of measured productivity.

The same shocks that drive fluctuations in economic activity – μ and b shocks – also explain much of the business-cycle frequency movements in inflation. This is not surprising in light of the New Keynesian Phillips curve. These shocks depress the level of output, and therefore real marginal costs, for a long period of time, and consequently lead to inflation below trend. Productivity shocks also play an important role, as positive shocks lead to lower real marginal costs, *ceteris paribus*. High frequency movements in inflation, e.g., due to oil price shocks, are captured by price mark-up shocks (λ_f). Conversely, movements in the inflation target (π_*), which are disciplined by the use of long-run inflation expectations in the SWπ model, capture low frequency inflation movements.

Figure 2.12 is also helpful in explaining the forecasts. For instance, the SWπ model forecasts above trend output growth throughout the forecast horizon largely because of b and μ shocks: as the economy recovers from the Great Recession, the negative impact of these shocks on the *level* of output diminishes, and this results in a boost in terms of *growth rates*. Because of their protracted effect on economic activity, these shocks also keep inflation lower than steady state.

7.2. Real-Time DSGE Density Forecasts During the Great Recession: A Post-Mortem

After having provided an ex-post rationalization of the 2008–2009 recession in the previous section, we now examine ex-ante forecasts of the SWπ model as well as two variants of the DSGE model with financial frictions discussed in Section 2.2, henceforth SWπ-FF. Figure 2.13 shows the DSGE models' and Blue Chip's forecasts for output growth (in Qo-Qpercent) obtained at three different junctures of the financial crisis that lead to the recession. The dates coincide with Blue Chip forecasts releases: (i) October 10, 2007, right after turmoil in financial markets had begun in August of that year; (ii) July 10, 2008, right before the default of Lehman Brothers; and (iii) January 10, 2009, at or near the apex of the crisis. Specifically, each panel shows the current real GDP growth vintage (black

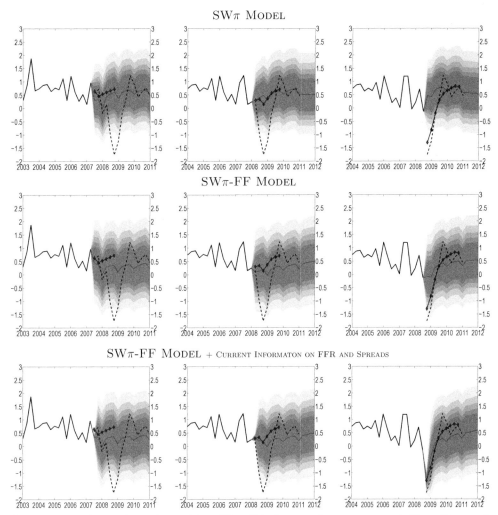

Figure 2.13 Predicting the crisis: model and Blue Chip forecasts for output growth. *Notes:* The panels show for each model/vintage the available real GDP growth data (black solid line), the DSGE model's multi-step (fixed origin) mean forecasts (red solid line) and bands of its forecast distribution (shaded blue areas; these are the 50, 60, 70, 80, and 90 percent bands, in decreasing shade), the Blue Chip forecasts (blue diamonds), and finally the actual realizations according to the last available vintage (May 2011, black dashed line). All the data are in percent, QoQ. (For interpretation of the references to color in this figure legend, the reader is referred to the web version of this book.)

line), the DSGE model's mean forecasts (red line) and percentile bands of the predictive distribution (shaded blue areas indicate 50% (dark blue), 60%, 70%, 80%, and 90% (light blue) bands), the Blue Chip forecasts (blue diamonds), and finally the actual realizations according to the May-2011 vintage (black dashed line).

In interpreting the results, the reader should bear in mind that the information used to generate the forecasts depicted in Figure 2.13 consists only of data that was available at the beginning of October 2007, July 2008, and January 2009, respectively. For instance, by January 10, 2009 the forecaster would have access to NIPA samples that end in 2008:Q3 data. The information set of the Blue Chip forecasters, on the other hand, contains additional information such as economic indicators for 2008:Q4, information from financial markets, and a plethora of qualitative information provided by the media, speeches of government officials, *etc.*

Each row of Figure 2.13 contains forecasts from a different model. We consider the SWπ model, the SWπ-FF model, and a specification that we label as SWπ-FF-Current. The two key differences between the SWπ and the SWπ-FF model are the introduction of financial frictions as in Bernanke et al. (1999) and the use of the Baa–10 year Treasury rate spread as an observable, which arguably captures distress in financial markets.[16] The difference between the SWπ-FF and the SWπ-FF-Current specification is that forecasts from the latter also utilize the Federal Funds rate and spreads of the most recent quarter, that is, of the quarter for which NIPA data are not yet available. For instance, the January 2009 SWπ-FF-Current forecast incorporates the average Federal Funds rate and the average spread for 2008:Q4. At any point in time, the information used to generate predictions from the SWπ-FF-Current model remains a subset of the information that has been available to the Blue Chip forecasters.

The October 10, 2007, Blue Chip Consensus forecasts for output are relatively upbeat, at or above 0.5% QoQ, that is, 2% annualized, as shown in the panels in the first column of Figure 2.13. The SWπ forecasts are less optimistic, especially in the short run. The model's mean forecasts for output growth are barely above zero in 2008:Q1, with a non-negligible probability of sustained negative growth (recession) throughout the year. The forecasts for the two SWπ-FF specifications are in line with those of the SWπ model, although a bit more subdued. Quarter by quarter, the SWπ-FF specifications assign a probability of 50% or more to the occurrence of negative growth. While the DSGE models capture the slowdown that occurred in late 2007 and early 2008, they do not anticipate the subsequent post-Lehman collapse of economic activity. The decline in real GDP that occurred in 2008:Q4 lies far in the tails of the predictive distribution generated by the SWπ model. While the DSGE models with financial frictions place more probability on growth rates below -1% than the SWπ model, the 2008:Q4 growth rate still falls outside of the 90% credible prediction intervals.

In July 2008 the Blue Chip forecast and the mean forecast for the SWπ model are roughly aligned. Both foresaw a weak economy – but not negative growth – in 2008, and a rebound in 2009. The two SWπ-FF specifications are less sanguine. Their forecasts

---

[16] Gilchrist and Zakrajsek (2012) use secondary market prices of corporate bonds to construct a credit spread index that, they argue, is a considerably more powerful predictor of economic activity than the measure of spreads we use. Their finding suggests that using an improved measure of spreads may further improve the SWπ-FF model's predictive ability.

for 2008 are only slightly more pessimistic than the Blue Chip forecast for 2008, but, unlike Blue Chip, the financial frictions models do not predict a strong rebound of the economy in 2009. While the two SWπ-FF deliver point forecasts of essentially zero growth in 2008:Q4, the models assign a lot of probability to strongly negative growth rates. As a consequence, the realized -1.7% growth rate in the last quarter of 2008 falls almost within the 90% credible interval associated with the predictive distribution.

By January 2009 the scenario has changed dramatically: Lehman Brothers has filed for bankruptcy a few months earlier (September 15, 2008), stock prices have fallen, financial markets are in disarray, and various current indicators have provided evidence that real activity was tumbling. None of this information was available to the SWπ model, which for the January 10, 2009, forecast round uses data up to 2008:Q3. Not surprisingly, the model is out of touch with reality with regard to the path of economic activity in 2008:Q4 and thereafter. It predicts a positive growth rate of 0.5% for the fourth quarter, while the actual growth rate is approximately -1.7%. The SWπ-FF model is less optimistic, it forecasts zero growth for 2008:Q4, but also misses the steep decline. The SWπ-FF uses spreads as an observable, but since the Lehman bankruptcy occurred toward the end of the third quarter, it had minor effects on the average Baa–10 year Treasury rate spread for 2008:Q3. As a consequence, the SWπ-FF model has little direct information on the turmoil in financial markets.

Finally, we turn to the forecasts from the SWπ-FF-Current specification, which uses 2008:Q4 observations on spreads and the Federal Funds rate. This model produces about the same forecast as Blue Chip for 2008:Q4. Unlike Blue Chip forecasters, the agents in the laboratory DSGE economy have not seen the Fed Chairman and the Treasury Secretary on television painting a dramatically bleak picture of the U.S. economy. Thus, we regard it as a significant achievement that the DSGE model forecasts and the Blue Chip forecasts are both around -1.3%. More importantly, we find this to be convincing evidence on the importance of using appropriate information in forecasting with structural models.

Figure 2.14 conducts the same post-mortem for inflation. On October 10, 2010, all three specifications generate similar forecasts of inflation. The mean quarterly forecasts are above 0.5% (2% annualized) in 2007, and slightly below 0.5% throughout the rest of the forecast horizon. Blue Chip forecasts are more subdued for 2007, and correctly so, but essentially coincide with the DSGE models' forecasts thereafter. The DSGE model point forecasts overstate inflation in 2009 and 2010. As the structural models miss the severity of the Great Recession, they also miss its impact on the dynamics of prices. In terms of density forecasts however, the forecasts of inflation are not as bad as those for output: In 2009 and 2010 the ex-post realizations of inflation are mostly within the 70% and 50% bands, respectively.

The July 10, 2008, Blue Chip forecasts for inflation increase quite a bit compared to 2007. The U.S. economy has just been hit by a commodity shock and, moreover, the Federal Reserve has lowered rates in response to the financial crisis, leading to Blue

SWπ MODEL

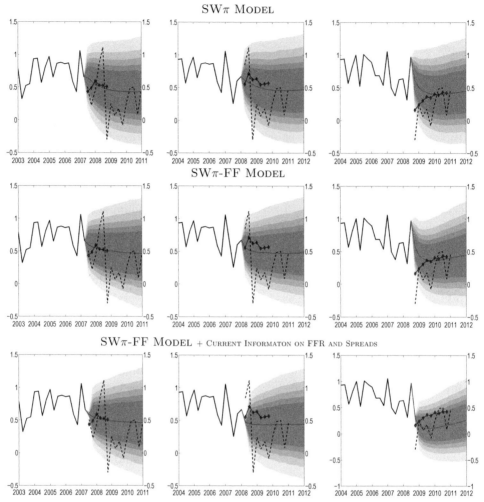

Figure 2.14 Predicting the crisis: model and Blue Chip forecasts for inflation. *Notes:* The panels show for each model/vintage the available real GDP growth data (black solid line), the DSGE model's multi-step (fixed origin) mean forecasts (red solid line) and bands of its forecast distribution (shaded blue areas; these are the 50, 60, 70, 80, and 90 percent bands, in decreasing shade), the Blue Chip forecasts (blue diamonds), and finally the actual realizations according to the last available vintage (May 2011, black dashed line) .All the data are in percent, QoQ. (For interpretation of the references to color in this figure legend, the reader is referred to the web version of this book.)

Chip quarterly inflation forecasts above 0.5% (2% annualized) throughout the forecast horizon. The mean DSGE model forecasts are instead slightly more subdued than in 2007, especially for the models with financial frictions. This occurs for two reasons. First, the DSGE models have no information on the recent rise in commodity prices. Second, the models perceive a weakness in aggregate activity and translate that into a moderate inflation outlook.

By 2008:Q3 inflation has risen following the commodity shock. Nonetheless, the January 10, 2009, inflation forecasts of the DSGE models are low. While all three models correctly assume the high 2008:Q3 inflation to be temporary, there exist significant differences in the inflation forecasts across models, which reflect their different assessment of the state of the economy. The SWπ and SWπ-FF models' mean forcasts for inflation are generally above the actuals for 2009 and 2010. Blue Chip consensus forecasts are — correctly — more subdued than these forecasts for 2008:Q4 and the first half of 2009, but are no different afterwards: quarterly inflation quickly reverts to 0.5% in their outlook. Conversely, the SWπ-FF-current model predicts inflation to remain low throughout the forecast horizon, which is consistent with the actual evolution of this variable in the aftermath of the Great Recession.

The examination of DSGE model forecasts during the 2008–2009 recession suggests that the DSGE models with financial frictions are preferable to the SWπ model. It turns out that this ranking is not stable over time. Figure 2.15 depicts RMSE differentials for the SWπ model and the SWπ-FF-Current model for $h = 4$-step-ahead forecasts (the results for model SWπ-FF are very similar). At each point in term the RMSEs are computed using the 12 previous quarters. A value greater than zero indicates that the financial-frictions model attains a lower RMSE. The figure indicates that on

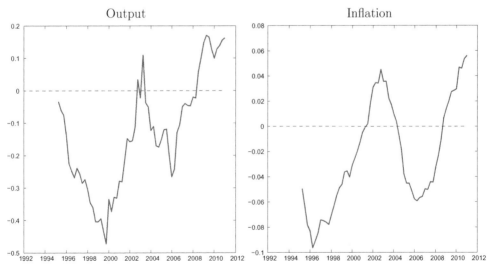

Figure 2.15 Difference in forecasting accuracy over time: SWπ and SWπFF-current. *Notes:* The figure shows the difference over time in 4-quarter-ahead rolling RMSEs between the SWπ and SWπFF-Current models for output growth and inflation. At each point in time, the RMSEs are computed using the previous 12 quarters, that is, the figure shows $RMSE_t(\text{SW}\pi) - RMSE_t(\text{SW}\pi\text{FF-Current})$, where $RMSE_t(\mathcal{M}_i) = \sqrt{\frac{1}{12}\sum_{j=0}^{11}\left(y_{t-j} - \hat{y}_{t-j|t-j-4}^{\mathcal{M}_i}\right)^2}$ and $\hat{y}_{t-j|t-j-4}^{\mathcal{M}_i}$ is the 4-quarter ahead forecast of y_{t-j} obtained using model $\mathcal{M}_i$, $\mathcal{M}_i = \{\text{SW}\pi, \text{SW}\pi\text{FF-Current}\}$.

average over the forecast period the model without financial frictions generates more accurate forecasts. However, during the recent financial crisis, the ordering is reversed. The SWπ-FF-Current model contains an additional mechanism that associates high spreads with low economic activity and helps the model to track and forecast aggregate output and inflation throughout the crisis.

7.3. Calibration of Density Forecasts

We previously presented a variety of interval and density forecasts. This begs the question of how accurate these density forecasts are. While, strictly speaking, predictive distributions in a Bayesian framework are subjective, the statistics reported below provide a measure of the extent to which the predicted probabilities of events are consistent with their observed frequencies. Dawid (1984) views this consistency as a minimal desirable property for probability forecasts. Bayarri and Berger (2004) refer to the notion that in repeated practical use of a sequential forecasting procedure the long-run average level of accuracy should be consistent with the long-run average reported accuracy as *frequentist principle*. The literature, see for instance Dawid (1982), refers to sequences of (subjective) density forecasts that adhere to the frequentist principle as *well calibrated*. To assess whether DSGE model density forecasts are well calibrated we generate histograms for probability integral transformations (PITs).

Starting with Dawid (1984) and Kling and Bessler (1989) the use of probability integral transformations (PITs) has a fairly long tradition in the literature on density forecast evaluation. The PIT of an observation $y^o_{i,T+h}$ based on its time T predictive distribution is

$$z_{i,h,T} = \int_{-\infty}^{y^o_{i,T+h}} p(y_{i,T+h}|Y_{1:T})dy_{i,T+h}. \tag{74}$$

Thus, the PIT is defined as the cumulative density of the random variable $y_{i,T+h}$ evaluated at the observation $y^o_{i,T+h}$. Based on the output of Algorithm 2 the PITs can be easily approximated by (recall that $\mathcal{I}\{x \geq a\}$ denotes the indicator function)

$$z_{i,h,T} \approx \sum_{j=1}^{n_{sim}} \mathcal{I}\{y^{(j)}_{i,T+h} \leq y_{i,T+h}\},$$

where $y_{i,T+h}$ is now the value of y_i observed in period $T + h$. It is straightforward to show that the marginal distribution of PITs is uniform. Consider a random variable X with density $F(x)$. Then

$$\mathbb{P}\{F(X) \leq z\} = \mathbb{P}\{X \leq F^{-1}(z)\} = F\left(F^{-1}(z)\right) = z$$

Building on results by Rosenblatt (1952), Diebold et al. (1998) show that for $h = 1$ the $z_{i,h,T}$'s are not just uniformly distributed, but they are also independent across time $T : z_{i,h,T} \sim iid\ \mathcal{U}[0, 1]$. For this reason, PITs are often called generalized residuals.

Below, we plot PIT histograms and informally assess the distance of the unconditional empirical distribution of the PITs from the uniform distribution. A more formal assessment, via posterior predictive checks, is provided in Herbst and Schorfheide (2011).[17] It is important to stress that the uniformity of PITs does not imply that a forecast is sharp, as shown in the following example. Abstracting from parameter uncertainty, suppose that y_t evolves according to

$$y_t = \theta y_{t-1} + u_t, \quad u_t \sim iidN(0, 1), \quad 0 \le \theta < 1. \tag{75}$$

Moreover, suppose that Forecaster F_1 reports the predictive density $N(\theta y_{t-1}, 1)$, whereas forecaster F_2 reports the density forecast $N\left(0, 1/(1 - \theta^2)\right)$. It is clear that as long as $\theta > 0$, F_1's forecast will be more precise than F_2's forecast because it exploits conditioning information that reduces the variance of the predictive distribution from $1/(1-\theta^2)$ to one. Nonetheless, both forecasts lead to PITs that are *unconditionally* uniformly distributed. The uniformity of the PITs associated with F_2 follows immediately. For F_1 it can be verified as follows. Let $\Phi_N(\cdot)$ denote the cdf of a $N(0, 1)$ random variable.

$$\mathbb{P}\left\{\Phi_N(y_t - \theta y_{t-1}) \le z\right\} = \mathbb{E}\left[\mathbb{P}\left\{\Phi_N(y_t - \theta y_{t-1}) \le z \mid y_{t-1}\right\}\right] = z.$$

The unconditional probability needs to be computed under the joint distribution of (y_t, y_{t-1}). It can be obtained by first conditioning on y_{t-1} and subsequently integrating out y_{t-1}, which leads to the first equality. The second equality follows from (75).

As we have seen in Section 5, DSGE model forecasts often do not exploit all the available information and therefore might not be as sharp as other forecasts. Nonetheless, it remains interesting to assess whether the predictive distributions are well-calibrated in the sense that PITs have an unconditional distribution that is approximately uniform. Figure 2.16 depicts histograms for PITs based on forecasts generated with the $SW\pi$ model using what we referred to as the "Blue Chip dates" (that is, the same sample used in the RMSE comparison with Blue Chip Consensus forecasts shown in the top panel of Figure 2.2, as well as in all subsequent RMSE comparison results). We group the PITs into five equally sized bins. Under a uniform distribution, each bin should contain 20% of the PITs, indicated by the solid horizontal lines in the figure. The empirical distribution looks quite different from a uniform distribution and the discrepancy increases with forecast horizon h. For output growth, an overly large fraction of PITs fall into the 0.4–0.6 bin. This indicates that the predictive distribution is too diffuse.

---

[17] As emphasized by Geweke and Whiteman (2006), Bayesian approaches to forecast evaluation are fundamentally different from frequentist approaches. In a Bayesian framework there is no uncertainty about the predictive density given the specified collection of models, because predictive densities are simply constructed by the relevant conditioning. Non-Bayesian approaches, see Corradi and Swanson (2006), tend to adopt the notion of a "true" data-generating process (DGP) and try to approximate the predictive density inherent in the DGP with a member of a collection of probability distributions indexed by a parameter θ. To the extent that the forecaster faces uncertainty with respect to θ, there is uncertainty about the density forecast itself, and non-Bayesian assessments try to account for this uncertainty.

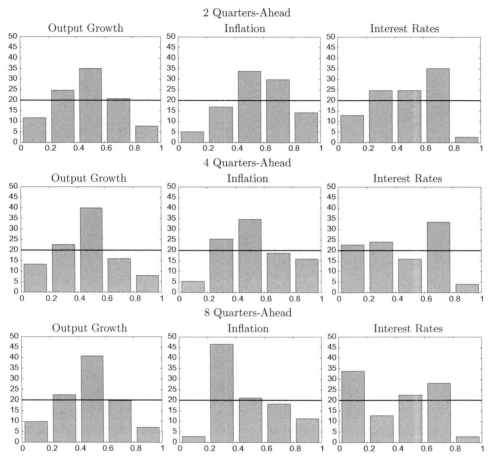

Figure 2.16 PITs: SWπ model (1992–2011). *Notes:* The figure computes PITs for 2, 4, and 8 quarters-ahead output growth, inflation, and interest rates forecasts for the SWπ model. The compuatation is done for the same vintages/forecast dates as the Blue Chip/DSGE comparison discussed in Section 4.3. All variables are expressed in terms of QoQ rates in percentage. Section 4.1 provides the details of the forecast comparison exercise.

One potential explanation is that all of the forecasts are generated post 1984 and most of them fall into the period of the so-called Great Moderation. The estimation sample, on the other hand, contains a significant fraction of observations from the pre-1984 period. Thus, the shock standard deviations, roughly speaking, are estimated to capture an average of the pre- and post-moderation volatility, which means that they tend to overpredict the volatility during the forecast period. While the empirical distribution of the output growth PITs is essentially symmetric, the PITs associated with inflation and interest rate forecasts have a slightly skewed distribution. The DSGE model assigns substantial probability to low inflation rates that never materialize. Vice versa, the model also assigns positive probability to relatively high interest rates that are not observed during the forecast period. Further results on the evaluation of density forecasts of medium-scale DSGE models can be found in Herbst and Schorfheide (2011) and Wolters (2010).

8. OUTLOOK

This chapter reviewed the recent literature on forecasting with DSGE models, discussed numerous useful algorithms, and provided empirical illustrations of the various methods considered. We presented some novel methods that allow modelers to incorporate external information and that may increase the accuracy of DSGE model forecasts. Moreover, we compared methods of generating forecasts conditional on desired interest rate paths, and studied the forecasting performance of DSGE models with and without financial frictions during the 2008–2009 recession. In closing, we provide some discussion of including non-linear and non-Gaussian features in DSGE models that are used for forecasting, we review empirical approaches that relax some of the DSGE model-implied restrictions to improve forecast accuracy; and lastly we briefly discuss future challenges for DSGE model-based forecasting.

8.1. Non-linear and Non-Gaussian Features in DSGE Models

Throughout this chapter we have generated forecasts from log-linearized DSGE models with Gaussian innovations. However, starting with the work of Fernández-Villaverde and Rubio-Ramírez (2007), an increasing number of researchers have applied likelihood-based estimation methods to DSGE models solved with non-linear techniques. To the extent that non-linearities, e.g., time-varying volatilities, kinks such as a zero-lower-bound constraint on the nominal interest rates, and business cycle asymmetries are empirically important features of macroeconomic time series, incorporating them into forecasting models is potentially beneficial. To date there have been few systematic studies of the forecasting performance of non-linearly solved DSGE models. The reason is that the estimation of non-linear DSGE models is much more time consuming than the estimation of linearized models, which makes it cumbersome to conduct recursive out-of-sample forecasting exercises.

We now discuss some non-Gaussian and non-linear features of DSGE models that are potentially useful for forecasting. We saw in Section 3.2 that the predictive distribution of the SWπ model were too diffuse. One potential explanation for this result is that the estimation sample contained a significant fraction of pre-Great-Moderation observations which inflates the estimated shock standard deviation that are used for predictions from 1992 onwards. Models with time-varying volatilities can potentially overcome this problem. In addition to low frequency changes in macroeconomic volatility, outliers can also contribute to excessively diffuse predictive distributions. One-step forecast errors as well as smoothed shock innovations often appear to be leptokurtic, that is, there are occasional outliers. In a model with Gaussian errors this tends to lead an upward bias in the standard deviation estimate.

The estimation of linearized DSGE models with student-t (instead of Gaussian) shocks is discussed in Chib and Ramamurthy (forthcoming) and Curdia et al. (2011). Justiniano and Primiceri (2008) replaced the homoskedastic shocks in a linearized DSGE model by shocks that exhibit stochastic volatility. Their approach is promising for forecasting applications because, which the exception of the time-variation in the shock standard deviation, their solution concept still delivers a linear state-space model which is fairly easy to estimate. The inclusion of stochastic volatility makes the implied predictive distribution of the model more adaptive to changes in macroeconomic volatility. Fernández-Villaverde et al. (2013) advocate to use higher perturbation methods to solve DSGE models with stochastic volatility. While this approach is conceptually more appealing and has a more solid approximation-theoretic foundation, it comes at a significant computational cost. Likelihood functions for DSGE models solved with higher-order perturbation methods need to be evaluated with numerical techniques, such as the particle filter in Fernández-Villaverde and Rubio-Ramírez (2007). For models without unobserved endogenous state variables and with time-varying volatility generated by Markov-switching shock standard deviations (Amisano and Tristani, 2011) show how to efficiently evaluate likelihood functions.

Macroeconomic instabilities not only manifest themselves in volatilities but also in levels of macroeconomic time series. Correctly capturing such level instabilities in DSGE models is likely to lead better conditional mean forecasts. Fernández-Villaverde and Rubio-Ramírez (2008) include autoregressive time-variation in the coefficients of the monetary policy rule and the parameters that determine the rigidity of nominal prices in the model economy. Schorfheide (2005) uses a Markov-switching process instead of the autoregressive process considered in Section 5.1 to model the evolution of the target inflation rate. More generally, Liu et al. (2011) explore the importance of regime switches for an estimated DSGE model.

While the above mentioned papers do not explicitly focus on the forecast performance of non-linear DSGE models, Pichler (2008) conducts a systematic study of the role of non-linearities for forecasting with a New Keynesian DSGE model with capital accumulation. His analysis consists of two parts. He shows that in simulations in which data are generated from a DSGE model that has been approximately solved with a second-order perturbation method, the forecasts from the non-linear version of the DSGE model are indeed more accurate than forecasts from a linearized DSGE model. On actual U.S. data, however, the result was reversed: the forecasts from the linearized model tended to be more precise than the forecast from the model approximated to second order.

The recent Great Recession also provides new impetus toward the study of non-linear models. As shown in Section 7.1, linear models such as SW can provide an ex-post rationalization of the crisis via (very large, as shown in Curdia et al. (2011)) shocks. While this explanation is not completely unreasonable, in that it points to sources of the crisis related to financial market imperfections, it is also far from satisfying. The hope is that non-linear models will be able to deliver a more compelling explanation for these events – and ideally help forecast future crisis. Recent work, see for instance the survey by Brunnermeier et al. (2012), suggests that non-linear models with financial frictions potentially offer some promise, at least in terms of explaining the crisis without requiring very large shocks. So far, to our knowledge none of these models have been taken to the data using either calibration or econometric methods however, and we do know anything about their forecasting ability. Estimation of non-linear models with financial frictions is therefore an interesting area of future research.

8.2. Beyond Forecasting with a Single DSGE Model

Thus far, we have focused on forecasts generated from specific DSGE models. In closing we briefly mention some strands of the literature that combine different DSGE models, relax some of the DSGE model restrictions to improve their forecast performance, or combine DSGE models with other classes of econometric models. The analysis in Section 7.2 suggests that there might be some gain from combining forecasts from different DSGE models, say one with and one without financial frictions. The most natural way of combining forecasts in a Bayesian framework is to conduct Bayesian model averaging. Suppose there are J models $M_j, j = 1, \ldots, J$, each of them having prior probability $\pi_{j,0}$. Provided that the model space is complete, i.e., all models that the forecaster regards as plausible are included among the J models, the posterior probability $\pi_{j,T}$ of model M_j is given by

$$\pi_{j,T} = \frac{\pi_{j,0} p(Y_{1:T}|M_j)}{\sum_{i=1}^{J} \pi_{i,0} p(Y_{1:T}|M_i)}, \tag{76}$$

where $p(Y_{1:T}|M_j)$ is the marginal data density that appeared as a normalization constant in Bayes Theorem in (30). The predictive distribution for $Y_{T+1:T+H}$ is given by the mixture

$$p(Y_{T+1:T+h}|Y_{1:T}) = \sum_{j=1}^{T} \pi_{j,T} p(Y_{T+1:T+h}|Y_{1:T}, M_j), \tag{77}$$

where the model-specific predictive densities $p(Y_{T+1:T+h}|Y_{1:T}, M_j)$ are given by (36). By applying Algorithm 2 to each of the J models and weighting the draws from the predictive densities by the posterior model probabilities, it is straightforward to generate draws from the predictive distribution. Based on these draws, one can calculate point, interval, and density forecasts. Empirical results from Bayesian and non-Bayesian model averaging procedures applied to a collection of DSGE models are reported in Wolters (2010).[18]

Potentially misspecified restrictions in DSGE models can lead to a poor forecasting performance. A number of methods have been proposed to relax DSGE model-implied restrictions. Ireland (2004) suggested to augment the DSGE model measurement

---

[18] To be precise, Wolters (2010) replaces the marginal likelihoods $\pi_{j,T}$ in (77) by predictive likelihoods because he combines models that are estimated on different sets of macroeconomic variables.

equation (35) by vector autoregressive measurement errors and (Canova, 2008) used measurement errors to relax DSGE-model-implied restrictions on trends, which are important for long-run forecasts. Curdia and Reis (2010) replaced the AR (1) processes for structural shocks that are used in most DSGE models by a more general vector autoregressive process.

Ingram and Whiteman (1994) were the first to use DSGE models to construct a prior distribution for vector autoregressions that is centered at the DSGE model-implied parameter restrictions. This approach has the advantage that the DSGE model restrictions are imposed in a non-dogmatic manner, allowing for modest violations of the DSGE model restrictions. Del Negro and Schorfheide (2004) developed this approach further and constructed a hierarchical Bayes model, called DSGE-VAR, that takes the form of a structural VAR and allows the researcher to simultaneously estimate the parameters of the DSGE model and the VAR. A hyperparameter determines the scale of the prior covariance matrix. If the prior covariance matrix is zero, then the DSGE model restrictions are dogmatically imposed on the VAR.

In the context of a small-scale DSGE model Del Negro and Schorfheide (2004) document that the best forecasting performance is obtained for an intermediate value of the hyperparameter that implies that prior distribution and likelihood of the VAR are about equally informative about the parameters. The DSGE-VAR produces substantially more accurate pseudo-out-of-sample forecasts than the underlying DSGE model. A similar empirical result is reported in Del Negro et al. (2007) for a variant of the Smets-Wouters model and in Warne et al. (2012) for the New Area Wide Model (NAWN) of the European Central Banks. Using the Smets and Wouters (2007) model to generate a prior distribution, Kolasa et al. (2010) found that the DSGE model actually outperforms their DSGE-VAR specification. The relative performance of DSGE-VARs and VARs with Minnesota prior is less clear-cut. Finally, Ghent (2009) generates forecasts from DSGE-VARs that have been constructed from different DSGE models. She finds the accuracy of the forecasts across model specifications to be very similar, which suggests that it might not be the particular economic structure, but rather general implications about the persistence of economic time series that gives rise to the improvement in forecast performance attained by DSGE-VARs.

An alternative way of combining VARs and DSGE models for macroeconomic forecasting applications is explored by Amisano and Geweke (2011). The authors consider a pool of macroeconomic models that incorporates, among others, DSGE models and VARs. A combined forecast is generated from a convex combination of the predictive densities associated with the models included in the pool. Roughly speaking, this convex combination takes the form

$$p(Y_{1:T}) = \prod_{t=1}^{T} \left(\sum_{j=1}^{J} \lambda_j p(y_t | Y_{1:t-1}, M_j) \right), \quad \sum_{j=1}^{J} \lambda_j = 1 \qquad (78)$$

and differs from the Bayesian model averaging approach described above in that the fore-caster does not have to specify the model space completely. The weights λ_j are estimated such that asymptotically as T gets large the Kullback–Leibler discrepancy between the convex combination of models and some underlying "data generating process" is min-imized. The authors find that while the DSGE model receives a non-trivial weight in the model mixture, the forecasting performance of the pool is substantially better than the forecasting performance of any of the individual models in the pool. Waggoner and Zha (2010) extend the Amisano–Geweke approach by allowing for time-varying model weights that follow a regime-switching process. Moreover, model parameters and mix-ture weights are estimated simultaneously rather than sequentially. The authors identify episodes in which the DSGE model is useful for macroeconomic forecasting and episodes in which the combined forecasts are dominated by the VAR. The same approach could be used to combine different DSGE models. As documented in Section 7.2, the relative ranking of DSGE models without and with financial frictions seems to shift over time.

Finally, there is a strand of literature that combines DSGE models and dynamic factor models (DFM). The goal of this literature is to link the DSGE model with a large cross section of macroeconomic indicators rather than a small set of seven or eight observables as was done in this chapter, and presents two potential advantages. First, the large set of macroeconomic variables might provide sharper inference about the current state of the economy. Second, this framework allows the modeler to assess the effect of structural shocks, e.g., monetary policy shocks, on variables that are not explicitly modeled in the DSGE model. The resulting empirical specification is called DSGE-DFM. It is essentially a DFM in which the latent factors are equated with the state variables of a DSGE model and follow the DSGE model-implied law of motion. The DSGE-DFM was first developed by Boivin and Giannoni (2006) and studied further by Kryshko (2010), who documents that the space spanned by the factors of a DSGE-DFM is very similar to the space spanned by factors extracted from an unrestricted DFM. Schorfheide et al. (2010) used a DSGE-DFM to generate DSGE-model-based forecasts for variables that do not explicitly appear in the DSGE model.

8.3. Future Challenges

While the literature on forecasting with DSGE models was practically non-existent a decade ago, it has become a vibrant area of research. A lot of progress has been made in the specification of DSGE models, as well as in the development of methods that enable the incorporation of real-time information, the relaxation of overly tight cross-equation restrictions, and the combination of DSGE models with other macroeconometric models. The progress is in part driven by the desire of central banks to incorporate modern macroeconomic equilibrium theory into their decision-making process. In this regard, the recent crisis with the emergence of non-conventional monetary policies and interest rates near the zero-lower bound has supplied new challenges for DSGE model-based forecasting that need to be tackled in future research. The results in Section 7.2 also suggest that financial markets data can contain valuable information for forecasting. A further challenge for DSGE model forecasters will be to exploit these data. In order to do that, it is first necessary to build models that have a shot at explaining these data, by itself a tall order. Non-linear models, which can generate time-varying risk premia, hold some promise in this dimension.

APPENDIX A. DETAILS FOR FIGURE 2.5

Table A-1 lists the RMSEs that are plotted in Figure 2.5 by study. The specific references for each study can be found in Table 2.3.

Table A-1 RMSEs for DSGE and AR(2) Models in Figure 2.5

Study	Model	$h = 1$			$h = 4$		
		GDP	INFL	INT	GDP	INFL	INT
RS	DSGE	0.496	0.224	0.130	0.448	0.287	0.335
	AR(2)	0.512	0.198	0.083	0.502	0.235	0.320
KRS	DSGE	0.485	0.240	0.108	0.477	0.255	0.335
	AR(2)	0.471	0.236	0.107	0.465	0.297	0.416
GEW	DSGE	0.610	0.290	0.138	0.385	0.350	0.405
	AR(2)	0.532	0.221	0.118	0.328	0.281	0.437
W-DS	DSGE	0.525	0.262	0.163	0.532	0.272	0.372
	AR(2)	0.491	0.257	0.121	0.523	0.331	0.402
W-FM	DSGE	0.494	0.321	0.133	0.586	0.330	0.391
	AR(2)	0.491	0.257	0.121	0.523	0.331	0.402
W-SW	DSGE	0.542	0.255	0.127	0.462	0.279	0.344
	AR(2)	0.491	0.257	0.121	0.523	0.331	0.402
W-Edo	DSGE	0.529	0.285	0.164	0.511	0.349	0.478
	AR(2)	0.491	0.257	0.121	0.523	0.331	0.402
EG	DSGE	0.550	0.180	0.110	0.510	0.200	0.100
	AR(2)	0.568	0.223	0.122	0.582	0.304	0.425
EKL	DSGE	0.448	0.294	0.208	0.502	0.292	0.465
	AR(2)	0.626	0.204	0.102	0.734	0.254	0.387
SW	DSGE	0.566	0.245	0.108	0.327	0.183	0.354
	AR(2)	0.546	0.229	0.126	0.352	0.289	0.467
DSSW	DSGE	0.664	0.249	0.123	0.657	0.243	0.394
	AR(2)	0.493	0.206	0.111	0.340	0.199	0.357
SSK	DSGE	0.510	0.220	0.177	0.410	0.190	0.532
	AR(2)	0.525	0.227	0.094	0.469	0.229	0.419

Table A-2 A Sample of Studies Reporting RMSEs for Medium-Scale DSGE Models: Part 1

Study	Real-Time Data Set?	Actuals for Forec. Eval. Used for DSGE Model	Actuals for Forec. Eval. Used for AR(2) Model	GDP Data Per Capita?	Forecast Multi-Averages?
RS	Yes	One-year after the forecasting origin	First final release	No	No
KRS	Yes	Fixed vintage (2009:Q1)	First final release	No	No
GEW	No	N/A	Fixed vintage (Jan 2008)	Yes	Yes (Output)
W-DS	Yes	Vintage released two quarters after	Same as original study	No	No
W-FM	Yes	Vintage released two quarters after	Same as original study	No	No
W-SW	Yes	Vintage released two quarters after	Same as original study	No	No
W-Edo	Yes	Vintage released two quarters after	Same as original study	No	No
EG	Yes	First final release	First final release	Yes	No
EKL	Yes	First final release	First final release	Yes	No
SW	No	N/A	Fixed vintage (Jan 2006)	Yes	Yes (Output)
DSSW	No	N/A	Fixed vintage (Apr 2005)	Yes	Yes (Output, Inflation)
SSK	No	N/A	Fixed vintage (Apr 2009)	Yes	No

Table A-2 Sample of Studies Reporting RMSEs for Medium-Scale DSGE Models: Part 2

Study	Forecast Origins	Forecasting Dates	Data for AR(2) Forecasting	Estimation Sample
RS	1994:Q1–2005:Q3	Middle of each quarter	Our realtime dataset (GB dates)	Most recent 60 quarters
KRS	1994:Q1–2007:Q4	Middle of each quarter	Our realtime dataset (GB dates)	Fixed starting point (1964:Q3)
GEW	1990:Q1–2007:Q1 (h = 1)	N/A	Vintage 4Q after last date of forecasting origin	Fixed starting point (1966:Q1)
W–DS	1984:Q1–2000:Q4	Greenbook	Use Faust and Wright dataset	Most recent 80 quarters
W–FM	1984:Q1–2000:Q4	Greenbook	Use Faust and Wright dataset	Most recent 80 quarters
W–SW	1984:Q1–2000:Q4	Greenbook	Use Faust and Wright dataset	Most recent 80 quarters
W–Edo	1984:Q1–2000:Q4	Greenbook	Use Faust and Wright dataset	Most recent 80 quarters
EG	1992:Q1(Jan)–2004:Q4(Dec)	Greenbook	Our realtime dataset (GB dates)	Fixed starting point (1965:Q1)
EKL	1996:Q3(Sep)–2002:Q4(Dec)	Greenbook	Our realtime dataset (GB dates)	Fixed starting point (1983:Q1)
SW	1990:Q1–2004:Q4 (h = 1)	N/A	Vintage 4Q after last date of forecasting origin	Fixed starting point (1966:Q1)
DSSW	1986:Q1–2000:Q2 (h = 1)	N/A	Vintage 4Q after last date of forecasting origin	Most recent 120 quarters
SSK	2001:Q1–2007:Q4 (h = 1)	N/A	Vintage 4Q after last date of forecasting origin	Fixed starting point (1984:Q1)

Table A-2 and A-2 contains details on the computation of AR(2) forecasts that are used to construct RMSE ratios.

ACKNOWLEDGMENTS

Schorfheide gratefully acknowledges financial support from the National Science Foundation under Grant SES 1061358. The completion of this project owes much to the outstanding research assistance of Minchul Shin (Penn), Raiden Hasegawa (FRB New York), and especially Daniel Herbst (FRB New York). We thank the editors, three anonymous referees, Fabio Canova, Keith Sill, as well as seminar participants at the 2012 AEA Meetings, the 2011 Asian Meetings of the Econometric Society, the 2011 Canon Institute for Global Studies Conference on Macroeconomic Theory and Policy, the National Bank of Poland conference on DSGE Models and Beyond," the Federal Reserve Bank of Minneapolis' Conference in Honor of Chris Sims and Tom Sargent, ECARES, the Federal Reserve Banks of Cleveland and Kansas City, and the Norges Bank for helpful comments and suggestions. We also thank Rochelle Edge and Refet Gurkaynak for giving and explaining us the real time data and Stefano Eusepi and Emanuel Monch for providing us with the survey data. The views expressed in this chapter do not necessarily reflect ect those of the Federal Reserve Bank of New York or the Federal Reserve System.

REFERENCES

Adolfson, M., Lindé, J., Villani, M., 2007a. Forecasting performance of an open economy dynamic stochastic general equilibrium model. Econometric Reviews 26 (2–4), 289–328.
Adolfson, M., Andersson, M.K., Lindé, J., Villani, M., Vredin, A., 2007b. Modern forecasting models in action: improving macroeconomic analyses at central banks. International Journal of Central Banking 3 (4), 111–144.
Amisano, G., Geweke, J., 2011. Prediction with Macroeconomic Models, Manuscript.
Amisano, G., Tristani, O., 2011. Exact likelihood computation for nonlinear DSGE models with heteroskedastic innovations. Journal of Economic Dynamics and Control 35 (12), 2167–2185.
An, S., Schorfheide, F., 2007a. Bayesian Analysis of DSGE Models. Econometric Reviews 26 (2–4), 113–172.
An, S., Schorfheide, F., 2007b. Bayesian analysis of DSGE models–rejoinder. Econometric Reviews 26 (2–4), 211–219.
Aruoba, S.B., Schorfheide, F., 2011. Sticky prices versus monetary frictions: an estimation of policy trade-offs. American Economic Journal: Macroeconomics, 3 (1), 60–90.
Bansal, R., Yaron, A., 2004. Risks for the Long-run: a potential resolution of asset pricing puzzles. Journal of Finance 59 (4), 1481–1509.
Bayarri, M., Berger, J., 2004. The Interplay of Bayesian and Frequentist Analysis. Statistical Science 19 (1), 58–80.
Beneš, J., Binning, A., Lees, K., 2008. Incorporating judgement with DSGE models, Manuscript, DP2008/10.
Bernanke, B., Gertler, M., Gilchrist, S., 1999. The financial accelerator in a quantitative business cycle framework. In: Taylor, J.B., Woodford, M. (Ed.), Handbook of Macroeconomics, vol. 1C. North Holland, Amsterdam.
Blake, A., 2012. Fixed Interest Rates over Finite Horizons, Bank of England Working Paper 454.
Boivin, J., Giannoni, M.P., 2006. DSGE Models in a Data Rich Enviroment, NBER Working Paper, 12772.
Brunnermeier, M.K., Eisenbach, T.M., Sannikov, Y., 2012. Macroeconomics with Financial Frictions: A Survey. Princeton University and FRB, New York, Manuscript.
Canova, F., 2008. Bridging Cyclical DSGE Models and the Raw Data, Working Paper.
Canova, F., 2009. What explains the great moderation in the US? A structural analysis. Journal of the European Economic Association 7 (4), 697–721.
Carlstrom, C., Fuerst, T., Paustian, M., 2012. How Inflationary is an Extended Period of Low Interest Rates, Manuscript.
Carter, C., Kohn, R., 1994. On Gibbs Sampling for State Space Models. Biometrika 81 (3), 541–553.

Chib, S., Ramamurthy, S., 2010. Tailored randomized block MCMC methods with application to DSGE models. Journal of Econometrics 155 (1), 19–38.

Chib, S., Ramamurthy, S., forthcoming. DSGE models with student-t errors, Econometric Reviews.

Christiano, L., Motto, R., Rostagno, M., 2003. The great depression and the Friedman-Schwartz hypothesis. Journal of Money, Credit and Banking 35, 1119–1197.

Christiano, L.J., Eichenbaum, M., Evans, C.L., 2005. Nominal rigidities and the dynamic effects of a shock to monetary policy. Journal of Political Economy 113 (1), 1–45.

Christiano, L., Motto, R., Rostagno, M., 2009. Financial Factors in Economic Fluctuations. Northwestern University and European Central Bank, Manuscript.

Christiano, L.J., Trabandt, M., Walentin, K., 2010. DSGE models for monetary policy analysis. In: Friedman, B.M., Woodford, M. (Ed.), Handbook of Monetary Economics, vol. 3. Elsevier, pp. 285–367.

Christoffel, K., Coenen, G., Warne, A., 2011. Forecasting with DSGE Models. In: Clements, M.P., Hendry, D.F., (Eds.), The Oxford Handbook of Economic Forecasting.

Clark, T., 2011. Real-time density forecasts from Bayesian vector autoregress with stochastic volatility. Journal of Business and Economic Statistics 29 (3), 327–341.

Clark, T.E., McCracken, M.W., 2012. Advances in forecast evaluation. In: Elliott, G., Timmermann, A. (Ed.), Handbook of Economic Forecasting, vol. 2. North Holland, Amsterdam.

Coenen, G., McAdam, P., Straub, R., 2008. Tax reform and labor market performance in the euro area: a simulation-based analysis using the new area-wide model. Journal of Economic Dynamics and Control 32 (8), 2543–2583.

Corradi, V., Swanson, N., 2006. Predictive Density Evaluation. In: Elliott, G., Granger, C., Timmermann, A. (Ed.), Handbook of Economic Forecasting. Handbooks in Economics 24, vol. 1. North Holland, Amsterdam, pp. 197–286.

Croce, M.M., 2008. Long-Run Productivity Risk: A New Hope for Production-Based Asset Pricing, SSRN Working Paper Series, ID 1106361.

Curdia, V., Reis, R., 2010. Correlated Disturbances and US Business Cycles. Columbia University and FRB New York (Manuscript).

Curdia, V., Del Negro, M., Greenwald, D., 2011. Rare Shocks. Great Recessions. Federal Reserve Bank of New York (Manuscript).

Dawid, A., 1982. The well-calibrated bayesian. Journal of the American Statistical Association 77 (379), 605–610.

Dawid, A., 1984. Statistical theory: the prequential approach. Journal of the Royal Statistical Society Series A 147 (2), 278–292.

DeGraeve, F., 2008. The external finance premium and the macroeconomy: US post-WWII evidence. Journal of Economic Dynamics and Control 32 (11), 3415–3440.

DeGraeve, F., Emiris, M., Wouters, R., 2009. A structural decomposition of the US yield curve. Journal of Monetary Economics 56 (4), 545–559.

DeJong, D.N., Ingram, B.F., Whiteman, C.H., 2000. A Bayesian approach to dynamic macroeconomics. Journal of Econometrics 98 (2), 203–223.

Del Negro, M., Eusepi, S., 2011. Fitting observed ination expectations. Journal of Economic Dynamics and Control 35, 2105–2131.

Del Negro, M., Schorfheide, F., 2004. Priors from general equilibrium models for VARs. International Economic Review 45 (2), 643–673.

Del Negro, M., Schorfheide, F., 2008. Forming Priors for DSGE models (and how it affects the assessment of nominal rigidities). Journal of Monetary Economics 55 (7), 1191–1208

Del Negro, M., Schorfheide, F., 2010. Bayesian macroeconometrics. In: van Dijk, H.K., Koop, G., Geweke, J. (Ed.), Handbook of Bayesian Econometrics. Oxford University Press.

Del Negro, M., Schorfheide, F., Smets, F., Wouters, R., 2007. On the fit of new Keynesian models. Journal of Business and Economic Statistics 25 (2), 123–162.

Diebold, F., Gunther, T., Tay, A., 1998. Evaluating density forecasts with applications to financial risk management. International Economic Review 39 (4), 863–883.

Doan, T., Litterman, R., Sims, C.A., 1984. Forecasting and conditional projections using realistic prior distributions. Econometric Reviews 3 (4), 1–100.

Durbin, J., Koopman, S.J., 2001. Time Series Analysis by State Space Methods. Oxford University Press.

Edge, R., Gürkaynak, R., 2010. How useful are estimated DSGE model forecasts for central bankers? Brookings Papers on Economic Activity, 41 (2), 209–259.

Edge, R., Kiley, M., Laforte, J.-P., 2009. A Comparison of Forecast Performance Between Federal Reserve Staff Forecasts, Simple Reduced-Form Models, and a DSGE Model, Federal Reserve Board of Governors Finance and Economics Discussion Paper Series 2009–2010.

Erceg, C.J., Levin, A.T., 2003. Imperfect credibility and inflation persistence. Journal of Monetary Economics 50, 915–944.

Faust, J., Gupta, A., 2012. Posterior Predictive Analysis for Evaluation DSGE Models, NBER, Work, p. 17906.

Faust, J., Wright, J., 2011. Forecasting Inflation. In: Elliott, G., Timmermann, A. (Ed.), Handbook of Economic Forecasting, vol. 2. Elsevier.

Fernández-Villaverde, J., Rubio-Ramírez, J.F., 2007. Estimating macroeconomic models: a likelihood approach. Review of Economic Studies 74 (4), 1059–1087.

Fernández-Villaverde, J., Rubio-Ramírez, J.F., 2008. How structural are structural parameters? In: Acemoglu, D., Rogoff, K., Woodford, M. (Eds.), NBER Macroeconomics Annual 2007, vol. 22. University of Chicago Press, Chicago, University of Chicago Press.

Fernández-Villaverde, J., Guerron-Quintana, P., Rubio-Ramírez, J.F., 2013. Macroeconomics and volatility: data, models, and estimation. In: Acemoglu, D., Arellano, M., Dekel, E. (Ed.), Advances in Economics and Econometrics: Theory and Applications, Tenth World Congress. Cambridge University Press, University of Chicago Press.

Geweke, J., Whiteman, C., 2006. Bayesian forecasting. In: Elliott, G., Granger, C., Timmermann, A. (Ed.), Handbook of Economic Forecasting. Handbooks in Economics, vol. 1. North Holland, Amsterdam, pp. 3–80.

Ghent, A.C., 2009. Comparing DSGE-VAR forecasting models: how big are the differences? Journal of Economic Dynamics and Control 33 (4), 864–882.

Giannone, D., Monti, F., Reichlin, L., 2010. Incorporating conjunctural analysis in structural models. In: Wieland, V. (Ed.), The Science and Practice of Monetary Policy Today, Springer, pp. 41–57.

Gilchrist, S., Zakrajsek, E., 2012. Credit spreads and business cycle fluctuations. American Economic Review 102 (4), 1692–1720.

Greenwood, J., Hercovitz, Z., Krusell, P., 1998. Long-run implications of investment-specific technological change. American Economic Review 87 (3), 342–36.

Herbst, E., 2010. Gradient and Hessian-based MCMC for DSGE Models, Manuscript.

Herbst, E., Schorfheide, F., 2011. Evaluating DSGE Model Forecasts of Comovements. University of Pennsylvania, Manuscript.

Ingram, B., Whiteman, C., 1994. Supplanting the minnesota prior- forecasting macroeconomic time series using real business cycle model priors. Journal of Monetary Economics 49 (4), 1131–1159.

Ireland, P.N., 2004. A method for taking models to the data. Journal of Economic Dynamics and Control 28 (6), 1205–1226.

Justiniano, A., Primiceri, G.E., 2008. The time-varying volatility of macroeconomic fluctuations. American Economic Review 98 (3), 604–641.

Justiniano, A., Primiceri, G.E., Tambalotti, A., 2009. Investment Shocks and Business Cycles, NBER Working Paper, 15570.

Karlsson, S., 2012. Forecasting with Bayesian VAR models. In: Elliott, G., Timmermann, A. (Ed.), Handbook of Economic Forecasting, vol. 2. North Holland, Amsterdam.

King, R.G., Plosser, C.I., Rebelo, S., 1988. Production, growth, and business cycles: I the basic neoclassical model. Journal of Monetary Economics 21 (2–3), 195–232.

Kling, J., Bessler, D., 1989. Calibration-based predictive distributions: an application of prequential analysis to interest rates, Money, Prices, and Output. Journal of Business 62 (4), 447–499.

Kohn, R., Giordani, P., Strid, I., 2010. Adaptive Hybrid Metropolis-Hastings Samplers for DSGE Models, Riksbank Manuscript.

Kolasa, M., Rubaszek, M., Skrzypczyński, P., 2010. Putting the New Keynesian DSGE Model to the Real-Time Forecasting Test, Working Paper.

Kryshko, M., 2010. Data-Rich DSGE and Dynamic Factor Models. University of Pennsylvania, Manuscript.

Laseen, S., Svensson, L.E., 2011. Anticipated alternative policy-rate paths in policy simulations. International Journal of Central Banking 7 (3), 1–35.

Leeper, E.M., Zha, T., 2003. Modest policy interventions. Journal of Monetary Economics 50 (8), 1673–1700.

Liu, Z., Waggoner, D.F., Zha, T., 2011. Sources of macroeconomic fluctuations: a regime-switching DSGE approach. Quantitative Economics 2 (2), 251–301.

Milani, F., Treadwell, J., 2011. The Effects of Monetary Policy News and Surprises, Manuscript.

Monti, F., 2010. Combining judgment and models. Journal of Money, Credit and Banking 42 (8), 1641–1662.

Otrok, C., 2001. On measuring the welfare costs of business cycles. Journal of Monetary Economics 45 (1), 61–92.

Owen, A.B., 2001. Empirical Likelihood. Chapman and Hall/CRC.

Pichler, P., 2008. Forecasting with DSGE models: the role of nonlinearities, The B.E. Journal of Macroeconomics 8 (1), 20.

Primiceri, G., 2006. Why inflation Rose and Fell: policymakers beliefs and US postwar stabilization policy. Quarterly Journal of Economics 121, 867–901.

Robertson, J.C., Tallman, E.W., Whiteman, C.H., 2005. Forecasting using relative entropy. Journal of Money, Credit, and Banking 37 (3), 383–401.

Rosenblatt, M., 1952. Remarks on a multivariate transformation. Annals of Mathematical Statistics 23 (3), 470–472.

Rubaszek, M., Skrzypczynski, P., 2008. On the forecasting performance of a small-scale DSGE model. International Journal of Forecasting 24 (3), 498–512.

Sargent, T.J., 1999. The Conquest of American Inflation. Princeton University Press, Princeton.

Schorfheide, F., 2000. Loss function-based evaluation of DSGE model. Journal of Applied Econometrics 15 (6), 645–670.

Schorfheide, F., 2005. Learning and monetary policy shifts. Review of Economic Dynamics 8 (2), 392–419.

Schorfheide, F., Sill, K., Kryshko, M., 2010. DSGE model-based forecasting of non-modelled variables. International Journal of Forecasting 26 (2), 348–373.

Silverman, B., 1986. Density Estimation for Statistics and Data Analysis. Chapman and Hall, New York.

Sims, C.A., 2002. Solving linear rational expectations models. Computational Economics 20 (1–2), 1–20.

Sims, C.A., Zha, T., 1998. Bayesian methods for dynamic multivariate models. International Economic Review 39 (4), 949–968.

Smets, F., Wouters, R., 2003. An estimated dynamic stochastic general equilibrium model of the euro area. Journal of the European Economic Association 1 (5), 1123–1175.

Smets, F., Wouters, R., 2005. Bayesian new neoclassical synthesis (NNS) models: modern tools for Central Banks. Journal of the European Economic Association 3 (2–3), 422–433.

Smets, F., Wouters, R., 2007. Shocks and frictions in US business cycles: a Bayesian DSGE approach. American Economic Review 97 (3), 586–606.

Waggoner, D., Zha, T., 1999. Conditional forecasts in dynamic multivariate models. Review of Economics and Statistics 81 (4), 639–651.

Waggoner, D.F., Zha, T., 2010. Confronting Model Misspecification in Macroeconomics. Federal Reserve Bank of Atlanta (Manuscript).

Warne, A., Coenen, G., Christoffel, K., 2012. Forecasting with DSGE-VAR Models. European Central Bank (Manuscript).

West, K.D., 2006. Forecast Evaluation. In: Elliott, G., Granger, C.W., Timmermann, A. (Ed.), Handbook of Economic Forecasting, vol. 1. North Holland, Amsterdam, pp. 100–134.

Wieland, V., Wolters, M.H., 2011. The diversity of forecasts from macroeconomic models of the US economy. Economic Theory 47, 247–292.

Wieland, V., Wolters, M.H., 2012. Forecasting and policy making. In: Elliott, G., Timmermann, A., Handbook of Economic Forecasting, vol. 2. Elsevier.

Wolters, M.H., 2010. Forecating under Model Uncertainty, Working Paper.

Wright, J., 2011. Evaluating Real-Time VAR Forecasts with an Informative Democratic Prior, Manuscript.

CHAPTER 3

Forecasting Output

Marcelle Chauvet[*] and Simon Potter[†]

[*]Department of Economics, University of California Riverside, CA 92521, USA
[†]Federal Reserve Bank of New York, 33 Liberty St., New York, NY 10045, USA

Contents

Abstract

This chapter surveys the recent literature on output forecasting, and examines the real-time forecasting ability of several models for U.S. output growth. In particular, it evaluates the accuracy of short-term forecasts of linear and nonlinear structural and reduced-form models, and judgmental forecasts of output growth. Our emphasis is on using solely the information that was available at the time the forecast was being made, in order to reproduce the forecasting problem facing forecasters in real-time. We find that there is a large difference in forecast performance across business cycle phases. In particular, it is much harder to forecast output growth during recessions than during expansions. Simple linear and nonlinear autoregressive models have the best accuracy in forecasting output growth during expansions, although the dynamic stochastic general equilibrium model and the vector autoregressive model with financial variables do relatively well. On the other hand, we find that most models do poorly in forecasting output growth during recessions. The autoregressive model based on the nonlinear dynamic factor model that takes into account asymmetries between expansions and recessions displays the best real time forecast accuracy during recessions. Even though the Blue Chip forecasts are comparable, the dynamic factor Markov switching model has better accuracy, particularly with respect to the timing and depth of output fall during recessions in real time. The results suggest that there are large gains in considering separate forecasting models for normal times and models especially designed for periods of abrupt changes, such as during recessions and financial crises.

Keywords

Real time, Evaluating forecasts, Macroeconomic forecasting, Nonlinear, Recession, DSGE models, Markov switching, Dynamic factor model, Vector autoregressive model

1. INTRODUCTION

Forecasting national output is one of the main objectives of private and government forecasters. The forecasts are keys inputs to the decision making of central banks, fiscal authorities, and private sector agents. For example, in assessing fiscal sustainability it is crucial to have good forecasts of the future path of national output. A wide range of approaches are used to produce the forecasts: at one end are judgmental methods that rely on the expertise of the individual forecaster to adjust forecasts produced by a suite of models and at the other end dynamic stochastic general equilibrium (DSGE) models that use modern economic theory to produce a forecast disciplined by economic theory.

In this chapter we provide a survey of a wide range of approaches to forecast output growth with a focus on recent forecast performance and models of interest to Central Bankers and time series econometricians. We start by giving some general background on the forecasting of output, then turn to the specific focus of the chapter. We then examine the forecasts of several models for U.S. output growth in the last 50 years, and compare their accuracy in real time. In particular, we evaluate short-term forecasts of linear and non-linear structural and reduced-form models, and judgmental-based forecasts of U.S. output growth. Our emphasis is on using solely the information that was available at the time the forecast was being made, in order to reproduce the forecasting problem in real time. This exercise is most compelling for policymakers and economic agents, who wish to know the economic situation and its short-run trends as they are occurring. This is especially the case in times of uncertainty around recessions and severe crises. The question we want to answer is whether existing models proved helpful in yielding accurate short-run forecasts of the dynamics of the economy, including during recessions.

1.1. Background

The concept of output most forecasted is Gross Domestic Product (GDP) from the national income accounts. GDP is the monetary value of the gross production of all finished goods and services within the borders of an economy. Gross National Product (GNP) is a related concept that measures the production attributable to all members of an economy without respect to their current location. Another related measure of economic activity is Gross Domestic Income (GDI), which is the sum of all income earned while producing goods and services within an economy's borders. As accounting concepts GDI and GDP are equal. However, in practice since GDP estimates are built from expenditure data and GDI estimates are derived from income data, there is usually a discrepancy between the two. These discrepancies can be large for real-time estimates of national output, especially around business cycle turning points (see e.g., Nalewaik, 2012). We will focus on GDP but will examine carefully the issues related to real-time estimates of GDP.

GDP can be split up into expenditure categories using the standard national account identity:

$$Y_t = C_t + I_t + G_t + X_t - M_t,$$

where Y_t is GDP during period t, C_t is consumption expenditures, I_t is gross investment (structures, capital equipment and change in inventories), G_t is direct government expenditures, X_t is exports, and M_t is imports.

Most of the effort in forecasting output focuses on real GDP, that is, nominal GDP deflated so that comparisons across time involve real changes in output rather than in the number of goods and services that can be purchased with a unit of currency. There are many ways to deflate nominal GDP to obtain a real measure. The best methods use chain weighting to produce an index of real output. This index can then be quoted in the value of the unit of account for a particular year but in practice the underlying real growth data come directly from the index. Chain-weighting is also applied to the individual components to produce indices of their real levels.[1] Unlike fixed-based year deflation this means that the individual component indices are not additive to the overall real output index and thus, the concept of growth contributions is used.

For most countries estimates of GDP are now produced at a quarterly frequency but some countries still only produce annual estimates. These estimates are designed to give the average flow of GDP during the quarter or the year. Initial estimates for GDP are usually produced in the quarter following the one being estimated but are subject to continuous revision after the initial estimates. Similar revisions occur in the related concepts of GNP and GDI. The origins of the revisions are a mixture of better source data and changes in national income concepts. For example, in 1999 chain-weighting was adopted for the U.S. national income accounts, changing the whole history of the GDP series.

In addition to standard quarter-ahead forecasts, GDP forecasts are often presented as year over year. That is, the average output in year $t + j$ over average output in year

---

[1] The chain-weighted method of measuring GDP growth entails two calculations of growth for each year, using the year itself and the preceding year as bases. The chain-weighted GDP growth for a year is then the average of these two growth rates. Since this method continually changes the relative weights of goods over time, it corrects potential distortion in growth when there are shifts in production from goods that have similar prices.

$t + j - 1$. This convention was based on the greater availability and at times greater accuracy of annual GDP estimates. The convention can produce some unusual effects if data for the current year are revised. We focus on models used to forecast quarterly U.S. GDP where the effect of data revisions is on the predictors rather than the prediction variable.

In many advanced countries the volatility of realized output growth fell in the last three decades. This has been documented by a number of authors, who find a structural break in its volatility in the mid-1980s (e.g., McConnell and Perez-Quiros, 2000; Kim and Nelson, 1999; Koop and Potter, 2000; Blanchard and Simon, 2000; Chauvet and Potter, 2001; van Dijk et al., 2002a; Chauvet and Gopli, 2003; Mills and Wang, 2003, etc.). A feature of the so-called Great Moderation in the United States was two very long business cycle expansions in the 1980s and 1990s. The 1990s expansion was followed by a very mild recession in 2001 when according to current estimates there were not two consecutive quarters of negative growth and the lowest four-quarter growth over the period including the recession was +0.4 percent. This so-called Great Moderation was associated with smaller absolute forecast errors of economic activity but in a relative sense the accuracy of many forecasts fell. As we show below this long period of relative calm made it very difficult for linear time series models to produce forecasts that captured some of the big swings in GDP growth starting in 2008. The "Great Moderation" in the advanced economies was followed by the Great Recession during which the absolute size of forecast errors increased dramatically as discussed in Section 3.3, and in more detail in Chauvet et al. (2013).

Many emerging market economies had suffered severe recessions in the last few decades. A pattern of drastic contractions and fast recoveries was repeated for many of those. However, only recently advanced economies have experienced such deep contractions, with many yet to recover to the previous level of real GDP. While linear time series models are not capable of forecasting large swings in GDP growth, some non-linear model perform well during these periods, as discussed in this chapter.

1.2. A Brief History and Survey of Recent Literature

The development of output forecasting was tightly related to the development of national income accounts and the availability of estimates of GDP and GNP. Prior to this the focus had been on forecasts of industrial output. Following the work of Tinbergen (1939, 1974) and Klein (1970) the approach was to estimate linear equations for different sectors of the economy that could be used to forecast aggregates measures such as GDP by use of the national income account identity.

The amount of economic theory used in the estimating equations varied and there was some debate about how to incorporate more formal time series models (Fair, 1970). The performance of these models was initially encouraging but a rigorous time series evaluation by Nelson (1972) showed that the large model for the U.S. developed at Penn, MIT, and the Federal Reserve Board was in many respects worse that the use of simple autoregressive time series models for forecasting.

In addition, the forecasting results from such large models were and continue to be judgmentally adjusted by their users. The judgment is applied to estimation of the current level of GDP (nowcasting) and to the path of GDP going forward. Some of this judgment uses expert knowledge of the construction of national income accounts to refine current quarter estimates while other forms of judgment rely on subjective assessments of the future course of the economy often informed by a suite of time series models that supplement the main model. While the judgmental approach to forecasting is very common, it is impossible to replicate so we rely on surveys of forecasters in real time to include judgmental forecasts in our assessment.

As noted above forecasts of GDP are important inputs to policy decisions. The rational expectations revolution of the 1970s highlighted a crucial conceptual issue with forecasts as inputs to policy decisions: if, as was the assumption, policy could affect outcomes then changes in policy might alter the time series properties of the data invalidating the use of the estimation sample for forecasting (The Lucas critique, Lucas, 1976). The poor forecast performance of the many large macro models in the 1970s gave support to this conceptual issue and led first to the use of vector autoregressions (VAR) and then to estimated DSGE models.

In its seminal paper, Sims (1980) criticizes large-scale macroeconometric models for failing to predict economic activity and inflation in face of the oil shocks in the 1970s. In addition, he argues that the identification of these models was based on restrictions that did not arise from economic theory or institutional facts. Sims proposes as alternative VARs to study economic data and relationships without imposing restrictions. This system of reduced form equations is used to obtain impulse response function of economic variables to shocks. Cooley and LeRoy (1985) criticize VARs arguing that identification of shocks and interpretation of impulse-response functions require structural assumptions. In response, Sims considers the possibility of weak identifying restrictions in order to achieve interpretation of impulse response functions, giving rise to structural VARs (SVARs).

Another response to the poor performance of large macroeconometric models in the 1970s was the construction of structural models based on microeconomic foundations that are not vulnerable to Lucas' Critique. Kydland and Prescott (1982) propose the Real Business Cycle (RBC) model based on principles of neoclassical growth models, in which real shocks are sources of economic fluctuations under flexible prices. The model assumes that agents' optimizing decisions follow rational expectations and are dynamically consistent. Later, Rotemberg and Woodford (1997) propose the New Keynesian DSGE model using a similar framework. Decisions are also based on microfoundations, but prices instead are set by monopolistic competitive firms and are not instantaneously adjusted.

In the last decade there has been substantial progress in the quantitative implementation and estimation of DSGE models. These models offer a coherent framework to characterize the behavior of the economy based on the interactions of microfounded decisions. The seminal work of Smets and Wouters (SW 2003, 2007) showed the feasibility of estimating large and richly specified DSGE models, and found that they can provide a good description of the U.S. macroeconomic data. This led to an increased interest by Central Banks in many countries in their application to policy analysis, particularly due to their story-telling implications.[2]

The next question was whether these models could also be used for forecasting. SW (2007) compare out-of-sample forecasts of the DSGE model with VAR, Bayesian vector autoregressive models (BVAR), and DSGE-VARs. Several authors have extended this approach to verify the forecasting ability of DSGE models for the U.S. and other countries, comparing the results also to judgmental-based forecasts, and to simple benchmarks such as univariate autoregressive processes or random walks.

Some examples are Adolfson et al. (2007a,b), Christoffel et al. (2008, 2011), and Liu et al. (2009). These studies compare out-of-sample results using revised, ex-post data. Some recent studies use real-time data such as Rubaszek and Skrzypczyński (2008), Kolasa et al. (2009), Edge et al. (2010), Wolters (2010), Edge and Gürkaynak (2010), Del Negro and Schorfheide (2013), and Wieland and Wolters (2011).

The general finding from the literature is that the DSGE forecasts are comparable or slightly superior to the ones obtained from VARs and BVAR, but not significantly different from simple benchmarks such as univariate autoregressive processes. Judgmental forecasts outperform DSGE, VAR, and BVAR or DSGE-VAR models in the short run (one or two quarters ahead). DSGE models show a better result in the medium run (three and four quarters ahead), but tests of equal forecast accuracy generally indicate that the differences in forecasts are not significantly different across models at these horizons. Interestingly, these results hold for the U.S., Euro area, and other countries.

Wolters (2010) additionally finds that structural models fail to forecast turning points (i.e., the beginning or end of a recession), large recessions, and booms, but display comparable accuracy to the judgmental and BVAR forecasts during "normal" times for medium-run horizons. This is also found by Del Negro and Schorfheide (2013) and Wieland and Wolters (2011). The former compares the real-time (pseudo out-of-sample) forecast ability of Blue Chip forecasts with the SW (2007) model and extensions that include financial frictions, or information on default risk and current interest rates in the last two decades, while the latter examines the real-time forecast accuracy of structural and reduced-form models with judgmental-based forecasts during the last five NBER-dated recessions. Both papers find that the model forecasts are outperformed by those from professional forecasts at short-run horizons but are comparable to them at medium-run horizons. Wieland and Wolters (2011), however, find that, with the exception of the 1980–1981 recession, the judgmental-based forecasts outperform the model-based ones for all other recessions, with the largest difference in forecasts being for the 2007–2009 recession and the smallest for the 2001 recession.

---

[2] Sims (2006), Tovar (2009), and Faust (2012) discuss some of the omissions of these models and important features that will enhance their contribution to discussion of policy analysis.

Regarding models used by Central Banks, Christoffel et al. (2011) compare the forecast accuracy of the New Area-Wide Model (NAWM), designed and used by the European Central Bank (ECB) for macroeconomic forecasts, with Bayesian DSGE-VARs, BVARs and reduced-form models.[3] They find that the DSGE-VAR model outperforms DSGE, NAWM, VAR, and BVAR models in forecasting output. Edge et al. (2010) compare the performance of Estimated Dynamic Optimization-based model (EDO) from the Federal Reserve Board (FRB) with VAR, BVAR, univariate autoregressive model, and the Greenbook and FRB forecasts. They find that the out-of-sample real-time forecasts of the EDO are comparable to the autoregressive model but generally not statistically different from it and the other models. However, as noticed by the authors, the models are evaluated for a period of relative stability, between 1996 and 2004.

Edge et al. (2010), Edge and Gürkaynak (2010), and Wang (2009) reach the same conclusions as the literature, but note the surprising evidence that the forecasting models or judgmental forecasts generally examined are very poor. This is exacerbated when long samples are considered. The models and judgmental-based results show modest nowcasting ability, but they display almost no forecasting ability from one-quarter ahead and on. As stressed by the authors, the comparison in the literature has been among poor forecasting methods.

The findings in the literature support the early evidence of Nelson (1972) that forecasts from simple autoregressive models are hard to beat by large-scale macroeconomic model. However, another strand of the literature has shown that the use of some variables in simple autoregressive processes or frontier time series models generally generate substantial gains in forecasting output growth.

Many papers find that some financial and macroeconomic series have significant predictive power for future economic activity across a number of countries.[4] Among those, the early work of Estrella and Hardouvelis (1991) and Stock and Watson (1993) find that the yield curve has the best short- and medium-run forecast power for output growth beyond the predictive power of several other variables including lagged output growth. The early literature is summarized in the comprehensive literature review of Stock and Watson (2003) and the more recent one focusing on the yield curve on the survey by Wheelock and Wohar (2009).

Some of the cutting-edge time series models and methods found to be useful to forecast economic activity are factor models, mixed frequency models, non-linear models,

---

[3] The literature finds that the BVAR model generally has good forecast accuracy for several variables in the system compared to other models, but not of real GDP growth.

[4] Some of the series that have been found to be good predictors of GDP growth are interest rates and spreads, stock prices, monetary aggregates, inflation, survey forecasts (e.g., NAPMC Purchasing managers' survey), the index of leading indicator and its components, such as vendor performance, contracts and orders for plants and equipment, housing permits, consumer expectations, change in manufacturers' unfilled durable goods orders, etc. Banegas (2011) finds that for emerging economies additional series that help predict output growth are portfolio investment flows, global commodity markets, and a cross-sectional firm size factor.

and forecasts combination. This list is not exhaustive as the literature is vast and dynamic, with innovations being proposed at a rapid pace. Below we discuss some of the recent developments.

A large number of papers have examined forecasts of macroeconomic variables using factor models, which are a parsimonious way of extracting large information on overall economic conditions. Stock and Watson (2002), Marcellino et al. (2003), and Forni et al. (2003) survey applications of these models in forecasting macroeconomic and financial variables. These and more recent studies find that factor models consistently beat univariate and multivariate autoregressive models and, often, judgmental forecasts both during expansions and recessions.

More recently, Wang (2009) compares the out-of-sample forecast performance for U.S. output growth of DSGE models with VARs and factor models. He finds that the factor model generally outperforms any other model in the short run, with significantly different gains. Lombardi and Maier (2011) study pseudo real-time forecasts of GDP for the euro area and its countries during the Great Moderation and Great Recession, comparing the performance of dynamic factor models and a model using survey indices (Purchasing Managers' Indices). Winter (2011) compares the short-term forecasting ability of factor models with several linear reduced-form models and private sector forecasts for recessions in general, and particularly the Great Recession in the Netherlands. Both papers conclude that the dynamic factor model displays the best forecast accuracy overall and during the recent crisis, and the difference in forecasts with the other models and judgmental forecasts is statistically significant.

Some advances in forecast methods include a recent growing literature on nowcasting and short-term forecasting GDP growth using mixed frequency models.[5] The idea is to explore information in more timely indicators that are available at a higher frequency to improve the forecast of quarterly output growth. Several papers use factor models cast in state space with mixed frequency to nowcast GDP growth in the U.S. or Euro area such as Marcellino and Schumacher (2008), Camacho et al. (2011,2012), Banbura and Runstler (2011), Giannone et al. (2004), Angelini et al. (2011), Giannone and Reichlin (2013), which are related to the methods of Trehan (1989), Mariano and Murasawa (2003), Evans (2005), Proietti and Moauro (2006), and Giannone et al. (2008). The general finding is that these models generally outperform nowcasts of GDP growth compared to models that use quarterly frequency only, and are comparable to judgmental forecasts in the United States and in the Euro area.[6]

Other authors apply the mixed frequency approach to univariate and multivariate autoregressive (VAR) processes. Clements and Galvao (2008) use the mixed data sampling

---

[5] Most macroeconomic data are released with at least one month lag, and many with longer delays. In addition, many series are revised substantially since their first release. This leads to a need to forecast the present and even the near past, which the literature has dubbed "nowcast."

[6] For a survey see Giannone and Reichlin (2013).

MIDAS method proposed by Ghysels et al. (2004, 2006) in autoregressive processes (AR). They find that MIDAS improves real-time forecasts of U.S. output growth compared to standard AR models at nowcasting and short horizons. Banbura et al. (2010), Kuzin et al. (2011) apply mixed frequency method to VAR and Schorfheide and Song (2012) to BVARs. They find that adding within-quarter monthly information improve VAR and BVAR forecasts. Kuzin et al. (2011) find additionally that the nowcasting and forecasting ability of the MIDAS and mixed-frequency VAR (MF-VAR) to quarterly GDP growth in the euro area are complements as the MIDAS does better for short horizons (up to five months), whereas MF-VAR are better for longer horizons (up to nine months).[7]

Aruoba et al. (2009) and Aruoba and Diebold (2010) propose a factor model with mixed frequency that include high-frequency data to measure economic activity.[8] These are the first frameworks that include frequencies higher than monthly. The approach is based on a linear small-data dynamic factor model to construct a high-frequency coincident indicator of business conditions, building on Stock and Watson (1989) and Mariano and Murasawa (2003).[9]

A popular forecasting approach is pooling of forecasts from several models. The common finding is that forecast combinations generate better results on average than forecasts from single models. Arguments in favor of pooling are that specification and selection of single forecast and nowcast models involve decisions on variable selection, model specification, estimation method, which all could lead to potential misspecification in theory. Timmermann (2006) studies the theoretical and empirical reasons behind the possible determinants of the advantages from combining forecasts, such as the correlation between forecast errors and the relative size of the forecast error variances of single models, model misspecification, and non-stationarities (see also Clements and Hendry, 2004). Recent empirical evidence favors forecast combination such as Clark and McCracken (2010), Assenmacher-Wesche and Pesaran (2008), Kuzin et al. (2013), or Aiolfi et al. (2011), amongst many others. Kuzin et al. (2013) find that forecast combination yields more robust forecasts than factor models for nowcasting and short-term forecasting output growth in several industrialized countries. Aiolfi et al. (2011) study forecast combinations of model-based forecasts from linear and non-linear univariate specifications, and multivariate factor-augmented models with judgmental survey forecasts and find that the leading forecasts are obtained from combining a simple equal-weighted average of survey and model-based forecasts.

Some recent papers show that a different type of aggregation can also be promising. In particular, aggregating forecasts of components, regions, or countries can lead to improved

---

[7] MIDAS are based on exponential lag polynomials coefficients, while the MF-VAR has unrestricted parameters.

[8] Real-time updates of the indicator is posted in the Philadelphia Fed website at http://www.philadelphiafed.org/research-and-data/real-time-center/business-conditions-index/

[9] Stock and Watson (1989) propose a widely popular low-dimensional linear dynamic factor model to construct coincident indicators of the U.S. economy.

performance compared to directly forecasting aggregated data. Frale et al. (2011) forecast output by aggregating forecasts of its components from the expenditure side, and Marcellino et al. (2003) produce nowcasts from aggregating member countries of the euro area. These papers find that forecasting aggregated components outperforms direct forecasts of aggregate output. Owyang et al. (2012) find that including state-level series to aggregate predictors at the national level improves the short-run forecast performance of the U.S. business cycle phase.

A large recent literature has shown that non-linearities in the dynamics of the economy can be quite important for forecasting. Non-linear models may reveal additional information and improve forecasts compared to frameworks that take into account only the average linear effect of one series on another. Many studies have shown that the largest forecasting errors in some series occur around the beginning or end of a recession, because it is at these times that the linear relationship may break down. This is especially the case for recessions, when most models yield large forecasts errors.

Recent methods have been advanced to provide a formal representation of non-linearities in economic series in a rigorous framework.[10] For example, the prewar emphasis on business cycles based on the idea of recurrent expansion and contraction phases has been formalized in the threshold models of Tong (1990) and Granger and Teräsvirta (1993), and in Hamilton's (1989) widely applied Markov switching model. There has also been lots of progress in modeling sophisticated versions of Probit models to forecast business cycle phases. These non-linear models are powerful tools for modeling recurrent phase changes as they capture potential asymmetries across phases, allowing expansions and contractions to display different amplitude, duration, or steepness.[11]

Diebold and Rudebusch (1996) propose a combination of the small scale dynamic factor model of Stock and Watson (1989) with Markov switching as in Hamilton (1989). Chauvet (1998) estimates such a multivariate dynamic factor model with Markov switching model to build a coincident indicator of the U.S. business cycle and probabilities that the economy is in a specific phase of the business cycle, and evaluates turning points of the 1990–1991 recession in real time.[12] Adding Markov switching to this framework allows analysis of asymmetries and recurrent breaks in a multivariate setting. The proposed model successfully signals recessions, which many models failed to predict in real time. Kim and Nelson (1998) estimate this model with Bayesian techniques and extending it to allow for time-varying probabilities.

---

[10] For a recent collection of papers on advances of nonlinear models see Ma and Wohar (forthcoming).

[11] In this paper we focus on forecasting output growth rather than on forecasting business cycle turning points. There is a vast literature in this area. Just to name a few see Stock and Watson (1993), Bernard and Gerlach (1998), Estrella and Mishkin (1998), Chauvet (1998), Anderson and Vahid (2001), Chauvet and Hamilton (2006), Chauvet and Piger (2008, 2013), Chauvet and Potter (2001, 2005), Chauvet et al. (2013), Chauvet and Senyuz (2012), Kauppi and Saikkonen (2008), and Nyberg (2010), etc. For a survey of threshold models see van Dijk et al. (2002b). A collection of recent papers describing techniques for building indicators of turning points can be found in Mazzi and Ozyildirim (forthcoming).

[12] The model uses the same coincident series as considered by the NBER: sales, personal income, industrial production, and employment.

Chauvet and Hamilton (2006) and Chauvet and Piger (2008) collect a large database of unrevised real-time data to reconstruct inferences that would have been generated if parameters had to be estimated based on data as they were originally released at each historical date. Chauvet and Hamilton (2006) examine the performance of the univariate Markov switching model of Hamilton (1989) and the dynamic factor model with Markov switching in Chauvet (1998) in forecasting U.S. business cycles in real time, while Chauvet and Piger (2008) compare the performance of a non-parametric algorithm and the parametric Markov-switching dynamic-factor model. These papers find that the recession probabilities from Markov-switching models perform quite well in estimation with real-time databases and are a successful tool in monitoring the U.S. business cycle.

More recently, Chauvet and Piger (2013) examine the real-time performance of the dynamic factor model with Markov switching in forecasting recessions, particularly the last one, using coincident series and different measures of employment. The recent recessions have been followed by jobless recoveries that led to great uncertainty regarding the recession end in real time. This paper evaluate the speed in identifying the beginning and end of recessions in real time when payroll employment or civilian employment are considered. They find that the model timely signaled the onset of recessions, including the Great Recession.[13] Altogether, these papers show that the dynamic factor model with regime switching is one of the most successful models in predicting business cycle phases in real time.

Recent innovations in Markov switching models include Kim et al. (2008), Chauvet (2010), Guerin and Marcellino (2011), Nalewaik (2011), Camacho et al. (2012), Chauvet and Su (2013), among others. Kim et al. (2008) extend Hamilton's model to allow for endogenous Markov regime switching and apply the framework to a volatility feedback model of stock returns. Chauvet (2010) proposes a 4-state Markov switching model to represent four phases of the US business cycle: recessions, recoveries, expansions, and slowdowns. Guerin and Marcellino (2011) propose a univariate Markov switching mixed data sampling (MS-MIDAS) extending Hamilton's (1989) model to allow the use of mixed-frequency data in Markov switching models. They find that the MS-MIDAS improve forecasts performance for U.S. output growth compared to the univariate MS model. Nalewaik (2011) uses a three state Markov switching model to capture transitions in economic activity from expansion to a short stall phase, and then to recession. The

---

[13] These authors find that the version of the model with payroll is quicker to call peaks, while the one with civilian employment is best for troughs. Notice that this is a model designed for identifying recessions based on coincident series, not a model for anticipating recessions based on leading series. For example, the model estimated with *coincident* series and payroll representing employment timely signaled in real time the onset of the Great Recession as December 2007 with information available in April 2008 (the earliest possible signal, given the lag in the availability of the data, would have been in March 2008). The real-time probabilities of recession were above 50% already in April 2008, and above 80% in July 2008. The probabilities stayed close to 100% during the whole financial crisis and the most of 2009, correctly signaling the intensity and duration of the recession. The real-time probabilities of recession are made publicly available on a monthly basis on Chauvet's website since 2006–2007 at: http://sites.google.com/site/marcellechauvet/probabilities-of-recession and on Piger's website at: http://pages.uoregon.edu/jpiger/us_recession_probs.htm.

model includes additional leading series as the yield curve, GDI, unemployment, and housing starts, and generates improved forecasts of output growth. Camacho et al. (2012) extend Chauvet (1998) Dynamic Factor Model with Markov Switching (DFMS) model to include ragged edges and mixed frequencies. The real-time analysis is not applied to forecast output growth, but phases of the business cycle.

Chauvet and Su (2013) propose a model with three Markov switching processes in order to simultaneously capture business cycle phases, structural breaks or outliers. Market economies undergo recurrent fluctuations and changes in the structure of aggregate activity. Models that do not take into account the evolving dynamics of the economy yield poor representation and forecast of economic activity. This has been specially the case with the Great Moderation in the mid 1980s and the recent Great Recession. Chauvet and Su's (2013) model successfully represents business cycle phases under structural and pulse breaks.

Finally, other recent models that have been used in a debate regarding the evolving dynamics of the economy related to the Great Moderation is the Time-Varying VAR (TVAR) model and the Markov switching VAR model (MS-VAR).[14] Cogley and Sargent (2001, 2005) and Primiceri (2005) use a reduced form TVAR that takes into account drifting parameters or heteroskedasticity while Sims and Zha (2006) study changes in monetary policy via MS-VAR models with discrete breaks that capture potential switching policy pre and post Volcker. The findings in these papers contrast regarding the nature of changes – whether they were abrupt as in depicted in MS-VAR models or more gradual as in TVAR models. Chauvet and Tierney (2009) use a non-parametric VAR model and find that there have been abrupt as well as gradual changes in shocks and in the dynamics of the U.S. economy in the last five decades. These models have not been widely used to predict output growth.[15]

On the other spectrum, there are judgmental methods that rely on the expertise of individual forecasters to fine-tune forecasts generated by a set of models. Most countries and some regions have survey of forecasters. For example, the ECB publishes the ECB Survey of Professional Forecasters, which is a quarterly survey of expectations of several key macroeconomic indicators, including real GDP growth. The Survey has been conducted since 1999 and it is based on forecasts from financial and non-financial institutions from the European Union.

In the U.S., the most popular ones are the Survey of Professional Forecasters (SPF) and the Blue Chip Indicators (BC). The Survey of Professional Forecasters is published by the Federal Reserve Bank of Philadelphia since 1990, taking over from the American

---

[14] Time-varying models have not been widely used to predict output growth. A possible reason suggested by Cogley in discussions of this paper is that since drifts in the parameters are gradual, TVAR models may not perform well around business cycle turning points, particularly if the recent Great Recession period is included.

[15] A possible reason in the case of TVAR models suggested by Cogley in discussions of this paper is that since drifts in the parameters are assumed to be gradual, TVAR models may not perform well around business cycle turning points, particularly if the recent Great Recession period is included.

Statistical Association and the National Bureau of Economic Research, which were publishing it since 1968. The SPF makes available the mean and median forecasts as well as the individual responses from each forecaster.

The Blue Chip Indicators is a poll of around top 50 forecast economists from banks, manufacturing industries, brokerage firms, and insurance companies. The poll has been conducted since 1976 and comprises several macro series, including real GDP growth. The survey contains forecasts from each member and the average (or consensus) of their forecasts. It also provides the average of the 10 highest and 10 lowest forecasts for each variable, and the median forecast. Finally, it also publishes a diffusion index that reflects changes in expectations that might take place before changes in the consensus forecast.

Another popular set of forecasts in the U.S. is the Greenbook of the Federal Reserve Board of Governors. The Greenbook is prepared as discussion material for each of the Federal Open Market Committee meetings. The Greenbook forecasts are based on assumptions about monetary policy and are put together by research economists from the Board of Governors. The forecasts are only publicly available after a lapse of 5 years.

1.3. Chapter Plan

In this chapter we focus on evaluating the real-time performance of several models in forecasting output growth over time as well as during expansions and recessions in a genuine out-of-sample exercise. As discussed in the previous section, there are a plethora of models that could be selected and, clearly choices have to be made in a literature this vast. In order to keep the task manageable, we focus on some popular structural, linear and non-linear multivariate models and apply them to U.S. output data.

Given that the literature has extensively compared the performance of DSGE models with VAR and BVAR models and found that these models have, on average, yielded poor forecasts, we focus also on comparing the forecast accuracy of structural models and state of the art reduced-form time series models, which could be more informative benchmarks.

We compare the forecast accuracy of the DSGE model of Smets and Wouters (2007) with linear and non-linear autoregressive models such as AR(2), Cumulative Depth of Recession by Beaudry and Koop (CDR 1993), VARs, BVARs, the univariate Markov switching model (MS), and the proposed autoregressive model associated with the Dynamic Factor Model with Markov Switching (AR-DFMS). Given the importance of the financial sector in explaining the recent crisis, we also study VARs with financial variables.[16]

The model-based forecasts are contrasted with the judgmental forecasts from the Blue Chip Indicators. The literature has found that the forecasts of U.S. output growth from the Survey of Professional Forecasters and Blue Chip are similar (see e.g., Wieland and

---

[16] For results of DSGE models with financial frictions, see the chapter by Del Negro and Schorfheide (2013) in this volume.

Wolters, 2011). On the other hand, the Greenbook forecasts are only available with a lag of 5 years. The latest forecasts available from the Philadelphia Fed website at the time this chapter was written were up to 2006.

We thus focus on comparisons with the Blue Chip Indicators representing judgmental forecasts, which allow analysis of forecasts using the same sample as the estimated models.[17] We also evaluate the forecast accuracy arising from equal-weight forecast combination as in Aiolfi et al. (2011).

As discussed in Edge et al. (2010), Edge and Gürkaynak (2010), and Wang (2009) the forecasts beyond two quarters from models or from professional forecasters generally examined in the literature are very poor. The models and judgmental forecasts have some nowcasting accuracy, but almost no forecasting ability from one-quarter ahead and on as they are beaten even by naïve constant growth models. In fact, these poor medium run forecast results is one reason why the nowcasting literature with mixed frequency has flourished (Giannone et al., 2008). In this chapter, we choose to focus on the comparison of informative short-run forecasts rather than discussing which models are best at scoring higher in uninformative medium or long-run results for output growth.

We find that recessions are generally harder to forecast than expansions for all models examined. The univariate AR(2) model, the MS model, and the forecast combination have the best forecast ability during expansions, significantly better than the DSGE model, and the VAR model with the term spread, but comparable to the BVAR (at two-quarter ahead horizon). The findings suggest that by using simple univariate linear autoregressive models of GDP growth, one would have gotten in real time as good as forecasts during expansions than any other model and the professional forecasters.

The Blue Chip forecasts of output growth are outperformed by the AR(2) and the MS models and the forecast combination during expansions and by the DFMS model during recessions. Although the Blue Chip forecasts are very similar to the ones from the DFMS model for the full sample, they are worse and significantly different during recession periods. Interestingly, the BC forecasts do not track well the variance of GDP growth, particularly at one-quarter horizon.

The autoregressive model associated with the non-linear dynamic factor model (AR-DFMS) displays the best real-time forecast accuracy for recessions. Even though the professional forecasters have information advantage over all models, the AR-DFMS model shows short-run improvements, particularly with respect to the timing and depth of recessions in real time. The reason for its successful performance is that this model uses not only information from GDP growth but also from monthly coincident series that signal a deterioration of the economy early on. The forecast ability of the model is also closely related to the dynamics of its real-time probabilities of recession, which increase around the beginning of recessions and remain high until around their trough. The

---

[17] The Greenbook forecasts are only available with a lag of 5 years. The latest forecasts available from the Philadelphia Fed website at the time this chapter was written were up to 2006.

accuracy of GDP growth forecasts from the AR–DFMS model is, thus, closely related to the ability of the model to forecast recessions in real time.

Combining all forecasts from the models and from the Blue Chip indicators using equal weight average results in slight better accuracy compared to the simple AR(2), but the differences in forecasts are not statistically significant. The forecast combination is outperformed by the AR-DFMS model and the BC forecasts for the full sample and during recessions at one and two-quarter horizons. The forecast combination is also outperformed by the CDR and MS models during recessions at the two-quarter horizon.

In summary, the results suggest that (a) it is hard to beat the univariate AR(2) model for short-term forecasts of U.S. real GDP growth, particularly for expansions. Its performance is followed by the MS model and the professional forecasts; (b) the DSGE models, VAR models, and BVAR models are commonly used but are outperformed by forecasts from simple autoregressive model during normal times; (c) it is harder to predict output growth during recessions than during expansions. Most models perform poorly in forecasting output growth during recessions. In particular, they miss the timing of output downfall and its intensity during recessions. The DFMS model yields the best forecasts as it allows for regime shifts and includes timely monthly information from several variables other than GDP; (d) pooling forecasts does not significantly improves precision compared to the autoregressive model during expansions. It is outperformed by several models during recessions, as it does not track well the volatility of GDP growth (particularly for two-quarters ahead).

Thus, we find that there are large gains in using distinct models to forecast output growth during normal times and models to forecast output growth during recessions. Although the DSGE and VAR models might be a useful story-telling tool to evaluate policy during normal times, there are substantial gains in forecasting output growth around recessions using non-linear models designed for periods of abrupt changes. By using and comparing forecasts from different models, especially those designed to handle regime changes and non-linearities, economic agents and Central Bankers can hedge against abrupt changes and obtain more informative forecasts at times of large uncertainty such as around business cycle turning points, when most linear models break down.

The chapter is organized as follows. Section 2 describes the forecasting models, and the Blue Chip Indicators. Section 3 describes the real-time data and studies the ability of the models and the professional forecasters in forecasting the economy in real time. Section 4 concludes.

2. FORECASTING MODELS

We examine the forecasts of GDP growth from the Blue Chip indicators, and seven linear and non-linear, structural and reduced form models. We consider a univariate linear autoregressive model (AR) as a benchmark, and two univariate non-linear models:

the Cumulative Depth of Recession model (CDR) from Beaudry and Koop (1993), and the Markov Switching model (MS). We also investigate the performance of four multivariate models: the structural DSGE model, several versions of the reduced-form linear VAR, BVAR, and the non-linear Dynamic Factor Model with Regime Switching model.

2.1. Benchmark Univariate Linear AR Model

Let y_t be the log of real GDP and $\Delta = 1 - L$, where L is the lag operator. The model is:

$$\Delta y_t = c + \phi_1 \Delta y_{t-1} + \cdots + \phi_p \Delta y_{t-p} + \varepsilon_t \quad \varepsilon_t \sim WN(0, \sigma^2). \tag{1}$$

Using Akaike and Schwarz information criteria, one-quarter ahead Theil inequality coefficients, and root mean squared forecast errors (RMSFE), we find that the best specification (order of p) for GDP growth is an AR(2) process. In addition, we estimate the model recursively with different lags using real-time data, and find that $p = 2$ is uniformly better in terms of AIC for most part of the sample. We use forecasts obtained from the AR(2) model as a benchmark to compare with the other models. This is the same benchmark used in Edge et al. (2010), Krane (2011), Wolters (2010), and Del Negro and Schorfheide (2013), and many others. The simple linear univariate AR(2) offers an interesting comparison with the more complicated models as it has been shown in several papers to have a comparable or better forecasting performance.

2.2. Current Depth of Recession

Beaudry and Koop (BK 1993) extend the autoregressive representation of output growth to allow for asymmetric persistence. The asymmetry is examined by allowing the depth of a current recession to have an impact in the path of future fluctuations. In BK's (1993) current depth of recession model (CDR) output growth is defined as the gap between the current level of output and its historical maximum level at horizon j. We extend our benchmark AR(2) model in Eq. (1) as:

$$\Delta y_t = c + \phi_1 \Delta y_{t-1} + \phi_2 \Delta y_{t-2} + \theta CDR_{t-1} + \varepsilon_{cdr,t} \tag{2}$$
$$CDR_t = \max(0, \{y_{t-j} - y_t\}_{j \geq 0}).$$

The lag $p = 2$ is also the selected specification in BK (1993), based on Akaike and Schwarz information criteria. The model implies that if current output growth is below the level value of the previous peak, the difference is positive and hence the economy is in recession. Otherwise the economy is in an expansion and the value of CDR_t is zero.

2.3. Judgmental Forecast: Blue Chip Economic Indicators

The Blue Chip Economic Indicator (BC) is a compilation of macroeconomic forecasts of the U.S. economy from about 50 major investment and commercial banks, financial and industrial firms, universities, and economic consulting firms. The quarterly forecasts are available on a monthly basis. The BC forecasts for GDP growth is the average of the panelists' projections and is released on the tenth of each month for responses based on information for the previous month. Before the official GDP growth observation for each quarter is released by the Bureau of Economic Analysis, the BC produces three forecasts for the quarter. For example, GDP growth in the first quarter of 2011 is forecast in the February 2011 survey based on information available as of the end of January; in the March 2011 survey based on information in the end of February; and in the April 2011 survey with information up to the end of March 2011.

2.4. Dynamic Stochastic General Equilibrium Model

In this chapter we consider the medium-scale DSGE model of Smets and Wouters' (SW 2007) to form forecasts of GDP growth. The description of the model in this section follows closely (SW 2007), Edge et al. (2010), and Del Negro and Schorfheide (2013). SW's (2007) framework is based on Christiano et al. (2005) model, and it consists of a real business cycle model with nominal and real rigidities. In addition to sticky prices and wages, it contains real rigidities in the form of habit formation in consumption, adjustment cost in investment in capital accumulation, and variable capacity utilization.

The model comprises households, firms, and a monetary authority. Households maximize a non-separable utility function with goods and labor effort over an infinite life horizon. Consumption is related to time-varying external habit. Labor is heterogeneous across households in the sense that there is a union that allows for some monopoly power over wages. This enables introduction of Calvo rigidities in wages. Households own capital and rent its services to firms. Their investment decisions are affected by capital adjustment costs: as rental price increases, capital utilization can be more intensive but at a variable cost.

There is monopolistic competition in the markets for intermediate goods. The firms rent labor via a union and capital from households to produce differentiated goods, setting their prices according to the Calvo model. These intermediate goods are aggregated into a final good by different firms in a perfectly competitive final-good sector. In addition to Calvo setting in prices and wages, prices that are not re-optimized are assumed to be partially indexed to past inflation. Thus, prices depend on current and expected marginal costs as well as past inflation. Marginal costs depend on the price of factor inputs. Similarly, wages are a function of current and expected marginal rates of substitution between leisure and consumption and past wage inflation.

Following Del Negro and Schorfheide (2013), we assume that the series used in the model contain a stochastic trend rather than a determinist trend as in SW. Thus, all series are detrended by $Z_t = e^{\gamma t + \frac{1}{1-\alpha}\tilde{z}_t}$, where γ is the steady state growth rate of the economy, α is the income share of capital net of markups and fixed costs, and

$\tilde{z}_t = \rho_z \tilde{z}_{t-1} + \sigma_z \varepsilon_{z,t}$. Hence, the growth rate of Z_t in deviation from γ is:

$$z_t = \ln\left(\frac{Z_t}{Z_{t-1}}\right) - \gamma = \frac{1}{1-\alpha}(\rho_z - 1)\tilde{z}_{t-1} + \frac{1}{1-\alpha}\sigma_z \varepsilon_{z,t}. \tag{3}$$

The detrended variables are expressed in log deviations from their non-stochastic steady state. Most of the resulting log-linearized equilibrium conditions are the same as in SW such as the Euler equation, the optimality condition for capital producers, the arbitrage condition between the return to capital and the riskless rate, and the optimality condition determining the rate of capital utilization. The only two equilibrium conditions that change under the assumption that technology has a unit root rather than a stationary trend are the equilibrium production function and the equilibrium resource constraint. These equations are reduced from the terms involving $\frac{1}{1-\alpha}\tilde{z}_t$.[18]

The model has seven observable variables. The observable variables are quarterly growth rate of real output, consumption, investment and real wage, and quarterly log hours worked, inflation, and nominal interest rates. The model is cast in state space form mapping these observable variables into the 14 endogenous variables. The stochastic behavior of the system of linear rational expectations equations is driven by seven exogenous disturbances: total factor productivity, investment-specific technology, risk premium, exogenous spending, price mark-up, wage mark-up, and monetary policy shocks.

The model is estimated using Bayesian methods, with the same priors as SW (2007). The priors are combined with the conditional density of the observables to obtain the posterior distribution. The moments and quantiles of the posterior distribution are obtained via Markov Chain Monte Carlo (MCMC) simulation, using the Random–Walk Metropolis algorithm. The sequences of draws from the posterior distribution can be used to obtain numerical approximations of the moments, and predictive density distribution. The model is estimated for a given data vintage, and the forecasts are obtained from the predictive distribution and posterior modes of each parameter.[19]

2.5. Vector Autoregressive Model

Let $\Delta \mathbf{Y}_t$ be a nx1 vector containing the values that n variables take at date t. The reduced form VAR is:

$$\Delta \mathbf{Y}_t = \mathbf{a} + \mathbf{A}_1 \Delta \mathbf{Y}_{t-1} + \cdots + \mathbf{A}_p \Delta \mathbf{Y}_{t-p} + \mathbf{u}_t \quad \mathbf{u}_t \sim (0, \Theta). \tag{4}$$

The assumption that $\Delta \mathbf{Y}_t$ follows a vector autoregression corresponds to the idea that p lags are sufficient to summarize all of the dynamic correlations among elements of $\Delta \mathbf{Y}_t$. Notice that the parameters of the reduced-form VAR include contemporaneous relations among the endogenous variables. To see this, let $\mathbf{x}_t$ be an $[(np+1) \times 1]$ vector containing

---

[18] For details on the equilibrium conditions and their derivation see Del Negro and Schorfheide (2013), and for a full version of the log-linearized version of the estimated model see SW (2003, 2007).

[19] For a detailed explanation see Del Negro and Schorfheide (2013).

a constant and the p lags of each of the elements of $\Delta \mathbf{Y}_t$ and $\mathbf{A}'$ be a $[n \times (np + 1)]$ matrix of coefficients:

$$\mathbf{x}_t \equiv \begin{bmatrix} 1 \\ \Delta \mathbf{Y}_{t-1} \\ \Delta \mathbf{Y}_{t-2} \\ \vdots \\ \Delta \mathbf{Y}_{t-p} \end{bmatrix} \quad \text{and} \quad \mathbf{A}' \equiv [\mathbf{a}\ \boldsymbol{\alpha}_1\ \boldsymbol{\alpha}_2 \cdots \boldsymbol{\alpha}_p].$$

The standard vector autoregressive system can then be written as:

$$\Delta \mathbf{Y}_t = \mathbf{A}' \mathbf{x}_t + \mathbf{u}_t, \tag{5}$$

where $\mathbf{u}_t$ is the vector of zero mean disturbances, which are independent of $\mathbf{x}_t$, or as:

$$\Delta y = (\mathbf{I}_M \otimes x)\alpha + u \tag{6}$$

with $\alpha = vec(A)$ and $u \sim N(0, \Theta \otimes \mathbf{I}_T)$. The least squares estimators (OLS) of $\mathbf{A}$ is:

$$\underset{[nx\{np+1\})]}{\hat{\mathbf{A}}'} = \left[\sum_{t=1}^{T} \Delta \mathbf{Y}_t \mathbf{x}_t'\right] \left[\sum_{t=1}^{T} \mathbf{x}_t \mathbf{x}_t'\right]^{-1},$$

From the regression of ΔY_{jt} on $\mathbf{x}_t$:

$$\Delta Y_{jt} = \boldsymbol{\alpha}_j \mathbf{x}_t + u_{jt} \tag{7}$$

we obtain the estimated coefficient vector:

$$\underset{[1x\{np+1\})]}{\hat{\boldsymbol{\alpha}}_j'} = \left[\sum_{t=1}^{T} \Delta Y_{jt} \mathbf{x}_t'\right] \left[\sum_{t=1}^{T} \mathbf{x}_t \mathbf{x}_t'\right]^{-1},$$

which corresponds to the jth row of $\hat{\mathbf{A}}'$. Given that only predetermined variables are on the right side of the equations, and that the error terms are serially uncorrelated, OLS estimates of the VAR coefficients are consistent. Further, if the disturbances are normal, OLS is efficient. In fact, VAR with same right-hand side variables is a Seemingly Unrelated Model (SUR), which implies that the estimates are efficient regardless on the contemporaneous correlations among the disturbances.

VARs have been widely used as a tool to study the relationship of economic series, the dynamic impact of shocks on the system of variables, and also for forecasting. It has also been used to compare actual data with data generated by DSGE models with calibrated parameters. VAR models are one of the tools used by Central Banks to conduct policy analysis and for economic forecasting.

We estimate a baseline VAR model with three series generally used in New Keynesian VARs: growth rate of real GDP, inflation rate, unemployment rate, and interest rates.

These are the same series used in several recent papers such as Koop and Korobilis (2010), Cogley and Sargent (2005), Primiceri (2005), and Koop et al. (2009), among many others.

Given the importance of the financial sector in the recent financial crisis, we also estimate alternative VARs using additionally several measures of term and default spreads (VAR-Fin). The details of the data are described in Section 3.3. The VARs are estimated with two lags.

2.6. Bayesian Vector Autoregressive Model

We also consider the BVAR proposed in Koop and Korobilis (2010). The model and series used are the same as in the baseline VAR discussed in the previous section, but it is estimated with Bayesian methods. The parameters of the model are assumed to be random variables associated with prior probabilities. The likelihood function of (6) can be obtained from the sampling density, $p(y|\alpha, \Theta)$.

Koop and Korobilis (2010) propose several alternative priors and estimation methods for BVARs. They show that all methods yield similar result.[20] We follow Koop and Korobilis (2010) and Del Negro and Schorfheide (2011) and use Minnesota priors. This implies that $\otimes$ is replaced by an estimate, and the prior for α assumes that:

$$\alpha \sim N(\underline{\alpha}_{nM}, \underline{V}_{nM}).$$

The Minnesota prior yields simple posterior distribution using the Normal distribution:

$$\alpha|y \sim N(\overline{\alpha}_{nM}, \overline{V}_{nM}),$$

where

$$\overline{V}_{nM} = [\underline{V}_{nM}^{-1} + (\hat{\Theta}^{-1} \otimes (x'x))]^{-1}$$

and

$$\overline{\alpha}_{nM} = \overline{V}_{nM}[\underline{V}_{nM}^{-1}\underline{\alpha}_{nM} + (\hat{\Theta}^{-1} \otimes x)'y].$$

The prior coefficient $\overline{\alpha}_{nM}$ is set to zero, including the first parameter of the lag of each variable (as the data considered are stationary). The variance-covariance matrix $\otimes$ is assumed to be diagonal with elements obtained from regressing each dependent variable on an intercept and four lags of all variables.[21]

The use of Minnesota priors allows simple analytical posterior and predictive results. The model is, thus, estimated using Monte Carlo integration. At each real-time recursive estimation 1000 parameters are drawn, and for the forecasts, 50 are drawn from the predictive density for each parameter draw (50 × 1000). The BVAR is estimated with four lags as in Koop and Korobilis (2010).

---

[20] Carriero et al. (2011) also find that choices related to priors, selection of hyper-parameters, and forecast construction do not affect substantially the point and density forecasting performance of BVAR models.

[21] The restrictions on coefficients become tighter at longer lags with prior variance depending on the inverse square of lag length.

2.7. Univariate Markov Switching Model

We apply the version of the univariate Markov switching model (MS) in Hamilton (1994) to predict output growth. As before, let Δy_t be the growth rate of real GDP:

$$\Delta y_t = \mu_{S_t} + \rho \Delta y_{t-1} + \cdots + \rho_r \Delta y_{t-r} + \varepsilon_t$$
$$\mu_{S_t} = \mu_0 + \mu_1 S_t \quad \mu_0 < 0 \tag{8}$$
$$\varepsilon_t \sim N(0, \sigma_\varepsilon^2).$$

$S_t = \{0, 1\}$ is an unobserved state variable that enables the parameter μ_{S_t} to switch between two regimes, following a first-order Markov process with transition probabilities $p_{ij} = \Pr[S_t = j | S_{t-1} = i]$, where $\sum_{j=0}^{1} p_{ij} = 1$, $i, j = 0, 1$. The growth rate of economic activity switches back and forth from μ_0 to $\mu_0 + \mu_1$. When $\mu_0 < 0$ and $\mu_0 + \mu_1 > 0$, the model captures business cycle phases representing economic contractions and economic expansions, respectively. The estimated model can be used to draw probabilities of the unobservable states representing business cycle phases, that is, filtered probabilities conditional on current information set I_t denoted $\Pr[S_t = j | I_t]$, or smoothed probabilities obtained by backward recursion based on the full sample information set I_T, denoted $\Pr[S_t = j | I_T]$.

McConnell and Perez-Quiros (2000) found evidence of a structural break in the volatility of U.S. economic growth towards stabilization in the first quarter of 1984. This result has been further investigated by many authors and the period post-1984 has been dubbed the Great Moderation.[22] One implication of this break, as discussed in Chauvet and Potter (2002, 2005) and Chauvet and Su (2013), among many others, is that the smoothed probabilities from the standard Markov switching model miss the U.S. recessions post-1984.[23] We augment the model by allowing y_t to follow two independent two-state Markov processes: one representing switches between economic recessions and expansions and the other that captures permanent structural breaks. The Markov process for detecting structural break has a switching drift and variance as proposed in Chib (1998):

$$\alpha_{D_t} = \alpha_0 (1 - D_t) + \alpha_1 D_t$$
$$\sigma_{D_t}^2 = \sigma_0^2 (1 - D_t) + \sigma_1^2 D_t,$$

where $D_t = 0$ if $t < t^*$ and $D_t = 1$ otherwise, and t^* is the break date. The transition probabilities for the Markov process are set to capture the endogenous permanent break as:

$$\Pr[D_t = 0 | D_{t-1} = 0] = q \quad 0 < q < 1$$
$$\Pr[D_t = 1 | D_{t-1} = 1] = 1.$$

---

[22] Chauvet and Popli (2003) find evidence of multitple structural volatility breaks in many industrialized countries.

[23] Extensions of the model that include other series (e.g., the DFMS model, or Nalewaik, 2011), or that explicitly takes into account pulse or dummy breaks (e.g., Kim and Nelson, 1999; Chauvet and Su, 2013 etc.) overcome this problem. For a discussion, see Chauvet and Su (2013).

The linear autoregressive dynamics or order $r = 1$ is found to be the best specification in characterizing business cycle phases, and in minimizing loss functions such as BIC and AIC criteria.

Following Hamilton (1994), forecasts from the univariate Markov switching model are obtained as follows. At first, suppose $\{S_t\}$ is observed. Then, the h-period ahead forecast for μ_{S_t} is:

$$E(\mu_{St+h}|S_t) = \mu_0 + \{\pi_1 + \lambda^m(S_t - \pi_1)\}(\mu_1 - \mu_0), \qquad (9)$$

where $\lambda \equiv (-1 + p_{11} + p_{00})$ and $\pi_1 = (1 - p_{00})/(1 - p_{11} + 1 - p_{00})$. The optimal forecast of $z_{t+h} = \rho \Delta y_{t-1+h} + \cdots + \rho_r \Delta y_{t-r+h} + \varepsilon_{t+h}$ is:

$$E(z_{t+h}|z_t, z_{t-1}, \ldots, z_{t-r+1}) = e_1' \Phi^h [z_t \ \ z_{t-1} \ \ \cdots \ \ z_{t-r+1}]', \qquad (10)$$

where e_1' corresponds to the first row of the (r x r) identity matrix and Φ is the (r x r) matrix of autoregressive coefficients. Substituting (9) and (10) in (8) we get:

$$\begin{aligned} E(y_{t+h}|S_t, I_t) = {} & \mu_0 + \{\pi_1 + \lambda^m(S_t - \pi_1)\}(\mu_1 - \mu_0) \\ & + e_1' \Phi^m[(y_t - \mu_{s_t}) \ \ (y_{t-1} - \mu_{s_{t-1}}) \ \ \cdots \ \ (y_{t-r+1} - \mu_{s_{t-r+1}})], \end{aligned} \qquad (11)$$

where I_t is the set of observables variables. Applying the law of iterated expectations to (11) we obtain the h-ahead forecast, which is based only on observable variables:

$$E(y_{t+h}|I_t) = \mu_0 + \{\pi_1 + \lambda^m[\Pr(S_t = 1|I_t) - \pi_1]\}(\mu_1 - \mu_0) + e_1' \Phi^m \tilde{\mathbf{y}}_t, \qquad (12)$$

where $\tilde{y}_{it} = y_{t-i+1} - \mu_0 \Pr(S_{t-i+1} = 0|I_t) - \mu_1 \Pr(S_{t-i+1} = 1|I_t)$ is the ith element of the (r x 1) vector $\tilde{\mathbf{y}}_t$.

2.8. Dynamic Factor Model with Markov Switching

We extend the dynamic factor model with regime switching approach in Chauvet (1998) to study the dynamics of output growth in a reduced-form multivariate setting, as explained below. This model takes into account the dynamic comovements of several variables and, therefore, captures pervasive cyclical fluctuations in various sectors of economic activity. Since recessions and expansions are caused by different shocks over time, the inclusion of different variables increases the ability of the model in representing and signaling phases of the business cycle. In addition, the combination of variables reduces measurement errors in the individual series and, consequently, the likelihood of false signaling turning points. Thus, this model allows representation of business cycle as the comovements of several sectors, with potential asymmetries in its phases, as suggested in Diebold and Rudebusch (1996).

The model is applied to variables that move contemporaneously with GDP. The series used are the same four coincident series used by the NBER Business Cycle Dating Committee to date recessions: employment, sales, personal income, and industrial production.

The model extracts the co-movements in these coincident series into a single unobserved common factor. This latent factor follows a two-state Markov switching process, capturing recession and expansion phases of the business cycle.

Let y_{it}^* be the log level of the ith series that move simultaneously with GDP, and Δy_{it}^* be the first difference of y_{it}^*.[24] The dynamic factor model with regime switching model (DFMS) is:

$$
\begin{bmatrix} \Delta y_{1t}^* \\ \Delta y_{2t}^* \\ \Delta y_{3t}^* \\ \Delta y_{4t}^* \end{bmatrix} = \begin{bmatrix} \lambda_1 \\ \lambda_2 \\ \lambda_3 \\ \lambda_4 \end{bmatrix} F_t + \begin{bmatrix} v_{1t} \\ v_{2t} \\ v_{3t} \\ v_{4t} \end{bmatrix}.
\tag{13}
$$

That is, the first difference of each series is modeled as an unobserved component common to each series, given by the dynamic factor F_t, and an idiosyncratic component to each series, given by v_{it}, $i = 1, \ldots, 4$. The factor loadings λ_i measure the sensitivity of the series to the dynamic factor.[25] The common component is assumed to follow a stationary autoregressive process:

$$
\varphi(L)(F_t - \mu_{S_t}^*) = \eta_t \quad \eta_t \sim N(0, \sigma_\eta^2)
\tag{14}
$$

$$
\mu_{S_t}^* = \mu_0^* + \mu_1^* S_t \qquad \mu_0^* < 0,
$$

where η_t is the common shock and $\varphi(L)$ is a lag polynomial with all roots outside the unit circle. The model separates out common signal underlying the observed variables from individual variations in each sector of the economic activity. The dynamic factor captures widespread simultaneous downturns and upturns of several sectors of the economy, which are the most important features of business cycles as proposed by the pioneer economists Burns and Mitchell's (1946). On the other hand, if only one of the variables declines (e.g., industrial production), this would not characterize a recession in the model, and it would be captured by the industrial production idiosyncratic term. A recession (expansion) will occur when all variables decrease (increase) at about the same time. That is, v_{it} and η_t are assumed to be mutually independent at all leads and lags, for all $i = 1, \ldots, 4$ variables, and $d_i(L)$ is diagonal.

The asymmetries across different states of the business cycle is modeled by allowing the intercept of the factor to switch regimes according to the Markov variable, $S_t^* = 0, 1$. That is, the economy can be either in an expansion state $(S_t^* = 1)$, where the mean growth rate is positive; or in a contraction phase $(S_t^* = 0)$, with a negative mean growth rate. The switches from one state to another is determined by the transition probabilities of the first-order two-state Markov process with transition probabilities $P(S_t^* = 1|S_{t-1}^* = 1) = p_{11}^*$

---

[24] The series used in estimating the model are the same coincident variables used by the NBER is calling recessions: sales, personal income, employment, and industrial production, as discussed in more detail in Section 3.2.

[25] The factor loading of one of the coincident series is set equal to one to provide a scale for the dynamic factor. This normalization is a necessary condition for identification of the factor. Notice that the choice of scale does not affect any of the time series properties of the dynamic factor or the correlation with its components.

and $P(S_t^* = 0|S_{t-1}^* = 0) = p_{00}^*$. Finally, the idiosyncratic components are assumed to follow a stationary autoregressive process:

$$d_i(L)v_{it} = u_{it} \quad u_{it} \sim i.i.d.N(0, \Omega). \tag{15}$$

The model yields estimated filtered and smoothed probabilities of the recessions and expansions at time t conditional on current data or the full sample, denoted $P(S_t^* = j|I_t)$ and $P(S_t^* = j|I_T)$, $j = 0, 1$, respectively, and the filtered and smoothed business cycle index, denoted $E(F_t|I_t)$ and $E(F_t|I_T)$, respectively. The results from dynamic factor models with Markov regime switching, as estimated in Chauvet (1998), Chauvet and Hamilton (2006), and Chauvet and Piger (2008, 2013) are not affected by the structural break in variance.

The DFMS business cycle index can be interpreted as a nowcast of business cycle, but it is not a direct forecast of GDP growth, as it neither includes this series nor projects it forward. We augment Eq. (1) with the probabilities of recession and the business cycle index in the AR-DFMS model:

$$\Delta y_t = c + \nu(L)\Delta y_t + \gamma(L)F_t + \delta(L)P(S_t = i|I_t) + \upsilon_t$$
$$\upsilon_t \sim WN(0, \sigma_\upsilon^2), \tag{16}$$

where $\nu(L)$, $\gamma(L)$, and $\delta(L)$ are lag polynomials, with the roots of $\nu(L)$ outside of the unit circle.[26]

Chauvet et al. (2013) also examine the marginal prediction of a linear version of the dynamic factor model in forecasting output growth. In this case, the AR(2) is augmented based on lags of factor that is produced as a linear combination of the coincident series Δy_{it}^*, and it does not include the term $P(S_t = i|I_t)$.

2.9. Forecast Combination

An interesting question is whether a combination of the model forecasts and subjective forecasts from the Blue Chip produces better results than the best single ones. This is particularly interesting, given that the set of information across some of the models are different and the judgmental and AR-DFMS model forecasts also include more timely monthly series. In addition, judgmental forecasts from the Blue Chip incorporate subjective information as well as expectations based on timely announcements of economic policy.

Aiolfi et al. (2011) find that the pooling that yields more accuracy gains is the combination model-based forecasts from linear and non-linear univariate specifications, and multivariate factor-augmented models with judgmental survey forecasts obtained achieved a simple equal-weighted average. We follow these authors and obtain the pooling of

---

[26] The standard errors are obtained using bootstrap.

forecasts $\hat{y}_{T+k|T}$ at horizon k as:

$$\hat{y}_{T+k|T} = \sum_{k=1}^{M} \hat{y}_{k,\,T+k|T},\qquad(17)$$

where M is the number of forecast combined.

3. FORECAST COMPARISON: REAL-TIME PERFORMANCE

Models that exhibit reasonable power in explaining the average linear dynamics of output over time may show poor performance during some events, such as recessions, or financial, currency, and banking crises, to name a few. Many papers have shown that the largest errors in forecasting output occur around business cycle turning points (see, e.g., Oh and Waldman, 1990; Beaudry and Koop, 1993; Chauvet and Guo, 2003). This has been particularly the case for recessions, which most models show a lesser forecast accuracy.

In this section we investigate the ability of models and professional forecasters to forecast the dynamics of output growth in real time as well as during expansions and recessions. We use unrevised real-time data that would have actually been available at any given point in time. The availability of these unrevised series allows analysis of the model performance at the time events were taking place.

We use annualized quarter-over-quarter changes in GDP growth, not annual growth rates, and focus on short horizons. Also, we obtain independent out-of-sample k-period ahead forecasts over the forecast period, in which the parameters of the model are recursively reestimated at each new observation T and the $T + k$ periods ahead forecasts are computed every time based on information at T.[27] As discussed in Tashman (2000), this disentangles potential impact on the forecast errors of special events associated with a unique origin and also reduces the sensitivity of the errors to rapid changes across phases of the business cycle. Most important, this emulates the real-time forecasting procedures of economic agents and Central Banks at that the time events were occurring.

3.1. Forecast Evaluation

We examine GDP growth forecasts of the five models described above and the judgmental-based forecasts from the Blue Chip indicators.[28] Summing up, the models examined and their acronyms are:

Model 1 – Benchmark AR(2)

Model 2 – Current Depth of Recession (CDR)

---

[27] We do not evaluate pseudo-out-of-sample forecasts in this paper. For a discussion of these results see Chauvet et al. (2013).

[28] The best specifications of the models in terms of the lags of the common factor and the idiosyncratic components were selected based on the Bayesian and Akaike Information Criteria, root mean squared error and Theil coefficient.

Model 3 – Dynamic Stochastic General Equilibrium (DSGE)

Model 4 – Vector Autoregressive Model (VAR)

Model 5 – Vector Autoregressive Model with Financial Variables (VAR-Fin)

Model 6 – Bayesian Vector Autoregressive Model (BVAR)

Model 7 – Univariate Markov Switching (MS)

Model 8 – AR-Dynamic Factor Model with Markov Switching (AR-DFMS)[29]

Judgmental Forecast - Blue Chip Indicators (BC)

Forecast Combination (FC)

We consider three loss functions: the RMSFE, Theil inequality coefficient (THEIL), and Pesaran and Timmermann (1992) sign test:

$$RMSFE = \sqrt{\frac{1}{N} \sum_{t=T+k}^{T+N} (\Delta \hat{y}_t - \Delta y_t)^2}$$

$$THEIL = \frac{\sqrt{\frac{1}{N} \sum_{t=T+k}^{T+N} (\Delta \hat{y}_t - \Delta y_t)^2}}{\sqrt{\frac{1}{N} \sum_{t=T+k}^{T+N} \Delta \hat{y}_t^2} + \sqrt{\frac{1}{N} \sum_{t=T+k}^{T+N} \Delta y_t^2}},$$

where T and N denote the number of observations in the estimation and forecast samples, respectively, k is the forecast horizon, $\Delta \hat{y}_t$ is the forecast and Δy_t is the observation. Note that Theil coefficient ranges between zero and one. For both loss functions zero is a perfect forecast. The RMSFE is scale-dependent while Theil is scale invariant. Although the dependent variable is the same across the models studied, we report both the total RMSFE of forecasts and the relative to the benchmark AR(2) model. We compute the RMSFE for the full sample, for expansion periods, and for recession periods as determined by the NBER Business Cycle Dating Committee.

Theil inequality coefficient can be decomposed into bias, variance, and covariance proportion:

Bias Proportion

$$\frac{\left(\frac{1}{N} \sum_{t=T+k}^{T+N} \Delta \hat{y}_t - \frac{1}{N} \sum_{t=T+k}^{T+N} \Delta y_t \right)^2}{\left(\frac{1}{N} \sum_{t=T+k}^{T+N} (\Delta \hat{y}_t - \Delta y_t)^2 \right)}$$

---

[29] A linear version of this model and its forecast are examined in Chauvet et al. (2013), and briefly discussed in Section 3.3.

Variance Proportion

$$\frac{[Stdev(\Delta \hat{y}_t) - Stdev(\Delta y_t)]^2}{\left(\frac{1}{N} \sum_{t=T+k}^{T+N} (\Delta \hat{y}_t - \Delta y_t)^2 \right)}$$

Covariance Proportion

$$\frac{2[1 - corr(\Delta \hat{y}_t, \Delta y_t)] Stdev(\Delta \hat{y}_t) Stdev(\Delta y_t)}{\left(\frac{1}{N} \sum_{t=T+k}^{T+N} (\Delta \hat{y}_t - \Delta y_t)^2 \right)}.$$

The bias and variance proportions measure, respectively, how far the mean and the variance of the forecast are from the mean and the variance of actual GDP growth. The covariance proportion is obtained by residual as the three components add up to one. Thus, the smaller the bias and variance proportions, the better the forecasts are. That is, ideally the largest fraction of the Theil coefficient should be from the covariance proportion.

We also consider the sign forecast test of Pesaran and Timmermann (1992). The test is based on the number of corrected predicted signs in the forecast series. Under the null hypothesis, the forecast $\Delta \hat{y}_{t+k}$ of the actual Δy_{t+k} have independent distributions, that is, the forecast values have no power to predict the sign of Δy_{t+k}. That is, it measures whether there is a significant difference between the observed probability of a correctly signed forecast and the estimate of this probability under the null. The corresponding statistic is:

$$S_n = \frac{(\hat{p} - p_*)}{[V(\hat{p}) - V(\hat{p}_*)]^{1/2}} \qquad S_n \xrightarrow{d} N(0, 1,),$$

where $\hat{p}$ is the sample estimate of the probability of a correctly signed forecast, $\hat{p}_*$ is the estimate of its expectation and $V(.)$ is their variance, obtained under the null.

3.2. Real-Time Data

In this section we provide a description of the data used in the estimation and forecasting process. The sample period used is determined by the common availability of all data.[30] All models are first estimated using data from 1964:Q2 to 1991:Q4. The models are recursively re-estimated for each quarter for the period starting in 1992:Q1 and ending in 2011:Q1 using only collected real-time realizations of the series as released at each quarter to generate k-quarter ahead forecasts.

The current U.S. real GDP series is obtained from the Bureau of Economic Analysis (BEA). All versions of the historical unrevised real-time GDP series released each month

---

[30] The real-time forecast sample is determined by limitations in the availability of some real-time variables for the DSGE model.

are collected and archived by the Federal Reserve Bank of Saint Louis and the Federal Reserve Bank of Philadelphia.[31] The quarterly real-time database used in this paper consists of realizations, or quarterly *vintages*, of the series as they would have appeared in the end of each quarter from 1992:Q1 to 2011:Q2. The sources and descriptions of other series used in the multivariate models are described below.

DSGE Model. We use the same series as SW (2007). Average weekly hours of production and non-supervisory employees for total private industries (HOUR), civilian employment (TCE), civilian non-institutional population (POP), and compensation per hour for the non-farm business sector (WAGE) are obtained from the Bureau of Labor Statistics (BLS). GDP deflator (GDPDEF), nominal personal consumption expenditures (NPCE), and nominal fixed private investment (NFPI) are obtained from the Bureau of Economic Analysis (BEA). The federal funds rate (FFR) is obtained from the Federal Reserve Board.

All nominal series are deflated using the GDP deflator. The series are transformed as in SW (2007). Real output, real consumption, real investment, and hours (times TCE/100) are in per capita terms obtained as 100 times the log of the ratio of these series to population. Inflation is the 100 times log first difference of the GDP deflator, and the annualized daily federal funds dates are converted to quarterly averages:

Real Output = 100xln ((GDP/GDPDEF)/POP);
Real Consumption = 100xln ((NCPE/GDPDEF)/POP)
Real Investment = 100xln ((NFPI/GDPDEF)/POP)
Real Wage = 100xln(WAGE/GDPDEF)
Hours = 100xln(WAGExTCE/100)/POP)
Inflation = 100xln(GDPDEF/GDPDEF(-1))
Interest Rates = FFR/4

The series are transformed into stationary according to the procedure described in sub-section 2.4.

VAR and BVAR Models. In addition to the GDP series used in all other models, the VAR and BVAR models use the same GDP price index and interest rates as in the DSGE model. However, the series are further differenced: inflation is the annualized second log difference of the GDP deflator, and interest rates are the first difference of the Federal Funds rate, as in Koop and Korobilis (2010).

We also consider as a fourth series in the baseline VAR model several versions of the default premium (i.e., the difference between bond yields with different credit ratings): the Baa and Aaa, Aaa and Treasury Bond 10- year, Baa minus Treasury-10 year. We also consider the term premium Treasury 10-year minus Treasury 5-year. The data are obtained from Haver-DLX.

---

[31] See Croushore and Stark (2001) for a description of the data and of the collection procedure. The data and information are available at http://www.phil.frb.org/research-and-data/real-time-center/real-time-data/data-files/ROUTPUT/

DFMS Model. The series used to estimate the DFMS model are U.S. monthly Industrial Production (IP) obtained from the Federal Reserve Board, Real Manufacturing and Trade Sales (MTS) and Real Personal Income excluding Transfer Payments (PILTP) obtained from the BEA, Payroll Employment (ENAP), and Total Civilian Employment (TCE) obtained from the BLS. These are the same four monthly variables used by the NBER Business Cycle Dating Committee in establishing the beginning and end of recession dates.

The real-time data used to estimate the DFMS model (PILTP, MTS, ENAP and IP) were obtained from a combination of the real-time datasets collected in Chauvet (1998), Chauvet and Hamilton (2006), Chauvet and Piger (2008), the Federal Reserve Bank of Philadelphia and the Federal Reserve Bank of Saint Louis archives. Real-time data for PILTP and MTS were hand collected as part of a larger real-time data collection project at the Federal Reserve Bank of St. Louis and first used in Chauvet and Piger (2008). The ENAP and IP data series were obtained from the Federal Reserve Bank of Philadelphia real-time data archive described in Croushore and Stark (2001). The real-time data for TCE were hand-collected as part of Chauvet (1998) and Chauvet and Hamilton (2006) and Chauvet and Piger's (2008) research, and some more recent data obtained from the Federal Reserve Bank of Saint Louis ALFRED archive.

Timing of Forecasts

The GDP series is first released based on preliminary and incomplete information, as it is the case of many macroeconomic variables. Multiple and often large revisions are implemented in subsequent releases in order to correct discrepancies caused by lags in the availability of primary data. There are three main releases of GDP for a quarter, which occur in the three subsequent months following that quarter. For example, the first release of GDP for the last quarter of a year occurs in the end of January of the following year, and is called "advance" version. The second release, named "second estimate" version, occurs in the end of February, and the "third estimate" release takes place in the end of March. After this "third estimate" release there are other revisions later onto include more complete information (annual or benchmark revisions, correction updates, etc.).

We use the "final" real-time release of GDP for each quarter.[32] Thus, the quarterly vintages are obtained from GDP data as available in the end of March, June, September and December of each year. For example, the vintage available in the first quarter of 1992 corresponds to GDP series for the fourth quarter of 1991 as available in March 1992, that is, the "final" estimate for this quarter. For each vintage the sample collected begins in the first quarter of 1964 and ends with the most recent data available for that vintage. The effective sample starts in 1964:Q2 after transforming the data in growth rates.

---

[32] We have also used the "advance" and "second" estimates. The results are discussed in Chauvet et al. (2013).

Table 3.1 Blue Chip Survey Dates and Forecasts

Blue Chip Survey Date	End of Estimation Sample T	Forecast Horizon		
		$k = 1$	$k = 2$	$k = 3$
Apr 1992	1991:Q4	1992:Q1	1992:Q2	1992:Q3
Jul 1992	1992:Q1	1992:Q2	1992:Q3	1992:Q4
Oct 1992	1992:Q2	1992:Q3	1992:Q4	1993:Q1
Jan 1992	1992:Q3	1992:Q4	1993:Q1	1993:Q2

As in Edge and Gürkaynak (2010), Edge et al. (2010), Krane (2011), and Del Negro and Schorfheide (2013), among others, we build vintages of real-time data available at the time of Blue Chip publication dates.[33] As explained in Section 2.3, the quarterly forecasts of the Blue Chip are available on a monthly basis and the surveys with forecasts of GDP growth are released on the tenth of each month for responses based on information for the previous month. We use the Blue Chip survey forecast for each quarter published in January, April, July, and October. For example, the forecast of GDP growth released in the April 10, 2008 survey is the k-quarter ahead forecast based on information as of the end of March 2008, which includes the "final" release of GDP for the fourth quarter of 2007. Hence, in this survey the "current" or "nowcast" forecast ($k = 0$) corresponds to GDP forecast of the fourth quarter of 2007, the one-quarter ahead ($k = 1$) is GDP growth projection for the first quarter of 2008, and the two-quarter ahead ($k = 2$) is projection for the second quarter of 2008, all based on the "final" release of GDP for 2007. Note in most cases, the vintage date for which the Blue Chip professional forecasters are surveyed falls after the release of the actual GDP by the BEA. As a result, the $k = 0$ forecast for the Blue Chip – which the Survey calls "one quarter ahead forecasts" in their publication – is actually the realized data for some dates. We, thus, focus instead on the comparison of the one and two quarter ahead forecasts of the BC with the $k = 1, 2$ of the models. Let $E(y_{T+k}|I_T)$ be the k-quarter ahead forecast of Δy_T made at T. The nowcast $k = 0$ is then $E(y_T|I_T)$, the one-quarter-ahead forecast $k = 1$ is $E(y_{T+1}|I_T)$, and the two quarter-ahead forecast $k = 2$ is $E(y_{T+2}|I_T)$.

We align the dates of the Blue Chip forecasts with the ones from the other models. That is, at each Blue Chip forecast survey, we use the data that were available on that date to estimate the AR(2), the CDR, the MS, the DSGE, and the DFMS models (see Table 3.1). The first forecast considered in the analysis is for 1992:Q1 (end of March/April

---

[33] For the DSGE model, the real-time dataset is from Edge and Gürkaynak (2010), updated in Del Negro and Schorfheide (2013), which were obtained from the Saint Louis Fed. The Blue Chip data are obtained from Del Negro and Schorfheide (2013).

1992 release using information up to the end of March) and the last one is for 2011:Q2 (end of June/July 2011 release using information up to the end of June).

For the real-time series used to estimate the DFMS model (PILTP, MTS, ENAP and IP), we use the *vintages* of these time series as they would have appeared at each month from April 1992 to June 2011. The series ENAP, IP, and PILTP are released for month $t - 1$ in month t. However, at time t, MTS is only available for month $t - 2$. We use MTS availability to restrict the month data to be included in a vintage estimation sample. That is, even though ENAP, IP, and PILTP are available for month $t - 1$ at time t, we only use at t their data up to $t - 2$ to balance it with the data for MTS. For example, ENAP, IP and PILTP are available up to February 1992 in the vintage for late March/early April 1992, but MTS is only available for January 1992. Thus, for this vintage we use all series up to January 1992.[34]

The DFMS model is estimated soon after the release of MTS data for that monthly vintage. For each vintage, the DFMS model is recursively estimated with the real-time data set, and monthly business cycle index and real-time probabilities of recessions are computed. The DFMS business cycle index can be interpreted as a nowcast of business cycle, but it is not a direct forecast of GDP growth, as it neither includes this series nor projects it forward. We use the business cycle index and the probabilities of recession as in Eq. (14) to obtain GDP growth forecasts from Eq. (17), pairing GDP with the ones used in BC and in the other models.

Note that this pairing generates information advantage for the Blue Chip forecast since the BC uses information all the way up to end of month prior to the survey date. For example, in the April 1992 survey, although the BC judgmental-based forecasts use the same GDP data as the models, they also include monthly information up to the end of March 1992. The DFMS model uses the same GDP data as the other models, but only monthly information up to January 1992.

We should stress that the estimation of all models are based solely on information that was available at each date, which aims to reproduce the forecasting problem of agents and Central Banks at the time the events were unfolding.

3.3. Real-Time Forecast Results

We examine the real-time GDP growth forecasts of the models described in section 3 and the judgmental-based forecasts from the Blue Chip indicators. As discussed earlier, our goal is to study short-term forecasts, as recent literature has shown that real-time forecasts of output growth from one-quarter and on are poor and uninformative (see, e.g., Wang,

---

[34] Although the DFMS model could be estimated using the only readily available information from ENAP and IP instead of waiting for the MTS data, we preferred to estimate the model with all series simultaneously, as the resulting indicator has been proved to be a reliable real-time indicator of business cycles (see Chauvet, 1998; Chauvet and Hamilton, 2006), and Chauvet and Piger (2008, 2013).

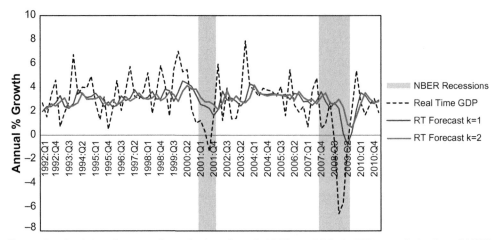

Figure 3.1 Real-time forecasts from the benchmark AR(2) model (—), GDP growth (- - -), and NBER recessions (shaded area).

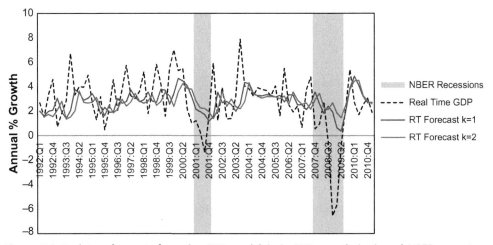

Figure 3.2 Real-time forecasts from the CDR model (—), GDP growth (- - -), and NBER recessions (shaded area).

2009; Edge et al., 2010; Edge and Gürkaynak, 2010). Hence we focus on steps up to two quarters ahead, using quarter-over-quarter growth changes in GDP.[35]

Figures 3.1–3.13 show actual GDP growth, and real-time out-of-sample forecasts for $k=1$ and $k=2$ from the models and from the Blue Chip, together with shaded areas

---

[35] Chauvet et al. (2013) examine longer horizons and different vintages and find that the qualitative results are similar to the ones found in this paper. In particular, the ranking of the models remains roughly the same – but the long run horizon forecasts are very poor for most models. In addition, using the "advance" and the "second" releases of GDP growth leads to an overall improved performance of the nonlinear time series models over the other ones.

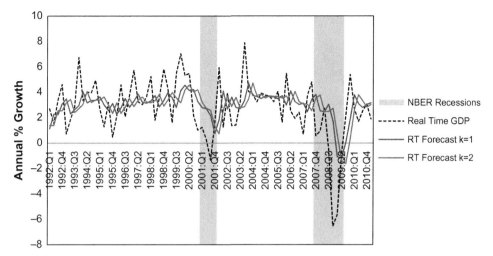

Figure 3.3 Real-time forecasts from the MS model (—), GDP growth (---), and NBER recessions (shaded area).

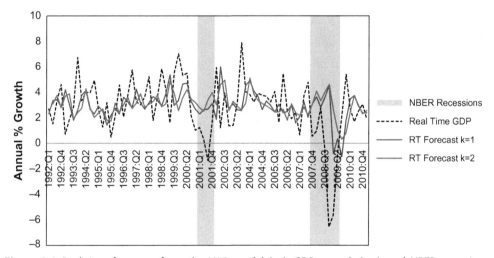

Figure 3.4 Real-time forecasts from the VAR model (—), GDP growth (---), and NBER recessions (shaded area).

for NBER recessions. We compute the Theil coefficient, the RMSFE, and Pesaran and Timmermann's (1992) test for the real-time out-of-sample period. We also report the RMSFE for output growth forecasts during recession and expansion periods as determined by the NBER.[36] Tables 3.2 and 3.3 report the loss functions for the different models.

[36] There are two recessions in the period analyzed. According to the NBER, the 2001 recession started in 2001:Q1 and ended in 2001:Q4. The 2007–2009 recession started in 2007:Q4 and ended in 2009:Q2.

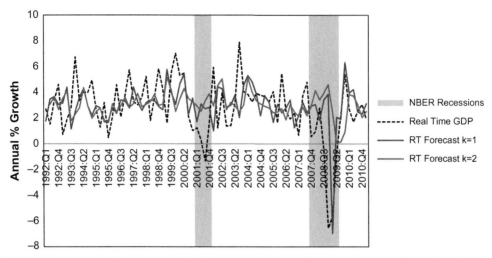

Figure 3.5 Real-time forecasts from the VAR-Fin Aaa-Baa model (—), GDP growth (- - -), and NBER recessions (shaded area).

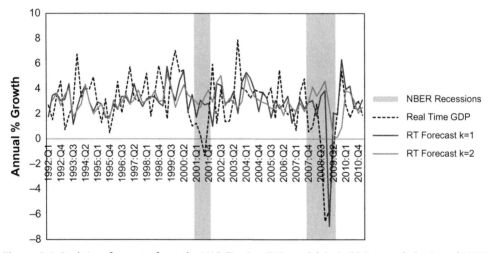

Figure 3.6 Real-time forecasts from the VAR-Fin Aaa-T10 model (—), GDP growth (- - -), and NBER recessions (shaded area).

3.3.1. Real-Time Out-of-Sample Period

The benchmark AR(2) model forecasts very well the mean of actual GDP growth, but does a poor job in predicting its volatility. This is reflected in the components of the Theil coefficient in Tables 3.1 and 3.2. The bias proportion is close to zero, but the variance proportion is around 50%, indicating that the model does not track well the variance of GDP growth.

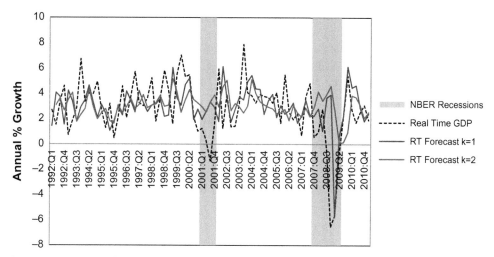

Figure 3.7 Real-time forecasts from the VAR-Fin Baa-T10 model (—), GDP growth (- - -), and NBER recessions (shaded area).

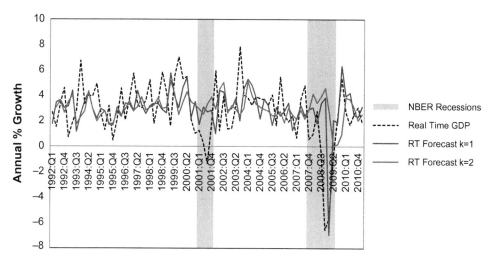

Figure 3.8 Real-time forecasts from the VAR-Fin T10-T5 model (—), GDP growth (- - -), and NBER recessions (shaded area).

The forecasts of the CDR model are similar to the benchmark autoregressive model, with the relative RMSFE close to one. However, the CDR model displays a slight reduction in the RMSFE for forecasts of output growth during recessions, and shows a modest improvement in tracking the variance of GDP growth. The variance proportion of the Theil coefficient is 43% and 46% for $k = 1$ and $k = 2$, respectively.

Both the benchmark and the CDR models have a very good accuracy in forecasting the mean of the series, with the bias proportion close to zero. Interestingly, the RMSFE

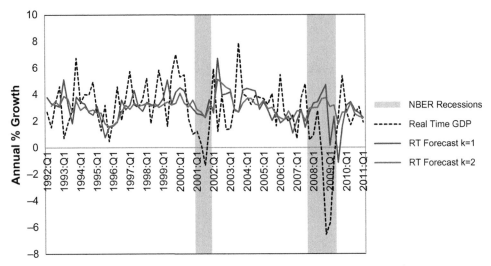

Figure 3.9 Real-time forecasts from the BVAR model (—), GDP growth (- - -), and NBER recessions (shaded area).

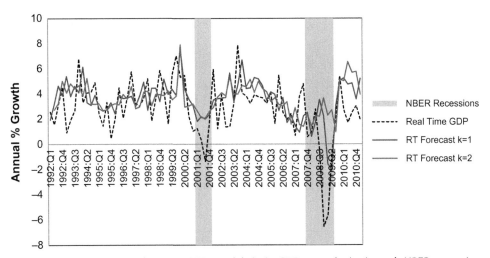

Figure 3.10 Real-time prediction DSGE model (—), GDP growth (- - -), and NBER recessions (shaded area).

for the simple univariate AR(2) model is lower compared to most multivariate models at the one and two-quarter horizons.

The performance of the univariate MS model is somewhat similar to the CDR and DSGE models with the relative RMSFE slightly below one for $k=1$ and $k=2$. The relative Theil coefficient of the MS model to the benchmark is below one for both horizons. However, the differences between these forecasts are not significant at the

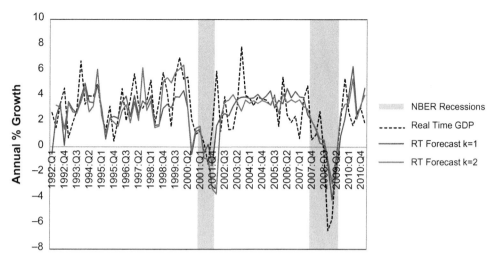

Figure 3.11a – Real-time Forecasts from the AR-DFMS model (—), GDP growth (- - -), and NBER recessions (shaded area).

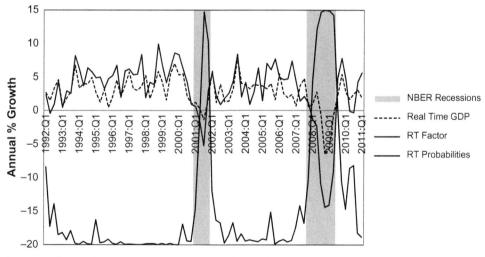

Figure 3.11b – Real-time Factor (—) and probabilities from the DFMS model (—), GDP growth (- - -), and NBER recessions (shaded area).

5% level using Diebold and Mariano's test (DM 1995). Nalewaik (2011) finds similar results extending Hamilton's model to consider three sates and additional series such as housing starts, GDI and unemployment rate. The forecasts are constructed similarly, based in Hamilton (1989,1994) as discussed in Section 2.7. The paper compares the results of this MS model with the Blue Chip forecasts, and finds that the performance varies across sub-samples and forecast horizons. In particular, it finds that for a longer sample starting

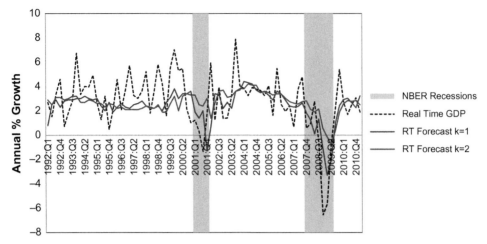

Figure 3.12 Real-time forecasts from the Blue Chip (—), GDP growth (- - -), and NBER recessions (shaded area).

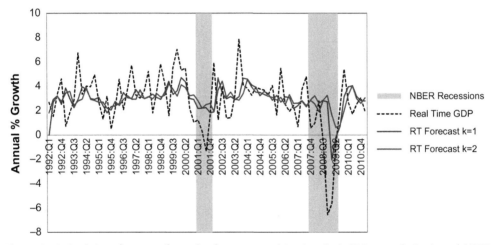

Figure 3.13 Real-time forecasts from the forecast combination (—) GDP growth (- - -), and NBER recessions (shaded area).

in 1981, the differences in forecasts are not statistically significant, but for a sample starting in 1993 there are gains at longer horizons ($k = 4, 5$).[37] However, as discussed earlier, the literature finds that the BC forecasts are not informative for GDP growth at horizons beyond two quarters. For example, Del Negro and Schorfheide (2013) also find that the RMSFEs of the DSGE model outperforms the BC forecasts at $k => 5$, while Edge et al. (2010), Edge and Gürkaynak (2010) find similar results for DSGE, VAR, and BVAR at long horizons. Edge and Gürkaynak (2010) and Wang (2009) show that these forecasts,

---

[37] The difference in forecast is also statistically different from the BC forecast for recession periods at four-quarter ahead.

Table 3.2 RMSFE, Theil Inequality, and PT Tests– Total and Relative to the Benchmark Real-Time Out-of-Sample One-Quarter Ahead Forecasts

Models	RMSFE			Theil Inequality Coefficient				
	Full Sample	Expansion	Recession	Total	Bias	Var	Cov	PT Test
AR(2)	2.150	1.752	3.735	0.322	0.003	0.471	0.526	3.819**
CDR	2.194	1.840	3.657	0.333	0.000	0.434	0.566	–
Relative	1.020	1.050	0.979	1.037				
DSGE	2.205	1.915	3.466	0.294	0.111	0.128	0.667	5.374**
Relative	1.025	1.093*	0.928	0.916*				1.407**
MS	2.111	**1.728**	3.644	0.311	0.010	0.390	0.600	5.437**
Relative	0.982	**0.986**	0.976	0.967				1.424**
BC	**1.923**	1.801	2.534	0.301	0.039	0.281	0.680	5.709**
Relative	**0.894****	1.028	0.679**	0.935				1.495**
AR-DFMS	**1.920**	1.879	**2.149**	**0.281**	0.007	0.075	0.918	4.500**
Relative	**0.893****	1.072	**0.575****	**0.874****				1.178**
BVAR	2.526	2.009	4.524	0.368	0.008	0.216	0.776	−0.269
Relative	1.175**	1.146**	1.211**	1.143**				−0.07**
VAR	2.452	1.985	4.296	0.360	0.005	0.249	0.746	2.527*
Relative	1.140**	1.133**	1.150**	1.120**				0.662**
VAR-Fin (Baa–Aaa)	2.349	1.966	3.929	0.335	0.007	0.111	0.882	3.818**
Relative	1.092*	1.122**	1.052	1.043				0.999
VAR-Fin (Aaa–T10)	2.441	2.000	4.209	0.355	0.006	0.199	0.795	2.527*
Relative	1.135**	1.142**	1.127**	1.105**				0.662**
VAR-Fin (Baa–T10)	2.367	2.002	3.897	0.338	0.007	0.110	0.883	3.818**
Relative	1.101**	1.142**	1.043	1.050				0.999
VAR-Fin (T10–T5)	2.425	1.879	4.471	0.357	0.004	0.274	0.721	4.312**
Relative	1.128**	1.072	1.197**	1.112**				1.129**
Forecast	2.101	1.757	3.517	0.312	0.004	0.397	0.598	5.437**
Combination	0.977	1.003	0.942	0.969				1.424**

Note: (*) and (**) denote that the difference between the loss function from the model and the benchmark is statistically significant at the 5% and 1% level, respectively, using Diebold and Mariano's (1995) test. Full sample is from 1992:Q1 – 2011:Q1. Recession (expansion) corresponds to periods of recession (expansion) phases as dated by the NBER. RMSFE stands for root mean squared forecast error, and PT for Pesaran and Timmermann's test (1992). The loss functions are given in absolute terms, and in relative terms compared to the AR(2) model. The models are: univariate autoregressive AR(2), Cumulative Depth of Recession (CDR), Dynamic Stochastic General Equilibrium (DSGE), Univariate Markov Switching (MS), Dynamic Factor with Markov Switching (AR-DFMS), Bayesian VAR (BVAR), Baseline VAR, and VARs including Baa-Aaa (VAR-Fin Baa-Aaa), Aaa-T10 (VAR-Fin Aaa-T10), Baa-T10 (VAR-Fin Baa-T10), and T10-T5 (VAR-Fin T10-T5). FC is the forecast combination. BC stands for the Blue Chip forecasts. The (-) entry in the last column indicates that the division is undefined.

however, are outperformed by simple autoregressive processes or naïve constant growth models and conclude that the comparison is among uninformative forecasts.

We find that the VAR models do not generally perform as well as the other models. The relative RMSFE with respect to the AR(2) benchmark for the BVAR and all VAR

Table 3.3 RMSFE, Theil Inequality, and PT Tests– Total and Relative to the Benchmark Real-Time Out-of-Sample Two-Quarter Ahead Forecasts

Models	RMSFE			Theil Inequality Coefficient				PT Test
	Full Sample	Expansion	Recession	Total	Bias	Var	Cov	
AR(2)	2.345	**1.796**	4.353	0.351	0.005	0.562	0.433	–
CDR	2.373	1.935	4.098	0.365	0.000	0.460	0.540	–
Relative	1.012	1.077*	0.941	1.039				
DSGE	2.436	1.934	4.346	0.326	0.114	0.219	0.667	–
Relative	1.039	1.077*	0.998	0.929				
MS	2.373	1.911	4.163	0.348	0.009	0.292	0.699	2.507*
Relative	1.012	1.064	0.956	0.990				
BC	**2.124**	1.850	3.307	0.330	0.005	0.485	0.511	5.400**
Relative	**0.905****	1.030	0.760**	0.938				
DFMS	2.137	2.062	**2.538**	**0.304**	0.001	0.025	0.973	5.234**
Relative	0.911*	1.148**	**0.583****	**0.866****				
BVAR	2.472	1.824	4.748	0.366	0.008	0.460	0.532	–
Relative	1.054	1.016	1.091**	1.043				
VAR	2.594	1.937	4.933	0.382	0.007	0.318	0.675	–
Relative	1.106**	1.079*	1.133**	1.087*				
VAR–Fin (Baa–Aaa)	2.593	1.955	4.886	0.381	0.007	0.292	0.701	–
Relative	1.105**	1.088**	1.122**	1.083*				
VAR–Fin (Aaa–T10)	2.559	1.901	4.888	0.375	0.008	0.320	0.671	–
Relative	1.091*	1.059	1.123**	1.069				
VAR–Fin (Baa–T10)	2.566	1.927	4.851	0.376	0.008	0.304	0.687	3.792**
Relative	1.094*	1.073*	1.114**	1.070				
VAR–Fin (T10–T5)	2.577	1.897	4.960	0.379	0.007	0.325	0.668	–
Relative	1.099**	1.057	1.139**	1.080*				
Forecast	2.293	1.773	4.212	0.342	0.007	0.530	0.463	–
Combination	0.978	0.988	0.968	0.972				–

Note: (*) and (**) denote that the difference between the loss function from the model and the benchmark is statistically significant at the 5% and 1% level, respectively, using Diebold and Mariano's (1995) test. Full sample is from 1992:Q1 – 2011:Q1. Recession (expansion) corresponds to periods of recession (expansion) phases as dated by the NBER. RMSFE stands for root mean squared forecast error, and PT for Pesaran and Timmermann's test (1992). The loss functions are given in absolute terms, and in relative terms compared to the AR(2) model. The models are: univariate autoregressive AR(2), Cumulative Depth of Recession (CDR), Dynamic Stochastic General Equilibrium (DSGE), Univariate Markov Switching (MS), Dynamic Factor with Markov Switching (AR-DFMS), Bayesian VAR (BVAR), Baseline VAR, and VARs including Baa-Aaa (VAR-Fin Baa-Aaa), Aaa-T10 (VAR-Fin Aaa-T10), Baa-T10 (VAR-Fin Baa-T10), and T10-T5 (VAR-Fin T10-T5). FC is the forecast combination. BC stands for the Blue Chip forecasts. The (-) entries in the last column indicate that the division is undefined.

models are greater than one for both horizons. The difference between the models' forecasts and the benchmark is significantly different from each other at the 1% level using DM's (1995) test for all but the BVAR model at $k = 2$. Interestingly, the BVAR does better than any other VAR at $k = 2$ and worse than any other VAR at $k = 1$.

The baseline VAR and VAR-Fin models generally have better accuracy at the two-quarter horizon than the one-quarter ahead horizon, according to the RMSFE. The inclusion of the term spread improves the forecast performance of the baseline VAR, but not as much as the default spread. For $k = 1$, the best accuracy among these models is for the VAR-Fin that includes the default risk Baa-Aaa, followed by the VAR-Fin Baa-T10, for both loss functions considered. For $k = 2$, the BVAR with no financial variable does best.

We find that the forecast accuracy of the multivariate DSGE model is similar to the univariate benchmark. For the full out-of-sample period the relative RMSFE for the DSGE model is slightly worse than the AR(2) at the one and two-quarter ahead horizon, but the difference between the models' forecasts is not significantly different from each other using DM test. This is in agreement with a vast literature on the forecast accuracy of DSGE, which finds that its forecasts are comparable or slightly superior to the ones obtained from VARs and BVAR, but not significantly different from simple benchmarks such as univariate autoregressive processes. The Theil coefficient indicates that the DSGE model forecasts relatively well the volatility of GDP fluctuations, with a variance proportion of only 13% for $k = 1$ and 22% for $k = 2$. Notice, however, that the DSGE model forecasts GDP growth with a bias, as shown in Figure 3.10 and Tables 3.1 and 3.2. The bias proportion of the Theil coefficient is 11% whereas all other models exhibit almost zero bias proportion.

Both loss functions for the AR-DFMS model are substantially lower than the one from the benchmark, and the difference is significant at the 1% or 5% level. For example, the RMSFE from the AR-DFMS model for $k = 1$ is only 1.920, considerably lower than any other specification examined, including the AR(2) (RMSFE = 2.150), the DSGE (RMSFE = 2.205), the univariate MS model (RMSFE = 2.111), and the best performing VAR for this horizon, the VAR-Fin Baa-Aaa (RMSFE = 2.349). Similar results are also found for the two-quarter ahead forecast horizon.

The AR-DFMS model also displays a very good ability in forecasting the volatility of GDP growth, outperforming all other models in this dimension. More specifically, the variance proportion of the Theil coefficient – which measures how far the forecast is from the variance of the actual series – is the smallest among all models. For $k = 1$, it is only 7.5%, whereas the variance proportion for the benchmark AR(2) is 47%. Other models that also track relatively well the volatility of GDP growth are the VAR-Fin Baa-T10 (10%), VAR-Fin Baa-Aaa (11%), and the DSGE (13%). However, for the two-quarter ahead forecast, the variance proportion for the AR-DFMS model is substantially lower than all other models (2.5%). This supports previous findings in the literature, in which the non-linearity of the Markov regime switching generates additional cyclical movements that are useful in replicating the variability of the business cycle.[38] The AR-DFMS model

---

[38] See, for example, Chauvet (1998, 2001), Chauvet and Hamilton (2006), Chauvet and Piger (2008), and Morley et al. (forthcoming).

also displays good forecasting accuracy of the mean growth rate of GDP, with a bias proportion almost zero.

The BC indicators are real-time judgmental forecasts made at each point at time and are not revised. The AR–DFMS model and the BC indicators have the best forecast accuracy relatively to all models to a large extent. Their performance is comparable, as their RMSFE associated with the one and two-quarter ahead forecasts are not significantly different from each other. Notice, however, that the difference between the Theil coefficient of the BC and the AR(2) model is not statistically significant for both horizons, whereas the relative forecast accuracy of the AR–DFMS to the benchmark is significant at the 1% level according to DM's test. This is in line with the evidence in Edge et al. (2010), Edge and Gürkaynak (2010), Wang (2009), Wieland and Wolters (2011), Del Negro and Schorfheide (2013), and Lundquist and Stekler (2011), who find that the judgmental-based results show modest nowcasting and short-run accuracy, but a lessen forecasting ability from one-quarter ahead and on.

The forecast combination has an overall improved accuracy compared to some models, but the AR–DFMS and the BC forecasts outperform the pooling. Notice that the forecast combination tracks relatively poorly the variance of output growth as measured by Theil coefficient.

Tables 3.2 and 3.3 also show the results for Pesaran and Timmerman's test. The null that there is a significant difference between the observed probability of a correctly signed forecast and the estimate of this probability is rejected at the 1% and 5% level for all models, except of the BVAR. This implies that the forecast from all other models have power to predict the sign of actual GDP growth.

The performance of the BVAR model, and the VAR to a lesser extent, is intriguing. However, it is somewhat in line with previous literature, which finds that the BVAR model generally yields good forecast accuracy for several variables in the system compared to other models, but not for real GDP growth. This is also the case for the VAR models (see, e.g., Christoffel et al., 2008; Edge et al., 2010; Wolters, 2010; Edge and Gürkaynak, 2010; Wieland and Wolters, 2011, etc.). Wieland and Wolters (2011) who also estimate a BVAR (4) find that this model forecasts output growth more accurately during the 1990–1991 and the 2001 recessions, but not as well when the sample includes the most recent recession. They reason that this might be related to the fact that the lag structure of the BVAR might work better during periods of lower volatility of output growth, such as during normal times and less volatile recessions as the 1990–1991 and the 2001 one.[39] This is supported in Clark (2011) who considers a BVAR with stochastic volatility. He finds that taking into account changes in the dynamics of volatility in the U.S. economy substantially improves the BVAR performance for density forecasts. A similar result is also found in a large-dimensional BVAR model with common stochastic volatility proposed in Carriero et al. (2012).

---

[39] Notice that our sample excludes the 1990–1991 recession.

3.3.2. Recession and Expansion Periods
Loss Functions

Tables 3.2 and 3.3 also show the RMSFE for real-time forecasts during expansion and recession periods. Some striking results are unveiled when the real-time out-of-sample period is divided across business cycle phases, as it allows examination of the sources of differences in loss functions. Some models that perform well for the full sample display poor accuracy for expansions or recessions. Some other models that do poorly in forecasting recessions do very well in forecasting expansions and vice versa.

Expansions. Interestingly, the benchmark AR(2) model has a very good forecast accuracy for expansions, ranking first for $k = 2$ and ranking second only to the univariate MS model for $k = 1$. At the one-quarter ahead forecast, the difference between the performance of the benchmark forecasts and some models is large and significant, such as for the DSGE, the BVAR, the baseline VAR, and all VAR–Fin models with the exception of the one that includes the term spread (VAR–Fin T10–T5). However, the accuracy of the benchmark model is not significantly different from the non-linear time series models CDR, MS, AR–DFMS, and from the BC forecasts. At the two-period ahead forecast, the AR(2) model has the lowest RMSFE of all forecasts including the ones from the BC, but the difference is not statistically significant for most models except for the AR–DFMS, which does better, and the VAR–Fin Baa–Aaa model, which does worse. Note that the BVAR and the VAR–Fin T10–T5 also perform well during expansions, but the relative RMSFE is not statistically significant.

We also consider pooling all forecasts from the models and from the Blue Chip indicators using equal weight average. We find that it results in slight better accuracy compared to the simple AR(2) for the full sample, but the differences in forecasts are not statistically significant. During expansion periods, the MS and AR(2) models are more accurate than the forecast combination at $k = 1$ but not at $k = 2$.

Overall, these findings imply that by using a simple univariate linear (AR(2)) or non-linear (MS) autoregressive model of GDP growth, one would have gotten in real time as good as forecasts during expansions than any other model and the professional forecasters. These simple models exhibit a very good ability to track the mean of GDP growth during normal times.

Recessions. The real-time performance of most models is generally poor in forecasting recessions. The RMSFEs are a lot larger during recessions compared to expansions and to the full out-of-sample period. This is the case for all models and the BC forecasts, which is consistent with several studies that show that recessions are harder to forecast than expansions.[40]

The performance of the benchmark AR(2) model is quite different for recessions compared to expansions and to the full sample. At both horizons, its forecast accuracy

---

[40] See, e.g., Chauvet and Guo (2003), Beaudry and Koop (1993), or Oh and Waldman (1990), among several others.

as measured by the RMSFE is worse than all but the VAR and BVAR models. The CDR model, which is designed to capture the depth of recessions, does better than the benchmark during recessions. However, their forecast accuracy is not significantly different at any significance level. This is also the case for the MS model.

The baseline VAR and the VAR-Fin models do not generally perform well in forecasting recessions, displaying the worst real-time accuracy at the one and two-quarter ahead horizons compared to all other models. The BVAR model, on one hand, has the best real-time accuracy performance of all eleven models considered and the BC forecast for $k = 2$, but on the other hand is the worst of all VAR models for $k = 1$.

Interestingly, the DSGE model forecasts of GDP growth at $k = 1$ fare relatively well during recessions compared to the benchmark AR(2), CDR, VAR, VAR-Fin, and BVAR models. On the other hand, at $k = 2$ the non-linear time series models such as the CDR, MS, and AR-DFMS do better than the benchmark, DSGE model, the VAR, VAR-Fin, and BVAR models. However, for both horizons, the difference in accuracy is only statistically significant for the VAR, VAR-Fin, and BVAR models. This is not a very informative conclusion, as the VAR models have very poor forecasting accuracy for recessions.

The best forecasting model for recessions is the AR-DFMS by a large difference compared to other models for both horizons. For example, its RMSFE (=2.149) is substantially lower compared to the AR(2), (RMSFE = 3.735), and it is about 50% to 66% lower than the RMSFE for the other models. For the two-quarter ahead horizon, the RMSFE (=2.538) for the AR-DFMS model is about only 51%–62% of the RMSFE of the other models.

The good performance of the AR-DFMS model in forecasting GDP growth during recessions is only comparable to the BC forecasts, although the model produces forecasts that are more accurate compared to the professional forecasts, with the difference in performance significant at any statistical level. The relative RMSFE during recessions for the AR-DFMS model is 0.848 of the BC forecast for $k = 1$, and 0.767 for $k = 2$.

We find that the forecast combination of all models and the BC is outperformed by the AR-DFMS model and the BC forecasts for the full sample and during recessions at one and two-quarter ahead. The forecast combination is also outperformed by the CDR and MS models during recessions at the two-quarter horizon.

Chauvet et al. (2013) examine the forecast ability of a linear version of the dynamic factor model, as discussed in Section 2.8. They find that this model yields forecasts that are comparable to the AR(2) model, and is outperformed by the AR-DMFS model. The comparative advantage of the AR-DFMS model to the linear DFMS and the other models considered is found to be mostly in the probability of recession terms obtained from monthly series (see Eq. (17)). Interestingly, although the forecasts of the univariate MS model are also based on probability of recessions, these are not as good forecasts as the ones from the AR-DMFS model. A possible reason is that the MS model is based only on information contained on quarterly GDP while the AR–DFMS is based on information from monthly coincident indicators of economic activity. The probabilities of recession from the DFMS model based on monthly coincident indicators timely signal recessions in real time, while the ones based solely on GDP growth yield delayed signals particularly for the last two recessions as GDP growth only mildly decreased *at their onset*.

Adding up, the accuracy of most models to output growth is relatively poor during recessions. Although the forecast ability of some models is good during expansions, most fail to forecast GDP growth during recessions. Some of the VAR-Fin models such as the one that includes the term spread T10-T5 and the BVAR do better than the DSGE model during expansions, but the gains are offset by their performance during recessions (which is the reason why their overall RMSFE for the full real-time sample is lower than the RMSFE for the DSGE model).

The best models for tracking future GDP growth during expansions are the univariate AR(2) and MS models, and the VAR-Fin T10-T5 model. For recessions, the best model is the AR–DFMS model and the BC forecasts.

The findings that the univariate autoregressive model has a good forecasting performance are in accord with Marcellino (2008). This chapter compares the accuracy of a large set of linear and non-linear models. It finds that carefully specified linear autoregressive ones (e.g., including linear trends) outperform most models.

Graphical Analysis

An analysis of the forecast dynamics of the models in Figures 3.1 to 3.13 gives a more comprehensive picture of their performance over time and across business cycle phases. As shown in the figures, the models display a better forecast ability to GDP growth during expansions compared to recessions. In particular, all models fail to forecast negative output growth during the 2001 recession, with the exception of the AR-DFMS model and the Blue Chip forecasts. The forecast accuracy differs substantially across models during the 2007–2009 recession, especially regarding the timing and intensity of the predicted fall in GDP growth in real time, as discussed below.

Figures 3.1 and 3.2 show the real-time forecasts for the AR(2) and the CDR models. These models track closely the future mean of GDP growth for both horizons, but not as well its volatility. This is particularly accentuated during the 2001 recession and the 2007–2009 recession. Both models show a small decline relatively to the actual decrease in GDP growth during these recessions. During the 2007–2010 recession, the CDR model forecasts only a mild decline in GDP but not negative growth, including during the financial crisis and the aftermath between 2008:Q3 and 2009:Q1. Actual unrevised GDP growth had a steep fall during this period, reaching −0.5 in 2008:Q3, −6.5 in 2008:Q4, and −5.6 in 2009:Q1. The AR(2) model forecasts a decline of 0.8% in 2009:Q2 at the one-quarter ahead horizon, and only a slow, positive growth at the two-quarter ahead horizon during the worst quarters of the recession.

Figure 3.3 plots the real-time forecasts for the MS model. As the other univariate models, the MS model tracks closely future GDP growth during expansions, but it also does better in forecasting its fluctuations as well. For both horizons, the MS model forecasts a deeper fall in GDP growth during recessions compared to the benchmark and CDR models (over -1.4% for the recent recession).

Figures 3.4 to 3.9 show the forecasts for the VAR, BVAR, and VAR-Fin models. These models have good forecast performance during expansions as well. As discussed earlier, their RMSFE is slightly worse for $k=1$ than the benchmark, but for $k=2$, their forecasts are not statistically significant different from the benchmark, the MS, and the DSGE models. The VAR and BVAR models perform better for the two-quarter ahead horizon.

Regarding recessions, the baseline VAR, all VAR-Fin, and the BVAR models basically miss the 2001 recession, forecasting an average growth during this period. However, their performance is very different for the most recent recession. The baseline VAR and the BVAR forecast a mild negative growth, but with the wrong timing. Both forecast negative growth one quarter after the end of the recession in 2009:Q2, although the baseline VAR also forecasts a mild fall in 2009:Q1 too.

The VAR-Fin models include variables that, on hindsight, were closely associated to the financial crisis in 2008. On effect, the inclusion of the default risk Aaa-Baa, Baa-T10 or Aaa-T10 in these models lead to forecast of a deep decline in GDP growth, but after the worst quarter of the crisis in 2008:Q4. The models correctly forecast a steep fall in GDP growth in 2009:Q1 and the strong recovery in 2009:Q4. Note that the inclusion of the term spread T10-T5 does not lead to a forecast of a dramatic fall in GDP during this period.

Figure 3.10 plots the real-time forecasts from the DSGE model. The model has reasonable forecast accuracy overall, although it presents the highest forecast bias compared to the other models – the DSGE has a bias proportion of 11% while all other models have this proportion equal or below 1%. Nevertheless, it tracks oscillations in GDP growth better than most models. The DSGE model also has a reasonable forecast accuracy during recessions. As most models, it does not forecast negative growth during the 2001 recession, and the severity of this recession is less than forecasted by all but the BVAR, VAR, and VAR-Fin models. With respect to the 2007–2009 recession, at the one-quarter ahead horizon the DSGE model forecasts a stronger negative growth in GDP during the 2007–2009 recession than the univariate models, but not as intense as forecasted by the other multivariate models. For $k=2$, however, the DSGE model completely miss the recession, predicting only a mild but positive decline in GDP growth during the worst part of the financial crisis.

Figure 3.11a shows the actual and output growth forecasts from the AR-DFMS model. The model forecasts display strong oscillations, following closely GDP growth overall, particularly during recessions. The AR-DFMS is the only model that forecasts the 2001 recession, with forecasts of negative growth matching the actual GDP data. This model also has a good performance in forecasting the 2007–2011 recession. It displays the best forecast of the timing and depth of the decline in GDP growth during this period at one and two-quarter ahead horizons. The forecasts start decreasing around the beginning of the recession, reach a trough with strong negative growth around the time of the financial crisis, and increase at around the time the recession ended.

The accuracy of the AR-DFMS forecasts is closely associated with the dynamics of the probabilities of recession and the Business Cycle Indicator obtained from this model (Figure 3.11b). The Business Cycle Indicator is highly correlated with GDP fluctuations, matching well its volatility particularly during recessions. The probabilities of recession closely match NBER expansion and recession phases. During periods in which the NBER classifies as expansions the probabilities of recession are close to zero. At around the time when the NBER recession starts, the probabilities of recessions rise substantially and remain high until around the end of the recessions as established by the NBER.[41]

For example, the model signaled in real time the onset of the Great Recession as December 2007 with information available in April 2008. The earliest possible signal, given the lag in the availability of the data, would have been in March 2008. The real-time probabilities of recession were above 50% already in April 2008, and above 80% in July 2008. The probabilities stayed close to 100% during the whole financial crisis and the most of 2009, correctly signaling the intensity of the recession. Notice, however, that for the period studied the trough dates from the model take place later compared to the NBER troughs. The model captures the "jobless recoveries" that have followed recent recessions. The accuracy of the forecasts of GDP growth from the AR-DFMS model is related to the ability of the model to forecast recessions in real time, as reflected in the probabilities of recessions and the Business Cycle Indicator shown in Figure 3.11b.

The Blue Chip indicator has a good accuracy for $k = 1$ and $k = 2$, outperforming the models except for the AR-DFMS, as discussed above. The BC indicator, as AR-DFMS model, forecasts negative growth at the one-quarter ahead horizon during the 2001 recession and 2007–2009 recession. However, the timing and intensity of the decline differ across forecast horizons to a large extent. For the 2007–2009 recession, the BC forecasts at the one-quarter horizon negative growth during and after the financial crisis, but the forecast depth is almost half of the actual decline in economic growth (Figure 3.12). At the two-quarter ahead horizon, the BC almost misses the recession – it forecasts decreasing but positive growth until 2008:Q4. When the Lehman Brothers failed, the forecasts were updated, and GDP growth was forecasted to be mildly negative in 2009:Q1 and 2009:Q2. At the two-quarter ahead horizon, the forecasting accuracy gets noticeably worse with the BC almost missing completely the recession. These results are in line with those of Edge and Gürkaynak (2010), Wieland and Wolters (2011), and Del Negro and Schorfheide

---

[41] Notice that this model is devised to timely signal turning points, not to forecast them. The model only includes coincident series, not leading economic variables. For an extension of this model, which uses nonlinear two dynamic factors of the yield curve and economic activity to forecast recessions, see Chauvet and Senyuz (2012).

(2013), who find that the forecasts from structural models and from the professional forecasters underpredicted recessions.

Finally, Figure 3.13 plots the forecast combination of all models and the BC forecasts. The pooling tracks relatively well output growth during expansions, but perform poorly during recessions. In particular, it misses the timing and intensity of recessions. This is partially explained by the fact that the pooling does not track well the volatility of GDP growth, which is particularly accentuated during recessions.

4. CONCLUSION

This chapter examines the real-time forecast accuracy of structural models and state of art reduced-form linear and non-linear time series models for U.S. output growth over time and across business cycle phases. We reproduce the forecast problem at each date that the forecast were being made in real time in the last two decades. We find that, for all models, recessions are a lot harder to forecast than expansions.

The best models for tracking future GDP growth during expansions are the AR(2) and the univariate Markov switching MS model, and the VAR model that includes the term spread. The latter and the BVAR do better than the DSGE model during expansions, but the gains are offset by their poor performance during recessions. Pooling forecasts lead to a good precision for expansions, but not as well for recessions.

In fact, we find that the accuracy of most models is relatively poor for recessions. Although the forecast ability of some models is good during expansions, most fail to forecast GDP growth during recessions. The DSGE model performance is similar to the benchmark AR(2) during recessions, but both do poorly during these periods. For recessions, the best forecast accuracy is for the non-linear multivariate AR-DFMS model and the BC forecasts. Even though the professional forecasters have information advantage over all models, the AR-DFMS model has better forecasting performance, as it is particularly advantageous by design for periods of sharp changes, such as during recessions and financial crises. The accuracy of the AR-DFMS forecasts is closely associated with the dynamics of the probabilities of recession and the business cycle indicator obtained from this model. The business cycle indicator is highly correlated with GDP fluctuations, matching well its volatility particularly during recessions. The probabilities of recession rise substantially at the beginning of recessions and remain high until around their end, as dated by the NBER. The accuracy of GDP growth forecasts from the AR-DFMS model is, thus, closely related to the ability of the model to forecast recessions in real time.

These findings imply that by using simple univariate linear autoregressive models of GDP growth, one would have gotten in real time as good as forecasts during expansions than any other model and the professional forecasters. These simple models exhibit a very good ability to track the mean of GDP growth during normal times. Although DSGE models do not score high in forecasting ability, they still appeal to policymakers as story telling tools for policy evaluation in-sample.

However, some models that display good forecast ability during normal times are not as good during periods of sharp changes, as they do not process information quickly. We find that there are large gains in using different models for recessions. Structural models and VARs are more suitable for forecasts during normal periods, although simple univariate autoregressive models do just as well. On the other hand, by using models designed to handle abrupt changes and non-linearities, such as the multivariate Markov switching model, economic agents and policymakers can hedge against those changes and obtain more reliable forecasts at times in which they are mostly needed.

ACKNOWLEDGMENTS

Ging Cee Ng (FRB New York), Raiden Hasegawa (FRB New York), and Daniel Herbst (FRB New York) provided excellent research assistance. We thank five anonymous referees, Allan Timmerman, Graham Elliott, Frederick Joutz, Timothy Cogley, James Morley, Mi Lu, and participants of the 2012 Conference in honor to Charles Nelson at the University of Washington, and of the 87th Conference of the Western Economic Association International in San Francisco for helpful comments and suggestions. We also thank Marco Del Negro and Frank Schorfheide for sharing some of the real-time data and codes used in the paper and allowing to cross-check our results. The views expressed in this chapter do not necessarily reflect those of the Federal Reserve Bank of New York or the Federal Reserve System.

REFERENCES

Adolfson, M., Linde, J., Villani, M., 2007a. Forecasting performance of an open economy dynamic stochastic general equilibrium model. Econometric Reviews 26 (2–4), 289–328.

Adolfson, M., Andersson, M., Linde, J., Villani, M., Vredin, A., 2007b. Modern forecasting models in action: improving macroeconomic analyses at central banks. International Journal of Central Banking 3, 111–144.

Aiolfi, M., Capistran, C., Timmermann, A., 2011. Forecast combinations. In: Clements, M., Hendry, D. (Eds.), The Oxford Handbook of Economic Forecasting. Oxford, 355–388.

Anderson, H.M., Vahid, F., 2001. Estimating the probability of a recession with nonlinear autoregressive leading indicator models. Macroeconomic Dynamics 5 (4), 482–505.

Angelini, E., Camba-Mendez, G., Giannone, D., Reichlin, L., Rünstler, G., 2011. Short-term forecasts of euro area GDP growth. Econometrics Journal, Royal Economic Society 14 (1), C25–C44.

Aruoba, S.B., Diebold, F.X., 2010. Real-time macroeconomic monitoring: real activity, inflation, and inter-actions. American Economic Review 100, 20–24.

Aruoba, S.B., Diebold, F.X., Scotti, C., 2009. Real-time measurement of business conditions. Journal of Business and Economic Statistics 27, 417–427.

Assenmacher-Wesche, K., Pesaran, M., 2008. Forecasting the Swiss Economy Using VECX* Models: An Exercise in Forecast Combination Across Models and Observation Windows. Working Papers 2008–03, Swiss National Bank.

Banbura, M., Runstler, G., 2011. A look into the factor model black box: publication lags and the role of hard and soft data in forecasting GDP. International Journal of Forecasting 27 (2), 333–346.

Banbura, M., Giannone, D., Reichlin, L., 2010. Large Bayesian VARs. Journal of Applied Econometrics 25 (1), 71–92.

Banegas, A., 2011. Predictability of Growth in Emerging Markets: Information in Financial Aggregates, Federal Reserve Board. Available at SSRN: <http://ssrn.com/abstract=1966076> or http://dx.doi.org/10.2139/ssrn.1966076.

Beaudry, P., Koop, G., 1993. Do recessions permanently change output? Journal of Monetary Economics 31, 149–163.

Bernard, H., Gerlach, S., 1998. Does the term structure predict recessions? The international evidence. International Journal of Finance and Economics 3 (3), 195–215.

Blanchard, O., Simon, J., 2000. The long and large decline in US output volatility. Brookings Papers on Economic Activity 1 (2001), 135–74.

Burns, Arthur F., Mitchell, Wesley C., 1946. Measuring Business Cycles. National Bureau of Economic Research, New York.

Camacho, M., Perez-Quiros, G., Poncela, P., 2011. Green Shoots in the Euro Area. A Real Time Measure. Working paper 1026, the Central Bank of Spain.

Camacho, M., Perez-Quiros, G., Poncela, P., 2012. Markov Switching Dynamic Factor Models in Real Time. Working Paper 1205, Bank of Spain.

Carriero, A., Clark, T., Marcellino, M., 2011. Bayesian VARs: Specification Choices and Forecasting Performance. CEPR WP 8273.

Carriero, A., Clark, T., Marcellino, M., 2012. Common Drifting Volatility in Large Bayesian VARs. CEPR WP 8894.

Chauvet, M., 1998. An econometric characterization of business cycle dynamics with factor structure and regime switches. International Economic Review 39 (4), 969–96.

Chauvet, M., 2001. A monthly indicator of Brazilian GDP. The Brazilian Review of Econometrics 21 (1), 1–15.

Chauvet, M., 2010. The Four Phases of the US Business Cycle. Working Paper. University of California Riverside.

Chauvet, M., Guo, J.T., 2003. Sunspots, animal spirits, and economic fluctuations. Macroeconomic Dynamics 7 (1), 77–103.

Chauvet, M., Hamilton, J., 2006. Dating business cycle turning points in real time. In: Van Dijk, Milas, Rothman (Eds.), Nonlinear Time Series Analysis of Business Cycles. Elsevier's Contributions to Economic Analysis series, pp. 1–54.

Chauvet, M., Piger, J., 2008. A comparison of the real-time performance of business cycle dating methods. Journal of Business Economics and Statistics 26 (1), 42–49.

Chauvet, M., Piger, J., 2013. Employment and the business cycle. Manchester School.

Chauvet, M., Popli, G., 2003. Maturing capitalism and stabilization: international evidence. Journal of Business and Economics 1 (12), 5–22.

Chauvet, M., Potter, S., 2001. Recent changes in the US business cycle. Manchester School 69 (5), 481–508.

Chauvet, M., Potter, S., 2002. Predicting recessions: evidence from the yield curve in the presence of structural breaks. Economics Letters 77 (2), 245–253.

Chauvet, M., Potter, S., 2005. Forecasting recessions using the yield curve. Journal of Forecasting 24 (2), 77–103.

Chauvet, M., Lu, M., Potter, S., 2013. Forecasting Output During Recessions and Crises. University of California Riverside. Working Paper.

Chauvet, M., Senyuz, Z., 2012. A Dynamic Factor Model of the Yield Curve as a Predictor of the Economy, Staff Working Papers in the Finance and Economics Discussion Series (FEDS), 2012-32, 1–45.

Chauvet, M., Su, Y., 2013. Robust Markov switching models. In: Wohar, M., Ma, J. (Eds.), Recent Advances in Estimating Nonlinear Models. Springer.

Chauvet, M., Tierney, H.L., 2009. Real time Changes in Monetary Policy. University of California Riverside, Working Paper.

Chib, S., 1998. Estimation and comparison of multiple change-point models. Journal of Econometrics 86 (22), 221–241.

Christiano, L.J., Eichenbaum, M., Evans, C.L., 2005. Nominal rigidities and the dynamic effects of a shock to monetary policy. Journal of Political Economy 113 (1), 1–45.

Christoffel, K., Coenen, G., Warne, A., 2008. The New Area-Wide Model of the Euro Area: Specification. Estimation Results and Properties. European Central Bank Working Paper, October 944.

Christoffel, K., Coenen, G., Warne, A., 2011. Forecasting with DSGE models. In: Clements, M., Hendry, D. (Eds.), Oxford Handbook on Economic Forecasting. Oxford University Press, pp. 89–128.

Clark, T., 2011. Real-time density forecasts from BVARs with stochastic volatility. Journal of Business and Economic Statistics 29, 327–341.

Clark, T.E., McCracken, M.W., 2010. Averaging forecasts from VARs with uncertain instabilities. Journal of Applied Econometrics 25 (1), 5–29.

Clements, M.P., Galvao, A., 2008. Macroeconomic forecasting with mixed frequency data: forecasting output growth in the United States. Journal of Business and Economic Statistics 26, 546–554.

Clements, M.P., Hendry, D.F., 2004. Pooling of forecasts. Econometrics Journal, Royal Economic Society 7 (1), 1–31.

Cogley, T., Sargent, T.J., 2001. Evolving post World War II US inflation dynamics. NBER Macroeconomics Annual 16, 331–373.

Cogley, T., Sargent, T.J., 2005. Drifts and volatilities: monetary policies and outcomes in the post WWII US. Review of Economic Dynamics 8, 262–302.

Cooley, T.F., LeRoy, S., 1985. Atheoretical macroeconometrics. A critique. Journal of Monetary Economics 16, 283–308.

Croushore, D., Stark, T., 2001. A real-time data set for macroeconomists. Journal of Econometrics 105, 111–30.

Del Negro, M., Schorfheide, F., 2011. Bayesian macroeconometrics. The Oxford Handbook of Bayesian Econometrics, pp. 293–389.

Del Negro, M., Schorfheide, F., 2013. DSGE model-based forecasting. In: Elliott, G., Timmermann, A. (Eds.), Handbook of Economic Forecasting, vol. 2. Elsevier.

Diebold, F.X., Mariano, R., 1995. Comparing Predictive Accuracy. Journal of Business and Economic Statistics 13, 253–263.

Diebold, F.X., Rudebusch, G.D., 1996. Measuring business cycles: a modern perspective. The Review of Economics and Statistics 78 (1), 67–77.

Edge, R., Gürkaynak, R., 2010. How useful are estimated DSGE model forecasts for central bankers? Brookings Papers on Economic Activity, 209–259 (Fall).

Edge, R.M., Kiley, M.T., Laforte, J.P., 2010. A comparison of forecast performance between federal reserve staff forecasts, simple forecasts, simple reduced-form models, and a DSGE model. Journal of Applied Econometrics 25, 720–754.

Estrella, A., Hardouvelis, G.A., 1991. The term structure as a predictor of real economic activity. Journal of Finance 46 (2), 555–576.

Estrella, A., Mishkin, F.S., 1998. Predicting US recessions: financial variables as leading indicators. Review of Economics and Statistics 80 (1), 45–61.

Evans, M.D.D., 2005. Where are we now? Real-time estimates of the macroeconomy. International Journal of Central Banking 1 (2), 129–175.

Fair, R.C., 1970. The estimation of simultaneous equation models with lagged endogenous variables and first order serially correlated errors. Econometrica 38 (3), 507–516.

Faust, J., 2012. DSGE models: I smell a rat (and it smells good). International Journal of Central Banking 8 (1), 53–64.

Forni, M., Hallin, M., Lippi, M., Reichlin, L., 2003. Do financial variables help forecasting inflation and real activity in the euro area? Journal of Monetary Economics 50, 1243–1255.

Frale, C., Marcellino, M., Mazzi, G., Proietti, T., 2011. EUROMIND: a monthly indicator of the euro area economic conditions. Journal of the Royal Statistical Society Series A 174, 439–470.

Ghysels, E., Santa-Clara, P., Valkanov, R., 2004. The MIDAS Touch: Mixed Data Sampling Regression Models. CIRANO Working Papers 2004s–20. CIRANO, Montreal, Canada.

Ghysels, E., Sinko, A., Valkanov, R., 2006. MIDAS regressions: further results and new directions. Econometric Reviews 26, 53–90.

Giannone, D., Reichlin, L., 2013. Nowcasting. In: Elliott, G., Timmermann, A. (Eds.), Handbook of Economic Forecasting, vol. 2. Elsevier.

Giannone, D., Reichlin, L., Sala, L., 2004. Monetary policy in real time. NBER Macroeconomics Annual 19, 161–224.

Giannone, D., Reichlin, L., Small, D., 2008. Nowcasting: the real-time informational content of macroeconomic data. Journal of Monetary Economics 55 (4), 665–676.

Granger, C.W.J., Teräsvirta, T., 1993. Modelling Nonlinear Economic Relationships. Oxford University Press, Oxford.

Guerin, P., Marcellino, M., 2011. Markov Switching MIDAS Models, CEPR WP 8234.

Hamilton, J.H., 1989. A new approach to the economic analysis of nonstationary time series and the business cycle. Econometrica 57 (2), 357–84.

Hamilton, J.H. (1994), State-space models. In: Engle, R., McFadden, D. (Eds.), Handbook of Econometrics, vol. 4. North-Holland.

Kauppi, H., Saikkonen, P., 2008. Predicting US recessions with dynamic binary response models. Review of Economics and Statistics 90, 777–791.

Kim, C.J., Nelson, C.R., 1998. Business cycle turning points, a new coincident index, and tests of duration dependence based on a dynamic factor model with regime switching. The Review of Economics and Statistics 80 (2), 188–201 (MIT Press).

Kim, Chang-Jin, Nelson, Charles R., 1999. Has the US economy become more stable? A Bayesian approach based on a Markov-switching model of business cycle. Review of Economics and Statistics 81 (4), 608–616.

Kim, C.J., Piger, J., Startz, R., 2008. Estimation of Markov regime-switching regression models with endogenous switching. Journal of Econometrics 143 (2), 263–273.

Klein, L.R., 1970. An Essay on Theory of Economic Prediction. Markham Publishing Company, Markham Economics Series, Chicago.

Kolasa, M., Rubaszek, M., Skrzypczynski, P., 2009. Putting the New Keynesian DSGE Model to the Real-Time Forecasting Test. European Central Bank Working Paper Series 1110, November.

Kolasa, M., Rubaszek, M., Skrzypczynski, P., 2012. Putting the new Keynesian DSGE model to the real-time forecasting test. Journal of Money, Credit and Banking 44 (7), 1301–1324.

Koop, G., Korobilis, D., 2010. Bayesian multivariate time series methods for empirical macroeconomics. Foundations and Trends in Econometrics 3 (4), 267–358.

Koop, G., Leon-Gonzalez, R., Strachan, R., 2009. On the evolution of monetary policy. Journal of Economic Dynamics and Control 33, 997–1017.

Krane, S.D., 2011. Professional forecasters' view of permanent and transitory shocks to GDP. American Economic Journal: Macroeconomics 3 (1), 184–211 (American Economic Association).

Kuzin, V., Marcellino, M., Schumacher, C., 2011. MIDAS versus mixed-frequency VAR: nowcasting GDP in the euro area. International Journal of Forecasting 27 (2), 529–542.

Kuzin, V., Marcellino, M., Schumacher, C., 2013. Pooling versus model selection for nowcasting GDP with many predictors: empirical evidence for six industrialized countries. Journal of Applied Econometrics 28 (3), 392–411.

Kydland, F.E., Prescott, E.C., 1982. Time to build and aggregate fluctuations. Econometrica 50 (6), 1345–1370.

Liu, G., Gupta, R., Schaling, E., 2009. A new-Keynesian DSGE model for forecasting the South African economy. Journal of Forecasting 28, 387–404.

Lombardi, M., Maier, P., 2011. Forecasting Economic Growth in the Euro Area during the Great Moderation and the Great Recession. European Central Bank Working Paper Series 1379, September.

Lucas, R., 1976. Econometric policy evaluation: a critique. Carnegie-Rochester Conference Series on Public Policy 1, 19–46.

Lundquist, K., Stekler, H.O., 2011. The Forecasting Performance of Business Economists During the Great Recession. Research Program on Forecasting. George Washington University Working Paper, pp. 2011–004.

Ma, J., Wohar, M. (Eds.), forthcoming. Recent Advances in Estimating Nonlinear Models. Springer Publishers.

Marcellino, M., 2008. A benchmark for models of growth and inflation. Journal of Forecasting 27, 305–340.

Marcellino, M., Schumacher, C., 2008. Factor-MIDAS for Now- and Forecasting with Ragged-Edge Data: A Model Comparison for German GDP. CEPR Discussion Papers 6708, C.E.P.R Discussion Papers.

Marcellino, M., Stock, J., Watson, M., 2003. Macroeconomic forecasting in the euro area: country-specific versus area-wide information. European Economic Review 47, 1–18.

Mariano, R.S., Murasawa, Y., 2003. A new coincident index of business cycles based on monthly and quarterly series. Journal of Applied Econometrics 18 (427), 443.

Mazzi, G., Ozyildirim, A. (Eds.), forthcoming. Handbook on Cyclical Composite Indicators, UN/Eurostat/ Statistic Netherlands.

McConnell, M.M., Perez-Quiros, G., 2000. Output fluctuations in the United States: what has changed since the early 1980s. The American Economic Review 90 (5), 1464–1476.

Mills, Terence C., Ping, Wang, 2003. Have output growth rates stabilised? Evidence from the G-7 economies. Scottish Journal of Political Economy 50 (3), 232–46.

Morley, J., Piger, J., Tien, P.L., forthcoming. Reproducing business cycle features: are nonlinear dynamics a proxy for multivariate information? Studies in Nonlinear Dynamics and Econometrics.

Nalewaik, J.J., 2011. Forecasting Recessions Using Stall Speeds. FEDS Working Paper 2011–24.

Nalewaik, J.J., 2012. Estimating probabilities of recession in real time using GDP and GDI. Journal of Money, Credit, and Banking 44, 235–253.

Nelson, C.R., 1972. The prediction performance of the FRB-MIT-PENN model of the US economy. American Economic Review 62, 902–917.

Nyberg, H., 2010. Dynamic probit models and financial variables in recession forecasting. Journal of Forecasting 29 (1–2), 215–230.

Oh, S., Waldman, M., 1990. The macroeconomic effects of false announcements. The Quarterly Journal of Economics 105 (4), 1017–34.

Owyang, M., Piger, J.M., Wall, H.J., 2012. Forecasting National Recessions Using State Level Data. Working Paper 2012–013A, Federal Reserve Bank of Saint Louis.

Pesaran, M.H., Timmermann, A., 1992. A simple nonparametric test of predictive performance. Journal of Business and Economic Statistics 10 (4), 461–465.

Primiceri, G., 2005. Time varying structural vector autoregressions and monetary policy. The Review of Economic Studies 72, 821–852.

Proietti, T., Moauro, F., 2006. Dynamic factor analysis with non linear temporal aggregation constraints. Applied Statistics 55, 281–300.

Rotemberg, J., Woodford, M., 1997. An optimization-based econometric framework for the evaluation of monetary policy. NBER Macroeconomics Annual 12, 297–346.

Rubaszek, M., Skrzypczyński, P., 2007. Can a Simple DSGE Model Outperform Professional Forecasters? National Bank of Poland Working Paper 43.

Rubaszek, M., Skrzypczyński, P., 2008. On the forecasting performance of a small-scale DSGE model. International Journal of Forecasting 24 (3), 498–512.

Schorfheide, F., Song, D.S., 2012. Real-Time Forecasting with a Mixed-Frequency VAR. Working Papers 701. Federal Reserve Bank of Minneapolis.

Sims, C., 1980. Macroeconomics and reality. Econometrica 48 (1), 1–48.

Sims, C., 2006. Comment on Del Negro, Schorfheide, Smets and Wouters. <http://sims.princeton.edu/yftp/DSSW806/DSseattleComment.pdf>.

Sims, C.A., Zha, T., 2006. Were there regime switches in US monetary policy? American Economic Review 96, 54–81.

Smets, F., Wouters, R., 2003. An estimated dynamic stochastic general equilibrium model of the euro area. Journal of the European Economic Association 1 (5), 1123–1175.

Smets, F., Wouters, R., 2007. Shocks and frictions in US business cycles: a Bayesian DSGE approach. American Economic Review 97 (3), 586–606.

Stock, J.H., Watson, M.W., 1989. New indexes of coincident and leading economic indicators. In: Blanchard, O., Fischer, S. (Eds.), NBER Macroeconomics Annual. MIT Press, Cambridge.

Stock, J.H., Watson, M.W., 1993. A procedure for predicting recessions with leading indicators: econometric issues and recent experience. In: Stock, J.H., Watson, M.W. (Eds.), Business Cycles, Indicators and Forecasting. University of Chicago Press for NBER, Chicago, pp. 255–284.

Stock, J., Watson, M., 2002. Macroeconomic forecasting using diffusion indexes. Journal of Business and Economic Statistics 20, 147–162.

Stock, J.H., Watson, M.W., 2003. Forecasting output and inflation: the role of asset prices. Journal of Economic Literature 41 (3), 788–829.

Tashman, L.J., 2000. Out-of-sample tests of forecasting accuracy: an analysis and review. International Journal of Forecasting 16 (4), 437–450.

Timmermann, A., 2006. Forecast Combinations. Elsevier, Handbook of Economic Forecasting.

Tinbergen, J., 1939. Business Cycles in the United States, 1919–1932 – Statistical Testing of Business-Cycle Theories. League of Nations, Economic Intelligence Service, Geneva.

Tinbergen, J., 1974. The Dynamics of Business Cycles: A Study in Economic Fluctuations. University of Chicago Press.

Tong, H., 1990. Non-Linear Time Series: A Dynamical System Approach. Oxford University Press.

Tovar, C., 2009. DSGE models and central banks, economics: the open-access. Open-Assessment E-Journal 3, 16.

Trehan, B., 1989. Forecasting Growth in Current Quarter Real GNP. Federal Reserve Bank of San Francisco Economic Review, 39–51 (Winter).

van Dijk, D., Osborn, D., Sensier, M., 2002a, Changes in the Variability of the Business Cycle in the G7 Countries. CGBCR Discussion Paper 16, University of Manchester, September.

van Dijk, D., Terasvirta, T., Franses, P.H., 2002b. Smooth transition autoregressive models—a survey of recent developments. Econometric Reviews 21 (1), 1–47.

Wang, M.C., 2009. Comparing the DSGE model with the factor model: an out-of-sample forecasting experiment. Journal of Forecasting 28–2, 167–182.

Wieland, V., Wolters, M.H., 2011. The diversity of forecasts from macroeconomic models of the US economy. Economic Theory 47, 247–292.

Winter, J., 2011. Forecasting GDP Growth in Times of Crisis: Private Sector Forecasts versus Statistical Models. De Nederlandsche Bank NV Working Paper 320, November.

Wolters, M., 2010. Forecasting Under Model Uncertainty. Goethe University Frankfurt Working Paper.

CHAPTER 4

Now-Casting and the Real-Time Data Flow

Marta Bańbura[*,††]**, Domenico Giannone**[†]**, Michele Modugno**[‡]** and Lucrezia Reichlin**[**]

[*]European Central Bank, Kaiserstrasse 29 60311 Frankfurt am Main, Germany
[†]Universite' libre de Bruxelles, ECARES, Av. Roosevelt 50, cp 114 1050 Bruxelles, Belgium
[‡]Universite' libre de Bruxelles, ECARES, Av. Roosevelt 50, cp 114 1050 Bruxelles, Belgium
[**]London Business School, Regent's Park, London NW1 4SA, UK

Contents

Abstract

The term now-casting is a contraction for now and forecasting and has been used for a long time in meteorology and recently also in economics. In this chapter we survey recent developments in economic now-casting with special focus on those models that formalize key features of how market participants and policymakers read macroeconomic data releases in real-time, which involves

[††]The opinions in this paper are those of the author and do not necessarily reflect the views of the European Central Bank.

monitoring many data, forming expectations about them and revising the assessment on the state of the economy whenever realizations diverge sizeably from those expectations.

Keywords

Macroeconomic news, Macroeconomic forecasting, High-dimensional data, Real-time data, Mixed frequency, Dynamic factor model, State-space models

1. INTRODUCTION

Now-casting is defined as the prediction of the present, the very near future and the very recent past. The term is a contraction for *now* and *forecasting* and has been used for a long time in meteorology and recently also in economics (Giannone et al., 2008).

Now-casting is relevant in economics because key statistics on the present state of the economy are available with a significant delay. This is particularly true for those collected on a quarterly basis, with Gross Domestic Product (GDP) being a prominent example. For instance, the first official estimate of GDP in the United States (US) or in the United Kingdom is published approximately one month after the end of the reference quarter. In the euro area the corresponding publication lag is 2–3 weeks longer. Now-casting can also be meaningfully applied to other target variables revealing particular aspects of the state of the economy and thereby followed closely by markets. An example is inflation, like in Modugno (2011).

The basic principle of now-casting is the exploitation of the information which is published early and possibly at higher frequencies than the target variable of interest in order to obtain an "early estimate" before the official figure becomes available. If the focus is on tracking GDP, one may look at its expenditure components, like for example personal consumption, which for the US is available at a monthly frequency, or variables related to the production side such as industry output. In addition, one may consider information contained in surveys or in forward looking indicators such as financial variables. The idea here is that both "hard" information like industrial production and "soft" information like surveys may provide an early indication of the current developments in economic activity. Surveys are particularly valuable because of their timeliness: they are the first monthly releases relating to the current quarter. Financial variables, which are available at very high frequency and, in principle, carry information on expectations of future economic developments, may also be useful although there is less empirical work on this topic (on this see Andreou et al., 2013) and the present chapter.

Until recently, the approach used in, for example, policy institutions to obtain an early estimate of GDP was based on judgment combined with simple models often called "bridge equations" (see Baffigi et al., 2004). Bridge equations are essentially regressions relating quarterly GDP growth to one or a few monthly variables (such as industrial production or surveys) aggregated to quarterly frequency. Since, typically, only partial monthly information is available for the target quarter, the monthly variables are forecasted using auxiliary models such as ARIMA. In order to exploit information from several monthly predictors bridge equations are sometime pooled (see, for example, Kitchen and Monaco, 2003).

Although part of this survey describes and evaluates this traditional approach to short-term forecasting, our focus is on models which provide a comprehensive solution to the problem of *now-casting*. In our definition *now-casting* is the exercise of reading, through the lenses of a model, the flow of data releases in real time. Ideally, a now-casting model should formalize key features of how market participants and policy makers read data in real time, which involves: monitoring many data releases, forming expectations about them and revising the assessment on the state of the economy whenever realizations diverge sizeably from those expectations.

Starting with Giannone et al. (2008) and Evans (2005), the literature has provided a formal statistical framework to embed the now-casting process defined in this broader sense. Key in this framework is to use a model with a state space representation. Such model can be written as a system with two types of equations: *measurement equations* linking observed series to a latent state process, and *transition equations* describing the state process dynamics. The latent process is typically associated with the unobserved state of the economy or sometimes directly with the higher frequency counterpart of the target variable. The state space representation allows the use of the Kalman filter to obtain projections for both the observed and the state variables. Importantly, the Kalman filter can easily cope with quintessential features of a now-casting information set such as different number of missing data across series at the end of the sample due to the non-synchronicity of data releases ("ragged"/"jagged" edge problem), missing data in the beginning of the sample due to only a recent collection of some data sources, and the data observed at different frequencies. Dealing with missing data at the beginning of the sample is particularly relevant for emerging markets where data collection efforts are relatively recent.

An important feature of the framework proposed by Giannone et al. (2008) is that it allows to interpret and comment various data releases in terms of the signal they provide on current economic conditions. This is possible because the Kalman filter generates projections for all the variables in the the model and therefore allows to compute, for each data release, a model-based surprise, the *news*. Bańbura and Modugno (2010) have shown formally how to link such news to the resulting now-cast revision. In this way, the data releases are weighted in a model-based rigorous way and the role of different categories of data – surveys, financial, production or labor market – in signaling changes in economic activity can be evaluated. We regard this as a major step ahead with respect to the traditional approach of bridge equations.

Since the market as well as policy makers typically watch and comment many data, essentially following the data flow throughout the quarter, the now-cast model should ideally be able to handle a high-dimensional problem. This is indeed one of the features of the econometric model proposed by Giannone et al. (2008). The motivation behind a data-rich approach is not necessarily the improvement in forecasting accuracy, but rather the ability to evaluate and interpret any significant information that may affect the now-cast.

In Giannone et al. (2008) the estimation procedure exploits the fact that relevant data series, although may be numerous, co-move quite strongly so that their dynamics can be captured by few common factors. In other words, all the variables in the information set are assumed to be generated by a dynamic factor model, which copes effectively with the so-called "curse of dimensionality" (large number of parameters relative to the sample size). The estimation method in Giannone et al. (2008) is the two-step procedure proposed by Doz et al. (2011), which is based on principal components analysis. More recent works, as, for example Bańbura and Modugno (2010), apply a quasi maximum likelihood for which Doz et al. (2012) have established the consistency and robustness properties when the size of the sample and the size of the cross-section are large.

The model of Giannone et al. (2008) was first implemented to now-cast GDP at the Board of Governors of the Federal Reserve in a project which started in 2003. Since then various versions have been built for different economies and implemented in other central banks, including the European Central Bank (ECB, 2008) and in other institutions as, for example, the International Monetary Fund (Matheson, 2011). There have been many other studies: for the United States (Lahiri and Monokroussos, 2011); for the aggregate euro area (Angelini et al., 2010, 2011; Bańbura and Modugno, 2010; Bańbura and Rünstler, 2011; Camacho and Perez-Quiros, 2010); for the single euro area countries, including France (Bessec and Doz, 2011; Barhoumi et al., 2010), Germany (Marcellino and Schumacher, 2010), Ireland (D'Agostino et al., 2008; Liebermann, 2012b), the Netherlands (de Winter, 2011), see also Rünstler et al. (2009); for China (Yiu and Chow, 2010); for the Czech Republic (Arnostova et al., 2011); for New Zealand (Matheson, 2010); for Norway (Aastveit and Trovik, 2012); for Switzerland (Siliverstovs and Kholodilin, 2012; Siliverstovs, 2012).

Results in the literature have provided support for several general conclusions. First, gains of institutional and statistical forecasts of GDP relative to the naïve constant growth model are substantial only at very short horizons and in particular for the current quarter. This implies that the ability to forecast GDP growth mostly concerns the current (and previous) quarter. Second, the automatic statistical procedure performs as well as institutional forecasts, which are the result of a process involving models and judgment. These results suggest that now-casting has an important place in the broader forecasting literature. Third, the now-casts become progressively more accurate as the quarter comes to a close and the relevant information accumulates, hence it is important to incorporate new data as soon as they are released. Fourth, the exploitation of timely data leads to improvement in the now-cast accuracy. In particular, the relevance of various data types is not only determined by the strength of their relationship with the target variable, as it is the case in traditional forecasting exercises, but also by their timeliness. Soft information has been found to be extremely important especially early in the quarter when hard information is not available. An extensive review of the literature, including empirical findings, is provided in the survey by Bańbura et al. (2011).

In this chapter we review different statistical approaches to now-casting in more detail and perform a new empirical exercise.

The focus of the review, as we stressed earlier, is on frameworks which provide a comprehensive approach to the problem of now-casting and are based on multivariate dynamic models that can be written in state space form. Although most applications are based on the dynamic factor model, we also review papers based on mixed frequency VARs (e.g., Giannone et al., 2009b and Kuzin et al., 2011) as they fit within the general framework. By contrast, partial models such as the traditional bridge equations capture only a limited aspect of the now-casting process. However, since these models are still used by practitioners, we include them in our review and discuss recent refinements such as MIDAS equations (used for now-casting by, e.g., Clements and Galvão, 2008, 2009; Kuzin et al., 2011).

In the empirical part, we propose and evaluate a daily dynamic factor model for now-casting US GDP with real-time data and provide illustrations on how it can be used for the reading of the real-time data flow, including not only variables available at a monthly frequency like in previous literature, but also daily financial variables and those weekly variables which are typically watched by the market.

The chapter is organized as follows. The second section defines the problem of now-casting in general and discusses different approaches used in the literature to deal with it. In the third section, we define the daily model and provide results for the empirical application. Section 4 concludes. Two appendixes contain, respectively, technical details on the implementation of the model and further empirical results.

2. NOW-CASTING: PROBLEM AND OVERVIEW OF APPROACHES

Now-casting essentially involves obtaining a projection of a variable of interest on the available information set, say Ω_v. Index v can be associated with time of a particular data release. The data vintage index v should not be confused with the model time index t. Due to frequent and non-synchronous statistical data releases v is of high frequency and is irregularly spaced. Several releases within a single day could occur.

Typically the variable of interest is an indicator collected at rather low frequency and subject to a significant publication lag. The aim is to obtain its "early estimate" on the basis of high frequency, more timely information. This has a number of implications regarding the features of the information set Ω_v. First, Ω_v could contain data collected at a wide range of frequencies, from daily to annual. Second, as different types of data are released in a non-synchronous manner and with different degrees of delay, the time of the last available observation differs from series to series. Key in now-casting is to use all the available information. This results in a so-called "ragged" or "jagged" edge of Ω_v. Finally, the information set could be very large.

Different solutions have been proposed to the problem of mixed frequency data, we review some of them in the context of now-casting in the following sections. We focus in particular on the approaches that treat the low frequency data as high frequency with periodically missing observations and specify the underlying model dynamics at high frequency. To this end, for the low frequency variables their high frequency unobserved "counterparts" are introduced. In this, the usual convention is to index the observations of low frequency variables by time indexes ts referring to the end of the respective observation intervals.

Before explaining the details, let us introduce some notation. For simplicity, in the main text we assume that the observation intervals for variables collected at low frequency are constant across time, i.e., each month or quarter would have a constant number of days. The case of irregular intervals is discussed in the Appendix. For some variable y, we will denote by y_t^k its "counterpart" defined at an observation interval of k periods. Note that it does not necessarily mean that the variable is collected at this interval. For example, we could have an indicator collected at monthly frequency expressed as a quarterly concept. In case y is collected at an interval k we will observe y_t^k for $t = k, 2k, 3k, \ldots$ In other words, for $k > 1$ the observations of y_t^k will be periodically missing. A vector of N variables, possibly defined at different observation intervals, will be denoted by $Y_t^{K_Y} = (y_{t,1}^{k_1}, y_{t,2}^{k_2}, \ldots, y_{t,N}^{k_N})'$. For each variable in the information set, the high frequency, possibly unobserved, construct will be denoted by $y_t = y_t^1$ and the corresponding vector of N variables by $Y_t = (y_{t,1}, y_{t,2}, \ldots, y_{t,N})'$.

Note that the time unit associated with t will depend on the particular framework. For some models t would correspond to months while for the others to days, for example. For a given economic concept, the corresponding k will depend on the time unit adopted for the model. For example, for industrial production, which is collected at monthly frequency, $k = 1$ in case of a monthly model and $k = 22$ (on average) if the model is specified at daily frequency. Typically some of the variables in Ω_v will be observed at high frequency, i.e., for some n we will have $k_n = 1$, but in general this is not a necessary condition.[1]

Given this notation, the information set can be defined as $\Omega_v = \{y_{t,n}^{k_n}, t = k_n, 2k_n, \ldots, T_n(v), n = 1, 2, \ldots, N\}$. $T_n(v)$ is a multiple of k_n and refers to the last observation of variable n in the data vintage v. Due to mixed frequency of the data-set and non-synchronous releases we will have in general $T_n(v) \neq T_m(v)$ for some $n \neq m$ leading to the ragged edge described above.

As some of the approaches will be focused on one particular variable of interest, without the loss of generality, we will assume that it is the first variable, $y_{t,1}^{k_1}$.

Scalar and vector random variables will be denoted by lower and upper case letters, respectively. Parameters will be denoted by Greek letters.

2.1. Temporal Aggregation

Since key element of now-casting methodology is dealing with mixed frequency data, the issue of temporal aggregation arises.

---

[1] For example, the model of Aruoba et al. (2009) in the current version is specified at daily frequency but the highest frequency of the data is weekly.

The focus of this chapter will be on the approaches in which the model is specified at high frequency. Therefore it is important to understand the relation between the high frequency variables, y_t, which for key economic concepts are unobserved, and the corresponding observed low frequency series, y_t^k, $k > 1$. The relation depends on whether the corresponding indicator is a flow or a stock variable and on how it is transformed before entering the model. As most of the now-casting applications are based on models specified for stationary variables,[2] y_t^k often corresponds to a (log-)differenced, at k interval, version of some raw series z_t^k. Let z_t denote the high frequency counterpart of z_t^k. For the stock variables, such as, e.g., price indexes, the following holds:

$$z_t^k = z_t, \quad t = k, 2k, \dots,$$

while for the flow variables, most notably GDP, we have:

$$z_t^k = \sum_{i=0}^{k-1} z_{t-i}, \quad t = k, 2k, \dots,$$

see, e.g., Harvey (1989). In case y_t^k is a differenced version of z_t^k, we have for the stock variables:

$$y_t^k = z_t^k - z_{t-k}^k = z_t - z_{t-k} = \sum_{i=0}^{k-1} \Delta z_{t-i} = \sum_{i=0}^{k-1} y_{t-i} = \sum_{i=0}^{k-1} \omega_i^{k,s} y_{t-i}, \quad t = k, 2k, \dots,$$

where $y_t = \Delta z_t$, $\omega_i^{k,s} = 1$ for $i = 0, 1, \dots, k-1$ and $\omega_i^{k,s} = 0$ otherwise. For the flow variables we have that

$$y_t^k = z_t^k - z_{t-k}^k = \sum_{i=0}^{k-1} z_{t-i} - \sum_{i=k}^{2k-1} z_{t-i}$$

$$= \sum_{i=0}^{k-1} (i+1) y_{t-i} + \sum_{i=k}^{2k-2} (2k - i - 1) y_{t-i} = \sum_{i=0}^{2k-2} \omega_i^{k,f} y_{t-i}, \quad t = k, 2k, \dots,$$

where $\omega_i^{k,f} = i+1$ for $i = 0, \dots, k-1$; $\omega_i^{k,f} = 2k - i - 1$ for $i = k, \dots, 2k-2$ and $\omega_i^{k,f} = 0$ otherwise. If z_t^k is a stationary flow variable the relation is the same as in the case of differenced stock variables.

Note that in case y_t^k is a log-differenced flow variable, we follow the approximation of Mariano and Murasawa (2003):

$$y_t^k = \log\left(z_t^k\right) - \log\left(z_{t-k}^k\right) = \log\left(\sum_{i=0}^{k-1} z_{t-i}\right) - \log\left(\sum_{i=k}^{2k-1} z_{t-i}\right)$$

$$\approx \sum_{i=0}^{k-1} \log\left(z_{t-i}\right) - \sum_{i=k}^{2k-1} \log\left(z_{t-i}\right) = \sum_{i=0}^{2k-2} \omega_i^{k,f} y_{t-i}, \quad t = k, 2k, \dots,$$

---

[2] See, e.g., Seong et al. (2007) for an approach with non-stationary data.

where $y_t = \Delta \log (z_t)$. The approximation allows to keep the observational constraints stemming from the temporal aggregation linear.[3] For example, for quarterly GDP in a monthly model we would have:

$$y_t^3 = y_t + 2y_{t-1} + 3y_{t-2} + 2y_{t-3} + y_{t-4}, \quad t = 3, 6, \ldots,$$

see, e.g., Bańbura et al. (2011), Bańbura and Modugno (2010), Kuzin et al. (2011) or Mariano and Murasawa (2003).

2.2. Joint Models in a State Space Representation

The key feature of this type of approaches is that a joint model for $Y_t^{K_Y}$ is specified and that it has a state space representation:

$$Y_t^{K_Y} = \mu + \zeta(\theta)X_t + G_t, \quad G_t \sim i.i.d.\ N(0, \Sigma_G(\theta)), \tag{1}$$

$$X_t = \varphi(\theta)X_{t-1} + H_t, \quad H_t \sim i.i.d.\ N(0, \Sigma_H(\theta)), \tag{2}$$

where the measurement equation (1) links the vector of observed variables, $Y_t^{K_Y}$, to a vector of possibly unobserved state variables, X_t, and the transition equation (2) specifies the dynamics of the latter (see, e.g., Harvey, 1989, for a comprehensive treatment of state space models). We do not add index t in order not to complicate the notation but both the matrices of the coefficients, $\zeta(\theta)$ and $\varphi(\theta)$, as well as the covariance matrices of the disturbances, $\Sigma_G(\theta)$ and $\Sigma_H(\theta)$, could be time-varying.

Given a model with a representation (1) and (2) and the parameters θ, the Kalman filter and smoother provide conditional expectations of the state vector on the information set Ω_v and the associated precision[4]:

$$X_{t|\Omega_v} = \mathbb{E}_\theta\left[X_t|\Omega_v\right], \quad P_{t|\Omega_v} = \mathbb{E}_\theta\left[\left(X_t - \mathbb{E}_\theta\left[X_t|\Omega_v\right]\right)\left(X_t - \mathbb{E}_\theta\left[X_t|\Omega_v\right]\right)'\right].$$

Importantly, the Kalman filter and smoother can efficiently deal with any missing observations in $Y_t^{K_Y}$ and provide the conditional expectation for those. Consequently, now–casts or forecasts can be easily obtained for the target variable and for the predictors. As in this framework the problems of mixed frequency and ragged edge are essentially missing data problems, they are easily solved by Kalman filter and smoother apparatus. Last but not least, joint state space representation also allows to derive model–based news of statistical data releases and to link them to the now–cast revision, see Section 2.3.

---

[3] Proietti and Moauro (2006) propose to use a non-linear smoothing algorithm to impose the temporal constraint exactly. Proietti (2011) further shows how to account for cross-sectional observational constraints.

[4] In case the disturbances are not Gaussian the Kalman smoother provides the minimum mean square linear (MMSLE) estimates.

$\zeta(\theta)P_{t|\Omega_v}\zeta(\theta)'$ is sometimes referred to as "filter uncertainty" (Giannone et al., 2008) as it captures the part of the uncertainty underlying the now-cast of $Y_t^{K_Y}$ that is associated with signal extraction.[5]

Different versions of the general model given by (1) and (2) have been considered in the literature.

2.2.1. Factor Model

As stressed above the real-time data flow is inherently high dimensional. As a consequence it is important to use a parsimonious model that allows to avoid parameter proliferation but at the same time is able to capture the salient features of the data. A dynamic factor model is particularly suitable in this context. In a dynamic factor model, each series is modeled as the sum of two orthogonal components: the first, driven by a handful of unobserved factors captures the joint dynamics and the second is treated as an idiosyncratic residual. If there is a high degree of co-movement among the series, the bulk of the dynamics of any series can be captured by the few factors. There is considerable empirical evidence that indeed this is the case for large panels of macroeconomic variables (see Sargent and Sims, 1977; Giannone et al., 2004; Watson, 2004 and, for a recent survey see Stock and Watson, 2011) and this is why we have chosen this modeling strategy here.

The most common version in the context of now-casting specifies that the high frequency variables, Y_t, have a factor structure and that the factors, F_t, follow a vector autoregressive (VAR) process:

$$Y_t = \mu + \Lambda F_t + E_t, \quad E_t \sim i.i.d. \, N(0, \Sigma_E), \tag{3}$$

$$F_t = \Phi(L)F_t + U_t, \quad U_t \sim i.i.d. \, N(0, \Sigma_U). \tag{4}$$

The latter feature can be particularly important for now-casting, as in the presence of ragged edge, both cross-sectional and "dynamic" information is useful. Σ_E is assumed to be diagonal but, as discussed below, the estimates are robust to violations of this assumption.

This is the type of model that Giannone et al. (2008) have proposed to now-cast GDP from a large set of monthly indicators. In their application Y_t contains only monthly (observed) variables, hence, Eqs. (3) and (4) constitute a state space representation and Kalman filter and smoother can be run to obtain the estimates of the factors. The now-casts are then obtained via a regression of GDP on temporally aggregated factor estimates:

$$y_{t,1}^{k_1} = \alpha + \beta F_{t|\Omega_v}^{k_1} + e_t^{k_1}, \quad t = k_1, 2k_1, \ldots, \tag{5}$$

Giannone et al. (2008) estimate the state space representation (3) and (4) by a so-called two-step procedure. In the first step, the parameters of the state space representation are

---

[5] Note that, for given set of parameters θ and for t sufficiently large, such that the Kalman smoother has approached its steady state, filter uncertainty can be considered time invariant in the sense that it will not depend on t but rather on the shape of the ragged edge in Ω_v with respect to the target quarter, see Bańbura and Rünstler (2011) for a formal explanation.

estimated using principal components derived from a "balanced" panel of Y_t as factor estimates. The balanced panel is obtained by considering only the sample for which all observations are available.[6] In the second step, factors are re-estimated by applying the Kalman smoother to the entire information set.

As stressed in the introduction, this approach has been widely used and applied for different countries. Bańbura and Rünstler (2011) and Angelini et al. (2010) modify it slightly by including quarterly variables into the state space representation using the temporal aggregator variables as explained below.

Doz et al. (2012) show that large systems like (3) and (4) can be also estimated by maximum likelihood. They use the Expectation Maximization (EM) algorithm to obtain the maximum likelihood estimates. The EM algorithm is a popular tool to estimate the parameters for models with unobserved components and/or missing observations, such as (3) and (4). The principle is to write the likelihood in terms of both observed and unobserved data, in this case the state variables, and to iterate between two operations: (i) compute the expectation of the log-likelihood (sufficient statistics) conditional on the data using the parameter estimates from the previous iteration and (ii) re-estimate the parameters through the maximization of the expected log-likelihood. In case of (3) and (4) this boils down to iterating the two-step procedure until convergence, at each step correcting for the uncertainty associated with the estimation of the common factors, see Watson and Engle (1983) and Shumway and Stoffer (1982).

Maximum likelihood has a number of advantages compared to the principal components and the two-step procedure. First it is more efficient for small systems. Second, it allows to deal flexibly with missing observations. Third, it is possible to impose restrictions on the parameters. For example, Bańbura and Modugno (2010) impose the restrictions on the loadings to reflect the temporal aggregation. Bańbura et al. (2011) introduce factors that are specific to groups of variables.

Doz et al. (2011, 2012) show consistency of the two-step and maximum likelihood estimates, respectively. The asymptotic properties are analyzed under different sources of misspecification: omitted serial and cross-sectional correlation of the idiosyncratic components, and non-normality. It is shown that the effects of misspecification on the estimation of the common factors is negligible for large sample size (T) and the cross-sectional dimension (N). We would like to stress here that large cross-section is just an asymptotic device to study the properties of the estimates when more data are included and hence it does not mean that robustness is achieved only when the number of variables approaches infinity. How large is large enough is an empirical question, and Monte Carlo exercises of Doz et al. (2011, 2012) show that substantial robustness is achieved already with a handful of variables.

---

[6] Reduced rank of the disturbances in the factor VAR is often imposed. As discussed in Forni et al. (2009) this feature enforces dynamic heterogeneity in the factor structure.

These results provide theoretical ground for the use of maximum likelihood estimation for factor models in now-casting since they point to its robustness to misspecification. Maximum likelihood estimation with the EM algorithm for a factor model adapted to the now-casting problem has been proposed by Bańbura and Modugno (2010) and this is the approach we use in the empirical application of this chapter. Camacho and Perez-Quiros (2010) and Frale et al. (2011), for example, have also applied maximum likelihood estimation although with a different implementation.

2.2.2. Model with Daily Data

Most of the now-casting applications have been based on monthly and quarterly variables. Modugno (2011) develops a model with daily, weekly, and monthly stock data for now-casting inflation. In this chapter, we generalize this framework by adding flow variables. As above we assume that the high frequency concepts follow a factor model (3) and (4). Consequently for nth variable defined at k_n interval we have:

$$y_{t,n}^{k_n} = \sum_{i=0}^{2k_n-2} \omega_i^{k_n,\cdot} y_{t-i,n} = \sum_{i=0}^{2k_n-2} \omega_i^{k_n,\cdot} \left(\Lambda_{n,\cdot} F_{t-i} + e_{t-i,n} \right),$$

where $\omega_i^{k_n,\cdot} = \omega_i^{k_n,f}$ for the flow variables and $\omega_i^{k_n,\cdot} = \omega_i^{k_n,s}$ for the stock variables. $\Lambda_{n,\cdot}$ denotes the nth row of Λ.

To limit the size of the state vector, temporal aggregator variables for F_t are constructed. We need separate aggregators for each frequency and for stock and flow variables, $F_t^{k,f}$ and $F_t^{k,s}$, $k = k_q, k_m, k_w$, where $k = k_q, k_m,$ and k_w refer to the (average) number of days in a quarter, month, and week, respectively.[7] These variables aggregate recursively F_t so that at the end of the respective period we have:

$$F_t^{k,\cdot} = \sum_{i=0}^{2k-2} \omega_i^{k,\cdot} F_{t-i}, \quad t = k, 2k, \ldots, \quad k = k_q, k_m, k_w.$$

The details on how the aggregators are constructed are provided in the Appendix.

Note that analogously to the common component, the idiosyncratic error in the measurement equation will be a moving average of the daily $e_{t,n}$. However, in the estimation we will assume that at k interval, at which it is defined, it is a white noise.

Another source of misspecification is due to conditional heteroskedasticity and fat tails which is typical of daily data. Fortunately, as discussed in Section 2.2, the factor model is robust to those misspecifications when the factors are extracted from many variables (see Doz et al., 2012). However, reducing misspecifications by explicitly modeling key data features might give sizeable advantages in finite samples. Important directions for future research, especially for daily data, consists in modeling stochastic volatility and rare big shocks, see Marcellino et al. (2012) and Curdia et al. (2012).

---

[7] In fact, we do not have quarterly stock variables in the data-set.

Let $Y_t^{k,\cdot}$ collect the variables observed at interval k (flows or stocks). The measurement equation can be written as follows:

$$
\begin{pmatrix}
Y_t^{k_q,f} \\
Y_t^{k_m,f} \\
Y_t^{k_m,s} \\
Y_t^{k_w,f} \\
Y_t^{k_w,s} \\
Y_t^{k_d}
\end{pmatrix}
=
\begin{pmatrix}
\tilde{\Lambda}^{q,f} & 0 & 0 & 0 & 0 & 0 \\
0 & \tilde{\Lambda}^{m,f} & 0 & 0 & 0 & 0 \\
0 & 0 & \Lambda^{m,s} & 0 & 0 & 0 \\
0 & 0 & 0 & \tilde{\Lambda}^{w,f} & 0 & 0 \\
0 & 0 & 0 & 0 & \Lambda^{w,s} & 0 \\
0 & 0 & 0 & 0 & 0 & \Lambda^{d}
\end{pmatrix}
\begin{pmatrix}
\tilde{F}_t^{k_q,f} \\
\tilde{F}_t^{k_m,f} \\
F_t^{k_m,s} \\
\tilde{F}_t^{k_w,f} \\
F_t^{k_w,s} \\
F_t
\end{pmatrix}
+ E_t^{K_Y}. \quad (6)
$$

For the flow variables an auxiliary aggregator variable, $\bar{F}_t^{k,f}$, is necessary: $\tilde{F}_t^{k,f\prime} = (F_t^{k,f\prime}\ \bar{F}_t^{k,f\prime})$ and $\tilde{\Lambda}^{\cdot,f} = (\Lambda^{\cdot,f}\ 0)$, see the appendix for details.

The coefficients of the transition equation are time-varying:

$$
\begin{pmatrix}
I_{2r} & 0 & 0 & 0 & 0 & \mathcal{W}_t^{k_q,f} \\
0 & I_{2r} & 0 & 0 & 0 & \mathcal{W}_t^{k_m,f} \\
0 & 0 & I_r & 0 & 0 & \mathcal{W}_t^{k_m,s} \\
0 & 0 & 0 & I_{2r} & 0 & \mathcal{W}_t^{k_w,f} \\
0 & 0 & 0 & 0 & I_r & \mathcal{W}_t^{k_w,s} \\
0 & 0 & 0 & 0 & 0 & I_r
\end{pmatrix}
\begin{pmatrix}
\tilde{F}_t^{k_q,f} \\
\tilde{F}_t^{k_m,f} \\
F_t^{k_m,s} \\
\tilde{F}_t^{k_w,f} \\
F_t^{k_w,s} \\
F_t
\end{pmatrix}
$$

$$
=
\begin{pmatrix}
\mathcal{I}_t^{k_q,f} & 0 & 0 & 0 & 0 & 0 \\
0 & \mathcal{I}_t^{k_m,f} & 0 & 0 & 0 & 0 \\
0 & 0 & \mathcal{I}_t^{k_m,s} & 0 & 0 & 0 \\
0 & 0 & 0 & \mathcal{I}_t^{k_w,f} & 0 & 0 \\
0 & 0 & 0 & 0 & \mathcal{I}_t^{k_w,s} & 0 \\
0 & 0 & 0 & 0 & 0 & \Phi
\end{pmatrix}
\begin{pmatrix}
\tilde{F}_{t-1}^{k_q,f} \\
\tilde{F}_{t-1}^{k_m,f} \\
F_{t-1}^{k_m,s} \\
\tilde{F}_{t-1}^{k_w,f} \\
F_{t-1}^{k_w,s} \\
F_{t-1}
\end{pmatrix}
+
\begin{pmatrix}
0 \\
0 \\
0 \\
0 \\
0 \\
U_t
\end{pmatrix},
\quad (7)
$$

where $\mathcal{W}_t^{\cdot,\cdot}$ contain appropriate aggregation weights and $\mathcal{I}_t^{\cdot,\cdot}$ are matrices of zeros and ones, see the appendix for details.[8]

The model is estimated by maximum likelihood using the EM algorithm, as explained in the appendix. Initial parameter values for the algorithm are obtained using principal components as factor estimates. To extract the principal components the missing observations are "filled in" using splines and then the data are filtered to reflect different aggregation intervals.

2.2.3. Mixed Frequency VAR
Another type of model that can be cast in a state space representation is a VAR. Different approaches have been considered to deal with the issue of mixed frequency. One solution, analogous to the approach explained above, is to specify that the high frequency concepts

---

[8] The transition equation is obtained by pre-multiplying (7) by the inverse of the left-hand side matrix.

follow a VAR:

$$\Psi(L)\Big(Y_t - \mu\Big) = E_t, \quad E_t \sim i.i.d. \ N(0, \Sigma_E)$$

and to derive the measurement equation using the (approximate) temporal aggregation relationships between the observed variables and Y_t as explained in Section 2.1, see, e.g., Mariano and Murasawa (2010). As in the case of factor models explained above, Kalman filter and smoother can be used to obtain the now-casts. Giannone et al. (2009b) and Kuzin et al. (2011) apply this type of model to now-cast euro area GDP with monthly indicators. Earlier applications include Zadrozny (1990) and Mittnik and Zadrozny (2004).

Another solution is sometimes referred to as "blocking," see, e.g., Chen et al. (2012). The model is specified at low frequency and the high frequency information is "distributed" into multiple series. For example, in a system with monthly and quarterly variables, blocking consists in having three different time series for each monthly variable, one for each of the three months of the quarter. For a detailed analysis of blocked linear systems see Chen et al. (2012). McCracken et al. (2013) use this approach for now-casting with a large Bayesian VAR.

VAR is a less parsimonious specification than a factor model. For large information sets two solutions to the curse of dimensionality problem could be adopted. Either the forecasts from many smaller systems could be combined or Bayesian shrinkage could be employed to avoid over-fitting in a large system, see Bańbura et al. (2010), Giannone et al. (2012) or Koop (2013) (see also the Chapter on Bayesian VAR in this volume by Karlsson, 2013). Recent papers that have used Bayesian shrinkage to handle large information sets in the context of now-casting are Bloor and Matheson (2011) and Carriero et al. (2012).

2.3. Now-Cast Updates and News

We argue that now-casting goes beyond producing a single prediction for a reference period. The aim is rather to build a framework for the reading of the flow of data releases in real time.

At each time that new data become available, a now-casting model produces an estimate of the variable of interest, say the current quarter growth rate of GDP, thereby providing a sequence of updates for this fixed event. Within a state space framework, the same model also produces forecasts for all variables we are interested in tracking so as to allow extracting the *news* or the "unexpected" component from the released data. Having model-based news for all variables allows obtaining the revision of the GDP now-cast as the weighted sum of those news where the weights are estimated by the model. The framework therefore provides a key for the understanding of changes in the estimates of current economic activity over time and helps evaluating the significance of each data publication.

Following Bańbura and Modugno (2010) we can explain these ideas formally.

Let us consider two consecutive data vintages, Ω_v and Ω_{v+1}. The information sets Ω_v and Ω_{v+1} can differ for two reasons: first, Ω_{v+1} contains some newly released figures, $\{y_{t_j,n_j}^{k_{n_j}}, j = 1, \ldots, J_{v+1}\}$, which were not available in Ω_v; second, some of the data might have been revised. To simplify the notation, in what follows we assume that no past observations for the variable of interest $y_{t,1}^{k_1}$ are contained in the release and that $k_{n_j} = 1$, $j = 1, \ldots, J_{v+1}$ so that $y_{t_j,n_j}^{k_{n_j}} = y_{t_j,n_j}$. The derivations can be modified to a general case in a straightforward manner. More importantly, we abstract from data revisions and therefore we have:

$$\Omega_v \subset \Omega_{v+1} \quad \text{and} \quad \Omega_{v+1}\backslash\Omega_v = \{y_{t_j,n_j}, j = 1, \ldots, J_{v+1}\},$$

hence the information set is "expanding." Note that since different types of data are characterized by different publication delays, in general we will have $t_j \neq t_l$ for some $j \neq l$.

Let us now look at the two consecutive now-cast updates, $\mathbb{E}\left[y_{t,1}^{k_1}|\Omega_v\right]$ and $\mathbb{E}\left[y_{t,1}^{k_1}|\Omega_{v+1}\right]$. The new figures, $\{y_{t_j,n_j}, j = 1, \ldots, J_{v+1}\}$, will in general contain some new information on $y_{t,1}^{k_1}$ and consequently lead to a revision of its now-cast. From the properties of conditional expectation as an orthogonal projection operator, it follows that:

$$\underbrace{\mathbb{E}\left[y_{t,1}^{k_1}|\Omega_{v+1}\right]}_{\text{new forecast}} = \underbrace{\mathbb{E}\left[y_{t,1}^{k_1}|\Omega_v\right]}_{\text{old forecast}} + \underbrace{\mathbb{E}\left[y_{t,1}^{k_1}|A_{v+1}\right]}_{\text{revision}},$$

where

$$A_{v+1} = (a_{v+1,1} \cdots a_{v+1,J_{v+1}})', \quad a_{v+1,j} = y_{t_j,n_j} - \mathbb{E}\left[y_{t_j,n_j}|\Omega_v\right], \quad j = 1, \ldots, J_{v+1}.$$

A_{v+1} represents the part of the release $\{y_{t_j,n_j}, j = 1, \ldots, J_{v+1}\}$, which is "orthogonal" to the information already contained in Ω_v. In other words, it is the "unexpected" (with respect to the model), part of the release. Therefore, we label A_{v+1} as the *news*. Note that it is the news and not the release itself that leads to now-cast revision. In particular, if the new numbers in Ω_{v+1} are exactly as predicted, given the information in Ω_v, or in other words "there is no news," the now-cast will not be revised.

We can further develop the expression for the revision, that is the difference between the new and the old now-cast, as:

$$\mathbb{E}\left[y_{t,1}^{k_1}|A_{v+1}\right] = \mathbb{E}\left[y_{t,1}^{k_1}A_{v+1}'\right]\mathbb{E}\left[A_{v+1}A_{v+1}'\right]^{-1}A_{v+1}.$$

In what follows we abstract from the problem of parameter uncertainty.

For the model written as (1) and (2) with a diagonal Σ_G, this can be further developed as:

$$\mathbb{E}\left[y_{t,1}^{k_1}a_{v+1,j}\right] = \zeta_{1,.}\mathbb{E}\left[\left(X_t - \mathbb{E}\left[X_t|\Omega_v\right]\right)\left(X_{t_j} - \mathbb{E}\left[X_{t_j}|\Omega_v\right]\right)'\right]\zeta_{n_j,.}', \quad \text{and}$$

$$\mathbb{E}\left[a_{v+1,j}a_{v+1,l}\right] = \zeta_{n_j,.}\mathbb{E}\left[\left(X_{t_j} - \mathbb{E}\left[X_{t_j}|\Omega_v\right]\right)\left(X_{t_l} - \mathbb{E}\left[X_{t_l}|\Omega_v\right]\right)'\right]\zeta_{n_l,.}' + \Sigma_{G,jl}1_{j=l},$$

where $\Sigma_{G,jl}$ is the element of the Σ_G from the jth row and lth column. Kalman filter and smoother provide appropriate expectations.

As a result, we can find a vector $\mathcal{D}_{v+1} = (\delta_{v+1,1}, \ldots, \delta_{v+1,J_{v+1}})$ such that the following holds:

$$\underbrace{\mathbb{E}\left[y_{t,1}^{k_1} | \Omega_{v+1}\right] - \mathbb{E}\left[y_{t,1}^{k_1} | \Omega_v\right]}_{\text{revision}} = \mathcal{D}_{v+1} A_{v+1} = \sum_{j=1}^{J_{v+1}} \delta_{v+1,j} \Big(\underbrace{y_{t_j, n_j} - \mathbb{E}\left[y_{t_j, n_j} | \Omega_v\right]}_{\text{news}} \Big). \quad (8)$$

In other words, the revision can be decomposed as a weighted average of the news in the latest release. What matters for the revision is both the size of the news as well as its relevance for the variable of interest, as represented by the associated weight $\delta_{v+1,j}$. Formula (8) can be considered as a generalization of the usual Kalman filter update equation (see, e.g., Harvey, 1989, Eq. (3.2.3a)) to the case in which "new" data arrive in a non-synchronous manner.

Note that filter uncertainty for $y_{t,1}^{k_1}$ decreases with the new release and the reduction can be decomposed along similar lines.

Relationship (8) enables us to trace sources of forecast revisions.[9] More precisely, in the case of a simultaneous release of several (groups of) variables it is possible to decompose the resulting forecast revision into contributions from the news in individual (groups of) series.[10] In addition, we can produce statements like, e.g., "after the release of industrial production, the forecast of GDP went up because the indicators turned out to be (on average) higher than expected".[11]

2.4. "Partial" Models

In contrast to approaches described in Section 2.2, the methodologies that we label as "partial" do not specify a joint model for the variable of interest and for the predictors. One limitation of partial models is that without a joint representation the model-based news of releases and their impact on the now-cast cannot be derived. Other drawbacks include the need for auxiliary models or for separate set of parameters for each data vintage. In spite of those limitations we review also partial models here because they have a long tradition in policy institutions, in particular central banks.

Again let us assume for simplicity that $k_n = 1$, $n \neq 1$ so that $y_{t,n}^{k_n} = y_{t,n}$. In other words, all the predictors are observed at the same, high frequency. The methodologies presented below typically can be generalized to relax this restriction.

The following "partial" models have been studied in the literature.

---

[9] Note, that the contribution from the news is equivalent to the change in the overall contribution of the series to the forecast (the measure proposed in Bańbura and Rünstler, 2011) when the correlations between the predictors are not exploited in the model. Otherwise, those measures are different. In particular, there can be a change in the overall contribution of a variable even if no new information on this variable was released. Therefore news is a better suited tool for analyzing the sources of forecasts revisions, see Bańbura and Modugno (2010) for the details.

[10] If the release concerns only one group or one series, the contribution of its news is simply equal to the change in the forecast.

[11] This holds of course for the indicators with positive entries in $\delta_{v+1,j}$.

2.4.1. Bridge Equations

In this type of model, the now-cast and forecasts of $y_{t,1}^{k_1}$ are obtained via the following regression:

$$y_{t,1}^{k_1} = \alpha + \beta y_{t,n}^{k_1} + e_t^{k_1}, \quad t = k_1, 2k_1, \ldots, \tag{9}$$

where $y_{t,n}^{k_1}$ is a predictor aggregated to the *lower* frequency, i.e., the frequency of the target variable. Hence the mixed frequency problem is solved by temporal aggregation of the predictors to the lower frequency. To handle ragged edge auxiliary models, such as ARMA or VAR, are used to forecast $y_{t,n}$ to close the target period of interest.

This is the "traditional" now-casting tool, popularly employed at central banks to obtain early estimates of GDP or its components. The predictors are typically monthly, see, e.g., Kitchen and Monaco (2003), Parigi and Golinelli (2007), Parigi and Schlitzer (1995) and Baffigi et al. (2004).

Equation (9) is typically estimated by the OLS. It can be further extended to include more predictors or the lags of the dependent variable. In case the information set is large, forecast combination is often performed (Kitchen and Monaco, 2003; Diron, 2008; Angelini et al., 2011; Rünstler et al., 2009). Bridge equations can be also combined in a so-called bottom-up approach where one now-casts GDP by aggregating the now-casts of its components exploiting national accounts identities (see Hahn and Skudelny, 2008; Drechsel and Scheufele, 2012; Baffigi et al., 2004).

Note that the model of Giannone et al. (2008) can be also interpreted as "bridging with factors" as the factor estimates obtained by the Kalman filter and smoother would be plugged into an equation similar to (9) to obtain the now-casts, cf. Eq. (5).

2.4.2. MIDAS-Type Equations

In contrast to the previous approach in a MIDAS-type model the predictors are included in the regression at their original observation frequency:

$$y_{t,1}^{k_1} = \alpha + \beta \Gamma(L, \theta) y_{t-h_n,n} + e_t^{k_1}, \quad t = k_1, 2k_1, \ldots, \tag{10}$$

where $\Gamma(L, \theta)$ is a lag polynomial. Since for large k_1 many lags of the explanatory variable might be required, key in this approach is that $\Gamma(L, \theta)$ is parsimoniously parameterised. Various versions have been proposed (Ghysels et al., 2003), including exponential Almon polynomial for which $\Gamma(L, \theta) = \sum_{m=1}^{M} \gamma(m, \theta) L^m$ with $\theta = (\theta_1, \theta_2)$ and $\gamma(m, \theta) = \frac{\exp(\theta_1 m + \theta_2 m^2)}{\sum_{m=1}^{M} \exp(\theta_1 m + \theta_2 m^2)}$. In contrast to approaches explained above, MIDAS-type regression implies that the temporal aggregation weights are data driven.

Regarding the problem of ragged edge, the solution in this type of approach can be thought of as re-aligning each time series. The time series with missing observations at the end of the sample are shifted forward in order to obtain a balanced data-set with the most recent information.[12] The parameters in Eq. (10) depend on h_n, which is determined by

---

[12] Re-aligning has been a popular strategy do deal with ragged-edge data (see, e.g., Altissimo et al., 2001, 2010 and de Antonio Liedo and Muoz, 2010).

the difference between the forecast target period and the period of the last observation of the predictor. As a consequence, separate models need to be estimated for different data vintages as the corresponding h_n vary. The case of $h_n < k_1$, i.e., when some data referring to the target quarter are available, is sometimes labeled as MIDAS with leads (Andreou et al., 2013).

Applications of this type of model to now-casting include Clements and Galvão (2008, 2009) or Kuzin et al. (2011) who use monthly indicators to forecast GDP. Recently, Andreou et al. (2013) also include daily financial variables to the equation. Equation (10) is typically estimated by non-linear least squares. Clements and Galvão (2008) propose how to add a lag of the low frequency variable in order to avoid a seasonal response of the dependent variable to the predictors. They use the Broyden–Fletcher–Goldfarg–Shanno method to obtain the estimates of the parameters.

The MIDAS equations suffer from the curse of dimensionality problem and can include only a handful of variables. Forecast combination is a popular strategy to deal with large information sets (see, e.g., Andreou et al., 2013).

As an alternative, Marcellino and Schumacher (2010) propose to now-cast GDP from the following equation:

$$y_{t,1}^{k_1} = \alpha + \beta \Gamma(L, \theta) F_{t-h_F|\Omega_v} + e_t^{k_1}, \quad t = k_1, 2k_1, \ldots,$$

where $F_{t|\Omega_v}$ are factors estimated from a set of monthly predictors following the methodology of Giannone et al. (2008) and h_F corresponds to the difference between the forecast target period and the latest observation in the predictor set.

As we have already remarked, in order to understand why and how now-casts change with the arrival of new information it is important to have a joint model that allows to form expectations and hence derive the news component of data releases and their impact on the now-cast. Attempts to circumvent the problem within partial models has to be necessarily based on a heuristic procedure. For example Ghysels and Wright (2009) construct news using market expectations. The latter are linked to the change in the forecast by estimating additional auxiliary regressions.

3. EMPIRICAL APPLICATION

The aim of the empirical application is to establish whether daily and weekly variables contribute to the precision of the now-cast of quarterly GDP growth and to use our framework to study the extent to which stock prices are connected with macroeconomic variables.

The now-casting framework is the appropriate one for studying the role of financial variables for macro forecasting since it takes into account the timeliness of financial information. Although the role of financial variables for the forecast of real economic conditions has been studied extensively in the forecasting literature (see Stock and Watson, 2003;

Forni et al., 2003), results are typically based on models which do not take into account the publication lags associated with different data series and therefore miss timeliness as an essential feature of financial information in real-time forecasting. What is more, most of the now-casting studies we have reviewed here are based on monthly models. Daily variables, when included, are first converted to monthly frequency hence their advantage due to timeliness might be partly lost (see, e.g., Giannone et al., 2008; Bańbura and Rünstler, 2011). This study corrects this feature by treating all data at their original frequency.

3.1. Data

We are considering 24 series of which only GDP is quarterly. Table 4.1 provides the list of variables, including the observation frequency and the transformation we have adopted. Among monthly data we include industrial production, labor market data, a variety of surveys but also price series, indicators of the housing market, trade and consumption statistics. The weekly series are initial jobless claims and the Bloomberg consumer comfort index. We have aimed at selecting the "headline" macroeconomic variables. Accordingly, the series we collected are marked on Bloomberg website as "Market Moving Indicators". The daily financial variables include S&P 500 stock price index, short- and long-term interest rates, effective exchange rate and the price of oil. To give an idea on the timeliness of each macroeconomic variable Table 4.1 also provides the publication delay, i.e., the difference (in days) between the end of the reference period and the date of the respective release for January 2011.[13] We can observe the typical pattern according to which soft data, notably surveys, are published more timely than the hard data.

Let us make some remarks about the criteria used for the selection of the macroeconomic variables. We only include the headlines of each macroeconomic report since these are the data followed by the market and extensively commented by the newspapers. For example, for the release of industrial production and capacity utilization we only include total indexes hence disregarding the sectoral disaggregation. The disaggregated data for each release were considered in Giannone et al. (2008) whose universe of data included around 200 time series. Bańbura and Modugno (2010) and Bańbura et al. (2011) analyze the marginal impact on the now-cast precision of disaggregated data and show that it is minimal, result which is supported by the observation that markets only focus on the headlines of each report. The same authors also show that the inclusion of disaggregated data does not deteriorate the performance of the model, supporting the results on the robustness of the factor model to data selection (see the empirical analysis in Bańbura et al., 2010 for longer horizons forecasting and the simulation study of Doz et al., 2011, 2012). In this chapter we have therefore decided to disregard them but the results just cited carry two important implications for empirical work in this field. First, the fact that

---

[13] The release dates typically vary from month to month. For example, industrial production is released between the 14th and 18th day of each month.

Table 4.1 Data

Number	Name	Frequency	Publication Delay (in Days After) Reference Period)	Transformation Log	Diff
1	Real Gross Domestic Product	Quarterly	28	×	×
2	Industrial Production Index	Monthly	14	×	×
3	Purchasing Manager Index, Manufacturing	Monthly	3		×
4	Real Disposable Personal Income	Monthly	29	×	×
5	Unemployment Rate	Monthly	7		×
6	Employment, Non-farm Payrolls	Monthly	7	×	×
7	Personal Consumption Expenditure	Monthly	29	×	×
8	Housing Starts	Monthly	19	×	×
9	New Residential Sales	Monthly	26	×	×
10	Manufacturers' New Orders, Durable Goods	Monthly	27	×	×
11	Producer Price Index, Finished Goods	Monthly	13	×	×
12	Consumer Price Index, All Urban Consumers	Monthly	14	×	×
13	Imports	Monthly	43	×	×
14	Exports	Monthly	43	×	×
15	Philadelphia Fed Survey, General Business Conditions	Monthly	−10		×
16	Retail and Food Services Sales	Monthly	14	×	×
17	Conference Board Consumer Confidence	Monthly	−5		×
18	Bloomberg Consumer Comfort Index	Weekly	4		×
19	Initial Jobless Claims	Weekly	4	×	×
20	S&P 500 Index	Daily	1	×	×
21	Crude Oil, West Texas Intermediate (WTI)	Daily	1	×	×
22	10-Year Treasury Constant Maturity Rate	Daily	1		×
23	3-Month Treasury Bill, Secondary Market Rate	Daily	1		×
24	Trade Weighted Exchange Index, Major Currencies	Daily	1		×

Notes: The publication delays are based on the data releases in January 2011. Negative numbers for surveys mean that they are released before the reference month is over.

including disaggregated data does not worsen forecasting performance says that, if for the problem at hand we were interested in commenting them, we could include them in the model without paying a cost in terms of larger forecast error. Second, including variables with little marginal forecasting power does not hurt results and therefore it is not necessary to select variables using criteria outside the model; the model itself attributes the appropriate weight to the different predictors.

An alternative approach consists in selecting the variables using statistical criteria as suggested in Boivin and Ng (2006) and Bai and Ng (2008). We do not consider it for a number of reasons. First, the algorithms for selecting predictors have been developed for balanced panels and hence they are not suitable in the context of now-casting since they are designed to account only for the quality of the signal but not for timeliness. Second, empirically it has been found that, if data are collinear, there is no major difference in the forecasting performance of models based on selected or all available predictors (see De Mol et al., 2008).[14] Finally and most importantly, because of collinearity among predictors, variable selection is inherently unstable, i.e., the set of predictors selected is very sensitive to minor perturbation of the data-set, such as adding new variables or extending the sample length (see De Mol et al., 2008). Similar instabilities have also been found in the context of model selection and model averaging (Ouysse, 2011; Stock and Watson, 2012).

The out-of-sample now-cast evaluations are performed on the basis of real-time data vintages for the series described in Table 4.1. This implies that at each date in which we produce a forecast we use the data that were available just before or on the same day. The real-time database has been downloaded from ALFRED, the US real-time database maintained by the Federal Reserve Bank of St. Louis.

Notice that most of the now-casting studies we reviewed earlier involve out-of-sample forecast evaluations in *pseudo* rather than in fully real time like here. Pseudo real-time forecast evaluation design mimics the real-time situation in the sense that the data publication delays are replicated following a realistic *stylized* publication calendar and that the model is estimated recursively. However, given the difficulties of obtaining real-time data vintages for many series, final revised data are used throughout the exercise. Hence the effects of data revisions, which for some variables can be sizable, are disregarded. As noted by, e.g., Croushore (2011) this could affect the results of forecast evaluation and comparison. The few studies with real-time data include, e.g., Camacho and Perez-Quiros (2010); Lahiri and Monokroussos (2011); Liebermann (2012a); Siliverstovs (2012).

3.2. Now-Casting GDP

In this section we study the model performance for real GDP now-casting from different perspectives. In particular, we analyze the evolution of the now-cast and its uncertainty

---

[14] This result also emerges from a careful reading of the empirical results of Boivin and Ng (2006).

in relation to releases of different categories of data. We focus on GDP since it is the variable that best summarizes the state of the economy.

The benchmark factor model described in Section 2.2.2 including the variables listed in Table 4.1 is estimated following Bańbura and Modugno (2010) and is specified with one factor only. Our choice is mainly motivated by simplicity and by the fact that results based on two factors are qualitatively similar to those based on one factor.[15] In order to shed light on the importance of high frequency data for the accuracy of the now-cast, we also construct two alternative models. The first is a factor model analogous to the benchmark model, but at monthly frequency and based on the information set that excludes the weekly and daily variables. The second is a small monthly factor model based on five (hard) indicators, namely real GDP, industrial production, real disposable income, retail sales and employment. This is the data-set used in Stock and Watson (1989) for estimating a coincident indicator for the US economy and it is also considered by the the NBER's Business Cycle Dating Committee.

We also compare the performance of the benchmark model to that of bridge equations. For the latter we estimate a separate regression of GDP on each of the 23 predictors. In each case we aggregate the monthly predictors to quarterly frequency as explained in Section 2.1.[16] As mentioned in Section 2, we use an auxiliary model to produce the forecast for the predictors over the "missing" months in the quarter of interest. To this end we estimate an autoregressive (AR) models on the series and use the BIC criteria to select the number of lags.

We finally report results for the survey of professional forecasters (SPF) which are available in the middle second month of each quarter.

Depending on when in the quarter we perform the now-cast update, the availability of information differs. For example, in the first month we only have very limited information on the current quarter, in particular no hard data. To assess how the accuracy of the now-cast improves as information on the current quarter accumulates, we evaluate the now-cast at different points within a quarter. Precisely, we produce the now-cast four times per month, on the 7th, 14th, 21st, and 28th, starting in the first month of the current quarter up to the first month of the following quarter.[17] Each time, the model is re-estimated in order to take into account parameter uncertainty.

---

[15] A more systematic approach to the choice of the number of factors is to set the parameterizations in a data driven fashion. This can be done in different ways: (a) minimizing recursive mean square forecast error; (b) averaging across all possible parameterizations; and (c) applying recursively information criteria. The literature typically indicates that results are robust across model parameterizations (see, for example Angelini et al., 2011) although some papers have advocated pooling across specifications (see Kuzin et al., 2013). Bańbura and Modugno (2010) note that the recent recession period saw larger differences between specifications in terms of forecast accuracy and advocate pooling.

[16] All the bridge equation models in this exercise are based on monthly variables. Accordingly, daily and weekly data are first averaged over month and the auxiliary models are run at monthly frequency. Partial monthly information is thus disregarded.

[17] As US GDP is typically released around the end of the first month of the following quarter.

The evaluation sample is 1995–2010. For most of the series the data vintages are available since January 1995, first date of our evaluation. For the data for which real-time vintages starting from January 1995 are not available, we use the oldest vintage available and we apply a "stylized" publication delay, as provided in Table 4.1.[18] The estimation is recursive, i.e., the first observation in the sample is fixed to the first business day of January 1983. Note that Bloomberg Consumer Comfort Index dates back only to 1985, however the EM algorithm used here can deal with series of different lengths.[19]

Figure 4.1 reports the Root Mean Squared Forecast Error (RMSFE) from the real-time now-casting exercise for the three specifications of the factor models, for the bridge equations and the SPF. The RMSFE is computed with respect to GDP in the final data vintage.[20] The factor model containing the complete data-set is labeled as "Benchmark," that including only GDP and monthly variables as "Monthly" and the small one with only hard data as "BCDC." For the bridge equations we report the RMSFE of the average forecast from the 23 equations (in Table A in the appendix we report the RMSFE for each single bridge equation model). The dots indicate the RMSFE of the SPF. On the horizontal axis we indicate the day and the month of the respective now-cast update.

Overall, the results confirm qualitatively the findings of earlier pseudo real-time exercises.

For example, as found in earlier work, Figure 4.1 shows that, as the information accumulates, the gains in forecast accuracy based on the factor model are substantial. In the next subsection, we show this point formally via a statistical test. Clearly, the ability of the model to incorporate increasingly richer information as time progresses is key for improving now-cast accuracy.

The SPF, published the second month of the quarter, has comparable performance to our model at that date. This confirms the results that model-based now-casts fair well in comparison to institutional or private sector forecasts (Giannone et al., 2008; de Winter, 2011) with real-time data.

The performance of the bridge equations is inferior, indicating sizable gains from adopting a joint multivariate modeling strategy. This result has been found in, e.g., Angelini et al. (2011), Angelini et al. (2010) or Rünstler et al. (2009).

Two other results emerge from the analysis. First, surveys appear to have an important role in improving the accuracy of the model at all points of time as the now-casts from the model based on only hard data are less accurate (on this point see also Giannone

---

[18] For example, retail sales vintages are available from June 2001 only. For the period January 1995–May 2001 we use the data figures as available in June 2001 vintage, but every time we produce a forecast we assume the publication lag of 14 days (cf. Table 4.1), i.e., on the 14th of each month we add the observation relating to the previous month.

[19] This can be an important feature as for many interesting new data sources (e.g., Google trends) only limited back-data is available. In addition, for many economies, even among headline indicators many have been collected only since recently.

[20] "Final" vintage corresponds to the data available in June 2011.

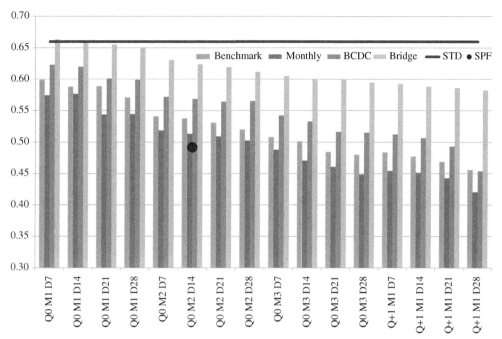

Figure 4.1 Root Mean Squared Forecast Error (RMSFE), GDP. *Notes:* Figure shows the Root Mean Squared Forecast Error (RMSFE) over period 1995–2010 for the model containing the complete dataset (Benchmark), the one that includes GDP and monthly variables only (Monthly), the one that uses the five hard variables considered by the NBER's Business Cycle Dating Committee (BCDC) and the RMSFEs of the average forecast produced by the bridge equations (Bridge) over the sample period 1995–2010. The forecast accuracy of the model is evaluated four times per month for four consecutive months (from the first month of the current quarter, Q0 M1 to the first month of the following quarter, Q+1 M1). The date of the update is indicated on the horizontal axis. The dot corresponds to the RMSFE for the survey professional forecasters (SPF).

et al., 2008; Bańbura and Rünstler, 2011; Lahiri and Monokroussos, 2011). Second, the inclusion of higher frequency data does not improve the results significantly.

Now-Casting After the Fall of Lehman Brothers

To further analyze the result that inclusion of daily and weekly variables does not improve now-cast accuracy, and as an illustration of how the sequence of news impacts the estimate of GDP and the associated uncertainty, we replicate a real-time now-cast from the benchmark specification of the GDP growth rate for the fourth quarter of 2008. Precisely, from October 1st 2008 until the end of January 2009, when the first official estimate of GDP was released, we produce daily updates of the now-cast, each time incorporating new data releases. This is a particularly interesting episode since it corresponds to the onset of the financial crisis following the bankruptcy of Lehman Brothers.

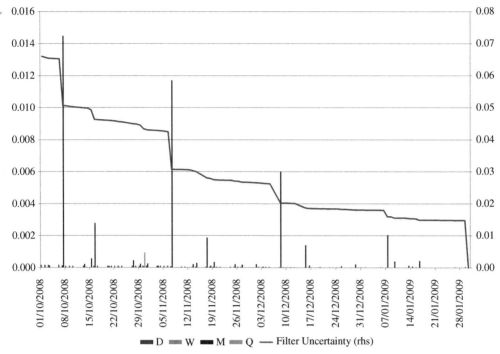

Figure 4.2 Filter uncertainty, GDP. *Notes:* Figure reports the evolution of filter uncertainty (RHS scale) and the contributions to its decline (LHS scale) for the GDP now-cast for fourth quarter of 2008. The data are grouped according to frequencies: daily ("D"), weekly ("W"), monthly ("M"), and quarterly ("Q"). The horizontal axis indicates the date of the now-cast update.

As explained in Section 2.3, the revisions of the GDP now-cast can be expressed as weighted sums of news from particular releases.[21] Similarly, the Kalman smoother output allows to decompose the gradual decline in filter uncertainty into contributions from particular (groups of) variables. For the purpose of the exercise we group the variables into the daily, weekly, monthly, and quarterly. As the decomposition is conditional on a given set of parameters, we produce all the updates using the parameters estimated over the sample 1983–2010.

Let us start with the filter uncertainty, see Figure 4.2. The chart indicates that macroeconomic monthly releases have the largest effects: the big spikes correspond to the release of the (monthly) employment situation report. Smaller spikes are experienced when industrial production is released. In contrast, daily and weekly data do not seem to have

[21] Recall that the decomposition does not take into account the effect of the revisions to back-data. Accordingly, the difference between two consecutive now-casts (based on vintages Ω_{v+1} and Ω_v) in the exercise is equal to the sum of the effect of the news and of the effect of data revisions. The latter is defined as the difference between the now-cast based on the data availability pattern of vintage Ω_v but with revised back-data as available in vintage Ω_{v+1} and the now-cast based on vintage Ω_v.

much of an impact. To understand whether this result is explained by the fact that the effect of daily data is spread over time, we have computed the cumulative effect of daily and weekly data on the uncertainty from the first day of the current quarter to the day of GDP release. For that period total uncertainty is reduced from 0.066 to 0.015 (the day of the GDP release it collapses to zero) and 92% of it is due to the macro variables while the daily variables account only for the remaining 8%. This confirms the finding of a negligible role of high frequency variables, notably daily financial data. Finally, the impact of GDP release for the previous quarter is very small. This is explained by timeliness: once "early" information on the current quarter is released and incorporated in the model, information on the previous quarter GDP becomes redundant for the now-cast of the current quarter.

Figure 4.3 reports the evolution of the now-cast itself and the contribution of the news component of the various data groups to the now-cast revision.

Industrial production for September (published mid October) has the largest impact and leads to a substantial downward revision. This negative news in October is confirmed

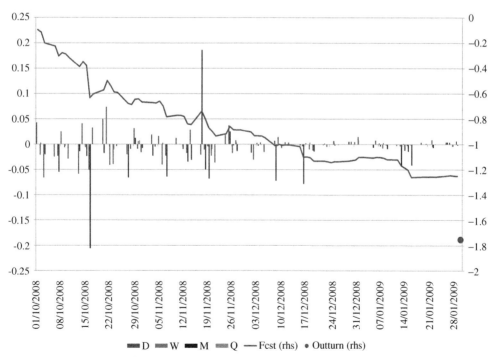

Figure 4.3 Contribution of news to now-cast revisions. *Notes:* Figure shows the evolution of the GDP now-cast (RHS scale) and how various data releases contribute to the now-cast revisions (LHS scale) for fourth quarter of 2008. The data are grouped according to frequencies: daily ("D"), weekly ("W"), monthly ("M"), and quarterly ("Q"). Dot indicates the outcome GDP growth (RHS scale, the latest vintage). The horizontal axis indicates the date of the now-cast update.

by subsequent data, both surveys and hard data. In fact, with all subsequent releases the tendency is for negative revisions.

News from daily financial variables are far from being small but they are volatile and lead to revisions in different directions. This explains the result of Figures 4.1 and 4.2. As will become clearer in the next section, it is the low frequency component of financial variables which is related to real economic activity while daily fluctuations might carry wrong signals.

Our results on the role of financial variables are in line with what has been found by Stock and Watson (2003) and Forni et al. (2003), who analyze the forecasting ability of financial variables for economic activity for longer horizon than ours and in models where they are aggregated at the monthly frequency and their timeliness is not exploited. A different conclusion is reached by Andreou et al. (2013) who find that financial variables have a sizeable impact on the now-cast accuracy of GDP.

With such different results obtained on the basis of different modeling approaches, more work is needed to reach a conclusion on this point. A difference between the application here and Andreou et al. (2013) is that the latter authors use a larger set of daily financial variables than the five we use.[22] However, results are hardly comparable since Andreou et al. (2013) treat monthly data such as surveys and the employment report, which we find very informative, as quarterly, thus disregarding their advantage in terms of timeliness.

Let us also observe that news from the weekly variables, unlike the daily financial news, are very small. Our conjecture for this finding is that initial jobless claims are rather noisy. This is line with the view of the NBER's Business Cycle Dating Committee, which does not use this series to determine the business cycle chronology (http://www.nber.org/cycles).

3.2.1. Does Information Help Improving Forecasting Accuracy? Monotonicity Tests

Figures 4.1–4.3 have shown heuristically that both out-of-sample and in-sample uncertainty decrease as more information becomes available. A natural way to formally test the decline in uncertainty as more data arrive is to apply the tests for forecast rationality proposed by Patton and Timmermann (2011) and based on the multivariate inequality tests in regression models of Wolak (1987, 1989). We rely on the first three tests of Patton and Timmermann (2011), and we report the p-values for the "Benchmark" model, the models "Monthly" and "BCDC" as well as the average p-value of the bridge equations.[23]

---

[22] To reduce the dimensionality of the large panel they consider, they extract a small set of principal components and/or apply forecast combination methods.

[23] We thank Allan Timmermann for suggesting these tests in our context.

Test 1: Monotonicity of the Forecast Errors

Let us define $\tilde{y}_t = y_{t,1}^{k_1}$ and $e_{t|\Omega_v} = \tilde{y}_t - \mathbb{E}\left[\tilde{y}_t|\Omega_v\right]$ as the forecast error obtained on the basis of the information set corresponding to the data vintage Ω_v and by $e_{t|\Omega_{v+1}}$ that obtained on the basis of a larger more recent vintage $v + 1$ and $v = 1, \ldots, V$.

The Mean Squared Errors (MSE) differential is $\Delta_v^e = \mathbb{E}\left[e_{t|\Omega_v}^2\right] - \mathbb{E}\left[e_{t|\Omega_{v+1}}^2\right]$.

The test is defined as follows:

$$H_0 : \mathbf{\Delta}^e \geq 0 \quad \text{vs} \quad H_1 : \mathbf{\Delta}^e \ngeq 0,$$

where the $(V - 1) \times 1$ vector of MSE-differentials is given by $\mathbf{\Delta}^e \equiv (\Delta_1^e, \ldots, \Delta_{V-1}^e)'$.

Test 2: Monotonicity of the Mean Squared Forecast

Define the mean squared forecast (MSF) for a given vintage as $\mathbb{E}\left[\tilde{y}_{t|\Omega_v}^2\right] = \mathbb{E}\left[\mathbb{E}[\tilde{y}_t^2|\Omega_v]\right]$ and consider the difference $\Delta_v^f = \mathbb{E}\left[\tilde{y}_{t|\Omega_v}^2\right] - \mathbb{E}\left[\tilde{y}_{t|\Omega_{v+1}}^2\right]$ and its associated vector $\mathbf{\Delta}^f$.

The test is:

$$H_0 : \mathbf{\Delta}^f \leq 0 \quad \text{vs} \quad H_1 : \mathbf{\Delta}^f \nleq 0.$$

The idea behind this test is that the variance of each observation can be decomposed as follows:

$$V\left(\tilde{y}_t\right) = V\left(\tilde{y}_{t|\Omega_v}\right) + \mathbb{E}\left[e_{t|\Omega_v}^2\right],$$

given that $\mathbb{E}\left[\tilde{y}_{t|\Omega_v}\right] = \mathbb{E}\left[\tilde{y}_t\right]$. Then a weakly decreasing pattern in MSE directly implies a weakly increasing pattern in the variance of the forecasts, i.e., $\mathbf{\Delta}^f \leq 0$.

Test 3: Monotonicity of Covariance Between the Forecast and the Target Variable

Here we consider the covariance between the forecast and the target variable for different vintages v and the difference: $\Delta_v^c = \mathbb{E}\left[\tilde{y}_{t|\Omega_v}\tilde{y}_t\right] - \mathbb{E}\left[\tilde{y}_{t|\Omega_{v+1}}\tilde{y}_t\right]$. The associated vector is defined as $\mathbf{\Delta}^c$ and the test is:

$$H_0 : \mathbf{\Delta}^c \leq 0 \quad \text{vs} \quad H_1 : \mathbf{\Delta}^c \nleq 0.$$

This test is closely related to the previous one. Indeed the covariance between the target variable and the forecast can be written as:

$$Cov\left[\tilde{y}_{t|\Omega_v}, \tilde{y}_t\right] = Cov\left[\tilde{y}_{t|\Omega_v}, \tilde{y}_{t|\Omega_v} + e_{t|\Omega_v}\right] = V\left(\tilde{y}_{t|\Omega_v}\right).$$

Consequently, a weakly increasing pattern in the variance of the forecasts implies a weakly increasing pattern in the covariances between the forecast and the target variable.

Results for the three tests are reported in Table 4.2. Monotonicity cannot be rejected by any of the three tests confirming the visual evidence of Figures 4.1 and 4.2. The results for the individual bridge equations are provided in the appendix.

Table 4.2 Monotonicity Tests

	$\Delta^e \geq 0$	$\Delta^f \leq 0$	$\Delta^c \leq 0$
Benchmark	0.50	0.49	0.50
Monthly	0.50	0.50	0.50
BCDC	0.50	0.50	0.50
Bridge	0.50	0.50	0.50

Notes: Table reports the *p*-values of three of monotonicity tests for, respectively, the forecast errors, the mean squared forecast and covariance between the forecast and the target variable. For the bridge equations the table reports the average *p*-value.

3.3. A Daily Index of the State of the Economy

To understand the working of the model, it is interesting to plot the estimated daily factor. Common factors extracted from a set of macroeconomic variables have become a popular tool to monitor business cycles conditions (see, e.g., Aruoba et al., 2009).[24] Our daily factor should be interpreted as a daily index of the underlying state of the economy, or rather its day-to-day change, which is to be distinguished from daily or intra-daily update of the estimate of quarterly GDP growth for the current quarter (the now-cast).

Figure 4.4a plots this daily index (re-scaled to facilitate the comparison) against GDP growth and shows that it tracks GDP quite well. The index is based on the latest data vintage and, as in the case of the filter uncertainty and news, on the parameters estimated over the sample 1983–2010.

By appropriate filtering, this index can be aggregated to reflect quarterly growth rate[25] and we can then consider the projection of GDP on this quarterly aggregate (Figure 4.4b). This is the common component of GDP growth and captures that part of GDP dynamics which co-moves with the series included in the model (monthly, weekly, and daily) while disregarding its idiosyncratic movements. The projection captures a large share of GDP dynamics suggesting that the common component, although it disregards the idiosyncratic residual, captures the bulk of GDP fluctuations.

3.4. Stock Prices

In this section we report some statistics on the degree of commonality of stock prices with macroeconomic variables.

---

[24] The Federal Reserve Bank of Philadelphia regularly publishes a daily index obtained by applying this framework to extract a daily common factor from the following indicators: weekly initial jobless claims; monthly payroll employment, industrial production, personal income less transfer payments, manufacturing and trade sales; and quarterly real GDP, see http://www.philadelphiafed.org/research-and-data/real-time-center/business-conditions-index/.

[25] As the filter weights we use $\omega_i^{k_q,f}$, $i = 0, 1, \ldots, 2k_q - 2$, as explained in Section 2.

(a)

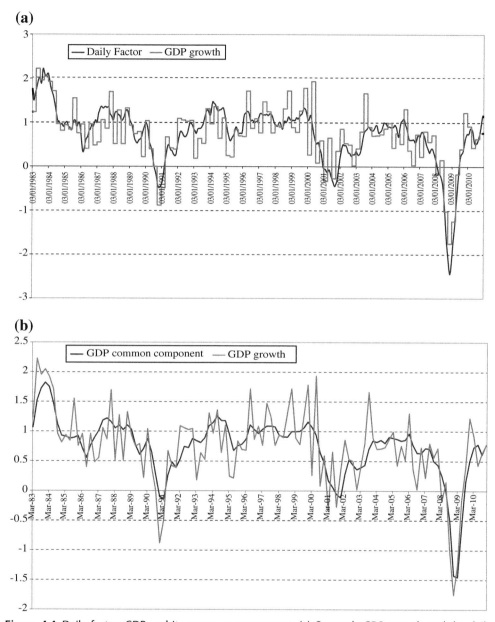

Figure 4.4 Daily factor, GDP and its common component. (a) Quarterly GDP growth and the daily factor. (b) Common component of GDP. *Notes:* The lower panel shows the GDP growth against its projection on the quarterly aggregation of the daily factor, i.e., against its common component.

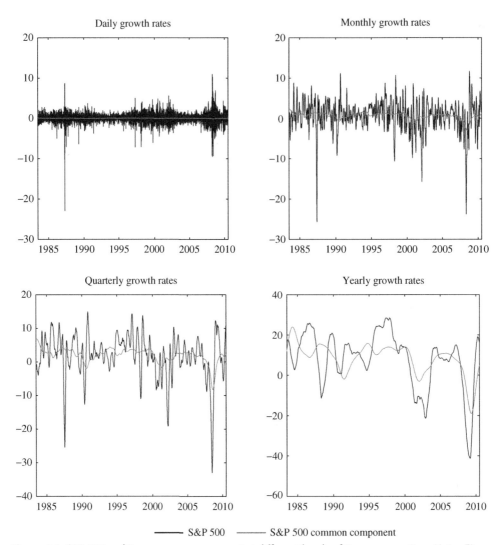

Figure 4.5 S&P 500 and its common component at different levels of time aggregation. *Notes:* Figure compares the S&P 500 and its common component at daily frequency filtered to match daily, monthly, quarterly, and yearly growth rates at the end of the respective periods.

First, we compute the common component of the S&P 500 index filtered to match daily, monthly, quarterly, and yearly growth rates at the end of the respective periods (Figure 4.5).[26] This is the signal of stock prices, extracting that part of their dynamics which is correlated with the macroeconomy. Figure 4.5 shows that the commonality is

[26] What we mean here by the monthly (quarterly and yearly) growth rate is the growth rate between the average last 22 (66 or 244) daily "level" observations and the average preceding 22 (66 or 244) observations. To obtain these growth rates we filter the daily growth rates using the weights $\omega_i^{k,f}$, $k = k_m$ ($k = k_q$ or $k = k_a$). Note that the resulting series is still at daily frequency.

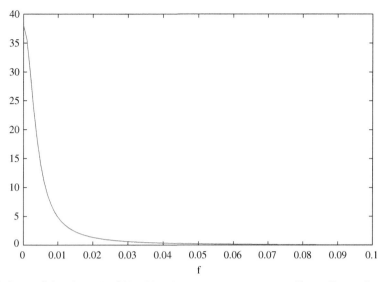

Figure 4.6 Spectral density ratio: S&P 500 vs its common component. *Notes:* Figure shows the ratio of spectral density of the common component to that of the S&P 500 of the series itself. *f* on the horizontal axis refers to the frequency.

not trivial when we consider longer term fluctuations, annual in particular, although the degree of commonality of the S&P 500 with the rest of the panel is less pronounced than what is estimated for GDP (Figure 4.4b). Clearly, although stock prices provide some false signals, they do go down in recessions.

Second, we compute the ratio of the spectral density of the common component to that of the series itself (at daily frequency).[27] Figure 4.6 shows that the bulk of commonality between the S&P 500 index and macroeconomic variables is at very low frequencies, i.e., the ratio of the variance of the common component relative to total is high at low frequencies. For a typical business cycle periodicity of eight years (corresponding to the frequency $f = 2\pi/(8*264) = 0.003$) we have a quite sizable "commonality," with the ratio of around 30%. This shows that low frequency components of stock prices are indeed related to macroeconomic fluctuations. Notice, however, that already for cycles with periodicity lower than yearly ($f > 2\pi/264 = 0.024$), the ratio is below 2%.

Our model can be developed further to express the common component of stock prices in terms of news and model-based weights of those news. We leave this for further work.

---

[27] The spectral density is derived from the estimated parameters of the model.

4. CONCLUSIONS AND DISCUSSION ON FURTHER DEVELOPMENTS

In this chapter we have reviewed different approaches to now-casting, including traditional tools used in policy institutions (bridge equations).

A key point of our discussion is that the traditional approach is limited since it does not provide a framework for the reading of the flow of data as they become available throughout the quarter and for the evaluation of their impact on the updates of the now-cast.

We have distinguished between an approach which is based on the specification of a joint model for the target variable and for the predictors – which can therefore be used to derive model-based *news* associated to different data releases and to assess their impact on the now-cast – and what we call "partial" models based on single equations.

In the discussion and application we have stressed that the essential ideas of now-casting have been developed in two papers, Evans (2005) and Giannone et al. (2008), which propose a model in which the state space representation is exploited in order to produce sequences of now-casts in relation to the real-time data flow. We have then discussed advances and refinements of this approach as well as different solutions to technical aspects of the real-time analysis: mixed frequency, "jagged"/"ragged" edges, high-dimensionality. On the latter aspect we have referred to theoretical work on factor models for high-dimensional data and, in particular to Doz et al. (2011, 2012). The latter paper provides the theoretical justification for using maximum likelihood estimation for a "large" factor model which is the approach followed in the empirical application as proposed by Bańbura and Modugno (2010) and Modugno (2011) and which we consider the state of the art in this field.

The empirical analysis we have presented, based on a daily model and a real-time evaluation, confirms early results on the role of surveys (see Bańbura et al., 2011, for a recent review) and indicates that daily financial variables do not help improving the precision of the GDP now-cast. A formal test on the role of expanding information for improving the accuracy of the GDP now-cast shows that, as more data become available during the quarter, the precision indeed increases thereby confirming previous heuristic evidence on this point.

As a by-product of our methodology we have constructed a daily index of economic activity and considered the projection of both GDP and the S&P 500 index of stock prices on this index. Results show that the projection explains the bulk of GDP dynamics while it explains much less of daily fluctuations of stock prices. On the other hand, the index explains low frequency movements of stock prices indicating that financial variables are linked to macroeconomic fundamentals.

We have limited the empirical application to GDP and stock prices although the methodology can be applied to the now-casting of any of the variables included in the model. Liebermann (2012a), for example, provides a detailed study on the now-casting of a large variety of key monthly macroeconomic releases. The same framework has also been used for now-casting inflation (Modugno, 2011) and for now-casting the components of GDP (Angelini et al., 2010).

Our review has focused on what we regard as essential contributions to the now-casting literature and has omitted some important papers. For example, we have focused only on point now-cast. Now-cast densities in a state space framework could be obtained both via a frequentist (Aastveit et al., 2011) or Bayesian (Marcellino et al., 2012) approach. Further, Aastveit et al. (2011) consider now-cast combination where different classes of models, including VARs, factor models, bridge equations are combined. This approach is interesting but it is not obvious how to use it to extract the *news* and relate them to the sequence of now-cast updates, the feature that we have stressed here as being a key element of now-casting. Also, we have omitted a discussion of the so-called bottom-up approach that imposes national account identities for obtaining coherent now-cast for GDP ad its main components. Empirically, in terms of forecasting accuracy there are no major advantages of this approach with respect to our direct approach. However, the forecasts of components of GDP might be useful for economic interpretation and "story telling." We refer the reader to Angelini et al. (2010) for the adaptation of our model in this context.

Let us also stress that we have focused on now-casting rather than on the construction of synthetic indicators of real economic activity, the so-called diffusion indexes. Those indexes were introduced by Stock and Watson (1989) in small-scale models with only monthly indicators and estimated by maximum likelihood. In large-scale models they have been developed by Altissimo et al. (2001, 2010) and Chicago Fed (2001) using principal component analysis. Mariano and Murasawa (2003) extended the framework of Stock and Watson (1989) to include quarterly GDP as well as monthly variables and recently Aruoba et al. (2009) have also included weekly initial jobless claims using the same framework.

Although models to construct early estimates of GDP using selected monthly data have been around for a long time in policy institutions, now-casting as we have defined it here is a recent field for academic research and it is therefore likely to see new developments in many aspects. Beside research on modeling high frequency data, such as financial, which we have mentioned in the text, research on the potential value of other sources of information like google search volumes (see for example Vosen and Schmidt, 2011) is also interesting and we are sure will be the object of future investigation.

Another idea for further research is to link the high frequency now-casting framework with a quarterly structural model in a model coherent way. Giannone et al. (2009a) have suggested a solution and other developments are in progress. A by-product of this analysis is that one can obtain real-time estimates of variables such as the output gap or the natural rate of interest which can only be defined theoretically on the basis of a structural model.

As a final remark, let us stress that the now-casting models we have considered here are all linear and with constant parameters. Our choice is motivated by the fact that the empirical knowledge at present is mostly limited to this class of models. However, the events of the last few years have challenged the predictive power of all models, including now-casting. Extensions of our framework, incorporating, e.g., time-varying features, might address some of these challenges and we consider this a promising area for future research (see e.g. Carriero et al., 2012, and Guerin and Marcellino, 2013).

APPENDIX: DETAILS ON THE STATE SPACE REPRESENTATION AND ESTIMATION

Aggregator Variables

We explain how the aggregator variables can be recursively obtained so that

$$F_t^{k,\cdot} = \sum_{i=0}^{2k-2} \omega_i^{k,\cdot} F_{t-i}, \quad t = k, 2k, \ldots, \quad k = k_q, k_m, k_w.$$

As for the flow variables, the summation in $F_t^{k,f}$ goes over the current and previous observation interval, we also need auxiliary variables, $\bar{F}_t^{k,f}$. $F_t^{k,f}$ can be obtained recursively as follows:

$$\tilde{F}_t^{k,f} = \begin{pmatrix} F_t^{k,f} \\ \bar{F}_t^{k,f} \end{pmatrix} = \begin{cases} \begin{pmatrix} \bar{F}_{t-1}^{k,f} + \omega_{k-1}^{k,f} F_t \\ 0 \end{pmatrix}, & t = 1, k+1, 2k+1, \ldots, \\ \begin{pmatrix} F_{t-1}^{k,f} + \omega_{R(k-t,k)}^{k,f} F_t \\ \bar{F}_{t-1}^{k,f} + \omega_{R(k-t,k)+k}^{k,f} F_t \end{pmatrix}, & \text{otherwise}, \end{cases}$$

where $R(\cdot, k)$ denotes the positive remainder of the division by k (e.g., $R(-1, k) = k-1$). For the stock variables only single aggregator variable is necessary and we have:

$$F_t^{k,s} = \begin{cases} \omega_{k-1}^{k,s} F_t, & t = 1, k+1, 2k+1, \ldots, \\ F_{t-1}^{k,s} + \omega_{R(k-t,k)}^{k,s} F_t, & \text{otherwise}. \end{cases}$$

This can be implemented via the transition equation (7) with the following $\mathcal{W}_t^{k,\cdot}$ and $\mathcal{I}_t^{k,\cdot}$:

$$\mathcal{W}_t^{k,f} = \begin{cases} \begin{pmatrix} -\omega_{k-1}^{k,f} \\ 0 \end{pmatrix}, & t = 1, k+1, \ldots, \\ \begin{pmatrix} -\omega_{R(k-t,k)}^{k,f} \\ -\omega_{R(k-t,k)+k}^{k,f} \end{pmatrix}, & \text{otherwise}, \end{cases}$$

$$\mathcal{I}_t^{k,f} = \begin{cases} \begin{pmatrix} 0 & I_r \\ 0 & 0 \end{pmatrix}, & t = 1, k+1, \ldots, \\ I_{2r}, & \text{otherwise}, \end{cases}$$

$$\mathcal{W}_t^{k,s} = -\omega_{R(k-t,k)}^{k,s}, \quad \mathcal{I}_t^{k,s} = \begin{cases} 0, & t = 1, k+1, \ldots, \\ I_r, & \text{otherwise}. \end{cases}$$

Different Number of Days Per Period

To deal with different number of days per month or quarter, for the flow variables we make an approximation that

$$z_t^k = \frac{k}{k_t} \sum_{i=0}^{k_t-1} z_{t-i}, \quad t = k_1, k_1 + k_{k_1+1}, \dots,$$

where k_t is the number of business days in the period (month or quarter) that contains day t and k is the average number of business days per period over the sample. This can be justified by the fact that data are typically working day adjusted. Consequently, $y_t^k = z_t^k - z_{t-k_t}^k$ becomes[28]

$$y_t^k = k \left(\sum_{i=0}^{k_t-1} \frac{i+1}{k_t} y_{t-i} + \sum_{i=k_t}^{k_t+k_{t-k_t}-2} \frac{k_t + k_{t-k_t} - i - 1}{k_{t-k_t}} y_{t-i} \right), \quad t = k_1, k_1 + k_{k_1+1}, \dots.$$

Hence we will have time-varying aggregation weights for the flow variables $\omega_{t,i}^{k,f} = k\frac{i+1}{k_t}$ for $i = 0, 1, \dots, k_t - 1$, $\omega_{t,i}^{k,f} = k\frac{k_t+k_{t-k_t}-i-1}{k_{t-k_t}}$ for $i = k_t, k_t + 1, \dots, k_t + k_{t-k_t} - 2$ and $\omega_{t,i}^{k,f} = 0$ otherwise. Formulas described above should be modified to reflect this.

Estimation by the EM Algorithm

We first explain the EM algorithm steps for a simpler state space representation, as given by (3) and (4), and then discuss how to modify the procedure for the more complicate representation (6) and (7).

For the state space representation (3) and (4) with one lag in the factor VAR we would have $\theta = (\mu, \Lambda, \Phi, \Sigma_E, \Sigma_U)$, where the only restriction is that Σ_E is diagonal. Let $T_v = \max_n T_v(n)$ denote the time index of the most recent observation in Ω_v. The log-likelihood can be written in terms of $Y = (Y_1, Y_2, \dots, Y_{T_v})$ and $F = (F_1, F_2, \dots, F_{T_v})$ as $l(Y, F; \theta)$. With some initial estimates of the parameters $\theta(0)$ the EM algorithm would proceed as follows:

$$\text{E-step:} \quad L(\theta, \theta(j)) = \mathbb{E}_{\theta(j)} \left[l(Y, F; \theta) | \Omega_v \right],$$
$$\text{M-step:} \quad \theta(j+1) = \arg\max_\theta L(\theta, \theta(j)).$$

The new parameter estimates in the M-step can be obtained in two steps, first $\Lambda(j + 1)$ and $\Phi(j + 1)$ are given by:

$$\Lambda(j+1) = \left(\sum_{t=1}^{T_v} \mathbb{E}_{\theta(j)} \left[Y_t F_t' | \Omega_v \right] \right) \left(\sum_{t=1}^{T_v} \mathbb{E}_{\theta(j)} \left[F_t F_t' | \Omega_v \right] \right)^{-1}, \qquad (11)$$

[28] If t is the last day of a period with k_t days then k_{t-k_t} refers to the number of days in the preceding period.

Table A Bridge Equations, RMSFEs and Monotonicity Tests

	IPTOT	PMI	DPRI	URATE	PYRLTOT	PCETOT	HSTAR	HSOLD	ORD	EXP	IMP	PHB
Q0 M1 D7	0.63	0.67	0.69	0.67	0.60	0.68	0.69	0.69	0.71	0.69	0.70	0.69
Q0 M1 D14	0.63	0.67	0.69	0.66	0.60	0.68	0.69	0.69	0.71	0.68	0.69	0.69
Q0 M1 D21	0.58	0.67	0.69	0.66	0.60	0.68	0.69	0.69	0.71	0.68	0.69	0.67
Q0 M1 D28	0.57	0.66	0.69	0.65	0.60	0.68	0.68	0.69	0.71	0.68	0.69	0.67
Q0 M2 D7	0.57	0.65	0.68	0.59	0.57	0.65	0.68	0.68	0.71	0.68	0.69	0.66
Q0 M2 D14	0.58	0.65	0.68	0.59	0.57	0.65	0.68	0.68	0.71	0.65	0.65	0.66
Q0 M2 D21	0.59	0.65	0.68	0.59	0.57	0.65	0.62	0.68	0.71	0.65	0.65	0.66
Q0 M2 D28	0.59	0.65	0.68	0.59	0.57	0.65	0.61	0.67	0.65	0.65	0.65	0.66
Q0 M3 D7	0.59	0.65	0.68	0.56	0.55	0.62	0.61	0.67	0.65	0.65	0.65	0.66
Q0 M3 D14	0.58	0.65	0.68	0.56	0.55	0.62	0.61	0.67	0.65	0.62	0.63	0.66
Q0 M3 D21	0.53	0.65	0.68	0.56	0.55	0.62	0.61	0.67	0.65	0.62	0.63	0.66
Q0 M3 D28	0.53	0.65	0.68	0.56	0.55	0.62	0.61	0.67	0.59	0.62	0.63	0.66
Q+1 M1 D7	0.53	0.65	0.69	0.55	0.54	0.59	0.61	0.67	0.58	0.62	0.63	0.66
Q+1 M1 D14	0.53	0.65	0.69	0.54	0.54	0.59	0.61	0.67	0.58	0.61	0.59	0.66
Q+1 M1 D21	0.50	0.65	0.69	0.54	0.54	0.59	0.59	0.67	0.58	0.61	0.59	0.66
Q+1 M1 D28	0.49	0.64	0.69	0.53	0.53	0.60	0.59	0.66	0.57	0.61	0.59	0.66

(Continued)

Table A Continued

	SALES	CONFCFB	PPIFG	CPITOT	BCC	ICSA	OIL	GS10	TB3	TWEXM	SP500
Q0 M1 D7	0.69	0.68	0.69	0.70	0.69	0.63	0.69	0.68	0.67	0.69	0.69
Q0 M1 D14	0.67	0.68	0.69	0.70	0.70	0.66	0.69	0.68	0.67	0.69	0.68
Q0 M1 D21	0.65	0.68	0.70	0.70	0.69	0.65	0.69	0.68	0.67	0.69	0.67
Q0 M1 D28	0.65	0.67	0.70	0.70	0.68	0.63	0.68	0.67	0.67	0.69	0.67
Q0 M2 D7	0.65	0.66	0.68	0.66	0.67	0.58	0.67	0.68	0.65	0.68	0.66
Q0 M2 D14	0.62	0.66	0.68	0.66	0.66	0.56	0.67	0.67	0.65	0.68	0.66
Q0 M2 D21	0.62	0.66	0.69	0.67	0.66	0.55	0.67	0.67	0.65	0.68	0.66
Q0 M2 D28	0.62	0.65	0.69	0.67	0.66	0.54	0.67	0.67	0.65	0.68	0.65
Q0 M3 D7	0.62	0.65	0.69	0.67	0.65	0.54	0.67	0.66	0.65	0.68	0.65
Q0 M3 D14	0.61	0.65	0.70	0.67	0.64	0.53	0.67	0.66	0.65	0.68	0.65
Q0 M3 D21	0.61	0.65	0.70	0.69	0.64	0.53	0.67	0.66	0.65	0.68	0.65
Q0 M3 D28	0.61	0.64	0.70	0.69	0.64	0.53	0.67	0.66	0.65	0.68	0.65
Q+1 M1 D7	0.61	0.64	0.70	0.69	0.64	0.53	0.67	0.66	0.65	0.68	0.65
Q+1 M1 D14	0.59	0.64	0.70	0.69	0.64	0.53	0.67	0.66	0.65	0.68	0.65
Q+1 M1 D21	0.59	0.64	0.70	0.69	0.64	0.53	0.67	0.66	0.65	0.68	0.65
Q+1 M1 D28	0.58	0.64	0.70	0.69	0.64	0.52	0.67	0.65	0.64	0.68	0.65

Notes: The upper part of the table reports the RMSFEs for each bridge equations over the sample period 1995–2010. The forecast accuracy of the model is evaluated four times per month (on the 7th, 14th, 21st, and 28th) for four consecutive months (from the first month of the current quarter, Q0 M1 to the first month of the following quarter, Q+1 M1).

$$\Phi(j+1) = \left(\sum_{t=1}^{T_v} \mathbb{E}_{\theta(j)}\big[F_t F'_{t-1}|\Omega_v\big]\right)\left(\sum_{t=1}^{T_v} \mathbb{E}_{\theta(j)}\big[F_{t-1}F'_{t-1}|\Omega_v\big]\right)^{-1}. \tag{12}$$

Second, given the new estimates of Λ and Φ, the covariance matrices can be obtained as follows:

$$\begin{aligned}
\Sigma_E(j+1) &= \text{diag}\left(\frac{1}{T_v}\sum_{t=1}^{T_v}\mathbb{E}_{\theta(j)}\Big[\big(Y_t - \Lambda(j+1)F_t\big)\big(Y_t - \Lambda(j+1)F_t\big)'|\Omega_v\Big]\right) \\
&= \text{diag}\left(\frac{1}{T_v}\left(\sum_{t=1}^{T_v}\mathbb{E}_{\theta(j)}\big[Y_t Y'_t|\Omega_v\big] - \Lambda(j+1)\sum_{t=1}^{T_v}\mathbb{E}_{\theta(j)}\big[F_t Y'_t|\Omega_v\big]\right)\right)
\end{aligned} \tag{13}$$

and

$$\Sigma_U(j+1) = \frac{1}{T}\left(\sum_{t=1}^{T_v}\mathbb{E}_{\theta(j)}\big[F_t F'_t|\Omega_v\big] - \Phi(j+1)\sum_{t=1}^{T_v}\mathbb{E}_{\theta(j)}\big[F_{t-1}F'_t|\Omega_v\big]\right), \tag{14}$$

see Watson and Engle (1983) and Shumway and Stoffer (1982). If Y_t did not contain missing observations ($\Omega_v = Y$), we would have that

$$\mathbb{E}_{\theta(j)}\big[Y_t Y'_t|\Omega_v\big] = Y_t Y'_t \quad \text{and} \quad \mathbb{E}_{\theta(j)}\big[Y_t F'_t|\Omega_v\big] = Y_t \mathbb{E}_{\theta(j)}\big[F'_t|\Omega_v\big],$$

which can be plugged to the formulas above. The expectations $\mathbb{E}_{\theta(j)}\big[F_t F'_t|\Omega_v\big]$, $\mathbb{E}_{\theta(j)}\big[F_t F'_{t-1}|\Omega_v\big]$ and $\mathbb{E}_{\theta(j)}\big[F_t|\Omega_v\big]$ can be obtained via the Kalman filter and smoother. When Y_t contains missing observations (11) and (13) become

$$\text{vec}\big(\Lambda(j+1)\big) = \left(\sum_{t=1}^{T_v}\mathbb{E}_{\theta(j)}\big[F_t F'_t|\Omega_v\big]\otimes \mathcal{S}_t\right)^{-1}\text{vec}\left(\sum_{t=1}^{T_v}\mathcal{S}_t Y_t \mathbb{E}_{\theta(j)}\big[F'_t|\Omega_v\big]\right) \tag{15}$$

and

$$\begin{aligned}
\Sigma_E(j+1) = \text{diag}\Bigg(\frac{1}{T_v}\sum_{t=1}^{T_v}\Big(&\mathcal{S}_t Y_t Y'_t \mathcal{S}'_t - \mathcal{S}_t Y_t \mathbb{E}_{\theta(j)}\big[F'_t|\Omega_v\big]\Lambda(j+1)'\mathcal{S}_t \\
&-\mathcal{S}_t\Lambda(j+1)\mathbb{E}_{\theta(j)}\big[F_t|\Omega_v\big]Y'_t\mathcal{S}_t + \mathcal{S}_t\Lambda(j+1)\mathbb{E}_{\theta(j)}\big[F_t F'_t|\Omega_v\big]\Lambda(j+1)'\mathcal{S}_t \\
&+(I_N - \mathcal{S}_t)\Sigma_E(j)(I_N - \mathcal{S}_t)\Big)\Bigg),
\end{aligned} \tag{16}$$

where $\mathcal{S}_t$ is a selection matrix, i.e., it is a diagonal matrix with ones corresponding to the non-missing observations in Y_t and zeros otherwise, see Bańbura and Modugno (2010).

For the daily model given by (6) and (7) the parameters are estimated using a modified version of the procedure just described. The necessary conditional expectations are provided by the Kalman filter and smoother applied to (6) and (7). $\Lambda^{\cdot\cdot}$ are estimated blockwise, by frequency and by stock or flow type, using a formula similar to (15) in which Y_t and F_t are replaced by the appropriate block of $Y_t^{K_Y}$ and the corresponding aggregator variable, respectively. The estimate of the covariance matrix of $E_t^{K_Y}$ follows from (16) with F_t and Λ replaced by the entire state vector and the entire matrix of coefficients in the measurement equation (6) respectively. Finally the estimates for Φ and Σ_U follow from (12) and (14) respectively, by taking the elements from the conditional covariances of the state vector corresponding to F_t.

Computation of the News

To compute the news we need the conditional covariances of X_t and X_{t-i}:

$$\mathbb{E}\left[\left(X_t - \mathbb{E}\left[X_t|\Omega_v\right]\right)\left(X_{t-i} - \mathbb{E}\left[X_{t-i}|\Omega_v\right]\right)'\right].$$

One way to obtain them is to extend the state vector by its i lags. However, if i is large this could lead to a prohibitively large state vector. Instead we use the direct formulas for the covariances by De Jong and Mackinnon (1988).

ACKNOWLEDGMENTS

The authors would like to thank the Editors, Graham Elliott and Allan Timmermann, and the Referees for their suggestions. This research is supported by the IAP research network grant nr. P7/06 of the Belgian government (Belgian Science Policy).

REFERENCES

Aastveit, K., Trovik, T., 2012. Nowcasting norwegian GDP: the role of asset prices in a small open economy. Empirical Economics 42 (1), 95–119.

Aastveit, K.A., Gerdrup, K.R., Jore, A.S., Thorsrud, L.A., 2011. Nowcasting GDP in Real-Time: A Density Combination Approach. Working Paper 2011/11, Norges Bank.

Altissimo, F., Bassanetti, A., Cristadoro, R., Forni, M., Hallin, M., Lippi, M., Reichlin, L., Veronese, G., 2001. EuroCOIN: A Real Time Coincident Indicator of the Euro Area Business Cycle. CEPR Discussion Papers 3108, C.E.P.R. Discussion Papers.

Altissimo, F., Cristadoro, R., Forni, M., Lippi, M., Veronese, G., 2010. New eurocoin: tracking economic growth in real time. The Review of Economics and Statistics 92 (4), 1024–1034.

Andreou, E., Ghysels, E., Kourtellos, A., 2013. Should macroeconomic forecasters look at daily financial data? Journal of Business & Economic Statistics 31 (2), 240–251.

Angelini, E., Bańbura, M., Rünstler, G., 2010. Estimating and forecasting the euro area monthly national accounts from a dynamic factor model. OECD Journal: Journal of Business Cycle Measurement and Analysis 2010 (1), 7.

Angelini, E., Camba-Méndez, G., Giannone, D., Reichlin, L., Rünstler, G., 2011. Short-term forecasts of euro area GDP growth. Econometrics Journal 14 (1), C25–C44.

Arnostova, K., Havrlant, D., Ruzicka, L., Toth, P., 2011. Short-term forecasting of Czech quarterly GDP using monthly indicators. Czech Journal of Economics and Finance 61 (6), 566–583.

Aruoba, S., Diebold, F.X., Scotti, C., 2009. Real-time measurement of business conditions. Journal of Business and Economic Statistics 27 (4), 417–427.

Baffigi, A., Golinelli, R., Parigi, G., 2004. Bridge models to forecast the euro area GDP. International Journal of Forecasting 20 (3), 447–460.

Bai, J., Ng, S., 2008. Forecasting economic time series using targeted predictors. Journal of Econometrics 146 (2), 304–317.

Bańbura, M., Modugno, M., 2010. Maximum Likelihood Estimation of Large Factor Model on Datasets with Arbitrary Pattern of Missing Data. Working Paper Series 1189, European Central Bank.

Bańbura, M., Rünstler, G., 2011. A look into the factor model black box: publication lags and the role of hard and soft data in forecasting GDP. International Journal of Forecasting 27 (2), 333–346.

Bańbura, M., Giannone, D., Reichlin, L., 2010. Large Bayesian VARs. Journal of Applied Econometrics 25 (1), 71–92.

Bańbura, M., Giannone, D., Reichlin, L., 2011. Nowcasting. In: Clements, M.P., Hendry, D.F. (Eds.), Oxford Handbook on Economic Forecasting. Oxford University Press, pp. 63–90.

Barhoumi, K., Darn, O., Ferrara, L., 2010. Are disaggregate data useful for factor analysis in forecasting French GDP? Journal of Forecasting 29 (1–2), 132–144.

Bessec, M., Doz, C., Prevision de court terme de la croissance du PIB francais laide de modeles facteurs dynamiques. Documents de Travail Numéro 2011/01 de la DG Tresor 1, France, Tresor Direction Gnral, Economie et Prevision.

Bloor, C., Matheson, T., 2011. Real-time conditional forecasts with Bayesian VARs: an application to New Zealand. The North American Journal of Economics and Finance 22 (1), 26–42.

Boivin, J., Ng, S., 2006. Are more data always better for factor analysis? Journal of Econometrics 132 (1), 169–194.

Camacho, M., Perez-Quiros, G., 2010. Introducing the euro-sting: short term indicator of euro area growth. Journal of Applied Econometrics 25 (4), 663–694.

Carriero, A., Clark, T.E., Marcellino, M., 2012. Real-Time Nowcasting with a Bayesian Mixed Frequency Model with Stochastic Volatility. Working Paper 1227, Federal Reserve Bank of Cleveland.

Chen, W., Anderson, B.D., Deistler, M., Filler, A., 2012. Properties of Blocked Linear Systems. Discussion Paper, Vienna University of Technology, Manuscript.

Chicago Fed, 2001. CFNAI Background Release. Discussion Paper. <http://www.chicagofed.org/economicresearchanddata/national/pdffiles/CFNAI bga.pdf>.

Clements, M.P., Galvão, A.B., 2008. Macroeconomic forecasting with mixed-frequency data. Journal of Business and Economic Statistics 26, 546–554.

Clements, M.P., Galvão, A.B., 2009. Forecasting US output growth using leading indicators: an appraisal using MIDAS models. Journal of Applied Econometrics 24 (7), 1187–1206.

Croushore, D., 2011. Frontiers of real-time data analysis. Journal of Economic Literature 49 (1), 72–100.

Curdia, V., Del Negro, M., Greenwald, D., 2012. Rare Shocks. Great Recessions. Discussion Paper, Federal Reserve Bank of New York, Manuscript.

D'Agostino, A., McQuinn, K., O'Brien, D., 2008. Now-casting Irish GDP. Research Technical Papers 9/RT/08, Central Bank & Financial Services Authority of Ireland (CBFSAI).

de Antonio Liedo, D., Muoz, E.F., 2010. Nowcasting Spanish GDP Growth in Real Time: "One and A Half Months Earlier". Banco de Espaa Working Papers 1037, Banco de Espaa.

De Jong, P., Mackinnon, M.J., 1988. Covariances for smoothed estimates in state space models. Biometrika 75 (3), 601–602.

De Mol, C., Giannone, D., Reichlin, L., 2008. Forecasting using a large number of predictors: is Bayesian shrinkage a valid alternative to principal components? Journal of Econometrics 146 (2), 318–328.

de Winter, J., 2011. Forecasting GDP Growth in Times of Crisis: Private Sector Forecasts Versus Statistical Models. DNB Working Papers 320, Netherlands Central Bank, Research Department.

Diron, M., 2008. Short-term forecasts of euro area real GDP growth: an assessment of real-time performance based on vintage data. Journal of Forecasting 27 (5), 371–390.

Doz, C., Giannone, D., Reichlin, L., 2011. A two-step estimator for large approximate dynamic factor models based on Kalman filtering. Journal of Econometrics 164 (1), 188–205.

Doz, C., Giannone, D., Reichlin, L., 2012. A maximum likelihood approach for large approximate dynamic factor models. Review of Economics and Statistics 94 (4), 1014–1024.

Drechsel, K., Scheufele, R., 2012. A Comparison of Bottom-Up Approaches and Direct Forecasts of German GDP in a Data-Rich Environment. Discussion Paper, Halle Institute for Economic Research (IWH), Manuscript.

ECB, 2008. Short-term forecasts of economic activity in the euro area. In: Monthly Bulletin. European Central Bank, April, pp. 69–74.

Evans, M.D.D., 2005. Where are we now? Real-time estimates of the macroeconomy. International Journal of Central Banking 1 (2).

Forni, M., Hallin, M., Lippi, M., Reichlin, L., 2003. Do financial variables help forecasting inflation and real activity in the euro area? Journal of Monetary Economics 50 (6), 1243–1255.

Forni, M., Giannone, D., Lippi, M., Reichlin, L., 2009. Opening the black box: structural factor models with large cross sections. Econometric Theory 25 (05), 1319–1347.

Frale, C., Marcellino, M., Mazzi, G.L., Proietti, T., 2011. EUROMIND: a monthly indicator of the euro area economic conditions. Journal of the Royal Statistical Society Series A 174 (2), 439–470.

Ghysels, E., Wright, J.H., 2009. Forecasting professional forecasters. Journal of Business and Economics Statistics 27 (4), 504–516.

Ghysels, E., Santa-Clara, P., Sinko, A., Valkanov, R., 2003. MIDAS Regressions: Further Results and New Directions. Working Paper, UNC and UCLA.

Giannone, D., Reichlin, L., Sala, L., 2004. Monetary policy in real time. In: Gertler, M., Rogoff, K. (Eds.), NBER Macroeconomics Annual. MIT Press, pp. 161–200.

Giannone, D., Reichlin, L., Small, D., 2008. Nowcasting: the real-time informational content of macroeconomic data. Journal of Monetary Economics 55 (4), 665–676.

Giannone, D., Monti, F., Reichlin, L., 2009a. Incorporating conjunctural analysis in structural models. In: Wieland, V. (Ed.), The Science and Practice of Monetary Policy Today. Springer, Berlin, pp. 41–57.

Giannone, D., Reichlin, L., Simonelli, S., 2009b. Nowcasting euro area economic activity in real time: the role of confidence indicators. National Institute Economic Review 210, 90–97.

Giannone, D., Lenza, M., Primiceri, G.E., 2012. Prior Selection for Vector Autoregressions. CEPR Discussion Papers 8755, C.E.P.R. Discussion Papers.

Guerin, P., Marcellino, M., 2013. Markov-switching MIDAS models. Journal of Business & Economic Statistics 31 (1), 45–56.

Hahn, E., Skudelny, F., 2008. Early Estimates of Euro Area Real GDP Growth – A Bottom Up Approach from the Production Side. Working Paper Series 975, European Central Bank.

Harvey, A., 1989. Forecasting, Structural Time Series Models and the Kalman Filter. Cambridge University Press.

Karlsson, S., 2013. Forecasting with Bayesian VAR models. In: Graham Elliott, A.T. (Ed.), Handbook of Economic Forecasting. North Holland.

Kitchen, J., Monaco, R.M., 2003. Real-time forecasting in practice: the US treasury Staff's real-time GDP forecast system. Business Economics, 10–19.

Koop, G., 2013. Forecasting with Medium and Large Bayesian VARs. Working Papers 1117, University of Strathclyde Business School, Department of Economics, Journal of Applied Econometrics 28 (2), 177—203.

Kuzin, V., Marcellino, M., Schumacher, C., 2011. MIDAS vs. mixed-frequency VAR: Nowcasting GDP in the euro area. International Journal of Forecasting 27 (2), 529–542.

Kuzin, V., Marcellino, M., Schumacher, C., 2013. Pooling Versus Model Selection For Nowcasting GDP With Many Predictors: Empirical Evidence For Six Industrialized Countries. Journal of Applied Econometrics 28 (3), 392–441.

Lahiri, K., Monokroussos, G., 2011. Nowcasting US GDP: The Role of ISM Business Surveys. SUNY at Albany Discussion Papers 11-01, University at Albany, SUNY.

Liebermann, J., 2012a. Real-Time Forecasting in a Data-Rich Environment. Discussion Paper 39452, MPRA Paper.

Liebermann, J., 2012b. Short-term forecasting of quarterly gross domestic product growth. Central Bank of Ireland Quarterly Bulletin 3, 74–84.

Marcellino, M., Schumacher, C., 2010. Factor MIDAS for nowcasting and forecasting with ragged-edge data: a model comparison for German GDP. Oxford Bulletin of Economics and Statistics 72 (4), 518–550.

Marcellino, M., Porqueddu, M., Venditti, F., 2012. Short-Term GDP Forecasting with a Mixed Frequency Dynamic Factor Model with Stochastic Volatility. Discussion Paper, European University Institute, Manuscript.

Mariano, R., Murasawa, Y., 2003. A new coincident index of business cycles based on monthly and quarterly series. Journal of Applied Econometrics 18, 427–443.

Mariano, R.S., Murasawa, Y., 2010. A coincident index, common factors, and monthly real GDP. Oxford Bulletin of Economics and Statistics 72 (1), 27–46.

Matheson, T.D., 2010. An analysis of the informational content of New Zealand data releases: the importance of business opinion surveys. Economic Modelling 27 (1), 304–314.

Matheson, T., 2011. New Indicators for Tracking Growth in Real Time. IMF Working Papers 11/43, International Monetary Fund.

McCracken, M.W., Sekhposyan, T., Owyang, M., 2013. Real-Time Forecasting with a Large, Mixed Frequency, Bayesian VAR. Manuscript.

Mittnik, S., Zadrozny, P.A., 2004. Forecasting Quarterly German GDP at Monthly Intervals Using Monthly IFO Business Conditions Data. CESifo Working Paper Series 1203, CESifo Group Munich.

Modugno, M., 2011. Nowcasting Inflation Using High Frequency Data. International Journal of Forecasting.

Ouysse, R., 2011. Comparison of Bayesian moving Average and Principal Component Forecast for Large Dimensional Factor Models. Discussion Papers 2012-03, The University of New South Wales, School of Economics.

Parigi, G., Golinelli, R., 2007. The use of monthly indicators to forecast quarterly GDP in the short run: an application to the G7 countries. Journal of Forecasting 26 (2), 77–94.

Parigi, G., Schlitzer, G., 1995. Quarterly forecasts of the Italian business cycle by means of monthly indicators. Journal of Forecasting 14 (2), 117–141

Patton, J.A., Timmermann, A., 2011. Forecast Rationality Tests Based on Multi-Horizon Bounds. CEPR Discussion Papers 8194, C.E.P.R. Discussion Papers.

Proietti, T., 2011. Estimation of common factors under cross-sectional and temporal aggregation constraints. International Statistical Review 79 (3), 455–476.

Proietti, T., Moauro, F., 2006. Dynamic factor analysis with non-linear temporal aggregation constraints. Journal of the Royal Statistical Society Series C 55 (2), 281–300.

Rünstler, G., Barhoumi, K., Benk, S., Cristadoro, R., Reijer, A.D., Jakaitiene, A., Jelonek, P., Rua, A., Ruth, K., Nieuwenhuyze, C.V., 2009. Short-term forecasting of GDP using large data sets: a pseudo real-time forecast evaluation exercise. Journal of Forecasting 28, 595–611.

Sargent, T.J., Sims, C.A., 1977. Business cycle modeling without pretending to have too much a-priori economic theory. In: Sims, C. (Eds.), New Methods in Business Cycle Research. Federal Reserve Bank of Minneapolis.

Seong, B., Ahn, S.K., Zadrozny, P.A., 2007. Cointegration Analysis with Mixed-Frequency Data. CESifo Working Paper 1939, CESifo Group Munich.

Shumway, R., Stoffer, D., 1982. An approach to time series smoothing and forecasting using the EM algorithm. Journal of Time Series Analysis 3, 253–264.

Siliverstovs, B., Kholodilin, K.A., 2012. Assessing the real-time informational content of macroeconomic data releases for now-/forecasting GDP: evidence for Switzerland. Journal of Economics and Statistics/Jahrbücher für Nationalökonomie und Statistik 232 (4), 429–444.

Siliverstovs, B., Kholodilin, K.A., 2012. Assessing the Real-Time Informational Content of Macroeconomic Data Releases for Now-/Forecasting GDP: Evidence for Switzerland. KOF Working Papers 10-251, KOF Swiss Economic Institute, ETH Zurich.

Stock, J.H., Watson, M.W., 1989. New Indexes of Coincident and Leading Economic Indicators. NBER Macroeconomics Annual 1989, vol. 4, NBER Chapters. National Bureau of Economic Research, Inc., pp. 351–409.

Stock, J.H., Watson, M.W., 2003. Forecasting output and inflation: the role of asset prices. Journal of Economic Literature 41 (3), 788–829.

Stock, J.H., Watson, M.W., 2011. Dynamic factor models. In: Clements, M.P., Hendry, D.F. (Eds.), Oxford Handbook on Economic Forecasting. Oxford University Press.

Stock, J.H., Watson, M.W., 2012. Generalized shrinkage methods for forecasting using many predictors. Journal of Business and Economics Statistics 30 (4), 481–493.

Vosen, S., Schmidt, T., 2011. Forecasting private consumption: survey-based indicators vs. Google trends. Journal of Forecasting 30 (6), 565–578.

Watson, M.W., 2004. Comment on Giannone, Reichlin, and Sala. In: Gertler, M., Rogoff, K. (Eds.), NBER Macroeconomics Annual. MIT Press, pp. 216–221.

Watson, M.W., Engle, R.F., 1983. Alternative algorithms for the estimation of dynamic factor, mimic and varying coefficient regression models. Journal of Econometrics 23, 385–400.

Wolak, F.A., 1987. An exact test for multiple inequality and equality constraints in the linear regression model. Journal of the American Statistical Association 82, 782–793.

Wolak, F.A., 1989. Testing inequality constraints in linear econometric models. Journal of Econometrics 31, 205–235.

Yiu, M.S., Chow, K.K., 2010. Nowcasting Chinese GDP: information content of economic and financial data. China Economic Journal 3 (3), 223–240.

Zadrozny, P., 1990. Estimating a Multivariate ARMA Model with Mixed-Frequency Data: An Application to Forecasting US GNP at Monthly Intervals. Working Paper Series 90-6, Federal Reserve Bank of Atlanta.

CHAPTER *5*

Forecasting and Policy Making

Volker Wieland[*] and Maik Wolters[†,‡]

[*]Goethe University of Frankfurt, Grüneburgplatz 1, Institute for Monetary and Financial Stability, House of Finance, 60323 Frankfurt am Main, Germany
[†]University of Kiel, Wilhelm-Seelig-Platz 1, 24118 Kiel, Germany
[‡]Kiel Institute for the World Economy, Hindenburgufer 66, 24105 Kiel, Germany

Contents

Handbook of Economic Forecasting, Volume 2A
ISSN 1574-0706, http://dx.doi.org/10.1016/B978-0-444-53683-9.00005-2
239

Abstract

Policymakers use forecasts to project the consequences of particular policy decisions for certain policy targets. This chapter investigates the use of economic forecasting in policy making by discussing practical examples, providing new empirical evidence and computing forecasts using different macroeconomic models. First, a theoretical framework is presented to differentiate the role of forecasts in simple feedback rules, optimal control policies, and forecast targeting. Then, we review institutional details of the forecasting process at fiscal authorities and central banks. We provide empirical evidence that central bank policy rate decisions in the United States and the Euro area are well described by interest rate rules responding to forecasts of inflation and economic activity rather than recent outcomes. Next, we provide a detailed exposition of methods for producing forecasts. We review forecasting models and provide practical applications. In particular, we illustrate how to use economic structure in interpreting forecasts and how to implement different conditioning assumptions regarding certain planned policy initiatives. Finally, we evaluate the accuracy of central bank and expert forecasts and investigate the interaction between forecasting and policy making by evaluating the performance and robustness of forecast-based policy rules under model uncertainty.

Keywords

Forecasting, Monetary policy, Fiscal policy, DSGE models, Conditional forecasts, Policy rules, Expectations, Business cycles, Robust policy

1. INTRODUCTION

Gouverner c'est prévoir

(Emile de Girardin, 1806–1881)

Implicit in any monetary policy action or inaction is an expectation of how the future will unfold, that is, a forecast.

(Greenspan, 1994, p. 241)

Forecasts play an important role in economic policy making, because the economic consequences of a policy decision made today only unfold over time and the new policy is typically intended to remain in place for some period. They are unavoidably fraught with uncertainty due to imperfect understanding and observation of the mechanisms and forces determining economic outcomes. Formal treatments of the proper use of forecasts in policy making go back to Theil (1958) building on Tinbergen (1952)'s theory of economic policy. Theil suggested that (i) the policy authorities have to predict impending changes in the economic environment; (ii) then they have to prepare forecasts of the effect of adjustments in the policy instrument; and (iii) based on these forecasts a plan of policy actions must be developed. The following practical example is still relevant today:

> "In the case of employment policy, it is necessary to obtain some idea as to the factors controlling next year's or next quarter's employment level. If this leads to a predicted employment, which is considered too low, the policymaker will try to find measures in order to increase the level; and then it is necessary to predict the effectiveness of alternative measures, i.e., of the reaction of variables, which are not controlled to changes in controlled variables. This leads to a plan of actions, which may be followed or abandoned in the light of subsequent events."

(Theil, 1958, p. 3)

Of course, forecasts can be usefully employed in many areas of economic policy. In this chapter we focus on the forecasting models and methods used in the context of monetary and fiscal policies for assessing their consequences for aggregate economic fluctuations. Central banks have long been concerned with estimating the transmission of changes in policy instruments such as the short-term nominal interest rate to target variables such as the rates of inflation and output growth. Their decisions are typically related to forecasts and adjusted frequently in response to new data, which induce forecast revisions. Fiscal policy has many tasks. Policymakers regularly need to decide on the size of the government budget, how to finance and how to spend it. They have multiple instruments at their disposal. Furthermore, budgetary forecasts are influenced in turn by economic developments. Occasionally, fiscal authorities also consider major reforms in taxation, debt or spending policies that require forward-looking impact assessments.

The role of forecasts in policy making is a very broad topic. Space requirements force us to omit many relevant and interesting theories, techniques, and applications. Wherever possible we refer to other sources for topics that are only treated in a cursory fashion in this chapter. Instead, we focus on a few specific and related questions. Section 2 begins with a recent practical example concerning the role of forecasts in policy making, namely prediction of the GDP impact of 2009 fiscal stimulus legislation in the United States. Then it presents a simple theoretical framework for linking forecasts with policy preferences and policy decisions. This framework applies the principles of Tinbergen and Theil's theory of forecasting and policy making to central bank interest rate decisions for macroeconomic stabilization purposes. Alternatively, a modified version of this framework with a fiscal sector could be used to analyze the role of fiscal policy in macroeconomic stabilization.

Section 3 reviews examples of forecasts produced at fiscal and monetary authorities. Particular emphasis is given to forecasts produced at the Federal Reserve and the European Central Bank (ECB) because they are used again in subsequent sections. In Section 4 we address the question whether policymakers adjust their decisions directly in response to economic forecasts. Answering this question requires an empirical investigation. Of course, it is easiest to search for such a link in an environment in which decision makers are exposed to a particular forecast on a regular basis and shortly thereafter make a policy decision that becomes public right away. Thus, it is most easily tested in the context of central bank interest rate policy. We show that interest rate setting by the Federal Reserve and the ECB is quite well explained by a response to forecasts.

Section 5 then reviews how to compute forecasts that account for the interaction with policy decisions. Thus, it focuses on the use of structural macroeconomic models for forecasting. These models incorporate explicit assumptions regarding the decision making of monetary and fiscal policymakers concerning variables such as government spending, taxes, transfers, central bank interest rates, and central bank money. Furthermore, they provide characterizations of the decision making and expectations formation of households and firms that indicate how they will change their behavior in response to systematic changes in policymaker decisions. We review models used at central banks, fiscal authorities and international institutions. Then we construct forecasts from a small projection model used at the International Monetary Fund (IMF) and from a medium-size Dynamic Stochastic General Equilibrium (DSGE) model that is similar to models now widely available to staff at monetary and fiscal authorities. Of specific interest to us are methods used for conditioning forecasts on particular planned policy initiatives. An application deals with projecting the GDP impact of U.S. fiscal stimulus legislation discussed in the practical example of Section 2. The section concludes with an assessment of forecast accuracy and a comparison of model and expert forecasts. Given the observed heterogeneity of forecasts, the chapter closes with a normative analysis of the performance and robustness of forecast-based policy rules under model uncertainty in Section 6. Section 7 concludes.

2. THE ROLE OF FORECASTS IN POLICY MAKING: A PRACTICAL EXAMPLE AND A THEORETICAL FRAMEWORK

2.1. A Practical Example: Forecasts in U.S. Fiscal Policy

To illustrate the interaction of forecasts and policy decisions, we consider the following example from the United States. On February 17, 2009, U.S. Congress enacted the American Recovery and Reinvestment Act (ARRA). It was a very unusual policy measure involving spending increases, transfers, and tax reductions on the scale of 787 billion U.S. dollars that were meant to stimulate economic activity following the global financial crisis. On January 7, 2009, the Congressional Budget Office (CBO) had published its regular Budget and Economic Outlook for the next 10 years. Its forecast for the remainder of 2009 implied a drop in real GDP of 2.2% followed by an increase of 1.5% in 2010. As usual, the CBO's near-term outlook was based on the assumption that "*current laws and policies governing federal spending and taxes do not change*" and therefore did "*not include the effects of a possible fiscal stimulus package.*"[1] On January 9, President Obama's advisers Christina Romer and Jared Bernstein circulated a report on the impact of the American Recovery and Reinvestment Plan predicting that such a plan could raise GDP by 3.6% above the baseline forecast within two years (Romer and Bernstein, 2009). Their calculations were based on measures of government spending and tax multipliers obtained from private sector forecasters and the Federal Reserve. Over the course of January and early February 2009, the CBO prepared several budgetary and economic impact forecasts of the stimulus legislation debated and eventually passed in the House of Representatives and the Senate in response to requests by members of U.S. Congress. On March 20, 2009, the CBO released an update of its budget and economic outlook taking into account the policy changes implied by the ARRA as well as new incoming economic data suggesting a more negative economic outlook than the data available for the January forecast.[2] On this basis, they predicted a steeper decline of real GDP in 2009 of −3.0% followed by an increase of 2.9% in 2010.

This example shows that economic policy is not only based on macroeconomic forecasts, but that the path of policy itself has a direct effect on projections of macroeconomic aggregates. Thus, forecasters need to base their predictions on specific assumptions regarding future policy. For example, professional forecasters and macroeconomists often use a particular future path for fiscal policy that they consider most likely to occur or an estimated feedback rule that accounts for the response of future policy to projected future economic conditions. Forecasters employed by policy institutions typically also

---

[1] See Congressional Budget Office, The Budget and Economic Outlook: Fiscal Years 2009 to 2019, January 2009.

[2] See Congressional Budget Office, A Preliminary Analysis of the President's Budget and an Update of CBO's Budget and Economic Outlook, March 20, 2009.

consider forecasts that are conditioned on unchanged policy as in the case of the CBO outlook. While such forecasts do not represent their best possible prediction of the future course of events, they are often used as a benchmark for the policy debate that helps set up desirable policy changes. Another important issue concerns the choice of economic model on which the forecast is to be conditioned. With regard to the ARRA, for example, a study by Cogan et al. (2010) using state-of-the-art New Keynesian models estimated much smaller multipliers than the models in Romer and Bernstein and predicted only about 1/6 of the GDP impact.[3]

2.2. A Simple Framework for Modeling the Interaction of Forecasts and Policy Decisions

In his formal treatment of economic policy, Tinbergen (1952) describes economic policy as the maximization of a collective ophelimity function by the government. This function contains a number of variables that the policymaker wants to influence but that are not directly under her control. These variables are called *targets*. Policy is implemented by manipulating variables that may be directly controlled by the policymaker – so-called control or instrument variables. Tinbergen (1952) differentiates between quantitative and qualitative policy changes. Qualitative changes imply a change in the economic structure. Examples are the dissolution of a monopoly, the introduction of a customs union or a monetary union. Thus, qualitative policy involves choosing from a finite number of policy alternatives. Quantitative policy changes are defined as adjusting certain policy parameters or instruments such as taxes, government expenditures or interest rates to achieve policy goals within a given economic structure. Conveniently, Tinbergen (1952) lists the following steps for the proper conduct of economic policy:

  i.   choose a collective preference indicator;
 ii.   deduce targets for economic policy from this indicator;
iii.   choose adequate instruments for achieving the targets;
 iv.   determine quantitative values of the instrument variables;
  v.   and formulate the connection between the targets and the instruments and the structure of the economy.

With regard to forecasts, Theil (1958, p. 3) stresses that

> *A realistic analysis of the relationship between forecasts and policy must be based on the assumption of several variables controlled and not controlled by the policymaker, of their interrelationships, (and) of the policymaker's preferences, which serve to formalize the optimality criterion.*

---

[3] A first working paper version was circulated shortly after the bill was passed in February.

In the following, we review central bank interest rate policy using Tinbergen's nomenclature and present a simple framework for linking forecasts with policy preferences and policy decisions aimed at controlling inflation and stabilizing economic fluctuations. Alternatively, a modified version of this framework with a fiscal sector could be used to analyze the role of fiscal policy in macroeconomic stabilization.

2.2.1. A Simple Model Linking Forecasts and Interest Rate Decisions: Policy Objective and Instrument

Typically, central banks do not publish an explicit objective function regarding collective economic welfare nor do they claim to optimize such a function.[4] Rather, a small number of targets or even a single principal target is specified by law. For example, the U.S Federal Reserve Act asks the U.S. central bank *"to promote effectively the goals of maximum employment, stable prices and moderate long-term interest rates."* The Fed itself clarifies that stable prices in the long-run are a pre-condition for the other two goals, while acknowledging a short-run tradeoff between inflation and employment stabilization.[5] As to the Euro area, the Maastricht treaty expresses a hierarchy of targets. *"The primary objective of the ESCB shall be to maintain price stability"* and *"without prejudice to the objective of price stability, the ESCB shall support the general economic policies in the community"*, which is explained further as a high level of employment and sustainable and non–inflationary growth. Many other central banks are tasked with a primary responsibility for price stability and publish a numerical target for the rate of inflation. According to Bernanke et al. (1999) *"inflation targeting is a framework for monetary policy characterized by the public announcement of official quantitative targets (or target ranges) over one or more time horizons, and by explicit acknowledgment that low, stable inflation is monetary policy's primary long-run goal"*.[6]

Research and technical policy analysis require a mathematical specification of central bank objectives in order to evaluate a particular policy. There is a long tradition of using *loss functions* that penalize squared deviations of the target variables from a desired value. For example, price stability could be measured with regard to squared deviations of the price level from a target value or target path. Inflation targeting, instead, may be evaluated in terms of inflation deviations from target. Other variables, such as output or employment deviations from natural rates or the variability of the change of interest rates are also often included in such loss functions. The following example captures the dual objective of the

---

[4] An exception is the procedure of the central bank of Norway. Objective functions that represent the bank's mandate and the board's policy preferences and the model used to produce forecasts and guide monetary policy are public and discussed in some in detail for example in Alstadheim et al. (2010).

[5] See "The Federal Reserve System: Purposes and Functions", www.federalreserve.gov.

[6] The ECB differentiates itself from inflation-targeting central banks by means of its two-pillar strategy, which involves a medium-term cross-check with monetary trends. Its numerical definition of price stability is an inflation rate below, but close to 2%.

Federal Reserve, though with output in place of employment:

$$L = E\left[\sum_{j=0}^{\infty} \beta^j[(\pi_{t+j} - \pi^*)^2 + \lambda(\gamma_{t+j} - \gamma_{t+j}^*)^2]|I_t\right]. \tag{1}$$

E denotes the expectations operator conditional on the policymaker's information set I_t in period t. π_t is the inflation rate and π^* is the inflation target.[7] γ_t denotes output, while γ_t^* refers to the associated target. Central banks typically associate γ_t^* with potential output, $\bar{\gamma}_t$, which is the long-run level of output consistent with stable inflation. It is important to recognize that potential output is an unobservable variable and central banks would have to rely on imprecise estimates in pursuing such an objective (cf. Orphanides and van Norden, 2002). There are two preference parameters. β is a discount factor, $(0 < \beta < 1)$, while $\lambda > 0$ indicates the weight assigned to output relative to inflation stabilization. Interestingly, this particular loss function also happens to approximate representative-household utility in a specific small-scale New Keynesian model (see Woodford, 2003).[8] Arguably, it does not reflect very well the hierarchical nature of objectives – i.e., price stability first – that is enshrined in many central bank laws.

Turning to the main instrument of monetary policy, nowadays most central banks use a short-term interest rate such as the federal funds rate in the United States.[9] Following Taylor (1993) it has become quite common to characterize central bank policy as an *interest rate rule* that responds to recent outcomes (or nowcasts) of target variables such as inflation and the output gap:

$$i_t = \bar{r} + \pi^* + \phi_\pi(\pi_t - \pi^*) + \phi_y(\gamma_t - \gamma_t^*). \tag{2}$$

Here, $\bar{r}$ refers to an equilibrium real interest rate, which together with the inflation target, sums to the equilibrium nominal rate. ϕ_π and ϕ_y constitute the central bank's response parameters. Using values of 2% for $\bar{r}$ and π^*, 1.5 for ϕ_π and 0.5 for ϕ_y, Taylor (1993) showed that the implied interest rate path matches Federal Reserve policy from 1987 to 1992 very well. However, he had not estimated this relationship. Rather, these values of the response coefficients had delivered good stabilization performance in a variety of models used in a major model- and policy-comparison exercise (see Bryant et al., 1993). Such performance evaluations follow Tinbergen's task list by using models of the relationship between policy instruments and targets (item (v)) to investigate the performance of interest rate rules (items (iii) and (iv)) with regard to a loss function that

---

[7] As to the Federal Reserve, Chairman Bernanke explained in 2009 that *"the longer-term projections of inflation may be interpreted [...] as the rate of inflation that FOMC participants see as most consistent with the dual mandate given to it by Congress – that is the rate of inflation that promotes maximum sustainable employment while also delivering reasonable price stability,"* (Bernanke, 2009) As of January 2012 the FOMC specified its target publicly.

[8] A positive value of the inflation target is often justified as a means for minimizing the impact of the zero lower bound on nominal interest rates on policy effectiveness (Coenen and Wieland, 2004).

[9] We abstract from other instruments used when interest policy is inhibited by the zero-lower-bound as in the course of the recent recession. See Wieland (2010) for a review of earlier research on policy instruments at the zero-bound.

is specified in terms of target variables such as Eq. (1), (items (i) and (ii)). Specifically, these evaluations used the weighted average of the unconditional variance of inflation and the output gap, that is the limiting case of Eq. (1) without discounting.[10]

Of course, just as central banks have typically avoided committing to a particular loss function, they have also abstained from announcing a fixed interest rate rule. Nevertheless, inflation targeting central banks such as the Bank of Canada and the Bank of England have used Taylor-style rules with forecasts early on in order to operationalize inflation-forecast targeting in model-based evaluations and projections (cf. Haldane, 1995; Amano et al., 1998; Batini and Haldane, 1999). Such a *forecast-based interest-rate rule* can be defined analogously to Eq. (2):

$$i_t = \bar{r} + \pi^* + \phi_{\pi,h}(E[\pi_{t+h}|I_t] - \pi^*) + \phi_{y,k}(E[y_{t+k} - y^*_{t+k}|I_t]), \tag{3}$$

where the subscripts h and k denote the forecast horizons of inflation and output forecasts, respectively. The policymaker's target is included in the expectation, assuming that policymakers aim at potential output. Similarly, its current value in Eq. (2) has to be understood as a nowcast.

2.2.2. The Macroeconomic Model

Item (v) on Tinbergen's list requires a particular *model* of the transmission of monetary policy to policy targets. As a simple example, we consider the following three-equation model in the spirit of Svensson (1997) and Orphanides and Wieland (2000b):

$$\pi_{t+1} = \pi_t + \kappa(y_t - \bar{y}_t) + \gamma z_{t+1} + \epsilon_{t+1} \tag{4}$$

$$y_{t+1} - \bar{y}_{t+1} = \alpha(y_t - \bar{y}_t) - \sigma(i_t - \pi_t - \bar{r}) + \delta z_{t+1} + \eta_{t+1} \tag{5}$$

$$z_{t+1} = \theta_1 \pi_t + \theta_2(y_t - \bar{y}_t) + \theta_3 z_t + \nu_{t+1}. \tag{6}$$

The model consists of a Phillips curve, which relates inflation to the output gap and an IS-curve which indicates the dependence of the output gap on the interest rate, that is the policy instrument. z_t serves as a stand-in for other, possibly endogenous, variables affecting output and inflation, and is determined according to the third equation in the model. $(\epsilon_{t+1}, \eta_{t+1}, \nu_{t+1})$ refer to normally-distributed economic shocks with mean zero and known variance. $(\alpha, \kappa, \gamma, \sigma, \delta, \theta_1, \theta_2, \theta_3)$ denote model parameters. Monetary policy suffers from a transmission lag. It takes two periods for a change of the interest rate to affect inflation.

This model may be estimated and then used as a testing ground for optimizing simple outcome- or forecast-based feedback rules as in the above-mentioned model comparison studies. Specifically, the policy response coefficients (ϕ_π, ϕ_y) and $(\phi_{\pi,h}, \phi_{y,k})$ in Eqs. (2) and (3), would be chosen to minimize the loss defined by (1) (or its limiting version without discounting) subject to the model defined by Eqs. (4), (5) and (6). For example, the

---

[10] See Taylor (1999) and Taylor and Wieland (2012) for similar studies.

comparison study in Taylor (1999) included a similar model by Rudebusch and Svensson (1999). The role of forecasts in such policy evaluations is consistent with Theil's proposition. Firstly, the forecast-based rule involves a policy response to the rational expectation/forecast of inflation and the output gap conditional on the macroeconomic model including the policy rule. Secondly, the optimization exercise with the outcome-based rule can be interpreted as a rational forecast of output and inflation variability conditional on the model and this particular rule. Of course, in the applications discussed later in this chapter, we will also consider state-of-the-art macro models that include forward-looking expectations by households and firms in the economic structure. In this case, policy optimization and associated forecasts will also need to differentiate the case of discretionary policy when private sector expectations do not incorporate policy commitments from the case when institutions are in place that allow for credible commitment.

2.2.3. Optimal Control Policy and Forecast Targeting

An alternative to simple policy rules is given by the *optimal control policy*. Optimal control would imply *choosing a path* of the policy instrument i_t that minimizes expected losses, defined by Eq. (1), subject to the model of the economy represented by Eqs. (4), (5), and (6) the information set I_t. Optimal control does not impose the particular functional form for policy implied by simple rules such as (2) and (3). However, given that the model considered is linear in the relevant state variables, $(\pi_t, y_t - \bar{y}_t, z_t)$, and the objective is quadratic in the target variables, (π, y), the optimal control policy turns out to be a linear function of the states:

$$ i_t = \bar{r} + \pi^* + \tilde{\phi}_\pi (\pi_t - \pi^*) + \tilde{\phi}_y(y_t - y_t^*) + \tilde{\phi}_z z_t, \tag{7} $$

where it is assumed that the policymaker observes potential output $\bar{y}_t$ and sets the target y_t^* accordingly. Contrary to the simple rules discussed above, the optimal control policy implies a direct interest rate response to all state variables, including z_t, which stands for many variables that affect output and inflation. The forecast-based rule incorporates an indirect response to all state variables via the inflation and output forecasts, but the functional form of this rule imposes additional restrictions on the coefficients relative to the optimal control policy. The optimal control coefficients $\tilde{\phi}_\pi$, $\tilde{\phi}_y$ and $\tilde{\phi}_z$ are non-linear functions of the structural model and loss function parameters $(\kappa, \gamma, \alpha, \sigma, \delta, \theta_1, \theta_2, \theta_3, \beta, \lambda)$. These coefficients are generally different from the response parameters in the simple rules, that is (ϕ_π, ϕ_y) and $(\phi_{\pi,h}, \phi_{y,k})$. Forecasts of future inflation and output deviations from the central bank's targets – conditional on the central bank's model and information set – are used in optimizing the path of the central bank interest rate.

No central bank has publicly announced that it strictly implements an optimal control policy and communicated all the preference and model parameters needed for the policy calculation. Svensson (1999, 2003) has proposed to mimic the optimal control policy by pursuing a so-called *forecast targeting rule*. This rule is expressed in forecasts of the target variables output and inflation, rather than directly implementable interest rate prescriptions. In his terminology the loss function with inflation and the output gap in Eq. (1) is referred to as flexible inflation targeting. He breaks the optimization problem in two steps. First, he derives the first-order conditions with respect to output and inflation conditional on the Phillips curve, Eq. (4), which determines the economic tradeoff between these two target variables. In the second step, the other model equations are used to derive the interest rate setting. This interest rate setting is equivalent to the optimal control policy defined by Eq. (7). Svensson (2003) shows that the optimality condition corresponds to,

$$E[\pi_{t+j+1} - \pi^*|I_t] = \frac{\lambda}{\beta\kappa}(\beta E[(y_{t+j+1} - y^*_{t+j+1}) - (y_{t+j} - y^*_{t+j})|I_t]), \quad j \geq 0, \qquad (8)$$

for the case when z_t is exogenous. This relationship between output and inflation forecasts provides an implicit definition of the optimal control policy. With regard to its practical implementation, Svensson (2003) recommends that "*the central bank staff construct the 'feasible' set of forecasts and instrument plans. The decision-making body ... then selects the combination of forecasts that 'look best' ..., the best compromise between stabilizing the inflation gap and the output gap*". This recommendation is similar but not identical to another often-used description of inflation forecast targeting, which states that central banks should set policy such that the implied inflation forecast is equal to the central bank's target at some given, constant horizon.

In the last 20 years a number of countries have adopted explicit inflation targeting regimes. They use forecasts extensively in their communication with markets. A possible description of their policy strategy is one in which the stance of policy is adjusted to ensure that the inflation rate is projected to return to target within an acceptable period (see, e.g., Leiderman and Svensson, 1995; Bernanke and Mishkin, 1997; Bernanke et al., 1999). The optimal control approach to inflation targeting – often referred to as forecast targeting – is developed in detail in Svensson (2010, 2011), Woodford (2007, 2011).

2.2.4. An Equivalence Result

Having presented several different approaches to the use of forecasts in policy design, namely simple outcome-based rules, simple forecast-based rules, optimal control policies, and forecast targeting rules, we close by noting an equivalence result that is obtained under restrictive conditions. Specifically, if the parameters γ and δ are set to zero, the other endogenous variable(s) denoted by z_t do not affect inflation or output. Thus, the optimal control policy takes the form of a simple outcome-based rule and can also be expressed as a forecast-based rule with the one-period ahead inflation forecast:

$$i_t = \bar{r} + \pi^* + \tilde{\phi}_\pi (\pi_t - \pi^*) + \tilde{\phi}_y(y_t - y^*_t), \quad \text{or} \qquad (9)$$

$$i_t = \bar{r} + \pi^* + \tilde{\phi}_{\pi,1}(E[\pi_{t+1}|I_t] - \pi^*) + \tilde{\phi}_{y,0}(y_t - y^*_t). \qquad (10)$$

In other words, there is one particular setting of the response parameters in the outcome-based rule, $(\tilde{\phi}_\pi, \tilde{\phi}_y)$, a different one in the forecast-based rule, $(\tilde{\phi}_{\pi,1}, \tilde{\phi}_{y,0})$, which render these rules identical to the optimal control policy. This setting could also be obtained by minimizing the loss function subject to the model and the particular form of the policy rule.

In sum, if the economic model exactly matches the true macroeconomic relations in the economy, then a central bank that implements the optimal control policy will achieve better or equal stabilization outcomes than simple outcome- or forecast-based rules. However, the optimal control solution is more complicated than either of the simple rules, making it more difficult to communicate to the public. Forecast targeting may help in organizing the implementation of an optimal control policy, but it does not provide an explicit prescription for the instrument setting that can be checked by the public as easily as simple rules. Forecast-based simple rules provide an avenue for taking into account additional information on the state and structure of the economy relative to outcome-based rules. Yet, given that the true structure is unknown, there is a risk that some of this information is misleading. Thus, it is of great interest to compare the robustness of different policy and forecasting approaches under model uncertainty as in (Levin et al., 2003). The interaction of forecast-based policy and economic fluctuations can be studied in structural macroeconomic models, which can also be used to search for efficient and robust policy prescriptions. We will return to this question in Section 6.

2.2.5. Preference and Forecast Asymmetries

The model we have considered features a quadratic loss function. This loss is symmetric, i.e., deviations of inflation or output above or below the respective target values are equally undesirable from the policymakers' perspective. In practice, central banks may treat such deviations asymmetrically. For example, they might react more aggressively to recessions by lowering interest rates to a greater extent than they would raise interest rates in the event of a boom of the same absolute magnitude. Such decision making would be consistent with an asymmetric loss function that penalizes negative deviations of output from potential more than positive deviations. The policy induced by such preferences would then induce an upward bias in inflation (see Nobay and Peel (2003) and Surico (2007) for analytical expositions and Surico for an empirical analysis of Federal Reserve policy).

An important consequence of asymmetric loss functions would be an asymmetry in forecasts. For example, Patton and Timmermann (2007) analyze Federal Reserve output growth forecasts and find that they are suboptimal under a symmetric loss function. However, the forecasts are optimal if overpredicting output growth is more costly than underpredicting it.

Asymmetric loss may also be an important feature of fiscal policy making and exert an influence on government budget forecasts. Empirical evidence is provided by Elliott et al. (2005). They analyze IMF and Organization for Economic Cooperation and Development (OECD) forecasts of budget deficits in the G7 countries. They argue that underestimating budget deficits yields different costs than overestimating budget deficits (see also Artis and Marcellino, 2001; Campbell and Ghysels, 1995). The shape of a forecast loss function might be influenced by political pressure of member countries or the budgetary discipline that these forecasts might impose. Elliott et al. (2005) find that the IMF and OECD forecasts systematically overpredict budget deficits, a finding which would be in line with the budgetary discipline argument. For some countries they find that underpredictions of budget deficits are viewed up to three times costlier than overpredictions. If policymakers in the member countries want to use these forecasts, but do not have the same loss function as the forecaster they would need to adjust the forecasts.

3. EXAMPLES OF FORECASTS PRODUCED AT FISCAL AUTHORITIES AND CENTRAL BANKS

Table 5.1 lists a number of forecasts that are of particular relevance for monetary and fiscal policy making and regularly published by policy institutions such as the Board of Governors of the Federal Reserve System, the CBO, the ECB, the European Commission, and other central banks and international organizations.

3.1. Forecasts for Fiscal Policy Purposes

As discussed in the introduction the *Budget and Economic Outlook* of the CBO is an essential part of the federal budgeting process in the United States. The forecasts are published every year in January and submitted to the House and Senate Committees on the Budget. The report is updated mid-year. In addition, the CBO publishes an analysis of the President's Budgetary Proposals for the upcoming fiscal year. The CBO forecasts play an important role in ensuring that the budgetary developments remain in accordance with any targeted deficit or surplus. Assumptions regarding future policy underlying the CBO's baseline forecast are based on rules established in The Balanced Budget and Emergency Deficit Control Act of 1985 (Public Law 99–177).[11] The baseline estimate assumes that existing policies and laws continue in the future. Specifically, direct spending and receipts are assumed to continue at the level prescribed by current law. Discretionary spending is assumed to continue at the level of current year spending adjusted for inflation and other factors. CBOs baseline projections are not intended to be a forecast of future budgetary outcomes, but are supposed to serve as a neutral benchmark. In addition, CBO publishes alternative scenarios that include changes in future policies.

In the European Union and the Euro area fiscal policy is conducted by national governments. However, the European Commission provides forecasts in a publication called European Economic Forecast. Forecasts are published twice a year with some

---

[11] The rules expired on September 30, 2006, but the CBO continues to follow the methodology prescribed in the law for establishing baseline projections.

Table 5.1 Examples of Important Forecasts

	U.S.	Euro Area	UK	International
Fiscal policy	CBO: Budget and Economic Outlook	European Commission: European Economic Forecast	Office for Budget Responsibility: Economic and Fiscal Outlook	
Monetary pol.	FRB (staff): Greenbook/Tealbook FOMC: FOMC minutes	Eurosystem (staff): Monthly Bulletin (ECB + National Central Banks)	Bank of England: Inflation Report	
General	Philadelphia Fed Survey of professional forecasters	ECB ECB Survey of Professional Forecasters		IMF World Economic Outlook OECD Economic Outlook

interim updates for the largest member states. Forecasts are computed for the individual countries, the Euro area, the EU, candidate countries, and some non-EU countries. The forecast covers 180 variables. Individual country forecasts are computed by country desks using different economic models and econometric tools. The forecasts for the Euro area and the EU are constructed by aggregating the country forecasts. The government of the United Kingdom recently founded a new Office for Budget Responsibility (OBR) in May 2010 that is tasked to assess public finances for each government budget similar to the CBO in the United States. It produces economic and fiscal forecasts and evaluates the long-run sustainability of public finances. Similar to the CBO the OBR publishes reports analyzing the accuracy of its own forecasting record.

3.2. Forecasts for Monetary Policy Purposes

In the following we provide a more detailed description of the production of forecasts at central banks. We focus especially on the Federal Reserve and the ECB, because we will use those forecasts later onto check whether they influence actual policy decisions. A more general though somewhat dated overview of forecasting practices at central banks is given in Robertson (2000).

3.2.1. Federal Reserve forecasts

The Federal Reserve publishes information on forecasts obtained via a regular poll of FOMC members, which include the Governors of the Federal Reserve System and the Presidents of the regional Federal Reserve Banks, prior to FOMC meetings. The semi-annual monetary policy reports to U.S. Congress (the so-called Humphrey–Hawkins reports) have presented information on the range and central tendency of FOMC members' forecasts since 1979. Since November 2007 the FOMC has compiled and released these forecast ranges and central tendencies four times a year. The central tendency excludes the three highest and three lowest projections. FOMC members are asked to predict economic growth, the unemployment rate, and core and overall price inflation as measured by the personal consumption expenditures deflator (PCE). Prior to 1998 the inflation forecasts concerned the consumer price index (CPI). The FOMC members' projections should be based on "*appropriate monetary policy*" that is defined "*as the future path of policy that the participant deems most likely to foster outcomes for economic activity and inflation that best satisfy his or her interpretation of the Federal Reserve's dual objectives of maximum employment and stable prices.*"[12] The horizon of the forecasts used to be for the current and next year. Since November 2007, FOMC members are asked to provide a projection for an additional year into the future as well as a long-run projection. This long-run projection implicitly provides information on FOMC perceptions regarding long-run

[12] See, for example, Minutes of the Federal Open Market Committee April 26–27, 2011, Summary of the Economic Projections, Page 1.

potential growth, the natural unemployment rate, and the FOMC's desired long-run inflation rate.

In addition, the staff of the Federal Reserve Board (FRB) in Washington, DC provides a forecast of economic developments for every meeting of the Federal Open Market Committee (FOMC). This document used to be called the Greenbook due to its green cover and is nowadays referred to as the Tealbook.[13] In contrast to the FOMC members' projections, the FRB staff forecasts are confidential. They are only meant to inform the discussion among FOMC members. The forecasts are made available to the public with a five-year lag. An online archive of past Greenbook data sets is available from the Federal Reserve Bank of Philadelphia.

The forecasts are conditioned on a specific future path of the federal funds rate – the primary policy instrument of the FOMC. It is often assumed that the federal funds rate will be kept constant at the most recent level. At other times a decreasing or increasing path is assumed, especially if a constant interest rate path would be implausible. We will discuss different conditioning assumptions in detail in Section 5.4.

As explained by Edge et al. (2010), Robertson (2000), and Reifschneider et al. (1997) the Federal Reserve staff forecast is a judgmental projection that is derived from quantitative data, qualitative information, different economic models, and various forecasting techniques. The forecast does not result from a mechanical run of any large-scale macroeconometric model; nor is it derived directly by add-factoring any such model. Instead, it relies heavily on the expertise of sector specialists and senior advisers. The Federal Reserve's structural macroeconomic model of the U.S. economy – the so-called FRB/U.S. model[14] – is only one of the tools used as an input into the deliberations that lead to the Greenbook/Tealbook projection. According to the above-mentioned descriptions of the FRB staff forecasting process, FRB/U.S. model forecasts are prepared at the same time as each Greenbook forecast and for the same projection horizon. Furthermore, the model forecast is conditioned on the same path for the federal funds rate as the Greenbook projection.

A forecast coordinator provides sector specialists with a set of conditioning assumptions and forecasts as a starting point. On this basis, staff economists that specialize on specific sectors create a first set of forecasts for a variety of economic variables. They might use a range of different statistical and econometric techniques and models and expert knowledge. Furthermore, all regional Federal Reserve Banks collect information on current regional conditions that are presented in the beige book and can also help in forming a view about the current state of the U.S. economy. Additionally, econometric methods that can process unbalanced data sets of differing frequency are used in creating an estimate of current conditions, in other words, a nowcast that can serve as a

---

[13] Until summer 2010 forecasts and monetary policy alternatives were summarized in two different documents: the Greenbook and the Bluebook. These are now merged in the Tealbook.

[14] See Brayton and Tinsley (1996) and Reifschneider et al. (1999) for descriptions of the FRB/U.S. model.

starting point for forecasts. The different assessments are aggregated with the help of the forecast coordinator and staff meetings into projections for output, inflation, and interest rates. Afterwards, individual sector forecasts are checked to be consistent with these aggregate forecasts. This process goes on until sectoral and aggregate forecasts converge (Reifschneider et al., 1997).

The Greenbook/Tealbook forecast contains a wide variety of variables that are grouped into expenditure, employment and production, income and savings and prices, and costs categories. There are also detailed projections of federal sector accounts. Real GDP and CPI-inflation are projected for major industrial and developing countries. The FRB/U.S. model is used to compute confidence intervals around the judgmental point forecast and alternative scenarios for some key aggregates like real GDP, the unemployment rate, and a core personal consumption expenditure price index. To this end, the core model is add-factored in order to replicate the final Greenbook point forecast over the forecast horizon. The add-factored version of the model is then used for various exercises, such as generating intervals around the Greenbook forecasts based on stochastic simulations and occasionally for producing longer-run forecasts at horizons beyond two years.

3.2.2. European Central Bank forecasts

As to the Euro area, the Eurosystem staff – that is, the staff of the ECB together with the staff of the Euro area national central banks – prepare macroeconomic projections twice a year. Furthermore, the ECB's staff prepares two additional projections per year so that Euro area projections are available at a quarterly frequency. These projections serve as an input to the ECB Governing Council meetings and are made public afterwards in the ECB's Monthly Bulletin. There is no public information on the personal forecasts of members of the ECB Governing Council.

The joint forecasting process of ECB staff and national central banks' (NCB) staff is described in European Central Bank (2001). This joint group is called the Working Group on Forecasting (WGF) and includes macroeconomic and econometric experts. They produce detailed macroeconomic projections under the responsibility and guidance of a Monetary Policy Committee (MPC). This committee consists of senior staff representatives of the ECB and the national central banks. National central banks compute forecasts of GDP growth, its components HICP inflation and the GDP deflator and possibly other variables in their countries. Country forecasts are then aggregated to Euro area forecasts in a process that involves several types of consistency checks. The forecast rounds done solely by the ECB staff are called macroeconomic projection exercises (MPEs) and the joint projections with the national central banks are called BMPEs (broad MPEs).

This process involves three steps: (i) setting the assumptions underlying the exercise; (ii) a process of overview at area-wide level with consistency checks and peer review of individual country results that leads to a set of projection figures; and (iii) preparation of a report for the Governing Council and the publication of the forecasts in the ECB's monthly bulletin.

With regard to conditioning assumptions, national central bank staff and ECB staff decide on a joint set of exogenous time paths for interest rates, exchange rates, the international environment, fiscal variables, and commodity prices. In particular, paths for interest rates and commodity prices are based on market expectations derived from futures rates.

Afterwards each national central bank computes a forecast for its country, whereas ECB staff prepare a set of projections for the individual countries as well as for the Euro area as a whole. The ECB's Euro area projection is a consistent aggregation of its country assessments. The national central banks use a variety of models, econometric methods and sectoral or country expertise. The combination of model-based and judgmental-based information may also vary across countries.

Then an iterative process of consistency checking between the ECB's area-wide forecast and the aggregation of the NCB forecasts is started. This process relies on meetings of NCB and ECB experts, and importantly, also on analysis using the area-wide macroeconomic model of the ECB research directorate.[15] In addition, consistency checks are conducted with respect to trade volumes and prices as well as financial flows and consolidated balance sheets of monetary financial institutions in the Euro area.

The resulting Eurosystem staff projections serve as an input to the ECBs Governing Councils meetings. Forecasts of variables that are published in the Monthly Bulletin include HICP inflation, real GDP growth and its main components over for the current and the next year. The projections are published in the form of uncertainty ranges corresponding to 57.5% probability bands.[16] Ranges are wider for longer forecast horizons reflecting the increased uncertainty. The ranges reflect uncertainty due to unforeseeable shocks and imprecise parameter estimates as well as departures from the conditioning assumptions of the baseline forecast. In addition specific scenarios deviating from the baseline conditioning assumptions are computed. For example, Eurosystem staff may compute a forecast where the growth rate for the United States is assumed to be much lower than in the baseline case or where the oil price is assumed to be higher. Many national central banks also publish the projections for their economies. Forecasts are published together with a written statement that explains economic developments and the surrounding uncertainty.

3.2.3. Inflation Targeting Central Banks

At inflation-targeting central banks such as, for example, the Reserve Bank of New Zealand, the Central Bank of Chile, the Bank of England, Sveriges Riksbank, or the Bank of Norway the inflation forecast takes center stage in the communication with

---

[15] A description of the area-wide model is available in Fagan et al. (2005). In 2008 this model was replaced with a New-Area-Wide model that is presented in Christoffel et al. (2008).

[16] By contrast, the ranges of FOMC forecasts published by the Federal Reserve indicate the level of disagreement between FOMC member point forecasts rather than economic uncertainty bands.

the public. Their forecasts are not just staff, but official forecasts. They are published and discussed regularly with the stated aim of influencing and anchoring private sector expectations. For example, announcing a certain inflation target and publishing an official forecast that illustrates that the central bank plans to do what is necessary to reach that target can induce price setters to adopt this forecast in their considerations.

While the Fed Greenbook and the Eurosystem forecasts are associated with the staff and not the policymakers, the official forecasts of inflation targeting central banks involve a much closer collaboration of staff and policymakers. The reason is that the inflation forecast typically serves as an intermediate policy target. In this context, the consequences of particular conditioning assumptions need to be considered especially carefully. We will discuss their consequences more thoroughly in Section 5.4.

A thorough review of forecasting practices at inflation targeting central banks is beyond this chapter.[17] To pick an example, we review the procedures employed at the Bank of England. Of course, there are differences in the forecasting processes employed by different inflation targeters. However, all of them publish detailed inflation forecasts that reflect the views of policymakers in an official document often called inflation report.

The published forecast of the Bank of England is the outcome of a joint forecasting process of staff and the Monetary Policy Committee (MPC).[18] In a series of meetings between the MPC and the bank's staff the forecasts are constructed, discussed and adjusted until they represent the views of the MPC. The forecast involves judgment as well as a variety of economic models.[19] The Bank of England mainly employs a suite of five models. The core model has been replaced in 2005 by the new Bank of England Quarterly Model (BEQM) (Bank of England, 1999, 2004). The suite of models includes small-open economy New Keynesian structural models, small vector autoregression models, single-equation regression models like Phillips curve models but also medium-scale DSGE models and larger-scale structural macroeconomic models. The BEQM is a macroeconometric model that combines a DSGE model that is consistently derived from microeconomic optimization behavior of households and firms with additional dynamics that reflect short-run correlations not matched by the core DSGE model. The BEQM is the main tool employed by the Bank of England staff and the MPC to construct the projections for the inflation reports. It serves as a reference point to organize discussions about recent and projected economic dynamics. However, the final projec-

---

[17] In this regard, the reader is referred to the chapter on inflation targeting in the Handbook of Monetary Economics by Svensson (2010).

[18] The MPC is the Bank's main policy-making committee not to be confused with the MPC committee in the Eurosystem, which involves staff experts charged with producing a joint forecast for the consideration of Euro area policymakers.

[19] In Section 5.4 we will demonstrate a formal approach to include judgment or off-model information via conditioning assumptions into structural model forecasts. Such a formal approach is used for example at the Central Bank of Norway (Bache et al., 2010). At most central banks, however, the process of including judgment and conditioning assumptions is less formal.

tions are not a mechanical output from the model, but include a high degree of judgment by the MPC.

The Bank of England's forecasts are presented as fan charts that represent uncertainty about future economic developments and the conditioning assumptions. The forecast horizon is up to three years ahead. The fan charts of the Bank of England offer more detail on the degree of uncertainty than the Eurosystem forecasts. First, confidence intervals are computed based on past forecast errors. Then the MPC comments on these intervals and they are adjusted accordingly to reflect asymmetric perceptions of upward and downward risks. In the case of upward risks, raising the interest rate would become more likely, than when the MPC's assessment points to symmetric uncertainty or downward risks to the inflation forecast. The adjustment of the uncertainty bands by the MPC could be useful to account for structural changes or additional variables not taken into account by the model and past forecast errors.

3.2.4. International Institutions

Other important forecasts that receive considerable attention by governments and the press are the IMF's World Economic Outlook, and the Organization for Economic Cooperation and Development (OECD) Economic Outlook. The IMF's World Economic Outlook includes analysis and projections of the main macroeconomic aggregates for all IMF member countries and is published twice a year. It is an integral element of the IMF's surveillance process. The OECD's Economic Outlook is a similar publication that covers the OECD member countries and is also published twice a year.

4. EMPIRICAL EVIDENCE THAT POLICYMAKERS' DECISIONS RESPOND TO FORECASTS

Do policymakers adjust their decisions in response to changes in the forecast? Answering this question requires an empirical investigation. Of course, it is easiest to search for such a link in an environment in which decision makers are exposed to a particular forecast on a regular basis and shortly thereafter make a policy decision that immediately becomes public. Thus, it is most easily tested in the context of central bank interest rate policy. We focus on the central banks in charge of the two most widely used currencies, the U.S. Federal Reserve and the ECB. After reviewing findings from the literature we conduct additional new empirical tests.

4.1. Federal Reserve Interest Rate Decisions

4.1.1. Literature

Central bank policy in the United States is primarily concerned with setting a target for the federal funds rate. Soon after Taylor (1993) showed that the federal funds rate path between 1987 and 1992 was matched very well by a simple rule that had been optimized in a model comparison exercise, Federal Reserve staff started preparing Taylor rule charts as part of the regular information package received by the FOMC (Kohn, 2007).[20] These charts included rules with Taylor's original coefficients on inflation and the output gap and rules with estimated coefficients similar to those in Judd and Rudebusch (1998). By 1997 this information also included rules based on (real-time) FOMC forecasts of inflation and unemployment that were shown to exhibit a better empirical fit than outcome-based rules by FRB economists Lindsey, Orphanides, and Wieland (1997).[21] In 2007 William Poole, then-President of the Federal Reserve Bank of St. Louis and member of the FOMC characterized the use of the Taylor rule by the FOMC as follows:

> The FOMC, and certainly John Taylor himself, view the Taylor rule as a general guideline. Departures from the rule make good sense when information beyond that incorporated in the rule is available. For example, policy is forward looking; which means that from time to time the economic outlook changes sufficiently that it makes sense for the FOMC to set a funds rate either above or below the level called for in the Taylor rule, which relies on observed recent data rather than on economic forecasts of future data.

(Poole, 2007, p. 6).

Many other studies have estimated Taylor-style rules using forecasts of U.S. data since the mid-1990s. Most of these studies included an interest-rate smoothing term (cf. Clarida et al., 1998, 2000).[22] Clarida et al. (2000), for example, compare forecast-based rules for the period before Paul Volcker's Fed chairmanship with the Volcker–Greenspan period using forecasts implied by U.S. data of 1997 vintage.

Many of the rules estimated in these studies are nested by following specification:

$$i_t = \rho i_{t-1} + (1 - \rho)[i^* + \beta(E_t \pi_{t+h_\pi} - \pi^*) + \gamma E_t y_{t+h_y}] + \epsilon_t, \tag{11}$$

where i_t denotes the nominal interest rate, π_t the rate of inflation and y_t the output gap, which is replaced with the unemployment rate in Lindsey et al. (1997) and Orphanides and Wieland (2008). Inflation and the nominal interest rate are measured at annual rates in percentage points. ρ, β and γ denote the response parameters. π^* is the inflation target and i^* the equilibrium nominal interest rate when inflation and output equal their respective target values. ϵ_t stands for a monetary policy shock, which captures deviations from the systematic policy response to output and inflation. The parameters h_π and h_y denote forecast horizons measured in quarters that correspond to the degree of forward-lookingness of the central bank. The policy rule (11) also nests Eqs. (2) and (3) from Section (2.2).

---

[20] One of the authors' of this chapter (Wieland) was the staff economist responsible for updating this rules package regularly for the FOMC from 1996 to 2000.

[21] This working paper was presented publicly at several occasions but not submitted for publication. It is available for download from www.volkerwieland.com.

[22] Sack and Wieland (2000) discuss several reasons why central banks tend to smooth interest rates. Rudebusch (2002) argues that a large and significant interest-rate smoothing coefficient is the result of a misspecified monetary policy rule. However, tests by English et al. (2003), Castelnuovo (2003), and Gerlach-Kristen (2004) provide further support for interest-smoothing.

Table 5.2 reports estimation results from the above-mentioned studies for rules corresponding to Eq. (11). Lindsey et al. (1997) identified a strong policy response to FOMC forecasts of inflation and unemployment with coefficients of 2.23 and −2.22, respectively. A rule-of-thumb for comparing the unemployment response coefficient with an output gap coefficient using Okun's law is to multiply with −0.5, which would imply an output gap coefficient near unity. Thus, the systematic policy response to inflation and output forecasts is quite a bit larger than the response to recent outcomes implied by the original Taylor rule coefficients of 1.5 and 0.5 respectively. However, the interest-rate-smoothing coefficient of 0.38 implies that the funds rate only adjusts partially towards this policy prescription within one quarter. Since FOMC forecasts were only produced semi-annually the estimation of Lindsey et al. (1997) only uses two observations per year. The forecast horizon is three quarters.[23]

Clarida et al. (2000) consider forecast horizons of one and four quarters for the rate of inflation, and a horizon of one quarter for the output gap. They use quarterly data of 1998 vintage and identify forecasts using generalized method of moments estimation.[24] Clarida et al. (2000) find that the interest rate response to inflation during the pre-Volcker period, that is from 1960 to 1979 was not sufficient to achieve stabilization. It fails the so-called Taylor principle. An increase of inflation (expectations) is followed by a less than one-to-one increase in the nominal interest rate and thus a decline in the real interest rate. Such a decline in the real rate of interest would further stimulate economic activity, generate additional output, and further upward pressure on prices resulting in faster inflation. For the Volcker–Greenspan era the inflation response coefficient is larger than 1 and consequently satisfies the Taylor principle. Over this period, the FOMC raised interest sufficiently in response to inflation forecasts so as to ensure a stabilizing impact on inflation. The response to the four-quarter ahead inflation forecast is estimated to be greater than the response to the one-quarter ahead inflation forecast.

Orphanides (2001) points out that actual policy decisions are better captured by using the data that was available to policymakers at that time. He analyzes the period from 1987 to 1992, the original sample considered by Taylor (1993). In a first step he compares interest rate rules for different forecast horizons using ex-post revised data. In this case, he finds that a specification with contemporaneous inflation and output gap estimates fits the data best. In a second step Orphanides uses Greenbook forecasts of inflation and the output gap to estimate the policy rule. With this real-time data specification he finds that policy rules with inflation and output gap forecasts fit the data better than with inflation and output gap nowcasts. In Table 5.2 we compare his results for one-quarter ahead and four-quarter ahead forecasts with real-time and revised data. Estimates with revised data overestimate the response to inflation. Estimates with one-quarter ahead

---

[23] The exact derivation of the constant-three-quarter ahead forecasts from the available FOMC forecasts is discussed in the next subsection.

[24] A possible justification for the differential horizons is that output affects inflation with a lag.

Table 5.2 Examples of Estimated Monetary Policy Parameters for Different Forecast Horizons

Source	Sample	h_π^a	h_y^a	ρ	β	γ
U.S.						
Lindsey et al. (1997): real-time	1988:Q1–1996:Q3	3	3	0.38[b]	2.23	−2.22[c]
Clarida et al. (2000)	1960:Q1–1979:Q2	1	1	0.68	0.83	0.27
Clarida et al. (2000)	1979:Q3–1996:Q4	1	1	0.79	2.15	0.93
Clarida et al. (2000)	1960:Q1–1979:Q2	4	1	0.73	0.86	0.34
Clarida et al. (2000)	1979:Q3–1996:Q4	4	1	0.78	2.62	0.83
Orphanides (2001): real-time	1987:Q1–1992:Q4	1	1	0.63	0.39	1.02
Orphanides (2001): revised	1987:Q1–1992:Q4	1	1	0.73	1.49	1.05
Orphanides (2001): real-time	1987:Q1–1992:Q4	4	4	0.56	1.62	0.82
Orphanides (2001): revised	1987:Q1–1992:Q4	4	4	0.95	3.72	2.96
Orphanides and Wieland (2008): real-time	1988:Q1–2007:Q3	3	3	0.39[b]	2.48	−1.84[c]
Euro Area						
Gerdesmeier and Roffia (2005): revised	1999:Q1–2003:Q1	4	0	0.81[d]	0.64	1.44
Gerdesmeier and Roffia (2005): real-time	1999:Q1–2003:Q1	4	0	0.98[d]	2.13	1.63
Gerdesmeier and Roffia (2005): real-time	1999:Q1–2003:Q1	8	0	0.95[d]	1.87	1.70
Gorter et al. (2008): real-time	1997:Q1–2006:Q4	4	4	0.89[d]	1.67	1.65
Gorter et al. (2008): revised	1997:Q1–2006:Q4	4	4	0.96[d]	0.04	0.86
Gerlach (2007)[e]	1999:Q2–2006:Q2	4	4	−0.79[f]	−0.60[g]	2.20[h]

Notes:

[a] The forecast horizons h_π and h_y always refer to a quarterly frequency regardless whether the data is monthly or quarterly.

[b] The interest rate lag corresponds to two quarters rather than one quarter.

[c] Lindsey et al. (1997) and Orphanides and Wieland (2008) use forecasts of the unemployment rate instead of the output gap. A rule-of-thumb for comparing the unemployment response coefficient with an output gap coefficient using Okun's law is to multiply with −0.5.

[d] The interest rate lag is one month rather than one quarter.

[e] Gerlach (2007) estimates an ordered probit model so that the size of the parameters is not directly comparable to the other results in the table. The equation includes in addition to the parameters in the table the lagged change in the interest rate and the exchange rate.

[f] Reaction to a one month lagged interest rate rather than one quarter.

[g] The negative inflation reaction found by Gerlach (2007) is not significant.

[h] Gerlach (2007) uses a measure of expected economic growth instead of the output gap.

forecasts do not fulfill the Taylor principle. However, the response to the four-quarter ahead inflation forecasts is stabilizing with an estimated parameter higher than unity. Orphanides (2001) also considers other forecast horizons and finds that the coefficient on inflation increases with the horizon, while the coefficient on the output gap decreases. He notes that the forward-looking specification captures the contours of the federal funds rate path considerably better.

Orphanides and Wieland (2008) have published updated and extended results regarding the interest rate rules in the Lindsey et al. (1997) study with FOMC forecasts. They confirm the earlier finding of a strong response of the funds rate to FOMC inflation and unemployment forecasts. Estimated values are surprisingly close to the Lindsey et al. estimates with 10 years of additional data. A rule with FOMC forecasts fits the data much better than an outcome-based rule. We will analyze and extend the estimation of Orphanides and Wieland (2008) in more detail in the next subsection.

4.1.2. New Empirical Estimates

On the occasion of the January 2010 meeting of the American Economic Association, Federal Reserve Chairman Ben Bernanke discussed the implications of Taylor-style policy rules for monetary policy during the housing bubble and the financial crisis and stated:

> . . . , *because monetary policy works with a lag, effective monetary policy must take into account the forecast values of the goal variables, rather than the current values. Indeed, in that spirit, the FOMC issues regular economic projections, and these projections have been shown to have an important influence on policy decisions (Orphanides and Wieland (2008)*
>
> **(Bernanke, 2010, p. 8).**

Thus, in the following we review and extend the Orphanides and Wieland (2008) study to shed further light on the finding that FOMC policy is best described with an interest rate rule based on FOMC forecasts. The range and a central tendency of the forecasts from the FOMC members are available in the Humphrey–Hawkins reports, which are presented in February and July of each year. As noted earlier, there is no information available on the FOMC's assessment of the output gap. For this reason, Orphanides and Wieland (2008) use the unemployment rate forecasts of the FOMC members as a measure of the level of economic activity. Assuming a constant NAIRU estimate, which is subsumed in the regression intercept, the unemployment rate forecast captures anticipated movements in the unemployment gap. Interestingly, Orphanides and Wieland (2008) also estimate rules with the GDP growth forecasts of FOMC, but find that the empirical fit then deteriorates relative to rules with the unemployment forecast.

The estimated rules require constant-horizon forecasts at the time of the policy decisions, which do not exactly correspond to the forecast horizon of the available FOMC forecasts. Constant horizon forecasts are computed by appropriately averaging available FOMC forecasts and recent outcome data. We illustrate the derivation of such constant-horizon forecasts in the context of our estimation of forecast-based rules in the Euro area in the next subsection. For the estimation with FOMC forecasts we follow Orphanides and Wieland (2008) in comparing rules with three-quarter ahead forecasts to rules with outcomes from the preceding quarter, with and without interest-rate smoothing. These rules are nested in the following specification:

$$i_t = \rho i_{t-1} + (1 - \rho)[\alpha + \beta E_t \pi_{t+h} + \gamma E_t u_{t+h}] + \epsilon_t. \tag{12}$$

It corresponds to Eq. (11) for $h = 3$ and $h = -1$. The intercept term $\alpha = i^* - \beta\pi^* - \gamma u^*$ includes the perceived equilibrium nominal interest rate, the inflation target and the perceived natural unemployment rate.

Figure 5.1 displays the fitted values of the rules with outcomes (dashed line) and forecasts (dotted line) relative to the actual funds rate target (solid line) decided at each of the February and July FOMC meetings from 1988 to 2010. The rules shown in the upper panel are estimated without interest-rate smoothing ($\rho = 0$ in Eq. (12)), while the rules in the lower panel include an estimated degree of interest-rate-smoothing ($\rho > 0$). The parameters are estimated based on the sample from 1988 to 2007. The implications of the rules are then simulated forward using the FOMC forecasts up to the end of 2010.

From the estimates without interest smoothing in the upper panel, it is directly apparent that the prescriptions from the forecast-based rule are much closer to actual decisions than those from the outcome-based rule. Not surprisingly, the interest rate rules with smoothing in the lower panel are closer the actual funds rate path. Even so, the forecast-based rule continues to fit better than the outcome-based rule. Orphanides and Wieland

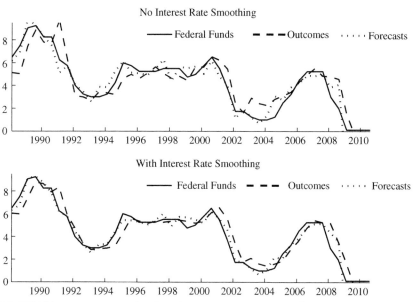

Figure 5.1 FOMC interest rate reaction functions: outcomes vs FOMC forecasts.

(2008) identify five periods during, which FOMC forecasts provide a better explanation of policy decisions. Around 1988 and 1994 the FOMC raised interest rates pre-emptively as it expected inflation to increase in the future. In those periods, the outcome-based rules respond more slowly, while the forecast-based rules fit almost exactly.

In 1990/1991 and in 2001 the FOMC decreased interest rates as it expected a downturn of the economy. The forecast-based rules capture this anticipation, while the fit of the outcome-based rules is not as good. Finally, in 2002/2003 the forecast-based policy rules indicate lower interest rates than the outcome-based rules, consistent with actual policy. As explained by Orphanides and Wieland (2008) the lower rate prescriptions are partly driven by a switch of the FOMC from forecasting CPI inflation, to forecasting PCE and then core PCE inflation. The PCE forecasts at the time suggested a threat of deflation. By contrast, private sector CPI forecasts would have implied higher interest rate prescriptions throughout this period. In sum, these episodes provide further support for forecast-based rules as a description of actual Federal Reserve Policy consistent with the earlier quotes of FOMC members Ben Bernanke and William Poole.

Table 5.3 reports the parameter values underlying the rules shown in Figure 5.1. In addition to the estimation results in Orphanides and Wieland (2008), we report on a specification that includes inflation forecasts together with unemployment outcomes. Policy rules with forecasts of inflation and outcomes of real economic activity have been considered in the literature because they account for the conventional wisdom that monetary policy changes are transmitted more quickly to economic activity than to inflation (see, e.g., Bernanke and Mihov, 1998).

Table 5.3 Interest Rate Rules with FOMC Forecasts of Inflation and Unemployment vs Outcomes: 1988–2007

	No Interest Smoothing			With Interest Smoothing		
	π_{t-1}, u_{t-1}	π_{t+3}, u_{t+3}	π_{t+3}, u_{t-1}	π_{t-1}, u_{t-1}	π_{t+3}, u_{t+3}	π_{t+3}, u_{t-1}
α	8.29	6.97	6.56	10.50	8.25	6.81
	(6.14, 10.79)	(5.22, 8.30)	(5.60, 7.61)	(5.07, 27.28)	(6.73, 10.24)	(5.56, 8.33)
β	1.54	2.34	2.20	1.29	2.48	2.23
	(0.98, 2.21)	(2.02, 2.57)	(1.96, 2.33)	(−0.64, 2.47)	(2.14, 2.65)	(1.91, 2.38)
γ	−1.40	−1.53	−1.40	−1.70	−1.84	−1.46
	(−1.91, −0.99)	(−1.75, −1.22)	(−1.60, −1.23)	(−3.93, −0.79)	(−2.17, −1.55)	(−1.67, −1.26)
ρ	0	0	0	0.69	0.39	0.24
				(0.24, 0.91)	(0.29, 0.54)	(0.04, 0.45)
R^2	0.75	0.92	0.94	0.85	0.96	0.95
$\bar{R}^2$	0.74	0.91	0.94	0.84	0.96	0.95

Notes: Parameters are estimated using non-linear least squares for the case $\rho \neq 0$. 95% confidence bands are shown in brackets and are computed using a moving block bootstrap with 5000 repetitions and a block size of 4 observations.

The parameter estimates indicate that all three specifications satisfy the Taylor principle. The reaction to inflation is highest for the specification with forecasts of inflation and the unemployment rate and lowest for the purely outcome-based rule. The response to unemployment is negative and quite large. For the specifications without interest-rate smoothing the fit in terms of R^2 and $\bar{R}^2$ is lowest for the outcome-based rule and highest for the rule with a response to the inflation forecast and unemployment outcome. For the specifications with interest-rate smoothing the fit is highest for the purely forecast-based rule and lowest for the purely outcome-based rule. In the latter case the parameters of the outcome-based rule are estimated with very large confidence bands, while the forecast-based rule is estimated much more precisely. Also, the degree of interest-rate smoothing is greater when using outcomes as regressors, which might be taken as a sign of misspecification.

These findings provide evidence that the FOMC bases its interest rate decisions on inflation forecasts, but are not as clear-cut regarding unemployment. Without interest-rate smoothing the fit for a rule with unemployment forecasts is very similar to the fit of a rule with unemployment outcomes, though with interest-rate smoothing the rule with unemployment forecasts fits better. In order to further test forecast- vs outcome-based rules we estimate the following specification, which nests both versions as limiting cases:

$$i_t = \rho i_{t-1} + (1-\rho)[\alpha + \beta((1-\phi_\pi)\pi_{t-1} + \phi_\pi E_t \pi_{t+3})$$
$$+ \gamma((1-\phi_u)u_{t-1} + \phi_u E_t u_{t+3})] + \epsilon_t. \tag{13}$$

The new parameters ϕ_π and ϕ_u indicate the relative importance of forecasts and outcomes of inflation and the unemployment rate. We impose the following constraints in estimation: $0 \le \phi_\pi \le 1$ and $0 \le \phi_u \le 1$. $\phi_\pi = 1$, for example, can then be interpreted as evidence that the Fed responds only to inflation forecasts and not outcomes. Orphanides and Wieland (2008) impose $\phi_\pi = \phi_u = \phi$, while we also allow these weights to differ. Table 5.4 reports the estimates obtained for ϕ, ϕ_π and ϕ_u.

When restricting the two weights to be equal, we find $\phi = 0.78$ and $\phi = 0.94$, without and with interest-rate smoothing, respectively. The point estimates are close to one indicating that forecasts are much more important than outcomes in explaining FOMC policy decisions. In both cases, the 95% confidence bands do not include $\phi = 0$. With interest-rate smoothing, $\phi = 1$ lies in the 95% confidence band.[25] Next, we allow for different weights on forecasts for inflation and unemployment. In the absence of interest-rate smoothing the weight on the inflation forecast increases further to $\phi_\pi = 0.87$. The weight on unemployment forecasts decreases to $\phi_u = 0.32$. This finding is in line with earlier results that for specifications without interest-rate smoothing a rule with inflation forecasts and unemployment outcomes yields the best fit. However, the specification

---

[25] We use a bootstrap algorithm to take account for the parameter restriction $0 \le \phi \le 1$. As we bootstrap blocks of four observations this allows in addition for serial correlation of the error term up to two years.

Table 5.4 The Relative Importance of Forecasts vs Outcomes: FOMC 1988–2007

	No Interest Smoothing		With Interest Smoothing	
	$\phi_\pi = \phi_u$	$\phi_\pi \neq \phi_u$	$\phi_\pi = \phi_u$	$\phi_\pi \neq \phi_u$
ϕ	0.78		0.94	
	(0.55, 0.84)		(0.67, 1.00)	
ϕ_π		0.87		0.93
		(0.61, 0.95)		(0.65, 1.00)
ϕ_u		0.32		1
		(0.00, 0.78)		(0.35, 1.00)
R^2	0.94	0.94	0.96	0.96
$\bar{R}^2$	0.93	0.94	0.96	0.96

Notes: Parameters are estimated using non-linear least squares. The parameters ϕ, ϕ_π and ϕ_u are restricted to be in the range of 0 to 1. 95% confidence bands are shown in brackets and are computed using a moving block bootstrap with 5000 repetitions and a block size of four observations.

with interest-rate smoothing yields even a higher $\bar{R}^2$. In this case, the weight on inflation forecasts is $\phi_\pi = 0.93$ and thus very close to 1. The 95% confidence band includes 1, but not 0. Furthermore, the point estimate for the unemployment forecast is on the upper bound: $\phi_u = 1$. While the 95% confidence band is wider than for inflation, it excludes 0. The latter results provide further evidence that FOMC policy decisions are based on forecast of inflation *and* unemployment rather than on outcomes.

In 2008, the Federal Reserve responded to the worsening of the financial crisis by rapidly lowering nominal interest rates towards near zero levels. Our out-of-sample simulation of forecast-based rules estimated with data through 2007 going forward throughout 2008 captures this policy response fairly well, though the initial decline in mid 2008 lags a bit behind actual decisions. Figure 5.2 displays the simulation up to the end of 2010 relative to the actual funds rate target. From 2009 onwards the FOMC has kept the funds rate at 25 basis points. Nominal interest rates cannot be lowered below zero – at least deposit rates – because savers can instead use cash, which pays an interest rate of zero, to store their savings. Since the economic outlook quickly deteriorated further at the end of 2008 and the beginning 2009, the interest rates prescribed by the feedback rules moved far into negative territory. As unemployment and unemployment forecasts increased drastically from about 6% to around 10%, the rules, which exhibit coefficients between 1.5 on outcomes and 2.3 on forecasts, suggested funds rate targets as low as -2% to -5%, respectively.

With the funds rate near zero, the Federal Reserve did not abstain from further action, but instead took measures that led to a rapid expansion of its balance sheet, including in particular massive direct purchases of assets such as government bonds and mortgage-backed securities, that are referred to as credit and quantitative easing. These policy actions are best understood as a continuation of Federal policy shifting from its usual

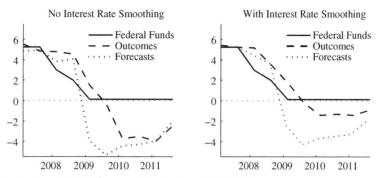

Figure 5.2 Outcome- vs FOMC forecast-based rules: 2005–2011.

policy instrument, the federal instrument, to quantity-based instruments when the funds rate reaches the zero lower bound. As proposed by Orphanides and Wieland (2000a) policy can be understood as a rule for the quantity of base money when the nominal interest rate is constrained at zero. The response coefficients of such a rule need to be adjusted appropriately taking into account parameters governing money demand and the degree of uncertainty about the effect of quantitative easing on output and inflation. An empirical comparison of the quantitative easing in the United States relative to the negative interest rates prescribed by the forecast-based policy rules would be of great interest but is beyond the present study. Of course, simply extending the estimation of the policy rule with 2009 and 2010 data without accounting for quantitative easing would incorrectly result in a downward bias of the estimated interest rate response coefficients.

4.2. ECB Interest Rate Decisions

4.2.1. Literature

As demonstrated by Gerlach and Schnabel (2000) average interest rates in the European Monetary Union (EMU) countries in the period leading up to the formation of EMU, that is from 1990 to 1998 moved very closely with average output gaps and inflation as suggested by the Taylor (1993) rule. The only exception noted by these authors was the period of the crisis of the European Monetary System (EMS) in 1992–93.

By now there are several studies that assess to what extent actual ECB decisions can be described by forecast- or outcome-based interest rate rules. Findings from several of these studies that are nested by Eq. (11) are reported in Table 5.2. ECB economists Gerdesmeier and Roffia (2005) provide a comprehensive study comparing rules estimated with real-time and final revised data of the Euro area as in Orphanides (2001). They use monthly Euro area data from 1999 to 2003.[26] Contrary to Orphanides (2001) they

---

[26] They use an average of five different output gap concepts: linear and quadratic trend measures, the HP Filter and the output gaps provided by the OECD and the European Commission (both are production function approaches). To get monthly output data they interpolate quarterly real GDP using a cubic spline.

find that estimates based on final revised data under-estimate the response coefficients. With real-time data Gerdesmeier and Roffia (2005) find a significant response to survey-based expectations for inflation and real economic activity, but not to outcomes of these variables. Thus, they provide evidence that the ECB is setting interest rates in a forward-looking manner.

Gorter et al. (2008) use Euro area Consensus Economics data for expected inflation and output growth. They compare estimates of forecast-based policy rules to outcome-based policy rules with monthly data from 1997 to 2006. They justify starting the sample in 1997 rather than in 1999 as interest rate setting was coordinated during the run-up to the currency union. They find that Euro area interest rates are better explained with responses to inflation and output growth forecasts than outcomes. The coefficient on inflation in the outcome-based policy rule is not significantly different from zero. Thus, their analysis corroborates Gerdesmeier and Roffia (2005) for a longer sample.

Gerlach (2007) estimates an ordered probit model on monthly data from 1999 to 2006 with measures of expected inflation and output growth taken from a poll of forecasters tabulated in "The Economist". He finds that expectations of economic growth play an important role in explaining the ECB's interest rate decisions, but not those regarding inflation. To shed further light on potential reasons for this finding, Gerlach (2007) constructs indicator variables from a word analysis of the ECB's assessment of economic conditions published in the ECB's monthly bulletin. He argues that the assessment in the official ECB report provides more accurate information about the Governing Council's view of the economy than external forecasts. He concludes from this analysis that the inflation increases that occured over the sample were viewed to be temporary by the ECB and therefore the Governing Council did not react to them with interest rate changes. By contrast, changes in output were viewed by the ECB as an indicator of future inflation. Thus, it reacted strongly to them consistent with a forecast-based approach to monetary policy. The negative interest-rate smoothing coefficient in Gerlach's ordered probit estimation has to be interpreted differently from the other studies that use ordinary least squares and instrumental variable regressions. It reflects that the interest rate is not adjusted every month. If the Governing Council decides to change the interest rate in one month the likelihood of another adjustment in the next month decreases.

Other studies on Euro area interest rate rules have been conducted by Fourans and Vranceanu (2004, 2007), Hayo and Hofmann (2006), Carstensen (2006) and Sauer and Sturm (2007). Further below, we will examine the role of Euro area staff forecasts in explaining ECB interest rates. These forecasts have not been used in any of the studies cited above.

4.2.2. New Empirical Estimates

Unfortunately, there are no publicly available ECB Governing Council projections for the Euro area. However, as discussed in Section 3 ECB staff projections for key Euro area variables are published four times a year in the ECB's monthly bulletin. The forecasts in March and September are computed by the ECB's staff and the forecasts for June and December by Eurosystem staff including experts from the national central banks. These staff projections are available from December 2000 onwards. They are published as ranges reflecting uncertainty derived from past forecasting errors and cover HICP inflation, real GDP, private consumption, government consumption, gross fixed capital formation, exports and imports. We have used the ECB staff forecasts of inflation and real GDP growth to estimate forecast- vs outcome-based policy rules for the Euro area similar to Orphanides (2001). Unfortunately, there is no data on output gap estimates or unemployment rates so as to estimate rules in the spirit of Orphanides and Wieland (2008). An important caveat is that we do not account for the ECB's declared practice of cross-checking the results of its economic outlook against medium-term monetary developments, the so-called monetary pillar of its strategy. Although Beck and Wieland (2007, 2008, 2009) have proposed a formal framework for including a cross-check against monetary trends in Taylor-style interest rate rules, a thorough empirical investigation is beyond the present chapter.

We estimate forecast-based and outcome-based policy rules nested by the following specification:

$$i_t = \rho i_{t-1} + (1 - \rho)[\alpha + \beta E_t \pi_{t+h} + \gamma E_t y_{t+h}] + \epsilon_t. \tag{14}$$

In doing so, we consider four-quarter ahead forecasts, ($h = 4$), and nowcasts, $h = 0$, for inflation and output growth. As in the case of the FOMC projections, constant-horizon forecasts need be computed by appropriately averaging available ECB staff forecasts of different horizons.

ECB staff projections concern average annual percentage changes and are published for the previous year, the current year and the following year. The December projections also include a forecast for the year after next year. As a result, the horizon of published projections varies over time. For example, the forecast of average inflation next year that is published in December is a four-quarter ahead forecast and denoted as $\pi_{t+4|t}$. The forecast for next year published in September instead is a five-quarter ahead forecast, $\pi_{t+5|t}$. Constant-horizon forecasts may then be deduced as follows: (i) the projections published in December have the right forecast horizon; (ii) the projections published in September for next year ($\pi_{t+5|t}$), and for the current year, $\pi_{t+1|t}$, can be appropriately averaged to obtain a four-quarter ahead forecast, $\pi_{t+4|t} = 0.25\pi_{t+1|t} + 0.75\pi_{t+5|t}$. Table 5.5 indicates how to derive the four-quarter ahead forecasts and the nowcasts needed for the regression analysis from the ECB staff forecasts published in the monthly bulletin in December, March, June, and September.

The resulting parameter estimates for outcome- and forecast-based interest rate rules are reported in Table 5.6.[27] These estimates confirm earlier findings in the literature that a

---

[27] The interest rate used in the estimation is the repo target rate.

Table 5.5 Computation of Four-Quarter Ahead Forecasts and Nowcasts

	Inflation	
December	$\pi_{t+4|t} = \pi_{t+4|t}$	$\pi_{t|t} = \pi_{t|t}$
March	$\pi_{t+4|t} = 0.75\pi_{t+3|t} + 0.25\pi_{t+7|t}$	$\pi_{t|t} = 0.25\pi_{t+3|t} + 0.75\pi_{t-1|t}$
June	$\pi_{t+4|t} = 0.5\pi_{t+2|t} + 0.5\pi_{t+6|t}$	$\pi_{t|t} = 0.5\pi_{t+2|t} + 0.5\pi_{t-2|t}$
September	$\pi_{t+4|t} = 0.25\pi_{t+1|t} + 0.75\pi_{t+5|t}$	$\pi_{t|t} = 0.75\pi_{t+1|t} + 0.25\pi_{t-3|t}$

	Output Growth	
December	$y_{t+4|t} = y_{t+4|t}$	$y_{t|t} = y_{t|t}$
March	$y_{t+4|t} = 0.75y_{t+3|t} + 0.25y_{t+7|t}$	$y_{t|t} = 0.25y_{t+3|t} + 0.75y_{t-1|t}$
June	$y_{t+4|t} = 0.5y_{t+2|t} + 0.5y_{t+6|t}$	$y_{t|t} = 0.5y_{t+2|t} + 0.5y_{t-2|t}$
September	$y_{t+4|t} = 0.25y_{t+1|t} + 0.75y_{t+5|t}$	$y_{t|t.} = 0.75y_{t+1|t} + 0.25y_{t-3|t}$

Notes: Forecast horizons correspond to the end quarter of expected average annual inflation and output growth rates.

Table 5.6 Rules with ECB Forecasts of Inflation and GDP Growth vs Outcomes: 2000–2010

	No Interest Smoothing			**With Interest Smoothing**		
	π_t, y_t	π_{t+4}, y_{t+4}	π_{t+4}, y_t	π_t, y_t	π_{t+4}, y_{t+4}	π_{t+4}, y_t
α	1.54	0.02	1.09	9.38	−2.11	−2.48
	(−1.86, 3.13)	(−1.68, 1.67)	(−0.14, 2.48)	(−2.10, 30.30)	(−6.11, 0.54)	(−4.75, 0.59)
β	0.28	1.26	0.58	−4.64	1.64	2.48
	(−0.55, 1.48)	(−0.10, 2.08)	(−0.34, 1.18)	(−17.42, 1.19)	(−0.08, 2.52)	(0.63, 3.81)
γ	0.47	0.20	0.43	2.07	0.93	0.21
	(0.16, 0.94)	(−0.38, 1.32)	(0.16, 0.87)	(0.40, 6.71)	(−0.04, 2.93)	(−0.15, 1.11)
ρ	0	0	0	0.89	0.81	0.78
				(0.62, 0.99)	(0.59, 0.91)	(0.50, 0.90)
R^2	0.63	0.46	0.65	0.94	0.95	0.94
$\bar{R}^2$	0.61	0.44	0.63	0.93	0.95	0.94

Notes: Parameters are estimated using non-linear least squares for the case $\rho \neq 0$. 95% confidence bands are shown in brackets and are computed using a moving block bootstrap with 5000 repetitions and a block size of 4 observations.

rule based on outcomes of inflation does not satisfy the Taylor principle. Unfortunately, the empirical fit of rules without interest-rate smoothing is rather weak. Rules with interest-smoothing fit better, but much of this improvement is due to a high coefficient on the lagged interest rate between 0.8 and 0.9. Among the rules with interest-rate smoothing, only the forecast-based rules satisfy the Taylor principle. Unfortunately the estimates are not very precise and the inflation response coefficient of the purely forecast-based policy rule is not significantly different from zero. However, both rules with inflation forecasts

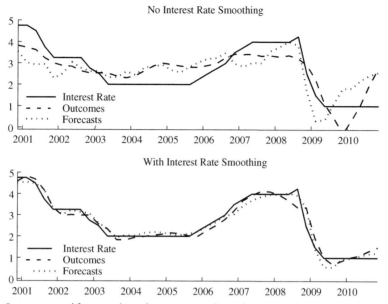

Figure 5.3 Outcome- and forecast-based monetary policy rules: Euro area.

exhibit very good empirical fit as measured by the R^2 and reasonable parameter values. By contrast, the parameters of the outcome-based rule are even less precisely estimated and the inflation coefficient is negative. These results suggest that rules with forecasts of inflation better describe ECB policy than rules with outcomes, but the findings are not as strong as in the case of the FOMC forecasts for the United States.

Figure 5.3 displays the fitted values of the estimated forecast-based (dotted line) and outcome-based (dashed line) policy rules relative to the actual path of Euro area short term interest rates (solid line, we use the repo rate target). Unfortunately, the empirical fit is not as impressive as in the case of the FOMC forecasts for the FOMC federal funds rate target in the United States. It is particularly poor in the case of the rules without interest-rate smoothing, which show big deviations from actual policy decisions. By contrast, the rule with interest-rate smoothing follows actual interest rates very closely. However, given that the interest-rate changes only slowly it is not so surprising that a rule with a high weight on last quarter's interest rate would seem to fit rather well. The graphical analysis does not bring forth big differences between forecast-based and outcome-based rules with interest-rate smoothing.

Finally, we estimate again a specification that allows for mixtures of forecast- and outcome-based rules with the pure versions as limiting cases. It is defined as follows:

$$i_t = \rho i_{t-1} + (1 - \rho)[\alpha + \beta((1 - \phi_\pi)E_t\pi_t + \phi_\pi E_t\pi_{t+4})$$
$$+ \gamma((1 - \phi_y)E_t y_t + \phi_y E_t y_{t+4})] + \epsilon_t. \tag{15}$$

Table 5.7 Policy Reactions to Forecasts and Outcomes: 2000–2010

	No Interest Smoothing		With Interest Smoothing	
	$\phi_\pi = \phi_u$	$\phi_\pi \neq \phi_u$	$\phi_\pi = \phi_u$	$\phi_\pi \neq \phi_u$
ϕ	0.44		1.00	
	(0.00,0.78)		(0.00,1.00)	
ϕ_π		0.42		1.00
		(0.00,1.00)		(0.00,1.00)
ϕ_y		0.48		1.00
		(0.00,1.00)		(0.12,1.00)
R^2	0.67	0.67	0.95	0.95
$\bar{R}^2$	0.63	0.63	0.95	0.95

Notes: Parameters are estimated using non-linear least squares. The parameters ϕ, ϕ_π and ϕ_u are restricted to be in the range of 0 to 1. 95% confidence bands are shown in brackets and are computed using a moving block bootstrap with 5000 repetitions and a block size of four observations.

The estimation results for the parameters governing the mixture of forecasts and outcomes are shown in Table 5.7. Again, the rules without interest-rate smoothing exhibit poor empirical fit. Therefore we focus on the rules with interest-rate smoothing. We find for all these specifications point estimates of $\phi = \phi_\pi = \phi_y = 1$. So, forecasts of inflation and output growth enter the policy rule, while outcomes do not play a role. However, due to the short sample most 95% confidence bands cover the whole range from 0 to 1. Only the confidence band for ϕ_y excludes 0, but includes 1. It is clear that all estimates for the Euro area have to be treated with caution because they are surrounded by high uncertainty due to the short sample. Additional data is needed. However, the point estimates suggest that forecasts of inflation and growth likely play a more important role for ECB decisions than recent nowcasts.

While the empirical literature reviewed in this section as well as our own estimation results provided overwhelming evidence that interest-rate setting at the Federal Reserve is conducted in a forward-looking manner and also delivered some indications that it might also be true for the ECB, these findings do not give an answer to the question whether forecast-based policy is desirable. Poole (1971) notes that desirability of forecast-based policy certainly depends on the accuracy of the forecasts. Thus, we will investigate different technical procedures for computing forecasts in the next section and then review the accuracy of such model-based forecasts together with expert forecasts such as the Greenbook in Section 5.6.

Furthermore, the simple framework for understanding the interaction of forecasts and policy presented previously in Section 2.2 suggests that the relative performance of forecast- versus outcome-based rules also depend on the structure of the economy. We will return to this question in Section 6.

5. COMPUTING FORECASTS THAT ACCOUNT FOR THE INTERACTION WITH POLICY DECISIONS

5.1. Forecasting Models used at Policy-Making Institutions

5.1.1. Non-Structural Time Series Models Versus Structural Macroeconomic Models

There are many purposes for producing forecasts at policy-making institutions and their staff use a variety of forecasting methods. Covering the full range of motives and techniques is beyond this chapter. Furthermore, there are some important uses and techniques that we will not discuss in detail because they are very well covered in other chapters of this Handbook.

For example, we do not review the nowcasting techniques used at policy institutions. The term "nowcast" refers to the estimate of the current state of the economy. It constitutes a first important step in any forecasting exercise because macroeconomic data only become available with some time lag. To give an example, the first release of U.S. GDP is published late in the first month following the quarter it refers to and updated releases are published subsequently. Rather than relying only on GDP numbers from earlier quarters, forecasters typically use other available information that is related to economic activity to construct an estimate. Data used include monthly series of GDP components such as industrial production or surveys and financial variables such as stock prices that contain information on perceptions regarding business conditions and economic growth. Typically, nowcasts are computed using non-structural time series models. They make it easier to incorporate high-frequency data. Current techniques include linear projections, bridge equations and dynamic factor models. For a more detailed review and applications of nowcasting techniques the reader is referred to the chapter on "Nowcasting with Daily Data" by Banbura et al. (2013).

Furthermore, simple non-structural time series models are widely used at policy institutions for predicting future developments in key variables of interest. They yield forecasts that are not easy to beat in terms of accuracy, in particular if they are initialized with efficient nowcasts. We do not discuss these forecasts in detail in this chapter because they cannot be used to assess the impact of planned changes in policy that are systematic in nature. In other words, such forecasting approaches are subject to the Lucas critique. Non-structural models assume that market participants respond to policy as they did in the past. Thus, non-structural forecasting techniques remain very useful for prediction in environments where policy will continue to be conducted in the same manner as in the past. For an exposition of different methods and a comparison of forecasting performance the reader is referred to the chapter by Faust and Wright (2013) on "Forecasting Inflation" in this Handbook. Recent comparisons of non-structural forecasting methods such as Bayesian VAR models with more sophisticated structural approaches can be found in Edge et al. (2010) and Wieland and Wolters (2011).

In the remainder of this section, we focus on the use of structural macroeconomic models for economic forecasting. These models incorporate explicit assumptions regarding the decision making of monetary and fiscal policymakers concerning variables such as government spending, taxes, transfers, central bank interest rates and central bank money. Furthermore, they provide characterizations of the decision making and expectations formation of households and firms that indicate how they will change their behavior in response to systematic changes in policymaker decisions. Thus, model equations and parameters have an economic interpretation that imposes particular parametric restrictions on the forecast relative to non-structural VAR models. In particular, we will use New Keynesian models which incorporate nominal rigidities such as staggered wage and price contracts that are important for analyzing short-run effects of monetary and fiscal policy.

We find it useful to distinguish between first- and second-generation New Keynesian models following Taylor and Wieland (2012) and Schmidt and Wieland (2012). First-generation models are characterized by nominal rigidities, rational expectations and policy rules. Second generation New Keynesian models developed from the late 1990s onwards explicitly implement all the restrictions resulting from optimizing behavior of representative households and firms subject to concretely specified constraints. They are typically referred to as New Keynesian DSGE models.

Small structural models typically consist of three to five equations representing key relationships such as a Phillips curve, an IS- or aggregate demand curve, and a monetary policy rule. Examples of first-generation small-scale New Keynesian models are Fuhrer and Moore (1995a), Fuhrer and Moore (1995b), Fuhrer (1997), and Batini and Haldane (1999). Small-scale New Keynesian DSGE models are presented by Rotemberg and Woodford (1997), Goodfriend and King (1997), and Woodford (2003).

5.1.2. Medium-size DSGE Models used at Policy Institutions

In recent years many policy institutions have built medium-size DSGE models that offer fairly detailed structural interpretations of the data. Such models are also used more and more as a central tool in the preparation of the main staff forecast at policy institutions.

For example, European Commission staff have been using a medium-size DSGE model with a detailed fiscal sector named QUEST for the analysis of Euro area fiscal stimulus and consolidation policies (see Ratto et al., 2009 and Roeger and in 't Veld, 2010). Staff of the IMF have developed a fairly large DSGE model, named GIMF, for the joint analysis of monetary and fiscal policies (see Freedman et al., 2010). Interestingly, the ECB has replaced its earlier, more traditional Area-Wide Model of Fagan et al. (2005) which featured largely backward-looking dynamics, with a New-Area-Wide Model (see Christoffel et al., 2008) of the DSGE variety in the ECB staff forecasting process.[28] The

---

[28] In addition, the model of Christiano et al. (2008), which includes a more detailed financial sector also plays an important role. The use of both models at the ECB is described in Smets et al. (2010)

Federal Reserve makes use of the FRB/EDO model of Edge et al. (2008),[29] though the FRB/U.S. model still remains its principal model for policy analysis. DSGE models used at other central banks include the ToTEM model of the Bank of Canada (Murchison and Rennison, 2006; Fenton and Murchison, 2006), and the RAMSES model used at the Swedish Riksbank (Adolfson et al., 2007b, 2008). All these models build on the medium-size DSGE model of Christiano et al. (2005). Christiano et al. extended the simple New Keynesian DSGE model and showed that such a medium-size DSGE model can match the VAR-based estimate of a monetary impulse response function. Typically, these models are estimated instead with Bayesian estimation methods as proposed and exemplified by Smets and Wouters (2003, 2007). In this manner they are able to explain the dynamics of a large number of macroeconomic times series.

An appealing feature of DSGE models is that they implement all restrictions arising from optimizing behavior of households and firms subject to clearly specified constraints. Thereby they go further in addressing the Lucas critique and offer useful input for fiscal and monetary policy making. DSGE models are less flexible than first-generation New Keynesian models in terms of freely introducing additional lags of endogenous variables to capture empirical dynamics. This lack of flexibility is typically made up for by introducing unrestricted serial correlation in the economic shock processes. The economic shocks themselves are typically derived within the context of microeconomic foundation and more meaningful than shocks that are simply added to behavioral equations as in some of the earlier-generation New Keynesian models. However, the unrestricted serial correlation of these shocks is similarly ad hoc as lags of endogenous variables in the earlier models. Even so, this feature has quickly been popularized in policy applications. The estimated degree of serial correlation importantly contributes to the forecasting power of the DSGE models. Several studies have shown that estimated DSGE models can generate forecasts of reasonable accuracy (Smets and Wouters, 2004, 2007 Adolfson et al., 2007a; Edge et al., 2010; Wang, 2009 Christoffel et al., 2010; Wieland and Wolters, 2011).

5.1.3. Large-Scale Macroeconomic Models used at Policy Institutions

Many policy-making institutions use even larger-scale models that contain many additional variables of interest to those institutions. The IMF and the European Commission, for example, have large multi-country models at their disposal. Another well known example is the FRB/U.S. model that has been used at the Federal Reserve since 1996 and contains many more data series for the U.S. economy than standard DSGE mod-

---

[29] The FRB-EDO features two production sectors, which differ with respect to the pace of technological progress. This structure can capture the different growth rates and relative prices observed in the data. Accordingly, the expenditure side is disaggregated as well. It is divided into business investment and three categories of household expenditure: consumption of non-durables and services, investment in durable goods and residential investment. The model is able to capture different cyclical properties in these four expenditure categories. The model is estimated using Bayesian techniques on eleven time series.

els. Typically, these models are not fully-fledged DSGE models. They may contain many additional ad hoc specifications as in the earlier-generation New Keynesian models.

The FRB/U.S. model has been documented in Brayton and Tinsley (1996) and Reifschneider et al. (1999). Individual equations or equation blocks are based on economic theory and inspired by the optimization problems of households and firms. However, they do not systematically enforce the restrictions implied by optimizing behavior subject to constraints as is done in DSGE models. The model aims to provide a good balance between data fit and economic theory. For example, the lag structure of adjustment cost processes is chosen to provide a good fit to the data and therefore polynomial adjustment processes are added to most equations (see Tinsley, 1993, for more details). While the equations can be interpreted structurally, the addition of polynomial adjustment cost processes makes this more difficult (Taylor, 1997). It contains – depending on the specific version – 50 stochastic equations that describe the economic behavior of different agents and 300 identities that define additional variables. By contrast, the FRB/EDO model – a DSGE model that has been developed at the Fed – contains only 11 observable and about 60 equations where most variables are treated as unobservable and are determined via the application of the Kalman Filter to the state space representation of the model.

One of the advantages of large econometric models is that they contain all important macroeconomic aggregates. For example, FRB/U.S. model breaks down aggregate demand into private consumption, fixed investment, inventory investment, net exports and government purchases. These broad categories are disaggregated even further. For example, spending on fixed investment is separated into equipment, non-residential structures and residential construction. Government spending is divided into six sub-components. Aggregate supply is also disaggregated. Potential output is modeled as a function of the labor force, crude energy use, and a composite capital stock, using a three-factor Cobb–Douglas production technology. While variables are assumed to move gradually to eliminate deviations from equilibrium values, they also respond to expected future equilibrium values. Expectations are also important in the financial sector. The long-term interest rate equals expected future short rates and a term premium. Real stock prices equal discounted expected future dividend payments. To estimate the model expectations are assumed to be formed by small VARs. However, for simulations one can choose whether to use the VAR-based expectations or a fully rational expectations-based version.

The forecasting accuracy of the FRB/U.S. model and the Fed's DSGE model (FRB/EDO) has been compared in Edge et al. (2010). Overall, the FRB/EDO model yields more precise forecasts, probably due to its more parsimonious parametrization. However, the forecasts from both models regarding key variables such as inflation are less accurate than the Greenbook forecasts. The superiority of the Greenbook forecasts may be due to the judgment used and information gleaned from other sources than the data series used by the models.

In the following, we will show how to employ structural models for identifying the sources of predicted dynamics of key macroeconomic variables and for interpreting forecasts. Since policymakers frequently request forecasts that are conditioned on particular plans for certain policy instruments, we will review techniques for computing such conditional forecasts. In doing so we show how to include judgment in model-based forecasts. Furthermore, we compare forecasts from smaller and larger models with other available forecasts and assess forecast accuracy. For a detailed technical presentation of the steps that need to be taken to produce forecasts with estimated structural macroeconomic models we refer the reader to the chapter on "DSGE Model-Based Forecasting" by Del Negro and Schorfheide (2013) in this Handbook. Furthermore, we would like to make the reader aware of a new model database and computational platform that makes small- medium- and even large-scale models available to the public and allows individual researchers to evaluate models developed and used at policy institutions (see Wieland et al. (2012) and www.macromodelbase.com).

5.2. Forecasts from a Small Structural Model: IMF's Small Quarterly Projection Model

We start by deriving forecasts from a particular small-scale structural New Keynesian model. The IMF's small quarterly projection model of the U.S. economy (Carabenciov et al., 2008) belongs to the first generation of New-Keynesian models. It is a closed economy model that captures the dynamics of output, inflation, a short term interest rate and the unemployment rate. According to the authors it offers a simple but plausible structure suited to forecasting and policy analysis at policy institutions. The main policy instrument considered is the central bank interest rate. It does not include fiscal variables. Similar models calibrated for different countries are currently used at several country desks at the IMF to help structure the dialogue with member countries.[30]

5.2.1. The Model

The core of the model consists of an IS-equation, a Phillips curve, a monetary policy rule and a version of Okun's law relating unemployment to the output gap:

$$y_t = \beta_1 y_{t-1} + \beta_2 E_t y_{t+1} - \beta_3 (i_t - E_t \pi_{t+1}) - \theta \eta_t + \epsilon_t^y, \tag{16}$$

$$\pi_t = \lambda_1 E_t \tilde{\pi}_{t+4} + (1 - \lambda_1)\tilde{\pi}_{t-1} + \lambda_2 y_{t-1} - \epsilon_t^\pi, \tag{17}$$

$$i_t = (1 - \gamma_1)[\gamma_2 (E_t \tilde{\pi}_{t+3}) + \gamma_3 y_t] + \gamma_1 i_{t-1} + \epsilon_t^i, \tag{18}$$

$$u_t = \alpha_1 u_{t-1} + \alpha_2 y_t + \epsilon_t^u, \tag{19}$$

$$BLT_t = B\bar{L}T_t - kE_t y_{t+4} + \epsilon_t^{BLT}, \tag{20}$$

$$\eta_t = \sum_{i=1}^{9} k_i \epsilon_{t-i}^{BLT}. \tag{21}$$

[30] See p. 7 of (Carabenciov et al., 2008) for more references.

All variables are expressed in terms of deviations from equilibrium values. Certain equilibrium values are modeled as stochastic processes (not shown), for example, potential output is driven by permanent level shocks as well as highly persistent shocks to its growth rate. Thus, y_t, which denotes output, is the deviation of the level of output from potential, that is the output gap.

The IS Eq. (16) relates the output gap to one lag and one lead of itself, the real interest rate, $i_t - E_t \pi_{t+1}$, bank lending conditions indicated by η_t, and a demand shock, ϵ_t^y. The Phillips curve Eq. (17) relates the quarterly inflation rate π_t, to the past and expected future four-quarter moving average of inflation (i.e., the year-on-year rate), $\tilde{\pi}_t$, the lagged output gap and a cost-push shock, ϵ_t^π. The interest rate rule (18) describes the determination of the short-term nominal interest rate i_t in response to the lagged rate, the output gap and deviations of inflation from target (normalized at zero) as well as a monetary policy shock ϵ_t^i. The equation for unemployment (19) is a version of Okun's law, linking the deviation of the unemployment rate from the equilibrium unemployment rate, u_t, to the output gap.

The model exhibits inertia in output and inflation dynamics and short-run real effects on monetary policy. In the long run, monetary policy only determines inflation. A novel feature of the model is the inclusion of linkages between financial intermediation and business cycle dynamics. Eqs. (20) and (21) serve to measure the degree of bank lending tightness, BLT_t, which impacts on aggregate demand. The corresponding empirical measure is obtained from survey answers regarding financial conditions from the Federal Reserve Board's quarterly Senior Loan Officer Opinion Survey on Bank Lending Practices. Banks are assumed to adjust their lending practices around an equilibrium value, $\bar{BLT}_t$, depending on their expectations about the real economy four quarters ahead and a financial shock ϵ_t^{BLT}. The equilibrium value of bank lending conditions follows a random walk. Banks are assumed to ease their lending conditions during economic upturns and tighten them during downturns. To link bank lending conditions to the real economy the lagged eight-quarter moving average of the financial shocks, η_t, enters the aggregate demand equation.

5.2.2. Forecasts

We have re-estimated the IMF projection model using U.S. data for real GDP, the CPI, the federal funds rate, the unemployment rate, and bank lending conditions (BLT) from 1994:Q1 to 2007:Q4. Our parameter estimates are very similar to those of Carabenciov et al. (2008). We have computed forecasts for all variables in the model including the unobservable equilibrium or natural values. The first set of forecasts uses information up to 2008:Q1. Then, we add data realizations sequentially and compute a set of forecasts up to four quarters ahead. We focus on point forecasts disregarding potential data revisions.

Figure 5.4 compares the forecasts (thin[2] blue lines) for quarterly real GDP growth, quarterly CPI inflation, the federal funds rate, and bank lending conditions to subsequent

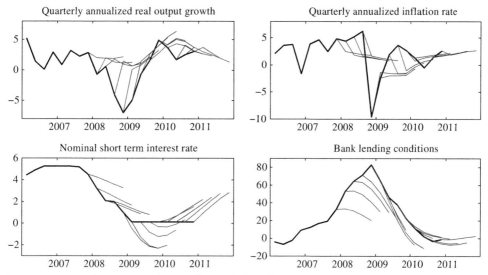

Figure 5.4 Quarterly GDP growth, CPI inflation, federal funds rates, and bank lending conditions: Data (thick black line) and forecasts (thin blue lines). (For interpretation of the references to color in this figure legend, the reader is referred to the web version of this book.)

data realizations (thick black lines). Despite its flexible formulation with various lags and permanent as well as temporary shocks, the IMF model has difficulties predicting output growth during the financial crisis and recession. Note, this is not a particular shortcoming of structural model forecasts but also applies to non-structural time series models and professional forecasts available from surveys. Perhaps, it is somewhat disappointing that the inclusion of data on bank lending tightness in the model does not help much in improving forecasts of the recession triggered by the financial crisis. On the positive side, forecasts are quite accurate from 2009:Q1 onwards and capture the initial recovery process surprisingly well. The initial recovery during 2009 and 2010 is predicted to be followed in the next year by growth rates broadly in line with average growth, which is estimated to be 2.6% in the sample.

The model correctly predicts inflation to fall during the recession, but it fails to capture the extreme decline in the fourth quarter of 2008. From 2009 onwards inflation projections are fairly precise. The projections of the federal funds rate explain why output growth estimates during the recovery turn out too optimistic. The model forecast does not enforce the zero bound on nominal interest rates. It allows rates to turn negative thereby incorporating too much stimulus to output. Imposing the zero-interest-floor on nominal interest rates would have resulted in less optimistic output forecasts. We will demonstrate a simple procedure for adjusting forecasts to take into account the zero-lower-bound in Section 5.4. We will discuss forecast accuracy during recessions in more detail in Section 5.6.

5.2.3. Unobservable Variables and Forecast Interpretation

The structural model includes unobservable variables such as potential output growth that help users interpret the economic forces driving the forecast. For example, the longer-term impact of the financial crisis on GDP may be judged by forecasts of the level and growth rate of potential output.

Figure 5.5 displays actual versus potential output and actual versus natural unemployment rates over the whole sample together with an out-of-sample forecast for 2011 and 2012. Potential output growth is first estimated to slow down around 2001 followed by a more severe slowdown in 2008. The growth rate of potential GDP is projected at about 0.5% at the end of the sample. While the output gap (not shown) is still in negative territory in 2010:Q4, it is projected to turn slightly positive in 2011, and remain near zero throughout 2012. Thus, it indicates no inflationary pressure from aggregate demand. Accordingly, year-on-year output growth is projected to slow down in 2012 towards 1.5%. This forecast is about 1 percentage point lower than the forecast we have obtained from non-structural time series models (not shown).

Relative to the estimated changes in potential output, the upward trend in the natural unemployment rate or NAIRU seems less extreme. It is projected at 7% by 2011. Thus, it explains only a smaller part of the increase in the unemployment rate. The model predicts unemployment to decline towards 8.40% by the end of 2011, which is slightly below the forecast we obtained from non-structural models (not shown).

This example shows that a structural model can help interpreting the forecast by projecting unobservable equilibrium-related concepts such as potential output and the natural rate. Of course, one might ask, what are the economics behind the sizeable impact

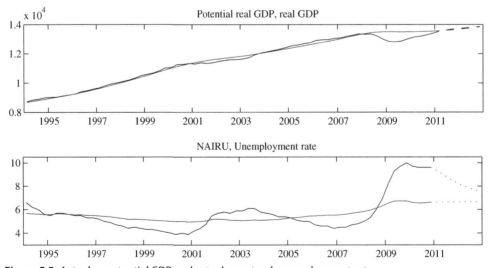

Figure 5.5 Actual vs potential GDP and actual vs natural unemployment rate.

on potential growth. While the assumed non-stationary stochastic process adds flexibility to the model, the model remains silent on the question to what extent the slowdown is due to lower capital utilization, a period of reduced investment or a preference shift towards leisure. Answers to such questions could be obtained from the type of medium-size DSGE model we will discuss in the next subsection.

5.2.4. Structural Shocks and Forecast Interpretation

Another unobservable element of structural models is given by the economic shocks. Structural shocks differ from estimation residuals. They require identification via parametric restrictions. Furthermore, in models with forward-looking terms identifying structural shocks requires computing the expectation of future variables so as to separate out the forecast error. Structural shocks may be interpreted as meaningful economic disturbances. Of course, the extent of useful interpretation depends on the economic foundations for the parametric restrictions in the model. Since the IMF projection model is not strictly micro-founded some of these shocks have little concrete interpretation. Even so, distinguishing aggregate demand shocks in the IS-curve from cost-push shocks in the Phillips curve and long-run supply shocks to potential output, helps understanding whether inflation is primarily driven by demand-pull factors, short-run cost-push shocks or productivity changes that may be related to technological improvements.

Figure 5.6 display the estimated series of structural shocks. The sequence of negative demand shocks between 2008 and 2010 indicates that according to this model an unexpected shortfall of demand (i.e., the shocks) caused an unexpected decline in GDP.

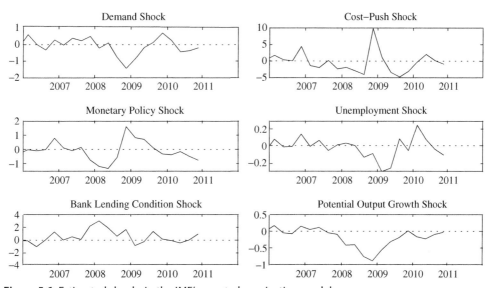

Figure 5.6 Estimated shocks in the IMF's quarterly projection model.

Furthermore, the sequence of positive monetary policy shocks in 2009 indicates that interest rates where higher than expected based on the policy rule, and therefore represented an additional cause for an unexpected decline in GDP. The sequence of negative shocks to potential GDP growth and the sequence of positive shocks to bank lending tightness also contribute to the unexpected drop in GDP.

In sum, these shocks reflect again the inability of the model to forecast the recession, but they help point to sources of the unexpected shortfall. The forecasting power of the model arises from predictable endogenous dynamics such as lags of output, inflation or interest rates, and from predictable exogenous dynamics such as the persistence of the bank lending tightness shocks. The sequence of positive monetary policy shocks in 2009 may be due to the omission of the zero bound. Including this constraint may therefore improve the forecasting performance.

The large positive cost-push shock in 2008:Q4 reflects the failure of forecasting the decline in inflation since this shock enters the Phillips curve negatively. According to this model the drop in inflation is largely due to a sudden decline in costs and to a lesser extent to the disinflationary impact of a shortfall of demand. Thus, without using data on energy prices the model indicates that the decline of energy costs was largely behind the drop in inflation in 2008:Q4. A sequence of positive shocks to unemployment in 2010 represents a source of unexpectedly high unemployment at the end of the recession according to this model.

Finally, one can explore the parameter estimates of the model to gauge the importance of different channels of influence in determining the forecast. One could also re-estimate the model for each forecast to investigate whether certain parameter values change a lot over time and thus spot structural changes. Here, we only point out the parameters governing the shock process to potential output. The estimates show that each quarter potential output growth equals 0.93 times the previous potential output growth rate plus 0.07 times steady-state growth. It thus takes a long time until potential output growth returns back to steady state. On the other hand, the estimation results show that the estimated variance of the growth rate of potential output is relatively high. In Figure 5.6 the lower right panel shows shocks to the potential output growth rate. A series of highly negative shocks led to the current extremely low estimates of potential output growth. Given the high variance of this shock series potential output could quickly adjust back to higher equilibrium growth rates once actual output growth increases.

5.3. Forecasts from a Medium-Scale New Keynesian DSGE Model for Monetary and Fiscal Policy Analysis

5.3.1. Brief Model Description

In the following, we will produce and interpret forecasts using a medium-scale DSGE model estimated in Cogan et al. (2010). Cogan et al. extended the Smets and Wouters (2007) model of the U.S. economy by introducing a share of households that consume current income. As a consequence, the model does not anymore exhibit Ricardian equivalence. The path of taxes and debt is not irrelevant. Tax and debt dynamics are modeled explicitly. Such an extension was proposed by Galí and Lopez-Salido (2007) in the context of a small New Keynesian model in order to better understand the consequences of fiscal policy, specifically changes in government purchases. Cogan et al. (2010) use this model to analyze the interaction of monetary policy and the U.S. ARRA fiscal stimulus at interest rates near the zero-lower bound. In the following, we refer to this model as the CCTW-SW model.

The CCTW-SW model contains a large number of frictions and structural shocks. Physical capital is included in the production function and capital formation is endogenous. Labor supply is modeled explicitly. Nominal frictions include sticky prices and wages and inflation and wage indexation. Real frictions include consumption habit formation, investment adjustment costs and variable capital utilization. Utility is non-separable in consumption and leisure. There exist fixed costs in production. The aggregator by Kimball (1995) is used which implies a non-constant elasticity of demand. The model includes equations for consumption, investment, price and wage setting as well as several identities. It contains seven structural shocks and it is fit to seven time series. Among the shocks are, total factor productivity, risk premium, investment-specific technology, wage mark-up, price mark-up, government spending and a monetary policy shock. All shock processes are serially correlated. Cogan et al. (2010) estimate a posterior mean of 26.5% of rule-of-thumb consumers and feedback equations for taxes that ensure a return to the steady-state debt to GDP ratio. A complete list and description of the equations is contained in Appendix A.

5.3.2. Forecasts

We have re-estimated the model with data from 1965:Q3 to 2007:Q4. On this basis, we have computed forecasts for all variables in the model including unobservable concepts like potential output and the natural rate of interest. We compute a sequence of forecasts starting in 2008:Q1 by adding subsequent data realizations sequentially up to the final set of forecasts as of 2011:Q1. Again, we focus on point forecasts.[31]

---

[31] We neglect that data revisions and current quarter observations are not observable when computing a forecast. We take the same data series and transform them in the same way as in Smets and Wouters (2007) with one exception: the hours per capita series. This series is non-stationary (see, e.g., Chang et al., 2007) and it is influenced by low frequency movements in government employment, schooling and the aging of the population that cannot be captured by a simple DSGE models. Thus, we follow (Francis and Ramey, 2009) and remove these trends by computing deviations of the hours per capita series using the HP filter with a weight of 16000 (compared to the standard weight of 1600 used for business-cycle frequency de-trending). Without this additional data treatment the Smets and Wouters model yields an unreasonable output gap that is largely negative for most parts of the sample. For each forecast we apply the HP-Filter only until the forecast starting point to prevent that this two-sided filter uses information about data points in the future.

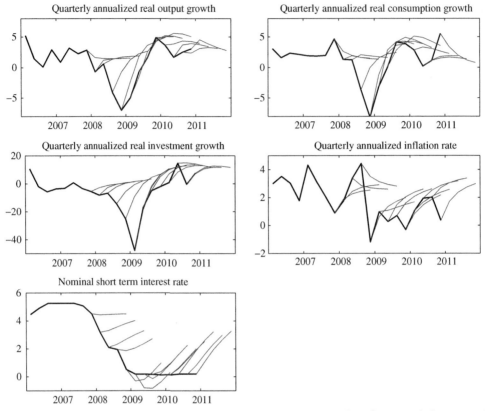

Figure 5.7 Real GDP growth, consumption growth, investment growth, inflation and the nominal interest rate: actual (black line) and forecasts (blue lines). (For interpretation of the references to color in this figure legend, the reader is referred to the web version of this book.)

Figure 5.7 displays forecasts for quarterly real output growth, consumption, investment, quarterly inflation[32] (annualized) and the federal funds rate.

The output growth forecasts are roughly similar to those computed with the small structural IMF model in the previous section. There is a strong comovement of output, consumption and investment. The fluctuations of investment growth are much larger than those of consumption growth. The model cannot predict the large recession in 2008–2009 and tends to predict a relatively quick return to the balanced growth path in

---

[32] The inflation rate is not directly comparable to the IMF model because the IMF model uses the CPI inflation rate, while the Smets and Wouters model uses the GDP deflator. To solve the problem that DSGE models contain only a very limited set of variables Schorfheide et al. (2010) propose to use auxiliary equations to link non-modeled variables to the state variables in the model. Predictions for the non-core variables are obtained by applying their measurement equations to DSGE model-generated forecasts of the state variables. In this way one can base forecasts of these non-core variables (including different definitions of inflation) on the structural representation of the model.

2008:Q3 while the recession actually deepened. Once the turning point has been reached in 2008:Q4 the recovery is predicted quite well. Forecasts are quite accurate from 2009 onwards even though growth turned out to be somewhat lower in 2010 than predicted by the model.

The forecast for investment growth is very persistent. Investment is predicted slightly below 12% for 2011. Afterwards, it is expected to decrease slowly to a substantially lower steady-state rate of about 2.4%, similar to GDP.[33]

The model cannot predict the spikes in inflation in 2008 and overpredicts inflation from 2009 to the end of 2010. The steady-state inflation rate is estimated to be 2.5% and thus higher than the most recent data observation. Accordingly, the model predicts increasing inflation rates reaching 1.8% in 2011 and 3% in 2012.

Federal funds rate forecasts violate the zero-lower bound in 2009. The difference of the model relative to the actual funds rate setting at 25 basis points manifests itself also in adverse monetary policy shocks. In contrast to the IMF model the steady-state interest rate is fixed and the interest rate forecast always predicts a return to the steady state.

Figure 5.8 shows actual real GDP relative to potential and the resulting output gap estimate. Values after 2011 are forecasts. Between 2005 and 2008 the output gap is positive. In 2009 it turns negative because real GDP declined, while potential output still increased. In 2010 the output gap comes close to zero as real GDP grew again and potential output declined. The forecast for the output gap is slightly above zero as real GDP is predicted to grow somewhat faster than potential GDP. In this model potential GDP and the output gap have a clear structural interpretation. While in the previous small structural model potential GDP was modeled as a trend, it is defined in the DSGE model as the level of output and expenditure that would be realized in the absence of price and wage rigidities and price and wage mark-up shocks.

5.3.3. Decomposition in Structural Shocks for Forecast Interpretation

To analyze which shocks played an important role during the financial crisis and recession, and to investigate which of them have a lasting impact over the forecast period, we derive a decomposition. Using the moving average representation of the model solution, we evaluate how much each type of shock contributes to a particular variable at each point in time over the sample and forecast periods. The model contains seven shocks: a risk premium shock, investment-specific technology shock, general technology shock, monetary policy shock and price and wage mark-up shocks. Figure 5.9 displays the decomposition of quarterly output growth (annualized). The bars for each period summarize the

---

[33] The high degree of persistence may be explained by the discrepancy between the average output growth rate and the much higher average investment growth rate observed in the data. The model enforces the same steady-state value and introduces persistence in investment to fit actual data series.

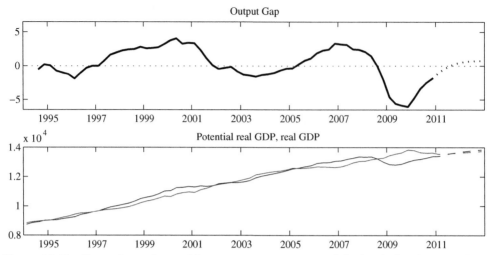

Figure 5.8 The figure shows the model consistent output gap and the level of real GDP and real potential GDP. Values after 2011 are forecasts. While real GDP is observable, the output gap and potential output are derived via the Kalman Filter.

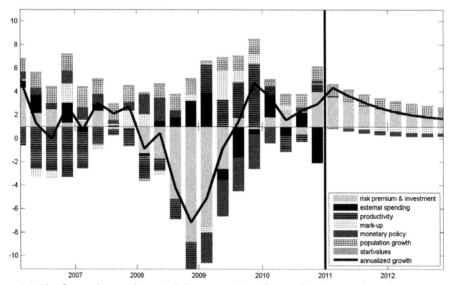

Figure 5.9 The figure shows a historical decomposition of annualized quarterly real output growth. The vertical line in 2011 indicates that values afterwards are forecasts. The black line show the output growth rate and the bars show the contribution of the different shocks, the population growth rate and initial values. The sum of the bars equals the output growth rate.

contributions of all shocks to output growth, some of them positive some negative. The areas with different textures identify the size of the contribution of each type of shock.

In addition to the shocks, the label of the chart refers to two more contributions to growth termed "starting values" and "population growth". The bars labeled starting values appear because data is not available for an infinite past history, and therefore shock realizations cannot be recovered from an infinite past. Thus, the "starting values" bar indicates the impact of the initial conditions. Their effect is negligible over the period shown in Figure 5.9.

DSGE models are usually defined in per capita terms. However, policymakers are more interested in aggregate growth rates. Therefore, the black solid-line indicates overall real GDP growth rather than per capita growth. Consequently, part of the GDP growth is due to population growth. This contribution is indicated by the "population growth" bars. As population growth is not defined in the model, we simply assume that the population continues to grow at the rate observed in 2009 and 2010. The horizontal axis indicates the steady-state per capita growth rate. For long-run forecasts the impact of the shocks will disappear and per capita growth will converge to this estimate of steady-state growth.

The positive and negative contributions from shocks, population growth and initial conditions sum up to the actual output growth rate (black line) over the sample period and to the predicted output growth rate over the forecast period. Interestingly, the deep recession of 2008 and 2009 is largely attributed to the combination of substantial (positive) risk premium shocks and negative investment shocks. The contribution of these two types of shocks is lumped in the left shaded area of the contribution bars.

In other words, the recession, which was not predicted by the model, is explained as being due to a sequence of unexpectedly high risk premia realizations together with unexpected shortfalls of investment demand. To the extent these shocks are estimated to persist, they also help predict future growth. Thus, even though the model does not utilize financial data other than federal funds rates, nor integrate asset prices and banking risk, it correctly points towards financial conditions and lack of investment as the cause of the recession. The risk premium shock is simply modeled as an exogenous premium in the return to bonds in the consumption equation, while the investment shock is modeled as a shock to the price of investment goods relative to consumption goods.

The other shocks have largely offsetting impacts on growth during the recession. The exogenous spending shock contributes positively to growth consistent with the observed improvement of the current account during this period. Throughout 2009 we observe contractionary monetary policy shocks. They arise because actual policy is constrained at the zero bound, while funds rate expectations turn negative throughout 2009 as prescribed by the policy rule's response to output and inflation conditions.

Over the forecast period from 2011 onwards, GDP growth returns to steady state as the impact of positive demand shocks dissipates. The main reason for the forecast staying above average growth over the forecast period are the investment-specific technology shocks. In the medium term the price-markup shocks reduce the output growth forecast somewhat. They reflect an exogenous price increase that causes inflation and depresses output.

5.4. Conditioning Forecasts on Specific Future Policy Decisions
5.4.1. Types of Conditioning Assumptions

Staff forecasts at policy institutions often form an important basis for discussions among decision makers. Frequently, they also request that staff forecasts be conditioned on a particular hypothetical path for future policy. Depending on the resulting forecasts, policymakers can then consider whether and how to change the policy instrument they are charged to use relative to the assumed baseline. There are a number of different underlying assumptions that may be used for generating such policy-conditioned forecasts: (i) unchanged policy; (ii) market-based expectations; (iii) a decision by policymakers on a preferred anticipated policy path; or (iv) an estimated or preferred policy rule.

i. *Unchanged policy.* For example, the baseline budget forecast of the U.S. Congressional Budget Office is always based on existing laws and regulations. Similarly, many central banks use staff forecasts that are based on a constant interest rate path. Such a simple benchmark path may be considered useful by members of a decision making committee for they can state their personal opinions relative to a seemingly purely technical benchmark. It should be understood, however, that a forecast based on unchanged fiscal or monetary policy is usually not the best possible forecast. It may not even be consistent with long-run stability. For example, the forecast of a particular budget deficit under existing laws and regulations may imply that government debt is unsustainable. Similarly, a constant central bank interest rate path may imply explosive dynamics. In fact, in rational expectations models it is essential for the existence of a short-run equilibrium that policy rates eventually adjust in an endogenous manner.

ii. *Market-based expectations.* An alternative conditioning assumption is given by market-based expectations of the relevant policy variable. These expectations may reflect market participants perceptions of the policy rule that best describes the systematic, predictable component of policymakers' decision making. An assumed future policy path based on market expectations avoids the lack of plausibility of the unchanged policy assumption. It also avoids difficulties and commitment issues arising in the construction of a path that reflects policymakers' expectations. However, market expectations may not be conditioned on a sufficiently stabilizing policy. Including this assumption directly in public policymaker forecasts, which then determine policy decisions, could mean that market expectations feed back on themselves. This may be stabilizing or not, but certainly complicates communication regarding the forecast.

iii. *Decision on preferred anticipated policy path.* A more consistent approach would be to ask policymakers first to decide on an anticipated path for the policy variable and then use this path to create a forecast. Whether or not such consistency is needed or even helpful for decision making is likely to depend on the particular role of the forecast in the policy making process. For example, if there is a debate in parliament about the likely budgetary impacts of certain fiscal initiatives it would appear perfectly suitable for the staff of the budget office to supply different forecasts conditioned on each policy proposal that is being debated. A different matter may be the forecast of central bank staff that plays a key role in central bank communication to the public as practiced primarily at inflation targeting central banks. In this case, it may be quite important to present the best possible forecast to the public. As such it should be conditioned on the most likely policy path that can be constructed based on the knowledge of decision maker preferences. It may be difficult to organize such a process but it is likely to improve communication with the public.

iv. *Policy rule.* Finally, another possibility would be to condition the forecast on a policy rule that captures the policymaker's past responses to important macroeconomic variables or a new rule that matches policymakers' preferences. Examples would be central bank interest rate rules such as those estimated in Section 4 of this chapter. Similarly, forecasts used for fiscal policy purposes could be based on particular feedback rules for government purchases, transfers or tax rates. However, policymakers might not be inclined to assign a particular rule such a prominent place in their deliberations. Furthermore, if members of a decision making committee disagree about specific policy objectives they will also disagree on the appropriate policy rules.

5.4.2. Experience with Different Conditioning Assumptions at Central Banks

A detailed discussion of the practices at central banks is available from Goodhart (2009). Table 5.8 lists conditioning assumptions used by several central banks.

Central banks have primarily used the first three approaches from the above list. Thus, they have used a constant interest rate path based on the latest interest rate level; expected future short-term interest rates implied by the yield curve, and a path that explicitly corresponds to the expectations of the monetary policy committee for future interest rates.

The choice between these three conditioning assumptions also appears to depend on whether the conditional forecast is only used internally or whether it is used to communicate policy to the public. While conditioning on a constant interest rate path might be a useful input in policy committee deliberations, it is less suited to be published to be understood as a forecast of likely future conditions. Publishing a forecast that is at odds with otherwise communicated expectations, such as long-run price stability, may confuse observers. Furthermore, in many situations it is very different from the path

Table 5.8 Conditioning Assumptions of Different Central Banks

Constant Path	Market-Based Expectations	Policy Committee-Based Expectations
US (most of the time)		
UK (1992–2004)	UK (since 2004)	
Sweden (until 2007)		Sweden (since 2007)
Euro area (until 2006:Q1)	Euro area (since 2006:Q2)	
		Norway (since 2006)
		New Zealand

that policymakers expect for the future and may want to signal to markets. Thus, not surprisingly, most central banks have eventually switched to other conditioning assumptions. Using market expectations of short-term interest rates is rather popular. Galí (2008) notes, however, that it might be difficult to disentangle expected short-term interest rates from liquidity and term premia.

An interest rate path that reflects explicitly the views of the monetary policy committee is the most complex choice. While it allows for the most consistent discussion and decision about interest rates, it might create some problems in practice. Perhaps, not all committee members can agree with it. It may be easier for smaller than larger committees to vote on a sequence of interest rates into the future. It may also be difficult to communicate that the path is to be understood by the public as an expectation and not a commitment of policymakers. However, so far central banks practicing this approach such as those of New Zealand or Norway have reported a positive experience.

The fourth option mentioned above, that is the assumption that central bank interest rates will follow an estimated rule capturing past practice or a rule that is conceived to be optimal, have not been used much in official forecasts. However, this assumption is nevertheless very common in policy analysis presented to central bank decision makers.

Using such a forecast as a basis for discussions among policymakers is appealing for two reasons. First, advantages of rule-based policy have been widely documented in economic research and using rules within forecasts would emphasize the systematic nature of the envisioned policy. Second, a policy rule provides a natural benchmark for discussions how to appropriately adjust the interest rate. The debate in the policy committee could focus on whether the path implied by the rule is appropriate or whether the rule fails to capture certain current developments and thus a deviation is in order.

A rule-based approach would also increase transparency in communicating policy decisions to the public. Policymakers can clearly distinguish between systematic responses to inflation and output and additional responses to other variables that are not included in the rule and comment on reasons for the latter. Already, interest rate prescriptions from different policy rules are routinely computed by the staff of central banks as an input for policy discussions of the decision-making committee.

5.4.3. Techniques for Computing Forecasts Conditional on an Exogenous Policy Path

Goodhart (2009) points out that a forecast conditional on an assumed future path for policy is a simulation rather than a forecast and should be interpreted as such. Such a procedure naturally assigns a role to structural macroeconomic models in computing and interpreting forecasts conditional on the exogenous policy path (for applications see for example Smets and Wouters (2004); Adolfson et al. (2007a) and Maih (2010)[34]).

---

[34] The focus in some of these papers is to use conditioning assumptions to include extra information in the model that potentially can improve the forecast.

In simulating unchanged-policy scenarios, it is important to incorporate technical restrictions that ensure the existence of unique equilibrium. Macroeconomic models typically exhibit explosiveness or equilibrium indeterminacy when the nominal interest rate does not respond in a stabilization fashion to inflation. Thus, most studies assume that the interest rate is held constant for a certain period and a policy rule kicks in afterwards to ensure the existence of a determinate equilibrium, or the uniqueness of such an equilibrium. Similarly, macroeconomic models that do not exhibit Ricardian equivalence such as the CCTW model require a stabilizing tax policy to ensure convergence to a steady-state debt to GDP ratio.

Given the above restrictions, the temporarily fixed policy period may be simulated by adjusting future policy shocks in a way to keep the policy variable on the assumed path. For example, a constant interest rate path that precedes a return to a policy rule with an endogenous response to inflation, output and the lagged interest rate, could be achieved by choosing policy shocks that exactly offset any reactions to inflation, the output gap and past interest rates over the chosen period.

There are two possibilities to adjust future shocks that have very different implications for the modeling of market participants' expectations. One approach is to assume that the agents in the model believe that the policy authority follows a rule. Policy shocks designed to keep the policy instrument constant are assumed not to be known to agents in advance. They are surprise shocks and do affect expectations only when they actually occur. Variables that are influenced by expectations about future values of the policy instrument change only gradually since agents do not know these shocks in advance, but only learn about them as they happen. Despite important limitations, this method has been used extensively in central bank circles to simulate constant interest rate scenarios.

First, this method does not provide a good benchmark scenario for policymakers, because it implies that effects of the constant policy assumptions via market expectations are negated. Expectations play a crucial role in macroeconomic policy transmission, and for this reason, feature importantly in DSGE models. These models have been build to analyze effects of policy on endogenous variables through expectations. Thus, it would appear counterproductive to abstract from these effects.

Furthermore, adjusting stochastic policy shocks is only reasonable as long as these adjusted shocks are in the range of historically observed policy shocks. Leeper and Zha (2003) call a policy intervention or shock modest if it "[...] does not significantly shift agents beliefs about policy regime and does not induce the changes in behavior that Lucas (1976) emphasizes." Concerning the constant interest rate scenarios considered at central banks, Smets and Wouters (2004) and Adolfson et al. (2007a) find that the surprise shocks needed in medium-sized DSGE models to keep the interest rate constant cannot be characterized as modest policy interventions, because they are often much larger than historically observed policy shocks.

The second option is to assume that agents in the model incorporate the assumed policy path in their expectation formation regarding future policy. They know the policy shocks that are necessary to keep the interest rate constant in advance. In a sense, the shocks used to adjust policy to the desired path are deterministic and often referred to with this term. Agents' consumption and investment decisions would be based on the anticipation of the exogenous policy path. This procedure accounts for the Lucas critique and all endogenous variables respond in a consistent manner. In forward-looking models, certain exogenous policy scenarios such as a constant interest rate path that lasts for a significant period may have substantial impacts on current values of those variables that are related to market participants expectations of future policy.[35]

5.5. DSGE Forecasts Conditioned on the 2009 Announcement of U.S. Fiscal Stimulus

To illustrate the conditioning of DSGE model forecasts on a particular policy path we use the CCTW-SW model to evaluate the impact of the U.S. fiscal stimulus in 2009 that was discussed earlier in Section 2.1. Specifically, we compute forecasts conditional on an exogenous path for government purchases. The particular path corresponds to the additional purchases announced with the legislation of the American Recovery and Reinvestment Act (ARRA) in February 2009. The values are taken from Table 5.3 in Cogan et al. (2010). They are given in the first column of said table titled "Increase in Federal Purchases". The additional purchases are highest in 2010 and 2011 but remain modest over all because much of the stimulus was allotted to transfers and tax reductions.

5.5.1. The Fiscal Sector of the CCTW-SW Model

Before proceeding to a discussion of the simulations, we review the fiscal sector and important related assumptions in the CCTW-SW model. A complete list and description of the equations of the log-linearized version of the model is contained in Appendix A.

Government purchases G_t appear in the resource constraint. Cogan et al. (2010) have added households that do not have access to financial markets and therefore cannot smooth consumption to the model of Smets and Wouters (2007). Such an extension was proposed by Galí et al. (2007) in the context of a small New Keynesian model in order to understand the consequences of fiscal shocks. Only a share $1 - \omega$ of households indexed by $j \in [0, 1 - \omega)$ makes optimizing, forward looking decisions and these households have

---

[35] Note, Galí (2008) shows in the context of constant interest rate simulations, that it is also possible to implement unchanged policy without adjusting policy shocks, but by choosing specific policy rules. These policy rules lead to determinacy while at the same time ensuring that the interest rate follows the desired conditional path. However, these policy rules are very different from conventional Taylor type rules. One example is the following rule: $i_t = i_t^* - \gamma i_{t-1}^* + \gamma (\pi_t + \sigma \Delta y_t)$, where i_t^* denotes the desired interest rate path, that includes terms from the IS-curve to fully offset any movements in inflation and the output gap. While using such a rule does not violate the Lucas critique, it does not seem plausible that agents would believe that the central bank pursues a completely different rule than in the past. Therefore, we will focus here on implementations where the central bank keeps following the same policy rule as in the past, but for some period deviates from it by adjusting policy shocks to hold the interest rate constant or on some other exogenous path.

access to financial markets. The remaining share ω of households indexed by $i \in [1-\omega, 1]$ – the rule-of-thumb consumers – do not have access to financial markets and simply consume their wage income less lump-sum tax payments.

In the absence of rule-of-thumb consumers, the model exhibits Ricardian equivalence, that is, with only permanent-income households that pay lump-sum taxes the timing of taxes and debt is irrelevant. In this case, the only restriction is the intertemporal government budget constraint, i.e., the discounted sum of government budget surpluses must cover the initial debt.

In the presence of rule-of-thumb consumers, the timing of taxes and debt matters. Thus, the CCTW-SW model includes the government budget identity:

$$P_t G_T + B_{t-1} = T_t + \frac{B_t}{R_t}, \tag{22}$$

where B_t refers to government bonds and T_t to lump-sum taxes. R_t denotes the nominal interest rate and P_t the nominal price level. Since the speed with which government debt is paid off matters for model dynamics, the model is closed with a log-linear fiscal policy rule suggested by Galí et al. (2007). This rule sets the percentage deviation of lump-sum taxes from steady state, t_t, in response to deviations of government debt, b_t, and government purchases, g_t:

$$t_t = \phi_b b_t + \phi_g g_t, \tag{23}$$

where ϕ_b and ϕ_g determine the elasticities of lump-sum taxes with respect to government debt and government spending.

These taxes are "lump sum" in the sense that they do not affect incentives to work, save or invest. They do, however, lower future after tax earnings and thereby wealth. Because of the absence of taxes that distort incentives, the model is not suited for analyzing the longer-term consequences of fiscal policy. However, it may well be used to analyze temporary changes in government purchases as in Cogan et al., 2010's analysis of the ARRA.[36]

5.5.2. ARRA Simulations by Conditioning on Policy Shocks

We consider both methods for conditioning on a policy path by adding suitably chosen shocks that are discussed in the preceding section. Of course, given that the ARRA legislation was announced and known to the public, the use of deterministic shocks that treat the additional government purchases as anticipated is much more appropriate than the stochastic shocks, which treat the additional purchases as surprises. Nevertheless, we

---

[36] Drautzburg and Uhlig (2011) show that if one takes incentive effects through increases in distortionary taxes into account in evaluating the impact of ARRA spending an increase in government spending would eventually reduce real GDP. They show that such a decrease of real GDP through increases in distortionary taxes can be long lasting. Cogan et al. (2013) go beyond an analysis of temporary changes in government purchases and taxes and analyze permanent changes in government purchases, transfers and distortionary taxes in the context of fiscal consolidation proposals for the U.S. economy.

simulate the stochastic case for comparison because it has been widely used at central banks in the context of interest rate policy. Our example will serve to illustrate that it is rarely appropriate.

The stochastic shock case is implemented in the DYNARE model solution software (see Juillard, 2001) and thus easily usable. The software computes the policy shocks that are necessary to keep government purchases on the proposed future path.

Figure 5.10 reports the forecasts obtained with the CCTW model from Section 5.3. The data goes through 2009:Q1 and the forecasts start in 2009:Q2, which is right after the ARRA legislation was passed. Coincidentally, the recession started to fade and the recovery gained ground in subsequent quarters.

The solid black line refers to the data and the solid gray line to the forecast without information on ARRA purchases. The dashed line indicates the forecast conditioned on ARRA purchases simulated with stochastic shocks. The dashed–dotted line reports the forecast conditioned on ARRA purchases simulated with anticipated shocks.

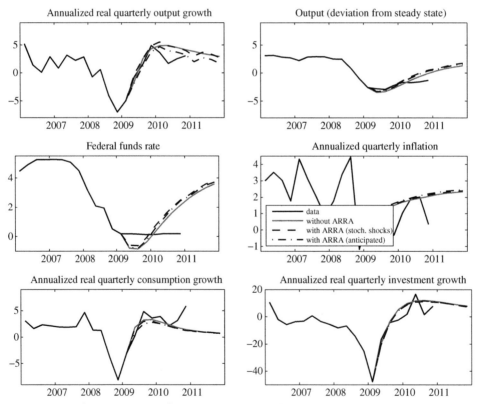

Figure 5.10 Conditioning 2009:Q2 forecasts on announced ARRA government purchases: Data (solid black line), forecast without ARRA (solid gray line), forecast with ARRA stochastic shocks (dashed line), forecast with ARRA anticipated (dashed-dotted line).

Generally, the inclusion of ARRA purchases does not change the forecast very much. The top-right panel indicates that the level of GDP is a bit higher throughout the forecast if ARRA purchases are included explicitly. Thus, it has a stimulative effect. However, both, consumption and investment growth are lower than in the forecast without ARRA. Increased government spending crowds out private spending. The stimulative effect is a bit larger in the simulation with stochastic shocks than in the simulation with anticipated deterministic shocks. The reason is that households reduce consumption initially more if they anticipate higher government spending to persist in the future. Given that the ARRA was public information, the simulation with stochastic shocks overstates the likely GDP impact of the fiscal stimulus.

For a thorough analysis of these methods in the context of simulating exogenous central bank interest rate paths the reader is referred to Galí (2008). He shows that different implementation strategies of an interest rate path lead to different projected output and inflation dynamics. This is due to a multiplicity of possible combinations of the real interest rate and expected inflation that lead to the same nominal interest rate. Thus, it is crucial to consider which is more appropriate in the particular situation the forecast is made and used in policy deliberations. Also, in terms of publishing forecasts it is important to explain the procedure used. "A complete description would need to include the nature and specification of the policy rule that will be followed in order to support the desired interest rate path." (Galí, 2008, p. 16). This might be difficult in practice and is an additional argument for basing central bank forecasts on a specific announced policy rule, rather than on a hypothetical interest rate path.

We close this section with a discussion of the interaction of monetary and fiscal policies at the zero lower bound on nominal interest rates. In the debate on the desirability of fiscal stimulus packages it has repeatedly been emphasized that fiscal stimulus has greater multiplier effects in the event when nominal interest rates are constrained at the zero interest rate floor. In this situation, fiscal stimulus does not induce an immediate increase in interest rates because the notional interest rate target of the central bank is in negative territory.

Indeed, the first panel in the second row of Figure 5.10 shows negative nominal interest rates in 2009. To investigate the impact of the zero lower bound on nominal interest rates we introduce this non-negativity constraint explicitly in the model structure.[37] Such a formulation is necessary to be able to determine the number of quarters for which the nominal interest would stay at the zero bound endogenously. As a consequence of the non-negativity constraint, the model needs to be solved by means of non-linear methods. We make use of the stacked-Fair-Taylor algorithm implemented in DYNARE (see Juillard, 1996).

Figure 5.11 reports the GDP impact (solid line) of the ARRA government purchases when the zero bound is implemented explicitly. The information shown in the figure is

---

[37] See Orphanides, Coenen, and Wieland (2004) for the functional form.

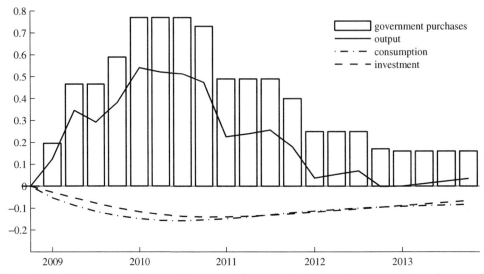

Figure 5.11 GDP, consumption, and investment forecasts: Anticipated government purchases and explicit zero bound on nominal interest rates.

the difference between the simulations with and without ARRA purchases using antici-pated shocks. The model forecast implies that the nominal interest rate (not shown) stays at zero for three quarters. The bars indicate quarterly ARRA purchases as a share of GDP. The GDP impact is lower than the government purchases throughout the simula-tion. In other words, the multiplier is below one. Private consumption and investment are reduced relative to the simulation without fiscal stimulus. The GDP impact of fiscal stimulus is only slightly greater than in the simulation without the zero bound.

Note, the data shown in Figure 5.10 indicates that the nominal interest rate stayed at zero longer than implied by the forecast with the explicit zero bound. However, this finding is consistent with output staying below the level predicted by the same forecasts, and thus monetary policy continuing to remain accommodative.

5.6. Forecast Comparison and Forecast Accuracy

Whether forecasts are useful for policy design depends on their accuracy. Thus, we com-pare the quality of inflation and output growth forecasts from the Fed's Greenbook and from the Survey of Professional Forecasters (SPF) with forecasts from the different types of macroeconomic models considered in the previous sections.

The SPF is a quarterly survey of professional macroeconomic forecasters conducted by the Federal Reserve Bank of Philadelphia. Typically, 30 to 50 respondents report projections of several key macroeconomic variables. The mean of the SPF forecasts is often more accurate than individual forecasts and can serve as an important source of information for policymakers regarding private sector expectations.

We first check whether forecasts are unbiased, then we will check how model-based forecasts compare in terms of accuracy to forecasts from professional forecasters and policy institutions. With regard to the latter, we focus on predictions around turning points because downturns and recoveries pose the greatest challenge for economic forecasters.

5.6.1. Forecast Bias

A good forecast should not be systematically higher or lower than the actual values of the forecasted variable if the forecast is based on a symmetric loss function. Otherwise there would be systematic forecast errors and the forecast would be biased. An exception is the case of an asymmetric loss function as we discussed in Section 2. But even if forecasts for fiscal or monetary policy purposes are based on asymmetric loss functions, it is still of interest to check whether forecasts are biased and to assess whether such a bias can be rationalized by assuming a specific asymmetric loss function.

Figure 5.12 plots a measure of the forecast bias for the Greenbook forecasts (solid line) and the mean forecast of the Survey of Professional forecasters (SPF, dotted line) and indicates how the bias varies over time.

The sample of Greenbook forecasts ends in 2005 as Greenbook data remains confidential for five years. We measure the forecast bias as the average of the forecast error: $1/T \sum_{t=1}^{T} E_t(y_{t+h}) - y_{t+h}$, where T denotes the number of forecasts that is taken into account, $E_t(y_{t+h})$ refers to the forecast for horizon h and y_{t+h} denotes the data realizations. We focus on quarterly annualized output growth and quarterly annualized inflation forecasts. The definition of data realizations is not a trivial choice as output growth data is revised substantially over time. GDP data is first released about one month after the end of the quarter to which the data refers, the so-called advance release. These data are then revised several times at the occasion of the preliminary release, final release, annual revisions, and benchmark revisions. We follow Faust and Wright (2009) and use the data point in the vintage that was released two quarters after the quarter to which the data refer to as revised data. For example, revised data for 2001:Q1 is obtained by selecting the entry for 2001:Q1 from the data vintage released in 2001:Q3. To study how the bias has changed over time we plot the average forecast error over a moving window of 40 quarterly observations, i.e., of 10 years.

The panels in Figure 5.12 show that Greenbook and SPF inflation forecasts exhibited an upward bias from about 1975 to 2000. Forecasters overestimated inflation by up to 1%. The bias is somewhat smaller for the Greenbook than for the SPF. The bias increases with the forecast horizon. The bias decreased in the 1990s and has disappeared for recent observations. Inflation bias would be consistent with asymmetric loss. The time-varying nature of this bias, however, may be more difficult to rationalize. Moreover the bias is similar for the Greenbook and the SPF forecasts. While the former is a forecast from a policy institution, which might weigh positive and negative forecast errors differently, it is more difficult to see why private sector forecasters would also weigh them asym-

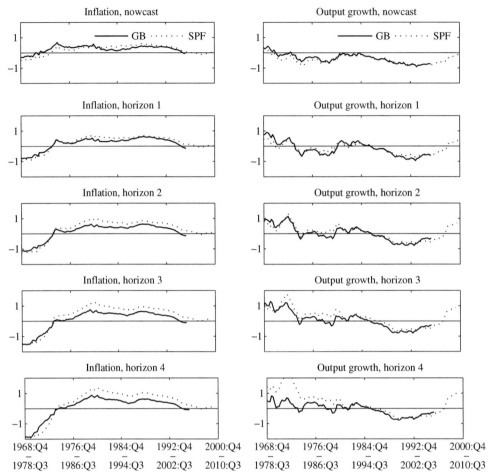

Figure 5.12 The graphs shows time variations in forecast bias. Bias is measured as the average forecast error of Greenbook (GB) and SPF forecasts over a moving window of 40 observations each. We use the data point in the vintage that was released two quarters after the quarter to which the data refer to as revised data. Inflation is defined as annualized quarterly inflation and output growth is defined as annualized quarterly output growth.

metrically. Another reason for this bias could be the great moderation. Inflation rates have decreased since the early 1980s. If forecasters use econometric models estimated on past data, it is likely that they included the high trend inflation from past data and thus overestimated future inflation.

Output growth forecasts are negatively biased for the 1990s. Output growth was very high especially in the late 1990s due to high productivity growth. This result is consistent with Patton and Timmermann (2007). They find that Greenbook forecast are suboptimal under a symmetric loss function. However, the forecasts are optimal if overpredicting output growth is more costly than underpredicting. They find that this asymmetry also depends on the level of output growth and is more important during periods of low growth. In such periods they find that overpredictions of GDP growth are more than three times as costly to the Fed as underpredictions, whereas in times of high growth overpredictions are only about 25% more costly than underpredictions. A reason for such a loss function might be that overpredicting output growth after a recession might incorrectly signal a strong recovery and could result in an overly tight monetary policy increasing the danger of falling back into a recession.

An alternative explanation is that a long period of unusually high output growth led to an under-prediction of growth rates with econometric models based on past data. At the end of the sample the bias is positive, especially for high forecast horizons, which might be influenced by data from the recent financial crisis. As we will show in more detail below, professional forecasters were not able to predict the deep recession of 2008–2009 and thus overpredicted growth rates.

A good forecast should not exhibit systematic errors unless the forecast is based on an asymmetric loss function. Theil notes:

> "If there are any errors in the forecasting process on which the measures taken are based, the measures themselves will in general be suboptimal. Hence a preliminary analysis of forecasts and especially of forecasting errors must be considered useful. Of course, forecasting in the field of economics is a hazardous enterprise, so that errors as such need not amaze us; but if it were possible to detect forecasting errors, which we might call 'systematic,' this could be helpful to find systematic failures in the adaptation of instruments, and it might be possible to indicate ways in which such failures can be avoided, at least approximately".

(Theil, 1958, p. 3)

To test whether the bias we found is significant and whether the forecasts are optimal in the sense that forecast errors are unpredictable, we use Mincer–Zarnowitz regressions (Mincer and Zarnowitz, 1969). We regress data realizations on a constant and the forecasts:

$$y_{t+h} = \alpha + \beta E_t(y_{t+h}). \qquad (24)$$

If the forecast error is unpredictable and thus the forecast unbiased, then $\alpha = 0$ and $\beta = 1$. If the intercept is different from zero, then the forecast has been systematically higher or lower than the actual data. If the slope is different from one then the forecast has systematically over- or underpredicted deviations from the mean (see, e.g., Edge and Gürkaynak, 2010).

We run the Mincer–Zarnowitz regression and estimate Newey–West standard errors with the number of lags equal to the forecast horizon to take into account serial correlation of overlapping forecasts. We conduct F-tests of the joint null hypothesis $\alpha = 0$ and $\beta = 1$. We run these tests for the moving window of 40 quarterly forecasts to check whether forecasting accuracy has changed over time.

Figure 5.13 plots the p-values of the test for forecast optimality for the Greenbook (solid line) and SPF (dotted line) forecasts. A p-value smaller than 0.05 indicates a rejection of the null hypothesis of optimal forecasts on the 5% level, which implies a significant bias. The p-values reflect the magnitude of the estimated bias shown previously. Greenbook

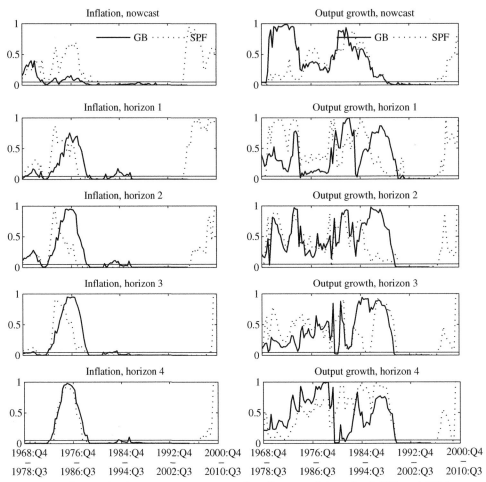

Figure 5.13 The graphs shows time variations in the efficiency of Greenbook (GB) and SPF forecasts measured by the p-value of a F-test of the joint null-hypothesis of optimal forecasts $\alpha = 0$ and $\beta = 1$ in the Mincer–Zarnowitz regression $y_{t+h} = \alpha + \beta E_t y_{t+h}$. A p-value smaller than 0.05 rejects the null hypothesis of optimal forecasts on the 5% level. A p-value larger than 0.05 shows that we cannot reject the null hypothesis of optimal forecasts. The straight horizontal line indicates a p-value of 0.05.

and SPF inflation forecasts are significantly biased from about 1980 to 2000, the time with the highest estimated inflation bias. The length of the bias period increases with the forecast horizon. More recently, the bias has disappeared from the SPF forecasts. Unfortunately, the Greenbook forecasts are not yet available for recent years to check whether they have also turned unbiased. Output growth forecasts are unbiased for large parts of the sample. Only the systematic under-prediction of output growth in the 1990s is statistically significant.

5.6.2. Information Content of Forecasts

While the previous statistics show whether a forecast can be improved by eliminating a systematic bias, they do not indicate whether forecasts contain much information about actual future economic developments, and therefore constitute valuable information for policymakers. One way to assess the information content of forecasts is to check how much of the variability of the data is explained by the forecasts. We use the R^2 from the Mincer–Zarnowitz regressions to evaluate the informational content of forecasts. The R^2 can be directly interpreted as the fraction of the variance in the data that is explained by the forecasts. This fraction will be always below 1 as there are shocks and idiosyncrasies that no economic model can capture. Figure 5.14 shows the R^2 from the rolling window regressions.

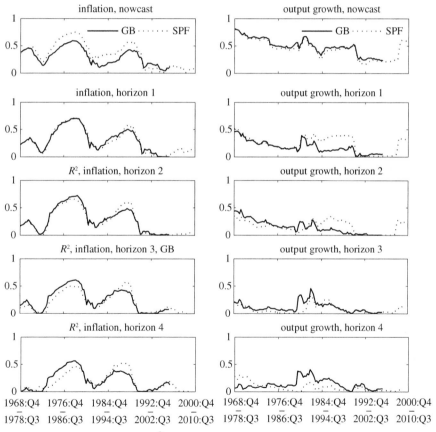

Figure 5.14 The graphs shows the R^2 in the Mincer-Zarnowitz regression $y_{t+h} = \alpha + \beta E_t y_{t+h}$ for Greenbook (GB) and SPF forecasts. A high value shows that a large fraction of the variance in the data is captured by the forecasts. A low value shows that forecasts can explain little of the variation of the forecasted variable.

The results are similar for the Greenbook and SPF forecasts. They show that the R^2 decreases with the forecast horizon. This finding indicates that it is more difficult to predict developments further ahead. Interestingly, the R^2 for the nowcasts is substantially below unity over the whole sample. The R^2 varies a lot over time taking values roughly between 0.1 and 0.6 for inflation. However, for the last 20 years the informational content of the inflation forecasts has dropped to values close to zero. A reason may be that the volatility of inflation has fallen to rather low level since the early 1990s. Inflation can now be characterized as idiosyncratic deviations from a low constant rate. Stock and Watson, 2007 show that the predictable, that is permanent component of inflation has been fairly high in the 1980s but has almost disappeared in the 1990s. The remaining fluctuations of inflation are not persistent and thus hardly predictable. Monetary policy may have been a key factor causing inflation to be difficult to forecast. Given a sufficiently high inflation response monetary policy might eliminate any lasting deviations from trend inflation or the inflation target (see, e.g., Benati, 2008; Gerlach and Tillmann, 2012, for some empirical evidence from inflation targeting central banks).

With regard to output growth, nowcasts explain a larger fraction of the variability of data realizations than in the case of inflation. However, the predictability of output growth quickly decreases with the forecast horizon and is close to zero for forecast horizons 2–4. Even the nowcast can only explain on average 50% of the variance of output growth data. This is not too surprising given the fact that output growth estimates are heavily revised even after the first data releases.[38] There is one period in the sample for which the informational content of output growth forecasts is especially low: the 1990s. For this period we also found a large forecast bias. Given the difficulties in forecasting output accurately beyond the nowcast, it is not surprising that policy institutions, and central banks in particular, put a lot of effort in estimating at least the current state of the economy relatively precisely.

5.6.3. Predicting Turning Points

In the following, we focus more closely on turning points in the business cycle. Forecasting performance during those periods is particularly important to policymakers. In doing so we will also compare the performance of model-based forecasts to Greenbook and SPF forecasts.

Wieland and Wolters (2011) investigate the accuracy of forecasts from the SPF, the Greenbook and six macroeconomic models during the five most recent U.S. recessions. The six macroeconomic models considered in their paper are three small-scale New Keynesian models, a Bayesian VAR model and two medium-scale DSGE models. The

---

[38] It would be interesting to compute the R^2 of the advance release of GDP in a Mincer–Zarnowitz regression. Even this first official estimate of GDP probably explains much less than 100% in the variability of revised GDP data.

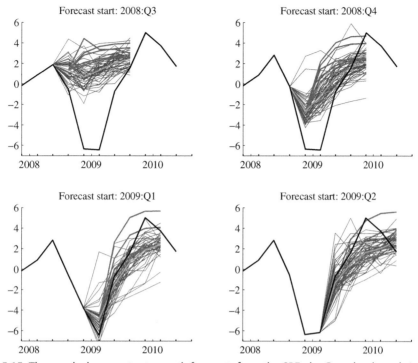

Figure 5.15 The graph shows output growth forecasts from the SPF, the Greenbook, and six macroeconomic models for the most recent U.S. recessions. The black line shows real-time data until the forecast starting point and revised data afterwards. The gray lines show individual forecasts from the SPF. The green line shows the mean of the SPF forecasts. The red lines show the model-based forecasts. (For interpretation of the references to color in this figure legend, the reader is referred to the web version of this book.)

models are estimated on real-time data vintages that were also available to professional forecasters at the time when forecasts were computed.[39]

Figure 5.15 shows output growth forecasts from the SPF, the Greenbook, and the six macroeconomic models for the 2008–2009 U.S. recessions. The black line shows real-time data until the forecast starting point and revised data afterwards. The grey lines correspond to individual forecasts from the SPF. The green line indicates the mean SPF forecast. The red lines are the model-based forecasts. Professional forecasters, on average failed to foresee the recession caused by the financial crisis, even as late as the third quarter of 2008. The mean SPF forecast indicates a slowdown in the fourth quarter followed by a return to higher growth in the first quarter of 2009. The model-based forecasts would

[39] The macroeconomic models are estimated on quarterly data and thus have a disadvantage for computing a nowcast as they cannot use within quarter information from higher frequency data. We eliminate this informational advantage by conditioning the model forecasts on the Greenbook nowcasts and for the most recent recession on the mean SPF nowcast.

not have performed any better. In fact, they do not indicate any impending decline in economic activity. In the fourth quarter of 2008, following the Lehman debacle, professional forecasters drastically revised their assessments downwards, and continued to do so in the first quarter of 2009. From 2009:Q2 onwards, the model-based forecasts perform quite well in predicting the recovery of the U.S. economy. From that point onwards, several of the models deliver predictions that are very similar to the mean SPF forecast and match up with the subsequent data releases well. Studying all the individual forecasts from the SPF, it is clear that not a single forecaster delivered a point forecast of the deep recession.

Figure 5.16 shows a similar figure for the 2001 recession. It confirms that model-based as well as SPF forecasts have difficulties predicting accurately beyond the nowcast. For this recession Greenbook projections are also available. The Greenbook projections (purple line) do not predict the recession any more accurately. In 2001:Q1 and 2001:Q2

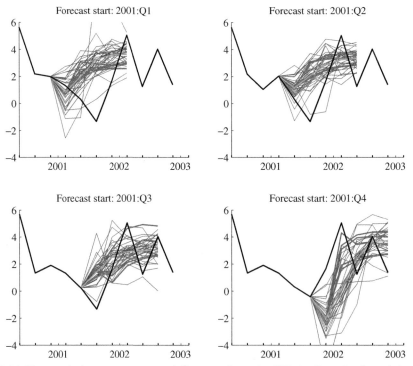

Figure 5.16 The graph shows output growth forecasts from the SPF, the Greenbook, and six macroeconomic models for the most recent US recessions. The black line shows real-time data until the forecast starting point and revised data afterwards. The grey lines show individual forecasts from the SPF. The green line shows the mean of the SPF forecasts. The purple line shows the Greenbook projection and the red lines show the model-based forecasts. (For interpretation of the references to color in this figure legend, the reader is referred to the web version of this book.)

the nowcast of most forecasters shows a decline in growth, which is relatively accurate. However, most forecasters predicted an increase in growth from horizon 1 onwards. Revised data shows that growth moved in the opposite direction towards negative growth rates. In 2001:Q3 model-based forecasts, SPF forecasts and Greenbook projections predicted a recovery. The actual recovery started one quarter later. In 2001:Q4 the recovery took place, but all forecasters missed it and predicted a much lower nowcast. This example reinforces that it is very difficult to predict recessions and business cycle turning points.

Forecasts during the recession in the early 1990s (not shown) indicate that forecasters also failed to predict this recession. However, once the downturn took place in 1990:Q4 SPF forecasters and Greenbook projections predict the recovery relatively well. The model-based forecasts show an upward bias similar to what we observed for the 2008:Q4 predictions. The recovery in 1991:Q1 and 1991:Q2 is predicted relatively precisely by the SPF forecasters and some of the model forecasts. Two of the models as well as the Federal Reserve predicted higher growth rates.

While model forecasts exhibited an upward bias compared to the professional forecasts for the 2008–2009 and the early 1990s recession, the mean SPF forecast is within the range of the model-based forecasts for the 2001 recession. Thus, stylized macroeconomic models perform not much worse than professional forecasters even though the number of data series used by models is only a small fraction of the data universe that experts can look at and judge to be important. Thus, once models are add-factored with such judgments they may do just as well or possibly even better than the expert forecasts. Similar graphs can be produced for inflation forecasts (not shown here). They tend to confirm that model-based forecasts are roughly in line with expert forecasts.

5.6.4. Comparing the Accuracy of Model-Based and Expert Forecasts

The results above show that economic forecasting is an extremely difficult endeavor. There are clearly limitations to the accuracy of forecasts especially around turning points that policymakers should be aware off. The policy process often relies on forecasts that are conditional on exogenous policy assumptions. As discussed in Section 5.4 structural models are well suited for such exercises. Given the limitations of forecasting the performance of structural models relative to expect forecasts such as the SPF and the Greenbook is of interest. Thus, we now investigate the relative performance more systematically. To this end, we compute the root mean squared prediction errors (RMSE) for all forecasts.

Table 5.9 reports the RMSE of the mean forecast of the six models, the Greenbook and the mean forecast of the SPF for inflation and output growth for the five most recent NBER defined U.S. recessions. The typical sample covers the period from four quarters prior to the trough determined by the NBER to four quarters after the trough.

In most cases model forecasts for inflation are on average somewhat less accurate than the Greenbook and mean SPF forecasts. The Greenbook forecasts are in turn more

Table 5.9 RMSEs of Forecasts Initialized with Expert Nowcasts

Sample/Horizon	Inflation			Output Growth		
	Mean	GB	SPF	Mean	GB	SPF
1980:1–1981:3						
0	1.67	1.67	1.52	5.05	5.05	—
1	2.59	1.25	1.81	5.83	6.65	—
2	2.59	1.66	1.92	4.83	5.54	—
3	1.73	1.77	2.23	5.20	6.11	—
4	3.22	2.21	2.56	4.05	5.32	—
1981:4–1983:4						
0	1.12	1.12	1.13	2.42	2.42	2.14
1	1.86	1.32	1.76	3.54	3.58	3.88
2	1.92	1.26	1.68	3.86	3.93	4.11
3	1.79	1.07	1.95	4.25	3.91	4.41
4	1.87	1.48	2.06	4.28	3.84	4.02
1990:1–1992:1						
0	0.73	0.73	1.09	1.27	1.27	1.12
1	1.03	0.84	0.98	2.47	2.09	1.45
2	1.23	0.95	1.01	2.82	2.34	2.06
3	1.20	1.06	1.19	2.94	2.31	2.54
4	1.16	1.02	1.19	2.69	2.18	2.37
2000:4–2002:4						
0	0.56	0.56	0.70	2.28	2.28	2.22
1	0.85	0.87	0.87	2.23	2.20	2.30
2	1.23	0.70	0.92	2.11	2.34	2.21
3	1.25	0.75	0.93	2.65	2.76	2.65
4	1.45	0.78	0.98	2.19	2.18	2.13
2007:4–2009:3						
0	1.11	—	1.11	1.94	—	1.94
1	1.10	—	1.03	4.21	—	3.30
2	1.28	—	1.10	4.89	—	4.11
3	1.51	—	1.24	5.32	—	4.80
4	1.65	—	1.40	5.70	—	5.39

accurate than the mean SPF forecast. Regarding output growth forecasts from models and professional forecasters are very similar. Only for the 2008–2009 recession the SPF forecasts are more accurate than the model forecasts. For all other recessions there is not much of a difference between model forecasts, Greenbook projections and SPF forecasts. Wieland and Wolters (2011) report that individual models perform worse than their mean forecast. This is also true for the SPF (see, e.g., Timmermann, 2006, on forecast averaging). Using a variety of different forecasting tools as currently practiced by many policy institutions is thus important to increase the accuracy of a final overall forecast.

6. EVALUATING THE PERFORMANCE OF POLICY RULES THAT RESPOND TO FORECASTS

Given the lack of accuracy of available model and expert forecasts and the heterogeneity resulting from reasonable differences in modeling assumptions, it is important to investigate whether policymaker decisions should explicitly and directly respond to changes in forecasts rather than recent data realizations. This question is of importance for many areas of policy making including monetary and fiscal policy. Answering this question requires simulating feedback rules in structural models that account for the interaction of economic forecasts with policy decisions. The type of models presented in the preceding section can be used for analyzing forecast-based feedback rules for monetary and fiscal policy instruments. Of course, space limitations in this chapter require us to select a particular example rather than covering a wide range of different policy instruments. Since we have provided new empirical evidence regarding direct responses of policy decisions to policymaker forecasts in the case of the U.S. Federal Open Market Committee (FOMC) in Section 4, we now also evaluate the performance of such rules for the federal funds rate in models of the U.S. economy.

Several authors (see, e.g., de Brouwer and Ellis, 1998; Laxton et al., 1993; Black et al., 1997) have analyzed the performance of forecast-based monetary policy rules in specific models. Using multiple models in parallel makes it possible to investigate the importance of different structural modeling assumptions for policy design.

To this end, we simulate rules with different horizons for inflation and output forecasts in three models: the small IMF quarterly projection model of the U.S. by Carabenciov et al. (2008); the medium-size DSGE model by Cogan et al. (2010) (CCTW-SW), and the linearized version of the FRB/U.S. model used by Levin et al. (2003); (see also Brayton and Tinsley, 1996, 1999). The version of the IMF-model we use is the one estimated in Section 5.2 with U.S. data from 1994:Q1 to 2007:Q4. The version of the CCTW-SW model is the one estimated in Section 5.2 with data from 1965:Q3 to 2007:Q4. For the FRB/U.S. model we use the same parameter values as in Levin et al., 2003. These parameters have been estimated at the Federal Reserve.

We compare the performance of policy rules across models and search for optimized rules given a loss-function of the policymaker. In this manner, we investigate whether the conventional wisdom that monetary policy should be forward-looking because of the existence of transmission lags is borne out by modern macroeconomic models. The exercise is similar in spirit to Levin et al. (2003) who optimize simple forecast-based policy rules for five different models of the U.S. economy.

6.1. Optimizing Forecast-Based Rules for Central Bank Interest Rates

We start by determining the optimal response coefficients and horizons concerning inflation and output gap forecasts in the following type of interest rate rule:

$$i_t = \rho i_{t-1} + (1 - \rho)[i^* + \beta(E_t\pi_{t+h_\pi} - \pi^*) + \gamma E_t y_{t+h_y}], \tag{25}$$

Here i_t denotes the nominal interest rate, π_t the average annual inflation rate, y_t the
output gap, π^* the inflation target and i^* the desired nominal interest rate when inflation
and output equal their respective targets. The nominal interest rate is measured at annual
rates in percentage points. The parameters h_π and h_y denote forecast horizons measured
in quarters.

6.1.1. Forecast Horizons and Equilibrium Determinacy

In searching for policies that deliver good stabilization performance we will focus on rules
that yield determinacy, i.e., a unique stationary rational expectations equilibrium. Rules
that lead to indeterminacy are not desirable because they may induce fluctuations unrelated to economic fundamentals. The models are too complex to identify determinacy
conditions analytically. Thus, we use numerical methods to check whether the models
exhibit determinacy for specific policy parameter combinations. Figure 5.17 shows determinacy regions for different combinations of the interest-rate smoothing and inflation
response coefficients under a range of forecast horizons. The output gap coefficient is
restricted to zero, ($\gamma = 0$). The shaded areas depict the determinacy regions.

   In the absence of interest-rate smoothing, ($\rho = 0$), the interest rate response to
inflation must simply be greater than one to ensure equilibrium determinacy. This condition, which implies that central banks act sufficiently to increase the real interest rate
in response to an increase in inflation, is well-known and often referred to as the Taylor
principle. For interest-rate rules that respond to recent outcomes of inflation ($h_\pi = 0$) the
determinacy regions are very large. The determinacy regions shrink with rising forecast
horizons ($h_\pi > 0$). Only the IMF-model is relatively immune to indeterminacy problems due to its high degree of intrinsic inflation persistence. Some studies have suggested
that interest-rate smoothing coefficients larger than one can yield a unique determinate
equilibrium. This is not the case in the models analyzed here. An interest rate coefficient
equal to or larger than one leads to explosive dynamics in all three models unless the
inflation response is lower than one.

   Figure 5.18 plots determinacy regions for rules with a unit reaction to the current
output gap ($\gamma = 1, h_y = 0$). Allowing for an additional response to the current output
gap increases the determinacy regions especially for moderate horizons of the inflation
forecast of up to four quarters. The output gap is an indicator of future inflation and can
increase the link between current and expected future inflation. This finding holds also
for an increase in the interest-rate smoothing coefficient. Both lead to a more stabilizing
policy and thus larger determinacy regions.

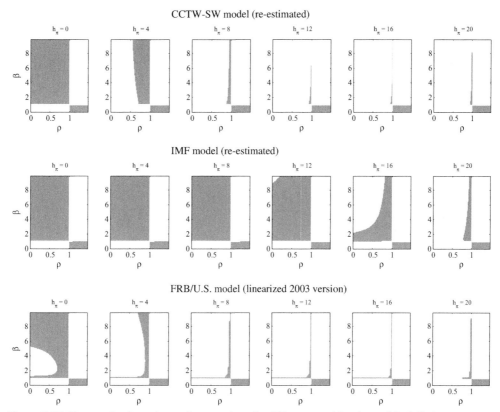

Figure 5.17 The graphs show determinacy regions for different combinations of the inflation response coefficient β and the interest-rate smoothing coefficient ρ. The response to the output gap is zero ($\gamma = 0$). For each specification of the inflation forecast horizon (0, 4, 8, 12, 16, and 20 quarters), multiple equilibira occur for all combinations of the parameters α and ρ that lie outside of the shaded area.

So far, our analysis has uncovered several conditions that render policy rules stabilizing: responding to current inflation or a near-term inflation forecast, an additional response to the output gap, and a substantial degree of interest-rate smoothing.

6.1.2. Optimizing Forecast-Based Rules

Having analyzed general conditions that lead to a unique stable equilibrium we now investigate rules with response coefficients optimized to a particular model. In optimizing coefficients we have in mind a policymaker who cares about stabilizing inflation and the output gap. Thus, we consider policymaker preferences that can be represented by a simple loss function of the following form:

$$L = var(\pi) + \lambda var(y), \tag{26}$$

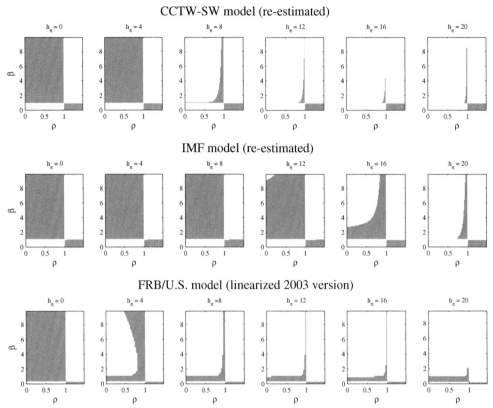

Figure 5.18 The graphs show determinacy regions for different combinations of the inflation response coefficient β and the interest-rate smoothing coefficient ρ. The response to the output gap is one ($\gamma = 1$). For each specification of the inflation forecast horizon (0, 4, 8, 12, 16, and 20 quarters), multiple equilibira occur for all combinations of the parameters α and ρ that lie outside of the shaded area.

where $var(.)$ denotes the unconditional variance and the weight $\lambda \geq 0$ indicates the policymaker's preference for reducing output variability relative to inflation variability. The loss function is a one-period version of the loss function in Eq. (1).

One might ask why not use a welfare function that is based on household utility (see, e.g., Schmitt-Grohé and Uribe, 2007). We use a traditional ad hoc loss function (this approach goes back to the work by Tinbergen, 1952; Theil, 1958), because only one of the three models considered here (CCTW-SW) would allow the derivation of a loss function from household utility. While the equations in the IMF-model and the FRB/U.S. model are based on economic theory, they are not rigorously derived from microeconomic optimization problems and thus the concept of a utility function is used only implicitly.[40]

---

[40] Furthermore, a utility-based welfare-function can be extremely model specific. Paez-Farrell (2010) shows that different theories of inflation persistence can result in a observationally equivalent Phillips curve, but imply different loss functions

We use numerical methods to compute optimal policy response coefficients and forecast horizons that minimize the weighted average of inflation and output gap variability, subject to an upper bound on interest rate variability. Only rules that yield determinacy are considered in the optimization.

We consider forecast horizons up to 20 quarters and restrict the policy parameters ρ, β and γ to the interval $[0, 3]$. The latter restriction is sometimes needed to avoid unreasonably high values for the inflation response coefficient (we found values above 100) that do not reduce the value of the loss function significantly more than an inflation response coefficient around three. Furthermore, we restrict the analysis to rules that imply a volatility of the first difference of the interest rate that is no greater than the value observed for the U.S. between 1983 and 2007.

Table 5.10 provides an overview of the characteristics and performance of optimized rules. For a range of values of λ, the weight on output gap variability in the loss function, the table reports the optimal horizons of inflation and output gap forecasts, h_π and h_y, and the optimal response coefficients on the lagged interest rate, inflation and the output gap, ρ, β and γ. The last column denoted by %ΔL indicates the percentage reduction in the value of the loss function under the optimal forecast-based rule relative to an optimized outcome-based rule. The value is always non-positive because the class of outcome-based rules ($h_\pi = 0$ and $h_y = 0$) is nested within the class of forecast-based rules. In the cases where the optimal forecast horizon is zero the value of %ΔL is zero.

The optimal forecast horizons are mostly below four quarters. One exception is the horizon of the output gap forecast in the CCTW-SW model when the policymaker places no weight on output stabilization ($\lambda = 0$). Other exceptions arise in the FRB/U.S. model, where the inflation forecast horizon can be rather high at four to five years. Even so, the reported loss function values indicate that responding to forecasts rather than outcomes does not yield major improvements in the stabilization of inflation and the output gap. This finding confirms Levin et al. (2003). The only model where basing policy on forecasts yields sizeable improvements is the IMF's model. The reason is probably the very high degree of inflation and output persistence in this model. In sum, forecast-based rules offer little advantage over outcome-based rules in the majority of the models.[41]

The optimal inflation response coefficient is often near or at the upper corner of the interval considered in the optimization, that is a value of 3.0. The response to the output gap increases with an increasing weight on output stabilization. It remains relatively low in the CCTW-SW model. In the IMF and FRB/U.S. models a positive response coefficient on the output is optimal even if the policymaker places no weight on the stabilization

---

and lead to different policy prescriptions. Therefore, optimal simple rules based on structural loss functions are not robust to model uncertainty.

[41] This result is also consistent with Levin et al. (1999) who find that complicated outcome-based rules, which include a large number of state variables and are thus similar to information encompassing forecast-based rules, yield only moderate stabilization gains over simple rules.

Table 5.10 Characteristics and Performance of Optimized Rules

Model	λ	h_π	h_y	ρ	β	γ	%ΔL
	0	0	20	0.87	3.00	0.00	−2.36
CCTW-SW	1/3	0	0	1.00	3.00	0.10	0.00
(re-estimated)	1	1	0	1.00	3.00	0.23	−0.06
	3	3	0	0.99	3.00	0.59	−0.33
	0	0	2	0.79	3.00	0.31	−13.71
IMF Model	1/3	1	3	0.82	2.60	3.00	−11.10
(re-estimated)	1	1	4	0.77	3.00	2.99	−30.77
	3	4	4	0.68	2.88	3.00	−30.92
	0	0	0	0.94	3.00	0.42	0.00
FRB/US	1/3	18	0	0.97	3.00	2.16	−3.78
(linearized, 2003)	1	18	0	0.97	3.00	2.97	−14.04
	3	16	0	0.98	3.00	3.00	−11.67

Notes: For each model and each value of the preference parameter λ, the table indicates the optimal forecast horizons for inflation and the output gap (h_π and h_y, respectively) and the optimal values of the policy coefficients ρ, β and γ. The table also indicates the percent change in the loss function (%ΔL) of the optimized rule compared to an optimal outcome-based rule. The interest rate rule is given by: $i_t = \rho i_{t-1} + (1 - \rho)[i^* + \beta(E_t\pi_{t+h_\pi} - \pi^*) + \gamma E_t y_{t+h_y}]$. The parameters ρ, β and γ are restricted to lie in the interval [0,3].

of the output gap ($\lambda = 0$), probably because it is an indicator of future inflation. The optimal interest-rate smoothing coefficient is close to unity.

Our findings do not support the conventional wisdom that central bank interest rates need to be set in response to forecasts rather than recent outcomes, because these rates influence output and inflation, i.e., the ultimate target variables, with a lag.[42] It would be useful to extend our analysis by including alternative assumptions regarding the expectations formation of market participants relative to rational expectations. Models with least-squares learning are available, for example, from Slobodyan and Wouters (2009) and Slobodyan and Wouters (2012).

6.2. Robustness Under Model Uncertainty

The heterogeneity of model-based forecasts documented in the preceding section underscores the great extent of model uncertainty faced by monetary and fiscal policymakers. Thus, even if certain rules perform very well in a given model, the question remains whether they are robust to such model uncertainty. We evaluate the robustness of the type of interest rate rules derived in the preceding sub-section by checking how they perform in competing models. In other words, we simulate a situation where the central

---

[42] Of course, this finding does not necessarily preclude the use of forecasts in communications to the public as practiced at many inflation targeting central banks even when central bank's decisions are driven by recent outcomes rather than forecasts of key macroeconomic variables.

bank can only use a simplified model that is an imperfect representation of the "true" world. The policymaker searches for an optimal rule in this misspecified model. The evaluation model represents the "true model of the economy", while the model used for the optimization of the policy parameters represents the "misspecified" model.

We conduct this exercise for outcome-based and forecast-based rules to find out which type of rules is more robust to model uncertainty. The exercise is similar to Levin et al. (2003) and Taylor and Wieland (2012). They evaluate the robustness of model-specific rules, respectively, across five and four models. Levin et al. (2003) find that rules that respond to a short horizon inflation forecast of up to one-year ahead and the current output gap and include a high degree of interest-rate smoothing are relatively robust to model uncertainty. Rules with longer forecast horizons are less robust in the sense that they lead to indeterminacy in a number of cases. Taylor and Wieland (2012) show that rules that are derived by averaging over the losses incurred in different models are generally more robust than model-specific rules.

First, we consider the robustness of outcome-based rules. Table 5.11 reports their performance across the three models. The first column? contains the weight on output variability in the loss function and the second column the name of the optimization model. The next three columns show the policy parameters of the rule to be evaluated. The last two columns indicate the loss and the percentage change in the loss function compared to a rule that has been optimized in the model that is used for the evaluation.

Most optimized rules exhibit a high degree of interest-rate smoothing and an inflation coefficient close to the upper bound of 3. The rules differ a lot with respect to the parameter on the output gap. It is rather small in the CCTW-SW model. In the FRB/U.S. model it rises to a value near 3.0 only when output and inflation variability receive equal weight in the loss function. In the IMF model, however, it mostly takes on values between 2 and 3. These differences in the policy parameters lead in most cases to the result that the optimized rule is not robust across the other two models. For example, taking the rule optimized for the Smets and Wouters model with $\lambda = 1/3$ yields a relative loss of 161.34% in the IMF model and a relative loss of 239.69% in the FRB/U.S. model.[43] Based on these results policymakers would probably be reluctant to rely on any rule that has been optimized in a single model only.

Table 5.12 reports the performance and robustness of forecast-based rules. We choose a forecast horizon of three quarters for inflation and the output gap as in the empirical estimation of forecast-based policy rules for the U.S. in Section 4.

Our findings indicate that model-specific rules are not robust to model uncertainty as suggested by Taylor and Wieland (2012), Model-specific rules are fine-tuned to a particular model and imply a substantial increase in loss in other models.

---

[43] In few cases the rules optimized in another model yield a slight improvement compared to the rule optimized in the evaluation model, but violate the imposed upper bound of the interest rate volatility. These rules are thus not desirable.

Table 5.11 Robustness of Outcome-Based Model-Specific Rules

λ	Model Used to Optimize the Rule	ρ	β	γ	Loss	%ΔL
	Evaluated in the CCTW–SW model					
0	IMF	0.79	2.23	1.73	46.79	6346.9
0	FRB	0.96	3.00	0.76	5.53	661.85
1/3	IMF	0.86	3.00	2.63	50.17	274.35
1/3	FRB	0.98	2.99	2.99	46.09	243.91
1	IMF	0.83	2.09	2.82	130.57	283.44
1	FRB	0.97	3.00	1.99	46.90	37.73
	Evaluated in IMF model					
0	CCTW-SW	0.87	3.00	0.00	1.18	18.97
0	FRB	0.96	3.00	0.76	1.61	59.28
1/3	CCTW-SW	0.99	3.00	0.22	3.11	161.34
1/3	FRB	0.98	2.99	2.99	2.14	179.83
1	CCTW-SW	0.99	3.00	0.53	4.03	137.06
1	FRB	0.97	3.00	1.99	2.80	64.71
	Evaluated in FRB/U.S. model					
0	CCTW-SW	0.87	3.00	0.00	5.62	80.13[a]
0	IMF	0.79	2.23	1.73	24.02	669.87
1/3	CCTW-SW	0.99	3.00	0.22	91.82	239.69
1/3	IMF	0.86	3.00	2.63	26.39	−2.36
1	CCTW-SW	0.99	3.00	0.53	216.89	217.08
1	IMF	0.83	2.09	2.82	62.97	−7.93

Notes: For each model and each value of the preference parameter λ, the table indicates the optimal policy parameters for inflation and output gap outcomes ($h_\pi = 0$ and $h_y = 0$). The table also indicates the loss and the percent change in the loss function (%ΔL) of a rule that has been optimized in another model compared to the rule that has been optimized in the same model that is used for the evaluation. A value of ∞ shows that this specific rule does not yield determinacy. The interest rate rule is given by: $i_t = \rho i_{t-1} + (1 - \rho)[i^* + \beta(E_t \pi_{t+h_\pi} - \pi^*) + \gamma E_t y_{t+h_y}]$. The parameters ρ, β and γ are restricted to lie in the interval [0,3]. We only consider rules that lead to a volatility of the first difference of the interest rate that is equal or lower to what can be empirically observed for the period 1983–2010.

[a] this rule violates the volatility restriction of the interest rate in the model that is used to evaluate the performance of the rule.

Rules responding to forecasts are even less robust than the outcome-based rules in the sense that they lead to indeterminacy in two cases. If we increase the forecast horizon to seven quarters equilibrium indeterminacy arises more frequently (not shown). For example, the rules optimized in the IMF model then always induce indeterminacy in the other two models.

In sum, we find that the advantages of forecast-based policy rules in terms of incorporating information on a wide range of state variables via the forecasts do not translate to

Table 5.12 Robustness of Model-Specific Rules with Forecast Horizon of Three Quarters

λ	Model Used to Optimize Rule	ρ	β	γ	Loss	%ΔL
	Evaluated in CCTW-SW model					
0	IMF	0.65	3.00	0.74	6.87	509.38[a]
0	FRB	0.95	3.00	0.51	3.95	248.70
1/3	IMF	0.77	3.00	1.81	34.25	155.77[a]
1/3	FRB	0.94	2.99	0.24	13.75	2.61
1	IMF	0.78	3.00	3.00	78.88	129.17[a]
1	FRB	0.98	2.85	3.00	69.02	100.50
	Evaluated in IMF model					
0	CCTW-SW	0.93	3.00	0.00	1.57	40.92
0	FRB	0.95	3.00	0.51	1.66	48.26
1/3	CCTW-SW	0.78	3.00	0.04	1.39	13.77
1/3	FRB	0.94	2.99	0.24	1.94	58.87
1	CCTW-SW	0.99	3.00	0.43	3.63	111.57
1	FRB	0.98	2.85	3.00	2.95	71.73
	Evaluated in FRB/U.S. model					
0	CCTW-SW	0.93	3.00	0.00	6.93	56.94
0	IMF	0.65	3.00	0.74	∞	∞
1/3	CCTW-SW	0.78	3.00	0.04	∞	∞
1/3	IMF	0.77	3.00	1.81	24.80	−65.63[a]
1	CCTW-SW	0.99	3.00	0.43	261.28	135.91
1	IMF	0.78	3.00	3.00	77.70	−29.84

Notes: The parameters are optimized for an inflation forecast horizon and an output gap horizon of three quarters ahead ($h_\pi = 3$ and $h_y = 3$, respectively). A value of ∞ shows that this specific rule does not yield determinacy.

[a] this rule violates the volatility restriction of the interest rate in the model that is used to evaluate the performance of the rule.

important gains in stabilization performance. By contrast, forecast-based rules are more prone to generate equilibrium indeterminacy. Rules that respond to longer-horizon forecasts perform worse across models. An important extension of this analysis would be to consider the performance of model-averaging rules as proposed by Taylor and Wieland (2012).

7. OUTLOOK

This chapter has been concerned with studying the link between economic forecasts and policy making, focusing in particular on the areas of monetary and fiscal policy.

Having presented a simple framework for linking forecasts with policy decisions, we then provided evidence that central bank interest rate decisions are well explained by a reaction to central bank forecasts. While there is a large literature on central bank reaction functions, it would be of great interest to shed more light on the relationship between fiscal forecasts and policy decisions. There is evidence that asymmetries may play an important role in explaining budgetary forecasts. Such asymmetric costs are likely to play an increasingly important role in the Euro area as supra-national efforts for exerting greater fiscal discipline on the national level take hold. An effective implementation of such fiscal discipline would require careful monitoring of the quality of fiscal forecasts.

A large part of this chapter has then been devoted to the study of structural models that can be used to compute forecasts that account for the interaction with policy decisions. We have also documented that model-based forecasts just like expert forecasts have missed the onset of the great recession in 2008–2009. In fact, models and experts generally have difficulty predicting recessions. On the positive side, models and experts provided reasonably useful forecasts of the recovery process. Using a small projection model from the IMF we found that information drawn from bank lending surveys helped explain the recent recession as a consequence of the global financial crisis. However, the bank lending information appeared not sufficiently predictable to improve the forecasting performance of the model. Of related interest is the evaluation of the forecasting performance of DSGE models with financial factors in the chapter on DSGE forecasting in this handbook by Del Negro and Schorfheide (2013). In this chapter we used a medium-size DSGE model with a fiscal sector to explore the use of alternative conditioning assumptions in predicting the GDP impact of the 2009 U.S. fiscal stimulus package. Our estimates indicate a fairly small stimulative effect of such measures.

Going forward, it is of eminent importance to develop the financial sector of DSGE models to better capture the experience of credit boom followed by credit bust that led to the global financial crisis and to integrate more realistic structural representations of the fragilities in financial intermediation. Hopefully, such modeling improvements will not only help explain past developments but also improve forecasting accuracy.

The diversity of model and expert forecasts suggests that forecast heterogeneity and learning dynamics might play an important role in propagating economic fluctuations. The structural forecasting models considered in this chapter, however, all rely on the assumption of homogenous and rational expectations. It is urgent to integrate heterogeneous expectations and learning in structural models and evaluate the forecasting performance of such models.

Furthermore, much work remains to be done in integrating the process in which policymakers learn from the data and revise their models of the economy formally in policy design.

Finally, the closing section on robustness of forecast-based policies under model uncertainty introduces a cautionary note. While forecasts play an important role in many economic policy decision-making processes caution should be exerted in basing policy explicitly on longer-run forecasts. Model uncertainty is a major practical problem. Research on Bayesian model averaging, robust control and worst-case analysis may help support more effective policy design that is robust to model uncertainty.

APPENDIX A.   A MEDIUM-SCALE DSGE MODEL

This appendix provides a description of the Smets and Wouters model with rule-of-thumb consumers estimated in Cogan et al. (2010).

The resource constraint is given by:

$$y_t = c_y c_t + i_y i_t + z_y z_t + g_t, \tag{27}$$

where output y_t is the sum of consumption, c_t, and investment, i_t, weighted with their steady-state ratios to output (c_y and i_y), the capital-utilization cost, which depends on the capital utilization rate, z_t, and government spending g_t. g_t follows an AR (1) process and is also affected by the technology shock. z_y equals $R_*^k k_y$, where k_y is the ratio of capital to output in steady state and R_*^k is the rental rate of capital in steady state.

A share $1 - \omega$ of households indexed by $j \in [0, 1 - \omega)$ makes optimizing, forward looking decisions and these households have access to financial markets. The remaining share ω of households indexed by $i \in [1 - \omega, 1]$ – the rule-of-thumb consumers – do not have access to financial markets and simply consume their wage income less lump-sum tax payments:

$$c_{i,t} = W_*^h L_* / C_* (w_t + L_t) - c_y^{-1} t_t, \tag{28}$$

where parameters with a $*$ subscript denote steady-state values. Combining the optimizing households' first order conditions for consumption and bond holdings yields the same consumption Euler equation as in Smets and Wouters (2007). Labor unions set the same nominal wage rate for both types of households. Hence, labor supply is equalized across the two groups. The consumption Euler equation for optimizing households is thus given by:

$$c_{j,t} = c_1 c_{j,t-1} + (1 - c_1) E_t(c_{j,t+1}) + c_2(l_t - E_t(l_{t+1})) - c_3(r_t - E_t(\pi_{t+1}) + \epsilon_t^b. \tag{29}$$

The parameters are $c_1 = (\lambda/\gamma)/(1+\lambda/\gamma)$, $c_2 = [(\sigma_c-1)(W_*^h L_*/C_*)]/[(\sigma_c(1+\lambda/\gamma)]$ and $c_3 = (1-\lambda/\gamma)/[(1+\lambda/\gamma)\sigma_c]$. λ governs the degree of habit formation, γ is the labor augmented steady growth rate, σ_c the inverse of the intertemporal elasticity of substitution. ϵ_t^b denotes an AR (1) shock process on the premium over the central bank controlled interest rate. Consumption of optimizing households is a weighted average of past and expected consumption due to habit formation. The consumption Euler equation depends on hours worked, l_t, because of the non-separability of utility. When consumption and hours are complements ($\sigma_c > 1$), consumption of optimizing households increases with current hours and decreases with expected hours next period. The real interest rate and the shock term affect aggregate demand by inducing intertemporal substitution in consumption. Overall consumption is a weighted average of consumption of both types of households:

$$c_t = (1 - \omega)c_{j,t} + \omega c_{i_t}. \tag{30}$$

The investment Euler equation is given by

$$i_t = i_1 i_{t-1} + (1 - i_1)E_t(i_{t+1}) + i_2 q_t + \epsilon_t^i, \tag{31}$$

where $i_1 = 1/(1 + \beta\gamma^{1-\sigma_c})$ and $i_2 = [1/(1 + \beta\gamma^{1-\sigma_c})\gamma^2\phi]$. β denotes the discount factor, ϕ the elasticity of the capital adjustment cost function, q_t Tobin's Q and ϵ_t^i an investment specific technology shock that follows an AR (1) process. Current investment is a weighted average of past and expected future investment due to the existence of capital adjustment costs. It is positively related to the real value of the existing capital stock. This dependence decreases with the elasticity of the capital adjustment cost function. The arbitrage equation for the real value of the capital stock is:

$$q_t = q_1 E_t(q_{t+1}) + (1 - q_1)E_t(r_{t+1}^k) - (r_t - E_t(\pi_{t+1}) + \epsilon_t^b), \tag{32}$$

where $q_1 = \beta\gamma^{-\sigma_c}(1 - \delta)$. r_t^k denotes the real rental rate of capital and δ the depreciation rate of capital. The real value of the existing capital stock is a positive function of its expected value next period and the rental rate on capital and a negative function of the real interest rate and the external finance premium.

The production process is assumed to be determined by a Cobb–Douglas production function with fixed costs:

$$y_t = \phi_p(\alpha k_t^s + (1 - \alpha)l_t + \epsilon_t^a). \tag{33}$$

k_t^s denotes effective capital (physical capital adjusted for the capital utilization rate), ϵ_t^a a neutral productivity shock that follows an AR (1) process and ϕ_p is one plus the share of fixed costs in production. Output is produced using capital and labor and is boosted by technology shocks. Capital used in production depends on the capital utilization rate and the physical capital stock of the previous period as new capital becomes effective with a lag of one quarter:

$$k_t^s = k_{t-1} + z_t. \tag{34}$$

Household income from renting capital services to firms depends on r_t^k and changing capital utilization is costly so that the capital utilization rate depends positively on the rental rate of capital:

$$z_t = (1 - \psi)/\psi r_t^k, \tag{35}$$

where $\psi \in [0, 1]$ is a positive function of the elasticity of the capital utilization adjustment cost function. The law of motion for physical capital is given by:

$$k_t = k_1 k_{t-1} + (1 - k_1)i_t + k_2 \epsilon_t^i, \tag{36}$$

where $k_1 = (1-\delta)/\gamma$ and $k_2 = (1-(1-\delta)/\gamma)(1+\beta\gamma^{1-\sigma_c})\gamma^2\phi$. The price mark-up μ_t^p equals the difference between the marginal product of labor and the real wage w_t:

$$\mu_t^p = \alpha(k_t^s - l_t) + \epsilon_t^a - w_t. \tag{37}$$

Monopolistic competition, Calvo-style price contracts, and indexation of prices that are not free to be chosen optimally combine to yield the following Phillips curve:

$$\pi_t = \pi_1\pi_{t-1} + \pi_2\pi_{t+1} - \pi_3\mu_t^p + \epsilon_t^p, \tag{38}$$

with $\pi_1 = \iota_p/(1+\beta\gamma^{1-\sigma_c}\iota_p)$, $\pi_2 = \beta\gamma^{1-\sigma_c}/(1+\beta\gamma^{1-\sigma_c}\iota_p)$, and $\pi_3 = 1/(1+\beta\gamma^{1-\sigma_c}\iota_p)[(1-\beta\gamma^{1-\sigma_c}\xi_p)(1-\xi_p)/\xi_p((\phi_p-1)\epsilon_p+1)]$. This Phillips curve contains not only a forward-looking but also a backward-looking inflation term because of price indexation. Firms that cannot adjust prices optimally either index their price to the lagged inflation rate or to the steady-state inflation rate. Note, this indexation assumption ensures also that the long-run Phillips curve is vertical. ξ_p denotes the Calvo parameter, ι_p governs the degree of backward indexation, ϵ_p determines the curvature of the Kimball (1995) aggregator. The Kimball aggregator complementarity effects enhance the price rigidity resulting from Calvo-style contracts. The mark-up shock ϵ_t^p follows an ARMA (1,1) process.

A monopolistic labor market yields the condition that the wage mark-up μ_t^w equals the real wage minus the marginal rate of substitution mrs_t:

$$\mu_t^w = w_t - mrs_t = w_t - \left(\sigma_l l_t + \frac{1}{1-\lambda/\gamma}(c_t - \lambda/\gamma c_{t-1})\right), \tag{39}$$

with σ_l being the Frisch elasticity of labor supply. The wage Phillips curve is given by:

$$w_t = w_1 w_{t-1} + (1-w_1)(E_t(w_{t+1}) + E_t(\pi_{t+1})) - w_2\pi_t + w_3\pi_{t-1} - w_4\mu_t^w + \epsilon_t^w, \tag{40}$$

where $w_1 = 1/(1+\beta\gamma^{1-\sigma_c})$, $w_2 = (1+\beta\gamma^{1-\sigma_c}\iota_w)/((1+\beta\gamma^{1-\sigma_c}))$, $w_3 = \iota_w/(1+\beta\gamma^{1-\sigma_c})$, and $w_4 = 1/(1+\beta\gamma^{1-\sigma_c})[(1-\beta\gamma^{1-\sigma_c}\xi_w)(1-\xi_w)/(\xi_w((\phi_w-1)\epsilon_w+1))]$. The parameter definition is analogous to the price Phillips curve.

Setting $\xi_p = 0$, $\xi_w = 0$, $\epsilon_t^p = 0$ and $\epsilon_t^w = 0$ one obtains the efficient flexible price and flexible wage allocation. The output gap x_t is defined as the log difference between output and flexible price output just like in the small-scale New-Keynesian models above.

The government purchases consumption goods g_t, issues bonds b_t and raises lump–sum taxes t_t. The government budget constraint is then given by:

$$b_t = R_*\left(b_{t-1}\pi_*^{-1} + g_t - t_t\right), \tag{41}$$

where R_* denotes the nominal steady-state interest rate and π_* the steady-state inflation rate. Fiscal policy follows a rule suggested by Galí et al., 2007:

$$t_t = \phi_b b_t + \phi_g g_t, \tag{42}$$

where ϕ_b and ϕ_g determine the elasticities of lump-sum taxes with respect to government debt and government spending.

The monetary policy rule reacts to inflation, the output gap and the change in the output gap and incorporates partial adjustment:

$$r_t = \rho r_{t-1} + (1 - \rho)(r_\pi \pi_t + r_x x_t) + r_{\Delta x_t}(x_t - x_{t-1}) + \epsilon_t^r. \tag{43}$$

ϵ_t^r is a monetary policy shock that follows an AR (1) process.

ACKNOWLEDGMENTS

Helpful comments by Allan Timmermann, Graham Elliott, Marta Banbura, Todd Clark, Kai Christoffel, William Gavin, Lutz Kilian, Mike Wickens, Jonathan Wright, participants at the Handbook of Economic Forecasting Conference at the Federal Reserve Bank of St. Louis and the Society for Computational Economics Conference 2012 in Prague, and two anonymous referees are gratefully appreciated. All remaining errors are our own. Wieland acknowledges research assistance support from the German Science Foundation, DFG Grant No. WI 2260/1-1 AOBJ 584949. Wolters thanks the Stanford Institute for Economic Policy Research (SIEPR) where he was a visiting scholar while part of this research was conducted.

REFERENCES

Adolfson, M., Andersson, M.K., Linde, J., Villani, M., Vredin, A., 2007a. Modern forecasting models in action: improving macroeconomic analyses at central banks. International Journal of Central Banking 3 (4), 111–144.

Adolfson, M., Laséen, S., Linde, J., Villani, M., 2007b. Bayesian estimation of an open economy DSGE model with incomplete pass-through. Journal of International Economics 72 (2), 481–511.

Adolfson, M., Laséen, S., Linde, J., Villani, M., 2008. Evaluating an estimated new Keynesian small open economy model. Journal of Economic Dynamics and Control 32 (8), 2690–2721.

Alstadheim, R., Bache, I.W., Holmsen, A., Maih, J., Risland., 2010. Monetary policy analysis in practice, Norges Bank Staff Memo No. 11.

Amano, R., Coletti, D., Macklem, T., 1998. Monetary rules when economic behaviour changes. In: Proceedings, Federal Reserve Bank of San Francisco (issue March).

Artis, M., Marcellino, M., 2001. Fiscal forecasting: the track record of the IMF, OECD and EC. Econometrics Journal 4, S20–S36.

Bache, I.W., Brubakk, L., Jore, A., Maih, J., Nicolaisen, J., 2010. Monetary policy analysis in practice – a conditional forecasting approach, Norges Bank Monetary Policy Staff Memo No. 8.

Banbura, M., Giannone, D., Modugno, M., Reichlin, L., 2013. Nowcasting and the real-time data flow. In: Elliott, G., Timmermann, A. (Eds.), Handbook of Economic Forecasting, vol. 2. Elsevier.

Bank of England, 1999. Economic Models at the Bank of England. Bank of England, London.

Bank of England, 2004. The New Bank of England Quarterly Model. Bank of England, London.

Batini, N., Haldane, A.G., 1999. Forward-looking rules for monetary policy. In: Taylor, J.B. (Ed.), Monetary Policy Rules. University of Chicago Press for National Bureau of Economic Research, Chicago, pp. 157–92.

Beck, G.W., Wieland, V., 2007. Money in monetary policy design: a formal characterization of ECB-style cross-checking. Journal of the European Economic Association 5 (2–3), 524–533.

Beck, G.W., Wieland, V., 2008. Central bank misperceptions and the role of money in interest rate rules. Journal of Monetary Economics 55 (1), S1–S17.

Beck, G.W., Wieland, V., 2009. Money in monetary policy design: monetary cross-checking in the New-Keynesian model. In: Wieland, V. (Ed.), The Science and Practice of Monetary Policy Today. Springer Science.

Benati, L., 2008. Investigating inflation persistence across monetary regimes. Quarterly Journal of Economics 123, 1005–1060.

Bernanke, B.S., 2009. Federal Reserve policies to ease credit and their implications for the Fed's balance sheet, speech at the National Press Club Luncheon, National Press Club, Washington, DC, February 18.

Bernanke, B.S., 2010. Monetary policy and the housing bubble. Speech at the Annual Meeting of the American Economic Association, Atlanta, Georgia, January 3.

Bernanke, B.S., Mihov, I., 1998. Measuring monetary policy. The Quarterly Journal of Economics 113 (3), 869–902.

Bernanke, B.S., Mishkin, F.S., 1997. Inflation targeting: a new framework for monetary policy? Journal of Economic Perspectives 11 (2), 97–116.

Bernanke, B.S., Laubach, T., Mishkin, F.S., Posen, A., 1999. Inflation targeting: lessons from the international experience. Princeton University Press, Princeton, NJ.

Black, R., Macklem, T., Rose, D., 1997. On policy rules for price stability. In: Macklem, T. (Ed.), Price stability, inflation targets and monetary policy. Ottawa, Bank of Canada.

Brayton, F., Tinsley, P., 1996. A guide to FRB/US: a macroeconometric model of the United States, FEDS Working Paper 96–42.

Bryant, R.C., Hooper, P., Mann, C.L. (Eds.), 1993. Evaluating Policy Regimes: New Research in Emprical Macroeconomics. Brookings Institution, Washington DC.

Campbell, B., Ghysels, E., 1995. Federal budget projections: A nonparametric assessment of bias and efficiency. Review of Economics and Statistics 77, 17–31.

Carabenciov, I., Ermolaev, I., Freedman, C., Juillard, M., Kamenik, O., Korshunov, D., Laxton, D., 2008. A small quarterly projection model of the US economy, IMF Working Paper No. 08/278.

Carstensen, K., 2006. Estimating the ECB policy reaction function. German Economic Review 7 (1), 1–34.

Castelnuovo, E., 2003. Taylor rules, omitted variables, and interest rate smoothing in the US. Economics Letters 81, 55–59.

Chang, Y., Doh, T., Schorfheide, F., 2007. Non-stationary hours in a DSGE model. Journal of Money, Credit and Banking 39 (6), 1357–1373.

Christiano, L.J., Eichenbaum, M., Evans, C.L., 2005. Nominal rigidities and the dynamic effects of a shock to monetary policy. Journal of Political Economy 113 (1), 1–45.

Christiano, L., Motto, R., Rostagno, M., 2008. Shocks, structures or monetary policies? the Euro area and US after 2001. Journal of Economic Dynamics and Control 32 (8), 2476–2506.

Christoffel, K., Coenen, G., Warne, A., 2008. The new area-wide model of the Euro area: a micro-founded open-economy model for forecasting and policy analysis, ECB Working Paper 944.

Christoffel, K., Coenen, G., Warne, A., 2010. Forecasting with DSGE models, ECB Working Paper 1185.

Clarida, R., Galí, J., Gertler, M., 1998. Monetary policy rules in practice: some international evidence. European Economic Review 42, 1003–1067.

Clarida, R., Galí, J., Gertler, M., 2000. Monetary policy rules and macroeconomic stability: evidence and some theory. Quarterly Journal of Economics 115 (1), 147–180.

Coenen, G., Wieland, V., 2004. Exchange rate policy and the zero bound on nominal interest rates. American Economic Review 94 (2), 80–84.

Cogan, J.F., Cwik, T., Taylor, J.B., Wieland, V., 2010. New Keynesian versus old Keynesian government spending multipliers. Journal of Economic Dynamics and Control 34, 281–295.

Cogan, J.F., Taylor, J.B., Wieland, V., Wolters, M.H., 2013. Fiscal consolidation strategies. Journal of Economic Dynamics and Control 37 (2), 404–421.

de Brouwer, G., Ellis, L., 1998. Forward-looking behaviour and credibility: some evidence and implications for policy, Rerserve Bank of Australia Research Discussion Papers 9803.

Del Negro, M., Schorfheide, F., 2013. DSGE model-based forecasting. In: Elliott, G., Timmermann, A. (Eds.), Handbook of Economic Forecasting, vol. 2. Elsevier.

Drautzburg, T., Uhlig, H., 2011. Fiscal stimulus and distortionary taxation, NBER Working Paper 17111.

Edge, R.M., Gürkaynak, R.S., 2010. How useful are estimated DSGE model forecasts for central bankers? Brookings Papers on Economic Activity, Economic Studies Program, The Brookings Institution 41 (Fall), 209–259.

Edge, R.M., Kiley, M.T., Laforte, J.-P., 2008. Natural rate measures in an estimated DSGE model of the US economy. Journal of Economic Dynamics and Control 32, 2512–2535.

Edge, R.M., Kiley, M.T., Laforte, J.-P., 2010. A comparison of forecast performance between federal reserve staff forecasts, simple reduced form models and a DSGE model. Journal of Applied Econometrics 25 (4), 720–754.

Elliott, G., Komunjer, I., Timmermann, A., 2005. Estimation and testing of forecast rationality under flexible loss. Review of Economic Studies 72, 1107–1125.

English, W.B., Nelson, W.R., Sack, B.P., 2003. Interpreting the significance of the lagged interest rate in estimated monetary policy rules. Contributions to Macroeconomics 4(1), Article 3.

European Central Bank, 2001. A guide to Eurosystem staff macroeconomic projection exercises.

Fagan, G., Henry, J., Mestre, R., 2005. An area-wide model for the Euro area. Economic Modelling 22, 39–59.

Faust, J., Wright, J.H., 2009. Comparing Greenbook and reduced form forecasts using a large realtime dataset. Journal of Business and Economic Statistics 27 (4), 468–479.

Faust, J., Wright, J., 2013. Forecasting inflation. In: Elliott, G., Timmermann, A. (Eds.), Handbook of Economic Forecasting, vol. 2. Elsevier.

Fenton, P., Murchison, S., 2006. ToTEM: the Bank of Canada's new projection and policy-analysis model. Bank of Canada Review Autumn, 5–18.

Fourans, A., Vranceanu, R., 2004. The ECB interest rate rule under the Duisenberg presidency. European Journal of Political Economy 20 (3), 579–595.

Fourans, A., Vranceanu, R., 2007. The ECB monetary policy: choices and challenges. Journal of Policy Modeling 29 (2), 181–194.

Francis, N., Ramey, V.A., 2009. Measures of per capita hours and their implications for the technology-hours debate. Journal of Money, Credit and Banking 41 (6), 1071–1097.

Freedman, C., Kumhof, M., Laxton, D., Muir, D., Mursula, S., 2010. Global effects of fiscal stimulus during the crisis. Journal of Monetary Economics 57, 506–526.

Fuhrer, J.C., 1997. Inflation/output variance trade-offs and optimal monetary policy. Journal of Money, Credit and Banking 29 (2), 214–234.

Fuhrer, J.C., Moore, G., 1995a. Inflation persistence. The Quarterly Journal of Economics 110 (1), 127–159.

Fuhrer, J.C., Moore, G., 1995b. Monetary policy trade-offs and the correlation between nominal interest rates and real output. The American Economic Review 85 (1), 219–239.

Galí, J., 2008. Are central banks' projections meaningful? CEPR Discussion Paper 8027.

Galí, J., Lopez-Salido, D., Valles, J., 2007. Understanding the effects of government spending on consumption. Journal of the European Economic Association 5, 227–270.

Gerdesmeier, D., Roffia, B., 2005. The relevance of real-time data in estimating reaction functions for the Euro area. North American Journal of Economics and Finance 3, 293–307.

Gerlach, S., 2007. Interest rate setting by the ECB, 1999–2006: words and deeds. International Journal of Central Banking 3 (3), 1–45.

Gerlach, S., Schnabel, G., 2000. The Taylor rule and interest rates in the EMU area. Economics Letters 67, 165–171.

Gerlach, S., Tillmann, P. 2012. Inflation targeting and inflation persistence in Asia-Pacific. Journal of Asian Economics 23, 360–373.

Gerlach-Kristen, P., 2004. Interest rates smoothing: monetary policy inertia or unobserved variables? Contributions to Macroeconomics 3(1), Article 5.

Goodfriend, M., King, R., 1997. The New Neoclassical synthesis and the role of monetary policy. In: NBER Macroeconomics Annual 1997, vol. 12. National Bureau of Economic Research, pp. 231–296.

Goodhart, C.A.E., 2009. The interest rate conditioning assumption. International Journal of Central Banking June, 85–108.

Gorter, J., Jacobs, J., de Haan, J., 2008. Taylor rules for the ECB using expectations data. Scandinavian Journal of Economics 110 (3), 473–488.

Greenspan, A., 1994. A discussion of the development of central banking. In: Capie, F., Goodhart, C., Fischer, S., Schnadt, N. (Eds.), The Future of Central Banking. Cambridge University Press, Cambridge.

Haldane, A.G., 1995. Rules, discretion and the United Kingdom's new monetary framework, Bank of England Working Paper No. 40.

Hayo, B., Hofmann, B., 2006. Comparing monetary policy reaction functions: ECB versus Bundesbank. Empirical Economics 31, 645–662.

Judd, J.P., Rudebusch, G.D., 1998. Taylor's rule and the Fed: 1970–1997. Federal Reserve Bank San Francisco Economic Review 3, 3–16.

Juillard, M., 1996. Dynare: a program for the resolution and simulation of dynamic models with forward variables through the use of a relaxation algorithm, CEPREMAP Working Paper 9602.

Juillard, M., 2001. Dynare: a program for the simulation of rational expectation models. Computing in Economics and Finance, 213.

Kimball, M., 1995. The quantitative analytics of the basic monetarist model. Journal of Money, Credit and Banking 27 (4), 1241–1277.

Kohn, D.L., 2007. John Taylor Rules. In: Speech at the Conference on John Taylor's Contributions to Monetary Theory and Policy, Federal Reserve Bank of Dallas, Dallas, Texas, October 12.

Laxton, D., Rose, D., Tetlow, R., 1993. Monetary policy, uncertainty and the presumption of linearity, mimeo. Bank of Canada.

Leeper, E., Zha, T., 2003. Modest policy interventions. Journal of Monetary Economics 50 (8), 1673–1700.

Leiderman, L., Svensson, L.E.O. (Eds.), 1995. Inflation targets. Centre for Economic Policy Research, London.

Levin, A.T., Wieland, V., Williams, J.C., 1999. Robustness of simple monetary policy rules under model uncertainty. In: Taylor, J.B. (Ed.), Monetary Policy Rules. University of Chicago Press, Chicago, pp. 263–299.

Levin, A., Wieland, V., Williams, J.C., 2003. The performance of forecast-based monetary policy rules under model uncertainty. The American Economic Review 93 (3), 622–645.

Lindsey, D., Orphanides, A., Wieland, V., 1997. Monetary policy under Federal Reserve Chairman Volcker and Greenspan: an exercise in description. Manuscript, March.

Lucas, R.E., 1976. Econometric policy evaluation: a critique. Carnegie-Rochester Conference Series on Public Policy 1 (1), 19–46.

Maih, J., 2010. Conditional forecasts in DSGE models, Norges Bank Working Paper No. 2010/07.

Mincer, J., Zarnowitz, V., 1969. The evaluation of economic forecasts. In: Mincer, J. (Ed.), Economic Forecasts and Expectations. NBER, New York.

Murchison, S., Rennison, A., 2006. ToTEM: The Bank of Canada's new quarterly projection model, technical Reports 97. Bank of Canada.

Nobay, A.R., Peel, D.A., 2003. Optimal discretionary monetary policy in a model of asymmetric central bank preferences. The Economic Journal 113, 657–665.

Orphanides, A., 2001. Monetary policy rules based on real-time data. American Economic Review 91, 964–985.

Orphanides, A., van Norden, S., 2002. The unreliability of output gap estimates in real time. Review of Economics and Statistics 84 (4), 569–583.

Orphanides, A., Wieland, V., 2000a. Efficient monetary policy design near price stability. Journal of the Japanese and International Economies 14, 327–365.

Orphanides, A., Wieland, V., 2000b. Inflation zone targeting. European Economic Review 44 (7), 1351–1387.

Orphanides, A., Wieland, V., 2008. Economic projections and rules of thumb for monetary policy. Federal Reserve Bank of St. Louis Review 90 (4), 307–324.

Paez-Farrell, J., 2010. Resuscitating the ad hoc loss function for monetary policy analysis. Working Paper Loughborough University.

Patton, A.J., Timmermann, A., 2007. Testing forecast optimality under unknown loss. Journal of the American Statistical Association 102, 1172–1184.

Poole, W., 1971. Rules-of-thumb for guiding monetary policy. In: Open Market Policies and Operating Procedures—Staff Studies. Board of Governors of the Federal Reserve System, Washington, DC.

Poole, W., 2007. Understanding the Fed. Federal Reserve Bank of St. Louis Review 89 (1), 3–13.

Ratto, M., Roeger, W., in 't Veld, J., 2009. QUEST III: an estimated open-economy DSGE model of the Euro area with fiscal and monetary policy. Economic Modelling 26 (1), 222–233.

Reifschneider, D.L., Stockton, D.J., Wilcox, D.W., 1997. Econometric models and the monetary policy process. Carnegie-Rochester Conference Series on Public Policy 47, 1–37.

Reifschneider, D., Tetlow, R., Williams, J.C., 1999. Aggregate disturbances, monetary policy and the macroeconomy: The FRB/US perspective. Federal Reserve Bulletin 85 (1), 1–19.

Robertson, J.C., 2000. Central bank forecasting: An international comparison. Economic Review Q2, 21–32.

Roeger, W., in 'tVeld, J., 2010. Fiscal stimulus and exit strategies in the EU: a model-based analysis. European Economy, Economic Papers no 426.

Romer, C., Bernstein, J., 2009. The job impact of the American Recovery and Reinvestment Plan, January 8.

Rotemberg, J.J., Woodford, M., 1997. An optimization-based econometric framework for the evaluation of monetary policy. NBER Macroeconomics Annual 12, 297–346.

Rudebusch, G.D., 2002. Term structure evidence on interest rate smoothing and monetary policy inertia. Journal of Monetary Economics 49, 1161–1187.

Rudebusch, G.D., Svensson, L.E.O., 1999. Policy rules for inflation targeting. In: Taylor, J.B. (Ed.), Monetary Policy Rules. Chicago University Press, Chicago, pp. 203–246.

Sack, B., Wieland, V., 2000. Interest-rate smoothing and optimal monetary policy: a review of recent empirical evidence. Journal of Economics and Business 52 (1–2), 205–228.

Sauer, S., Sturm, J.-E., 2007. Using Taylor rules to understand European Central Bank monetary policy. German Economic Review 8 (3), 375–398.

Schmidt, S., Wieland, V., 2012. The New Keynesian approach to Dynamic General Equilibrium Modeling: Models, methods and macroeconomic policy evalation. In: Dixon, P.B., Jorgenson, D.W. (Eds.), Handbook of Computable General Equilibrium Modeling, vol. 1. Elsevier. (Chapter 22).

Schmitt-Grohé, S., Uribe, M., 2007. Optimal simple and implementable monetary and fiscal rules. Journal of Monetary Economics 54, 1702–1725.

Schorfheide, F., Sill, K., Kryshko, M., 2010. DSGE model-based forecasting of non-modelled variables. International Journal of Forecasting 26 (2), 348–373.

Slobodyan, S., Wouters, R., 2009. Estimating a medium-scale DSGE model with expectations based on small forecasting models, mimeo. CERGE-EI and National Bank of Belgium.

Slobodyan, S., Wouters, R., 2012. Learning in an estimated medium-scale DSGE model. Journal of Economic Dynamics and Control 36 (1), 26–46.

Smets, F., Wouters, R., 2003. An estimated dynamic stochastic general equilibrium model of the Euro area. Journal of the European Economic Association. 5 (09), 1123–1175.

Smets, F., Wouters, R., 2004. Forecasting with a Bayesian DSGE model: an application to the Euro area. Journal of Common Market Studies 42 (4), 841–867.

Smets, F., Wouters, R., 2007. Shocks and frictions in US business cycles: a Bayesian DSGE approach. The American Economic Review 97 (3), 586–606.

Smets, F., Christoffel, K., Coenen, G., Motto, R., Rostagno, M., 2010. DSGE models and their use at the ECB. Journal of the Spanish Economic Association 1 (1–2), 51–65.

Stock, J., Watson, M.W., 2007. Why has US inflation become harder to forecast? Journal of Money, Credit and Banking 39 (1), 3–33.

Surico, P., 2007. The fed's monetary policy rule and US inflation: the case of asymmetric preferences. Journal of Economic Dynamics and Control 31, 305–324.

Svensson, L.E.O., 1997. Inflation forecast targeting: implementing and monitoring inflation targets. European Economic Review 41 (6), 1111–1146.

Svensson, L.E.O., 1999. Inflation targeting as a monetary policy rule. Journal of Monetary Economics 43 (3), 607–654.

Svensson, L.E.O., 2003. What is wrong with Taylor rules? Using judgment in monetary policy through targeting rules. Journal of Economic Literature 41, 426–477.

Svensson, L.E., 2010. Inflation targeting. In: Friedman, B.M., Woodford, M. (Eds.), Handbook of Monetary Economics, vol. 3. Elsevier, pp. 1237–1302 (Chapter 22).

Svensson, L.E.O., 2011. Practical monetary policy: examples from Sweden and the United States. Brookings Papers on Economic Activity Fall, 289–332.

Taylor, J.B., 1993. Discretion versus policy rules in practice. Carnegie-Rochester Conference Series on Public Policy 39, 195–214.

Taylor, J., 1997. Econometric models and the monetary policy process. A comment. Carnegie-Rochester Conference Series on Public Policy 47, 39–42.

Taylor, J.B., 1999. A historical analysis of monetary policy rules. In: Taylor, J.B. (Ed.), Monetary Policy Rules. Chicago University Press, Chicago.

Taylor, J.B., Wieland, V., 2012. Surprising comparative properties of monetary models: Results from a new monetary model base. Review of Economics and Statistics 94 (3), 800–816.

Theil, H., 1958. Economic Forecasts and Policy. North-Holland, Amsterdam.

Timmermann, A., 2006. Forecast combinations. In: Elliott, G., Granger, C.W.J., Timmermann, A. (Eds.), Handbook of Economic Forecasting. North Holland, Amsterdam, pp. 135–196.

Tinbergen, J., 1952. Contributions to Economic Analysis, On the Theory of Economic Policy, vol. I. Amsterdam.

Tinsley, P., 1993. Fitting both data and theories: polynominal adjustment costs and error-correction decision rules, FEDS Working Paper 93–21.

Wang, M.-C., 2009. Comparing the DSGE model with the factor model: an out-of-sample forecasting experiment. Journal of Forecasting 28 (2), 167–182.

Wieland, V., 2010. Quantitative easing: A rationale and some evidence from Japan. In: Reichlin, L., West, K. (Eds.), NBER International Seminar on Macroeconomics 2009. NBER and University of Chicago Press.

Wieland, V., Wolters, M.H., 2011. The diversity of forecasts from macroeconomic models of the US economy. Economic Theory 47 (2–3), 247–292.

Wieland, V., Cwik, T., Müller, G.J., Schmidt, S., Wolters, M.H., 2012. A new comparative approach to macroeconomic modeling and policy analysis. Journal of Economic Behavior and Organization 83 (3), 523–541.

Woodford, M., 2003. Interest and Prices: Foundations of a Theory of Monetary Policy. Princeton University Press.

Woodford, M., 2007. The case for forecast targeting as a monetary policy strategy. Journal of Economic Perspectives 21 (4), 3–24.

Woodford, M., 2011. Principled policymaking in an uncertain world. Mimeo, Columbia University.

Forecasting Financial Variables

CHAPTER 6

Forecasting Stock Returns

David Rapach[*] and Guofu Zhou[†]

[*]John Cook School of Business, Saint Louis University, 3674 Lindell Boulevard, St. Louis, MO 63108, USA
[†]Olin School of Business, Washington University in St. Louis, St. Louis, MO 63130, USA

Contents

Abstract

We survey the literature on stock return forecasting, highlighting the challenges faced by forecasters as well as strategies for improving return forecasts. We focus on U.S. equity premium forecastability and illustrate key issues via an empirical application based on updated data. Some studies argue that, despite extensive in-sample evidence of equity premium predictability, popular predictors from the literature fail to outperform the simple historical average benchmark forecast in out-of-sample tests. Recent studies, however, provide improved forecasting strategies that deliver statistically and economically significant out-of-sample gains relative to the historical average benchmark. These strategies – including economically motivated model restrictions, forecast combination, diffusion indices, and regime shifts – improve forecasting performance by addressing the substantial model uncertainty and parameter instability surrounding the data-generating process for stock returns. In addition to the U.S. equity premium, we succinctly survey out-of-sample evidence supporting U.S. cross-sectional and international stock return forecastability. The significant evidence of stock return forecastability

Handbook of Economic Forecasting, Volume 2A
ISSN 1574-0706, http://dx.doi.org/10.1016/B978-0-444-53683-9.00006-4

worldwide has important implications for the development of both asset pricing models and investment management strategies.

Keywords

Equity premium, Economic variables, Technical indicators, Forecast combination, Diffusion index, Regime shifts, Asset pricing model, Asset allocation, Business cycle

1. INTRODUCTION

Forecasting stock returns is a fascinating endeavor with a long history. From the standpoint of practitioners in finance, asset allocation requires real-time forecasts of stock returns, and improved stock return forecasts hold the promise of enhancing investment performance. It is thus not surprising that finance practitioners employ a plethora of variables in an attempt to forecast stock returns. Academics in finance are also keenly interested in stock return forecasts, since the ability to forecast returns has important implications for tests of market efficiency; more generally, understanding the nature of stock return forecastability helps researchers to produce more realistic asset pricing models that better explain the data.

While stock return forecasting is fascinating, it can also be frustrating. Stock returns inherently contain a sizable unpredictable component, so that the best forecasting models can explain only a relatively small part of stock returns. Furthermore, competition among traders implies that once successful forecasting models are discovered, they will be readily adopted by others; the widespread adoption of successful forecasting models can then cause stock prices to move in a manner that eliminates the models' forecasting ability (e.g., Lo, 2004; Timmermann and Granger, 2004; Timmermann, 2008). However, rational asset pricing theory posits that stock return predictability can result from exposure to time-varying aggregate risk, and to the extent that successful forecasting models consistently capture this time-varying aggregate risk premium, they will likely remain successful over time.

Along this line, there is a common misconception that stock return predictability is contrary to market efficiency. The canonical random walk model, used historically by many modelers and popularized to the broader public by Malkiel (1973, 2011), implies that future stock returns are unpredictable on the basis of currently available information. While the random walk model is consistent with market efficiency, so is a predictable return process, insofar as predictability is consistent with exposure to time-varying aggregate risk. According to the well-known Campbell and Shiller (1988a) present-value decomposition, deviations in the dividend-price ratio from its long-term mean signal changes in expected future dividend growth rates and/or expected future stock returns; changes in the latter represent time-varying discount rates and return predictability.[1] In this context, fluctuations in aggregate risk exposure that produce time-varying discount

---

[1] See Koijen and Van Nieuwerburgh (2011) for a survey on the relationship between the present-value identity and stock return predictability.

rates and return predictability are entirely compatible with market efficiency. In other words, only when the risk-adjusted time-varying expected return – after further adjusting for transaction costs and other trading frictions (e.g., liquidity and borrowing constraints, research costs) – is nonzero can we say that a market is inefficient.

Theoretically, asset returns are functions of the state variables of the real economy, and the real economy itself displays significant business-cycle fluctuations. If the quantity and price of aggregate risk are linked to economic fluctuations, then we should expect time-varying expected returns and return predictability, even in an efficient market. For instance, if agents become more risk averse during economic contractions when consumption and income levels are depressed, then they will require a higher expected return on stocks near business-cycle troughs to be willing to take on the risk associated with holding stocks; variables that measure and/or predict the state of the economy should thus help to predict returns (e.g., Fama and French, 1989; Campbell and Cochrane, 1999; Cochrane, 2007, 2011). Indeed, an important theme of this chapter is that stock return predictability is closely tied to business-cycle fluctuations.

While rational asset pricing is consistent with return predictability, theory does impose certain bounds on the maximum degree of return predictability that is consistent with asset pricing models. To the extent that return predictability exceeds these bounds, this can be interpreted as evidence for mispricing or market inefficiencies stemming from, for example, information processing limitations and/or the types of psychological influences emphasized in behavioral finance. Since information processing limitations and psychological influences are likely to be exacerbated during rapidly changing economic conditions, return predictability resulting from market inefficiencies is also likely linked to business-cycle fluctuations.

The degree of stock return predictability is ultimately an empirical issue. There is ample in-sample evidence that U.S. aggregate stock market returns are predictable using a variety of economic variables. While thorny econometric issues complicate statistical inference, such as the well-known Stambaugh (1986, 1999) bias, there is an apparent consensus among financial economists that, on the basis of in-sample tests, stock returns contain a significant predictable component (Campbell, 2000). Bossaerts and Hillion (1999) and Goyal and Welch (2003, 2008), however, find that the predictive ability of a variety of popular economic variables from the literature does not hold up in *out-of-sample* forecasting exercises, a finding eerily reminiscent of Meese and Rogoff (1983) in the context of exchange rate predictability. Under the widely held view that predictive models require out-of-sample validation,[2] this finding casts doubt on the reliability of stock return predictability.

The unreliability of return predictability, however, can result from the econometric methods themselves; as pointed out by Lamoureux and Zhou (1996), many studies of return predictability implicitly use a strong prior on predictability. Moreover, in

---

[2] Campbell (2008, p. 3) succinctly expresses the prevailing view: "The ultimate test of any predictive model is its out-of-sample performance."

highlighting the importance of out-of-sample tests for analyzing return predictability, Pesaran and Timmermann (1995) demonstrate the relevance of *model uncertainty* and *parameter instability* for stock return forecasting. Model uncertainty recognizes that a forecaster knows neither the "best" model specification nor its corresponding parameter values. Furthermore, due to parameter instability, the best model can change over time. Given the connection between business-cycle fluctuations and stock return predictability, it is not surprising that model uncertainty and parameter instability are highly relevant for stock return forecasting, as these factors are also germane to macroeconomic forecasting.

The substantial model uncertainty and parameter instability surrounding the data-generating process for stock returns render out-of-sample return predictability challenging to uncover. Fortunately, recent studies provide forecasting strategies that deliver statistically and economically significant out-of-sample gains, including strategies based on:

- *economically motivated model restrictions* (e.g., Campbell and Thompson, 2008; Ferreira and Santa-Clara, 2011);
- *forecast combination* (e.g., Rapach et al., 2010);
- *diffusion indices* (e.g., Ludvigson and Ng, 2007; Kelly and Pruitt, forthcoming; Neely et al., 2012);
- *regime shifts* (e.g., Guidolin and Timmermann, 2007; Henkel et al., 2011; Dangl and Halling, 2012).

These forecasting strategies produce out-of-sample gains largely by accommodating model uncertainty and parameter instability. We focus on these strategies in this chapter, discussing their implementation and how they improve stock return forecasts.

We illustrate relevant issues concerning the formation and evaluation of stock return forecasts via an empirical application based on forecasting the U.S. equity premium with updated data. In addition to significantly outperforming the simple historical average benchmark forecast according to the conventional mean squared forecast error (MSFE) statistical criterion, we show that the forecasting approaches cited above generate sizable utility gains from an asset allocation perspective.

Although we present the leading themes of this chapter in the context of forecasting the U.S. equity premium, we also survey the evidence on stock return forecastability in international markets. Ang and Bekaert (2007) provide compelling in-sample evidence of stock return predictability for France, Germany, the United Kingdom, and the United States. We discuss recent studies that furnish out-of-sample evidence of return predictability for these and other industrialized countries. In addition, we survey studies that explore out-of-sample stock return predictability along cross-sectional dimensions, including portfolios sorted by size, book-to-market value, and industry.[3]

While stock return forecasting will always be extremely challenging – and we will likely never explain more than a small part of returns – the take-away message of this

---

[3] While not focusing on forecasting *per se*, Hawawini and Keim (1995) and Subrahmanyam (2010) provide informative surveys on international and cross-sectional stock return predictability.

chapter is that methods are available for reliably improving stock return forecasts in an economically meaningful manner. Consequently, investors who account for stock return predictability with available forecasting procedures significantly outperform those who treat returns as entirely unpredictable.

The remainder of this chapter is organized as follows. Section 2 provides a benchmark by discussing the degree of stock return predictability that we should expect theoretically in a predictive regression framework. Section 3 surveys the literature on U.S. aggregate stock market return forecastability; this section also contains the empirical application based on forecasting the U.S. equity premium. Section 4 discusses the evidence on stock return forecastability in international and cross-sectional contexts. Section 5 concludes.

2. WHAT LEVEL OF PREDICTABILITY SHOULD WE EXPECT?

Stock return predictability is typically examined via the following predictive regression model:

$$r_{t+1} = \alpha + \beta x_t + \epsilon_{t+1}, \tag{1}$$

where r_{t+1} is the return on a broad stock market index in excess of the risk-free interest rate (or equity premium or excess stock return) from the end of period t to the end of period $t + 1$, x_t is a variable available at the end of t used to predict the equity premium (such as the dividend-price ratio), and ϵ_{t+1} is a zero-mean disturbance term. Given an asset pricing model, how much predictability should we expect in (1)?

An asset pricing model is almost always uniquely determined by its stochastic discount factor (SDF, or state-price density or pricing kernel), which is a random variable m_{t+1} that satisfies

$$E(R_{j,t+1}m_{t+1}|I_t) = 1, \quad j = 1, \ldots, N, \tag{2}$$

where $R_{j,t+1}$ is the gross return on asset j and I_t is the information available at t. A particular asset pricing model entails a specification of m_{t+1} (e.g., Cochrane, 2005).[4] Assume that the risk-free rate is constant; this assumption is not a problem, since the risk-free rate changes little relative to stock returns. Ross (2005, p. 56) shows that the regression R^2 in (1) has an elegant upper bound:

$$R^2 \leq R_f^2 \text{Var}(m_t), \tag{3}$$

where R_f is the (gross) risk-free rate and m_t is the SDF for a given asset pricing model. Following Ross (2005) by using an annualized risk-free rate of 3.5%, an annualized standard deviation of 20% for the U.S. aggregate stock market, and an upper bound on market risk aversion equaling five times the observed market risk aversion on asset returns, the R^2 bound in (3) is approximately 8% for monthly returns. This bound, however, is

---

[4] The SDF corresponds to the representative investor's intertemporal marginal rate of substitution in consumption–based asset pricing models.

too loose to be binding in applications. For example, in their well-known study, Fama and French (1988) report monthly R^2 statistics of 1% or less for predictive regression models based on dividend-price ratios, and Zhou (2010) reports monthly R^2 statistics of less than 1% for individual predictive regressions based on 10 popular economic variables from the literature.

Incorporating insights from Kan and Zhou (2007), Zhou (2010) refines the Ross (2005) R^2 bound so that it is more relevant for empirical research. The default SDF, which, by construction, also satisfies (2) and thus prices the N risky assets, is given by

$$m_{0,t} = \mu_m + (1_N - \mu_m\mu)'\Sigma^{-1}(R_t - \mu), \tag{4}$$

where R_t is the vector of gross returns on the N risky assets, μ (Σ) is the mean vector (covariance matrix) for R_t, $E(m_t) = \mu_m$, and 1_N is an N-vector of ones.[5] Let $z_t = (z_{1,t}, \ldots, z_{K,t})'$ denote a K-vector of state variables corresponding to a specific asset pricing model and consider the following linear regression model:

$$m_{0,t} = a + b'z_t + e_t, \tag{5}$$

where b is a K-vector of slope coefficients. For a linear regression model, we have $E(e_t) = 0$ and $\text{Cov}(e_t, z_t) = 0$, by construction. Under the slightly stronger assumption that $E(e_t|z_t) = 0$,[6] Zhou (2010) proves the following result, which tightens the Ross (2005) bound:

$$R^2 \le \rho^2_{z,m_0} R^2_f \text{Var}[m_t(z_t)], \tag{6}$$

where ρ_{z,m_0} is the multiple correlation between the state variables z_t and the default SDF $m_{0,t}$. This R^2 bound thus improves the Ross (2005) bound by a factor of ρ^2_{z,m_0}. Since ρ_{z,m_0} is typically small in practice, the reduction in the R^2 bound is substantial. For example, Kan and Zhou (2007) report ρ_{z,m_0} values ranging from 0.10 to 0.15 using either the aggregate market portfolio or 25 Fama–French size/value-sorted portfolios for R_t in (4) and consumption growth and the surplus consumption ratio as the state variables in (5), where the latter correspond to the state variables for the well-known Campbell and Cochrane (1999) consumption-based asset pricing model with habit formation. For these ρ_{z,m_0} values and Ross's (2005) assumptions, the R^2 bound ranges from 0.08% to 0.18%. These values for the R^2 bound are so low that predictive regressions based on a number of popular predictors – even though they have monthly R^2 statistics of 1% or less – actually violate the theoretical bounds implied by the Campbell and Cochrane (1999) model.

The upshot of this analysis is that, from the perspective of asset pricing models, we should expect only a limited degree of stock return predictability. Indeed, a seemingly

---

[5] We assume that μ is not proportional to 1_N and that the N risky assets are not redundant (so that Σ is non-singular).
[6] This assumption does not appear to be too restrictive. A sufficient condition for $E(e_t|z_t) = 0$ is that the returns and state variables are jointly elliptically distributed. The t-distribution is a special case of the elliptical distribution, and Tu and Zhou (2004) show that the t-distribution fits return data well.

"small" monthly R^2 of 1% or less can nevertheless signal "too much" return predictability and the existence of market inefficiencies from the standpoint of existing asset pricing models. Predictive models that claim to explain a large part of stock return fluctuations imply either that existing asset pricing models are grossly incorrect or that massive market inefficiencies exist (along with substantial risk-adjusted abnormal returns); both of these implications appear unlikely. In general, such high return predictability is simply too good to be true and should be viewed with appropriate suspicion. This does not mean that we should throw up our hands and give up on stock return forecasting; instead, it means that the ability to forecast even a seemingly small part of stock return fluctuations on a reasonably consistent basis is no mean feat.

Furthermore, as shown asymptotically by Inoue and Kilian (2004) and in Monte Carlo simulations by Cochrane (2008), if our ultimate aim is to determine whether we can reject the null hypothesis that the population parameter $\beta \neq 0$ in (1), in-sample tests will typically be more powerful than out-of-sample tests. Intuitively, unlike in-sample tests, out-of-sample tests cannot utilize the entire available sample when estimating the parameters used to generate return predictions; in-sample tests inherently make more observations available for estimating parameters, thereby increasing estimation efficiency and test power.[7] The greater number of available observations for in-sample parameter estimation can also lead to higher in-sample R^2 statistics relative to out-of-sample R^2 statistics (Campbell and Thompson, 2008). The monthly R^2 statistics in the neighborhood of 1% cited previously in the context of the R^2 bound refer to in-sample estimation of predictive regressions. Out-of-sample R^2 statistics will frequently be even lower, reiterating the fundamental notion that we should expect only a limited degree of stock return forecastability.

Although we should expect a limited degree of stock return forecastability, it is important to realize that a little goes a long way. That is, even an apparently small degree of return predictability can translate into substantial utility gains for a risk-averse investor who does not affect market prices (e.g., Kandel and Stambaugh, 1996; Xu, 2004; Campbell and Thompson, 2008). We illustrate this for U.S. equity premium forecasts in Section 3.

3. U.S. AGGREGATE STOCK MARKET RETURN FORECASTABILITY

This section first provides an overview of the academic literature on aggregate U.S. stock market return forecastability, highlighting recently proposed strategies for significantly improving stock return forecasts. After discussing key issues involving the evaluation of

---

[7] If we are interested in testing the null hypothesis that return predictability exists at some point in the sample, Clark and McCracken (2005) show that out-of-sample tests can be more powerful than conventional in-sample tests in the presence of structural breaks near the end of the sample; also see Rossi (2005). We discuss the importance of accounting for structural breaks when forecasting stock returns in Section 3. See the chapter by Barbara Rossi in this volume for a detailed survey of recent advances in forecasting in the presence of structural breaks.

stock return forecasts, it presents the empirical application based on forecasting the U.S. equity premium using updated data. The empirical application illustrates a number of relevant issues regarding the formation and evaluation of stock return forecasts.

3.1. Overview of Return Forecastability

Academic investigation of U.S. aggregate stock market return forecastability begins with Cowles's (1933) seminal paper, "Can Stock Market Forecasters Forecast?" Cowles (1933) constructs a portfolio using Dow Jones industrial average (DJIA) market index forecasts made in editorials by William Peter Hamilton during his 26-year (1903–1929) tenure as editor of the *Wall Street Journal*. Hamilton bases his forecasts on Charles Dow's then-popular Dow Theory – a type of technical analysis – of which Hamilton was a strong proponent. The portfolio based on Hamilton's forecasts generates a lower annualized average return than a buy-and-hold portfolio based on the DJIA (12% and 15.5%, respectively). Similarly, Cowles (1933) finds that portfolios based on broad market recommendations from 24 individual financial publications for 1928–1932 fail to outperform a passive investment in the DJIA by 4% on average on an annualized basis. Cowles (1933) also concludes that the performances of the most successful of the 24 individual portfolios do not differ substantially from what would be expected from pure chance.[8] In sum, Cowles (1933) answers the question posed in his title in the negative.

A spate of prominent studies during the 1960s examines the forecasting power of various technical indicators, including popular filter rules, moving averages, and momentum oscillators. Technical indicators seek to provide insights into future returns on the basis of patterns in past prices. Analyzing a variety of broad market indices, Alexander (1961, 1964) reports that portfolios based on certain filter rules earn higher returns than buy-and-hold portfolios that invest in the indices. However, after switching the focus from broad market indices to individual stocks, studies by Cootner (1962), Fama and Blume (1966), and Jensen and Benington (1970), among others, present evidence that portfolios constructed from filter rules (and technical indicators more generally) frequently fail to outperform buy-and-hold portfolios, especially after accounting for transaction costs. These negative findings proved influential in the ascendancy of the efficient market hypothesis – in the form of the random walk model – among academic researchers, as epitomized by Fama's (1970) influential survey and the first edition of Malkiel's (1973) book, *A Random Walk Down Wall Street*.[9]

---

[8] In an early – and labor-intensive – Monte Carlo experiment, Cowles (1933) simulates random recommendations by randomly drawing numbered cards to reach this conclusion.

[9] More recent studies, including Brock et al. (1992), Brown et al. (1998), Lo et al. (2000), and Neely et al. (2012), provide evidence that certain technical indicators provide useful signals for forecasting stock returns. However, using White's (2000) "reality check" bootstrap, Sullivan et al. (1999, 2001) show that data snooping can account for some of the predictive ability of technical indicators. (We discuss data snooping in more detail in Section 3.4.) See Park and Irwin (2007) for a survey of the technical analysis literature.

Starting in the late 1970s, a vast literature compiles evidence that numerous economic variables predict monthly, quarterly, and/or annual U.S. aggregate stock returns in the predictive regression framework given by (1). The most popular predictor in this literature is the dividend–price ratio (Rozeff, 1984; Campbell and Shiller, 1988a, 1998; Fama and French, 1988, 1989; Cochrane, 2008; Lettau and Van Nieuwerburgh, 2008; Pástor and Stambaugh, 2009). Other economic variables that evince predictive ability include the earnings–price ratio (Campbell and Shiller, 1988b, 1998), book-to-market ratio (Kothari and Shanken, 1997; Pontiff and Schall, 1998), nominal interest rates (Fama and Schwert, 1977; Breen et al., 1989; Ang and Bekaert, 2007), interest rate spreads (Campbell, 1987; Fama and French, 1989), inflation (Nelson, 1976; Campbell and Vuolteenaho, 2004), dividend-payout ratio (Lamont, 1998), corporate issuing activity (Baker and Wurgler, 2000; Boudoukh et al., 2007), consumption-wealth ratio (Lettau and Ludvigson, 2001), stock market volatility (Guo, 2006), labor income (Santos and Veronesi, 2006), aggregate output (Rangvid, 2006), output gap (Cooper and Priestly, 2009), expected business conditions (Campbell and Diebold, 2009), oil prices (Driesprong et al., 2008), lagged industry portfolio returns (Hong et al., 2007), and accruals (Hirshleifer et al., 2009).[10] Fama's (1991) sequel survey reflects the growing evidence for stock return predictability in predictive regressions. This evidence also spurred the development of general equilibrium asset pricing models that feature rational time-varying expected returns (e.g., Campbell and Cochrane, 1999; Bansal and Yaron, 2004).

The evidence for U.S. aggregate stock return predictability is predominantly in-sample. In-sample tests of return predictability in the context of predictive regressions are complicated by the well-known Stambaugh (1986, 1999) bias. This bias arises when the predictor is highly persistent and the predictor and return innovations are correlated. Importantly, the Stambaugh bias potentially leads to substantial size distortions when testing the null hypothesis of no predictability, $\beta = 0$, using a conventional t-statistic approach. A number of studies develop procedures for improving inference in predictive regressions with persistent predictors, including Amihud and Hurvich (2004), Lewellen (2004), Torous et al. (2005), Campbell and Yogo (2006), Amihud et al. (2009), and Pástor and Stambaugh (2009).[11] Furthermore, the evidence for stock return predictability using valuation ratios frequently appears stronger at longer horizons. Studies investigating long-horizon predictability typically employ overlapping return observations. Overlapping observations induce severe serial correlation in the disturbance term in predictive regressions, potentially creating additional size distortions in conventional tests. Studies that analyze the statistical implications of predictive regressions with overlapping returns and develop econometric procedures for making more reliable inferences include Hodrick (1992), Goetzmann and Jorion (1993), Nelson and Kim (1993), Valkanov (2003), Boudoukh et al. (2008), Britten-Jones et al. (2011), and Hjalmarsson (2011).

---

[10] The cited studies are representative and do not constitute an exhaustive list.

[11] Cavanaugh et al. (1995) is an important precursor to studies of predictive regressions with persistent predictors.

Despite the formidable econometric difficulties surrounding in-sample predictive regression tests, Campbell (2000, p. 1512) observes that "most financial economists appear to have accepted that aggregate returns do contain an important predictable component."

Bossaerts and Hillion (1999), Goyal and Welch (2003, 2008), Brennan and Xia (2005), and Butler et al. (2005) argue that the in-sample evidence of return predictability is not robust to out-of-sample validation. The study by Goyal and Welch (2008), which won the 2008 Michael Brennan Best Paper Award for the *Review of Financial Studies*, has been especially influential in this regard. Considering a variety of economic variables from the literature, Goyal and Welch (2008) show that out-of-sample equity premium forecasts based on the bivariate predictive regression, (1), fail to consistently outperform the simple historical average benchmark forecast in terms of MSFE. The historical average forecast assumes that $\beta = 0$ in (1) and corresponds to the constant expected equity premium (or random walk with drift) model, implying that the information in x_t is not useful for predicting the equity premium. A multiple regression forecasting model that includes all potential predictors – the "kitchen sink" forecast – also performs much worse than the historical average forecast; this is not surprising, since it is well known that, due to in-sample overfitting, highly parameterized models typically perform very poorly in out-of-sample forecasting. Overall, Goyal and Welch (2008) conclude that predictive regressions are unstable and that conventional forecasting models fail to outperform the historical average.

Fortunately, a collection of recent studies shows that certain forecasting approaches improve upon conventional predictive regression forecasts and significantly outperform the historical average forecast in out-of-sample tests. These approaches improve forecasting performance by addressing the substantial model uncertainty and parameter instability characterizing the data-generating process for stock returns.

3.1.1. Economically Motivated Model Restrictions

The first approach for improving forecasting performance imposes economically motivated restrictions on predictive regression forecasts of stock returns. Recall the bivariate predictive regression model given by (1),

$$r_{t+1} = \alpha_i + \beta_i x_{i,t} + \epsilon_{i,t+1}, \tag{7}$$

where r_{t+1} is now the log excess stock return and the i subscript indexes one of K potential return predictors ($i = 1, \ldots, K$). An equity premium forecast based on (7) is naturally computed as

$$\hat{r}_{i,t+1} = \hat{\alpha}_{i,t} + \hat{\beta}_{i,t} x_{i,t}, \tag{8}$$

where $\hat{\alpha}_{i,t}$ and $\hat{\beta}_{i,t}$ are ordinary least squares (OLS) estimates of α_i and β_i, respectively, in (7) based on data from the start of the available sample through t. As discussed in Section 2, since out-of-sample forecasts can only utilize data up to the time of forecast formation, these parameter estimates will be less efficient than their in-sample counterparts.

The limited available estimation sample – and given that stock returns contain a sizable unpredictable component – means that the forecasting model parameters are potentially very imprecisely estimated, which can lead to poor forecasting performance. In response, Campbell and Thompson (2008) recommend imposing sign restrictions on $\hat{\beta}_{i,t}$ and $\hat{r}_{i,t+1}$ in (8). In particular, theory typically suggests the sign of β_i in (7); if $\hat{\beta}_{i,t}$ has an unexpected sign, then we set $\hat{\beta}_{i,t} = 0$ in (8) when forming the forecast. In addition, risk considerations usually imply a positive expected equity premium, so that we set the forecast equal to zero if $\hat{r}_{i,t+1} < 0$ in (8). Such sign restrictions reduce parameter estimation uncertainty and help to stabilize predictive regression forecasts. Campbell and Thompson (2008) find that, in contrast to unrestricted bivariate predictive regression forecasts, restricted predictive regression forecasts based on a number of economic variables outperform the historical average forecast.

Campbell and Thompson (2008), Campbell (2008), and Ferreira and Santa-Clara (2011) consider other types of restrictions on stock return forecasts involving valuation ratios. We focus on Santa-Clara's (2011) sum-of-the-parts method. By definition, the gross return on a broad market index is

$$R_{t+1} = \frac{P_{t+1} + D_{t+1}}{P_t} = CG_{t+1} + DY_{t+1}, \tag{9}$$

where P_t is the stock price, D_t is the dividend, $CG_{t+1} = P_{t+1}/P_t$ is the gross capital gain, and $DY_{t+1} = D_{t+1}/P_t$ is the dividend yield. The gross capital gain can be expressed as

$$CG_{t+1} = \frac{(P_{t+1}/E_{t+1})}{(P_t/E_t)} \frac{E_{t+1}}{E_t} = \frac{M_{t+1}}{M_t} \frac{E_{t+1}}{E_t} = GM_{t+1} GE_{t+1}, \tag{10}$$

where E_t denotes earnings, $M_t = P_t/E_t$ is the price-earnings multiple, and $GM_{t+1} = M_{t+1}/M_t$ ($GE_{t+1} = E_{t+1}/E_t$) is the gross growth rate of the price-earnings multiple (earnings). Using (10), the dividend yield can be written as

$$DY_{t+1} = \frac{D_{t+1}}{P_{t+1}} \frac{P_{t+1}}{P_t} = DP_{t+1} GM_{t+1} GE_{t+1}, \tag{11}$$

where $DP_t = D_t/P_t$ is the dividend-price ratio. Based on (10) and (11), the gross return in (9) becomes

$$R_{t+1} = GM_{t+1} GE_{t+1} (1 + DP_{t+1}), \tag{12}$$

which for the log return can be expressed as

$$\log(R_{t+1}) = gm_{t+1} + ge_{t+1} + dp_{t+1}, \tag{13}$$

where gm_{t+1} (ge_{t+1}) is the log growth rate of the price-earnings multiple (earnings) and dp_t is the log of one plus the dividend-price ratio.

Ferreira and Santa-Clara (2011) use (13) as the basis for a stock return forecast. Since price-earnings multiples and dividend-price ratios are highly persistent and nearly random walks, reasonable forecasts of gm_{t+1} and dp_{t+1} based on information through t are zero and dp_t, respectively. Earnings growth is nearly entirely unpredictable, apart from a low-frequency component (van Binsbergen and Koijen, 2010), so that Ferreira and Santa-Clara (2011) employ a 20-year moving average of log earnings growth through t, $\overline{ge}_t^{20}$, as a forecast of ge_{t+1}. Their sum-of-the-parts equity premium forecast is then given by

$$\hat{r}_{t+1}^{SOP} = \overline{ge}_t^{20} + dp_t - r_{f,t+1}, \tag{14}$$

where $r_{f,t+1}$ is the log risk-free rate, which is known at the end of t.[12] Comparing (14) to (8), it is evident that the sum-of-the-parts forecast is a predictive regression forecast that restricts the slope coefficient to unity for $x_{i,t} = dp_t$ and sets the intercept to $\overline{ge}_t^{20} - r_{f,t+1}$.[13] Ferreira and Santa-Clara (2011) show that their sum-of-the-parts forecast significantly outperforms the historical average forecast. Furthermore, Monte Carlo simulations indicate that the sum-of-the-parts forecast improves upon conventional predictive regression forecasts by substantially reducing estimation error.

Bayesian approaches provide another avenue for incorporating economically reasonable restrictions via prior views. Along this line, a number of important studies, including Kandel and Stambaugh (1996), Barberis (2000), Wachter and Warusawitharana (2009), and Pástor and Stambaugh (2012), employ Bayesian methods to examine the implications of prior views on return predictability and estimation risk for optimal portfolio choice. An important result emerging from these studies is that return predictability significantly affects asset allocation, even for investors with relatively skeptical priors beliefs on the existence of return predictability.

3.1.2. Forecast Combination

Rapach et al. (2010) consider another approach for improving equity premium forecasts based on forecast combination. Since Bates and Granger's (1969) seminal paper, it has been know that combining forecasts across models often produces a forecast that performs better than the best individual model. As emphasized by Timmermann (2006), forecast combination can be viewed as a diversification strategy that improves forecasting performance in the same manner that asset diversification improves portfolio performance. Intuitively, from the standpoint of equity premium forecasting, particular forecasting models capture different aspects of business conditions; furthermore, the predictive power of individual models can vary over time, so that a given model provides informative

---

[12] Ferriera and Santa-Clara (2011) report complete results for the log return, but they note that their results are similar for the log excess return.

[13] While Ferreira and Santa-Clara (2011) focus on log returns, we can compute a simple (instead of log) return forecast as follows. Let $gr_{m,t+1}$ ($gr_{e,t+1}$) denote the net growth rate of the price-earnings multiple (earnings). Using these definitions, (12) becomes $R_{t+1} = (1 + gr_{m,t+1})(1 + gr_{e,t+1})(1 + DP_{t+1})$. Multiplying out the right-hand-side and treating all cross-product terms as approximately zero, we have $R_{t+1} = 1 + gr_{m,t+1} + gr_{e,t+1} + DP_{t+1}$. Treating the price-earnings multiple and dividend-price ratio as approximately random walks, a simple excess return forecast is given by $\overline{gr}_{e,t}^{20} + DP_t$ minus the risk-free rate, where $\overline{gr}_{e,t}^{20}$ is a 20-year moving average of earnings growth through t. This forecast is analogous to (14). We use this simple excess return forecast for the asset allocation exercise in our empirical application in Section 3.3.

signals during certain periods but predominantly false signals during others. If the individual forecasts are relatively weakly correlated, a combination of the individual forecasts should be less volatile, thereby stabilizing the individual forecasts, reducing forecasting risk, and improving forecasting performance in environments with substantial model uncertainly and parameter instability (e.g., Hendry and Clements, 2004; Clements and Hendry, 2006; Timmermann, 2006).

A combination (or pooled) forecast takes the form of a weighted average of the individual forecasts given by (8) for $i = 1, \ldots, K$:

$$\hat{r}_{t+1}^{POOL} = \sum_{i=1}^{K} \omega_{i,t} \hat{r}_{i,t+1}, \tag{15}$$

where $\{\omega_{i,t}\}_{i=1}^{K}$ are the combining weights based on information available through t and $\sum_{i=1}^{K} \omega_{i,t} = 1$. Simple combining schemes frequently perform surprisingly well. The simplest scheme sets $\omega_{i,t} = 1/K$ for all i to give the mean combination forecast. This is analogous to a "naïve" portfolio rule that places equal weight on each asset. The advantage of simple rules is that they do not require the estimation of combining weights. Similarly to the situation discussed previously with respect to parameter estimation, it is typically difficult to precisely estimate weights for more elaborate combining schemes.

Nevertheless, it can be beneficial to "tilt" the combining weights toward certain individual forecasts, although it is advisable to hew relatively closely to equal weights. In line with this idea, Rapach et al. (2010) compute a discount MSFE (DMSFE) combination forecast that computes weights based on the forecasting performance of individual models over a holdout out-of-sample period (Stock and Watson, 2004):

$$\omega_{i,t} = \phi_{i,t}^{-1} / \sum_{k=1}^{K} \phi_{k,t}^{-1}, \tag{16}$$

where

$$\phi_{i,t} = \sum_{s=m}^{t-1} \theta^{t-1-s} (r_{s+1} - \hat{r}_{i,s+1})^2, \tag{17}$$

$m + 1$ delineates the start of the holdout out-of-sample period, and θ is a discount factor. The DMSFE forecast thus attaches greater weight to individual predictive regression forecasts with lower MSFE (better forecasting performance) over the holdout out-of-sample period. When $\theta = 1$, there is no discounting, so that all observations are treated equally when computing MSFE over the holdout out-of-sample period, while $\theta < 1$ allows for greater emphasis on recent forecasting performance.[14] Rapach et al. (2010) show

---

[14] When the individual forecasts are uncorrelated, $\theta = 1$ corresponds to the optimal combination forecast derived by Bates and Granger (1969). More generally, when individual forecasts are correlated, the optimal weights depend on the correlations. Given the difficulties in precisely estimating the parameters for optimal weights, theoretically optimal weights frequently do not perform well in practice. See Timmermann (2006) for a detailed treatment of theoretically optimal combining weights and their practical limitations.

that simple and DMSFE combination forecasts of the quarterly U.S. equity premium consistently outperform the historical average.

It is curious that the simple combination forecast performs much better than the kitchen sink forecast, since both approaches entail the estimation of K slope coefficients. Rapach et al. (2010) show that the simple combination forecast can be interpreted as a "shrinkage" forecast that circumvents the in-sample overfitting problem plaguing highly parameterized forecasting models. Consider the multiple predictive regression model underlying the kitchen sink forecast, which, for transparency, we express in deviation form:

$$r_{t+1} - \bar{r} = \sum_{i=1}^{K} \beta_i^{KS}(x_{i,t} - \bar{x}_i) + \epsilon_{t+1}, \tag{18}$$

where $\bar{r}$ and $\bar{x}_i$ are the sample means based on data available at the time of forecast formation for r_t and $x_{i,t}$, respectively. The kitchen sink forecast is then given by

$$\hat{r}_{t+1} = \bar{r} + \sum_{i=1}^{K} \hat{\beta}_i^{KS}(x_{i,t} - \bar{x}_i), \tag{19}$$

where $\hat{\beta}_i^{KS}$ is the OLS estimate of β_i^{KS} in the multiple regression, (18), using data available at the time of forecast formation. The simple combination forecast can be expressed as

$$\hat{r}_{t+1} = \bar{r} + (1/K) \sum_{i=1}^{K} \hat{\beta}_i(x_{i,t} - \bar{x}_i), \tag{20}$$

where $\hat{\beta}_i$ is the OLS slope coefficient estimate for the bivariate regression of r_{t+1} on $(x_{i,t} - \bar{x})$ based on data available at the time of forecast formation. Comparing (20) to (19), we see that the simple combination forecast replaces $\hat{\beta}_i^{KS}$ in (19) with $(1/K)\hat{\beta}_i$. This stabilizes the forecast via two channels: (1) reducing estimation variability by substituting the bivariate regression slope coefficient estimates for the multiple regression estimates; (2) shrinking the forecast toward the historical average forecast by premultiplying each slope coefficient by $1/K$. Stabilization permits the combination forecast to incorporate information from a host of economic variables while avoiding in-sample overfitting.

In a similar spirit to forecast combination, Cremers (2002) uses Bayesian model averaging to incorporate information from a multitude of potential predictors in a predictive regression framework. In essence, Bayesian model averaging provides an alternative procedure for shrinking the slope coefficients in (19), where the degree of shrinkage is now governed by the posterior probabilities that each of the predictors appears in the model (as well as the prior distributions for the slope coefficients). The slope coefficients for predictors with "low" posterior inclusion probabilities receive greater shrinkage toward zero, thereby stabilizing the forecast and preventing overfitting. For the 1969–1998 forecast evaluation period, Cremers (2002) finds that monthly U.S. equity premium forecasts based on Bayesian model averaging slightly outperform the historical average benchmark, while they substantially outperform forecasts based on models selected via conventional information criteria such as the AIC and SIC.

3.1.3. Diffusion Indices

Ludvigson and Ng (2007), Kelly and Pruitt (forthcoming), and Neely et al. (2012) adopt a diffusion index approach to improve equity premium forecasting. Diffusion indices provide a means for conveniently tracking the key co-movements in a large number of potential return predictors. The diffusion index approach assumes a latent factor model structure for the (demeaned) potential predictors:

$$x_{i,t} = \lambda_i' f_t + e_{i,t} \quad (i = 1, \ldots, K), \tag{21}$$

where f_t is a q-vector of latent factors, λ_i is a q-vector of factor loadings, and $e_{i,t}$ is a zero-mean disturbance term. A strict factor model assumes that the disturbance terms are contemporaneously and serially uncorrelated, while an "approximate" factor model permits a limited degree of contemporaneous and/or serial correlation in $e_{i,t}$ (e.g., Bai, 2003). Under (21), co-movements in the predictors are primarily governed by fluctuations in the relatively small number of factors ($q \ll K$).

For either the strict or approximate factor model, the latent factors can be consistently estimated by principal components (e.g., Bai, 2003; Stock and Watson, 2006). Estimates of the latent factors then serve as regressors in the following predictive regression model:

$$r_{t+1} = \alpha_{DI} + \beta_{DI}' f_t + \epsilon_{t+1}, \tag{22}$$

where β_{DI}' is a q-vector of slope coefficients. The basic intuition behind (22) is the following. All of the K predictors, $x_{i,t}$ ($i = 1, \ldots, K$), potentially contain relevant information for forecasting r_{t+1}; however, as previously discussed, individual predictors can also provide noisy signals. Rather than using the $x_{i,t}$ variables directly in a predictive regression, we use the factor structure in (21) to identify the important common fluctuations in the potential predictors – as represented by f_t – thereby filtering out the noise in the individual predictors – as captured by $e_{i,t}$. The factor structure thus generates a more reliable signal from a large number of predictors to employ in a predictive regression.

An equity premium forecast based on (22) is given by

$$\hat{r}_{t+1}^{DI} = \hat{\alpha}_{DI,t} + \hat{\beta}_{DI,t}' \hat{f}_{t,t}, \tag{23}$$

where $\hat{f}_{t,t}$ is the principal component estimate of f_t based on data available through t and $\hat{\alpha}_{DI,t}$ and $\hat{\beta}_{DI,t}$ are OLS estimates of α_{DI} and β_{DI}, respectively, in (22) from regressing $\{r_s\}_{s=2}^{t}$ on a constant and $\{\hat{f}_{s,t}\}_{s=1}^{t-1}$. Implementation of this approach requires the specification of q, the number of latent factors. From a forecasting perspective, it is advisable to keep q relatively small, again to avoid an overparameterized forecasting model.

Ludvigson and Ng (2007) analyze diffusion index models along the lines of (22) for quarterly data and factors extracted from 209 macroeconomic and 172 financial variables. In addition to detecting significant in-sample predictive power for the estimated factors, Ludvigson and Ng (2007) find that diffusion index forecasts of the quarterly U.S. equity premium substantially outperform the historical average forecast.

Neely et al. (2012) use a diffusion index approach to forecast the monthly U.S. equity premium. They extract factors from a set of 14 economic variables from the literature and 14 technical indicators computed from moving average, momentum, and volume-based rules. Selecting the number of factors using the adjusted R^2, Neely et al. (2012) show that the diffusion index forecast significantly outperforms the historical average, as well as the 28 predictive regression forecasts based on the individual economic variables and technical indicators. At present, their diffusion index approach based on both economic variables and technical indicators appears to provide the best monthly U.S. equity premium forecast.

An interesting extension of the diffusion index approach relies on "targeted" predictors (Bai and Ng, 2008).[15] From a forecasting standpoint, a potential drawback to the diffusion index model is that the estimated factors are designed to explain the co-variation among the individual predictors themselves, without explicitly taking into account the relationship between the predictors and the targeted variable that we want to forecast. Kelly and Pruitt (2012) develop a three-pass regression filter (3PRF) to estimate the factors that are the most relevant for forecasting the target. In an application of the 3PRF approach, Kelly and Pruitt (forthcoming) use factors extracted from an array of disaggregated valuation ratios to generate out-of-sample U.S. equity premium forecasts that significantly outperform the historical average forecast.

3.1.4. Regime Shifts

A fourth approach for improving equity premium forecastability centers on regime shifts. This approach recognizes that the data-generating process for stock returns is subject to parameter instability, in line with the results of Paye and Timmermann (2006) and Rapach and Wohar (2006a), who find significant evidence of parameter instability in predictive regression models of U.S. aggregate stock returns using the structural break tests of Bai and Perron (1998, 2003), Hansen (2000), and Elliott and Müller (2006).[16]

One strategy for modeling breaks follows the pioneering work of Hamilton (1989) by assuming that parameters take on different values as the economy switches between a relatively small number of latent states.[17] In the context of stock return predictability, it is natural to expect such states, corresponding, for example, to bull/bear markets or

---

[15] See the chapter by Serena Ng in this volume for a detailed analysis of targeted predictors.

[16] Paye and Timmermann (2006) also find significance evidence of structural breaks in predictive regression models of aggregate returns for other G-7 countries.

[17] Ang and Timmermann (2012) provide an insightful survey of regime switching in financial markets.

business-cycle expansions/recessions. Consider the following Markov-switching predictive regression model:

$$r_{t+1} = \alpha_{S_{t+1}} + \beta'_{S_{t+1}} x_t + \sigma_{S_{t+1}} u_{t+1}, \tag{24}$$

where S_{t+1} is a first-order Markov-switching process representing the state of the economy, x_t is a vector of predictors, and u_{t+1} is a zero-mean variate with unit variance. S_{t+1} can take integer values between 1 and m, corresponding to the state of the economy, where the transition between states is governed by an $m \times m$ matrix with typical element

$$p_{ij} = \Pr(S_t = j | S_{t-1} = i) \quad (i, j = 1, \ldots, m). \tag{25}$$

Since the state of the economy is unobservable, (24) cannot be estimated using conventional regression techniques. Hamilton (1989) develops a non-linear iterative filter that can be used to estimate the parameters of Markov-switching models via maximum likelihood and make inferences regarding the state of the economy.

Conditional on the parameter estimates in (24), a forecast of r_{t+1} for $m = 2$ is given by

$$\hat{r}^{MS}_{t+1} = \Pr(S_{t+1} = 1 | I_t)(\hat{\alpha}_{1,t} + \hat{\beta}'_{1,t} x_t) + \Pr(S_{t+1} = 2 | I_t)(\hat{\alpha}_{2,t} + \hat{\beta}'_{2,t} x_t), \tag{26}$$

where $\Pr(S_{t+1} = j | I_t)$ is the probability that $S_{t+1} = j$ given information available through t (which is produced by the estimation algorithm) and $\hat{\alpha}_{j,t}$ and $\hat{\beta}_{j,t}$ are the estimates of α_j and β_j, respectively, in (24) using data available through t for $j = 1, 2$. Intuitively, (26) diversifies across forecasts from the two possible regimes. In periods where it is difficult to determine next period's state, $\Pr(S_{t+1} = 1 | I_t) \approx \Pr(S_{t+1} = 2 | I_t) \approx 0.5$, so that approximately equal weights are placed on the two regime forecasts; if there is strong evidence based on data through t that $S_{t+1} = 1$ $(S_{t+1} = 2)$, then much more weight is placed on the first (second) regime forecast. In this way, the Markov-switching forecast accommodates structural breaks in model parameters while accounting for the uncertainty inherent in identifying the state of the economy.

Guidolin and Timmermann (2007) estimate a multivariate four-regime Markov-switching model for U.S. stock and bond returns via maximum likelihood, where the dividend yield serves as a predictor.[18] Characterizing the four states as "crash," "slow growth," "bull," and "recovery," they present statistical evidence favoring a four-regime structure. Most relevant from our perspective, they also find that real-time asset allocation decisions guided by Markov-switching model forecasts of stock and bond returns yield substantial utility gains relative to asset allocation decisions based on constant expected excess return forecasts.[19]

---

[18] An equation similar to (24) with $m = 4$ is part of Guidolin and Timmermann's (2007) multivariate model.

[19] Ang and Bekaert (2002) find that regime switching has important implications for optimal portfolio choice for an investor allocating across equities in the United States, the United Kingdom, and Germany.

Henkel et al. (2011) estimate (24) as part of a two-regime Markov-switching vector autoregressive process that includes the dividend–price ratio, short-term nominal interest rate, term spread, and default spread in x_t. They estimate their model via Bayesian methods and find that the two states correspond closely to NBER-dated business-cycle expansions and recessions, with in-sample return predictability highly concentrated during recessions. They also show that monthly U.S. equity premium forecasts based on (26) outperform the historical average benchmark in terms of MSFE, and, like the in-sample results, out-of-sample return predictability is concentrated during economic downturns. Overall, the results in Henkel et al. (2011) suggest that the historical average forecast is sufficient during "normal" times, while economic variables provide useful signals for forecasting returns during contractionary episodes.

Markov-switching models appear to be most popular type of non-linear model for forecasting stock returns. Other well-known non-linear specifications include threshold models, where regimes are defined by the values taken by observable transition variables relative to threshold parameters, and neural nets; see Franses and van Dijk (2000), Teräsvirta (2006), White (2006), and González-Rivera and Lee (2009) for informative surveys of non-linear forecasting models. Guidolin et al. (2009) analyze the circumstances under which non-linear forecasting models of stock returns are likely to be useful.[20]

Instead of parameters switching among a relatively small number of states via a Markov-switching process, time-varying parameter (TVP) models allow for parameters to evolve from period to period, so that each period can be viewed as a new regime. Dangl and Halling (2012) specify the following TVP predictive regression model:

$$r_{t+1} = \alpha_t + \beta_t' x_t + \epsilon_{t+1}, \tag{27}$$

$$\begin{pmatrix} \alpha_t \\ \beta_t \end{pmatrix} = \begin{pmatrix} \alpha_{t-1} \\ \beta_{t-1} \end{pmatrix} + \begin{pmatrix} w_{1,t} \\ w_{2,t} \end{pmatrix}, \tag{28}$$

where

$$\epsilon_t \sim N(0, \sigma^2), \tag{29}$$

$$w_t \sim N(0, W_t), \tag{30}$$

and $w_t = (w_{1,t}, w_{2,t}')'$. According to (28), the intercept and slope coefficients in the predictive regression (27) evolve as (driftless) random walks. After placing restrictions on W_t to limit the parameter space, the TVP model given by (27)-(30) can be estimated using the Kalman filter and maximum likelihood.

---

[20] Non- or semi-parametric modeling represents another approach for approximating general functional forms for the relationship between expected returns and predictors. See Chen and Hong (2010) for recent promising results on equity premium forecasting using a non-parametric approach. Aït-Sahalia and Brandt (2001) employ semi-parametric methods to directly relate predictors of stock return moments to optimal portfolio weights.

An equity premium forecast based on the TVP model is given by

$$\hat{r}_{t+1}^{TVP} = \hat{\alpha}_{t,t} + \hat{\beta}_{t,t}' x_t, \tag{31}$$

where $\hat{\alpha}_{t,t}$ and $\hat{\beta}_{t,t}$ are estimates of α_t and β_t, respectively, in (27) based on data available through t. The TVP forecast in (31) allows for forecasting model coefficients to evolve in a very general way, so that the TVP forecast can respond to changes in economic structure resulting from a myriad of factors, including changes in technology, institutions, and policy. Dangl and Halling (2012) employ Bayesian methods to estimate (27)–(30) for the monthly U.S. equity premium. They find that forecasts based on (31) significantly outperform the historical average, and, similarly to Henkel et al. (2011), the out-of-sample gains are concentrated during recessions.[21]

Pettenuzzo and Timmermann (2011) adopt a Bayesian approach that allows for a few large breaks in predictive regression model coefficients, rather than assuming that the coefficients constantly evolve according to (30). Pettenuzzo and Timmermann (2011) are primarily interested in the implications of infrequent structural breaks for optimal portfolio choice. Indeed, they show that structural breaks in predictive regressions have important implications for investors with long horizons and that ignoring breaks can result in sizable welfare losses.

3.2. Forecast Evaluation

MSFE is the most popular metric for evaluating forecast accuracy, and it is not surprising that MSFE is routinely reported in studies of stock return forecastability. This raises two important issues. The first relates to statistical tests of equal MSFE when comparing forecasts from nested models, while the second concerns the adequacy of the MSFE criterion itself.

To fix ideas, suppose that a sample of T observations for r_t and $x_{i,t}$ is available. We divide the total sample into an initial in-sample estimation period comprised of the first n_1 observations and an out-of-sample period comprised of the last $n_2 = T - n_1$ observations. One-step ahead equity premium forecasts are computed over these last n_2 observations using (8). The MSFE for the predictive regression forecast over the forecast evaluation period is given by

$$\text{MSFE}_i = (1/n_2) \sum_{s=1}^{n_2} (r_{n_1+s} - \hat{r}_{i,n_1+s})^2. \tag{32}$$

To analyze out-of-sample stock return predictability, the accuracy of the predictive regression forecast is compared to the historical average benchmark forecast, which assumes constant expected excess returns,

---

[21] Since they consider a large number of potential predictors, Dangl and Halling (2012) also employ Bayesian model averaging along the line of Cremers (2002) in constructing out-of-sample forecasts for their TVP model structure.

$$\bar{r}_{t+1} = (1/t) \sum_{s=1}^{t} r_t, \tag{33}$$

and its MSFE is given by

$$\text{MSFE}_0 = \left(1/n_2\right) \sum_{s=1}^{n_2} \left(r_{n_1+s} - \bar{r}_{n_1+s}\right)^2. \tag{34}$$

The out-of-sample R^2 (Campbell and Thompson, 2008) is a convenient statistic for comparing MSFEs. It is analogous to the conventional in-sample R^2 and measures the proportional reduction in MSFE for the predictive regression forecast relative to the historical average:

$$R_{OS}^2 = 1 - (\text{MSFE}_i/\text{MSFE}_0). \tag{35}$$

Obviously, when $R_{OS}^2 > 0$, the predictive regression forecast is more accurate than the historical average in terms of MSFE ($\text{MSFE}_i < \text{MSFE}_0$).

While R_{OS}^2 measures the improvement in MSFE for the predictive regression forecast vis-á-vis the historical average, we are also interested in determining whether the improvement is statistically significant; that is, we are interested in testing $H_0 : \text{MSFE}_0 \le \text{MSFE}_i$ against $H_A : \text{MSFE}_0 > \text{MSFE}_i$, corresponding to $H_0 : R_{OS}^2 \le 0$ against $H_A : R_{OS}^2 > 0$.[22] The well-known Diebold and Mariano (1995) and West (1996) statistic for testing the null of equal MSFE (or equal predictive ability) is given by

$$DMW_i = n_2^{0.5} \bar{d}_i \hat{S}_{d_i,d_i}^{-0.5}, \tag{36}$$

where

$$\bar{d}_i = \left(1/n_2\right) \sum_{s=1}^{n_2} \hat{d}_{i,n_1+s}, \tag{37}$$

$$\hat{d}_{i,n_1+s} = \hat{u}_{0,n_1+s}^2 - \hat{u}_{i,n_1+s}^2, \tag{38}$$

$$\hat{u}_{0,n_1+s} = r_{n_1+s} - \bar{r}_{n_1+s}, \tag{39}$$

$$\hat{u}_{i,n_1+s} = r_{n_1+s} - \hat{r}_{i,n_1+s}, \tag{40}$$

$$\hat{S}_{d_i,d_i} = \left(1/n_2\right) \sum_{s=1}^{n_2} \left(\hat{d}_{i,n_1+s} - \bar{d}_i\right)^2. \tag{41}$$

The DMW_i statistic is equivalent to the t-statistic corresponding to the constant for a regression of $\hat{d}_{i,n_1+s}$ on a constant for $s = 1, \ldots, n_2$. When comparing forecasts from non-nested models, Diebold and Mariano (1995) and West (1996) show that DMW_i has a standard normal asymptotic distribution, so that it is straightforward to test $H_0 : \text{MSFE}_0 \le \text{MSFE}_i$ against $H_A : \text{MSFE}_0 > \text{MSFE}_i$ by comparing the sample statistic to 1.282, 1.645, and 2.326 for the 10%, 5%, and 1% significance levels, respectively.

---

[22] Corradi and Swanson (2006), West (2006), and the chapter by Todd Clark and Michael McCracken in this volume provide instructive surveys of statistical tests of relative forecast accuracy.

Clark and McCracken (2001) and McCracken (2007), however, show that DMW_i has a non-standard asymptotic distribution when comparing forecasts from nested models. In the context of predictive regressions, out-of-sample tests of stock return predictability entail a comparison of nested forecasts, since the predictive regression model, (7), reduces to the constant expected excess return model when $\beta_i = 0$. For nested forecast comparisons, the asymptotic distribution of DMW_i is a function of Brownian motion and depends on two parameters: (1) $\pi = n_2/n_1$; (2) the dimension of the set of predictors, x_t (which is one for a bivariate predictive regression). Clark and McCracken (2001) and McCracken (2007) provide tabulated critical values for a variety of parameter values that are relevant in applied research. A stark feature of the asymptotic critical values is that they frequently shift markedly to the left relative to standard normal critical values. For example, consider a bivariate predictive regression model and $\pi = 2$, which corresponds to reserving the first third of the total sample for the initial in-sample period. From Table 6.1 in McCracken (2007), the 10%, 5%, and 1% critical values are 0.281, 0.610, and 1.238, respectively, which are well below their standard normal counterparts. The implication is that tests of equal predictive ability based on conventional critical values can often be severely undersized, leading to tests with very low power to detect out-of-sample return predictability. In short, it is crucial to use appropriate critical values when testing for stock return forecastability; otherwise, statistically significant evidence of out-sample return predictability can easily be missed.

Clark and West (2007) adjust DMW_i to produce a modified statistic, $MSFE\text{-}adjusted$, for comparing nested model forecasts that has an asymptotic distribution well approximated by the standard normal. The $MSFE\text{-}adjusted$ statistic also performs well in finite-sample simulations. Clark and West (2007) thus provide a very convenient method for assessing statistical significance when comparing nested forecasts that obviates the need to look up a new set of critical values for each application. The $MSFE\text{-}adjusted$ statistic is straightforward to compute by first defining

$$\tilde{d}_{i,n_1+s} = \hat{u}^2_{0,n_1+s} - \left[\hat{u}^2_{i,n_1+s} - \left(\bar{r}_{n_1+s} - \hat{r}_{i,n_1+s}\right)^2\right], \tag{42}$$

and then regressing $\tilde{d}_{i,n_1+s}$ on a constant for $s = 1, \ldots, n_2$; $MSFE\text{-}adjusted$ is the t-statistic corresponding to the constant. Recent studies of stock return forecastability that employ the $MSFE\text{-}adjusted$ statistic include Rapach et al. (2010), Kong et al. (2011), Dangl and Halling (2012), and Neely et al. (2012).[23]

While MSFE is overwhelmingly the most popular measure of forecast accuracy, it is not necessarily the most relevant metric for assessing stock return forecasts. Leitch

---

[23] The Diebold and Mariano (1995) and West (1996) DMW_i and Clark and West (2007) $MSFE\text{-}adjusted$ statistics are tests of population-level predictability. There is a subtle but important distinction between population-level and finite-sample predictability. Section 3 of the chapter by Todd Clark and Michael McCracken in this volume discusses this distinction and recently proposed procedures for testing finite-sample predictability that have potentially important implications for analyzing stock return forecastability.

Table 6.1 Monthly U.S. Equity Premium Out-of-Sample Forecasting Results Based on Individual Economic Variables, 1957:01–2010:12

Economic Variable	Overall		Expansion		Recession	
	R^2_{OS} (%)	Δ (annual %)	R^2_{OS} (%)	Δ (annual %)	R^2_{OS} (%)	Δ (annual %)
Panel A: Unrestricted predictive regression forecasts						
log (DP)	−0.05 [0.10]	0.87	−1.24 [0.42]	−1.47	2.41 [0.00]	11.87
log (DY)	−0.37 [0.07]	1.18	−2.28 [0.40]	−1.98	3.56 [0.00]	16.17
log (EP)	−1.88 [0.28]	0.57	−2.21 [0.31]	−0.41	−1.20 [0.38]	4.99
log (DE)	−2.04 [0.97]	−0.44	−1.26 [0.80]	0.06	−3.67 [0.97]	−2.73
SVAR	0.32 [0.17]	−0.11	−0.02 [0.50]	−0.37	1.01 [0.16]	1.08
BM	−1.74 [0.31]	−0.72	−2.56 [0.44]	−2.01	−0.04 [0.28]	5.12
NTIS	−0.91 [0.41]	−0.21	0.50 [0.03]	0.72	−3.82 [0.94]	−4.71
TBL	−0.01 [0.09]	1.53	−0.84 [0.30]	0.24	1.71 [0.10]	7.58
LTY	−1.17 [0.12]	1.29	−2.37 [0.38]	−0.21	1.32 [0.11]	8.38
LTR	−0.08 [0.20]	0.57	−0.85 [0.63]	−0.35	1.52 [0.05]	4.74
TMS	0.06 [0.16]	1.15	−0.40 [0.34]	0.01	1.00 [0.09]	6.49
DFY	−0.04 [0.59]	0.29	−0.06 [0.64]	0.00	−0.01 [0.48]	1.48
DFR	−0.01 [0.38]	0.39	0.12 [0.25]	0.15	−0.28 [0.48]	1.53
INFL	−0.09 [0.50]	0.34	0.10 [0.22]	0.19	−0.48 [0.66]	1.16
Panel B: Predictive regression forecasts with Campbell and Thompson (2008) restrictions						
log (DP)	0.15 [0.07]	0.87	−0.92 [0.38]	−1.47	2.36 [0.00]	11.87
log (DY)	0.17 [0.04]	1.18	−1.33 [0.40]	−1.98	3.26 [0.00]	16.17
log (EP)	−0.82 [0.24]	0.57	−1.19 [0.30]	−0.41	−0.06 [0.32]	4.99
log (DE)	−1.74 [0.98]	0.01	−1.19 [0.78]	0.01	−2.88 [0.98]	0.00
SVAR	0.00 [−]	−0.26	0.00 [−]	−0.36	0.00 [−]	0.18
BM	−1.17 [0.29]	−0.72	−1.68 [0.40]	−2.01	−0.13 [0.30]	5.12
NTIS	−0.91 [0.41]	−0.21	0.50 [0.03]	0.72	−3.82 [0.94]	−4.71
TBL	0.21 [0.10]	1.53	−0.25 [0.27]	0.24	1.16 [0.10]	7.58
LTY	−0.01 [0.09]	1.29	−0.67 [0.29]	−0.21	1.36 [0.07]	8.38
LTR	0.22 [0.12]	0.63	−0.47 [0.52]	−0.36	1.64 [0.03]	5.15
TMS	0.12 [0.15]	1.15	−0.42 [0.37]	0.01	1.23 [0.06]	6.49
DFY	−0.01 [0.50]	0.29	−0.03 [0.55]	0.00	0.01 [0.45]	1.48
DFR	−0.16 [0.49]	0.56	0.09 [0.27]	0.15	−0.68 [0.66]	2.51
INFL	−0.06 [0.46]	0.34	0.10 [0.22]	0.19	−0.38 [0.63]	1.16

Notes: R^2_{OS} measures the percent reduction in mean squared forecast error (MSFE) for the predictive regression forecast based on the economic variable given in the first column relative to the historical average benchmark forecast. Brackets report *p*-values for the Clark and West (2007) *MSFE-adjusted* statistic for testing the null hypothesis that the historical average MSFE is less than or equal to the predictive regression MSFE against the alternative that the historical average MSFE is greater than the predictive regression MSFE (corresponding to $H_0: R^2_{OS} \leq 0$ against $H_A: R^2_{OS} > 0$). Average utility gain (Δ) is the portfolio management fee (in annualized percent return) that an investor with mean–variance preferences and risk aversion coefficient of five would be willing to pay to have access to the predictive regression forecast based on the economic variable given in the first column relative to the historical average benchmark forecast. 0.00 indicates less than 0.005. R^2_{OS} statistics and average utility gains are computed for the entire 1957:01–2010:12 forecast evaluation period and separately for NBER-dated expansions and recessions.

and Tanner (1991) consider why many firms purchase professional forecasts of economic and financial variables that frequently fail to outperform forecasts from simple time-series models in terms of MSFE. They argue that forecast profitability is a more relevant metric for assessing forecasts, helping to explain the value of professional forecasts to firms.[24] Comparing professional and simple time-series model forecasts of interest rates, for which profitability is readily measured, Leitch and Tanner (1991) find that professional forecasts are often more profitable. Furthermore, there is a weak relationship between MSFE and forecast profitability. Among the conventional forecast error measures that they analyze, only the direction-of-change metric appears significantly correlated with forecast profitability. Henriksson and Merton (1981), Cumby and Modest (1987), and Pesaran and Timmermann (1992) provide statistical tests of directional forecasting ability, and academic researchers often employ these tests when analyzing stock return forecasts (e.g., Breen et al., 1989; Pesaran and Timmermann (2002, 2004); Marquering and Verbeek, 2004).

In line with the conclusions of Leitch and Tanner (1991), academic researchers also frequently analyze stock return forecasts with profit- or utility-based metrics, which provide more direct measures of the value of forecasts to economic agents. In these exercises, stock return forecasts serve as inputs for *ad hoc* trading rules or asset allocation decisions derived from expected utility maximization problems. A leading utility-based metric for analyzing U.S. equity premium forecasts is the average utility gain for a mean-variance investor. Consider a mean-variance investor with relative risk aversion γ who allocates her portfolio between stocks and risk-free bills based on the predictive regression forecast (8) of the equity premium.[25] At the end of t, the investor allocates the following share of her portfolio to equities during $t + 1$:

$$a_{i,t} = \left(\frac{1}{\gamma}\right) \left(\frac{\hat{r}_{i,t+1}}{\hat{\sigma}_{t+1}^2}\right), \tag{43}$$

where $\hat{\sigma}_{t+1}^2$ is a forecast of the variance of stock returns.[26] Over the forecast evaluation period, the investor realizes the average utility,

$$\hat{v}_i = \hat{\mu}_i - 0.5\gamma\hat{\sigma}_i^2, \tag{44}$$

where $\hat{\mu}_i$ ($\hat{\sigma}_i^2$) is the sample mean (variance) of the portfolio formed on the basis of $\hat{r}_{i,t+1}$ and $\hat{\sigma}_{t+1}^2$ over the forecast evaluation period. If the investor instead relies on the historical

---

[24] Also see Granger and Machina (2006) and Batchelor (2011).

[25] For asset allocation exercises, we use simple (instead of log) returns, so that the portfolio return is given by the sum of the individual portfolio weights multiplied by the asset returns.

[26] Under the assumption of constant return volatility, the variance of stock returns can be estimated using the sample variance computed from a recursive window of historical returns. To allow for a time-varying variance, a rolling window or some type of GARCH model can be used. Campbell and Thompson (2008) estimate $\hat{\sigma}_{t+1}^2$ using the sample variance computed from a five-year rolling window of historical returns. See Andersen et al. (2006) for an extensive survey of return volatility forecasting. Note that a general expected utility maximization problem for an investor requires a forecast of the entire conditional distribution of future returns, including conditional mean and volatility forecasts.

average forecast of the equity premium (using the same variance forecast), she allocates the portfolio share,

$$a_{0,t} = \left(\frac{1}{\gamma}\right)\left(\frac{\bar{r}_{t+1}}{\hat{\sigma}^2_{t+1}}\right), \tag{45}$$

to equity during $t+1$ and, over the forecast evaluation period, realizes the average utility,

$$\hat{v}_0 = \hat{\mu}_0 - 0.5\gamma\hat{\sigma}_0^2, \tag{46}$$

where $\hat{\mu}_0$ ($\hat{\sigma}_0^2$) is the sample mean (variance) of the portfolio formed on the basis of $\bar{r}_{t+1}$ and $\hat{\sigma}^2_{t+1}$ over the forecast evaluation period. The difference between (44) and (46) represents the utility gain accruing to using the predictive regression forecast of the equity premium in place of the historical average forecast in the asset allocation decision. This utility gain, or certainty equivalent return, can be interpreted as the portfolio management fee that an investor would be willing to pay to have access to the information in the predictive regression forecast relative to the information in the historical average forecast alone. Marquering and Verbeek (2004), Campbell and Thompson (2008), Cooper and Priestly (2009), Rapach et al. (2010), Ferreira and Santa-Clara (2011), Dangl and Halling (2012), and Neely et al. (2012) all detect sizable utility gains for mean-variance investors who rely on equity premium forecasts based on economic variables relative to the historical average forecast.

Kandel and Stambaugh (1996), Guidolin and Timmermann (2007), Pettenuzzo and Timmermann (2011), and Cenesizoglu and Timmermann (2011) measure utility gains for investors with power utility defined over wealth who optimally allocate among assets, and they also find significant economic gains accruing to equity premium forecasts based on economic variables. Similarly to Leitch and Tanner (1991), Cenesizoglu and Timmermann (2011) find a weak relationship between MSFE and utility gains. Hong et al. (2007) examine whether equity premium forecasts based on lagged industry portfolio returns possess market timing ability. They consider a portfolio that allocates all of the portfolio to equities (Treasury bills) if the equity premium forecast is positive (negative). For investors with power utility, portfolios formed using equity premium forecasts based on lagged industry returns generate sizable utility gains relative to portfolios relying on equity premium forecasts that ignore lagged industry returns.

3.3. Empirical Application

3.3.1. Monthly U.S. Equity Premium Forecastability

We next consider an application based on forecasting the monthly U.S. equity premium that illustrates many of the concepts and methodologies discussed in Sections 3.1 and 3.2. We use updated data from Goyal and Welch (2008) spanning 1926:12–2010:12.[27]

---

[27] We thank Amit Goyal for kindly providing the data on his web page at http://www.hec.unil.ch/agoyal/. The data and their sources are described in detail in Goyal and Welch (2008). Other than the economic variables compiled by

The equity premium is the log return on the S&P 500 (including dividends) minus the log return on a risk-free bill.[28] Fourteen popular economic variables serve as candidate predictors:

1. **Log dividend-price ratio** [log (DP)]: log of a 12-month moving sum of dividends paid on the S&P 500 index minus the log of stock prices (S&P 500 index).
2. **Log dividend yield** [log (DY)]: log of a 12-month moving sum of dividends minus the log of lagged stock prices.
3. **Log earnings-price ratio** [log (EP)]: log of a 12-month moving sum of earnings on the S&P 500 index minus the log of stock prices.
4. **Log dividend-payout ratio** [log (DE)]: log of a 12-month moving sum of dividends minus the log of a 12-month moving sum of earnings.
5. **Stock variance** $(SVAR)$: monthly sum of squared daily returns on the S&P 500 index.
6. **Book-to-market ratio** (BM): book-to-market value ratio for the DJIA.
7. **Net equity expansion** $(NTIS)$: ratio of a 12-month moving sum of net equity issues by NYSE-listed stocks to the total end-of-year market capitalization of NYSE stocks.
8. **Treasury bill rate** (TBL): interest rate on a three-month Treasury bill (secondary market).
9. **Long-term yield** (LTY): long-term government bond yield.
10. **Long-term return** (LTR): return on long-term government bonds.
11. **Term spread** (TMS): long-term yield minus the Treasury bill rate.
12. **Default yield spread** (DFY): difference between BAA- and AAA-rated corporate bond yields.
13. **Default return spread** (DFR): long-term corporate bond return minus the long-term government bond return.
14. **Inflation** $(INFL)$: calculated from the CPI (all urban consumers); we use $x_{i,t-1}$ in (7) for inflation to account for the delay in CPI releases.

We first compute bivariate predictive regression forecasts of the equity premium based on (8) for each predictor. We use 1926:12–1956:12 as the initial in-sample estimation period, so that we compute out-of-sample forecasts for 1957:01–2010:12 (648 observations). The forecasts employ a recursive (or expanding) estimation window, meaning that the estimation sample always starts in 1926:12 and additional observations are used as they become available. Forecasting model parameters are also frequently estimated with a rolling window, which drops earlier observations as additional observations

---

Goyal and Welch (2008), Han et al. (forthcoming), and Neely et al. (2012) recently showed that technical indicators are valuable as predictors in predictive regression forecasts of stock returns, a new finding in academic research.

[28] When performing asset allocation exercises, we measure the equity premium as the simple aggregate market return minus the simple risk-free rate.

become available. Rolling estimation windows are typically justified by appealing to structural breaks, although a rolling window generally will not be an optimal estimation window in the presence of breaks. Pesaran and Timmermann (2007) and Clark and McCracken (2009) show that, from an MSFE perspective, it can be optimal to employ pre-break data when estimating forecasting models, a manifestation of the classic bias-efficiency tradeoff. More generally, they demonstrate that the optimal window size is a complicated function of the timing and size of breaks. Since these parameters are difficult to estimate precisely, recursive estimation windows frequently perform better in terms of MSFE than rolling windows or windows selected on the basis of structural break tests when forecasting stock returns.[29]

The 1957:01–2010:12 forecast evaluation period covers most of the postwar era, including the oil price shocks of the 1970s; the deep recession associated with the Volcker disinflation in the early 1980s; the long expansions of the 1960s, 1980s, and 1990s; and the recent Global Financial Crisis and concomitant Great Recession. The selection of the forecast evaluation period is always somewhat arbitrary. Hansen and Timmermann (2012) recently develop an out-of-sample test of forecasting ability that is robust to the in-sample/out-of-sample split.[30]

Table 6.1 reports results for out-of-sample horse races pitting the individual bivariate predictive regression forecasts against the historical average. Panels A and B of Table 6.1 give results for unrestricted predictive regression forecasts and predictive regression forecasts that implement the Campbell and Thompson (2008) sign restrictions described in Section 3.1.1, respectively.[31] In addition to the full 1957:01–2010:12 forecast evaluation period, we present results computed separately during NBER-dated business-cycle expansions and recessions.[32]

The R_{OS}^2 statistics in the second column of Table 6.1, Panel A succinctly convey the message of Goyal and Welch (2008): individual predictive regression forecasts frequently fail to beat the historical average benchmark in terms of MSFE. Indeed, 12 of the 14 R_{OS}^2 statistics are negative in the second column of Panel A, indicating that the predictive regression forecast has a higher MSFE than the historical average. For the two predictors with a positive R_{OS}^2 (SVAR and TMS), the Clark and West (2007) p-values reported in the

[29] We confirmed this in our application. Rossi and Inoue (2012) develop out-of-sample tests of forecasting ability that are robust to the estimation window size.

[30] Section 5 of the chapter by Todd Clark and Michael McCracken in this volume examines issues relating to the choice of in-sample/out-of-sample split when evaluating forecasts. In Figures 6.1 and 6.3, we employ a graphical device from Goyal and Welch (2003, 2008) to assess the consistency of out-of-sample predictive ability.

[31] Specifically, the Campbell and Thompson (2008) restrictions entail setting the slope coefficient used to generate the bivariate predictive regression forecast to zero if the sign of the estimated slope coefficient differs from its theoretically expected sign, and a non-negativity constraint is imposed by setting the forecast to zero if the predictive regression forecast is negative.

[32] The NBER business-cycle peak and trough dates defining expansions and recessions are available at http://www.nber.org/cycles.html. The U.S. economy was in recession for approximately 17% of the months during 1957:01–2010:12.

brackets are greater than 0.10, so that these economic variables do not display statistically significant out-of-sample predictive ability at conventional levels.[33]

Figure 6.1 further illustrates the generally poor performance of the conventional predictive regression forecasts. The black line in each panel depicts the cumulative difference in squared forecast errors for the historical average forecast vis-á-vis the predictive regression forecast:

$$\text{CDSFE}_{i,\tau} = \sum_{s=1}^{\tau} (r_{n_1+s} - \bar{r}_{n_1+s})^2 - \sum_{s=1}^{\tau} (r_{n_1+s} - \hat{r}_{i,n_1+s})^2, \qquad (47)$$

for $\tau = 1, \ldots, n_2$. Goyal and Welch (2003, 2008) recommend this highly informative graphical device to assess the ability of a predictive regression forecast to consistently outperform the historical average. The figure can be conveniently used to determine if the predictive regression forecast has a lower MSFE than the historical average for any period by simply comparing the height of the curve at the beginning and end points of the segment corresponding to the period of interest: if the curve is higher (lower) at the end of the segment relative to the beginning, then the predictive regression forecast has a lower (higher) MSFE than the historical average during the period. A predictive regression forecast that always outperforms the historical average will thus have a slope that is positive everywhere. Of course, realistically, this ideal will not be reached in practice, but the closer the curve is to this ideal the better. The black lines in Figure 6.1 all fall far short of the ideal. All of the lines are predominantly negatively sloped or flat, with relatively short and infrequent positively sloped segments. In fact, numerous segments are steeply and negatively sloped, indicating that the historical average substantially outperforms the predictive regression forecasts during these periods. At best, the predictive regression forecasts provide episodic—or "elusive" (Timmermann, 2008) – evidence of out-of-sample stock return predictability.[34] In sum, Figure 6.1, along with the R_{OS}^2 statistics in the second column of Table 6.1, Panel A, support a bearish view of predictive regression forecasts of the U.S. equity premium.

Closer inspection of Figure 6.1 reveals a pattern to the episodic nature of equity premium forecastability. In a number of instances, the curves are relatively steeply and positively sloped during and around NBER-dated recessions (depicted by the vertical bars in Figure 6.1), indicating that out-of-sample stock return predictability is largely a recessionary phenomenon. Additional evidence of this is provided in the fourth and sixth

---

[33] Interestingly, three of the economic variables with negative R_{OS}^2 statistics in Table 6.1 – log (DP), log (DY), and TBL – actually have p-values less than or equal to 0.10, so that we reject the null that $R_{OS}^2 \leq 0$ in favor or $R_{OS}^2 > 0$ at conventional levels, even though the sample R_{OS}^2 is negative. This is a manifestation of the Clark and McCracken (2001) and McCracken (2007) result discussed in Section 3.2.

[34] Giacomini and Rossi (2010) provide a measure of relative local forecasting performance and tests of the stability of forecasting gains (also see Giacomini and Rossi, 2009). Their tests, however, require rolling estimation windows when comparing nested forecasts, while we focus on recursive estimation windows in our application.

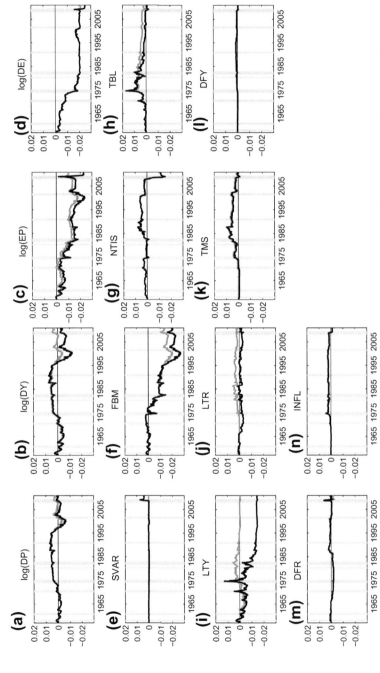

Figure 6.1 Cumulative differences in squared forecast errors, monthly U.S. equity premium out-of-sample forecasts based on individual economic variables, 1957:01–2010:12. Black (gray) lines in each panel delineate the cumulative difference in squared forecast errors for the historical average forecast relative to the unrestricted predictive regression forecast (predictive regression forecast with Campbell and Thompson (2008) restrictions imposed) based on the economic variable given in the panel heading. Vertical bars depict NBER-dated recessions. (For interpretation of the references to color in this figure legend, the reader is referred to the web version of this book.)

columns of Table 6.1, Panel A, which report R^2_{OS} statistics computed separately during expansions and recessions, respectively. For seven of the predictors, the R^2_{OS} statistics move from being negative (and typically below -1%) during expansions to 1% or above during recessions. Furthermore, five of these R^2_{OS} statistics are significant at conventional levels during recessions according to the Clark and West (2007) p-values, despite the decreased number of available observations. The difference in relative out-of-sample forecasting performance across business-cycle phases is particularly evident for log (DP) and log (DY), where the R^2_{OS} statistics go from -1.24% and -2.28% during expansions to 2.41% and 3.56%, respectively, during recessions.

Up to this point, we have analyzed equity premium forecasts in terms of MSFE. As discussed in Section 3.2, however, MSFE is not necessarily the most relevant metric for assessing stock return forecasts. The third column of Table 6.1, Panel A reports average utility gains (in annualized percent return) for a mean-variance investor with relative risk coefficient of five who allocates among equities and risk-free bills using predictive regression forecasts in place of the historical average.[35] Relative to the R^2_{OS} statistics in the second column, the predictive regression forecasts appear significantly more valuable according to the average utility gains, with 10 of the 14 economic variables offering positive gains. The annualized gain is above 0.5% for seven of the economic variables, meaning that the investor would be willing to pay more than 50 basis points to have access to the information in the predictive regression forecasts compared to the historical average forecast. The utility gains are greater than 100 basis points for log (DY), TBL, LTY, and TMS. Similarly to the pattern in the R^2_{OS} statistics, the average utility gains are typically higher during recessions than expansions (see the fifth and seventh columns of Table 6.1, Panel A). In fact, the differences in forecasting performance as measured by the utility gains are more pronounced than for the R^2_{OS} statistics. For 12 of the 14 predictors, the average utility gain is higher during recessions than expansions, and the differences are especially large for log (DP) and log (DY), where the average utility gains increase from -1.47% and -1.98% during expansions to 11.87% and 16.17%, respectively, during recessions. Overall, the average utility gains in Table 6.1, Panel A provide stronger support for stock return forecastability, highlighting the need to supplement standard statistical criteria with more direct value-based measures when analyzing out-of-sample stock return predictability.[36]

Panel B of Table 6.1 presents R^2_{OS} statistics and average utility gains for predictive regression forecasts that impose the Campbell and Thompson (2008) sign restrictions. Comparing the second column of Panel B to Panel A, we see that the theoretically motivated restrictions generally improve the predictive regression forecasts in terms of MSFE.

---

[35] The results are qualitatively similar for other reasonable risk aversion coefficient values. We follow Campbell and Thompson (2008) and estimate the variance of stock returns using the sample variance computed from a five-year rolling window of historical returns.

[36] An important outstanding issue is assessing the statistical significance of average utility gains; see McCracken and Valente (2012) for insightful initial theoretical results.

Eleven of the 14 R_{OS}^2 statistics in Panel B are greater than their Panel A counterparts, and the R_{OS}^2 statistics turn from negative to positive for log (DP), log (DY), TBL, and LTR as we move from Panel A to B. The R_{OS}^2 statistics in the fourth and sixth columns of Panel B help to explain the overall increase in forecast accuracy corresponding to the restrictions. The R_{OS}^2 statistics in the sixth column of Panels A and B are reasonably similar; if anything, there is a tendency for the restrictions to decrease the R_{OS}^2 statistics during recessions. In contrast, the R_{OS}^2 statistics become substantially less negative during expansions for a number of predictors, especially log (DP) and log (DY) (see the fourth column of Panels A and B). The restrictions thus appear to improve overall forecasting performance by ameliorating the underperformance of the predictive regression forecasts during expansions. The results in Panel B indicate that the restrictions have relatively little effect on forecasting performance as measured by the average utility gains.

Figure 6.2, which graphs the individual bivariate predictive regression forecasts, sheds additional light on the role of sign restrictions. The sign restrictions on the estimated slope coefficients for the predictive regression forecasting models are rarely binding.[37] Instead, as shown in Figure 6.2, the predictive regression forecasts are negative for many periods for a number of predictors, so that it is the sign restrictions on the predictive regression forecasts themselves that are relevant. For example, the predictive regression forecasts based on valuation ratios – log (DP), log (DY), log (EP), and BM – are often negative during the mid-to-late 1990s. The corresponding lines in Figure 6.1 are predominantly steeply and negatively sloped during this period, indicating that the predictive regression forecasts perform very poorly relative to the historical average. The gray lines in Figure 6.1 correspond to differences in cumulated squared forecast errors for the historical average forecast relative to the restricted predictive regression forecasts. The gray lines for the valuation ratios lie above the black lines starting in the mid–1990s, so that the restrictions are particularly useful in improving forecasting performance around this time. In general, the sign restrictions stabilize the predictive regression forecasts by truncating them from below, helping to avoid more implausible equity premium forecasts.

Panel A of Table 6.2 reports R_{OS}^2 statistics and average utility gains for monthly equity premium forecasts based on multiple economic variables, with no sign restrictions placed on the forecasts. Figure 6.3 graphs the cumulative differences in squared forecast errors for the historical average forecast relative to forecasts based on multiple economic variables, while Figure 6.4 depicts the forecasts themselves.

The first forecast in Table 6.2, the kitchen sink, corresponds to a multiple predictive regression model that includes all 14 economic variables as regressors. Confirming the results in Goyal and Welch (2008) and Rapach et al. (2010), the kitchen sink forecast performs very poorly according to the MSFE metric, with an R_{OS}^2 of -8.43% over the

---

[37] The major exception is $SVAR$, where theory suggests $\beta_i > 0$, but the estimated slope coefficient is always negative. This is evident from the R_{OS}^2 of exactly zero for $SVAR$ in Panel B.

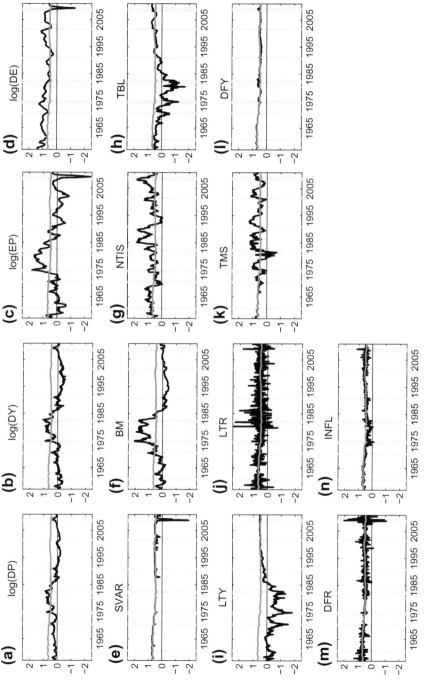

Figure 6.2 Monthly U.S. equity premium out-of-sample forecasts (in percent) based on individual economic variables, 1957:01–2010:12. Black (gray) lines delineate unrestricted predictive regression forecasts based on the economic variable given in the panel heading (historical average forecast). Vertical bars depict NBER-dated recessions. (For interpretation of the references to color in this figure legend, the reader is referred to the web version of this book.)

Table 6.2 Monthly U.S. Equity Premium Out-of-Sample Forecasting Results Based on Multiple Economic Variables, 1957:01–2010:12

Method	Overall		Expansion		Recession	
	R_{OS}^2 (%)	Δ (annual %)	R_{OS}^2 (%)	Δ (annual %)	R_{OS}^2 (%)	Δ (annual %)
Panel A: Unrestricted forecasts						
Kitchen sink	−8.43 [0.42]	0.24	−9.41 [0.68]	−1.60	−6.38 [0.28]	8.94
SIC	−5.61 [0.99]	−1.77	−5.80 [1.00]	−3.24	−5.21 [0.79]	5.00
POOL-AVG	0.44 [0.03]	1.25	0.12 [0.21]	0.41	1.10 [0.01]	5.14
POOL-DMSFE	0.51 [0.02]	1.52	0.08 [0.25]	0.40	1.39 [0.01]	6.76
Diffusion index	0.68 [0.01]	1.65	−1.00 [0.27]	−1.46	4.15 [0.00]	16.42
Sum-of-the-parts	0.93 [0.01]	2.47	0.29 [0.13]	0.27	2.24 [0.01]	12.87
Panel B: Forecasts with nonnegativity restrictions						
Kitchen sink	−2.57 [0.59]	0.24	−3.38 [0.64]	−1.60	−0.89 [0.45]	8.94
SIC	−4.47 [0.99]	−1.77	−4.73 [0.99]	−3.24	−3.03 [0.85]	5.00
POOL-AVG	0.44 [0.03]	1.25	0.12 [0.21]	0.41	1.10 [0.01]	5.14
POOL-DMSFE	0.51 [0.02]	1.52	0.08 [0.25]	0.40	1.39 [0.01]	6.76
Diffusion index	0.70 [0.01]	1.65	−0.68 [0.24]	−1.46	3.47 [0.00]	16.42
Sum-of-the-parts	0.99 [0.00]	2.47	0.31 [0.12]	0.27	2.40 [0.00]	12.87

Notes: R_{OS}^2 measures the percent reduction in mean squared forecast error (MSFE) for the forecasting method given in the first column relative to the historical average benchmark forecast. Brackets report *p*-values for the Clark and West (2007) *MSFE-adjusted* statistic for testing the null hypothesis that the historical average MSFE is less than or equal to the forecasting method MSFE against the alternative that the historical average MSFE is greater than the forecasting method MSFE (corresponding to $H_0: R_{OS}^2 \leq 0$ against $H_A: R_{OS}^2 > 0$). Average utility gain (Δ) is the portfolio management fee (in annualized percent return) that an investor with mean-variance preferences and risk aversion coefficient of five would be willing to pay to have access to the forecasting method relative to the historical average benchmark forecast. 0.00 indicates less than 0.005. R_{OS}^2 statistics and average utility gains are computed for the entire 1957:01–2010:12 forecast evaluation period and separately for NBER-dated expansions and recessions.

full forecast evaluation period. The line in Figure 6.3, Panel A is nearly always negative sloped, showing that the kitchen sink forecast consistently underperforms the historical average in terms of MSFE. Panel A of Figure 6.4 indicates that the kitchen sink forecast is highly volatile, more so than any of the individual bivariate predictive regression forecasts (note the difference in the vertical axis scales in Figures 6.2 and 6.4, Panel A). The monthly kitchen sink forecast reaches nearly 4% – implying an annualized expected equity premium of nearly 48% – and falls below −4% – implying an annualized expected equity premium near −50%. These extreme values are highly implausible, clearly demonstrating the in-sample overfitting problem that causes highly parameterized models to produce large forecast errors; such errors are stringently penalized by the MSFE criterion. Despite the very poor performance of the kitchen sink forecast in terms of MSFE, it does deliver a positive overall average utility gain, although the gain is less than 25 basis points on an annualized basis. This again illustrates how different evaluation criteria can lead to different conclusions regarding stock return forecasting performance.

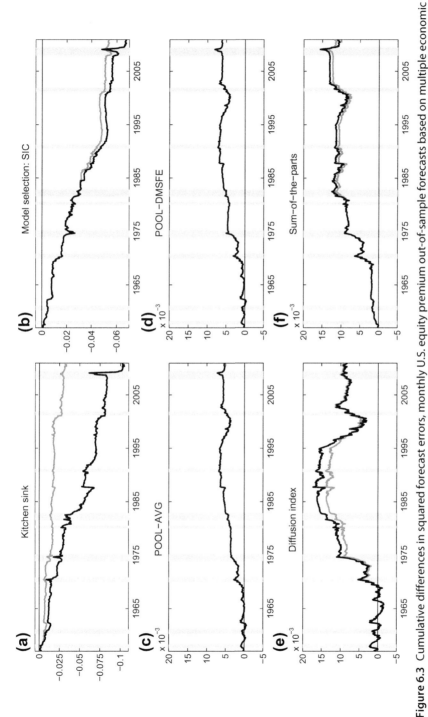

Figure 6.3 Cumulative differences in squared forecast errors, monthly U.S. equity premium out-of-sample forecasts based on multiple economic variables, 1957:01–2010:12. Black (gray) lines in each panel delineate the cumulative difference in squared forecast errors for the historical average forecast relative to the forecasting method given in the panel heading (forecasting method with nonnegativity restrictions imposed). Vertical bars depict NBER-dated recessions. (For interpretation of the references to color in this figure legend, the reader is referred to the web version of this book.)

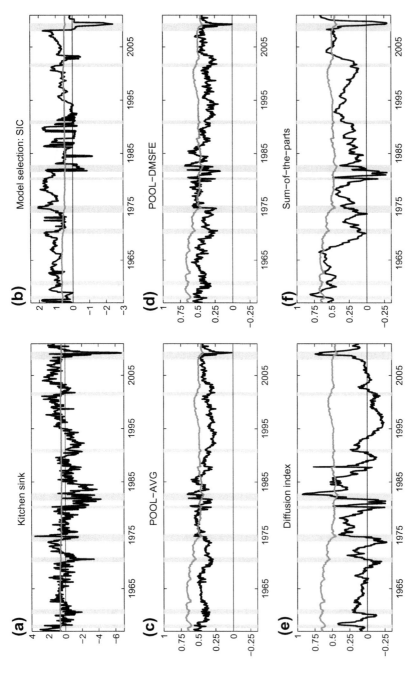

Figure 6.4 Monthly U.S. equity premium out-of-sample forecasts (in percent) based on multiple economic variables, 1957:01–2010:12. Black (gray) lines delineate forecasts based on the forecasting method given in the panel heading (historical average forecast). Vertical bars depict NBER-dated recessions. (For interpretation of the references to color in this figure legend, the reader is referred to the web version of this book.)

In the spirit of Pesaran and Timmermann (1995) and Bossaerts and Hillion (1999), the next forecast in Table 6.2 selects the forecasting model using the SIC, from among the 2^K possible specifications for the $K = 14$ potential predictors, based on data available at the time of forecast formation.[38] The idea is to use the SIC to guard against in-sample overfitting, since the SIC penalizes models with more parameters. While the R^2_{OS} increases for the full forecast evaluation period for the SIC relative to the kitchen sink forecast, it is still well below zero (-5.61%), and Figure 6.3, Panel B indicates that it is consistently outperformed by the historical average. Panel B of Figure 6.4 shows that, while the SIC forecast is less volatile than the kitchen sink forecast (as expected), it remains quite volatile, so that the SIC forecast still appears to be plagued by in-sample overfitting. The SIC forecast also fails to outperform the historical average in terms of average utility gain.

The last four forecasts considered in Table 6.2 employ three of the recently proposed approaches for improving equity premium forecasts reviewed in Section 3.1. The first two of these forecasts are combination forecasts based on (15), which we implement in two ways: (1) a simple combining scheme, $\omega_{i,t} = 1/K$ for $i = 1, \ldots, K$ (POOL-AVG); (2) combining weights that depend on recent forecasting performance, (16) for $\theta = 0.75$ (POOL-DMSFE).[39] The next forecast is the diffusion index forecast given by (23), where we use the first principal component extracted from the 14 economic variables. The final forecast is the sum-of-the-parts forecast in (14).

The results in Table 6.2, Panel A demonstrate the usefulness of recently proposed forecasting strategies. The POOL-AVG, POOL-DMSFE, diffusion index, and sum-of-the parts forecasts all deliver positive R^2_{OS} statistics for the full 1957:01–2010:12 forecast evaluation period, and each of the corresponding Clark and West (2007) p-values indicates significance at the 5% level.[40] The R^2_{OS} statistics for these four forecasts range from 0.44% (POOL-AVG) to 0.93% (sum-of-the-parts), all of which are larger than any of the R^2_{OS} statistics for the individual bivariate predictive regression forecasts in the second column of Table 6.1. In marked contrast to Figure 6.1 and Panels A and B of Figure 6.3, these four forecasts produce out-of-sample gains on a quite consistent basis over time, as demonstrated in Panels C–F of Figure 6.3. The POOL-AVG and POOL-DMSFE forecasts, in particular, deliver very consistent gains, with slopes in Figure 6.3 that are nearly always positive. Although the lines are briefly negatively sloped during the late 1990s, the deterioration in performance during this time is much milder than that exhibited by a number of the individual bivariate predictive regression forecasts in Figure 6.1 (not to mention the kitchen sink and SIC forecasts in Panels A and B of Figure 6.3). While it generates a higher R^2_{OS} for the full forecast evaluation period, the diffusion index forecast

---

[38] We obtain similar results for other information criteria, such as the AIC.

[39] We use 1947:01–1956:12 as the initial holdout out-of-sample period when computing the POOL-DMSFE forecast.

[40] Strictly speaking, Clark and West (2007) analyze the *MSFE-adjusted* statistic for forecasts generated from linear predictive regressions estimated via OLS. The POOL-AVG, POOL-DMSFE, and sum-of-the-parts forecasts do not exactly conform to this structure, so that we use the *MSFE-adjusted* statistic as an approximation to statistical significance.

performs more erratically than the combination forecasts, with a much sharper dropoff during the late 1990s. The sum-of-the-parts forecast generates a higher R^2_{OS} for the full evaluation period than the combination and diffusion index forecasts, while providing less (more) consistent gains than the combination forecasts (diffusion index forecast). The POOL-AVG, POOL-DMSFE, diffusion index, and sum-of-the-parts forecasts also generate sizable average utility gains for the 1957:01–2010:12 forecast evaluation period, ranging from 125 to 247 basis points on an annualized basis. These four forecasts thus perform well according to both MSFE and direct utility-based criteria.

Panels C–F of Figure 6.4 provide insight into the success of the POOL-AVG, POOL-DMSFE, diffusion index, and sum-of-the-parts forecasts. Relative to many of the individual bivariate predictive regression forecasts in Figure 6.2 and the kitchen sink and SIC forecasts in Panels A and B of Figure 6.4, these four forecasts tend to be considerably more stable (again, note the differences in vertical axis scales). Stabilization is accomplished by shrinkage for the combination forecasts (Section 3.1.2), by filtering noise from predictors for the diffusion index forecast (Section 3.1.3), and by reducing estimation error for the sum-of-the-parts forecast (Section 3.1.1). Such stabilization is necessary due to the substantial model uncertainty and parameter instability surrounding stock return forecasting. Successful stock return forecasting strategies incorporate information from multiple economic variables – information ignored by the historical average forecast – but in a manner that accommodates model uncertainty and parameter instability, thereby producing return forecasts that are economically plausible.

Supporting the economic plausibility of the POOL-AVG, POOL-DMFSE, diffusion index, and sum-of-the parts forecasts, the behavior of these forecasts appears linked to business-cycle fluctuations in Figure 6.4. In particular, during the mid–1970s and 1990–1991 recessions, and especially the severe recession of the early 1980s, the forecasts descend to distinct local minima near business-cycle peaks and then increase sharply during the course of recessions, reaching distinct local maxima near business-cycle troughs.[41] This countercyclical pattern in expected returns is very much in line with the time-varying risk aversion explanation of return predictability in Fama and French (1989), Campbell and Cochrane (1999), and Cochrane (2007, 2011), among others: economic agents have relatively low risk aversion at the end of economic expansions – and therefore require a lower equity risk premium – but agents' risk aversion increases during contractions as income and consumption levels fall – necessitating a higher equity risk premium. While the behavior of the diffusion index forecasts also conforms to this pattern during the recent Great Recession, the behavior of the POOL-AVG, POOL-DMSFE, and sum-of-the-parts forecasts diverges somewhat from this pattern during this period, as the latter three forecasts typically decline over the course of the recession and subsequently increase sharply after the cyclical trough in 2009:06. This could be due to the severe disruptions

---

[41] Some of the bivariate predictive regression forecasts in Figure 6.2 also exhibit this pattern, in particular, $\log(DP)$, $\log(DY)$, and *TMS*.

in financial markets and unprecedented policy interventions associated with the Global Financial Crisis and very weak economic recovery from the Great Recession.

The last four columns of Table 6.2, Panel A show that the out-of-sample gains, in terms of both the R^2_{OS} statistics and average utility gains, are concentrated during recessions for the POOL-AVG, POOL-DMSFE, diffusion index, and sum-of-the-parts forecasts. The R^2_{OS} statistics are positive for three of these four forecasts during expansions (the exception is the diffusion index), but none of these is significant at conventional levels. The R^2_{OS} statistics range from 1.10% (POOL-AVG) to 4.15% (diffusion index) during recessions, and all of these statistics are significant at the 1% level, despite the reduced number of available observations. The average utility gain during recessions is a very substantial 16.42% for the diffusion index. The economically plausible behavior of the POOL-AVG, POOL-DMSFE, diffusion index, and sum-of-the-parts forecasts over the business cycle accords with the substantial out-of-sample gains associated with these forecasts during recessions.[42]

Panel B of Table 6.2 reports results for forecasts based on multiple economic variables with non-negativity restrictions, where we set the forecast to zero if a given method produces a negative forecast. By stabilizing the relatively volatile kitchen sink and SIC forecasts, the non-negativity restrictions substantially increase the R^2_{OS} statistics for these forecasts, although they remain well below zero. The non-negativity constraints are never binding for the POOL-AVG and POOL-DMSFE forecasts (see Figure 6.4, Panels C and D), so that the R^2_{OS} statistics are identical for these forecasts across Panels A and B. For the diffusion index and sum-of-the-parts forecasts, the non-negativity restrictions only lead to slight increases in the R^2_{OS} statistics. Overall, non-negativity restrictions have limited impact on the performance of the POOL-AVG, POOL-DMSFE, diffusion index, and sum-of-the-parts forecasts, presumably due to the stabilizing nature of these strategies.[43]

While positive, the R^2_{OS} statistics for the POOL-AVG, POOL-DMSFE, diffusion index, and sum-of-the-parts forecasts in the second column of Table 6.2 seem small at first blush. As discussed in Section 2, however, theory predicts that the predictable component in the monthly equity premium will be small. Moreover, the monthly R^2_{OS} statistics for these four forecasts, while below 1%, still represent excessive stock return predictability from the standpoint of leading asset pricing models, making them economically relevant.

The average utility gains in Table 6.2 point to substantial economic value for the POOL-AVG, POOL-DMSE, diffusion index, and sum-of-the-parts forecasts. Nevertheless, an important word of caution is in order. The mean-variance investor for whom we

[42] Of course, we identify enhanced return predictability during recessions *ex post*, since the NBER dates business-cycle peaks and troughs retrospectively. As discussed in Section 3.1.4, Markov-switching models provide a natural framework for switching between forecasting models according to estimated probabilities of the state of the economy, helping to exploit enhanced return predictability during recessions in real time. Another possibility is to rely on a real-time index of business conditions, such as Aruoba et al. (2009), to guide switching between forecasts over the business cycle.

[43] Since the asset allocation exercise places a lower bound of zero on the equity portfolio weight, the average utility gains are identical across Panels A and B of Table 6.2.

compute utility gains is assumed to have a constant relative risk aversion coefficient over time. To the extent that return predictability is generated by time-varying risk aversion over the business cycle, the utility gains computed under the assumption of constant risk aversion only obtain for a "small" (i.e., non-representative) investor who does not affect market prices. In essence, a non-representative investor can exploit the return predictability created by the time-varying risk aversion of the representative investor.[44]

3.3.2. U.S. Equity Premium Forecastability at Longer Horizons

Since the literature on in-sample return predictability frequently analyzes predictability at longer horizons, we also compute R^2_{OS} statistics and average utility gains for quarterly and annual (non-overlapping) forecasts.[45] Results for quarterly equity premium forecasts based on individual bivariate prediction regressions are reported in Table 6.3. The R^2_{OS} statistics for the unrestricted predictive regression forecasts in Panel A are reasonably similar to the corresponding statistics for the monthly forecasts in Table 6.1. The average utility gains in Table 6.3, Panel A are often more sizable than those in Table 6.1, Panel A, so that the economic significance of out-of-sample return predictability appears stronger at we move from a monthly to quarterly horizon. Following the pattern in Table 6.1, return predictability at the quarterly horizon is concentrated during business-cycle recessions for the valuation ratios and *TMS*. When we impose Campbell and Thompson (2008) restrictions in Table 6.3, Panel B, log (*DP*) and log (*DY*) both have positive and significant R^2_{OS} statistics, and the R^2_{OS} for log (*DY*) is well above 1%.

Table 6.4 reports results for quarterly forecasts based on multiple economic variables. Panel A (B) reports results for unrestricted forecasts (forecasts with non-negativity restrictions imposed). The R^2_{OS} statistics and average utility gains for the quarterly kitchen sink and SIC forecasts in both panels of Table 6.4 deteriorate relative to the corresponding monthly values in Table 6.2. In contrast, the R^2_{OS} statistics and average utility gains increase for the POOL-AVG, POOL-DMSFE, diffusion index, and sum-of-the-parts forecasts as we move from a monthly to quarterly horizon (and the R^2_{OS} statistics remain significant). In both panels of Table 6.4, the R^2_{OS} statistics for the POOL-DMSFE, diffusion index, and sum-of-the-parts forecasts are now all greater than 1%, and the latter two are above 2%. Similarly to Table 6.2, imposing non-negativity restrictions on the quarterly forecasts substantially improves the R^2_{OS} statistics for the kitchen sink and SIC forecasts, although the R^2_{OS} statistics both remain well below zero, while the restrictions have little effect on the POOL-AVG, POOL-DMSFE, diffusion index, and sum-of-the-parts forecasts.

Table 6.5 reports results for individual bivariate prediction regression forecasts (Panel A), as well as forecasts based on multiple economic variables (Panel B), at an annual

---

[44] This brings to mind Warren Buffett's well-known quote: "We simply attempt to be fearful when others are greedy and to be greedy only when others are fearful."

[45] Quarterly and annual data are also available from Amit Goyal's web page at http://www.hec.unil.ch/agoyal/.

Table 6.3 Quarterly U.S. Equity Premium Out-of-Sample Forecasting Results Based on Individual Economic Variables, 1957:1–2010:4

Economic Variable	Overall		Expansion		Recession	
	R^2_{OS} (%)	Δ (annual %)	R^2_{OS} (%)	Δ (annual %)	R^2_{OS} (%)	Δ (annual %)
Panel A: Unrestricted predictive regression forecasts						
log (DP)	−0.80 [0.07]	2.40	−6.92 [0.43]	−1.88	7.23 [0.00]	19.19
log (DY)	0.36 [0.07]	3.00	−4.71 [0.47]	−1.19	7.02 [0.00]	19.39
log (EP)	−6.51 [0.26]	1.61	−10.19 [0.36]	−0.05	−1.68 [0.29]	7.43
log (DE)	−4.93 [0.97]	−0.02	−2.98 [0.75]	−0.17	−7.48 [0.97]	0.57
SVAR	−0.47 [0.92]	0.27	−0.40 [0.93]	0.18	−0.57 [0.80]	0.50
BM	−6.87 [0.20]	0.19	−13.53 [0.45]	−1.59	1.87 [0.13]	6.43
NTIS	−5.38 [0.48]	−1.12	1.01 [0.02]	0.44	−13.76 [0.95]	−7.32
TBL	−0.56 [0.16]	2.38	−1.96 [0.31]	0.36	1.28 [0.19]	10.22
LTY	−3.43 [0.20]	2.25	−5.62 [0.36]	0.17	−0.55 [0.22]	10.39
LTR	−0.72 [0.38]	0.14	0.70 [0.14]	0.20	−2.58 [0.73]	−0.33
TMS	−0.12 [0.25]	1.44	−1.71 [0.49]	−0.24	1.95 [0.13]	7.77
DFY	0.15 [0.31]	1.33	0.00 [0.40]	0.51	0.34 [0.33]	4.04
DFR	−4.79 [0.95]	−1.71	−1.93 [0.51]	−0.24	−8.54 [0.98]	−7.33
INFL	0.16 [0.33]	1.89	−0.25 [0.72]	−0.35	0.70 [0.23]	10.64
Panel B: Predictive regression forecasts with Campbell and Thompson (2008) restrictions						
log (DP)	0.66 [0.04]	2.40	−3.90 [0.42]	−1.88	6.66 [0.00]	19.19
log (DY)	1.48 [0.03]	3.00	−2.68 [0.38]	−1.19	6.94 [0.00]	19.39
log (EP)	−2.22 [0.21]	1.61	−4.68 [0.36]	−0.05	1.00 [0.22]	7.43
log (DE)	−4.22 [0.97]	0.04	−2.74 [0.71]	−0.10	−6.17 [0.98]	0.66
SVAR	−0.07 [0.87]	0.27	−0.01 [0.52]	0.18	−0.16 [0.91]	0.50
BM	−3.75 [0.22]	0.19	−6.68 [0.42]	−1.59	0.09 [0.21]	6.43
NTIS	−5.34 [0.48]	−1.12	1.03 [0.02]	0.44	−13.70 [0.95]	−7.32
TBL	0.50 [0.14]	2.38	−0.74 [0.30]	0.36	2.12 [0.16]	10.22
LTY	0.09 [0.11]	2.25	−1.43 [0.25]	0.17	2.08 [0.15]	10.39
LTR	−0.31 [0.30]	0.14	0.86 [0.13]	0.20	−1.85 [0.66]	−0.33
TMS	0.10 [0.23]	1.44	−1.63 [0.49]	−0.24	2.37 [0.09]	7.77
DFY	0.15 [0.31]	1.33	0.00 [0.40]	0.51	0.34 [0.33]	4.04
DFR	−0.13 [0.60]	−0.01	0.27 [0.25]	0.00	−0.64 [0.91]	−0.03
INFL	0.17 [0.32]	1.89	−0.23 [0.70]	−0.35	0.70 [0.23]	10.64

Notes: R^2_{OS} measures the percent reduction in mean squared forecast error (MSFE) for the predictive regression forecast based on the economic variable given in the first column relative to the historical average benchmark forecast. Brackets report *p*-values for the Clark and West (2007) *MSFE-adjusted* statistic for testing the null hypothesis that the historical average MSFE is less than or equal to the predictive regression MSFE against the alternative that the historical average MSFE is greater than the predictive regression MSFE (corresponding to $H_0: R^2_{OS} \leq 0$ against $H_A: R^2_{OS} > 0$). Average utility gain (Δ) is the portfolio management fee (in annualized percent return) that an investor with mean-variance preferences and risk aversion coefficient of five would be willing to pay to have access to the predictive regression forecast based on the economic variable given in the first column relative to the historical average benchmark forecast. 0.00 indicates less than 0.005. R^2_{OS} statistics and average utility gains are computed for the entire 1957:1–2010:4 forecast evaluation period and separately for NBER-dated expansions and recessions.

Table 6.4 Quarterly U.S. Equity Premium Out-of-Sample Forecasting Results Based on Multiple Economic Variables, 1957:1–2010:4

Method	Overall		Expansion		Recession	
	R^2_{OS} (%)	Δ (annual %)	R^2_{OS} (%)	Δ (annual %)	R^2_{OS} (%)	Δ (annual %)
Panel A: Unrestricted forecasts						
Kitchen sink	−29.82 [0.76]	0.01	−25.89 [0.43]	−2.07	−34.97 [0.85]	8.22
SIC	−19.16 [0.95]	−3.64	−15.27 [0.59]	−4.40	−24.28 [0.97]	−1.31
POOL-AVG	0.73 [0.09]	1.74	0.40 [0.20]	0.98	1.15 [0.13]	4.42
POOL-DMSFE	1.09 [0.05]	2.27	0.23 [0.26]	0.68	2.22 [0.05]	8.41
Diffusion index	2.10 [0.01]	3.40	−3.58 [0.23]	−1.26	9.56 [0.00]	21.81
Sum-of-the-parts	2.02 [0.03]	3.61	0.24 [0.22]	0.63	4.35 [0.03]	15.34
Panel B: Forecasts with nonnegativity restrictions						
Kitchen sink	−10.35 [0.77]	0.01	−8.06 [0.45]	−2.07	−13.34 [0.87]	8.22
SIC	−15.37 [0.91]	−3.64	−12.36 [0.55]	−4.40	−19.31 [0.95]	−1.31
POOL-AVG	0.73 [0.09]	1.74	0.40 [0.20]	0.98	1.15 [0.13]	4.42
POOL-DMSFE	1.09 [0.05]	2.27	0.23 [0.26]	0.68	2.22 [0.05]	8.41
Diffusion index	2.06 [0.01]	3.40	−2.09 [0.23]	−1.26	7.51 [0.00]	21.81
Sum-of-the-parts	2.26 [0.02]	3.61	0.51 [0.18]	0.63	4.55 [0.02]	15.34

Notes: R^2_{OS} measures the percent reduction in mean squared forecast error (MSFE) for the forecasting method given in the first column relative to the historical average benchmark forecast. Brackets report *p*-values for the Clark and West (2007) *MSFE-adjusted* statistic for testing the null hypothesis that the historical average MSFE is less than or equal to the forecasting method MSFE against the alternative that the historical average MSFE is greater than the forecasting method MSFE (corresponding to H_0: $R^2_{OS} \leq 0$ against H_A: $R^2_{OS} > 0$). Average utility gain (Δ) is the portfolio management fee (in annualized percent return) that an investor with mean-variance preferences and risk aversion coefficient of five would be willing to pay to have access to the forecasting method relative to the historical average benchmark forecast. 0.00 indicates less than 0.005. R^2_{OS} statistics and average utility gains are computed for the entire 1957:1–2010:4 forecast evaluation period and separately for NBER-dated expansions and recessions.

horizon. Among the unrestricted individual forecasts, only log (*DP*) has a positive R^2_{OS} (1.76%). Campbell and Thompson (2008) restrictions generally raise the R^2_{OS} statistics for the individual forecasts – the R^2_{OS} increases to 3.51% for log (*DP*) – although the majority remain negative. Nearly all of the average utility gains for the individual forecasts increase as we move from Table 6.3 to Table 6.5, so that out-of-sample return predictability again becomes more economically significant as the forecasting horizon lengthens.

The R^2_{OS} statistics for the kitchen sink and SIC forecasts are substantially lower in Table 6.5 vis-á-vis Table 6.4, indicating that the accuracy of these forecasts continues to deteriorate as the horizon lengthens. The kitchen sink and SIC forecasts also produce negative average utility gains at an annual horizon. In line with the previous pattern, the R^2_{OS} statistics for the POOL-AVG, POOL-DMSFE, diffusion index, and sum-of-the parts forecasts increase as we move from a quarterly horizon in Table 6.4 to an annual horizon in Table 6.5. The R^2_{OS} statistics for both the diffusion index and sum-of-the parts forecasts are now well above 5% (and the R^2_{OS} for the former is above 7%). The average utility gains fall somewhat for the POOL-AVG, POOL-DMSFE, and sum-of-the parts

Table 6.5 Annual U.S. Equity Premium Out-of-Sample Forecasting Results, 1957–2010

Economic Variable or Method	Unrestricted		Campbell and Thompson (2008) Restrictions		Nonnegativity Restrictions	
	R^2_{OS} (%)	Δ (annual %)	R^2_{OS} (%)	Δ (annual %)	R^2_{OS} (%)	Δ (annual %)
Panel A: Forecasts based on individual economic variables						
log (DP)	1.76 [0.09]	4.13	3.51 [0.07]	4.13	—	—
log (DY)	−17.34 [0.21]	4.28	−1.26 [0.13]	4.28	—	—
log (EP)	−4.18 [0.16]	1.30	0.76 [0.09]	1.30	—	—
log (DE)	−7.89 [0.95]	−0.66	−0.05 [0.84]	0.02	—	—
SVAR	−2.34 [0.94]	−0.02	0.00 [−]	0.02	—	—
BM	−8.16 [0.17]	1.63	−4.99 [0.14]	1.63	—	—
NTIS	−16.89 [0.71]	−1.32	−16.89 [0.71]	−1.32	—	—
TBL	−4.86 [0.20]	2.88	0.95 [0.14]	2.88	—	—
LTY	−9.13 [0.18]	2.46	0.74 [0.11]	2.46	—	—
LTR	−6.35 [0.04]	1.92	−5.03 [0.04]	1.92	—	—
TMS	−0.34 [0.22]	1.48	0.00 [0.22]	1.48	—	—
DFY	−2.07 [0.97]	0.00	−0.01 [0.91]	0.02	—	—
DFR	−4.69 [0.58]	−0.04	−4.34 [0.57]	−0.04	—	—
INFL	−1.06 [0.70]	−0.22	−1.06 [0.70]	−0.22	—	—
Panel B: Forecasts based on multiple economic variables						
Kitchen sink	−99.18 [0.70]	−2.93	—	—	−57.39 [0.66]	−2.93
SIC	−45.37 [0.56]	−1.02	—	—	−32.74 [0.53]	−1.02
POOL-AVG	3.11 [0.07]	1.36	—	—	3.11 [0.07]	1.36
POOL-DMSFE	1.71 [0.17]	1.29	—	—	1.71 [0.17]	1.29
Diffusion index	7.14 [0.03]	4.89	—	—	6.98 [0.03]	4.89
Sum-of-the-parts	5.60 [0.04]	2.85	—	—	5.85 [0.04]	2.85

Notes: R^2_{OS} measures the percent reduction in mean squared forecast error (MSFE) for the predictive regression forecast based on the economic variable or forecasting method given in the first column relative to the historical average benchmark forecast. Brackets report *p*-values for the Clark and West (2007) *MSFE-adjusted* statistic for testing the null hypothesis that the historical average MSFE is less than or equal to the predictive regression or forecasting method MSFE against the alternative that the historical average MSFE is greater than the predictive regression or forecasting method MSFE (corresponding to H_0: $R^2_{OS} \leq 0$ against H_A: $R^2_{OS} > 0$). Average utility gain (Δ) is the portfolio management fee (in annualized percent return) that an investor with mean–variance preferences and risk aversion coefficient of five would be willing to pay to have access to the predictive regression forecast or forecasting method relative to the historical average benchmark forecast. 0.00 indicates less than 0.005.

forecasts in Table 6.5 relative to Table 6.4, while the average utility gain increases to a very sizable 4.89% for the diffusion index forecast in Table 6.5.

Focusing on the POOL-AVG, POOL-DMSFE, diffusion index, and sum-of-the-parts forecasts, larger R^2_{OS} statistics – and, hence, greater out-of-sample return predictability according to the MSFE criterion – are available at longer horizons. This increase in out-of-sample return predictability accords with in-sample results from the literature. The theoretical bounds on return predictability discussed in Section 2, however, also increase as the horizon lengthens, so that new economic information is not necessarily available at longer horizons.

3.4. Data Snooping

Data-snooping concerns naturally arise when considering a large number of potential predictors of stock returns. Lo and MacKinlay (1990b), Foster et al. (1997), and Ferson et al. (2003) analyze data snooping in the context of in-sample tests of stock return predictability. White (2000) develops a "reality check" bootstrap to control for data snooping when testing whether any forecast from a group of competing forecasts significantly outperforms a benchmark forecast. White's (2000) procedure is based on a test statistic that is a function of the maximum of the average loss differentials between the benchmark forecast and each competing forecast. A p-value for the maximum statistic is computed via a non-parametric stationary bootstrap that resamples from the original time series of loss differentials.[46] As emphasized by Clark and McCracken (2012), however, the asymptotic properties of the non-parametric stationary bootstrap do not generally apply when all of the competing forecasting models nest the benchmark model. This is relevant for testing out-of-sample stock return predictability. It is often the case that all of the competing forecasts essentially nest the benchmark, since the benchmark typically corresponds to a constant expected return model that excludes the information in the predictors that appear in the competing forecasts, similarly to our application in Section 3.3.

Inoue and Kilian (2004) derive the asymptotic distribution of the maximum Diebold and Mariano (1995) and West (1996) statistic,

$$\max DMW = \max_{i=1,\ldots,K} DMW_i, \tag{48}$$

where DMW_i is given by (36), under the null hypothesis that $\beta_i = 0$ in (7) for all $i = 1, \ldots, K$. This provides an asymptotic framework for controlling for data snooping when testing for out-of-sample stock return predictability. While Inoue and Kilian (2004) focus on asymptotic results, they observe that potential finite-sample size distortions can be handled in practice by bootstrap methods. Using annual data for 1927–1999, Rapach and Wohar (2006b) use a data-snooping-robust bootstrap procedure to test whether nine popular economic variables evince significant out-of-sample predictive ability for S&P

---

[46] Hansen (2005) develops a more powerful refinement of the White (2000) reality check.

500 and CRSP equal-weighted aggregate returns for the 1964–1999 forecast evaluation period. Rapach and Wohar (2006b) compute bootstrapped critical values for

$$\max \; MSE\text{-}F = \max_{i=1,\dots,K} \; MSE\text{-}F_i, \tag{49}$$

where $MSE\text{-}F_i = n_2^{0.5} \bar{d}_i / \text{MSFE}_i$ is a more powerful version of DMW_i from Clark and McCracken (2001). To implement the bootstrap, a pseudo sample of stock return observations matching the original sample size is generated under the null of no predictability by estimating (7) with $\beta_i = 0$ and resampling (with replacement) from the fitted residuals. Autoregressive (AR) processes are estimated for each of the predictors, $x_{i,t}$ ($i = 1, \dots, K$), and a pseudo sample of predictor observations is built up by resampling from the fitted AR process residuals. Importantly, the residuals for the return and predictor processes are drawn in tandem, thereby preserving the contemporaneous correlations in the original data. The maximum statistic is computed for the pseudo sample and stored. Repeating this process many times, bootstrapped critical values are computed from the empirical distribution of maximum statistics. Rapach and Wohar (2006b) find that maximum statistics are significant at conventional levels according to the bootstrapped critical values, signaling that out-of-sample stock return predictability is reasonably robust to data snooping.

Clark and McCracken (2012) recently prove that a wild fixed-regressor bootstrap delivers asymptotically valid critical values for the max DMW and max $MSE\text{-}F$ statistics when comparing multiple forecasts that nest a benchmark. The wild fixed-regressor bootstrap accommodates conditional heteroskedasticity and performs well in finite-sample simulations. The bootstrap is straightforward to implement and provides a theoretically justified bootstrap procedure for controlling for data snooping in tests of out-of-sample stock return predictability.

To implement the wild fixed-regressor bootstrap, a general model that includes all possible predictors is estimated. A pseudo sample of return observations is generated under the null of no predictability by setting $r_t^* = \hat{\alpha}_{0,T} + \eta_t \hat{\epsilon}_t$, where r_t^* is the pseudo observation for r_t, $\hat{\alpha}_{0,T}$ is the sample mean of r_t, η_t is a draw from the standard normal distribution, and $\hat{\epsilon}_t$ is the fitted residual from the general model. Simulating the disturbance term using $\eta_t \hat{\epsilon}_t$ makes this a wild bootstrap. The predictors, $x_{i,t}$ ($i = 1, \dots, K$), from the original sample also serve as the observations for the predictors in the pseudo sample, making this a fixed-regressor bootstrap. By generating a large number of pseudo samples for r_t and storing the maximum statistics for each pseudo sample, an empirical distribution of maximum statistics is built up that can be used to compute critical values or a p-value for the maximum statistic corresponding to the original sample.

As mentioned in Section 3.1.3, Neely et al. (2012) calculate monthly U.S. equity premium forecasts using individual bivariate predictive regression models based on 14 economic variables and 14 technical indicators, as well as a diffusion index forecast, (23), that employs principal components to extract a small number of factors from the 28 predictors. Since they consider a large number of forecasting models, each of which nests the historical average benchmark, Neely et al. (2012) use the Clark and McCracken (2012) wild fixed-regressor bootstrap to assess the significance of the max MSE-F statistic. The bootstrapped p-value is 0.03, so that the significant evidence of equity premium predictability is not readily ascribed to data snooping.

4. STOCK RETURN FORECASTABILITY ALONG OTHER DIMENSIONS

4.1. International Stock Returns

While the literature on aggregate stock return predictability focuses on U.S. returns, a number of studies investigate return predictability for other countries. Papers examining stock return predictability for countries outside of the United States include Cutler et al. (1991), Harvey (1991), Bekaert and Hodrick (1992), Campbell and Hamao (1992), Ferson and Harvey (1993), Solnik (1993), Rapach et al. (2005), Ang and Bekaert (2007), Cooper and Priestly (2009), Della Corte et al. (2010), Hjalmarsson (2010), Kellard et al. (2010), and Henkel et al. (2011). All of these studies estimate in-sample predictive regressions for individual country returns using a variety of domestic and/or U.S. economic variables as predictors. The consensus from these studies is that stock returns are predictable worldwide. In an examination of lead-lag relationships in monthly international stock returns – in the spirit of studies investigating such relationships in portfolios of individual U.S. stocks sorted on size, analyst coverage, volume, and/or industry (e.g., Lo and MacKinlay, 1990a; Brennan et al., 1993; Chordia and Swaminathan, 2000; Hou, 2007) – Rapach et al. (forthcoming) find that lagged U.S. returns predict non-U.S. returns, but that the reverse generally does not hold.

Fewer studies consider out-of-sample tests of international stock return predictability. Among the previously cited studies, Solnik (1993); Rapach et al. (2005), Cooper and Priestly (2009), Della Corte et al. (2010), Hjalmarrson (2010), Kellard et al. (2010), Henkel et al. (2011), and Rapach et al. (forthcoming) conduct out-of-sample tests. Solnik (1993) forms predictive regression forecasts of monthly aggregate stock returns for eight developed countries using domestic dividend yields, short- and long-term nominal interest rates, and a January dummy as predictors. He finds that a dynamic trading strategy that allocates across stocks in the eight countries based on the predictive regression forecasts significantly outperforms a strategy that assumes constant expected returns.

Rapach et al. (2005) investigate out-of-sample stock return predictability for 12 developed countries using up to 10 domestic economic variables as predictors for each country. Nominal interest rates exhibit the most consistent forecasting ability across the 12 countries. Cooper and Priestly (2009) test out-of-sample monthly stock return predictability for the United States and the other G-7 countries using predictive regression forecasts based on domestic output gaps. They detect significant evidence of return forecastability using the R^2_{OS} and MSE-F_i statistics, and they find positive average utility gains for a mean-variance investor with relative risk aversion coefficient of three.

Della Corte et al. (2010) analyze the forecasting power of Lettau and Ludvigson's (2001) consumption-wealth ratio in long spans of annual data for stock returns in the United States, the United Kingdom, Japan, and France. After accounting for "look ahead" bias in the estimation of the long-run consumption-wealth relationship (Brennan and Xia, 2005; Hahn and Lee, 2006), they fail to find significant evidence of out-of-sample return predictability using the R^2_{OS} and $MSE\text{-}F_i$ statistics. According to a variety of performance measures, however, portfolios formed from return forecasts that incorporate information from the consumption-wealth ratio substantially outperform portfolios that ignore the consumption-wealth ratio. This again illustrates the importance of supplementing conventional statistical measures of forecast accuracy with direct profit- and/or utility-based metrics. Again highlighting the value of economically motivated model restrictions, Della Corte et al. (2010) also find that imposing restrictions on predictive regression forecasts á la Campbell and Thompson (2008) improves forecasting performance.

Hjalmarsson (2010) analyzes bivariate predictive regression forecasts of monthly stock returns for a large number of primarily developed countries, where the individual bivariate predictive regressions use the dividend-price ratio, earnings-price ratio, short-term nominal interest rate, and term spread as predictors. Overall, Hjalmarsson (2010) finds that the interest rate variables, especially the term spread, display the most out-of-sample predictive ability. Interestingly, Hjalmarsson (2010) shows that forecasts generated from pooled predictive regressions that impose slope homogeneity restrictions typically produce higher R^2_{OS} statistics than conventional predictive regression forecasts. While the slope homogeneity restrictions are unlikely to be literally true, their imposition permits more efficient parameter estimation that can lead to improved forecasting performance in terms of MSFE. This is another example of the usefulness of sensible model restrictions for forecasting stock returns.

Kellard et al. (2010) compare stock return predictability in the United States and United Kingdom on the basis of dividend-price ratios. They find that the dividend-price ratio exhibits stronger out-of-sample forecasting ability in terms of MSFE in the United Kingdom vis-á-vis the United States, and they attribute the difference to the higher proportion of dividend-paying firms in the United Kingdom. As discussed in Section 3.1.4, Henkel et al. (2011) document strong evidence of out-of-sample stock return predictability in the United States using a regime-switching predictive regression based on popular economic variables from the literature. However, they find weaker evidence that regime switching produces out-of-sample gains in other G-7 countries.

Finally, Rapach et al. (forthcoming) find that lagged U.S. stock returns have substantial out-of-sample predictive power for returns in non-U.S. developed countries. Bivariate predictive regression forecasts based on lagged U.S. returns deliver monthly R^2_{OS} statistics of up to nearly 4% for non-U.S. returns over the 1985:01–2010:12 out-of-sample period, and lagged U.S. returns produce especially sizable out-of-sample gains during the recent Global Financial Crisis.

4.2. Cross-Sectional Stock Returns

In addition to U.S. aggregate stock returns, an ample literature examines return predictability for component portfolios of the aggregate market, including portfolios sorted by market capitalization, book-to-market value, and industry. Ferson and Harvey (1991, 1999), Ferson and Korajczyk (1995), and Kirby (1998), among others, estimate in-sample predictive regressions for component portfolios based on the same types of predictors used in studies of aggregate market return predictability.

Analysis of out-of-sample return predictability for component portfolios, however, is relatively rare. Avramov (2002) adopts a Bayesian approach to investigate return predictability for six size/value-sorted portfolios based on 14 popular economic variables from the literature. Avramov (2002) employs Bayesian model averaging to account for model uncertainty, and he finds that Bayesian model averaging forecasts of monthly component portfolio returns outperform forecasts based on the constant expected component portfolio return assumption in terms of MSFE. In addition, asset allocation exercises reveal sizable utility gains for investors who incorporate return predictability, although it is crucial to account for model uncertainty in the asset allocation decision to realize these gains. Subsequently, Avramov (2004) also uses a Bayesian approach to investigate optimal asset allocation across the 25 Fama-French size/value-sorted portfolios and industry portfolios, respectively, with a smaller set of five economic variables serving as return predictors. For a wide range of prior beliefs, allowing for time variation in monthly expected component portfolio returns produces substantial out-of-sample asset allocation gains relative to assuming constant expected component portfolio returns.

Kong et al. (2011) compute combination forecasts of monthly returns for the 25 Fama-French portfolios from individual bivariate predictive regression forecasts based on the 14 economic variables from Section 3.3 and lagged size/value-sorted portfoilo returns. R_{OS}^2 statistics are positive for all 25 of the combination forecasts of component portfolio returns, and 22 of the R_{OS}^2 statistics are significant at the 5% level according to the Clark and West (2007) test. Furthermore, out-of-sample component return predictability is notably stronger during business-cycle recessions vis-á-vis expansions, similarly to the situation for U.S. aggregate market returns. Return forecastability is also substantially stronger for portfolios comprised of small, value firms; for example, the monthly R_{OS}^2 is 5.73% (0.36%) for the S1/BM5 (S5/BM1) portfolio comprised of firms with the lowest market capitalization and highest book-to-market value (highest market capitalization and lowest book-to-market value). In asset allocation exercises, Kong et al. (2011) show that a variety of component-rotation portfolios based on combination forecasts of component returns outperform portfolios based on historical average forecasts of component returns. Component-rotation portfolios based on the combination forecasts also exhibit significant alpha (after controlling for the three Fama-French factors), as well as significant timing ability according to Lo's (2008) test.[47]

Rapach et al. (2011) compute diffusion index forecasts of 33 industry portfolio returns by extracting the first two principal components from the same 14 economic variables and lagged industry portfolio returns. R_{OS}^2 statistics are positive for nearly all industries, and 26 are significant at conventional levels based on the Clark and West (2007) test. Textiles, apparel, furniture, printing, and publishing, and transportation equipment are among the most predictable industries, with monthly R_{OS}^2 statistics above 3%. In addition, industry-rotation portfolios that utilize diffusion index forecasts of industry returns generate sizable utility gains relative to historical average forecasts for an investor with power utility.

Another interesting forecasting application in the cross-sectional domain is Han et al. (forthcoming), who examine the use of technical indicators to inform asset allocation decisions across portfolios sorted by volatility. They find that moving-average rules generate investment timing portfolios that substantially outperform a buy-and-hold strategy. Furthermore, the timing portfolios have negative or little risk exposures to the three Fama-French factors, signaling abnormal returns from the perspective of the Fama-French three-factor model, with annual alphas exceeding 20% for high-volatility portfolios.

5. CONCLUSION

The key themes of this chapter can be summarized as follows:

- Theory tells us that the predictable component in stock returns will be small and that monthly R_{OS}^2 statistics below 1% can be economically relevant. Forecasting models that purport to explain a large portion of stock return fluctuations imply substantial risk-adjusted abnormal returns and are simply too good to be true.
- As forcefully demonstrated by Goyal and Welch (2008), conventional predictive regression forecasts of stock returns fail to consistently outperform the simple historical average forecast in terms of MSFE. Model uncertainty and parameter instability render conventional predictive regression forecasts unreliable.
- Recently proposed strategies significantly improve upon conventional predictive regression forecasts. These procedures, which improve forecasting performance by accommodating model uncertainty and parameter instability, include economically motivated model restrictions, forecast combination, diffusion indices, and regime shifts.
- Inferences concerning out-of-sample stock return predictability typically involve comparisons of nested forecasts. Unless statistical tests designed for nested forecast

---

[47] Although not employing a predictive regression framework *per se*, Tu (2010) finds that responding to regime switching between "bull" and "bear" markets substantially improves portfolio performance for an investor allocating across the 25 Fama-French portfolios.

comparisons are used, significant evidence of stock return forecastability can easily be missed.

- It is important to supplement conventional statistical criteria of forecast accuracy with direct profit- or utility-based criteria, since the two types of measures are not necessarily strongly related. In particular, utility-based measures can indicate clear economic significance, even if conventional statistical measures fail to detect out-of-sample gains.
- Stock return forecastability is strongly linked to business-cycle fluctuations, with a substantially greater degree of forecastability evident during recessions vis-á-vis expansions.
- In addition to the U.S. aggregate market, there is significant out-of-sample evidence of stock return predictability for countries outside of the United States, as well as component portfolios of the U.S. market. Exploiting the out-of-sample predictability in international and cross-sectional returns can produce sizable utility gains from an asset allocation perspective.

We conclude by suggesting avenues for future research. The literature on stock return forecasting primarily relies on popular economic variables as predictors. However, other variables that potentially contain relevant information for forecasting stock returns have received less attention. Such variables include options, futures, and other derivative prices; microstructure measures of liquidity; and institutional trading variables such as trading volumes and money flows for mutual and hedge funds. Furthermore, recent studies find significant in-sample evidence of a positive relationship between expected returns and risk (e.g., Guo and Whitelaw, 2006; Lanne and Saikkonen, 2006; Lundblad, 2007; Bali, 2008). It would be interesting to examine whether these approaches could be used to generate reliable out-of-sample stock return forecasts based on the expected return-risk relationship; Ludvigson and Ng (2007) report promising results in this direction. Finally, learning appears to play an important role in stock return predictability (e.g., Timmermann, 1993, 1996; Pástor and Veronesi, 2009). Theoretical models that explain how investors form return forecasts in light of available information and respond to their forecasting errors serve as promising building blocks for forecasting models based on learning.

ACKNOWLEDGMENTS

We are grateful to Graham Elliott and Allan Timmermann (Editors), two anonymous referees, Massimo Guidolin, Lutz Kilian, Michael McCracken, Ľuboš Pástor, and participants at the Handbook of Economic Forecasting conference hosted by the Federal Reserve Bank of St. Louis for very helpful comments.

REFERENCES

Aït-Sahalia, Y., Brandt, M.W., 2001. Variable selection for portfolio choice. Journal of Finance 56, 1297–1351.

Alexander, S., 1961. Price movement in speculative markets: trends or random walks. Industrial Management Review 2, 7–26.

Alexander, S., 1964. Price movement in speculative markets: trends or random walks, number 2. Industrial Management Review 5, 25–46.

Amihud, Y., Hurvich, C.M., 2004. Predictive regressions: a reduced-bias estimation method. Journal of Financial and Quantitative Analysis 39, 813–841.

Amihud, Y., Hurvich, C.M., Wang, Y., 2009. Multi-predictor regressions: hypothesis testing. Review of Financial Studies 22, 413–434.

Andersen, T.G., Bollerslev, T., Christoffersen, P.C., Diebold, F.X. 2006. Volatility and Correlation Forecasting. In: Elliott, G., Granger, C.W.J., Timmermann, A. (Eds.), Handbook of Economic Forecasting, vol. 1. Elsevier, Amsterdam.

Ang, A., Bekaert, G., 2002. International asset allocation with regime shifts. Review of Financial Studies 15, 1137–1187.

Ang, A., Bekaert, G., 2007. Return predictability: is it there? Review of Financial Studies 20, 651–707.

Ang, A., Timmermann, A., 2012. Regime changes and financial markets. Annual Review of Financial Economics 4, 313-337.

Aruoba, S.B., Diebold, F.X., Scotti, C., 2009. Real-time measurement of business conditions. Journal of Business and Economic Statistics 27, 417–427.

Avramov, D., 2002. Stock return predictability and model uncertainty. Journal of Financial Economics 64, 423–458.

Avramov, D., 2004. Stock return predictability and asset pricing models. Review of Financial Studies 17, 699–738.

Bai, J., 2003. Inferential theory for factor models of large dimensions. Econometrica 71, 135–171.

Bai, J., Ng, S., 2008. Forecasting economic time series using targeted predictors. Journal of Econometrics 146, 304–317.

Bai, J., Perron, P., 1998. Estimating and testing linear models with multiple structural changes. Econometrica 66, 47–78.

Bai, J., Perron, P., 2003. Computation and analysis of multiple structural change models. Journal of Applied Econometrics 18, 1–22.

Baker, M., Wurgler, J., 2000. The equity share in new issues and aggregate stock returns. Journal of Finance 55, 2219–2257.

Bali, T.G., 2008. The intertemporal relation between expected returns and risk. Journal of Financial Economics 87, 101–131.

Bansal, R., Yaron, A., 2004. Risks for the long run: a potential resolution of asset pricing puzzles. Journal of Finance 59, 1481–1509.

Barberis, N., 2000. Investing for the long run when returns are predictable. Journal of Finance 55, 225–264.

Batchelor, R., 2011. Accuracy versus profitability. Foresight: The International Journal of Applied Forecasting 21, 10–15.

Bates, J.M., Granger, C.W.J., 1969. The combination of forecasts. Operational Research Quarterly 20, 451–468.

Bekaert, G., Hodrick, R.J., 1992. Characterizing predictable components in excess returns on equity and foreign exchange markets. Journal of Finance 47, 467–509.

van Binsbergen, J.H., Koijen, R.S.J., 2010. Predictive regressions: a present-value approach. Journal of Finance 65, 1439–1471

Bossaerts, P., Hillion, P., 1999. Implementing statistical criteria to select return forecasting models: what do we learn? Review of Financial Studies 12, 405–428.

Boudoukh, J., Michaely, R., Richardson, M.P., Roberts, M.R., 2007. On the importance of measuring payout yield: implications for empirical asset pricing. Journal of Finance 62, 877–915.

Boudoukh, J., Richardson, M.P., Whitelaw, R.F., 2008. The myth of long-horizon predictability. Review of Financial Studies 21, 1577–1605.

Breen, W., Glosten, L.R., Jagannathan, R., 1989. Economic significance of predictable variation in stock index returns. Journal of Finance 44, 1177–1189.

Brennan, M.J., Jegadeesh, N., Swaminathan, B., 1993. Investment analysis and the adjustment of stock prices to common information. Review of Financial Studies 6, 799–824.

Brennan, M.J., Xia, Y., 2005. *tay*'s as good as *cay*. Finance Research Letters 2, 1–14.

Britten-Jones, M., Neuberger, A., Nolte, I., 2011. Improved inference in regression with overlapping observations. Journal of Business, Finance, and Accounting 38, 657–683.

Brock, W., Lakonishok, J., LeBaron, B., 1992. Simple technical trading rules and the stochastic properties of stock returns. Journal of Finance 47, 1731–1764.

Brown, S.J., Goetzmann, W.N., Kumar, A., 1998. The Dow Theory: William Peter Hamilton's track record reconsidered. Journal of Finance 53, 1311–1333.

Butler, A.W., Grullon, G., Weston, J.P., 2005. Can managers forecast aggregate market returns? Journal of Finance 60, 963–986.

Campbell, J.Y., 1987. Stock returns and the term structure. Journal of Financial Economics 18, 373–399.

Campbell, J.Y., 2000. Asset pricing at the millennium. Journal of Finance 55, 1515–1567.

Campbell, J.Y., 2008. Viewpoint: estimating the equity premium. Canadian Journal of Economics 41, 1–21.

Campbell, J.Y., Cochrane, J.H., 1999. By force of habit: a consumption-based explanation of aggregate stock market behavior. Journal of Political Economy 107, 205–251.

Campbell, J.Y., Hamao, Y., 1992. Predictable stock returns in the United States and Japan: a study of long-term capital market integration. Journal of Finance 47, 43–69.

Campbell, J.Y., Shiller, R.J., 1988a. The dividend-price ratio and expectations of future dividends and discount factors. Review of Financial Studies 1, 195–228.

Campbell, J.Y., Shiller, R.J., 1988b. Stock prices, earnings, and expected dividends. Journal of Finance 43, 661–676.

Campbell, J.Y., Shiller, R.J., 1998. Valuation ratios and the long-run stock market outlook. Journal of Portfolio Management 24, 11–26.

Campbell, J.Y., Thompson, S.B., 2008. Predicting excess stock returns out of sample: can anything beat the historical average? Review of Financial Studies 21, 1509–1531.

Campbell, J.Y., Vuolteenaho, T., 2004. Inflation illusion and stock prices. American Economic Review 94, 19–23.

Campbell, J.Y., Yogo, M., 2006. Efficient tests of stock return predictability. Journal of Financial Economics 81, 27–60.

Campbell, S.D., Diebold, F.X., 2009. Stock returns and expected business conditions: a half century of direct evidence. Journal of Business and Economic Statistics 27, 266–278.

Cavanaugh, C.L., Elliott, G., Stock, J.H., 1995. Inference in models with nearly non-stationary regressors. Econometric Theory 11, 1131–1147.

Cenesizoglu, T., Timmermann, A., 2011. Do return prediction models add economic value? Manuscript, HEC Montreal and University of California at San Diego.

Chen, Q., Hong, Y., 2010. Predictability of equity returns over different time horizons: a non-parametric approach. Cornell University, Manuscript.

Chordia, T., Swaminathan, B., 2000. Trading volume and cross-autocorrelations in stock returns. Journal of Finance 55, 913–935.

Clark, T.E., McCracken, M.W., 2001. Test of equal forecast accuracy and encompassing for nested models. Journal of Econometrics 105, 85–110.

Clark, T.E., McCracken, M.W., 2005. The power of tests of predictive ability in the presence of structural breaks. Journal of Econometrics 124, 1–31.

Clark, T.E., McCracken, M.W., 2009. Improving forecast accuracy by combining recursive and rolling forecasts. International Economic Review 50, 363–395.

Clark, T.E., McCracken, M.W., 2012. Reality checks and comparisons of nested predictive models. Journal of Business and Economic Statistics 30, 53–66.

Clark, T.E., West, K.D., 2007. Approximately normal tests for equal predictive accuracy in nested models. Journal of Econometrics 138, 291–311.

Clements, M.P., Hendry, D.F., 2006. Forecasting with breaks. In: Elliott, G., Granger, C.W.J., Timmermann, A. (Eds.), Handbook of Economic Forecasting, vol. 1. Elsevier, Amsterdam.

Cochrane, J.H., 2005. Asset Pricing revised ed. Princeton University Press, Princeton, NJ.

Cochrane, J.H., 2007. Financial markets and the real economy. In: Mehra, R. (Ed.), Handbook of the Equity Premium. Elsevier, Amsterdam.

Cochrane, J.H., 2008. The dog that did not bark: a defense of return predictability. Review of Financial Studies 21, 1533–1575.

Cochrane, J.H., 2011. Presidential address: discount rates. Journal of Finance 66, 1047–1108.

Cooper, I., Priestly, R., 2009. Time-varying risk premiums and the output gap. Review of Financial Studies 22, 2801–2833.

Cootner, P.H., 1962. Stock prices: random vs. systematic changes. Industrial Management Review 3, 24–45.

Corradi, V., Swanson, N.R., 2006. Predictive density evaluation. In: Elliott, G., Granger, C.W.J., Timmermann, A. (Eds.), Handbook of Economic Forecasting, vol. 1. Elsevier, Amsterdam.

Cowles, A., 1933. Can stock market forecasters forecast? Econometrica 1, 309–324.

Cremers, K.J.M., 2002. Stock return predictability: a Bayesian model selection perspective. Review of Financial Studies 15, 1223–1249.

Cumby, R.E., Modest, D.M., 1987. Testing for market timing ability: a framework for forecast evaluation. Journal of Financial Economics 19, 169–189.

Cutler, D.M., Poterba, J.M., Summers, L.H., 1991. Speculative dynamics. Review of Economic Studies 58, 529–546.

Dangl, T., Halling, M., 2012. Predictive regressions with time-varying coefficients. Journal of Financial Economics, forthcoming.

Della Corte, P., Sarno, L., Valente, G., 2010. A century of equity premium predictability and the consumption-wealth ratio: an international perspective. Journal of Empirical Finance 17, 313–331.

Diebold, F.X., Mariano, R.S., 1995. Comparing predictive accuracy. Journal of Business and Economic Statistics 13, 253–263.

Driesprong, G., Jacobsen, B., Maat, B., 2008. Striking oil: another puzzle? Journal of Financial Economics 89, 307–327.

Elliott, G., Müller, U., 2006. Efficient tests for general persistent time variation in regression coefficients. Review of Economic Studies 73, 907–940.

Fama, E.F., 1970. Efficient capital markets: a review of theory and empirical work. Journal of Finance 25, 383–417.

Fama, E.F., 1991. Efficient capital markets: II. Journal of Finance 46, 1575–1617.

Fama, E.F., Blume, M.E., 1966. Filter rules and stock-market trading. Journal of Business 39, 226–241.

Fama, E.F., French, K.R., 1988. Dividend yields and expected stock returns. Journal of Financial Economics 22, 3–25.

Fama, E.F., French, K.R., 1989. Business conditions and expected returns on stocks and bonds. Journal of Financial Economics 25, 23–49.

Fama, E.F., Schwert, G.W., 1977. Asset returns and inflation. Journal of Financial Economics 5, 115–146.

Ferreira, M.I., Santa-Clara, P., 2011. Forecasting stock market returns: the sum of the parts is more than the whole. Journal of Financial Economics 100, 514–537.

Ferson, W.E., Harvey, C.R., 1991. The variation in economic risk premiums. Journal of Political Economy 99, 385–415.

Ferson, W.E., Harvey, C.R., 1993. The risk and predictability of international equity returns. Review of Financial Studies 6, 527–566.

Ferson, W.E., Harvey, C.R., 1999. Conditioning variables and the cross section of stock returns. Journal of Finance 54, 1325–1360.

Ferson, W.E., Korajczyk, R.A., 1995. Do arbitrage pricing models explain the predictability of stock returns? Journal of Business 68, 309–349.

Ferson, W.E., Sarkissian, S., Simin, T.T., 2003. Spurious regressions in financial economics? Journal of Finance 58, 1393–1413.

Foster, F.D., Smith, T., Whaley, R.E., 1997. Assessing goodness-of-fit of asset pricing models: the distribution of the maximum R^2. Journal of Finance 52, 591–607.

Franses, P.H., van Dijk, D., 2000. Non-linear Time Series Models in Empirical Finance. Cambridge University Press, Cambridge, United Kingdom.

Giacomini, R., Rossi, B., 2009. Detecting and predicting forecast breakdowns. Review of Economic Studies 76, 669–705.

Giacomini, R., Rossi, B., 2010. Forecast comparisons in unstable environments. Journal of Applied Econometrics 25, 595–620.

Goetzmann, W.N., Jorion, P., 1993. Testing the predictive power of dividend yields. Journal of Finance 48, 663–679.

González-Rivera, G., Lee, T.-H., 2009. Nonlinear time series in financial forecasting. In: Meyer, R.A. (Ed.), Encyclopedia of Complexity and Systems Science. Springer, New York.

Goyal, A., Welch, I., 2003. Predicting the equity premium with dividend ratios. Management Science 49, 639–654.

Goyal, A., Welch, I., 2008. A comprehensive look at the empirical performance of equity premium prediction. Review of Financial Studies 21, 1455–1508.

Granger, C.W.J., Machina, M.J. 2006. Forecasting and decision theory. In: Elliott, G., Granger, C.W.J., Timmermann, A. (Eds.), Handbook of Economic Forecasting, vol. 1. Elsevier, Amsterdam.

Guidolin, M., Hyde, S., McMillan, D., Ono, S., 2009. Non-linear predictability in stock and bond returns: when and where is it exploitable? International Journal of Forecasting 25, 373–399.

Guidolin, M., Timmermann, A., 2007. Asset allocation under multivariate regime switching. Journal of Economic Dynamics and Control 31, 3503–3544.

Guo, H. 2006. On the out-of-sample predictability of stock market returns. Journal of Business 79, 645–670.

Guo, H., Whitelaw, R.F., 2006. Uncovering the risk-return relation in the stock market. Journal of Finance 61, 1433–1463.

Hahn, J., Lee, H., 2006. Interpreting the predictive power of the consumption-wealth ratio. Journal of Empirical Finance 13, 183–202.

Hamilton, J.D., 1989. A new approach to the economic analysis of nonstationary time series and the business cycle. Econometrica 57, 357–384.

Han, Y., Yang, K., Zhou, G., forthcoming. A new anomaly: the cross-sectional profitability of technical analysis. Journal of Financial and Quantitative Analysis.

Hansen, B.E., 2000. Testing for structural change in conditional models. Journal of Econometrics 97, 93–115.

Hansen, P.R. 2005. A test for superior predictive ability. Journal of Business and Economic Statistics 23, 365–380.

Hansen, P.R., Timmermann, A., 2012. Choice of sample split in out-of-sample forecast evaluation. European University Institute Working Paper, ECO 2012/10.

Harvey, C.R., 1991. The world price of covariance risk. Journal of Finance 46, 111–157.

Hawawini, G., Keim, D.B., 1995. On the predictability of common stock returns: world-wide evidence. In: Jarrow, R., Maksimovic, V., Ziemba, W. (Eds.), Handbooks in Operations Research and Management Science, vol. 9. Elsevier, Amsterdam.

Hendry, D.F., Clements, M.P., 2004. Pooling of forecasts. Econometrics Journal 7, 1–31.

Henkel, S.J., Martin, J.S., Nadari, F., 2011. Time-varying short-horizon predictability. Journal of Financial Economics 99, 560–580.

Henriksson, R.D., Merton, R.C., 1981. On market timing and investment performance, II: statistical procedures for evaluating forecasting skills. Journal of Business 54, 513–533.

Hirshleifer, D., Hou, K., Teoh, S.H., 2009. Accruals, cash flows, and aggregate stock returns. Journal of Financial Economics 91, 389–406.

Hjalmarsson, E., 2010. Predicting global stock returns. Journal of Financial and Quantitative Analysis 45, 49–80.

Hjalmarrson, E., 2011. New methods for inference in long-horizon regressions. Journal of Financial and Quantitative Analysis 46, 815–839.

Hodrick, R.J., 1992. Dividend yields and expected stock returns: alternative procedures for inference and measurement. Review of Financial Studies 5, 357–386.

Hong, H., Torous, W., Valkanov, R., 2007. Do industries lead stock markets? Journal of Financial Economics 83, 367–396.

Hou, K., 2007. Industry information diffusion and the lead-lag effect in stock returns. Review of Financial Studies 20, 1113–1138.

Inoue, A., Kilian, L. 2004. In-sample or out-of-sample tests of predictability: which one should we use? Econometric Reviews 23, 371–402.

Jensen, M.C., Benington, G.A., 1970. Random walks and technical theories: some additional evidence. Journal of Finance 25, 469–482.

Kan, R., Zhou, G., 2007. A new variance bound on the stochastic discount factor. Journal of Business 79, 941–961.

Kandel, S., Stambaugh, R.F., 1996. On the predictability of stock returns: an asset-allocation perspective. Journal of Finance 51, 385–424.

Kellard, N.M., Nankervis, J.C., Papadimitriou, F.I., 2010. Predicting the equity premium with dividend ratios: reconciling the evidence. Journal of Empirical Finance 17, 539–551.

Kelly, B., Pruitt, S., 2012. The three-pass regression filter: a new approach to forecasting using many predictors. University of Chicago Booth School of Business Working Paper No. 11–19.

Kelly, B., Pruitt, S., forthcoming. Market expectations in the cross section of present values. Journal of Finance.

Kirby, C., 1998. The restrictions on predictability implied by rational asset pricing models. Review of Financial Studies 11, 343–382.

Koijen, R.S.J., Van Nieuwerburgh, S., 2011. Predictability of returns and cash flows. Annual Review of Financial Economics 3, 467–491.

Kong, A., Rapach, D.E., Strauss, J.K., Zhou, G., 2011. Predicting market components out of sample: asset allocation implications. Journal of Portfolio Management 37, 29–41.

Kothari, S.P., Shanken, J., 1997. Book-to-market, dividend yield, and expected market returns: a time-series analysis. Journal of Financial Economics 44, 169–203.

Lamont, O., 1998. Earnings and expected returns. Journal of Finance 53, 1563–1587.

Lamoureux, C.G., Zhou, G., 1996. Temporary components of stock returns: what do the data tell us? Review of Financial Studies 9, 1033–1059.

Lanne, M., Saikkonen, P., 2006. Why is it so difficult to uncover the risk-return tradeoff in stock returns? Economics Letters 92, 118–125.

Leitch, G., Tanner, J.E., 1991. Economic forecast evaluation: profit versus the conventional error measures. American Economic Review 81, 580–590.

Lettau, M., Ludvigson, S.C., 2001. Consumption, aggregate wealth, and expected stock returns. Journal of Finance 56, 815–849.

Lettau, M., Van Nieuwerburgh, S., 2008. Reconciling the return predictability evidence. Review of Financial Studies 21, 1607–1652.

Lewellen, J., 2004. Predicting returns with financial ratios. Journal of Financial Economics 74, 209–235.

Lo, A.W., 2004. Reconciling efficient markets with behavioral finance: the adaptive markets hypothesis. Journal of Investment Consulting 7, 21–44.

Lo, A.W., 2008. Where do alphas come from? A new measure of the value of active investment management. Journal of Investment Management 6, 1–29.

Lo, A.W., MacKinlay, A.C., 1990a. When are contrarian profits due to stock market overreaction? Review of Financial Studies 3, 175–205.

Lo, A.W., MacKinlay, A.C., 1990b. Data-snooping biases in tests of financial asset pricing models. Review of Financial Studies 3, 431–467.

Lo, A.W., Mamaysky, H., Wang, J., 2000. Foundations of technical analysis: computational algorithms, statistical inference, and empirical implementation. Journal of Finance 55, 1705–1765.

Ludvigson, S.C., Ng, S., 2007. The empirical risk-return relation: a factor analysis approach. Journal of Financial Economics 83, 171–222.

Lundblad, C., 2007. The risk return tradeoff in the long run: 1836–2003. Journal of Financial Economics 85, 123–150.

Malkiel, B.G., 1973. A Random Walk Down Wall Street first ed. Norton, New York.

Malkiel, B.G., 2011. A Random Walk Down Wall Street revised ed. Norton, New York.

Marquering, W., Verbeek, M., 2004. The economic value of predicting stock index returns and volatility. Journal of Financial and Quantitative Analysis 39, 407–429.

McCracken, M.W., 2007. Asymptotics for out of sample tests of Granger causality. Journal of Econometrics 140, 719–752.

McCracken, M.W., Valente, G., 2012. Testing the economic value of asset return predictability. Federal Reserve Bank of St. Louis Working Paper 2012-049A.

Meese, R.A., Rogoff, K.S., 1983. Empirical exchange rate models of the seventies: do they fit out of sample? Journal of International Economics 14, 3–24.

Neely, C.J., Rapach, D.E., Tu, J., Zhou, G., 2012. Forecasting the equity risk premium: the role of technical indicators. Federal Reserve Bank of St. Louis Working Paper 2010–008E.

Nelson, C.R., 1976. Inflation and the rates of return on common stock. Journal of Finance 31, 471–483.

Nelson, C.R., Kim, M.J., 1993. Predictable stock returns: the role of small sample bias. Journal of Finance 48, 641–661.

Park, C.-H., Irwin, S.H., 2007. What do we know about the profitability of technical analysis? Journal of Economic Surveys 21, 786–826.

Pástor, L., Stambaugh, R.F., 2009. Predictive systems: living with imperfect predictors. Journal of Finance 64, 1583–1628.

Pá stor, L., Stambaugh, R.F., 2012. Are stocks really less volatile in the long run? Journal of Finance 67, 431–478.

Pástor, L., Veronesi, P., 2009. Learning in financial markets. Annual Review of Financial Economics 1, 361–381.

Paye, B.S., Timmermann, A., 2006. Instability of return prediction models. Journal of Empirical Finance 13, 274–315.

Pesaran, M.H., Timmermann, A., 1992. A simple nonparametric test of predictive performance. Journal of Business and Economic Statistics 10, 461–465.

Pesaran, M.H., Timmermann, A., 1995. Predictability of stock returns: robustness and economic significance. Journal of Finance 50, 1201–1228.

Pesaran, M.H., Timmermann, A., 2002. Market timing and return prediction under model instability. Journal of Empirical Finance 9, 495–510.

Pesaran, M.H., Timmermann, A., 2004. How costly is it to ignore breaks when forecasting the direction of a time series? International Journal of Forecasting 20, 411–425.

Pesaran, M.H., Timmermann, A., 2007. Selection of estimation window in the presence of breaks. Journal of Econometrics 137, 134–161.

Pettenuzzo, D., Timmermann, A., 2011. Predictability of stock returns and asset allocation under structural breaks. Journal of Econometrics 164, 60–78.

Pontiff, J., Schall, L.D., 1998. Book-to-market ratios as predictors of market returns. Journal of Financial Economics 49, 141–160.

Rangvid, J., 2006. Output and expected returns. Journal of Financial Economics 81, 595–624.

Rapach, D.E., Strauss, J.K., Tu, J., Zhou, G. 2011. Out-of-sample industry return predictability: evidence from a large number of predictors. Manuscript, Saint Louis University, Singapore Management University, and Washington University in St. Louis.

Rapach, D.E., Strauss, J.K., Zhou, G., 2010. Out-of-sample equity premium prediction: combination forecasts and links to the real economy. Review of Financial Studies 23, 821–862.

Rapach, D.E., Strauss, J.K., Zhou, G., forthcoming. International stock return predictability: what is the role of the United States? Journal of Finance.

Rapach, D.E., Wohar, M.E., 2006a. Structural breaks and predictive regression models of aggregate US stock returns. Journal of Financial Econometrics 4, 238–274.

Rapach, D.E., Wohar, M.E. 2006b. In-sample vs. out-of-sample tests of stock return predictability in the context of data mining. Journal of Empirical Finance 13, 231–247.

Rapach, D.E., Wohar, M.E., Rangvid, J., 2005. Macro variables and international stock return predictability. International Journal of Forecasting 21, 137–166.

Ross, S.A., 2005. Neoclassical Finance. Princeton University Press, Princeton, NJ.

Rossi, B., 2005. Optimal tests for nested model selection with underlying parameter instabilities. Econometric Theory 21, 962–990.

Rossi, B., Inoue, A., 2012. Out-of-sample forecast tests robust to the window size choice. Journal of Business and Economic Statistics 30, 432-453.

Rozeff, M.S., 1984. Dividend yields are equity risk premiums. Journal of Portfolio Management 11, 68–75.

Santos, T., Veronesi, P., 2006. Labor income and predictable stock returns. Review of Financial Studies 19, 1–44.

Solnik, B., 1993. The performance of international asset allocation strategies using conditioning information. Journal of Empirical Finance 1, 33–55.

Stambaugh, R.F., 1986. Biases in regressions with lagged stochastic regressors. University of Chicago Graduate School of Business Working Paper No. 156.

Stambaugh, R.F., 1999. Predictive regressions. Journal of Financial Economics 54, 375–421.

Stock, J.H., Watson, M.W., 2004. Combination forecasts of output growth in a seven-country data set. Journal of Forecasting 23, 405–430.

Stock, J.H., Watson, M.W., 2006. Forecasting with many predictors. In: Elliott, G., Granger, C.W.J., Timmermann, A. (Eds.), Handbook of Economic Forecasting, vol. 1. Elsevier, Amsterdam.

Subrahmanyam, A., 2010. The cross-section of expected stock returns: what have we learnt from the past twenty-five years of research? European Financial Management 16, 27–42.

Sullivan, R., Timmermann, A., White, H., 1999. Data-snooping, technical trading rule performance, and the bootstrap. Journal of Finance 54, 1647–1691.

Sullivan, R., Timmermann, A., White, H., 2001. Dangers of data mining: the case of calendar effects in stock returns. Journal of Econometrics 105, 249–286.

Teräsvirta, T. 2006. Forecasting economic variables with nonlinear models. In: Elliott, G., Granger, C.W.J., Timmermann, A. (Eds.), Handbook of Economic Forecasting, vol. 1. Elsevier, Amsterdam.

Timmermann, A., 1993. How learning in financial markets generates excess volatility and predictability of stock returns. Quarterly Journal of Economics 108, 1135–1145.

Timmermann, A., 1996. Excess volatility and predictability of stock prices in autoregressive dividend models with learning. Review of Economic Studies 63, 523–557

Timmermann, A., 2006. Forecast combinations. In: Elliott, G., Granger, C.W.J., Timmermann, A. (Eds.), Handbook of Economic Forecasting, vol. 1. Elsevier, Amsterdam.

Timmermann, A., 2008. Elusive return predictability. International Journal of Forecasting 24, 1–18.

Timmermann, A., Granger, C.W.J., 2004. Efficient market hypothesis and forecasting. International Journal of Forecasting 20, 15–27.

Torous, W., Valkanov, R., Yan, S., 2005. On predicting stock returns with nearly integrated explanatory variables. Journal of Business 77, 937–966.

Tu, J., 2010. Is regime switching in stock returns important in portfolio decisions? Management Science 56, 1198–1215.

Tu, J., Zhou, G., 2004. Data-generating process uncertainty: what difference does it make in portfolio decisions? Journal of Financial Economics 72, 385–421.

Valkanov, R., 2003. Long-horizon regressions: theoretical results and applications. Journal of Financial Economics 68, 201–232

Wachter, J.A., Warusawitharana, M., 2009. Predictable returns and asset allocation: should a skeptical investor time the market? Journal of Econometrics 148, 162–178.

West, K.D., 1996. Asymptotic inference about predictive ability. Econometrica 64, 1067–1084.

West, K.D. 2006. Forecast evaluation. In: Elliott, G., Granger, C.W.J., Timmermann, A. (Eds.), Handbook of Economic Forecasting, vol. 1. Elsevier, Amsterdam.

White, H., 2000. A reality check for data snooping. Econometrica 68, 1097–1126.

White, H. 2006. Approximate nonlinear forecasting methods. In: Elliott, G., Granger, C.W.J., Timmermann, A. (Eds.), Handbook of Economic Forecasting, vol. 1. Elsevier, Amsterdam.

Xu, Y., 2004. Small levels of predictability and large economic gains. Journal of Empirical Finance 11, 247–275.

Zhou, G., 2010. How much stock return predictability can we expect from an asset pricing model? Economics Letters 108, 184–186.

renewcommand06.0

CHAPTER 7

Forecasting Interest Rates

Gregory Duffee

Johns Hopkins University, 440 Mergenthaler Hall, 3400 N. Charles St., Baltimore, MD 21218, USA

Contents

Abstract

This chapter discusses what the asset-pricing literature concludes about the forecastability of interest rates. It outlines forecasting methodologies implied by this literature, including dynamic, no-arbitrage term structure models and their macro-finance extensions. It also reviews the empirical evidence concerning the predictability of future yields on Treasury bonds and future excess returns to holding these bonds. In particular, it critically evaluates theory and evidence that variables other than current bond yields are useful in forecasting.

Keywords

Term structure, Affine models, Predicting bond returns, Predicting bond yields

1. INTRODUCTION

How are interest rates on Treasury securities likely to change during the next month, quarter, and year? This question preoccupies financial market participants, who attempt to profit from their views. Policymakers also care. They attempt to predict future rates (and attempt to infer market participants' predictions) to help choose appropriate monetary and fiscal policies. More relevant for this chapter, academics use interest rate forecasts to help predict related variables, such as real rates, inflation, and macroeconomic activity. They also build term structure models that link interest rate forecasts to the dynamics of risk premia.

This chapter describes and evaluates an approach to forecasting that is grounded in finance. Interest rates are functions of asset prices, thus their dynamics can be studied using tools of asset pricing theory. The theory is particularly powerful when applied to Treasury yields, since the underlying assets have fixed payoffs (unlike, say, stocks). Nonetheless, there are known limitations to this approach, and important questions that remain open.

The most immediate implication of finance theory is that investors' beliefs about future prices are impounded into current prices. Therefore forecasts made at time t should be conditioned on the time-t term structure. An incontrovertible conclusion of the literature is that the time-t term structure contains substantial information about future changes in the slope and curvature of the term structure. It is less clear whether the term structure has information about future changes in the overall level of the term structure. This chapter argues that according to the bulk of the evidence, the level is close to a martingale.

Overfitting is always a concern in forecasting. Again, this chapter takes a finance-based approach to addressing this issue. Forecasts of future interest rates are also forecasts of future returns to holding bonds. Forecasts that imply substantial predictable variation in expected excess returns to bonds (i.e., returns less the risk-free return) may point to overfitting. For example, big swings in expected excess returns from 1 month to the next are hard to reconcile with risk-based explanations of expected excess returns.

Gaussian dynamic term structure models are the tool of choice to describe joint forecasts of future yields, future returns, and risk premia. These models impose no-arbitrage restrictions. Sharpe ratios implied by estimated models are helpful in detecting overfitting, and restrictions on the dynamics of risk premia are a natural way to address overfitting. One of the important open questions in the literature is how these restrictions should be imposed. The literature takes a variety of approaches that are largely data-driven rather than driven by economic models of attitudes towards risk.

Macroeconomic variables can be added to a dynamic term structure model to produce a macro-finance model. From the perspective of forecasting interest rates, this type of extension offers many opportunities. It allows time-t forecasts to be conditioned on information other than the time-t term structure. In addition, the dynamics of interest rates are tied to the dynamics of the macro variables, allowing survey data on their expected values to be used in estimation. Finally, macro-finance models allow restrictions on risk premia to be expressed in terms of fundamental variables such as economic activity and consumption growth.

Unfortunately, standard economic explanations of risk premia fail to explain the behavior of expected excess returns to bonds. In the data, mean excess returns to long-term Treasury bonds are positive. Yet traditional measures of risk exposure imply that Treasury bonds are not assets that demand a risk premium. Point estimates of their consumption betas are negative and point estimates of their CAPM betas are approximately zero. Moreover, although expected excess returns to bonds vary over time, these variations are unrelated to interest rate volatility or straightforward measures of economic growth. These facts are a major reason why applied models of bond risk premia shy away from approaches grounded in theory.

Recent empirical work concludes that some macro variables appear to contain substantial information about future excess returns that is not captured by the current term structure. Some, but not all, of this evidence is consistent with a special case of macro-finance models called hidden-factor models. The only original contribution of this chapter is to take a skeptical look at this evidence. Based on the analysis here, it is too soon to conclude that information other than the current term structure is helpful in forecasting future interest rates, excess returns, and risk premia.

2. FORECASTING METHODS FROM A FINANCE PERSPECTIVE

Figure 7.1 displays a panel of yields derived from prices of nominal Treasury bonds. The displayed yields are, for the most part, not yields on actual Treasury securities. The figure displays zero-coupon bond yields. These yields are the objects of interest in most academic work. The Treasury Department issues both zero-coupon and coupon bonds. The former are Treasury bills, which have original maturities no greater than a year. The latter are Treasury notes and bonds. Academics typically use zero-coupon yields interpolated from yields on Treasury securities. (This chapter uses the terms "yield" and "interest rate" interchangeably.) The interpolation is inherently noisy. Bekaert et al. (1997) estimate that the standard deviation of measurement error is in the range of seven to nine basis points of annualized yield for maturities of at least a year.

The yields in Figure 7.1 are yields on actual 3-month Treasury bills, zero-coupon yields on hypothetical bonds with maturities from 1 to 5 years constructed by the Center for Research in Security Prices (CRSP), and the yield on a zero-coupon hypothetical

10-year bond constructed by staff at the Federal Reserve Board following the procedure of Gurkaynak et al. (2007). Yields are all continuously compounded. The CRSP data are month-end from June 1952 through December 2010. Until the 1970s, the maturity structure of securities issued by the Treasury did not allow for reliable inference of the 10-year zero-coupon yield. The first observation used here is January 1972.

A glance at the figure suggests that yields are co-integrated. More precisely, spreads between yields on bonds of different maturities are mean-reverting, but the overall level of yields is highly persistent. A robust conclusion of the literature is that Standard tests cannot reject the hypothesis of a unit root in any of these yields. From an economic perspective it is easier to assume that yields are stationary and highly persistent rather than truly non-stationary. Econometrically these alternatives are indistinguishable over available sample sizes.

By contrast, another robust conclusion of the literature is that spreads are stationary. For example, the handbook chapter of Martin et al. (1996) shows there is a single co-integrating vector in Treasury yields. Not surprisingly, early academic attempts to model the dynamic behavior of bond yields used co-integration techniques. It is helpful to set up some accounting identities before discussing the logic and limitations of a co-integration approach to forecasting.

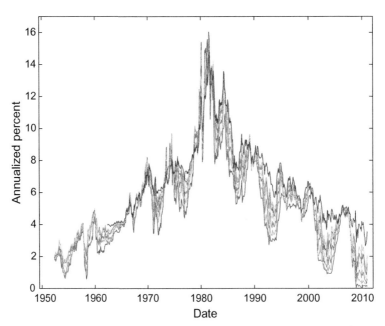

Figure 7.1 Yields on nominal Treasury zero-coupon bonds. The maturities range from 3 months to 10 years.

2.1. Notation and Accounting Identities

Consider a zero-coupon bond that matures at $t + n$ with a payoff of a dollar. Denote its time-t price and yield by

$$P_t^{(n)} : \text{Price}$$

$$p_t^{(n)} : \text{Log price}$$

$$y_t^{(n)} : \text{Continuously compounded yield}, \; y_t^{(n)} \equiv -\frac{1}{n} p_t^{(n)}.$$

The superscript refers to the bond's remaining maturity. Denote the return to the bond from t to $t + 1$, when its remaining maturity is $n - 1$, by

$$R_{t,t+1}^{(n)} : \text{gross return to the bond from } t \text{ to } t + 1, \; R_{t,t+1}^{(n)} \equiv P_{t+1}^{(n-1)} / P_t^{(n)}$$

$$r_{t,t+1}^{(n)} : \text{log return}, \; r_{t,t+1}^{(n)} \equiv \log R_{t,t+1}^{(n)}.$$

The log return to the bond in excess of the log return to a one-period bond is denoted

$$xr_{t,t+1}^{(n)} : \text{log excess return}, \; xr_{t,t+1}^{(n)} \equiv r_{t,t+1}^{(n)} - y_t^{(1)}.$$

The yield on a bond can be related to future bond returns in two useful ways. The first links the bond's current yield to the bond's yield next period and the excess return to the bond. The relation is

$$y_t^{(n)} = y_t^{(1)} + \frac{n-1}{n}\left(y_{t+1}^{(n-1)} - y_t^{(1)}\right) + \frac{1}{n} xr_{t,t+1}^{(n)}. \tag{1}$$

This is an accounting identity; the $t + 1$ realizations on the right side must equal the time-t value on the left. For example, a higher yield at $t+1$ implies a lower price at $t+1$, and thus a lower realized excess return. The second accounting identity links the current yield to the sum, during the life of the bond, of one-period yields and excess returns:

$$y_t^{(n)} = \frac{1}{n} \sum_{j=0}^{n-1} y_{t+j}^{(1)} + \frac{1}{n} \sum_{j=0}^{(n-1)} xr_{t+j,t+j+1}^{(n-j)}. \tag{2}$$

In words, holding a bond's yield constant, a higher average short rate over the life of the bond corresponds to lower realized excess returns.

Conditional expectation versions of these identities are

$$y_t^{(n)} = y_t^{(1)} + \frac{n-1}{n}\left(E_t\left(y_{t+1}^{(n-1)}\right) - y_t^{(1)}\right) + \frac{1}{n}E_t\left(xr_{t,t+1}^{(n)}\right) \tag{3}$$

and

$$y_t^{(n)} = \frac{1}{n}E_t\left(\sum_{j=0}^{n-1} y_{t+j}^{(1)}\right) + \frac{1}{n}E_t\left(\sum_{j=0}^{(n-1)} xr_{t+j,t+j+1}^{(n-j)}\right). \tag{4}$$

These conditional expectations are also identities. They hold regardless of the information set used for conditioning, as long as the set contains the yield $y_t^{(n)}$. In particular, these equations hold for investors' information sets and econometricians' information sets, which may differ.

2.2. Co-integration

Campbell and Shiller (1987) motivate a co-integration approach to modeling the term structure. They make the simplifying assumption that the weak form of the expectations hypothesis holds. Then the conditional expectation (4) can be written as

$$y_t^{(n)} = \frac{1}{n} E_t \left(\sum_{j=0}^{n-1} y_{t+j}^{(1)} \right) + c^{(n)}, \tag{5}$$

where $c^{(n)}$ is a maturity-dependent constant. The spread between the yield on an n-period bond and the one-period yield is then, after some manipulation,

$$S_{n,1} \equiv y_t^{(n)} - y_t^{(1)} = \sum_{j=1}^{n-1} (n-j) E_t \left(y_{t+j}^{(1)} - y_{t+j-1}^{(1)} \right) + c^{*(n)}. \tag{6}$$

Spreads are sums of expected first differences of one-period yields. Therefore spreads are $I(0)$ if one-period yields are $I(1)$.

Campbell and Shiller examine monthly observations of 1-month and 20-year bond yields over the period 1959 to 1983. They cannot reject the hypotheses that yields are $I(1)$ and the spread is $I(0)$. Hence they advocate an error-correction model (ECM) to fit yield dynamics. For a vector of bond yields y_t and a linearly independent vector of spreads S_t, an ECM(p) representation is

$$\Delta y_t = \sum_{i=1}^{p-1} \Theta_i \Delta y_{t-i} + B S_t + \epsilon_{t+1}, \tag{7}$$

where Θ_i and B are matrices. The intuition is straightforward and does not depend on the weak form of the expectations hypothesis. Investors impound their information about future short-term rates in the prices (and hence yields) of long-term bonds. If investors have information about future rates that is not captured in the history of short-term rates, then yield spreads will help forecast changes in short-term rates.

The first application of this type of model to forecasting interest rates is Hall et al. (1992). Researchers continue to pursue advances in this general methodology. When many yields are included in the cross-section, the dimension of the estimated model is high. This can lead to overfitting and poor out-of-sample forecasts. Bowsher and Meeks (2008) use cubic splines to fit the cross-section. The knots of the spine are modeled with an ECM. Almeida et al. (2012) take a similar approach, interpreting the splines as a way to model partially segmented markets across Treasury bonds.

The ECM approach is based on asset-pricing theory. However, the theory is not pushed to its sensible conclusion. Spreads help forecast future yields because investors put their information into prices. The ECM approach does not recognize that period-t bond prices (yields) are determined based on *all* information that investors at t have about future interest rates.

2.3. The Term Structure as a First-Order Markov Process

Asset prices incorporate all information available to investors. This fact leads to a more parsimonious approach to modeling interest rates than an ECM. We first look at the general statement of the result, then consider some special cases and caveats.

Assume that all of the information that determines investors' forecasts at t can be summarized by a p-dimensional state vector x_t. More precisely, x_t contains all information investors at t use to predict one-period bond yields and excess returns to multi-period bonds for all future periods $t+1, t+2$ and so on. Substitute this assumption into the identity (4) to produce

$$y_t^{(n)} = \frac{1}{n}\left(\sum_{j=1}^{n-1} E\left(y_{t+j}^{(1)}|x_t\right)\right) + \frac{1}{n}\left(\sum_{j=1}^{(n-1)} E\left(xr_{t+j-1,t+j}^{(n-j)}|x_t\right)\right). \tag{8}$$

It is trivial to see that the yield on the left side cannot be a function of anything other than the state vector, since only x_t shows up on the right side. Hence we can write

$$y_t^{(n)} = y(x_t; n).$$

This is simply a statement that investors determine the price of the n-period bond based on the predictions of short rates during the life of the bond and expected returns to the bond in excess of these short rates.

Stack time-t yields on bonds with different maturities in a vector y_t. These yields are a function of the state vector

$$y_t = f\left(x_t; \mathcal{N}\right),$$

where the maturities of the bonds are in the vector $\mathcal{N}$. The key step in the derivation is to assume there exists an inverse function such that

$$x_t = f^{-1}\left(y_t; \mathcal{N}\right). \tag{9}$$

The inverse function exists if yields contain the same information as x_t. Therefore the rank of $\partial f/\partial x_t'$ must be p. A necessary condition is that there are at least p yields in the vector y_t. There are standard technical conditions associated with this result, but the intuition is straightforward. If each element of x_t has its own unique effect on the time-t

yield curve, the yield curve can be inverted to infer x_t. Put differently, the time-t yield curve contains all information necessary to predict future values of x_t, and thus future yield curves. This allows us to write

$$E_t(y_{t+k}) = g\left(y_t; \mathcal{N}\right) \qquad (10)$$

for some function $g(\cdot)$ that is determined by the mappings from factors to expected future one-period yields and excess bond returns.

A slightly simplistic interpretation of (10) is that both x_t and y_t must follow first-order Markov processes. Intuitively, x_t is Markov because it is defined as the set of information relevant to forming conditional expectations for all future horizons. If information at time t other than x_t were helpful in predicting future values of x_t, then investors could use that additional information to refine their conditional expectations of future yields. Similarly, everything investors know about expected future yields shows up in the period-t term structure. This intuition does not quite correspond to the statement that x_t and y_t are Markov because (10) says nothing about conditional higher moments. For example, the vector x_t need not contain all information relevant to forming conditional co-variances among yields. Collin-Dufresne and Goldstein (2002) construct a general framework in which state variables that drive variations in conditional volatilities of yields do not affect the cross section of yields.

Some readers may find it useful to compare this statement with the expectations hypothesis. The weak form of the expectation hypothesis states that time-t forward rates differ from expected future yields by maturity-dependent constants. Forecasting with the weak form requires a parameterized model, but it is a trivial model: the only unknown parameters are the constants. When we step outside the weak form of the expectations hypothesis, we recognize that forward rates incorporate both expected future yields and time-varying expected excess returns. Equation (8) puts structure on expected excess returns by requiring that they depend on at most p state variables. Equation (9) implicitly says that by looking at the entire yield curve, we can disentangle shocks to expected excess returns from shocks to expected future yields. Disentangling these shocks requires estimation of the function $g(\cdot)$ in (10).

There is a potentially important hole in this derivation. It is possible that some cancellation may occur on the right side of (8). In other words, there may be a state variable that has equal and opposite effects on expected future short rates and expected future excess bond returns. This will reduce the dimension of the state vector that determines yields. "Hidden factor models," introduced by Duffee (2011a) and Joslin et al. (2010), capture this idea. State variables that drive this kind of variation drop out of the left side, hence the period-t cross-section of yields does not contain all information relevant to forecasting future yields. We defer considering hidden factor models until Section 5.3.

2.4. Methodological Implications

The previous argument has an important implication for the choice of forecasting methodology. When forming forecasts as of time-t, the use of information other than time-t yields requires a compelling justification. Such information includes yields dated prior to t, measures of inflation, central bank policy announcements, and economic activity. All of these variables are related to future yields. They may also be key components of the fundamental economic determinants of yields. But all of the information in these variables is already embedded in the time-t yield curve.

One way to justify using non-yield information is ease of estimation. To take an extreme example, we can form a forecast of next year's average 3-month Treasury bond yield either by estimating a model or by reading a forecast off of survey responses of financial market participants. The latter approach is easier and probably more accurate. Unfortunately, samples of survey data for interest rate forecasts are not as long as those for forecasts of important macro variables such as inflation. Moreover, surveys typically ask questions about only one or two maturities on the yield curve. Section 5.1 discusses alternate uses of survey data.

A less extreme example is parameter stability over time. If there is a good reason to believe that the mapping from current yields to expected future yields is unstable over time, while the mapping from, say, current inflation to expected future yields is stable, then it makes sense to use inflation data to forecast yields. The literature contains considerable evidence for parameter instability in term structure models, but it is silent on the relative stability of forecasts using yields versus forecasts using other variables.

Another justification for the use of non-yield information is that we may believe investors at time t were using the wrong model to forecast yields. For example, they may have ignored a variable that we, as econometricians looking back in time, know is important. Yet another justification is the belief that the length of the state vector that drives expectations exceeds the number of available yields in the cross-section. Finally, measurement error can obscure the information in observed time-t yields. In practice, this is implausible because the measurement error in yields is very small relative to the measurement error in other relevant variables, such as observed inflation and output growth.

It is also important to recognize that a Markov process for yields does not imply that yields follow a first-order VAR. Markov processes may be non-linear. For example, there may be occasional regime shifts in yield dynamics. When yields follow a Markov process, the time-t regime can be backed out of time-t yields. But extracting this information requires a regime-shifting model rather than a VAR(1).

Even if a VAR(1) is a reasonable model of yields, we must decide how to compress the information in the cross-section of yields. Yields on bonds of similar maturities are very highly correlated. Therefore a standard approach is to extract common factors from yields and apply a VAR to the factors. This procedure is the subject of the next section.

3. REGRESSION APPROACHES TO FORECASTING TREASURY YIELDS

For forecasting purposes, an important difference between Treasury yields and macro variables such as GDP is the role of the cross-section. Since yields on bonds of different maturities are highly correlated, it does not make much sense to estimate unrelated forecasting regressions for each yield.[1] An almost universal approach to regression-based forecasting of Treasury yields is to first compress the cross-section into a low-dimensional vector, then use regressions to forecast elements of the vector. Forecasts of individual yields are determined by the cross-sectional mapping from the vector to the individual yield. We begin with the compression technique of principal components.

3.1. Principal Components of Yields

Following the spirit of Litterman and Scheinkman (1991), researchers often summarize term structures by a small set of linear combinations of yields.[2] An uncontroversial conclusion of the term structure literature is that the first few principal components of the covariance matrix of yields capture almost all of the variation in the term structure. Table 7.1 illustrates this for the sample 1972 through 2010. The table reports the unconditional standard deviations of the seven bond yields over this sample. It also reports the standard deviations of the residuals after taking out the first n principal components. Standard deviations of residuals from using three principal components range from five to eleven basis points of annualized yields, which is roughly the same range as the measurement error described by Bekaert et al. (1997).

These first three principal components are commonly called "level," "slope," and "curvature," respectively. The motivation behind the labels is illustrated in Figure 7.2, which is constructed from the sample 1972 through 2010. A change in the first principal component corresponds to a roughly level change in yields of different maturities. A change in the second component moves short-maturity yields in the opposite direction of long-maturity yields. A change in the third component moves the short end and the long end together, away from intermediate maturities.

The figure includes loadings on the fourth and fifth components. From the scale of the figure, it is clear that level, slope, and curvature account for almost all of the variation in term structure shapes. Therefore forecasting future Treasury term structures is, for most purposes, equivalent to forecasting the first three principal components of yields.

Equation (10) requires that expectations of future yields are determined by current yields. We implement this in a regression setting by forecasting future principal components with current principal components. One method uses separate regressions for each future horizon k. Carriero et al. (2012) follow this path. In this chapter a VAR(1) is the primary tool for forecasting. Section 2.4 makes it clear that 10 does not imply that the

---

[1] However, the important early contribution to forecasting of Fama and Bliss (1987) adopts this method.

[2] Litterman and Scheinkman use factor analysis rather than principal components.

Table 7.1 Cross-Sectional Fitting Errors Using Principal Components

Number of Components	3 mon	1 yr	2 yr	3 yr	4 yr	5 yr	10 yr
0	322.2	319.7	310.3	298.9	290.0	281.3	250.8
1	75.3	44.0	16.3	18.8	30.2	38.9	65.0
2	21.4	14.5	14.6	12.4	9.4	6.4	22.1
3	5.0	10.9	6.1	6.2	8.1	6.4	7.4
4	0.5	3.4	6.0	5.0	5.2	5.6	1.9
5	0.2	0.3	2.6	4.9	4.4	5.1	1.2

Notes: Principal components of zero-coupon nominal bond yields are calculated for the sample January 1972 through December 2010. The maturities range from 3 months to 10 years. The table reports cross-sectional residuals from using the first n components to fit the cross-section of yields, from $n = 0$ to $n = 5$. The values for $n = 0$ are the sample standard deviations of the yields. Standard deviations measured in basis points of annualized yields.

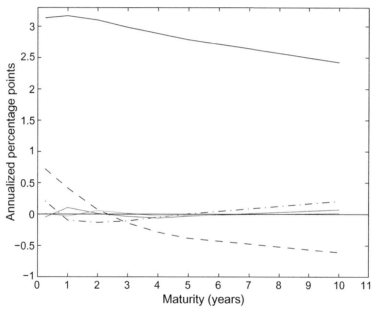

Figure 7.2 Principal components of nominal bond yields. The figure displays loadings of yields on their first five principal components, multiplied by the sample standard deviations of the components. The first, second, and third principal components, termed "level," "slope," and "curvature," are displayed with solid, dashed, and dotted-dashed lines. The data sample is January 1972 through December 2010.

yield curve follows a VAR(1) process. Nonetheless, it is the most obvious model with which to generate forecasts across various horizons that are consistent with each other. A VAR(1) applied to principal components allows us to use time-t principal components to predict time-$(t + k)$ principal components. The mapping from principal components to yields translates these forecasts to expected future yields.

We want to limit the number of principal components included in the VAR to avoid overfitting. The time-t term structure is almost entirely described by level, slope, and curvature, but it does not necessarily follow that a VAR(1) that includes only these first three principal components is an appropriate model.[3] Other principal components may have information about expected future values of level, slope, and curvature. Cochrane and Piazzesi (2005) point out that a factor does not need to have a large effect on the time-t term structure in order to play an important role in time-t expectations of future yields and expected returns. Roughly, the factor could have partially offsetting effects on the right side of (8). Therefore the appropriate number of principal components to include in the VAR is an empirical question.

3.2. Forecasting Principal Components

How much information is in the time-t term structure about future values of level, slope, and curvature? Stack the first five principal components of the term structure in the vector $\tilde{\mathcal{P}}_t$ and denote individual principal components by $\tilde{\mathcal{P}}_{i,t}$. A tilde represents observed data, which may be contaminated by measurement error or market imperfections. The forecasting regressions are

$$\tilde{\mathcal{P}}_{i,t+k} - \tilde{\mathcal{P}}_{i,t} = b_0 + b_1' \tilde{\mathcal{P}}_t + e_{i,t,t+k}$$

Table 7.2 reports results for forecasts of the first three principal components. The regressions are estimated for two sample periods and 1-month, 3-month, and 12-month horizons. Of course, the longer-horizon regressions are superfluous if we are confident that the VAR(1) is an accurate description of monthly yield dynamics. Only non-overlapping observations are used for the last two horizons. Overlapping observations contain somewhat more information. They also can have large discrepancies between finite-sample and asymptotic statistical properties, especially in a near unit-root setting. The choice here is to give up some of the information in the sample in exchange for more reliable test statistics.

There in conclusions to draw from Table 7.2. First, there is no statistical evidence that changes in the first principal component (level) are forecastable. For both the 1952–2010 and 1970–2010 samples, tests of the hypothesis that all five coefficients of b_1 are zero cannot be rejected at the 5 covariance matrix of the parameter estimates is adjusted for generalized heteroskedasticity. Only one p-value is less than 10 sample. This p-value should not be given much weight since there are only 38 observations for this regression.

Second, slope and curvature are unquestionably forecastable. The p-values are approximately zero for both sample periods and all forecasting horizons. At the quarterly horizon, about 20 (30) of the variation in slope (curvature) is predictable.

---

[3] Principal components are unconditionally orthogonal, but not necessarily conditionally orthogonal. Therefore a VAR(1) process for principal components will generally not equal a set of univariate AR(1) processes for the individual components.

Table 7.2 Predicting Level, Slope, and Curvature with the Term Structure

| | First PC | | | Second PC | | | Third PC | |
| | R^2 | 1–5 Test | R^2 | 1–5 Test | 4–5 Test | R^2 | 1–5 Test | 4–5 Test |
Freq								
1952 through 2010 sample								
M	0.016	0.219	0.077	0.000	0.946	0.125	0.000	0.048
Q	0.038	0.192	0.198	0.000	0.842	0.300	0.000	0.011
A	0.143	0.247	0.549	0.000	0.229	0.496	0.000	0.993
1972 through 2010 sample								
M	0.029	0.125	0.082	0.002	0.784	0.089	0.000	0.246
Q	0.055	0.160	0.220	0.000	0.580	0.255	0.000	0.005
A	0.161	0.062	0.582	0.000	0.439	0.469	0.000	0.406

Notes: Principal components of month-end observations of nominal bond yields are constructed for the specified samples. Changes in these principal components from month t to months $t + 1$, $t + 3$, and $t + 12$ are forecast in-sample with OLS using the month-t values of the first five principal components. The table reports R^2s of these regressions and p-values of tests of the hypothesis that all five coefficients are zero. For forecasts of the second and third principal components, the table also reports p-values of tests of the hypothesis that the coefficients on the fourth and fifth principal components are zero. The tests use the White heteroskedasticity-consistent covariance matrix.

The 1952 through 2010 sample uses yields with maturities of 3 months and one through 5 years. For this sample the forecasting regressions use 702 monthly observations from 1952:7 through 2010, 234 quarterly observations from 1952:Q3 through 2010:Q4, and 58 annual observations from 1953 through 2010. The 1972 through 2010 sample adds a 10-year maturity. For this sample the regressions use 467 monthly, 155 quarterly, and 38 annual observations.

Third, factors other than the first three do not contribute much to forecasts of slope and curvature. For slope forecasts, tests of the hypothesis that the coefficients on the fourth and fifth principal components equal zero do not come close to rejection. The statistical evidence for curvature forecasts is mixed. In particular, these components appear to help predict quarter ahead curvature. But recall from Figure 7.2 that curvature contributes relatively little to variations in the term structure over time. Moreover, the incremental R^2 of the fourth and fifth principal components to curvature forecasts is economically small; between three and five percentage points at the quarterly horizon. (These details are not reported in any table.)

These results, combined with the idea that parsimonious dynamic models are better than complicated models, suggest that a reasonable forecasting model is a VAR(1) for level, slope, and curvature, combined with restriction that level is a random walk, unforecastable by any of the principal components. The mapping from these factors to observed yields is

$$\tilde{y}_t^{(n)} = \sum_{i=1}^{3} \beta_{i,n} \tilde{\mathcal{P}}_{i,t} + \epsilon_{n,t}. \tag{11}$$

The residual picks up cross-sectional variation in yields that is unexplained by the first three principal components. Duffee (2011b) takes this approach in forecasting future yields and concludes that the model works well in pseudo out-of-sample forecasting, relative to various other forecasting methods.

The conclusion that the level is unforecastable may appear to rely heavily on a misspecified model. There have been important shifts in the data-generating process of short rates during the past 50 years. The most prominent is the Federal Reserve's monetarist experiment from 1979 to 1983. Stationary regime-shifting processes can appear non-stationary from the perspective of a model that does not include regime shifts.

A comprehensive analysis of regime shifts is beyond the scope of this chapter. However, it is worth noting that the unpredictability of the level factor is robust to allowing for a simple kind of structural change. In results not detailed in any table, I estimate a VAR(1) on the first three principal components of yields for the sample 1952 through 2010. Chow-type dummies are included for the period 1979:1 through 2003:12. The results overwhelmingly reject the null hypothesis of constant coefficients over the full sample. In particular, during the monetarist period the level factor exhibits strong mean reversion, both economically and statistically. But outside of this monetarist period, the hypothesis that the level is unpredictable is not rejected at the 10.

3.3. Related Models

The previous subsection describes a simple model of the term structure. Three principal components follow a VAR(1), and yields are related to the principal components through the cross-sectional mapping (11). This model does not attempt to impose any no-arbitrage conditions, other than the Markov intuition of Section 2.3. Researchers have developed other models with VAR(1) factor dynamics and mappings from factors to yields that also ignore no-arbitrage considerations.

Perhaps the best-known of these models is the contribution of Diebold and Li (2006). They build a dynamic version of the term structure introduced by Nelson and Siegel (1987). The cross-section of the term structure is summarized by the level, slope, and curvature factors of the Nelson–Siegel model. These three factors are assumed to follow a VAR(1). Diebold and Li find that the dynamics with the best pseudo out-of-sample properties are those without any feedback among the factors. In other words, level, slope, and curvature follow univariate AR(1) processes. The forecast accuracy of their model is discussed in Section 3.5.

Other methods for compressing the information in yields can also be combined with a VAR(1). Perhaps the simplest approach is to choose a few bonds with maturities across the term structure – say, 3 months, 2 years, and 10 years – and use the yields on these bonds as factors. This method ignores information in other bond yields. Other methods use information from the entire term structure. For example, the knot points of the cubic spline used by Bowsher and Meeks (2008) could be fit to a VAR(1) instead of the ECM model described in Section 2.2. Almeida and Vicente (2008) use Legendre polynomials to describe the cross-section of yields and fit them to a VAR(1).

The Markov logic of Section 2.4 implies that there is a high bar to including non-yield variables in forecasting regressions. Simply noting that expected future yields should depend on, say, inflation or macroeconomic activity is not sufficient. Since this information is already in contemporaneous yields, including both yields and macro variables in a regression is a recipe for overfitting, in both in-sample and pseudo out-of-sample forecasts.

Perhaps not surprisingly, this logic is routinely ignored. A popular forecasting approach uses a VAR that includes both compressed information from the term structure and compressed information from a large panel of macro variables. Recent examples are Koopman and van der Wel (2011) and Favero et al. (2012). Empirical evidence linking macro variables with term structure forecasts is discussed in Section 5. Much of the empirical work involving macro variables and the term structure focuses on forecasting future returns to bonds rather than future yields. The equivalence of these perspectives is discussed next.

3.4. Predictable Excess Returns

Forecasts of future yields using current yields (and perhaps other variables) are necessarily also forecasts of expected log returns to bonds. A derivation based on Campbell et al. (1991) makes this point starkly. The relevant accounting identity is

$$
y_{t+1}^{(n-1)} - y_t^{(n)} = \frac{1}{n-1}\left(y_t^{(n)} - y_t^{(1)}\right) - \frac{1}{n-1}xr_{t,t+1}. \tag{12}
$$

Campbell et al. (1991) use this equation as a test of the weak form of the expectations hypothesis by taking time-t expectations, then fixing the expected excess return to a constant. They test whether the OLS coefficient on the first term on the right side equals one, and conclusively reject the hypothesis.

The left side is the change in the yield on a bond from t to $t + 1$. For reasonably long maturities (say, a 5-year bond), variations over time in the left side are very close to variations in the first principal component – the level – of the term structure. Therefore according to the results of Table 7.2, the left side is close to unforecastable with time-t yields. Since the left side equals the right side, the right side must also be unforecastable with time-t yields. The first term on the right side is a measure of the slope of the term structure, which varies widely over time; recall Figure 7.1. Since the sum on the right is unforecastable, the second term, excess returns to the bond, must also be strongly forecastable and positively correlated with the slope of the term structure.

This implication is confirmed with excess return regressions. Monthly simple returns to maturity-sorted portfolios of Treasury bonds are available from CRSP. Excess returns are constructed by subtracting the return to the shortest-maturity portfolio, which contains bonds with maturities less than 6 months. Excess returns for horizons longer than a month are constructed by compounding simple returns to the portfolios, then subtracting the compounded return to the shortest-maturity portfolio.

Excess returns from month t to $t+k$ are regressed on the first five principal components of the term structure at month t. Formally, the regressions have the form

$$\tilde{R}^e_{i,t,t+k} = b_0 + b'_1 \tilde{\mathcal{P}}_t + e_{p,t,t+k}, \tag{13}$$

where the notation on the left side indicates the observed simple excess return to portfolio i from t to $t+k$. As in Table 7.2, the regressions are estimated for monthly, quarterly, and annual horizons, and only non-overlapping observations are used for the last two horizons.

Point estimates for two portfolios are displayed in Table 7.3. There are two strong conclusions to draw from the results. First, the level of the term structure is unrelated to future excess returns. None of the t-statistics comes close to rejecting the hypothesis that the point estimate is zero. Second, a less-steep slope (larger value of the second principal component) corresponds to lower future excess returns. A one standard deviation increase in the second principal component corresponds to a decrease of about 0.25 next month's

Table 7.3 Forecasting Excess Returns to Treasury Bonds with the Yield Curve

Freq	Maturity Bucket	PC 1	PC 2	PC 3	PC 4	PC 5
1952 through 2010 sample						
M	2–3 years	0.028	−0.110	−0.068	0.050	−0.027
		(0.54)	(−2.06)	(−1.97)	(1.43)	(−0.47)
M	5–10 years	0.041	−0.257	−0.139	0.199	−0.011
		(0.44)	(−3.03)	(−2.08)	(2.60)	(−0.12)
Q	5–10 years	0.206	−0.730	−0.573	0.183	−0.056
		(0.67)	(−2.26)	(−3.26)	(0.87)	(−0.17)
A	5–10 years	0.861	−2.799	−0.833	−0.187	−1.254
		(1.13)	(−3.86)	(−1.48)	(−0.22)	(−1.49)
1972 through 2010 sample						
M	2–3 years	0.012	−0.117	−0.082	0.082	−0.081
		(0.18)	(−1.84)	(−1.59)	(1.20)	(−0.96)
M	5–10 years	0.005	−0.285	−0.151	0.237	−0.217
		(0.04)	(−2.73)	(−1.63)	(1.88)	(−1.70)
Q	5–10 years	0.137	−0.847	−0.572	0.630	−0.057
		(0.37)	(−2.58)	(−2.19)	(1.49)	(−0.10)
A	5–10 years	0.396	−2.639	−1.103	−0.027	−2.096
		(0.40)	(−2.77)	(−1.58)	(−0.02)	(−1.96)

Notes: Excess returns to maturity-sorted portfolios of Treasury bonds from month t to month $t+k$ are regressed on the month-t values of the first five principal components of the Treasury term structure. The horizons are one month, one quarter, and one year. Only non-overlapping observations are used. Returns are expressed in have unit standard deviation. The table reports parameter estimates and asymptotic t-statistics. The covariance matrices of parameter estimates are adjusted for generalized heteroskedasticity.

Table 7.4 R^2s of Excess-Return Forecasting Regressions

Sample Period	Maturity Bucket	Month	Quarter	Annual
1952–2010	2–3 years	0.030	0.075	0.252
1972–2010	2–3 years	0.040	0.098	0.243
1964–2003	2–3 years	0.036	0.097	0.526
1952–2010	5–10 years	0.050	0.107	0.309
1972–2010	5–10 years	0.064	0.132	0.343
1964–2003	5–10 years	0.058	0.129	0.525

Notes: Excess returns to maturity-sorted portfolios of Treasury bonds from month t to month $t + k$ are regressed on the month-t values of the first five principal components of the Treasury term structure. The horizons are one month, one quarter, and one year. Only non-overlapping observations are used. The table reports R^2s for various combinations of sample periods and maturity-sorted portfolios.

excess return to bonds with maturities between 5 and 1 years. The coefficients scale almost linearly in the return horizon, at least up to the annual horizon considered here.

Less clear are the links between other principal components and future excess returns. There is reasonably strong statistical evidence that greater curvature (an increase in short-maturity and long-maturity yields, a decrease in intermediate-maturity yields) predicts lower excess returns. The magnitude of the predictability is about half of that associated with the slope of the term structure. Three of the four t-statistics for the 1952–2010 sample allow rejection at the 5 hypothesis that the coefficient is zero.

Table 7.4 reports the R^2s of these and related forecasting regressions. At the monthly horizon, roughly 5 variation in excess returns is predictable. The figure rises to roughly 10 horizons are intriguing. For the two sample periods emphasized in this chapter, the R^2s are between 25 and 304 and also includes results for the sample 1964 through 2003, which matches the sample period studied by Cochrane and Piazzesi (2005). They report R^2s up to 44 predicted by five forward rates. In Table 7.4 the R^2s for the 1964 through 2003 sample exceed 50 slightly different than those used by Cochrane and Piazzesi (2005) and because the regressions use non-overlapping observations. There is unquestionably overfitting in these regressions, since only 39 observations are explained by five variables. But the annual regression for 1972 through 2010 has fewer observations and yet a much smaller R^2. Section 7 discusses this result in detail. In this section it suffices to note that the high R^2s realized over the sample period of Cochrane and Piazzesi are not matched in the full sample.

3.5. Forecast Accuracy Evaluation

At this point it is appropriate to discuss how we should evaluate forecasting models. In this Handbook, Clark and Michael (2013) emphasize the important role of pseudo out-of-sample forecasts in econometric evaluation of forecasting models. They discuss two reasons for this focus. First, forecasting models are often used to forecast (truly) out of sample, thus evaluation methodologies that mimic this procedure are sensible. Second, in-sample overfitting via data-mining is often detected with pseudo out-of-sample tests.

Both explanations apply to forecasts of bond yields, and pseudo out-of-sample forecast accuracy plays a major role in much of the relevant research. Two particularly influential contributions to the term structure literature recommend specific models based on their pseudo out-of-sample performance. Duffee (2002) and Diebold and Li (2006) conclude that their respective term structure models have pseudo out-of-sample forecasts of future yields that are more accurate than random walk forecasts. Their results are a major reason why much of the subsequent forecasting literature has explored variants of their models.

Unfortunately, neither conclusion is robust. Carriero (2011) finds the Diebold–Li model performs poorly out-of-sample for the period 1983 through 2009, a result driven by the forecast errors in the latter part of the sample. Duffee (2011b) finds that forecasts from both models are inferior to random walk forecasts when the data samples in the original papers are expanded to include more recent observations. In other words, the pseudo out-of-sample performance of the models differs substantially from the true out-of-sample performance. Only the passage of additional time will reveal whether the conclusions of Duffee (2002) and Diebold and Li (2006) are examples of pseudo out-of-sample data-mining or whether the models' recent performance is anomalous.

This chapter advocates a different tool for evaluation: the conditional Sharpe ratio. The main advantage of the conditional Sharpe ratio is that it is a tool for ex ante evaluation of a forecast. Unlike out-of-sample forecasting errors, Sharpe ratios do not depend on sampling error inherent in out-of-sample realizations.

The conditional Sharpe ratio for asset or portfolio i over the horizon from t to $t+k$ is

$$s_{i,t,t+k} = \frac{E_t\left(R^e_{i,t,t+k}\right)}{\sqrt{\mathrm{Var}_t\left(R^e_{i,t,t+k}\right)}}. \tag{14}$$

Fitted conditional Sharpe ratios that are implausibly large are evidence of overfitting. For the forecasting regressions (13), the numerator of (14) is the fitted value of the regression. If the return innovations are homoskedastic, the denominator is the standard deviation of the regression's residuals.

Figure 7.3 displays fitted values of (14) for the portfolio of Treasury bonds with maturities between 5 and 10 years. The fitted values are from monthly regressions for the sample 1952 through 2010. The sample mean conditional Sharpe ratio is only 0.06, or about 0.24 when multiplied by the square root of 12 to put it in annual terms. The fitted Sharpe ratios fluctuate substantially over time, reaching a maximum of 1.3 (4.7 in annual terms) and a minimum of −1.0 (−3.3 in annual terms), both during the Fed's monetarist experiment period. Since conditional volatilities were relatively high during this same period, the assumption of homoskedasticity exaggerates the fluctuations in conditional

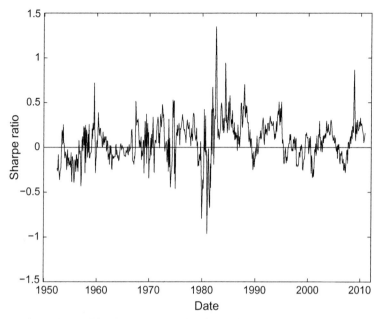

Figure 7.3 Conditional monthly Sharpe ratios. The figure displays fitted conditional Sharpe ratios from month t to month $t+1$ for a portfolio of Treasury bonds with maturities between 5 and 10 years. Monthly excess returns are predicted using the first five principal components of Treasury yields. The Sharpe ratios are calculated assuming that conditional standard deviations of excess returns are constant over time.

Sharpe ratios. But even outside of this period, the patterns in Figure 7.3 are hard to reconcile with our intuition about risk premia. For example, in the late 1960s and early 1970s, fitted conditional Sharpe ratios frequently flip back and forth from about one to minus one (in annual terms).

Although fitted Sharpe ratios can reveal overfitting, it is not easy to address the problem using finance theory at the level of accounting identities discussed in Section 2. If, say, a shrinkage principle is used to reduce the predictability of excess returns, the accounting identities (3) and (4) imply that forecasts of future yields will be affected in some way. But the effects could work through conditional variances of expected future yields, covariances among expected future yields, or co-variances between expected future yields and current expected excess returns. There is insufficient structure to distinguish among these possibilities. For this additional structure, we turn to term structure models that impose no-arbitrage restrictions on yield dynamics.

4. A DYNAMIC TERM STRUCTURE FRAMEWORK

This section presents the workhorse no-arbitrage framework used for forecasting. It first appears in Ang and Piazzesi (2003). In contrast to the early term structure models that are expressed in a continuous-time setting, the setting here builds on the discrete-time model of Backus and Zin (1994). The key assumptions are that interest rate dynamics are linear and homoskedastic with Gaussian shocks. Before presenting the model, it is worth discussing why a model with such obviously counterfactual assumptions lays a central role in the literature.

It is easy to find evidence of non-linear, non-Gaussian dynamics. For example, Figure 7.1 shows that conditional variances of yields vary substantially through time, reaching their peak during the monetarist experiment of 1979 through 1982. Gray (1996) concludes that a model of time-varying mean reversion and time-varying GARCH effects fits the dynamics of the short-term interest rate. The figure also shows that the zero bound imposes non-linear dynamics on yields that bind in the last 2 years of the sample. Unfortunately, tractability must sometimes trump truth in dynamic term structure models. Dynamic term structure models describe the evolution of bond prices over time. This description requires (a) a method for computing bond prices that satisfy no-arbitrage; and (b) transition densities of prices from t to $t + \tau$. Researchers naturally restrict their attention to models for which (a) and (b) are computationally feasible.

The best-known class of models with tractable bond pricing is the affine class of Duffie and Kan (1996). This class includes both homoskedastic (Gaussian) and heteroskedastic models. Dai and Singleton (2000) and Duffee (2002) combine this affine class with linear dynamics of the underlying state vector to produce the "completely affine" and "essentially affine" classes respectively. One of the conclusions in Duffee (2002) is that only the Gaussian models in this class are sufficiently flexible to generate plausible forecasts of future yields. Gaussian no-arbitrage models are easy to understand and use, and can generate complicated yield dynamics. Although the models have fixed conditional variances, this is typically not a concern of the forecasting literature. This literature focuses on predicting yields and excess returns rather than constructing conditional second moments.

Recent research has attempted to find alternatives to the Gaussian class. Cheridito et al. (2007) extend the essentially affine class to give non-Gaussian versions greater flexibility. A non-linear tweak to the completely affine class is introduced by Duarte (2004). The quadratic class, which has non-linear dynamics, is developed by Leippold and Wu (2002) and Ahn et al. (2002). Dai et al. (2007) and Ang et al. (2008) construct models with regime switches along certain dimensions. A fairly general non-linear framework with affine pricing is developed by Le et al. (2010).

These and other approaches show promise, but none has gained much traction in the applied literature. The limited existing evidence suggests that further exploration is warranted. For example, Almeida et al. (2011) find that a stochastic volatility model in the extended affine class generates more accurate in-sample forecasts of yields than a comparable Gaussian model. Almeida and Vicente (2008) draw favorable conclusions about the forecast accuracy of no-arbitrage models that describe the term structure with Legendre polynomials. But as of this writing, the workhorse framework is the Gaussian essentially affine setting.

4.1. The Framework

The continuously-compounded nominal one-period interest rate is r_t. This can also be written as $y_t^{(1)}$, the yield on a one-period bond. The short rate is a function of a length-p state vector, denoted x_t. The function is

$$r_t = \delta_0 + \delta_1' x_t. \tag{15}$$

The state vector has first-order Markov dynamics

$$x_{t+1} = \mu + K x_t + \Sigma \epsilon_{t+1}, \quad \epsilon_{t+1} \sim N(0, I). \tag{16}$$

Without loss of generality, Σ is lower triangular. The parameters of (16) are common knowledge. An implication of this assumption is that an econometrician cannot hope to uncover a trading strategy with expected returns that exceed the compensation required for bearing the strategy's risk. All expected excess returns must be explained by risk compensation.

Using the notation of Section 2.1, no-arbitrage implies

$$P_t^{(n)} = E_t \left(M_{t+1} P_{t+1}^{(n-1)} \right), \tag{17}$$

where M_{t+1} is the strictly positive pricing kernel, or stochastic discount factor (SDF). The SDF is assumed to have the log-linear form

$$\log M_{t+1} = -r_t - \Lambda_t' \epsilon_{t+1} - \frac{1}{2} \Lambda_t' \Lambda_t. \tag{18}$$

The vector Λ_t is the compensation investors require to face the unit normal shocks ϵ_{t+1}. The price of risk is a function of the state vector, thus it varies over time according to

$$\Sigma \Lambda_t = \lambda_0 + \lambda_1 x_t. \tag{19}$$

The left side of (19) is the compensation investors require to face shocks to the state vector. Bonds are priced using the equivalent martingale dynamics

$$x_{t+1} = \mu^q + K^q x_t + \Sigma \epsilon_{t+1}^q, \tag{20}$$

where the equivalent martingale parameters are

$$\mu^q = \mu - \lambda_0, \quad K^q = K - \lambda_1. \tag{21}$$

The discrete-time analogues of the restrictions in Duffie and Kan (1996) imply that zero-coupon bond prices can be written as

$$p_t^{(n)} = \mathbb{A}_n + \mathbb{B}_n' x_t. \tag{22}$$

The loading of the log price on the state vector is

$$\mathbb{B}'_n = -\delta'_1 \left(I - K^q\right)^{-1} \left(I - \left(K^q\right)^n\right) \tag{23}$$

and the constant term satisfies the difference equation

$$\mathbb{A}_1 = -\delta_0, \quad \mathbb{A}_{n+1} = -\delta_0 + \mathbb{A}_n + \mathbb{B}'_n \mu^q + \frac{1}{2}\mathbb{B}'_n \Sigma \Sigma' \mathbb{B}_n. \tag{24}$$

Zero-coupon yields are written as

$$y_t^{(n)} = A_n + B'_n x_t, \tag{25}$$

$$A_n = -\frac{1}{n}\mathbb{A}_n, \quad B_n = -\frac{1}{n}\mathbb{B}_n. \tag{26}$$

The log excess return to an n-period bond from t to $t+1$ is

$$xr_{t,t+1}^{(n)} = \mathbb{B}'_{n-1}\left(\lambda_0 + \lambda_1 x_t\right) - \frac{1}{2}\mathbb{B}'_{n-1}\Sigma\Sigma'\mathbb{B}_{n-1} + \mathbb{B}'_{n-1}\Sigma\epsilon_{t+1}. \tag{27}$$

To understand this equation, begin with the final term on the right side, which is the return shock. The state-vector shock is $\Sigma\epsilon_{t+1}$. An n-period bond at t is an $(n-1)$-period bond at $t+1$, and the sensitivity of its log price to the state vector is $\mathbb{B}_{n-1}$. Investors require compensation to face innovations in the state vector. The risk compensation for holding the bond is the first term on the right, which is the exposure to the state-vector shock times the conditional compensation for the shock. The middle term on the right is a Jensen's inequality adjustment for log returns.

4.2. Empirical Estimation

Assume that we observe a panel of zero-coupon Treasury bonds. There are T time series observations of $d \geq p+1$ yields, stacked in vectors $\tilde{y}_t$, $t = 1, T$. Recall the tilde denotes observed yields, which here must be distinguished from model-implied yields. The maturities of the bonds are $n_1, \ldots, n_d$, which are fixed across time. There must be at least $p+1$ yields to identify the model's parameters. Using the language of the Kalman filter, the measurement equation is

$$\tilde{y}_t = \mathbf{A} + \mathbf{B}x_t + \eta_t, \quad \eta_t \sim N(0, \Omega). \tag{28}$$

The mapping from the state vector to yields satisfies no-arbitrage, or

$$\mathbf{A} = \left(A_{n_1} \ldots A_{n_d}\right)',$$

$$\mathbf{B} = \left(B_{n_1} \ldots B_{n_d}\right)',$$

where A_n and B_n are defined by (26). The error term in (28) accounts for deviations from the exact no-arbitrage prices. The interpretation of this term that is consistent with the no-arbitrage formulas is measurement error. In reality, it also picks up model misspecification, such as too few common factors, and components of yields related to market imperfections. Another way to write the measurement equation is

$$\tilde{y}_t = y_t + \eta_t, \tag{29}$$

$$y_t = \mathbf{A} + \mathbf{B}x_t. \tag{30}$$

The notation y_t, without the tilde, indicates yields uncontaminated by measurement error (or model misspecification and market imperfections).

The model can be estimated with maximum likelihood (ML) using the Kalman filter. Because the state vector is latent (i.e., not tied to anything observable), the model is unidentified unless identifying restrictions are imposed. Examples of identifying restrictions are discussed next.

4.3. What are the Factors?

What determines the dynamic behavior of the term structure? Although this is an important question, it is vacuous in the context of the simple factor model here. The question is effectively asking how we should interpret elements of the state vector. But the state vector is arbitrary. An observationally equivalent model is produced by scaling, rotating, and translating the state vector. Associated with each rotation is a different set of parameters of the transition equation (16) and the measurement equation (28).

Define such a transformation as

$$x_t^* = \underbrace{\Gamma_0}_{p \times 1} + \underbrace{\Gamma_1}_{p \times p} x_t, \tag{31}$$

where Γ_1 is non-singular. Following Dai and Singleton (2000), an observationally equivalent model replaces x_t with x_t^*, and replaces the parameters of (16) with

$$K^* = \Gamma_1 K \Gamma_1^{-1}, \quad \mu^* = \Gamma_1 \mu + (I - K^*)\Gamma_0, \quad \Sigma^* = \left(\Gamma_1 \Sigma \Sigma' \Gamma_1'\right),$$

where $(\cdot)$ indicates a Cholesky decomposition. Similarly, the parameters of the equivalent-martingale dynamics (20) are replaced with

$$K^{q*} = \Gamma_1 K^q \Gamma_1^{-1}, \quad \mu^{q*} = \Gamma_1 \mu^q + \left(I + K^{q*}\right)\Gamma_0.$$

There are many ways to identify the state vector and thus identify the model's parameters. One way is to restrict the K matrix to a diagonal matrix, set μ to zero, and set the diagonal elements of Σ equal to one. These define a rotation, translation, and scaling, respectively.[4] Another approach equates the state vector with linear combinations of yields.

---

[4] This is slightly stronger than identification, since it imposes the restriction that the eigenvalues of K are real.

Consider any $p \times d$ matrix $\mathcal{L}$ with rank p. (Recall $p < d$.) Premultiply (30) by $\mathcal{L}$ to produce

$$\mathcal{L}y_t = \mathcal{L}\mathbf{A} + \mathcal{L}\mathbf{B}x_t. \tag{32}$$

As long as $\mathcal{L}\mathbf{B}$ is invertible, the left side of equation (32) defines a new state vector. A simple example is a diagonal $\mathcal{L}$ with p diagonal elements equal to one and the remainder equal to zero. This choice produces a state vector equal to p "true" yields, or yields uncontaminated by measurement error. Normalization restrictions for arbitrary $\mathcal{L}$ are described in Joslin et al. (2011).

Another useful choice of $\mathcal{L}$ is based on principal components of yields. For a given data sample, the first p principal components can be written as

$$\tilde{\mathcal{P}}_t = \mathcal{L}\tilde{y}_t,$$

where $\mathcal{L}$ is a $p \times d$ matrix of loadings of the sample principal components on the observed yields. Figure 7.2 is a graphical illustration of this matrix for one sample. Then the factors correspond to "level," "slope," and so on. Regardless of the choice of $\mathcal{L}$, this kind of state vector rotation emphasizes that the term structure model is really a model of one set of derivative instruments (yields) explaining another set of derivative instruments (more yields).

4.4. No-Arbitrage Restrictions and Sharpe Ratios

No-arbitrage restrictions ensure that bonds are priced consistently with each other: equal risk receives equal compensation. The restrictions say nothing about the appropriate magnitude of the compensation, or how it should vary over time. Additional restrictions can be imposed on a no-arbitrage model to put more structure on risk premia. With this Gaussian model, the polar cases are unrestricted risk premia – the vector λ_0 and the matrix λ_1 in (19) are free parameters – and risk-neutrality, which sets both to zero.

It might seem natural to estimate the model with unrestricted risk premia, but Joslin et al. (2011) and Duffee (2011b) show that this version of the no-arbitrage model is of no value in forecasting. There are two pieces to the argument, and both are worth describing in some detail.

Joslin et al. (2011) conclude that no-arbitrage restrictions, in the absence of restrictions on risk premia, have no bite when estimating conditional expectations of future values of the state vector. These conditional expectations are determined by the parameters μ and K of the true, or physical measure, dynamics (16). No-arbitrage restrictions boil down to the existence of equivalent martingale dynamics, given by (20). When risk premia are unrestricted, the parameters μ^q and K^q of the equivalent martingale dynamics are unrelated to their physical-measure counterparts. Although the two measures share volatility parameters, in a Gaussian setting these parameters do not affect ML estimates of μ and K. If the state vector is rotated to, say, the first p principal components of yields, then the ML estimates of μ and K are essentially indistinguishable from VAR estimates.

No-arbitrage restrictions *do* affect the mapping from the state vector to yields; in other words, they bite. Absent the no-arbitrage restrictions, the parameters **A** and **B** of the measurement equation (28) are restricted only by normalization requirements. But Duffee (2011b) points out that these parameters can be estimated with extremely high precision even if no-arbitrage restrictions are not imposed, since the measurement equation amounts to a regression of yields on other yields. The R^2s of such regressions are very close to one. In practice, imposing the restrictions even when they are true does not improve estimates of the measurement equation.

In a nutshell, the Gaussian no-arbitrage model, absent additional restrictions on risk premia, offers no advantages over a simple regression-based approach. First estimate a VAR on the first p principal components, then estimate cross-sectional regressions of yields on the components. Nonetheless, the no-arbitrage model is valuable because the estimated properties of risk premia, and hence fitted conditional Sharpe ratios, can be used to evaluate the reasonableness of the regression-based approach.

This analysis of Sharpe ratios goes beyond the fitted Sharpe ratios (14) calculated with forecasting regressions. The forecasting regressions produce Sharpe ratios for portfolios of Treasury bonds. This contrasts sharply with a no-arbitrage model, which can be used to determine Sharpe ratios for any dynamic trading strategy in fixed income, including all strategies that attain the maximum Sharpe ratio.

With the log-normal SDF, the maximum conditional Sharpe ratio for simple returns is

$$s_t^{max} = \sqrt{e^{\Lambda_t' \Lambda_t} - 1}. \tag{33}$$

Duffee (2010) explains why bond portfolios do not attain this maximum Sharpe ratio. The intuition is that an asset with the maximum Sharpe ratio has a return that is perfectly negatively correlated with the SDF. Log returns to bonds can be perfectly negatively correlated with the log of the SDF. If the SDF and bond returns both have low volatility, this is almost the same as a perfect negative correlation in levels. But with high volatilities, there can be a substantial wedge between Sharpe ratios of bonds and the maximum Sharpe ratio implied by a Gaussian term structure model. The higher the Sharpe ratios for bond portfolios, the more volatile is the SDF, and therefore the larger the wedge there is between Sharpe ratios for bond portfolios and the maximum Sharpe ratio.

Fitted maximum Sharpe ratios for high-dimensional Gaussian models can be unrealistically high. Using a data sample of Treasury yields from 1971 to 2008, Duffee (2010) estimates Gaussian no-arbitrage models with two, three, four, and five factors. No restrictions are placed on risk premia. He calculates a monthly mean of (33) for each model. Annual-horizon maximum Sharpe ratios are about 2.7 for the four-factor model, a number that seems quite large until it is compared to the five-factor model figure of about 10^{30}. Sharpe ratios for two-factor and three-factor models are reasonable.

This Sharpe ratio evidence points to overfitting with a four-factor model and severe overfitting with a five-factor model. One simple way to solve the overfitting problem is to simply build forecasting models with only three factors, sacrificing the ability to capture more obscure information in the term structure. Another approach is to impose restrictions on risk premia dynamics.

4.5. Restrictions on Risk Premia Dynamics

Restrictions on risk premia increase the precision of estimates of physical dynamics (16). The reason is that equivalent-martingale dynamics (20) are estimated with high precision, and risk premia restrictions tighten the relation between physical and equivalent-martingale dynamics. Thus imposing correct restrictions on risk premia should improve forecast accuracy.

Risk premia are determined by the p-vector λ_0 and the $p \times p$ matrix λ_1. The compensation investors receive for facing a unit shock to element i of the state vector is an affine function of the state vector. The constant term of this risk compensation is element i of the vector λ_0, while the sensitivity of risk compensation to the state vector is row i of λ_1.

There are many ways to impose restrictions on the elements of λ_0 and λ_1. One is to set to zero any parameters that are statistically indistinguishable from zero. A more formal frequentist approach is adopted by Christensen et al. (2010) and Joslin et al. (2010), who use various information criteria. Bauer (2011) adopts a Bayesian approach to estimating these parameters. Another is to apply a shrinkage principle, setting the parameters to a weighted average of their unrestricted estimates and their risk-neutral value of zero. A simple example of this is in Cochrane and Piazzesi (2008). Duffee (2010) takes yet another approach, estimating parameters subject to a restriction on maximum Sharpe ratios.

Another common approach imposes *a priori* restrictions on the elements of λ_0 and λ_1 based on a combination of tractability and beliefs about risk premia. For example, both Cochrane and Piazzesi (2008) and Duffee (2011a) assume that only shocks to the level of the term structure have time-varying risk compensation. For Duffee's chosen factor rotation, this restriction implies that only one row of λ_1 is non-zero. Cochrane and Piazzesi go further and choose a rotation for which a single factor drives time-variation in a single price of risk. A qualitatively similar approach is taken by Ang et al. (2008), who choose a factor rotation such that risk premia depend only on one of the factors. A weaker assumption that does not rely on a specific factor rotation is that the rank of λ_1 is less than p. Joslin et al. (2011) describe how to impose this restriction in ML estimation.

An indirect method of imposing restrictions on risk premia dynamics is to impose restrictions on the physical dynamics (16). One example is Christensen et al. (2011), which is a dynamic model of the three factors of Nelson and Siegel (1987).[5] The version

---

[5] Christensen et al. (2011) slightly modify the Nelson-Siegel factors to satisfy no-arbitrage. Their model does not fit into the framework of Section 4 because it is written in continuous time. The version in Diebold and Li (2006) is in discrete time, but does not satisfy no-arbitrage.

of their model with the most accurate forecasts imposes the restrictions that the factors all follow univariate autoregressive processes. These restrictions implicitly restrict risk premia dynamics.

Noticeably absent from this discussion of risk premia is any mention of fundamental determinants of risk compensation. The framework of Section 4 abstracts from consumption, inflation, output growth, and all other macroeconomic variables. With a yields-only model, it is difficult to impose restrictions that motivated by workhorse asset-pricing models of risk premia. The model must be extended to include macroeconomic variables.

5. MACRO-FINANCE MODELS

The primary motivation behind macro-finance models is to ground term structure dynamics in the dynamics of variables, such as inflation, that are viewed as fundamental determinants of yields. A secondary motivation is to improve forecasts of yields out-of-sample by reducing the overfitting problem.

Macro-finance models typically follow Ang and Piazzesi (2003) by expanding the measurement equation of the yields-only framework. Assume we observe some variables at time t, stacked in a vector $\tilde{f}_t$. In principle, this vector may contain any variable other than the price of a fixed-income derivative. Usually it contains macro variables, but it may also contain survey data.

The macro-finance measurement equation is

$$\begin{pmatrix} \tilde{y}_t \\ \tilde{f}_t \end{pmatrix} = \begin{pmatrix} \mathbf{A}_y \\ \mathbf{A}_f \end{pmatrix} + \begin{pmatrix} \mathbf{B}_y \\ \mathbf{B}_f \end{pmatrix} x_t + \eta_t. \tag{34}$$

No-arbitrage restrictions apply to the vector $\mathbf{A}_y$ and the matrix $\mathbf{B}_y$. No such restrictions apply to the vector $\mathbf{A}_f$ and the matrix $\mathbf{B}_f$, although other restrictions may be imposed.

The key assumption built into (34) is that the same state vector that determines the cross-section of yields also determines the additional variables. This is a practical rather than a theoretical restriction. In theory, even if the term structure and the additional variables had nothing to do with each other, the state vector could be expanded to include the necessary state variables. But in practice, researchers use state vectors with three, four, or five factors.

5.1. Survey Data

One of the most promising applications of the macro-finance framework has nothing to do with uncovering the fundamental determinants of yields or risk premia. Instead, it uses information from surveys to improve estimates of the model's dynamics. Investors' expectations of future interest rates are measured directly with surveys. These survey-based expectations can be included in $\tilde{f}_t$. The model's parameters can then be estimated while imposing the restriction that the survey expectations equal the model's expectations plus noise, as in Kim and Orphanides (2005).

An extension of this approach is Chernov and Mueller (2012). They include both observed inflation and survey expectations of future inflation to a yields–only model. Including inflation forces yields to share dynamics with inflation, and including inflation expectations helps to pin down those shared dynamics. Their use of survey data is consistent with the results of Ang et al. (2007), who find that surveys produce more accurate forecasts of inflation than models.

5.2. The Factors of Macro-Finance Models

An important conceptual difficulty with macro–finance models is that the macro variables of interest, such as inflation, aggregate consumption, and output growth, are not spanned by the term structure. Recall from (32) that the length-p state vector can be rotated into p linearly independent combinations of "true" yields. The only requirement is that the mapping from the original state vector to the linear combinations is invertible. This result implies that, aside from cross-sectional measurement error, regressions of the macro factors on p linear combinations of contemporaneous yields should produce R^2s of one.

We do not observe variables in the absence of the cross-sectional error. The equivalent regressions using observed variables tell us about the magnitude of this error. For typical variables included in macro-finance models, the R^2s are on the wrong side of $1/2$. To illustrate the problem, consider quarterly observations of Treasury yields, inflation, per capita consumption growth, and industrial production growth. Quarter-t inflation is measured by the log change in the CPI from the final month of quarter $t-1$ to the final month of quarter t. Per capita consumption growth is measured by the log change in real consumption per person on non–durables and services from quarter $t-1$ to quarter t. Consumption data are constructed following Piazzesi and Schneider (2007). Bond yields are for maturities of 3 months and 1 through 5 years. The sample period is 1952:Q2 through 2010:Q4.

Table 7.5 reports R^2s of cross-sectional regressions of the macro variables on the first five principal components of the Treasury yields. The implicit macro-finance model is one with five factors. The R^2s range from 3 percent (inflation). As mentioned above, one interpretation of these low R^2s is measurement error. We know from Section 3.1 that the measurement error of yields is tiny relative to the variability of yields over this sample. Thus if the five-factor model is correctly specified, the observed macro variables are primarily noise.

This seems implausible. But there is more direct evidence that the problem is misspecification. If yields are measured perfectly and the macro variables are measured with noise, then p linear combinations of yields contain all information relevant to forecasting future values of the macro variables. Lags of the macro variables should have no additional explanatory power. To test this implication, one-quarter ahead values of inflation, consumption growth, and industrial production growth are first predicted with five principal components of yields, then with just the lagged value of the macro variable. Finally, all six explanatory variables are included.

Table 7.5 Explaining Macroeconomic Variables with the Term Structure

	Cross Section	Forecasting, Principal Components	Forecasting, Univariate	T-Statistic
Inflation	0.451	0.429	0.376	3.54
Consumption growth	0.090	0.110	0.143	4.69
IP growth	0.032	0.081	0.146	3.87

Notes: The term structure at the end of quarter t is summarized by its first five principal components. CPI inflation is measured from the last month of quarter $t-1$ to the last month of quarter t. Industrial production growth is measured similarly. Log aggregate per capita consumption growth is measured from quarter $t-1$ to quarter t. The table reports R^2s of regressions of the macro variables on the five principal components of the term structure. Regressions are both cross-sectional and one-quarter ahead forecasts. Univariate R^2s are for AR(1) regressions of the macro variables. The column labeled "T-statistic" is the t-statistic on the lagged macro variable when it is included in a forecasting regression with the five principal components. It is adjusted for generalized heteroskedasticity. The data sample is 1952:Q2 through 2010:Q4.

Table 7.5 reports R^2s for the first two regressions and reports t-statistics on the lagged macro variable for the third regression. The hypothesis that the term structure contains all information relevant for forecasting future values is overwhelmingly rejected for all three macro variables. In fact, the term structure has less information about future inflation and industrial production growth than is contained in the single lag of the forecasted variable.

At first glance, a sensible interpretation of this evidence is that the macro variables all contain some component that is orthogonal to term structure dynamics. But there is another interpretation, suggested by regressions that forecast excess bond returns. Following the logic that the state vector can be rotated into linear combinations of yields, all information about future excess bond returns should be contained in current yields.

Recent evidence undercuts this implication. Cooper and Priestly (2009) finds that the output gap forecasts excess bond returns even when information from the term structure is included in the forecasting regression. Ludvigson and Ng (2009, 2010) construct principal components of more than 130 macroeconomic and financial time series. They use the first eight principal components to predict excess bond returns. Cieslak and Povala (2011) construct a weighted average of past inflation, where the weights decline very slowly. Empirically, both the principal components and the measure of past inflation contain substantial information about future excess returns that is not contained in the term structure.

We take a close look at some of this evidence in Section 7. In the next subsection we take the evidence at face value and consider its implications.

5.3. Hidden Factors

Duffee (2011a) and Joslin et al. (2010) develop a restricted form of Gaussian no-arbitrage models called hidden factor models. A key feature of a hidden factor model is that no linear combinations of yields can serve as the model's state vector. Mathematically, the matrix $\mathcal{L}\mathbf{B}$ in (32) is not invertible for any choice of $\mathcal{L}$. Somewhat less formally, the term structure of bond yields is not a first-order Markov process. Investors have information about future yields and future excess returns that is not impounded into current yields.

The intuition behind a hidden factor model is easily expressed using equation (8). If there is some state variable (or linear combination of state variables) that has equal and opposite effects on time-t expectations of future short-term rates and time-t expectations of future excess returns, that state variable (or linear combination) will not affect the time-t term structure. Put differently, the state vector that determines yields is smaller than the state vector that determines expected future yields. Duffee (2011a) shows that a single parameter restriction on the Gaussian no-arbitrage model produces a hidden factor.

Hidden factors can, in principle, explain all of the results in Table 7.5, as long as the factor (s) that are hidden from the term structure are revealed in macroeconomic data. For example, imagine that economic growth suddenly stalls. Investors anticipate that short-term rates will decline in future months. But investors' risk premia also rise because of the downturn. These effects move long-term bond yields in opposite directions. If they happen to equal each other in magnitude, the current term structure is unaffected. Nothing in the term structure predicts what happens next to either economic growth or bond yields. However, the lower economic growth will predict higher future excess bond returns.

This kind of story motivates the empirical approach of Joslin et al. (2010), who build a model with two hidden factors that are revealed in economic activity and inflation. Duffee (2011a) takes a different approach, using only yields and filtering to infer the presence of a hidden factor. Both conclude hidden factors are important, as do Chernov and Mueller (2012), who use survey expectations of inflation to reveal such a factor. This preliminary evidence indicates that hidden factor models should be taken seriously.

However, this evidence can also be used as a poor justification for data-mining. The spanning requirement of models without hidden factors reduces significantly the ability of researchers to fish for variables that forecast excess returns. Hidden factors remove this constraint. If a researcher finds a variable that has statistically significant forecast power when information from the term structure is included in the forecasting regression, they can simply say that yet another hidden factor is uncovered.

Even with hidden factor models, data-mining would not be an important problem if we understood the economic fundamentals behind risk premia in the bond market. Armed with this knowledge, we could require that the only variables used to forecast excess returns be those linked to the fundamental determinants of risk premia. Unfortunately, the state of the art in term structure research tells us little about these fundamental determinants.

6. ECONOMIC FUNDAMENTALS AND RISK PREMIA

The workhorse models used in finance to explain risk premia are extensions of the classic case of a representative agent with power utility and an aggregate consumption endowment. An asset's conditional expected excess return depends on the return's conditional covariance with consumption growth (power utility and habit formation as in Campbell and Cochrane (1999)) and with the return to total wealth (recursive utility as in Epstein and Zin (1989)). To help judge whether these models can explain the dynamics of bond risk premia, this section presents two types of empirical evidence. The first subsection looks at consumption and CAPM betas. The second considers whether time-varying expected excess returns are related to macroeconomic conditions.

6.1. Bond Return Betas

This empirical analysis uses quarterly returns to match up with quarterly observations of consumption growth. Excess bond returns are measured by the return to a portfolio of Treasury bonds with maturities between 5 and 10 years. Quarter-end to quarter-end returns are simple returns cumulated from monthly returns from CRSP. The simple return to a 3-month T-bill is subtracted to form excess returns. Excess returns to the aggregate stock market are constructed in the same way, using the CRSP value-weighted index.

Table 7.6 reports correlations among these excess returns and log per capita consumption growth. The table also includes the same series of quarterly inflation and log growth in industrial production that are used in Section 5.2. The sample is 1952:Q2 through 2010:Q4. The most important information in the table is that at the quarterly frequency, excess Treasury bond returns are countercyclical. The correlations with consumption growth and industrial production growth are both negative.

This pattern may surprise some readers. The influential handbook chapter of Campbell (2003) reports that the correlation between excess bond returns and consumption growth is slightly positive for the U.S., although the evidence for other countries is mixed. Campbell uses the "beginning of period" assumption for consumption growth. In Table 7.6 that is the correlation between excess bond returns and the lead of consumption growth,

Table 7.6 Sample Correlations, 1952 Through 2010

	Excess Bond Ret	Excess Stock Ret	Δc_t	Δc_{t+1}	ΔIP_t	ΔIP_{t+1}	π_t
Excess bond return	1.00						
Excess stock return	0.06	1.00					
Δc_t	−0.13	0.20	1.00				
Δc_{t+1}	0.07	0.26	0.38	1.00			
ΔIP_t	−0.28	0.04	0.50	0.26	1.00		
ΔIP_{t+1}	−0.13	0.36	0.42	0.52	0.38	1.00	
π_t	−0.29	−0.15	−0.25	−0.30	−0.13	−0.19	1.00

Notes: Excess returns to a portfolio of long-term Treasury bonds and the aggregate stock market are measured from the end of quarter $t-1$ to the end of quarter t. Contemporaneous per capita consumption growth is the log change in aggregate per capita consumption from quarter $t-1$ to quarter t, Δc_t. Industrial production growth and CPI inflation are both log changes from the final month of quarter $t-1$ to the final month of quarter t, ΔIP_t and π_t respectively. The sample period is 1952:Q2 through 2010:Q4.

which is slightly positive. The motivation behind the beginning of period assumption is that aggregate stock returns are more closely correlated with future consumption growth than contemporaneous consumption growth. The usual interpretation is that the shock underlying the aggregate stock return is not fully incorporated into measured consumption until the next quarter. But that is not the case for the shock underlying bond returns; the immediate reaction of both consumption and industrial production is much stronger than the one-quarter ahead reaction.

The table also reports that the correlation between aggregate stock returns and aggregate bond returns is close to zero. This fact, combined with the negative correlation with consumption growth, spells trouble for simple consumption-based models of the term structure. On average, the nominal yield curve in the U.S. slopes up. This shape implies that expected excess returns to Treasury bonds are positive. But these correlations suggest that the risk premium should be negative.

More formal evidence is in Table 7.7, which reports results of regressing excess bond returns on either contemporaneous consumption growth or contemporaneous aggregate stock returns. The table also reports the sample mean of excess returns. Over the full sample 1952 through 2010, the consumption beta of excess bond returns is around minus one, while the stock market beta is almost exactly zero. Neither coefficient is statistically different from zero. Results are also displayed for the first and second halves of the sample. In one sense, these samples differ substantially from each other: the mean excess return in the first half is weakly negative, while the mean excess return in the second half is strongly positive. Yet in both cases, the coefficients are statistically indistinguishable from zero, the consumption beta is negative, and the stock market beta is almost zero. The table also contains results for a fairly homogeneous sample period, the Greenspan era of 1987 through 2006. The consumption beta over this period is about -1.8, while mean excess returns remain strongly positive.

There are, of course, a variety of ways to reconcile these betas with a positively-sloped term structure. For example, it is possible that conditional betas covary with conditional risk premia in a manner that generates both unconditionally positive mean excess returns and unconditionally negative consumption betas. In addition, the aggregate stock return is not the return to total wealth. It is possible that the beta with respect to the return to total wealth is positive even though the beta with respect to the stock market is zero. Moreover, there are alternative utility-based models that introduce heterogeneous agents, heterogeneous goods, and different utility specifications. An evaluation of these approaches is outside the scope of this chapter. The handbook chapter Duffee (2013) discusses in detail some of the theory and evidence relating the term structure and the macroeconomy.

6.2. Predictable Variation of Excess Bond Returns

Beginning with Kessel (1965) and Van Horne (1965), economists have proposed various theories of time-varying expected excess bond returns. Naturally, many theories imply that this variation is correlated with the state of the economy. Here we look at some empirical evidence to help us evaluate the theories.

Table 7.7 Consumption and CAPM Betas for Excess Bond Returns

Sample	Constant	Consumption Growth	Aggregate Stock Return
1952:2–2010:4	0.40		
	(1.91)		
	0.77	−0.86	
	(2.41)	(−1.81)	
	0.36		0.02
	(1.64)		(0.63)
1952:2–1980:4	−0.15		
	(−0.67)		
	0.29	−0.88	
	(0.66)	(−1.40)	
	−0.27		0.07
	(−1.14)		(1.93)
1981:1–2010:4	0.92		
	(2.90)		
	1.11	−0.51	
	(2.52)	(−0.65)	
	0.94		−0.01
	(2.88)		(−0.27)
1986:1–2007:4	0.74		
	(2.64)		
	1.47	−1.76	
	(3.06)	(−1.97)	
	0.85		−0.06
	(2.99)		(−1.38)

Notes: Excess returns to a portfolio of long-term Treasury bonds and the aggregate stock market are measured from the end of quarter $t − 1$ to the end of quarter t. Contemporaneous consumption growth is the log change in aggregate per capita consumption from quarter $t − 1$ to quarter t, Δc_t. The table reports coefficients of regressions of excess bond returns on either consumption growth or stock returns. Asymptotic t-statistics, in parentheses, use a Newey–West adjustment with two lags. The units are percent per quarter.

For this exercise, monthly excess returns to nominal Treasury bonds are defined as the simple return to a portfolio of bonds with maturities between 5 and 10 years less the return to a portfolio with maturities under 6 months. The data are from CRSP. The forecasting regressions take the form

$$\tilde{R}^e_{bond,t,t+1} = b_0 + b_1' \tilde{X}_t + e_{bond,t,t+1}, \tag{35}$$

where $\tilde{X}_t$ is a vector of variables known at t. The focus on monthly returns is somewhat at odds with much of the recent literature that follows Cochrane and Piazzesi (2005) by studying annual returns. But the goal here is not to generate large R^2s, but rather to judge the statistical significance of predictability. When necessary, here we follow the intuition

Table 7.8 Predictability of Excess Returns to Bonds and Stocks

Predictors	Sample	Adj. R^2	Test Stat	Sign
A. Excess bond returns				
Slope	1952:7 – 2010:12	0.0256	0.002	Pos
Conditional SD of yields	1962:3 – 2010:12	0.0007	0.486	Pos
Log change of industrial prod.	1952:7 – 2010:12	0.0016	0.111	Neg
12-month average of log change of industrial prod.	1952:7 – 2010:12	0.0007	0.225	Neg
8 principal components of of macro/financial variables	1964:2 – 2008:1	0.0864	0.000	–
"Real activity" principal component of macro/financial variables	1964:2 – 2008:1	0.0161	0.002	Neg
Log change of industrial prod.	1964:2 – 2008:1	0.0066	0.017	Neg
B. Excess stock returns				
Slope	1952:7 – 2010:12	0.0047	0.066	Pos
Log change of industrial prod.	1952:7 – 2010:12	−0.0012	0.774	Pos
8 principal components of of macro/financial variables	1964:2 – 2008:1	0.0408	0.000	–
"Real activity" principal component of macro/financial variables	1964:2 – 2008:1	0.0018	0.245	Neg

Notes: Monthly excess returns to long-term nominal Treasury bonds and the aggregate stock market are regressed on a variety of predetermined variables. The column labeled "Test Stat" is the *p*-value of the test that the coefficient(s) are all zero. The covariance matrix of the estimated coefficients uses the Newey–West adjustment for five lags of moving average residuals. For regressions with a single predictor, the sign of the estimated coefficient is reported.

of Hodrick (1992) by predicting monthly returns with annual averages of predictors rather than predicting annual returns with month-*t* values of the predictors.

Panel A of Table 7.8 reports the results of a variety of forecasting regressions. Consistent with the evidence in Tables 7.3 and 7.4, the statistical evidence for predictability using information in the term structure is overwhelming. The slope of the term structure, measured by the 5-year yield less the 3-month yield, is positively correlated with future excess returns.

Although excess returns are clearly predictable, a couple of obvious choices of macroeconomic determinants of risk premia have no predictive power. A measure of the conditional standard deviation of long-term bond yields is constructed using squared daily changes in yields. This measure has no ability to forecast excess bond returns; the *p*-value is about 0.5. (Owing to the availability of daily observations of long-term yields, the sample period for this regression begins with 1962.) Many theories imply that risk premia are countercyclical. Yet over the 1952–2010 period, lagged changes in log industrial production have no ability to forecast excess returns, whether the changes are from month $t - 1$ to month t or from month $t - 12$ to month t.

The next regression uses the eight principal components of macroeconomic and financial times series constructed by Ludvigson and Ng (2010). Their data are available for 1964 through 2007. Table 7.8 reports that when these eight principal components are used to forecast monthly excess returns, the adjusted R^2 is more than 8 coefficients are jointly zero is rejected at any conceivable confidence level. Note that this regression does not include any information from the term structure. This evidence concerns the overall forecast power of the eight principal components, not their incremental explanatory power.

Although this evidence is certainly encouraging to researchers searching for links between risk premia and the macroeconomy, there are three important caveats. First, it is not clear how to map much of this predictability to specific macroeconomic concepts. Ludvigson and Ng call the first principal component "real activity" because it is highly correlated with standard measures of real activity. For example, its correlation with log-differenced industrial production exceeds 0.8. But relatively little of the forecast power of the principal components comes from the measure of real activity. Table 7.8 reports that the adjusted R^2 using only the first principal component is about 1.6 components is more problematic.

Second, the sample period 1964 through 2007, although very long, may be anomalous. Table 7.8 uses this shorter sample to redo the forecasting regression with industrial production growth. With the shorter sample, the p-value for growth in industrial production drops from 0.5 to 0.02. Since the first principal component is highly correlated with the growth in industrial production, this result suggests that the predictability associated with Ludvigson and Ng's real activity factor may be sample-specific.

Third, the predictability of excess bond returns is not accompanied by similar predictability of excess stock returns. In models that link time-varying bond risk premia to the macroeconomy, this variation is typically accompanied by varying equity risk premia. But Panel B of Table 7.8 reports that the shape of the term structure contains little information about future aggregate equity excess returns. These regressions take the same form as (35), with excess stock returns replacing excess bond returns on the left side. The eight principal components of macroeconomic and financial variables collectively have substantial forecasting power, but the coefficients on the principal components do not line up with those that forecast bond returns. The correlation between the fitted values of the regressions is only 0.39. For the aggregate stock excess return, the coefficient on real activity is statistically indistinguishable from zero.

7. A ROBUSTNESS CHECK

Is there really information about future excess returns that is not captured by the current term structure? Section 5.2 briefly discusses empirical evidence that macroeconomic variables have incremental explanatory power. We take a closer look at that evidence here. We also consider one of the results in Cochrane and Piazzesi (2005), hereafter CP. The material in this section is new to the literature.

In an influential paper, CP find that 5 month-t forward rates constructed with yields on bonds with maturities of one through 5 years contain substantial information about excess bond returns over the next year (the end of month t to the end of month $t+12$). Their evidence is surprising along many dimensions. In particular, they conclude that lags of forward rates (dated $t-1$ and earlier) contain information about the excess returns that is not in month t forward rates.

As CP note, this result is inconsistent with the logic that the time-t term structure contains all information relevant to forecasting future yields and excess returns. In this sense, the evidence is similar to the evidence that macro variables help predict excess returns. Hidden factors help justify the macro evidence. But even if there are hidden factors (a theoretical development not available to CP), it is hard to understand why the information is hidden from the time-t term structure but not hidden in earlier term structures. CP suggest measurement error in yields that is averaged away by including additional lags of yields.

Rather than examine the annual horizon returns of CP, here we look at monthly returns. Consider forecasting monthly excess returns using both the time t term structure and lagged information, as in

$$\tilde{R}^e_{bond,t,t+1} = b_0 + b_1' \tilde{\mathcal{P}}_t + b_2' \sum_{i=0}^{11} \tilde{F}_{t-i} + e_{bond,t,t+1}. \tag{36}$$

In (36), the notation $\tilde{F}_t$ refers to a vector of forward rates observed at month t,

$$\tilde{F}_t = \left(\tilde{F}_{0,1,t} \ \tilde{F}_{1,2,t} \ \tilde{F}_{2,3,t} \ \tilde{F}_{3,4,t} \ \tilde{F}_{4,5,t} \right)',$$

where $\tilde{F}_{j-1,j,t}$ is the forward rate from year $j-1$ to year j as of month t. The notation $\tilde{\mathcal{P}}_t$ refers to the vector of five principal components of the term structure. If the principal components are excluded from this regression, it is the Hodrick (1992) version of the regressions in CP. Instead of using month-t forward rates to forecast annual excess returns, the sum of the previous 12 months of forward rates is used to forecast monthly excess returns. The excess bond return is for a portfolio of Treasury bonds with maturities between 5 and 10 years.

The regression is estimated for the 1964 through 2003 sample studied by CP and for the full 1952 through 2010 sample. Two versions are estimated. One excludes the forward rates and the other includes both sets of explanatory variables. Results are in Table 7.9, as are other results that are discussed below.

When the forward rates are excluded, the R^2 for the 1964 through 2003 sample is 5.8 reported in the last line of Table 7.4. Including lagged forward rates raises the R^2 to 11.0 coefficients on the forward rates are all zero is overwhelmingly rejected. However, over

Table 7.9 The Incremental Explanatory Power of Lagged Term Structures

Forecasted Variable	Five Principal Components	Principal Components and Average Forward Rates	Test of Forwards
1964 through 2003 sample			
Excess returns	0.058	0.110	0.001
First PC (level)	0.020	0.066	0.023
Second PC (slope)	0.079	0.098	0.336
Third PC (curve)	0.129	0.147	0.098
1952 through 2010 sample			
Excess returns	0.050	0.066	0.094
First PC (level)	0.016	0.028	0.322
Second PC (slope)	0.077	0.097	0.101
Third PC (curve)	0.125	0.145	0.015

Notes: The month-t term structure is summarized in two ways: the first five principal components of yields and five forward rates from year ahead $j-1$ to year ahead j, $j = 1, \ldots, 5$. The forward rates are then averaged over months $t - 11, \ldots, t$. This term structure information is used to predict excess returns to a portfolio of Treasury bonds from month t to $t+1$. It is also used to predict changes in the level, slope, and curvature of the term structure (first three principal components) from t to $t+1$. The table reports R^2s for the forecasting regressions. It also reports the p-value of a test that the averaged forward rates have no incremental explanatory power when the five principal components are included in the regression. The covariance matrices of the parameter estimates are adjusted for generalized heteroskedasticity.

the full sample, the incremental explanatory power of the forward rates is modest; the comparable R^2s are 5.0 percent and 6.6 hypothesis that the coefficients on the forward rates are all zero cannot be rejected at the 5.

These results are qualitatively similar to the forecasting regression R^2s in Table 7.4 and discussed in Section 3.4. In Table 7.4, five principal components of yields are used to predict excess returns at horizons of 1, 3, and 12 months. The R^2s for 1 month are approximately the same for the three sample periods 1952–2010, 1972–2010, and 1964–2003. The same result holds for the 3-horizon. But at the annual horizon, the 1964 through 2003 period stands out, with R^2s that are about 20 percentage points greater than the R^2s for the other two periods. The results of Table 7.9 explain the discrepancy, at least in a mechanical sense. Over the 1964 to 2003 sample, lagged term structures have incremental predictive power for monthly excess returns. Thus the forecast power of lagged term structures is unusual in a statistical sense: it is overwhelmingly significant over most of the 1952 through 2010 sample, but insignificant over the entire period.

The forecast power of lagged term structures is unusual in another way. Recall the discussion in Section 3.2 that future changes in the level of the term structure are unforecastable with the current term structure. Only changes in the slope and curvature are forecastable. Yet over the 1964 through 2003 sample, lagged forward rates predict future changes in the level.

Table 7.10 The Incremental Explanatory Power of Macroeconomic Variables

Forecasted Variable	Five Yield PCs	Yield PCs and Macro PCs	Test of Macro PCs
1964:1 through 2007:12 sample			
Excess returns	0.058	0.138	0.000
First PC (level)	0.021	0.140	0.000
Second PC (slope)	0.080	0.117	0.056
Third PC (curve)	0.130	0.159	0.232

Forecasted Variable	Five Yield PCs	Yield PCs and Past Inflation	Test of Past Inflation
1971:11 through 2009:12 sample			
Excess returns	0.065	0.106	0.000
First PC (level)	0.027	0.056	0.000
Second PC (slope)	0.078	0.079	0.406
Third PC (curve)	0.130	0.131	0.757

Notes: The month-t term structure is summarized by the first five principal components of yields. These principal components are used to predict excess returns to a portfolio of Treasury bonds from month t to $t+1$. Other predictors are the eight principal components of many macroeconomic time series, constructed by Ludvigson and Ng (2010), and a weighted average of past inflation constructed by Cieslak and Povala (2011). These variables are also used to predict changes in the level, slope, and curvature of the term structure (first three principal components) from t to $t+1$. The table reports R^2s for the forecasting regressions. It also reports the p-value of a test that other predictors have no incremental explanatory power when the five principal components are included in the regressions. The covariance matrices of the parameter estimates are adjusted for generalized heteroskedasticity.

The evidence is again in Table 7.9. The relevant regressions replace the excess return on the left side of (36) with changes in the first three principal components of yields. Over the sample period of CP, the null hypothesis that lagged forward rates have no incremental explanatory power for changes in the level is rejected at the 3 curvature are not rejected. Over the full sample period, lagged forward rates have no ability to forecast the level of yields.

The level of the term structure is a random walk: it exhibits no mean reversion. But during the period 1964 through 2003, lagged term structures contained information about future increments to the level. This is why the lags have incremental explanatory power for excess returns. The next major result of this section is that the same statement applies to macro variables known to forecast excess returns.

Denote the eight principal components of macro and financial variables constructed by Ludvigson and Ng (2010) by $\tilde{\mathcal{M}}_t$.[6] The excess return forecasting regression is

$$\tilde{R}^e_{bond,t,t+1} = b_0 + b_1'\tilde{\mathcal{P}}_t + b_2'\tilde{\mathcal{M}}_t + e_{bond,t,t+1}. \tag{37}$$

The sample period is 1964 through 2007.

The first panel of Table 7.10 reports the results. When the Ludvigson–Ng data are excluded, the R^2 is 5.5 are included, the R^2 jumps to 13.8 the coefficients on the principal

---

[6] Thanks to the authors for making their data available.

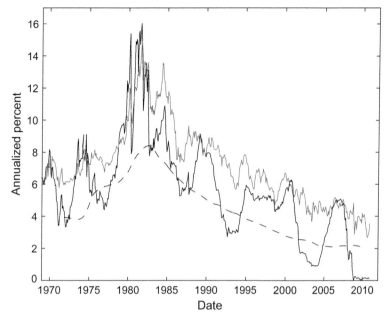

Figure 7.4 Treasury bond yields and a backward-looking measure of long-run inflation. The figure plots yields on 3-month and 10-year zero-coupon Treasury bonds. It also plots a weighted average of past inflation, denoted τ^{CPI}, constructed by Cieslak and Povala (2011).

components are all zero is overwhelmingly rejected. The next set of regressions replace the excess return on the left side of (37) with changes in level, slope, and curvature. The macro/financial factors have substantial incremental forecast power for the level of the term structure and none for either slope or curvature.

Next, replace the macro/financial principal components with the measure of lagged inflation constructed by Cieslak and Povala (2011).[7] The sample period is 1972 through 2009, determined by the availability of the inflation measure. The results are in the second panel of Table 7.10. Including this single predictive variable raises the R^2 of excess returns from 6.5 that the coefficient is zero is overwhelmingly rejected. The same result holds for forecasts of changes in the level of the term structure. Again, the variable has no incremental explanatory power for slope or curvature.

These results raise two important questions about the robustness of the results of Ludvigson and Ng (2009, 2010) and Cieslak and Povala (2011). First, how reliable is the statistical inference? Drawing correct inferences about the finite-sample behavior of a random walk process is often difficult. Consider, for example, Figure 7.4, which displays the 3-month yield, the 5-year yield, and the lagged inflation measure of Cieslak and Povala. Over the sample period 1970 through 2010, the level of yields rises steadily for 12 years, then drops for the next 30 years. The behavior of the lagged inflation measure is similar.

---

[7] Thanks to the authors for making their data available.

This kind of pattern can easily produce spurious predictability. Both Ludvigson and Ng (2009, 2010) and Cieslak and Povala (2011) are concerned about statistical reliability, and employ pseudo out-of-sample tests. But true out-of-sample tests require patience.

Second, what kind of hidden-factor story is consistent with this evidence? Macro stories are typically cyclical. But to explain the patterns here, a hidden-factor story has to explain why macro news today corresponds to an expected future permanent shock to short rates. Moreover, the shock has to temporarily change risk premia in the opposite direction.

To answer the question posed at the beginning of the section: perhaps not. There are good theoretical and empirical reasons to be skeptical of the evidence that there is information about expected excess returns beyond that contained in bond yields.

8. CONCLUDING COMMENTS

Finance theory provides some specific guidance when forming forecasts of future interest rates. Nonetheless, important questions remain open. The Holy Grail of this literature is a dynamic model that is parsimonious owing to economically-motivated restrictions. The requirement of no-arbitrage is motivated by economics, but by itself it is too weak to matter. Economic restrictions with bite require, either directly or indirectly, that risk premia dynamics be tied down by economic principles. There no consensus in the literature about how this should be done. To date, no restrictions that come out of our workhorse models of asset pricing appear to be consistent with the observed behavior of Treasury bond yields.

Another open question is whether any variables contain information about future interest rates that is not already in the current term structure. Recent empirical work suggests that both lagged bond yields and certain macroeconomic variables have incremental information, but this chapter argues that the robustness of these results is not yet known. A closely related question is whether changes in the overall level of the term structure are forecastable. Again, recent empirical work suggests (at least implicitly) they are forecastable, but the nature of this forecastability raises some statistical and economic problems that are not yet resolved.

ACKNOWLEDGMENTS

Thanks to two anonymous referees and many seminar participants for helpful comments and conversations.

REFERENCES

Ahn, Dong-Hyun, Dittmar, Robert F., Gallant, Ronald A., 2002. Quadratic term structure models: theory and evidence. Review of Financial Studies 15, 243–288.
Almeida, Caio, Graveline, Jeremy J., Joslin, Scott, 2011. Do interest rate options contain information about excess returns? Journal of Econometrics 164, 35–44.

Almeida, Caio, Simonsen, Axel, Vicente, José, 2012. Forecasting bond yields with segmented term structure models. Working Paper, Central Bank of Brazil.

Almeida, Caio, Vicente José, 2008. The role of no-arbitrage on forecasting: Lessons from a parametric term structure model. Journal of Banking and Finance 32, 2695-2705.

Ang, Andrew, Bekaert, Geert, Wei, Min, 2007. Do macro variables, asset markets or surveys forecast inflation better? Journal of Monetary Economics 54, 1163–1212.

Ang, Andrew, Bekaert, Geert, Wei, Min, 2008. The term structure of real rates and expected inflation. Journal of Finance 63, 797–849.

Ang, Andrew, Piazzesi, Monika, 2003. A no-arbitrage vector autoregression of term structure dynamics with macroeconomic and latent variables. Journal of Monetary Economics 50, 745–787.

Backus, David K., Zin, Stanley E., 1994. Reverse engineering the yield curve. NBER Working Paper, 4676.

Bauer, Michael D., 2011. Term premia and the news. Federal Reserve Bank of San Francisco, Working Paper, 2011-03.

Bekaert, Geert, Hodrick, Robert J., Marshall, David A., 1997. On biases in tests of the expectations hypothesis of the term structure of interest rates. Journal of Financial Economics 44, 309–348.

Bowsher, Clive G., Meeks, Roland, 2008. The dynamics of economic functions: modelling and forecasting the yield curve. Working Paper, Federal Reserve Bank of Dallas.

Campbell, John Y., 2003. Consumption-based asset pricing, in George Constantinides. in: Harris, Milton, Stulz, Rene (Eds.), Handbook of the Economics of Finance, vol. 1B. North-Holland, Amsterdam, pp. 803–887.

Campbell, John Y., Cochrane, John H., 1999. By force of habit: a consumption-based explanation of aggregate stock market behavior. Journal of Political Economy 107, 205–251.

Campbell, John Y., Shiller, Robert J., 1987. Cointegration and tests of present value models. Journal of Political Ecoomy 95, 1062–1088.

Campbell, John Y., Shiller, Robert J., 1991. Yield spreads and interest rate movements: a bird's eye view. Review of Economic Studies 58, 495–514.

Carriero, Andrea, 2011. Forecasting the yield curve using priors from no-arbitrage affine term structure models. International Economic Review 52, 425–460.

Carriero, Andrea, Kapetanios, George, Marcellino, Massimiliano, 2012. Forecasting government bond yields with large Bayesian vector autoregressions. Journal of Banking and Finance 36, 2026–2047

Cheridito, Patrick, Filipović, Damir, Kimmel, Robert L., 2007. Market price of risk specifications for affine models: Theory and evidence. Journal of Financial Economics 83, 123–170.

Chernov, Mikhail, Mueller, Philippe, 2012. The term structure of inflation expectations. Journal of Financial Economics 106, 367-394.

Christensen, Jens H.E., Diebold, Francis X., Rudebusch, Glenn D., 2011. The affine arbitrage-free class of Nelson-Siegel term structure models. Journal of Econometrics 164, 4–20.

Christensen, Jens H.E., Lopez, Jose, Rudebusch, Glenn D., 2010. Inflation expectations and risk premiums in an arbitrage-free model of nominal and real bond yields. Journal of Money, Credit, and Banking 42, 143–178.

Cieslak, Anna, Povala, Pavol, 2011. Understanding bond risk premia. Working Paper, Kellogg School of Management.

Clark, Todd E., McCracken, Michael W., 2013. Advances in Forecast Evaluation. This Handbook.

Cochrane, John H., Piazzesi, Monika, 2005. Bond risk premia. American Economic Review 95, 138–160.

Cochrane, John H., Piazzesi, Monika, 2008. Decomposing the yield curve. Working Paper, Chicago Booth.

Collin-Dufresne, Pierre, Goldstein, Robert S., 2002. Do bonds span the fixed income markets? Theory and evidence for unspanned stochastic volatility. Journal of Finance 57, 1685–1730

Cooper, Ilan, Priestly, Richard, 2009. Time-varying risk premiums and the output gap. Review of Financial Studies 22, 2801–2833.

Dai, Qiang, Singleton, Kenneth J., 2000. Specification analysis of affine term structure models. Journal of Finance 55, 1943–1978.

Dai, Qiang, Singleton, Kenneth J., Yang, Wei, Regime shifts in a dynamic term structure model of US treasury bond yields. Review of Financial Studies 20, 1669–1706.

Diebold, Francis X., Li, Canlin, 2006. Forecasting the term structure of government bond yields. Journal of Econometrics 130, 337–364.

Duarte, Jefferson, 2004. Evaluating an alternative risk preference in affine term structure models. Review of Financial Studies 17, 379–404.

Duffee, Gregory R., 2002. Term premia and interest rate forecasts in affine models. Journal of Finance 57, 405–443.

Duffee, Gregory R., 2010. Sharpe ratios in term structure models. Working Paper, Johns Hopkins.

Duffee, Gregory R., 2011a. Information in (and not in) the term structure. Review of Financial Studies 24, 2895–2934.

Duffee, Gregory R., 2011b. Forecasting with the term structure: the role of no-arbitrage restrictions. Working Paper, Johns Hopkins.

Duffee, Gregory R., 2013. Bond pricing and the macroeconomy. In: Constantinides, G.M., Harris, M., Stulz, R. (Eds.), Handbook of the Economics of Finance, vol 2B. Elsevier, pp. 907–967.

Duffie, Darrell, Kan, Rui, 1996. A yield-factor model of interest rates. Mathematical Finance 6, 379–406.

Epstein, Larry G., Zin, Stanley E., 1989. Substitution, risk aversion, and the temporal behavior of consumption and asset returns: a theoretical framework. Econometrica 57, 937–969.

Fama, Eugene F., Bliss, Robert R., 1987. The information in long-maturity forward rates. American Economic Review 77, 680–692.

Favero, Carlo A., Niu, Linlin, Sala, Luca, 2012. Term structure forecasting: no-arbitrage restrictions versus large information set. Journal of Forecasting 31, 124–156.

Gray, Stephen F., 1996. Modeling the conditional distribution of interest rates as a regime-switching process. Journal of Financial Economics 42, 27–62.

Gurkaynak, Refet S., Sack, Brian, Wright, Jonathan H., 2007. The US treasury yield curve: 1961 to the present. Journal of Monetary Economics 54, 2291–2304.

Hall, Anthony D., Anderson, Heather M., Granger, Clive W.J., 1992. Review of Economics and Statistics 74, 116–126.

Hodrick, Robert J., 1992. Dividend yields and expected stock returns: alternative procedures for inference and measurement. Review of Financial Studies 5, 357–386.

Joslin, Scott, Priebsch, Marcel, Singleton, Kenneth J., 2010. Risk premiums in dynamic term structure models with unspanned macro risks. Working Paper, Stanford GSB.

Joslin, Scott, Singleton, Kenneth J., Zhu, Haoxiang, 2011. A new perspective on Gaussian dynamic term structure models. Review of Financial Studies 24, 926–970.

Kessel, Reuben A., 1965. The cyclical behavior of the term structure of interest rates. NBER, Occasional Paper 91.

Kim, Don H., Orphanides, Athanasios, 2005. Term structure estimation with survey data on interest rate forecasts. FEDS working Paper, 2005-48, Federal Reserve Board.

Koopman, Siem Jan, van der Wel, Michel, 2011. Forecasting the US term structure of interest rates using a macroeconomic smooth factor dynamic model. Working Paper, Tinbergen Institute.

Le, Ahn, Singleton, Kenneth J., Dai, Qiang, 2010. Discrete-time affine^Q term structure models with generalized market prices of risk. Review of Financial Studies 23, 2184–2227.

Leippold, Markus, Wu, Liuren, 2002. Asset pricing under the quadratic class. Journal of Financial and Quantitative Analysis 37, 271–295.

Litterman, Robert, Scheinkman, Jose, 1991. Common factors affecting bond returns. Journal of Fixed Income 1, 54–61.

Ludvigson, Sydney C., Ng, Serena, 2009. Macro factors in bond risk premia. Review of Financial Studies 22, 5027–5067.

Ludvigson, Sydney C., Ng, Serena, 2010. A factor analysis of bond risk premia. In: Ullah, A., Giles, D. (Eds.), Handbook of Empirical Economics and Finance. Chapman and Hall, Boca Raton, FL, pp. 313–372.

Martin, Vance, Hall, Anthony D., Pagan, Adrian R., 1996. Modelling the term structure. In : Maddala, G.S., Rao, C.R. (Eds.), Handbook of Statistics, vol. 14, pp. 91–118.

Nelson, Charles R., Siegel, Andrew F., 1987. Parsimonious modeling of yield curves. Journal of Business 60, 473–489.

Piazzesi, Monika, Schneider, Martin, 2007. Equilibrium yield curves. NBER Macroeconomics Annual 2006, MIT Press, Cambridge, MA, 389–442.

Van Horne, James, 1965. Interest-rate risk and the term structure of interest rates. Journal of Political Economy 73, 344–351.

CHAPTER 8

Forecasting the Price of Oil

Ron Alquist[*], Lutz Kilian[†], and Robert J. Vigfusson[‡]

[*]Bank of Canada, Ottawa, ON, Canada
[†]University of Michigan, Ann Arbor, MI, USA
[‡]Federal Reserve Board, Washington, DC, USA

Contents

Handbook of Economic Forecasting, Volume 2A
ISSN 1574-0706, http://dx.doi.org/10.1016/B978-0-444-53683-9.00008-8

Abstract

We address some of the key questions that arise in forecasting the price of crude oil. What do applied forecasters need to know about the choice of sample period and about the tradeoffs between alternative oil price series and model specifications? Are real and nominal oil prices predictable based on macroeconomic aggregates? Does this predictability translate into gains in out-of-sample forecast accuracy compared with conventional no-change forecasts? How useful are oil futures prices in forecasting the spot price of oil? How useful are survey forecasts? How does one evaluate the sensitivity of a baseline oil price forecast to alternative assumptions about future oil demand and oil supply conditions? How does one quantify risks associated with oil price forecasts? Can joint forecasts of the price of oil and of U.S. real GDP growth be improved upon by allowing for asymmetries?

Keywords

Oil, No-change forecast, Futures price, Economic fundamentals, Asymmetries, Structural change, Structural oil market models, Predictability, Forecast scenarios, Risk

1. INTRODUCTION

There is widespread agreement that unexpected large and persistent fluctuations in the price of oil are detrimental to the welfare of both oil-importing and oil-producing economies, making reliable forecasts of the price of crude oil of interest for a wide range of applications. For example, central banks and private sector forecasters view the price of oil as one of the key variables in generating macroeconomic projections and in assessing macroeconomic risks. Of particular interest is the question of the extent to which the price of oil is helpful in predicting recessions. For example, Hamilton (2009), building on the analysis in Edelstein and Kilian (2009), provides evidence that the recession of late 2008 was amplified and preceded by an economic slowdown in the automobile industry and a deterioration in consumer sentiment.

Not only are more accurate forecasts of the price of oil likely to improve the accuracy of forecasts of macroeconomic outcomes, but, in addition, some sectors of the economy depend directly on forecasts of the price of oil for their business. For example, airlines rely on such forecasts in setting airfares, automobile companies decide their product menu and set product prices with oil price forecasts in mind, and utility companies use oil price forecasts in deciding whether to expand capacity or to build new plants. Likewise, homeowners rely on oil price forecasts in deciding the timing of their heating oil purchases or whether to invest in energy-saving home improvements.

Finally, forecasts of the price of oil (and the price of its derivatives such as gasoline or heating oil) are important in modeling purchases of energy-intensive durables goods such as automobiles or home heating systems.[1] They also play a role in generating projections of energy use, in modeling investment decisions in the energy sector, in predicting carbon emissions and climate change, and in designing regulatory policies such as the imposition of automotive fuel standards or gasoline taxes.[2]

This chapter provides a comprehensive analysis of the problem of forecasting the price of crude oil. In Section 2 we compare alternative measures of the price of oil. In Section 3 we discuss the rationales of alternative specifications of the oil price variable in empirical work. Section 4 studies the extent to which the nominal price of oil and the real price of oil are predictable based on macroeconomic aggregates. We document strong evidence of predictability in population. Predictability in population, however, need not translate into out-of-sample forecastability. The latter question is the main focus of Sections 5 through 10.

In Sections 5, 6 and 7, we compare a wide range of out-of-sample forecasting methods for the nominal price of oil. For example, it is common among policymakers to treat the price of oil futures contracts as the forecast of the nominal price of oil. We focus on the ability of daily and monthly oil futures prices to forecast the nominal price of oil in real time compared with a range of simple time series forecasting models. We find some evidence that the price of oil futures has additional predictive content compared with the current spot price at the 12-month horizon; the magnitude of the reduction in the mean-squared prediction error (MSPE) is modest even at the 12-month horizon, however, and there are indications that this result is sensitive to small changes in the sample period and in the forecast horizon. There is no evidence of significant forecast accuracy gains at shorter horizons, and at the long horizons of interest to policymakers, oil futures prices are clearly inferior to the no-change forecast.

Similarly, a forecasting model motivated by the analysis in Hotelling (1931), and a variety of simple time series regression models are not successful at significantly lowering the MSPE at short horizons. There is strong evidence, however, that recent percent changes in the nominal price of industrial raw materials (other than crude oil) can be used to substantially and significantly reduce the MSPE of the nominal price of oil at horizons of 1 and 3 months, building on insights in Barsky and Kilian (2002). The gains may be as large as 22% at the 3-month horizon. Similar short-run gains also are possible based on models that extrapolate the current nominal price of oil at the rate of recent percent changes in the dollar exchange rate of major broad-based commodity exporters such as Canada or Australia, consistent with insights provided in Chen et al. (2010).

By comparison, the predictive success of expert survey forecasts of the nominal price of oil proved disappointing. Only the one-quarter-ahead U.S. Energy Information

---

[1] See, e.g., Kahn (1986), Davis and Kilian (2011).
[2] See, e.g., Goldberg (1998), Allcott and Wozny (2011), Busse et al. (2011), Kellogg (2010).

Administration (EIA) forecast significantly improves on the no-change forecast and none of the expert forecasts we studied significantly improves on the MSPE of the no-change forecast at the 1-year horizon. Finally, forecasts obtained by adjusting the current price of oil for survey inflation expectation do little to improve accuracy at horizons up to 1 year, but outperform the no-change forecast by a wide margin at horizons of several years. Section 8 summarizes the lessons to be drawn from our analysis for forecasting the nominal price of oil.

Although the nominal price of crude oil receives much attention in the press, the variable most relevant for economic modeling is the real price of oil. Section 9 compares alternative forecasting models for the real price of oil. We provide evidence that reduced-form autoregressive and vector autoregressive models of the global oil market are more accurate than the random walk forecast of the real price of oil at short horizons. Even after taking account of the constraints on the real-time availability of these predictors, the MSPE reductions can be substantial in the short run. The accuracy gains tend to diminish at longer horizons, however, and, beyond 1 year, the no-change forecast of the real price of oil typically is the predictor with the lowest MSPE. Moreover, the extent of the MSPE reductions depends on the definition of the oil price series. The lessons to be drawn from this evidence are discussed in Section 10.

An important limitation of reduced-form forecasting models from a policy point of view is that they provide no insight into what is driving the forecast and do not allow the policymaker to explore alternative hypothetical forecast scenarios. In Section 11, we illustrate how recently developed structural vector autoregressive models of the global oil market may be used to generate conditional projections of how the oil price forecast would deviate from the unconditional forecast baseline, given alternative scenarios about future oil demand and oil supply conditions such as a surge in speculative demand triggered by Iran, a resurgence of the global business cycle, or an increase in U.S. oil production.

Section 12 focuses on the problem of jointly forecasting U.S. macroeconomic aggregates such as real GDP growth and the price of oil. Of particular interest is the forecasting ability of non-linear transformations of the price of oil such as the nominal net oil price increase or the real net oil price increase. The net oil price increase is a censored predictor that assigns zero weight to net oil price decreases. There is little evidence that this type of asymmetry is reflected in the responses of U.S. real GDP to innovations in the real price of oil, as documented in Kilian and Vigfusson (2011a,b), but Hamilton (2011) suggests that the net oil price increase specification is best thought of as a parsimonious forecasting device. We provide a comprehensive analysis of this conjecture.

Point forecasts of the price of oil are important, but they fail to convey the large uncertainty associated with oil price forecasts. This uncertainty can be captured by predictive densities. In Section 13 we discuss various approaches of conveying the information in the predictive density including measures of price volatility and of tail conditional expectations with particular emphasis on defining appropriate risk measures. Section 14 contains a discussion of directions for future research. The concluding remarks are in Section 15.

2. ALTERNATIVE OIL PRICE MEASURES

Figure 8.1 plots three alternative measures of the nominal price of oil. The longest available series is the West Texas Intermediate (WTI) price of crude oil. WTI is a particular grade of crude oil. The WTI price refers to the price of WTI oil to be delivered to Cushing, Oklahoma, and serves as a benchmark in pricing oil contracts. It is available in real time. An alternative measure of the oil price is the price paid by U.S. refiners purchasing crude oil. Data on the U.S. refiners' acquisition cost for domestically produced oil, for imported crude oil and for a composite of these series are available starting in 1974.1. These data become available only with a delay and are subject to revisions (see Baumeister and Kilian, 2012a).

Figure 3.1 highlights striking differences in the time series process for the price of oil prior to 1973 and after 1973. The WTI data until 1973 tend to exhibit a pattern resembling a step-function. The price remains constant for extended periods, followed by large adjustments. The U.S. wholesale price of oil for 1948-1972 used in Hamilton (1983) is very similar to the WTI series. As discussed in Hamilton (1983, 1985) the peculiar pattern of crude oil price changes during this period is explained by the specific

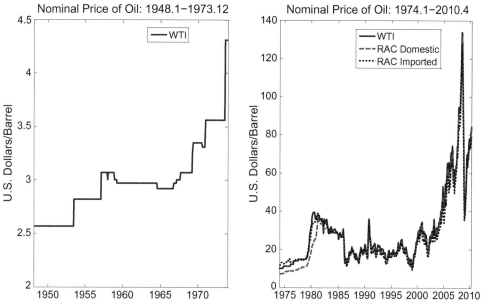

Figure 8.1 The nominal price of crude oil. *Notes*: WTI stands for the West Texas Intermediate price of crude oil and RAC for the U.S. refiners' acquisition cost.

regulatory structure of the oil industry during 1948-72. Each month the Texas Railroad Commission and other U.S. state regulatory agencies would forecast demand for oil for the subsequent month and would set the allowable production levels for wells in the state to meet demand. As a result, much of the cyclically endogenous component of oil demand was reflected in shifts in quantities rather than prices. The commission was generally unable or unwilling to accommodate sudden disruptions in oil production, preferring instead to exploit these events to implement sometimes dramatic price increases (Hamilton, 1983, p. 230).

Whereas the WTI price is a good proxy for the U.S. price for oil during 1948-72, when the U.S. was largely self-sufficient in oil, it becomes less representative after 1973, when the share of U.S. imports of oil rapidly expanded. The price discrepancy between unregulated foreign oil and regulated domestic oil created increasing pressure to deregulate the domestic market. As regulatory control weakened in the mid-1970s, adjustments to the WTI price became much more frequent and smaller in magnitude, as shown in the right panel of Figure 8.1. By the mid-1980s, the WTI had been deregulated to the point that there was strong comovement between all three oil price series most of the time.

Figure 8.2 shows the corresponding oil price data adjusted for U.S. CPI inflation. The left panel reveals that in real terms the price of oil had been falling considerably since the late 1950s. That decline was corrected only by the sharp rise in the real price of oil in 1973/74. There has been no pronounced trend in the real price of oil since 1974, but considerable volatility. The definition of the real price of oil is of lesser importance after 1986.

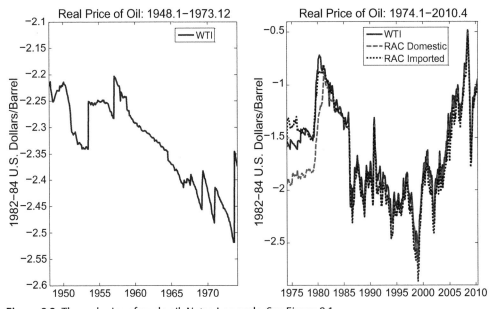

Figure 8.2 The real price of crude oil. *Notes*: Log scale. See Figure 8.1.

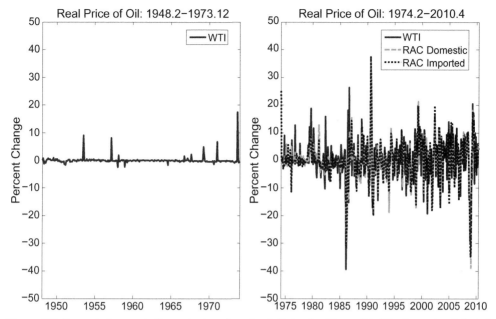

Figure 8.3 Percent changes in the real price of crude oil. *Notes:* See Figure 8.1. All price series deflated by the U.S. CPI for all urban consumers, seasonally adjusted.

Prior to 1986, one key difference is that the refiners' acquisition cost for imported crude oil fell in 1974–76, whereas the real WTI price rose. A second key difference is that the real WTI price spiked in 1980, whereas the real price of oil imports remained largely stable. This pattern was only reversed with the outbreak of the Iran–Iraq War in late 1980.

Figure 8.3 once more highlights the striking differences between the pre- and post-1973 period. It shows the percent growth rate of the real price of oil. A major structural change in the distribution of the price of oil in late 1973 is readily apparent.[3] Whereas the pre-1973 period is characterized by long periods of low volatility interrupted by infrequent large positive price spikes, the post-1973 period is characterized by high month-to-month volatility. It has been suggested that perhaps this volatility has increased systematically after the collapse of OPEC in late 1985. The answer is somewhat sensitive to the exact choice of dates. If one were to date the OPEC period as 1973.10-1985.12, for example, there is no evidence of an increase in the variance of the percent change in the real WTI price of oil. The volatility in the OPEC period is virtually identical to that in the post-OPEC period of 1986.1-2010.6. Shifting the starting date of the OPEC period to 1974.1, in contrast, implies a considerable increase in volatility

---

[3] In related work, Dvir and Rogoff (2010) present formal evidence of a structural break in the process driving the annual real price of oil in 1973. Given this evidence of instability, combining pre- and post-1973 real oil price data is not a valid option.

after 1985. Extending the ending date of the OPEC period to include the price collapse in 1986 induced by OPEC actions, on the other hand, renders the volatility much more similar across subperiods. Finally, combining the earlier starting date and the later ending date, there is evidence of a reduction in the real price volatility after the collapse of OPEC rather than an increase. Below we therefore treat the post-1973 data as homogeneous.

Which price series is more appropriate for the analysis of post-1973 data depends in part on the purpose of the study. The WTI price data (as well as other measures of the domestic U.S. price of oil) are questionable to the extent that these prices were regulated until the mid-1980s and do not reflect the true scarcity of oil or the price actually paid by U.S. refiners. The main advantage of the WTI price is that it is available in a timely manner and not subject to data revisions. The refiners' acquisition cost for imported crude oil provides a good proxy for oil price fluctuations in global oil markets, but may not be representative for the price that U.S. refineries paid for crude oil. The latter price may be captured better by a composite of the acquisition cost of domestic and imported crude oil, neither of which, however, is available before January 1974. The real price of oil imports also is the price relevant for theories interpreting oil price shocks as terms-of-trade shocks. Theories that interpret oil price shocks as allocative disturbances, on the other hand, require the use of retail energy prices, for which the composite refiners' acquisition cost may be a better proxy than the refiners' acquisition cost of oil imports. Below we will consider several alternative oil price series.[4]

3. ALTERNATIVE OIL PRICE SPECIFICATIONS

Although an increasing number of empirical studies of the post-1973 data focus on the real price of oil, many other studies have relied on the nominal price of oil. One argument for the use of nominal oil prices has been that the nominal price of oil – unlike the real price of oil – is considered exogenous with respect to U.S. macroeconomic conditions and hence linearly unpredictable on the basis of lagged U.S. macroeconomic conditions.[5] This argument may have some merit for the pre-1973 period, but it is implausible for the post-1973 period. If the U.S. money supply unexpectedly doubles, for example, then, according to standard macroeconomic models, so will all nominal prices denominated in dollars (including the nominal price of oil), leaving the relative price or real price of crude oil unaffected (see Gillman and Nakov, 2009). Clearly, one would not want to interpret such an episode as an oil price shock involving a doubling of the nominal price of oil. Indeed, economic models of the impact of the price of oil on the U.S. economy correctly predict that such a nominal oil price shock should have no effect on the U.S.

---

[4] For further discussion of the trade-offs between alternative oil price definitions from an economic point of view see Kilian and Vigfusson (2011b).

[5] For a review of the relationship between the concepts of (strict) exogeneity and predictability in linear models see Cooley and LeRoy (1985).

economy because theoretical models inevitably are specified in terms of the real price of oil, which has not changed in this example.

Another argument in the literature has been that the nominal price of oil can be considered exogenous after 1973 because it is set by OPEC. This interpretation is without basis. First, there is little evidence to support the notion that OPEC has been successfully acting as a cartel in the 1970s and early 1980s, and the role of OPEC has diminished further since 1986 (see, e.g., Skeet, 1988; Smith, 2005; Almoguera et al., 2011). Second, even if we were to accept the notion that an OPEC cartel sets the nominal price of oil, economic theory predicts that this cartel price will endogenously respond to U.S. macroeconomic conditions. This theoretical prediction is consistent with anecdotal evidence of OPEC oil producers raising the price of oil (or equivalently lowering oil production) in response to unanticipated U.S. inflation, low U.S. interest rates, and the depreciation of the dollar. Moreover, as observed by Barsky and Kilian (2002), economic theory predicts that the strength of the oil cartel itself (measured by the extent to which individual cartel members choose to deviate from cartel guidelines) will be positively related to the state of the global business cycle (see Green and Porter, 1984). Thus, both nominal and real oil prices must be considered endogenous with respect to the global economy, unless proven otherwise.

A third and distinct argument has been that consumers of refined oil products choose to respond to changes in the nominal price of oil rather than the real price of oil, perhaps because the nominal price of oil is more visible. In other words, consumers suffer from money illusion. There is no direct empirical evidence in favor of this behavioral argument at the micro level. Rather the case for this specification, if there is one, has to be based on the predictive success of such models; a success that, however, has yet to be demonstrated empirically. We will address this question in Section 12.

Even proponents of using the nominal price in empirical models of the transmission of oil price shocks have concluded that there is no stable dynamic relationship between percent changes in the nominal price of oil and in U.S. macroeconomic aggregates. There is evidence from in-sample fitting exercises, however, of a predictive relationship between U.S. real GDP and suitable non-linear transformations of the nominal price of oil. The most successful of these transformations is the net oil price increase measure of Hamilton (1996, 2003). Let s_t denote the nominal price of oil in logs and Δ the difference operator. Then the net oil price increase is defined as:

$$\Delta s_t^{+,net} \equiv \max \left[0, s_t - s_t^* \right],$$

where s_t^* is the highest oil price in the preceding 12 months or, alternatively, the preceding 36 months. This transformation involves two distinct ideas. One is that consumers in oil-importing economies respond to increases in the price of oil only if the increase is large relative to the recent past. If correct, the same logic by construction should apply to decreases in the price of oil, suggesting a net change transformation that is symmetric in increases and decreases.

The second idea implicit in Hamilton's definition is that consumers do not respond to net decreases in the price of oil, allowing us to omit the net decreases from the model. In other words, consumers respond asymmetrically to net oil price increases and to net oil price decreases, and they do so in a very specific fashion. Although there are theoretical models that imply the existence of an asymmetry in the response of the economy to oil price increases and decreases, these models do not imply the specific non-linear structure embodied in the net increase measure nor do they imply that the net decrease measure should receive zero weight. Nevertheless, Hamilton's nominal net oil price increase variable has become one of the leading specifications in the literature on predictive relationships between the price of oil and the U.S. economy. Hamilton (2011), for example, interprets this specification as capturing non-linear changes in consumer sentiment in response to nominal oil price increases.[6]

As with other oil price specifications there is reason to expect lagged feedback from global macroeconomic aggregates to the net oil price increase. Whereas Hamilton (2003) made the case that net oil price increases in the 1970s, 1980s, and 1990s were capturing exogenous events in the Middle East, Hamilton (2009) concedes that the net oil price increase of 2003-08 was driven in large part by a surge in the demand for oil. Kilian (2009a,b, 2010), on the other hand, provides evidence based on structural vector autoregressive (VAR) models that in fact most net oil price increases have contained a large demand component driven by global macroeconomic conditions, even prior to 2003. This finding is also consistent with the empirical results in Kilian and Murphy (2013) and Baumeister and Peersman (forthcoming), among others.

For now we set aside all non-linear transformations of the price of oil and focus on linear forecasting models for the nominal price of oil and for the real price of oil. Non-linear joint forecasting models for U.S. real GDP and the price of oil based on net oil price increases are discussed in Section 12.

4. GRANGER CAUSALITY TESTS

Much of the existing work on predicting the price of oil has focused on testing for the existence of a predictive relationship from macroeconomic aggregates to the price of oil. In the absence of structural change, the existence of predictability in population is a necessary precondition for out-of-sample forecastability (see Inoue and Kilian, 2004a). Within the linear VAR framework the absence of predictability from one variable to another in population may be tested using Granger non-causality tests. We distinguish between predictability for the nominal price of oil and for the real price of oil. These are

---

[6] The behavioral rationale for the net oil price increase measure applies equally to the nominal price of oil and the real price of oil. Although Hamilton (2003) applied this transformation to the nominal price of oil, several other studies have recently explored models that apply the same transformation to the real price of oil (see, e.g., Kilian and Vigfusson, 2011a; Herrera et al., 2011).

potentially quite different questions. For example, if the U.S. CPI is predictable and the nominal price of oil is not, then one could find that changes in the real price of oil are predictable simply because inflation is predictable. On the other hand, if the real price of oil is unpredictable, but the U.S. CPI is predictable, then one would expect to be able to forecast the nominal price simply because inflation is predictable. Finally, the real price of oil, the nominal price of oil, and the U.S. CPI may all be predictable to varying degrees.

4.1. Nominal Oil Price Predictability

4.1.1. The Pre-1973 Evidence

Granger causality from macroeconomic aggregates to the price of oil has received attention in part because Granger non-causality is one of the testable implications of strict exogeneity. The notion that the percent change in the nominal price of oil may be considered exogenous with respect to the U.S. economy was bolstered by evidence in Hamilton (1983), who observed that there is no apparent Granger causality from U.S. domestic macroeconomic aggregates to the percent change in the nominal price of oil during 1948-1972. Of course, the absence of Granger causality is merely a necessary condition for strict exogeneity. Moreover, a failure to reject the null of no Granger causality is at best suggestive; it does not establish the validity of the null hypothesis. Hamilton's case for the exogeneity of the nominal price of oil with respect to the U.S. economy therefore rested primarily on the unique institutional features of the oil market during this period, discussed in Section 2, and on historical evidence that unexpected supply disruptions under this institutional regime appear to be associated with exogenous political events in the Middle East, allowing us to treat the resulting price spikes as exogenous with respect to the U.S. economy. Even if we accept Hamilton's interpretation of the pre-1973 period, the institutional conditions that Hamilton (1983) appeals to ceased to exist in the early 1970s. The question that matters for our purposes is to what extent there is evidence that oil prices can be predicted from macroeconomic aggregates in the post-1973 period.

4.1.2. The Post-1973 Evidence

There is widespread agreement among oil economists that, starting in 1973, nominal oil prices must be considered endogenous with respect to U.S. macroeconomic variables (see, e.g., Kilian, 2008a). This fact alone is not sufficient, however, for the nominal price of oil to be predictable on the basis of lagged U.S. macroeconomic aggregates. If the nominal price of oil instantaneously incorporates information about expected U.S. macroeconomic conditions, as suggested by some rational expectations models, this could render the nominal price of oil linearly unpredictable on the basis of lagged U.S. macroeconomic aggregates. This line of reasoning is familiar from the analysis of stock and bond prices as well as exchange rates.[7]

---

[7] Hamilton (1994 p. 306) illustrates this point in the context of a model of stock prices and expected dividends.

A recent study by Kilian and Vega (2010) helps resolve this question. Kilian and Vega find no evidence of systematic feedback from news about a wide range of U.S. macroeconomic aggregates to the nominal price of oil at any horizon between 1 day and 1 month. This lack of evidence is in sharp contrast to the results obtained for other asset prices based on the same sample, so a lack of power of the procedure employed by Kilian and Vega cannot explain the absence of significant feedback from U.S. macroeconomic news to the nominal price of oil. These two results in conjunction allow us to rule out contemporaneous feedback from U.S. macroeconomic aggregates to the nominal price of oil and imply that lagged U.S. macroeconomic aggregates must have predictive power in population, if the nominal price of oil is indeed endogenous with respect to these macroeconomic aggregates.

Predictability in the context of linear vector autoregressions may be tested using Granger causality tests. Table 8.1 investigates the evidence of Granger causality from selected nominal U.S. and global macroeconomic predictors to the nominal price of oil. All results are based on pairwise vector autoregressions. The lag order is fixed at 12. We consider four alternative nominal oil price series. The evaluation period is 1975.2–2009.12. There are several reasons to expect the dollar-denominated nominal price of oil to respond to changes in nominal U.S. macroeconomic aggregates. One channel

Table 8.1 Marginal Significance Levels for Predictability from Selected Nominal Aggregates to Nominal Price of Oil Since 1973

Predictors	WTI	RAC Oil Imports	RAC Domestic Oil	RAC Composite
Monthly Predictors:				
U.S. CPI	**0.072**	**0.024**	0.234	**0.097**
U.S. M1	**0.057**	**0.003**	**0.000**	**0.000**
U.S. M2	0.101	0.184	**0.014**	**0.062**
CRB Industrial Raw Materials Price Index	**0.000**	**0.000**	**0.001**	**0.002**
CRB Metals Price Index	**0.004**	**0.009**	**0.001**	**0.011**
U.S. 3-Month T-Bill Rate	0.232	0.438	0.361	0.377
Trade-Weighted U.S. Exchange Rate	0.736	0.725	0.490	0.706
Australian/U.S. Exchange Rate	0.223	0.207	0.176	0.172
Canadian/U.S. Exchange Rate	**0.022**	**0.003**	0.155	**0.019**
New Zealand/U.S. Exchange Rate	0.548	0.667	0.218	0.438
South African/U.S. Exchange Rate	0.184	0.208	**0.082**	0.123

Notes: p-values for Wald tests of Granger non-causality causality based on heteroskedasticity-robust variance estimator. Boldface indicates significance at the 10% level. All test results are based on bivariate VAR(12) models. The evaluation period is 1975.2-2009.12. RAC stands for U.S. refiners' acquisition cost and CRB for the Commodity Research Bureau. All variables but the interest rate are expressed in percent changes. Interest rates are expressed in changes. In some cases, one needs to consider the possibility of cointegration in levels. In those cases, all rejections above remain significant if we follow Dolado and Lütkepohl (1996) in conducting a lag-augmented Granger non-causality test.

of transmission is purely monetary and operates through U.S. inflation. For example, Gillman and Nakov (2009) stress that changes in the nominal price of oil must occur in equilibrium just to offset persistent shifts in U.S. inflation, given that the price of oil is denominated in dollars. Indeed, the Granger causality tests in Table 8.1 indicate significant lagged feedback from U.S. headline CPI inflation to the percent change in the nominal price of oil except for the domestic refiners' acquisition cost, consistent with the findings in Gillman and Nakov (2009). The evidence of predictability is weaker for the domestic oil price series than for the price of oil imports.

Gillman and Nakov view changes in inflation in the post-1973 period as rooted in persistent changes in the growth rate of money.[8] Thus, an alternative approach of testing the hypothesis of Gillman and Nakov (2009) is to focus on Granger causality from monetary aggregates to the nominal price of oil. Given the general instability in the link from changes in monetary aggregates to inflation, one would not necessarily expect changes in monetary aggregates to have much predictive power for the price of oil, except perhaps in the 1970s (see Barsky and Kilian, 2002). Table 8.1 nevertheless shows that there is statistically significant lagged feedback from narrow measures of money such as M1 to all four nominal oil price measures. The evidence for broader monetary aggregates such as M2 is weaker, with only two tests statistically significant.

A third approach to testing for a role for U.S. monetary conditions relies on the fact that rising dollar-denominated non-oil commodity prices are thought to presage rising U.S. inflation. To the extent that oil price adjustments are more sluggish than adjustments in other industrial commodity prices, one would expect changes in nominal Commodity Research Bureau (CRB) spot prices to Granger cause changes in the nominal price of oil. Indeed, Table 8.1 indicates highly statistically significant lagged feedback from CRB sub-indices for industrial raw materials and for metals. This evidence is also consistent with rising non-oil commodity prices being an indicator of shifts in the global demand for industrial commodities, in which case the predictability of the nominal price would arise because of the predictability of the real price of oil.

In contrast, neither short-term interest rates nor trade-weighted exchange rates have significant predictive power for the nominal price of oil. According to the Hotelling model, one would expect the nominal price of oil to grow at the nominal rate of interest if the marginal extraction cost is zero, providing yet another link from U.S. macroeconomic aggregates to the nominal price of oil.[9] Table 8.1, however, shows no evidence

---

[8] For an earlier exposition of the role of monetary factors in determining the price of oil see Barsky and Kilian (2002). Both Barsky and Kilian (2002) and Gillman and Nakov (2009) view the shifts in U.S. inflation in the early 1970s as caused by persistent changes in the growth rate of the money supply, but there are important differences in emphasis. Whereas Barsky and Kilian stress the effects of unanticipated monetary expansions on real domestic output, on the demand for oil and hence on the real price of oil, Gillman and Nakov stress that the relative price of oil must not decline in response to a monetary expansion, necessitating a higher nominal price of oil, consistent with anecdotal evidence on OPEC price decisions (see, e.g., Kilian, 2008b). These two explanations are complementary.

[9] Specifically, we use the 3-month, 6-month, and 12-month constant-maturity Treasury bill rates from the Federal Reserve Board's website http://federalreserve.gov/releases/H15/data.htm

of statistically significant feedback from the 3-month T-Bill rate to the price of oil. This finding is not surprising as the price of oil was not even approximately growing at the rate of interest (see Figure 8.1). Nor is there evidence of significant feedback from lagged changes in the trade-weighted nominal U.S. exchange rate. This does not necessarily mean that all bilateral exchange rates lack predictive power. In related work, Chen et al. (2010) show that the floating exchange rates of small commodity exporters (including Australia, Canada, New Zealand, South Africa and Chile) with respect to the dollar in some cases have remarkably robust forecasting power for the global prices of their commodity exports. The explanation presumably is that these exchange rates are forward looking and embody information about future movements in commodity export markets that cannot easily be captured by other means.

Although Chen et al.'s analysis cannot be extended to oil exporters such as Saudi Arabia because Saudi Arabia's exchange rate has not been floating freely, the bilateral dollar exchange rates of Australia, Canada, New Zealand, and South Africa may serve as a proxy for expected broad-based movements in industrial commodity prices that may also be helpful in predicting changes in the nominal price of oil. According to Chen et al., the share of non-agricultural commodity exports is largest in South Africa, followed by Australia, Canada, and New Zealand. In general, the larger the share of non-agricultural exports, the higher one would expect the predictive power for industrial commodities to be. For the price of oil, the share of energy exports such as crude oil, coal, and natural gas may be an even better indicator of predictive power, suggesting that Canada should have the highest predictive power for the price of oil, followed by Australia, South Africa, and New Zealand. Table 8.1 shows strong evidence of predictability for the bilateral exchange rate of Canada, consistent with the intuition that the share of oil in commodity exports matters. There is no such evidence for the other commodity exporters. Moreover, when using the dollar exchange rate of the Japanese Yen and of the British Pound as a control group, there is no significant evidence of Granger causality from exchange rates to the price of oil.[10]

4.1.3. Reconciling the Pre- and Post-1973 Evidence on the Predictability of the Nominal Price of Oil

Table 8.1 suggests that indicators of U.S. inflation have significant predictive power for the nominal price of oil. This result is in striking contrast to the pre-1973 period. As shown in Hamilton (1983) using quarterly data and in Gillman and Nakov (2009) using monthly data, there is no significant Granger causality from U.S. inflation to the percent change in the nominal price of oil in the 1950s and 1960s. This difference in results is suggestive of a structural break in late 1973 in the predictive relationship between the price of oil and the U.S. economy. One reason that the pre-1973 predictive regressions

---

[10] Although the U.K. has been exporting crude oil from the late 1970s until recently, its average share of petroleum exports is too low to consider the U.K. a commodity exporter (see Kilian et al., 2009).

differ from the post-1973 regressions is that prior to 1973 the nominal price of oil was adjusted only at discrete intervals (see Figure 8.1). Because the nominal oil price data were generated by a discrete-continuous choice model, conventional autoregressive or moving average time series processes are inappropriate for these data and tests of the predictability of the price of oil based on such models have to be viewed with caution.

This problem with the pre-1973 data may be ameliorated by deflating the nominal price of oil, which renders the oil price data continuous and more amenable to VAR analysis (see Figure 8.2). Additional problems arise, however, when combining oil price data generated by a discrete-continuous choice process with data from the post-Texas Railroad Commission era that are fully continuous. Concern over low power has prompted many applied researchers to combine oil price data for the pre-1973 and post-1973 period in the same model when studying the predictive relationship from macroeconomic aggregates to the price of oil. This approach is obviously inadvisable when dealing with nominal oil price data. Perhaps less obviously, this approach is equally unappealing when dealing with vector autoregressions involving the real price of oil. The problem is that the nature and speed of the feedback from U.S. macroeconomic aggregates to the real price of oil differs by construction, depending on whether the nominal price of oil is temporarily fixed or not. This instability manifests itself in a structural break in the predictive regressions commonly used to test for lagged potentially non-linear feedback from the real of price of oil to real GDP growth (see, e.g., Balke et al., 2002). The p-value for the null hypothesis that there is no break in 1973.Q4 in the coefficients of this predictive regression is 0.001 (see Kilian and Vigfusson, 2011b).[11] For that reason, regression estimates of the relationship between the real price of oil and domestic macroeconomic aggregates obtained from the entire post-war period are not informative about the strength of these predictive relationships in post-1973 data.[12] In the analysis of the real price of oil below we therefore restrict the evaluation period to start no earlier than 1974.1.

4.2. Real Oil Price Predictability in the Post-1973 Period

It is well established in natural resource theory that the real price of oil increases in response to low expected real interest rates and in response to high real aggregate output. Any analysis of the role of expected real interest rates is complicated by the fact that inflation expectations are difficult to pin down, especially at longer horizons, and that the relevant horizon for resource extraction is not clear. We therefore focus on the predictive power of fluctuations in real aggregate output. Table 8.2 reports p-values for tests of the

---

[11] Even allowing for the possibility of data mining, this break remains statistically significant at the 5% level.

[12] This situation is analogous to that of combining real exchange rate data for the pre- and post-Bretton Woods periods in studying the speed of mean reversion toward purchasing power parity. Clearly, the speed of adjustment toward purchasing power parity will differ if one of the adjustment channels is shut down, as was the case under the fixed exchange rate system, than when both prices and exchange rates are free to adjust, as has been the case under the floating rate system. Thus, regressions on long time spans of real exchange rate data produce average estimates that by construction are not informative about the speed of adjustment after the end of the Bretton Woods system.

Table 8.2 Marginal Significance Levels for Predictability from Selected Real Aggregates to Real Price of Oil Since 1973

Predictors	WTI		RAC Oil Imports		RAC Domestic Oil		RAC Composite	
Quarterly Predictors:	*p*=4	*p*=8	*p*=4	*p*=8	*p*=4	*p*=8	*p*=4	*p*=8
U.S. Real GDP								
LT	0.615	0.765	0.419	0.269	0.268	0.269	0.323	0.268
HP	0.594	0.705	0.401	0.883	0.304	0.630	0.343	0.691
DIF	0.746	0.457	0.386	0.567	0.234	0.668	0.271	0.620
World Industrial Production[a]								
LT	**0.014**	0.108	**0.050**	0.149	**0.016**	0.130	**0.024**	0.135
HP	0.578	0.909	0.821	0.909	0.499	0.912	0.534	0.900
DIF	0.518	0.846	0.734	0.869	0.564	0.823	0.595	0.851
Monthly Predictors:	*p*=12	*p*=24	*p*=12	*p*=24	*p*=12	*p*=24	*p*=12	*p*=24
Chicago Fed National Activity Index (CFNAI)	0.489	0.781	0.696	0.960	0.409	0.864	0.393	0.923
U.S. Industrial Production								
LT	0.179	0.126	0.195	0.512	**0.023**	0.184	**0.031**	0.193
HP	0.199	0.205	0.243	0.746	**0.045**	0.234	**0.052**	0.298
DIF	**0.061**	0.148	0.169	0.266	**0.024**	0.193	**0.027**	0.757
OECD+6 Industrial Production[b]								
LT	**0.001**	**0.004**	**0.002**	**0.019**	**0.002**	**0.012**	**0.001**	**0.015**
HP	**0.093**	0.196	**0.069**	0.486	**0.074**	0.249	**0.040**	0.404
DIF	**0.061**	0.148	0.169	0.266	**0.024**	0.193	**0.027**	0.757
Global Real Activity Index[c]	**0.034**	**0.002**	**0.082**	**0.007**	**0.006**	**0.002**	**0.016**	**0.005**

Notes: p-values for Wald tests of Granger non-causality based on heteroskedasticity-robust variance estimator. Boldface indicates significance at the 10% level. The evaluation period is 1976.2–2009.12 and 1976.II–2009.IV, respectively, unless noted otherwise. LT denotes linear detrending. HP denotes HP filtering with smoothing parameter $\lambda = 1600$ and $\lambda = 129600$, respectively (see Ravn and Uhlig, 2002), and DIF denotes first differencing. The CFNAI and the global real activity index are constructed to be stationary. RAC stands for U.S. refiners' acquisition cost. All test results are based on bivariate $VAR(p)$ models. In the baseline specification the real price of oil is expressed in log levels, while the output variable is suitably transformed to remove trends. Similar results are obtained when both variables are detrended by the same method.

[a] Data source: U.N. Monthly Bulletin of Statistics. These data end in 2008.III because the U.N. has temporarily suspended updates of this series, resulting in a shorter evaluation period.

[b] Data source: OECD Main Economic Indicators.

[c] Data source: Updated version of the index developed in Kilian (2009a).

hypothesis of Granger non-causality from selected measures of real aggregate output to the real price of oil.

A natural starting point is U.S. real GDP. Economic theory implies that U.S. real GDP and the real price of oil are mutually endogenous and determined jointly. For example, one would expect an unexpected increase in U.S. real GDP, all else equal, to increase the flow demand for crude oil and hence the real price of oil. Unless the real price of oil is forward looking and already embodies all information about future U.S. real GDP, a reasonable conjecture therefore is that lagged U.S. real GDP should help predict the real price of oil. Recent research by Kilian and Murphy (2013) has shown that the real price of oil indeed contains an asset price component, but that this component most of the time explains only a small fraction of the historical variation in the real price of oil. Thus, we would expect fluctuations in U.S. real GDP to predict the real price of oil at least in population. Under the assumption that the joint process can be approximated by a linear vector autoregression, this implies the existence of Granger causality from U.S. real GDP to the real price of oil

Notwithstanding this presumption, Table 8.2 indicates no evidence of Granger causality from U.S. real GDP growth to the real price of oil. This finding is robust to alternative methods of detrending and alternative lag orders. In the absence of instantaneous feedback from U.S. real GDP to the real price of oil, a finding of Granger non-causality from U.S. real GDP to the real price of oil – in conjunction with evidence that the real price of oil Granger causes U.S. real GDP – would be consistent with the real price of oil being strictly exogenous with respect to U.S. real GDP. It can be shown, however, that the evidence of reverse Granger causality from the real price of oil to U.S. real GDP is not much stronger, suggesting that the test is simply not informative because of low power. In fact, this is precisely the argument that prompted some researchers to combine data from the pre-1973 and post-1973 period – a strategy that we do not recommend for the reasons discussed in Section 4.1.3.

Another likely explanation of the failure to reject the null of no predictability is model misspecification. It is well known that Granger causality in a bivariate model may be due to an omitted third variable, but equally relevant is the possibility of Granger non-causality in a bivariate model arising from omitted variables (see Lütkepohl, 1982). This possibility is more than a theoretical curiosity in our context. Recent models of the determination of the real price of oil after 1973 have stressed that this price is determined in global markets (see, e.g., Kilian, 2009a; Kilian and Murphy, 2013). In particular, the demand for oil depends not merely on U.S. demand, but on global demand. The bivariate model for the real price of oil and U.S. real GDP by construction omits fluctuations in real GDP in the rest of the world. The relevance of this point is that offsetting movements in real GDP abroad can easily obscure the effect of changes in U.S. real GDP and eclipse the dynamic relationship of interest, lowering the power of the Granger causality test. Only when real GDP fluctuations are highly correlated across countries would we expect U.S. real GDP to be a good proxy for world real GDP.[13] In addition, as the U.S. share in world GDP evolves, by construction so do the predictive correlations underlying Table 8.2. In this regard, Kilian and Hicks (forthcoming) have documented dramatic changes in the PPP-adjusted share in GDP of the major industrialized economies and of the main emerging economies in recent years that cast further doubt on the U.S. real GDP results in Table 8.2. For example, China, and India combined have almost as high a share in world GDP today as the United States.

A closely related third point is that fluctuations in real GDP are a poor proxy for business-cycle driven fluctuations in the demand for oil. It is well known, for example, that in recent decades the share of services in U.S. real GDP has greatly expanded at the cost of manufacturing and other sectors. Clearly, real GDP growth driven by the non-service sector will be associated with disproportionately higher demand for oil and other industrial commodities than real GDP growth in the service sector. This provides one more reason why one would not expect a strong or stable predictive relationship between U.S. real GDP and the real price of oil.

An alternative quarterly predictor that partially addresses these last two concerns is quarterly world industrial production from the *U.N. Monthly Bulletin of Statistics.* This series has recently been introduced by Baumeister and Peersman (forthcoming) in the context of modeling the demand for oil. Although there are serious methodological concerns regarding the construction of any such index, as discussed in Beyer et al. (2001), one would expect this series to be a better proxy for global fluctuations in the demand for crude oil than U.S. real GDP. Indeed, Table 8.2 shows evidence of Granger causality from world industrial production to all four real oil price series for the LT model specification with four lags. Likewise, for the LT specification with eight lags, the reduction in p-values compared with U.S. real GDP is dramatic. The fact that there is evidence of predictability only for the linearly detrended series is consistent with the view, expressed in Kilian (2009b), that the demand for industrial commodities such as crude oil is subject to long swings. Detrending methods such as HP filtering or first differencing eliminate much of this low frequency covariation in the data, making it more difficult to detect predictability.

Additional insights may be gained by focusing on monthly rather than quarterly predictors in the lower panel of Table 8.2. The first contender is the Chicago Fed National Activity Index (CFNAI). This is a broad measure of monthly real economic activity in the United States obtained from applying principal components analysis to a wide range of monthly indicators of real activity expressed in growth rates (see Stock and Watson, 1999).

---

[13] For example, the conjunction of rising growth in emerging Asia with unchanged growth in the U.S. all else equal would cause world GDP growth and hence the real price of oil to increase, but would imply a zero correlation between U.S. real GDP growth and changes in the real price of oil. Alternatively, slowing growth in Japan and Europe may offset rising growth in the U.S., keeping the real price of oil stable and implying a zero correlation of U.S. growth with changes in the real price of oil. This does not mean that there is no feedback from lagged U.S. real GDP. Indeed, with lower U.S. growth the increase in the real price of oil would have slowed in the first example and without offsetting U.S. growth the real price of oil would have dropped in the second example.

As in the case of quarterly U.S. real GDP, there is no evidence of Granger causality. If we rely on U.S. industrial production as the predictor, the p-values drop across the board. There even is statistically significant evidence of feedback to the real price of oil for some specifications, but the evidence is weak, especially for the import price. There are no monthly data on world industrial production, but the OECD provides an industrial production index for OECD economies and six selected non-OECD countries. As expected, the rejections of Granger non-causality become much stronger when we focus on OECD+6 industrial production. Table 8.2 indicates strong and systematic Granger causality, especially for the LT specification. Even OECD+6 industrial production, however, is an imperfect proxy for business-cycle driven fluctuations in the global demand for industrial commodities such as crude oil.

An alternative is the index of global real activity recently proposed in Kilian (2009a). This index does not rely on any country weights and has global coverage. It has been constructed with the explicit purpose of capturing unexpected fluctuations in the broad-based demand for industrial commodities associated with the global business cycle in the context of structural oil market models.[14] It also is a good predictor of the real price of oil. The last row of Table 8.2 indicates strong evidence of Granger causality from this index to the real price of oil, regardless of the definition of the oil price series. That evidence becomes even stronger, once we allow for 2 years' worth of lags rather than 1 year. This finding mirrors the point made in Hamilton and Herrera (2004) that it is essential to allow for a rich lag structure in studying the dynamic relationship between the economy and the price of oil.

Although none of the proxies for global fluctuations in demand is without limitations, we conclude that there is a robust pattern of Granger causality, once we correct for problems of model misspecification and of data measurement that undermine the power of the test. This conclusion is further strengthened by evidence in Kilian and Hicks (forthcoming) based on distributed lag models that revisions to professional real GDP growth forecasts have significant predictive power for the real price of oil during 2000.11-2008.12 after weighting each country's forecast revision by its share in PPP weighted world real GDP. Predictability in population, of course, does not necessarily imply out-of-sample

---

[14] This index is constructed from ocean shipping freight rates. The idea of using fluctuations in shipping freight rates as indicators of shifts in the global real activity dates back to Isserlis (1938) and Tinbergen (1959). The panel of monthly freight-rate data underlying the global real activity index was collected manually from *Drewry's Shipping Monthly* using various issues since 1970. The data set is restricted to dry cargo rates. The earliest raw data are indices of iron ore, coal and grain shipping rates compiled by *Drewry's*. The remaining series are differentiated by cargo, route and ship size and may include in addition shipping rates for oilseeds, fertilizer and scrap metal. In the 1980s, there are about 15 different rates for each month; by 2000 that number rises to about 25; more recently that number has dropped to about 15. The index was constructed by extracting the common component in the nominal spot rates. The resulting nominal index is expressed in dollars per metric ton, deflated using the U.S. CPI and detrended to account for the secular decline in shipping rates. For this paper, this series has been extended based on the Baltic Exchange Dry Index, which is available from Bloomberg. The latter index, which is commonly discussed in the financial press, is essentially identical to the nominal data underlying the Kilian (2009a) index, but only available since 1985.

forecastability in practice (see Inoue and Kilian, 2004a). Not only is the objective of predictability testing fundamentally different from that of forecasting out of sample, but the smaller samples available for the construction of forecasting models necessitate simpler models and cause estimates to be less precise. In addition, structural changes in the data generating process could potentially undermine a model's out-of-sample accuracy. The next sections therefore examine alternative approaches to forecasting the nominal and the real price of oil out-of-sample.

5. SHORT-HORIZON FORECASTS OF THE NOMINAL PRICE OF OIL

The most common approach to forecasting the nominal price of oil is to treat the price of the oil futures contract of maturity h as the h-period forecast of the price of oil.[15] In particular, many central banks and the International Monetary Fund (IMF) use the price of NYMEX oil futures as a proxy for the market's expectation of the spot price of crude oil. A widespread view is that prices of NYMEX futures contracts are not only good proxies for the expected spot price of oil, but also better predictors of oil prices than econometric forecasts. Forecasts of the spot price of oil are used as inputs in the macroeconomic forecasting exercises that these institutions produce. For example, the European Central Bank (ECB) employs oil futures prices in constructing the inflation and output-gap forecasts that guide monetary policy (see Svensson, 2005). Likewise the IMF relies on futures prices as a predictor of future spot prices (see, e.g., International Monetary Fund 2005, p. 67; 2007, p. 42). Futures-based forecasts of the price of oil also play a role in policy discussions at the Federal Reserve Board. This is not to say that forecasters do not recognize the potential limitations of futures-based forecasts of the price of oil. Nevertheless, the perception among many macroeconomists, financial analysts and policymakers is that oil futures prices, imperfect as they may be, are the best available forecasts of the spot price of oil. Such attitudes have persisted notwithstanding recent empirical evidence to the contrary and notwithstanding the development of theoretical models aimed at explaining the lack of predictive ability of oil futures prices and spreads (see, e.g., Knetsch, 2007; Alquist and Kilian, 2010).

Interestingly, the conventional wisdom in macroeconomics and finance is at odds with long-held views about storable commodities in agricultural economics. For example, Peck (1985) emphasized that "expectations are reflected nearly equally in current and in futures prices. In this sense cash prices will be nearly as good predictions of subsequent

---

[15] Futures contracts are financial instruments that allow traders to lock in today a price at which to buy or sell a fixed quantity of the commodity at a predetermined date in the future. Futures contracts can be retraded between inception and maturity on a futures exchange such as the New York Mercantile Exchange (NYMEX, now CME Group). This exchange offers institutional features that allow traders to transact anonymously. These features reduce individual default risk and ensure homogeneity of the traded commodity, making the futures market a low-cost and liquid mechanism for hedging against and for speculating on oil price risks. The NYMEX light sweet crude contract traditionally has been the most liquid and largest volume market for crude oil trading.

cash prices as futures prices," echoing in turn the discussion in Working (1942) who was critical of the "general opinion among economists that prices of commodity futures are . . . the market expression of consciously formed opinions on probable prices in the future" whereas "spot prices are not generally supposed to reflect anticipation of the future in the same degree as futures prices." Working specifically criticized the error of "supposing that the prices of futures . . . tend to be more strongly influenced by these anticipations than are spot prices." The next section investigates the empirical merits of these competing views in the context of oil markets.

5.1. Forecasting Methods Based on Monthly Oil Futures Prices

Alquist and Kilian (2010) recently provided a comprehensive evaluation of the forecast accuracy of models based on monthly oil futures prices using data ending in 2007.2, superseding earlier analysis by Wu and McCallum (2005), among others. Below we update their analysis until 2009.12 and expand the range of alternative forecasting models under consideration.[16] In this subsection, attention is limited to forecast horizons of up to 1 year. Let $F_t^{(h)}$ denote the current nominal price of the futures contract that matures in h periods, S_t the current nominal spot price of oil, and $E_t[S_{t+h}]$ the expected future spot price at date $t+h$ conditional on information available at t.

A natural benchmark for forecasts based on the price of oil futures is provided by the random walk model without drift. This model implies that changes in the spot price are unpredictable, so the best forecast of the spot price of crude oil is simply the current spot price:

$$\hat{S}_{t+h|t} = S_t \quad h = 1, 3, 6, 9, 12 \tag{1}$$

This forecast is also known as the no-change forecast. In contrast, the common view that oil futures prices are the best available predictor of future oil prices implies the forecasting model:

$$\hat{S}_{t+h|t} = F_t^{(h)} \quad h = 1, 3, 6, 9, 12 \tag{2}$$

A closely related approach to forecasting the spot price of oil is to use the spread between the futures price and the spot price as an indicator of whether the price of oil is likely to go up or down. If the futures price equals the expected spot price, the spread should be an indicator of the expected change in spot prices. We explore the forecasting accuracy of the spread based on several alternative forecasting models. The simplest model is:

$$\hat{S}_{t+h|t} = S_t \left(1 + \ln\left(F_t^{(h)}/S_t\right)\right), \quad h = 1, 3, 6, 9, 12 \tag{3}$$

---

[16] Because the Datastream data for the daily WTI spot price of oil used in Alquist and Kilian (2010) were discontinued, we rely instead on data from the Energy Information Administration and from Bloomberg. As a result the estimation window for the forecast comparison is somewhat shorter in some cases than in Alquist and Kilian (2010).

To allow for the possibility that the spread may be a biased predictor, it is common to relax the assumption of a zero intercept:

$$\hat{S}_{t+h|t} = S_t \left(1 + \hat{\alpha} + \ln\left(F_t^{(h)}/S_t\right)\right), \quad h = 1, 3, 6, 9, 12 \tag{4}$$

Alternatively, one can relax the proportionality restriction:

$$\hat{S}_{t+h|t} = S_t \left(1 + \hat{\beta} \ln\left(F_t^{(h)}/S_t\right)\right), \quad h = 1, 3, 6, 9, 12 \tag{5}$$

Finally, one can relax both the unbiasedness and proportionality restrictions:

$$\hat{S}_{t+h|t} = S_t \left(1 + \hat{\alpha} + \hat{\beta} \ln\left(F_t^{(h)}/S_t\right)\right), \quad h = 1, 3, 6, 9, 12 \tag{6}$$

Here $\hat{\alpha}$ and $\hat{\beta}$ denote least-squares estimates obtained in real time from recursive regressions.

Our empirical analysis is based on daily prices of crude oil futures on the NYMEX from the commercial provider *Price-Data.com*. The time series begins in March 30, 1983, when crude oil futures were first traded on the NYMEX, and extends through December 31, 2009. Contracts are for delivery at Cushing, Oklahoma. Trading ends four days prior to the 25th calendar day preceding the delivery month. If the 25th is not a business day, trading ends on the third business day prior to the last business day before the 25th calendar day. A common problem in constructing monthly futures prices of a given maturity is that an h-month contract may not trade on a given day. We use as the end-of-month value the price of the h-month futures contract which trades closest to the last trading day of this month among all daily contracts in that month. Our approach is motivated by the objective of computing in a consistent manner end-of-month time series of oil futures prices for different maturities. This allows us to match up end-of-month spot prices and futures prices as closely as possible. The daily spot price data are obtained from the webpage of the Energy Information Administration and refer to the price of West Texas Intermediate crude oil available for delivery at Cushing, Oklahoma.

Table 8.3 assesses the predictive accuracy of various forecasting models against the benchmark of a random walk without drift for horizons of 1, 3, 6, 9, and 12 months. The forecast evaluation period is 1991.1-2009.12 with suitable adjustments, as the forecast horizon is varied. The assessment of which forecasting model is most accurate may depend on the loss function of the forecaster (see Elliott and Timmermann, 2008). We report results for the MSPE ratio relative to the no-change forecast and for the relative frequency with which a forecasting model correctly predicts the sign of the change in the spot price based on the success ratio statistic of Pesaran and Timmermann (2009). We also formally test the null hypothesis that a given candidate forecasting model is as accurate as the no-change forecast against the alternative that the candidate model is more accurate than the no-change forecast. It should be noted that commonly used tests of equal predictive accuracy for nested models (including the tests we rely on in this chapter) by

Table 8.3 1-Month, 3-Month, 6-Month, 9-Month, and 12-Month Ahead Forecast Error Diagnostics for Nominal WTI Price

$\hat{S}_{t+h\mid t}$	h=1 MSPE Ratio	h=1 Success Ratio	h=3 MSPE Ratio	h=3 Success Ratio	h=6 MSPE Ratio	h=6 Success Ratio	h=9 MPSE Ratio	h=9 Success Ratio	h=12 MPSE Ratio	h=12 Success Ratio
S_t	20.325	N.A.	95.451	N.A	222.28	N.A.	282.32	N.A.	302.54	N.A.
$F_t^{(h)}$	0.988	0.465	0.998	0.465	0.991	0.509	0.978	0.548	0.941	**0.557**
$S_t\left(1+\hat{\alpha}+\hat{\beta}\ln\left(F_t^{(h)}/S_t\right)\right)$	1.001	0.539	1.044	0.531	1.051	0.535	1.042	0.583	1.240	0.537
$S_t\left(1+\hat{\beta}\ln\left(F_t^{(h)}/S_t\right)\right)$	0.995	**0.531**	0.990	0.474	0.978	0.535	0.989	**0.553**	1.052	0.528
$S_t\left(1+\hat{\alpha}+\ln\left(F_t^{(h)}/S_t\right)\right)$	1.002	0.513	1.026	0.518	1.024	0.544	1.019	0.561	1.281	0.528
$S_t\left(1+\ln\left(F_t^{(h)}/S_t\right)\right)$	0.988	0.465	0.998	0.465	0.995	0.509	0.985	0.548	0.950	**0.557**
$S_t\left(1+\Delta s_t\right)^h$	1.397	0.504	2.325	0.535	8.580	0.539	29.179	0.509	179.77	0.496
$S_t\left(1+\hat{\alpha}\right)$	1.006	0.531	1.032	0.561	1.057	0.557	1.066	0.447	1.093	0.407
$S_t\left(1+\Delta\hat{s}_t^{(h)}\right)$	1.397	0.504	1.678	0.539	2.225	0.504	2.816	0.487	3.746	0.439
$S_t\left(1+i_{t,h}\right)^{h/12}$	N.A.	N.A.	1.000	0.575	1.002	0.575	N.A.	N.A.	0.998	0.566
$S_t(1+\Delta e_t^{AUS})^h$	0.865	0.513	0.811	**0.553**	1.071	**0.561**	1.352	**0.583**	1.678	**0.583**
$S_t(1+\Delta e_t^{CAN})^h$	0.930	0.478	0.918	0.496	0.966	0.526	0.990	0.539	1.144	0.504
$S_t(1+\Delta\bar{e}_{t,h}^{AUS})$	**0.865**	0.513	**0.872**	**0.579**	1.080	**0.662**	1.148	**0.618**	1.180	**0.610**
$S_t(1+\Delta\bar{e}_{t,h}^{CAN})$	**0.931**	0.478	**0.926**	0.526	**0.917**	**0.601**	1.022	**0.592**	1.185	0.544

(Continued)

Table 8.3 Continued

$\hat{S}_{t+h\mid t}$	h=1		h=3		h=6		h=9		h=12	
	MSPE Ratio	Success Ratio	MSPE Ratio	Success Ratio	MSPE Ratio	Success Ratio	MPSE Ratio	Success Ratio	MPSE Ratio	Success Ratio
$S_t(1 + \Delta p_t^{CRB,ind})^h$	0.913	**0.583**	0.802	**0.605**	0.976	**0.614**	1.402	**0.570**	1.846	**0.566**
$S_t(1 + \Delta p_t^{CRB,met})^h$	1.031	**0.579**	0.942	**0.636**	1.574	**0.592**	3.374	**0.561**	7.170	0.548
$S_t(1 + \Delta \bar{p}_t^{CRB,ind,(h)})$	**0.913**	**0.583**	**0.782**	**0.601**	1.055	**0.583**	1.076	0.553	1.035	0.548
$S_t(1 + \Delta \bar{p}_t^{CRB,met,(h)})$	1.031	**0.579**	**0.750**	**0.601**	1.219	**0.623**	1.304	0.575	1.278	0.539

Notes: The forecast evaluation period is 1991.1–2009.12. The initial estimation window is 1986.1–1990.12. For regressions based on 6-month futures prices the estimation window begins in 1986.1; for the 9-month futures price in 1986.12; for the 12-month futures price in 1989.1. $F_t^{(h)}$ is the futures price that matures in h periods; $i_{t,m}$ is the m month interest rate; S_t is the percent change in S_t in the most recent month; and $\Delta \bar{s}_t^{(h)}$ is the percent change in the spot price over the most recent h months. All MSPE results are presented as ratios relative to the benchmark no-change forecast model, for which we report the level of the MSPE. The success ratio is defined as the fraction of forecasts that correctly predict the sign of the change in the price of oil. Results that are statistically significant at the 10% level are shown in boldface. All tests of statistical significance refer to pairwise tests of the null of equal predictive accuracy with the no-change forecast. Comparisons of non-nested models without estimated parameters are based on the DM-test of Diebold and Mariano (1995) using N(0,1) critical values; the results for other non-nested comparisons are obtained by bootstrapping. Nested model comparisons with estimated parameters are obtained by bootstrapping the DM-test statistic as in Clark and McCracken (2005a) and Killian (1999). The sign test in the last column is based on Pesaran and Timmermann, 2009. This test cannot be applied when there is no variability in the predicted sign.

construction are tests of the null of no predictability in population rather than tests of equal out-of-sample MSPEs (see, e.g., Inoue and Kilian (2004a,b); Clark and McCracken, 2010). This means that these tests will reject the null of equal predictive accuracy more often than they should under the null, suggesting caution in interpreting test results that are only marginally statistically significant. We will discuss this point in more detail further below. This concern does not affect non-nested forecast accuracy comparisons.

Row (2) of the results in Table 8.3 shows that the oil futures price has lower MSPE than the no-change forecast at all horizons considered, but the differences are small and none of the differences is statistically significant. For all practical purposes, the forecasts are equally accurate. Nor do futures forecasts have important advantages when it comes to predicting the sign of the change in the nominal price of oil. Only at the 12-month horizon is the success ratio significant at the 10% level. The improvement in this case is 5.7%. At the 1-month and 3-month horizon, the success ratio of the futures price forecast actually is inferior to tossing a coin. Similarly, rows (3)-(6) in Table 8.3 show no systematic difference between the MSPE of the spread-based forecasts and that of the random walk forecast. In no case is there a statistically significant reduction in the MSPE from using the spread model. In the rare cases in which one of the spread models significantly helps predict the direction of change, the gains in accuracy are quite moderate. No spread model is uniformly superior to the others.

We conclude that there is no compelling evidence that, over this sample period, monthly oil futures prices were more accurate predictors of the nominal price of oil than simple no-change forecasts. Put differently, a forecaster using the most recent spot price would have done just as well in forecasting the nominal price of oil. This finding is broadly consistent with the empirical results in Alquist and Kilian (2010). To the extent that some earlier studies have reported evidence more favorable to oil futures prices, the difference in results can be traced to the use of shorter samples.[17]

5.2. Other Forecasting Methods

The preceding subsection demonstrated that simple no-change forecasts of the price of oil tend to be about as accurate in the MSPE sense as forecasts based on oil futures prices, but this does not rule out that there are alternative predictors with even lower MSPE. Next we broaden the range of forecasting methods to include some additional predictors that are of practical interest. One approach is the use of parsimonious regression-based forecasting models of the spot price of crude oil. Another approach is to adjust the no-change forecast on the basis of readily available macroeconomic indicators. For example, we may exploit the implication of the standard Hotelling (1931) model that the price of oil should grow at the rate of interest. Similarly parsimonious forecasting models may be

---

[17] Although we have focused on the WTI price of oil, qualitatively similar results would also be obtained on the basis of Brent spot and Brent futures prices, which are available from the same data sources. The evaluation period for the Brent price series, however, is shorter, casting doubt on the reliability of the results, which is why we focus on the WTI data.

constructed by adjusting the no-change forecast for recent percent changes in bilateral exchange rates or in non-oil industrial commodity prices.

5.2.1. Alternative Atheoretical Forecasting Models

One alternative is the double-differenced forecasting model proposed in Hendry (2006). Hendry observed that, when time series are subject to infrequent trend changes, the no-change forecast may be improved upon by extrapolating today's oil price at the most recent growth rate:

$$\hat{S}_{t+h|t} = S_t \left(1 + \Delta s_t\right)^h \quad h = 1, 3, 6, 9, 12 \tag{7}$$

where Δs_t denotes the percent growth rate between $t-1$ and t. In other words, we apply the no-change forecast to the growth rate rather than the level. Although there are no obvious indications of structural change in our sample period, it is worth exploring this alternative method, given the presence of occasional large fluctuations in the price of oil. Row (7) in Table 8.3 shows that the double-differenced specification does not work well in this case. Especially at longer horizons, this forecasting method becomes erratic and suffers from very large MSPEs. Nor is this method particularly adept at predicting the sign of the change in the nominal price of oil.

Yet another strategy is to extrapolate from recent trends. Given that oil prices have been persistently trending upward (or downward) at times, it is natural to consider a random walk model with drift. One possibility is to estimate this drift recursively, resulting in the forecasting model:

$$\hat{S}_{t+h|t} = S_t \left(1 + \hat{\alpha}\right) \quad h = 1, 3, 6, 9, 12 \tag{8}$$

Alternatively, a local drift term may be estimated using rolling regressions:

$$\hat{S}_{t+h|t} = S_t(1 + \Delta \bar{s}_t^{(h)}) \quad h = 1, 3, 6, 9, 12, \tag{9}$$

where $\hat{S}_{t+h|t}$ is the forecast of the spot price at $t+h$; and $\Delta \bar{s}_t^{(h)}$ is the percent change in the spot price over the most recent h months. This local drift model postulates that traders extrapolate from the spot price's recent behavior when they form expectations about the future spot price. The local drift model is designed to capture "short-term forecastability" that arises from local trends in the oil price data. Rows (8)–(9) in Table 8.3 document that allowing for a drift typically increases the MSPE and in no case significantly lowers the MSPE relative to the no-change forecast, whether the drift is estimated based on rolling regressions or is estimated recursively. Nor does allowing for a drift significantly improve the ability to predict the sign of the change in the nominal price of oil.

5.2.2. Parsimonious Economic Forecasting Models

An alternative approach to forecasting the nominal price of oil is to rely on economic predictors. One forecast rule is motivated by Hotelling's (1931) model, which predicts that the price of an exhaustible resource such as oil appreciates at the risk-free rate of interest, provided the marginal extraction cost is zero:

$$\hat{S}_{t+h|t} = S_t(1 + i_{t,h})^{h/12} \quad h = 3, 6, 12, \tag{10}$$

where $i_{t,h}$ refers to the annualized interest rate at the relevant maturity h.[18] Although the Hotelling model may seem too stylized to generate realistic predictions, we include it in this forecast accuracy comparison. We employ the Treasury bill rate as a proxy for the risk free rate. Row (10) in Table 8.3 shows no evidence that adjusting the no-change forecast for the interest rate significantly lowers the MSPE. The Hotelling model is better at predicting the sign of the change in the nominal price of oil than the no-change forecast, although we cannot assess the statistical significance of the improvement, given that there is no variability at all in the sign forecast.

An alternative approach builds on the insights of Chen et al. (2010) we discussed earlier and uses recent percent changes in the bilateral nominal dollar exchange rate of selected commodity exporters to extrapolate the current price of oil:

$$\hat{S}_{t+h|t} = S_t(1 + \Delta e_t^i)^h \quad h = 1, 3, 6, 9, 12, \tag{11}$$

where $i \in \{Canada, Australia\}$. To conserve space we do not include results for New Zealand and South Africa, but note that the latter results are typically statistically insignificant and indicate little evidence of forecast ability. Table 8.3 shows that model (11) based on the Canadian dollar and the Australian dollar exchange rate yield reductions in the MSPE as high as 19% at short horizons, but these gains are not statistically significant. There is evidence that the Australian exchange rate has significant predictive power for the sign of the change in the nominal price of oil at horizons 3, 6, 9, and 12. We also considered the alternative specification

$$\hat{S}_{t+h|t} = S_t(1 + \Delta \bar{e}_{t,h}^i) \quad h = 1, 3, 6, 9, 12, \tag{12}$$

based on the percent change in the exchange rate over the most recent h months, where $i \in \{Canada, Australia\}$ as before. This specification helps smooth the exchange rate changes. The use of model (12) improves the directional accuracy of both exchange rate models. It also implies statistically significant short-run MSPE reductions as high as 13% up for the Australian dollar and as high as 8% for the Canadian dollar. The MSPE reductions for the Canadian dollar remain significant at the 6-month horizon. We conclude that forecasting models for the nominal price of oil based on bilateral exchange-rates have some predictive power at horizons up to 1 year, provided we focus on broad-based commodity exporters such as Canada and Australia.

A third approach is to explore the forecasting value of recent percent changes in non-oil CRB commodity prices, building on insights about the link between oil and

---

[18] Assuming perfect competition, no arbitrage, and no uncertainty, oil companies extract oil at a rate that equates: (1) the value today of selling the oil less the costs of extraction; (2) and the present value of owning the oil, which, given the model's assumptions, is discounted at the risk free rate. In competitive equilibrium, oil companies extract crude oil at the socially optimal rate.

non-oil commodity prices discussed in Barsky and Kilian (2002) and Kilian (2009b), among others. One such forecasting model is

$$\hat{S}_{t+h|t} = S_t(1 + \Delta p_t^{com})^h \quad h = 1, 3, 6, 9, 12, \; com \in \{ind, met\}. \tag{13}$$

It can be shown that model (13) does not produce statistically significant reductions in the MSPE, presumably because month-to-month changes in commodity prices tend to be noisy. In fact, model (13) tends to worsen the MSPE ratio at long horizons, although it significantly improves directional accuracy at horizons up to 9 months for metals prices and up to 12 months for prices of industrial raw materials. An alternative model specification is based on the percent change in the CRB price index over the most recent h months:

$$\hat{S}_{t+h|t} = S_t(1 + \Delta \bar{p}_{t,h}^{com}) \quad h = 1, 3, 6, 9, 12, \quad com \in \{ind, met\}. \tag{14}$$

Model (14) is designed to capture persistent changes in commodity prices in the recent past. This specification is less successful at predicting the direction of change at horizons beyond 6 months, but can yield significant reductions in the MSPE at short horizons. For example, the model using metals prices significantly lowers the MSPE at horizon 3 and the model using prices of industrial raw materials significantly reduces the MSPE at horizons 1 and 3. The MSPE reductions may be as large as 25% at horizon 3.

We conclude that forecasting models extrapolating persistent changes in CRB industrial commodity prices significantly reduce the MSPE of the nominal price of oil relative to the no-change forecast at short horizons. Beyond the 3-month horizon, based on the MSPE criterion, the no-change forecast for all practical purposes remains the most accurate model for forecasting the nominal price of oil in real time. Based on directional accuracy somewhat more favorable results are obtained. The model based on persistent changes in recent commodity prices model is significantly more accurate than the no-change forecast even at the 6-month horizon. These results are encouraging in that they demonstrate that even very simple models may outperform the random walk for the nominal price of oil.

5.3. Short-Horizon Forecasts Based on Daily Oil Futures Prices

Following the extant literature, our analysis so far has relied on monthly data for oil futures prices and spreads constructed from daily observations. The construction of monthly data allows one to compare the accuracy of these forecasts to that of alternative forecasts based on data only available at monthly frequency. A complementary approach is to utilize all daily oil futures prices and compare their forecasting accuracy to the no-change forecast only. This alternative approach makes use of all oil-futures price data and hence may have more accurate size and higher power. It is not without drawbacks, however. Ideally, one would like to compare the price of a futures contract for delivery in h months with the price of delivery exactly h months later, where one month corresponds to 21 business days. That price, however, is not observed. The spot price quoted on the day of delivery

Table 8.4 Short-Horizon Forecasts of the Nominal WTI Price of Oil from Daily Oil Futures Prices since January 1986

	Start of evaluation period: January 1986									
	h=1		*h*=3		*h*=6		*h*=9		*h*=12	
	MSPE	SR	MSPE	SR	MSPE	SR	MSPE	SR	MSPE	SR
$F_t^{(h)}$	0.963	0.522	0.972	0.516	0.973	0.535	0.964	0.534	0.929	0.562
	(0.009)	(0.040)	(0.053)	(0.072)	(0.077)	**(0.002)**	(0.063)	**(0.001)**	**(0.001)**	**(0.000)**

Notes: There are 5968, 5926, 5861, 5744, and 5028 daily observations at horizons of 1 through 12 months, respectively. Following Leamer's (1978) rule for adjusting the threshold for statistical significance with changes in the sample size, *p*-values below about 0.0035 are considered statistically significant and are shown in boldface.

instead will be the price for delivery sometime in the month following the date on which the futures contract matures. In fact, the date of delivery associated with a given spot price can never be made exact. We therefore follow the convention of evaluating futures price forecasts against the spot price prevailing when the futures contract matures. A reasonable case can be made that this is what practitioners view as the relevant forecasting exercise.

Note that the daily data are sparse in that there are many days for which no price quotes exist. We eliminate these dates from the sample and stack the remaining observations similar to the approach taken in Kilian and Vega (2010) in the context of modeling the impact of U.S. macroeconomic news on the nominal price of oil. Table 8.4 summarizes our findings. The MSPE ratios in Table 8.4 indicate somewhat larger gains in forecasting accuracy from using oil futures prices than in Table 8.3. There are a number of caveats, however. First, the *h*-month oil futures forecasts are not forecasts for a horizon of *h* months as in Table 8.3, but rather for a horizon that may vary arbitrarily between *h* and *h* + 1 months. For example, an oil futures contract quoted on August 13 for delivery starting on October 1 would be considered a 1-month contract for the purpose of Table 8.4, but so would an oil-futures contract quoted on August 25 for delivery starting on October 1. This is an inherent limitation of working with daily oil futures price data. This concern suggests caution in interpreting short-horizon results, but obviously becomes less important as *h* increases. A second concern is that the sample period spanned by the daily data extends back to January 1986, whereas the data in Table 8.3 start in 1990. This difference is not driving the results in Table 8.4. It can be shown that making the sample period compatible with that in the earlier tables would yield substantively identical results.

The third and most important concern is the statistical significance of the results in Table 8.4. Given that the sample size in Table 8.4 is larger than in Table 8.3 by a factor of about 10, care must be exercised in interpreting the *p*-values. As is well known, for sufficiently large sample sizes, any null hypothesis is bound to be rejected at conventional significance levels, making it inappropriate to apply the same significance level as in Table 8.3. In recognition of this problem, Leamer (1978 p. 108-120) proposes a rule for constructing sample-size dependent critical values. For example, for the F-statistic, the appropriate level of statistical significance is $\alpha = 1 - fcdf\left((t-1) \times (t^{(1/t)} - 1), 1, t\right)$. For $t = 216$, as in Table 8.3, this rule of thumb implies a threshold for rejecting the null hypothesis of $\alpha = 0.0209$. In contrast, for $t = 5968$ the same rule implies a much higher threshold of $\alpha = 0.0032$. Applying this rule to the p-values in Table 8.4, none of the MSPE reductions is statistically significant except at the 12-month horizon. The MSPE ratio at the 12-month horizon of 0.93 is similar to the ratio of 0.94 reported in Table 8.3 based on monthly data. There also is evidence that at horizons 6, 9 and 12, the oil futures price has statistically significant directional accuracy, but the gains are quantitatively negligible except perhaps at horizon 12.

These results lead us to revise somewhat our earlier findings. We conclude that there is statistically significant evidence that oil futures prices improve on the accuracy of the no-change forecast of the nominal price of oil at the 1-year horizon, but not at shorter horizons. The magnitude of these gains in accuracy is modest – at least by the standards of the literature on forecasting macroeconomic aggregates such as inflation rates. Moreover, there are indications that this result is sensitive to changes in the sample period and may not be robust as more data accumulate. After eliminating the data beyond March 2008, for example, the MSPE ratio of the 12-month futures price exceeds 1 and only when extending the sample period beyond July 2008 is the MSPE reduction statistically significant. This result, together with the lack of evidence for slightly shorter or slightly longer futures contracts, suggests caution in interpreting the evidence for the 12-month contract in Table 8.4.

6. LONG-HORIZON FORECASTS OF THE NOMINAL PRICE OF OIL BASED ON OIL FUTURES PRICES

For oil industry managers facing investment decisions or for policymakers pondering the medium-term economic outlook a horizon of 1 year is too short. Crude oil futures may have maturities as long as 7 years. Notwithstanding the low liquidity of oil futures markets at such long horizons, documented in Alquist and Kilian (2010), it is precisely these long horizons that many policymakers focus on. For example, Greenspan (2004a) explicitly referred to the 6-year oil futures contract in assessing effective long-term supply prices. For similar statements also see Greenspan (2004b), Gramlich (2004), and Bernanke (2004). In this section we focus on forecasting the nominal price of oil at horizons up to 7 years.

It can be shown that the daily data are too sparse at horizons beyond 1 year to allow the construction of time series of end-of-month observations for oil futures prices. However, we can instead evaluate each daily futures price quote for contracts of any given maturity against the spot price that is realized on the day the contract expires. We already used this approach in Table 8.4 for horizons up to 1 year. One drawback of extending this approach to longer horizons is that the evaluation period for long-horizon contracts may exclude many of the particularly informative observations at the end of our sample period. Another drawback is that long-horizon futures prices are sparsely quoted, greatly reducing the sample size as the horizon is lengthened. For that reason, one would expect the results to be far less reliable than the earlier short-horizon results. Nevertheless, they provide the only indication we have of the usefulness of oil futures prices at the horizons at which they are employed by many policymakers.

Table 8.5 shows the results for horizons of 2, 3, 4, 5, 6, and 7 years. In sharp contrast with Table 8.4 the MSPE ratios are consistently above 1, indicating that oil futures prices are less accurate than the no-change forecast. In no case is there evidence of significant reductions in the MSPE. The test for directional accuracy is statistically significant at the 2 year horizon, but not at longer horizons. In fact, in many cases the success ratios at longer horizons are distinctly worse than tossing a coin. Table 8.5 provides no evidence in support of the common practice at central banks of appealing to the price of long-horizon oil futures contracts as an indication of future spot prices. In particular, at a horizon of 6 years, which figures prominently in policy statements and speeches, central bankers would have been much better off relying on the no-change forecast than on oil futures prices.

An interesting question is whether the poor accuracy of forecasts from oil futures prices beyond 1 year simply reflects a sharp drop-off in the liquidity of oil futures markets at longer horizons. This does not appear to be the case. Figure 8.4 plots two measures of the liquidity of the oil futures market by horizon. Open interest is the total number of futures contracts, either long or short, that have been entered into for a given delivery

Table 8.5 Long-Horizon Forecasts of the Nominal WTI Price of Oil from Daily Oil Futures Prices

h(in years)	Starting Date	Sample Size	MSPE	SR
2	11/20/90	3283	1.159	0.515
			(1.000)	**(0.000)**
3	05/29/91	515	1.168	0.518
			(0.996)	(0.281)
4	11/01/95	194	1.212	0.294
			(1.000)	(N.A.)
5	11/03/97	154	1.280	0.247
			(1.000)	(N.A.)
6	11/03/97	134	1.158	0.276
			(0.999)	(N.A.)
7	11/21/97	22	1.237	0.500
			(0.957)	(N.A.)

Notes: Following Leamer's (1978) rule for adjusting the threshold for statistical significance with changes in the sample size, *p*-values below 0.0044 for a horizon of 2 years are considered statistically significant and are shown in boldface.

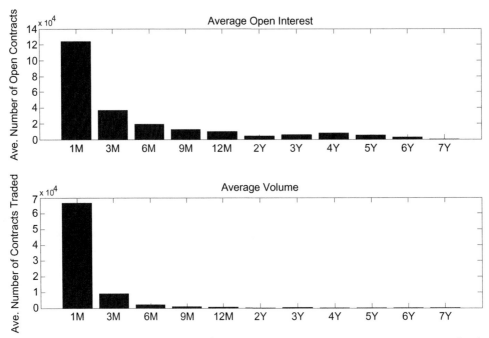

Figure 8.4 Measures of liquidity in the oil futures market (by Maturity). *Notes*: Computations by the authors based on CRB data.

month and have not yet been offset by another transaction or by physical delivery of the oil. It measures the total number of contracts outstanding for delivery in a specific month. Volume is the total number of contracts traded during a specific period of time. Contracts are denoted in units of 1,000 barrels of crude oil. Although both average open interest and average trading volume drop off quickly with increasing maturity, it is not the case that average liquidity at the daily frequency is discontinuously lower at horizons beyond 1 year than at the 12-month horizon. Rather the decline in average liquidity is smooth.

One concern with the results in Table 8.5 is that the most traded oil futures contracts are the June and December contracts. This suggests focusing on the most liquid daily contracts rather than averaging results across all daily contracts, as we did in Table 8.5. Below we report sensitivity analysis for this subset of daily oil futures contracts. Because long-term futures contracts only became available in recent years and because their use greatly reduces the effective sample size, we focus on June and December contracts with maturities of 1, 2, and 3 years. Based on the evaluation period of 1998–2010, we find that 1-year contracts have an MSPE ratio of 0.91 compared with the no-change forecast, 2-year contracts an MSPE ratio of 1.01 and 3-year contracts an MSPE ratio of 1.27. These results are qualitatively similar to those in Table 8.5 for the same maturities, suggesting that there are no gains in forecast accuracy from restricting the sample.

Finally, we note that these results may not have been apparent in the years when longer-term oil futures contracts were first introduced. As recently as in the late 1990s, a forecaster employing the same methods that we used in this section, would have found that the monthly price of oil futures contracts with 1-year maturity is much more accurate than the no-change forecast, although the MSPE reductions declined steadily throughout the 1990s, as more information became available, and the ratio has oscillated about 1 since then. Even 2- and 3-year daily contracts, which were introduced much more recently, initially seemed to forecast more accurately than the no-change forecast, but these MSPE reductions have been reversed more recently. Given that the forecast errors become more highly serially correlated, the higher the data frequency, very long samples are required for reliable estimates of relative MSPEs. Clearly, an evaluation period of 15 years, for example, is insufficient to learn about the forecasting ability of oil futures prices, as illustrated by the repeated sharp reversals in forecast rankings over time. Even our results must be considered tentative and could be reversed as more data become available.

One possible explanation for the unexpectedly low out-of-sample accuracy of oil futures-based forecasts may be the presence of transaction costs impeding arbitrage. An alternative forecasting strategy in which one uses the futures price only if the futures spread exceeds 5% in absolute terms and uses the spot price otherwise, yields MSPE reductions between 0% and 6% at short horizons. Notably the MSPE reductions at horizons of 3 and 6 months are statistically significant in both the daily and the monthly data. At horizons beyond 1 year, this alternative method is much less accurate than the no-change forecast, however. We conclude that the evidence from daily futures prices is broadly consistent with the earlier evidence from monthly data.

7. SURVEY FORECASTS OF THE NOMINAL PRICE OF OIL

A comparison of alternative oil price forecasts would not be complete without evidence on survey expectations of the nominal price of oil. Given the significance of crude oil to the international economy, it is surprising that there are few organizations that produce monthly forecasts of spot prices. In the oil industry, where the spot price of oil is critical to investment decisions, producers tend to make annual forecasts of spot prices for horizons as long as 15-20 years, but these are not publicly available. The U.S. Department of Energy's EIA has published quarterly forecasts of the nominal price of oil since 1983. The *Economist Intelligence Unit* has produced annual forecasts since the 1990s for horizons of up to 5 years. None of these sources provides monthly forecasts.

One common source of monthly forecasts of the price of crude oil is *Consensus Economics Inc.*, a U.K.-based company that compiles private sector forecasts in a variety of countries. Initially, the sample consisted of more than 100 private firms; it now contains about 70 firms. Of interest to us are the survey expectations for the 3- and 12-month-ahead spot price of West Texas Intermediate crude oil, which corresponds to the type

Table 8.6 Accuracy of Survey and Expert Forecasts Relative to No-Change Forecast

	h=3		h=12		h=60	
	MSPE Ratio	Success Ratio	MSPE Ratio	Success Ratio	MSPE Ratio	Success Ratio
$\hat{S}_{t+h\|t} = S_{t,h}^{CE}$	1.519	0.447	0.944	**0.539**	–	–
$\hat{S}_{t+h\|t} = S_{t,h}^{EIA}$	**0.918**	0.417	0.973	**0.562**	–	–
$\hat{S}_{t+h\|t} = S_t(1 + \pi_{t,h}^{MSC})$	–	–	1.047	0.566[a]	–	–
$\hat{S}_{t+h\|t} = S_t(1 + \pi_{t,h}^{SPF})$	–	–	1.016	0.579[a]	**0.855**	0.811[a]

Notes: Boldface indicates statistical significance at the 10% level.

[a] No significance test possible due to lack of variation in success ratio. SPF denotes the Survey of Professional Forecasters, EIA the Energy Information Administration and CE denotes Consensus Economics Inc. $\pi_{t,h}$ stands for the expected inflation rate between t and $t + h$.

and grade delivered under the NYMEX futures contract. The survey provides the arithmetic average, the minimum, the maximum, and the standard deviation for each survey month beginning in October 1989 and ending in December 2009. We use the arithmetic mean at the relevant horizon:

$$\hat{S}_{t+h|t} = S_{t,h}^{CE} \quad h = 3, 12. \tag{15}$$

Table 8.6 reveals that this survey forecast does not significantly reduce the MSPE relative to the no-change forecast and may increase the MSPE substantially. The survey forecast is particularly poor at the 3-month horizon. At the 12-month horizon the survey forecast has a lower MSPE than the no-change forecast, but the gain in accuracy is not statistically significant. There also is a statistically significant but negligible gain in directional accuracy.[19]

Further analysis shows that until 2008.12 the consensus survey forecast had a much higher MSPE than the no-change forecast at both the 3-month and 12-month horizons. This pattern changes only toward the end of the sample. There is evidence that the accuracy of the consensus survey forecasts improves at the 12-month horizon, especially in 2009 as the oil market recovers from its collapse in the second half of 2008. It appears that professional forecasters correctly predicted a long-term price recovery in this instance, although they were not successful at predicting the timing of the 2009 recovery. Notwithstanding these caveats, there is no compelling evidence overall that survey forecasts outperform the no-change forecast. Figure 8.5 shows that these professional

[19] The CE forecast is typically released in the second week of each month. We evaluate this forecast against the realization of the nominal price of oil h months after the end of the month in which the forecast is released. This corresponds to the way that *Consensus Economics Inc.* interprets its forecasts. For example, the January 10 release of the 3-month forecast is intended to be a forecast for the price at the end of April.

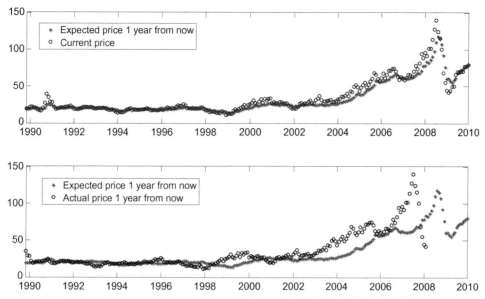

Figure 8.5 Consensus economics expectations of nominal price of oil (Dollars/Barrel): 1989.10–2009.12. *Notes*: Computations by the authors based on data from Consensus Economics Inc.

oil price forecasts most of the time are below the current price of oil. The upper panel of Figure 8.5 shows that professional forecasters tend to smooth the predicted path relative to the current price. This smoothing is especially apparent during large oil price fluctuations such as those in 1990/91, in 1999/2000, and in 2003-2009. This tendency contributes to the large and persistently negative forecast errors shown in the lower panel of Figure 8.5. It also helps explain why the consensus forecast typically fails to improve on the no-change forecast in Table 8.6.

One possible explanation of the less than satisfactory accuracy of these survey forecasts is that professional macroeconomic forecasters may not be experts on the oil market. Figure 8.6 focuses on an alternative time series of 1-quarter and 4-quarters-ahead forecasts of the U.S. nominal refiners' acquisition cost for imported crude oil:

$$\hat{S}_{t+h|t} = S_{t,h}^{EIA} \quad h = 3, 12. \tag{16}$$

These forecasts were collected from the U.S. Energy Information Administration's *Short-term Economic Outlook*, which is published by the U.S. Department of Energy. Given the difference in frequency and oil price definition the results are not strictly speaking comparable with our earlier analysis of the monthly WTI price. Nevertheless, these data are illuminating. Figure 8.6 illustrates that even these expert forecasts generally underpredicted the price of crude oil between 2004 and mid-2008, especially at longer horizons, while overpredicting it following the collapse of the price of oil in mid-2008 and underpredicting it again more recently. A natural question is how the EIA forecasts

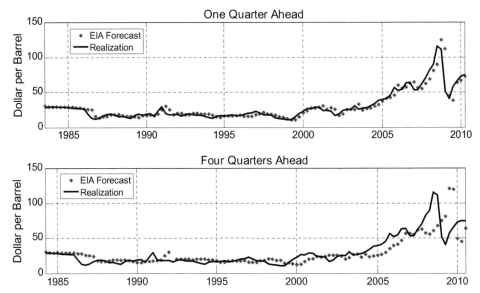

Figure 8.6 EIA forecasts of the U.S. refiners' acquisition cost for imported crude oil 1983.Q1-2009.Q4. *Notes*: The quarterly price forecasts were collected manually from the EIA's *Short-Term Economic Outlook* and compared with the ex-post realizations of the average quarterly nominal refiners' acquisition cost for imported crude oil. The plot shows the price realizations together with the EIA forecasts made for the same point in time one and four quarters earlier.

compare to the no-change forecast on the basis of the EIA's preliminary data releases for the current refiners' acquisition cost for imported crude oil. The latter data are provided by the same source. The *DM* test for equal predictive accuracy in Table 8.6 suggests that the MSPE ratio of 0.92 for the one-quarter-ahead forecast is statistically significant at the 10% level, but the MSPE ratio of 0.97 for the four-quarters-ahead forecast is not. We conclude that even the EIA has had at best modest success in forecasting the nominal price of oil in the short run and even less success at the 1-year horizon.

Professional surveys tend to focus on short forecast horizons. Although there are no long monthly or quarterly time series of long-horizon professional forecasts of the nominal price of oil, survey data on long-run inflation expectations may be used to construct surprisingly accurate real-time forecasts of the nominal price of oil at horizons of several years. The proposal is to forecast the nominal price of crude oil by extrapolating the current price at the rate of expected inflation. This amounts to treating changes in the real price of oil as unpredictable.[20] Measures of inflation expectations may be obtained from surveys of professional forecasts, even for very long horizons. Here we use the expected inflation rate at the 5-year horizon from the *Survey of Professional Forecasters*.

$$\hat{S}_{t+h|t} = S_t(1 + \pi_{t,h}^{SPF}) \quad h = 12, 60. \tag{17}$$

[20] This proposal builds on insights in Anderson et al. (2011) about how households form expectations about gasoline prices.

Table 8.6 shows that this forecast is quite accurate with an MSPE ratio of only 0.855. The p-value for the null hypothesis of equal predictive accuracy is 0.000. The success ratio of 0.811 is also extraordinarily high.[21] The reason for these strong improvements in forecast accuracy is that at long horizons the inflation component of the nominal price of oil becomes very large. In other words, it is a fairly safe bet that the nominal price of oil must increase in nominal terms over a 5-year horizon. This simple forecasting rule is also much more accurate than the forecast implied by the 5-year oil futures price.

In contrast, at a horizon of 1 year, the effect of inflation on the nominal price is fairly small. As a result, forecasts based on inflation expectations show only modest gains in directional accuracy and have lower MSPEs than the no-change forecast. This is true whether we use the *Survey of Professional Forecasters* or the *Michigan Survey of Consumers* (see Table 8.6). The fact that these results are weaker than those obtained using inflation measures in Granger causality tests may simply reflect that there was not much variation in inflation expectations in our evaluation period, but considerable variation historically.

8. WHAT HAVE WE LEARNED ABOUT FORECASTING THE NOMINAL PRICE OF OIL?

Section 4 provided strong evidence that the nominal price of oil is predictable in population. An obvious concern is how useful this insight is when it comes to forecasting the nominal price of oil out of sample. There are many reasons why full-sample evidence of predictability need not translate into more accurate out-of-sample forecasts (see, e.g., Inoue and Kilian, 2004a). One reason is the inevitable bias-variance trade-off in out-of-sample forecasting. Another reason is that evidence of predictability on average over the full sample may obscure the disappearance of this predictability in the latter part of the sample (see Clark and McCracken, 2005b). For example, Barsky and Kilian (2002) observed that the 1970s were characterized by major shifts in monetary aggregates, whereas monetary aggregates remained much more stable following the Volcker disinflation. Hence, it would not be surprising to see the predictive content of monetary aggregates diminish after the mid-1980s.

In the presence of structural change, evidence of Granger causality in historical data would be of little relevance to applied forecasters interested in exploiting this predictability. This makes it important to assess the out-of-sample accuracy of models of the same set of predictors we considered in Section 4. To further complicate matters, some of the predictors studied in Section 4 cannot be evaluated out of sample without addressing the real-time data limitations faced by applied forecasters. A good example is U.S. M1. Among those predictors that lend themselves to real-time forecasts of the nominal price of oil, we found that inflation-based models are far less accurate out of sample than in the

---

[21] The Pesaran–Timmermann test for directional accuracy cannot be applied because there is no variability in the predicted sign, making it impossible to judge the statistical significance of the success ratio.

full sample. It is all the more remarkable therefore that the forecast accuracy gains for the models based on industrial commodity prices (and to a lesser extent for models based on selected bilateral exchange rates) are large and as statistically significant out of sample as they were in the Granger causality analysis of Section 4. In fact, we found significant pre-dictability out-of-sample for the model based on the Australian exchange rate even in the absence of Granger causality in the full sample. One possible explanation of this finding is that predictability increased in the second part of the sample rather than decreased.

   One interpretation of the success of these forecasting models is that persistent increases in indices of non-oil industrial commodity prices reflect global demand pressures that affect all industrial commodities (see Barsky and Kilian, 2002; Kilian, 2009a), which in turn are reflected in the dollar exchange rates of broad-based commodity exporters such as Australia and Canada. This interpretation is consistent with additional evidence we will present in Section 9. It suggests some caution in using these forecasting models during times when the price of oil is primarily influenced by other demand or supply shocks. A case in point would be a major oil supply disruption causing an oil price spike. To the extent that the price of oil sometimes is driven by shocks not associated with the global business cycle, one would expect the accuracy gains from using model (14) to be smaller. On the other hand, events such as major oil supply disruptions or speculative frenzies in oil markets are rare, which explains why the forecasting model in question performs well over the full sample.

9. SHORT-HORIZON FORECASTS OF THE REAL PRICE OF OIL

Our analysis in Section 4 suggests that we stand a better chance of forecasting the real price of oil out-of-sample using monthly data, given the availability of more appropriate predictors at the monthly frequency. A natural benchmark for all forecasting models of the real price of oil is again the no-change forecast. At short horizons, inflation is expected to be at best moderate and ex ante there is every reason to expect the high forecast accuracy of the random walk model without drift relative to many less parsimonious regression models to carry over to the real price of oil.[22] On the other hand, in forecasting the real price of oil we may rely on additional economic structure and on additional predictors that could potentially improve forecast accuracy. This section explores a number of such models. We consider two alternative measures of the real price of oil: The U.S. refiners' acquisition cost for imported crude oil, which may be thought of as a proxy for the price of oil in global oil markets, and the WTI price; in both cases the deflator is the U.S. CPI.

---

[22] Such a finding would not necessarily imply that the real price of oil actually follows a random walk. It could merely reflect the fact that the bias-variance tradeoff favors parsimonious forecasting models in small samples. The local-to-zero asymptotic approximation of predictive models suggests that using the no-change forecast may lower the asymptotic MSPE even relative to the correctly specified non-random walk model, provided the local drift parameter governing the predictive relationship is close enough to zero (see, e.g., Inoue and Kilian, 2004b; Clark and McCracken, 2010).

9.1. Real U.S. Refiners' Acquisition Cost for Imported Crude Oil
9.1.1. Unrestricted AR, ARMA, and VAR Models

A useful starting point is a forecast accuracy comparison of selected monthly autoregressive (AR) and autoregressive-moving average (ARMA) models for the real price of oil in log levels and in log differences. Both classes of models are evaluated in terms of their ability to predict the log level of the real price of oil in recursive settings. Estimation starts in 1973.2, and the evaluation period is 1991.12-2009.8 to facilitate direct comparisons with VAR models of the global market for crude oil in this and the next section.[23] All MSPE results are expressed as fractions of the MSPE of the no-change forecast. Some models are based on fixed lag orders of 12 or 24, whereas others rely on the Schwarz Information Criterion (SIC) or the Akaike Information Criterion (AIC) for lag order selection (see Inoue and Kilian, 2006; Marcellino et al., 2006). We search over $p \in \{0, ..., 12\}$. The forecast accuracy results are robust to allowing for a larger upper bound.

There are no theoretical results in the forecasting literature on how to assess the null of equal predictive accuracy when comparing iterated AR or ARMA forecasts to the no-change forecast. In particular, the standard tests discussed in Clark and McCracken (2001, 2005a) or Clark and West (2007) are only designed for direct forecasts. Below we assess the significance of the MSPE reductions based on bootstrap p-values for the MSPE ratio constructed under the null of a random walk model without drift.[24] The upper panel of Table 8.7 suggests that AR and ARMA models in log levels have lower recursive MSPE than the no-change forecast at short horizons. The accuracy gains may approach 17% in some cases and are highly statistically significant. Beyond the 6-month horizon, all gains in forecast accuracy evaporate. There also are statistically significant gains in directional accuracy at horizons 1 and 3, and in some cases at horizon 6. There is little to choose between the AR(12), ARMA(1,1), AR(SIC) and AR(AIC) specifications overall. The AR(24) model has slightly better directional accuracy at longer horizons, but at the cost of a higher MSPE ratio.

The next panel of Table 8.7 shows the corresponding forecasting models in log differences. Note that after imposing the unit root, the autoregressive lag order is reduced by one. For example, an ARMA(1,1) model in levels corresponds to an MA(1) model in differences. We find that models in log differences generally are about as accurate as models in log levels. There is robust evidence of statistically significant MSPE reductions at horizons 1 and 3 and there are statistically significant gains in directional accuracy at horizons of up to 6 months in some cases. There is little to choose between the five forecasting models in log differences. We conclude (1) that forecasting the real price of oil based on models in log levels is by no means inferior to forecasting based on models in log differences; (2) that simple AR or ARMA models with fixed lag orders perform quite

[23] The refiners' acquisition cost was extrapolated back to 1973.2 as in Barsky and Kilian (2002).
[24] Because there is no reason to expect the limiting distribution of the DM test statistic to be pivotal in this context, we bootstrap the average loss differential instead.

Table 8.7 Recursive Forecast Error Diagnostics for the Real Price of Oil from Unrestricted AR and ARMA Models

		Evaluation Period: 1991.12-2009.8								
		h=1		h=3		h=6		h=9		h=12	
		MSPE	SR	MSPE	SR	MSPE	SR	MSPE	SR	MSPE	SR
RAC	AR(12)	**0.849**	**0.599**	**0.921**	**0.552**	**0.969**	0.522	1.034	0.441	1.022	0.517
Imports	AR(24)	**0.898**	**0.576**	**0.978**	**0.557**	1.008	**0.565**	1.056	0.446	1.058	0.453
	AR(SIC)	**0.826**	**0.613**	**0.936**	0.557	1.015	0.488	1.039	0.515	1.007	0.532
	AR(AIC)	**0.842**	**0.613**	**0.940**	**0.562**	**0.983**	0.483	1.013	0.500	0.989	0.527
	ARMA(1,1)	**0.837**	**0.580**	**0.932**	0.514	**0.982**	0.493	1.006	0.510	0.992	0.527
RAC	ARI(11)	**0.856**	**0.604**	**0.939**	**0.571**	1.003	0.517	1.095	0.471	1.091	0.512
Imports	ARI(23)	**0.898**	**0.561**	**0.978**	0.538	1.009	**0.546**	1.068	0.500	1.068	0.508
	ARI(SIC)	**0.833**	**0.594**	**0.951**	**0.605**	1.041	0.546	1.053	0.505	1.016	0.527
	ARI(AIC)	**0.849**	**0.604**	**0.958**	**0.605**	1.008	**0.556**	1.042	0.500	1.015	0.527
	ARIMA(0,1)	**0.841**	**0.599**	**0.945**	**0.581**	1.009	**0.546**	1.032	0.515	1.017	0.512
WTI	AR(12)	**0.972**	0.500	**0.974**	0.533	1.011	0.459	1.037	0.441	1.034	0.478
	AR(24)	1.035	0.486	**0.994**	0.500	**0.995**	0.502	1.008	0.461	1.019	0.473
	AR(SIC)	**0.947**	0.505	**0.979**	0.491	1.022	0.464	1.052	0.471	1.058	0.508
	AR(AIC)	**0.949**	0.505	**0.980**	0.491	1.022	0.464	1.046	0.471	1.047	0.508
	ARMA(1,1)	**0.956**	0.500	**0.982**	0.491	1.010	0.473	1.036	0.476	1.040	0.508
WTI	ARI(11)	**0.978**	0.505	**0.985**	0.529	1.032	0.517	1.081	0.456	1.083	0.433
	ARI(23)	1.034	0.524	**0.988**	0.538	**0.988**	**0.594**	1.016	0.534	1.026	0.522
	ARI(SIC)	**0.944**	0.528	**0.971**	**0.571**	1.013	0.546	1.023	0.505	1.020	0.517
	ARI(AIC)	**0.947**	0.524	**0.976**	0.552	1.018	0.517	1.031	0.466	1.026	0.488
	ARIMA(0,1)	**0.952**	0.524	**0.975**	**0.600**	1.009	0.527	1.021	0.500	1.019	0.517

Notes: ARI and ARIMA, respectively, denote AR and ARMA models in log differences. The SIC and AIC are implemented with an upper bound of 12 lags. MSPE is expressed as a fraction of the MSPE of the no-change forecast. SR stands for success ratio. The p-values for the sign test are computed following Pesaran and Timmermann (2009); those for the test of equal MSPEs are computed by bootstrapping the VAR model under the null, adapting the bootstrap algorithm in Kilian (1999). Boldface indicates statistical significance at the 10% level.

well; and (3) that the no-change forecast of the real price of oil can be improved upon at horizons of 1 month and 3 months, but generally not at horizons beyond half a year.

All models in Table 8.7 have in common that the information set is restricted to past values of the real price of oil. The question we turn to next is whether suitably chosen macroeconomic predictors can be used to improve further on the no-change forecast. Recently, a number of structural vector autoregressive models of the global market for crude oil have been proposed (see, e.g., Kilian, 2009a). These models produce empirically plausible estimates of the impact of demand and supply shocks on the real price of oil. A natural conjecture is that such models may also have value for forecasting the real price of oil. Here we focus on the reduced-form representation of the VAR (p) model in Kilian and Murphy (2013). The variables in this model include the percent change in global crude oil production ($\Delta prod_t$), the global real activity measure we already discussed in Section 4 (rea_t), the log of the real price of oil (r_t), and a proxy for the change in global above-ground crude oil inventories (ΔI). The model is $B(L)y_t = e_t$, where $B(L) = 1 - B_1 L - \ldots - B_p L^p$, e_t is white noise, and $y_t = \left(\Delta prod_t, rea_t, r_t, \Delta I_t \right)'$. The sample period is 1973.2-2009.8. For further discussion of the data see Kilian and Murphy (2013). The model may be consistently estimated without taking a stand on whether the real price of oil is I(0) or I(1) (see Sims et al., 1990). We focus on recursive rather than rolling regression forecasts throughout this section. This approach makes sense in the absence of structural change, given the greater efficiency of recursive regressions and the small sample size.[25]

A natural starting point for the forecast accuracy comparison is the unrestricted VAR model. An obvious concern with forecasting from unrestricted vector autoregressions is that these highly parameterized models are subject to considerable estimation uncertainty which tends to inflate the out-of-sample MSPE. For that reason unrestricted VAR models are rarely used in applied forecasting. They nevertheless provide a useful point of departure. The upper panel of Table 8.8 shows results for unrestricted VAR models with 12 lags. Column (1) corresponds to the four-variable model used in Kilian and Murphy (2013). Table 8.8 shows that this unrestricted VAR forecast has lower recursive MSPE than the no-change forecast at all horizons but one and non-trivial directional accuracy.[26] Despite the lack of parsimony, the reductions in the MSPE are somewhat larger than for the AR and ARMA models in Table 8.7. Bootstrap p-values for the MSPE ratio constructed under the null of a random walk model without drift indicate statistically significant reductions in the MSPE at horizons 1, 3, and 6. At longer horizons it becomes harder to beat the no-change forecast benchmark and there are no statistically significant reductions in the MSPE. There also is evidence of statistically significant gains in directional accuracy at horizons 1 and 3.

The forecasting success of the VAR approach clearly depends on the choice of variables and of the lag length. The remaining columns of the upper panel of Table 8.8 show analogous results for five other unrestricted VAR (12) models obtained by dropping one or more of the variables included in model (1). None of these models performs as well as the original four-variable model with two exceptions. The bivariate model (4) which includes only the change in oil inventories and the real price of oil has slightly lower MSPE than the four-variable VAR (12) model and similar directional accuracy, as does

[25] Rolling regression forecasts would not protect us from structural change in any case. It has been shown that the presence of structural breaks at unknown points in the future invalidates the use of forecasting model rankings obtained in forecast accuracy comparisons whether one uses rolling or recursive regression forecasts (see Inoue and Kilian, 2006).

[26] It also outperforms the random walk model with drift in both of these dimensions, whether the drift is estimated recursively or as the average growth rate over the most recent h months. These results are not shown to conserve space.

Table 8.8 Recursive Forecast Error Diagnostics for the Real Price of Oil from Unrestricted VAR Models

Model:			(1)		(2)		(3)		(4)		(5)		(6)	
Price	p	h	MSPE	SR	MSPE	SR	MSPE	SR	MSPE	SR	MSPE	SR	MSPE	SR
RAC	12	1	**0.814**	**0.561**	**0.876**	**0.594**	**0.863**	**0.613**	**0.801**	**0.613**	**0.863**	**0.580**	**0.798**	**0.585**
Imports		3	**0.834**	**0.567**	**0.960**	**0.562**	**0.947**	**0.576**	**0.833**	**0.614**	**0.944**	0.524	**0.833**	**0.586**
		6	**0.940**	0.546	1.011	0.507	**0.991**	0.536	**0.920**	0.551	0.996	0.527	**0.922**	0.511
		9	1.047	0.564	1.085	0.534	1.060	0.539	0.999	0.544	1.063	0.471	1.000	0.569
		12	0.985	**0.632**	1.055	0.562	1.036	0.567	**0.948**	**0.617**	1.045	0.503	**0.931**	**0.647**
RAC	24	1	**0.961**	**0.561**	**0.954**	**0.552**	**0.912**	**0.580**	**0.892**	**0.571**	**0.912**	**0.561**	**0.895**	**0.561**
Imports		3	**1.081**	**0.614**	1.151	**0.591**	**1.048**	**0.619**	**0.924**	**0.591**	**1.005**	**0.548**	**0.978**	**0.605**
		6	1.298	**0.604**	1.271	**0.585**	1.078	**0.594**	1.052	0.546	1.073	0.522	1.129	**0.585**
		9	1.476	**0.583**	1.441	**0.593**	1.153	**0.632**	1.150	0.431	1.158	0.422	1.255	**0.593**
		12	1.415	**0.647**	1.407	**0.612**	1.137	**0.642**	1.137	0.468	1.169	0.458	1.208	**0.617**
WTI	12	1	**0.896**	0.519	**0.981**	0.467	**0.976**	0.481	**0.893**	0.547	**0.983**	0.505	**0.882**	0.547
		3	**0.843**	0.538	**0.979**	0.524	**0.968**	0.548	**0.877**	0.552	**0.994**	0.529	**0.841**	0.548
		6	**0.988**	0.517	1.035	0.541	1.011	0.551	**0.984**	0.541	1.037	0.464	**0.973**	0.541
		9	1.053	0.534	1.080	0.485	1.049	0.510	1.021	0.564	1.067	0.441	1.014	0.539
		12	1.007	0.562	1.062	0.498	1.041	0.498	0.988	**0.602**	1.059	0.438	**0.968**	**0.592**
WTI	24	1	**1.109**	0.509	1.118	0.491	**1.053**	0.538	**1.011**	0.552	1.063	0.500	**1.013**	0.509
		3	**1.112**	**0.581**	1.185	0.552	**1.017**	0.562	**0.970**	0.562	1.049	0.481	**0.962**	**0.619**
		6	1.369	**0.570**	1.312	0.541	1.030	**0.594**	1.107	0.483	1.075	0.488	1.127	**0.589**
		9	1.455	0.564	1.340	0.520	1.060	0.583	1.160	0.446	1.106	0.490	1.153	**0.583**
		12	1.369	0.562	1.378	0.503	1.054	**0.592**	1.167	0.478	1.119	0.478	1.086	**0.602**

Notes: MSPE is expressed as a fraction of the MSPE of the no-change forecast. SR stands for success ratio. The *p*-values for the sign test are computed following Pesaran and Timmermann (2009); those for the test of equal MSPEs are computed by bootstrapping the VAR model under the null, adapting the bootstrap algorithm in Kilian (1999). Boldface indicates statistical significance at the 10% level. Model (1) includes all four variables used in the VAR model of Kilian and Murphy (2010); model (2) excludes oil inventories; model (3) excludes both oil inventories and oil production; model (4) excludes real activity and oil production; model (5) excludes real activity and oil inventories; and model (6) excludes oil production.

the trivariate model (6) specification that drops oil production from the baseline model. The differences are negligible, however.

The next panel of Table 8.8 suggests that including 24 lags in the unrestricted model tends to reduce the MSPE reductions. All VAR(24) models but model (2) still significantly improve on the MSPE of the no-change forecast at horizons 1 and 3, but their MSPE ratio tends to exceed unity at longer horizons. Likewise, all six VAR(24) models yield statistically significant gains in directional accuracy at short horizons. Only the four VAR(24) models that include the global real activity variable in the model, however, retain their superior directional accuracy at all horizons. Unlike in the corresponding

VAR(12) models, the gains in directional accuracy are statistically significant at all horizons.

We conclude that there is important predictive information in the change in oil inventories and in global real activity in particular, whereas the inclusion of oil production growth appears less important for forecasting. Moreover, based on the MSPE metric, suitably chosen VAR models systematically outperform the no-change forecast at short horizons. At horizons of 9 and 12 months, the no-change forecast remains unbeaten, except based on the sign metric. Beyond 1 year, none of these VAR forecasting models systematically outperforms the no-change forecast.

It is important to keep in mind, however, that Table 8.8 may overstate the statistical significance of the short-horizon MSPE reductions. One indication of this problem is that Table 8.8 sometimes indicates statistically significant rejections of the no-change forecast benchmark even when the MSPE ratio exceeds 1, indicating that the VAR has a strictly higher recursive MSPE. The reason for this counterintuitive result is that, as discussed earlier, standard tests of equal predictive accuracy do not test the null of equal out-of-sample MSPEs, but actually test the null of no predictability in population – much like the Granger causality tests we applied earlier – as pointed out by Inoue and Kilian (2004a). This point is readily apparent from the underlying proofs of asymptotic validity as well as the way in which critical values are simulated.

The distinction between population predictability and out-of-sample predictability does not matter asymptotically under fixed parameter asymptotics, but fixed parameter asymptotics typically provide a poor approximation to the finite-sample accuracy of forecasting models. Under more appropriate local asymptotics (designed to mimic the weak predictive power of many regressors) it can be shown that the null of no predictability in population is distinct from the null of equal out-of-sample MSPEs. It is always easier to reject the former than the latter. In other words, conventional tests of equal predictive accuracy test the wrong null hypothesis and may spuriously reject the no-change forecast in favor of the alternative. This is the deeper reason for the very low p-value obtained, for example, for model (1) with 24 lags at horizon 3. The intuition for this rejection is that under the null that the real price of oil is unpredictable one would expect much higher MSPE ratios than 1.047, so the fact that the MSPE of the VAR model is so close to 1 actually is evidence in favor of the VAR model being the population model.

Which model is the population model, of course, is irrelevant for the question of which model generates more accurate forecasts in finite samples, so we have to interpret this rejection with some caution. This type of insight recently has prompted the development of alternative tests of equal predictive accuracy based on local-to-zero asymptotic approximations to the predictive regression. Clark and McCracken (2010) for the first time proposed a correctly specified test of the null of equal out-of-sample MSPEs. Their analysis is limited to direct forecasts from much simpler forecasting models, however, and cannot be applied in Table 8.8.[27] This caveat suggests that we discount only marginally statistically significant rejections of the no predictability null hypothesis in Table 8.8 and focus on the highly statistically significant test results. The tests for directional accuracy are not affected by this concern.

9.1.2. Real-Time Forecasts

The results so far are encouraging in that they suggest that VAR models (even more so than AR or ARMA models) may produce useful short-horizon forecasts of the real price of oil. An important caveat regarding the results in Tables 8.7 and 8.8 is that the forecast accuracy comparison is not conducted in real time. There are two rather distinct concerns. One is that not all useful predictors may be available to the forecaster in real time. The other concern is that many predictors and indeed some measures of the price of oil are subject to data revisions. This caveat applies even to the no-change forecast. For example, the refiners' acquisition cost data become available only with a delay of about 3 months and the CPI data used to deflate the refiners' acquisition cost become available only with a 1-month delay.

Additional caveats apply to the VAR evidence. Although the dry cargo shipping rate data underlying the real activity index are available in real time and not subject to revisions, the construction of the real activity index involves real-time CPI data as well real-time estimates of the trend in real shipping rates. Moreover, the data on global crude oil production only become available with a delay of 4 months and the data used to approximate global crude oil inventories with a delay of 5 months. This is less of a concern for the oil production data which tend to evolve rather smoothly than for the more volatile data on changes in crude oil inventories for which there is no good real-time proxy. How imposing these real-time data constraints alters the relative accuracy of no-change benchmark model compared with VAR models is not clear a priori because both the benchmark model and the alternative model are affected.

The first study to investigate this question is Baumeister and Kilian (2012a) who recently developed a real-time data set for the variables in question. They find (based on a data set extending until 2010.6) that VAR forecasting models of the type considered in this section can also generate substantial improvements in real-time forecast accuracy. The MSPE reduction for unrestricted VAR models may be as high as 25% at the 1-month horizon and as high as 9% at the 3-month horizon. At longer horizons the MSPE reductions diminish even for the most accurate VAR models. Beyond 1

---

[27] The size problem of conventional tests of equal predictive accuracy gets worse, when the number of extra predictors under the alternative grows large relative to the sample size. This point has also been discussed in a much simpler context by Anatolyev (2012) who shows that modifying conventional test statistics for equal predictive accuracy may remove these size distortions. Also see Calhoun (2011a). Related results can be found in Calhoun (2011b) who shows that standard tests of equal predictive accuracy for nested models such as Clark and McCracken (2001) or Clark and West (2007) will choose the larger model too often when the smaller model is more accurate in out-of-sample forecasts and also proposes alternative asymptotic approximations based on many predictors. None of the remedies is directly applicable in the context of Tables 8.7, 8.8 and 8.9, however.

year, the no-change forecast usually has lower MSPE than the VAR model. Baumeister and Kilian also show that VAR forecasting models based on Kilian and Murphy (2013) exhibit significantly improved directional accuracy. The improved directional accuracy persists even at horizons at which the MSPE gains have vanished. The success ratios range from 0.51 to 0.60, depending on the model specification and horizon. These results are broadly consistent with the evidence based on ex-post revised data in Table 8.8.

9.2. Real WTI Price

The lower panels of Tables 8.7 and 8.8 show the corresponding results based on the real WTI price of oil instead of the real U.S. refiners' acquisition cost for imported crude oil. These results are not intended to validate those in the upper panels of Tables 8.7 and 8.8, given the inherent differences in the definition of the oil price data; rather they are of independent and complementary interest. The estimation and evaluation period is unchanged to allow direct comparisons. The nominal WTI price is available without delay and is not subject to revisions, reducing concerns over the real-time availability of the oil price data.

Table 8.7 provides robust evidence that AR and ARMA models improve on the no-change forecast of the real WTI price of oil at horizons 1 and 3 with the exception of models with 24 lags. The largest MSPE reductions are only 5%, however, and all such accuracy gains vanish at longer horizons. The results for the unrestricted VAR(12) models in Table 8.8 paint a similar picture with MSPE reductions as high as 16% at horizon 3. Unrestricted VAR(24) models, on the other hand, are far less accurate. We conclude that the definition of the real price of oil matters for the degree of forecastability, but the overall patterns are similar.

Broadly similar results are obtained for a real-time data set extending to 2010.6 (see Baumeister and Kilian, 2012a). Unlike for the real refiners' acquisition cost, the differences between real-time forecasts of the real WTI price and forecasts based on ex-post revised data tend to be small. In both cases, there are substantial gains in out-of-sample forecast accuracy up to a horizon of about 1 year, corroborating and strengthening the qualitative results in Table 8.8.

9.3. Restricted VAR Models

Although the results for the unrestricted VAR models in Tables 8.7 and 8.8 are encouraging, there is reason to believe that alternative estimation methods may reduce the MSPE of the VAR forecast even further. One candidate is the use of Bayesian estimation methods. In the VAR model at hand a natural starting point would be to shrink all lagged parameters toward zero under the maintained assumption of stationarity. This leaves open the question of how to determine the weights of the prior relative to the information in the likelihood. Giannone et al. (2010) recently proposed a simple and theoretically founded data-based method for the selection of priors in recursively estimated Bayesian VARs (BVARs). Their recommendation is to select priors using the marginal

Table 8.9 Recursive MSPE Ratios for the Real Price of Oil from Bayesian VAR Models

		Evaluation Period: 1991.12-2009.8											
Model:		(1)		(2)		(3)		(4)		(5)		(6)	
p	*h*	RAC	WTI	RAC	WTI	RAC	WTI	RAC	WTI	RAC	WTI	RAC	WTI
12	1	**0.800**	**0.892**	**0.825**	**0.938**	**0.828**	**0.945**	**0.798**	0.896	**0.827**	**0.951**	**0.795**	0.883
	3	0.876	0.886	**0.929**	**0.954**	**0.930**	**0.957**	0.855	0.890	**0.921**	**0.972**	0.867	0.870
	6	0.967	0.990	**0.988**	**1.008**	**0.987**	**1.006**	0.943	0.985	**0.971**	**1.011**	0.962	0.984
	9	1.052	1.036	**1.053**	**1.036**	**1.054**	**1.037**	1.033	1.037	**1.031**	**1.029**	1.050	1.036
	12	1.004	1.005	**1.024**	**1.024**	**1.028**	**1.028**	0.994	1.008	**1.015**	**1.022**	1.004	1.003
24	1	**0.801**	**0.894**	**0.826**	**0.939**	**0.828**	**0.947**	**0.800**	**0.902**	**0.829**	**0.952**	**0.795**	**0.886**
	3	**0.883**	**0.875**	**0.939**	**0.945**	**0.944**	**0.948**	**0.860**	**0.877**	**0.924**	**0.958**	**0.876**	**0.859**
	6	**0.993**	**0.990**	**1.012**	**1.007**	**1.015**	**1.000**	**0.955**	**0.980**	**0.970**	**0.991**	**0.991**	**0.986**
	9	**1.095**	**1.038**	**1.093**	**1.034**	**1.096**	**1.032**	**1.044**	**1.028**	**1.028**	**1.005**	**1.097**	**1.037**
	12	**1.059**	**1.002**	**1.073**	**1.016**	**1.078**	**1.018**	**1.016**	**1.010**	**1.026**	**1.008**	**1.058**	**0.998**

Notes: The Bayesian VAR forecast relies on the data-based procedure proposed in Giannone et al. (2010) for selecting the optimal degree of shrinkage in real time. MSPE is expressed as a fraction of the MSPE of the no-change forecast. Boldface indicates MSPE ratios lower than for the corresponding unrestricted VAR forecasting model in Tables 8.12 and 8.14. RAC refers to the U.S. refiners' acquisition cost for imported crude oil and WTI to the price of West Texas Intermediate crude oil. Model (1) includes all four variables used in the VAR model of Kilian and Murphy (2010); model (2) excludes oil inventories; model (3) excludes both oil inventories and oil production; model (4) excludes real activity and oil production; model (5) excludes real activity and oil inventories; and model (6) excludes oil production.

data density (i.e., the likelihood function integrated over the model parameters), which only depends on the hyperparameters that characterize the relative weight of the prior and the information in the data. They provide empirical examples in which the forecasting accuracy of that model in recursive settings is not only superior to unrestricted VAR models, but is comparable to that of single-equation dynamic factor models (see Stock and Watson, 1999).

Table 8.9 compares the forecasting accuracy of this approach with that of the unrestricted VAR models considered in Table 8.8. In all cases, we shrink the model parameters toward a white noise prior mean with the desired degree of shrinkage being determined by the data-based procedure in Giannone et al. (2010). For models with 12 lags, there is no strong evidence that shrinkage estimation reduces the MSPE. Although there are some cases in which imposing Bayesian priors reduces the MSPE slightly, in other cases it increases the MSPE slightly. For models with 24 lags, however, shrinkage estimation often greatly reduces the MSPE ratio and typically produces forecasts about as accurate as forecasts from the corresponding model with 12 lags. As in Table 8.8, there is evidence of MSPE reductions at horizons at short horizons. For example, model (1) with 12 lags yields MSPE reductions of 20% at horizon 1, 12% at horizon 3, and 3% at horizon 6 with no further gains at longer horizons. Model (1) with 24 lags yields gains of 20%, 12% and 1%, respectively. Again, it can be shown that similar gains in accuracy are feasible even using real-time data at horizons as high as 12 months with corresponding gains in directional accuracy (see Baumeister and Kilian, 2012a).

10. WHAT HAVE WE LEARNED ABOUT FORECASTING THE REAL PRICE OF OIL?

As we discussed in the context of nominal oil prices, it is important to assess the out-of-sample accuracy of models that help predict the real price of oil based on full-sample regressions. Table 8.2 demonstrated overwhelming evidence of population predictability of the real price of oil based on the Kilian (2009a) measure of global real activity. The evidence in column (3) of Table 8.8 demonstrates that the same model also achieves large reductions in the out-of-sample MSPE. These reductions are statistically significant, according to standard tests of equal predictive accuracy. We conclude that measures of global real activity are useful for reducing the MSPE of in-sample as well as out-of-sample forecasts of the real price of oil.

One obvious concern is that the forecasting success of the models in Tables 8.7, 8.8, and 8.9 may merely reflect our ability to forecast inflation. For example, if the U.S. CPI is predictable and the nominal price of oil is not, one should be able to predict changes in the real price of oil to the extent that inflation is predictable. It is clear that this phenomenon cannot explain our results. Inflation does not move nearly enough to explain the large observed variation in the real price, so even if one were to generate perfect short-run inflation forecasts, one would obtain a poor forecast of the real price of oil. It can be shown that our VAR models do a much better job at forecasting the real price of oil than would forecasting models based on expected inflation. In fact, it is easy to see that a forecast of the real price of oil constructed by subtracting expected inflation from the current price of oil not only would have failed to predict the surge in the real price of oil between 2003 and mid-2008, but would have predicted a decline in the real price of oil instead. Another illustration of this point is provided in Baumeister and Kilian (2012a), who contrast the performance of alternative real-time forecasts of the real price of oil generated in 2010.12. On the contrary, our results suggest that the nominal price of oil is predictable because the real price of oil is predictable. In fact, it is possible to adjust the forecast of the real price of oil generated by the VAR models of Section 9 for expected inflation to produce a forecast of the nominal price of oil that is more accurate than the no-change forecast.

It can also be shown that extrapolating the current nominal price of oil based on recent percent changes in the price of industrial raw materials, adjusted for expected inflation, produces a forecast of the real price of oil that is as accurate in the short run as the forecasts of the real price of oil from VAR models – and more accurate than forecasts based on the oil futures spread adjusted for expected inflation (see Baumeister and Kilian, 2012a). The fact that these models perform similarly is no accident. The VAR models that are successful at beating the no-change forecast in the short run are consistent with economic models in which the real price of oil responds to changes in global real activity and other real variables such as changes in crude oil inventories. Both of these variables may be viewed as leading indicators of the real price of oil. Likewise models based on recent percent changes in the price index for non-oil industrial raw materials will capture the effect of persistent changes in the global business cycle on the real price of oil, because shifts in the demand for all industrial raw materials are also associated with shifts in the demand for crude oil. The advantage of the VAR approach is that it allows for a broader set of determinants of the real price of oil, making it potentially more robust.

Finally, we note that the evidence in favor of VAR forecasts also is consistent with the result that simple autoregressive models outperform the no-change forecast of the real price of oil. The latter models may be viewed as approximations to the marginalized VAR processes. The chief advantage of VAR models over AR models is their superior directional accuracy.

11. STRUCTURAL VAR FORECASTS OF THE REAL PRICE OF OIL

So far we have considered reduced-form VAR forecasting models. VAR models can also be useful for studying how baseline forecasts of the real price of oil must be adjusted under hypothetical forecasting scenarios. This does require the structural shocks in the VAR model to be identified, however. Recent research has shown that historical fluctuations in the real price of oil can be decomposed into the effects of distinct oil demand and oil supply shocks including a forward-looking or speculative element in the real price of oil (see, e.g., Kilian and Murphy, 2013). Changes in the composition of these shocks over time help explain why conventional regressions of macroeconomic aggregates on the price of oil tend to be unstable. They also are potentially important in interpreting oil price forecasts.

In Section 9 we showed that recursive forecasts of the real price of oil based on the type of oil market VAR model originally proposed by Kilian and Murphy (2013) for the purpose of structural analysis are superior to simple no-change forecasts at least at short horizons. The case for the use of VAR models, however, does not rest on their predictive accuracy alone. Policymakers expect oil price forecasts to be interpretable in light of an economic model. They also expect forecasters to be able to generate projections conditional on a variety of hypothetical economic scenarios. Questions of interest include, for example, what effects an unexpected slowing of Asian growth would have on the forecast of the real price of oil; or what the effect would be of an unexpected decline in global oil production associated with peak oil. Answering questions of this type is impossible using reduced-form time series models. It requires a fully structural VAR model.

In this section we illustrate how to generate such projections from the structural moving average representation of the VAR model of Kilian and Murphy (2013) estimated on data extending to 2009.8. The methodology resembles that discussed in Baumeister and Kilian (2012b).[28] The structural model allows the identification of three shocks of economic interest: (1) a shock to the flow of the production of crude oil ("flow supply shock"), (2) a shock to the flow demand for crude oil ("flow demand shock") that reflects unexpected fluctuations in the global business cycle, and (3) a shock to the demand for oil inventories arising from forward-looking behavior not otherwise captured by the model ("speculative demand shock"). The structural demand and supply shocks in this model are identified by a combination of sign restrictions and bounds on impact price elasticities. This model is set-identified, but the admissible models can be shown to be quite similar, allowing us to focus on one such model with little loss of generality. We focus on the same model that Kilian and Murphy use as the basis for their historical decompositions.

There is a strict correspondence between standard reduced-form VAR forecasts and forecasts from the structural moving average representation. The reduced-form forecast corresponds to the expected real price of oil conditional on all future shocks being zero. Departures from this benchmark can be constructed by feeding pre-specified sequences of future structural shocks into the structural moving-average representation. A forecast scenario is defined as a sequence of future structural shocks. The implied movements in the real price of oil relative to the baseline forecast obtained by setting all future structural shocks to zero correspond to the revision of the reduced-form forecast implied by this scenario.

Here we consider three scenarios of economic interest. Additional scenarios are discussed in Baumeister and Kilian (2012b). The forecast horizon is 24 months for illustrative purposes. The first scenario involves a successful stimulus to U.S. oil production, as had been considered by the Obama administration prior to the 2010 oil spill in the Gulf of Mexico. Here we consider the likely effects of a 20% increase in U.S. crude oil output in 2009.9, after the estimation sample of Kilian and Murphy (2013) ends. This is not to say that such a dramatic and sudden increase would be feasible, but that it would be an optimistic scenario. Such a U.S. oil supply stimulus would translate to a 1.5% increase in world oil production, which is well within the variation of historical data. We simulate the effects of this production increase by calibrating a one-time structural oil supply shock such that the impact response of global oil production growth in 2009.9 is 1.5%. All other future structural shocks are set to zero. Figure 8.7 shows that the resulting reduction in the real price of oil expressed in percent changes relative to the baseline forecast is negligible. Even a much larger U.S. oil supply stimulus would do little to affect the forecast of the real price of oil, suggesting that policies aimed at creating such a stimulus will be ineffective at lowering the real price of oil.

The second scenario involves a recovery of global demand for oil and other industrial commodities. We ask how an unexpected surge in the demand for oil similar to that

---

[28] Related work in a different context also includes Waggoner and Zha (1999).

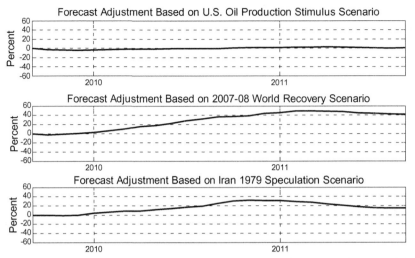

Figure 8.7 Forecasting scenarios for the real price of oil based on the structural VAR model of Kilian and Murphy (2013): Conditional projections expressed relative to baseline forecast. *Notes*: All results are based on the structural oil market model of Kilian and Murphy (2013). The U.S. oil production stimulus involves a 20% increase in U.S. oil production in 2009.9, which translates to a 1.5% increase in world oil production. For this purpose, a one-time structural oil supply shock is calibrated such that the impact response of global oil production is 1.5%. The 2007-08 world recovery scenario involves feeding in as future shocks the sequence of flow demand shocks that occurred in 2007.1–2008.6. The Iran 1979 speculation scenario involves feeding in as future shocks the speculative demand shocks that occurred between 1979.1 and 1980.2 and were a major contributor to the 1979/80 oil price shock episode.

occurring during 2007.1-2008.6, but starting in 2009.9, would affect the real price of oil. This scenario involves feeding into the structural moving average representation future flow demand shocks corresponding to the sequence of flow demand shocks that occurred in 2007.1-2008.6, while setting all other future structural shocks equal to their expected value of zero. Figure 8.7 shows a persistent increase in the real price of oil starting in early 2010 that peaks in early 2011 about 50% above the price of oil in 2009.8. Taking the no-change forecast as the benchmark, for example, this means that the peak occurs at a price of about 100 dollars.

Finally, we consider the possibility of a speculative frenzy such as occurred starting in mid-1979 after the Iranian Revolution (see Kilian and Murphy, 2013). This scenario involves feeding into the model future structural shocks corresponding to the sequence of speculative demand shocks that occurred between 1979.1 and 1980.2 and were a major contributor to the 1979/80 oil price shock episode. Figure 8.7 shows that this event would raise the baseline forecast temporarily by as much as 30%. Most of the effects would have dissipated by mid-2011.

These results, while necessarily tentative, illustrate how structural models of oil markets may be used to assess the sensitivity of reduced-form forecasts to specific economic events, possibly in conjunction with the formal risk measures discussed in Section 13. Conditional projections, of course, are only as good as the underlying structural models. Our example highlights the importance of refining these models and of improving structural forecasting methods, perhaps in conjunction with Bayesian methods of estimating VAR forecasting models.

12. THE ABILITY OF OIL PRICES TO FORECAST U.S. REAL GDP

One of the main reasons why the price of oil is considered important by many macroeconomists is its perceived predictive power for U.S. real GDP. Assessing that predictive power requires a joint forecasting model for the price of oil and for domestic real activity. In this section we first examine the forecasting accuracy of linear models and then examine a variety of non-linear forecasting models. The baseline results are for the U.S. refiners' acquisition cost for imported crude oil. Toward the end of the section we discuss how these results are affected by other oil price choices. Our discussion draws on results in Kilian and Vigfusson (2013).

12.1. Linear Autoregressive Models

A natural starting point is a linear $VAR(p)$ model for the real price of oil and for U.S. real GDP expressed in quarterly percent changes. The general structure of the model is $x_t = B(L)x_{t-1} + e_t$, where $x_t \equiv [\Delta r_t, \Delta y_t]'$, r_t denotes the log of real price of oil, y_t the log of real GDP, Δ is the difference operator, e_t the regression error, and $B(L) = B_1 + B_2 L + B_3 L^2 + \ldots + B_p L^{p-1}$. The benchmark model for real GDP growth is the $AR(p)$ model obtained with

$$B(L) = \begin{pmatrix} \times & \times \\ 0 & B_{22}(L) \end{pmatrix}.$$

The specification of the components of $B(L)$ marked as $\times$ is irrelevant for this forecasting model. We determined the lag order of this benchmark model based on a forecast accuracy comparison involving all combinations of horizons $h \in \{1, \ldots, 8\}$ and lag orders $p \in \{1, \ldots, 24\}$. The $AR(4)$ model for real GDP growth proved to have the lowest MSPE or about the same MSPE as the most accurate model at all horizons. The same $AR(4)$ benchmark model has also been used by Hamilton (2003) and others, facilitating comparisons with existing results in the literature.

We compare the benchmark model with two alternative models. One model is the unrestricted $VAR(p)$ model obtained with

$$B(L) = \begin{pmatrix} B_{11}(L) & B_{12}(L) \\ B_{21}(L) & B_{22}(L) \end{pmatrix}.$$

Table 8.10 MSPE Ratios of Linear Autoregressive Models Relative to the AR(4) Benchmark Model: Cumulative U.S. Real GDP Growth Rates

	Real RAC Price of Imports		Nominal RAC Price of Imports	
Horizon	Oil Price Endogenous	Oil Price Exogenous	Oil Price Endogenous	Oil Price Exogenous
1	1.09	1.09	1.10	1.10
2	1.03	1.03	1.04	1.04
3	0.99	**0.98**	1.00	**0.99**
4	**0.97**	**0.96**	**0.98**	**0.97**
5	**0.96**	**0.95**	**0.97**	**0.95**
6	**0.95**	**0.94**	**0.95**	**0.94**
7	**0.92**	**0.92**	**0.92**	**0.92**
8	**0.92**	**0.92**	**0.92**	**0.92**

Notes: The benchmark model is an AR(4) for U.S. real GDP growth. The first alternative is a VAR(4) model for real GDP growth and the percent change in the price of oil that allows for unrestricted feedback from U.S. real GDP growth to the price of oil. The second alternative is a restricted VAR(4) model that treats the price of oil as exogenous. Boldface indicates gains in accuracy relative to the benchmark model. No tests of statistical significance have been conducted, given that these models are economically indistinguishable.

The other is a restricted VAR model of the form

$$B(L) = \begin{pmatrix} B_{11}(L) & 0 \\ B_{21}(L) & B_{22}(L) \end{pmatrix}.$$

The restriction $B_{12}(L) = 0$ is implied by the hypothesis of exogenous oil prices. Although that restriction is not literally true, in Section 4 we observed that in linear models the predictive content of U.S. real GDP for the real price of oil, while not zero, appears to be weak. Thus, a natural conjecture is that the added parsimony from imposing zero feedback from lagged real GDP to the real price of oil may help reduce the out-of-sample MSPE of multi-step-ahead real GDP forecasts.

The real price of oil is obtained by deflating the refiners' acquisition cost for imported crude oil by the U.S. CPI. All three models are estimated recursively on data starting in 1974.Q1. The initial estimation period ends in 1990.Q1, right before the invasion of Kuwait in August of 1990. The forecast evaluation ends in 2010.Q1. The maximum length of the recursive sample is restricted by the end of the data and the forecast horizon. We evaluate the MSPE of each model for the cumulative growth rates at horizons $h \in \{1, ..., 8\}$, corresponding to the horizons of interest to policymakers.

The first column of Table 8.10 shows that, at horizons of three quarters and beyond, including the real price of oil in the autoregressive models may reduce the MSPE for real GDP growth by up to 8% relative to the AR(4) model for real GDP growth. The unrestricted VAR(4) model for the real price of oil is about as accurate as the restricted VAR(4) model in the second column. Imposing exogeneity marginally reduces the MSPE at some horizons, but the differences are all negligible. This fact is remarkable given the

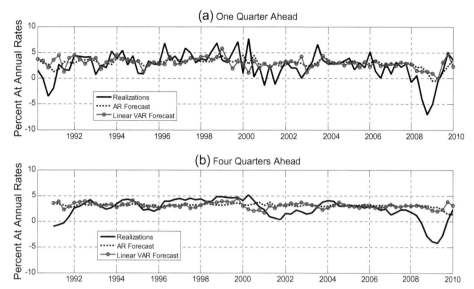

Figure 8.8 VAR forecasts of cumulative real GDP growth based on the real price of oil: U.S. refiners' acquisition cost for imports. *Notes*: The benchmark model is an AR(4) for real GDP growth. The alternative is an unrestricted linear VAR(4) model for real GDP growth and the percent change in the real price of oil. The price of oil is defined as the U.S. refiners' acquisition cost for imports.

greater parsimony of the model with exogenous oil prices. We conclude that there are no significant gains from imposing exogeneity in forecasting from linear models. Next consider a similar analysis for the nominal price of oil. Although the use of the nominal price of oil in predicting real GDP is not supported by standard economic models, it is useful to explore this alternative approach in light of the discussion in Section 3. Table 8.10 shows that the unrestricted VAR(4) model based on the real price of oil is consistently at least as accurate as the same model based on the nominal price of oil. We conclude that in linear models there are no gains in forecast accuracy from replacing the real price of oil by the nominal price. Imposing exogeneity, as shown in the last column, again makes little difference.

MSPE ratios are informative about relative forecasting accuracy, but are not informative about how accurate these models are in practice. Figure 8.8 focuses on the ability of recursively estimated AR(4) and VAR(4) models based on the real price of oil imports to predict the recessions of 1991, 2001, and 2007/8. The upper panel plots the one-quarter-ahead forecasts against the forecast realizations. AR and VAR forecasts are generally quite similar. Neither model is able to forecast the large economic declines in 1990/91, 2001, and 2008/09. The forecast accuracy deteriorates further at the one-year horizon, as shown in the lower panel.

One possible explanation is that this forecast failure simply reflects our inability to forecast more accurately the real price of oil. Put differently, the explanation could be that the real GDP forecasts would be more accurate if only we had more accurate forecasts of the real price of oil. Conditioning on realized values of the future price of oil, however, does not greatly improve the forecast accuracy of the linear VAR model for cumulative real GDP growth, so this explanation can be ruled out. An alternative explanation could be that the predictive relationship between the price of oil and domestic macroeconomic aggregates is time-varying. One source of time variation is that the share of energy in domestic expenditures has varied considerably over time. This suggests that we replace the percent change in the real price of oil in the linear VAR model by the percent change in the real price of oil weighted by the time-varying share of oil in domestic expenditures, building on the analysis in Edelstein and Kilian (2009). Hamilton (2009) reported some success in employing a similar strategy.[29] Another source of time variation may be changes in the composition of the underlying oil demand and oil supply shocks, as discussed in Kilian (2009a). Finally, yet another potential explanation investigated below is that the linear forecasting model may be inherently misspecified. Of particular concern is the possibility that non-linear dynamic regression models may generate more accurate out-of-sample forecasts of cumulative real GDP growth.

12.2. Non-Linear Dynamic Models

In this regard, Hamilton (2003) suggested that the predictive relationship between oil prices and U.S. real GDP is non-linear in that (1) oil price increases matter only to the extent that they exceed the maximum oil price in recent years and that (2) oil price decreases do not matter at all. This view was based on the in-sample fit of a single-equation predictive model of the form:

$$\Delta y_t = \alpha + \sum_{i=1}^{4} \beta_i \Delta y_{t-i} + \sum_{i=1}^{4} \delta_i \Delta s_{t-i}^{net,+,3yr} + u_t, \tag{18}$$

where s_t denotes the log of the nominal price of oil and $\Delta s_t^{net,+,3yr}$ the corresponding 3-year net increase in the nominal price of oil.

Hamilton's line of reasoning has prompted many researchers to construct asymmetric responses to positive and negative oil price innovations from censored oil price VAR models. Censored oil price VAR models refer to linear VAR models for $[\Delta s_t^{net,+,3yr}, \Delta y_t]'$, possibly augmented by other variables. Recently, Kilian and Vigfusson (2011a) have shown that impulse response estimates from VAR models involving censored oil price variables are inconsistent. Specifically, that paper demonstrated, first, that asymmetric

[29] In related work, Ramey and Vine (2010) propose an alternative adjustment to the price of gasoline that reflects the time cost of queuing in gasoline markets during the 1970s. That adjustment as well serves to remove a non-linearity in the transmission process. Both the non-linearity postulated in Edelstein and Kilian (2009) and that postulated in Ramey and Vine (2010) is incompatible with the specific non-linearity embodied in the models of Mork (1989) and Hamilton (1996,2003). In fact, the aforementioned papers rely on linear regressions after adjusting the energy price data.

models of the transmission of oil price shocks cannot be represented as censored oil price VAR models and are fundamentally misspecified whether the data generating process is symmetric or asymmetric. Second, standard approaches to the construction of structural impulse responses in this literature are invalid, even when applied to correctly specified models. Instead, Kilian and Vigfusson proposed a modification of the procedure discussed in Koop et al. (1996). Third, standard tests for asymmetry based on the slope coefficients of single-equation predictive models are neither necessary nor sufficient for judging the degree of asymmetry in the structural response functions, which is the question of ultimate interest to users of these models. Kilian and Vigfusson proposed a direct test of the latter hypothesis and showed empirically that there is no statistically significant evidence of asymmetry in the response functions for U.S. real GDP.

Hamilton (2011) agrees with Kilian and Vigfusson on the lack of validity of impulse response analysis from censored oil price VAR models, but suggests that non-linear predictive models such as model (18) may still be useful for out-of-sample forecasting. Indeed, the predictive model (18) can be consistently estimated by OLS and used to form one-quarter-ahead forecasts. We explore the forecasting accuracy of this strategy below. We consider both one-quarter-ahead forecasts of real GDP growth and forecasts of the cumulative real GDP growth rate several quarters ahead. The latter forecasts require a generalization of the single-equation forecasting approach proposed by Hamilton (2011).

In implementing this approach, there are several potentially important modeling choices to be made. First, even granting the presence of asymmetries in the predictive model, one question is whether the predictive model should be specified as

$$\Delta y_t = \alpha + \sum_{i=1}^{4} \beta_i \Delta y_{t-i} + \sum_{i=1}^{4} \delta_i \Delta s_{t-i}^{net,+,3yr} + u_t, \tag{18}$$

as in Hamilton (2003), or rather as

$$\Delta y_t = \alpha + \sum_{i=1}^{4} \beta_i \Delta y_{t-i} + \sum_{i=1}^{4} \gamma_i \Delta s_{t-i} + \sum_{i=1}^{4} \delta_i \Delta s_{t-i}^{net,+,3yr} + u_t, \tag{19}$$

as in Balke et al. (2002) or Herrera et al. (2011), for example. The latter specification encompasses the linear reduced-form model as a special case. If $\gamma_i = 0 \forall i$, or, alternatively, if the slopes γ_i are close enough to zero, the more parsimonious non-linear predictive model (18) will have lower out-of-sample MSPE in finite samples than the unrestricted encompassing model (19). Below we explore the merits of imposing $\gamma_i = 0 \forall i$ not only in the context of single-equation models designed for one-step-ahead forecasting, but for multivariate non-linear models as well.

A second point of contention is whether non-linear forecasting models should be specified in terms of the nominal price of oil or the real price of oil. For linear models, a strong economic case can be made for using the real price of oil. For non-linear models, the situation is less clear, as noted by Hamilton (2011). Because the argument for using net oil price increases is behavioral, one specification appears as reasonable as the other. Below we therefore will consider models specified in real as well as in nominal oil prices.

A third issue that arises only in constructing iterated forecasts for higher horizons is how to specify the process governing the price of oil. The case can be made that treating this process as exogenous with respect to real GDP might help reduce the out-of-sample MSPE, even if that restriction is incorrect. Below we therefore consider specifications with and without imposing exogeneity.

In Table 8.11, we investigate whether there are MSPE reductions associated with the use of censored oil price variables at horizons $h \in \{1, ..., 8\}$, drawing on the analysis in Kilian and Vigfusson (2011b) and Kilian and Vigfusson (2013). For completeness, we also include results for the percent increase specification proposed in Mork (1989), the forecasting performance of which has not been investigated to date. We consider non-linear models based on the real price of oil as in Kilian and Vigfusson and non-linear models based on the nominal price of oil as in Hamilton (2003). The unrestricted multivariate non-linear forecasting model takes the form

$$\Delta r_t = \alpha_1 + \sum_{i=1}^{4} B_{11,i} \Delta r_{t-i} + \sum_{i=1}^{4} B_{12,i} \Delta y_{t-i} + e_{1,t}$$

$$\Delta y_t = \alpha_2 + \sum_{i=1}^{4} B_{21,i} \Delta r_{t-i} + \sum_{i=1}^{4} B_{22,i} \Delta y_{t-i} + \sum_{i=1}^{4} \delta_i \tilde{r}_{t-i} + e_{2,t} ,$$

(20)

where $\tilde{r}_t \in \left\{ \Delta r_t^{net,+,3yr}, \Delta r_t^{net,+,1yr}, \Delta r_t^{+} \right\}$, $\Delta r_t^{+} \equiv \Delta r_t I(\Delta r_t > 0)$ as in Mork (1989), and $I(\cdot)$ denotes the indicator function. Analogous non-linear forecasting models may be constructed based on the nominal price of oil, denoted in logs as s_t:

$$\Delta s_t = \alpha_1 + \sum_{i=1}^{4} B_{11,i} \Delta s_{t-i} + \sum_{i=1}^{4} B_{12,i} \Delta y_{t-i} + e_{1,t}$$

$$\Delta y_t = \alpha_2 + \sum_{i=1}^{4} B_{21,i} \Delta s_{t-i} + \sum_{i=1}^{4} B_{22,i} \Delta y_{t-i} + \sum_{i=1}^{4} \delta_i \tilde{s}_{t-i} + e_{2,t} ,$$

(20')

where $\tilde{s}_t \in \left\{ \Delta s_t^{net,+,3yr}, \Delta s_t^{net,+,1yr}, \Delta s_t^{+} \right\}$.

In addition, we consider a restricted version of models (20) and (20') which imposes the hypothesis that the price of oil is exogenous such that:

$$\Delta r_t = \alpha_1 + \sum_{i=1}^{4} B_{11,i} \Delta r_{t-i} + e_{1,t}$$

$$\Delta y_t = \alpha_2 + \sum_{i=1}^{4} B_{21,i} \Delta r_{t-i} + \sum_{i=1}^{4} B_{22,i} \Delta y_{t-i} + \sum_{i=1}^{4} \delta_i \tilde{r}_{t-i} + e_{2,t}$$

(21)

and

$$\Delta s_t = \alpha_1 + \sum_{i=1}^{4} B_{11,i} \Delta s_{t-i} + e_{1,t}$$

$$\Delta \gamma_t = \alpha_2 + \sum_{i=1}^{4} B_{21,i} \Delta s_{t-i} + \sum_{i=1}^{4} B_{22,i} \Delta \gamma_{t-i} + \sum_{i=1}^{4} \delta_i \tilde{s}_{t-i} + e_{2,t} \; . \tag{21'}$$

Alternatively, we may restrict the feedback from lagged percent changes in the price of oil, as suggested by Hamilton (2003). After imposing $B_{21,i} = 0 \forall i$, the baseline non-linear

Table 11a MSPE Ratios of Nonlinear Dynamic Models Relative to the AR(4) Benchmark Model Cumulative U.S. Real GDP Growth Rates

	Real Refiners' Acquisition Cost for Imported Crude Oil					
	Unrestricted Model (20)			Exogenous Model (21)		
		Hamilton Net Increase			Hamilton Net Increase	
Horizon	Mork Increase	1 Year	3 Year	Mork Increase	1 Year	3 Year
1	1.14	1.21	**0.98**	1.15	1.21	**0.98**
2	1.13	1.10	**0.83**	1.13	1.10	**0.83**
3	1.07	1.05	**0.79**	1.07	1.04	**0.79**
4	1.08	**0.99**	**0.76**	1.07	**0.99**	**0.76**
5	1.09	**0.94**	**0.75**	1.09	**0.93**	**0.74**
6	1.10	**0.92**	**0.77**	1.09	**0.91**	**0.77**
7	1.10	**0.92**	**0.79**	1.09	**0.91**	**0.78**
8	1.10	**0.92**	**0.81**	1.09	**0.91**	**0.80**

	Nominal Refiners' Acquisition Cost for Imported Crude Oil					
	Unrestricted Model (20')			Exogenous Model (21')		
		Hamilton Net Increase			Hamilton Net Increase	
Horizon	Mork Increase	1 Year	3 Year	Mork Increase	1 Year	3 Year
1	1.12	1.20	1.08	1.12	1.20	1.08
2	1.10	1.07	**0.87**	1.09	1.07	**0.87**
3	1.04	1.01	**0.81**	1.03	1.01	**0.81**
4	1.04	**0.96**	**0.77**	1.04	**0.96**	**0.77**
5	1.05	**0.92**	**0.77**	1.04	**0.92**	**0.77**
6	1.05	**0.91**	**0.79**	1.04	**0.91**	**0.79**
7	1.05	**0.91**	**0.82**	1.04	**0.91**	**0.81**
8	1.06	**0.92**	**0.83**	1.05	**0.91**	**0.83**

Notes: The benchmark model is an AR(4) for U.S. real GDP growth. The nonlinear dynamic models are described in the text. Boldface indicates gains in accuracy relative to benchmark model. The exogenous model suppresses feedback from lagged real GDP growth to the current price of oil.

Table 11b MSPE Ratios of Nonlinear Dynamic Models Relative to the AR(4) Benchmark Model
Cumulative U.S. Real GDP Growth Rates

	Real Refiners' Acquisition Cost for Imported Crude Oil					
	Restricted Model (22)			Restricted Exogenous Model (23)		
		Hamilton Net Increase			Hamilton Net Increase	
Horizon	Mork Increase	1 Year	3 Year	Mork Increase	1 Year	3 Year
1	1.14	1.12	**0.91**	1.14	1.12	**0.91**
2	1.12	1.05	**0.80**	1.11	1.05	**0.80**
3	1.07	1.01	**0.77**	1.07	1.01	**0.78**
4	1.04	**0.97**	**0.76**	1.03	**0.96**	**0.75**
5	1.03	**0.93**	**0.75**	1.02	**0.93**	**0.75**
6	1.02	**0.91**	**0.77**	1.00	**0.91**	**0.77**
7	1.01	**0.91**	**0.79**	1.00	**0.90**	**0.78**
8	1.01	**0.91**	**0.80**	1.01	**0.90**	**0.79**

	Nominal Refiners' Acquisition Cost for Imported Crude Oil					
	Restricted Model (22')			Restricted Exogenous Model (23')		
		Hamilton Net Increase			Hamilton Net Increase	
Horizon	Mork Increase	1 Year	3 Year	Mork Increase	1 Year	3 Year
1	1.12	1.12	1.01	1.12	1.12	1.01
2	1.09	0.02	**0.84**	1.08	1.02	**0.83**
3	1.04	**0.98**	**0.79**	1.03	**0.97**	**0.79**
4	1.01	**0.94**	**0.76**	1.00	**0.94**	**0.76**
5	**0.99**	**0.92**	**0.77**	**0.98**	**0.91**	**0.77**
6	**0.99**	**0.91**	**0.80**	**0.97**	**0.90**	**0.79**
7	**0.98**	**0.90**	**0.81**	**0.97**	**0.90**	**0.80**
8	**0.98**	**0.91**	**0.83**	**0.97**	**0.90**	**0.82**

Notes: The benchmark model is an AR(4) for U.S. real GDP growth. The nonlinear dynamic models are described in the text. Boldface indicates gains in accuracy relative to benchmark model. The restricted model suppresses feedback from lagged percent changes in the price of oil to current real GDP growth, as proposed by Hamilton (2003, 2011). The restricted exogenous model combines this restriction with that of exogenous oil prices, further increasing the parsimony of the model.

forecasting model reduces to:

$$\Delta r_t = \alpha_1 + \sum_{i=1}^{4} B_{11,i} \Delta r_{t-i} + \sum_{i=1}^{4} B_{12,i} \Delta y_{t-i} + e_{1,t}$$

$$\Delta y_t = \alpha_2 + \sum_{i=1}^{4} B_{22,i} \Delta y_{t-i} + \sum_{i=1}^{4} \delta_i \tilde{r}_{t-i} + e_{2,t} .$$

(22)

and

$$\Delta s_t = \alpha_1 + \sum_{i=1}^{4} B_{11,i}\Delta s_{t-i} + \sum_{i=1}^{4} B_{12,i}\Delta y_{t-i} + e_{1,t}$$

$$\Delta y_t = \alpha_2 + \sum_{i=1}^{4} B_{22,i}\Delta y_{t-i} + \sum_{i=1}^{4} \delta_i \tilde{s}_{t-i} + e_{2,t} \,.$$

(22′)

Finally, we can combine the restrictions $B_{12,i} = 0 \forall i$ and $B_{21,i} = 0 \forall i$, resulting in forecasting models (23) and (23′):

$$\Delta r_t = \alpha_1 + \sum_{i=1}^{4} B_{11,i}\Delta r_{t-i} + e_{1,t}$$

$$\Delta y_t = \alpha_2 + \sum_{i=1}^{4} B_{22,i}\Delta y_{t-i} + \sum_{i=1}^{4} \delta_i \tilde{r}_{t-i} + e_{2,t}$$

(23)

and

$$\Delta s_t = \alpha_1 + \sum_{i=1}^{4} B_{11,i}\Delta s_{t-i} + e_{1,t}$$

$$\Delta y_t = \alpha_2 + \sum_{i=1}^{4} B_{22,i}\Delta y_{t-i} + \sum_{i=1}^{4} \delta_i \tilde{s}_{t-i} + e_{2,t} \,.$$

(23′)

At the one-quarter horizon, real GDP growth forecasts from model (22′) and (23′) only depend on the second equation, which is equivalent to using Hamilton's model (1). All models are estimated by least squares, as is standard in the literature. The forecasts are constructed by Monte Carlo integration based on 10,000 draws. The estimation and evaluation periods are the same as in Table 8.10.

Table 8.11 displays the MSPE ratios for all eight models by horizon. All results are normalized relative to the AR(4) model for real GDP growth. No tests of statistical significance have been conducted, given the computational cost of such tests. The first result is that no non-linear model is substantially more accurate than the AR(4) benchmark model at the one-quarter horizon except for models (22) and (23) with the 3-year net oil price increase. For the latter models, the reduction in MSPE is 9%. At the one-year horizon, the reduction in MSPE reaches 24% and 25% respectively. The accuracy gains at the two-year horizon are about 20%. Second, models that combine Hamilton's assumptions with that of exogenous oil prices and embed all these assumptions in a multivariate dynamic framework, help improve forecast accuracy at short horizons. Third, neither the percent increase model based on Mork (1989) nor the 1-year net increase model motivated by Hamilton (1996) is more accurate than the AR(4) benchmark at the one-quarter horizon. This is true regardless of whether the price of oil is specified in nominal or real terms and regardless of what additional restrictions we impose. At longer horizons, there is weak evidence that some of these specifications reduce the MSPE at some horizons, but in no case as much as for the three-year net oil price increase. Fourth, there is a clear ranking between 3-year net increase models based on the real price of oil and the corresponding models based on the nominal price of oil. Forecasts from models 22 and 23 based on the real price of oil are more accurate, especially at short horizons, than forecasts from models (22′) and (23′) based on the nominal price.

An obvious question of interest is to what extent allowing for nonlinearities improves our ability to forecast major economic downturns in the U.S. The one-quarter ahead results in the upper panel of Figure 8.9 indicate that the 3-year net increase models are quite successful at forecasting the 2008 recession, about half of which is forecast by models 23 and (23′), whereas their performance during other episodes is less impressive. The corresponding lower panel in Figure 8.9 shows that models 23 and (23′) are equally successful at forecasting the downturn of 2008 and the subsequent recovery four quarters ahead. If anything, these nonlinear models appear too successful in that their forecasting success in 2008 implies a comparatively minor role for the financial crisis. This success, however, comes at the price that these models forecast a number of economic declines in the pre-crisis period that did not materialize. For example, the net increase model

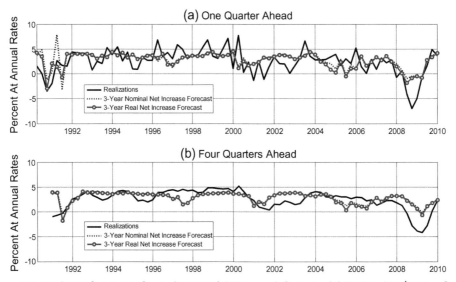

Figure 8.9 Nonlinear forecasts of cumulative real GDP growth from models (23) and (23′) U.S. refiners' acquisition cost for imports. Notes: One forecasting model is a suitably restricted VAR(4) model for real GDP growth and the percent change in the real price of oil augmented by four lags of the 3-year real net oil price increase. The other model is a similarly restricted VAR(4) model for real GDP growth and the percent change in the nominal price of oil augmented by four lags of the 3-year nominal net oil price increase.

incorrectly forecast much lower growth than materialized in 1997 and in 2005/06, and it missed the beginning of the economic decline of 1990/91.

Plots of the recursive MSPE of these nonlinear models show that much of the forecasting success of nonlinear models is driven by one episode, namely the economic collapse in 2008/09 following the financial crisis. This point is illustrated in Figure 8.10. The left panel of Figure 8.10 is based on the nominal PPI used in Hamilton's original analysis; the right panel shows the corresponding results for the nominal refiners' acquisition cost for crude oil imports. The plot of the cumulative recursive MSPE for the PPI model (23′) reveals that the overall gain in accuracy in this example is almost driven entirely by the 2008/09 recession. Excluding this episode, model (23′) has higher MSPE than the linear AR model nearly throughout the evaluation period. Given this evidence a strong case can be made that few forecasters would have had the courage to stick with the predictions of this nonlinear model given the sustained failure of the model in the years leading up to the financial crisis. The corresponding results for the refiners' acquisition cost for imported crude oil in the right panel are somewhat more favorable, but also reveal a tendency of the net oil price increase model to have a higher recursive MSPE prior to the financial crisis than the AR(4) benchmark model for real GDP growth.

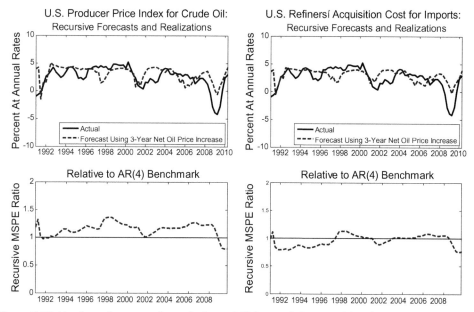

Figure 8.10 Nonlinear forecasts of cumulative real GDP growth from model (23′). Notes: The nonlinear forecasting model is a suitably restricted VAR(4) model for real GDP growth and the percent change in the nominal price of crude oil augmented by four lags of the corresponding 3-year nominal net oil price increase.

The unusually good fit of the 3-year net increase model in 2008/08 combined with the tendency of this model to incorrectly predict recessions prior to the crisis, is an indication of potential out-of-sample overfitting. It is usually thought that out-of-sample forecasts protect against overfitting. This intuition may fail in small samples because, under quadratic loss, the ability of the nonlinear model to predict correctly one extreme event (such as the sharp economic decline associated with the financial crisis) may more than offset repeated smaller forecast errors of the same nonlinear model during earlier episodes. Given that the financial crisis occurred immediately after a major surge in the price of oil, but itself was presumably not caused by that oil price surge, the obvious concern is that net increase models may have forecast the 2008 recession for the wrong reasons.[30] Only additional data will ultimately resolve the question of how much the low MSPE of the net increase model in Table 8.11 owes to overfitting. If the near-simultaneous occurrence of the financial crisis and the oil price surge is coincidental, then the forecasting accuracy of the nonlinear model can be expected to worsen, as the sample is extended. If the forecasting success of the nonlinear model were to persist even after the financial crisis is over, this would add credibility to the nonlinear real GDP growth forecasts.

The same concern regarding the financial crisis episode arises to varying degrees with other oil price series. Table 8.12 provides a systematic comparison of the performance of nonlinear forecasting models relative to the AR(4) benchmark model for real GDP growth for different oil price series and evaluation periods. To conserve space, we focus on models 23 and which tend to be the most accurate nonlinear forecasting models. Table 8.12 shows that the relative MSPE of nonlinear forecasting models can be highly sensitive to the choice of oil price series. The first two columns of Table 8.12 focus on the evaluation period 1990.Q1-2010.Q1. Column (1) shows that, for eight of ten model specifications, the one-quarter ahead nonlinear forecasting model proposed by Hamilton (2011) fails to outperform the AR(4) benchmark model for real GDP. Only for the real refiners' acquisition cost for imported crude oil and for the nominal WTI specification are there any gains in forecast accuracy. In particular, the nominal PPI specification favored by Hamilton (2011) on the basis of in-sample diagnostics is less accurate than the AR benchmark model. Much more favorable results are obtained at the one-year horizon in column (2) of Table 8.12. In the latter case, all nonlinear forecasting models yield sizable reductions in the MSPE. However, almost all evidence of forecast accuracy gains vanishes once the financial crisis episode is excluded, as shown in columns (3) and (4) of Table 8.12, suggesting once again an element of overfitting. Some nonlinear forecasting models have more than 60% higher MSPE than the AR benchmark model in that case. We conclude

---

[30] While the case can be made that higher oil prices contributed to the U.S. housing crisis, as discussed in Hamilton (2009, p. 255–257), for example, few observers would view higher oil prices as the primary cause of the subsequent financial market meltdown.

Table 8.12 MSPE Ratios for Cumulative U.S. Real GDP Growth Rate Relative to AR(4) Benchmark Model: Models (23) and (23′) for Alternative Oil Price Specifications and Evaluation Periods

	Oil Price Series	1990.Q1-2010.Q1 Horizon		1990.Q1-2007.Q4 Horizon	
		h=1	h=4	h=1	h=4
Real	RAC imports	**0.91**	**0.75**	1.12	1.14
	RAC composite	1.16	**0.81**	1.50	1.33
	RAC domestic	1.22	**0.82**	1.56	1.23
	WTI	1.04	**0.77**	1.24	**0.97**
	PPI	1.23	**1.86**	1.64	1.50
Nominal	RAC imports	1.01	**0.76**	1.23	1.05
	RAC composite	1.25	**0.80**	1.59	1.16
	RAC domestic	1.22	**0.83**	1.50	1.12
	WTI	**0.91**	**0.80**	1.01	**0.94**
	PPI	1.23	**0.80**	1.59	1.23

Notes: To conserve space, we focus on the most accurate nonlinear forecasting models. The models are described in the text. Boldface indicates gains in accuracy relative to AR(4) benchmark model for real GDP growth. The out-of-sample evaluation period for $h = 4$ starts three quarters later by construction than for $h = 1$.

that the evidence that nonlinear oil price transformation help forecast cumulative U.S. real GDP growth is mixed at best.[31]

12.3. Does Using Pre-1974 Data Help in Forecasting Real GDP?

In Section 4.2.3 we made the case that using pre-1974 data in studying the predictive relationship between the price of oil and U.S. real GDP is inadvisable. This argument has not prevented some researchers from fitting forecasting models on samples dating back to 1949. Indeed, one can make the case that in forecasting the reduction in the variance of the model estimates from using these additional data may in practice outweigh any biases caused by ignoring structural breaks. For example, Hamilton (2011) reports the one–quarter-ahead MSPE ratio of his preferred forecasting model (18) with four lags of the 3-year net increase in the nominal PPI with the coefficients estimated on data for 1949.Q2 to 2001.Q3 relative to a model motivated by the analysis in Kilian and Vigfusson (2011a) with six lags of real GDP growth, six lags of the percent change in the oil price, and six lags of the net oil price increase. The latter model is estimated on data for 1974.Q1-2007.Q4. The out-of-sample MSPE of both models is evaluated over 2008.Q1 to 2010.Q1. The resulting MSPE ratio is 0.24.

---

[31] The results in Tables 8.11 and 8.12

This result is not directly comparable to our analysis for three reasons. First, it is based on split-sample analysis rather than recursive analysis for model (18). Second, the relevant benchmark for our out-of-sample comparisons is the AR(4) model for real GDP growth, not the much less parsimonious model discussed in Kilian and Vigfusson (2011a). Third, Hamilton' out-of-sample evaluation window includes only two years of data, whereas we evaluate the model over a 20-year period. Moreover, the specific 2 years of data that Hamilton focuses on when evaluating the model correspond to the financial crisis episode, which we showed to be to the time period most favorable to Hamilton's model.

It is straightforward to conduct an exercise in the same spirit as Hamilton's such that the results can be compared directly to those in Table 8.12. When we conducted this additional analysis, we found that the one-quarter-ahead MSPE ratio of Hamilton's 3-year net increase model (18) recursively estimated on data back to 1949.Q2 and evaluated on the 1990.Q1-2010.Q1 period is 1.02 compared with an AR(4) model for real GDP estimated on post-break data. This compares with a ratio of 1.23 for the same model estimated on post-break data, as reported in Table 8.12, indicating that using the longer sample does improve the one-quarter-ahead MSPE, but does not overturn our conclusion that the AR(4) for real GDP growth is more accurate out of sample than Hamilton's model.[32] We also found that the MSPE ratio of the corresponding 4-quarter ahead iterated forecast increases from 0.80 in Table 8.12 to 0.85, if we include the pre-1973 data in the recursive estimation of the model, indicating that the longer estimation sample lowers the model's forecast accuracy. Finally, when the nonlinear model in question is estimated based on data back to 1949.Q2, but we exclude the financial crisis period from the evaluation sample, the recursive MSPE ratios increase to 1.36 one quarter ahead and 1.53 four quarters ahead. In short, our results are robust to extending the estimation sample back to 1949.Q2.

12.4. Non-Parametric Approaches

Our approach in this section has been parametric. Alternatively, one could have used non-parametric econometric models to investigate the forecasting ability of the price of oil for real GDP. In related work, Bachmeier et al. (2008) used the integrated conditional moment test of Corradi and Swanson (2002, 2007) to investigate whether oil prices help forecast real GDP growth one-quarter-ahead. The advantage of this approach is that — while imposing linearity under the null – it allows for general non-linear models under the alternative; the disadvantage is that the test is less powerful than the parametric approach if the parametric structure is known. Bachmeier et al. report a p-value of 0.20 for the null that nominal net increases in the WTI price of oil do not help forecast U.S. real GDP. The p-value for percent changes in the WTI price of crude oil is 0.77. Similar results

---

[32] The corresponding one-quarter-ahead MSPE ratio during the 1990.Q1-2007.Q4 evaluation period is 1.36 and the ratio during 2008.Q1-2010.Q1 is 0.32, consistent with our earlier remarks on the special nature of this 2-year period.

are obtained for real net increases and for percent changes in the real WTI price. These findings are broadly consistent with ours. Bachmeier et al. (2008) also report qualitatively similar results using a number of fully non-parametric approaches. An obvious caveat is that their analysis is based on data since 1949, which is not appropriate for the reasons discussed earlier, and ends before the 2008/09 recession. Using their non-parametric techniques on our much shorter sample period does not seem advisable, because there is no way of controlling the size of the test.

13. THE ROLE OF OIL PRICE VOLATILITY

Point forecasts of the price of oil are important, but they fail to convey the uncertainty associated with oil price forecasts. That uncertainty is captured by the predictive density. Figure 8.11 plots the 12-month-ahead predictive density for the real price of oil as of 2009.12, generated from the no-change forecasting model. Although it is obvious that there is tremendous uncertainty about the future real price of oil, even when using the best available forecasting methods, it is less obvious how to convey and interpret that information. For example, standard questions in the financial press about whether the price of oil *could* increase to $200 a barrel, at the risk of being misunderstood, inevitably and always must be answered in the affirmative because the predictive distribution has unbounded support. That answer, however, is vacuous because it does not convey how likely such an event is or by how much the price of oil is expected to exceed the $200 threshold in that event.

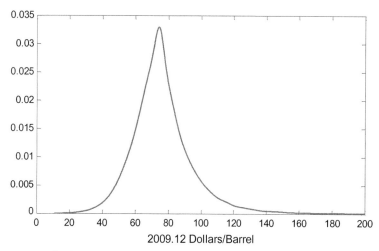

Figure 8.11 12-Month-ahead predictive density of the real WTI price of oil as of 2009.12 based on no-change forecast.

13.1. Nominal Oil Price Volatility

One seemingly natural way of summarizing the information in the predictive distribution is to report the variability of the forecasts. Interest in oil price volatility measures arises, for example, from financial analysts interested in pricing options and from portfolio managers interested in diversifying risks. Given that at short horizons CPI inflation is negligible, it is customary in financial applications to focus on nominal oil price volatility. One approach to measuring oil price volatility is to rely on the implied volatilities of put and call options, which are available from January 1989 on. Implied volatility measures are computed as the arithmetic average of the daily implied volatilities from the put and call options associated with a futures contract of a given maturity. The upper panel of Figure 8.12 shows the 1-month implied volatility time series for 2001.1-2009.12, computed from daily CRB data, following the same procedure as for the spot and futures prices in Section 5. Alternatively, we may use daily percent changes in the nominal WTI price of oil to construct measures of realized volatility, as shown in the second panel of Figure 8.12 (see, e.g., Bachmeier et al., 2008). Finally, yet another measure of volatility can be constructed from parametric GARCH or stochastic volatility models. The bottom panel of Figure 8.12 shows the 1-month-ahead conditional variance obtained from recursively

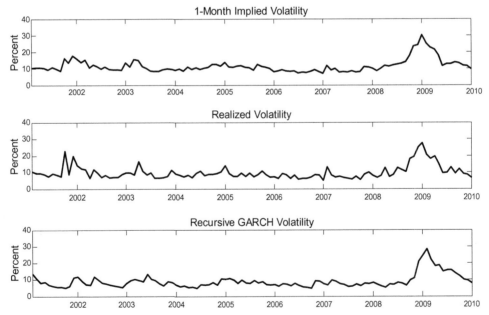

Figure 8.12 Alternative measures of nominal oil price volatility. *Notes*: The GARCH volatility estimate is for the percent change in the nominal WTI price. The realized volatility was obtained from daily WTI prices. The implied volatility measure refers to the arithmetic average of the daily implied volatilities from at-the-money put and call options associated with 1-month oil futures contracts and was constructed by the authors from CRB data. All volatility estimates are monthly and expressed as standard deviations, following the convention in the literature.

estimated Gaussian GARCH(1,1) models.[33] The initial estimation period is 1974.1-2000.12. The estimates are based on the percent change in the nominal WTI price; the corresponding results for the real WTI price are almost indistinguishable at the 1-month horizon.[34]

Figure 8.12 plots all three volatility measures on the same scale. Although the volatility estimates agree that by far the largest peak in volatility occurred near the end of 2008, there are important differences. For example, the implied volatility measure increases steadily starting in early 2008 and peaks in December 2008. Realized volatility also peaks in December 2008, but does not increase substantially the second half of 2008. Finally, GARCH volatility is even slower to increase in 2008 and only peaks in January 2009. This ranking is consistent with the view that implied volatility is the most forward-looking volatility measure and GARCH volatility the most backward-looking volatility estimate (and hence the least representative measure of real time volatility). Similarly, the implied volatility and realized volatility measures indicate substantial secondary spikes in volatility in 2001/02 and 2003, whereas the spikes in the GARCH volatility estimate are much smaller and occur only with a delay.

It may seem that fluctuations in oil price volatility, defined in this manner, would be a good indicator of changes in oil price risks. It is important not to equate risk and uncertainty, however. Whereas the latter may be captured by the volatility of oil price forecasts, the former cannot. The standard risk that financial markets in oil-importing economies are concerned with is the risk of excessively high oil prices. That risk in general will be at best weakly correlated with the volatility of oil price forecasts because any reduction in risk, as the price of oil falls, all else equal, will be associated with increased oil price volatility. This is why in 1986, for example, oil price volatility increased, as OPEC collapsed and the price of oil dropped sharply, whereas by all accounts consumers were pleased with lower oil prices and the diminished risk of an OPEC-induced supply disruption. Hence, standard volatility measures are of limited use as summary statistics for the predictive distribution of oil price forecasts. We defer to Section 13.3 a more detailed exposition of how appropriate risk measures may be computed from the predictive distribution of the price of oil.

13.2. Real Oil Price Volatility

Interest in the volatility of oil prices also has been prompted by research aimed at establishing a direct link from oil price volatility to business cycle fluctuations in the real economy.

---

[33] The standard GARCH model is used for illustrative purposes. An alternative would be a GARCH-in-Mean model. Given that oil is only one of many assets handled by portfolio managers, however, it is not clear that the GARCH-in-Mean model for single-asset markets is appropriate in this context, while more general multivariate GARCH models are all but impossible to estimate reliably on the small samples available for our purposes (see, e.g., Bollerslev et al., 1992).

[34] We deliberately focus on oil price volatility at the 1-month horizon. Although from an economic point of view volatility forecasting at longer horizons would be of great interest, the sparsity of options price data makes it difficult to extend the implied volatility approach to longer horizons. Likewise, GARCH volatility estimates quickly converge to the unconditional variance at longer horizons.

For example, Bernanke (1983) and Pindyck (1991) showed that the uncertainty of the price of oil (measured by the volatility of the price of oil) matters for investment decisions if firms contemplate an irreversible investment, the cash flow of which depends on the price of oil. An analogous argument holds for consumers considering the purchase of energy-intensive durables such as cars. Real options theory implies that, all else equal, an increase in expected volatility will cause marginal investment decisions to be postponed, causing a reduction in investment expenditures. Kellogg (2010) provides evidence that such mechanisms are at work in the Texas oil industry, for example.

Unlike in empirical finance, the relevant volatility measure in these models is the volatility of the real price of oil at horizons relevant to purchase and investment decisions, which is typically measured in years or even decades rather than days or months, making standard measures of short-term nominal price volatility inappropriate. Measuring the volatility of the real price of oil at such long forecast horizons is inherently difficult given how short the available time series are, and indeed researchers in practice have typically asserted rather than measured these shifts in real price volatility or they have treated short-horizon volatility as a proxy for longer-horizon volatility (see, e.g., Elder and Serletis, 2010).[35] This approach is unlikely to work. Standard monthly or quarterly GARCH model cannot be used to quantify changes in the longer-run expected volatility of the real price of oil because GARCH forecasts of the conditional variance quickly revert to their time invariant unconditional expectation, as the forecasting horizon increases. If volatility at the economically relevant horizon is constant by construction, it cannot explain variation in real activity over time, suggesting that survey data may be better suited for characterizing changes in forecast uncertainty over time. Some progress in this direction may be expected from ongoing work conducted by Anderson et al. (2011) based on the distribution of Michigan consumer expectations of 5-year-ahead gasoline prices. For further discussion of this point also see Kilian and Vigfusson (2011b).

13.3. Quantifying Oil Price Risks

Although oil price volatility shifts play a prominent role in discussions of the impact of oil price shocks, it is important to keep in mind that volatility measures are not in general useful measures of the price risks faced by either producers or consumers of crude oil (or of refined products). Consider an oil producer capable of producing crude oil from existing wells as long as the price of oil exceeds his marginal cost of $25 a barrel. One risk faced by that oil producer is that he will go out of business if the price of oil falls below that threshold. Excessively high oil prices, in contrast, are of no concern until they

---

[35] In rare cases, the relevant forecast horizon may be short enough for empirical analysis. For example, Kellogg (2010) makes the case that for the purpose of drilling oil wells in Texas, as opposed to Saudi Arabia, a forecast horizon of only 18 months is adequate. Even at that horizon, however, there are no oil-futures options price data that would allow the construction of implied volatility measures. Kellogg (2010) therefore converts the 1-month volatility to 18-month volatilities based on the term structure of oil futures. That approach relies on the assumption that oil futures prices are reliable predictors of future oil prices.

reach the point of making replacement technologies economically viable. That might be the case at a threshold of $120 a barrel, for example, at which price major oil producers risk inducing the large-scale use of alternative technologies with adverse consequences for the long-run price of crude oil.[36] Thus, the oil producer will care about the risk of the price of oil not being contained in the range between $25 and $120, and the extent to which he is concerned with violations of that range depends on his risk aversion, which need not be symmetric in either direction.[37] There is no reason why oil producers should necessarily be concerned with a measure of the variability of the real price of oil. In fact, it can be shown that risk measures are not only quantitatively different from volatility measures, but in practice may move in the opposite direction.

Likewise, a consumer of retail motor gasoline (and hence indirectly of crude oil) is likely to be concerned with the price of gasoline exceeding what he can afford to spend each month (see Edelstein and Kilian, 2009). The threshold at which consumers might trade in their SUV more energy-efficient car is near $3 a gallon perhaps. The threshold at which commuters may decide to relocate closer to their place of work might be at a price near $5 a gallon. The possibility that the price of gasoline could fall below $2, in contrast, is of comparatively little consequence to consumers' economic choices, making the volatility of oil prices and related statistics such as the value at risk irrelevant to the typical consumer.

In both examples above, the appropriate specification of these agents' decision problem is in terms of upside and downside price risks. The literature on risk management postulates that risk measures must satisfy two basic requirements. One requirement is that the measure of risk must be related to the probability distribution $F(\cdot)$ of the random variable of interest; the other requirement is that it must be linked to the preferences of the user, typically parameterized by a loss function (see Machina and Rothschild, 1987). Except in special cases these requirements rule out commonly used measures of risk based on the predictive distribution alone such as the sample moments, sample quantiles or the value at risk. In deriving appropriate risk measures that characterize the predictive distribution for the real price of oil, it is useful to start with the loss function. A reasonably general class of loss functions $l(\cdot)$ that encompasses the two empirical examples above is:

$$l(R_{t+h}) = \begin{cases} a(\underline{R} - R_{t+h})^{\alpha} & \text{if } R_{t+h} < \underline{R} \\ 0 & \text{if } \underline{R} \leq R_{t+h} \leq \bar{R} \\ (1-a)(R_{t+h} - \bar{R})^{\beta} & \text{if } R_{t+h} > \bar{R}, \end{cases}$$

where R_{t+h} denotes the real price of oil in dollars h periods from date t, $0 \leq a \leq 1$ is the weight attached to downside risks, and $\alpha \geq 0$ and $\beta \geq 0$ are determined by the user's degree of risk aversion. Risks are associated with the event of R_{t+h} exceeding an upper

[36] A similar irreversible shift in OECD demand occurred after the oil price shocks of the 1970s when fuel oil was increasingly replaced by natural gas. The fuel oil market never recovered, even as the price of this fuel fell dramatically in the 1980s and 1990s (see Dargay and Gately, 2010).

[37] The threshold of $120 in this example follows from adjusting the cost estimates for shale oil production in Farrell and Brandt (2006) for the cumulative inflation rate since 2000.

threshold of $\bar{R}$ or falling below the lower threshold of $\underline{R}$. It can be shown that under this loss function, the expected loss is a weighted average of upside and downside risks of the form

$$E(l) = -aDR_\alpha + (1-a)UR_\beta,$$

where

$$DR_\alpha \equiv -\int_{-\infty}^{\underline{R}} (\underline{R} - R_{t+h})^\alpha dF(R_{t+h}), \quad \alpha \geq 0$$

$$UR_\beta \equiv \int_{\bar{R}}^{\infty} (R_{t+h} - \bar{R})^\beta dF(R_{t+h}), \quad \beta \geq 0$$

are the downside risk and upside risk, respectively. This definition encompasses a variety of risk definitions familiar from the finance literature. For example, for the special case of $\alpha = \beta = 0$ these expressions reduce to the (target) probabilities $DR_0 = -\Pr(R_{t+h} < \underline{R})$ and $UR_0 = \Pr(R_{t+h} > \bar{R})$ and for the special case of $\alpha = \beta = 1$ they reduce to the probability weighted expected shortfall $DR_1 = E(R_{t+h} - \underline{R}|R_{t+h} < \underline{R})\Pr(R_{t+h} < \underline{R})$ and the probability weighted expected excess $UR_1 = E(R_{t+h} - \bar{R}|R_{t+h} > \bar{R})\Pr(R_{t+h} > \bar{R})$. Note that the latter definition not only is concerned with the likelihood of a tail event, but also with how far the real price of oil is expected to be in the tail. The latter term is also known as the expected shortfall (or expected excess). The expectations and probabilities in question in practice can be estimated by their sample equivalent.[38]

This digression highlights that the volatility of the real price of oil in general is not the relevant statistic for the analysis of risks. In particular, if and only if the loss function is quadratic and symmetric about zero, the variance of the price of oil about zero provides an adequate summary statistic for the risk in oil price forecasts. Even that target variance, however, is distinct from conventionally used measures of oil price volatility, defined as the variance about the sample mean of the predictive distribution. The latter measure under no circumstances can be interpreted as a risk measure because it depends entirely on the predictive distribution of the price of oil and not at all on the user's preferences.

Risk measures can be computed for any predictive distribution. Estimates of predictive distributions for iterated forecasts may be constructed by applying standard bootstrap methods (possibly adapted to allow for conditional heteroskedasticity) to the serially uncorrelated errors of the estimated regression model and iteratively constructing the bootstrap realizations of the multi-step-ahead forecast. When evaluating the distribution of direct forecasts rather than iterated forecasts, additional complications may arise. Applying standard bootstrap methods to the sequence of one-step-ahead forecast errors

---

[38] Measures of risk of this type were first introduced by Fishburn (1977), Holthausen (1981), Artzner et al. (1999), and Basak and Shapiro (2001) in the context of portfolio risk management and have become a standard tool in recent years (see, e.g., Engle and Brownlees, 2010). For a general exposition of risk measures and risk management in a different context see Kilian and Manganelli (2007, 2008).

obtained from fitting the direct forecasting model to historical data requires the fore-cast errors to be serially uncorrelated. This will typically be the case when constructing forecasts at horizon $h = 1$. For example, when fitting a random walk model of the form $s_{t+1} = s_t + \varepsilon_{t+1}$, the forecast errors at horizon 1 may be resampled using standard bootstrap methods as in the case of iterated forecasts.

At longer horizons, however, the construction of direct multi-horizon forecasts from the random walk model is more involved. One option is to fit the forecasting model on non-overlapping observations and proceed as for $h = 1$. This approach is simple, but tends to involve a considerable reduction in estimation precision. For example, in constructing the predictive distribution of 1-year-ahead no-change forecasts from monthly data, one would construct for the current month the sequence of year-on-year percent changes relative to the same month in the preceding year and approximate the predictive distri-bution by resampling this sequence of year-on-year forecast errors. The other option is to construct forecast errors from overlapping observations and to recover the underlying white noise errors by fitting an $MA(h-1)$ process to the sequence of h-step-ahead forecast errors. This allows the construction of bootstrap approximations of the predictive density by first resampling the serially uncorrelated white noise residuals using suitable bootstrap methods and then constructing bootstrap replicates of the h-month-ahead forecast errors from the implied moving averages. Below we implement this approach in the context of a 12-month-ahead no-change forecast of the real WTI price of oil. The risk mea-sures are constructed directly from the bootstrap estimate of the predictive distribution, as discussed above.

Figure 8.13 plots the risk that the price of oil (expressed in 2009.12 dollars) exceeds $80 1 year later ($\bar{R} = 80$) and the risk that it drops below $45 1 year later ($\underline{R} = 45$). These thresholds have been chosen for illustrative purposes. The upper panel of Figure 8.13 plots the upside and downside risks for $\alpha = \beta = 0$, whereas the lower panel plots the corresponding results for $\alpha = \beta = 1$. Note that by convention the downside risks have been defined as a negative number to improve the readability of the plots. Although the upside risks and downside risks respond to sustained changes in the conditional mean forecast by construction, the relationship is not one-for-one. Figure 8.13 shows that the ex ante probability of the real price of oil exceeding $80 1 year later was small except during 2005-08 and after mid-2009; high probabilities of the real price of oil falling below $45 occurred only in 2001-04 and 2009. The lower panel shows the corresponding probability-weighted expected excess and expected shortfall measures. For $\alpha = \beta = 1$, the upside risks in 2007-08 become disproportionately larger relative to earlier upside risks and relative to the downside risks. Regardless of the choice of α and β, the balance of risks since mid-2009 has been tilted in the upside direction. Recent upside risks are comparable to those in 2006.

It is immediately evident that the three standard volatility measures in Figure 8.12 are not good proxies for either of the two risks shown in Figure 8.13. For example, in

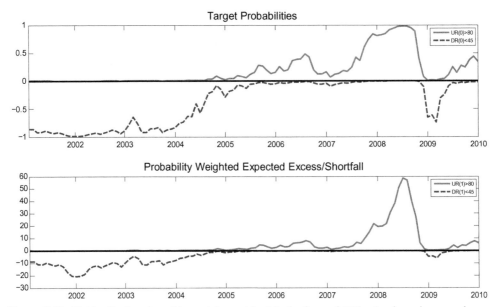

Figure 8.13 12-Month-ahead upside and downside risks in the real WTI price based on no-change forecast. *Notes*: Risks are defined in terms of the event that the price of oil (in 2009.12 dollars) exceeds 80 dollars or falls below 45 dollars. For further discussion of these risk measures see Kilian and Manganelli (2007).

the second half of 2008 volatility skyrockets while the upside risk plummets. The upside risk peaks in mid-2008, when the real price of oil peaked, but volatility only peaks in December 2008 or January 2009, when the real price of oil had reached a trough, much to the relief of oil consumers. Moreover, the spikes in volatility in 2001/02 and 2003 are not mirrored by increases in upside risk, while the sustained increase in upside risk after 2004 is not mirrored by a sustained increase in volatility. Nor is volatility systematically related to downside oil price risks. Although both downside risks and volatility peak in 2001/02, the sustained increase in volatility in early and mid-2008 is not mirrored by an increase in downside risk. Furthermore, the decline in downside risks during 2004 and 2005 is not reflected in systematic changes in volatility.

It is worth emphasizing that none of these 12-month-ahead risk forecasts provided any warning of the collapse of the real price of oil in late 2008. To the extent that this collapse was unpredictable based on past data, this is not surprising. The problem is not with the risk measures but rather with the underlying predictive distribution that these risk measures have been applied to. In fact, none of the available forecasting methods provided an advance warning of the collapse of the real price of oil in late 2008, although some of the more accurate forecasting models predicted a decline in the real price.

14. AVENUES FOR FUTURE RESEARCH

There are a number of directions for future research on forecasting oil prices. One relates to the use of additional industry-level predictors not commonly considered by economists. Although crude oil is one of the more homogeneous commodities traded in global markets, not all refineries may process all grades of crude oil. Moreover, different grades of crude oil yield different mixes of refined products. Hence, shifts in the demand for one type of refined product, say, diesel fuel, have implications for the product mix of refined products (diesel, gasoline, kerosene, heating oil, etc.) and hence for the demand for different grades of crude oil, depending on the capacity utilization rates of different refineries. Situations can arise in which excess demand for one grade of crude oil may result in rising prices, while excess supply of another grade of crude oil is associated with falling prices.[39] Models that incorporate information about such spreads or about the underlying determinants of demand have the potential of improving forecasts of the price of a given grade of crude oil (see, e.g., Verleger Jr., 1982, 2011).

A second issue of interest is the role played by heterogenous oil price and gasoline price expectations in modeling the demand for energy-intensive durables (see Anderson et al., 2011). There is strong evidence that not all households share the same expectations, casting doubt on standard rational expectations models with homogeneous agents. This also calls into question the use of a single price forecast in modeling purchasing decisions in the aggregate. This problem is compounded to the extent that different market participants (households, refiners, oil producers) in the same model may have very different risk assessments based on the same predictive oil price distribution. Both of these effects may undermine the predictive power of the price of oil for macroeconomic aggregates as well as the explanatory power of theoretical models based on oil price forecasts.

Third, we have deliberately refrained from exploring the use of factor models for forecasting the price of oil. In related work, Zagaglia (2010) reports some success in using a factor model in forecasting the nominal price of oil at short horizons, although his evaluation period only covers early 2003 to early 2008 given his data limitations, and it is unclear how sensitive the results would be to extending the evaluation period. An obvious concern is that there are no price reversals over the evaluation period, so any predictor experiencing sustained growth is likely to have some forecasting power. Moreover, we have shown in Section 5 that much simpler forecasting models appear capable of generating equally substantial reductions in the MSPE of the nominal price of oil at short horizons and do so for extended periods. The more important problem from an economic point of view, in any case, is forecasting the real price of oil. It seems

---

[39] A case in point is the persistent divergence of the Brent price and WTI price of crude oil in 2011. This unusual divergence can be explained by a combination of factors including (1) an excess supply of Canadian crude oil in the United States, given the lack of infrastructure for selling Canadian crude oil elsewhere, (2) a shortage of light sweet crude oil in the EU due to the recent Libyan production shortfall, and (3) increased demand for diesel fuel (caused in part by environmental policies) driving up the demand for light sweet crude oil in Europe.

unlikely that approximate factor models could be used to forecast the real price of oil. The variables that matter most for the determination of the real price of oil are global. Short of developing a comprehensive worldwide data set of real aggregates at monthly frequency, it is not clear whether there are enough predictors available for reliable real-time estimation of the factors. For example, drawing excessively on U.S. real aggregates as in Zagaglia (2010) is unlikely to be useful for forecasting the global price of oil for the reasons discussed in Section 4. Using a cross-section of data on energy prices, quantities, and other oil-market related indicators may be more promising, but almost half of the series used by Zagaglia are specific to the United States and unlikely to be representative of global markets.

15. CONCLUSIONS

Although there are a fair number of papers dealing with the problem of predicting the price of oil, it is difficult to reconcile the seemingly conflicting results in this literature. The problem is not only the precise definition of the oil price variable, but whether the price of oil is expressed in nominal or in real terms, what estimation and evaluation periods are chosen, how the forecast accuracy is evaluated, whether the conditional mean, conditional variance or conditional density is being forecast, whether the analysis is conducted in-sample or out-of-sample, whether the methods are parametric or non-parametric, and whether tests of statistical significance are provided or not. The most common problem in the literature is that results are sensitive to the choice of the sample period and vanish when the sample period is extended.

In this chapter, our objective has been to provide a benchmark based on data that include the recent collapse of the price of oil in late 2008 and its subsequent recovery. We started by discussing problems with combining data from the pre-1973 and post-1973 period, highlighting the need to discard the pre-1973 data because these data cannot be represented by standard time series models. We documented a structural break in the time series process of both the nominal and the real price of oil in late 1973. We also noted the presence of a structural break in the dynamic correlations between changes in the real price of oil and U.S. real GDP growth. This structural break invalidates predictive regressions based on data extending back further than 1973.

A natural starting point for our analysis was the question of whether changes in the price of oil are inherently unpredictable, as is sometimes claimed. We provided strong evidence that after 1973 changes in the nominal price of oil are predictable in population. The most successful predictors are recent percent changes in U.S. consumer prices and monetary aggregates as well as global non-oil industrial commodity prices. We also found strong evidence that after 1973 the real price of oil is predictable in population based on fluctuations in global real output. We illustrated how problems of omitted variables and of measurement can obscure this predictive relationship. We emphasized the importance of accounting for structural changes in the composition of real output, of using measures with broad geographic coverage, and of using methods of detrending that can capture long swings in the demand for industrial commodities.

These results demonstrate that neither the nominal nor the real price of oil follows a random walk in population. Predictability in population, however, need not translate into out-of-sample forecast accuracy. One concern is that in small samples simple parsimonious forecasting models such as the no-change forecast often have lower MSPE than forecasts from larger-dimensional models suggested by economic theory. This may occur even if the large-dimensional model is correctly specified, provided the increase in the forecast variance from estimating the unknown parameters of the correctly specified model exceeds the reduction in the (squared) forecast bias from eliminating the model misspecification.

We provided evidence that this concern is unwarranted. We showed that suitably designed unrestricted vector autoregressive models estimated recursively on ex-post revised data tend to have lower out-of-sample MSPE than the no-change forecast of the real price of oil at horizons up to 12 months in some cases. The largest MSPE reductions occur at horizons 1 and 3. The MSPE reductions may be as high as 20%. The same models also have statistically significant directional accuracy at horizons up to 1 year. In addition, there is strong evidence that recursively estimated AR and ARMA models have lower MSPE than the no-change forecast, especially at horizons of 1 and 3 months. At horizons beyond 1 year, the no-change forecast of the real price of oil typically is the predictor with the lowest MSPE. These results are robust to the use of real time data.

Likewise, it is possible to forecast the nominal price of oil out of sample. There is strong evidence of statistically significant MSPE reductions in forecasting the nominal price of oil at horizons of 1 and 3 months based on recent percent changes in the price of non-oil industrial raw materials, for example. The reductions in the out-of-sample MSPE at the 3-month horizon are 22%. Similarly, information in recent changes in the dollar exchange rate of Canada and Australia helps reduce the MSPE of the forecast of the nominal price of oil at horizons up to 6 months. Both models also exhibit statistically significant directional accuracy. Finally, there is evidence that simply adjusting the no-change forecast for the real price of oil for expected inflation yields much more accurate forecasts of the nominal price of oil than the no-change forecast at horizons of several years. The same inflation-based model provides few if any accuracy gains at short or intermediate horizons, however.

More commonly used methods of forecasting the nominal price of oil based on the price of oil futures or the spread of the oil futures price relative to the spot price cannot be recommended. There is no reliable evidence that oil futures prices significantly lower the MSPE relative to the no-change forecast at short horizons, and long-term futures prices often cited by policymakers are distinctly less accurate than the no-change forecast. One possible explanation for the unexpectedly low out-of-sample accuracy of oil futures-based forecasts may be the presence of transaction costs impeding arbitrage. An alternative forecasting strategy in which one uses the futures price only if the futures spread exceeds 5% in absolute terms and uses the spot price otherwise, yields MSPE reductions between 0% and 6% at short horizons (some of which are statistically significant), but performs much worse than the no-change forecast at longer horizons. Likewise professional and government forecasts of the nominal price of oil do not significantly improve on the no-change forecast, except in some cases in the short run, and can be much less accurate.

One of the main reasons for the importance that many macroeconomists attach to the price of oil is its perceived predictive power for U.S. real GDP. We assessed this predictive power based on a joint forecasting model for the price of oil and for domestic real activity. We showed that there are only small gains in using the price of oil in forecasting cumulative real GDP growth from VAR models. This finding is robust to whether the price of oil is specified in nominal or in real terms and whether it is treated as exogenous or as endogenous. More importantly, bivariate linear autoregressive models fail to predict major economic downturns. One possible explanation of this forecast failure is that the predictive relationship is non-linear. We therefore evaluated and compared a wide range of non-linear joint forecasting models for the price of oil and real GDP growth. Except for the 3-year net oil price increase specification, we found no evidence at all of substantially improved forecast accuracy for real GDP growth. Even for the 3-year net increase model, the evidence was mixed at best. For example, we found no evidence that the nominal PPI 3-year net increase model is more accurate than linear models for real GDP growth at the one-quarter horizon. A multivariate generalization of the model proposed by Hamilton (2003, 2011) tended to provide MSPE gains of up to 20% relative to the AR(4) benchmark model at longer horizons. Even more accurate results were obtained with some alternative oil price series. All these forecasting successes, however, were driven mainly by the 2008/09 recession. Excluding that episode from the evaluation period, all nonlinear forecasting models were less accurate than the benchmark AR(4) model for real GDP growth at the one-quarter horizon, and only two of ten nonlinear models showed any improvement relative to the AR(4) model at the four-quarter horizon.

This evidence suggests that there is reason to be skeptical of the seeming forecasting success of many nonlinear models during the recent financial crisis. If these forecasts are to be believed, the financial crisis played a small role in the economic decline of 2008/09, which does not seem economically plausible. An alternative explanation is that the evaluation sample is too short for reliable inference. We observed that the net oil price increase model has a tendency to predict economic declines anytime the price of oil has increased substantially. Although such predictions repeatedly proved incorrect, most notably in 2005/06, the ability of some 3-year net increase models to forecast the extreme decline in U.S. real GDP in 2008/09 under quadratic loss more than compensates for earlier forecasting errors and hence accounts for their higher average out-of-sample forecast accuracy when the evaluation period includes the financial crisis.

We also discussed the use of structural forecasting models for the real price of oil. An important limitation of reduced-form forecasting models of the real price of oil from a policy point of view is that they do not allow the user to explore alternative hypothetical forecasting scenarios. We illustrated how recently developed structural vector autoregressive models of the global oil market not only generate quite accurate out-of-sample forecasts, but may be used to generate projections of how the oil price forecast would deviate from the unconditional baseline forecast, conditional on alternative economic scenarios such as a surge in speculative demand similar to previous historical episodes, a resurgence of the global business cycle, or increased U.S. oil production. The proposed method allows users to assess the risks associated with reduced-form oil price forecasts.

Finally, we showed that oil price volatility measures commonly used to characterize predictive densities for the price of oil are not adequate measures of the risks faced by market participants. We demonstrated how appropriate risk measures can be constructed. Those risk measures, however, are only as good as the underlying forecasting models. Although the best forecasting models are substantially more accurate at short horizons than the no-change forecast of the price of oil, it is fair to say that even the best available forecasting methods are far from accurate and substantial uncertainty remains about the evolution of the price of oil in nominal and in real terms.

ACKNOWLEDGMENTS

We thank Christiane Baumeister for providing access to the global industrial production data. We thank Domenico Giannone for providing the code generating the Bayesian VAR forecasts. We have benefited from discussions with Christiane Baumeister, Mike McCracken, James Hamilton, Ana María Herrera, Ryan Kellogg, Simone Manganelli, and Keith Sill, as well as comments from two anonymous referees and the editors. We thank David Finer and William Wu for assisting us in collecting some of the data. The views in this paper are solely the responsibility of the authors and should not be interpreted as reflecting the views of the Board of Governors of the Federal Reserve System or of the Bank of Canada or of any other person associated with the Federal Reserve System or with the Bank of Canada.

REFERENCES

Allcott, H., Wozny N., 2011. Gasoline Prices, Fuel Economy, and the Energy Paradox. Mimeo, MIT.
Almoguera, P.A., Douglas, C., Herrera, A.M., 2011. Testing for the cartel in OPEC: noncooperative collusion or just noncooperative? Oxford Review of Economic Policy 27, 144–168.
Alquist, R., Kilian, L., 2010. What do we learn from the price of crude oil futures? Journal of Applied Econometrics 25, 539–573.
Anatolyev, S., 2012. Inference in regression models with many regressors. Journal of Econometrics 170, 368–382.
Anderson, S., Kellogg, R., Sallee, J., 2011. What Do Consumers Believe About the Price of Gasoline? Mimeo, Department of Economics, University of Michigan.
Artzner, P., Delbaen, F., Eber, J.-M., Heath, D., 1999. Coherent measures of risk. Mathematical Finance 9, 203–228.

Bachmeier, L., Li, Q., Liu, D., 2008. Should oil prices receive so much attention? An evaluation of the predictive power of oil prices for the US economy. Economic Inquiry 46, 528–539.

Balke, N.S., Brown, S.P.A., Yücel, M.K., 2002. Oil price shocks and the US economy: where does the asymmetry originate? Energy Journal 23, 27–52.

Barsky, R.B., Kilian, L., 2002. Do we really know that oil caused the great stagflation? A monetary alternative. In: Bernanke, B.S., Rogoff, K. (Eds.), NBER Macroeconomics Annual 2001. MIT Press, Cambridge, MA, pp. 137–183.

Basak, S., Shapiro, A., 2001. Value-at-risk based management: optimal policies and asset prices. Review of Financial Studies 14, 371–405.

Baumeister, C., Kilian, L., 2012a. Real-time forecasts of the real price of oil. Journal of Business and Economic Statistics 30, 326–336.

Baumeister, C., Kilian, L., 2012b. Real-Time Analysis of Oil Price Risks using Forecast Scenarios. Mimeo, Department of Economics, University of Michigan.

Baumeister, C., Peersman, G., 2012. The role of time-varying price elasticities in accounting for volatility changes in the crude oil market. Journal of Applied Econometrics.

Bernanke, B.S., 1983. Irreversibility, uncertainty, and cyclical investment. Quarterly Journal of Economics 98, 85–106.

Bernanke, B.S, 2004. Oil and the Economy. Speech presented at Darton College, Albany, GA. <http://www.federalreserve.gov/boarddocs/speeches/2004/20041021/default.htm>.

Beyer, A., Doornik, J.A., Hendry, D.F., 2001. Constructing historical euro-zone data. Economic Journal 111, 308–327.

Bollerslev, T., Chou, R.Y., Kroner, K.F., 1992. ARCH modeling in finance. Journal of Econometrics 52, 5–59.

Busse, M., Knittel, C., Zettelmeyer, F., 2011. Pain at the Pump: How Gasoline Prices Affect Automobile Purchasing. Mimeo, Northwestern University.

Calhoun, G., 2011a. Hypothesis testing in linear regression when k/n is large. Journal of Econometrics 165, 163–174.

Calhoun, G., 2011b. Out of Sample Comparisons of Overfit Models. Mimeo, Department of Economics, Iowa State University.

Carlton, A.B., 2010. Oil Prices and Real-Time Output Growth. Mimeo, Department of Economics, University of Houston.

Chen, Y.-C., Rogoff, K., Rossi, B., 2010. Can exchange rates forecast commodity prices? Quarterly Journal of Economics 125, 1145–1194.

Clark, T.E., McCracken, M., 2001. Tests of equal predictive accuracy and encompassing for nested models. Journal of Econometrics 105, 85–101.

Clark, T.E., McCracken, M., 2005a. Evaluating direct multistep forecasts. Econometric Reviews 24, 369–404.

Clark, T.E., McCracken, M., 2005b. The power of tests of predictive ability in the presence of structural breaks. Journal of Econometrics 124, 1–31.

Clark, T.E., McCracken, M., 2010. Nested Forecast Model Comparisons: A New Approach to Testing Equal Accuracy. Mimeo, Federal Reserve Bank of St. Louis.

Clark, T.E., West, K.D., 2007. Approximately normal tests for equal predictive accuracy in nested models. Journal of Econometrics 138, 291–311.

Cooley, T.F., LeRoy, S., 1985. Atheoretical macroeconometrics: a critique. Journal of Monetary Economics 16, 283–308.

Corradi, V., Swanson, N.R., 2002. A consistent test for nonlinear out of sample predictive accuracy. Journal of Econometrics 110, 353–381.

Corradi, V., Swanson, N.R., 2007. Nonparametric bootstrap procedures for predictive inference based on recursive estimation schemes. International Economic Review 48, 67–109.

Dargay, J.M., Gately, D., 2010. World oil demand's shift toward faster growing and less price-responsive products and regions. Energy Policy 38, 6261–6277.

Davis, L.W., Kilian, L., 2011. The allocative cost of price ceilings in the US residential market for natural gas. Journal of Political Economy 119, 212–241.

Diebold, F.X., Mariano, R.S., 1995. Comparing predictive accuracy. Journal of Business and Economic Statistics 13, 253–263.

Dolado, J.J., Lütkepohl, H., 1996. Making wald tests work for cointegrated VAR systems. Econometric Reviews 15, 369–386.

Dvir, E., Rogoff, K., 2010. Three Epochs of Oil. Mimeo, Harvard University.

Edelstein, P., Kilian, L., 2009. How sensitive are consumer expenditures to retail energy prices? Journal of Monetary Economics 56, 766–779.

Elder, J., Serletis, A., 2010. Oil price uncertainty. Journal of Money, Credit and Banking 42, 1138–1159.

Elliott, G., Timmermann, A., 2008. Economic forecasting. Journal of Economic Literature 46, 3–56.

Engle, R.F., Brownlees, C.T., 2010. Volatility, Correlation and Tails for Systemic Risk Measurement. Stern School of Business. Mimeo, New York University.

Farrell, A.E., Brandt, A.R., 2006. Risks of the oil transition. Environmental Research Letters 1, 1–6.

Fishburn, P.C., 1977. Mean-risk analysis with risk associated with below-target returns. American Economic Review 67, 116–26.

Giannone, D., Lenza, M., Primiceri, G., 2010. Prior Selection for Vector Autoregressions. Department of Economics. Mimeo, Free University of Brussels.

Gillman, M., Nakov, A., 2009. Monetary effects on nominal oil prices. North American Journal of Economics and Finance 20, 239–254.

Goldberg, P., 1998. The Effects of the corporate average fuel economy standards in the US. Journal of Industrial Economics 46, 1–33.

Gramlich, E.M., 2004. Oil Shocks and Monetary Policy. Annual Economic Luncheon, Federal Reserve Bank of Kansas City, Kansas City, Missouri.

Green, E.J., Porter, R.H., 1984. Noncooperative collusion under imperfect price information. Econometrica 52, 87–100.

Greenspan, A., 2004a. Energy Remarks by Chairman Alan Greenspan Before the Center for Strategic and International Studies. Washington, DC. <http://www.federalreserve.gov/boarddocs/speeches/2004/20040427/default.htm>.

Greenspan, A., 2004b. Oil, Speech presented at the National Italian American Foundation. Washington, DC. <htttp://www.federalreserve.gov/boarddocs/speeches/2004/200410152/default.htm>.

Hamilton, J.D., 1983. Oil and the macroeconomy since world war II. Journal of Political Economy 91, 228–248.

Hamilton, J.D., 1985. Historical causes of postwar oil shocks and recessions. Energy Journal 6, 97–116.

Hamilton, J.D., 1994. Time Series Analysis. Princeton University Press, Princeton, NJ.

Hamilton, J.D., 1996. This is what happened to the Oil Price–Macroeconomy Relationship. Journal of Monetary Economics 38, 215–220.

Hamilton, J.D., 2003. What is an oil shock? Journal of Econometrics 113, 363–398.

Hamilton, J.D., 2009. Causes and consequences of the oil shock of 2007–08. Brookings Papers on Economic Activity, vol. 1. Springer, pp. 215–261.

Hamilton, J.D., 2011. Nonlinearities and the macroeconomic effects of oil prices. Macroeconomic Dynamics 15, 364–378.

Hamilton, J.D., Herrera, A.M., 2004. Oil shocks and aggregate economic behavior: the role of monetary policy. Journal of Money, Credit and Banking 36, 265–286.

Hendry, D., 2006. Robustifying forecasts from equilibrium-correction systems. Journal of Econometrics 135, 399–426.

Herrera, A.M., Lagalo, L.G., Wada, T., 2011. Oil price shocks and industrial production: is the relationship linear? Macroeconomic Dynamics 15, 472–497.

Holthausen, D.M., 1981. A risk-return model with risk and return measured in deviations from target return. American Economic Review 71, 182–88.

Hotelling, H., 1931. The economics of exhaustible resources. Journal of Political Economy 39, 137–175.

Inoue, A., Kilian, L., 2004a. In-sample or out-of-sample tests of predictability: which one should we use? Econometric Reviews 23, 371–402.

Inoue, A., Kilian, L., 2004b. Bagging Time Series Models. CEPR Discussion Paper No. 4333.

Inoue, A., Kilian, L., 2006. On the selection of forecasting models. Journal of Econometrics 130, 273–306.

International Monetary Fund, 2005. World Economic Outlook. Washington, DC.

International Monetary Fund, 2007. World Economic Outlook. Washington, DC.

Isserlis, L., 1938. Tramp shipping cargoes and freights. Journal of the Royal Statistical Society 101 (1), 53–134.

Kahn, J.A., 1986. Gasoline prices and the used automobile market: a rational expectations asset price approach. Quarterly Journal of Economics 101, 323–340.

Kellogg, R., 2010. The Effect of Uncertainty on Investment: Evidence from Texas Oil Drilling. Mimeo, Department of Economics, University of Michigan.

Kilian, L., 1999. Exchange rates and monetary fundamentals: what do we learn from long-horizon regressions? Journal of Applied Econometrics 14, 491–510.

Kilian, L., 2008a. The economic effects of energy price shocks. Journal of Economic Literature 46 (4), 871–909.

Kilian, L., 2008b. Exogenous oil supply shocks: how big are they and how much do they matter for the US economy? Review of Economics and Statistics 90, 216–240.

Kilian, L., 2009a. Not all oil price shocks are alike: disentangling demand and supply shocks in the crude oil market. American Economic Review 99, 1053–1069.

Kilian, L., 2009b. In: James, D., Hamilton (Eds.), Comment on Causes and Consequences of the Oil Shock of 2007–08. Brookings Papers on Economic Activity, vol. 1. Springer, pp. 267–278.

Kilian, L., 2010. Explaining fluctuations in US gasoline prices: a joint model of the global crude oil market and the US retail gasoline market. Energy Journal 31, 87–104.

Knetsch, T.A., 2007. Forecasting the price of oil via convenience yield predictions. Journal of Forecasting 26, 527–549.

Kilian, L., Hicks, B., forthcoming. Did unexpectedly strong economic growth cause the oil price shock of 2003–2008? Journal of Forecasting.

Kilian, L., Manganelli, S., 2007. Quantifying the risk of deflation. Journal of Money, Credit and Banking 39, 561–590.

Kilian, L., Manganelli, S., 2008. The central banker as a risk manager: estimating the federal reserve's preferences under greenspan. Journal of Money, Credit and Banking 40, 1103–1129.

Kilian, L., Murphy, D., 2013. The Role of Inventories and Speculative Trading in the Global Market for Crude Oil. Mimeo, University of Michigan.

Kilian, L., Rebucci, A., Spatafora, N., 2009. Oil shocks and external balances. Journal of International Economics 77, 181–194.

Kilian, L., Vega, C., 2010. Do energy prices respond to US macroeconomic news? A test of the hypothesis of predetermined energy prices. Review of Economics and Statistics 93, 660–671.

Kilian, L., Vigfusson, R.J., 2011a. Are the responses of the US economy asymmetric in energy price increases and decreases? Quantitative Economics 2, 419–453.

Kilian, L., Vigfusson, R.J., 2011b. Nonlinearities in the oil price-output relationship. Macroeconomic Dynamics 15, 337–363.

Kilian, L., Vigfusson, R.J., 2013. Do oil price increases help forecast US real GDP? The role of nonlinearities and asymmetries. Journal of Business and Economic Statistics 31, 78–93.

Koop, G., Pesaran, M.H., Potter, S.M., 1996. Impulse response analysis in nonlinear multivariate models. Journal of Econometrics 74, 119–147.

Leamer, E.E., 1978. Specification Searches: Ad hoc Inference with Nonexperimental Data. Wiley-Interscience, New York.

Lütkepohl, H., 1982. Non-causality due to omitted variables. Journal of Econometrics 19, 367–378.

Machina, M.J., Rothschild, M., 1987. Risk. In: Eatwell, J., Millgate, M., Newman, P. (Eds.), The New Palgrave Dictionary of Economics. MacMillan, London, pp. 203–205.

Marcellino, M., Stock, J.H., Watson, M.W., 2006. A comparison of direct and iterated multistep AR methods for forecasting macroeconomic time series. Journal of Econometrics 135, 499–526.

Mork, K.A., 1989. Oil and the macroeconomy. When prices go up and down: an extension of Hamilton's results. Journal of Political Economy 97, 740–744.

Peck, A.E., 1985. Economic role of traditional commodity futures markets. In: Peck, A.E. (Ed.), Futures Markets: Their Economic Role. American Enterprise Institute for Public Policy Research, Washington, DC, pp. 1–81.

Pesaran, M.H., Timmermann, A., 2009. Testing dependence among serially correlated multicategory variables. Journal of the American Statistical Association 104, 325–337.

Pindyck, R.S., 1991. Irreversibility, uncertainty and investment. Journal of Economic Literature 29, 1110–1148.

Ramey, V.A., Vine, D.J., 2010. Oil, Automobiles, and the US economy: how much have things really changed. NBER Macroeconomics Annual 25, 333–368.

Ravazzolo, F., Rothman, P., 2013. Oil and US GDP: a real time out-of-sample examination. Journal of Money, Credit and Banking 45, 449–463.

Ravn, M.O., Uhlig, H., 2002. On adjusting the Hodrick-Prescott filter for the frequency of observations. Review of Economics and Statistics 84, 371–380.

Sims, C.A., Stock, J.H., Watson, M.W., 1990. Inference in linear time series models with some unit roots. Econometrica 58, 113–144.

Skeet, I., 1988. OPEC: Twenty-Five Years of Prices and Politics. Cambridge University Press, Cambridge.

Smith, J.L., 2005. Inscrutable OPEC? Behavioral tests of the cartel hypothesis, Energy Journal 26, 51–82.

Stock, J.H., Watson, M.W., 1999. Forecasting inflation. Journal of Monetary Economics 44, 293–335.

Svensson, L.E.O., 2005. Oil Prices and ECB Monetary Policy. Briefing Paper for the Committee on Economic and Monetary Affairs of the European Parliament.

Tinbergen, J., 1959. Tonnage and freight. In: Jan Tinbergen Selected Papers. North Holland, Amsterdam, pp. 93–111.

Verleger, Jr., P.K., 1982. The determinants of official OPEC crude prices. Review of Economics and Statistics 64, 177–183.

Verleger, Jr., P.K., 2011. The margin, currency, and the price of oil. Business Economics 46, 71–82.

Waggoner, D.F., Zha, T., 1999. Conditional forecasts in dynamic multivariate models. Review of Economics and Statistics 81, 639–651.

Working, H., 1942. Quotations on commodity futures as price forecasts. Econometrica 16, 39–52.

Wu, T., McCallum, A., 2005. Do Oil Futures Prices Help Predict Future Oil Prices? Federal Reserve Bank of San Francisco Economic Letter, pp. 2005–38.

Zagaglia, P., 2010. Macroeconomic factors and oil futures prices: a data-rich model. Energy Economics 32, 409–417.

CHAPTER *9*

Forecasting Real Estate Prices

Eric Ghysels[*], Alberto Plazzi[†], Rossen Valkanov[‡], and Walter Torous[**]

[*]UNC, Department of Economics and Kenan-Flagler Business School, Gardner Hall, Chapel Hill, NC 27599-3305, USA
[†]University of Lugano and Swiss Finance Institute, Institute of Finance, Via Buffi 13, Lugano 6904, Switzerland
[‡]Rady School of Management, UCSD, Pepper Canyon Hall, 9500 Gilman Drive, La Jolla, CA 92093, USA
[**]The Center for Real Estate, Massachusetts Institute of Technology, Cambridge, MA, 02139.

Contents

Abstract

This chapter reviews the evidence of predictability in U.S. residential and commercial real estate markets. First, we highlight the main methodologies used in the construction of real estate indices, their underlying assumptions and their impact on the stochastic properties of the resultant series. We then survey the key empirical findings in the academic literature, including short-run persistence and long-run reversals in the log changes of real estate prices. Next, we summarize the ability of local as well as aggregate variables to forecast real estate returns. We illustrate a number of these results by relying on six aggregate indexes of the prices of unsecuritized (residential and commercial) real estate and REITs. The effect of leverage and monetary policy is also discussed.

Keywords

Real estate, Predictability, Market efficiency, REIT

1. INTRODUCTION

The importance of real estate as an asset class cannot be overstated. Its total value in the U.S. at the end of 2011 was about $25 trillion, of which more than $16 trillion was in residential properties.[1] By comparison, at the end of the same year, the capitalization of the U.S. stock market was in the neighborhood of $18 trillion. Moreover, recent history suggests that fluctuations in real estate prices, whether in bubble or burst mode, have the potential to buoy up or wreak havoc on the financial sector and the rest of the economy. Some of that impact is due to leverage and the fact that real estate is the easiest asset to borrow against, especially from a household's perspective. Indeed, in 2011, about $12 trillion of outstanding mortgage debt had been issued against the value of residential real estate.[2] But the connection between real estate and the macroeconomy is not a bubbles-only phenomenon. Case et al. (2005) show that variations in real estate prices have had a significant effect on aggregate consumption in the U.S., in fact more significant than the stock market, even before the recent volatility in the residential market. Reinhart and Rogoff (2009) document this to be the case more universally across a number of countries and over longer time periods. From an economic perspective, understanding what drives real estate values is no less important than is understanding the pricing dynamics of other asset classes, such as stocks, bonds, commodities, and currencies.

The real estate market is different from other financial markets in several important aspects. It is characterized by extreme heterogeneity due to the location and physical attributes of a property. Participants in that market face large transaction costs, carrying costs, illiquidity, and tax considerations. They also face large search costs stemming from real estate's heterogeneity. Investors have just limited possibility of exploiting forecast decreases in property values, because of the impossibility to short sale a specific asset and the absence of liquid real estate futures contracts.[3] These large frictions suggest that the real estate market might generally not be efficient in the sense that other financial markets

---

[1] The source is the Flow of Funds Accounts. This estimate obtains summing the value of Households real estate (Table B.100, line 4) with that of Non-financial Corporate Business (Table B.102, line 3).

[2] The source is the Flow of Funds Accounts, Total Mortgages (Table L.217), obtained as the sum of Home and Multifamily residential.

[3] There are some recently launched indexes that track the performance of residential and commercial mortgage backed securities. These indices allow investors to take short positions in assets that are undoubtedly correlated with the aggregate real estate portfolio. Shorting the construction sector of the economy is another indirect way of shorting real estate.

are (e.g., Fama, 1970). But before we can talk about market efficiency, which implies that some investors are able to take advantage of profit opportunities, we first must investigate whether price changes are in fact statistically predictable.

The presence of frictions does not imply that predicting real estate returns is an easy task. In practice, the opposite is true. An illustration of this fact can be gleaned from the transcripts of the Federal Open Market Committee's (FOMC) 2006 discussions, which were held at the peak of the recent housing bubble. This was a time when a growing consensus amongst economists that residential prices were inflated coincided with a growing uncertainty about their future direction. The transcripts reveal that most FOMC participants shared the opinion that we were in for a "a soft landing or a period of stabilization after several years of strong price appreciation."[4] Now, with the benefit of a hindsight and the Great Recession behind us, we know that this prediction was considerably off the mark. Long-horizon forecasts can be equally challenging to make. One such forecast was formulated by Mankiw and Weil (1989), who argued that the rise of housing prices in the 1970s and 1980s was mostly due to the Baby Boom generation entering the residential market. Based on these findings and reasoning that future demand for housing will decrease over the next 20 years, the authors predicted that "real housing prices will fall substantially – indeed, real housing prices may well reach levels lower than those experienced at any time in the past 40 years." Now, 20 or more years after Mankiw and Weil (1989) formulated this forecast, we have observed that the trends and volatility in the housing market were driven by factors other than demographic fundamentals.

In this chapter, we review the literature on return predictability in real estate markets. Many of the papers on this topic involve the use of indices at the city, regional, or national level rather than individual property prices. This is due to one obvious reason: real estate transactions are very infrequent. Hence, as a starting point, we discuss the construction and underlying assumptions behind some of the most widely used residential and commercial real estate indices. The distinction between residential and commercial properties is important as they tend to have different dynamics and return properties (Geltner and Miller, 2006). The difference is not surprising as a household's decision to purchase a home – presumably driven not only by investment considerations but also by the need to consume a housing unit – is quite different from that of an investor looking to purchase a retail property (Flavin and Yamashita, 2002). Perhaps the most transparent residential index is the median sales price, versions of which are provided by the Census Bureau and the National Association of Realtors (NAR). While it is easy to construct and interpret, it does not adjust for the quality of properties that are on the market and thus confounds fluctuations in prices with fluctuations in real estate attributes. The fact that it is not a "constant quality" index makes it less desirable than some of the alternatives, which specifically adjust for property attributes. Examples of constant-quality indices include, for

---

[4] Excerpts from the transcript of the Meeting of the Federal Open Market Committee, May 10, 2006, available at http://www.federalreserve.gov/monetarypolicy/files/FOMC20060510meeting.pdf.

residential properties, the Case–Shiller and the Federal Housing Finance Agency (FHFA) repeat-sales prices and, for commercial properties, the National Council of Real Estate Investment Fiduciaries's Transaction-Based (TBI) hedonic prices. We discuss these and other indices in some detail in Section 2, because their statistical properties are determined as much by assumptions behind their construction as by market forces. Understandably, much creative energy and papers have been devoted to this topic. Without reliable indices, empirical research in real estate is virtually impossible.

To get a glimpse into the aggregate real estate data, in Figures 9.1 and 9.2 we plot three residential and three commercial indices that have been widely used in the literature and whose properties we will analyze in this chapter. It is immediately clear that the three time series in Figure 9.1 do not exhibit the same dynamics despite the fact that they are all intended to measure the same price appreciation of houses in the U.S. For instance, the growth rate (not the level) of the Case–Shiller index has a serial correlation of 0.939. Some of that serial correlation is due to the way the index is constructed and some of it is undoubtedly due to economic frictions. The same statistic for the growth rate of the Census median price is −0.517. Similarly dramatic differences are evident in Figure 9.2, where the price of a real estate investment trusts (REIT) portfolio exhibits volatility that dwarfs that of the other two indices. Before we can use these time series, we have to understand how they are constructed, what they measure, and whether they are suitable

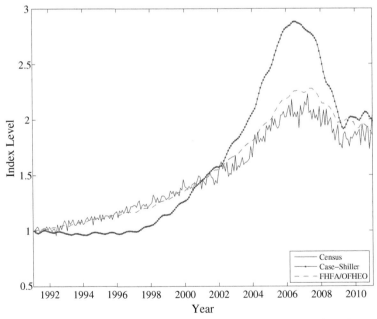

Figure 9.1 Residential Real Estate Indices. Time series plot of the Census Median, Case–Shiller Composite 10, and OFHEO. All series are are sampled quarterly and normalized at one in 1991:Q1.

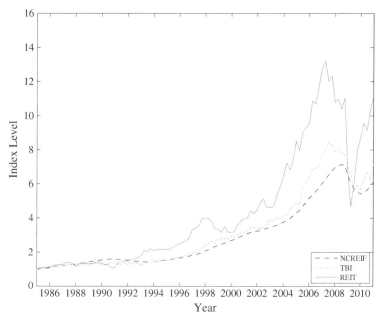

Figure 9.2 Commercial Real Estate Indices. Time series plot of the NCREIF All, TBI All, and CRSP/Ziman REIT All indices. All series are sampled quarterly and normalized at one in 1984:Q4.

for forecasting. In Section 2.1, we discuss the various types of real estate indices, provide details behind their constructions and, in Section 2.2, we present their summary statistics.

Predictive regressions in the real estate literature in many respects mirror those in other asset classes. The forecasted quantity, often future price changes or returns, is regressed on a set of predetermined variables, which are chosen to test a set of economic hypotheses. The presence of return forecastability is interpreted either as evidence of market inefficiencies (Fama, 1970) or of time-varying risk premia in otherwise efficient markets. However, predictive regressions are inherently reduced-form expressions and cannot identify the economic reasons underlying the forecastability without further modeling restrictions (Fama and French, 1988a).

It is useful to divide predictive regressions into three categories based on the predictors and maintained hypotheses. First, if the predictor is lagged returns as in Gau (1984, 1985), Linneman (1986), Guntermann and Smith (1987), Rayburn et al. (1987), Case and Shiller (1989), McIntosh and Henderson (1989), Gyourko and Voith (1992), Kuo (1996), Hill et al. (1997, 1999), Gu (2002), and Schindler (2011), this is a test of weak-form market efficiency. However, simple serial dependence tests in real estate are complicated by the fact that the price changes of some indices are serially correlated by construction, making it difficult to disentangle spurious correlations from actual market inefficiencies. The evidence of weak-form market efficiency is presented in Section 3.1.

Second, valuation ratios – such as the rent–price ratio or price–income ratio – are often used as predictors (e.g., Hamilton and Schwab, 1985; Meese and Wallace, 1994; Geltner and Mei, 1995; Capozza and Seguin, 1996; Lamont and Stein, 1999; Malpezzi, 1999; Himmelberg et al., 2005; Campbell et al., 2009; Gallin, 2008). We review predictive regression with valuation ratios in Section 3.2. Such regressions are motivated either by the valuation ratios' ability to detect deviations and slow adjustments toward an equilibrium or because they proxy for time variation in expected returns. Overall, the evidence supports the view that valuation ratios are not able to capture all the variation in the conditioning set.

Third, a richer set of hypotheses can be tested by including property- and/or region-specific economic variables, whose aim is to proxy for demand and supply shocks in the real estate market. Such predictors, used, amongst others, by Rosen (1984), Linneman (1986), Skantz and Strickland (1987), Case and Shiller (1990), Abraham and Hendershott (1996), Pace et al. (2000), MacKinnon and Zaman (2009), and Plazzi et al. (2010), include demographic variables, income variables, construction costs, and zoning restrictions. One can argue that these regressions account more fully for the heterogeneity in real estate investments. The evidence from these regressions is reviewed in Section 3.3.

Real estate data present some unique challenges in forecasting settings. First, the predictive results have to take into account high transaction costs, which in real estate can be 6%, or even higher, of the property value. In addition to the statistical significance, the coefficient estimate must be large enough to cover those costs. Second, the available real estate data is relatively short in its duration and is observed at a monthly or quarterly frequency.[5] Sparse datasets are available from the 1970s, but most empirical work is done with series starting from the 1980s or later. The lack of longer and higher-frequency data renders estimation and hypothesis testing difficult. Third, the in-sample fit of predictive regressions is often traced to dichotomous variables for geographical location, coastal proximity, or whether a commercial property is of a certain type (apartments, retail space, offices, or industrial buildings). While these fixed-effects are important in accounting for the heterogeneity of the asset, they are not predictors in the usual sense of the word. They do not change over time and cannot be the source of time series predictability. Fourth, the predictability evidence is mainly based on in-sample statistics. It is rarely evaluated with mean squared prediction errors (MSPE) or other out-of-sample analysis (West, 2006), mainly because of the severe data limitations. Finally, and related to the previous point, parameter stability and the robustness of the forecasting model are rarely investigated (e.g., Rossi, 2013).

A real-estate-related market that does not suffer from the high transaction costs and infrequent observations issues is that of publicly-traded real estate investment trusts. REITs are exchange-traded funds that derive most of their income from real estate

---

[5] A notable exception is Eichholtz (1997), whose bi-annual residential index of Amsterdam properties spans the period 1628–1973.

investments and whose returns provide a remarkably clean venue for testing whether or not real estate returns are forecastable. The REIT market has been given particular attention in the real estate literature and we are also devoting special attention to it in Section 4. The focus on REITs is attributable to the fact that their returns have less measurement error and are observable at higher frequency than other real estate investments. Hence, econometric issues arising in the estimation and forecasting of returns can largely be addressed.[6] However, empirical work with REITs does have its limitations. For instance, investing in a REIT is not the same as investing in the underlying commercial property market. The risk-return characteristics of the investments might be different. Ross and Zisler (1991) document that REITs have the risk-return profile of small-cap stocks and co-move more with the stock market rather than the underlying real estate market.

We supplement the summary of existing findings with our own set of predictive regressions estimated with three residential and three commercial real estate indices at the national (U.S.) level with monthly and quarterly data from 1991 to the end of 2010. We choose to work mainly with aggregate indices as they are available over a long time span and allow us to keep a common set of predictors. Some cross-sectional results are provided using metropolitan level data for residential properties. Following the literature, we run various specifications of the predictive regressions. For all non-REIT indices, the data restrict us to stay with in-sample comparisons. However, with REITs, we are able to estimate a more complete (and interesting) predictive system, to adjust the estimates for known small-sample biases, to impose relevant economic restrictions, to look for predictability at various horizons, and out-of-sample. These results are discussed in Sections 3 and 4.

The data and empirical methods that we survey are remarkably diverse. As a way of providing a bird's eye view of this body of work, in Table 9.1 we summarize most of the covered papers along with the main findings pertaining to returns forecastability. The papers differ not only in their econometric approach, but also in the type of properties they investigate (residential, commercial, REITs), the geographical coverage of the data, the time span, and the conditioning variables. Despite all these differences, a common set of findings emerges from this literature, most of which we are able to observe in our aggregate predictive regressions. These stylized facts can be summarized as follows:

- Price changes of repeat-sales and hedonic indices are very positively serially correlated at monthly and quarterly frequency, whereas median price indices exhibit negative serial correlation. The serial correlation of REIT returns is similar to that of small-cap stocks.
- Transaction costs and other frictions are too large for the serial correlation to translate into economic gains for the non-REIT and REIT data.

---

[6] These issues stem from the fact that the predictor is often a near-integrated process whose innovations are correlated with the innovations of returns (Cavanagh et al., 1995; Stambaugh, 1999).

Table 9.1 Summary of Literature

Papers	Conditioning Variables	Predictability Evidence
	Real Estate (Residential and Commercial)	
Gau (1984, 1985; Vancouver, 1971–1980); Linneman (1986; Philadelphia, 1975–1978); Guntermann and Smith (1987; 57 MSAs, 1968–1982); Rayburn et al. (1987; Memphis, 1970–1984)	Lagged returns/abnormal returns	Y/N (insufficient to cover transaction costs)
Case and Shiller (1989; 4 cities, 1970–1986); Hill et al. (1999; CS (1989) data); Kuo (1996, CS (1989) data); Schindler (2011; CS national and 20 MSAs; 1987–2009)	Lagged returns/abnormal returns	Y
Capozza et al. (2004; U.S. metropolitan areas, 1979–1995)	Geographic, demographic, and economic variables	Y/N (income, population growth, and construction costs are important factors)
Gyourko and Voith (1992; aggregate indices, 1971–1989); Glaeser et al. (2008; aggregate indices, 1982–2007)	Long-term mean reversion in prices	Y/N (less mean reversion in markets with more elastic housing supply)
Gu (2002; U.S. indices, 1975–1999); Crawford and Fratantoni (2003; U.S. indices, 1979–2001)	Lagged returns/regime switching	Y/N (instability across locations and time periods)
McIntosh and Henderson (1989; Dallas-Forth Worth; 1979–1985)	Lagged returns	N

(Continued)

Table 9.1 Continued

Papers	Conditioning Variables	Predictability Evidence
	Real Estate (Residential and Commercial)	
Capozza and Seguin (1996; U.S. indices, 1960–1990), Meese and Wallace (1994; county data, 1970–1988)	Rent–price	Y
Campbell et al. (2009; U.S. indices, 1975–2007), Gallin (2008; U.S. index, 1970–2005)		
Geltner and Mei (1995; U.S. indices, 1975–1992)		
Ghysels et al. (2007, 21 MSAs, 1985–2000), Plazzi et al. (2010; 53 MSAs, 1994–2001)	Rent–price, geographic, demographic, and economic variables	
Favilukis et al. (2013; U.S., 1991–2010); Mian and Sufi (2009; U.S., 2002–2009)	Rent–price, credit supply	Y
Lamont and Stein (1999; U.S. metropolitan areas, 1984–1994)	Loan-to-value	Y
Malpezzi (1999; U.S. metropolitan areas, 1979–1996)	price-to-income	Y
Abraham and Hendershott (1996; U.S. indices, 1977–1992)	Geographic, demographic, and economic variables	Y/N (mostly pronounced in areas with more elastic housing supply)
Zhong-Guo (1997; U.S. indices, 1970–1994)	sales volume	Y
MacKinnon and Zaman (2009; U.S. index, 1984–2007)	REIT returns, bond returns, rent–price	Y/N

(Continued)

Table 9.1 *Continued*

Papers	Conditioning Variables	Predictability Evidence
	REITs	
Liu and Mei (1992, 1994; U.S., 1972–1989);	Dividend-price ratio and other macro variables	Y
Mei and Gao (1995; U.S., 1962–1990); Nelling and Gyourko (1998; U.S., 1975–1995);	Returns	Y/N (insufficient to cover transaction costs)
Cooper et al. (1999; U.S., 1973–1995); Serrano and Hoesli (2010; 10 countries, 1990–2007);	Returns	Y
Stevenson (2002; 11 countries, 1977–2000); Graff and Young (1997; U.S., 1987–1996) Serrano and Hoesli (2007; U.S., 1978–2006)	Returns to other asset classes	Y

Notes: The table summarizes many of the papers that document predictability in real estate returns (residential, commercial, and REITs). In the first column, in parenthesis after the year of the paper, we report the market for which the analysis is conducted followed by the sample period. The conditioning variables used in each group of papers are listed in the middle column. The last column reports whether the results support strong (Y), weak (N), or mixed (Y/N) evidence of return predictability.

- Valuation ratios, such as the rent–price ratio or the income-price ratio, have some predictive power, in-sample. It is mostly attributable to time varying expected returns rather than to exploitable market inefficiencies.
- Variables, such as construction costs, demographic changes, and regulatory restrictions, have a sizeable impact on future real estate returns. However, the out-of-sample properties of these forecasts are largely unexplored.
- For REITs, there is weak in-sample evidence of return predictability and stronger evidence for rent-growth predictability. The evidence for out-of-sample predictability is not strong.
- Leverage is positively related to future returns.

We should point out that several of these results obtain in pooled regressions with more cross-sectional than time series observations. Hence, their "predictive" nature should be taken with some caution. This is a general theme in real estate research, as the lack of good time series data prevents us from applying the standard forecasting toolbox. For instance, it precludes the use of what some might consider to be the ultimate forecast evaluation tool: out-of-sample predictive measures, such as the MSPE comparison. The MSPE analysis is mostly asymptotic in nature and, as West (2006) points out, is not useful for studies with only a handful of observations for out-of-sample evaluation. However, the lack of a long time series data also raises a host of new interesting questions, such as how to use the richness of the cross-section in formulating and evaluating forecasts.

There is also a growing literature investigating the portfolio implications of investing in housing, as in Ross and Zisler (1991), Goetzmann (1993), Flavin and Yamashita (2002), and Cauley et al. (2007). Recent papers by Lustig and Van Nieuwerburgh (2005), Campbell and Cocco (2007), and Piazzesi et al. (2007) investigate the connection between housing, consumption, and asset pricing. Becker and Shabani (2010) examine the implications of large household debt (a mortgage) on investment decisions. As a next step, it would be interesting to incorporate predictable real estate returns in the optimal investment decision of households. The portfolio setting would provide a natural measure of the economic importance of real estate return predictability in absolute terms and relative to the predictability of stock and bond returns. A first step in that direction is the work of MacKinnon and Zaman (2009) and Plazzi et al. (2010).

Following the recent real estate crisis, two research areas have generated considerable interest. First, there has been renewed attention on the role of leverage on house price dynamics. Theoretical work by Stein (1995), McDonald (1999), Spiegel (2001), and Ortalo-Magn'e and Rady (2006) and the empirical findings of Linneman and Wachter (1989), Genesove and Mayer (1997), Lamont and Stein (1999), Brown (2000), Aoki et al. (2004), and Favilukis et al. (2011) suggest that leveraged properties are more sensitive to economic shocks. The main amplifying channel in those papers is due to the fact that a household's ability to borrow is directly tied to asset values. While not all of the papers we discuss in that section contain direct evidence of real estate predictability, they all suggest that leverage is an important determinant of house price dynamics. On a related topic, Mian and Sufi (2009, 2011) and Favilukis et al. (2013) analyze the effect of the recent credit expansion on real estate prices. We review this literature in Section 5.1. Second, the recent real estate crisis has focused attention on the effect of monetary policy on real estate prices, which we survey in Section 5.2. Section 6 concludes and offers directions for current and future research.

2. THE REAL ESTATE DATA

In this section, we summarize the availability of U.S. real estate data.[7] The focus is on price indices, which can naturally be categorized, based on the construction methodology, into four groups: median-price indices, repeat-sales indices, hedonic indices, and stock-market-based indices. In each category, the indices can track either residential or commercial properties.[8] In Section 2.1, when introducing the various indices, we pay particular attention to the way they are constructed and the effect of the construction on subsequent forecasting regressions. Section 2.2 presents summary statistics for several well-known indices that will be used in the rest of this chapter.

2.1. Real Estate Index Definitions

2.1.1. Median Price Indices

Median price indices track the price at which the median priced home within a particular area trades in a given period. At present, residential median-price indices are provided for U.S. single-family homes by the Federal Housing Finance Agency, the Census Bureau (new homes),[9] and by the National Association of Realtors (existing homes).[10] They are all available at monthly frequency, but the sample spans vary.

The appeal of median price indices stems from the ease with which they can be computed and their unambiguous interpretation. However, they ignore potentially important changes in the characteristics of the dwellings being sold. In particular, if high-quality and low-quality homes are put on the market at different times, the corresponding median prices may exhibit spurious time series fluctuations due mainly to differences in the quality of the properties. Moreover, it is reasonable to expect the mix of homes sold to be correlated with local economic conditions as more expensive homes will tend to be put on the market in expansionary times. These considerations suggest that a median price index provides not only a noisy but also a systematically biased estimate of the behavior

---

[7] While we try to cover as much ground as possible, the increasing interest in real estate and the lower cost of information acquisition have resulted in an increase of available data sources.

[8] A third useful categorization is to decompose a property value into land and improvements. While we do not analyze land data in our article, aggregate, state-level, and MSA-level price indices for land are provided by the Lincoln Institute following the work of Davis and Heathcote (2007). See http://www.lincolninst.edu/.

[9] See http://www.census.gov/const/www/newressalesindex.html.

[10] See http://www.realtor.org/.

of home prices in a particular market. Because of this, attempts have been made to keep the quality of the median house constant through time when constructing these indices. Corrections also include stratification methods, which adjust for compositional changes in the transactions, as in Prasad and Richards (2008).

By far, the two most popular methods to explicitly control for quality and infrequent trading of real estate properties are repeat-sales regressions and hedonic models, which we review next.

2.1.2. Repeat-Sales Indices

Repeat-sales indices use information about homes that transact at least twice during the sample period to infer market-wide price movements. Let $P_{i,t}$ be the price of home i at the end of period t, and $p_{i,t}$ its logarithmic transformation. The standard repeat-sales approach models $p_{i,t}$ as the sum of two components:

$$p_{i,t} = p_{m,t} + e_{i,t}, \tag{1}$$

where $p_{m,t}$ denotes the aggregate real estate index – an equally-weighted portfolio of properties – and $e_{i,t}$ is a property-specific mean–zero stochastic drift. Shocks to $e_{i,t}$, denoted by $\varepsilon_{i,t} = e_{i,t} - e_{i,t-1}$, are assumed to be i.i.d. both cross-sectionally as well as over time, with finite variance σ_ε^2.

We are interested in obtaining estimates of $p_{m,t}$ using a sample of I individual property transaction prices, but we don't have observations for the same property in each period. Instead, we have information for home i, $i = \{1, \ldots, I\}$, on the date of its initial purchase t_i, the date of its first sale $t_i + T_i$, with $T_i \geq 1$, and the corresponding prices. The subscript i captures the fact that the transaction dates t_i and $t_i + T_i$ are dwelling-specific. Then, following (1), the log return during the $[t_i; t_i + T_i]$ period can be expressed as:

$$p_{i,t_i+T_i} - p_{i,t_i} = p_{m,t_i+T_i} - p_{m,t_i} + \sum_{\tau=t_i+1}^{t_i+T_i} \varepsilon_{i,\tau}. \tag{2}$$

Motivated by this expression, the standard repeat-sales regression (RSR) approach of Bailey et al. (1963) consists of estimating via ordinary least squares the following cross-sectional regression

$$y_i = \beta X_i + u_i, \tag{3}$$

where the dependent variable y_i is the holding period return for home i, or $y_i = p_{i,t_i+T_i} - p_{i,t_i}$. The regressor X_i is a dummy variable that contains values for each time period, except for the first. It equals 1 on the first sale date $t_i + T_i$, -1 on the purchase date t_i, and 0 otherwise. If the purchase period t_i coincides with the first period of the sample, then the purchase date dummy is omitted. If there are a total of $T + 1$ periods, then the $T \times 1$ vector $\widehat{\beta}$ provides an estimate of the log price of the aggregate index, or $\widehat{p}_{m,t} = \widehat{\beta}_t$. The value of the log price in the initial period is normalized to zero.

The OLS estimator of (3) is, however, not efficient. In particular, the variance of the error term $u_i = \sum_{\tau=t_i+1}^{t_i+T_i} \varepsilon_{i,\tau}$ increases linearly with the interval of time between the two transaction dates, or $\sigma_{u_i}^2 = T_i \sigma_\varepsilon^2$. As a result, the OLS estimator overweighs the information on transactions that occur after longer time intervals, ignoring the larger noise embedded in their price changes. In this context, the best linear unbiased estimator (BLUE) is a GLS estimator of (3) where each observation is weighted by the inverse of the square root of its holding period. The resultant error terms are now i.i.d. and the system satisfies the Gauss–Markov conditions. This GLS estimator coincides with the maximum likelihood estimator when we assume normality of the underlying ε_is (Goetzmann, 1992 and references therein).

Case and Shiller (1987) extend model (1) to allow for the presence of noise in individual home prices. Formally, the log price of property i is expressed as

$$p_{i,t} = p_{m,t} + e_{i,t} + n_{i,t}, \tag{4}$$

where $n_{i,t}$ is a normal i.i.d. noise factor with finite variance σ_n^2, which captures imperfections in the housing market. The variance σ_n^2 is constant across properties because it is determined by market-wide conditions. The three components are assumed to be uncorrelated amongst each other at all leads and lags. Iterating Eq. (4) over the transaction period $[t_i; t_i + T_i]$, we obtain that $\sigma_{u_i}^2$ now equals the sum of a fixed component, $2\sigma_n^2$, plus a component, which is linearly increasing in the length of the holding period, $T_i \sigma_\varepsilon^2$. The weighted repeat sales (WRS) method of Case and Shiller (1987) adapts the GLS estimator to account for the presence of this constant term in the variance of the error. Its construction is based on a three-step procedure. In the first step, regression (3) is estimated by OLS and the corresponding residuals $\hat{u}_i$ are stored. The second step consists of a weighted least square regression of these residuals squared on a constant and on the time interval between transactions. The constant term of this regression represents an estimate of $2\sigma_n^2$ whereas the slope is an estimate of σ_ε^2. In the third step, a GLS regression of (3) is run where each observation is weighted by the inverse of the square root of the corresponding fitted value from the second step.

Using this methodology, Case and Shiller (1987) construct real estate price indices for Atlanta, Chicago, Dallas, and San Francisco/Oakland relying on nearly 40,000 pairs of transactions over the 1970–1986 period. Compared to median-based indices, the resultant series do not exhibit marked seasonal patterns and display considerable cross-sectional and time series fluctuations. Further, the weighting implied by the WRS has a substantial effect on the quarter-to-quarter changes in the index compared to the RSR approach. The improvement is largely attributable to the common component in the error variance, σ_n^2, being quite substantial, on the order of 6% to 7%. By looking at the ratio between the standard deviation of the estimated index and the average standard error of the estimates, they also show that their WRS index captures quite precisely the level of aggregate prices and its annual differences. Quarterly differences, on the other hand, are quite noisy and poorly estimated.

A variant of the Case and Shiller (1987) methodology has been proposed by Goetz-mann and Spiegel (1995). They document that including an intercept term in the matrix X of dummy variables helps reduce biases in the estimation. This fixed "non-temporal" component in housing returns most likely relates to property-specific improvements occurring at the time of a sale, which can be as high as 2% to 3% of the investment. Alternative repeat-sales methodologies include shrinkage-type estimators and Bayesian approaches (e.g., Kuo, 1996 and Goetzmann, 1992). Goetzmann (1992) compares the performance of various RSR estimators using simulation on a cross-section of common stocks during a given year. He finds that there seems to be little, if any, advantage to using anything more sophisticated than the GLS estimator when focusing on monthly data and the number of repeat sales observations is large enough relative to the number of intervals estimated.

An appealing feature of the repeat-sales estimator is the fairly limited amount of variables that are required to construct the index, consisting at the very least of prices changes and dates of individual property transactions. Measures of homes characteristics and quality are not directly used in the estimation but may be needed to identify and exclude properties, which have undergone major quality changes – such as renovations, expansions, or re-zoning – between transactions. The estimation procedure is compu-tationally tractable, and standard econometric procedures can be used to construct the relevant statistics.

On the other hand, repeat-sales estimators make use of just a limited number of trans-actions as the information on homes that transacted once is neglected. Also, homes that are sold repeatedly may not be representative of the population as a whole, thus giving rise to a selection bias problem (Clapp and Tirtiroglu, 1991; Gatzlaff and Haurin, 1998; Quigley, 1995; Korteweg and Sorensen, 2011). From a statistical perspective, the estimation may be inaccurate because of the singularity or near-singularity of the matrix X. This will occur when no or very few transactions are available in a given period. The practical solution in such a case is to omit the redundant columns, and to calculate the index over longer time intervals. Single-period returns are then assigned the average return during those periods. The accuracy of the index increases at lower frequencies, but autocorrelation is induced in the higher frequency returns. This issue has no clear solution and tends to be more relevant as we attempt to construct indices in thin markets where the number of properties is large relative to the turnover.

An additional concern is represented by spurious autocorrelation in returns arising from overlapping information. Due to the presence of the house-specific noise compo-nent, the estimates of p_m may exhibit serial correlation in first differences even if house prices truly follow a random walk. The sign of this serial correlation is not clear and depends on the timing of the sales of the homes relied upon, but it tends to be negative over short time intervals.[11] Longer (1-year) returns are instead more precisely estimated and generally display positive autocorrelation. The autocorrelation properties of the index returns are clearly of importance when analyzing predictability, an issue we will return to in Section 3.1.[12] Lastly, the β estimates and thus the whole time series of the index may change as new information becomes available and the coefficients in (3) are re-estimated. These revisions may be substantial, on the order of one to two percentage points on an annual basis (Abraham and Schauman, 1991). Moreover, they tend to be insensitive to sample size, with systematic and persistent dynamics (Clapp and Giaccotto, 1999; Clapham et al., 2006). The revision of the index also renders out-of-sample tests hard to evaluate, as the original series is no longer available.

For the residential real estate market, the most well-known repeat-sales indices are the S&P/Case–Shiller Home Price Indices and the HPI Index constructed by the Federal Housing Finance Agency.[13] The S&P/Case–Shiller Home Price Indices are based on the repeat-sales methodology as modified by Case and Shiller (1987) (see Standard and Poor's, 2008). The index tracks monthly changes in the value of single-family homes both nationally as well as in 20 individual metropolitan areas. The indices are calculated monthly using a 3-month moving average and published with a 2-month lag. The national index is a quarterly indicator for the nine U.S. Census divisions, and captures approximately 75% of the U.S. residential housing stock by value.[14] For the national index, for most of the MSAs indices, and for the Composite 10 index the data begins in 1986, while all remaining metropolitan indices and the Composite 20 begin in 2000. To account for sample selection, sales that occur within 6-months of one another are excluded owing to the likelihood that the homes have been renovated.

The methodology behind the repeat-sales indices provided by the Federal Housing Finance Agency (FHFA) is a variant of Case and Shiller (1987). The difference is that the second step also involves a quadratic term in the regression of squared residuals on the time interval between transactions. The indexes are based on data of conventional conforming mortgage transactions obtained from Freddie Mac and Fannie Mae. The HPI provides a broader geographic coverage with respect to the Case–Shiller index owing to the national operations of the two government sponsored housing enterprises. However, this comes at a cost as mortgage transactions on attached and multi-unit properties, properties financed by government insured loans, and properties financed by mortgages exceeding

---

[11] Webb (1981a,b,c) show that under some conditions the autocorrelation in return errors approaches −0.5 as the number of observations goes to infinity.

[12] Another concern is that, as noted by Goetzmann (1992), RSR methods estimate the average cross-sectional log return (geometric average), which is lower than the log of the arithmetic average return by Jensen's inequality. This issue is not alleviated by augmenting the number of observations.

[13] Another popular series is the Conventional Mortgage Home Price Index (CMPHI) jointly created by Freddie Mac and Fannie Mae based on mortgages purchased or securitized. See http://www.alliemae.org/cmhpi.html.

[14] Time series data and further information on the index construction can be found at the website http://www.standardandpoors.comand http://www.macromarkets.com/index.shtml.

the conforming loan limits determining eligibility for purchase by Freddie Mac or Fannie Mae (such as sub-prime mortgages) are excluded. Further details about its construction are provided by Calhoun (1996). Monthly indices for the U.S. and Census divisions based on sales price data are available since January 1991. Quarterly indices estimated using both sales prices and appraisal data for the U.S., Census divisions, and metropolitan areas start in the first quarter of 1975.

Competing repeat-sales indexes for the aggregate and local U.S. residential market starting in 1975 are also available from CoreLogic. They are constructed based on a broad universe (about 50 million) of mortgages, and cover about 98% of all U.S. Zip codes. Unfortunately, the data are not publicly available. For a recent application using the CoreLogic series, see Favilukis et al. (2013). Recently, repeat-sale indices have also been introduced into commercial real estate markets. Prominent among these are the Moodys/REAL commercial property price index (CPPI) and the CoStar commercial repeat sales index (CCRSI).

It is important to emphasize that these indices only track price appreciation. That is, they only account for changes in prices and ignore any intermediate cash flow over the period the home is being held. These cash flows include explicit or implicit rent, tax effects, and maintenance costs. Clearly, true measures of (excess) returns to real estate must reflect all inflows and outflows arising from the trading and management of a dwelling. An average implied rent and a rent-to-price ratio series for the Case–Shiller and FHFA indices has been constructed by the Lincoln Institute based on the methodology of Davis et al. (2008).[15]

2.1.3. Hedonic Indices

Repeat sales models measure movements in property prices in a given location over time. They do not shed light on what specific factors determine these prices at a given point in time. To answer this question, we turn our attention to hedonic pricing models. In hedonic models, the price of a property is expressed as a function of a set of characteristics, which determine its quality (such as square footage, number of bedrooms, etc.) and other factors (such as proximity to a school).[16] This relation may arise as the equilibrium outcome of a competitive market with heterogenous goods whose characteristics enter the agent's utility function (Rosen, 1974).

An important classification of hedonic models pertains to the functional form relating the property price and its characteristics. The standard semi-log formulation assumes a linear specification of the type

$$p_{i,t} = \beta Z_i + \delta D + \epsilon_{i,t}, \tag{5}$$

---

[15] The data are downloadable at http://www.lincolninst.edu/resources/.

[16] For an extensive discussion of hedonic models, see Hill (2011). An early application of hedonic models to commercial real estate is Hoag (1980) who investigates the risk and return characteristics of industrial real estate.

where $p_{i,t}$ is the log transaction price of property i in period t, Z_i is a $C \times 1$ vector of property attributes (also known as hedonic variables) including a constant term, and D is a $T - 1 \times 1$ vector of time dummies, one for each period except the first. The OLS estimates of (β, δ) in (5) are obtained by pooling the information of all transactions and have an immediate interpretation. The estimates of β measure the marginal utility an investor derives from having one additional unit of a characteristic, also known as a shadow price. The parameter estimates of δ capture, by contrast, the period-specific change in log price once the effect of property characteristics has been accounted for. Similar to repeat-sales models, the vector $\widehat{\delta}$ is then regarded as an estimate of the log price of the quality-adjusted aggregate index, or $\widehat{p}_{m,t} = \widehat{\delta}_t$. The value of the log price in the initial period is again normalized to zero.

Semi-log hedonic models are often preferred for their ease of estimation. Standard errors and statistical tests are easily computed. Linear models are, however, clearly prone to model mis-specification. Several researchers have explored alternative specifications, which allow for greater flexibility through non-parametric functional forms or second-order expansions (see Halvorsen and Pollakowski, 1981; Wallace, 1996; and Clapp, 2004). These models have been found to provide superior out-of-sample predictive performance compared to linear ones (Pace and Ronald Barry, 1993), but their estimation requires the availability of large datasets and shadow prices are not easily obtainable.

Another key element in the implementation of hedonic models is the choice of the appropriate set of characteristics. The most commonly used characteristics are lot size, square footage, number of bedrooms, number of bathrooms, and age (Wallace, 1996; Sirmans et al., 2006). Others include garage space and the presence of air conditioning, a swimming pool, and a fireplace. In general, this list is dictated by data availability. Data on properties characteristics, along with owners' own assessment of their values, can be found in the Panel Study of Income Dynamics (PSID), which starts in 1968. Moreover, several variables that may affect pricing such as the amount of traffic noise and sunlight exposure are not directly measurable or observable. This renders hedonic models prone to both omitted variable and selection bias, as missing observations for some characteristics may lead to data censoring toward, for example, high quality buildings. As in any regression-type approach, the maintained assumption for consistency of the estimates is that the included variables are not correlated with omitted determinants.[17] A perhaps comforting result is the evidence that shadow prices for the same characteristics resulting from the estimation of the semi-log model on different databases appear to be rather stable (Sirmans et al., 2006). In addition, location identifiers (such as zip codes, location dummies for proximity to the ocean or nearby lakes) are usually included in the regression in order to account for unobserved heterogeneity, as in Campbell et al. (2011).

---

[17] Shiller (2008) argues that hedonic models are subject to the risk that researchers "cherry pick" the functional form and characteristics to obtain the desired results. This argument, however, applies broadly to all empirical studies.

Repeat sales models can be viewed a special case of hedonic pricing models. To see this, consider a property i, which sold twice, say at times t_1 and t_2, and apply the hedonic pricing model, expression (5), at each of these time points assuming the shadow prices of the property's attributes as well as the sizes of the attributes themselves do not change between sales:

$$p_{i,t_1} = \beta Z_i + \delta_{t_1} D_{t_1} + \epsilon_{i,t_1}$$
$$p_{i,t_2} = \beta Z_i + \delta_{t_2} D_{t_2} + \epsilon_{i,t_2}.$$

Subtracting these expressions gives

$$p_{i,t_2} - p_{i,t_1} = \delta_{t_2} D_{t_2} - \delta_{t_1} D_{t_1} + \epsilon_{i,t_2} - \epsilon_{i,t_1}$$
$$= \delta_{t_2} D_{t_2} - \delta_{t_1} D_{t_1} + v_i.$$

If we assume a sale occurred at t_2 and assign $D_{t_2} = -1$ and a purchase at t_1 and set $D_{t_1} = +1$, the latter expression above corresponds to the repeat sales model given in expression (3).

Several studies compare the relative performance of hedonic and repeat-sales models. Meese and Wallace (1997) exploit the fact that repeat-sales estimators can be viewed as constrained versions of a dynamic hedonic model in which it is assumed that (i) homes that sold twice are representative of the whole market and (ii) the shadow prices of the attributes are constant over time and therefore cancel out in the construction of the index. They reject both of these assumptions using data on transactions prices and characteristics for 50,000 homes located in the cities of Oakland and Fremont, California. In addition, they find that repeat-sales indices tend to be very volatile. They attribute this behavior to sample selection bias, non-constancy of the characteristics' shadow prices, and sensitivity to small-sample problems, which all make these approaches less suitable to study efficiency in local markets. Surprisingly, they find that the time series properties of the readily-available median sales price index were very close to those of a hedonic Fisher Ideal index. Similar conclusions are reached by Clapp (2002) looking at the empirical distribution of prediction errors using data for Dade Country, Florida.

As in the case for repeat-sales models, hedonic models provide estimates of the average log return, and not of the log return of the average property. They rely on the assumption that the set of houses that transact is representative of the market as a whole. If instead the sample of house sold varies with economic conditions, the resultant indices may be systematically biased. The magnitude of this bias can be analyzed by comparing hedonic models with price indices based on censored regression procedures, as in Gatzlaff and Haurin (1997, 1998).

An alternative way of constructing hedonic-based indices, which does not require data on properties characteristics is to take advantage of appraisal valuations. Appraisals are estimates of the current value of a property provided either by the owner (so called "internal appraisals") or by a professional agent ("external appraisals"). The key insight here is that while an appraisal value may represent a noisy estimate of a property's true market value, it serves as a valuable hedonic variable, summarizing a building's characteristics, which are either observable, such as its size, or are unobservable, such as its quality. For the U.S. commercial real estate market, a popular index, which is based primarily on appraisal values is the National Property Index (NPI) constructed by the National Council of Real Estate Investment Fiduciaries, NCREIF.[18] NCREIF assets are institutional-grade commercial properties managed by investment fiduciaries on behalf of tax-exempt investors, mostly pension funds. The commercial properties are acquired in the private market for investment purposes only.[19] Based on the information provided by its members, NCREIF constructs quarterly indices for the aggregate commercial real estate as well as indices disaggregated by property type and region. The indices are value-weighted by each property market value, and include cash flows from net operating income and capital expenditures. The series for the U.S., industrial properties, retail properties, and offices start in the first quarter of 1978, while the index for apartments is available from 1984.

A well-known drawback of using appraisal valuations is that the resultant returns respond with a lag to changes in actual market values and are much smoother (Fisher, 2005). The Transaction-Based Index (TBI) constructed by the MIT Center for Real Estate uses the information on transaction prices of properties sold from the NCREIF database to provide a more timely measure of market movements.[20] The index is based on the two-stage methodology of Fisher et al. (2007), which combines the information of infrequent transaction prices with that of frequent appraisal valuations. In the first stage, quarterly transaction data are used to estimate a hedonic price model in which corresponding transaction prices are regressed against properties' lagged appraisal values as well as several dummy variables controlling for time, property type, and location. The estimated coefficients from this regression are then used in a second stage to construct predicted prices based on the appraisal values and other characteristics of those properties that did not transact in a given quarter.[21] In order to construct the aggregate TBI Index, the first-stage estimates are then applied to a representative property mirroring the average characteristics of the data. The methodology can also be used to construct pseudo-market prices for individual properties, as in Plazzi et al. (2011). The nation-wide

---

[18] See http://www.ncreif.org/data.aspx.

[19] When a property is sold or is subject to a change of use, it exits the database. Due to changes in its composition and the type of assets included, the NPI index may therefore not be representative of the commercial real estate market as a whole.

[20] See http://web.mit.edu/cre/research/credl/tbi.html.

[21] The methodology also accounts for transaction sample selection bias in the first stage using a Heckman (1979) two-step approach and applies Bayesian noise filtering technique to reduce the effect of noise in the quarterly series due to the limited number of transactions. See Fisher et al. (2007) for further details on this estimation procedure.

index is available quarterly from 1984:Q1, while property-specific indices for apartments, industrial properties, retail properties, and offices start in 1994:Q1.[22]

2.1.4. Hybrids

A combination of two or more types of indices might attenuate the deficiencies in the individual approaches. Along those lines, Case et al. (1991), Case and Quigley (1991), Quigley (1995), Meese and Wallace (1997) combine repeat-sales and non-parametric hedonic methodologies in the construction of hybrid indices. The specification of Case and Quigley's (1991) hybrid model is appealingly simple. It involves estimating the repeal-sales model (3) and the hedonic model (5) jointly in a GMM system of equations.

Hill et al. (1997) improve upon the estimation of Case and Quigley (1991) hybrid model. More specifically, they use hedonic regressions to estimate the effect of depreciation (the shadow price of a building's age) and impose a first-order autoregressive process for the error term to capture sluggish adjustments to economic shocks. They then jointly estimate a repeat-sales regression consistent with this error structure via maximum-likelihood and document substantial efficiency gains in terms of lower standard errors and narrower interval estimates for the resultant index. Hybrid indices seem to offer improvements over either the repeat-sales or the purely hedonic models (Case et al., 1991 and Meese and Wallace, 1997), which illustrates well the fact that the adoption of one particular model to the exclusion of all others is likely to result in the suboptimal use of information. The intuition for this results is analogous to that in the forecast combinations literature (Timmermann, 2006).

2.1.5. Stock Market-Based Indices

Institutions and individuals can take positions in the commercial real estate market by investing in publicly-traded REIT companies. Market-based indices can be obtained from the trading of individual REIT stocks. These indices are usually constructed as value-weighted averages of firm-specific REIT returns. The two standard data sources here are the CRSP/Ziman Real Estate Data Series and the FTSE NAREIT U.S. Real Estate Index Series. Both indices track the performance of the U.S. market and provide disaggregated information across REIT types (equity, mortgage, and hybrids). The CRSP Index is available from 1979, while the NAREIT data starts in 1972. The CRSP Index also provides separate indices for Apartments, Industrial and Offices, and Retail.

A few caveats are, however, in order when using REIT data. First, the overall value of the 163 REITs traded at the end of 2010 was about $366 billion, and thus represent quite a small fraction of the approximately $10 trillion estimated value of non-residential real estate market. Hence, REITs may not constitute a representative sample of the U.S. commercial real estate market as a whole. Second, the number of traded REITs varies

---

[22] The starting date for the property-specific indices is motivated by the need of a sufficient number of transactions to estimate the model parameters separately within each property.

considerably over time, from about 100 trusts in the early 1980s to slightly less than 200 during the mid 2000s. Third, the market is characterized by a few large companies and many smaller REITs. This description is consistent with the fact that in 2009 the average market cap of REITs was $1.37 billion, while the median market cap was only $0.618 billion. An investment in REITs exposes investors to the risks inherent in small-cap stocks. Finally, many REIT companies have a significant amount of debt and thus the return series reflect the profit for the equity stake of investing in real estate. Since equity is nothing but a call option on the value of assets (Merton, 1974), higher debt levels amplify the effect of shocks to the value of the asset (property). Hence, we expect REITs returns to exhibit higher mean and volatility compared to those of the commercial real estate market.

2.1.6. Other Methods

The non-observability of the true underlying price process has also prompted some researchers to apply filtering techniques to extract the information of true prices embedded in noisy transaction prices. Engle et al. (1985) use an EM algorithm (based upon Kalman filtering and smoothing) to estimate unobservable rent–price ratios, by relying on hedonic prices and a present value model between prices and future rents. For forecasting real house prices in the U.K., a Kalman filter model with time-varying coefficients has been used by Brown et al. (1997). Giaccotto and Clapp (1992) use Monte Carlo simulation to show that Bayesian-type techniques based on a Kalman filter should be preferred by appraisers to estimate current true prices.

Finally, the increasing availability of large databases has led researchers to explore the use of spatial econometric techniques that control for geographical and temporal dependence in real estate prices.[23] Spatial dependence refers to the fact that properties, which are in geographical proximity to each other will tend to be subject to similar shocks. Moreover, the location of a dwelling may play an important role in its pricing due to the presence of factors such as proximity to schools, parks, and malls. We would then expect the error components in hedonic regressions to be more correlated the closer the two properties are to each other. In contrast, temporal dependence refers to the fact that the parameters of hedonic models (the attribute prices) may change over time. This is similar to modeling time-varying coefficients in standard regression analysis. Error terms, which refer to transactions occurring in distant periods are then likely to be less correlated. Explicitly accounting for these two sources of correlation helps reduce the bias and improves the efficiency of the estimators. Application of spatial models to housing can be found in Can (1992), Pace et al. (1998, 2000), Caplin et al. (2008), Nappi–Choulet and Maury (2009).

---

[23] See Anselin (1988) for a book treatment of spatial regressions.

2.2. Summary Statistics

Residential: For residential properties, we have three data sources – one median price index and two repeat-sales indices. First, the Census Bureau provides median and average prices of U.S. residential properties at monthly frequency. Second, Standard and Poor's/Case–Shiller (Case–Shiller) construct repeat-sales prices that are available at various frequencies and aggregation levels. A national index is constructed quarterly and a monthly version for the 10 largest metropolitan areas (C10) is also available. In addition, we compute a monthly equally-weighted average across all available areas at a point in time and label it as "EW" Third, the Federal Housing Finance Agency's (FHFA) repeat-sales House Price Index is available monthly (Purchase Only) and quarterly (All Transactions) at the national level. All three series track price appreciation in nominal, as opposed to real, house prices. We compute log price changes of all indices, which cannot be interpreted as returns in the usual sense of the term since the levels do not account for rents. Rent-to-price data for the Case–Shiller and FHFA data are from the Lincoln Institute at quarterly frequency. These data are also used to obtain growth in rents. Unfortunately, we do not have access to residential hedonic price data. To facilitate the comparison across data sources, we sample all series starting in 1991 (or later, depending on the series availability). The exception is REITs, for which we use a sample starting from January 1980.

In Panel A of Table 9.2, we report summary statistics – annualized means, annualized standard deviations, skewness, and AR(1) coefficient – for log price changes of all indices as well as the rent growth rate and the rent-to-price ratios. The average growth rate of the Census median sales index and of the repeat-sales series are all in the neighborhood of 3%. However, the standard deviation of the median sales index, at 8.8%, is significantly higher than the 2.0% to 5.1% observed for the Case–Shiller and FHFA indices.[24] All indices are negatively skewed, but the skewness in repeat-sales indices is larger in absolute value.

From a time series perspective, the most significant difference between the median and the repeat-sales indices is the level of time-dependence. Changes in log levels of the Census series are significantly negatively correlated, with an AR(1) coefficient of −0.522. The Case–Shiller C10 and EW monthly log changes exhibit an AR(1) coefficient of 0.938 and 0.929, respectively. To a significant extent, this dependence reflects the fact that, as explained above, the Case–Shiller indices are constructed as a 3-month moving average of an underlying series. Indeed, if we take the quarterly index, the AR(1) coefficient is significantly lower (0.613). The FHFA monthly and quarterly log changes also have large positive AR(1) coefficients of 0.756 and 0.708, respectively.

The average rent growth rate for the repeat-sale indices is 3%. The series exhibit very little volatility and high serial correlation (0.900). The rent-to-price ratio is 4.5%

---

[24] It is worth noticing that over the 1963–2010 period for which Census data are available, the return standard deviation is even higher at 13%.

Table 9.2 Summary Statistics

	Begin date	Returns/Price Changes				Dividend/Rent Growth				Dividend/Rent-to-Price Ratio			
		Mean	Std	Skew	AR(1)	Mean	Std	Skew	AR(1)	Mean	Std	Skew	AR(1)
Panel A: Residential Real Estate													
Census													
Median (M)	Jan 1991	0.034	0.088	−0.425	−0.522	−	−	−	−	−	−	−	−
Average (M)	Jan 1991	0.032	0.080	0.136	−0.192	−	−	−	−	−	−	−	−
Case–Shiller													
U.S. (Q)	1991:Q1	0.029	0.051	−1.362	0.613	0.030	0.007	−0.941	0.900	0.045	0.013	−0.989	0.987
C10 (M)	Mar 1991	0.034	0.033	−0.773	0.938	−	−	−	−	−	−	−	−
EW (M)	Mar 1991	0.029	0.029	−1.594	0.929	−	−	−	−	−	−	−	−
OFHEO													
U.S. (Q)	1991:Q1	0.032	0.026	−0.911	0.756	0.030	0.007	−0.941	0.900	0.045	0.009	−0.765	0.994
U.S. (M)	Feb 1991	0.031	0.020	−1.165	0.708	−	−	−	−	−	−	−	−
Panel B: Commercial Real Estate													
NCREIF													
All (Q)	1991:Q1	0.068	0.052	−1.888	0.801	−	−	−	−	−	−	−	−
Apt (Q)	1991:Q1	0.081	0.051	−2.402	0.821	−	−	−	−	−	−	−	−
Ind (Q)	1991:Q1	0.071	0.053	−1.747	0.809	−	−	−	−	−	−	−	−
Off (Q)	1991:Q1	0.060	0.065	−1.563	0.742	−	−	−	−	−	−	−	−
Rtl (Q)	1991:Q1	0.074	0.045	−0.938	0.750	−	−	−	−	−	−	−	−
TBI													
All (Q)	1991:Q1	0.090	0.096	−0.850	0.087	0.021	0.053	−0.388	0.365	0.056	0.024	−0.825	0.971
Apt (Q)	1994:Q2	0.098	0.090	−0.430	0.256	0.020	0.104	3.097	0.206	0.052	0.032	−0.218	0.980
Ind (Q)	1994:Q2	0.097	0.115	−0.463	0.053	0.018	0.106	−0.044	0.163	0.058	0.025	−0.310	0.948
Off (Q)	1994:Q2	0.095	0.090	−0.670	0.415	0.021	0.098	−0.446	0.569	0.047	0.027	−0.242	0.971
Rtl (Q)	1994:Q2	0.089	0.089	1.120	0.184	0.027	0.062	0.912	0.421	0.065	0.027	−0.340	0.967

(*Continued*)

Table 9.2 *Continued*

	Begin date	Returns/Price Changes				Dividend/Rent Growth				Dividend/Rent-to-Price Ratio			
		Mean	Std	Skew	AR(1)	Mean	Std	Skew	AR(1)	Mean	Std	Skew	AR(1)
CPPI													
All (Q)	Jan 2001	0.011	0.075	−1.354	0.452	—	—	—	—	—	—	—	—
Apt (Q)	2001:Q1	0.034	0.114	−1.324	0.193	—	—	—	—	—	—	—	—
Ind (Q)	2001:Q1	0.022	0.113	−1.793	0.256	—	—	—	—	—	—	—	—
Off (Q)	2001:Q1	0.022	0.109	−1.716	0.006	—	—	—	—	—	—	—	—
Rtl (Q)	2001:Q1	0.031	0.093	−1.249	0.376	—	—	—	—	—	—	—	—
REITs													
All (Q)	Jan 1980	0.104	0.179	−1.730	0.146	0.018	0.077	−1.700	−0.050	0.067	0.051	0.384	0.957
Apt (Q)	Jan 1980	0.114	0.190	−1.081	0.090	0.053	0.185	0.884	−0.090	0.072	0.083	0.452	0.970
Ind & Off (Q)	Jan 1980	0.066	0.225	−1.816	0.111	−0.039	0.191	−1.357	−0.099	0.071	0.076	1.173	0.940
Rtl (Q)	Jan 1980	0.121	0.200	−1.818	0.144	0.025	0.124	−4.494	−0.078	0.065	0.055	0.453	0.947
Panel C: Stock, T-bill, Inflation, Industrial Production													
CRSP VW (M)	Jan 1980	0.107	0.163	−1.096	0.114	0.050	0.047	2.159	0.082	0.027	0.038	0.580	0.992
RTB (M)	Jan 1980	−0.021	0.038	−0.046	0.885	—	—	—	—	—	—	—	—
CPI (M)	Jan 1980	0.034	0.012	−0.486	0.555	—	—	—	—	—	—	—	—
TSP (M)	Jan 1980	0.015	0.010	−0.410	0.924	—	—	—	—	—	—	—	—
CP (M)	Jan 1980	0.013	0.020	0.340	0.783	—	—	—	—	—	—	—	—
IPG (M)	Jan 1980	0.019	0.025	−1.096	0.294	—	—	—	—	—	—	—	—

Notes: Annualized mean, annualized standard deviation, skewness, and first-order autoregressive coefficient for returns/price changes, rent/dividend growth, and rent/dividend-price ratio of aggregate real estate indices and conditioning variables. For residential real estate (Panel A), the indices are the Census Median and Average; the Case–Shiller aggregate U.S., Composite 10 (C10), and equally-weighted average of available MSA indices (EW); the FHFA/OFHEO quarterly All-Transactions and monthly Purchase Only indices. Rent growth and the rent–price ratio for the Case–Shiller and OFHEO indices are from the Lincoln Institute. For commercial real estate (Panel B), the indices are from NCREIF, TBI, CPPI, and CRSP/Ziman REIT for the aggregate market (All) and separately for apartments (Apt), industrial properties (Ind), offices (Off), and retail properties (Rtl). In Panel C, the Financial and Macro Variables are the CRSP Value–Weighted NYSE/AMEX/NASDAQ index, the 3–month Treasury bill minus its 12-month moving average (RTB), the return on the CPI index (CPI), the term spread as difference between the 5–year and 3–month yields (TSP), the Cochrane–Piazzesi (2005) interest rate factor (CP), and industrial production growth (IPG). Begin date reports the first return observation. The monthly (M) or quarterly (Q) frequency of each index is also denoted.

for both indices. Its standard deviation is very small compared to that of the log price changes, but it is extremely persistent, with AR(1) coefficients of 0.987 (Case–Shiller) and 0.994 (FHFA). Given that these estimates are downward-based (Andrews, 1993), there is little doubt that these series are close to non-stationary. The high level of persistence in the rent-to-price ratio is similar to that observed in valuation ratios (dividend-price, earnings-price) of the U.S. stock market (Welch and Goyal, 2008). The average return from residential real estate can be computed by adding the average price appreciation and the average rent-to-price ratio. Over our sample, it is 7.6% for both repeat-sales indices.

Commercial: Commercial properties naturally fall into one of four categories: apartments (Apt), industrial properties (Ind), offices (Off), and retail properties (Rtl). Indices are available for each of these categories as well as for the overall commercial real estate market. The first source of commercial real estate values is the NPI from the National Council of Real Estate Investment Fiduciaries (NCREIF). An alternative hedonic index, based on the work by Fisher et al. (2007), is the TBI.

Repeat-sales commercial real estate indices are relatively new. One such index, the Moodys/REAL commercial property price index (CPPI) provides monthly data at the aggregate level and quarterly series by property type from 2001 to the present.[25] While this time span is too short for forecasting exercises, we include the CPPI for completeness and provide summary statistics. We have no doubt that repeat-sales indices will play a growing role in commercial real estate.

REIT is a value-weighted index of all publicly-traded REITs in the CRSP–Ziman database. Using monthly returns with and without dividends, we construct its dividend-price ratio and dividend growth rate (see Appendix A.2 for details). Since REIT is a stock-market based index, it presents a unique opportunity to investigate the performance and predictability of commercial real estate returns without the complications inherent in hedonic and repeat-sales indices. It is therefore not surprising that many academic papers have been written on REIT return predictability and so we will also devote special attention to this market.

Panel B of Table 9.2 contains summary statistics for the NPI, TBI, CPPI, and REIT indices. Whenever available, we also report summary statistics for rent growth rates (or dividend growth, in the case of REITs) and rent-to-price ratios (dividend-price ratios, for REITs). With the exception of CPPI, all return series include cash flows distributions (net rents or dividends).

The TBI index shows a higher average return than the TBI (9.0% versus 6.8%) and a higher standard deviation (9.6% versus 5.2%). Since the two indexes are based on the same data, the increased volatility of the TBI is attributable to the reduced impact of the

[25] The CPPI tracks same-property realized round-trip price changes based on transactions data provided by Real Estate Analytics, LLC (REAL). The RCA database aims at collecting price information for every commercial property transaction in the U.S. over $2,500,000 in value. Thus, it reflects a more extensive set of properties than those in the NCREIF portfolio. See Geltnerand Pollakowski (2007) and http://mit.edu/cre/research/credl/rca.html.

smoothness coming from appraisal valuations. Indeed, the AR(1) coefficient of the NPI is 0.80, about one order of magnitude larger than that for the TBI (0.087). The low serial correlation in the return series makes the TBI particularly appealing from an economic perspective. The rent growth rate of the TBI exhibits moderate serial dependence (AR(1) coefficient of 0.365) whereas its rent-to-price ratio is extremely persistent (AR(1) coefficient of 0.971). The changes in the log CPPI have a very low average mean of 1.1%. This is mostly due to the sample over which these statistics were calculated.[26] The CPPI series are also quite volatile and exhibit moderate dependence (AR(1) of 0.452).

The average REIT returns, at the bottom of Panel B, Table 9.2, have a mean of about 10.4% and a standard deviation of 17.9%. These numbers are higher than for the other commercial real estate indices. By comparison, during the common 1991–2010 period, which is used in our forecasting regressions, the return mean and volatility for the All-property index are respectively 0.105 and 0.202. Since REIT is a stock index, it is useful to compare its return and volatility with that of the market-wide portfolio return. The CRSP value-weighted portfolio return has an average of 10.7% and a standard deviation of 16.3% over a similar period, which implies a higher Sharpe ratio than that of REITs. REIT returns have a relatively higher serial correlation of 0.146, which is in line with that of small-cap stocks in the U.S. stock market.

Conditioning Variables: The conditioning variables we select proxy for time variation in the state of the economy and thus in the prevailing investment opportunity set. These variables have also been shown to successfully capture time variation in expected returns of the aggregate U.S. stock market and bond returns. These include the lagged aggregate stock market (Campbell and Vuolteenaho, 2004), its dividend-price ratio (Fama and French, 1988b; Lettau and Van Nieuwerburgh, 2008), the relative 3-month Treasury bill calculated as the current rate minus its 12-month moving average (Hodrick, 1992), the inflation rate (Fama and Schwert, 1977), the term spread as difference between the 5-year and 3-month log yields (Fama and French, 1989), the Cochrane and Piazzesi (2005) tent-shaped combination of forward rates, and industrial production growth (Fama, 1990). Summary statistics, reported in the bottom panel of Table 9.2, show a wide range of persistence with AR(1) coefficients ranging from 0.29 for Industrial Production growth to as high as 0.92 for the Term Spread. Details on the data source and construction are provided in Appendix A.2.

3. FORECASTING REAL ESTATE RETURNS

The extensive predictability literature in finance and real estate considers variations of the following linear predictive regression:

$$r_{t+1} = \alpha + \beta' X_t + \epsilon_{t+1}, \tag{6}$$

[26] Unfortunately, a longer time span is not available.

where r_{t+1} is a return (or price change) and X_t is a vector of variables, observable at time t. Predictability in r_{t+1} may arise because of two distinct economic reasons. First, it might be due to market inefficiency if some available information is not incorporated in prices in a timely manner by market participants (e.g., Fama, 1970). Second, predictability might be due to time-variation in expected returns (e.g., Campbell and Shiller, 1988). Unfortunately, the existence of predictability in a reduced-form regression (6) does not allow us to trace its economic provenance. Also, the existence of predictability does not necessarily imply that the market is inefficient in the usual sense of the term (Fama, 1970). For a market to be inefficient, investors should be able to exploit some of the serial dependence. This point is discussed in detail by Case and Shiller (1989) in the context of residential real estate.

Linear models are deceptively simple. An extensive literature has investigated their statistical properties (estimation and inference) and out-of-sample predictive performance (Rapach and Zhou, 2013 in this Handbook). Statistical complications arise because the predictor X_t is often persistent and its innovations are correlated with ϵ_{t+1}, which induces bias in the estimation of β (Stambaugh, 1999). Moreover, excessive noise in the returns series renders hypothesis testing unreliable. We will revisit some of these issues below.

In this section, we review the literature on real estate predictability. We also report estimates from our own predictive regressions using the indices introduced above. The discussion is organized around the kind of predictive information that is included in X_t and the implied hypotheses.

3.1. Serial Dependence in Real Estate Returns and Weak-Form Market Efficiency

We start off with the simplest information set X_t, that of past returns, r_t. In this case, regression (6) tests for serial correlation in returns and weak-form market efficiency. Several studies in the real estate literature find that returns (or price changes) exhibit positive serial correlation, including Gau (1984, 1985), Linneman (1986), Guntermann and Smith (1987), Rayburn et al. (1987), Case and Shiller (1989), McIntosh and Henderson (1989), Gyourko and Voith (1992), Kuo (1996), Hill et al. (1997, 1999), Gu (2002), and Schindler (2011). However, the evidence on whether this predictability can be exploited for financial gains is less clear.

In one of the earliest papers of weak-form efficiency for the U.S. real estate market, Gau (1985) investigates the persistence in monthly returns to commercial real estate in Vancouver during the 1971–1980 period. Rather than using simple returns, he works with abnormal returns, defined as returns adjusted for various sources of systematic risk. The cross-sectional risk-adjustments alter the unconditional mean of the returns series, but have little effect on their dynamics. Gau (1985) finds that the forecasting errors from predicting abnormal returns using past price information are too small to be exploitable by a trading strategy. Linneman (1986) uses hedonic prices, also adjusted for risk, to test for market efficiency in the Philadelphia residential market. He finds evidence of serial dependence in the data, but concludes that the predictability is insufficient "to cover the high transaction costs associated with transacting real estate." Guntermann and Smith (1987) apply a portfolio approach to uncover the autocorrelation of aggregate unanticipated total returns to residential real estate in 57 MSAs using the Federal Housing Administration data over the 1968–1982 sample. Their study is one of the first to explicitly take into account rental income in computing returns. They document positive predictability over horizons of 1 to 3 years, and negative autocorrelation at the 4- to 10-year horizon. This pattern is consistent with short-run momentum and long-run reversal. Consistent with Linneman (1986), the persistence is not large enough for various trading rules to appear profitable once transaction costs are considered. Rayburn et al. (1987) and McIntosh and Henderson (1989) reach similar conclusions using different datasets and methodologies.

In an influential study, Case and Shiller (1989) test for weak-form efficiency in four U.S. singe-family markets: Atlanta, Chicago, Dallas, and San Francisco/Oakland. They do so using their weighted repeat sales (WRS) index (Case and Shiller, 1987). To reduce errors-in-variables issues, they randomly partition their sample of transactions into two groups and obtain two corresponding WRS indices for each of the four cities. They then regress quarterly observations on the annual return in one index on the 1-year lagged annual return of the other index. This approach, which can be seen as instrumental variables (IV), produces consistent, albeit biased, estimates of the autoregressive coefficient.[27] Case and Shiller (1989) document substantial predictability in real and excess returns to housing, with predictive R^2 ranging from 0.11 to as high as 0.48 corresponding to average trading profits between 1% and 3%. They also find it much harder to forecast individual properties returns using the city-wide index, due to the large amount of noise-to-signal ratio in such data. Out-of-sample performance deteriorates considerably due to measurement error in estimating the aggregate index using only a subset of the sample. Moreover, the random partitioning approach implies that the estimates and forecasts will change if we alter the partitioning of the data.

Hill et al. (1999) and Schindler (2011) provide some additional evidence on the Case and Shiller (1989) data. Hill et al. (1999) reject the hypothesis of a random walk in these price series using the methodology in Hill et al. (1997). The test is based on the idea that a random walk process for prices would induce heteroskedasticity in repeat-sales indices. They also show that the GLS procedure of Case and Shiller (1989) can be improved upon by accounting for a stationary, autoregressive component in house prices. Schindler (2011) provides recent evidence of predictability in the

---

[27] To reduce the bias arising from noisy instruments, Kuo (1996) proposes an alternative Bayesian approach to estimate an AR(2) model based on repeat-sales. His setup explicitly models the unknown true indices as random variables and hence does not necessitate partitioning the repeat-sales sample. The corresponding posterior means of the AR(2) coefficients suggest that repeat-sales indices are more dependent than what found in previous studies.

Case–Shiller real and nominal log nominal price changes, computed for the national and 20 metropolitan areas indices. Not surprisingly, he finds strong evidence for dependence in the price changes, with some indices exhibiting strong positive autocorrelation even at 24 monthly lags. Perhaps more surprising is his finding that, after comparing different buy-and-hold and dynamic trading strategies, the author concludes that in some markets the persistence in the data is large enough to be exploitable. It is worth mentioning that the markets with the largest gains from the trading strategies – Los Angeles, Las Vegas, San Diego, and San Francisco – are also the markets that have exhibited the largest bubbles. Hence, it is not clear whether these strategies would fare equally well out-of-sample.

Gu (2002) studies the autocorrelation properties of quarterly returns to the Conventional Mortgage Home Price Index (CMHPI) for all U.S. states, the District of Columbia, nine Census Divisions, and an aggregate index for the U.S. during the 1975–1999 period. He finds that the degree of persistence and the sign of correlation varies geographically as well as over time. The findings in Gu (2002) also point to the difficulty of comparing the results of weak-form efficiency studies in real estate using information from different markets, datasets (some aggregated, others not), sample periods, and methodologies.

A growing literature uses regime switching models to capture real estate price dynamics.[28] In a regime switching model, the time series properties of a series depend on the realization of an underlying state variable.[29] Moreover, it is reasonable to expect substantial variation in regimes across different areas and property types owing to the reliance of real estate to local economic and geographic conditions. Shifts in house price dynamics may arise, for example, because of a changing relationship between housing, income, and interest rates (see, e.g., Muellbauer and Murphy, 1997; Boz and Mendoza, 2010; and Favilukis et al., 2011) or from the interaction between credit-constrained households, lenders, and developers (Spiegel, 2001).[30]

Theoretically, the entire conditional density of a process may depend on the current state realization. In practice, for tractability, the empirical applications have mainly adopted

[28] Following the influential work of Hamilton (1989), regime switching models have been extensively used in the macroeconomic and finance literature to capture non-linearities in exchange rates (Engel and Hamilton, 1990), interest rates (Gray, 1996; Garcia and Perron, 1996; Bansal and Zhou, 2002), stock returns (Perez-Quiros and Timmermann, 2001; Granger and Hyung, 2004; Guidolin and Timmermann, 2008), GDP growth (Diebold and Rudebusch, 1999), and GNP growth (Hamilton, 1989).

[29] Using Monte Carlo simulations, Van Nordena and Vigfusson (1998) provide evidence that regime-switching tests for bubbles suffer from a downward bias distortion even with relatively large samples – i.e., they reject the null of no bubble too often – but display considerable power in detecting non-stationarities. This makes them suitable to capture the persistent real estate cycles.

[30] Similarly, Guirguis et al. (2005) find evidence of parameters instability in the relationship between real estate prices and the fraction of the population aged between 25 and 35, real disposable income, stock of owner-occupied dwellings, the expected nominal capital gains, the nominal post-tax mortgage interest rate. They interpret this fact as evidence of structural changes and suggest the use of time-varying coefficient methods coupled with Kalman filter.

first-order autoregressive regime switching models:

$$r_t = c_{s_t} + \phi_{s_t} r_{t-1} + \epsilon_t, \tag{7}$$

where $\epsilon_t \sim N(0, \sigma_{s_t}^2)$. In this context, returns follow an AR(1) process whose intercept, slope, and error variance depend on the realization of the regime variable s_t. Thus, the data-generating process is subject to jumps in the unconditional mean, persistence, and level of volatility. The choice of the number of regimes n that better describes the data is usually chosen by likelihood ratio tests or information criteria. However, due to the availability of relatively short time series, most of the existing studies rely on low-order models with two or three regimes (Crawford and Fratantoni, 2003). The fact that prices of direct investments in real estate are available at low frequency – monthly, at the very best – also complicates the detection of short-lived regimes. The estimates are obtained using maximum likelihood (Hamilton, 1994).

Among the empirical studies, Crawford and Fratantoni (2003) compare the in-sample and out-of-sample forecasting performance of regime switching models to that of ARIMA processes and GARCH models on the annualized growth rates in the state-level OFHEO quarterly return series from 1979 until 2001. Their approach parallels that of Perez-Quiros and Timmermann (2001) for the stock market. The authors document considerable heterogeneity in the time series properties of residential returns across states. For example, past returns explain only 6% of the variance of returns to Ohio but about 75% in the case of California. Their data exhibits a strong degree of persistence and non-linearity in the volatility process, which is modeled as an EGARCH. They also observe that the time series patterns seem to be better captured by a two-states regime model, which deliver much lower in-sample RMSEs and R^2. Out-of-sample, however, ARMA models display better forecasting properties (lower MSFE), probably due to the tendency of regime switching models to overfit in-sample.[31] Interestingly, this last finding is consistent with Gu's (2002) analysis on CMHPI data.

Another stream of papers makes a connection between a high degree of positive serial correlation in returns and bubbles in real estate markets. For example, Gyourko and Voith (1992) analyze autocorrelation in median house prices for 56 MSAs during 1971–1989. They find significant differences in autocorrelations across areas, which they interpret as evidence of market inefficiency. At the same time, they argue that a global component drives residential prices and that "the national economy strongly influences local housing markets." Glaeser et al. (2008) use the FHFA/OFHEO data to show that large price increases in residential properties were almost entirely experienced in cities where housing supply is more inelastic. Hence, they argue that boom-bust housing cycles are largely driven by housing supply rather than demand shocks.

---

[31] Perez-Quiros and Timmermann (2001) document that even when the data are generated by a regime switching process, simple autoregressive models may provide better short-term forecasts.

The stylized facts that emerge from this literature can therefore be summarized as follows: (i) most residential indices exhibit serial correlation in log price changes; (ii) the serial correlation is positive at horizons up to a few years; (iii) at longer horizons, we observe a reversal, or a negative serial correlation in returns; (iv) the economic significance of this serial correlation and whether it can be exploited by market participants is still an open question.

To illustrate these findings, we run simple autoregressive tests, which are mostly descriptive in nature. The goal is to replicate some of the key dynamics outlined above for returns in the aggregate residential and commercial real estate markets. As we don't have access to the disaggregated data used in the construction of the indices, we cannot replicate the more involved estimation specifications. We consider the following long-horizon regression:

$$r_{t+1:t+T} = \alpha(T) + \beta(T)r_{t-T+1:t} + \varepsilon_{t+1:t+T}, \tag{8}$$

where $r_{t+1:t+T}$ is the log change of a price index over T periods. For $T = 1$, Eq. (8) collapses to an AR(1) model. Long-horizon return regressions (8) are used frequently in empirical finance to investigate the behavior or equity returns at various horizons (e.g., Fama and French, 1988a). Versions have also been used in the residential real estate literature by Guntermann and Smith (1987) and in the commercial real estate literature by Plazzi et al. (2010). Under the null hypothesis that the price process has no predictable component, $\beta(T)$ should be zero at all horizons. Deviations from the null hypothesis imply that there are predictable dynamics at different horizons.

In Figure 9.3, we provide the results from this regression estimated for four indices, two residential and two commercial. We choose indices that exhibit various degrees of serial correlation. For residential, we use the median and FHFA/OFHEO indices,[32] whereas for commercial, the comprehensive TBI, and REIT indices. For all regressions, we plot the least squares estimates of $\beta(T)$, $T = 1, \ldots, 48$ months with a solid line along with two times the Newey and West (1987) standard errors (dotted line), based on T lags. The Census median index exhibits negative serial correlation at short horizons. As the horizon increases, the correlation turns positive between 12 and 24 months and then reverts to zero. With the exception of the short-horizon negative correlation, we cannot reject the null that the Census median forecast changes are uncorrelated. The picture is quite different for the repeat-sales FHFA/OFHEO data. We observe a strong degree of serial correlation at short and medium horizons. The $\beta(T)$ estimates are positive and significant for horizons up to 30 months. Then, the serial correlation turns negative but insignificant.

The TBI index is not serially correlated at the very short horizon. The estimates of $\beta(T)$ turn significantly positive for horizons between 6 and 18 months. Then, similarly to the FHFA/OFHEO index, we observe a reversal and a negative, albeit not

---

[32] The Case–Shiller is even more serially correlated than the FHFA/OFHEO index. This is due to its construction, which takes a three-month average of an underlying repeat-sales index.

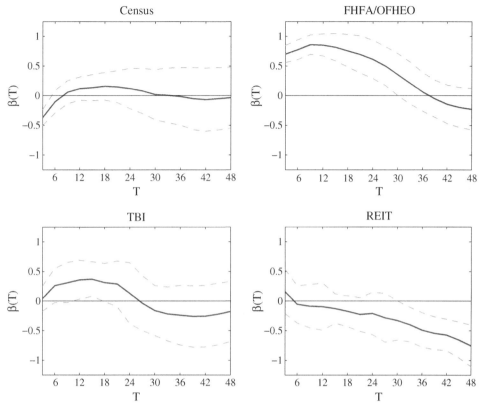

Figure 9.3 Long-Horizon Return Autocorrelations. The thick solid line reports the OLS slope coefficients $\beta(T)$ in the regression of T-month overlapping returns on a constant and their T-period lagged value, $r_{t+1:t+T} = \alpha + \beta(T)r_{t-T+1:t} + \epsilon_{t+1:t+T}$. The dashed lines denote the point estimate plus or minus two Newey and West (1987) HAC standard errors based on T lags. The plots are (in clockwise order, starting from top left) for the Census Median index quarterly sampled, FHFA/OFHEO Quarterly series, REIT All quarterly sampled, and TBI All. The X-axis reports the horizon T in months. The sample period is as in Table 9.2.

significant, correlation in long–horizon returns. Finally, the REIT index exhibits a positive but insignificant correlation at the 1–month horizon, which is typical for small–cap stocks (Campbell et al., 1997). As the horizon increases, we notice a negative drift in the estimates, which turns significant after about 30 months. This is consistent with the model in Fama and French (1988a), who show that in the presence of a small mean reverting component in returns, the estimate of $\beta(T)$ will be negative at long horizons. This evidence supports the presence of a small predictable component in REIT prices.

The results in Figure 9.3 show the main salient findings in the real estate literature, namely positive serial correlation in the price changes at short horizons of up to 2 to 3 years and reversals at horizons beyond 3 years. In the case of the FHFA/OFHEO and

TBI indices, the positive serial correlation is due partly to the construction of the index, as discussed in Section 2.1, and partly to market inefficiencies in real estate markets. The construction of an index that captures a quality-adjusted price without introducing artificial dynamics remains an important topic of research. The current indices, especially those that are filtered, are appropriate for capturing the state of the real estate market. However, their excessive serial correlation does not make them suitable for forecasting exercises. Moreover, the majority of the studies cited above reach the conclusion that high transaction costs render the observed predictability hard to exploit by market participants.

3.2. Predictability Based on Valuation Ratios

Valuation ratios, such as the dividend-price, the book-to-market, and the earnings-price, have a long-standing tradition as predictors of equity returns (see Rapach and Zhou, 2013 in this Handbook and references therein). Analogous ratios have been used in the real estate literature, some of which are the rent-to-price (Hamilton and Schwab, 1985; Meese and Wallace, 1994; Geltner and Mei, 1995; Capozza and Seguin, 1996; Campbell et al., 2009; Himmelberg et al., 2005; Gallin, 2008; Plazzi et al., 2010), the loan-to-value (Lamont and Stein, 1999), and the price-to-income ratio (see, e.g., Malpezzi, 1990, 1999). The economic reason for the use of ratios as predictors of future returns is straightforward and hinges on the plausible assumption that the variables used to form the ratios are co-integrated in logs (Engle and Granger, 1987). To see that, consider the log rent–price ratio. If log rents and log prices are co-integrated, then the log rent–price ratio must be a mean-reverting process. If at time t, the ratio is higher than its unconditional mean, the mean reversion implies that either expected returns would be high or that expected growth in rents would be low, or a combination of the two (Campbell et al., 2009; Plazzi et al., 2010). Similar logic applies to most valuation ratios.

To understand the appeal of the rent–price ratio to forecast either future rent growth or future returns, it is useful to introduce some notation. Let H_t denote rents net of all operating expenses of a property and P_t denotes its current price. Then the rent–price ratio is H_t/P_t and we denote its log transformation by $hp_t \equiv \ln(H_t) - \ln(P_t)$. It is also known as the capitalization, or cap, rate of the property. We will use the terms rent–price ratio and cap rate interchangeably from now on. Following Campbell and Shiller (1988), Campbell et al. (2009), and Plazzi et al. (2010) show that hp_t can be expressed as

$$
hp_t = k + E_t \left[\sum_{j=0}^{\infty} \rho^j r_{t+1+j} \right] - E_t \left[\sum_{j=0}^{\infty} \rho^j \Delta h_{t+1+j} \right], \tag{9}
$$

where r_{t+1+j} is the future return of the property, Δh_{t+1+j} is the future growth in its rents, and k and ρ are linearization constants. In other words, fluctuations in the log cap rate must be able to predict either future returns, or future growth in rents, or both.

Expression (9) is the basis for the following long-horizon regressions:

$$r_{t+1:t+T} = \beta_r(T)hp_t + \tau^r_{t+1:t+T} \tag{10}$$

$$\Delta h_{t+1:t+T} = \beta_d(T)hp_t + \tau^d_{t+1:t+T}, \tag{11}$$

where $r_{t+1:t+T} \equiv \Sigma^T_{j=1} r_{t+j}$ and $\Delta h_{t+1:t+T} \equiv \Sigma^T_{j=1} \Delta h_{t+j}$ approximate, respectively, the first and second term in (9) for a large T.[33] These approximations are appealing because $r_{t+1:t+T}$ and $\Delta h_{t+1:t+T}$ represent the log T-period return and rent growth, respectively. The forecasting regressions are estimated at various horizons, ranging from one period $(T = 1)$ to several years ahead. The framework above has been used to investigate predictability of residential, commercial, and REIT returns. Given the extensive literature about REITs, we devote more attention to that literature in a separate section.

One might wonder why should the cap rate alone predict future real estate returns. Shouldn't other variables, such as construction costs, local economic conditions, zoning laws, and demographic trends be part of the set of explanatory variables? The assumption that the cap rate is the only conditioning variable is equivalent to assuming that all other economic factors are successfully summarized by that one quantity. In other words, this ratio captures all relevant economic fluctuations and it is the sole state variable. To the extent that some of the current economic information is not embedded in that ratio, the model will be misspecified.

Most of the literature focuses on return (or price appreciation) predictability in expression (10). A notable exception is the work of Hamilton and Schwab (1985). They find a significant negative relation between the rent–price ratio (not in logs) and future growth in rents. Using aggregate REIT data, our regressions support their findings (Section (4)).

Meese and Wallace (1994), Capozza and Seguin (1996), Gallin (2008), and Campbell et al. (2009) are some of the studies testing for return predictability within the above framework while Himmelberg et al. (2005) offer a slightly broader approach. Gallin (2008) estimates Eqs. (10) and (11) using quarterly repeat-sales index data from 1970:Q1 to 2005:Q4. The two equations are estimated separately at 4-years-ahead horizons $(T = 16)$. He finds that the rent–price ratio has a positive relation with future returns and a negative relation with future rent growth rates, as predicted by expression (9). In his work, the coefficient $\beta_d(T)$ in the rent growth regression is statistically significant, whereas $\beta_r(T)$ in the return regression is not. Hence, from a statistical perspective, the evidence of rent–price predicting future returns is tenuous. Meese and Wallace (1994) formulate a different test, which they carry out with transaction level data for Alameda and San Francisco counties in Northern California. They find evidence of short-run violations but long-run consistency with the present value relation and argue that high transaction costs might be the reason behind the differences across horizons. Capozza and Seguin (1996) point out that the predictive power of the cap rate is best observed

---

[33] The constant ρ is usually close to unity.

Table 9.3 Correlation Matrix

	Census Median	CS10	FHFA/OFHEO	NCREIF	TBI	REIT
Census Median	1					
CS10	0.148	1				
FHFA/OFHEO	0.029	0.803	1			
NCREIF	0.080	0.425	0.335	1		
TBI	0.029	0.340	0.329	0.604	1	
REIT	0.334	0.374	0.181	0.280	0.220	1

Notes: Correlation matrix of quarterly returns to the Census Median, Case–Shiller Composite 10, FHFA/OFHEO U.S. Monthly, NCREIF All, TBI All, and REIT All indices during the common 1991:Q2-2010:Q4 sample period.

once they account for other cross-sectional differences in rental versus owner-occupied housing. They use a pooled sample of 64 metropolitan areas across the U.S. from 1960 to 1990 and most of the data is from the decennial Census of Housing and Population.

In a recent work, Campbell et al. (2009) also use expression (9) as a starting point of their analysis. Rather than assuming that future returns are an adequate proxy for expected returns, the authors follow Campbell (1991) and use vector autoregression (VAR) to forecast the future quantities in (9). One of the forecasting variables is the log rent–price ratio. Based on the VAR estimates, they document predictable variations in expected returns and expected rent growth for 23 metropolitan markets, four regional markets, and the national housing market over the 1975–2007 period with quarterly data. Consistent with the results of Gallin (2008), the rent–price ratio explains a larger fraction of the variability of expected returns than of expected rent growth. This is true for the entire sample and even during the boom subsample of 1997 to 2007. However, the statistical significance of the return predictability is not compelling. To illustrate the degree of real estate predictability by the log rent–price ratio, we run short-horizon equivalents of regression (10). The data are sampled at quarterly frequency and $T = 1$, which implies that we forecast returns one quarter ahead. We include the lagged return in addition to the lagged log rent–price ratio in the regressions because of the high degree of serial correlation documented in the previous section. The regressions are estimated for residential properties with the Census, Case–Shiller, and FHFA/OFHEO databases, and for commercial properties with the NCREIF, TBI, and REIT indices.

The residential results are presented in Table 9.4, Panel B.[34] When included as a stand-alone variable, the log rent–price ratio is a rather weak predictor of future returns for all

[34] We cannot run the residential regressions at monthly horizons, because the rent–price ratio data is only available quarterly.

Table 9.4 Forecasting Residential Real Estate

Panel A: Monthly

	Census			Case–Shiller			FHFA/OFHEO		
r	−0.569		−0.573	0.938		0.863	0.725		0.593
	(−11.894)		(−12.211)	(26.222)		(21.141)	(10.592)		(7.097)
r_m		0.058	0.061		0.017	0.007		0.017	0.013
		(1.067)	(1.203)		(0.885)	(1.063)		(1.372)	(1.755)
dp_m		−0.005	−0.010		−0.016	−0.003		−0.007	−0.004
		(−1.115)	(−1.393)		(−5.542)	(−1.592)		(−5.182)	(−3.395)
RTB		−0.055	−0.073		0.491	0.041		0.234	0.070
		(−0.227)	(−0.300)		(2.876)	(0.990)		(3.210)	(2.081)
CPI		0.013	0.003		0.259	0.200		0.237	0.030
		(0.019)	(0.004)		(1.431)	(3.554)		(1.911)	(0.253)
TSP		0.224	0.359		−0.118	0.062		−0.163	0.017
		(0.788)	(1.032)		(−0.819)	(1.399)		(−2.080)	(0.344)
CP		−0.153	−0.137		0.251	0.029		0.186	0.050
		(−0.691)	(−0.550)		(2.801)	(0.880)		(3.788)	(1.340)
IPG		0.370	0.464		0.076	−0.029		−0.081	−0.051
		(0.768)	(1.279)		(0.717)	(−0.535)		(−1.058)	(−0.905)
R^2	0.317	0.005	0.332	0.881	0.250	0.893	0.501	0.136	0.543

(*Continued*)

Table 9.4 *Continued*

Panel B: Quarterly

	Census					Case–Shiller					FHFA/OFHEO				
hp	0.011	0.008			−0.005	0.000	0.017			0.015	0.006	0.009			0.000
	(0.379)	(0.255)			(−0.153)	(−0.007)	(1.342)			(0.941)	(0.239)	(0.883)			(−0.015)
r		−0.523			−0.620		0.765			0.480		0.661			0.535
		(−7.262)			(−7.596)		(9.834)			(5.397)		(9.260)			(3.267)
dp_m			−0.008		−0.030			−0.046		−0.034			−0.020		−0.012
			(−0.769)		(−2.414)			(−6.521)		(−4.388)			(−4.929)		(−1.805)
r_m			0.005		0.081			0.052		0.008			0.006		−0.012
			(0.070)		(1.332)			(1.211)		(0.468)			(0.300)		(−0.710)
RTB				−0.050	0.116				1.460	0.882				0.747	0.343
				(−0.093)	(0.217)				(1.882)	(2.290)				(2.417)	(1.594)
CPI				0.125	−0.304				0.579	0.509				−0.121	−0.351
				(0.121)	(−0.362)				(1.996)	(4.132)				(−0.645)	(−1.858)
TSP				0.001	0.501				−0.417	0.329				−0.624	−0.128
				(0.002)	(0.937)				(−0.651)	(1.187)				(−1.876)	(−0.652)
CP				0.011	0.160				0.709	0.348				0.567	0.267
				(0.029)	(0.429)				(1.525)	(1.870)				(2.640)	(1.418)
IPG				0.065	0.011				−0.035	−0.241				−0.067	−0.020
				(0.306)	(0.041)				(−0.148)	(−1.043)				(−0.423)	(−0.148)
R^2	0.001	0.273	0.002	0.001	0.334	0.000	0.559	0.255	0.268	0.670	0.002	0.409	0.140	0.197	0.484

Notes: OLS slope estimates of the regression of returns on the Census Median, Case–Shiller Composite 10, and FHFA/OFHEO U.S. Monthly indices on a constant (not reported) and the following lagged conditioning variables: the return and rent–price ratio of the index (r and hp respectively), the return and dividend–price ratio of the aggregate stock market (r_m and dp_m respectively), and the financial and macro variables as defined in Table 9.2. The rent–price ratio used for the Census Median in Panel B is the average between the Case–Shiller and FHFA/OFHEO rent–price ratios. In Panel A, the horizon is monthly from February 1991 until December 2010. In panel B, the horizon is quarterly from 1991:Q2 until 2010:Q4. In parenthesis below the estimates, Newey and West (1987) HAC t-statistics based on four lags are reported.

three series. The coefficient is positive for the Census and FHFA/OFEHO series but is far from being statistically significant, and is essentially zero for the Case–Shiller index. In the subsequent specification, we add lagged returns as a control variable. The results from the Census data are now the most discouraging, from a predictability perspective. The point estimate for lagged log rent–price ratio is 0.008 with a Newey–West t-statistic of 0.255. This lack of predictability might be due to the fact that the Census median returns series do not adjust for the quality of properties. Some evidence pointing in that direction is presented in the next subsection. The Case–Shiller and FHFA/OFHEO estimates are positive, as suggested by Malpezzi (1999), but still statistically insignificant. The large R^2s of 0.559 and 0.409 are mostly due to the serial correlation in returns, which is captured by the lagged return term, r.

In Table 9.5, we display the predictive regressions results for commercial real estate returns based on quarterly observations over the same 1991:Q2-2010:Q4 period. The specifications are directly comparable with those for residential properties in Table 9.4, and the results are very much in agreement. More precisely, we observe a positive relation between the log rent–price ratio and future commercial real estate returns. While the point estimates are slightly larger for all three indices, and especially for the TBI, the Newey–West t-statistics are in the range of -0.121 to 1.494 when no other conditioning variables are included and in the range of 0.964 to 1.532 when controlling for lagged returns. The inability to reject the null of no predictability might be due to a lack of power of our test, especially given the presence of noise in the returns series. We will be able to explore the lack of power direction a bit further in the case of REITs, as we have market-based monthly observations over a longer time span. In sum, these results suggest that while there is a positive relation between the log rent–price ratio and future returns, as suggested by expression (6), it is not statistically significant in our samples. Admittedly, short-horizon predictability, even if it were present, is hard to detect in real estate indices that are so serially correlated.

The price–income ratio is suggested by Malpezzi (1999) as another predictor of real estate price changes. The underlying assumption behind this approach is the presence of an equilibrium relationship between house prices and household income. A temporary deviation of the price–income ratio above its long-run mean implies that either future prices will have to come down, the income level has to increase, or both. Malpezzi (1999) tests this prediction on repeat-sales and hedonic indexes on residential housing data at the MSA level. He documents that a one-unit increase in the distance between the price–income ratio and its equilibrium level is associated with a 2.7% drop in housing prices in the subsequent year. He also finds that other variables, such as mortgage rates, population growth and housing regulations, have an effect on future prices beyond the lags of the price–income. For instance, the stringency of the regulatory environment raises prices consistently, suggesting that supply shocks are important in determining house price dynamics (Glaeser et al., 2008). An inelastic housing supply is also suggested by the

Table 9.5 Forecasting Commercial Real Estate

	NCREIF					TBI					REITs				
	(1)	(2)	(3)	(4)	(5)	(1)	(2)	(3)	(4)	(5)	(1)	(2)	(3)	(4)	(5)
hp/dp	−0.003	0.011				−0.007		0.031		0.031	0.003	0.070	0.109		0.136
	(−0.121)	(0.985)				(−1.139)		(0.917)		(0.964)	(0.123)	(1.494)	(1.532)		(1.620)
r		0.819					0.363			0.057		−0.254	0.257		0.016
		(13.330)					(2.066)			(0.460)		(−1.871)	(1.727)		(0.113)
r_m			−0.053					−0.026		−0.035		−0.031	0.016		0.025
			(−3.553)					(−2.057)		(−1.545)		(−1.236)	(0.405)		(0.506)
dp_m			0.059					0.005		0.093		0.000	0.365		0.260
			(1.328)					(0.397)		(1.137)		(0.002)	(1.428)		(1.229)
RTB				0.698	0.570				1.098	1.481				1.630	0.729
				(2.076)	(2.405)				(1.512)	(1.793)				(1.231)	(0.518)
CPI				0.630	0.357				0.509	0.551				3.521	3.885
				(2.407)	(2.033)				(1.009)	(1.032)				(1.486)	(1.544)
TSP				−1.265	−0.309				−0.640	−0.658				0.073	0.918
				(−2.635)	(−0.870)				(−0.857)	(−0.997)				(0.033)	(0.444)
CP				0.099	0.073				0.193	0.334				0.748	−0.850
				(0.282)	(0.391)				(0.348)	(0.534)				(0.640)	(−0.573)
IPG				0.759	0.499				1.116	1.182				1.262	1.748
				(3.101)	(1.826)				(2.643)	(2.848)				(0.950)	(1.228)
R^2	0.001	0.650	0.371	0.588	0.767	0.024	0.027	0.074	0.253	0.317	0.022	0.082	0.088	0.179	0.270

Notes: OLS slope estimates of the regression of returns on the NCREIF All, TBI All, and REIT All indices on a constant (not reported) and lagged conditioning variables. Variables definition follows from Table 9.4. The horizon is quarterly from 1991:Q2 until 2010:Q4. In parenthesis below the estimates, Newey and West (1987) HAC t-statistics based on four lags are reported.

evidence that higher growth rates of population and income are associated with future price changes. The effect of supply shocks, however, hinges crucially on the assumption about the ability of households to move. If this can happen freely, shocks to supply do not have an impact on house prices (Van Nieuwerburgh and Weill, 2010). Finally, higher mortgage rates predict lower price changes.

The vast majority of studies on real estate predictability estimate regressions (10) and/or (11) by OLS, equation by equation. However, if future returns and future rent growth are correlated (and there is no reason to believe that they are not), then equation-by-equation OLS regressions suffer from an omitted-variables bias. This argument has been made by Lettau and Ludvigson (2001) and Koijen and Van Binsbergen (2010) in the context of stock returns. The reason is that, in the presence of a correlation, the rent-to-price ratio is not sufficient to capture the time variation in the predicted variables and may understate their degree of time-variation. The same point has been made by Plazzi et al. (2010) in the case of commercial real estate predictability. To circumvent this issue, Plazzi et al. (2010) assume a first-order autoregressive process for the unobserved expected returns and expected rent growth and link it to the reduced form OLS regression coefficient in the rent-to-price ratio regression. They estimate the parameters of the underlying processes on a panel of quarterly returns to apartments, industrial properties, offices, and retail properties for 53 MSAs over the 1994–2003 period. Because of the added structure in the predictive regressions, they are able to identify and estimate substantial variations in both expected returns and expected rent growth in the time series and across property types (in the 2–20% range).

While the use of valuation ratios in predictive regressions has its appeal, an obvious drawback is that the predictive ratio might not be capturing all time variation in the conditioning information set. This is yet another reason to suspect that the results for such regressions may suffer from omitted-variable bias. But even if a ratio were a sufficient proxy for the time variation in economic conditions, the reduced form version of regressions (10) and (11) do not allow us to understand the economic forces that are behind the predictive relation. Is the forecastability due to demographic changes or other demand shocks? Or is it driven by supply shocks, such as tighter real estate regulations and zoning laws? What role, if any, do slowly-adjusting construction costs play? Those questions can only be answered if additional conditioning variables are introduced in the predictive regressions.

3.3. Predictability Based on Economic Variables

There is considerable evidence that economic variables, other than past returns or valuation ratios, are associated with future appreciations in property values, as shown by Rosen (1984), Linneman (1986), Skantz and Strickland (1987), Case and Shiller (1990), Abraham and Hendershott (1996), Pace et al. (2000), MacKinnon and Zaman (2009), Plazzi et al. (2010), among others. The empirical framework in most of these papers is the predictive regression (6) with conditioning information X_t that includes demographic variables (population growth, percentage of population within a certain age), income and employment variables, construction costs, housing starts, tax rates, zoning restrictions, and other regulatory variables. The selection of the conditioning information is dictated by the data, the level of aggregation, and the methodology.

Linneman (1986) uses data from the Annual Housing Survey for the Philadelphia residential market in 1975 and 1978 to test whether a wide set of property characteristics are associated with future changes in property values. He regresses 1975 residential values on a broad set of structural and neighborhood characteristics and finds that the 1975 residuals are significantly correlated with 1978 property prices.

Linneman's (1986) work is one of the first to document persistence in changes in residential values. However, it is not a predictive model in the strict sense of the term. In regression (6), we are looking to relate systematic changes in X_t with future returns. Most of the property characteristics in his hedonic model are fixed-effects and do not change with time. In an interesting study, Skantz and Strickland (1987) investigate house price dynamics following an unexpected disaster, Houston's widespread flood on July 26, 1979, which affected several subdivisions of the city. They find that prices in the flooded subdivision did not decrease immediately after the flood, which suggests that residential values already reflected the higher flood risk. They also document that house prices started to adjust downwards a year after the event, mainly because of an increase in flood insurance premia. The fact that, net of insurance premia costs, home prices are not affected by a natural disaster is a compelling evidence in favor of market efficiency.

Case and Shiller (1990) test for predictability in the excess total returns (returns minus the T-bill rate) of four metropolitan areas (Atlanta, Chicago, Dallas, San Francisco) with a number of conditioning variables including lagged returns. The return data is computed from repeat-sales indices, rental data from the 1970 Census, and residential rent from the Bureau of Labor Statistics. The larger information set allows the authors to test a stronger version of the market efficiency hypothesis than in Case and Shiller (1989). The dataset is at quarterly frequency, from 1970 to 1986. The conditioning variables, the majority of which are available at metropolitan level, are: the rent–price ratio, the mortgage payment–income ratio, construction costs–price ratio, employment growth rate, real per capital income growth, growth rate in construction costs, percentage change in adult population (between ages 25 and 44), the percentage change in marginal tax rate, and housing starts divided by the population. The forecasting variable of interest is the excess return over the next four quarters. Case and Shiller (1990) show that the economic predictors are able to capture a significant fraction of the fluctuations in future real estate returns; their fully-specified predictive regressions have an R^2 of 0.336 to as much as 0.615 (their Tables 7–9). From the included variables, real per capita income growth and the increase in the adult population are strongly positively related with future annual excess returns. The sign is consistent with economic intuition, namely, improved

Table 9.6 Forecasting REITs

Estimation, Horizon	Panel A: Real Returns											
	All			Apt			Ind & Off			Rtl		
	β_r	$t(\beta_r)$	R^2	β_r	$t(\beta_r)$	R^2	β_r	$t(\beta_r)$	R^2	β_r	$t(\beta_r)$	R^2
						Overlapping						
OLS, $T = 1$	0.001	0.035	0.002	0.000	0.013	0.001	−0.012	−0.791	0.001	0.003	0.189	0.002
OLS, $T = 3$	0.031	0.820	0.009	0.022	0.967	0.010	−0.020	−0.547	0.001	0.039	0.998	0.012
OLS, $T = 6$	0.117	1.490	0.039	0.080	1.652	0.040	0.000	−0.005	0.000	0.129	1.660	0.045
OLS, $T = 12$	0.280	1.684	0.092	0.200	1.968	0.110	0.031	0.182	0.002	0.321	1.872	0.119
GMM, $T = \{1, 3, 6, 12\}$	0.013	1.126	−	0.010	1.421	−	−0.004	−0.328	−	0.017	1.435	−
						Non-Overlapping						
OLS, $T = 1$	0.001	0.041	0.002	0.000	0.014	0.001	−0.012	−0.841	0.001	0.003	0.235	0.002
OLS, $T = 3$	0.014	0.345	0.009	0.009	0.338	0.009	−0.031	−0.865	0.001	0.026	0.614	0.014
OLS, $T = 6$	0.024	0.309	0.013	0.023	0.508	0.017	−0.080	−1.139	0.004	0.041	0.520	0.019
OLS, $T = 12$	0.062	0.504	0.027	0.057	0.671	0.037	−0.112	−0.644	0.003	0.126	0.837	0.049
GMM, $T = \{1, 3, 6, 12\}$	0.009	1.397	−	0.003	1.607	−	−0.001	−0.128	−	0.008	1.410	−

Estimation, Horizon	Panel B: Real Dividend Growth											
	All			Apt			Ind & Off			Rtl		
	β_r	$t(\beta_r)$	R^2	β_r	$t(\beta_r)$	R^2	β_r	$t(\beta_r)$	R^2	β_r	$t(\beta_r)$	R^2
						Overlapping						
OLS, $T = 1$	−0.015	−3.232	0.029	−0.026	−2.266	0.042	−0.046	−4.125	0.071	−0.020	−2.298	0.026
OLS, $T = 3$	−0.051	−3.465	0.094	−0.081	−2.912	0.118	−0.125	−5.628	0.212	−0.063	−2.765	0.078
OLS, $T = 6$	−0.119	−3.361	0.162	−0.182	−3.101	0.201	−0.255	−5.231	0.325	−0.137	−2.671	0.139
OLS, $T = 12$	−0.261	−3.551	0.230	−0.384	−3.483	0.320	−0.541	−4.994	0.447	−0.263	−2.458	0.193
GMM, $T = \{1, 3, 6, 12\}$	−0.018	−9.716	−	−0.031	−7.156	−	−0.045	−9.366	−	−0.025	−6.828	−
						Non-Overlapping						
OLS, $T = 1$	−0.015	−2.753	0.029	−0.026	−2.097	0.042	−0.046	−4.062	0.071	−0.020	−2.210	0.026
OLS, $T = 3$	−0.049	−3.063	0.095	−0.082	−2.002	0.145	−0.127	−4.198	0.210	−0.059	−2.149	0.079
OLS, $T = 6$	−0.120	−3.586	0.170	−0.205	−2.514	0.280	−0.271	−4.760	0.388	−0.154	−2.228	0.173
OLS, $T = 12$	−0.230	−4.629	0.213	−0.396	−3.354	0.417	−0.488	−4.547	0.525	−0.295	−2.367	0.231
GMM, $T = \{1, 3, 6, 12\}$	−0.019	−6.696	−	−0.035	−5.677	−	−0.055	−9.179	−	−0.023	−3.227	−

Notes: Slope coefficients of the regressions of T-month real returns (Panel A) and real dividend growth (Panel B) on the aggregate CRSP/Ziman All-Equity REIT index (All) and separately for apartments (Apt), industrial properties and offices (Ind & Off), and retail properties (Rtl) on a constant (not reported) and lagged log dividend-price ratio. OLS results are shown for separate monthly horizons. The table also reports the one-month two-stage GMM estimates, which impose the present value constraint (Eq. (16)) across equations and the short-long horizon relationship (Eq. (15)) across horizons $T = \{1, 3, 6, 12\}$. The coefficients are bias-adjusted following Stambaugh, 1999. The t-statistics are Newey and West (1987) based on four lags for non-overlapping and T lags for overlapping returns. The sample is monthly from December 1980 until December 2010.

Table 9.7 Forecasting REITs In-Sample and Out-Of-Sample

| Forecaster | Real Returns | | | | | Real Dividend-Growth | |
	IS	OOS unc	OOS sign(β_r)	OOS $\hat{r} > 0$	OOS both	IS	OOS unc
			Panel A: Monthly				
dp	0.181	−0.686	−0.571	−0.321	−0.205	2.866	−1.873
r_m	4.760	4.022	4.022	1.885	1.885	0.572	0.985
dp_m	0.005	−0.637	−0.572	−0.324	−0.260	0.008	−1.160
RTB	0.071	−2.005	0.000	−1.565	0.000	0.058	−2.015
CPI	0.641	−3.105	0.000	−3.075	0.000	0.047	−1.846
TSP	0.313	−0.488	−0.488	−0.406	−0.406	0.559	−10.616
CP	0.250	−0.385	−0.318	0.211	0.278	1.739	−4.108
IP	2.805	−0.227	0.327	−0.985	−0.411	2.320	−1.920
Combined	2.093	0.187	0.620	−0.226	0.241	6.862	0.291
			Panel B: Quarterly				
dp	0.919	−6.189	−6.160	−4.337	−4.308	9.366	−15.520
r_m	0.470	1.463	2.218	0.770	1.526	0.230	−0.319
dp_m	0.121	−2.406	−2.406	−1.284	−1.284	0.002	−1.442
RTB	0.031	−3.792	0.000	−3.704	0.000	0.258	−0.290
CPI	0.690	−6.142	−0.445	−6.373	−0.445	0.268	0.297
TSP	2.156	−1.007	−1.007	0.749	0.749	0.602	−15.706
CP	0.798	0.638	0.649	0.638	0.649	2.536	−3.415
IP	2.240	1.059	2.156	−0.162	1.150	3.116	−3.049
Combined	2.093	−1.319	−0.166	−1.270	−0.045	6.862	−0.266
			Panel C: Semi-Annual				
dp	3.862	−15.211	−15.185	−9.784	−9.757	16.217	−40.390
r_m	0.480	0.377	0.611	0.377	0.611	0.016	−1.645
dp_m	0.450	−3.825	−3.825	−2.314	−2.314	0.002	−2.137
RTB	0.001	−4.650	0.000	−4.650	0.000	0.526	−0.418
CPI	0.001	−3.694	−0.017	−3.694	−0.017	0.658	0.912
TSP	2.955	−0.984	−0.984	−0.522	−0.522	1.076	−19.220
CP	0.193	1.216	1.095	1.216	1.095	5.412	−5.349
IP	1.240	−1.267	2.143	−1.888	1.469	5.580	−5.200
Combined	2.093	−2.625	−1.340	−2.164	−0.890	6.862	−2.492

Notes: In-sample (IS) and Out-Of-Sample (OOS) R^2, as defined in Eq. (17), for the predictive regression of real returns and real dividend growth to the aggregate CRSP/Ziman All-Equity REIT index at the monthly (Panel A), quarterly (Panel B), and semi-annual (Panel C) frequency. The forecasters are defined as in Table 9.5. "Combined" refers to the average forecast across all forecasters. Specification "unc" is the unconstrained regression; specification "sign(β_r)" and "$r > 0$" replace the forecast with the unconditional mean when the slope coefficient or the forecast, respectively, are negative; specification "both" imposes both constraints. The OOS results are based on a 180-month burn-in period. The full sample is monthly observations from December 1980 until December 2010.

economic conditions and demographic booms both put demand pressure on house prices. Two measures of fundamental value, the price-rent ratio and construction costs divided by price, also forecast future returns with a positive sign. To put things in perspective, the rent–price ratio alone has an in-sample R^2 of 0.109 (Tables 9.8 and 9.9). Variables such as the growth rate of employment, marginal individual income tax rate, and houses starts are also found to be important predictors. Overall, the addition of control variables increases the in-sample R^2 from about 10% to as much as 60%, thus rejecting the hypothesis of a semi-strongly efficient market. Their analysis is, however, in-sample and the pooled regression (across cities) use overlapping observations and do not explicitly account for cross-sectional correlation in the residuals.

Abraham and Hendershott (1996) explore the systematic predictability patterns of residential properties and link them to supply shocks. They express the growth in real estate prices as a linear function of lagged state variables such as the growth in real construction costs, the growth in real income per working age adult, the growth in employment, and the change in real after-tax rate. The error term of this regression is interpreted as a deviation from a market equilibrium and, therefore, a proxy for a bubble as it reflects adjustment dynamics and data noise. Working on the repeat-sales house price indices from Freddie Mac–Fannie Mae for 30 MSAs, they find that coastal and inland cities are more pronounced in those markets. Their results imply that predictability in the residential market is to some degree related to measures of local supply elasticity such as the availability of desirable land.

The papers thus far have focused on predictability in the residential market. Similar studies have been conducted with commercial real estate data. For instance, MacKinnon and Zaman (2009) analyze the predictability of returns to direct real estate investment, proxied by the TBI index, and REITs in the context of a long-horizon asset allocation problem.[35] Their in-sample analysis reveals that TBI returns are predictable by variables such as lagged REIT returns, bond returns, and the T-bill interest rate, while cap rates and employment growth show only limited predictive power. This result is noteworthy especially because, as we saw in Table 9.2, price changes in the TBI index are close to uncorrelated. The mean-reversion in direct real estate investment makes it a less risky asset for long-horizon investors. As a result, for reasonable target values of the total portfolio expected return, the fraction of wealth invested in commercial properties is found to be no lower than 17%. Interestingly, in their application, the correlation between REITs and TBI returns is high enough to make REITs a redundant asset class when investors have access to direct investment in commercial properties.

The interaction between prices, vacancy rates, transactions volume, housing stock, and rents have also been investigated. For example, Wheaton and Torto (1988) consider deviations from equilibrium and adjustment dynamics between vacancy and rents in the office market. They find a statistically significant and qualitatively strong relationship between current excess vacancy and future real rent changes, even when accounting

[35] For a recent investigation on the European market, see Fugazza et al. (2007).

for the possibility in trends in the structural vacancy rates. Zhong-Guo (1997) uses a vector autoregression (VAR) error correction model to analyze the joint relationship between sales volume and median sales prices from the National Association of Realtors. Granger-causality tests indicate that sales affect price significantly, but home prices affect sales only weakly. DiPasquale and Wheaton (1994) show that the Tax Reform Act of 1986 had economically significant supply and demand effects on the rental properties markets. Based on their estimates, they predicted that, over the next 10 years, real rents should have increased by 8% as a direct result of the legislation. These numbers are economically meaningful, especially given the low variability of rents over the decades preceding the 1986 legislation.

Evidence for predictability in commercial real estate returns and rent growth is also provided by Plazzi et al. (2010) using three principal components extracted from the level and change in population, employment, per-capita income, and construction costs. In particular, either the first or first and second principal components – which load on the level and growth in population and income as well as on construction costs – are found to be significant at the 1% level or better across all four property types. When the cap rate and a coastal dummy are also included, the adjusted R^2 in the returns predictive regressions range from 17% (for offices) to 37% for retail properties. In the rental growth predictive regressions, the adjusted R^2 are from 8% for offices to 14% for apartments. Interestingly, the cap rate remains significant even after the inclusion of these principal components, which suggests that the valuation ratio it is truly capturing time-varying dynamics rather than mere cross-sectional differences. Consistent with the findings in Abraham and Hendershott (1996), Plazzi et al. (2010) document cross-sectional differences in predictability depending on density and land-use restrictions. Evidence of return predictability is drawn primarily from locations characterized by lower population density and less stringent land-use restrictions. By contrast, rent growth predictability is more likely observed in locations characterized by higher population density and more severe land-use restrictions.

We revisit the predictability of aggregate real estate indices by conditioning variables other than lagged returns or log rent–price ratio. Panels A and B of Table 9.4 present various specifications of regression (6), estimated with monthly and quarterly residential data. In Panel A, we observe that the inclusion of the stock market's dividend-price ratio (dp_m), which is a proxy for the state of the equity market, has a negative effect on future residential returns. The effect is statistically significant for the Case–Shiller and FHFA/OHFEO indices. The relative T-Bill rate and the Cochrane and Piazzesi (2005) bond factor are significant for the repeat-sales indices. In the fourth, most comprehensive specification, the inclusion of lagged returns and all other economic variables reveals that, at monthly horizons, the data is simply too serially correlated for any of the additional predictors to be statistically significant.

In the quarterly predictability regressions, Panel B of Table 9.4, we observe that several economic variables are statistically significant in explaining future fluctuations in real estate price changes. More specifically, for the Case–Shiller index, the stock market's dividend-price ratio, the relative T-Bill rate, inflation, and the Cochrane and Piazzesi (2005) bond factor are significant at the 10% confidence level or better. The results for the FHFA/OFHEO are similar, albeit less significant. In all specifications, the log rent–price ratio is insignificant. Also, the Census median price index remains the least forecastable of the three indices.

In Table 9.5, we present the equivalent results for commercial properties at quarterly frequency. As in the previous table, the stock market's log dividend price ratio is negative and significantly related to future returns of the NCREIF and TBI indices. In the third specification of the regressions, higher industrial production growth leads to higher future changes in the same two indices. In the case of NCREIF, the term spread is also statistically significant but its point estimate is negative. The NCREIF is the most forecastable index, with as much as 70.9% of its changes being predicted, in-sample, by the economic variables. For the TBI, the explanatory power drops to 25.5%. REIT returns are the least predictable, as the joint explanatory power of all predictor yields an adjusted R^2 of 15.4%.

A recurring theme in the extant real estate literature is that the predictability of returns varies across geographic regions (e.g., Case and Shiller, 1989; Gyourko and Voith, 1992; Abraham and Hendershott, 1996; Gu, 2002; Crawford and Fratantoni, 2003; Fratantoni and Schuh, 2003; Capozza et al., 2004, and Hill, 2004). In a particularly exhaustive study of 62 metropolitan areas from 1979 to 1995, Capozza et al. (2004) note that "the dynamic properties of housing markets are specific to the given time and location being considered." The economic sources of heterogeneity in predictive regressions are the same ones that determine house price dynamics, namely, demographic changes, regulations and zoning restrictions, local economic conditions, as well as heterogeneous responses to global macro-economic shocks. While differences in datasets, variable definitions, and methodologies make it hard to compare results across studies, quantifying the predictive ability of economic variables across metropolitan areas is of clear interest.

To illustrate the cross-sectional differences, we run predictive regressions similar to the ones discussed in Tables 9.4 and 9.5, but with MSA-level (rather than national) indices. To do so, we compute quarterly log price changes of 25 MSA regions from FHFA/OHFEO over the 1991–2010 period. For each region, we regress the one-period-ahead price changes on the same set of conditioning variables that were used in Table 9.4. In other words, we run 25 MSA-level regressions, whose coefficient estimates, t-statistics, and R^2s are comparable to those for the aggregate FHFA/OFHEO index, reported in the very last column of Table 9.4. Rather than tabulating a large number of statistics, in Figure 9.4, we summarize the average predictive coefficients on each variable across regions (top-left panel), the average t-statistics (top right), the number of significant coefficients across regions (bottom left), and the average R^2 (bottom right).

The average coefficient on lagged returns is about 0.2, with an average t-statistic of nearly 2, and is statistically significant in 13 out of the 25 metropolitan areas. Interestingly,

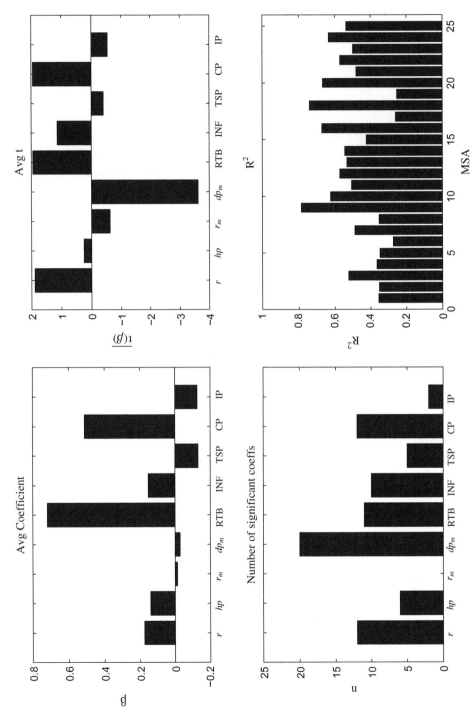

Figure 9.4 Predicting Residential Real Estate MSA Returns. Summary of the predictive regression of each of the 25 MSAs OFHEO Purchase Only quarterly return series on a constant, its own (lagged) return, the aggregate OFHEO rent-to-price ratio, and macro and financial variables as defined in Table 9.4. The regressors are all jointly included as in the largest specification of Tables 9.4 and 9.5. For each regressor (except the constant) across MSA, the figure shows in the top left panel the average slope coefficient, in the top right panel the average t-statistic, and in the bottom left panel the number of t-statistics greater than two in absolute value. The bottom right panel displays the R^2 for each regression. The list of MSAs is reported in Appendix A.1. The sample is quarterly observations from 1991:Q2 until 2010:Q4.

the most strongly significant predictors in the top-right panel – the lagged return, the market dividend-price ratio, and the RTB – are the same ones that were significant in the aggregate regressions (Table 9.4). Here, an additional predictor, the CP factor, displays a comparable importance. The same four variables appear as the most frequently significant across metropolitan areas, with the addition of inflation, suggesting that their average t-statistics are not driven by a few outliers. The fact that inflation and industrial production do not reach (on average) statistical significance might indicate the need for MSA-specific measures of economic activity. Our regressions, which are designed to capture common movements across MSAs price changes (because the predictors are the same across MSAs), show that at least some of the time-variation in residential returns is attributable to systematic, market-wide fluctuations. Abraham and Hendershott (1996), Capozza et al. (2004), and Del Negro and Otrok (2007) report similar findings. The average R^2 is 49%, in line with the 48% value documented for the national series. There is, however, considerable dispersion in the individual regressions R^2 (bottom-right plot), ranging from 25% for St. Louis, MO-IL to as high as 79% for Los Angeles-Long Beach-Glendale, CA.

As a more direct test of the presence of common factors in the cross-section of 25 MSAs, we extract the first 10 principal components of their covariance matrix. In the top panel of Figure 9.5, we plot the fraction of the total variance explained by each of these components. Strikingly, the first principal component explains slightly less than 70% of the covariance, while the other components are much less important. This evidence supports the findings in Figure 9.4 and the assertion that macro-economic fluctuations are behind some of the time-variation, at least over our sample period. Of course, a significant part of the unexplained variance is due to local factors. The bottom panel in the figure displays the fraction explained by the first component over the 2001–2010 period, estimated with a 40-quarter rolling window basis. Interestingly, the common component increased significantly during the 2008–2010 period, undoubtedly as a result of the bust of the residential real estate bubble and the subsequent financial crisis.

4. REITs

A real estate corporation is considered to be a REIT for tax-purposes if it distributes at least 90% of its taxable income as dividends.[36] This unambiguous link between cash flows from commercial real estate and dividends makes REITs particularly suitable for

---

[36] In order to qualify as a REIT, a company must comply with certain provisions within the U.S. Internal Revenue Code. As required by the tax code, a REIT must: Be an entity that is taxable as a corporation; Be managed by a board of directors or trustees; Have shares that are fully transferable; Have no more than 50% of its shares held by five or fewer individuals during the last half of the taxable year; Invest at least 75% of its total assets in qualifying real estate assets, which include interests in real property, interests in mortgages on real property, or shares in other REITs; Derive at least 75% of its gross income from real estate related services, such as rents from real property or interest on mortgages financing real property; Have no more than 25% of its assets consist of stock in taxable REIT subsidiaries; Pay annually at least 90% of its taxable income in the form of shareholder dividends.

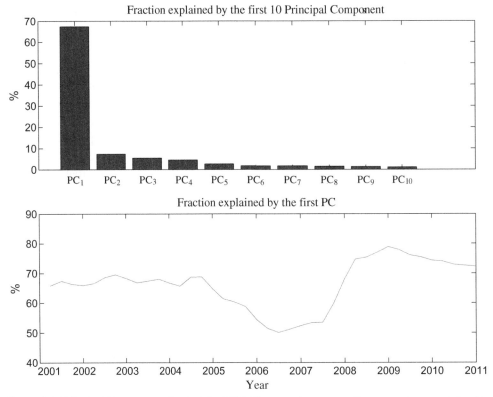

Figure 9.5 Principal Component Analysis by MSA. The top plot reports the percentage explained by the first 10 principal components extracted from the covariance matrix of returns to the 25 MSAs OFHEO Purchase Only quarterly series. The bottom plot shows the percentage explained by the first component based on 40-quarter rolling windows. The full sample is quarterly observations from 1991:Q2 until 2010:Q4.

predictability tests. In addition, REITs are traded on the U.S. stock exchange, are relatively liquid, and have small transaction costs relative to other real estate investments.

We devote particular attention to REITs for two additional reasons. First, the data is available at higher frequency and over a longer time span than other datasets. This allows us to correct the parameter estimates for well-known, small-sample biases and to cast the predictive system in a GMM framework. Cross-equations restrictions, imposed by the model, may provide further efficiency gains in the estimation. These improvements will ultimately allow us to verify whether more precise parameter estimates and better in-sample fit obtain by using longer and less noisy series. Second, the longer sample allows us to investigate the (pseudo) out-of-sample performance of the forecasts. Thus far, most of the discussion had focused on estimation and in-sample performance. However, as is well-known in the stock market forecasting literature, in-sample fit does not necessarily translate into successful out-of-sample performance (Welch and Goyal, 2008). The disconnect between in-sample and out-of-sample results is likely due to parameter estimation error, structural breaks (Rossi, 2013 in this Handbook) or more general model misspecifications. We investigate the out-of-sample predictability of REITs by also incorporating some new insights.

The literature on REIT predictability is voluminous. A partial list of the works on the topic include Liu and Mei (1992), Mei and Liu (1994), Li and Wang (1995), Mei and Gao (1995), Nelling and Gyourko (1998), Liu and Mei (1998), Brooks and Tsolacos (2001, 2003), and Serrano and Hoesli (2007, 2010). The empirical approach in most of these studies can be framed into the following predictive system:

$$r_{t+1} = \mu_r + \beta_r x_t + \tau^r_{t+1} \tag{12}$$

$$\Delta d_{t+1} = \mu_d + \beta_d x_t + \tau^d_{t+1} \tag{13}$$

$$x_{t+1} = \mu_x + \phi x_t + \tau^{dp}_{t+1}. \tag{14}$$

The one-period regressions are sometimes augmented by investigating the predictability of long-horizon returns $r_{t+1:t+T} \equiv T^{-1} \Sigma^T_{j=1} r_{t+j}$ and dividend growth $\Delta d_{t+1:t+T} \equiv T^{-1} \Sigma^T_{j=1} \Delta d_{t+j}$, as in Eqs. (10) and (11) above. The conditioning variable x_t is usually the log dividend-price ratio. Multiple predictors are also considered, in which case β_r, β_d, and x_t are vectors.

In many instances, the predictor x_t is highly persistent and its innovations are correlated with the return innovations. In other words, ϕ is close to unity and the correlation between τ^{dp}_{t+1} and τ^r_{t+1} is non-zero. If that were the case, Cavanagh et al. (1995) and Stambaugh (1999) have shown that the OLS estimator of β_r is biased. The larger (in absolute value) the correlation between the innovations, the larger is the bias. This result is of relevance in real estate predictive regressions, as the predictor is often a valuation ratio, the T-bill rate, or a yield spread, which are all persistent. Several approaches of dealing with the small-sample bias have been suggested in the literature. We discuss the Stambaugh (1999) bias-correction below.

Liu and Mei (1992) is one of the earlier studies to investigate the predictability of U.S. REIT returns. Using monthly data from 1972 to 1989, they document that the log cap rate on REITs and the T-Bill, and to a lesser extent the dividend-price ratio of the aggregate stock market, forecast 1-month-ahead REIT returns. The corresponding adjusted R^2 for REITs at 0.175 is found to be much higher than the 0.087 value for the overall market, and comparable to the 0.165 R^2 of a portfolio of small-cap stocks. This makes economic sense as REITs fall, on average, in the small-caps category of stocks. In a follow-up study, Mei and Liu (1994) find that market-timing trading strategies based on the predictors in Liu and Mei (1992) outperform a buy-and-hold portfolio strategy for REIT firms in an out-of-sample test. In particular, they report an R^2 of the conditioning model relative to the unconditional mean of 0.136 for a portfolio of real estate building companies stocks, and lower R^2s at 0.109 and 0.083 in the case of the mREIT and eREIT portfolios, respectively. Similar predictability is however not present for common stocks. In a recent work, Serrano and Hoesli (2010) document that REITs returns in more mature and well-established REIT markets – most notably the U.S., the Netherlands, and Australia – are more predicable than are local stock market returns. Trading strategies based on the forecasting regressions outperform a buy-and-hold benchmark portfolio in all ten countries, and the gains exceed the transaction costs in about half of them. In sum, these studies suggest that predictability in real estate returns might be exploitable.

Several papers have gone beyond the simple univariate, linear forecasting models of Eqs. (12)–(14). For example, the results in Serrano and Hoesli (2007) indicate that neural networks models outperform linear regressions (time varying coefficient regressions and VAR systems) in forecasting equity REIT returns, when the models jointly include stock, bond, real estate, size, and book-to-market factors. Similar findings based on European data can be found in Brooks and Tsolacos (2003). Although there is no consensus in the literature as to what forecasting technique works best, increasing the complexity of the model seems in general to provide some in-sample improvements in forecasting accuracy.

Performance continuation and reversals are also related to the time series properties of asset returns and have been the subject of many studies in the financial economics literature. For securitized real estate, Mei and Gao (1995) examine serial persistence of weekly returns and argue that a contrarian-based strategy is profitable only if transaction costs are ignored. Analogous results based on monthly observations can be found in Nelling and Gyourko (1998), who document that the extant predictability is strongest after 1992 following the major reforms in the REITs market. Using a filter-based rule, Cooper et al. (1999) show that a contrarian strategy is in many cases more profitable than its associated execution costs. Graff and Young (1997) use different frequencies and find positive momentum effects with yearly data, evidence of performance reversals with monthly data, and no evidence of momentum or reversals with quarterly data. Finally, Stevenson (2002) provides international evidence of momentum effects over short- and medium-term horizons, as well as little support for price reversals.

To highlight and update the results we just discussed, we test for predictability using the monthly equity REIT series from the CRSP/Ziman database during the full 1980–2010 period. We construct monthly dividends using total and without-dividends returns as in Fama and French (1988b). The dividend series is then calculated as sum of the current and past 11 months dividends. The log dividend-price ratio is defined as the log dividend minus the log of the level in the current month. The left-hand side variables are the real log return and dividend growth, deflated by the CPI Index.[37] We also look

---

[37] Working with nominal or excess returns yield very similar results.

at the results for the REIT portfolios of companies that hold mainly apartment buildings (Apt), industrial buildings and offices (Ind & Off), and retail properties (Rtl), as they may exhibit different predictability properties.

Table 9.6 presents OLS estimates of Eqs. (12) and (13) for all REITs, Apt, Ind & Off, and Rtl. The predictive regressions are estimated over horizons of $T = \{1, 3, 6, 12\}$ months. Some studies compute long-horizon returns by overlapping one-period returns, whereas others consider non-overlapping windows. We provide both sets of results. Panel A displays the estimates for the return regressions (12) and Panel B displays those for the dividend-growth regression (13). It is well-known that the persistence of the dividend-price ratio (ϕ in (14) close to one) and a negative correlation of the predictor innovations with those of returns (correlation of τ_{t+1}^r and τ_{t+1}^{dp}) induce significant small-sample bias in the OLS estimates in regression (12) (Stambaugh, 1999). Therefore, the displayed coefficient estimates are adjusted for the small-sample bias using Stambaugh's (1999) correction. In the non-overlapping results, the t-statistics are calculating with Newey and West (1987) standard errors with four lags. In the overlapping data, the number of lags equals the number of overlapping observations T.

In Panel A of Table 9.6, the positive OLS estimates of β_r at various horizons show that the log dividend-yield is positively related to future REIT returns. This is true for the entire REIT portfolio and especially for retail properties. Interestingly, industrial and office properties exhibit little predictability at any horizon. Plazzi et al. (2010) document a similar finding, namely, that industrial and office property returns are the least predictable, using a different dataset. As the horizon increases, we observe an increase in the t-statistics. For overlapping returns, they reach customary significance levels at the yearly horizon. This result supports the claim in previous studies that returns are predictable at long horizons. However, we observe that the non-overlapping long-horizon results are not significant, which raises the possibility that the high t-statistics might be the product of distorted inference, due to the severe serial correlation, induced by the overlap (Valkanov, 2003).

The OLS estimates of β_d in Panel B are negative, as implied by the log-linearized expression (9). The point estimates are larger in magnitude than those in Panel A and, more importantly, they are statistically significant, with t-statistics for overlapping REITs in the -3.5 range. For industrial and office properties, the predictability is even more significant as the t-statistics are about -5. This finding mirrors the Plazzi et al. (2010) results that those properties exhibit the most predictable rent growth rates. It is comforting to observe that estimates and t-statistics using overlapping and non-overlapping dividend growth data yield very similar results. The R^2 in the overlapping and non-overlapping regressions is 0.2 for all REITs and as high as 0.4 to 0.5 for industrial and office properties. The strong ability of the dividend-price ratio to predict REITs dividend growth rates is in sharp contrast with the findings for the aggregate stock market (Lettau and Van Nieuwerburgh, 2008). This difference may be partly attributable to the strict payout policy that makes REITs dividends less prone to artificial smoothing, or to the nature of REIT cash flows.

The mixed predictability results of returns might be due to the lack of statistical power of our tests. Recent work by Lettau and Van Nieuwerburgh (2008) suggests that estimation and inference in long-horizon regressions can be improved by noting that the predictive system (12), (13), (14) implies the following time series restriction relating one-period and T-period slope coefficients:

$$\beta_r(T) = \beta_r \left(\frac{1 - \phi^T}{1 - \phi} \right) \quad \text{and} \quad \beta_d(T) = \beta_d \left(\frac{1 - \phi^T}{1 - \phi} \right). \tag{15}$$

In addition, the Campbell and Shiller (1988) present-value identity imposes a restriction between the predictive regression coefficients:

$$\beta_r - \beta_d = 1 - \rho\phi, \tag{16}$$

where ρ is the log-linearization coefficient. This expression is nothing but a restatement of the fact that, owing to the variability of dp, we must observe either return predictability, dividend growth predictability, or both. These observations suggest that more efficient estimates of β_r and β_d can be obtained through a GMM estimator, which imposes the above restrictions across different horizons T, as in Lettau and Van Nieuwerburgh (2008) and Plazzi et al. (2010).

In Table 9.6 we report the one-month coefficients β_r and β_d, estimated with GMM using horizons of $\{1, 3, 6, 12\}$ months. The estimates of β_r in Panel A remain positive and statistically insignificant for all REITs and for the various property types. The estimates of β_d (Panel B) are negative and smaller in magnitude than those in the unrestricted OLS regressions. However, their t-statistics have increased both with overlapping and non-overlapping data. The OLS and GMM results point to the same three conclusions. First, there is a positive but largely insignificant in-sample relation between the log dividend-price ratio and future returns. Second, the log dividend-price ratio forecasts dividend growth rates with a negative sign and the estimates are statistically significant. Finally, industrial and office properties seem to exhibit the least returns predictability and the most dividend growth predictability. This last finding merits further attention as it might provide further insights about the underlying economic sources behind the trade-off in predictability between returns and dividend growth rates.

The empirical discussions were thus far framed around in-sample fit in predictive regressions. However, the ultimate test of such regressions resides in whether they can produce accurate out-of-sample forecasts. Recently, the stock market predictability literature has found that significant predictors do not necessarily produce accurate out-of-sample forecasts. For instance, Welch and Goyal (2008) have documented that stock return predictors do not outperform the simple unconditional mean in a (pseudo) out-of-sample comparison. As a measure of relative forecasting accuracy, Welch and Goyal

(2008) use the out-of-sample (as opposed to in-sample) R^2 defined as:

$$R_{OOS}^2 = 1 - \frac{\sum_{t=1}^{T} (r_t - \widehat{r}_{t|t-1})}{\sum_{t=1}^{T} (r_t - \overline{r}_{t|t-1})}, \tag{17}$$

where $\widehat{r}_{t|t-1}$ and $\overline{r}_{t|t-1}$ are the predicted value and the historical average return, respectively, estimated using information up to and including time $t - 1$.

We take this opportunity to look at the out-of-sample predictive power of conditioning variables in REIT regressions. In addition to the log dividend-price ratio, we consider the same commonly-used predictors that were discussed in Tables 9.3 and 9.4.[38] We conduct the out-of-sample comparison by splitting the sample in two periods. A first 180-month period, corresponding to the 1980–1995 sample, is used to estimate first the forecasting model. Then, the estimates from that sample are taken to form the first forecasts of returns and dividend growth for January, 1996. Subsequently, we include the January 1996 observations to re-estimate the models and formulate forecasts for February, 1996 and so on until December, 2010. We do this at horizons of $T = \{1, 3, 6\}$ months. Given the limited time series, longer horizons are not possible.

In Panel A of Table 9.7, we present the monthly in-sample (column "IS") and out-of-sample (column "OOS unc") R^2s. The "unc" stands for "unconstrained" to differentiate those results from some constrained ones, discussed below. From the definition of R_{OOS}^2 in Eq. (17), positive values imply that the model delivers a lower mean square forecasting error (MSFE) than the unconditional mean. Looking down the IS column for real returns, we notice that several predictors have in-sample predictive power. However, the OOS unc column reveals that, with the exception of the lagged stock market return, the OOS R^2 are all negative. In other words, the MSFEs of all but one forecasting variable are higher than that of the unconditional mean. A combined forecast, obtained by equally-weighting all eight predictions, does well in-sample but its out-of sample performance barely beats the unconditional mean (last row in Panel A).

Campbell and Thompson (2008) show that imposing economic constraints on the OOS forecasts of stock market returns results in significant improvements in their OOS R^2. Following their work, we consider several non-linear constraints. The first one (column "sign (β_r)") restricts the estimated coefficient in a given period to have the expected sign.[39] The second constraint (column "OOS $\widehat{r} > 0$") imposes non-negativity of the forecasted real return. In column "OOS both," the forecast must satisfy both constraints. In periods when a constraint is violated, the historical average is used instead as a forecast.[40] The OOS results from the three constraints are displayed in Table 9.7. Imposing

---

[38] For the Cochrane and Piazzesi (2005) factor, we construct out-of-sample estimates by re-estimating the coefficients using only information available up to time $t - 1$.

[39] For the dividend-price ratio, the Campbell and Shiller (1988) decomposition implies a positive coefficient. For the other variables, we impose the same positivity constraint, although the guidance from economic theory is less clear. The sign constraints are broadly consistent with the prior of counter-cyclical risk premia.

[40] Other types of constraints could be imposed to enhance forecastability. See, for example, Pettenuzzo et al. (2011).

the sign (β_r) constraint brings several of the negative OOS R^2s into positive territory and increases the OOS R^2s of the combined forecast. The $\hat{r} > 0$ and joint constraints lead to modest improvements in the predictions. In Panels B and C, we present the results at quarterly and semi-annual horizons and observe several differences with respect to the monthly results. The log dividend-price ratio, which was insignificant at monthly frequency, is more significant in-sample. In Panel C, its in-sample R^2s is as high as 3.862 percent. Similar increases in IS R^2s occur for dp_m, and TSP. However, this in-sample fit does not translate into OOS performance. Indeed, the MSFE of dp is 15.211 percent higher than that of the unconditional mean. Some predictors, such as the CP factor, exhibit improvement in OOS forecasting power. Imposing the constraints does not help the log dividend-yield but does lead to a better performance of IP.

The results in Tables 9.6 and 9.7 all point toward weak evidence of in-sample predictability at long horizons. Econometric refinements, designed to reduce bias and increase efficiency of the estimates, do not alter significantly this conclusion. The OOS forecasting exercise suggests that most of the predictors yield MSFEs similar to or higher than the unconditional mean. This is true whether or not we impose economic constraints. The in-sample significance of our predictive results appears somewhat smaller than documented in previous studies. This difference may be partly due to the fact that our sample includes the particularly volatile 2007 to 2010 period and to the downward bias adjustment. Perhaps the most novel result in the tables is that the dividend growth of REITs is forecastable in-sample, although the OOS results are, once again, much weaker.

5. REAL ESTATE, LEVERAGE, AND MONETARY POLICY

5.1. The Effect of Leverage

The relation between real estate prices and leverage is a natural one, especially in the residential market. While in principle any asset could be used as collateral, housing is by far the easiest asset to borrow against. At the peak of the recent U.S. residential bubble, about $12 trillion of outstanding mortgage debt had been issued against the value of properties, which at the time were worth in the neighborhood of $25 trillion (Case, 2007). In the UK, Aoki et al. (2004) report that about 80% of all household borrowing is secured on housing. High levels of home borrowing are bound to have an effect on house price dynamics and some of the studies that analyze this relationship are Linneman and Wachter (1989), Stein (1995), Lamont and Stein (1999), Spiegel (2001), Aoki et al. (2004), Ortalo-Magn'e and Rady (2006), Lustig and Van Nieuwerburgh (2005), Favilukis et al. (2011).

Stein (1995) proposes a static fully-rational model that explains the joint relationship between house prices, trading volume, and leverage. In his framework, households must repay any existing loan and make a down-payment prior of moving to a new home. If households experience a negative exogenous shock to their income, the home-equity portion for families with a high level of leverage may not be enough to meet the down-payment of a larger house. These households may therefore decide not to move, thus creating a decrease in demand, which further depresses prices.[41] On the contrary, following a positive income shock, these financially constrained families prefer to move to their desired location promptly, thus increasing prices and volume. Stein's (1995) model implies that the mix of leverage and liquidity constraints amplifies the effect of changes in asset values on the demand for housing. In cities where a large fraction of families are highly leveraged, the impact of fundamental shocks on house prices will be significantly higher, thus giving rise to self-reinforcing effects. As a result, home prices would display pronounced boom-to-bust cycles, which may appear incompatible with a efficient capital market dynamics.[42]

McDonald (1999), Spiegel (2001), and Ortalo-Magn'e and Rady (2006) are three additional papers that investigate the theoretical links between leverage and real estate prices. Spiegel (2001) shows that the presence of credit constraints can lead to construction cycles. As an implication of his model, he shows that leverage and developer construction decisions forecast time variation in expected housing returns. Ortalo-Magn'e and Rady (2006) propose a life-cycle model in which households differ in their income and thus ability to afford down-payment on a home. Young agents are constrained in their ability to borrow to purchase their first "starter" home. Moreover, changes in the price of starter homes shift the agents' demand for trade-up homes, thus establishing a link between the price of a starter homes and the price of trade-up homes. While the modeling assumptions are different from Stein's (1995), the two papers rely on the same amplifying effects of leverage and emphasize the role of down-payments and liquidity constraints.

The empirical predictions of Stein (1995) are investigated by Lamont and Stein (1999) whose main focus in on the effect of leverage on future house price fluctuations. Working on a sample of 44 metropolitan areas available at annual frequency between 1984 and 1994, they look at the fraction of all owner-occupants with an outstanding mortgage balance to house value ratio greater than 80%. This measure is meant to capture the relative presence of "constrained mover" families, which play a destabilizing effect in Stein's (1995) model. Lamont and Stein (1999) find that leverage plays an important role in predicting future real estate prices in two distinct ways. First, lenders and borrowers may be willing to take on high leveraged positions just if they foresee house prices to rise. Consistent with this expectation hypothesis, high leverage today is found to positively correlate with future price appreciation. In their sample, real estate prices are predictable by lagged price changes, with a positive sign, and negatively by the lagged

---

[41] Alternatively, they may also try to list their home for a relatively high price as this represents a low-cost alternative. This would explain why even in falling markets there is some inertia in the decrease of prices.

[42] The model's main predictions hold as long as the market for renting does not represent a costless alternative than buying a new home. Tax and moral hazard reasons suggest that renting is not a perfect substitute for direct ownership, so that the most efficient way to consume new housing is owner-occupied. The magnitude of these effects can be big as a large fraction of all home sales are to repeat buyers.

price–income ratio. These effects suggest that housing prices are driven by local economic conditions, short-run momentum, and long-run reversal to fundamentals.

A second important finding of Lamont and Stein (1999) is the economically and statistically large effect of leverage when it is interacted with changes in income. While shocks to income seem to be fully absorbed by real estate prices within 4 years, there are considerable cross-sectional differences in the response of house prices depending on the initial distribution of debt levels. In high-leverage cities, housing prices react quickly to an income shock and overshoot in the short-run. This effect peaks in the fourth year, when prices start to mean-revert to their new long-run level. By contrast, low-leverage cities display a more gradual response to the same economic shock and a smooth transition to the new equilibrium level. These effects are consistent with the main prediction of Stein (1995). Even if the level of leverage in an area is ultimately an endogenous variable, their analysis suggests a causal relationship, which runs from changes in leverage to house price fluctuations. An empirical limitation of the their findings, however, is that they use homeowners' estimates of their home value rather than true market prices.

Several other methods have been used to quantify the effect of leverage on the demand for residential and commercial properties. Linneman and Wachter (1989) document that wealth and income constraints lead to a lower probability of home ownership. Using data from the Federal Reserve Board's 1977 Survey of Consumer Credit and the 1983 Survey of Consumer Finances, they show that mortgage market innovations tend to relax financial constrains. However, the authors do not investigate price effects as a function of the constraints. Genesove and Mayer (1997) use data from the Boston condominium market in the early 1990s to show that an owner's level of leverage determines his behavior as a seller and might have an impact on transaction prices. They find that leveraged owners tend to set a higher asking price, their properties stay longer on the market, and conditional on selling, the transaction price is higher than that of less leveraged owners. These findings are broadly consistent with the predictions of Stein (1995) and Ortalo-Magn'e and Rady (2006). Brown (2000) compares the performance of highly-leveraged mortgage REITs (typically 80% leverage or more) to those of less leveraged properties held by property management companies. In the period of the late 1980s and early 1990s, which was characterized by large declines in commercial real estate values, he finds that the leveraged mortgage REITs were net sellers of highly leveraged assets, whereas equity REITs were net buyers. Moreover, the returns of mortgage REITs were significantly more negative that those of equity REITs. The overall evidence of the 1989 and 1990 period suggests that high levels of debt forced mortgage REITs to sell assets at fire sale prices, thus resulting in large losses.

Recently, Favilukis et al. (2011) formulate an elegant general equilibrium overlapping-generation model in which heterogeneous agents derive utility from a durable consumption good and housing and face stochastic life-cycle earnings. Two frictions are at play in their model. First, the households face borrowing constraints in the form of a down-payment as well as transaction costs. A "financial market liberalization" FML, corresponds to a relaxation of these constraints. Second, financial markets are incomplete, which implies that both idiosyncratic and aggregate risks cannot be perfectly insured. This rich framework represents an ideal laboratory to investigate the ability of FML and foreign capital inflows of producing the swings in housing markets, aggregate quantities, and consumption that are observed in U.S. data. The model is indeed able to generate endogenous swings in rent-to-price ratios largely as a response to a financial market liberalization. A positive shock to FML – i.e., an easing of collateral requirements and lower transaction costs – increases risk-sharing as allows households to borrow more aggressively against unexpected shocks to their wealth. This, in turn, decreases risk premia and increase prices. The opposite pattern is observed during a reversal of FML. The authors also show that low interest rates, which are the result of an inflow of foreign capital into the domestic bond market, play a comparatively small role in driving house prices fluctuations. The reason is that the decrease in interest rates is almost offset by an increase in risk premia due to the fact that domestic savers are pulled out of the bond market by foreign purchases, and are therefore more exposed to systematic equity and housing risk. The demand pressure on Treasuries from capital inflows keeps interest rates low thus balancing the decrease in precautionary savings from FML, but does not constitute the ultimate cause of the housing boom and bust.

The model in Favilukis et al. (2011) is also capable of generating plausible amounts of real estate predictability for both excess returns and rent growth. High rent–price ratios forecast higher future (excess) returns, as a result of the improved risk-sharing above mentioned. As a point in case, the R^2 from predicting 1-year excess returns implied by the model is about 3%, which increases to 10% at the 5-year horizon. High rent–price ratios also forecast higher future rental growth rates, contrary to the main prediction of standard present-value models. The authors argue that this empirical regularity can only be understood in a general equilibrium context, in which a negative economic shock can simultaneously drive discount rates up and residential investment down. As a result of a shrinking supply of housing, future rental growth rates increase. This positive correlation between risk premia and expected rental growth is at the root of the positive coefficient in the predictive regression.

Favilukis et al. (2013) provide further evidence in line with the predictions of the model by taking an empirical look at the determinants of residential real estate dynamics in the U.S. and several other countries. They document that a measure of credit supply of the banking sector is by far the most powerful explanatory variable of contemporaneous real house price growth during the 2000–2010 decade internationally, and for the U.S. also in the longer 1991–2010 period. This variable is meant to capture an easing of credit constraints, such as an increase in loan-to-value ratios and in the availability of new mortgage contracts, a reduction of fees, and laxer documentation requirements. They show that credit supply is also a powerful *forecaster* of both future house prices and rent-to-price ratios, with R^2s exceeding 0.40 in predictive regressions of one- to four-quarter ahead. These results still hold when credit supply is purged from endogenous shocks by controlling for expected economic conditions, which suggests the existence of a causality link running from exogenous shocks in the tightness of credit supply to subsequent movements in house prices. In contrast, capital flows, interest rates, and GDP growth are found not to be statistically significant determinants of current and future real house price dynamics, both in the U.S. as well as internationally.

A similar argument is found in Mian and Sufi (2009), who investigate the links between credit supply, leverage, and housing prices in the 2007 subprime crisis. Using zip-code level data, they find that mortgage origination during the 2002–2005 period was stronger in zip codes with a larger fraction of sub-prime applicants. The same areas, however, exhibit a sharp decrease in income and employment growth in both absolute and relative terms with respect to other zip codes in the same county. Thus, more mortgages originated in zip codes with worsening relative prospects. Mian and Sufi (2009) also test whether the increase in credit has been driven by expectations of future house price appreciation. Their identification strategy exploits the index of housing supply elasticity based on land-topology metrics developed by Saiz (2010). House price growth in elastic MSAs is expected not to exceed the inflation rate for house construction costs, as supply can quickly accommodate any increased demand (Glaeser et al., 2008). Historically, the bulk of house price appreciations have been concentrated in MSAs with inelastic supply. Based on this evidence, one would expect not to observe any increase in lending in elastic MSAs areas, as these do not have good prospects for house price appreciations. Contrary to this prediction, even zip codes in elastic MSAs with a greater fraction of sub-prime lenders experienced an increase in the relative fraction of originated mortgages sold for securitization and a positive relative mortgage origination growth. These results are supportive of a supply-based hypothesis, one in which the increased in credit supply through more relaxed lending practices, a decrease in the price of debt (the subprime-prime spread), and an increase in securitization in high subprime zip codes all lead to a reduction in denial rates and to an increase in house prices. Moreover, 2002–2005 was the only period in the last 18 years when house prices where negatively correlated to income growth, and thus to fundamentals. Also, it was a period of great expansion of the sub-prime lending industry.

In a companion paper, Mian and Sufi (2011) document that, from 2002 to 2006, the average homeowner extracted about 25 to 30 cents of every dollar increase in his home equity. This home-equity-based borrowing channel is much stronger for more financially constrained households, such as younger, low quality borrowers, and high credit card users. They estimate that, on aggregate, about 53% of the increase in homeowners' debt from 2002 to 2006, or about \$1.25 trillion, was due to home-equity borrowing. Defaults of these existing homeowners represented 39% of total new defaults in the U.S. during the same period. Their results point at the importance of a feedback effect, resulting from an increase in collateral values and impacting the availability of new credit, and are consistent with the aggregate evidence of a wealth effect in Case et al. (2011).

Overall, these studies corroborate the claim that exogenous economic shocks lead to larger price fluctuations in leveraged properties. The work of Lamont and Stein (1999) and Brown (2000) suggests that the amplification mechanism derives from the fact that, in real estate, the ability to borrow is directly linked to asset values. An exogenous decrease in those values can lead to a reduction in asset demand, as the borrowing capacity has decreased. However, more research is needed to document whether positive and negative economic shocks lead to an asymmetric response in prices. The analysis in Mian and Sufi (2009) and Favilukis et al. (2013) leads to the conclusion that the supply of (subprime) credit in the mid-2000s fueled to a large extent the subsequent house price increases.

5.2. Monetary Policy and Real Estate

Under the premise that monetary policy can stimulate economic activity by reducing borrowing costs, and given that the real estate market is heavily reliant on credit, it is reasonable to ask what is the effect of monetary policy shocks on real estate prices and sales volume. An emerging literature is looking at this question, with recent contributions by Fratantoni and Schuh (2003), Aoki et al. (2004), Iacoviello (2005), Ahearne et al. (2005), Del Negro and Otrok (2007), Hamilton (2008), Iacoviello and Neri (2010).

At the aggregate level, Iacoviello (2005) shows that house prices and GDP respond negatively to tight monetary policy in the U.S. with quarterly data from 1974 to 2003. To explore the role of borrowing constraints in the observed link between house prices and monetary policy, Iacoviello (2005) uses a new-Keynesian model with collateral constraints tied to real estate values for firms, as in Kiyotaki and Moore (1997). The importance of collateral to lower borrowing costs is also considered by Aoki et al. (2004), who note that house prices may have a direct effect on consumption via the credit market. Their theoretical model is supported by the empirical evidence in Case et al. (2005, 2011) that price changes in real estate have a large impact on aggregate consumption. In the Aoki et al. (2004) model, a house represents collateral for homeowners, and borrowing on a secured basis against ample housing collateral is generally cheaper than borrowing against little collateral or on an unsecured basis, such as a personal loan or credit card. Therefore, an increase in housing prices makes more collateral available to homeowners, which in turn encourages them to borrow more to finance their desired level of consumption and housing investment. Looking at structural changes in the UK's retail financial market, they also show that cheaper access to home equity means that, for a given house price increase, more borrowing will be devoted to consumption relative to housing investment. The response of consumption to an unanticipated change in interest rates will therefore be larger, and the response of house prices and housing investment will be smaller. Ahearne et al. (2005) find that the links between monetary policy shocks and real estate prices are observed more generally across eighteen developed economies.

Due to the geographical heterogeneity of real estate, it is unlikely that a monetary policy shock will have the same effect on all regional markets. In fact, it has been documented that the impact of monetary actions varies across regions (Carlino and Robert, 1999; Carlino and DeFina, 1998) and is a function of local economic conditions. It is therefore possible that the response of real estate prices to monetary policy shocks may differ across regions in magnitude and duration. Based on this premise, Fratantoni and Schuh (2003) quantify the importance of regional heterogeneity in housing markets with respect to monetary policy shocks. They start off with a model in which the monetary authority sets the global monetary policy and the mortgage rate serves as the central channel for monetary transmission. At the regional level, income, housing investment, and housing prices are determined by households and firms. Fratantoni and Schuh (2003) contrast the standard method of estimating the effect of monetary policy with one in which regional heterogeneity matters. Following the standard approach first, the authors estimate a structural VAR model of log non-housing deflator, log housing deflator, log per-capita non-housing GDP, log real per-capita housing investment, FED funds rate, and a nominal rate on a 30-year mortgage during the 1966–1998 period. Their VAR estimates suggest that a monetary shock has a significantly larger and more rapid effect on the housing than non-housing sector and that monetary policy accounts for a large fraction of fluctuations in the housing sector. However, since housing supply and demand are determined locally, this motivates their regional heterogeneous-agent VAR (HAVAR) analysis.

A HAVAR model involves the estimation of regional VARs, which are then aggregated at a national level. The authors show that aggregating these VARs induces non-linearities in the form of time variation (aggregation across heterogeneous regions) and state dependence, due to prevailing economic conditions at the time of the monetary policy intervention. They estimate their model on MSA-level data of housing starts (from the Bureau of Labor Statistics), housing prices (from the FHFA repeat sales transactions), and state-level income (from the Census Bureau). Using a balanced panel of 27 MSAs over 1986:Q3 to 1996:Q2, they estimate unrestricted VARs via OLS and look at the effect of monetary policy tightening, defined as a transitory 100-basis points shock to the FED funds rate, on regional income, housing investment, and house appreciation. The resulting impulse-response functions show that the magnitude and duration of the regional responses vary widely across areas. For instance, monetary tightening is moderately less effective when the economy is experiencing a coastal housing boom. Their key finding is that there are economically and statistically significant differences between the dynamic responses of the HAVAR model they develop and the conventional VAR approach. Peak responses to monetary shocks can vary by more than 1%, and mean lags, by more than 1 year, depending on local conditions.

In a complementary work, Del Negro and Otrok (2007) use a dynamic factor model to decompose house price movements into regional shocks and a common national component. The motivation for the decomposition is the considerable empirical heterogeneity in the growth rate of house prices across states. They use the FHFA/OFHEO data during the 1986–2005 period. The dynamic factor model is estimated via Bayesian methods and the common component is identified from the idiosyncratic movements. Del Negro and Otrok (2007) find that, historically, fluctuations in housing prices have been mainly driven by local factors. Interestingly, growth rates of housing are far less correlated across states than are growth rates in real per capita income. This heterogeneity is due to the fact that states have different exposures to the common business cycle. However, in the more recent period, many states display an increase in house prices due to the national factor. The authors investigate whether this increased correlation may be due to monetary policy intervention. Interestingly, the impact of monetary policy shocks on house prices is found to be fairly small. Thus, the authors conclude that the Fed expansionary policy was not behind the recent boom in house prices.

Hamilton (2008) uses a new, high-frequency measure of monetary policy shocks – daily innovations in the 1- and 2-month-ahead futures contracts – and traces out its effect on the housing market. More specifically, he estimates the response of new homes sold (reported by the Census Bureau) following monetary policy shocks. The main finding in the empirical analysis, which is carried out at the aggregate level, is that sales respond with a considerable lag to monetary shocks. He attributes the delay of several months to heterogeneity in search time across households. It would be interesting to extend Hamilton's (2008) approach and investigate the impact of Fed policy shocks on real estate prices. However, it is fair to say that this, and the other papers in this literature, suggests that monetary policy actions have an important role to play in understanding real estate price fluctuations.

6. CONCLUDING REMARKS

How difficult is it to predict changes in real estate prices? In this chapter, we revisit this question from the perspective of the academic real estate literature. However, before we can even tackle the question of predictability, we must step back and address an even more basic issue: constructing reliable real estate price indices in light of the fact that the underlying asset is extremely heterogeneous, faces high transaction costs, and is inherently illiquid. Various indices have been proposed and all have limitations. Recently much interest has focused on repeat-sales indices, both for commercial and residential properties. However, while these indices may be suitable for capturing the current state of the market, they might not necessarily be ideal for forecasting future *market* prices.

Researchers have explored a variety of predictors of real estate price changes beyond simple autoregressive models. A partial list of the most successful forecasting variables include valuation ratios such as the rent-to-price and income-to-price ratios; local economic variables, such as the employment rate, income growth, construction costs;

demographic trends such as population growth; local space market variables such as housing starts, vacancy rates, and transactions volume; proxies for zoning restrictions; and measures of leverage and monetary policy action. The interpretation and success of the predictive models varies considerably as do the datasets on which they have been tested. From a statistical perspective, evaluating the accuracy of real estate forecasts is a challenge: the lack of a sufficiently long time series of price data has prevented researchers from conducting meaningful out-of-sample MSFE comparisons. Most of the reported evidence is in-sample and exploits cross-sectional differences. However, from an economic perspective, whether the profits from exploiting predictable patterns in real estate prices are enough to cover transaction and search costs is still an unresolved issue.

A notable exception is the REITs market, for which exchange-traded returns are available for a relatively long timespan. In-sample results highlight some predictability of REIT returns, especially at yearly horizons. Significantly more predictability is observed in the growth rates of their cashflows. Out-of-sample predictions of REIT returns mimic those of the aggregate stock market, where unconstrained forecasts perform relatively poorly, although economic constraints may provide some improvements. Linking REITs returns to those of the underlying properties may be an interesting application to trace the origin of the extant predictability.

7. APPENDIX A. DATA SOURCES

A.1. Real Estate Data

Residential: The Census Median and Average Sales Prices of New Homes Sold are obtained from the Census.[43] The S&P/Case–Shiller indexes are the NSA series from Macromarkets.[44] FHFA/OFHEO NSA Purchase only monthly and All-Transactions quarterly indexes are from the Federal Housing Finance Agency website.[45]

The 25 metropolitan areas in the FHFA/OFHEO Purchase Only Indexes tape are: Atlanta-Sandy Springs-Marietta, GA; Baltimore-Towson, MD; Chicago-Joliet-Naperville, IL (MSAD); Cleveland-Elyria-Mentor, OH; Dallas-Plano-Irving, TX (MSAD); Denver-Aurora-Broomfield, CO; Edison-New Brunswick, NJ (MSAD); Houston-Sugar Land-Baytown, TX; Los Angeles-Long Beach-Glendale, CA (MSAD); Miami-Miami Beach-Kendall, FL (MSAD); Minneapolis-St.Paul-Bloomington, MN-WI; Nassau-Suffolk, NY (MSAD); New York-White Plains-Wayne, NY-NJ (MSAD); Oakland-Fremont-Hayward, CA (MSAD); Philadelphia, PA (MSAD); Phoenix-Mesa-Glendale, AZ; Pittsburgh, PA; Riverside-San Bernardino-Ontario, CA; St. Louis, MO-IL; San Diego-Carlsbad-San Marcos, CA; Santa Ana-Anaheim-Irvine, CA (MSAD); Seattle-Bellevue-Everett, WA (MSAD); Tampa-St. Petersburg-Clearwater, FL;

---

[43] http://www.census.gov/const/uspricemon.pdf.
[44] http://www.macromarkets.com/csi_housing/sp_caseshiller.asp.
[45] http://www.fhfa.gov/Default.aspx?Page=87.

Warren-Troy-Farmington Hills, MI (MSAD); Washington-Arlington-Alexandria, DC-VA-MD-WV (MSAD).

Commercial: NCREIF indexes are from the NCREIF website.[46] The TBI and the Moody's/REAL Commercial Property Price Index (CPPI) are from the MIT center for real estate.[47] REIT indexes are from the CRSP/Ziman All-Equity tape.

A.2. Financial and Macro Variables

The aggregate stock market is the value-weighted NYSE/AMEX/NASDAQ index. The dividend-price ratio is constructed following Fama and French (1988b) as sum of current and previous 11-month (or 3 quarters, for quarterly data) dividends over the current price index. The 3-month rate is the Fama Risk-free rate, the average of bid and ask. The inflation rate is the return to the CPI index. The Cochrane and Piazzesi (2005) factor is constructed using Fama-Bliss Discount Bond Yields. The source for all these series is the Center for Research in Security Prices (CRSP). Industrial Production is obtained from the Federal Reserve Bank of St. Louis.

REFERENCES

Abraham, Jesse M., Hendershott, Patric H., 1996. Bubbles in metropolitan housing markets. Journal of Housing Research 7, 191–207.

Abraham, Jesse M., Schauman, William S. 1991. New evidence on home prices from Freddie Mac repeat sales. Real Estate Economics 19, 333–352.

Ahearne, Allan, Ammer, John, Doyle, Brian, Kole, Linda, Martin, Robert, 2005. House prices and monetary policy: a cross-country study. International Finance Discussion Paper 841, Board of Governors of the Federal Reserve System.

Andrews, D.W.K., 1993. Exactly median-unbiased estimation of first order autoregressive unit root models. Econometrica 61, 139–165.

Anselin, Luc, 1988. Spatial Econometrics: Methods and Models. Kluwer Academic Publishers, Dordrecht, The Netherlands.

Aoki, Kosuke, Proudman, James, Vlieghe, Gertjan, 2004. House prices, consumption, and monetary policy: a financial accelerator approach. Journal of Financial Intermediation 13, 414–435

Bailey, Martin J., Muth, Richard F., Nourse, Hugh O., 1963. A regression method for real estate price index construction. Journal of the American Statistical Association 58, 933–942.

Bansal, Ravi, Zhou, Hao, 2002. Term structure of interest rates with regime shifts. The Journal of Finance 57, 1997–2043.

Becker, T., Shabani, R., 2010. Outstanding debt and the household portfolio. Review of Financial Studies 23, 2900–2934.

Boz, Emine, Mendoza, Enrique G., 2010, Financial innovation, the discovery of risk, and the U.S. credit crisis. NBER Working Paper 16020.

Brooks, Chris, Tsolacos, Sotiris, 2001. Forecasting real estate returns using financial spreads. Journal of Property Research 18, 235–248.

Brooks, Chris, Tsolacos, Sotiris, 2003. International evidence on the predictability of returns to securitized real estate assets: econometric models versus neural networks. Journal of Property Research 20, 133–155.

Brown, David T., 2000. Liquidity and liquidation: evidence from real estate investment trusts. The Journal of Finance 55, 469–485.

---

[46] http://www.ncreif.org/tbi-returns.aspx.

[47] http://web.mit.edu/cre/.

Brown, Jane P., Song, Haiyan, McGillivray, Alan, 1997. Forecasting UK house prices: a time varying coefficient approach. Economic Modelling 14, 529–548.

Calhoun, Charles A., 1996. OFHEO house price indexes: HPI technical description. Discussion paper Office of Federal Housing Enterprise Oversight, Washington, DC.

Campbell, Davis, Davis, Morris, Gallin, Joshua, Martin, Robert, 2009. What moves housing markets: a variance decomposition of the price-rent ratio. Journal of Urban Economics 66, 90–102.

Campbell, J., Cocco, J., 2007. How do house prices affect consumption? evidence from micro data. Journal of Monetary Economics 54, 591–621.

Campbell, J.Y., 1991. A variance decomposition for stock returns. Economic Journal 101, 157–179.

Campbell, John Y., Giglio, Stefano, Pathak, Parag, 2011. Forced sales and house prices. American Economic Review 101, 2108–2131.

Campbell, John Y., Lo, Andrew W., Craig MacKinlay, A., 1997. The Econometrics of Financial Markets. Princeton, Princeton University Press.

Campbell, John Y., Shiller, Robert J., 1988. The dividend-price ratio and expectations of future dividends and discount factors. Review of Financial Studies 1, 195–228.

Campbell, John Y., Thompson, Samuel B., 2008. Predicting excess stock returns out of sample: can anything beat the historical average? Review of Financial Studies 21, 1509–1531.

Campbell, John Y., Vuolteenaho, Tuomo, 2004. Bad beta, good beta. American Economic Review 94, 1249–1275.

Can, A., 1992. Specification and estimation of hedonic housing prices models. Regional Science and Urban Economics 22, 453–474.

Caplin, Andrew, Chopra, Sumit, Leahy, John, LeCun, Yahn, Trivikraman Thampy, 2008. Machine learning and the spatial structure of house prices and housing returns. Working Paper.

Capozza, Dennis R., Hendershott, Patric H., Mack, Charlotte, 2004. An anatomy of price dynamics in illiquid markets: analysis and evidence from local housing markets. Real Estate Economics 32, 1–32.

Capozza, D.R., Seguin, P., 1996. Expectations, efficiency, and euphoria in the housing market. Regional Science and Urban Economics 26, 369–386.

Carlino, Gerard A., DeFina, Robert H., 1998. The differential regional effects of monetary policy. Reviview of Economics and Statistics 80, 572–587.

Carlino, Gerard A., DeFina, Robert H., 1999. Do states respond differently to changes in monetary policy? Business Review, 17–27.

Case, Bradford, Pollakowski, Henry, Wachter, Susan, 1991. On choosing among house price index methodologies. AREUEA Journal 19, 286–307.

Case, Bradford, Quigley, John M., 1991. The dynamics of real estate prices. Reviview of Economics and Statistics 73, 50–58.

Case, Karl E., 2007. The value of land in the United States: 1975–2005. In: Ingram, Gregory, Hong, Yu-Hung (Eds.), Land Policies and Their Outcomes, Lincoln Institute of Land Policy.

Case, Karl E., Quigley, J.M., Shiller, R., 2005. Comparing wealth effects: the stock market versus the housing market. Advances in Macroeconomics 5, 1.

Case, Karl E., Quigley, J.M., Shiller, R., 2011. Wealth effects revisited 1978–2009. NBER Working Paper, No 16848.

Case, Karl E., Shiller, Robert J., 1987. Prices of single-family homes since 1970: new indexes for four cities. New England Economic Review, 46–56.

Case, Karl E., Shiller, Robert J., 1989. The efficiency of the market for single-family homes. The American Economic Review 1, 125–137.

Case, Karl E., Shiller, Robert J., 1990. Forecasting prices and excess returns in the housing market. Real Estate Economics 18, 253–273.

Cauley, S., Pavlov, A., Schwartz, E., 2007. Homeownership as a constraint on asset allocation. Journal of Real Estate Finance and Economics 34, 283–311.

Cavanagh, C., Elliott, G., Stock, J., 1995. Inference in models with nearly integrated regressors. Econometric Theory 11, 1131–1147.

Clapham, Eric, Englund, Peter, Quigley, John M., Redfearn, Christian L., 2006. Revisiting the past and settling the score: index revision for house price derivatives. Real Estate Economics 34, 275–302.

Clapp, John M., 2004. A semiparametric method for estimating local house price indices. Real Estate Economics 32, 127–160.

Clapp, John M., Giaccotto, Carmelo, 1999. Revisions in repeat-sales price indexes: here today, gone tomorrow? Real Estate Economics 27, 79–104.

Clapp, John M., 2002. Evaluating house price forecasts. Journal of Real Estate Research 24, 1–26.

Clapp, John M., Tirtiroglu, Dogan, 1991. Housing price indices based on all transactions compared to repeat subsamples. Real Estate Economics 19, 270–285.

Cochrane, John H., Piazzesi, Monika, 2005. Bond risk premia. American Economic Review 95, 138–160.

Cooper, Michael, Downs, David H., Patterson, Gary A., 1999. Real estate securities and a filter-based, short-term trading strategy. Journal of Real Estate Research 18, 313–334.

Crawford, Gordon W., Fratantoni, Michael C., 2003. Assessing the forecasting performance of regime-switching. ARIMA and GARCH models of house prices. Real Estate Economics 31, 223–243.

Davis, Morris, Lehnert, Andreas, Martin, Robert F., 2008. The rent–price ratio for the aggregate stock of owner-occupied housing. Review of Income and Wealth 54, 279–284.

Davis, Morris A., Heathcote, Jonathan, 2007. The price and quantity of residential land in the united states. Journal of Monetary Economics 54, 2595–2620.

Del Negro, Marco, Otrok, Christopher, 2007. 99 luftballons: monetary policy and the house price boom across US states. Journal of Monetary Economics 54, 1962–1985.

Diebold, Francis X., Rudebusch, Glenn D., 1999. Business cycles: durations, dynamics, and forecasting. In: Measuring Business Cycles: A Modern Perspective. Princeton, New Jersey, Princeton University Press, pp. 117–143.

DiPasquale, Denise, Wheaton, William C., 1994. Housing market dynamics and the future of housing prices. Journal of Urban Economics 35, 1–27.

Eichholtz, Piet, 1997. A long run house price index: the herengracht index, 1628–1973. Real Estate Economics 25, 175–192.

Engel, Charles, Hamilton, James D., 1990. Long swings in the dollar: are they in the data and do markets know it? The American Economic Review 80, 689–713.

Engle, Robert, Granger, Cliff, 1987. Co-integration and error-correction: representation, estimation, and testing. Econometrica 55, 251–276.

Engle, R., Lilien, D., Watson, M., 1985. A dymimic model of housing price determination. Journal of Econometrics 28, 307–326.

Fama, Eugene, 1970. Efficient capital markets: a review of theory and empirical work. Journal of Finance 25, 383–417.

Fama, Eugene, French, Kenneth, 1988a. Permanent and temporary components of stock prices. The Journal of Political Economy 96, 246–273.

Fama, E., Schwert, G.W., 1977. Asset returns and inflation. Journal of Financial Economics 5, 115–146.

Fama, Eugene F., 1990. Stock returns, expected returns, and real activity. The Journal of Finance 45, 1089–1108.

Fama, Eugene F., French, Kenneth R., 1988b. Dividend yields and expected stock returns. Journal of Financial Economics 22, 3–25.

Fama, Eugene F., French, Kenneth R., 1989. Business conditions and expected returns on stocks and bonds. Journal of Financial Economics 25, 23–49.

Favilukis, Jank, Kohn, David, Ludvigson, Sidney, Van Nieuwerburgh, Stijn, 2013. International capital flows and house prices: theory and evidence. Housing and the financial crisis, NBER Book Series (chapter 8).

Favilukis, Jank, Ludvigson, Sidney, Van Nieuwerburgh, Stijn, 2011. Macroeconomic implications of housing wealth, housing finance, and limited risk-sharing in general equilibrium. NBER Working Paper.

Fisher, Jeffrey, 2005, US Commercial real estate indices: the NCREIF property index. Discussion Paper BIS Papers No 21.

Fisher, Jeff, Geltner, David, Pollakowski, Henry, 2007. A quarterly transactions-based index of institutional real estate investment performance and movements in supply and demand. The Journal of Real Estate Finance and Economics 34, 5–33.

Flavin, Marjorie, Yamashita, Takashi, 2002. Owner-occupied housing and the composition of the household portfolio. American Economic Review 92, 345–362.

Fratantoni, Michael, Schuh, Scott, 2003. Monetary policy, housing, and heterogeneous regional markets, Journal of Money, Credit and Banking 35, 557–589.

Fugazza, Carolina, Guidolin, Massimo, Nicodano, Giovanna, 2007. Investing for the longrun in European real estate. The Journal of Real Estate Finance and Economics 34, 35–80. http://dx.doi.org/10.1007/s11146-007-9002-5.

Gallin, J., 2008. The long-run relationship between house prices and rents. Real Estate Economics 36, 635–668.

Garcia, Ren, Perron, Pierre, 1996. An analysis of the real interest rate under regime shifts. Review of Economics and Statistics 78, 111–125.

Gatzlaff, Dean H., Haurin, Donald R., 1997. Sample selection bias and repeat-sales index estimates. The Journal of Real Estate Finance and Economics 14, 33–50.

Gatzlaff, Dean H., Haurin, Donald R., 1998. Sample selection and biases in local house value indices. Journal of Urban Economics 43, 199–222.

Gau, George W., 1984. Weak form tests of the efficiency of real estate investment markets. Financial Review 19, 301–320.

Gau, George W., 1985. Public information and abnormal returns in real estate investment. Real Estate Economics 13, 15–31.

Geltner, D., Mei, J., 1995. The present value model wtih time-varying discount rates: implications for commercial property valuation and investment decisions. Journal of Real Estate Finance and Economics 11, 119–135.

Geltner, David, Pollakowski, Henry, 2007. A Set of Indexes for Trading Commercial Real Estate Based on the Real Capital Analytics Transaction Prices Database, MIT/CREDL, available at <http://web.mit.edu/cre/research/credl/rca/MIT-RCA-wp.pdf>.

Geltner, David M., Miller, Norman G., 2006. Commercial Real Estate Analysis and Investments. South-Western Educational Publishing, Cincinnati.

Genesove, D., Mayer, 1997. Equity and time to sale in the real estate market. The American Economic Review 87, 255–269.

Ghysels, Eric, Plazzi, Alberto, Valkanov, Rossen, 2007. Valuation in the U.S. commercial real estate. European Financial Management 13, 472–497.

Giaccotto, Carmelo, Clapp, John, 1992. Appraisal-based real estate returns under alternative market regimes. Real Estate Economics 20, 1–24.

Glaeser, Edward L., Gyourko, Joseph, Saiz, Albert, 2008. Housing supply and housing bubbles. Journal of Urban Economics 64, 198–217.

Goetzmann, William, 1992. The accuracy of real estate indices: repeat sale estimators. Journal of Real Estate Finance and Economics 5, 5–53.

Goetzmann, W., 1993. The single family home in the investment portfolio. Journal of Real Estate Finance and Economics 6, 201–222.

Goetzmann, William N., Spiegel, Matthew, 1995. Non-temporal components of residential real estate appreciation. Review of Economics and Statistics 77, 199–206.

Graff, Richard A., Young, Michael S., 1997. Serial persistence in REIT returns. Journal of Real Estate Research 14, 183–214.

Granger, Clive W.J., Hyung, Namwon, 2004. Occasional structural breaks and long memory with an application to the S&P 500 absolute stock returns. Journal of Empirical Finance 11, 399–421.

Gray, Stephen F., 1996. Modeling the conditional distribution of interest rates as a regimeswitching process. Journal of Financial Economics 42, 27–62.

Gu, Anthony Y., 2002. The predictability of house prices. Journal of Real Estate Research 24, 213–233.

Guidolin, Massimo, Timmermann, Allan, 2008. International asset allocation under regime switching, skew, and kurtosis preferences. Review of Financial Studies 21, 889–935.

Guirguis, Hany S., Giannikos, Christos I., Anderson, Randy I., 2005. The US housing market: asset pricing forecasts using time varying coefficients. The Journal of Real Estate Finance and Economics 30, 33–53.

Guntermann, Karl L., Smith, Richard L., 1987. Efficiency of the market for residential real estate. Land Economics 63, 34–45.

Gyourko, Joseph, Voith, Richard, 1992. Local market and national components in house price appreciation. Journal of Urban Economics 32, 52–69.

Halvorsen, Robert, Pollakowski, Henry O., 1981. Choice of functional form for hedonic price equations. Journal of Urban Economics 10, 37–49.

Hamilton, Bruce W., Schwab, Robert M., 1985. Expected appreciation in urban housing markets. Journal of Urban Economics 18, 103–118.

Hamilton, James D., 1989. A new approach to the economic analysis of nonstationary time series and the business cycle. Econometrica 57, 357–384.

Hamilton, James D., 1994. Time Series Analysis. Princeton, New Jersey, Princeton University Press.

Hamilton, James D., 2008. Daily monetary policy shocks and new home sales. Journal of Monetary Economics 55, 1171–1190.

Heckman, James, 1979. Sample selection bias as a specification error. Econometrica 47, 153–161.

Hill, Robert, 2011, Hedonic price indexes for housing. OECD Statistics Working Papers, 2011/01, OECD Publishing. Available at http://dx.doi.org/10.1787/5kghzxpt6g6f-en.

Hill, R., Carter, C.F. Sirmans, Knight, John R., 1997. Estimating capital asset price indexes. Review of Economics and Statistics 79, 226–233.

Hill, R., Carter, C.F. Sirmans, Knight, John R., 1999. A random walk down main street? Regional Science and Urban Economics 29, 89–103.

Hill, Robert J., 2004. Constructing price indexes across space and time: the case of the European union. The American Economic Review 94, 1379–1410.

Himmelberg, C., Mayer, C., Sinai, T., 2005. Assessing high house prices: bubbles, fundamentals, and misperceptions. Journal of Economic Perspectives 19, 67–92.

Hoag, J.W., 1980. Towards idices of real estate value and return. Journal of Finance 35, 569–580.

Hodrick, R.J., 1992. Dividend yields and expected stock returns: alternative procedures for inference and measurement. Review of Financial Studies 5, 357–386.

Iacoviello, Matteo, 2005. House prices, borrowing constraints, and monetary policy in the business cycle. American Economic Review 95, 739–764.

Iacoviello, Matteo, Neri, Stefano, 2010. Housing market spillovers: evidence from an estimated dsge model. American Economic Journal: Macroeconomics 2, 125–164.

Kiyotaki, Nobuhiro, Moore, John, 1997. Credit cycles. Journal of Political Economy 105, 211–248.

Koijen, Ralph, Van Binsbergen, Jules H., 2010. Predictive regressions: a present-value approach. Journal of Finance 65, 1439–1471.

Korteweg, Arthur, Sorensen, Morten, 2011, Estimating loan-to-value and foreclosure behavior. NBER Working Paper No. 17882.

Kuo, Chiong-Long, 1996. Serial correlation and seasonality in the real estate market. The Journal of Real Estate Finance and Economics 12, 139–162.

Lamont, Owen, Stein, Jeremy, 1999. Leverage and house-price dynamics in US Cities. RAND Journal of Economics 30, 498–514.

Lettau, Martin, Ludvigson, Sydney, 2001. Consumption, aggregate wealth, and expected stock returns. The Journal of Finance 56, 815–849.

Lettau, Martin, Van Nieuwerburgh, Stijn, 2008. Reconciling the return predictability evidence. Review of Financial Studies 21, 1607–1652.

Li, Yuming, Wang, Ko, 1995. The predictability of REIT returns and market segmentation. Journal of Real Estate Research 10, 471–482.

Linneman, Peter, 1986. An empirical test of the efficiency of the housing market. Journal of Urban Economics 20, 140–154.

Linneman, Peter, Wachter, Susan, 1989. The Impacts of Borrowing Constraints on Home ownership. Real Estate Economics 17, 389–402.

Liu, Crocker H., Mei, Jianping, 1992. The predictability of returns on equity REITs and their co-movement with other assets. The Journal of Real Estate Finance and Economics 5, 401–418.

Liu, C.H., Mei, J., 1998. The predictability of international real estate markets, exchange rate risks, and diversification consequences. Real Estate Economics 26, 3–39.

Lustig, Hanno N., Van Nieuwerburgh, Stijn G., 2005. Housing collateral, consumption insurance, and risk premia: an empirical perspective. The Journal of Finance 60, 1167–1219.

MacKinnon, Gregory H., Zaman, Ashraf Al, 2009. Real estate for the long term: the effect of return predictability on long-horizon allocations. Real Estate Economics 37, 117–153.

Malpezzi, S., 1990. Urban housing and financial markets: some international comparisons. Urban Studies 27, 971–1022.

Malpezzi, Stephen, 1999. A simple error correction model of house prices. Journal of Housing Economics 8, 27–62.

Mankiw, Gregory, Weil, David, 1989. The baby boom, the baby bust, and the housing market. Regional Science and Urban Economics 19, 235–258.

McDonald, John F., 1999. Optimal leverage in real estate investment. Journal of Real Estate Finance and Economics 18, 239–252.

McIntosh, Willard, Henderson, Glenn V., 1989. Efficiency of the office properties market. The Journal of Real Estate Finance and Economics 2, 61–70.

Meese, Richard, Wallace, Nancy, 1994. Testing the present value relation for housing prices: should i leave my house in San Francisco? Journal of Urban Economics 35, 245–266.

Meese, Richard A., Wallace, Nancy E., 1997. The construction of residential housing price indices: a comparison of repeat-sales. Hedonic-regression, and hybrid approaches. The Journal of Real Estate Finance and Economics 14, 51–73.

Mei, Jianping, Gao, Bin, 1995. Price reversal, transaction costs, and arbitrage profits in the real estate securities market. The Journal of Real Estate Finance and Economics 11, 153–165.

Mei, Jianping, Liu, Crocker H., 1994. The predictability of real estate returns and market timing. The Journal of Real Estate Finance and Economics 8, 115–135.

Merton, Robert, 1974. On the pricing of corporate debt: the risk structure of interest rates. Journal of Finance 29, 449–470.

Mian, Atif, Sufi, Amir, 2009. The consequences of mortgage credit expansion: evidence from the US mortgage default crisis. Quarterly Journal of Economics 124, 1449–1496.

Mian, Atif, Sufi, Amir, 2011. House prices, home-equity-based borrowing, and the US household leverage crisis. American Economic Review 101, 2132–2156.

Muellbauer, John, Murphy, Anthony, 1997. Booms and busts in the UK housing market. The Economic Journal 107, 1701–1727.

Nappi-Choulet Pr, Ingrid, Maury, Tristan-Pierre, 2009. A Spatiotemporal autoregressive price index for the Paris office property market. Real Estate Economics 37, 305–340.

Nelling, Edward, Gyourko, Joseph, 1998. The predictability of equity REIT returns. Journal of Real Estate Research 16, 251–268.

Newey, Whitney K., West, Kenneth D., 1987. A simple positive semi-definite. Heteroskedasticity and autocorrelation consistent covariance matrix. Econometrica 55, 703–708.

Ortalo-Magn'e, François, Rady, Sven, 2006. Housing market dynamics: on the contribution of income shocks and credit constraints. Review of Economic Studies 73, 459–485.

Pace, R., Ronald Barry, Kelley, Clapp, J., Rodriguez, M., 1998. Spatiotemporal autoregressive models of neighborhood effects. Journal of Real Estate Finance and Economics 17, 14–33.

Pace, R., Ronald Barry, K., Gilley, O., Sirmans, C.F., 2000. A method for spatial-temporal forecasting with an application to real estate prices. International Journal of Forecasting 16, 229–246.

Pace, R., Ronald Barry, Kelley, 1993. Nonparametric methods with applications to hedonic models. The Journal of Real Estate Finance and Economics 7, 185–204.

Perez-Quiros, Gabriel, Timmermann, Allan, 2001. Business cycle asymmetries in stock returns: evidence from higher order moments and conditional densities. Journal of Econometrics 103, 259–306.

Pettenuzzo, D., Timmermann, A., Valkanov, R., 2011. Return predictability under equilibrium constraints on the equity premium. UCSD Working Paper.

Piazzesi, M., Schneider, M., Tuzel, S., 2007. Housing, consumption and asset pricing. Journal of Financial Economics 83, 531–569.

Plazzi, Alberto, Torous, Walter, Valkanov, Rossen, 2010. Expected returns and expected growth in rents of commercial real estate. Review of Financial Studies 23, 3469–3519.

Plazzi, Alberto, Torous, Walter, Valkanov, Rossen, 2011. Exploiting property characteristics in commercial real estate portfolio Allocation. Journal of Portfolio Management 35, 39–50.

Prasad, Nalini, Richards, Anthony, 2008. Improving median housing price indexes through stratification. Journal of Real Estate Research 30, 45–72.

Quigley, J.M., 1995. A simple hybrid model for estimating real estate price indexes. Journal of Housing Economics 4, 1–12.

Rapach, D., Zhou, G., 2013. Forecasting stock returns. To appear in: Timmermann, A., Elliott, G. (Eds.), Handbook of Economic Forecasting, vol. II.

Rayburn, William, Devaney, Michael, Evans, Richard, 1987. A test of weak-form efficiency in residential real estate returns. Real Estate Economics 15, 220–233.

Reinhart, Carmen, Rogoff, Kenneth, 2009. This Time is Different: Eight Centuries of Financial Folly. Princeton, New Jersey, Princeton University Press.

Rosen, Kenneth T., 1984. Toward a model of the office building sector. Real Estate Economics 12, 261–269.

Rosen, Sherwin, 1974. Hedonic prices and implicit markets: product differentiation in pure competition. Journal of Political Economy 82, 34–55.

Ross, S., Zisler, R., 1991. Risk and return in real estate. Journal of Real Estate Finance and Economics 4, 175–1990.

Rossi, B., 2013. Handbook of economic forecasting. In: Advances in Forecasting under Instabilities, Elsevier-North Holland.

Saiz, Albert, 2010. The geographic determinants of housing supply. The Quarterly Journal of Economics 125, 1253–1296.

Schindler, Felix, 2011. Predictability and persistence of the price movements of the S&P/case–shiller house price indices, The Journal of Real Estate Finance and Economics, 1–47.

Serrano, Camilo, Hoesli, Martin, 2007. Forecasting EREIT returns. Journal of Real Estate Portfolio Management 13, 293–309.

Serrano, Camilo, Hoesli, Martin, 2010. Are securitized real estate returns more predictable than stock returns? Journal of Real Estate Finance and Economics 41, 170–192.

Shiller, Robert, 2008, Derivative markets for home prices. NBER Working Paper 13962.

Sirmans, G., MacDonald, Lynn, Macpherson, David, Zietz, Emily, 2006. The value of housing characteristics: a meta analysis. The Journal of Real Estate Finance and Economics 33, 215–240.

Skantz, Terrance R., Strickland, Thomas H., 1987. House prices and a flood event: an empirical investigation of market efficiency. Journal of Real Estate Research 2, 75–83.

Spiegel, Matthew, 2001. Housing return and construction cycles. Real Estate Economics 29, 521–551.

Stambaugh, Robert, 1999. Predictive regressions. Journal of Financial Economics 54, 375–421.

Standard and Poor's, 2008. S&P/case–shiller home price indices index methodology. Discussion paper. Standard and Poor's, New York. Available at <http://www.standardandpoors.com/home/en/us>.

Stein, Jeremy C., 1995. Prices and trading volume in the housing market: a model with down-payment effects. The Quarterly Journal of Economics 110, 379–406.

Stevenson, Simon, 2002. Momentum effects and mean reversion in real estate securities. Journal of Real Estate Research 23, 47–64.

Timmermann, A., 2006, Handbook of economic forecasting. In: Forecast Combinations. North-Holland, pp. 135–178.

Valkanov, Rossen, 2003. Long-horizon regressions: theoretical results and applications. Journal of Financial Economics 68, 201–232.

Van Nieuwerburgh, Stijn, Weill, Pierre-Olivier, 2010. Why has house price dispersion gone up? Review of Economic Studies 77, 1567–1606.

Van Norden, Simon, Vigfusson, Robert, 1998. Avoiding the pitfalls: can regime-switching tests reliability detect bubbles? Studies in Nonlinear Dynamics & Econometrics 3, 1–22.

Wallace, Nancy E., 1996. Hedonic-based price indexes for housing: theory, estimation, and index construction. Economic Review 3, 34–48.

Webb, Cary, 1981a. A discrete random walk model for price levels in real estate. Working Paper, Department of Mathematics, Chicago State University.

Webb, Cary, 1981b. The expected accuracy of a real estate price index. Working Paper, Department of Mathematics. Chicago State University.

Webb, Cary, 1981c. Trading activity and the variance of an index number. Working Paper, Department of Mathematics, Chicago State University.

Welch, Ivo, Goyal, Amit, 2008. A comprehensive look at the empirical performance of equity premium prediction. Review of Financial Studies 21, 1455–1508.

West, K.D., 2006. Handbook of economic forecasting. In: Forecast Evaluation. North-Holland, pp. 101–133.

Wheaton, William C., Torto, Raymond, 1988. Vacany rates and the future of office rents. AREUEA Journal 19, 430–436.

Zhong-Guo, Zhou, 1997, Forecasting sales and price for existing single-family homes: a VAR model with error correction. Journal of Real Estate Research 14, 155.

CHAPTER 10

Forecasting with Option-Implied Information

Peter Christoffersen[*,†], Kris Jacobs[‡,**], and Bo Young Chang[††]

[*]Rotman School of Management, University of Toronto, Canada
[†]Copenhagen Business School and CREATES, Denmark
[‡]Bauer College of Business, University of Houston, USA
[**]Tilburg University, Netherlands
[††]Financial Markets Department, Bank of Canada, Canada

Contents

Handbook of Economic Forecasting, Volume 2A
ISSN 1574-0706, http://dx.doi.org/10.1016/B978-0-444-53683-9.00010-6

Abstract

This chapter surveys the methods available for extracting information from option prices that can be used in forecasting. We consider option-implied volatilities, skewness, kurtosis, and densities. More generally, we discuss how any forecasting object that is a twice differentiable function of the future realization of the underlying risky asset price can utilize option-implied information in a well-defined manner. Going beyond the univariate option-implied density, we also consider results on option-implied covariance, correlation and beta forecasting, as well as the use of option-implied information in cross-sectional forecasting of equity returns. We discuss how option-implied information can be adjusted for risk premia to remove biases in forecasting regressions.

Keywords

Volatility, Skewness, Kurtosis, Density forecasting, Risk-neutral

1. INTRODUCTION

In this chapter, we provide an overview of techniques used to extract information from derivatives, and document the usefulness of this information in forecasting. The premise of this chapter is that derivative prices contain useful information on the conditional density of future underlying asset returns. This information is not easily extracted using econometric models of historical values of the underlying asset prices, even though historical information may also be useful for forecasting, and combining historical information with information extracted from derivatives prices may be especially effective.

1.1. Options and Other Derivative Securities

A derivative contract is an asset whose future payoff depends on the uncertain realization of the price of an underlying asset. Many different types of derivative contracts exist: futures and forward contracts, interest rate swaps, currency and other plain-vanilla swaps, credit default swaps (CDS) and variance swaps, collateralized debt obligations (CDOs) and basket options, European style call and put options, and American style and exotic options. Several of these classes of derivatives, such as futures and options, exist for many different types of underlying assets, such as commodities, equities, and equity indexes.

Because of space constraints, we are not able to discuss all the available techniques and empirical evidence of predictability for all available derivatives contracts. We therefore use three criteria to narrow our focus. First, we give priority to larger and more liquid markets, because they presumably are of greater interest to the reader, and the extracted information is more reliable. Second, we focus on methods that are useful across different types of securities. Some derivatives, such as basket options and CDOs, are multivariate in nature, and as a result techniques for information extraction are highly specific to these securities. While there is a growing literature on extracting information from these derivatives, the literature on forecasting using this information is as yet limited, and we therefore do not focus on these securities. Third, some derivative contracts such as forwards and futures are linear in the return on the underlying security, and therefore their payoffs are too simple to contain enough useful and reliable information relative to non-linear contracts. This makes these securities less interesting for our purpose. Other securities, such as exotic options, have path-dependent payoffs, which may make information extraction cumbersome.

Based on these criteria, we mainly focus on European-style options. European-style options hit the sweet spot between simplicity and complexity and will therefore be the main, but not the exclusive, focus of our survey.[1] Equity index options are of particular interest, because the underlying risky asset (a broad equity index) is a key risk factor in the economy. They are among the most liquid exchange-traded derivatives, so they have reliable and publicly available prices. The fact that the most often-used equity index options are European-style also makes them tractable and computationally convenient.[2] For these reasons, the available empirical literature on equity index options is also the most extensive one.

Forecasting with option-implied information typically proceeds in two steps. First, derivative prices are used to extract a relevant aspect of the option-implied distribution of the underlying asset. Second, an econometric model is used to relate this option-implied

---

[1] Note that for American options the early exercise premium can usually be estimated (using binomial trees for example). By subtracting this estimate from the American option price, a synthetic European option is created, which can be analyzed using the techniques we study in this chapter.

[2] Most studies use options on the S&P 500 index, which are European. Early studies used options on the S&P 100, which was the most liquid market at the time. These options are American.

information to the forecasting object of interest. For example, the Black–Scholes model can be used to compute implied volatility of an at-the-money European call option with 30 days to maturity. Then, a linear regression is specified with realized volatility for the next 30 days regressed on today's implied Black–Scholes volatility. We will focus on the first step in this analysis, namely extracting various information from observed derivatives prices. The econometric issues in the second step are typically fairly standard and so we will not cover them in any detail.

Finally, there are a great number of related research areas we do not focus on, even though we may mention and comment on some of them in passing. In particular, this chapter is not a survey of option valuation models (see Whaley, 2003), or of the econometrics of option valuation (see Garcia et al., 2010), or of volatility forecasting in general (see Andersen et al., 2006). Our chapter exclusively focuses on the extraction of information from option prices, and only to the extent that such information has been used or might be useful in forecasting.

1.2. Risk Premia

Risk premia play a critical role when forecasting with option-implied information. Here we briefly outline the impact of risk premia, using the simplest possible example of a derivatives contract, a forward. A forward contract requires the seller to deliver to the buyer the underlying asset with current spot price, S_0, on a prespecified future date, T, at a prespecified price, F_0, to be paid at date T. In the absence of taxes, short-sale constraints and assuming that investors can lend and borrow at the same risk-free rate, r, the no-arbitrage price of the forward contract on a financial asset is simply

$$F_0 = S_0 \exp(rT),\tag{1}$$

assuming continuous compounding. The simplicity of this contract makes it well-suited to explore the impact of risk premia. Consider using forward prices as predictors of the future realized spot price, S_T. Again, for simplicity, assume that the price evolves as a Brownian motion with risk premium μ and volatility σ. The distribution of the future spot price is log-normal in this case and the expected future spot price is

$$E_0[S_T] = S_0 \exp\left((r + \mu)T\right).$$

Using the no-arbitrage condition (1), we get

$$E_0[S_T] = F_0 \exp\left(\mu T\right).\tag{2}$$

Equation (2) is a very simple example of how a derivatives contract can contain useful information about future values of the underlying security. Similar intuition holds for more complex derivatives, such as options, but the relationship between the derivatives price and the future underlying is more complex. As explained above, the simplicity of

(2) is why we do not extensively discuss the extraction of information from forward contracts in this chapter.[3] Equation (1) indicates that the forward price, F_0, is a simple linear function of the underlying asset price, S_0, and therefore information from F_0 is not likely to be more useful than S_0 itself.

Equation (2) illustrates that unless the asset's risk premium μ is equal to zero, the forward price will be a biased forecast of the future spot price of the asset. In standard asset pricing models, the risk premium μ of the asset will be positive if the asset price is positively correlated with overall wealth in the economy, implying that $F_0 < E_0[S_T]$, so that the forward price will be a downward-biased forecast of the future spot price. In a standard forecasting regression, the bias will show up in the intercept if μ does not change over time. If μ is time-varying, the bias may show up in the slope coefficient. Notice that what is critical here is that μ is not directly observable, so that we cannot easily correct the future spot price for the risk premium.

While for more complex derivatives the relation between the derivatives price, the expected price of the underlying, and the risk premium will typically be more complex, the same intuition holds: the presence of a risk premium will impact on information extracted from options. Also, while our example addresses the first moment of the under-lying security, the derivatives-implied estimate of the higher moments of the return on the underlying security are also biased by the presence of risk premia.

While risk premia are not directly observable, they can be estimated, by combining the prices of the derivative and the underlying contract, but this typically requires additional assumptions. We therefore proceed in two steps. In Sections 2–4, we work exclusively under the so-called risk-neutral or pricing measure where risk premia are zero. We subsequently discuss the incorporation of risk premia into option-implied forecasts in Section 5.

1.3. Chapter Overview

This chapter addresses forecasting future realizations using several option-implied objects: volatility, skewness and kurtosis, and the return density.[4] There is a recent and quite distinct literature on forecasting expected equity returns (over time and in the cross-section) using higher option-implied moments, and we also discuss this evidence in some detail.

Note that the available evidence on forecasting with option-implied volatility is more extensive than the evidence using skewness and kurtosis. There are several reasons for this.

---

[3] In certain markets futures contracts trade in the hours after today's closing and/or before tomorrow's opening of the spot market. In this case the futures price can serve as a more useful predictor of future spot prices than yesterday's closing spot price simply because the futures price is observed more recently. The futures price will still be a biased forecast as Eq. (2) shows, but the bias will be small if the maturity, T, of the futures contract is small and/or if the risk-premium, μ, is small. If trading in the futures markets can be done more cheaply and efficiently than in the underlying spot market then futures prices may lead spot prices at short horizons as well.

[4] The option-implied first moment is equal to the risk-free rate and so not used in forecasting.

On the one hand, it is more straightforward to estimate option-implied volatility compared to option-implied higher moments. More subtly, option-implied forecasts are more likely to be informative about future moments when risk premia are small, and there is growing evidence that volatility risk premia are smaller than the risk premia for higher moments, in particular for skewness.

The chapter proceeds as follows. Section 2 discusses methods for extracting volatility and correlation forecasts from option prices. Section 3 focuses on constructing option-implied skewness and kurtosis forecasts. Section 4 covers techniques that enable the forecaster to construct the entire density, thus enabling event probability forecasts for example. Sections 2–4 cover model-based as well as model-free approaches. When discussing model-based techniques, we discuss in each section the case of two workhorse models, Black and Scholes (1973) and Heston (1993), as well as other models appropriate for extracting the object of interest. Sections 2–4 use the option-implied distribution directly in forecasting the physical distribution of returns. Section 5 discusses the theory and practice of allowing for risk premia and thus converting option-implied forecasts to physical forecasts. Section 6 concludes.

2. EXTRACTING VOLATILITY AND CORRELATION FROM OPTION PRICES

Volatility forecasting is arguably the most widely used application of option-implied information. When extracting volatility information from options, model-based methods were originally more popular, but recently model-free approaches have become much more important. We will discuss each in turn.

2.1. Model-Based Volatility Extraction

In this section we will review the most commonly used option valuation model for volatility extraction, namely the Black and Scholes (1973) model. The Black–Scholes model only contains one unknown parameter, volatility, which is constant, and so extracting an option-implied volatility forecast from this model is straightforward. We will also review the Heston (1993) model. The Heston model allows for stochastic volatility, which can be correlated with returns, but it contains multiple parameters and so it is more cumbersome to implement. Finally, we will use an argument from Hull and White (1987) to show how the Black–Scholes model is related to a special case of the Heston model. This relationship suggests why the Black–Scholes model continues to be widely used for extracting option-implied volatility.

2.1.1. Black–Scholes Implied Volatility
Black and Scholes (1973) assume a constant volatility geometric Brownian motion risk-neutral stock price process of the form

$$dS = rSdt + \sigma Sdz,$$

where again r is the risk-free rate, σ is the volatility of the stock price, and dz is a normally distributed innovation.[5] Given this assumption, the future log stock price is normally distributed and the option price for a European call option with maturity T and strike price X can be computed in closed form using

$$C^{BS}\left(T, X, S_0, r; \sigma^2\right) = S_0 N(d) - X \exp\left(-rT\right) N\left(d - \sigma\sqrt{T}\right),\tag{3}$$

where S_0 is the current stock price, $N\left(\cdot\right)$ denotes the standard normal CDF, and where

$$d = \frac{\ln\left(S_0/X\right) + T\left(r + \frac{1}{2}\sigma^2\right)}{\sigma\sqrt{T}}.\tag{4}$$

European put options can be valued using put-call parity

$$P_0 + S_0 = C_0 + X \exp\left(-rT\right)$$

which can be derived from a no-arbitrage argument alone and so is not model dependent.

The Black–Scholes option pricing formula has just one unobserved parameter, namely volatility, denoted by σ. For any given option with market price, C_0^{Mkt}, the formula therefore allows us to back out the value of σ, which is implied by the market price of that option,

$$C_0^{Mkt} = C^{BS}\left(T, X, S_0, r; BSIV^2\right).\tag{5}$$

The resulting option-specific volatility, $BSIV$, is generically referred to as implied volatility (IV). To distinguish it from other volatility measures implied by options, we will refer to it as Black–Scholes IV, thus the $BSIV$ notation.

Although the Black–Scholes formula in (3) is clearly non-linear, for at-the-money options, the relationship between volatility and option price is virtually linear as illustrated in the top panel of Figure 10.1.

In general the relationship between volatility and option prices is positive and monotone. This in turn implies that solving for $BSIV$ is quick. The so-called option Vega captures the sensitivity of the option price w.r.t. changes in volatility. In the Black–Scholes model it can be derived as

$$Vega_{BS} = \frac{\partial C_0^{BS}}{\partial \sigma} = S_0\sqrt{T}N'(d),$$

where d is as defined in (4) and where $N'\left(d\right)$ is the standard normal probability density function.

---

[5] Throughout this chapter we assume for simplicity that the risk-free rate is constant across time and maturity. In reality it is not and the time-zero, maturity-dependent risk-free rate, $r_{0,T}$ should be used instead of r in all formulas. Recently, the overnight indexed swap rate has become the most commonly used proxy for the risk-free rate. See Hull (2011, Chapter 7).

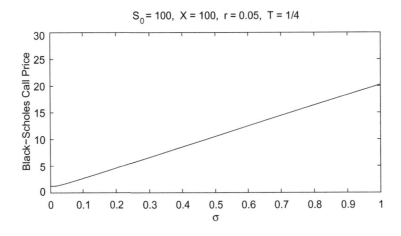

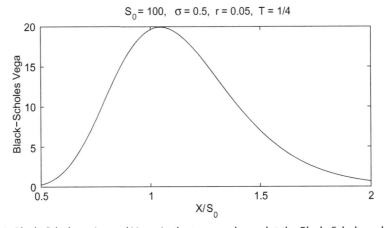

Figure 10.1 Black–Scholes price and Vega. In the top panel, we plot the Black–Scholes call price as a function of volatility for an at-the-money option with a strike price of 100 and 3 months to maturity. The risk-free interest rate is 5% per year. In the bottom panel we plot the Black–Scholes Vega as a function of moneyness for a call option with a volatility of 50% per year.

The bottom panel of Figure 10.1 plots the Black–Scholes Vega as a function of moneyness. Note that the sensitivity of the options with respect to volatility changes is largest for at-the-money options. This in turn implies that changes in at-the-money option prices are the most informative about changes in expected volatility.

In Figure 10.2 we plot *BSIV*s for out-of-the-money S&P 500 call and put options quoted on October 22, 2009. In the top panel of Figure 10.2 the *BSIV*s on the vertical axis are plotted against moneyness (X/S_0) on the horizontal axis for three different maturities.

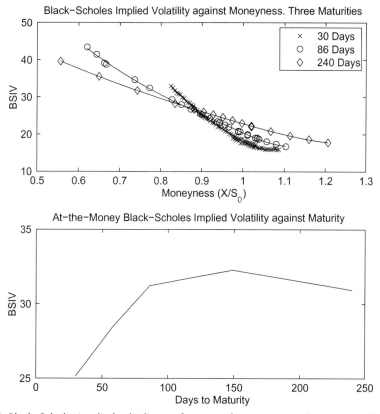

Figure 10.2 Black–Scholes implied volatility as a function of moneyness and maturity. In the top panel, we plot Black–Scholes implied volatility (*BSIV*) against moneyness, X/S_0, for various out-of-the-money S&P 500 options quoted on October 22, 2009. In the bottom panel we plot at-the-money *BSIV* against days to maturity (DTM).

The index-option *BSIV*s in the top panel of Figure 10.2 display a distinct downward sloping pattern commonly known as the "smirk" or the "skew." The pattern is evidence that the Black–Scholes model is misspecified. Deep out-of-the-money (OTM) put options ($X/S_0 \ll 1$) have much higher *BSIV*s than other options which from Figure 10.1 implies that they are more expensive than the Black–Scholes model, which assumes lognormality, would suggest. Only a distribution with a fatter left tail (that is negative skewness) would be able to generate these much higher prices for OTM puts. This finding will lead us to consider models that account for skewness and kurtosis in Section 3.

The bottom panel of Figure 10.2 shows that the *BSIV* for at-the-money options ($X/S_0 \approx 1$) tends to be larger for long-maturity than short-maturity options. This is evidence that volatility changes over time although it is assumed constant in the Black–Scholes model. We therefore consider models with stochastic volatility next.

2.1.2. Stochastic Volatility

For variances to change over time, we need a richer setup than the Black–Scholes model. The perhaps most widely used stochastic volatility model is Heston (1993),[6] who assumes that the price of an asset follows the so-called square-root process[7]

$$dS = rSdt + \sqrt{V}Sdz_1 \tag{6}$$
$$dV = \kappa\left(\theta - V\right)dt + \sigma_V\sqrt{V}dz_2,$$

where the two innovations are correlated with parameter ρ.

At time zero, the variance forecast for horizon T can be obtained as

$$VAR_0\left(T\right) \equiv E_0\left[\int_0^T V_t dt\right] = \theta T + \left(V_0 - \theta\right)\frac{\left(1 - e^{-\kappa T}\right)}{\kappa}. \tag{7}$$

The horizon-T variance $VAR_0\left(T\right)$ is linear in the spot variance V_0. Notice how the mean-reversion parameter κ determines the extent to which the difference between current spot volatility and long run volatility, $\left(V_0 - \theta\right)$, affects the horizon T forecast. The smaller the κ, the slower the mean reversion in volatility, and the higher the importance of current volatility for the horizon T forecast. Recall that in this and the subsequent two sections we set all risk premia to zero and work with the risk-neutral distribution. All expectations are therefore computed using the risk-neutral distribution as well.

Figure 10.3 shows the volatility term structure in the Heston model, namely

$$\sqrt{VAR_0\left(T\right)/T} = \sqrt{\theta + \left(V_0 - \theta\right)\frac{\left(1 - e^{-\kappa T}\right)}{\kappa T}}, \tag{8}$$

using $\theta = 0.09$ and $\kappa = 2$. $V_0 = 0.36$ (dashed line) corresponds to a high current spot variance and $V_0 = 0.01$ (solid line) corresponds to a low current spot variance.

A similar approach could be taken for the wide range of models falling in the affine class to which the Heston model belongs. Duffie et al. (2000) provide an authoritative treatment of a general class of continuous time affine models. For examples of discrete time affine models, see Heston and Nandi (2000) and Christoffersen et al. (2006).

Hull and White (1987) show that in the case where volatility is uncorrelated with returns $(\rho = 0)$,[8] we can think of the stochastic volatility option price as the expected value of the Black–Scholes price

$$C^{SV} = E_0\left[C^{BS}\left(T, X, S_0, r; \frac{1}{T}\int_0^T V_t dt\right)\right],$$

---

[6] Heston's model is based on earlier stochastic volatility models by Hull and White (1987), Scott (1987), Wiggins (1987), and Melino and Turnbull (1990).

[7] Christoffersen et al. (2010b) investigate the empirical performance of stochastic volatility models with alternative drift and diffusion specifications.

[8] They also assume that volatility does not carry a separate risk premium. We will discuss the volatility risk premium in Section 5.

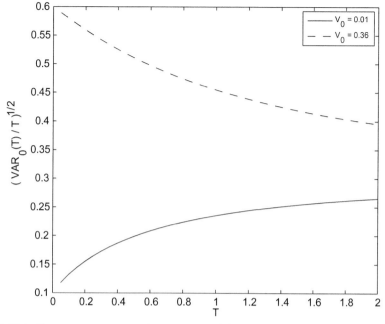

Figure 10.3 Volatility term structures in the Heston model. We plot the volatility term structure in the Heston model defined as

$$\sqrt{VAR_0\left(T\right)/T} = \sqrt{\theta + \left(V_0 - \theta\right)\frac{\left(1 - e^{-\kappa T}\right)}{\kappa T}},$$

where $\theta = 0.09$ and $\kappa = 2$. $V_0 = 0.36$ (dashed line) corresponds to a high current spot variance and $V_0 = 0.01$ (solid line) corresponds to a low current spot variance.

where the conditional expectation is taken over the distribution of future integrated variance. We saw in Figure 10.1 that the Black–Scholes formula is close to linear in volatility for at-the-money options and we therefore have that

$$C^{SV} \approx C^{BS}\left(T, X \approx S_0, S_0, r; E_0\left[\frac{1}{T}\int_0^T V_t dt\right]\right), \tag{9}$$

which holds only approximately because we are using variance and not volatility here.

The important practical implication of this result is that – even when volatility is stochastic – we can invert the Black–Scholes formula for an at-the-money option to easily obtain a decent forecast of the average variance between now and maturity of the option

$$BSIV\left(X \approx S_0\right) \approx \sqrt{E_0\left[\frac{1}{T}\int_0^T V_t dt\right]} \tag{10}$$

when returns and volatility are uncorrelated.

Using only at-the-money options to extract volatility forecasts omits potentially important information from other strikes. Furthermore, we would like to be able to generate option-based forecasts at horizons different from the ones corresponding to available option maturities. This can be done by estimating the parameters in the Heston model. Note that whereas the Black–Scholes model only has one parameter, σ, the Heston model has four parameters, namely κ, θ, σ_V, and ρ, in addition to the spot variance, V_0. Estimation of the parameters and spot volatility in the model can be done using a data set of returns, but also using option prices. Bakshi et al. (1997) re-estimate the model daily treating V_0 as a fifth parameter to be estimated along with the structural parameters θ, κ, ρ, and σ_V. Bates (2000) and Christoffersen et al. (2009) keep the structural parameters fixed over time. They make use of an iterative two-step option valuation error minimization procedure where in the first step the structural parameters are estimated for a given path of $\{V_t\}_{t=1}^N$. In the second step V_t is estimated each period keeping the structural parameters fixed. Iterating between the first and second step provides the final estimates of structural parameters and spot volatilities. Alternatively, a more formal filtering technique can be used, which is econometrically more complex.

The complications involved in estimating the parameters and filtering the unobserved spot volatility in models such as Heston's – as well as the parametric assumptions required – have motivated the analysis of model-free volatility extraction to which we now turn.

2.2. Model-Free Volatility Extraction

2.2.1. Theory and Implementation

Under the assumptions that investors can trade continuously, interest rates are constant, and the underlying futures price is a continuous semi-martingale, Carr and Madan (1998) show that the expected value of the future realized variance can be computed as

$$E_0\left[\int_0^T V_t dt\right] = 2 \int_0^\infty \frac{C_0^F(T, X) - \max\left(F_0 - X, 0\right)}{X^2} dX, \tag{11}$$

where F_0 is the forward price of the underlying asset and $C^F(T, X)$ is a European call option on the forward contract.

Britten-Jones and Neuberger (2000) show that the relationship also holds when V_t is replaced by the instantaneous squared return

$$E_0\left[\int_0^T (dS_t/S_t)^2 dt\right] = 2 \int_0^\infty \frac{C_0^F(T, X) - \max\left(F_0 - X, 0\right)}{X^2} dX. \tag{12}$$

Jiang and Tian (2005) generalize this result further and show that (12) holds even if the price process contains jumps.

When relying on options on the underlying spot asset rather than on the forward contract, the expected variance between now and horizon T is

$$VAR_0\left(T\right) = 2\int_0^\infty \frac{C_0\left(T, e^{-rT}X\right) - \max\left(S_0 - X, 0\right)}{X^2}\,dX.$$

Jiang and Tian (2005, 2007) discuss the implementation of (12). In particular, they discuss potential biases that can arise from:

1. Truncation errors: the integration is performed over a finite range of strike prices instead of from 0 to ∞.
2. Discretization errors: the integral over strikes is replaced by a sum.
3. Limited availability of strikes: the range of available strikes is narrow and/or has large gaps.

In practice, a finite range, $X_{\max} - X_{\min}$, of discrete strikes are available. Jiang and Tian (2005) use the trapezoidal integration rule

$$VAR_0\left(T\right) \approx \sum_{i=1}^m \left\{ \frac{\left[C_0^F\left(T, X_i\right) - \max\left(F_0 - X_i, 0\right)\right]}{X_i^2} \right. $$
$$\left. + \frac{\left[C_0^F\left(T, X_{i-1}\right) - \max\left(F_0 - X_{i-1}, 0\right)\right]}{X_{i-1}^2} \right\} \Delta X, \qquad (13)$$

where $\Delta X = \left(X_{\max} - X_{\min}\right)/m$, and the discrete (evenly spaced) strikes $X_i = X_{\min} + i\Delta X$.

In order to reduce the discretization error, ΔX needs to be reasonably small. Jiang and Tian (2005) fill in gaps in strikes by applying a cubic spline to the $BSIV$s of traded options, and demonstrate using a Monte Carlo experiment that this approach works well. To overcome truncation problems, Jiang and Tian (2005) use a flat extrapolation outside of the strike price range, whereas Jiang and Tian (2007) use a linear extrapolation with smooth pasting. Figlewski (2010) proposes further modifications, including: (i) a fourth degree rather than a cubic spline, (ii) smoothing, which does not require the interpolation function to fit the traded option prices exactly, and (iii) the application of extreme value functions for the tails of the distribution.

2.2.2. The VIX Volatility Index

The VIX volatility index is published by the Chicago Board of Options Exchange (CBOE). It is probably the best-known and most widely used example of option–implied information. It has become an important market indicator and it is sometimes referred to as "The Investor Fear Gauge"(Whaley, 2000).

The history of the VIX nicely illustrates the evolution in the academic literature, and the increasing prominence of model-free approaches rather than model-based approaches.

Prior to 1993, the VIX was computed as the average of the *BSIV* for four call and four put options just in- and out-of-the-money, with maturities just shorter and longer than thirty days. (See Whaley, 2000 for a detailed discussion.) Since 2003, the new VIX relies on a model-free construction, and relies on the following general result.[9]

Consider first a variance swap, which is a contract that at time T pays integrated variance between time 0 and T less a strike price, X_{VS}. The strike is set so that the value of the variance swap is zero when written at time 0

$$e^{-rT} E_0 \left[\frac{1}{T} \int_0^T V_t dt - X_{VS} \right] = 0.$$

Consider next a stock price process with a generic dynamic volatility specification

$$dS = rSdt + \sqrt{V_t} S dz.$$

From Ito's lemma we have

$$d \ln (S) = \left(r - \frac{1}{2} V_t \right) dt + \sqrt{V_t} dz$$

so that

$$\frac{dS}{S} - d \ln (S) = \frac{1}{2} V_t dt.$$

This relationship shows that variance can be replicated by taking positions sensitive to the price, S, and the log price, $\ln(S)$, of the underlying asset.[10] Demeterfi et al. (1999) use this expression for the variance to derive the replicating cost of the variance swap as

$$VAR_0 (T) = E_0 \left[\int_0^T V_t dt \right] = 2E_0 \left[\int_0^T \frac{dS}{S} - d \ln(S) \right] = 2E_0 \left[\int_0^T \frac{dS}{S} - \ln \left(\frac{S_T}{S_0} \right) \right].$$
(14)

Consider now an arbitrary stock price level, S_*, usually chosen to be close to the forward price. Demeterfi et al. (1999) show that

$$VAR_0 (T) = 2 \left[rT - \left(\frac{S_0}{S_*} e^{rT} - 1 \right) - \ln \left(\frac{S_*}{S_0} \right) \right.$$
$$\left. + \int_0^{S_*} \frac{e^{rT}}{X^2} P (X, T) dX + \int_{S_*}^\infty \frac{e^{rT}}{X^2} C (X, T) dX \right],$$
(15)

where P and C are put and call prices. Now, if we let $S_* = F_0$, then because $F_0 = S_0 e^{rT}$ the terms to the left of the integrals cancel and we can write

$$VAR_0 (T) = 2e^{rT} \left[\int_0^{F_0} \frac{1}{X^2} P (X, T) dX + \int_{F_0}^\infty \frac{1}{X^2} C (X, T) dX \right].$$
(16)

[9] The VIX calculation assumes a stock price process where the drift and diffusive volatility are arbitrary functions of time. These assumptions encompass for example implied tree models in which volatility is a function of stock price and time. See Dupire (1994) for a discussion of this type of model.

[10] The idea of using log contracts to hedge volatility risk was first introduced by Neuberger (1994).

However, if we set $S_* = X_0$ where X_0 is close to F_0, but not exactly F_0, then a second-order Taylor approximation of the log function around $\frac{F_0}{X_0}$ gives

$$rT - \left(\frac{S_0}{X_0}e^{rT} - 1\right) - \ln\left(\frac{X_0}{S_0}\right) = \left(\frac{F_0}{X_0} - 1\right) + \ln\left(\frac{F_0}{X_0}\right) \approx -\frac{1}{2}\left[\frac{F_0}{X_0} - 1\right]^2. \quad (17)$$

The CBOE implementation of the VIX (CBOE, 2009) is based on (15) and (17), and is given by

$$VIX = 100\sqrt{\frac{2}{T}\sum_i \frac{\Delta X_i}{X_i^2}e^{rT}O\left(X_i\right) - \frac{1}{T}\left[\frac{F_0}{X_0} - 1\right]^2}, \quad (18)$$

where X_0 is the first strike below F_0, $\Delta X_i = \left(X_{i+1} - X_{i-1}\right)/2$, and $O\left(X_i\right)$ is the midpoint of the bid-ask spread for an out-of-the-money call or put option with strike X_i. Note that the VIX is reported in annual percentage volatility units and that compared to (15), it is an average as opposed to an integrated variance. See Jiang and Tian (2007) for more details on how (18) can be derived from (15).

The CBOE computes VIX using out-of-the-money and at-the-money call and put options. It calculates the volatility for the two available maturities that are the nearest and second-nearest to 30 days. Then they either interpolate, if one maturity is shorter and the other is longer than 30 days, or otherwise extrapolate, to get a 30-day index.

It is noteworthy that the implementation of this very popular index requires several ad hoc decisions, which could conceivably affect the results. See for example Andersen and Bondarenko (2007), Andersen and Bondarenko (2009), and Andersen et al. (2011) for potential improvements to the VIX methodology. The latter paper shows that the time-varying range of strike prices available for the VIX calculation affects its precision and consequently suggests an alternative measure based on corridor variance, which uses a consistent range of strike prices over time.

Besides the underlying modeling approach, another important change was made to the computation of the VIX in 1993. Since 1993, the VIX is computed using S&P 500 option prices. Previously, it was based on S&P 100 options. Note that the CBOE continues to calculate and disseminate the original-formula index, known as the CBOE S&P 100 Volatility Index, with ticker VXO. This volatility series is sometimes useful because it has a price history going back to 1986.

The popularity of the VIX index has spawned the introduction of alternative volatility indexes in the U.S. and around the world. Table 10.1 provides an overview of VIX-like volatility indexes around the world. Table 10.1 also contains other option-implied indexes to be discussed below.

Table 10.1 Volatility Indexes Around the World

Country	Exchange	Index	Underlying	Maturity	Launch Date	Method
U.S.	Chicago Board Options Exchange (CBOE)	VIX	S&P 500	1 month	Sep 2003 (previous index renamed VXO, 1993-)	Demeterfi et al. (1999) (VIX methodology)
U.S.	CBOE	VXV	S&P 500	3 months	Nov 2007	VIX
U.S.	CBOE	VXO	S&P 100	1 month	1993	Whaley (1993)
U.S.	CBOE	VXD	DJIA	1 month	Mar 2005	VIX
U.S.	CBOE	VXN	Nasdaq 100	1 month		VIX
U.S.	CBOE	VXAZN, VXAPL, VXGS, VXGOG, VXIBM	Stocks: Amazon, Apple, Goldman Sachs, Google, IBM	1 month	Jan 2011	VIX
U.S.	CBOE	EVZ, GVZ, OVX, VXEEM, VXSLV, VXFXI, VXGDX, VXEWZ, VXXLE	ETFs: EuroCurrency, gold, crude oil, emerging markets, silver, China, gold miners, Brazil, energy sector	1 month	2008	VIX
U.S.	CBOE	ICJ, JCJ, KCJ	S&P 500	As of May 2011, KCJ – Jan 2012, ICJ – Jan 2013, JCJ – Jan 2014, the tickers are to be recycled as they expire	Jul 2009	Skintzi and Refenes (2005)
Australia	Australian Securities Exchange	S&P/ASX 200 VIX (ASX code: XVI)	S&P/ASX 200 (XJO)	1 month	Sep 2010	VIX
Belgium	Euronext	VBEL	BEL 20	1 month	Sep 2007	VIX
Canada	TMX	S&P/TSX 60 VIX (VIXC)	S&P/TSX 60	1 month	Oct 2010	VIX

(Continued)

Table 10.1 *Continued*

Country	Exchange	Index	Underlying	Maturity	Launch Date	Method
Europe	Eurex	VSTOXX	Euro STOXX 50	30, 60, 90,..., 360 days	Apr 2005 (30 days); May 2010 (60–360 days)	VIX
France	Euronext	VCAC	CAC 40	1 month	Sep 2007	VIX
Germany	Deutsche Borse	VDAX-NEW	DAX	1 month	Apr 2005 (previously VDAX, Dec 1994)	VIX
Hong Kong	Hong Kong Futures Exchange	VHSI	HSI	1 month	Feb 2011	VIX
India	National Stock Exchange of India	India VIX	NIFTY	1 month	Jul 2010	VIX
Japan	CSFI, Univ. of Osaka	CSFI – VXJ	Nikkei 225	1 month	Jul 2010	VIX
Mexico	Mexican Derivatives Exchange	VIMEX	Mexican Stock Exchange Price and Quotation Index (IPC)	3 months	Apr 2006	Fleming et al. (1995)
Netherlands	Euronext	VAEX	AEX	1 month	Sep 2007	VIX
South Africa	Johannesburg Stock Exchange	New SAVI	FTSE/JSE Top40	3 months	2010 (previously SAVI, 2007–)	VIX
South Korea	Korea Exchange	V-KOSPI	KOSPI200	1 month	Apr 2009	VIX
Switzerland	Six Swiss Exchange	VSMI	SMI	1 month	Apr 2005	VIX
UK	Euronext	VFTSE	FTSE 100	1 month	Jun 2008	VIX

2.3. Comparison of Option-Implied Volatility Methods

A large number of studies test the ability of option-implied volatility in forecasting the future volatility of the underlying asset. An extensive review of the literature on this topic has been conducted by Poon and Granger (2003). Older studies covered in Poon and Granger (2003) typically used different combinations of *BSIV*s (e.g., ATM, vega-weighted, volume-weighted, etc.), whereas more recent studies focus more on model-free estimates, *MFIV*. Overall, the evidence indicates that *BSIV* and *MFIV* are biased predictors of the future volatility of the underlying asset.

A plausible reason for the bias is that neither *BSIV* or *MFIV* takes into account the non-zero volatility risk premium in option prices. We will discuss this issue in more detail in Section 5. Poteshman (2000) and Chernov (2007) find that the bias disappears when volatility is extracted from option pricing models that allow for volatility risk premiums such as Heston (1993), and when jump-diffusion models are used in forecasting. However, there is no evidence that the unbiased estimates outperform *BSIV* or *MFIV* in forecasting. Despite the bias, *BSIV* and *MFIV* continue to be preferred to the volatility estimates from Heston (1993) or jump-diffusion models in volatility forecasting.

Another possible source of bias is the fact that volatility is the square root of variance so that even if a particular variance forecast is unbiased its square root need not be an unbiased forecast of ex-post volatility because of the non-linearity of the square root function. This is the bias arising from the approximation in (10).

Comparing *BSIV* and *MFIV* in their forecasting performance, two recent studies arrive at two opposite conclusions. Jiang and Tian (2005) find that *MFIV* subsumes all information in *BSIV* whereas Andersen and Bondarenko (2007) find the opposite result. Thus, there is no consensus on which one of these two predictors work better. It is likely that *BSIV* will perform relatively well when only a few strike prices are available and when they are close to the current underlying asset price. The *MFIV* measure is more demanding in terms of the richness of strike prices required in implementation, which ultimately may hamper its performance if only a few strike prices are available or if the strike prices far from the current spot price are illiquid. In general, tightly parametric methods are likely to work well when the data are scarce, so long as the parametric assumptions are reasonable. Non-parametric methods are much more likely to do well in data rich environments. This logic is likely to hold in the various applications we consider below in this section and in subsequent sections as well.

2.4. Applications of Option-Implied Volatility Forecasts

In their survey, Poon and Granger (2003) consider papers that compare volatility forecasts from GARCH models and simple historical squared return averages with option-implied volatility forecasts. Out of 34 relevant studies, 26 found that option-implied volatility forecasts outperformed simple historical averages. Out of 18 relevant studies, 17 found that option-implied volatility forecasts outperformed GARCH based forecasts. The case

Table 10.2 Forecasting Monthly Realized Variance Using Black–Scholes Implied Variance

Intercept	RV_M	RV_W	RV_D	$BSIV^2$	Adj. R^2
Panel A: Foreign exchange data					
0.0061	0.2186	0.0981	0.1706	–	26.0
(0.0011)	(0.1138)	(0.1438)	(0.0828)		
0.0022	–	–	–	0.8917	40.7
(0.0011)				(0.0884)	
0.0021	−0.1483	0.0769	0.0765	0.8733	41.1
(0.0011)	(0.1178)	(0.1284)	(0.0754)	(0.1419)	
Panel B: S&P 500 data					
0.0053	0.6240	−0.3340	0.6765	–	53.0
(0.0025)	(0.1132)	(0.1039)	(0.1007)		
−0.0050	–	–	–	1.0585	62.1
(0.0027)				(0.0667)	
−0.0052	0.0378	−0.1617	0.3177	0.9513	64.0
(0.0027)	(0.1311)	(0.0943)	(0.1026)	(0.1391)	
Panel C: Treasury bond data					
0.0031	0.3600	0.1112	0.1389	–	32.5
(0.0005)	(0.1106)	(0.1143)	(0.0744)		
0.0023	–	–	–	0.5686	35.0
(0.0006)				(0.0641)	
0.0018	0.0462	0.1835	0.0817	0.3933	40.4
(0.0006)	(0.1254)	(0.1086)	(0.0710)	(0.0882)	

Note: We reproduce parts of Table 1 from Busch et al. (2011), who regress total realized variance (*RV*) for the current month on the lagged monthly (subscript *M*), weekly (subscript *W*) and daily (subscript *D*) realized variance. Black–Scholes implied variance ($BSIV^2$) is introduced in univariate regressions as well as an additional regressor in the RV regressions. Panel A contains USD/DM FX data for 1987–1999, Panel B contains S&P 500 data for 1990–2002, and Panel C contains Treasury bond data for 1990–2002. Standard errors are in brackets.

for option-implied volatility forecasts thus seems strong at least when the alternative is historical models based on daily (or lower-frequency) returns only.

More recently, researchers have compared the forecasting power of option-implied versus realized volatility measures constructed from intraday returns. Table 10.2 reproduces results from Busch et al. (2011), who regress total realized variance (*RV*) for the current month on the lagged daily, weekly and monthly realized variance, and subsequently use $BSIV^2$ as a regressor. Realized daily variance is computed using intraday returns. Panel A contains USD/DM FX data for 1987–1999, Panel B contains S&P 500 data for 1990–2002, and Panel C contains Treasury bond data for 1990–2002.

The results in Table 10.2 are striking. Option-implied variance has an adjusted R^2 of 40.7% for FX, 62.1% for S&P 500 and 35% for Treasury bond data. This compares with

R^2 of 26%, 53% and 32.5% respectively for the RV based model.[11] The simple $BSIV^2$ forecast is thus able to compete with some of the most sophisticated historical return-based forecasts. The Treasury bond options contain wild-card features that increase the error in option-implied variance in this market. The fact that $BSIV^2$ performs worse in this case is therefore not surprising.

Table 10.2 also suggests that there is some scope for forecast combination between option-implied and return-based forecasts. The third row in each panel of Table 10.2 combines the RV and the $BSIV^2$ forecast. The increase in R^2 compared with the $BSIV^2$-only case is minor for FX, better for S&P 500 and largest for Treasury bond data. These results suggest that when the option data provide biased forecasts – perhaps due to risk premia or early exercise premia – then combining the option-implied forecast with return-based forecasts can be helpful.

Table 10.3 contains a summary of existing empirical results. We now discuss these empirical results for different underlying assets.

2.4.1. Equity Market Applications

The main market of interest in volatility forecasting has been the equity market, particularly stock market indexes. Most studies find that option-implied volatility contains useful information over traditional predictors based on historical prices, and that option-implied volatility by itself often outperforms historical volatility.

Almost all studies find that option-implied index volatility is useful in forecasting the volatility of the stock market index, a notable exception being Canina and Figlewski (1993). However, the evidence is mixed regarding the unbiasedness and efficiency of the option-implied estimates. Fleming et al. (1995), Fleming (1998), and Blair et al. (2001) find that $BSIV$ is an efficient, but biased, predictor, whereas Day and Lewis (1992) find that $BSIV$ is an unbiased, but inefficient, predictor. Christensen and Prabhala (1998) find that $BSIV$ is unbiased and efficient. Busch et al. (2011) find that $BSIV$ is an efficient and unbiased predictor of equity index variance.

Jiang and Tian (2005) find that model-free option-implied volatility ($MFIV$) is biased, but efficient, subsuming all information in $BSIV$. Andersen and Bondarenko (2007) find a different result using a new measure of implied volatility, called Corridor IV (CIV). They compare the forecasting performance of the broad and narrow CIV, which are substitutes of the $MFIV$ and $BSIV$ respectively, and find that the narrow CIV ($BSIV$) is biased, but subsumes the predictive content of the broad CIV ($MFIV$).

Latané and Rendleman (1976), Chiras and Manaster (1978), Beckers (1981), and Lamoureux and Lastrapes (1993) find that $BSIV$ is useful in forecasting the volatility of individual stocks. Swidler and Wilcox (2002) focus on bank stocks, and find that $BSIV$ outperforms historical predictors.

---

[11] Busch et al. (2011) also consider forecasting variance using smooth RV and jump components as separate regressors. These models sometimes perform better than the basic RV models.

Table 10.3 Forecasting with Option-Implied Volatility

Authors	Year	Market	Predictor	To Predict	Method	Conclusion
Fackler and King	1990	Commodity	Mean, vol	Mean, vol	Average of closest-to ATM put and call IV	Prediction is reliable for corn and live cattle, but overstates volatility of soybean and understates mean of hog prices
Kroner, Kneafsey, and Claessens	1995	Commodity	Vol	Vol	Barone-Adesi and Whaley (1987)	Combination of IV and historical outperforms
Jorion	1995	Currency	Vol	Vol	Black (1976) at the money	IV outperforms historical, but biased
Taylor and Xu	1995	Currency	Vol	Vol	Barone-Adesi and Whaley (1987)	IV outperforms historical
Pong, Shackleton, Taylor, and Xu	2004	Currency	Vol	Vol	OTC quotes	IV as accurate as historical at 1 and 3 month horizons, but not better
Christoffersen and Mazzotta	2005	Currency	Vol, density, interval	Vol, density, interval	Malz (1997)	Unbiased and accurate forecast
Day and Lewis	1992	Equity	Vol	Vol	Dividend adjusted BS + Whaley (1982)	Add IV to GARCH and EGARCH. Both are unbiased, but inconclusive as for the relative performance
Harvey and Whaley	1992	Equity	Vol	Vol	Cash-dividend adjusted binomial	IV predicts, but arbitrage profits are not possible, thus consistent with market efficiency

(*Continued*)

Table 10.3 *Continued*

Authors	Year	Market	Predictor	To Predict	Method	Conclusion
Canina and Figlewski	1993	Equity	Vol	Vol	Binomial tree adjusting for dividends and early exercise	IV does not predict
Fleming, Ostdiek, and Whaley	1995	Equity	Vol	Vol	Cash-dividend adjusted binomial, old VIX from Whaley (1993)	Biased, but useful for forecasting
Christensen and Prabhala	1998	Equity	Vol	Vol	BS	IV outperforms historical
Fleming	1998	Equity	Vol	Vol	Modified binomial model of Fleming and Whaley (1994)	IV is an upward biased forecast, but contains relevant information
Blair, Poon, Taylor	2001	Equity	Vol	Vol	VIX	VIX forecasts best and high-frequency intraday returns add no incremental information
Poon and Granger	2003	Equity	Vol	Vol	N/A	Review of volatility forecasting, table with summary of literature
Jiang and Tian	2005	Equity	Vol	Vol	Britten-Jones and Neuberger (2000), cubic spline	MFIV subsumes all information in BSIV and historical volatility
Ang, Hodrick, Xing, and Zhang	2006	Equity	Vol	Cross-section of stock returns	VIX	Innovation in VIX is a priced risk factor with a negative price of risk

(Continued)

Table 10.3 *Continued*

Authors	Year	Market	Predictor	To Predict	Method	Conclusion
Andersen and Bondarenko	2007	Equity	Vol	Vol	Corridor implied volatility (CIV)	Broad CIV related to MFIV. Narrow CIV related to BSIV. Narrow CIV is a better volatility predictor than MFIV or BSIV
Bollerslev, Tauchen, and Zhou	2009	Equity	Variance risk premium	Equity risk premium	VIX	VRP predicts stock market return
Bekaert, Hoerova, and Lo Duca	2010	Equity	Variance risk premium	Equity risk premium	VIX	A lax monetary policy decreases risk aversion after about five months. Monetary authorities react to periods of high uncertainty by easing monetary policy
Zhou	2010	Equity	Variance risk premium	Equity risk premium	VIX	VRP predicts a significant positive risk premium across equity, bond, and credit markets in the short-run (1–4 months)
Bakshi, Panayotov, and Skoulakis	2011	Equity	Forward variances	(i) Growth in measures of real economic activity, (ii) Treasury bill returns, (iii) stock market returns, and (iv) changes in variance swap rates	Forward variances extracted from the prices of exponential claims of different maturities (Carr and Lee (2008))	The forward variances predict (i) growth in measures of real economic activity, (ii) Treasury bill returns, (iii) stock market returns, and (iv) changes in variance swap rates

(Continued)

Table 10.3 *Continued*

Authors	Year	Market	Predictor	To Predict	Method	Conclusion
Feunou, Fontaine, Taamouti, and Tedongap	in press	Equity	Term structure of implied volatility	Equity risk premium, variance risk premium	VIX	Term structure of implied volatility predicts both equity risk premium and variance risk premium
DeLisle, Doran, and Peterson	2011	Equity	Vol	Cross-section of stock returns	VIX	Result in Ang et al. (2006) holds when volatility is rising, but not when volatility is falling
Latané and Rendleman	1976	Equity (individual)	Vol	Vol	Vega-weighted average of individual stock option BSIVs	Outperforms historical
Chiras and Manaster	1978	Equity (individual)	Vol	Vol	BSIV	Risk-free return using option trading strategies
Beckers	1981	Equity (individual)	Vol	Vol	Weighted average BSIV vs. at-the-money BSIV	At-the-money BSIV predicts better than weighted average of BSIVs
Sheikh	1989	Equity (individual)	Vol	Split announcement and ex-dates	Roll (1977), American option with dividends	No relative increase in IV of stocks announcing splits, but increase is detected at the ex-date.
Lamoureux and Lastrapes	1993	Equity (individual)	Vol	Vol	Hull and White (1987) stochastic volatility option pricing model	IV contains incremental information to historical
Swidler and Wilcox	2002	Equity (individual)	Vol	Bank stock volatility	OldVIX	IV outperforms historical

(Continued)

Table 10.3 *Continued*

Authors	Year	Market	Predictor	To Predict	Method	Conclusion
Banerjee, Doran, and Peterson	2007	Equity (individual)	Vol	Return of characteristic-based portfolios	VIX	Strong predictive ability
Diavatopoulos, Doran, Fodor, and Peterson	2008	Equity (individual)	Idiosyncratic volatility	Future cross-sectional stock returns		Strong positive link
Doran, Fodor, and Krieger	2010	Equity (individual)	Vol	Abnormal return after analyst recommendation change	Simulate Bates (1996b) SVJ model	Information in option markets leads analyst recommendation changes
Demiguel, Plyakha, Uppal, and Vilkov	2011	Equity (individual)	Vol, skew, correlation, variance risk premium	Portfolio selection	Bakshi et al. (2003) for volatility and skew, Driessen et al. (2009) for correlation, Bollerslev et al. (2011) for VRP	Exploiting information contained in the volatility risk premium and option-implied skewness increases substantially both the Sharpe ratio and certainty-equivalent return
Amin and Ng	1997	FI	Vol	Volatility of interest rate	Heath et al. (1992)	Predicts well. Shows how to combine IV with historical
Busch, Christensen, and Nielsen	2011	FI, equity, currency	Vol	Realized volatility, jump	Numerical inversion of Black (1976)	Prediction in all three markets

Harvey and Whaley (1992) test if *BSIV* itself can be predicted and find that *BSIV* is predictable, but conclude that since arbitrage profits are not possible in the presence of transaction costs, this predictability is not inconsistent with market efficiency. Poon and Granger (2003) provide a comprehensive survey of volatility forecasting in general.

A few studies investigate if option-implied volatility can predict variables other than volatility, such as stock returns and bond spreads. Banerjee et al. (2007) find that the VIX predicts returns on portfolios sorted on book-to-market equity, size, and beta. Doran et al. (2010) find that information in option prices leads analyst recommendation changes.

2.4.2. Other Markets

Fackler and King (1990) and Kroner et al. (1995) study the forecasting ability of implied volatility in commodity markets. Fackler and King (1990) compare the option-implied distribution with the empirical distribution of the futures prices of corn, live cattle, soybean, and hogs between 1985 and 1988. They find that there are differences among markets in terms of reliability of the option-implied distribution. The option-implied distribution matched the empirical distribution closely for corn and live cattle while the option-implied distribution over-predicted the variability of soybean prices and under-predicted the location of hog prices. Kroner et al. (1995) focuses on volatility forecasting over a 225-day horizon for cocoa, cotton, corn, gold, silver, sugar, and wheat prices. They find that a combination of time-series based predictors and option-implied volatility predicts better than either of the predictors alone.

For currencies, Jorion (1995) and Xu and Taylor (1995) find that *BSIV* outperforms historical predictors. Pong et al. (2004) compare *BSIV* to predictors based on historical intraday data in currency markets, and find that historical predictors outperform *BSIV* for 1-day and 1-week horizons, whereas *BSIV* is at least as accurate as historical predictors for 1-month and 3-month horizons. Christoffersen and Mazzotta (2005) also find that the implied volatility yields unbiased and accurate forecast of exchange rate volatility.

Cao et al. (2010) consider the use of option-implied forecasts of volatility for the purpose of credit default swap valuation.

As mentioned above, Busch et al. (2011) investigate assets in three different markets: the S&P 500, the currency market, using the USD/DM exchange rate, and the fixed income market, using the 30-year U.S. Treasury bond. They find that the $BSIV^2$ contains incremental information about future variance in all three markets, relative to continuous and jump components of intraday prices. $BSIV^2$ is an efficient predictor in all three markets and is unbiased in foreign exchange and stock markets (see Table 10.2). Amin and Ng (1997) also find that implied volatility from Eurodollar futures options forecasts a large part of the realized interest rate volatility.

2.4.3. Forecasting the Cross-Section of Expected Stock Returns

Ang et al. (2006) have a very different focus, investigating the performance of the VIX as a pricing factor: they find that the VIX is a priced risk factor with a negative price of risk, so that stocks with higher sensitivities to the innovation in VIX exhibit on average future lower returns. Delisle et al. (2010) find that the result in Ang et al. (2006) holds when volatility is rising, but not when volatility is falling.

Diavatopoulos et al. (2008) find that implied idiosyncratic volatility can forecast the cross-section of stock returns.

The cross-sectional forecasting exercises that use option-implied information are potentially very promising, but of course they are fundamentally different from the traditional use of option information in time-series forecasting.

2.5. Extracting Correlations from Option-Implied Volatilities

Certain derivatives contain very rich information on correlations between financial time series. This is especially the case for basket securities, written on a basket of underlying securities, such as CDOs. As mentioned in the introduction, because of space constraints we limit our survey to options.

We now discuss the extraction of information on correlations for two important security classes, currency and equity. In both cases, some additional assumptions need to be made. Despite the differences in assumptions, in both cases correlations are related to option-implied volatilities. This is not entirely surprising, as correlation can be thought of as a second co-moment. Implied correlation information on equities is particularly relevant, because equity as an asset class is critically important for portfolio management. Table 10.4 contains a summary of existing empirical results on the use of option-implied correlations in forecasting.

2.5.1. Extracting Correlations from Triangular Arbitrage

Using the U.S. dollar, \$, the British Pound, £, and the Japanese Yen, ¥, as an example, from triangular arbitrage in FX markets we know that

$$S_{\$/£} = S_{\$/¥} S_{¥/£}.$$

From this it follows that for log returns

$$R_{\$/£} = R_{\$/¥} + R_{¥/£}.$$

From this we get that

$$VAR_{\$/£} = VAR_{\$/¥} + VAR_{¥/£} + 2COV(R_{\$/¥}, R_{¥/£})$$

so that the correlation must be

$$CORR(R_{\$/¥}, R_{¥/£}) = \frac{\left(VAR_{\$/£} - VAR_{\$/¥} - VAR_{¥/£}\right)}{2VAR_{\$/¥}^{1/2} VAR_{¥/£}^{1/2}}.$$

Provided we have option-implied variance forecasts for the three currencies, we can use this to get an option-implied covariance forecast. See Walter and Lopez (2000) and Campa and Chang (1998) for applications.

Table 10.4 Forecasting with Option-Implied Correlation

Authors	Year	Market	Predictor	To Predict	Method	Conclusion
Siegel	1997	Currency	Correlation	Correlation: USD/DM/GBP	Garman and Kohlhagen (1983)	Outperforms forecast based on historical correlation
Campa and Chang	1998	Currency	Correlation	Correlation between USD/DM and USD/JPY	From relationship between implied volatilities of three exchange rates	Outperforms forecast based on historical correlation
Walter and Lopez	2000	Currency	Correlation	Correlation: USD/DM/JPY, USD/DM/CHF	From relationship between implied volatilities of three exchange rates	Useful for USD/DM/JPY, not for USD/DM/CHF, so may not be useful in general
Skintzi and Refenes	2005	Equity (individual)	Correlation	Correlation	Implied correlation based on IV of index and individual stocks	Although the implied correlation index is a biased forecast of realized correlation, it has a high explanatory power, and it is orthogonal to the information set compared to a historical forecast
Driessen, Maenhout, and Vilkov	2009	Equity (individual)	Correlation	Correlation	Stock prices follow a geometric Brownian motion with constant drift and possibly stochastic diffusion. Assume that a single-state variable drives all pairwise correlations	The entire index variance risk premium can be attributed to the high price of correlation risk

(Continued)

Table 10.4 *Continued*

Authors	Year	Market	Predictor	To Predict	Method	Conclusion
Buss and Vilkov	2012	Equity (individual)	Correlation and factor betas	Factor betas	Stock prices follow a multifactor model. Assume that a single-state variable drives all pairwise correlations	Most efficient and unbiased predictor of beta
Chang, Christof-fersen, Jacobs, and Vainberg	2012	Equity (individual)	Beta, moments	Beta	Formula based on implied vol and skew of index and individual stocks	Forecasts future beta
Demiguel, Plyakha, Uppal, and Vilkov	2011	Equity (individual)	Vol, skew, correla-tion, variance risk pre-mium	Portfolio selection	Bakshi et al. (2003) for volatility and skew, Driessen et al. (2009) for correlation, Bollerslev et al. (2011) for VRP	Exploiting information contained in the volatility risk premium and option-implied skewness increases substantially both the Sharpe ratio and certainty-equivalent return
Longstaff, Santa-Clara, and Schwartz	2003	FI	Correlation	Correlation	Caps and swaptions	Implied correlation is lower than historical correlation. Significant mispricings detected
De Jong, Driessen, and Pelsser	2004	FI	Correlation	Correlation	Caps and swaptions	Implied correlation is different from historical correlation. Significant mispricings detected

Siegel (1997) finds that option-implied exchange rate correlations for the DM/GBP pair and the DM/JPY pair predict significantly better than historical correlations between 1992 and 1993. Campa and Chang (1998) also find that the option-implied correlation for USD/DM/JPY predicts better than historical correlations between 1989 and 1995. The evidence in Walter and Lopez (2000), however, is mixed. They find that the option-implied correlation is useful for USD/DM/JPY (1990–1997), but much less useful for USD/DM/CHF (1993–1997), and conclude that the option-implied correlation may not be worth calculating in all instances.

Correlations have been extracted from options in fixed income markets. Longstaff et al. (2001) and De Jong et al. (2004) provide evidence that forward rate correlations implied by cap and swaption prices differ from realized correlations.

2.5.2. *Extracting Average Correlations Using Index and Equity Options*

Skintzi and Refenes (2005) and Driessen et al. (2009) propose the following measure of average option-implied correlation between the stocks in an index, I,

$$\rho_{ICI} = \frac{VAR_I - \sum_{j=1}^n w_j^2 VAR_j}{2 \sum_{j=1}^{n-1} \sum_{i>j}^n w_i w_j VAR_i^{1/2} VAR_j^{1/2}}, \tag{19}$$

where w_j denotes the weight of stock j in the index.

Note that the measure is based on the option-implied variance for the index, VAR_I, and the individual stock variances, VAR_j. Skintzi and Refenes (2005) use options on the DJIA index and its constituent stocks between 2001 and 2002, and find that the implied correlation index is biased upward, but is a better predictor of future correlation than historical correlation. Buss and Vilkov (2012) use the implied correlation approach to estimate option-implied betas and find that the option-implied betas predict realized betas well. DeMiguel et al. (2011) use option-implied information in portfolio allocation. They find that option-implied volatility and correlation do not improve the Sharpe ratio or certainty-equivalent return of the optimal portfolio. However, expected returns estimated using information in the volatility risk premium and option-implied skewness increase both the Sharpe ratio and the certainty-equivalent return substantially. The CBOE has recently introduced an Implied Correlation Index (ICI) for S&P 500 firms based on (19).

3. EXTRACTING SKEWNESS AND KURTOSIS FROM OPTION PRICES

The *BSIV* smirk patterns in Figure 10.2 revealed that index options imply negative skewness not captured by the normal distribution. As discussed in Rubinstein (1994), prior to 1987, this pattern more closely resembled a symmetric "smile." Rubinstein (1985) documents systematic deviations from Black–Scholes for individual equity options. Other underlying assets such as foreign exchange rates often display symmetric smile patterns in

BSIV implying evidence of excess kurtosis rather than negative skewness. In this section we consider methods capable of generating option-implied measures of skewness and kurtosis, which can be used as forecasts for subsequent realized skewness and kurtosis. We will begin with model-free methods for higher moment forecasting because they are the most common.

3.1. Model-Free Skewness and Kurtosis Extraction

This section first develops the general option replication approach of which higher-moment extraction is a special case. We will then briefly consider other approaches.

3.1.1. The Option Replication Approach

Building on Breeden and Litzenberger (1978), Bakshi and Madan (2000), and Carr and Madan (2001) show that any twice continuously differentiable function, $H(S_T)$, of the terminal stock price S_T, can be replicated (or spanned) by a unique position of risk-free bonds, stocks and European options. Let $H\left(S_0\right) - H'\left(S_0\right) S_0$ denote units of the risk-free discount bond, which of course is independent of S_T. Let $H'\left(S_0\right)$ denote units of the underlying risky stock, which is trivially linear in S_T, and let $H''\left(X\right) dX$ denote units of (non-linear) out-of-the-money call and put options with strike price X, then we have

$$H\left(S_T\right) = \left[H\left(S_0\right) - H'\left(S_0\right) S_0\right] + H'\left(S_0\right) S_T$$
$$+ \int_0^{S_0} H''\left(X\right) \max\left(X - S_T, 0\right) dX$$
$$+ \int_{S_0}^{\infty} H''\left(X\right) \max\left(S_T - X, 0\right) dX. \tag{20}$$

This result is clearly very general. A derivation can be found in Carr and Madan (2001). From a forecasting perspective, for any desired function $H\left(\cdot\right)$ of the future realization S_T there is a portfolio of risk-free bonds, stocks, and options whose current aggregate market value provides an option-implied forecast of $H\left(S_T\right)$.

Let the current market value of the bond be e^{-rT}, and the current put and call prices be $P_0\left(T, X\right)$ and $C_0\left(T, X\right)$ respectively, then we have

$$E_0\left[e^{-rT} H\left(S_T\right)\right] = e^{-rT}\left[H\left(S_0\right) - H'\left(S_0\right) S_0\right] + S_0 H'\left(S_0\right)$$
$$+ \int_0^{S_0} H''\left(X\right) P_0\left(T, X\right) dX$$
$$+ \int_{S_0}^{\infty} H''\left(X\right) C_0\left(T, X\right) dX, \tag{21}$$

Bakshi et al. (2003) (BKM hereafter) apply this general result to the second, third, and fourth power of log returns. To provide added intuition for the replicating option portfolios we consider higher moments of simple returns instead where $H\left(S_T\right) = \left(\frac{S_T - S_0}{S_0}\right)^2$, $H\left(S_T\right) = \left(\frac{S_T - S_0}{S_0}\right)^3$, and $H\left(S_T\right) = \left(\frac{S_T - S_0}{S_0}\right)^4$.

We can use OTM European call and put prices to derive the quadratic contract as[12]

$$M_{0,2}\left(T\right) \equiv E_0\left[e^{-rT}\left(\frac{S_T - S_0}{S_0}\right)^2\right]$$

$$= \frac{2}{S_0^2}\left[\int_0^{S_0} P_0\left(T, X\right) dX + \int_{S_0}^{\infty} C_0\left(T, X\right) dX\right]. \tag{22}$$

The cubic contract is given by

$$M_{0,3}\left(T\right) \equiv E_0\left[e^{-rT}\left(\frac{S_T - S_0}{S_0}\right)^3\right]$$

$$= \frac{6}{S_0^2}\left[\int_0^{S_0}\left(\frac{X - S_0}{S_0}\right) P_0\left(T, X\right) dX\right.$$

$$\left. + \int_{S_0}^{\infty}\left(\frac{X - S_0}{S_0}\right) C_0\left(T, X\right) dX\right] \tag{23}$$

and the quartic contract is given by

$$M_{0,4}\left(T\right) \equiv E_0\left[e^{-rT}\left(\frac{S_T - S_0}{S_0}\right)^4\right]$$

$$= \frac{12}{S_0^2}\left[\int_0^{S_0}\left(\frac{X - S_0}{S_0}\right)^2 P_0\left(T, X\right) dX + \int_{S_0}^{\infty}\left(\frac{X - S_0}{S_0}\right)^2 C_0\left(T, X\right) dX\right]. \tag{24}$$

Notice how the quadratic contract – which is key for volatility – simply integrates over option price levels. The cubic contract – which is key for skewness – integrates over option prices multiplied by moneyness, $\frac{X - S_0}{S_0} = \frac{X}{S_0} - 1$. The quartic contract – which is key for kurtosis – integrates over the option prices multiplied by moneyness squared. High option prices imply high volatility. High OTM put prices and low OTM call prices imply negative skewness (and vice versa). High OTM call and put prices at extreme moneyness imply high kurtosis.

[12] When using log returns instead, we get

$$M_{0,2}\left(T\right) = \int_0^{S_0}\frac{2\left(1 + \ln\left[S_0/X\right]\right)}{X^2} P\left(T, X\right) dX + \int_{S_0}^{\infty}\frac{2\left(1 - \ln\left[X/S_0\right]\right)}{X^2} C\left(T, X\right) dX.$$

We can now compute the option-implied volatility, skewness, and kurtosis (for convenience we suppress the dependence of M on T) as

$$VOL_0\left(T\right) \equiv \left[VAR_0\left(T\right)\right]^{1/2} = \left[e^{rT}M_{0,2} - M_{0,1}^2\right]^{1/2} \tag{25}$$

$$SKEW_0\left(T\right) = \frac{e^{rT}M_{0,3} - 3M_{0,1}e^{rT}M_{0,2} + 2M_{0,1}^3}{\left[e^{rT}M_{0,2} - M_{0,1}^2\right]^{\frac{3}{2}}} \tag{26}$$

$$KURT_0\left(T\right) = \frac{e^{rT}M_{0,4} - 4M_{0,1}e^{rT}M_{0,3} + 6e^{rT}M_{0,1}^2M_{0,2} - 3M_{0,1}^4}{\left[e^{rT}M_{0,2} - M_{0,1}^2\right]^2}, \tag{27}$$

where[13]

$$M_{0,1} \equiv E_0\left[\left(\frac{S_T - S_0}{S_0}\right)\right] = e^{rT} - 1. \tag{28}$$

BKM provide a model-free measure of implied variance, like the Britten-Jones and Neuberger (2000) measure in Eq. (12). BKM compute the variance of the holding period return, whereas Britten-Jones and Neuberger (2000) compute the expected value of realized variance. These concepts of volatility will coincide if the log returns are zero mean and uncorrelated.

Using S&P 500 index options from January 1996 through September 2009, Figure 10.4 plots the higher moments of log returns for the 1-month horizon using the BKM approach.

Not surprisingly, the volatility series is very highly correlated with the VIX index, with a correlation of 0.997 between January 1996 and September 2009. The annualized volatility varied between approximately 0.1 and 0.4 before the subprime crisis of 2008, but its level shot up to an unprecedented level of around 0.8 at the onset of the crisis, subsequently reverting back to its previous level by late 2009. The estimate of skewness is negative for every day in the sample, varying between minus three and zero. Interestingly, skewness did not dramatically change during the subprime crisis, despite the fact that option-implied skewness is often interpreted as the probability of a market crash or the fear thereof. The estimate of kurtosis is higher than three (i.e., excess kurtosis) for every day in the sample, indicating that the option-implied distribution has fatter tails than the normal distribution. Its level did not dramatically change during the sub-prime crisis, but the time series exhibits more day-to-day variation during this period.

The estimation of skewness and kurtosis using the BKM method is subject to the same concerns discussed by Jiang and Tian (2005, 2007), in the context of volatility estimation. Chang et al. (2012) present Monte Carlo evidence on the quality of skewness estimates when only discrete strike prices are available. Fitting a spline through the implied volatilities and integrating the spline, following the methods of Jiang and Tian (2005,

---

[13] Throughout the chapter *KURT* denotes raw and not excess kurtosis.

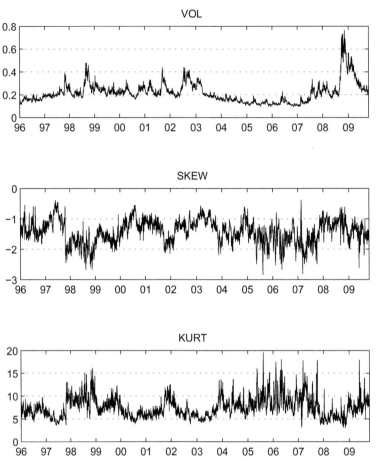

Figure 10.4 Option-implied moments for 1-month S&P 500 returns. We plot the volatility, skewness, and kurtosis implied by S&P 500 index options using the methodology in Bakshi et al. (2003).

2007), seems to work well for skewness too, and dominates simple integration using only observed contracts.

In February 2011, the CBOE began publishing the CBOE S&P 500 Skew Index. The Skew Index is computed using the methodology in BKM described in this section combined with the interpolation/extrapolation method used in the VIX calculation described in Section 2.2.2. See CBOE (2011) for details.

3.1.2. Other Model-Free Measures of Option-Implied Skewness
Many empirical studies on option-implied skewness use the asymmetry observed in the implied volatility curve in Figure 10.2, often referred to as the smirk, to infer skewness of the option-implied distribution. There are many variations in the choice of options

used to measure the asymmetry of the implied volatility curve. The most popular method involves taking the difference of the out-of-the-money put *BSIV* and out-of-the-money call *BSIV*. This measure, proposed by Bates (1991), reflects the different extent to which the left-hand tail and the right-hand tail of the option-implied distribution of the underlying asset price deviate from the lognormal distribution. Another approach is to take the difference between the out-of-the-money put *BSIV* and at-the-money put (or call) *BSIV* as in Xing et al. (2010). This measure only looks at the left-hand side of the distribution, and is often used in applications where the downside risk of the underlying asset is the variable of interest. Another variable that is also shown to be somewhat related to implied skewness is the spread of implied volatility of call and put options with the same maturity and same strike (Cremers and Weinbaum (2010) and Bali and Hovakimian (2009)).

Recently, Neuberger (2012) has proposed a model-free method that extends the variance swap methodology used to compute the VIX index. He shows that just as there is a model-free strategy to replicate a variance swap, a contract that pays the difference between option-implied variance and realized variance, there is also a model-free strategy to replicate a skew swap, a contract that pays the difference between option-implied skew and realized skew.

3.2. Model-Based Skewness and Kurtosis Extraction

In this section we first review two models that are based on expansions around the Black–Scholes model explicitly allowing for skewness and kurtosis. We then consider an alternative model-based approach specifying jumps in returns, which imply skewness and kurtosis.

3.2.1. Expansions of the Black–Scholes Model

Jarrow and Rudd (1982) propose an option pricing method where the density of the security price at option maturity, T, is approximated by an alternative density using the Edgeworth series expansion. If we choose the lognormal as the approximating density, and use the shorthand notation for the Black–Scholes model

$$C_0^{BS}(T, X) \equiv C^{BS}(T, X, S_0, r; \sigma^2),$$

then the Jarrow–Rudd model is defined by

$$C_0^{JR}(T, X) \approx C_0^{BS}(T, X) - e^{-rT} \frac{(K_3 - K_3(\Psi))}{3!} \frac{d\psi(T, X)}{dX}$$
$$+ e^{-rT} \frac{(K_4 - K_4(\Psi))}{4!} \frac{d^2\psi(T, X)}{dX^2}, \tag{29}$$

where K_j is the jth cumulant of the actual density, and $K_j(\Psi)$ is the cumulant of the lognormal density, $\psi(T, X)$, so that

$$\psi(T, X) = \left(X\sigma\sqrt{T2\pi}\right)^{-1} \exp\left\{-\frac{1}{2}\left(d - \sigma\sqrt{T}\right)^2\right\}$$

$$\frac{d\psi(T, X)}{dX} = \frac{\psi(T, X)\left(d - 2\sigma\sqrt{T}\right)}{X\sigma\sqrt{T}}$$

$$\frac{d^2\psi(T, X)}{dX^2} = \frac{\psi(T, X)}{X^2\sigma^2 T}\left[\left(d - 2\sigma\sqrt{T}\right)^2 - \sigma\sqrt{T}\left(d - 2\sigma\sqrt{T}\right) - 1\right]$$

and where d is as defined in (4).

In general we have the following relationships between cumulants and moments

$$K_2 = VAR, \quad K_3 = K_2^{3/2} SKEW, \quad K_4 = K_2^2\left(KURT - 3\right).$$

For the lognormal density we have the following moments

$$VAR(\Psi) = K_2(\Psi) = \exp\left(2\left(\ln(S_0) + \left(r - \frac{1}{2}\sigma^2\right)T\right) + \sigma^2 T\right)\left(\exp(\sigma^2 T) - 1\right)$$

$$SKEW(\Psi) = K_3(\Psi)/K_2^{3/2}(\Psi) = \left(\exp(\sigma^2 T) + 2\right)\sqrt{\exp(\sigma^2 T) - 1}$$

$$KURT(\Psi) = K_4(\Psi)/K_2^2(\Psi) + 3 = \exp(4\sigma^2 T)$$
$$+ 2\exp(3\sigma^2 T) + 3\exp(2\sigma^2 T) - 3.$$

These expressions can be solved for the cumulants, $K_3(\Psi)$ and $K_4(\Psi)$, which are needed in Eq. (29) above.

The Jarrow–Rudd model in (29) now has three parameters left to estimate, namely, σ, K_3, and K_4 or equivalently σ, $SKEW$ and $KURT$. In principle these three parameters could be solved for using three observed option prices. These parameters would then provide option-implied forecasts of volatility, skewness and kurtosis in the distribution of $\ln(S_T)$. Alternatively they could be estimated by minimizing the option valuation errors on a larger set of observed option prices. Christoffersen and Jacobs (2004) discuss the choice of objective function in this type of estimation problems.

As an alternative to the Edgeworth expansion, Corrado and Su (1996) consider a Gram–Charlier series expansion,[14] in which

$$C_0^{CS}(T, X) = C_0^{BS}(T, X) + Q_3 SKEW + Q_4 (KURT - 3),$$
(30)

where

$$Q_3 = \frac{1}{3!} S_0 \sigma \sqrt{T} \left(\left(2\sigma\sqrt{T} - d\right) N'(d) + \sigma^2 T N(d) \right);$$

$$Q_4 = \frac{1}{4!} S_0 \sigma \sqrt{T} \left(\left(d^2 - 1 - 3\sigma\sqrt{T}\left(d - \sigma\sqrt{T}\right)\right) N'(d) + \sigma^3 T^{3/2} N(d) \right),$$

where $N'(d)$ is again the standard normal probability density function. Note that Q_3 and Q_4 represent the marginal effect of skewness and kurtosis respectively and note that d is as defined in (4). In the Corrado–Su model $SKEW$ and $KURT$ refer to the distribution of log return shocks defined by

$$Z_T = \left[\ln S_T - \ln(S_0) - \left(r - \frac{1}{2}\sigma^2\right) T \right] / \left(\sigma\sqrt{T} \right)$$

Again, option-implied volatility, skewness, and kurtosis can be estimated by minimizing the distance between $C_0^{CS}(T, X)$ and a sample of observed option prices or by directly solving for the three parameters using just three observed option prices.

3.2.2. Jumps and Stochastic Volatility

While the Black and Scholes (1973) and stochastic volatility option pricing models are often used to extract volatility, the study of higher moments calls for different models. The Black–Scholes model assumes normality, and therefore strictly speaking cannot be used to extract skewness and kurtosis from the data, although patterns in Black–Scholes implied volatility are sometimes used to learn about skewness.

Stochastic volatility models such as Heston (1993) can generate skewness and excess kurtosis, but fall short in reconciling the stylized facts on physical higher moments with the dynamics of higher option-implied moments (Bates, 1996b and Pan, 2002). Instead, generalizations of the Black and Scholes (1973) and Heston (1993) setup are often used, such as the jump-diffusion model of Bates (1991) and the stochastic volatility jump-diffusion (SVJ) model of Bates (1996b).

In Bates (2000), the futures price F is assumed to follow a jump-diffusion of the following form

$$dF/F = -\lambda \bar{k} dt + \sqrt{V} dz_1 + k dq,$$
(31)
$$dV = \kappa (\theta - V) dt + \sigma_V \sqrt{V} dz_2,$$

---

[14] See also Backus et al. (1997).

where q is a Poisson counter with instantaneous intensity λ, and where k is a lognormally distributed return jump

$$\ln\left(1+k\right) \sim N\left[\ln\left(1+\overline{k}\right) - \delta^2/2, \delta^2\right].$$

As in Heston (1993), the return and variance diffusion terms are correlated with coefficient ρ.

Bates (2000) derives the nth cumulant for horizon T to be

$$K_n\left(T\right) = \left[\frac{\partial^n A\left(T; \Phi\right)}{\partial \Phi^n} + \frac{\partial^n B\left(T; \Phi\right)}{\partial \Phi^n} V\right]_{\Phi=0} + \lambda T\left[\frac{\partial^n C\left(\Phi\right)}{\partial \Phi^n}\right]_{\Phi=0}$$

where

$$A\left(T; \Phi\right) = -\frac{\kappa\theta T}{\sigma_V^2}\left(\rho\sigma_V\Phi - \kappa - D\left(\Phi\right)\right)$$

$$-\frac{2\kappa\theta}{\sigma_V^2}\ln\left[1 + \frac{1}{2}\left(\rho\sigma_V\Phi - \kappa - D\left(\Phi\right)\right)\frac{1 - e^{D(\Phi)T}}{D\left(\Phi\right)}\right],$$

$$B\left(T; \Phi\right) = \frac{-\left[\Phi^2 - \Phi\right]}{\rho\sigma_V\Phi - \kappa + D\left(\Phi\right)\left(\frac{1+e^{D(\Phi)T}}{1-e^{D(\Phi)T}}\right)}, \text{ and}$$

$$C\left(\Phi\right) = \left[\left(1+\overline{k}\right)^\Phi e^{\frac{1}{2}\delta^2[\Phi^2-\Phi]} - 1\right] - \overline{k}\Phi, \text{ and where}$$

$$D\left(\Phi\right) = \sqrt{\left(\rho\sigma_V\Phi - \kappa\right)^2 - 2\sigma_V^2\left\{\frac{1}{2}[\Phi^2 - \Phi]\right\}}.$$

From the cumulants we can compute the conditional moments for the log futures returns for holding period T using

$$VAR_0\left(T\right) = K_2\left(T\right), \quad SKEW_0\left(T\right) = K_3\left(T\right)/K_2^{3/2}\left(T\right),$$
$$KURT_0\left(T\right) = K_4\left(T\right)/K_2^2\left(T\right) + 3.$$

Besides higher moments such as skewness and kurtosis, this model yields parameters describing the intensity and size of jumps, which can potentially be used to forecast jump-like events such as stock market crashes and defaults.

There is an expanding literature estimating models like (31) as well as more general models with jumps in volatility using returns and/or options. See for instance Bates (2000), Bates (2008), Andersen et al. (2002), Pan (2002), Huang and Wu (2004), Eraker et al. (2003), Broadie et al. (2009), Li et al. (2008), and Chernov et al. (2003).

3.3. Comparison of Methods

The list of studies on option-implied skewness and kurtosis is much shorter than those on option–implied volatility. In fact, we do not know of any study that compares different estimation methods. The real challenge in evaluating these methods is the fact that we do not have a good estimate of ex-post realized skewness and kurtosis because higher moments are hard to estimate accurately from time series of prices or returns. For example, the estimates of skewness and kurtosis of the S&P 500 return will be markedly different if we use a sample period that contains a stock market crash compared to one that does not. Without a proper realized measure, it is difficult to compare different methods empirically.

The method that is used most widely at the moment is the model-free methodology of Bakshi et al. (2003). This method has the advantage of being model-free and simple to implement. However, it is sensitive to the choice of extrapolation method applied to the tails of the distribution where there is no traded option price. Another limitation of this method is that the moments are risk-neutral, so the estimates are likely to be biased.

Model-based methods such as Heston (1993) and Bates (2000) allow us to compute physical moments and risk-neutral moments separately. Therefore, the physical moment estimates from these models are potentially unbiased although they can still be biased if the model is misspecified. The disadvantages of these methods are that they are restricted by the model specifications and that they are harder to implement.

3.4. Applications of Option-Implied Skewness and Kurtosis Forecasts

As discussed in Section 2.4, many studies use option-implied volatility to forecast the volatility of the underlying asset. A few studies have used option-implied skewness and kurtosis to forecast the returns on the underlying, as well as cross-sectional differences in stock returns. Table 10.5 contains a summary of existing empirical results.

3.4.1. Time Series Forecasting

Bates (1991) investigates the usefulness of jump parameters estimated using a jump diffusion model for forecasting the stock market crash of 1987. He also forecasts using a skewness premium constructed from prices of out-of-the-money puts and calls. Bates (1996a) examines option-implied skewness and kurtosis of the USD/DM and USD/JPY exchange rates between 1984 and 1992, and finds that the option-implied higher moments contain significant information for the future USD/DM exchange rate, but not for the USD/JPY rate. The option-implied higher moments are again estimated both using a model-based approach, using a jump-diffusion dynamic, but also using a model-free measure of the skewness premium.

Navatte and Villa (2000) extract option-implied moments for the CAC 40 index using the Gram–Charlier expansion. They find that the moments contain a substantial amount of information for future moments, with kurtosis contributing less forecasting power than skewness and volatility.

Carson et al. (2006) find that the implied volatility skew has strong predictive power in forecasting short-term market declines. However, Doran et al. (2007) find that the predictability is not economically significant.

Table 10.5 Forecasting with Option-Implied Skewness and Kurtosis

Authors	Year	Market	Predictor	To Predict	Method	Conclusion
Bates	1996	Currency	Skew, kurt	Skew, kurt of USD/DM, USD/JPY, 1984–1992	Jump diffusion	The implicit abnormalities (e.g., moments) predict future abnormalities in log-differenced USD/DM futures prices, but not USD/JPY
Bates	1991	Equity	Skew premium, jump–diffusion parameters	Crash of 1987	Jump diffusion	Risk-neutral distribution of stock market return negatively skewed 1 year before the crash, but no strong crash fears during 2 months immediately preceding the crash
Navatte and Villa	2000	Equity	Vol, skew, kurt	Moments of CAC 40 index	Gram–Charlier	Implied moments contain substantial amount of information, which decreases with the moment's order
Doran, Carson, and Peterson	2006	Equity	Skew	Stock market crash	Barone–Adesi and Whaley (1987)	Implied volatility skew has significant forecasting power for assessing the degree of market crash risk

(Continued)

Table 10.5 *Continued*

Authors	Year	Market	Predictor	To Predict	Method	Conclusion
Agarwal, Bakshi, and Huij	2009	Equity	Vol, skew, kurt	Cross-section of hedge fund returns	Bakshi et al. (2003)	Innovations in implied market vol, skew, kurt are all priced risk factors for hedge fund returns
Chang, Christof-fersen, and Jacobs	2013	Equity	Vol, skew, kurt	Cross-section of stock returns	Bakshi et al. (2003)	Negative relationship between the sensitivity to innovation in option-implied skewness of the S&P 500 index and future cross-section of stock returns
Doran, Peterson, and Tarrant	2007	Equity (individual)	Skew	Crashes and spikes upward	Barone–Adesi and Whaley (1987)	Reveal crashes and spikes with significant probability, but not economically significant
Diavatopoulos, Doran, Fodor, and Peterson	2008	Equity (individual)	Skew, kurt prior to earnings announce-ments	Stock and option returns	Bakshi et al. (2003)	Both have strong predictive power

(Continued)

Table 10.5 *Continued*

Authors	Year	Market	Predictor	To Predict	Method	Conclusion
Bali and Hov-akimian	2009	Equity (individual)	Realized–implied volatility, call-put IV spread	Cross-section of stock returns		Negative relationship with realized-implied volatility. Positive relationship with call-put IV spread
Conrad, Dittmar, and Ghysels	2013	Equity (individual)	Vol, skew, kurt	Cross-section of stock returns	Bakshi et al. (2003)	Average stock returns are negatively related to lagged implied volatility and skewness, and positively related to lagged implied kurtosis in the cross section of firms
Cremers and Weinbaum	2010	Equity (individual)	Call-put IV spread	Cross-section of stock returns	BSIV	Positive relationship
Doran and Krieger	2010	Equity (individual)	Volatility skew	Return	Five skew measures based on ATM, ITM, OTM IV and traded volume	Discourage the use of skew-based measures for forecasting equity returns without fully parsing the skew into its most basic components

(Continued)

Table 10.5 *Continued*

Authors	Year	Market	Predictor	To Predict	Method	Conclusion
Rehman and Vilkov	2010	Equity (individual)	Skew	Return	Bakshi et al. (2003)	Positive relationship
Xing, Zhao, and Zhang	2010	Equity (individual)	Volatility skew	Cross–section of stock returns	OTM put IV – ATM call IV (highest volume, highest open-interest, or volume or open-interest weighted)	Stocks with steepest smirks underperform stocks with least pronounced smirks
Demiguel, Plyakha, Uppal, and Vilkov	2011	Equity (individual)	Vol, skew, correlation, variance risk premium	Portfolio selection	Bakshi et al. (2003) for volatility and skew, Driessen et al. (2009) for correlation, Bollerslev et al. (2011) for VRP	Exploiting information contained in the volatility risk premium and option-implied skewness increases substantially both the Sharpe ratio and certainty-equivalent return

For individual stocks, Diavatopoulos et al. (2012) look at changes in implied skewness and kurtosis prior to earnings announcements and find that both have strong predictive power for future stock and option returns. DeMiguel et al. (2011) propose using implied volatility, skewness, correlation and variance risk premium in portfolio selection, and find that the inclusion of skewness and the variance risk premium improves the performance of the portfolio significantly.

3.4.2. Forecasting the Cross-Section of Expected Stock Returns

Two recent studies investigate if option-implied higher moments of the S&P 500 index help explain the subsequent cross-section of returns. Chang et al. (2013) investigate the cross-section of all stocks in the CRSP database, whereas Agarwal et al. (2009) investigate returns on the cross-section of hedge fund returns. Both studies use the model-free moments of BKM described in Section 3.1. Both studies find strong evidence that stocks with higher sensitivity to the innovation in option-implied skewness of the S&P 500 index exhibit lower returns in the future. Agarwal et al. (2009) also find a positive relationship between a stock's sensitivity to innovations in option-implied kurtosis of the S&P 500 index and future returns.

Several recent studies find a cross-sectional relationship between the option-implied skew of individual stocks and their subsequent returns. Xing et al. (2010) define skew as the difference in implied volatilities between out-of-the-money puts and at-the-money calls. They find that steeper smirks are associated with lower future stock returns. Doran and Krieger (2010) decompose the volatility skew into several components. They find that future stock returns are positively related to the difference in volatilities between at-the-money calls and puts, and negatively related to a measure of the left skew of the implied volatility curve. These results are consistent with those found in Cremers and Weinbaum (2010), Bali and Hovakimian (2009), and Xing et al. (2010). More importantly, the results in Doran and Krieger (2010) indicate that different measures of implied skewness can lead to different empirical results on the relationship between implied skewness and the cross-section of future stock returns.

Conrad et al. (2013) and Rehman and Vilkov (2010) both use the model-free skewness of Bakshi et al. (2003), but report conflicting results on the relationship between implied skewness and the cross-section of future stock returns. Conrad et al. (2013) find a negative relationship while Rehman and Vilkov (2010) find a positive one. One difference between these two empirical studies is that Conrad et al. (2013) use average skewness over the last three months whereas Rehman and Vilkov (2010) use skewness measures computed only on the last available date of each month. Again, these conflicting results indicate that the relationship between equity skews and the cross-section of future stocks returns is sensitive to variations in empirical methodology.

3.4.3. Option-Implied Betas

Section 2.5 above documents how option-implied correlation can be extracted from option data. Given the assumptions, correlations are a function of option-implied volatilities. Chang et al. (2012) provide an alternative approach, assuming that firm-specific risk has zero skewness. In this case it is possible to derive an option-implied beta based on the option-implied moments of firm j and the market index I as follows

$$\beta_j = \left(\frac{SKEW_j}{SKEW_I} \right)^{1/3} \left(\frac{VAR_j}{VAR_I} \right)^{1/2}, \tag{32}$$

where VAR and $SKEW$ can be computed from index options and from equity options for firm j using (25) and (26). Chang et al. (2012) find that, similar to the evidence for implied volatilities, historical betas and option-implied betas both contain useful information for forecasting future betas.

4. EXTRACTING DENSITIES FROM OPTION PRICES

There are many surveys on density forecasting using option prices. See Söderlind and Svensson (1997), Galati (1999), Jackwerth (1999), Jondeau and Rockinger (2000), Bliss and Panigirtzoglou (2002), Rebonato (2004), Taylor (2005), Bu and Hadri (2007), Jondeau et al. (2007), Figlewski (2010), Fusai and Roncoroni (2008), and Markose and Alentorn (2011). We describe the details of only a few of the most popular methods in this section, and refer the readers interested in the details of other methods to these surveys. We start by discussing model-free estimation, and subsequently discuss imposing more structure on the problem using no-arbitrage restrictions or parametric models.

4.1. Model-Free Estimation

Breeden and Litzenberger (1978) and Banz and Miller (1978) show that the option-implied density of a security can be extracted from a set of European-style option prices with a continuum of strike prices. This result can be derived as a special case of the general replication result in (20), see for instance Carr and Madan (2001).

The value of a European call option, C_0, is the discounted expected value of its payoff on the expiration date T. Under the option-implied measure, $f_0(S_T)$, the payoff is discounted at the risk-free rate

$$C_0(T, X) = e^{-rT} \int_0^\infty \max\{S_T - X, 0\} f_0(S_T) \, dS_T = e^{-rT} \int_X^\infty (S_T - X) f_0(S_T) \, dS_T. \tag{33}$$

We can take the partial derivative of C_0 with respect to the strike price X to get

$$\frac{\partial C_0(T, X)}{\partial X} = -e^{-rT} \left[1 - \tilde{F}_0(X) \right], \tag{34}$$

which yields the cumulative distribution function (CDF)

$$\tilde{F}_0(X) = 1 + e^{rT}\frac{\partial C_0(T, X)}{\partial X} \text{ so that } \tilde{F}_0(S_T) = 1 + e^{rT}\frac{\partial C_0(T, X)}{\partial X}\bigg|_{X=S_T}. \tag{35}$$

The conditional probability density function (PDF) denoted by $f_0(X)$ can be obtained by taking the derivative of (35) with respect to X.

$$f_0(X) = e^{rT}\frac{\partial^2 C_0(T, X)}{\partial X^2} \text{ so that } f_0(S_T) = e^{rT}\frac{\partial^2 C_0(T, X)}{\partial X^2}\bigg|_{X=S_T}. \tag{36}$$

As noted above, put-call parity states that $S_0 + P_0 = C_0 + Xe^{-rT}$, so that if we use put option prices instead, we get

$$\tilde{F}_0(S_T) = e^{rT}\frac{\partial P_0(T, X)}{\partial X}\bigg|_{X=S_T} \text{ and } f_0(S_T) = e^{rT}\frac{\partial^2 P_0(T, X)}{\partial X^2}\bigg|_{X=S_T}. \tag{37}$$

In practice, we can obtain an approximation to the CDF in (35) and (37) using finite differences of call or put option prices observed at discrete strike prices

$$\tilde{F}_0(X_n) \approx 1 + e^{rT}\left(\frac{C_0(T, X_{n+1}) - C_0(T, X_{n-1})}{X_{n+1} - X_{n-1}}\right) \tag{38}$$

or

$$\tilde{F}_0(X_n) \approx e^{rT}\left(\frac{P_0(T, X_{n+1}) - P_0(T, X_{n-1})}{X_{n+1} - X_{n-1}}\right). \tag{39}$$

Similarly, we can obtain an approximation to the PDF in (36) and (37) via

$$f_0(X_n) \approx e^{rT}\frac{C_0(T, X_{n+1}) - 2C_0(T, X_n) + C_0(T, X_{n-1})}{(\Delta X)^2} \tag{40}$$

$$f_0(X_n) \approx e^{rT}\frac{P_0(T, X_{n+1}) - 2P_0(T, X_n) + P_0(T, X_{n-1})}{(\Delta X)^2}. \tag{41}$$

In terms of the log return, $R_T = \ln S_T - \ln S_0$, the CDF and PDF are

$$\tilde{F}_{0,R_T}(x) = F_0(e^{x+\ln S_0}) \quad \text{and} \quad f_{0,R_T}(x) = e^{x+\ln S_0}f_0(e^{x+\ln S_0}).$$

The most important constraint in implementing this method is that typically only a limited number of options are traded in the market. This approximation method can therefore only yield estimates of the CDF and the PDF at a few points in the domain. This constraint has motivated researchers to develop various ways of imposing more structure on the option-implied density. In some cases the additional structure exclusively derives from no-arbitrage restrictions, in other cases a parametric model is imposed. We now survey these methods in increasing order of structure imposed.

4.2. Imposing Shape Restrictions

Aït-Sahalia and Duarte (2003) propose a model-free method of option-implied density estimation based on local polynomial regressions that incorporates shape restrictions on the first and the second derivatives of the call pricing function. Again, let $f_0(S_T)$ be the conditional density, then the call option prices are

$$C_0(T, X) = e^{-rT} \int_0^{+\infty} \max(S_T - X, 0) f_0(S_T) \, dS_T.$$

By differentiating the call price C with respect to the strike X, we get

$$\frac{\partial C_0(T, X)}{\partial X} = -e^{-rT} \int_X^{+\infty} f_0(S_T) \, dS_T.$$

Since $f_0(S_T)$ is a probability density, it is positive and integrates to one. Therefore,

$$-e^{-rT} \le \frac{\partial C_0(T, X)}{\partial X} \le 0. \tag{42}$$

By differentiating the call price twice with respect to the strike price, we obtain as before

$$\frac{\partial^2 C_0(T, X)}{\partial X^2} = e^{-rT} f_0(X) \ge 0. \tag{43}$$

Two additional restrictions can be obtained using standard no arbitrage bounds of the call option prices,

$$\max(0, S_0 - X e^{-rT}) \le C_0(T, X) \le S_0.$$

Li and Zhao (2009) develop a multivariate version of the constrained locally polynomial estimator in Aït-Sahalia and Duarte (2003) and apply it to interest rate options.

4.3. Using Black–Scholes Implied Volatility Functions

The simple but flexible ad hoc Black–Scholes (*AHBS*) model in which the density forecast is constructed from Black–Scholes implied volatility curve fitting is arguably the most widely used method for option-implied density forecasting, and we now describe it in some more detail. The density construction proceeds in two steps.

First, we estimate a second-order polynomial or other well-fitting function for implied Black–Scholes volatility as a function of strike and maturity. This will provide the following fitted values for *BSIV*. We can write

$$BSIV(T, X) = a_0 + a_1 X + a_2 X^2 + a_3 T + a_4 T^2 + a_5 XT. \tag{44}$$

Second, using this estimated polynomial, we generate a set of fixed-maturity implied volatilities across a grid of strikes. Call prices can then be obtained using the Black–Scholes functional form

$$C_0^{AHBS}(T, X) = C_0^{BS}\left(T, X, S_0, r; BSIV(T, X)^2\right). \tag{45}$$

Once the model call prices are obtained the option-implied density can be obtained using the second derivative with respect to the strike price.

$$f_0(S_T) = e^{rT} \left. \frac{\partial^2 C_0^{AHBS}(T, X)}{\partial X^2} \right|_{X=S_T}.$$

Shimko (1993) was the first to propose this approach to constructing density forecasts from smoothed and interpolated *BSIV*s. Many variations on the Shimko approach have been proposed in the literature, and strictly speaking most of these are not entirely model-free, because some parametric assumptions are needed. The differences between these variations mainly concern three aspects of the implementation (see Figlewski, 2010 for a comprehensive review):

1. Choice of independent variable: the implied volatility function can be expressed as a function of strike (X), or of moneyness (X/S), or of option delta. See Malz (1996).
2. Choice of interpolation method: implied volatilities can be interpolated using polynomials (Shimko, 1993; Dumas et al., 1998) or splines which can be quadratic, cubic (Bliss and Panigirtzoglou, 2002), or quartic (Figlewski, 2010). Malz (1997), Rosenberg (1998), Weinberg (2001), and Monteiro et al. (2008) propose different alternatives.
3. Choice of extrapolation method: for strikes beyond the range of traded options, one can use extrapolation (Jiang and Tian, 2005, 2007), truncation (Andersen and Bondarenko, 2007, 2009 and Andersen et al., 2011), or alternatively a parametric density function can be used. For instance Figlewski (2010) and Alentorn and Markose (2008) propose the Generalized Extreme Value distribution. Lee (2004), Benaim and Friz (2008, 2009) derive restrictions on the slope of the implied volatility curve at the tails based on the slope's relationship to the moments of the distribution.

Figure 10.5 shows the CDF and PDF obtained when applying a smoothing cubic spline using *BSIV* data on 30-day OTM calls and puts on the S&P 500 index on October 22, 2009 together with the CDF and PDF of the lognormal distribution. The model-free estimate of the option-implied distribution is clearly more negatively skewed than the lognormal distribution. Note that we only depict the distribution for available strike prices and thus do not extrapolate beyond the lowest and highest strikes available.

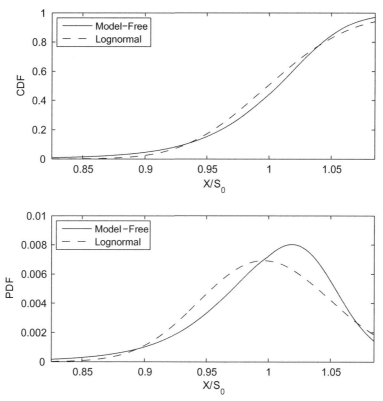

Figure 10.5 Option-implied distribution from BSIV curve fitting vs. lognormal. We plot the CDF and PDF obtained from applying a cubic spline (solid lines) using data for S&P 500 index options with thirty days to expiration on October 22, 2009, together with the CDF and PDF of the lognormal distribution (dashed lines).

Related approaches are proposed by Madan and Milne (1994), who use Hermite polynomials, and Abadir and Rockinger (2003), who propose the use of hypergeometric functions. Empirical studies using these approaches include Abken et al. (1996), Jondeau and Rockinger (2000), Flamouris and Giamouridis (2002), Rompolis and Tzavalis (2008), and Giacomini et al. (2009).

Many alternative approaches have been proposed including (1) Implied binomial trees (Rubinstein, 1994) and its extensions (Jackwerth, 1997, 2000; Jackwerth and Rubinstein, 1996; Jackwerth, 2000; and Dupont, 2001); (2) Entropy (Stutzer, 1996; Buchen and Kelly, 1996); (3) Kernel regression (Aït-Sahalia and Lo, 1998, 2000); (4) Convolution approximations (Bondarenko, 2003); and (5) Neural networks (Healy et al., 2007). However, Black–Scholes implied volatility curve fitting remains the simplest and most widely used method.[15]

[15] See for example Christoffersen and Jacobs (2004) and Christoffersen et al. (in press).

4.4. Static Distribution Models

As discussed above in Section 3.2.1, Jarrow and Rudd (1982) propose an Edgeworth expansion of the option-implied distribution around the lognormal density and Corrado and Su (1996) propose a related Gram–Charlier expansion, which we also discussed above. These methods can be used to produce density forecasts as well as moment forecasts.

If we alternatively assume that S_T is distributed as a mixture of two lognormals, then we get

$$f_0\left(S_T\right) = w\psi\left(S_T, \mu_1, \sigma_1, T\right) + \left(1 - w\right)\psi\left(S_T, \mu_2, \sigma_2, T\right). \tag{46}$$

The forward price for maturity T imposes the constraint

$$F_0 = w\mu_1 + \left(1 - w\right)\mu_2,$$

where μ_1 and μ_2 are parameters to be estimated, subject to the above constraint, along with the remaining parameters w, σ_1 and σ_2. The resulting option pricing formula is simply a weighted average of BS option prices:

$$C_0^{Mix}\left(T, X\right) = wC^{BS}\left(T, X, \mu_1, r; \sigma_1^2\right) + \left(1 - w\right)C^{BS}\left(T, X, \mu_1, r; \sigma_2^2\right).$$

Most applications assume a mixture of two or three lognormals. The resulting mixture is easy to interpret, especially when it comes to predicting events with a small number of outcomes. The moments can be obtained from

$$E_0\left[S_T^n\right] = w\mu_1^n \exp\left(\frac{1}{2}\left(n^2 - n\right)\sigma_1^2 T\right) + \left(1 - w\right)\mu_2^n \exp\left(\frac{1}{2}\left(n^2 - n\right)\sigma_2^2 T\right).$$

The distribution is thus flexible enough to capture higher moments such as skewness and kurtosis. See for instance Ritchey (1990), Bahra (1997), and Melick and Thomas (1997) as well as Taylor (2005).

Alternative parametric distributions have been entertained by Bookstaber and McDonald (1991), who use a generalized beta distribution of the second kind, Sherrick et al. (1996), who use a Burr III distribution, Savickas (2002), who uses a Weibull distribution, and Markose and Alentorn (2011), who assume a Generalized Extreme Value (GEV) distribution. Other distributions used include generalized Beta functions (Aparicio and Hodges, 1998, and Liu et al., 2007), generalized Lambda distribution (Corrado, 2001), generalized Gamma distribution (Tunaru and Albota, 2005), skewed Student t (De Jong and Huisman 2000), Variance Gamma (Madan et al., 1998), and Lévy processes (Matache et al., 2005).

4.5. Dynamic Models with Stochastic Volatility and Jumps

There is overwhelming evidence that a diffusion with stochastic volatility (Heston, 1993), a jump-diffusion with stochastic volatility (Bates, 1996b), or an even more complex model for the underlying with jumps in returns and volatility is a more satisfactory description of the data than a simple Black–Scholes model. Nevertheless, these models are not the most popular choices in forecasting applications. This is presumably due to the significantly higher computational burden, which is especially relevant in a forecasting application, which requires frequent re-calibration of the model.

The advantage of assuming a stochastic volatility model with jumps is that the primitives of the model include specification of the dynamic of the underlying at a frequency which can be chosen by the researcher. This not only adds richness to the model in the sense that it allows the multiperiod distribution to differ from the one-period distribution, it also allows consistent treatment of options of different maturities, and it ensures that the estimation results can be related in a straightforward way to estimation results for the underlying security.

In affine SVJ models closed-form solutions are available for the conditional characteristic function for the log stock price at horizon T defined by

$$\Upsilon_0 \left(i\phi, T \right) \equiv E_0[\exp \left(i\phi \ln \left(S_T \right) \right)].$$

The characteristic function can be used to provide call option prices as follows:

$$C_0(T, X) = S_0 P_1 \left(T, X \right) - X e^{-rT} P_2 \left(T, X \right), \tag{47}$$

where P_1 and P_2 are obtained using numerical integration of the characteristic function. The cumulative density forecast implied by the model is directly provided by $P_2 \left(T, X \right)$ and the density forecast can be obtained from

$$f_0 \left(S_T \right) = \left. \frac{\partial P_2 \left(T, X \right)}{\partial X} \right|_{X = S_T},$$

which must be computed numerically.[16]

4.6. Comparison of Methods

Many studies have compared the empirical performance of different density estimation methods. Jondeau and Rockinger (2000) compare semi-parametric methods based on Hermite and Edgeworth expansions, single and mixture lognormals, and methods based on jump diffusion and stochastic volatility models, and recommend using the mixture of lognormals model for short-run options, and the jump-diffusion model for long-run options. Coutant et al. (2001) compare Hermite expansion, maximum entropy, mixture of lognormals, and a single lognormal methods and conclude that all methods do better than a single lognormal method. They favor the Hermite expansion method due to its numerical speed, stability, and accuracy. Bliss and Panigirtzoglou (2002) compare

---

[16] In recent work, Andersen et al. (2012) estimate SVJ models by minimizing option implied volatility errors subject to fitting the historical path of realized volatility.

double-lognormal and smoothed implied volatility function, focusing on the robustness of their parameter estimates, and conclude that the smoothed implied volatility function method dominates the double-lognormal method. Campa et al. (1998) and Jackwerth (1999) compare various parametric and non-parametric methods, and conclude that the estimated distributions obtained using different methods are rather similar.

In summary, these and many other papers compare different estimation methods, and arrive at conclusions that are not always consistent with one another. Since the resulting densities are often not markedly different from each other when using different estimation methods, it makes sense to use methods that are computationally easy and/or whose results are easy to interpret given the application at hand. Because of computational ease and the stability of the resulting parameter estimates, the smoothed implied volatility function method is a good choice for many purposes. The jump-diffusion model is useful if the event of interest is a rare event such as stock market crash. The lognormal-mixture is particularly useful when dealing with situations with a small number of possible outcomes, such as elections.

4.7. Applications of Option-Implied Density Forecasts

Table 10.6 contains a summary of the existing empirical studies using option-implied densities (OID) in forecasting. Several early studies focus on the markets for commodities and currencies. Silva and Kahl (1993) extend Fackler and King (1990) and test two hypotheses: (i) the OID becomes more reliable as commodity option markets mature, and (ii) the reliability of the OID can be improved by using a distribution-free approach rather than a model based on lognormal assumption. They find evidence supporting their first hypothesis, and also find that the lognormal approach is better than the distribution-free approach. Melick and Thomas (1997) estimate the distribution of crude oil futures price during the Persian Gulf crisis, assuming a mixture of three lognormal distributions to capture the fact that there were mainly three possible outcomes to the crisis. They find that the OID was consistent with market commentary at the time, which predicted a major disruption in oil prices. They also find that the lognormal mixture model performed better in characterizing the data than the standard lognormal model. More recently, Høg and Tsiaras (2011) compare the performance of (i) OID, (ii) time-series based densities, and (iii) risk-adjusted OID, in forecasting the crude oil prices during 1990–2006 period. They find that the risk-adjusted OID (also referred to as physical or real-world density) outperforms the other two approaches.

The OID has also been applied to currency markets. Leahy and Thomas (1996) estimate densities from Canadian dollar futures options around the referendum on Quebec sovereignty in October 1995, using the mixture of lognormals model as in Melick and Thomas (1997). They find that the OID immediately preceding the day of the referendum was consistent with three possible outcomes: no surprise, surprising defeat of the sovereignty proposal, and a surprising victory. They conclude that the use of lognormal rather than the mixture model based densities in circumstances in which there are a few possible outcomes can obscure interesting features of the data. Malz (1997) uses model-free OIDs to explore the forward rate bias. Malz finds that option-implied volatility, skewness, and kurtosis have considerable explanatory power for excess returns on forward exchange rates. Campa and Chang (1996), Malz (1996), and Haas et al. (2006) examine the information content of exchange rate OIDs around the ERM crises of 1992. All three studies find that option-implied measures provide useful information for policy makers. Haas et al. (2006) find that time-series based measures are also useful. Campa et al. (2002) apply the intensity of realignment and credibility measures developed in Campa and Chang (1996) to the "crawling peg" between the Brazilian Real and the U.S. dollar as well as a realignment of the "maxibands" between 1994 and 1999. They conclude that the OID is a better indicator of such events in currency management relative to macroeconomic or interest-rate based indicators. Campa et al. (1998) and Bodurtha and Shen (1999) study the USD/DM and USD/JPY relationship. Campa et al. (1998) find a positive correlation between skewness and the spot rate, which means that the stronger the currency, the more expectations are skewed towards a further appreciation of that currency. Bodurtha and Shen (1999) show that investors should consider both historical and implied volatility covariance parameter estimates in their Value-at-Risk computations.

Using equity options, Gemmill and Saflekos (2000) study the predictive power of the OIDs around four stock market crashes and three British elections between 1987 and 1997 using FTSE-100 index options. They cannot reject the hypothesis that the OIDs reflect market sentiment, but sentiment as measured has little forecasting ability. Mizrach (2006) examines whether the collapse of Enron was expected in option markets, and find that option markets remained far too optimistic about the stock until just weeks before Enron's bankruptcy filing. Shackleton et al. (2010) estimate S&P 500 index densities using various methods, and find that the risk-adjusted OID has the best performance. Recently, Kostakis et al. (2011) use estimated densities for portfolio selection. They find that the risk-adjusted OID improves the risk-adjusted return of the portfolio when compared with the portfolio formed based only on historical return distributions.

4.8. Event Forecasting Applications

There is a significant and expanding literature on prediction markets. The primary purpose of these markets is to forecast future events, and the contracts are designed to facilitate extracting information used in forecasting. This literature is covered in detail in Snowberg et al. (in press) and is therefore not discussed here. We instead focus on the prediction of events using option data, where the primary function of the traded options is not prediction itself. In this literature, which naturally overlaps with the density forecasting work discussed above, estimation methods vary greatly depending on the events to be forecast. We therefore do not describe details of the estimation methods but instead focus our attention on empirical results. Table 10.7 contains a summary of relevant empirical studies.

Table 10.6 Forecasting using Option-Implied Densities

Authors	Year	Market	Predictor	To Predict	Method	Conclusion
Silva and Kahl	1993	Commodity	PDF	PDF of soybean, corn	Log-normal vs. linear interpolation of CDF	Option-implied density of soybean became more reliable from 1985–1987 to 1988–1990 as option market matured
Melick and Thomas	1997	Commodity	PDF from American options	Crude oil price during the Gulf crisis	Mixture of two or three lognormals	Option-implied density was consistent with the market commentary at the time, which predicted a major disruption in oil price. Lognormal mixture worked better than lognormal
Høg and Tsiaras	2011	Commodity	PDF	PDF	Generalized Beta of the second kind (GB2), risk-neutral to physical using statistical recalibration	Outperforms historical
Leahy and Thomas	1996	Currency	PDF from American options	Canadian dollar around Quebec referendum	Mixture of three lognormals	Option prices were consistent with market commentary
Campa and Chang	1996	Currency	PDF, intensity of realignment and credibility measures	ERM target-zone credibility and devaluation	Arbitrage bounds	Devaluation predicted with different time lags from a week to a year

(Continued)

Table 10.6 *Continued*

Authors	Year	Market	Predictor	To Predict	Method	Conclusion
Malz	1996	Currency	PDF from American options	PDF and realignment probability of GBP/DM	Jump diffusion	Useful for defense of target zones against speculative attack
Malz	1997	Currency	PDF, moments	Excess return puzzle in currency markets	IV in function of ATM IV, risk reversal price, and strangle price	Tests International CAPM using risk-neutral moments as explanatory variables and shows that they have considerably greater explanatory power for excess returns in currency markets
Campa, Chang, and Reider	1998	Currency	PDF from American options	PDF of USD/DM and USD/JPY	Compare cubic splines, implied binomial trees, mixture of normals	Use trimmed binomial tree
Bodurtha and Shen	1999	Currency	PDF of correlation	Covariance VaR of DM and JPY	Whaley (1982)	Implied correlation provides incremental explanatory power over historical-based correlation estimates
Campa, Chang, and Refalo	2002	Currency	PDF, Intensity and credibility measure of Campa and Chang (1996)	PDF and realignment probability of Brazilian Real/USD, 1991–1994	Shimko (1993) IV in quadratic function of strike	Anticipate realignments of exchange rate bands

(Continued)

Table 10.6 *Continued*

Authors	Year	Market	Predictor	To Predict	Method	Conclusion
Haas, Mittnik, and Mizrach	2006	Currency	PDF	PDF, central bank credibility during ERM crisis	Mixture of normals	Both historical and option-based forecasts are useful
Gemmill and Saflekos	2000	Equity	PDF	PDF, four crashes, three British elections	Mixture of two lognormals	Little forecasting ability
Mizrach	2006	Equity	PDF	Enron's collapse	Mixture of lognormals	Market remained too optimistic until just weeks before the collapse
Shackleton, Taylor, and Yu	2010	Equity	PDF	PDF, S&P 500 index return	Calibration of jump-diffusion model, statistical transformation from risk-neutral to physical	Compare historical, risk-neutral, and risk-transformed physical PDF. Performance depends on forecast horizon
Kostakis, Panigirt- zoglou, and Skiadopou- los	2011	Equity	PDF	Portfolio selection	Smoothed IV smile + Barone-Adesi and Whaley (1987)	Improved portfolio performance

Table 10.7 Forecasting with Option-Implied Event Probabilities

Melick and Thomas	1997	Commodity	PDF from American options	Crude oil price during the Gulf crisis	Mixture of two or three lognormals	Option prices were consistent with market commentary. Use of lognormal model would have overestimated the probability and price impact of a major disruption
Leahy and Thomas	1996	Currency	PDF from American options	Canadian dollar	Mixture of three lognormals	Option prices were consistent with the market commentary
Campa and Chang	1996	Currency	PDF; Intensity of realignment and credibility measures	ERM target-zone credibility and devaluation	Arbitrage bounds	Devaluation predicted with different time lags from a week to a year
Malz	1996	Currency	PDF from American options	PDF and realignment probability of GBP/DM	Jump diffusion	Useful for defense of target zones against speculative attack

(Continued)

Table 10.7 *Continued*

Authors	Year	Market	Predictor	To Predict	Method	Conclusion
Campa, Chang, and Refalo	2002	Currency	PDF, intensity of realignment and credibility measures	PDF and realignment probability of Brazilian Real/USD, 1991–1994	Shimko (1993) IV in quadratic function of strike	Anticipate realignments of exchange rate bands
Haas, Mittnik, and Mizrach	2006	Currency	PDF	PDF, central bank credibility during ERM crisis	Mixture of normals	Both historical and option based forecasts are useful
Bates	1991	Equity	Jump-diffusion parameters	Crash of 1987	Jump diffusion	Risk-neutral distribution negatively skewed 1 year before the crash, but no strong crash fears during 2 months immediately preceding the crash
Gemmill and Saflekos	2000	Equity	PDF	PDF, four crashes, three British elections	Mixture of two lognormals	Little forecasting ability
Doran, Carson, and Peterson	2006	Equity	Skew	Crash	Barone–Adesi and Whaley (1987)	Implied volatility skew has significant forecasting power for assessing the degree of market crash risk

(Continued)

Table 10.7 *Continued*

Authors	Year	Market	Predictor	To Predict	Method	Conclusion
Mizrach	2006	Equity	PDF	Enron's collapse	Mixture of lognormals	Market remained too optimistic until just weeks before the collapse
Sheikh	1989	Equity (individual)	Volatility	Split announcement and ex-dates	Roll (1977), American option with dividends	No relative increase in IV of stocks announcing splits, but increase is detected at the ex-date
Jayaraman, Mandelker, and Shastri	1991	Equity (individual)	Premia on call options	Information leakage prior to merger announcement	BSIV	Implied volatility increases prior to the announcement of the first bid for the target firm and decreases significantly at the announcement date
Barone-Adesi, Brown, and Harlow	1994	Equity (individual)	Probability and timing of acquisitions	Probability and timing of acquisitions	Propose model of probability weighted IV	Cannot predict success or timing of acquisition
Cao, Chen, and Griffin	2005	Equity (individual)	Call volume imbalance	Takeover announcement day return	Regression	Takeover targets with the largest preannouncement call-volume imbalance increases experience the highest announcement day returns
Bester, Martinez, and Rosu	2011	Equity (individual)	Merger success probability	Merger success probability	New option pricing model with merger	Better prediction compared to naive method

Many stock market events are of great interest from a forecasting perspective, including stock market crashes and individual corporate events such as earnings announcements, stock splits, and acquisitions. Bates (1991) is perhaps the best known study of whether and how stock market index option prices reveal the market's expectation of future stock market crashes. He studies the behavior of S&P 500 futures options prices prior to the crash of October 1987, and finds unusually negative skewness in the option-implied distribution of the S&P 500 futures between October 1986 and August 1987, leading to the conclusion that the crash was expected. He finds, however, that the same indicators do not exhibit any strong crash fears during the 2 months immediately preceding the crash. There are few other studies investigating if index option prices can predict stock market crashes. Doran et al. (2007) find that the option skew is useful in predicting stock market crashes and spikes, but conclude that the value of this predictive power is not always economically significant. Overall therefore, there is some evidence in favor of predictability, but the evidence is not conclusive.

Mizrach (2006) finds that option prices did not reflect the risk of Enron until just weeks before the firm's bankruptcy filing in 2001. Other studies examine corporate events other than crashes, and the results of these studies are more positive. Jayaraman et al. (1991), Barone-Adesi et al. (1994), Cao et al. (2005), and Bester et al. (2011) all test the forecasting ability of variables in the option market (e.g., prices, trading volume, etc.) prior to corporate acquisitions. Jayaraman et al. (1991) find that implied volatilities increase prior to the announcement of the first bid for the target firm and decrease significantly at the announcement date, indicating that the market identifies potential target firms prior to the first public announcement of the acquisition attempt. Cao et al. (2005) find that takeover targets with the largest preannouncement call-volume imbalance increases experience the highest announcement day returns. As for the probability of success and timing of announced acquisitions, Bester et al. (2011) show that their option pricing model yields better predictions compared to a "naive" method, although Barone-Adesi et al. (1994) find no evidence that option prices predict the timing of announced acquisitions.

5. ALLOWING FOR RISK PREMIA

So far in the chapter we have constructed various forecasting objects using the so-called risk-neutral or pricing measure implied from options. When forecasting properties of the underlying asset, we ideally want to use the physical measure and not the risk-neutral measure, which is directly embedded in option prices. Knowing the mapping between the two measures is therefore required. A fully specified option valuation model provides a physical measure for the underlying asset return as well as a risk-neutral measure for derivatives valuation, and therefore implicitly or explicitly defines the mapping. In this section we explore the mapping between measures. We will use superscript Q to denote the option-implied density used above, and superscript P to denote the physical density of the underlying asset.

5.1. Complete Markets

Black and Scholes (1973) assume a physical stock price process of the form

$$dS = (r + \mu) \, S dt + \sigma S dz, \tag{48}$$

where μ is the equity risk premium. In the Black–Scholes model a continuously rebalanced dynamic portfolio consisting of one written derivative, C, and $\frac{\partial C}{\partial S}$ shares of the underlying asset has no risk and thus earns the risk-free rate. This portfolio leads to the Black–Scholes differential equation.

In the complete markets world of Black–Scholes the option is a redundant asset, which can be perfectly replicated by trading the stock and a risk-free bond. The option price is independent of the degree of risk-aversion of investors because they can replicate the option using a dynamic trading strategy in the underlying asset. This insight leads to the principle of risk-neutral valuation where all derivative assets can be valued using the risk-neutral expected payoff discounted at the risk free rate. For example, for a European call option we can write

$$C_0 \left(T, X \right) = \exp \left(-rT \right) E_0^Q \left[\max \left\{ S_T - X, 0 \right\} \right]. \tag{49}$$

Using Ito's lemma on (48) we get

$$d \ln \left(S \right) = \left(r + \mu - \frac{\sigma^2}{2} \right) dt + \sigma \, dz,$$

which implies that log returns are normally distributed

$$f_0^P \left(\ln \left(S_T \right) \right) = \frac{1}{\sqrt{2\pi\sigma^2 T}} \exp \left(\frac{-1}{2\sigma^2 T} \left(\ln \left(S_T \right) - \ln \left(S_0 \right) - \left(r + \mu - \frac{\sigma^2}{2} \right) T \right)^2 \right).$$

Under the risk-neutral measure, $\mu = 0$, and we again have the lognormal density, but now with a different mean

$$f_0^Q \left(\ln \left(S_T \right) \right) = \frac{1}{\sqrt{2\pi\sigma^2 T}} \exp \left(\frac{-1}{2\sigma^2 T} \left(\ln \left(S_T \right) - \ln \left(S_0 \right) - \left(r - \frac{\sigma^2}{2} \right) T \right)^2 \right),$$

which can be used to compute the expectation in (49).

In a Black–Scholes world, the option-implied density forecast will therefore have the correct volatility and functional form but a mean biased downward because of the equity premium, μ. Since the risk-neutral mean of the asset return is the risk-free rate, the option price has no predictive content for the mean return.

5.2. Incomplete Markets

The Black–Scholes model is derived in a complete market setting where risk–neutralization is straightforward. Market incompleteness arises under the much more realistic assumptions of market frictions arising for example from discrete trading, transactions costs, market illiquidity, price jumps and stochastic volatility or other non-traded risk factors.

5.2.1. Pricing Kernels and Investor Utility

In the incomplete markets case we can still assume a pricing relationship of the form

$$C_0\left(T, X\right) = \exp\left(-rT\right) E_0^Q\left[\max\left\{S_T - X, 0\right\}\right]$$
$$= \exp\left(-rT\right) \int_X^\infty \max\left\{\exp\left(\ln\left(S_T\right)\right) - X, 0\right\} f_0^Q\left(\ln\left(S_T\right)\right) dS_T.$$

But the link between the option-implied and the physical distributions is not unique and a pricing kernel M_T must be assumed to link the two distributions. Define

$$M_T = \exp\left(-rT\right) \frac{f_0^Q\left(\ln\left(S_T\right)\right)}{f_0^P\left(\ln\left(S_T\right)\right)},$$

then we get

$$C_0\left(T, X\right) = \exp\left(-rT\right) E_0^Q\left[\max\left\{S_T - X, 0\right\}\right]$$
$$= E_0^P\left[M_T \max\left\{S_T - X, 0\right\}\right].$$

The pricing kernel (or stochastic discount factor) describes how in equilibrium investors trade off the current (known) option price versus the future (stochastic) payoff.

The functional form for the pricing kernel can be motivated by a representative investor with a particular utility function of terminal wealth. Generally, we can write

$$M_T \propto U'\left(S_T\right),$$

where $U'\left(S_T\right)$ is the first-derivative of the utility function.

For example, assuming exponential utility with risk-aversion parameter γ we have

$$U\left(S\right) = -\frac{1}{\gamma} \exp\left(-\gamma S\right)$$

so that $U'\left(S\right) = \exp\left(-\gamma S\right)$, and

$$f_0^Q\left(S_T\right) = \exp\left(rT\right) M_T f_0^P\left(\ln\left(S_T\right)\right) = \frac{\exp\left(-\gamma\left(S_T\right)\right) f_0^P\left(S_T\right)}{\int_0^\infty \exp\left(-\gamma\left(S\right)\right) f_0^P\left(S\right) dS},$$

where the denominator ensures that $f_0^Q\left(S_T\right)$ is a proper density.

Assuming instead power utility, we have

$$U\left(S\right) = \frac{S^{1-\gamma} - 1}{1 - \gamma}, \tag{50}$$

so that $U'\left(S\right) = S^{-\gamma}$, and

$$f_0^Q\left(S_T\right) = \frac{S_T^{-\gamma} f_0^P\left(S_T\right)}{\int_0^\infty S^{-\gamma} f_0^P\left(S\right) dS}.$$

Importantly, these results demonstrate that any two of the following three uniquely determine the third: (1) the physical density; (2) the risk-neutral density; (3) the pricing kernel. We refer to Hansen and Renault (2010) for a concise overview of various pricing kernels derived from economic theory.

The Black–Scholes model can be derived in a discrete representative investor setting where markets are incomplete. Brennan (1979) outlines the sufficient conditions on the utility function and return distribution to obtain the Black–Scholes option pricing result.

5.2.2. Static Distribution Models

Liu et al. (2007) show that if we assume a mixture of lognormal option-implied distribution as in (46) and furthermore a power utility function with relative risk aversion parameter γ as in (50) then the physical distribution will also be a mixture of lognormals with the following parameter mapping

$$\mu_i^P = \mu_i \exp\left(\gamma\sigma_i^2 T\right) \quad \text{for } i = 1, 2$$

$$w^P = \left[1 + \frac{1 - w}{w}\left(\frac{\mu_2}{\mu_1}\right)^\gamma \exp\left(\frac{1}{2}\left(\gamma^2 - \gamma\right)\left(\sigma_2^2 - \sigma_1^2\right) T\right)\right]^{-1},$$

where σ_1^2 and σ_2^2 do not change between the two measures.

The physical moments can now be obtained from

$$E_0^P\left[S_T^n\right] = w^P\left(\mu_1^P\right)^n \exp\left(\frac{1}{2}\left(n^2 - n\right)\sigma_1^2 T\right) + \left(1 - w^P\right)\left(\mu_2^P\right)^n \exp\left(\frac{1}{2}\left(n^2 - n\right)\sigma_2^2 T\right).$$

Keeping $\mu_1, \mu_2, w, \sigma_1^2$ and σ_2^2 fixed at their option-implied values, the risk aversion parameter γ can be estimated via maximum likelihood on returns using the physical mixture of lognormals defined by the parameter mapping above. Liu et al. (2007) also investigate other parametric distributions. See Fackler and King (1990) and Bliss and Panigirtzoglou (2004) for related approaches.

5.2.3. Dynamic Models with Stochastic Volatility

The Heston model allows for stochastic volatility implying that the option, which depends on volatility, cannot be perfectly replicated by the stock and bond. Markets are incomplete in this case and the model therefore implicitly makes an assumption on the pricing kernel or the utility function of the investor. Heston (1993) assumes that the price of an asset follows the following physical process

$$dS = (r + \mu V) S dt + \sqrt{V} S dz_1 \tag{51}$$
$$dV = \kappa^P (\theta^P - V) dt + \sigma_V \sqrt{V} dz_2,$$

where the two diffusions are allowed to be correlated with parameter ρ. The mapping between the physical parameters in (51) and the option-implied parameters in (6) is given by

$$\kappa = \kappa^P + \lambda, \theta = \theta^P \frac{\kappa^P}{\kappa},$$

where λ is the price of variance risk.

Christoffersen et al. (in press) show that the physical and option-implied processes in (51) and (6) imply a pricing kernel of the form

$$M_T = M_0 \left(\frac{S_T}{S_0} \right)^\gamma \exp \left(\delta T + \eta \int_0^T V(s) ds + \xi (V_T - V_0) \right), \tag{52}$$

where ξ is a variance preference parameter.[17] The risk premia μ and λ are related to the preference parameters γ and ξ via

$$\mu = -\gamma - \xi \sigma_V \rho$$
$$\lambda = -\rho \sigma_V \gamma - \sigma_V^2 \xi.$$

In order to assess the implication of the price of variance risk, λ, for forecasting we consider the physical expected integrated variance

$$VAR_0^P (T) = \theta^P T + (V_0 - \theta^P) \frac{\left(1 - e^{-\kappa^P T} \right)}{\kappa^P}$$
$$= \theta \frac{\kappa}{\kappa - \lambda} T + \left(V_0 - \theta \frac{\kappa}{\kappa - \lambda} \right) \frac{\left(1 - e^{-(\kappa - \lambda) T} \right)}{\kappa - \lambda}.$$

Under the physical measure the expected future variance in the Heston (1993) model of course differs from the risk-neutral forecast in (7) when $\lambda \neq 0$. If an estimate of λ can be obtained, then the transformation from option-implied to physical variance forecasts is trivial.

---

[17] Christoffersen et al. (2010a) provide a general class of pricing kernels in a discrete time setting with dynamic volatility and non-normal return innovations.

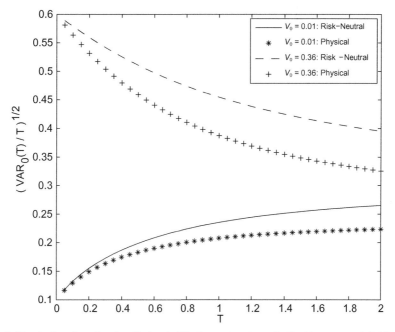

Figure 10.6 Physical and option-implied volatility term structures in the Heston model. Lines with '*' and '+' markers denote physical forecasts. The dashed line with $V_0 = 0.36$ shows the option-implied forecast from a a high current spot variance and the solid line with $V_0 = 0.01$ shows the option-implied forecasts from a low current spot variance.

In Figure 10.6 we plot the physical volatility term structure per year defined by

$$\sqrt{VAR_0^P(T)/T} = \sqrt{\theta\frac{\kappa}{\kappa - \lambda} + \left(V_0 - \theta\frac{\kappa}{\kappa - \lambda}\right)\frac{\left(1 - e^{-(\kappa - \lambda)T}\right)}{(\kappa - \lambda)T}} \qquad (53)$$

along with the option-implied term structure from (8). We use parameter values as in Figure 10.3, where $\theta = 0.09, \kappa = 2$, and $\lambda = -1.125$, which implies that $\theta/\theta^P = \frac{\kappa - \lambda}{\kappa} = (1.25)^2$, which corresponds to a fairly large variance risk premium. Figure 10.6 shows the effect of a large volatility risk premium on the volatility term structure. For short horizons and when the current volatility is low, the effect of the volatility risk premium is relatively small. However for long horizons the effect is much larger.

5.2.4. Model-Free Moments

Bakshi et al. (2003) also assume power utility with parameter γ, and show that option-implied and physical moments for the market index are approximately related as follows

$$VAR^Q \approx VAR^P \left(1 - \gamma SKEW^P \left(VAR^P\right)^2\right)$$

$$SKEW^Q \approx SKEW^P - \gamma(KURT^P - 3)\left(VAR^P\right)^2.$$

Given a reasonable estimate for γ it is thus possible to convert option-implied estimates for VAR^Q and $SKEW^Q$ into physical moment forecasts, VAR^P and $SKEW^P$, without making explicit assumptions on the functional form of the distribution.

5.3. Pricing Kernels and Risk Premia

There is a related literature focusing on estimating pricing kernels from P and Q densities rather than on forecasting. Jackwerth (2000) estimates pricing kernels using Q-densities obtained from one day of option prices, and P-densities using returns for the previous month. Christoffersen et al. (in press) estimate pricing kernels using the entire return sample by standardizing returns by a dynamic volatility measure. Some authors assume that Q is time varying while P is constant over time. Aït-Sahalia and Lo (2000) use 4 years of data to estimate P when constructing pricing kernels. Rosenberg and Engle (2002) use returns data over their entire sample 1970–1995 to construct estimates of the pricing kernel.

Interestingly, recent evidence suggests that key features of the pricing kernel such as risk premia are useful for forecasting returns. This is not surprising, because as we saw above, the pricing kernel is related to preferences, and therefore changes in the pricing kernel may reflect changes in risk aversion, or, more loosely speaking, in sentiment.

For example, Bollerslev et al. (2009), Bekaert et al. (2010), and Zhou (2010) find strong evidence that the variance risk premium, $VAR^Q - VAR^P$, can predict the equity risk premium. Bollerslev et al. (2012) report evidence on this from a set of international equity markets. Bakshi et al. (2011) compute the forward variance, which is the implied variance between two future dates, and find that the forward variance is useful in forecasting stock market returns, T-bill returns, and changes in measures of real economic activity. A related paper by Feunou et al. (in press) finds that the term structure of implied volatility can predict both the equity risk premium and variance risk premium.

Risk premia can be estimated in various ways. Parametric models can be used to jointly calibrate a stochastic model of stock and option prices with time-variation in the Q and P densities. For instance, Shackleton et al. (2010) and Pan (2002) calibrate stochastic volatility models to options and asset prices. In recent work, Ross (in press) suggests a methodology for estimating physical volatility using option prices in a representative investor setting. Alternatively, (model-free) option-implied moments can be combined with separately estimated physical moments to compute risk premia. In this case, the question arises how to estimate the physical moments. The literature on the optimal type of physical information to combine with option-implied information is in its infancy. However, we have extensive knowledge about the use of different types of physical information from the literature on forecasting with historical information as chronicled in this volume of the Handbook of Economic Forecasting as well as previous volumes.

6. SUMMARY AND DISCUSSION

The literature contains a large body of evidence supporting the use of option-implied information to predict physical objects of interest. In this chapter we have highlighted some of the key tools for extracting forecasting information using option-implied moments and distributions.

These option-implied forecasts are likely to be most useful when:

- The options market is highly liquid so that market microstructure biases do not adversely affect the forecasts. In illiquid markets bid-ask spreads are wide and furthermore, option quotes are likely to be based largely on historical volatility forecasts so that the option quotes add little or no new information.
- Many strike prices are available. In this case, model-free methods can be used to extract volatility forecasts without assuming particular volatility dynamics or return distributions.
- Many different maturities are available. In this case the option-implied forecast for any desired horizon can be constructed with a minimum of modeling assumptions.
- The underlying asset is uniquely determined in the option contract. Most often this is the case, but in the case of Treasury bond options for example, many different bonds are deliverable, which in turn complicates option-based forecasting of the underlying return dynamics.
- Options are European, or in the case of American options, when the early exercise premium can be easily assessed. The early exercise premium must be estimated and subtracted from the American option price before using the method surveyed in this chapter. Estimating the early exercise premium thus adds noise to the option-implied forecast.
- The underlying asset has highly persistent volatility dynamics. In this case time-series forecasting models may be difficult to estimate reliably.
- The underlying asset undergoes structural breaks. Such breaks complicate the estimation of time-series models and thus heighten the role for option-implied forecasts.
- The focus is on higher moments of the underlying asset return. The non-linear payoff structure in option contracts makes them particularly attractive for higher-moment forecasting.
- Risk premia are small. Risk premia may bias the option-implied forecasts but option-based forecasts may nevertheless contain important information not captured in historical forecasts.

Related to the last bullet point, we have also summarized the key theoretical relationships between option-implied and physical densities, enabling the forecaster to take into account risk premia and convert the option-implied forecasts to physical forecasts. We hasten to add that it is certainly not mandatory that the option-implied information is mapped into the physical measure to generate forecasts. Some empirical studies have found that transforming option-implied to physical information improves forecasting performance in certain situations (see Shackleton et al., 2010 and Chernov, 2007) but these results do not necessarily generalize to other types of forecasting exercises.

We would expect the option-implied distribution or moments to be biased predictors of their physical counterparts, but this bias may be small, and attempting to remove it can create problems of its own, because the resulting predictor is no longer exclusively based on forward-looking information from option prices, but also on backward-looking information from historical prices as well as on assumptions on investor preferences.

More generally, the existence of a bias does not prevent the option-implied information from being a useful predictor of the future object of interest. Much recent evidence on variance forecasting for example (see our Table 1 which is Table 1 in Busch et al. (2011)) strongly suggests that this is indeed the case empirically.

Going forward, developing methods for combining option-implied and historical return-based forecasts would certainly be of use – in particular when risk-premia may be present. In certain applications, for example volatility forecasting, forecasts can be combined in a simple regression framework or even by using equal weighting. In other applications, such as density forecasting, more sophisticated approaches are needed. Timmermann (2006) provides a thorough overview of available techniques.

Most of the empirical literature has been devoted to volatility forecasting using simple Black–Scholes implied volatility. Clearly, much more empirical research is needed to assess the more sophisticated methods for computing option-implied volatility as well as the other forecasting objects of interest including skewness, kurtosis, and density forecasting.

ACKNOWLEDGMENT

We would like to thank the Bauer Chair at the University of Houston and SSHRC for financial support. The authors can be reached by emailing peter.christoffersen@rotman.utoronto.ca, kjacobs@bauer.uh.edu, and bchang@bankofcanada.ca

REFERENCES

Abadir, K., Rockinger, M., 2003. Density functionals, with an option-pricing application. Economic Theory 19, 778–811.

Abken, P.A., Madan, D.B., Ramamurtie, S., 1996. Estimation of risk-neutral and statistical densities by hermite polynomial approximation: with an application to eurodollar futures options. Federal Reserve Bank of Atlanta, Working Paper.

Agarwal, V., Bakshi, G., Huij, J., 2009. Do higher-moment equity risks explain hedge fund returns? University of Maryland, Working Paper.

Aït-Sahalia, Y., Duarte, J., 2003. Nonparametric option pricing under shape restrictions. Journal of Econometrics 116, 9–47.

Aït-Sahalia, Y., Lo, A.W., 1998. Nonparametric estimation of state-price densities implicit in financial asset prices. Journal of Finance 53, 499–547.

Aït-Sahalia, Y., Lo, A.W., 2000. Nonparametric risk management and implied risk aversion. Journal of Econometrics 94, 9–51.

Alentorn, A., Markose, S., 2008. Generalized extreme value distribution and extreme economic value at risk (EE-VaR). In: Kontoghiorghes, E.J., Rustem, B., Winker, P. (Eds.), Computational Methods in Financial Engineering, Springer-Verlag, 47–71.

Amin, K.I., Ng, V.K., 1997. Inferring future volatility from the information in implied volatility in eurodollar options: a new approach. Review of Financial Studies 10, 333–367.

Andersen, T.G., Benzoni, L., Lund, J., 2002. An empirical investigation of continuous-time equity return models. Journal of Finance 57, 1239–1284.

Andersen, T.G., Bollerslev, T., Christoffersen, P.F., Diebold, F.X., 2006. Volatility and correlation forecasting. In: Elliott, G., Granger, C.W.J., Timmermann, A. (Eds.), Handbook of Economic Forecasting, Elsevier Science, 778–878.

Andersen, T.G., Bondarenko, O., 2007. Construction and interpretation of model-free implied volatility. In: Nelken, I. (Ed.), Volatility as an Asset Class, Risk Publications, 141–184.

Andersen, T.G., Bondarenko, O., 2009. Dissecting the pricing of equity index volatility. Northwestern University, Working Paper.

Andersen, T.G., Bondarenko, O., Gonzalez-Perez, M.T., 2011. A corridor fix for VIX: developing a coherent model-free option-implied volatility measure. Northwestern University, Working Paper.

Andersen, T.G., Fusari, N., Todorov, V., 2012. Parametric inference, testing, and dynamic state recovery from option panels with fixed time span. Northwestern University, Working Paper.

Ang, A., Hodrick, R.J., Xing, Y., Zhang, X., 2006. The cross-section of volatility and expected returns. Journal of Finance 61, 259–299.

Aparicio, S.D., Hodges, S., 1998. Implied risk-neutral distribution: a comparison of estimation methods. University of Warwick, Working Paper.

Backus, D., Foresi, S., Li, K., Wu, L., 1997. Accounting for biases in Black-Shcholes. New York University, Working Paper.

Bahra, B., 1997. Implied risk-neutral probability density functions from option prices: theory and application. Bank of England, Working Paper.

Bakshi, G., Cao, C., Chen, Z., 1997. Empirical performance of alternative option pricing models. Journal of Finance 52, 2003–2049.

Bakshi, G., Kapadia, N., Madan, D., 2003. Stock return characteristics, skew laws, and the differential pricing of individual equity options. Review of Financial Studies 16, 101–143.

Bakshi, G., Madan, D., 2000. Spanning and derivative-security valuation. Journal of Financial Economics 55, 205–238.

Bakshi, G., Panayotov, G., Skoulakis, G., 2011. Improving the predictability of real economic activity and asset returns with forward variances inferred from option portfolios. Journal of Financial Economics 100, 475–495.

Bali, T.G., Hovakimian, A., 2009. Volatility spreads and expected stock returns. Management Science 55, 1797–1812.

Banerjee, P.S., Doran, J.S., Peterson, D.R., 2007. Implied volatility and future portfolio returns. Journal of Banking and Finance 31, 3183–3199.

Banz, R.W., Miller, M.H., 1978. Prices for state-contingent claims: some estimates and applications. Journal of Business 51, 653–672.

Barone-Adesi, G., Brown, K.C., Harlow, W.V., 1994. On the use of implied volatilities in the prediction of successful corporate takeovers. In: Chance, D.M., Trippi, R.R. (Eds.), Advances in Futures and Options Research, Emerald Group Publishing, 147–165.

Barone-Adesi, G., Whaley, R.E., 1987. Efficient analytic approximation of American option values. Journal of Finance 42, 301–320.

Bates, D.S., 1991. The crash of '87: was it expected? The evidence from options markets. Journal of Finance 46, 1009–1044.

Bates, D.S., 1996a. Dollar jump fears, 1984–1992: Distributional abnormalities implicit in currency futures options. Journal of International Money and Finance 15, 65–93.

Bates, D.S., 1996b. Jumps and stochastic volatility: exchange rate processes implicit in Deutsche mark options. Review of Financial Studies 9, 69–107.

Bates, D.S., 2000. Post-'87 crash fears in the S&P 500 futures option market. Journal of Econometrics 94, 181–238.

Bates, D.S., 2008. The market for crash risk. Journal of Economic Dynamics and Control 32, 2291–2321.

Beckers, S., 1981. Standard deviations implied in option prices as predictors of future stock price variability. Journal of Banking and Finance 5, 363–381.

Bekaert, G., Hoerova, M., Lo Duca, M., 2010. Risk, uncertainty, and monetary policy. National Bureau of Economic Research, Working Paper.

Benaim, S., Friz, P., 2008. Smile asymptotics II: models with known moment generating function. Journal of Applied Probability 45, 16–32.

Benaim, S., Friz, P., 2009. Regular variation and smile asymptotics. Mathematical Finance 19, 1–12.

Bester, C.A., Martinez, V.H., Rosu, I., 2011. Option prices and the probability of success of cash mergers. University of Chicago, Working Paper.

Black, F., 1976. The pricing of commodity contracts. Journal of Financial Economics 3, 167–179.

Black, F., Scholes, M., 1973. The pricing of options and corporate liabilities. Journal of Political Economy 81, 637–654.

Blair, B.J., Poon, S.-H., Taylor, S.J., 2001. Forecasting S&P 100 volatility: the incremental information content of implied volatilities and high-frequency index returns. Journal of Econometrics 105, 5–26.

Bliss, R.R., Panigirtzoglou, N., 2002. Testing the stability of implied probability density functions. Journal of Banking and Finance 26, 381–422.

Bliss, R.R., Panigirtzoglou, N., 2004. Option-implied risk aversion estimates. Journal of Finance 59, 407–446.

Bodurtha, J.N.J., Shen, Q., 1999. Historical and implied measures of value at risk: the DM and Yen case. University of Michigan, Working Paper.

Bollerslev, T., Gibson, M., Zhou, H., 2011. Dynamic estimation of volatility risk premia and investor risk aversion from option-implied and realized volatilities. Journal of Econometrics 160, 235–245.

Bollerslev, T., Marrone, J., Xu, L., Zhou, H., 2012. Stock return predictability and variance risk premia: statistical inference and international evidence. Duke University, Working Paper.

Bollerslev, T., Tauchen, G., Zhou, H., 2009. Expected stock returns and variance risk premia. Review of Financial Studies 22, 4463–4492.

Bondarenko, O., 2003. Estimation of risk-neutral densities using positive convolution approximation. Journal of Econometrics 116, 85–112.

Bookstaber, R.M., McDonald, J.B., 1991. Option pricing for generalized distributions. Communications in Statistics - Theory and Methods 20, 4053–4068.

Breeden, D.T., Litzenberger, R.H., 1978. Prices of state-contingent claims implicit in option prices. Journal of Business 51, 621–651.

Brennan, M.J., 1979. The pricing of contingent claims in discrete time models. Journal of Finance 34, 53–68.

Britten-Jones, M., Neuberger, A., 2000. Option prices, implied price processes, and stochastic volatility. Journal of Finance 55, 839–866.

Broadie, M., Chernov, M., Johannes, M., 2009. Understanding index option returns. Review of Financial Studies 22, 4493–4529.

Bu, R., Hadri, K., 2007. Estimating option implied risk-neutral densities using spline and hypergeometric functions. Econometrics Journal 10, 216–244.

Buchen, P.W., Kelly, M., 1996. The maximum entropy distribution of an asset inferred from option prices. Journal of Financial and Quantitative Analysis 31, 143–159.

Busch, T., Christensen, B.J., Nielsen, M.O., 2012. The role of implied volatility in forecasting future realized volatility and jumps in foreign exchange, stock, and bond markets. Journal of Econometrics 160, 48–57.

Buss, A., Vilkov, G., 2012. Measuring equity risk with option-implied correlations. Review of Financial Studies, 25, 3113–3140.

Campa, J.M., Chang, P., Reider, R.L., 1998. Implied exchange rate distributions: evidence from OTC option markets. Journal of International Money and Finance 17, 117–160.

Campa, J.M., Chang, P.H.K., 1996. Arbitrage-based tests of target-zone credibility: evidence from ERM cross-rate options. The American Economic Review 86, 726–740.

Campa, J.M., Chang, P.H.K., 1998. ERM realignment risk and its economic determinants as reflected in cross-rate options. The Economic Journal 108, 1046–1066.

Campa, J.M., Chang, P.H.K., Refalo, J.F., 2002. An options-based analysis of emerging market exchange rate expectations: Brazil's Real plan, 1994–1999. Journal of Development Economics 69, 227–253.

Canina, L., Figlewski, S., 1993. The informational content of implied volatility. Review of Financial Studies 6, 659–681.

Cao, C., Chen, Z., Griffin, J.M., 2005. Informational content of option volume prior to takeovers. Journal of Business 78, 1073–1109.

Cao, C., Yu, F., Zhong, K., 2010. The information content of option-implied volatility for credit default swap valuation. Journal of Financial Markets 13, 321–343.

Carr, P., Lee, R., 2008. Robust replication of volatility derivatives. New York University, Working Paper.

Carr, P., Madan, D., 1998. Towards a theory of volatility trading. In: Jarrow, R.A. (Ed.), Volatility: New Estimation Techniques for Pricing Derivatives, RISK Publications, 417–427.

Carr, P., Madan, D., 2001. Optimal positioning in derivative securities. Quantitative Finance 1, 19–37.

Carson, J.M., Doran, J.S., Peterson, D.R., 2006. Market crash risk and implied volatility skewness: evidence and implications for insurer investments. Florida State University, Working Paper.

CBOE, 2009. The CBOE volatility index - VIX. Technical Report.

CBOE, 2011. The CBOE skew index - SKEW. Technical Report.

Chang, B.-Y., Christoffersen, P., Jacobs, K., 2013. Market skewness risk and the cross-section of stock returns. Journal of Financial Economics 107, 46–68.

Chang, B.-Y., Christoffersen, P., Jacobs, K., Vainberg, G., 2012. Option-implied measures of equity risk. Review of Finance 16, 385–428.

Chernov, M., 2007. On the role of risk premia in volatility forecasting. Journal of Business and Economic Statistics 25, 411–426.

Chernov, M., Gallant, A.R., Ghysels, E., Tauchen, G., 2003. Alternative models for stock price dynamics. Journal of Econometrics 116, 225–257.

Chiras, D.P., Manaster, S., 1978. The information content of option prices and a test of market efficiency. Journal of Financial Economics 6, 213–234.

Christensen, B.J., Prabhala, N.R., 1998. The relation between implied and realized volatility. Journal of Financial Economics 50, 125–150.

Christoffersen, P., Elkamhi, R., Feunou, B., Jacobs, K., 2010a. Option valuation with conditional heteroskedasticity and nonnormality. Review of Financial Studies 23, 2139–2183.

Christoffersen, P., Heston, S.L., Jacobs, K., 2006. Option valuation with conditional skewness. Journal of Econometrics 131, 253–284.

Christoffersen, P., Heston, S.L., Jacobs, K., 2009. The shape and term structure of the index option smirk: why multifactor stochastic volatility models work so well. Management Science 55, 1914–1932.

Christoffersen, P., Heston, S.L., Jacobs, K., in press. Capturing option anomalies with a variance-dependent pricing kernel. Review of Financial Studies.

Christoffersen, P., Jacobs, K., 2004. The importance of the loss function in option valuation. Journal of Financial Economics 72, 291–318.

Christoffersen, P., Jacobs, K., Mimouni, K., 2010b. Volatility dynamics for the S&P 500 evidence from realized volatility, daily returns and option prices. Review of Financial Studies 23, 3141–3189.

Christoffersen, P., Mazzotta, S., 2005. The accuracy of density forecasts from foreign exchange options. Journal of Financial Econometrics 3, 578–605.

Conrad, J., Dittmar, R.F., Ghysels, E., 2013. Ex ante skewness and expected stock returns. Journal of Finance 68, 85–124.

Corrado, C.J., 2001. Option pricing based on the generalized lambda distribution. Journal of Futures Markets 21, 213–236.

Corrado, C.J., Su, T., 1996. Skewness and kurtosis in S&P 500 index returns implied by option prices. Journal of Financial Research 19, 175–192.

Coutant, S., Jondeau, E., Rockinger, M., 2001. Reading PIBOR futures options smiles: the 1997 snap election. Journal of Banking and Finance 25, 1957–1987.

Cremers, M., Weinbaum, D., 2010. Deviations from put-call parity and stock return predictability. Journal of Financial and Quantitative Analysis 45, 335–367.

Day, T.E., Lewis, C.M., 1992. Stock market volatility and the information content of stock index options. Journal of Econometrics 52, 267–287.

De Jong, C., Huisman, R., 2000. From skews to a skewed-t. Erasmus Research Institute of Management, Working Paper.

De Jong, F., Driessen, J., Pelsser, A., 2004. On the information in the interest rate term structure and option prices. Review of Derivatives Research 7, 99–127.

Delisle, R.J., Doran, J.S., Peterson, D.R., 2010. Implied systematic moments and the cross-section of stock returns. Washington State University, Working Paper.

Demeterfi, K., Derman, E., Kamal, M., Zou, J., 1999. More than you ever wanted to know about volatility swaps. Quantitative Strategies Research Notes, Goldman Sachs.

DeMiguel, V., Plyakha, Y., Uppal, R., Vilkov, G., 2011. Improving portfolio selection using option-implied volatility and skewness. London Business School, Working Paper.

Diavatopoulos, D., Doran, J., Peterson, D., 2008. The information content in implied idiosyncratic volatility and the cross-section of stock returns: evidence from the option markets. Journal of Futures Markets 28, 1013–1039.

Diavatopoulos, D., Doran, J.S., Fodor, A., Peterson, D., 2012. The information content of implied skewness and kurtosis changes prior to earnings announcements for stock and option returns. Journal of Banking and Finance 36, 786–802.

Doran, J.S., Fodor, A., Krieger, K., 2010. Option market efficiency and analyst recommendations. Journal of Business Finance and Accounting 37, 560–590.

Doran, J.S., Krieger, K., 2010. Implications for asset returns in the implied volatility skew. Financial Analysts Journal 66, 65–76.

Doran, J.S., Peterson, D.R., Tarrant, B.C., 2007. Is there information in the volatility skew? Journal of Futures Markets 27, 921–959.

Driessen, J., Maenhout, P.J., Vilkov, G., 2009. The price of correlation risk: evidence from equity options. Journal of Finance 64, 1377–1406.

Duffie, D., Pan, J., Singleton, K., 2000. Transform analysis and asset pricing for affine jump-diffusions. Econometrica 68, 1343–1376.

Dumas, B., Fleming, J., Whaley, R.E., 1998. Implied volatility functions: empirical tests. Journal of Finance 53, 2059–2106.

Dupire, B., 1994. Pricing with a smile. Risk 7, 18–20

Dupont, D.Y., 2001. Extracting risk-neutral probability distributions from option prices using trading volume as a filter. Economics Series, Institute for Advanced Studies.

Eraker, B., Johannes, M., Polson, N., 2003. The impact of jumps in volatility and returns. Journal of Finance 58, 1269–1300.

Fackler, P.L., King, R.P., 1990. Calibration of option-based probability assessments in agricultural commodity markets. American Journal of Agricultural Economics 72, 73–83

Feunou, B., Fontaine, J.-S., Taamouti, A., Tedongap, R., in press. The equity premium and the maturity structure of uncertainty. Review of Finance.

Figlewski, S., 2010. Estimating the implied risk neutral density for the U.S. market portfolio. In: Bollerslev, T., Russell, J.R., Watson, M. (Eds.), Volatility and Time Series Econometrics: Essays in Honor of Robert F. Engle, Oxford University Press, 323–353.

Flamouris, D., Giamouridis, D., 2002. Estimating implied PDFs from American options on futures: a new semiparametric approach. Journal of Futures Markets 22, 1096–9934.

Fleming, J., 1998. The quality of market volatility forecasts implied by S&P 100 index option prices. Journal of Empirical Finance 5, 317–345.

Fleming, J., Ostdiek, B., Whaley, R.E., 1995. Predicting stock market volatility: a new measure. Journal of Futures Markets 15, 265–302.

Fleming, J., Whaley, R.E., 1994. The value of wildcard options. Journal of Finance 49, 215–236.

Fusai, G., Roncoroni, A., 2008. Implementing Models in Quantitative Finance: Methods and Cases. Springer, Berlin.

Galati, G. (Ed.)., 1999. Proceedings of a Workshop on Estimating and Interpreting Probability Density Functions. Bank for International Settlements.

Garcia, R., Ghysels, E., Renault, E., 2010. The econometrics of option pricing. In: Aït-Sahalia, Y., Hansen, L.P. (Eds.), Handbook of Financial Econometrics, North Holland, 479–552.

Garman, M.B., Kohlhagen, S.W., 1983. Foreign currency option values. Journal of International Money and Finance 2, 231–237.

Gemmill, G., Saflekos, A., 2000. How useful are implied distributions? Evidence from stock index options. Journal of Derivatives 7, 83–98.

Giacomini, E., Härdle, W., Krätschmer, V., 2009. Dynamic semiparametric factor models in risk neutral density estimation. Advances in Statistical Analysis 93, 387–402.

Haas, M., Mittnik, S., Mizrach, B., 2006. Assessing central bank credibility during the ERM crises: comparing option and spot market-based forecasts. Journal of Financial Stability 2, 28–54.

Hansen, L.P., Renault, E., 2010. Pricing kernels and stochastic discount factors. In: Rama Cont (Ed.), Encyclopedia of Quantitative Finance, Chapter 19–009, John Wiley Sons.

Harvey, C.R., Whaley, R.E., 1992. Market volatility prediction and the efficiency of the S&P 100 index option market. Journal of Financial Economics 31, 43–73.

Healy, J.V., Dixon, M., Read, B.J., Cai, F.F., 2007. Non-parametric extraction of implied asset price distributions. Physica A: Statistical Mechanics and its Applications 382, 121–128.

Heath, D., Jarrow, R., Morton, A., 1992. Bond pricing and the term-structure of interest rates: a new methodology. Econometrica 60, 77–105.

Heston, S.L., 1993. A closed-form solution for options with stochastic volatility with applications to bond and currency options. Review of Financial Studies 6, 327–343.

Heston, S.L., Nandi, S., 2000. A closed-form GARCH option valuation model. Review of Financial Studies 13, 585–625.

Høg, E., Tsiaras, L., 2011. Density forecasts of crude oil prices using option-implied and arch-type models. Journal of Futures Markets 31, 727–754.

Huang, J.-Z., Wu, L., 2004. Specification analysis of option pricing models based on time-changed Lévy processes. Journal of Finance 59, 1405–1440.

Hull, J.C., 2011. Options, Futures, and Other Derivatives, 8th edition, Pearson Prentice Hall.

Hull, J.C., White, A., 1987. The pricing of options on assets with stochastic volatilities. Journal of Finance 42, 281–300.

Jackwerth, J.C., 1997. Generalized binomial trees. Journal of Derivatives 5, 7–17.

Jackwerth, J.C., 1999. option-implied risk-neutral distributions and implied binomial trees. Journal of Derivatives 7, 66–82.

Jackwerth, J.C., 2000. Recovering risk aversion from option prices and realized returns. Review of Financial Studies 13, 433–451.

Jackwerth, J.C., Rubinstein, M., 1996. Recovering probability distributions from option prices. Journal of Finance 51, 1611–1631.

Jarrow, R., Rudd, A., 1982. Approximate option valuation for arbitrary stochastic processes. Journal of Financial Economics 10, 347–369.

Jayaraman, N., Mandelker, G., Shastri, K., 1991. Market anticipation of merger activities: an empirical test. Managerial and Decision Economics 12, 439–448.

Jiang, G.J., Tian, Y.S., 2005. The model-free implied volatility and its information content. Review of Financial Studies 18, 1305–1342.

Jiang, G.J., Tian, Y.S., 2007. Extracting model-free volatility from option prices: an examination of the VIX index. Journal of Derivatives 14, 35–60.

Jondeau, E., Poon, S.-H., Rockinger, M., 2007. Financial Modeling Under Non-Gaussian Distributions. Springer-Verlag, London.

Jondeau, E., Rockinger, M., 2000. Reading the smile: the message conveyed by methods which infer risk neutral densities. Journal of International Money and Finance 19, 885–915.

Jorion, P., 1995. Predicting volatility in the foreign exchange market. Journal of Finance 50, 507–528.

Kostakis, A., Panigirtzoglou, N., Skiadopoulos, G., 2011. Market timing with option-implied distributions: a forward-looking approach. Management Science, 1110–1346.

Kroner, K.F., Kneafsey, K.P., Claessens, S., 1995. Forecasting volatility in commodity markets. Journal of Forecasting 14, 77–95.

Lamoureux, C.G., Lastrapes, W.D., 1993. Forecasting stock-return variance: toward an understanding of stochastic implied volatilities. Review of Financial Studies 6, 293–326.

Latané, H.A., Rendleman Jr., R.J., 1976. Standard deviations of stock price ratios implied in option prices. Journal of Finance 31, 369–381.

Leahy, M.P., Thomas, C.P., 1996. The sovereignty option: the Quebec referendum and market views on the Canadian dollar. International Finance Discussion Papers, Board of Governors of the Federal Reserve System.

Lee, R.W., 2004. The moment formula for implied volatility at extreme strikes. Mathematical Finance 14, 469–480.

Li, H., Wells, M.T., Yu, C.L., 2008. A Bayesian analysis of return dynamics with Lévy jumps. Review of Financial Studies 21, 2345–2378.

Li, H., Zhao, F., 2009. Nonparametric estimation of state-price densities implicit in interest rate cap prices. Review of Financial Studies 22, 4335–4376.

Liu, X., Shackleton, M.B., Taylor, S.J., Xu, X., 2007. Closed-form transformations from risk-neutral to real-world distributions. Journal of Banking and Finance 31, 1501–1520.

Longstaff, F.A., Santa-Clara, P., Schwartz, E.S., 2001. The relative valuation of caps and swaptions: theory and empirical evidence. Journal of Finance 56, 2067–2109.

Madan, D.B., Carr, P.P., Chang, E.C., 1998. The variance gamma process and option pricing. European Finance Review 2, 79–105.

Madan, D.B., Milne, F., 1994. Contingent claims valued and hedged by pricing and investing in a basis. Mathematical Finance 4, 223–245.

Malz, A.M., 1996. Using option prices to estimate realignment probabilities in the European monetary system: the case of sterling-mark. Journal of International Money and Finance 15, 717–748.

Malz, A.M., 1997. Option-implied probability distribution and currency excess returns. Staff Reports, Federal Reserve Bank of New York.

Markose, S., Alentorn, A., 2011. The generalized extreme value distribution, implied tail index, and option pricing. Journal of Derivatives 18, 35–60.

Matache, A., Nitsche, P., Schwab, C., 2005. Wavelet Galerkin pricing of American options on Lévy driven assets. Quantitative Finance 5, 403–424.

Melick, W.R., Thomas, C.P., 1997. Recovering an asset's implied PDF from option prices: an application to crude oil during the Gulf crisis. Journal of Financial and Quantitative Analysis 32, 91–115.

Melino, A., Turnbull, S.M., 1990. Pricing foreign currency options with stochastic volatility. Journal of Econometrics 45, 239–265.

Mizrach, B., 2006. The Enron bankruptcy: when did the options market in Enron lose its smirk? Review of Quantitative Finance and Accounting 27, 365–382.

Monteiro, A.M., Tutuncu, R.H., Vicente, L.N., 2008. Recovering risk-neutral probability density functions from options prices using cubic splines and ensuring nonnegativity. European Journal of Operational Research 187, 525–542.

Navatte, P., Villa, C., 2000. The information content of implied volatility, skewness and kurtosis: empirical evidence from long-term CAC 40 options. European Financial Management 6, 41–56.

Neuberger, A., 1994. The log contract. Journal of Portfolio Management 20, 74–80.

Neuberger, A., 2012. Realized skewness. Review of Financial Studies 25, 3423–3455.

Pan, J., 2002. The jump-risk premia implicit in options: evidence from an integrated time-series study. Journal of Financial Economics 63, 3–50.

Pong, S., Shackleton, M.B., Taylor, S.J., Xu, X., 2004. Forecasting currency volatility: a comparison of implied volatilities and AR(FI)MA models. Journal of Banking and Finance 28, 2541–2563.

Poon, S.-H., Granger, C., 2003. Forecasting volatility in financial markets: a review. Journal of Economic Literature 41, 478–539.

Poteshman, A.M., 2000. Forecasting future volatility from option prices. University of Illinois at Urbana-Champaign, Working Paper.

Rebonato, R., 2004. Volatility and Correlation: The Perfect Hedger and the Fox. John Wiley and Sons.

Rehman, Z., Vilkov, G., 2010. Risk-neutral skewness: return predictability and its sources. Goethe University, Working Paper.

Ritchey, R.J., 1990. Call option valuation for discrete normal mixtures. Journal of Financial Research 13, 285–296.

Roll, R., 1977. An analytic valuation formula for unprotected American call options on stocks with known dividends. Journal of Financial Economics 5, 251–258.

Rompolis, L.S., Tzavalis, E., 2008. Recovering risk neutral densities from option prices: a new approach. Journal of Financial and Quantitative Analysis 43, 1037–1053.

Rosenberg, J.V., 1998. Pricing multivariate contingent claims using estimated risk-neutral density functions. Journal of International Money and Finance 17, 229–247.

Rosenberg, J.V., Engle, R.F., 2002. Empirical pricing kernels. Journal of Financial Economics 64, 341–372.

Ross, S.A., in press. The recovery theorem. Journal of Finance.

Rubinstein, M., 1985. Nonparametric tests of alternative option pricing models using all reported trades and quotes on the 30 most active CBOE option classes from August 23, 1976 through August 31, 1978. Journal of Finance 40, 455–480.

Rubinstein, M., 1994. Implied binomial trees. Journal of Finance 49, 771–818.

Savickas, R., 2002. A simple option-pricing formula. Financial Review 37, 207–226.

Scott, L.O., 1987. Option pricing when the variance changes randomly: theory, estimation, and an application. Journal of Financial and Quantitative Analysis 22, 419–438.

Shackleton, M.B., Taylor, S.J., Yu, P., 2010. A multi-horizon comparison of density forecasts for the S&P 500 using index returns and option prices. Journal of Banking and Finance 34, 2678–2693.

Sherrick, B.J., Garcia, P., Tirupattur, V., 1996. Recovering probabilistic information from option markets: tests of distributional assumptions. Journal of Futures Markets 16, 545–560.

Shimko, D.C., 1993. Bounds of probability. Risk Magazine 6, 33–37.

Siegel, A.F., 1997. International currency relationship information revealed by cross-option prices. Journal of Futures Markets 17, 369–384.

Silva, E.M., Kahl, K.H., 1993. Reliability of soybean and corn option-based probability assessments. Journal of Futures Markets 13, 765–779.

Skintzi, V.D., Refenes, A.N., 2005. Implied correlation index: a new measure of diversification. Journal of Futures Markets 25, 171–197.

Snowberg, E., Wolfers, J., Zitzewitz, E., in press. Prediction markets for economic forecasting. In: Elliott, Timmermann, A. (Eds.), Handbook of Economic Forecasting, vol. 2. Elsevier Science.

Söderlind, P., Svensson, L., 1997. New techniques to extract market expectations from financial instruments. Journal of Monetary Economics 40, 383–429.

Stutzer, M., 1996. A simple nonparametric approach to derivative security valuation. Journal of Finance 51, 1633–1652.

Swidler, S., Wilcox, J.A., 2002. Information about bank risk in options prices. Journal of Banking and Finance 26, 1033–1057.

Taylor, S.J., 2005. Asset Price Dynamics, Volatility, and Prediction. Princeton University Press.

Timmermann, A., 2006. Forecast combinations. In: Elliott, G., Granger, C.W.J., Timmermann, A. (Eds.), Handbook of Economic Forecasting. North Holland, Amsterdam, 135–196.

Tunaru, R., Albota, G., 2005. Estimating risk neutral density with a generalized gamma distribution. City University London, Working Paper.

Walter, C., Lopez, J.A., 2000. Is implied correlation worth calculating? Evidence from foreign exchange options and historical data. Federal Reserve Bank of San Francisco, Working Paper.

Weinberg, S.A., 2001. Interpreting the volatility smile: an examination of the information content of option prices. International Finance Discussion Papers, Board of Governors of the Federal Reserve System.

Whaley, R.E., 1982. Valuation of American call options on dividend-paying stocks: empirical tests. Journal of Financial Economics 10, 29–58.

Whaley, R.E., 1993. Derivatives on market volatility: hedging tools long overdue. Journal of Derivatives 1, 71–84.

Whaley, R.E., 2000. The investor fear gauge. Journal of Portfolio Management 26, 12–17.

Whaley, R.E., 2003. Derivatives. In: Constantinides, G., Harris, M., Stulz, R. (Eds.), Handbook of the Economics of Finance: Volume 1B Financial Markets and Asset Pricing. Elsevier North-Holland Publishing, 1129–1206.

Wiggins, J. B., 1987. Option values under stochastic volatility: theory and empirical estimates. Journal of Financial Economics 19, 351–372.

Xing, Y., Zhang, X., Zhao, R., 2010. What does the individual option volatility smirk tell us about future equity returns? Journal of Financial and Quantitative Analysis 45, 641–662.

Xu, X., Taylor, S. J., 1995. Conditional volatility and the informational efficiency of the PHLX currency options market. Journal of Banking and Finance 19, 803–821.

Zhou, H., 2010. Variance risk premia, asset predictability puzzles, and macroeconomic uncertainty. Finance and Economics Discussion Series, Board of Governors of the Federal Reserve System.

CHAPTER 11

Prediction Markets for Economic Forecasting

Erik Snowberg[*], Justin Wolfers[†] and Eric Zitzewitz[‡]

[*]Division of Humanities and Social Sciences, California Institute of Technology and National Bureau of Economic Research (NBER), USA
[†]University of Michigan and Center for Economic Policy Research (CEPR), CESifo, IZA, and NBER, USA
[‡]Dartmouth College and NBER, USA

Contents

Abstract

Prediction markets – markets used to forecast future events – have been used to accurately forecast the outcome of political contests, sporting events, and, occasionally, economic outcomes. This chapter summarizes the latest research on prediction markets in order to further their utilization by economic forecasters. We show that prediction markets have a number of attractive features: they quickly incorporate new information, are largely efficient, and are impervious to manipulation. Moreover, markets generally exhibit lower statistical errors than professional forecasters and polls. Finally, we show how markets can be used to both uncover the economic model behind forecasts, as well as test existing economic models.

Keywords

Prediction markets, Economic derivatives, Options, Commodities, Political events, Economic models

Handbook of Economic Forecasting, Volume 2A
ISSN 1574-0706, http://dx.doi.org/10.1016/B978-0-444-53683-9.00011-8

1. INTRODUCTION

Market prices, in the form of gambling odds, have been used to forecast events since at least the beginning of the sixteenth century. The use of such prices had a heyday in the early twentieth century, when gambling odds on elections were printed daily in newspapers such as *The New York Times*. This was followed by a decline in popularity, due largely to the advent of scientific polling (Rhode and Strumpf, 2004,2008). Scientific interest in market prices as tools for forecasting was kindled in the second half of the twentieth century by the efficient markets hypothesis and experimental economics (Plott and Sunder, 1982, 1988; Berg et al., 2008). This scientific foundation, coupled with advances in telecommunications – which allowed prices to be shared in real time across companies and the globe – has led to resurgent interest in using markets for forecasting (Snowberg et al., 2007b).[1]

Despite this long history, and markets' proven track-record of providing accurate forecasts of uncertain events, prediction markets – markets used to forecast future events – are largely unused in economic forecasting. There are some exceptions: the difference in yields between inflation protected and standard government bonds is used to forecast inflation, and futures contracts are sometimes used to forecast commodity prices, such as the price of oil. However, as other chapters in this volume reveal, these uses are accompanied by concerns about what else, other than information about future events, may be lurking in market prices (Alquist and Vigfusson, 2013; Duffee, 2013; Wright and Faust, 2013; Zhou and Rapach, 2013).

This chapter brings together the latest research on prediction markets to further their utilization by economic forecasters. We begin by providing a description of standard types of prediction markets, and an heuristic framework useful in understanding why prediction markets do, and sometimes do not, make useful predictions. We then show that, in practice, prediction markets often have a number of attractive features: they quickly incorporate new information, are largely efficient, and impervious to manipulation. Moreover, markets generally out-perform professional forecasters and polls. Finally, we argue that examining co-movement in market prices, through, for example, event studies, can be used to shed light on the underlying economic model of market participants. We conclude with a short list of open questions that may be of particular interest to economic forecasters.

2. TYPES OF PREDICTION MARKETS

A prediction market is generally implemented as a wager (or contract) that pays off if a particular outcome, such as an economic indicator taking a particular value y, occurs. Assuming that both the efficient markets hypothesis holds, and that the market acts as

---

[1] See Wolfers and Zitzewitz (2008a) for an overview, and Tziralis and Tatsiopoulos (2007) for an exhaustive literature review.

Table 11.1 Contract Types: Estimating Uncertain Quantities or Probabilities

Contract	Example	Details	Reveals Market Expectation of...
Winner-takes-all	Outcome y: Level of initial unemployment claims (in thousands).	Contract costs $\$p$. Pays \$1 if and only if event y occurs. Bid according to the value of $\$p$.	Probability that outcome y occurs.
Index	Contract pays \$1 for every 1,000 initial unemployment claims.	Contract pays $\$\,y$.	Mean value of outcome y: $\mathbb{E}[y]$.
Spread	Contract pays even money if initial unemployment claims are greater than y^*.	Contract costs \$1. Pays \$2 if $y > y^*$. Pays \$0 otherwise. Bid according to the the value of y^*	Median value of outcome y.

Notes: Adapted from Table 11.1 in Wolfers and Zitzewitz (2004).

a risk-neutral representative trader, the price of the contract will be the best estimate of various parameters tied to the probability of that outcome. While these assumptions are clearly too stark, in many settings the biases from violations are quite small, and in practice, the predictions extracted under these assumptions have been shown to be quite reliable.[2]

Table 11.1 summarizes three standard types of contracts. These contracts can be used to elicit the probability of a particular outcome occurring, or, if the outcome takes on numerical values, the expected mean or median.

Following the nomenclature introduced in Wolfers and Zitzewitz (2004), a "winner-takes-all" contract costs some amount $\$p$, and pays off, say, \$100, if y, initial unemployment claims (in thousands), are reported to be between $y = 330$ and $y = 340$. Under the assumptions above, the price represents the market's expectation of the probability that initial unemployment claims will be in this range. A family of such contracts with payoffs tied to all likely values of the event can elicit the entire distribution of the market's beliefs. For example, a set of contracts, one of which pays off if initial unemployment claims are

---

[2] The literature has considered two possible divergences. When prediction market security outcomes are correlated with a priced asset market factor, such as the overall level of the stock market, prices can be above objective probabilities if a prediction market security offers hedging value. In most applications, differences between risk-neutral and objective probabilities are smaller (see, e.g., Snowberg et al., 2007a; Wolfers and Zitzewitz, 2008b). A second issue is that when beliefs differ, a market may aggregate beliefs in a different way than is statistically optimal. Wolfers and Zitzewitz (2006) find, however, that under most reasonable assumptions about risk-aversion, prices are close to the wealth-weighted mean belief (see also, Manski, 2006; Gjerstad, 2005; Ottaviani and Sørensen, 2010).

between 310 and 320, another that pays off if they are between 320 and 330, and so on, recovers the markets' pdf (integrated over bins of 10,000) of initial unemployment claims.[3]

However, if a researcher is interested in simply obtaining moments of the market's distribution, an "index" contract may be more useful. Such a contract has an unknown payoff tied to the value of the outcome. Continuing the example from above, if y is initial unemployment claims (in thousands), the price for this contract represents the market's expectation of the outcome: $\mathbb{E}[y]$. Higher-order moments can be elicited by using multiple index contracts. For example, by adding a contract that pays off the square of initial unemployment claims y^2, one can recover the variance of the market's beliefs: $\mathbb{E}[y^2] - \mathbb{E}[y]^2$.

Finally, a "spread" contract allows a researcher to elicit a robust measure of the central tendency of the market's beliefs. These contracts, which are familiar to bettors on basketball and American football, feature a fixed cost and fixed payoff if an indicator is below the spread value; however, the spread's value y^* changes as contracts are bought and sold. That is, if the payoff is twice the cost, say \$2 and \$1, respectively, the value of the spread y^* is allowed to vary until an equal number of contracts are bought and sold. The value of the spread y^* is thus the median of the market's distribution. By varying the cost and payoff of the contract, it is possible to elicit other percentiles. For example, a contract that costs \$4 and pays \$5 when $y > y^*$ elicits the value y^* such that the market believes $\text{Prob}(y < y^*) = 0.8$.

We should note that although all of the contracts discussed above have been utilized to some extent, winner-take-all contracts on a single event are by far the most popular form of prediction markets. This is largely because such contracts are straightforward for market participants to understand. More research is needed to understand the benefits, and limitations, of other forms of contracts and families of those contracts.

2.1. Formats for Administering Prediction Markets

Most prediction markets, like those available on the industry standard Intrade.com, are implemented like equity markets. That is, buyers and sellers interact through a continuous double auction. However, a number of other designs have been suggested, and, in some cases gained traction. The major variations are play-money markets, pari-mutuel markets, and market scoring rules.

Due to concerns about speculation and manipulation, the U.S. Commodities Futures Trading Commission has tightly regulated prediction markets (Arrow et al., 2008). Thus, many markets, especially internal corporate markets, have been established using play money (Bell, 2009). For example, Lumenlogic, a leading provider of prediction markets to businesses, and the Hollywood Stock Exchange, which seeks to forecast entertainment-related outcomes, have chosen to run their exchanges using a virtual currency that can

---

[3] The techniques contained in Bakshi and Madan (2000) and Carr and Madan (2001) may be especially useful in analyzing such a family of contracts.

either be traded in for prizes, or amassed for prestige. Existing research suggests that these virtual currency prediction markets can be as accurate as real-money markets, but more research is needed (Servan-Schreiber et al., 2004).

Economic Derivatives, large-scale markets run by Goldman Sachs and Deutsche Bank that were tied directly to macroeconomic outcomes, such as initial unemployment claims and non-farm payrolls, were run as occasional, pari-mutuel markets. This structure, familiar from gambling on horse races, allows traders to buy or sell contracts on specific ranges of the economic indicator – similar to the example index contract above. However, the price is not determined until the auction closes – although estimated prices are displayed based on the price that would prevail if no more orders were posted. Once the market is closed and the outcome is realized, pari-mutuel markets split the total amount wagered among those who wagered on the correct range. If, for example, the actual initial unemployment claims (in thousands) were between $y = 330$ and $y = 340$, then each contract on that range would split the total amount wagered on all ranges.[4] Like the example of index contracts given above, a pari-mutuel market structure will recover the full pdf of the market's beliefs. However, the pari-mutuel market does this with a single market, rather than the numerous index contracts that would need to be set up.[5]

Finally, market scoring rules (Hanson, 2003, 2007) have shown great promise in the lab, and have been used by Microsoft and other corporations for their internal markets (Abramowicz, 2007). This format starts with a simple scoring rule – which rewards a single person for the accuracy of his or her prediction – and allows other entrants to essentially purchase the right to the reward when they believe they have a more accurate prediction. This format is used largely to reduce speculation and deal with problems that typically arise from thin markets. However, like standard scoring rules, market scoring rules require a market maker to subsidize the reward for accurate predictions. Still, in some situations, this may be a small price to pay for the added benefits.

3. WHY PREDICTION MARKETS WORK

Three inter-related facets lead to prediction markets' ability to produce accurate, reliable forecasts. First, the market mechanism is essentially an algorithm for aggregating information. Second, as superior information will produce monetary rewards, there is a financial incentive for truthful revelation. Third, and finally, the existence of a market provides longer-term incentives for specialization in discovering novel information and trading on it. While these facets are inherent in any market, other forecasting mechanisms, such as polling, or employing professional forecasters, lack one or more of them. For example,

---

[4] The Economic Derivatives market used a more sophisticated algorithm to determine prices in such a way to maximize trades. For a more detailed description of the design of these markets see Gürkaynak and Wolfers (2005).

[5] Plott (2000) gives an example using a similar structure inside of a large business to produce a full pdf sales forecast.

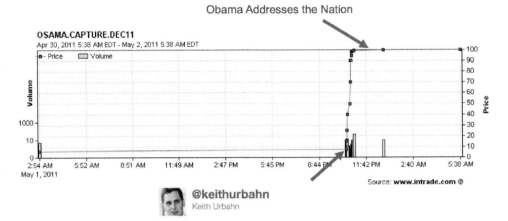

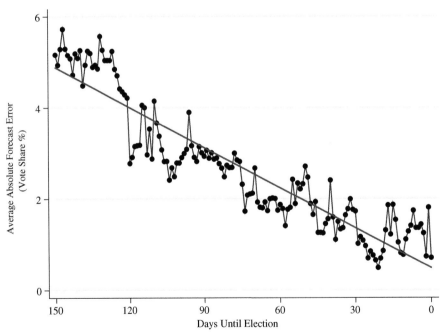

Figure 11.1 Information is incorporated quickly, and continuously across time. *Notes:* Second panel based on data from the IEM, 1988–2000, available at < http://www.biz.uiowa.edu/iem>. Adapted from Wolfers and Zitzewitz (2004).

polling lacks incentives for truthful revelation, and professional forecasters may have other motivations than simply forecast accuracy (Ottaviani and Sørensen, 2012).

This section documents several examples of how these facets lead to desirable characteristics in practice, such as the rapid incorporation of information, a lack of arbitrage opportunities, and a resistance to manipulation. We then turn to a brief overview of design flaws that may lead markets to fail, and conclude this section with a discussion of more speculative uses of prediction markets. The next section compares prediction market accuracy to other available methods.

As an illustration of the speed at which prediction markets incorporate new information, consider the killing of Osama bin Laden. At 10:25 p.m. Eastern time on May 1, 2011, Keith Urbahn, the former chief of staff to Defense Secretary Donald Rumsfeld used the social media service Twitter to announce, "So I'm told by a reputable person they have killed Osama Bin Laden. Hot Damn." The first panel of Figure 11.1 shows the reaction of a prediction market tracking the probability that Osama bin Laden would be captured or killed by December 31, 2011. Within moments of Urbahn's statement, the price of this contract, which generally saw very little trading, started to rise. Within 25 minutes of this initial announcement, the probability implied by this contract had risen from 7% to nearly 99%. This final estimate was eight minutes before any mainstream media outlet "broke the story" of bin Laden's death.

Moreover, prediction markets continuously incorporate new information. The second panel of Figure 11.1 shows the accuracy of election forecasts from the Iowa Electronic Markets (IEM), an academic-run prediction market based at the University of Iowa, across time. The figure shows quite clearly that as the election approaches, and more information is revealed about likely outcomes, the forecast error decreases steadily.[6]

Prediction markets also evince little evidence of arbitrage opportunities. Contracts within a single exchange are generally arbitrage linked. For example, a rapid increase in the price of a contract tied to the victory of a particular political candidate is generally accompanied by decreases in the prices of contracts linked to other candidates, so the implied probability of *someone* winning an election stays quite close to 100%. Although the general winnowing of prediction market companies in the 2000s makes it more difficult to compare prices across exchanges, Figure 11.2 shows that in 2003 the prices of different contracts tied to Arnold Schwarzenegger becoming the governor of California exhibited significant variation, but moved in lockstep.[7]

Additionally, prediction markets are quite difficult to manipulate. Attempts by party bosses to manipulate the price of their candidates in turn of the century gambling markets

---

[6] Additionally, the error is generally smaller than polls across time, see Figures 11.6 and 11.7, and the surrounding discussion.

[7] There was an arbitrage opportunity in 7 of the 105 time periods for which we have data, and the average size the arbitrage opportunity was 1.17 points. However, as positions cannot be moved across exchanges, executing on that opportunity would require holding a long position on one exchange, and a short position on the other until expiry. That is, one must hold $200 in positions for the duration of the contract in order gain $1 in arbitrage.

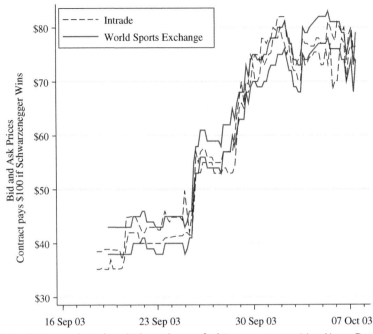

Figure 11.2 Prediction markets show little evidence of arbitrage opportunities. *Notes:* Data underlying lower line for each data source are bids, data underlying upper line for each data source are asks. Prices collected electronically every 4 hours by David Pennock, adapted from Wolfers and Zitzewitz (2004).

were largely unsuccessful, as were more recent attempts by candidates themselves (Rhode and Strumpf, 2008; Wolfers and Leigh, 2002). More recent, and systematic, attempts at manipulation yielded only brief transitory effects on prices. Rhode and Strumpf (2008) placed random $500 bets (the largest allowed) on the IEM and found that prices quickly returned to pre-manipulation levels. Camerer (1998) placed large bets in pari-mutuel horse racing markets (which he cancelled moments before the race) to see if this would create a bandwagon effect of follow-on bets. It did not. Finally, evidence from experimental prediction markets, run in the lab, show similar results. In a first experiment where some participants were incentivized to try to manipulate prices, there was little evidence that these participants were successful (Hanson et al., 2006). A second experiment based incentives on whether or not observers of the market price could be manipulated. Similarly, there was little evidence that manipulators affected the beliefs of observers (Hanson et al., 2011). Indeed, manipulators may increase the accuracy of prediction markets by providing more liquidity (Hanson and Oprea, 2009).

Anecdotal reports of attempts at manipulation abound, and reports indicate they have generally been unsuccessful. One exception we are aware of is manipulation of a contract tied to Hillary Clinton's probability of winning the presidency in 2008, conditional on winning the Democratic nomination. A single, large trader bought contracts on Intrade.com at prices that implied Clinton was much more electable by the general electorate than her Democratic competitors. While the manipulator was able to keep prices high for a significant period of time, the profit opportunity was noticed and discussed by other traders, resulting in huge losses for the large trader. Moreover, the manipulated price garnered only one mention in the mainstream media.[8]

Finally, in most cases, prediction markets seem to satisfy at least the weak form of the efficient markets hypothesis. That is, there is no evidence that trading on past prices can result in a profit. This has been explicitly demonstrated for prediction markets by Leigh et al. (2003), Tetlock (2004), and Berg et al. (2006). In particular, Leigh et al. (2003) test prediction markets related to the demise of Sadaam Hussein, and find that an augmented Dickey–Fuller test cannot reject the null that those markets follow a random walk. They also find that a KPSS test rejects the null that prices are trend-stationary. Berg et al. (2006) also finds that prices in the Iowa Electronic Markets follow a random walk. Finally, Tetlock (2004) finds some evidence of mispricing in prediction markets concerning sporting events, including evidence of over-reaction to news. However, the mispricing is not large enough to allow for profitable trading strategies. Moreover, Tetlock (2004) finds no evidence of mispricing in prediction markets about financial events on the same exchange. More evidence about the efficiency of prediction markets can be found in the large literature on gambling markets. This literature generally finds that betting markets are weakly efficient (discussed in several chapters of Vaughn and Leighton, 2005; Hausch and Ziemba, 2007).

3.1. Why They (Sometimes) Fail

Although prediction markets generally function quite well, design flaws sometimes prevent reliable forecasts. These flaws generally lead to a lack of noise traders (or thin markets) that reduces incentives for discovering, and trading on the basis of, private information (Snowberg et al., 2005). In order to attract noise traders, the subject of a prediction market must be interesting and information must be widely dispersed.

Prediction market contracts must be well specified, so that it is clear when they will (and will not) pay off. However, this specificity may be in tension with making a contract interesting for traders. For example, in 2003, Intrade ran markets that asked, "Will there be a UN Resolution on Iraq (beyond #1441)?" and "Will Saddam be out of office by June 30?" The former is clearly better specified, but the latter had much higher trading volume. Moreover, even the former has some ambiguity: what does it mean for a UN Resolution to be "on" Iraq?

Noise traders may quite rationally choose not to trade in markets where there is a high degree of insider information. For example, despite the high intrinsic interest in who a Supreme Court nominee will be, markets on this topic have routinely failed. This may be due to the fact that most traders are aware that there are very few people with actual information on who the President's choice will be. This anecdote underlines the

---

[8] A summary of this (successful) attempt at manipulation can be found in Zitzewitz (May 30, 2007).

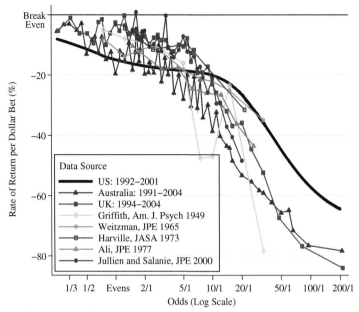

Figure 11.3 The favorite–longshot bias is the most prominent pricing anomaly in sports betting. *Notes:* Adapted from Snowberg and Wolfers (2010).

importance of prohibiting insider trading: for instance, a market to predict the Institute for Supply Management's (ISM's) business confidence measure would be unlikely to function if it were well known that ISM employees were trading in it.

An extreme form of information not being widely dispersed is when there is no information at all to aggregate. For example, prediction markets on whether weapons of mass destruction (WMDs) would be found in Iraq predicted they would very likely be found. The false confidence that could be inspired by such an estimate ignores the fact that there was no information being aggregated by these markets. That is to say, it was unlikely that anyone in Iraq who might actually have some information (perhaps based on rumors, past experience, or informal discussions with friends and relatives in the government) about whether Iraq's WMD program was likely to exist or not was trading in these markets.

Finally, it is unclear to what extent prices in prediction markets may be affected by behavioral biases. The most prominent, and well-understood, pricing anomaly in sports betting is the favorite–longshot bias. This pattern, shown across many studies and countries by Figure 11.3, comes from long–shots being overbet and favorites being underbet relative to their risk-neutral probabilities of victory.[9] Thus, interpreting the prices of gambles on horses as probabilities will tend to underestimate a horse's probability of victory when

---

[9] As the favorite-longshot bias is a divergence between risk-neutral implied probabilities and actual probabilities, it is also related to pricing phenomena in options markets, see Rubinstein (1994); Tompkins et al. (2008).

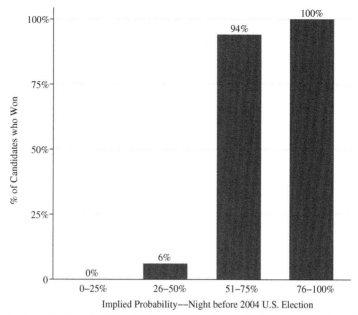

Figure 11.4 The favorite–longshot bias is also apparent in prediction markets. *Notes:* Data pools 50 markets on the state-by-state outcome of the electoral college, and 34 markets on U.S. Senate races on Intrade.com (then: Tradesports.com).

that probability is very high, and tend to overestimate a horse's probability of victory when that probability is very low.

A similar pattern is documented in 2004 U.S. election markets from Intrade.com in Figure 11.4. Almost all of the contracts that traded above a price of 50 won, and almost all of those that traded below a price of 50 lost, implying that those markets that predicted a high probability of one candidate winning underpredicted the actual probability of victory, while those that predicted a low probability of victory overpredicted the actual probability.

Recent work has attributed the favorite-longshot bias in gambling markets to behavioral phenomena, with Jullien and Salanié (2000) attributing it to asymmetries in the way traders value gains and losses, and Snowberg and Wolfers (2010) attributing it to misperceptions of probabilities. Regardless of the underlying explanation, a good rule of thumb is to use extreme caution when interpreting results based on contracts that imply a risk-neutral probability between 0 and 10%, or 90%, and 100%.

3.2. Bleeding Edge Design

The stories of failure above lead to some straightforward rules for designing prediction markets: make sure the question is well-defined, that there is dispersed information about the question, and that there is sufficient interest in the question to ensure liquidity.

However, such simple guidelines leave much to be desired. For example, what if the question is inherently difficult to define, or there simply is not sufficient interest in the question? These problems have been confronted by corporations using prediction markets, and although there is little academic work on their experiences, we do our best to summarize those experiences here.[10]

Corporations are attracted to prediction markets as they can potentially pass unbiased information from a company's front-line employees to senior management.[11] However, many questions of interest to executives are not widely interesting, nor are there many employees that have relevant information. This creates a lack of liquidity in markets, perhaps leading to no trading, or, worse, inaccurate predictions. Microsoft has responded to this problem by using a market-making algorithm, which is a variation of the market scoring rules described above (Berg and Proebsting, 2009). The market maker's function in a prediction market is similar to that in any other equity market: it buys and sells when other market participants are not available. However, unlike most market-makers, market-making algorithms are less concerned with making money, and often prefer to lose money if it is likely to increase informational efficiency.

Separately, Hewlett-Packard has used a structure similar to a pari-mutuel market in which a small number of participants are forced to take bets. This implementation is particularly interesting as the market designers use other information about the market participants, such as their risk attitudes and social connections, to enhance the market's efficiency. For example, if three participants who are known to be friends all bet heavily on the same potential outcome, the market interprets these bets as being based on redundant information, and lowers the impact of each bet on the overall price (Chen and Krakovsky, 2010).

One of the most prominent corporate applications of prediction markets has been to manage R&D portfolios. This is done through "idea markets," which allow employees to buy stock in particular ideas in order to determine which idea(s) are likely to be most profitable for the company. However, the price of the contract depends only on supply and demand, and is not tied to any actual outcome (such as profit if the product is eventually launched). These markets are sometimes described as "preference markets," and they are similar to pure beauty contests (Marinovic et al., 2011). Thus, there is the risk of divergence between the question of interest, and what the market can answer. Indeed, GE, one of the most prominent users of idea markets has found that the originators of ideas trade aggressively to raise the price of their idea and lower the price of other's ideas (Spears et al., 2009).

Despite the theoretical problems associated with such markets, and the lack of a clear way to evaluate their performance, they are increasingly popular. This has driven a range

---

[10] Firms whose internal prediction markets have been mentioned in the public domain include Abbott Labs, Arcelor Mittal, Best Buy, Chrysler, Corning, Electronic Arts, Eli Lilly, Frito Lay, General Electric, Hewlett-Packard, Intel, InterContinental Hotels, Masterfoods, Microsoft, Motorola, Nokia, Pfizer, Qualcomm, Siemens, and TNT (Cowgill et al., 2009). The results of these markets are rarely reported, as they often entail sensitive information.

[11] Side benefits, such as creating a sense of empowerment and fun among a company's front line employees have also been reported, see Strumpf (2009).

of experiments with different designs. These experiments vary many of the fine details of market structure, and hence are not easily summarized. Details can be found in Lavoie (2009), Spears et al. (2009), Dahan et al. (2010). An unusually detailed description of the design and evaluation of a prediction market to help with technology assessment can be found in Gaspoz (2011).

A final design constraint is the uncertain legal and regulatory environment surrounding prediction markets (Arrow et al., 2008). The current legal situation is summarized in Bell (2009). Companies are likely best served by consulting with a professional purveyor of prediction market services, a list of which can be found in Berg and Proebsting (2009).

4. FORECAST ACCURACY

The most notable feature of prediction markets is the accuracy of the forecasts they produce. We illustrate this accuracy through a number of case studies, beginning with an examination of the sole, large-scale, prediction market run on macro-economic outcomes, the Economic Derivatives markets mentioned earlier. We supplement this with case studies from businesses and politics, where prediction markets have been more extensively studied, and arguably, have had a much larger impact.

4.1. Macro Derivatives

For a few years, beginning in October 2002, Goldman Sachs and Deutsche Bank operated markets tied directly to macro-economic outcomes.[12] These markets, described as "Economic Derivatives," allowed investors to purchase options with payoffs that depended on growth in non-farm payrolls, retail sales, levels of the ISM's manufacturing diffusion index (a measure of business confidence) and initial unemployment claims, among others. The payoffs in these markets were tied to particular data releases, and thus allowed investors to hedge against specific, event-based, risk. The performance of these markets was analyzed by Gürkaynak and Wolfers (2005); this subsection summarizes their main results.

The forecasts gleaned from these markets can be compared with a survey based forecast released by Money Market Services, which typically averages predictions across approximately 30 forecasters, as in Figure 11.5.[13] Visual inspection shows that the market-based forecast is weakly more accurate than the survey-based forecast, and this is verified by a numerical analysis.

Table 11.2 examines both the mean absolute error and mean squared error of both forecasts, normalized by the average forecast error from past surveys. The normalization makes the data across all four series sufficiently comparable to pool all data in the fifth

---

[12] These markets no longer exist, presumably because the trading volume was not sufficiently high as to make them profitable.

[13] Money Market Services was acquired by Informa in 2003, so some of the survey-based data comes from Action Economics and Bloomberg.

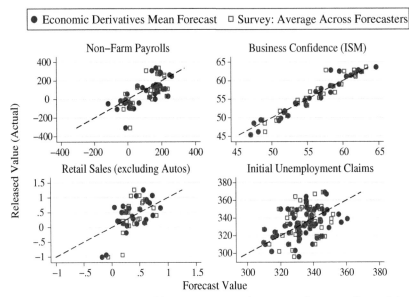

Figure 11.5 Macro derivatives are weakly more accurate than survey forecasts. *Notes:* Adapted from Gürkaynak and Wolfers (2005).

column. For all four series, the market-based forecast is more accurate than the survey-based forecast. Across all series, relying on the market-based forecast would have reduced forecast errors by approximately 5.5% of the average forecast error over the preceding decade. With the small number of observations in each series, the differences are rarely statistically significant, however, the differences in the pooled data are statistically significant at the 5% level.[14]

Table 11.3 examines the forecasting power of each predictor. The first panel reports the correlation of each forecast with actual outcomes. As all of the correlations are quite high, it is clear that both sources have substantial unconditional forecasting power. The middle panel implements (Harvey et al., 1998) tests of forecast encompassing, and finds that we can reject the null that the market encompasses the survey for Business confidence and initial unemployment claims; we can also reject the null that the survey encompasses the market for business confidence. Additionally, the p-values on the test of the null that the survey encompasses the market for retail sales and initial unemployment claims are 0.11 and 0.16, respectively. Thus, it is clear that both the market and the survey provide some unique information.

The final panel follows Fair and Shiller (1990) in using a regression-based test of the information content of each forecast. The results are striking: for all four series the coefficient on the market based forecast is statistically indistinguishable from one, and the coefficient on the survey-based forecast is only statistically different from zero in one

---

[14] Bootstrapped standard errors produce very similar results.

Table 11.2 Economic Derivatives have Slightly Smaller Errors than Forecasters

	Non-farm Payrolls	Business Confidence (ISM)	Retail Sales (Ex Autos)	Initial Unemp. Claims	Pooled Data
Panel A: Mean Absolute Error					
Economic derivatives	0.723	0.498	0.919	0.645	0.680
	(.097)	(.090)	(.123)	(.061)	(.044)
Survey of forecasters	0.743	0.585	0.972	0.665	0.719
	(.098)	(.093)	(.151)	(.063)	(.046)
Difference	−0.021	−0.087*	−0.053	−0.020	−0.039**
	(.034)	(.043)	(.060)	(.023)	(.018)
Panel B: Mean Squared Error					
Economic derivatives	0.823	0.481	1.222	0.654	0.753
	(.240)	(.257)	(.262)	(.126)	(.088)
Survey of forecasters	0.862	0.593	1.512	0.690	0.848
	(.268)	(.296)	(.364)	(.130)	(.114)
Difference	−0.039	−0.112	−0.289	−0.037	−0.095**
	(.061)	(.082)	(.208)	(.040)	(.018)
Sample Size (Oct. 2002–Jul. 2005)	33	30	26	64	153

Notes: ***, **, * denote statistically significant Diebold and Mariano (1995) / West (1996) tests, implemented as recommended by West (2006), at the 1%, 5%, and 10% level. Standard errors in parentheses. Forecast errors normalized by historical standard error of survey-based forecasts. Adapted from Table 11.1 in Gürkaynak and Wolfers (2005).

series, where it is (perversely) negative. That is, conditioning on the market-based forecast renders the survey-based forecast uninformative. Pooling the data across all four series only reinforces this general pattern.

While the market-based forecasts perform better than the survey of forecasters according to most of the statistical criteria examined here, these criteria may not be the most relevant. It is still an open question whether a particular trading strategy, similar to Leitch and Tanner (1991), would fare better or worse using information from forecasters or prediction markets.

4.2. Politics

Prediction markets first gained notoriety for their ability to predict election outcomes. Researchers at the University of Iowa began markets tracking various candidates' vote shares, and chances of victory, in 1988. This experimental market, called the Iowa Electronic Market (IEM), proved to be incredibly accurate. Figure 11.6 summarizes the predictions of the IEM and compares them with the predictions of polls from Gallup. The figure shows that markets were slightly better predictors than polls the day before the election.

Table 11.3 Economic Derivatives have Slightly Smaller Errors than Forecasters

	Non-farm Payrolls	Business Confidence (ISM)	Retail Sales (Ex Autos)	Initial Unemp. Claims	Pooled Data
Panel A: Correlation of Forecast with Actual Outcomes					
Economic derivatives	0.700	0.968	0.653	0.433	0.631
	(.126)	(.047)	(.151)	(.114)	(.063)
Survey of forecasters	0.677	0.961	0.544	0.361	0.576
	(.130)	(.052)	(.168)	(.117)	(.066)
Panel B: Encompassing Tests (based on absolute error)					
Economic derivatives	−0.048	0.194*	0.123	−0.260***	−0.062
encompasses survey	(.157)	(.113)	(.267)	(.089)	(.075)
Survey of forecasters	0.081	−0.269**	−0.471	−0.125	0.096
encompasses market	(.159)	(.110)	(.326)	(.089)	(.081)
Panel C: Horse Race Regression (Fair–Shiller)					
$Actual_t = \alpha + \beta * EconomicDerivatives_t + \gamma * SurveyForecast_t (+ surveyfixedeffects)$					
Economic derivatives	1.06	0.91**	1.99**	1.64***	1.25***
	(.78)	(.37)	(.79)	(.60)	(.29)
Survey of forecasters	−0.14	0.17	−1.03	−1.21*	−0.24
	(.89)	(.38)	(1.10)	(.68)	(.30)
Adjusted R^2	0.46	0.93	0.40	0.20	0.99
Sample Size (Oct. 2002–Jul. 2005)	33	30	26	64	153

Notes: ***,**,* denote statistically significant coefficients at the 1%, 5% and 10% level with standard errors in parentheses. Forecast errors normalized by historical standard error of survey-based forecasts. Adapted from Table 11.1 in Gürkaynak and Wolfers (2005).

However, markets are statistically more accurate than polls in the run-up to the election itself. Over the run-up, markets have half the forecast error of polls (Berg et al., 2006; Berg and Rietz, 2006; Berg et al., 2008).

However, as Erikson and Wlezien (2008) notes, there are well-known biases in polls that can and should be controlled for. For example, both parties' candidates usually see their poll numbers climb immediately after their party's convention. Rothschild (2009) compares the forecasts from polls, de-biased in real time, with prediction market prices adjusted for the favorite-longshot bias (discussed above) over the 2008 Presidential election.[15] The results are summarized in Figure 11.7, which considers prediction markets and polls tied to the outcome of the presidential election in each of the 50 states.

---

[15] To de-bias polls, Rothschild (2009) follows Erikson and Wlezien (2008), which finds the optimal projection from polls at the same point in previous election cycles and eventual elections, and applies that projection to polls from the current electoral cycle.

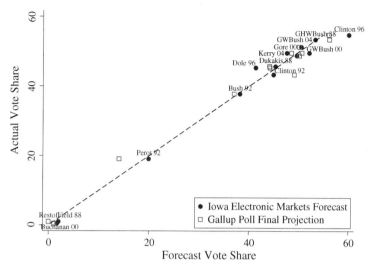

Figure 11.6 Prediction markets are more accurate even the night before an election. *Notes:* Market forecast is closing price on election eve; Gallup forecast is final pre-election projection.

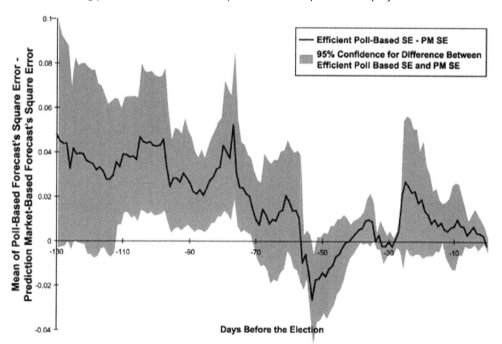

Figure 11.7 Prediction markets are generally more accurate than polls, even after removing known biases. *Notes:* Each data point is the difference in mean-squared error between two different types of forecast over the 50 electoral college races in 2008. Each forecast is generated by taking raw data from a poll or prediction market and utilizing the most efficient transformation from raw data into forecasts, as outlined in Rothschild (2009).

Table 11.4 Comparing the Information in Prediction Markets and Polls

	Horse Race Regression (Fair-Shiller) $VoteShare = \alpha + \beta * Poll + \gamma * MarketPrices$		
	All Observations	**Before Labor Day**	**Less-certain Races**
De-biased Gallup Poll	0.296***	0.458***	0.195
	(.060)	(.100)	(.164)
De-biased Prediction Market Prices	0.759***	0.754***	0.788***
	(.072)	(.099)	(.099)
N	8,361	4,354	3,167

Notes: ***, **, * denote statistical significance at the 1%, 5% and 10% level with robust standard errors in parentheses. Table uses the data from Rothschild (2009), with prediction market prices converted into expected vote shares using past trends. Less-certain races are those where neither candidate has a (projected) 90% chance of winning. More details of the procedure for de-biasing polls and prediction market prices can be found in Rothschild (2009).

As the figure shows, the mean squared error of polls is much higher, sometimes statistically significantly so, over the first 70 days of the election cycle. For the second half, polls and markets switch places (twice), and one is not clearly better than the other. However, as shown in Table 11.4, in Fair and Shiller (1990) type horse–race regressions, prediction markets encapsulate all of the information in polls when contracts that indicate a probability of 90% of one or the other candidate winning that state are dropped from the sample. When these markets are included, the coefficient on the forecast from the prediction market is still statistically significant and close to one, but the coefficient on de-biased polls is statistically different from zero. Taking all of this evidence together, raw prediction market prices provide superior forecasts to raw polls, but polls may contain some additional information, especially in races where one candidate dominates.

4.3. Business

Corporations have aggressively used prediction markets to help with their internal forecasts. As noted in Section 3.2, there is little academic evidence of their impact. However, three important exceptions deserve a mention here.

First, in a seminal study, Chen and Plott (2002) ran eight prediction markets within Hewlett-Packard to forecast important variables like quarterly printer sales. These results showed that the markets were more accurate than the company's official forecasts. This improvement in accuracy was obtained even though the markets had closed, and final prices were known, at the time the official forecast was made.

Second, Cowgill et al. (2009) analyze data from 270 markets run inside of Google. While the markets were, in general, quite accurate, and often provided forecasts that would have been difficult to obtain in anything other than an ad hoc way, there were identifiable biases in some market prices. In particular, when markets involved the performance of

Google as a company, optimistic outcomes were forecast to be more likely to happen than they actually were. Moreover, this "optimistic bias" was more pronounced among traders who were newer employees, and on days when Google's stock appreciated.

Third, and finally, Berg et al. (2009) ran several prediction markets to predict Google's market cap at the end of the first day of trading. Notably, these predictions could be compared to the auction that Google used in setting its IPO price. The prediction market fared quite well: its prediction was 4% above the actual market cap, while the IPO price was 15% below. Had the company set its IPO price based on the prediction market price, they would have earned $225 million more in their IPO.

5. DISCOVERING ECONOMIC MODELS

The information from prediction markets has also proven quite useful in augmenting event studies (Snowberg et al., 2011). This use of prediction markets may be of particular interest to economic forecasters, as they reveal pieces of the economic model underlying the markets' reaction to various types of information. We show first how prediction markets can be used to measure the uncertainty surrounding an event, before exploring two examples of prediction market event studies. The first example measures the expected impact of the second Iraq war on oil prices, while the second example examines the impact of politics on broad stock market indices.

5.1. Disagreement and Uncertainty

Consumers of economic forecasts care not just about the mean prediction, but the uncertainty attached to it as well. As professional forecasters generally only give mean forecasts, it has become common practice to report *disagreement* – the standard error of economic forecasters' forecasts – as a proxy for uncertainty. This practice is theoretically founded: Laster et al. (1999) show that, under reasonable assumptions, the distribution of forecasts will match the distribution of beliefs. However, data from prediction markets show that disagreement between forecasters is a poor proxy for uncertainty.

Markets, such as the economic derivative markets above, allow one to recover the entire distribution of the markets beliefs. In turn, this may be used to calculate the *uncertainty* – the standard deviation – of market based forecasts. Gürkaynak and Wolfers (2005) show that this measure is very close to the rout-mean standard error (RMSE) of the market-based (mean) forecast, so the market's uncertainty seems to be well calibrated. However, Figure 11.8 shows that disagreement tends to be much smaller than actual uncertainty.

Moreover, there is generally a poor correlation between disagreement and uncertainty. Table 11.5 regresses uncertainty on disagreement. Panel A shows a statistically significant, positive correlation between the two measures for all series except ISM. The fifth column shows that the coefficients are jointly quite significant, suggesting a strong,

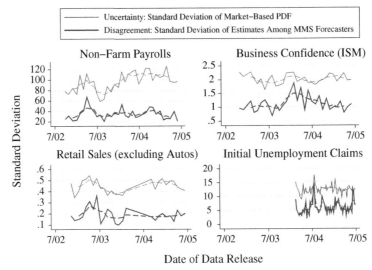

Figure 11.8 Uncertainty is generally greater than disagreement. *Notes:* Dashed lines show 5-period, centered, moving averages. Adapted from Gürkaynak and Wolfers (2005).

Table 11.5 Disagreement Among Forecasters is a Poor Proxy for Uncertainty

	Non-farm Payrolls	Business Confidence (ISM)	Retail Sales (Ex Autos)	Joint Significance (F-test)
Panel A: Contemporaneous Relationship				
$Uncertainty_t = \alpha + \beta * Disagreement_t$				
Disagreement	0.66**	−0.03	0.44**	0.27***	$p = .0002$
	(.29)	(.12)	(.16)	(.07)	
Constant	73.6***	2.04***	0.36***	10.86***	
	(10.39)	(.13)	(.03)	(.47)	
Adjusted R^2	0.11	−0.03	0.20	0.17	
Panel B: Low Frequency – 5 Period, Centered, Moving Averages				
$Smoothed\ Uncertainty_t = \alpha + \beta * Smoothed\ Disagreement_t$				
Disagreement	0.55	0.10	0.65***	.32**	$p = .15$
	(.47)	(.10)	(.24)	(.06)	
Constant	77.7***	1.89***	0.32***	10.5***	
	(16.8)	(.11)	(.05)	(.37)	
Adjusted R^2	0.01	−0.002	0.23	0.32	

Notes: ***, **, * denote statistically significant regression coefficients at the 1%, 5% and 10% level with standard errors in parentheses. Adapted from Table 11.5 in Gürkaynak and Wolfers (2005).

contemporaneous relationship. Panel B focuses on lower-frequency variation. There is still a correlation between the two series, but it is substantially lower. Note that the correlation is likely overstated as standard errors here are not corrected for the autocorrelation generated by smoothing. The joint test now fails to achieve statistical significance at conventional levels. Together, these results suggest that disagreement is poorly calibrated to actual forecast error, and that it is a poor proxy for uncertainty.

5.2. War

Wars can have large economic impacts, and, in the post WWII era, usually have a fairly long buildup. However, as each war is unique, it is difficult to build wars into economic forecasts, even when the probability of war is very high. In particular, it is quite difficult to make conditional forecasts in anything other than an ad hoc way, as much of the information available may be tainted by political considerations, and, moreover, such a large-scale event may have general equilibrium effects that are poorly understood.

Prediction market event studies present the possibility of improving economic forecasts when such a unique event becomes likely. By tracking the probability of such an event through a prediction market, and correlating movements in the prediction market with asset prices, it becomes possible to understand the market's assessment of how such an event will affect outcomes such as the price of oil, or the returns to securities.

Leigh et al. (2003) performed a prediction market event study in the buildup to the second Iraq war. Its prospective analysis showed that every 10% increase in the probability of war lead to a $1 increase in the spot price of oil. As shown in Figure 11.9, they used

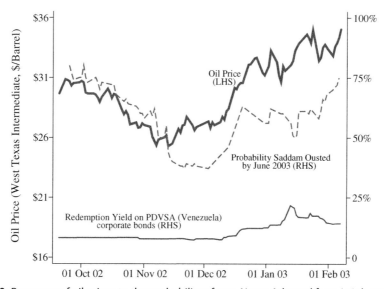

Figure 11.9 Response of oil prices to the probability of war. *Notes:* Adapted from Leigh et al. (2003).

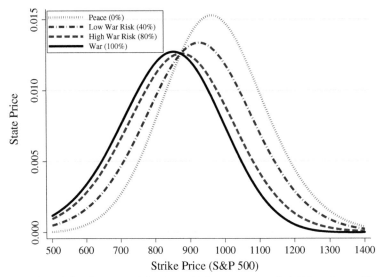

Figure 11.10 Predicted distributions of the S&P 500 for various probabilities of war. *Notes:* Adapted from Wolfers and Zitzewitz (2008b).

a prediction market, run by Intrade.com, that measured the probability that Saddam Hussein would be out of office by a certain date as the probability of war a few months before that date.[16] As can be seen from the figure, as the probability of war fluctuated, so did the spot price of oil.

Moreover, the S&P 500 dropped 1.5% for every 10% increase in the probability of war. This implied that the market anticipated that a war would decrease stock prices by 15 percentage points. A further analysis of S&P 500 options revealed that the distribution of potential outcomes was quite negatively skewed. Option prices suggested there was a 70% probability that war would have a moderately negative effect of 0 to −15 percentage points, a 20% probability of a −15 to −30 percentage-point effect, and a 10% chance of even larger declines. Figure 11.10 presents this information in a slightly disaggregated way: for each of four probabilities of war, it shows the full state-price distribution. It is clear that in the case of certain war (the thick, solid line), the mode of the state-price distribution is substantially shifted from what it would be under a zero chance of war (the thin, dashed line). Moreover, in certain war, the markets predicted a non-negligible probability that the S&P 500 would fall below 500 (Wolfers and Zitzewitz, 2008b).

The striking magnitude of this effect stands in contrast with the conventional wisdom, based in part on studies such as Cutler et al. (1989), that political and military news explain only a small portion of market movements. In contrast, Wolfers and Zitzewitz (2008b) finds that, "[O]ver 30% of the variation in the S&P and 75% of the variation in spot oil prices between September 2002 and February 2003 can be explained econometrically by

---

[16] This is a reasonable proxy – out of office was defined as no longer controlling the center of Baghdad.

changes in the probability of war (and, for oil, the Venezuelan crisis)." The authors note that it is possible to reconcile this result with the conventional wisdom by noting that typically when economically important events happen, they are often near certainties. That is to say, if the actual declaration of war comes when the market's assessment of the probability of war is already 95%, then any correlated market movements must be scaled by a factor of 20 to appreciate the full economic magnitude of the event. However, determining the markets' assessment of the probability of war immediately preceding an event is quite difficult without prediction markets.

Additionally, prediction markets can be constructed to measure the overall economic cost of a military intervention. For example, to determine the state price distribution of the S&P 500, a researcher could combine S&P 500 futures with a prediction market on the probability of war, as shown in Figure 11.10. A cleaner design would be to issue options on the S&P 500 that pay off only if the U.S. has gone to war, with all transactions reversed if the U.S. does not go to war. By combining these options with prediction markets tied directly to whether or not the U.S. goes to war, and, for example, the level of troop deployments in the case of war, one could recover state price distributions under different military scenarios. This (largely theoretical) use of prediction markets has been described as "decision markets" or, more spectacularly, "futarchy" (Hanson, 1999; Berg and Rietz, 2003; Hahn and Tetlock, 2005; Hanson, 2011).[17]

5.3. Politics

Prediction markets can also help to determine the effect of more routine political events, such as elections. A large literature in political science, economics, and the popular press argues about the effect of various candidates and parties, and the policies they endorse, on the economy. Despite some evidence that broad stock market indices in the U.S. may perform up to 20% better under Democrats than Republicans (Santa-Clara and Valkanov, 2003), political considerations are rarely reflected in economic forecasts.

This is at least partly due to the fact that there is no academic consensus on even the direction of the effect of political outcomes on economic variables. However, markets exhibit much more consistency. In particular, by using a prediction market event study on election night 2004, Snowberg et al. (2007a) show that broad stock market indices rose approximately 2% on news of Bush's victory over Kerry. Moreover, this effect seems to be relatively consistent across time, as, using data from 1880 to 2004, the same authors show that a Republican victory caused a broad-based market index to rise by approximately 2.5%.

Figure 11.11 shows the price of a prediction market that paid off if Bush won in 2004, expressed as risk-neutral probabilities, and the value of a near-month S&P 500 future over

---

[17] Malhotra and Snowberg (2009) provide an example of how to use a decision market to pick the presidential candidate that would maximize a particular party's chance of winning.

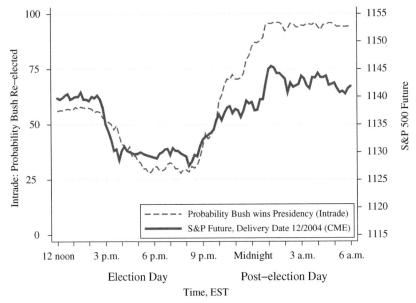

Figure 11.11 Prediction markets uncover the market's reaction to political changes. *Notes:* Adapted from Snowberg et al. (2007a).

election night 2004. The prices of these two securities track each other quite closely. The probability of Bush's re-election starts near 55%, and declines by about 30% on flawed exit polls showing Kerry with a lead in some swing states. At approximately the same time, the S&P 500 future decreases in value by approximately 0.7%. Thus, this particular event study indicates that a Bush victory would increase the value of the S&P 500 by 0.7%/30% = 2.3%. As early vote totals were released, showing the faults of the earlier poll results, Bush's probability of re-election climbed 65%, and the S&P rose by about 1.3%. Thus, this event study indicates that a Bush victory would increase the S&P 500 by 1.3%/65% = 2%.

A first differences regression essentially averages together a large number of event studies. In particular, estimates of

$$\Delta(\log(\text{FinancialVariable}_t)) = \alpha + \beta\Delta(\text{Re} - \text{electionProbability}_t) + \varepsilon_t$$

are shown for a number of different financial variables in Table 11.6. Estimates based on 10-minute and 30-minute differences are consistent, although the results based on 30-minute differences have slightly larger coefficients, reflecting the fact that the prediction market was slower to incorporate information than financial markets, as is apparent from Figure 11.11. As can be seen from the table, a Bush victory increased all three major U.S. stock indices by 2–2.5%. Consistent with expectations of expansionary fiscal policies, the Dollar and Bond Yields rose, as did near-term expectations of the price of oil.

Table 11.6 High-Frequency Data from Prediction Markets Allows for Precise Estimates of the Effect of Elections on Economic Variables

		10-Minute First Differences		30-Minute First Differences	
		Estimated Effect of Bush Presidency	n	Estimated Effect of Bush Presidency	n
Dependent Variable: $\Delta(Log(FinancialIndex))$					
S & P 500		0.015***	104	0.021***	35
		(.004)		(.005)	
Dow Jones Industrial Average		0.014***	84	0.021***	29
		(.005)		(.006)	
Nasdaq 100		0.017***	104	0.024***	35
		(.006)		(.008)	
U.S. Dollar (vs. Trade-weighted basket)		0.004	93	0.005**	34
		(.003)		(.003)	
Dependent Variable: $\Delta(Price)$					
Light Crude Oil Futures	December '04	1.110***	88	1.706***	29
		(.371)		(.659)	
	December '05	0.652*	85	1.020	28
		(.375)		(.610)	
	December '06	-0.580	63	-0.666	21
		(.783)		(.863)	
Dependent Variable: $\Delta(Yield)$					
2-Year T-Note Future		0.104*	84	0.108***	30
		(.058)		(.036)	
10-Year T-Note Future		0.112**	91	0.120**	31
		(.050)		(.046)	

Notes: ***, **, * denote statistically significant regression coefficients at the 1%, 5%, and 10% level with robust standard errors in parentheses. The sample period is noon Eastern Time on 11/2/2004 to six a.m. on 11/3/2004. Election probabilities are the most recent transaction prices, collected every ten minutes from Intrade.com (then TradeSports.com), S& P, Nasdaq, and foreign exchange futures are from the Chicago Mercantile Exchange; Dow and bond futures are from the Chicago Board of Trade, while oil futures data are from the New York Mercantile Exchange. Equity, bond, and currency futures have December 2004 delivery dates. Yields are calculated for the Treasury futures using the daily yields reported by the Federal Reserve for 2- and 10-year Treasuries, and projecting forward and backward from the bond market close at 3 p.m. using future price changes and the future's durations of 1.96 and 7.97 reported by CBOT. The trade-weighted currency portfolio includes six currencies with CME-traded futures (the Euro, Yen, Pound, Australian, and Canadian Dollars, and the Swiss Franc). Adapted from Table 11.1 in Snowberg et al. (2007a).

Were this just a one-off result, it would make little sense to add political changes to a forecasting model. However, as Figure 11.12 and Table 11.7 show, Republican elections routinely lead to an increase of about 2.5% in a broad equity market index. The first panel of the figure, and first column of the table, show the relationship between the change in probability of a Republican President over election night and the change in a

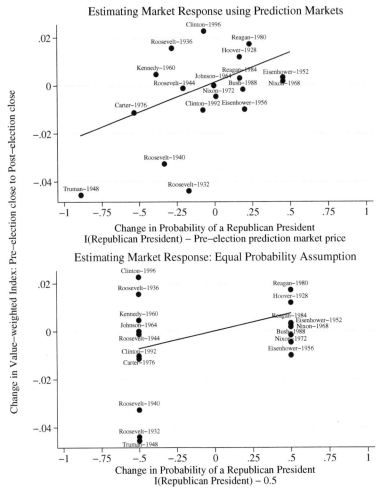

Figure 11.12 Prediction markets uncover the market's reaction to political changes. *Notes:* Adapted from Snowberg et al. (2011).

broad-based market index from market close the day before the election, to market close the day after.[18] That is, the table contains an estimate of

$$\Delta(\text{MarketIndex}_t) = \alpha + \beta \Delta(\text{RepublicanPresident}_t) + \varepsilon_t,$$

$$\text{where} \Delta(\text{RepublicanPresident}_t) = \mathbb{I}(\text{RepublicanPresident}_t) - P(\text{RepublicanElection}_t)$$

[18] Equity index values are from Schwert's (1990) daily equity returns data, which attempts to replicate returns on a value-weighted total return index, supplemented by returns on the CRSP-value-weighted portfolio since 1962. The prediction market prices come from the curb exchange on Wall Street, where exchanges on various political candidates ran up until shortly after WWII (Rhode and Strumpf, 2004).

Table 11.7 Prediction Markets Identify the Effect of Elections on Markets

	Dependent Variable: Stock Returns from Election-eve Close to Post-election Close		
ΔP(RepublicanPresident)	0.0297**		0.0249***
(*From Prediction Markets*)	(.118)		(.0082)
$\mathbb{I}$(RepublicanPresident) $- 0.5$		0.0128	
(*As in Santa-Clara and Valkanov*)		(.0089)	
Constant	−0.0102	−0.0027	0.0014
	(.0059)	(0.0040)	(0.0028)
Sample	1928–1996	1928–1996	1880–2004
N	18	18	32

Notes: ***, **, * denote statistical significance at the 1%, 5% and 10% level with robust standard errors in parentheses. Adapted from Table 11.5 in Snowberg et al. (2007a).

where $\mathbb{I}$(RepublicanElected$_t$) takes a value of one if a Republican was elected in year t, and zero otherwise, and P(RepublicanElection$_t$) is the expected probability of a Republican victory, according to the price of an historical prediction market (from Rhode and Strumpf (2004)) the night before the election.

The second panel of the figure, and second column of the table, show the role of prediction markets in this estimate. Lacking prediction market data, Santa-Clara and Valkanov (2003) simply fix P(RepublicanElection$_t$) $= 0.5$ for all years from which they have data: 1928–1996. This results in the smaller, statistically insignificant estimate found in the second column of Table 11.7. The third column of the same table contains data from all years available in Snowberg et al. (2007a), and shows a precisely estimated, stable effect of the election of a Republican president of about 2.5%. The contribution of prediction markets is clear: a more precise estimate of the probability of one or the other candidate winning allows for a better estimate of the effect of political candidates on financial markets.

6. CONCLUSION

Over the last half decade, many economists, and the public, have re-evaluated the efficiency of financial markets. While these re-evaluations have not been favorable to markets, it is important to keep in mind the alternative (Zingales, 2010). In the case of forecasting, the alternative is often professional forecasters, polls, pundits, or a combination of the three. As we have shown in these paper, prediction markets out-perform both professional forecasters and polls in a variety of statistical tests.

We have shown that prediction markets have many of the properties expected under the efficient markets hypothesis. In particular, they are difficult to manipulate, lack significant arbitrage opportunities, aggregate information quickly and in a seemingly efficient manner. Evidence of efficiency can be seen in the macro-derivatives markets, which out-perform professional forecasters, or in political prediction markets, which out-perform polls.

However, prediction markets are not a panacea. In particular, care must be taken when designing prediction markets to ensure they are interesting, well-specified, and are not subject to excessive insider information. More pernicious problems come from behavioral biases, such as those underlying the favorite-longshot bias, and knowing when there is dispersed information that can be aggregated.

With that said, we believe the real promise of prediction markets comes not from their ability to predict particular events. Rather, the real promise lies in using these markets, often several at a time, to test particular economic models, and use these models to improve economic forecasts.

ACKNOWLEDGMENT

We dedicate this chapter to the memory of John Delaney, founder and CEO of Intrade.com. An innovator and source of inspiration for many prediction market researchers, he will be sorely missed.

REFERENCES

Abramowicz, Michael, 2007. The hidden beauty of the quadratic market scoring rule: a uniform liquidity market maker, with variations. The Journal of Prediction Markets 1 (2), 111–125.

Alquist, Ron, Rober, Vigfusson, J., 2013. Forecasting oil prices. In: Handbook of Economic Forecasting, vol. 2. Elsevier: Handbooks in Economics Series.

Arrow, Kenneth, J., Forsythe, Robert, Gorham, Michael, Hahn, Robert, Hanson, Robin, Ledyard, John, O., Levmore, Saul, Litan, Robert, Milgrom, Paul, Nelson, Forrest, D., Neumann, George, R., Ottaviani, Marco, Schelling, Thomas, C., Shiller, Robert, J., Smith, Vernon, L., Snowberg, Erik, Sunstein, Cass, R., Tetlock, Paul, C., Tetlock, Philip, E., Varian, Hal, R., Wolfers, Justin, Zitzewitz, Eric, 2008. The promise of prediction markets. Science 320 (5878), 877–878.

Bakshi, Gurdip, Madan, Dilip, 2000. Spanning and derivative-security valuation. Journal of Financial Economics 55 (2), 205–238.

Bell, Tom, W., 2009. Private prediction markets and the law. The Journal of Prediction Markets 3 (1), 89–110.

Berg, Henry, Proebsting, Todd, A., 2009. Hanson's automated market maker. The Journal of Prediction Markets 3 (1), 45–59.

Berg, Joyce, E., Rietz, Thomas, A., 2003. Prediction markets as decision support systems. Information Systems Frontiers 5 (1), 79–93.

Berg, Joyce, E., Rietz, Thomas, A., 2006. The iowa electronic market: lessons learned and answers year-ned. In: Hahn, Robert, Tetlock, Paul (Eds.), Information Markets: A New Way of Making Decisions in the Public and Private Sectors. AEI-Brookings Joint Center, Washington, D.C.

Berg, Joyce, Forrest, Nelson, Rietz, Thomas, 2006. Accuracy and Forecast Standard Error in Prediction Markets. University of Iowa, mimeo.

Berg, Joyce, Forsythe, Robert, Nelson, Forrest, Rietz, Thomas, 2008. Results from a dozen years of election futures markets research. In: Plott, Charles, R., Smith, Vernon, L. (Eds.), The Handbook of Experimental Economics Results. Handbooks in Economics series, Elsevier.

Berg, Joyce, E., Neumann, George, R., Rietz, Thomas, A., 2009. Searching for google's value: using prediction markets to forecast market capitalization prior to an initial public offering. Management Science 55 (3), 348–361.

Camerer, Colin, F., 1998. Can asset markets be manipulated? A field experiment with racetrack betting. Journal of Political Economy 106 (3), 457–482.

Carr, Peter, Madan, Dilip, 2001. Optimal positioning in derivative securities. Quantitative Finance 1 (1), 19–37.

Chen, Kay-Yut, Krakovsky, Marina, 2010. Secrets of the Moneylab: How Behavioral Economics Can Improve Your Business. Portfolio Penguin.

Chen, Kay-Yut, Plott, Charles, R., 2002. Information Aggregation Mechanisms: Concept, Design and Implementation for a Sales Forecasting Problem. California Institute of Technology Social Science Working Paper #1131.

Cowgill, Bo, Wolfers, Justin, Zitzewitz, Eric, 2009. Using Prediction Markets to Track Information Flows: Evidence from Google. Dartmouth College, memeo.

Cutler, David, M., Poterba, James, M., Summers, Lawrence, H., 1989. What moves stock prices? Journal of Portfolio Management 15 (3), 4–12.

Dahan, Ely, Soukhoroukova, Arina, Spann, Martin, 2010. New product development 2.0: preference marketshow scalable securities markets identify winning product concepts and attributes. Journal of Product Innovation Management 27 (7), 937–954.

Diebold, Francis, X., Mariano, Robert, S., 1995. Comparing predictive accuracy. Journal of Business and Economic Statistics 13 (3), 134–144.

Duffee, Gregory, 2013. Forecasting interest rates. In: Timmermann, Allan, Elliott, Graham (Eds.), Handbook of Economic Forecasting, vol. 2. Handbooks in Economics series, Elsevier.

Erikson, Robert, S., Wlezien, Christopher, 2008. Are political markets really superior to polls as election predictors? Public Opinion Quarterly 72 (2), 190–215.

Fair, Ray, C., Shiller, Robert, J., 1990. Comparing information in forecasts from econometric models. American Economic Review 80 (3), 375–389.

Gaspoz, Cédric. 2011. Prediction Markets Supporting Technology Assessment. Self-published.

Gjerstad, Steven, 2005. Risk Aversion, Beliefs, and Prediction Market Equilibrium. University of Arizona, mimeo.

Gürkaynak, Refet, Wolfers, Justin, 2005. Macroeconomic derivatives: an initial analysis of market-based macro forecasts, uncertainty, and risk. In: Frankel, Jeffrey, A. and Pissarides, Christopher, A. (Eds.), NBER International Seminar on Macroeconomics 2005, MIT Press, Cambridge, MA, pp. 11–50.

Hahn, Robert, W., Tetlock, Paul, C., 2005. Using information markets to improve public decision making. Harvard Journal of Law and Public Policy 28, 213–289.

Hanson, Robin, 1999. Decision markets. IEEE Intelligent Systems 14 (3), 16–19.

Hanson, Robin, 2003. Combinatorial information market design. Information Systems Frontiers 5 (1), 107–119.

Hanson, R., 2007. Logarithmic market scoring rules for modular combinatorial information aggregation. The Journal of Prediction Markets 1 (1), 3–15.

Hanson, Robin. 2011. Shall we vote on values, but bet on beliefs? Journal of Political Philosophy forthcoming.

Hanson, Robin, Oprea, Ryan, 2009. A manipulator can aid prediction market accuracy. Economica 76 (302), 304–314.

Hanson, Robin, Oprea, Ryan, Porter, David, 2006. Information aggregation and manipulation in an experimental market. Journal of Economic Behavior & Organization 60 (4), 449–459.

Hanson, Robin, Opera, Ryan, Porter, David, Hibbert, Chris, Tila, Dorina, 2011. Can Manipulators Mislead Prediction Market Observers? George Mason University, mimeo.

Harvey, David, I., Leybourne, Stephen, J., Newbold, Paul, 1998. Tests for forecast encompassing. Journal of Business & Economic Statistics 16 (2), 254–259.

Hausch, Donald, Ziemba, William (Eds.), 2007. Handbook of Sports and Lottery Markets. Handbooks in Finance series, Elsevier.

Jullien, Bruno, Salanié, Bernard, 2000. Estimating preferences under risk: the case of racetrack bettors. Journal of Political Economy 108 (3), 503–530.

Laster, D., Bennett, P., Geoum, In Sun, 1999. Rational bias in macroeconomic forecasts. Quarterly Journal of Economics 114 (1), 293–318.

Lavoie, Jim, 2009. The innovation engine at rite-solutions: lessons from the CEO. Journal of Prediction Markets 3 (1), 1–11.

Leigh, Andrew, Wolfers, Justin, Zitzewitz, Eric, 2003. What do Financial Markets Think of the War with Iraq? NBER Working Paper #9587.

Leitch, Gordon, Tanner, Ernest, J., 1991. Economic forecast evaluation: profits versus the conventional error measures. The American Economic Review 81 (3), 580–590.

Malhotra, Neil, Snowberg, Erik, 2009. The 2008 Presidential Primaries through the Lens of Prediction Markets. California Institute of Technology, mimeo.

Manski, Charles, F., 2006. Interpreting the predictions of prediction markets. Economics Letters 91 (3), 425–429.

Marinovic, Iván, Ottaviani, Marco, Sørenson, Peter Norman, 2011. Modeling idea markets: between beauty contests and prediction markets. In: Williams, Leighton Vaughn (Ed.), Prediction Markets, Routledge.

Ottaviani, Marco, Sørensen, Peter, N, 2010. Aggregation of Information and Beliefs: Asset Pricing Lessons from Prediction Markets. Northwestern University, mimeo.

Ottaviani, Marco, Sørensen, Peter Norman, 2012. Forecasters' objectives and strategies. In: Handbook of Economic Forecasting, vol. 2. Elsevier: Handbooks in Economics series.

Plott, Charles, R., Shyam Sunder, 1988. Rational expectations and the aggregation of diverse information in laboratory security markets. Econometrica, pp. 1085–1118.

Plott, Charles, R., 2000. Markets as information gathering tools. Southern Economic Journal 67 (1), 2–15.

Plott, Charles, R., Sunder, Shyam, 1982. Efficiency of experimental security markets with insider information: an application of rational-expectations models. The Journal of Political Economy 90 (4), 663–698.

Rhode, Paul, W., Strumpf, Koleman, S., 2004. Historical presidential betting markets. Journal of Economic Perspectives 18 (2), 127–142.

Rhode, Paul, W., Strumpf, Koleman, S., 2008. Historical Election Betting Markets: An International Perspective. University of Arizona, mimeo.

Rothschild, David, 2009. Forecasting elections comparing prediction markets, polls, and their biases. Public Opinion Quarterly 73 (5), 895–916.

Rubinstein, Mark, 1994. Implied binomial trees. Journal of Finance 69 (3), 771–818.

Santa-Clara, Pedro, Valkanov, Rossen, 2003. The presidential puzzle: political cycles and the stock market. The Journal of Finance 58 (5), 1841–1872.

Schwert, G. William, 1990. Indexes of US Stock Prices from 1802–1987. Journal of Business 63 (3), 399–426.

Servan-Schreiber, Emile, Wolfers, Justin, Pennock, David, M., Galebach, Brian, 2004. Prediction markets: does money matter? Electronic Markets 14 (3), 243–251.

Snowberg, Erik, Wolfers, Justin, 2010. Explaining the favorite-longshot bias: is it risk-love or misperceptions? Journal of Political Economy 118 (4), 723–746.

Snowberg, Erik, Wolfers, Justin, Zitzewitz, Eric, 2005. Information (In)efficiency in Prediction Markets. In: Williams, Leighton Vaughn (Ed.), Information Efficiency in Betting Markets, Cambridge Unversity Press, pp. 366–386.

Snowberg, Erik, Wolfers, Justin, Zitzewitz, Eric, 2007a. Partisan impacts on the economy: evidence from prediction markets and close elections. The Quarterly Journal of Economics 122 (2), 807–829.

Snowberg, Erik, Wolfers, Justin, Zitzewitz, Eric, 2007b. Prediction markets: from politics to business (and back). In: Hausch, Donald, Ziemba, William (Eds.), Handbook of Sports and Lottery Markets, Elsevier: Handbooks in Finance series, pp. 385–402.

Snowberg, Erik, Wolfers, Justin, Zitzewitz, Eric, 2011. How prediction markets can save event studies. In: Williams, Leighton Vaughn (Ed.), Prediction Markets, Routledge.

Spears, Brian, LaComb, Christina, Interrante, John, Barnett, Janet, Senturk-Dogonaksoy, Deniz, 2009. Examining trader behavior in idea markets: an implementation of ge's imagination markets. The Journal of Prediction Markets 3 (1), 17–39

Strumpf, Koleman, S., 2009. Introduction to special issue on corporate applications of prediction markets. Journal of Prediction Markets 3 (1), i–vii.

Tetlock, Paul., 2004. How efficient are information markets? Evidence from an Online Exchange. Columbia University, mimeo.

Tompkins, Robert, G., Ziemba, William, T., Hodges, Stewart D., 2008. The favorite-longshot bias in S&P 500 and FTSE 100 index futures options: the return to bets and the cost of insurance. In: Hausch, Donald, B., Ziemba, William, T., (Eds.), Handbook of Sports and Lottery Markets. Handbooks in Finance series, Elsevier.

Tziralis, George, Tatsiopoulos, Ilias, 2007. Prediction markets: an extended literature review. The Journal of Prediction Markets 1 (1), 75–91.

Vaughn, Williams, Leighton, (Eds.), 2005. Information Efficiency in Betting Markets. Cambridge Unversity Press.

West, Kenneth, D., 1996. Asymptotic inference about predictive ability. Econometrica 64 (5), 1067–1084.

West, Kenneth, D., 2006. Forecast evaluation. In Elliott, Graham, Granger, Clive, W.J., Timmermann, Allan (Eds.), Handbook of Economic Forecasting, vol. 1. Elsevier, pp. 99–134, chapter 3.

Wolfers, Justin, Leigh, Andrew, 2002. Three tools for forecasting federal elections: lessons from 2001. Australian Journal of Political Science 37 (2), 223–240.

Wolfers, Justin, Zitzewitz, Eric, 2004. Prediction markets. Journal of Economic Perspectives 18 (2), 107–126.

Wolfers, Justin, Zitzewitz, Eric, 2006. Interpreting Prediction Market Prices as Probabilities. NBER Working Paper Series 12200.

Wolfers, Justin, Zitzewitz, Eric, 2008a. Prediction markets in theory and practice. In: Blume, Larry, Durlauf, Steven (Eds.), The New Palgrave Dictionary of Economics, second ed. Palgrave, London.

Wolfers, Justin, Zitzewitz, Eric, 2008b. Using markets to inform policy: the case of the iraq war. Economica 76 (302), 225–250.

Wright, Jonathan, Faust, Jon, 2013. Forecasting inflation. In: Elliott, Graham, Timmermann, Allan (Eds.), Handbook of Economic Forecasting, vol. 2. Handbooks in Economics series, Elsevier.

Zhou, Guofo, Rapach, David, 2013. Forecasting stock returns. In: Timmermann, Allan, Elliott, Graham (Eds.), Handbook of Economic Forecasting, vol. 2. Handbooks in Economics series, Elsevier.

Zingales, Luigi, 2010. Learning to live with not-so-efficient markets. Daedalus 139 (4), 31–40.

Zitzewitz, Eric., May 30, 2007. Manipulation can Affect Prices. MidasOracle.org, http://www.midasoracle.org/2007/05/30/manipulation-can-affect-prices/.

INDEX

Printed and bound by CPI Group (UK) Ltd, Croydon, CR0 4YY

08/05/2025

01864967-0003